THE FOURTH BOOK OF MOSES, (

NUMBERS

VOLUME 6

THE PREACHER'S OUTLINE & SERMON BIBLE®

THE FOURTH BOOK OF MOSES, CALLED

NUMBERS

VOLUME 6

THE PREACHER'S OUTLINE & SERMON BIBLE®

OLD TESTAMENT

KING JAMES VERSION

Leadership Ministries Worldwide
Chattanooga TN

The Preacher's Outline & Sermon Bible® is written for God's people to use in their preparation for preaching and teaching. Leadership Ministries Worldwide wants God's people to use *The Preacher's Outline & Sermon Bible®*. The purpose of the copyright is to prevent the reproduction, misuse, and abuse of the material.

May our Lord bless us all as we preach, teach, and write for Him, fulfilling His great commission to make disciples of all nations.

Please address all requests for information or permission to:

Leadership Ministries Worldwide
PO Box 21310
Chattanooga, TN 37424-0310
Ph.# (423) 855-2181 FAX (423) 855-8616 E-Mail outlinebible@compuserve.com
http://www.outlinebible.org

Library of Congress Catalog Card Number: 96-75921
International Standard Book Number: 1-57407-118-1

Printed in the United States of America

Publisher & Distributor

DEDICATED:

To all the men and women of the world
who preach and teach the Gospel of our
Lord Jesus Christ
and
To the Mercy and Grace of God.

- Demonstrated to us in Christ Jesus our Lord.

  "In whom we have redemption through His blood, the forgiveness of sins, according to the riches of His grace." (Eph. 1:7)

- Out of the mercy and grace of God His Word has flowed. Let every person know that God will have mercy upon him, forgiving and using him to fulfill His glorious plan of salvation.

  "For God so loved the world, that he gave his only begotten Son, that whosoever believeth in him should not perish, but have everlasting life. For God sent not his Son into the world to condemn the world; but that the world through him might be saved." (Jn 3:16-17)

  "For this is good and acceptable in the sight of God our Saviour; who will have all men to be saved, and to come unto the knowledge of the truth." (I Tim. 2:3-4)

&

The Preacher's Outline and Study Bible®
is written for God's people to use
in their study and teaching of God's Holy Word.

OUR VISION, PASSION & PURPOSE:

- To share the Word of God with the world.
- To help the believer, both minister and layman alike, in his understanding, preaching, and teaching of God's Word.
- To do everything we possibly can to lead men, women, boys, and girls to give their hearts and lives to Jesus Christ and to secure the eternal life which He offers.
- To do all we can to minister to the needy of the world.
- To give Jesus Christ His proper place, the place which the Word gives Him. Therefore — No work of Leadership Ministries Worldwide will ever be personalized.

9/99

Outline Bible Resources

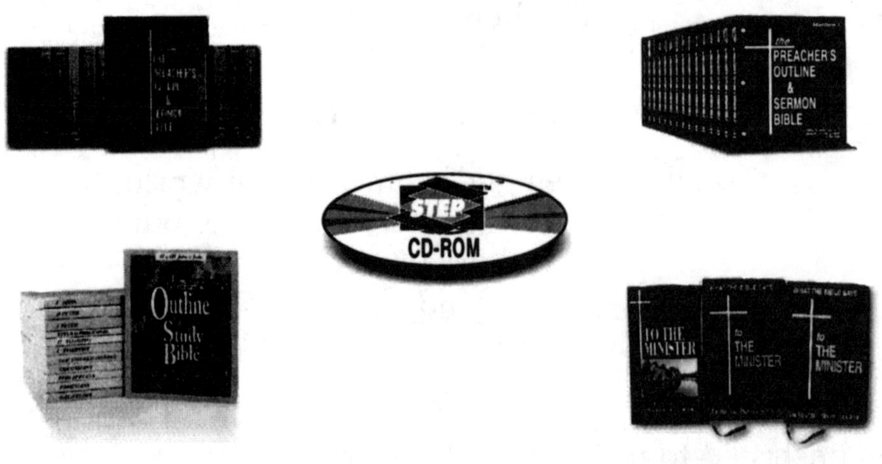

This material, like similar works, has come from imperfect man and is thus susceptible to human error. We are nevertheless grateful to God for both calling us and empowering us through His Holy Spirit to undertake this task. Because of His goodness and grace **The Preacher's Outline & Sermon Bible®** - New Testament is complete in 14 volumes, and the Old Testament volumes release periodically. **The Minister's Handbook** is available and *OUTLINE* Bible materials are releasing electonically on **POSB-CD** and our **Web site**.

God has given the strength and stamina to bring us this far. Our confidence is that, as we keep our eyes on Him and grounded in the undeniable truths of the Word, we will continue working through the Old Testament volumes and the second series known as **The Teacher's Outline & Study Bible™**. The future includes helpful *Outline Bible* books and **Handbook** materials for God's dear servants.

To everyone everywhere who preaches and teaches the Word, we offer this material firstly to Him in whose name we labor and serve, and for whose glory it has been produced.

Our daily prayer is that each volume will lead thousands, millions, yes even billions, into a better understanding of the Holy Scriptures and a fuller knowledge of Jesus Christ the incarnate Word, of whom the Scriptures so faithfully testify.

> As you have purchased this volume, you will be pleased to know that a small portion of the price you have paid has gone to underwrite and provide similar volumes in other languages (Russian, Korean, Spanish and others yet to come) — To a preacher, pastor, lay leader, or Bible student somewhere around the world, who will present God's message with clarity, authority, and understanding beyond their own. *Amen.*

For information and prices, kindly contact your *OUTLINE* Bible bookseller or:

Leadership Ministries Worldwide

P.O. Box 21310, 515 Airport Road, Suite 107
Chattanooga, TN 37424-0310
(423) 855-2181 FAX (423) 855-8616
E-Mail - outlinebible@compuserve.com
www.outlinebible.org — *FREE* download materials 3/99

ACKNOWLEDGMENTS AND BIBLIOGRAPHY

Every child of God is precious to the Lord and deeply loved. And every child as a servant of the Lord touches the lives of those who come in contact with him or his ministry. The writing ministry of the following servants have touched this work, and we are grateful that God brought their writings our way. We hereby acknowledge their ministry to us, being fully aware that there are so many others down through the years whose writings have touched our lives and who deserve mention, but the weaknesses of our minds have caused them to fade from memory. May our wonderful Lord continue to bless the ministry of these dear servants, and the ministry of us all as we diligently labor to reach the world for Christ and to meet the desperate needs of those who suffer so much.

THE REFERENCE WORKS

Archer, Gleason L. Jr. *A Survey of Old Testament Introduction*. Chicago, IL: Moody Bible Institute of Chicago, 1974.

Atlas of the World. Hammond Concise Edition. Maplewood, NJ: Hammond Incorporated, MCMXCIII.

Baker's Dictionary of Theology. Everett F. Harrison, Editor-in-Chief. Grand Rapids, MI: Baker Book House, 1960.

Barker, William P. *Everyone in the Bible*. Westwood, NJ: Fleming H. Revell Co., 1966.

Brown, Francis. *The New Brown-Driver-Briggs-Gesenius Hebrew-English Lexicon*. Peabody, MA: Hendrickson Publishers, 1979.

Cruden's Complete Concordance of the Old & New Testament. Philadelphia, PA: The John C. Winston Co., 1930.

Dake, Finis Jennings. *Dake's Annotated Reference Bible, The Holy Bible*. Lawrenceville, GA: Dake Bible Sales, Inc., 1963.

Funk & Wagnalls Standard Desk Dictionary. Lippincott & Crowell, Publishers, 1980, Vol.2.

Geisler, Norman. *A Popular Survey of the Old Testament*. Grand Rapids, MI: Baker Book House, 1977.

Good News Bible. Old Testament: © American Bible Society, 1976. New Testament: © American Bible Society, 1966, 1971, 1976. Collins World.

Good News for Modern Man, the New Testament. New York, NY: American Bible Society, 1971.

Good, Joseph. *Rosh HaShanah and the Messianic Kingdom to Come*. Pt. Arthur, TX: Hatikva Ministries, 1989.

Harrison, Roland Kenneth. *Introduction to the Old Testament*. Grand Rapids, MI: Eerdmans Publishing Company, 1969.

Josephus, Flavius. *Complete Works*. Grand Rapids, MI: Kregel Publications, 1981.

Kelley, Page H. *Exodus: Called for Redemptive Mission*. January Bible Study. Nashville, TN: Convention Press, 1977.

Kohlenberger, John R. III. *The Interlinear NIV Hebrew-English Old Testament*. Grand Rapids, MI: Zondervan Publishing House, 1987.

Kouffman, Donald T. *The Dictionary of Religious Terms*. Westwood, NJ: Fleming H. Revell Co., 1967.

Life Application® Bible. Wheaton, IL: Tyndale House Publishers, Inc., 1991.

Lindsell, Harold and Woodbridge, Charles J. *A Handbook of Christian Truth*. Westwood, NJ: Fleming H. Revell Company, A Division of Baker Book House, 1953.

Lipis, Joan R. *Celebrate Passover Haggadah*. San Francisco, CA: Purple Pomegranate Productions, 1993.

Living Quotations For Christians. Edited by Sherwood Eliot Wirt and Kersten Beckstrom. New York, NY: Harper & Row, Publishers, 1974.

Lockyer, Herbert. *All the Books and Chapters of the Bible*. Grand Rapids, MI: Zondervan Publishing House, 1966.

Lockyer, Herbert. *All the Men of the Bible*. Grand Rapids, MI: Zondervan Publishing House, 1958.

Lockyer, Herbert. *All the Miracles of the Bible*. Grand Rapids, MI: Zondervan Publishing House, 1961.

Lockyer, Herbert. *All the Parables of the Bible*. Grand Rapids, MI: Zondervan Publishing House, 1963.

Lockyer, Herbert. *The Women of the Bible*. Grand Rapids, MI: Zondervan Publishing House, 1967.

Martin, Alfred. *Survey of the Scriptures*, Part I, II, III. Chicago, IL: Moody Bible Institute of Chicago, 1961.

McDowell, Josh. *Evidence That Demands A Verdict*, Vol.1. San Bernardino, CA: Here's Life Publishers, Inc., 1979.

Merrill F. Unger & William White, Jr. *Nelson's Expository Dictionary of the Old Testament*. Nashville, TN: Thomas Nelson Publishers, 1980.

Miller, Madeleine S. & J. Lane. *Harper's Bible Dictionary*. New York, NY: Harper & Row Publishers, 1961.

Nave, Orville J. *Nave's Topical Bible*. Nashville, TN: The Southwestern Company. Copyright © by J.B. Henderson, 1921.

New American Standard Bible, Reference Edition. La Habra, CA: The Lockman Foundation, 1975.

New Bible Dictionary, 3rd Edition. Leicester, England: Universities & Colleges Christian Fellowship, 1996.

New International Version Study Bible. Grand Rapids, MI: Zondervan Bible Publishers, 1985.

New Living Translation, Holy Bible. Wheaton, IL: Tyndale House Publishers, Inc., 1996.

NIV Exhaustive Concordance. (Grand Rapids, MI: Zondervan Corporation, 1990).

Orr, William. *How We May Know That God Is*. Wheaton, IL: Van Kampen Press, No date given.

Owens, John Joseph. *Analytical Key to the Old Testament,* Vols.1, 2, 3. Grand Rapids, MI: Baker Book House, 1989.

Payne, J. Barton. *Encyclopedia of Biblical Prophecy*. New York, NY: Harper & Row, Publishers, 1973.

Pilgrim Edition, Holy Bible. New York, NY: Oxford University Press, 1952.

Ridout, Samuel. *Lectures on the Tabernacle*. New York, NY: Loizeaux Brothers, Inc., 1914.

Roget's 21st Century Thesaurus, Edited by Barbara Ann Kipfer. New York, NY: Dell Publishing, 1992.

Rosen, Ceil and Moishe. *Christ In The Passover*. Chicago, IL: Moody Press, 1978.

Slemming, C.W. *Made According To Pattern*. Fort Washington, PA: Christian Literature Crusade, 1983.

Smith, William. *Smith's Bible Dictionary*. Peabody, MA: Hendrickson Publishers, No date given.

Soltau, Henry W. *The Holy Vessels And Furniture Of The Tabernacle*. Grand Rapids, MI: Kregel Publications, 1971.

Soltau, Henry W. *The Tabernacle The Priesthood And The Offerings*. Grand Rapids, MI: Kregel Publications, 1972.

Stone, Nathan J. *Names of God*. Chicago, IL: Moody Press, 1944.

Strong, James. *Strong's Exhaustive Concordance of the Bible*. Nashville, TN: Thomas Nelson, Inc., 1990.

Strong, James. *The Tabernacle Of Israel*. Grand Rapids, MI: Kregel Publications, 1987.

ACKNOWLEDGMENTS AND BIBLIOGRAPHY (continued)

The Amplified Bible. Scripture taken from THE AMPLIFIED BIBLE, Old Testament copyright © 1965, 1987 by the Zondervan Corporation. The Amplified New Testament copyright © 1958, 1987 by The Lockman Foundation. Used by permission.

The Evangelical Dictionary of Theology. Elwell, Walter A., Editor. Grand Rapids, MI: Baker Book House, 1984.

The Hebrew-Greek Key Study Bible, New International Version. Spiros Zodhiates, Th.D., Executive Editor. Chattanooga, TN: AMG Publishers, 1996.

The Holy Bible in Four Translations. Minneapolis, MN: Worldwide Publications. Copyright © The Iversen-Norman Associates: New York, NY, 1972.

The Interlinear Bible, Vol.1, 2, & 3, Translated by Jay P. Green, Sr. Grand Rapids, MI: Baker Book House Company, 1976.

The International Standard Bible Encyclopaedia, Edited by James Orr. Grand Rapids, MI: Eerdmans Publishing Company, 1939.

The NASB Greek/Hebrew Dictionary and Concordance. (La Habra, CA: The Lockman Foundation, 1988).

The New Compact Bible Dictionary, Edited by T. Alton Bryant. Grand Rapids, MI: Zondervan Publishing House, 1967. Used by permission of Zondervan Publishing House.

The New Scofield Reference Bible, Edited by C.I. Scofield. New York, NY: Oxford University Press, 1967.

The New Thompson Chain Reference Bible. Indianapolis, IN: B.B. Kirkbride Bible Co., Inc., 1964.

The Open Bible. Nashville, TN: Thomas Nelson Publishers, 1975.

The Quest Study Bible. New International Version. Grand Rapids, MI: Zondervan Publishing House, 1994.

The Zondervan Pictorial Encyclopedia of the Bible, Vol.1. Merrill C. Tenney, Editor. Grand Rapids, MI: Zondervan Publishing House, 1982.

Theological Wordbook of the Old Testament, Edited by R. Laird Harris. Chicago, IL: Moody Bible Institute of Chicago, 1980.

W.E. Vine, Merrill F. Unger, William White, Jr. *Vine's Complete Expository Dictionary of Old and New Testament Words*. Nashville, TN: Thomas Nelson Publishers, 1985.

Webster's Seventh New Collegiate Dictionary. Springfield, MA: G. & C. Merriam Company, Publishers, 1971.

Wilson, William. *Wilson's Old Testament Word Studies*. McLean, VA: MacDonald Publishing Company, No date given.

Wood, Leon. *A Survey of Israel's History*. Grand Rapids, MI: Zondervan Publishing House, 1982.

Young, Edward J. *An Introduction to the Old Testament*. Grand Rapids, MI: Eerdmans Publishing Company, 1964.

Young, Robert. *Young's Analytical Concordance to the Bible*. Grand Rapids, MI: Eerdmans Publishing Company, No date given.

Zehr, Paul M. *Glimpses of the Tabernacle*. Lancaster, PA: Mennonite Information Center, 1976.

THE COMMENTARIES

Ashley, Timothy R. *The Book of Numbers*. "The New International Commentary on the Old Testament." Grand Rapids, MI: Eerdmans Publishing Co., 1993.

Barclay, William. *The Old Law & The New Law*. Edinburgh, Scotland: The Saint Andrew Press, 1972.

Barnes' Notes, Exodus to Esther. F.C. Cook, Editor. Grand Rapids, MI: Baker Book House, No date given.

Burroughs, P.E., D.D. *Old Testament Studies*. Nashville, TN: Sunday School Board, Southern Baptist Convention, 1915.

Bush, George. *Numbers*. Minneapolis, MN: Klock & Klock Christian Publishers, Inc., 1981.

Gill, John. *Gill's Commentary*, Vol.1. Grand Rapids, MI: Baker Book House, 1980.

Henry, Matthew. *Matthew Henry's Commentary*, 6 Volumes. Old Tappan, NJ: Fleming H. Revell Co., No date given.

Heslop, William G. *Nuggets from Numbers*. Grand Rapids, MI: Kregel Publications, 1975.

Jones, Kenneth E. *The Book of Numbers*. "Shield Bible Study Series." Grand Rapids, MI: Baker Book House, 1972.

Keil-Delitzsch. *Commentary on the Old Testament*, Vol.1. Grand Rapids, MI: Eerdmans Publishing Company, No date given.

Mackintosh, C.H. *Notes on Numbers*. Neptune, NJ: Loizeaux Brothers, 1965.

Maclaren, Alexander. *Expositions of Holy Scripture*, 11 Vols. Grand Rapids, MI: Eerdmans Publishing Company, 1952-59.

McGee, J. Vernon. *Thru The Bible*, Vol.1. Nashville, TN: Thomas Nelson Publishers, 1981.

Noordtzij, A. *Bible Student's Commentary, Numbers*. Grand Rapids, MI: Zondervan Publishing House, 1983.

Olford, Stephen. *The Tabernacle, Camping With God*. Neptune, NJ: Loizeaux Brothers, 1971.

Philip, James. *Mastering the Old Testament, Vol.4: Numbers*. Dallas, TX: Word Publishing, 1987.

Pink, Arthur W. *The Ten Commandments*. Grand Rapids, MI: Baker Books, 1994.

Poole, Matthew. *Matthew Poole's Commentary on the Holy Bible*. Peabody, MA: Hendrickson Publishers, No date given.

Saphir, Adolph. *Christ and Israel*. Grand Rapids, MI: Kregel Publications, No date given.

Spurgeon, C.H. *Spurgeon's Sermon Notes. Genesis to Malachi*. Westwood, NJ: Fleming H. Revell Co., No date given.

The Biblical Illustrator, Leviticus—Numbers. Edited by Exell, Joseph S. Grand Rapids, MI: Baker Book House, 1966.

The Complete Biblical Library: The Old Testament. Volume 3: Study Bible, Leviticus–Numbers. Springfield, MO: World Library Press, Inc., 1995.

The Expositor's Bible Commentary, Vol.2. Gaebelein, Frank E., Editor. Grand Rapids, MI: Zondervan Publishing House, 1990.

The Interpreter's Bible, 12 Vols. New York, NY: Abingdon Press, 1956.

The Pulpit Commentary. 23 Volumes. Edited by H.D.M. Spence & Joseph S. Exell. Grand Rapids, MI: Eerdmans Publishing Company, 1950.

Thomas, W.H. Griffith. *Through the Pentateuch Chapter by Chapter*. Grand Rapids, MI: Eerdmans Publishing Company, 1957.

Wenham, Gordon J. *The Book of Numbers*. "The New International Commentary on the Old Testament." Grand Rapids, MI: Eerdmans Publishing Co., 1981.

MISCELLANEOUS ABBREVIATIONS

&	=	And
Arg.	=	Argument
Bckgrd.	=	Background
Bc.	=	Because
Circ.	=	Circumstance
Concl.	=	Conclusion
Cp.	=	Compare
Ct.	=	Contrast
Dif.	=	Different
e.g.	=	For example
Et.	=	Eternal
f.	=	Following
Govt.	=	Government
Id.	=	Identity or Identification
Illust.	=	Illustration
K.	=	Kingdom, K. of God, K. of Heaven, etc.
No.	=	Number
N.T.	=	New Testament
O.T.	=	Old Testament
Pt.	=	Point
Quest.	=	Question
Rel.	=	Religion
Resp.	=	Responsibility
Rev.	=	Revelation
Rgt.	=	Righteousness
Thru	=	Through
V.	=	Verse
Vs.	=	Verses
Vs.	=	Versus

How To Use... The Preacher's Outline & Sermon Bible™

A *Your **Scripture Passage** always printed out* B *Your **Sermon Outline** located next to each verse* C *A Wealth of **Practical Commentary** Material* D ***Illustrations** and **Applications** for every audience* E ***Support Scripture** thoroughly researched & written out*	***First***: Glance at the **Subject Heading**. Think about it for a moment. ***Then***: Glance at the **Subject Heading** & the **Major Points** together. ***Now***: Glance at both the **Major Points** & **Subpoints** while reading the Scripture. Note how the points are beside the applicable verse—simply stating what the Scripture is saying—in Outline form. ***Finally***: Read the **Commentary**. KEY: Note that the *major point numbers* in the *outline* match those in the *commentary*.

MATTHEW 6:1-4

Outline	Scripture	Scripture (cont.)	Outline
	CHAPTER 6 **K. The Right Motive for Giving,**DS1 **6:1-4** A	hypocrites do in the synagogues and in the streets, that they may have glory of men. Verily I say unto you, They have their reward.	hypocrites c. Reward: Recognition by men only B
1 Alms—doing good & giving a. Warning: Do not seek recognition b. The reason: God will not reward	Take heed that ye do not your alms before men, to be seen of them: otherwise ye have no reward of your Father which is in heaven.	3 But when thou doest alms, let not thy left hand know what thy right hand doeth:	**3 The right motive** a. Giving unconsciously
		4 That thine alms may be in secret: and thy Father	b. Giving quietly—privately—secretly
2 The wrong motive a. Giving for recognition b. Characteristic of	2 Therefore when thou doest thine alms, do not sound a trumpet before thee, as the	which seeth in secret himself shall reward thee openly.	**4 The reasons** a. Father sees in secret b. Father rewards openly

DIVISION IV

THE TEACHINGS OF THE MESSIAH TO HIS DISCIPLES: THE GREAT SERMON ON THE MOUNT, 5:1-7:29

K. The Right Motive for Giving, 6:1-4

(6:1-4) **Introduction—Motive**: what a man does matters greatly to God. God expects men to be kind and to do good in the world: to help others both through personal involvement and through giving generously and sacrificially.

But there is something else that God expects, something of critical importance: God expects a man to have *the right motive*. Just why a man does good and shows kindness matters greatly to God. It matters so much that a person's eternal fate is determined by his motive. Because of this, Christ warns us about right and wrong motives.

1. Alms—doing good and giving (v.1).
2. The wrong motive (v.2).
3. The right motive (v.3-4).
4. The reason (v.4).

C

1 (6:1) **Alms—Service—Giving**: there is the giving of alms—doing good and giving to others. The word "alms" means righteous acts; giving in order to meet the needs of the poor. To the Jew, giving alms and righteousness meant the same thing. Giving alms was the greatest thing a Jew could do; it was the first act of religion. It was considered to be the very embodiment of righteousness, so much so that the two words began to be used synonymously. Giving alms merited and assured one of righteousness and salvation. (See note 5—Mt.5:6.) Christ warned there is great danger in giving and doing alms. Take heed and guard yourself. Do not give for recognition, or you will lose your reward.

Thought 1. There are two important lessons in this verse.

D

1) Man must guard and be alert to the deception of giving and doing good before men. A person's heart can be deceived. The sin creeps up on man; it is insidious and subtle. It will keep a person from receiving anything from God.
2) A person must give alms and do good. It is a duty of the Christian. In this passage alone Christ says four times, "Do alms."

E

"But all their works they do for to be seen of men" (Mt.23:5).

"Beware of the scribes, which desire to walk in long robes, and love greetings in the markets, and the highest seats in the synagogues, and the chief rooms at feasts" (Lk.20:46).

"

Woe is unto me, if I preach not the gospel

" **(1 Cor.9:16)**

TABLE OF CONTENTS

THE FOURTH BOOK OF MOSES, CALLED
NUMBERS

AUTHOR: Moses, the great lawgiver and prophet of God. Moses was the great leader who led the Israelites from Egyptian slavery and through the wilderness wanderings. The evidence is strong, very strong, that Moses is the author.

1. The Book of Numbers itself claims to have been written by Moses.

> **"And the Lord spake unto Moses in the wilderness of Sinai, in the tabernacle of the congregation, on the first day of the second month, in the second year after they were come out of the land of Egypt, saying" (Num.1:1).**
>
> **"These are the journeys of the children of Israel, which went forth out of the land of Egypt with their armies under the hand of Moses and Aaron. And Moses wrote their goings out according to their journeys by the commandment of the Lord: and these are their journeys according to their goings out" (Num.33:1-2).**

2. Jesus Christ Himself said that Moses was the author and stated that it was Moses who had actually lifted up the serpent in the wilderness.

> **"And as Moses lifted up the serpent in the wilderness, even so must the Son of man be lifted up" (Jn.3:14; cp. Num.21:9).**
>
> **"And Moses made a serpent of brass, and put it upon a pole, and it came to pass, that if a serpent had bitten any man, when he beheld the serpent of brass, he lived" (Num.21:9).**

3. The New Testament mentions several events in Numbers that associate them with Moses.

> **"I [God] have seen, I [God] have seen the affliction of my people which is in Egypt, and I have heard their groaning, and am come down to deliver them. And now come, I will send thee into Egypt. This Moses whom they refused, saying, Who made thee a ruler and a judge? the same did God send to be a ruler and a deliverer by the hand of the angel which appeared to him in the bush. He brought them out, after that he had showed wonders and signs in the land of Egypt, and in the Red sea, and in the wilderness forty years" (Acts 7:34-36).**
>
> **"Moreover, brethren, I would not that ye should be ignorant, how that all our fathers were under the cloud, and all passed through the sea; And were all baptized unto Moses in the cloud and in the sea; And did all eat the same spiritual meat; And did all drink the same spiritual drink: for they drank of that spiritual Rock that followed them: and that Rock was Christ. But with many of them God was not well pleased: for they were overthrown in the wilderness" (1 Cor.10:1-5).**
>
> **"And Moses verily was faithful in all his house, as a servant, for a testimony of those things which were to be spoken after; But Christ as a son over his own house; whose house are we, if we hold fast the confidence and the rejoicing of the hope firm unto the end. Wherefore (as the Holy Ghost saith, To day if ye will hear his voice, Harden not your hearts, as in the provocation, in the day of temptation in the wilderness: When your fathers tempted me, proved me, and saw my works forty years" (Heb.3:5-9).**

4. Without exception, the Old Testament always refers to Moses as the author of the Pentateuch, the first five books of the Bible (Ex.17:14; 24:4; 34:27; Num.33:1-2; Josh.1:7-8; 8:31-32; 1 Ki.2:3; 8:9, 53; 2 Ki.10:31; 14:6; Ezra 6:18; Neh.13:1; Dan.9:11-13; Mal.4:4).

5. Without exception, the New Testament always refers to Moses as the author of the Pentateuch, which includes Numbers (Mt.8:4; 19:7-8; 23:2; Mk.1:44; 7:10; 10:3-4; 12:19, 26; Lk.5:14; 16:29-31; 20:37; 24:27, 44; Jn.1:17; 3:14; 5:45-46; 6:32; 7:19, 22-23; Acts 3:22; 13:39; 15:1, 5, 21; 26:22; 28:23; Ro.10:5, 19; 1 Cor.9:9; 2 Cor.3:15).

For several centuries now there has been a popular theory surrounding the Bible that is called "the documentary hypothesis." This theory says there are four major sources for the Pentateuch, each of which was written sometime between 900-400 B.C. These sources are said to be...

- *J* (for Jehovah or Yahweh). This represents the writer or source that used the Hebrew name *Jehovah* or *Yahweh* for God throughout the Pentateuch.
- *E* (for Elohim). This represents the writer or source that used the Hebrew name *Elohim* for God.
- *D* (for Deuteronomist). This represents the writer or source that recorded the different accounts of the law throughout the Pentateuch.
- *P* (for Priestly). This represents the writer or source that recorded the information dealing with the *priests*.

The first person to suggest the theory of "the documentary hypothesis" was a French physician, Jean Astruc, in 1752. Note that he was a physician, not a theologian. The theory was later picked up by the German historian and Biblical writer, J.G. Eichhorn in 1787. However, "the documentary hypothesis" was not thoroughly developed and popularized until Julius Wellhausen who lived from 1844-1918 (Victor Hamilton. *The Book of Genesis*, Chapters 1-17, p.13).

The Expositor's Bible Commentary has an excellent statement in answer to the critics of the Mosaic authorship:

> "Many of the arguments given by [critical] scholars may be countered by evidence from within the Bible and from what we now know concerning patterns of writing in the ancient world that run directly counter to the basic postulates of standard critical theory. But the most telling distinction between nonevangelical scholars and evangelical scholars is one's starting point. When a person begins with the...divine inspiration of Scripture and...inerrancy, then the dates of Scripture are read quite differently than if one does not begin with a belief in the inspiration, authority, and inerrancy of Scripture....

INTRODUCTION TO NUMBERS

"We may conclude...that the essential content of the book did come from Moses, the servant of the Lord. His name is repeatedly in the book; he is the principal human protagonist in the book; and he is the one with the training, opportunity, motivation, and opportunity to produce the book. It is almost axiomatic to observe that God brings good out of even the most grim, the most dismal situations. We may reckon that one of the good things that came out of the ghastly waste of life and energy of the condemned, rebellious first generation of the Hebrew people was the opportunity the desert experience afforded Moses, prince and prophet of God, to write the books that are associated so strongly with his name.

"If Moses was the principal writer of the Book of Numbers, then we may assert that he would have written these accounts over a lengthy period that included the stay of Israel in the Desert of Sinai as well as on their encampments enroute to the plains of Moab. Much of the unevenness of style may be occasioned by the periodic nature of the writing. But the unity of the book overrides its uneven style. The Book of Numbers may be regarded as *The Memoirs of Moses in the Desert Years*."[1]

DATE: Moses obviously wrote Numbers sometime between 1445-1406 B.C., perhaps closer to 1406 B.C. This much is known: Numbers covers thirty-eight of the forty years of wilderness wanderings. The history of Numbers picks up in the 13th month after the Exodus from Egyptian slavery and ends with the forty years of wandering. Therefore, the book could not have been completed until after Israel's wanderings in the desert. (See *Introduction, Date—Genesis, Volume 1 or 2* for more discussion.) However, the book was completed sometime before Moses died (Dt.31:24).

TO WHOM WRITTEN: the people of Israel and all people in general. However it is important to note this fact: there are at least two groups of believers seen in the Book of Numbers. The first group is the first generation of believers who were delivered from Egyptian slavery by the miraculous power of God. But this group of believers failed God miserably. They became gripped with a spirit of unbelief and rebellion, complaining and grumbling against God and His dear servant Moses. As a result, they were condemned to die in the desert wilderness. They were barred from the promised land and never allowed to enter it.

The other group seen in the Book of Numbers is the second generation of believers, the sons and daughters of the first generation. When the first generation rebelled against God, God did not hold the children accountable, not any child twenty years old or younger. God had condemned the first generation to wander about in the desert wilderness until the last adult had died. The forty years of wilderness wanderings were used by God to discipline and strengthen the children, teaching them not to follow after their parents in unbelief and rebellion. The children were taught the great hope of the promised land, to diligently seek after the inheritance promised by God. The events covered in the great Book of Numbers stood as a strong warning to the second generation of believers, a warning not to imitate their parents in unbelief and rebellion. The great Book of Numbers also stands as a strong warning to every believer of every generation, a warning not to follow in the steps of unbelief and rebellion against God.

PURPOSE: three purposes are seen in the great Book of Numbers.

1. The *Historical Purpose*: to give a permanent record of Israel's *Wilderness Wanderings*, of the people's journey from Mt. Sinai to the border of the promised land of Canaan. This period of history covered about 38½ years of the 40 year period known as the *wilderness wanderings*. It was during this period that the first generation of believers died out under the judgment of God. But of paramount importance is this fact: it was during the *wilderness wanderings* that God took the children—the second generation of believers—and trained them. God prepared them—toughened, strengthened, and disciplined them—to conquer and inherit the promised land.

2. The *Doctrinal or Spiritual Purpose*: several doctrinal or spiritual lessons are clearly seen as the great Book of Numbers is studied.

   a. We learn more and more about endurance and hope, about how to grow in endurance and hope as we march to the promised land of God.

   "For whatsoever things were written aforetime were written for our learning, that we through patience and comfort of the scriptures might have hope" (Ro.15:4).

   b. We learn that we must not lust nor set our hearts on evil things as the Israelites did.

   "Now these things were our examples, to the intent we should not lust after evil things, as they also lusted" (1 Cor.10:6).

   c. We learn that any of us can fall into unbelief and rebellion, complaining and grumbling. Even Moses did (Num.20:1-13). This stands as a clear warning to us all: we can arouse God's judgment to strike out against us, just as it did against Moses and the Israelites.

   "Neither be ye idolaters, as *were* some of them; as it is written, The people sat down to eat and drink, and rose up to play. Neither let us commit fornication, as some of them committed, and fell in one day three and twenty thousand. Neither let us tempt Christ, as some of them also tempted, and were destroyed of serpents. Neither murmur ye, as some of them also murmured, and were destroyed of the destroyer. Now all these things happened unto them for ensamples: and they are written for our admonition, upon whom the ends of the world are come" (1 Cor.10:7-11).

---

1 *The Expositor's Bible Commentary*, Vol.2. Frank E. Gaebelein, Editor. (Grand Rapids, MI: Zondervan Publishing House, 1990), p.665, 668.

INTRODUCTION TO NUMBERS

"Wherefore (as the Holy Ghost saith, To day if ye will hear his voice, Harden not your hearts, as in the provocation, in the day of temptation in the wilderness: When your fathers tempted me, proved me, and saw my works forty years. Wherefore I was grieved with that generation, and said, They do alway err in *their* heart; and they have not known my ways. So I sware in my wrath, They shall not enter into my rest.) Take heed, brethren, lest there be in any of you an evil heart of unbelief, in departing from the living God" (Heb.3:7-12).

"While it is said, To day if ye will hear his voice, harden not your hearts, as in the provocation. For some, when they had heard, did provoke: howbeit not all that came out of Egypt by Moses. But with whom was he grieved forty years? *was it* not with them that had sinned, whose carcases fell in the wilderness? And to whom sware he that they should not enter into his rest, but to them that believed not? So we see that they could not enter in because of unbelief. Let us therefore fear, lest, a promise being left *us* of entering into his rest, any of you should seem to come short of it" (Heb.3:15-4:1).

(See Introduction, *Special Features*—Numbers for other doctrinal and spiritual lessons, especially points 1, 3, 7, 11, 12, 13, 14, 15, 16, 17, 18, 19, 21, 23.)

3. The *Christological or Christ-Centered Purpose*: the great Book of Numbers points to Jesus Christ.
   a. Jesus Christ is the fulfillment of the atoning sacrifice. (See outline and notes—Num.6:13-20; 7:10-88; 9:1-14; 21:4-20; 15:1-29; 19:1-22; 21:1-35; 28:1-29:40.)

"The next day John seeth Jesus coming unto him, and saith, Behold the Lamb of God, which taketh away the sin of the world" (Jn.1:29).

"But Christ being come an high priest of good things to come, by a greater and more perfect tabernacle, not made with hands, that is to say, not of this building; Neither by the blood of goats and calves, but by his own blood he entered in once into the holy place, having obtained eternal redemption *for us*. For if the blood of bulls and of goats, and the ashes of an heifer sprinkling the unclean, sanctifieth to the purifying of the flesh: How much more shall the blood of Christ, who through the eternal Spirit offered himself without spot to God, purge your conscience from dead works to serve the living God?" (Heb.9:11-14).

   b. Jesus Christ is the Light of the world as symbolized by the Lampstand. (See outline and notes—Num.8:1-4.)

"In him was life; and the life was the light of men" (Jn.1:4).

"Then spake Jesus again unto them, saying, I am the light of the world: he that followeth me shall not walk in darkness, but shall have the light of life" (Jn.8:12).

"I am come a light into the world, that whosoever believeth on me should not abide in darkness" (Jn.12:46).

   c. Jesus Christ is the coming Deliverer—the great Star and Scepter—who will conquer all enemies and rule over them, sitting upon the very throne of David and of God Himself. (See outline and notes—Num.24:17-19.)

"These things I have spoken unto you, that in me ye might have peace. In the world ye shall have tribulation: but be of good cheer; I have overcome the world" (Jn.16:33).

"For as in Adam all die, even so in Christ shall all be made alive. But every man in his own order: Christ the firstfruits; afterward they that are Christ's at his coming. Then *cometh* the end, when he shall have delivered up the kingdom to God, even the Father; when he shall have put down all rule and all authority and power." (1 Cor.15:22-24).

"To him that overcometh will I grant to sit with me in my throne, even as I also overcame, and am set down with my Father in his throne" (Rev.3:21).

"Of the increase of *his* government and peace *there shall be* no end, upon the throne of David, and upon his kingdom, to order it, and to establish it with judgment and with justice from henceforth even for ever. The zeal of the LORD of hosts will perform this" (Is.9:7; cp. Is.53:12).

"Behold, the days come, saith the LORD, that I will raise unto David a righteous Branch, and a King shall reign and prosper, and shall execute judgment and justice in the earth" (Jer.23:5; cp. Dan.7:14).

SPECIAL FEATURES:

1. Numbers is "A Great Book that Focuses upon the Promised Land of God." What is *the promised land* of God? What is the inheritance God promised to Abraham and his descendants (believers)? What does Scripture say? Because of the importance of the promised land in *Numbers*, the subject is being mentioned here as point 1 of the *Special Features*. But because of the length of the point, it is actually being discussed in point 26 of the *Special Features*.

2. Numbers is "The Great Book on the Believer's Pilgrimage." As the believer marches through this life, he encounters trial after trial and temptation after temptation. Life is full of pitfalls and enemies that oppose his reaching the promised land of God. Numbers takes the pilgrimage of Israel and pictures the believer's pilgrimage through life as he faces trials and temptations, pitfalls and enemies. The subject of the entire book is the pilgrimage of the Israelites as they march to the promised land of God. The very subjects of the outlines of Numbers clearly show this.

3. Numbers is "A Great Book on the History of Salvation." Through trial after trial, this great book shows how God saves His people and leads them to the promised land of God.

4. Numbers is "A Great Book that Covers the Only Acceptable Approach and Worship of God." There is a right way and a wrong way to approach and worship God. This is stressed time and again: the only acceptable way to approach and

worship God is through the atoning sacrifice, a symbol of God's dear Son, the Lord Jesus Christ. (See outline and notes—Num.6:22-27; 7:10-88; 8:1-4; 9:1-14; 15:1-16; 19:1-22; 28:1-29:40.)

5. Numbers is "The Great Book that Distinguishes—Covers the Differences—Between the Priests and the Levites." (See outline and notes—Num.1:47-54; 3:1-51; 8:5-26; 18:1-32; 26:57-62.)

6. Numbers is "The Great Book of Census Records." All together, six census polls were taken:

⇒ There were two major census polls taken of the nation as a whole (see outline and notes—Num.1:1-2:34; 26:1-56).
⇒ There were three census polls taken of the Levites (see outline and notes—Num.3:1-39; 4:21-49; 26:57-62).
⇒ There was one census taken of the firstborn sons of the nation (see outline and note—Num.3:40-51).

7. Numbers is "A Great Book on the Preparation for the March to the Promised Land of God: A Symbol of Heaven and of Spiritual Conquest and Rest." (See outline and notes—Num.1:1-10:36; 26:1-36:13.)

8. Numbers is "The Great Book that Covers the Tragic, Devastating Failure of Israel: The Book that Shows Why People Forfeit Their Right to Enter the Promised Land of God." (See outline and notes—Num.11:1-14:45.)

9. Numbers is "The Great Book that Covers the Long, Difficult *Wilderness Wanderings* of Israel." This is a picture of the *Believer's Pilgrimage* through this world as he prepares to enter the promised land of God. (See outline and notes—Num.1:1-36:13.)

10. Numbers is "The Great Book that Covers the Interesting Story of Balaam, His Donkey, and His Encounters with God." (See outline and notes—Num.22:1-25:18.)

11. Numbers is "A Great Book that Covers the Very Heart of the Nazarite Vow." The Nazarite vow was a very special provision for the person who longed to draw closer to God. (See outline and notes—Num.6:1-27.)

12. Numbers is "The Great Book on Holiness." It demonstrates the utter necessity to live a holy life—a righteous life, a life totally set apart to God. Every chapter either stresses or illustrates the obligation of the believer to live a holy life, a life totally set apart to God.

13. Numbers is "A Great Book of Types, Symbols, and Pictures of God's Dear Son, the Lord Jesus Christ." (See chart on Types, Symbols, and Pictures.) A large number of types are clearly seen, focusing upon such major subjects as these:

⇒ The atoning sacrifice of Jesus Christ as the Savior of the world (see outline and notes—Num.6:13-20; 7:10-88; 9:1-14; 21:4-20; 15:1-29; 19:1-22; 21:1-35; 28:1-29:40).
⇒ The symbol of Christ, the Light of the world (see outline and notes—Num.8:1-4).
⇒ The symbol of Christ as the Coming Deliverer—the great Star and Scepter—who will conquer all enemies and rule over them (see outline and notes—Num.24:17-19).

14. Numbers is "A Book that Reveals the Chilling Reality of God's Justice and Judgment." God chastises and disciplines believers when they sin. Moreover, He condemns and executes judgment upon evil unbelievers who rebel and sin beyond repentance. (See outline and notes—Num.11:1-14:45; 16:1-50; 20:7-13; 21:1-35; 25:1-18.)

15. Numbers is "A Great Book that Demonstrates the Awesome Importance of Intercessory Prayer." Time and again the great prayer warrior Moses is seen interceding for God's mercy in times of terrible stress, and God is seen intervening. God saved His people because of prayer. The lesson is forceful: God hears the desperate cry of those who cry out to Him. Intercession works. (See outline and notes—Num.21:4-20, esp. 7; 11:1-3; 11:4-35; 12:13-16; 13:1-14:45,, esp. 10-25; 16:1-50, esp. 1-15; 20:2-6; 21:4-20, esp. 7; 27:14-17.)

16. Numbers is "The Great Book that Demonstrates the Breathtaking Guidance of God." God guides His people day by day. To teach this wonderful truth, God gave Israel the *pillar of cloud* or the *fiery cloud* by day and by night. This was a cloud that symbolized God's presence. The cloud hung right above the Tabernacle. At night it glowed like fire so the people could see and have a continued, unbroken assurance of God's presence. God guided His people by moving the cloud when it was time for the Israelites to march and by stopping the cloud over a particular spot when it was time for the people to set up camp. (See outline and notes—Num.8.15-23; 10:11-12; 10:33-34; cp. 11:25; 12:5, 10, 14:14; 16:42.)

17. Numbers is "The Great Book that Reveals the Amazing Mercy and Grace of God." Time and again, God had mercy and showered His grace upon His people despite their terrible unbelief and disobedience. He chastised them in order to correct them and to keep them from damaging themselves beyond repair. But in every case, He had mercy and bestowed His grace upon them. He gave them another chance. This He did until they went beyond repentance and repair, went to a point when they would never turn to follow Him wholeheartedly. Up to this point, God had mercy upon them. Numbers is the great book revealing the mercy and grace of God. (Every chapter and every event reveals the mercy and grace of God, but special occasions would be these: Num. 11:1-14:45; 16:1-50; 17:11-13; 19;1-22; 20:2-13; 21:4-9; 21:33-35; 22:1-25:18; 27:12-25; 28:1-29:40; 31:1-54; 33:1-56; 34:1-29; 35:1-34.)

18. Numbers is "The Great Book that Stresses the Word of God." "The Lord spoke" is used over 150 times in twenty-plus ways throughout the book. This fact points strongly to the inspiration of Numbers, that the great book is "God-inspired" (2 Tim.3:16).

19. Numbers is "A Great Book that Shows the Absolute Necessity of Obedience." Disobedience results in judgment. This great book exposes the disobedient heart and behavior of Israel and the judgment that fell upon them. This alone shows the great importance of obedience. But more than this, the positive message of obedience is magnificently demonstrated in the life of Moses and even in the behavior of the Israelites when they were faithful. Practically every page of Numbers stresses obedience. The fact that the people obeyed "just as the Lord commanded" is stated over thirty times.

20. Numbers is "A Great Book that Unfolds the History of Redemption." Every page stresses this one glorious fact: God saves and delivers His people day by day as they march to the promised land of God. He strengthens His dear people to conquer all the trials and enemies of life. He gives them whatever provisions are necessary to reach the destination of the promised land. It is His redemptive power—His salvation and deliverance—that assures the believer's inheritance, the inheritance of heaven, of living eternally with God in the new heavens and earth.

21. Numbers is "One of the Great Books Written as a Strong Warning to People."

INTRODUCTION TO NUMBERS

"For whatsoever things were written aforetime were written for our learning, that we through patience and comfort of the scriptures might have hope" (Ro.15:4).

"Now these things were our examples, to the intent we should not lust after evil things, as they also lusted" (1 Cor.10:6).

"Now all these things happened unto them for ensamples: and they are written for our admonition, upon whom the ends of the world are come" (1 Cor.10:11).

22. Numbers is "The Great Book that Reveals the Overwhelming Patience of God." God is patient, long-suffering. Patience is one of the basic traits of God's character, and He demonstrated His patience time and again with His erring people. There is a verse in Numbers that describes God's patience in descriptive terms. In fact, the verse describes the full nature of God that comes into play when dealing with us:

> **"The LORD *is* longsuffering, and of great mercy, forgiving iniquity and transgression, and by no means clearing *the guilty,* visiting the iniquity of the fathers upon the children unto the third and fourth *generation*" (Num. 14:18.** See *Special Features*, pt.17—*Introduction to Numbers* for more discussion.)

23. Numbers is "The Great Book with an Uninspiring Title." The English name comes from the Greek title of the book (Arithmoi). This title was obviously given to the book because of the census records found throughout (Chapters 1-4, 26). "In the wilderness" is the Hebrew title given to the book, being taken from Chapter 1:5. *Numbers* sounds more like a math book than a spiritual book. Nevertheless, *Numbers* is a very spiritual book, one of the *greatest spiritual books* ever written. It is the history of the believer's pilgrimage upon earth as he marches to the promised land of God and of heaven. Just glance at the major subjects covered by this great book:

I. THE PREPARATION FOR THE MARCH TO THE PROMISED LAND, 1:1-10:36
II. THE TRAGIC, DEVASTATING FAILURE OF ISRAEL: WHY PEOPLE FORFEIT THEIR RIGHT TO ENTER THE PROMISED LAND, 11:1-14:45
III. THEFORTY LONG YEARS OF WILDERNESS WANDERINGS: A PICTURE OF THE BELIEVER'S PILGRIMAGE THROUGH THIS WORLD AS HE PREPARES TO ENTER THE PROMISED LAND, 15:1-25:18
IV. THE PREPARATION FOR THE MARCH TO ENTER THE PROMISED LAND, 26:1-36:13

24. Numbers is "The Great Book that Exposes the Terrible Evil of Unbelief and Rebellion, of Complaining and Grumbling." This was the constant sin of Israel, the sin that led to their tragic, devastating judgment. They were barred from ever entering the promised land of God. They never received their inheritance because of the sins of unbelief and rebellion against God. Even Moses himself lost the right to enter the promised land. Neither he nor the first generation of believers ever knew the spiritual rest and the conquering power of God over the enemies of the promised land. (See outline and notes—Num.11:1-14:45; 16:1-50; 20:2-13; 21:4-20; 25:1-18; 32:1-42; 33:5-49.)

25. Numbers is "A Great Book of Instructive and Practical Laws." Note these subjects:

⇒ The Basic Laws That Keep God's People United and Pure: How God's People Must Live Pure Lives, 5:1-31
⇒ The Special Provision Instituted for Drawing Closer to God—the Nazarite Vow and the Special Benediction of God upon His People: The Importance and Seriousness of Vows, 6:1-27
⇒ Event 1—God Gave Various Laws to Help Govern His People: Being Reassured and Prepared for the Promised Land, 15:1-41
⇒ Event 4—God Spelled Out the Service of the Priests and Levites: The Duties, Support, and Tithing of God's Ministers, 18:1-32
⇒ Event 5—God Gave the Law to Govern the Offering of the Red Heifer and the Cleansing Water: A Symbol of Christ, His Sacrifice and Cleansing Power, 19:1-22
⇒ The Basic Law that Gave Women an Inheritance in the Promised Land: Five Women of Enormous Courage, Faith, and Hope, 27:1-11
⇒ The Offerings and Sacrifices Commanded by the LORD: The Picture of Man's Need to Continually Approach and Worship God through the Atonement Secured by the Sacrifice (a Symbol of God's Dear Son, the LORD Jesus Christ), 28:1-29:40
⇒ The Laws that Govern Vows: The Obligation to Keep Vows and to Consider Others in Making Vows, 30:1-16
⇒ The Women Who Inherited Property: A Picture of Strong Faith in the Promised Land—a Symbol of Spiritual Conquest and Rest and of Heaven, 37:1-13

26. Numbers is "A Great Book that Focuses upon the Promised Land of God." What is *the promised land* of God? What is the inheritance God promised to Abraham and his descendants (believers)? What does Scripture say? As stated earlier, because of the importance of the promised land in *Numbers*, the subject was mentioned as point 1 of the *Special Features*. But because of the length of the point, it is actually being discussed here in point 26.

Scripture teaches that God promised to give Abraham and his descendants the *promised land* of Canaan (Gen.12:1). God actually promised land to Abraham. But note:

⇒ The land was only promised: it lay out in the future; it was not to be immediately possessed. The land was just what believers have called it for centuries, *the promised land*. It was to be the great hope of Abraham. This is the reason the land of Canaan is referred to as *the promised land*.

All Abraham had to go on was the promise of God, on what God had said. Abraham had to step out in faith and believe God's Word—His promise—about *the promised land*. Note several facts about this great promise to Abraham.

a. *The promised land* definitely refers to Palestine, the land of Israel. This is clearly stated by God time and again.

1) Note God's promise to Abraham.

"And Abram passed through the land unto the place of Sichem, unto the plain of Moreh. And the Canaanite was then in the land. And the LORD appeared unto Abram, and said, Unto thy seed will I give this land: and there builded he an altar unto the LORD, who appeared unto him" (Gen.12:6-7).

"And the LORD said unto Abram, after that Lot was separated from him, Lift up now thine eyes, and look from the place where thou art northward, and southward, and eastward, and westward: for all the land which thou seest, to thee will I give it, and to thy seed for ever....Arise, walk through the land in the length of it and in the breadth of it: for I will give it unto thee" (Gen.13:14-15, 17).

"And he said unto him, I am the LORD that brought thee out of Ur of the Chaldees, to give thee this land to inherit it....In the same day the LORD made a covenant with Abram, saying, Unto thy seed have I given this land, from the river of Egypt unto the great river, the river Euphrates: the Kenites, and the Kenizzites, and the Kadmonites, and the Hittites, and the Periozzites, and the Rephaims, and the Amorites, and the Canaanites, and the Girgashites, and the Jebusites" (Gen.15:7, 18-21).

"And I will give unto thee, and to thy seed after thee, the land wherein thou art a stranger, all the land of Canaan, for an everlasting possession: and I will be their God" (Gen.17:8).

2) Note God's promise to Abraham's son, Isaac.

"Sojourn in this land, and I will be with thee, and will bless thee; for unto thee, and unto thy seed, I will give all these countries, and I will perform the oath which I sware unto Abraham thy father" (Gen.26:3).

3) Note God's promise to Abraham's grandson, Jacob.

"And, behold, the LORD stood above it, and said, I am the LORD God of Abraham thy father, and the God of Isaac: the land whereon thou liest, to thee will I give it, and to thy seed" (Gen.28:13).

"And the land which I gave Abraham and Isaac, to thee I will give it, and to thy seed after thee will I give the land" (Gen.35:12).

b. *The promised land* definitely refers to heaven. The promised land of Canaan is a symbol (a type, a picture, an illustration) of heaven, of God's promise to the believer that he will inherit heaven, the new heavens and earth. Note two facts:

1) God's promised land refers to *the whole world*. It is *the whole world* that Abram and believers are to *inherit*.

"For the promise, that he should be the heir of the world, was not to Abraham, or to his seed, through the law, but through the righteousness of faith" (Ro.4:13).

The inheritance of the whole world could only refer to the *new heavens and earth*—the new universe—that God is going to recreate in the end time. It could not refer to a corruptible universe that is deteriorating, wasting away, and running down, that would eventually cease to exist millions of years from now—cease to exist just by the natural process of time. (See outlines and notes—2 Pt.3:1-18 for more discussion.)

"But the day of the Lord will come as a thief in the night; in the which the heavens shall pass away with a great noise, and the elements shall melt with fervent heat, the earth also and the works that are therein shall be burned up. Seeing then that all these things shall be dissolved, what manner of persons ought ye to be in all holy conversation and godliness. Looking for and hasting unto the coming of the day of God, wherein the heavens being on fire shall be dissolved, and the elements shall melt with fervent heat? Nevertheless we, according to his promise, look for new heavens and a new earth, wherein dwelleth righteousness" (2 Pt.3:10-13).

"And I saw a new heaven and a new earth: for the first heaven and the first earth were passed away; and there was no more sea. And I John saw the holy city, new Jerusalem [the capital of the new universe], coming down from God out of heaven, prepared as a bride adorned for her husband. And I heard a great voice out of heaven saying, Behold, the tabernacle of God is with men, and he will dwell with them, and they shall be his people, and God himself shall be with them, and be their God. And God shall wipe away all tears from their eyes; and there shall be no more death, neither sorrow, nor crying, neither shall there be any more pain: for the former things are passed away" (Rev.21:1-4).

"Of old hast thou laid the foundation of the earth: and the heavens are the work of thy hands. They shall perish, but thou shalt endure: yea, all of them shall wax old like a garment; as a vesture shalt thou change them, and they shall be changed: but thou art the same, and thy years shall have no end" (Ps.102:25-27).

"And all the host of heaven shall be dissolved, and the heavens shall be rolled together as a scroll: and all their host shall fall down, as the leaf falleth off from the vine, and as a falling fig from the fig tree" (Is.34:4).

"Lift up your eyes to the heavens, and look upon the earth beneath: for the heavens shall vanish away like smoke, and the earth shall wax old like a garment, and they that dwell therein shall die in like manner: but my salvation shall be for ever, and my righteousness shall not be abolished" (Is.51:6).

"For, behold, I create new heavens and a new earth: and the former shall not be remembered, nor come into mind" (Is.65:17).

"For as the new heavens and the new earth, which I will make, shall remain before me, saith the LORD, so shall your seed and your name remain" (Is.66:22).

2) God's promised land refers to *a* heavenly *country* and *a heavenly city*. It is a heavenly home—a heavenly country and city that are eternal—that Abraham and believers are to inherit. Note how clearly Scripture states this:

"By faith Abraham, when he was called to go out into a place which he should after receive for an inheritance, obeyed; and he went out, not knowing whither he went. By faith he sojourned in the land of promise, as in a strange country, dwelling in tabernacles with Isaac and Jacob, the heirs with him of the same promise: for he looked for a city which hath foundations, whose builder and maker is God....These all died in faith, not having received the promises, but having seen them afar off, and were persuaded of them, and embraced them, and confessed that they were strangers and pilgrims on the earth. For they that say such things declare plainly that they seek a country. And truly, if they had been mindful of that country from whence they came out, they might have had opportunity to have returned. But now they desire a better country, that is, an heavenly: wherefore God is not ashamed to be called their God: for he hath prepared for them a city" (Heb.11:8-10, 13-16).

"But ye are come unto mount Sion, and unto the city of the living God, the heavenly Jerusalem, and to an innumerable company of angels" (Heb.12:22).

"For here have we no continuing city [a perfect heavenly city], but we seek one to come" (Heb.13:14).

"And I John saw the holy city, new Jerusalem, coming down from God out of heaven, prepared as a bride adorned for her husband. And I heard a great voice out of heaven, saying, Behold, the tabernacle of God is with men, and he will dwell with them, and they shall be his people, and God himself shall be with them, and be their God. And God shall wipe away all tears from their eyes; and there shall be no more death, neither sorrow, nor crying, neither shall there be any more pain: for the former things are passed away" (Rev.21:2-4).

"And he carried me away in the spirit to a great and high mountain, and showed me that great city, the holy Jerusalem, descending out of heaven from God" (Rev.21:10).

c. *The promised land* represented many things to Abraham.

1) The promised land was the assurance of *a personal inheritance*: the possession of a new country, of his own property with all its good land, wealth, and rights. Abraham believed that he would live in a new city within his own land and country—all given by God Himself. And the land was to be forever, for it was promised by the eternal God Himself.

Note this, for it is important: Abraham's hope was for a permanent, eternal city and country. True, he was physically journeying all throughout the promised land of Canaan, believing that God was going to give him and his seed (descendents) the land of Canaan. But while he was journeying, his hope was for the permanent, eternal city and country of God. Abraham knew that God's promised land referred to the heavenly as well as to the earthly land. Note how clearly Scripture states this:

⇒ **"For all the land which thou seest, to thee will I give it, and to thy seed for ever" (Gen.13:15).**

God's promise included the eternal, permanent possession of the promised land, and Abraham knew this.

⇒ **"By faith he sojourned in the land of promise, as in a strange country, dwelling in tabernacles with Isaac and Jacob, the heirs with him of the same promise: for he looked for a city which hath foundations, whose builder and maker is God" (Heb.11:9-10).**

This refers to the heavenly Jerusalem, the capital of the new heavens and earth (cp. Heb.12:22; 13:14. See pt.2 above. Also see note—Rev.21:2.)

⇒ **"These all died in faith, not having received the promises, but having seen them afar off, and were persuaded of them, and embraced them, and confessed that they were strangers and pilgrims on the earth. For they that say such things declare plainly that they seek a country. And truly, if they had been mindful of that country from whence they came out, they might have had opportunity to have returned. But now they desire a better country, that is, an heavenly: wherefore God is not ashamed to be called their God: for he hath prepared for them a city" (Heb.11:13-16).**

Note v.15: it clearly states that Abraham's mind was on the heavenly and eternal country. If it had not been, he would have returned to his former home. He would have never wandered about, suffering the hardships he bore.

Thought 1. Note how the promise given to Abraham parallels the promise given to the believer. Abraham was to inherit *the promised land* if he turned away from the world and followed God. We are to inherit *the promised* land *of heaven* if we turn away from the world and follow God. *The promised land* is a symbol, a type, a picture of heaven.

(1) The promise given to Abraham.

"And I will give unto thee, and to thy seed after thee, the land wherein thou art a stranger, all the land of Canaan, for an everlasting possession; and I will be their God" (Gen.17:8).

(2) The promise given to the believer.

"In my Father's house are many mansions: if it were not so, I would have told you. I go to prepare a place for you. And if I go and prepare a place for you, I will come again, and receive you unto myself; that where I am, there ye may be also" (Jn.14:2-3).

"For we know that if our earthly house of this tabernacle were dissolved, we have a building of God, an house not made with hands, eternal in the heavens" (2 Cor.5:1).

"For our conversation [citizenship] is in heaven; from whence also we look for the Saviour, the Lord Jesus Christ: who shall change our vile body, that it may be fashioned like unto his glorious body, according to the working whereby he is able even to subdue all things unto himself" (Ph.3:20-21).

"By faith Abraham, when he was called to go out into a place which he should after receive for an inheritance, obeyed; and he went out, not knowing whither he went. By faith he sojourned in the land of promise, as in a strange country, dwelling in tabernacles with Isaac and Jacob, the heirs with him of the same promise: for he looked for a city which hath foundations, whose builder and maker is God" (Heb.11:8-10).

"These all died in faith, not having received the promises, but having seen them afar off, and were persuaded of them, and embraced them, and confessed that they were strangers and pilgrims on the earth. For they that say such things declare plainly that they seek a country. And truly, if they had been mindful of that country from whence they came out, they might have had opportunity to have returned. But now they desire a better country, that is, an heavenly: wherefore God is not ashamed to be called their God: for he hath prepared for them a city" (Heb.11:13-16).

"Blessed be the God and Father of our Lord Jesus Christ, which according to his abundant mercy hath begotten us again unto a lively hope by the resurrection of Jesus Christ from the dead, to an inheritance incorruptible, and undefiled, and that fadeth not away, reserved in heaven for you, who are kept by the power of God through faith unto salvation ready to be revealed in the last time" (1 Pt.1:3-5).

"Blessed are they that do his commandments, that they may have right to the tree of life, and may enter in through the gates into the city [New Jerusalem]" (Rev.22:14).

2) The promised land was the assurance of *conquest and rest, of spiritual victory and spiritual rest*. The promised land was to bring a God-given peace and security, freedom and liberty, deliverance and salvation to Abraham. The promised land meant victory and rest to Abraham, a God-given victory and rest...

- from having to wander about.
- from never being settled.
- from restlessness.
- from being exposed to all kinds of trials, dangers, threats, attacks, slavery, and bondage that comes from having no settled home within this world, from having no place that is given and protected by God Himself.

To Abraham, the promised land was the assurance of victory and rest, the conquest and triumph over all enemies, a victory and rest that was to be given by God Himself.

Thought 1. Note how the spiritual victory and rest promised to Abraham represents the spiritual rest promised to the believer (see note—Heb.4:1 for more discussion).

(1) The promise given to Abraham.

"And I will make of thee a great nation, and I will bless thee, and make thy name great; and thou shalt be a blessing: and I will bless them that bless thee, and curse him that curseth thee: and in thee shall all families of the earth be blessed" (Gen.12:2-3).

"After these things the word of the LORD came unto Abram in a vision, saying, Fear not, Abram: I am thy shield, and thy exceeding great reward" (Gen.15:1).

"That in blessing I will bless thee, and in multiplying I will multiply thy seed as the stars of the heaven, and as the sand which is upon the sea shore; and thy seed shall possess the gate of his enemies; and in thy seed shall all the nations of the earth be blessed; because thou hast obeyed my voice" (Gen.22:17-18).

(2) The promise given to the believer.

"Take my yoke upon you, and learn of me; for I am meek and lowly in heart: and ye shall find rest unto your souls" (Mt.11:29).

"And I heard a voice from heaven saying unto me, Write, Blessed are the dead which die in the Lord from henceforth: yea, saith the Spirit, that they may rest from their labours; and their works do follow them" (Rev.14:13).

"Let us therefore fear, lest, a promise being left us of entering into his rest, any of you should seem to come short of it. For unto us was the gospel preached, as well as unto them: but the word preached did not profit them, not being mixed with faith in them that heard it. For we which have believed do enter into rest" (Heb.4:1-3).

"Let us labour therefore to enter into that rest, lest any man fall after the same example of unbelief" (Heb.4:11).

"And he said, My presence shall go with thee, and I will give thee rest" (Ex.33:14).

"And I said, Oh that I had wings like a dove! for then would I fly away, and be at rest" (Ps.55:6).

"Return unto thy rest, O my soul; for the LORD hath dealt bountifully with thee" (Ps.116:7).

"To whom he said, This is the rest wherewith ye may cause the weary to rest; and this is the refreshing: yet they would not hear" (Is.28:12).

3) The promised land was the assurance of *God's own presence*, that is, of God's love, care, provision, and protection. Abram was bound to know this: if God was going to give him the promised land, then God must love and care for him. God would therefore provide and protect him no matter what lay ahead. God—His strong presence—would be with him through all the trials and struggles of life.

Thought 1. Abraham's assurance of God's presence symbolizes the believer's experience. The believer can be assured of God's presence: of God's love, care, provision, and protection.

(1) The promise given to Abraham.

"And I will give unto thee, and to thy seed after thee, the land wherein thou art a stranger, all the land of Canaan, for an everlasting possession; and I will be their God" (Gen.17:8).

"And, behold, I am with thee, and will keep thee in all places whither thou goest, and will bring thee again into this land; for I will not leave thee, until I have done that which I have spoken to thee of" (Gen.28:15).

(2) The promise given to the believer.

"When thou goest out to battle against thine enemies, and seest horses, and chariots, and a people more than thou, be not afraid of them: for the LORD thy God is with thee, which brought thee up out of the land of Egypt" (Dt.20:1).

"When thou passest through the waters, I will be with thee; and through the rivers, they shall not overflow thee: when thou walkest through the fire, thou shalt not be burned; neither shall the flame kindle upon thee" (Is.43:2).

"But seek ye first the kingdom of God, and his righteousness; and all these things shall be added unto you" (Mt.6:33).

"Lo, I am with you alway, even unto the end of the world" (Mt.28:20).

"Let your conversation be without covetousness; and be content with such things as ye have: for he hath said, I will never leave thee, nor forsake thee" (Heb.13:5).

ALPHABETICAL INDEX
TYPES, SYMBOLS, AND PICTURES
THE BOOK OF NUMBERS

What is a biblical type or symbol? Simply put, a *biblical type* is a "foreshadowing" of what was to come at a later time in history. Through a person, place or thing a biblical type points toward a New Testament fulfillment.

In addition to biblical types, there are what we may call *biblical pictures*. A biblical picture is a lesson that we can see in the Scriptures *without distorting the truth*. The study of biblical types and pictures is a valuable study in that it helps us apply the truth of the Scriptures in our lives. Scripture itself tells us this:

> **"Now all these things happened unto them for examples: and they are written for our admonition, upon whom the ends of the world are come" (1 Cor.10:11).**
>
> **"For whatsoever things were written aforetime were written for our learning, that we through patience and comfort of the scriptures might have hope" (Ro.15:4).**

For quick and easy reference, every type or picture in Numbers has been alphabetized and cross-referenced with similar subjects. To further assist one's study, Scripture references are also included.

TYPES, SYMBOLS, AND PICTURES ALPHABETICAL INDEX

PERSON/PLACE/THING	SCRIPTURE, OUTLINE, & DISCUSSION
Burned, Wholly: the Red Heifer Was to Be Wholly Burned, All Its Parts	Num.19:1-10, esp. v.5
Burnt Offering, the	Num.6:3-12; 15:1-16; 28:11-15; (see also Lev. 1:1-17; 6:8-13; 8:18-21; 16:24)
Camp, Outside the: Red Heifer Was to Be Put to Death	Num.19:1-10, esp. v.3
Censers	Num.16:36-40
Census of the Firstborn and Their Replacement by the Levites, the (See Firstborn, Census of…)	Num.3:40-51
Cities of Refuge (See Refuge…)	Num.35:9-29
Clean Person Was to Gather Up the Ashes of the Sacrifice and Keep Them In a Clean Place Outside the Camp (See Ashes of the Sacrifice…)	Num.19:1-10, esp. v.9-10
Cleansing of Everyone Who Had Anything to Do with the Sacrifice Had to Cleanse Himself And His Clothes	Num.19:1-10, esp. v.7-8
Cleansing of the Levites	Num.8:5-26
Cleansing Water: Unclean Person Had to Be Purified with the Cleansing Water On the Third And Seventh Days	Num.19:11-16, esp. v.12
Clothes, Tearing of	Num.14:1-10, esp. v.6
Clothes, Washing of the Levites'	Num.8:5-26
Cloud, Pillar of	Num.9:15-23
Coming Deliverer, the (See Deliverer…)	Num.24:14-19
Compromise of Gad and Reuben	Num.32:1-42
Conquest of the Midianites (See Midianites…)	Num.31:1-54
Contact with a Dead Body (See Dead Body…)	Num.6:3-12; (see also Lev. 10:4-5)
Day of Atonement, the	Num.29:7-11; (see also Lev. 16:1-34; Lev.23:27)
Dead Body, Contact with	Num.6:3-12; (see also Lev. 10:4-5)
Death	Num.19:11-16
Death, Contact with: A Person Who Had Been In Contact with Death Defiled the Lord's Tabernacle: He Was to Be Cut Off	Num.19:11-16, esp. v.13
Dedication of the Levites (See Levites….)	Num.8:5-26
Deliverer, Coming the	Num.24:14-19

TYPES, SYMBOLS, AND PICTURES
ALPHABETICAL INDEX

PERSON/PLACE/THING	SCRIPTURE, OUTLINE, & DISCUSSION
Dividing the Inheritance of the Promised Land (See Promised Land, Inheritance of...)	Num.26:53-56
Drink Offering, the	Num.6:13-20; 15:1-16, esp. v.7
Egypt	Num. 3:5-13; 9:1-14; (see also Lev. 11:44-47; 19:33-34)
Everyone Who Had Anything to Do with the Sacrifice Had to Cleanse Himself And His Clothes. (See Cleansing of...)	Num.19:1-10, esp. v.7-8
Fellowship Offering, the Nazarite Burning His Hair (See Nazarite Burning...)	Num.6:13-20
Fellowship or Peace Offering, the (See Peace Offering...)	Num.6:13-20; 15:1-16; (see also Lev. 3:1-17)
Festival of Firstfruits, the (See Firstfruits...)	Num.28:26-31; (see also Lev. 23:9-14)
Festival of Tabernacles or Booths or Shelters, the (See Tabernacles...)	Num.29:12-38; (see also Lev. 23:33-34)
Festival of Trumpets, the (See Trumpets...)	Num.29:1-6; (see also Lev. 23:23-25)
Firstborn, Census of (See Census of the Firstborn...)	Num.3:40-51
Firstfruits	Num.15:17-21
Firstfruits, Festival of	Num.28:26-31; (see also Lev. 23:9-14)
Garments of Aaron: Putting Aaron's Garments on Eleazar	Num.20:23-29
Gathered to His People	Num.20:23-29
Grain Offering	Num.15:1-16; (see also Lev. 2:3)
Great Army of God's People Marched Forth Division by Division—as Commanded (See Army of God...)	Num.10:13-28
Great March to the Promised Land Finally Begins (See March...)	Num.10:11-36
Guilt Offering, the	Num.6:3-12; (see also Lev. 5:14-6:7)
Hair, the Nazarite Burning His (See Nazarite Burning...)	Num.6:13-20
High Priest, the	Num.3:5-13; 4:1-20; (see also Lev.16:3, 6)
Israel	Num.23:1-12
Israel's Shocking Military Error against Midian. (See Israel, Error against...)	Num.31:14-18
Israel, Attack Upon (by the Amorites)	Num.21:21-32
Israel, Error against Midian	Num.31:14-18

TYPES, SYMBOLS, AND PICTURES
ALPHABETICAL INDEX

TYPES, SYMBOLS, AND PICTURES
ALPHABETICAL INDEX

PERSON/PLACE/THING	SCRIPTURE, OUTLINE, & DISCUSSION
Priest Loosening the Woman's Hair, the (See Woman's Hair...)	Num.5:11-31, esp. v.18
Priest, the. the Test to Vindicate the Priest, to Prove That He Was God's Choice	Num.17:2-5
Promised Land, Inheritance of	Num.26:53-56
Promised Land, the	Num.1:1-2:34; 5:1-31; 34:1-15
Putting Aaron's Garments on Eleazar (See Garments of Aaron...)	Num.20:23-29
Red Heifer Was to Be Put to Death Outside the Camp. (See Camp, Outside the...)	Num.19:1-10, esp. v.3
Red Heifer Was to Be Wholly Burned, All Its Parts. (See Burned, Wholly...)	Num.19:1-10, esp. v.5
Red Heifer Was to Have No Defect or Blemish (See Perfection of...)	Num.19:1-10, esp. v.2
Red Heifer, an Unused	Num.19:1-10, esp. v.2
Red Heifer, Offering of the	Num.19:1-22
Red Heifer, Offering of: Was Established as A Permanent Law for Israel and for All Foreigners Among Them.	Num.19:1-10, esp. v.10
Red Heifer: Some Blood of the Red Heifer Was to Be Sprinkled Seven Times at the Front of the Tabernacle. (See Blood Sprinkled Seven Times...)	Num.19:1-10, esp. v.4
Refuge, Cities of	Num.35:9-29
Rest, Spiritual	Num.28:9-10
Shaving of the Levites' Heads	Num.8:5-26
Showbread, the Twelve Loaves of	Num.8:1-4
Sin Offering, the	Num.6:3-12; 28:11-15; (see also Lev. 4:1-5:13. 6:24-30; 8:14-17; 9:2; 9:15; 10:17; 16:3-22)
Skin Disease (See Leprosy...)	Num.5:1-4; 12:13-16; (see also Lev. 13:1-59)
Spoils Taken from the Defeated Enemy	Num.31:25-54
Staff of Aaron	Num.17:6-9
Sunrise on the Tabernacle's Entrance (See Tabernacle, Sunrise on...)	Num.3:14-39
Sweet Aroma, the (See Aroma...)	Num.28:1-2; 28:3-8; (see also Lev. 1:9; 8:21; 16:27-28)
Sword (the) of the Angel of the Lord (See Angel of the Lord...)	Num.22:22-35

TYPES, SYMBOLS, AND PICTURES ALPHABETICAL INDEX

CHRONOLOGICAL INDEX
TYPES, SYMBOLS, AND PICTURES
THE BOOK OF NUMBERS

What is a biblical type or symbol? Simply put, a *biblical type* is a "foreshadowing" of what was to come at a later time in history. Through a person, place or thing a biblical type points toward a New Testament fulfillment.

In addition to biblical types, there are what we may call *biblical pictures*. A biblical picture is a lesson that we can see in the Scriptures *without distorting the truth*. The study of biblical types and pictures is a valuable study in that it helps us apply the truth of the Scriptures in our lives. Scripture itself tells us this:

> **"Now all these things happened unto them for examples: and they are written for our admonition, upon whom the ends of the world are come" (1 Cor.10:11).**
>
> **"For whatsoever things were written aforetime were written for our learning, that we through patience and comfort of the scriptures might have hope" (Ro.15:4).**

PERSON/PLACE/THING	SCRIPTURE, OUTLINE, & DISCUSSION
Promised Land, the	Num.1:1-2:34; 5:1-31; 34:1-15
Tabernacle, the	Num.1:47-54; 4:1-20; (see also Lev.17:3-9)
Egypt	Num.3:5-13; 9:1-14; (see also Lev. 11:44-47; 19:33-34)
High Priest, the	Num.3:5-13; 4:1-20; (see also Lev.16:3, 6)
Sunrise on the Tabernacle's Entrance	Num.3:14-39
Census of the Firstborn and Their Replacement by the Levites, the	Num.3:40-51
Leprosy or Infectious Skin Disease	Num.5:1-4; 12:13-16; (see also Lev. 13:1-59)
Priest Loosening the Woman's Hair, the	Num.5:11-31, esp. v.18
Contact with a Dead Body	Num.6:3-12; (see also Lev. 10:4-5)
Sin Offering, the	Num.6:3-12; 28:11-15; (scc also Lev. 4:1-5:13. 6:24-30; 8:14-17; 9:2; 9:15; 10:17; 16:3-22)
Burnt Offering, the	Num.6:3-12; 15:1-16; 28:11-15; (see also Lev. 1:1-17; 6:8-13; 8:18-21; 16:24)
Guilt Offering, the	Num.6:3-12; (see also Lev. 5:14-6:7)
Nazarite Burning His Hair under the Fellowship Offering	Num.6:13-20
Drink Offering, the	Num.6:13-20; 15:1-16, esp. v.7
Fellowship Offering, the Nazarite Burning His Hair	Num.6:13-20
Fellowship or Peace Offering, the	Num.6:13-20; 15:1-16; (see also Lev. 3:1-17)
Twelve Loaves of Showbread	Num.8:1-4
Lampstand, the	Num.8:1-4; (see also Lev. 24:1-4)

TYPES, SYMBOLS, AND PICTURES
CHRONOLOGICAL INDEX

PERSON/PLACE/THING	SCRIPTURE, OUTLINE, & DISCUSSION
Shaving of the Levites' Heads	Num.8:5-26
Levites Had to be Sprinkled with the Water of Cleansing, Shave Their Whole Heads, and Wash Their Clothes	Num.8:5-26
Cleansing of the Levites	Num.8:5-26
Dedication of the Levites	Num.8:5-26
Passover, the	Num.9:1-14; (see also Lev. 23:5)
Pillar of Cloud.	Num.9:15-23
Great March to the Promised Land Finally Begins	Num.10:11-36
Great Army of God's People Marched Forth Division by Division—as Commanded	Num.10:13-28
Appeal of Moses to His Brother-In-Law to Join the March to the Promised Land	Num10:29-32
Ark or Chest, the	Num.10:33-34; (see also Exodus 25:10-22; 40:20; 35:12; 37:1-5; 39:35; 40:3, 20-21)
Joshua	Num.13:1-25; 27:18
Tearing of Clothes.	Num.14:1-10, esp. v.6
Grain Offering	Num.15:1-16; (see also Lev. 2:3)
Firstfruits	Num.15:17-21
Censers	Num.16:36-40
Test to Vindicate the Priest, to Prove That He Was God's Choice	Num.17:2-5
Aaron's Staff	Num.17:6-9
An Unused Red Heifer	Num.19:1-10, esp. v.2
Red Heifer Was to Have No Defect or Blemish	Num.19:1-10, esp. v.2
Red Heifer Was to Be Put to Death Outside the Camp.	Num.19:1-10, esp. v.3
Blood (of the Red Heifer) Was Sprinkled Seven Times at the Front of the Tabernacle.	Num.19:1-10, esp. v.4
Red Heifer Was to Be Wholly Burned, All Its Parts.	Num.19:1-10, esp. v.5
Priest (the) Was to Burn Some Cedar Wood, Hyssop And Scarlet Wool with the Red Heifer.	Num.19:1-10, esp. v.6
Everyone Who Had Anything to Do with the Sacrifice Had to Cleanse Himself And His Clothes.	Num.19:1-10, esp. v.7-8

TYPES, SYMBOLS, AND PICTURES CHRONOLOGICAL INDEX

TYPES, SYMBOLS, AND PICTURES
CHRONOLOGICAL INDEX

Festival of Firstfruits, the	Num.28:26-31; (see also Lev. 23:9-14)
Festival of Trumpets, the	Num.29:1-6; (see also Lev. 23:23-25)
Day of Atonement, the	Num.29:7-11; (see also Lev. 16:1-34; Lev.23:27)
Festival of Tabernacles or Booths or Shelters, the	Num.29:12-38; (see also Lev. 23:33-34)
Conquest of the Midianites	Num.31:1-54
Israel's Shocking Military Error against Midian.	Num.31:14-18
Spoils Taken from the Defeated Enemy	Num.31:25-54
Compromise of Gad and Reuben	Num.32:1-42
Wilderness Wanderings	Num.33:5-49
Cities of Refuge	Num.35:9-29
Moses	Num.36:13; (see also Lev. 1:1; 8:1-5)

OUTLINE OF NUMBERS

THE PREACHER'S OUTLINE & SERMON BIBLE® is *unique*. It differs from all other Study Bibles & Sermon Resource Materials in that every Passage and Subject is outlined right beside the Scripture. When you choose any *Subject* below and turn to the reference, you have not only the Scripture, but you discover the Scripture and Subject *already outlined for you—verse by verse*.

For a quick example, choose one of the subjects below and turn over to the Scripture, and you will find this marvelous help for faster, easier, and more accurate use.

In addition, every point of the Scripture and Subject is *fully developed in a Commentary with supporting Scripture* at the bottom of the page. Again, this arrangement makes sermon preparation much easier and faster.

Note something else: The Subjects of Numbers have titles that are both Biblical and *practical*. The practical titles sometimes have more appeal to people. This *benefit* is clearly seen for use on billboards, bulletins, church newsletters, etc.

A suggestion: For the *quickest* overview of Numbers, first read *all the major titles* (I, II, III, etc.), then come back and read the subtitles.

OUTLINE OF NUMBERS

PART I: THE FIRST GENERATION OF ISRAELITES OR BELIEVERS

I. THE PREPARATION FOR THE MARCH TO THE PROMISED LAND, 1:1-10:36

A. The Organization of Israel—the First Census: Mobilizing God's People for the March to the Promised Land, 1:1-2:34
B. The Organization of the Priests, the Levites, and the Firstborn—the Second and Third Census Records: Called to Be Assistants, 3:1-51
C. The Organization of the Mature Levites and Their Duties—the Fourth Census: Knowing One's Job and Doing It, 4:1-49
D. The Basic Laws That Keep God's People United and Pure: God's People Must Live Pure Lives, 5:1-31
E. The Special Provision Instituted for Drawing Closer to God—the Nazarite Vow and the Special Benediction of God: The Importance and Seriousness of Vows, 6:1-27
F. The Spontaneous Offerings at the Dedication of the Tabernacle: Supporting God's Work and Approaching Him Exactly as He Says, 7:1-89
G. The Placement of the Lampstand and the Setting Apart of the Levites to Serve God: Standing Forth as Lights and Servants of God, 8:1-26
H. The Three Special Provisions of God: God's Great Deliverance, His Guidance, and His Call to Arise and Follow Him, 9:1-10:10
I. The Great March to the Promised Land Finally Begins: A Picture of the Believer Finally Beginning His March to the Promised Land of Heaven, 10:11-36

II. THE TRAGIC, DEVASTATING FAILURE OF ISRAEL: WHY PEOPLE FORFEIT THEIR RIGHT TO ENTER THE PROMISED LAND, 11:1-14:45

A. The First Tragic Failure Seen in the People: Distrusting God—Complaining and Grumbling, Craving and Lusting, 11:1-35
B. The Second Tragic Failure Seen in Two Leaders, Miriam and Aaron: Distrusting God—Criticizing and Questioning the Call of God's Servant, 12:1-16
C. The Final Tragic Failure that Dooms the People—the Twelve Spies and Their Mixed Report: Distrusting God—Being Negative, Fearful, and Defeated, Disbelieving and Rebelling against God, 13:1-14:45

III. THE FORTY LONG YEARS OF WILDERNESS WANDERINGS: A PICTURE OF THE BELIEVER'S PILGRIMAGE THROUGH THIS WORLD AS HE PREPARES TO ENTER THE PROMISED LAND 15:1-25:18

A. Event 1—God Gave Various Laws to Help Govern His People: Being Reassured and Prepared for the Promised Land, 15:1-41
B. Event 2: A Dangerous Rebellion by Korah and His Allies: God Judges All Grumbling and Unbelief, All Rebellion and Unauthorized Approaches, 16:1-50
C. Event 3—The Budding of Aaron's Staff: The Test to Vindicate God's Priest and His Ministry (a Symbol of Christ or of the Minister), 17:1-13
D. Event 4—God Spelled Out the Service of the Priests and Levites: The Duties, Support, and Tithing of God's Ministers, 18:1-32

E. Event 5—God Gave the Law to Govern the Offering of the Red Heifer and the Cleansing Water: A Symbol of Christ, His Sacrifice and Cleansing Power, 19:1-22
F. Event 6—the Last Year of Israel in the Wilderness: Five Sad Events, 20:1-29
G. Event 7—the First Military Victories and the Bronze Snake: A Picture of Desperate Vows, of Christ the Savior, and of God's Protection and Victory, 21:1-35
H. Event 8—the Story of Balaam, His Donkey, and His Three Encounters with God (Part 1): A Picture of the Unseen, Unknown Attempts by the Powers of Darkness to Defeat God's People, 22:1-41
I. Event 9—the Story of Balaam and the Seven Startling Oracles or Prophecies Pronounced by Him: The Blessings of God and a Glimpse into the Future, 23:1-24:25
J. Event 10: The Ultimate Rebellion of God's People and the End of the Forty Years of Wilderness Wanderings: Apostasy—Turning to Worldliness, to the Worship of Sex and Other Gods, 25:1-18

PART II: THE SECOND GENERATION OF ISRAELITES OR BELIEVERS

IV. THE PREPARATION FOR THE MARCH INTO THE PROMISED LAND, 26:1-36:13

A. The Organization of the Second Generation—the Second Nationwide Census: Mobilizing God's People to Enter and Inherit the Promised Land, 26:1-65
B. The Basic Law that Gave Women an Inheritance in the Promised Land: Five Women of Enormous Courage, Faith, and Hope, 27:1-11
C. The Appointment of Joshua as the Successor to Moses: A Strong Picture of God Preparing the Believer for Death, 27:12-23
D. The Offerings and Sacrifices Commanded by the Lord: A Picture of Man's Need to Continually Approach and Worship God through the Atonement Secured by the Sacrifice (a Symbol of God's Dear Son, the Lord Jesus Christ), 28:1-29:40
E. The Laws that Govern Vows: The Obligation to Keep Vows and to Consider Others in Making Vows, 30:1-16
F. The Conquest of the Most Dangerous and Threatening Enemies, the Midianites: A Picture of Conquering the Seductive, Immoral Enemies of the World, 31:1-54
G. The Settlement East of the Jordan River: A Picture of Compromise, Selfishness, Covetousness, Disloyalty, and Half-Hearted Commitment, 32:1-42
H. The Review of the Wilderness Wanderings and a Strong Charge to Take Possession of the Promised Land: A Picture of God's Faithfulness and Man's Failure, 33:1-56
I. The Boundaries of Canaan, the Promised Land: The Great Gift and Assurance of God—His People Will Inherit the Promised Land, 34:1-29
J. The Inheritance of the Levites and the Cities of Refuge: The Provision of God for His Ministers and for All Who Need Refuge from the Storms and Threats of Life, 35:1-34
K. The Women Who Inherited Property: A Picture of Strong Faith in the Promised Land of God, 36:1-13

DIVISION I

THE PREPARATION FOR THE MARCH TO THE PROMISED LAND, 1:1-10:36

(1:1—10:36) **DIVISION OVERVIEW—Wilderness Wanderings, Overview of—Israel, Wilderness Wanderings of—Numbers, Book of, Title**: *Numbers*—what an unappealing, uninteresting title. *Numbers* sounds more like a math book than a spiritual journey. Yet, this is exactly what this great book is: one of the greatest spiritual journeys ever taken by a body of believers.

Numbers is the spiritual journey (pilgrimage) of Israel as they marched to the promised land of God. There are actually two generations of Israelites dealt with throughout this journey. The first generation of Israelites were those who had been delivered from the slavery of Egypt (a symbol of the world). To these believers God gave the great principles necessary for inheriting the promised land of God—if they would just follow God with their whole hearts. (See outline and note—Ex.19:5-9; Deeper Study # 1—Ex.19:5-6 for more discussion.)

The first generation is seen preparing and beginning their journey to the promised land with great excitement and joy. But they soon develop a terrible spirit of unbelief and rebellion, complaining and grumbling. Consequently, the judgment of God falls. They are condemned to wander about in the desert for forty long, exhausting years, wander about until they all die (all except Joshua and Caleb). They are barred from the promised land, never to receive the glorious inheritance promised by God.

The second generation of Israelites were the sons and daughters of the parents who had sinned so terribly. Only the adults twenty years old or older were judged and condemned to die in the desert wilderness. All the children were spared. It was these—the second generation of believers—whom God prepared to enter the promised land. He used the forty years of wilderness wanderings to teach, strengthen, discipline, and toughen the children so they would be spiritually prepared to enter the promised land and claim the glorious inheritance promised by God. Their history is covered in the last ten chapters (26:1-35:13).

The history of the first generation is vividly pictured in the first twenty-five chapters (1:1-25:18). The great book of *Numbers* opens with the first generation preparing for their march to the promised land. Excitement and joy—a sense of adventure, anticipation, and hope—flood their hearts. They are about to embark on the most wonderful journey of their lives, to receive the glorious inheritance of the promised land of God Himself.

THE PREPARATION FOR THE MARCH TO THE PROMISED LAND, 1:1-10:36

G. The Placement of the Lampstand and the Setting Apart of the Levites to Serve God: Standing Forth as Lights and Servants of God, 8:1-26

H. The Three Special Provisions of God: Acknowledging God's Great Deliverance, His Guidance, and His Call to Arise and Follow Him, 9:1-10:10

I. The Great March to the Promised Land Finally Begins: A Picture of the Believer Finally Beginning His March to the Promised Land of Heaven, 10:11-36

THE FOURTH BOOK OF MOSES, CALLED NUMBERS

CHAPTER 1

I. THE PREPARATION FOR THE MARCH TO THE PROMISED LAND, 1:1-10:36

A. The Organization of Israel—the First Census: Mobilizing God's People for the March to the Promised Land, 1:1-2:34

1. The strong emphasis: "The LORD spoke"—guided, directed His people (statement used over 150 times in 20 plus ways)
   a. Spoke in the Tent of Meeting
   b. Spoke in the desert wilderness
   c. Spoke 13 months after the deliverance from Egyptian slavery

2. The military census: The people of God must prepare for warfare
   a. To take a census of all Israelites: Listing every man by name
   b. To identify all men able to serve in the army—20 years old & above

3. The selection of leaders: Some must be willing to serve as leaders
   a. Tribe of Reuben: Elizur
   b. Tribe of Simeon: Shelumiel
   c. Tribe of Judah: Nahshon
   d. Tribe of Issachar: Nethanel
   e. Tribe of Zebulun: Eliab
   f. Tribe from Joseph
      1) Tribe of Ephraim: Elishama
      2) Tribe of Manasseh: Gamaliel
   g. Tribe of Benjamin: Abidan
   h. Tribe of Dan: Ahiezer
   i. Tribe of Asher: Pagiel
   j. Tribe of Gad: Eliasaph
   k. Tribe of Naphtali: Ahira
   l. These were the tribal leaders, the chiefs or heads of the clans of Israel

And the LORD spake unto
Moses in the wilderness
of Sinai, in the tabernacle of
the congregation, on the first
day of the second month,
in the second year after they
were come out of the land
of Egypt, saying,
2 Take ye the sum of all the
congregation of the children
of Israel, after their families,
by the house of their fathers,
with the number of their
names, every male by their
polls;
3 From twenty years old and
upward, all that are able to
go forth to war in Israel: thou
and Aaron shall number
them by their armies.
4 And with you there shall be
a man of every tribe; every
one head of the house of his
fathers.
5 And these are the names of
the men that shall stand with
you: of the tribe of Reuben;
Elizur the son of Shedeur.
6 Of Simeon; Shelumiel the
son of Zurishaddai.
7 Of Judah; Nahshon the son
of Amminadab.
8 Of Issachar; Nethaneel the
son of Zuar.
9 Of Zebulun; Eliab the son
of Helon.
10 Of the children of Joseph:
of Ephraim; Elishama
the son of Ammihud: of
Manasseh; Gamaliel the son
of Pedahzur.
11 Of Benjamin; Abidan the
son of Gideoni.
12 Of Dan; Ahiezer the son
of Ammishaddai.
13 Of Asher; Pagiel the son
of Ocran.
14 Of Gad; Eliasaph the son
of Deuel.
15 Of Naphtali; Ahira the
son of Enan.
16 These were the renowned of the congregation,
princes of the tribes of their
fathers, heads of thousands
in Israel.
17 And Moses and Aaron
took these men which are
expressed by their names:
18 And they assembled all
the congregation together on
the first day of the second
month, and they declared
their pedigrees after their
families, by the house of
their fathers, according to the
number of the names, from
twenty years old and
upward, by their polls.
19 As the LORD commanded
Moses, so he numbered them
in the wilderness of Sinai.
20 And the children of
Reuben, Israel's eldest son,
by their generations, after
their families, by the house
of their fathers, according to
the number of the names, by
their polls, every male from
twenty years old and
upward, all that were able to
go forth to war;
21 Those that were numbered of them, even of the
tribe of Reuben, were forty
and six thousand and five
hundred.
22 Of the children of
Simeon, by their generations, after their families, by
the house of their fathers,
those that were numbered of
them, according to the number of the names, by their
polls, every male from twenty years old and upward, all
that were able to go forth to
war;
23 Those that were numbered of them, even of the
tribe of Simeon, were fifty
and nine thousand and three
hundred.
24 Of the children of Gad,
by their generations, after
their families, by the house
of their fathers, according to
the number of the names,
from twenty years old and
upward, all that were able to
go forth to war;
25 Those that were numbered of them, even of the
tribe of Gad, were forty and
five thousand six hundred
and fifty.
26 Of the children of Judah,
by their generations, after
their families, by the house
of their fathers, according to
the number of the names,

4. The results of the census: Every believer must believe God & serve in the army of God
   a. The leaders compiling the census
      1) All men 20 years old or older were listed by name, one by one
      2) The census was taken just as the LORD commanded in the Desert of Sinai
   b. The number of men from each tribe who were able to serve in the army
      1) The tribe of Reuben: 46,500
      2) The tribe of Simeon: 59,300
      3) The tribe of Gad: 45,650
      4) The tribe of Judah: 74,600

from twenty years old and upward, all that were able to go forth to war;
27 Those that were numbered of them, even of the tribe of Judah, were threescore and fourteen thousand and six hundred.

5) The tribe of Issachar: 54, 400

28 Of the children of Issachar, by their generations, after their families, by the house of their fathers, according to the number of the names, from twenty years old and upward, all that were able to go forth to war;
29 Those that were numbered of them, even of the tribe of Issachar, were fifty and four thousand and four hundred.

6) The tribe of Zebulun: 57,400

30 Of the children of Zebulun, by their generations, after their families, by the house of their fathers, according to the number of the names, from twenty years old and upward, all that were able to go forth to war;
31 Those that were numbered of them, even of the tribe of Zebulun, were fifty and seven thousand and four hundred.

7) The tribe of Ephraim: 40, 500

32 Of the children of Joseph, namely, of the children of Ephraim, by their generations, after their families, by the house of their fathers, according to the number of the names, from twenty years old and upward, all that were able to go forth to war;
33 Those that were numbered of them, even of the tribe of Ephraim, were forty thousand and five hundred.

8) The tribe of Manasseh: 32,200

34 Of the children of Manasseh, by their generations, after their families, by the house of their fathers, according to the number of the names, from twenty years old and upward, all that were able to go forth to war;
35 Those that were numbered of them, even of the tribe of Manasseh, were thirty and two thousand and two hundred.

9) The tribe of Benjamin: 35,400

36 Of the children of Benjamin, by their generations, after their families, by the house of their fathers, according to the number of the names, from twenty years old and upward, all that were able to go forth to war;
37 Those that were numbered of them, even of the tribe of Benjamin, were thirty and five thousand and four hundred.

10) The tribe of Dan: 62,700

38 Of the children of Dan, by their generations, after their families, by the house of their fathers, according to the number of the names, from twenty years old and upward, all that were able to go forth to war;
39 Those that were numbered of them, even of the tribe of Dan, were threescore and two thousand and seven hundred.

11) The tribe of Asher: 41,500

40 Of the children of Asher, by their generations, after their families, by the house of their fathers, according to the number of the names, from twenty years old and upward, all that were able to go forth to war;
41 Those that were numbered of them, even of the tribe of Asher, were forty and one thousand and five hundred.

12) The tribe of Naphtali: 53,400

42 Of the children of Naphtali, throughout their generations, after their families, by the house of their fathers, according to the number of the names, from twenty years old and upward, all that were able to go forth to war;
43 Those that were numbered of them, even of the tribe of Naphtali, were fifty and three thousand and four hundred.

c. The accuracy & total of the men
   1) The men were counted by Moses & Aaron & the twelve leaders of Israel
   2) The men were counted by families

44 These are those that were numbered, which Moses and Aaron numbered, and the princes of Israel, being twelve men: each one was for the house of his fathers.
45 So were all those that were numbered of the children of Israel, by the house of their fathers, from twenty years old and upward, all that were able to go forth to war in Israel;

   3) The total number: 603,550

46 Even all they that were numbered were six hundred thousand and three thousand and five hundred and fifty.

5. The setting apart of the

47 But the Levites after the

Levites to the sacred task of the Tabernacle: Some must serve God in special ministries

a. They were excluded from the military

b. They were placed in charge of the Tabernacle
   1) In charge of materials & furnishings
   2) In charge of transporting it
   3) In charge of taking it down & erecting it

c. They were in charge of protecting the Tabernacle: To execute anyone who went near, profaned, or plundered it (a symbol of the church)

d. They were to camp around the Tabernacle
   1) To set their tents by divisions with each man under his own standard
   2) The purpose:
      • To prevent God's wrath from falling upon the people due to their neglect of the Tabernacle & their allowing it to be abused or robbed
      • To teach people to approach God with fear & reverence

6. The placement of the Tabernacle in the center of the camp: All must know that God dwells in the midst of His people & guides them as they march to the promised land

7. The placement of the tribes around the Tabernacle, each man under his banner: Each believer must take his place under the standard of Christ & stand fast under the banner of God's family

a. On the east:
   1) The division of Judah
      • The leader: Nahshon
      • Division number: 74,600

tribe of their fathers were not
numbered among them.
48 For the LORD had spoken
unto Moses, saying,
49 Only thou shalt not number the tribe of Levi, neither
take the sum of them among
the children of Israel:
50 But thou shalt appoint
the Levites over the tabernacle of testimony, and over all
the vessels thereof, and over
all things that belong to it:
they shall bear the tabernacle, and all the vessels thereof; and they shall minister
unto it, and shall encamp
round about the tabernacle.
51 And when the tabernacle
setteth forward, the Levites
shall take it down: and when
the tabernacle is to be
pitched, the Levites shall set
it up: and the stranger that
cometh nigh shall be put to
death.
52 And the children of
Israel shall pitch their tents,
every man by his own camp,
and every man by his own
standard, throughout their
hosts.
53 But the Levites shall
pitch round about the tabernacle of testimony, that there
be no wrath upon the congregation of the children of
Israel: and the Levites shall
keep the charge of the tabernacle of testimony.
54 And the children of
Israel did according to all
that the LORD commanded
Moses, so did they.

CHAPTER 2

And the LORD spake unto
Moses and unto Aaron, saying,
2 Every man of the children
of Israel shall pitch by his
own standard, with the
ensign of their father's
house: far off about the tabernacle of the congregation
shall they pitch.
3 And on the east side
toward the rising of the sun
shall they of the standard of
the camp of Judah pitch
throughout their armies: and
Nahshon the son of Ammi-
nadab shall be captain of the
children of Judah.
4 And his host, and those
that were numbered of them,
were threescore and fourteen
thousand and six hundred.
5 And those that do pitch
next unto him shall be the
tribe of Issachar: and
Nethaneel the son of Zuar
shall be captain of the children of Issachar.
6 And his host, and those
that were numbered thereof,
were fifty and four thousand
and four hundred.
7 Then the tribe of Zebulun:
and Eliab the son of Helon
shall be captain of the children of Zebulun.
8 And his host, and those
that were numbered thereof,
were fifty and seven thousand and four hundred.
9 All that were numbered in
the camp of Judah were an
hundred thousand and
fourscore thousand and six
thousand and four hundred,
throughout their armies.
These shall first set forth.
10 On the south side shall
be the standard of the camp
of Reuben according to their
armies: and the captain of
the children of Reuben shall
be Elizur the son of Shedeur.
11 And his host, and those
that were numbered thereof,
were forty and six thousand
and five hundred.
12 And those which pitch
by him shall be the tribe of
Simeon: and the captain of
the children of Simeon shall
be Shelumiel the son of
Zurishaddai.
13 And his host, and those
that were numbered of them,
were fifty and nine thousand
and three hundred.
14 Then the tribe of Gad:
and the captain of the sons of
Gad shall be Eliasaph the
son of Reuel.
15 And his host, and those
that were numbered of them,
were forty and five thousand
and six hundred and fifty.
16 All that were numbered
in the camp of Reuben were
an hundred thousand and
fifty and one thousand and
four hundred and fifty,
throughout their armies. And
they shall set forth in the second rank.
17 Then the tabernacle of
the congregation shall set
forward with the camp of the
Levites in the midst of the
camp: as they encamp, so
shall they set forward, every

   2) The division of Issachar
      • The leader: Nethanel
      • Division number: 54,400
   3) The division of Zebulun
      • The leader: Eliab
      • Division number: 57,400
   4) The total of the three divisions: 186,400
   5) The marching position: In the forefront—to lead the way

b. On the south
   1) The division of Reuben
      • The leader: Elizur
      • Division number: 46,500
   2) The division of Simeon
      • The leader: Shelumiel
      • Division number 59, 300
   3) The division of Gad
      • The leader: Eliasaph
      • Division number: 45,650
   4) The total of three divisions: 151,450
   5) The marching position: Second in line

c. In the center: The Tabernacle & the Levites—marched in the same order as they camped

d. On the west
   1) The division of Ephraim
      • The leader: Elishama
      • Division number: 40,500
   2) The division of Manasseh
      • The leader: Gamaliel
      • Division number: 32,200
   3) The division of Benjamin
      • The leader: Abidan
      • Division number: 35,400
   4) The total of the these divisions: 108,100
   5) The marching position: Third in line
e. On the north
   1) The division of Dan
      • The leader: Ahiezer
      • Division number: 62,700

man in his place by their standards.

18 On the west side shall be the standard of the camp of Ephraim according to their armies: and the captain of the sons of Ephraim shall be Elishama the son of Ammihud.

19 And his host, and those that were numbered of them, were forty thousand and five hundred.

20 And by him shall be the tribe of Manasseh: and the captain of the children of Manasseh shall be Gamaliel the son of Pedahzur.

21 And his host, and those that were numbered of them, were thirty and two thousand and two hundred.

22 Then the tribe of Benjamin: and the captain of the sons of Benjamin shall be Abidan the son of Gideoni.

23 And his host, and those that were numbered of them, were thirty and five thousand and four hundred.

24 All that were numbered of the camp of Ephraim were an hundred thousand and eight thousand and an hundred, throughout their armies. And they shall go forward in the third rank.

25 The standard of the camp of Dan shall be on the north side by their armies: and the captain of the children of Dan shall be Ahiezer the son of Ammishaddai.

26 And his host, and those that were numbered of them, were threescore and two thousand and seven hundred.

27 And those that encamp by him shall be the tribe of Asher: and the captain of the children of Asher shall be Pagiel the son of Ocran.

28 And his host, and those that were numbered of them, were forty and one thousand and five hundred.

29 Then the tribe of Naphtali: and the captain of the children of Naphtali shall be Ahira the son of Enan.

30 And his host, and those that were numbered of them, were fifty and three thousand and four hundred.

31 All they that were numbered in the camp of Dan were an hundred thousand and fifty and seven thousand and six hundred. They shall go hindmost with their standards.

32 These are those which were numbered of the children of Israel by the house of their fathers: all those that were numbered of the camps throughout their hosts were six hundred thousand and three thousand and five hundred and fifty.

33 But the Levites were not numbered among the children of Israel; as the LORD commanded Moses.

34 And the children of Israel did according to all that the LORD commanded Moses: so they pitched by their standards, and so they set forward, every one after their families, according to the house of their fathers.

   2) The division of Asher
      • The leader: Pagiel
      • Division number: 41,500
   3) The division of Naphtali
      • The leader: Ahira
      • Division number: 53,400
   4) The total of the three divisions: 157,600
   5) The marching position: Fourth in line
f. The accuracy & total of the men
   1) The way they were counted: By families
   2) The total numbered: 603,550
   3) The Levites were not counted

8. The obedience of God's people: Every believer must do everything God commands
   a. They camped as God commanded
   b. They marched as God commanded

DIVISION I

THE PREPARATION FOR THE MARCH TO THE PROMISED LAND, 1:1-10:36

A. The Organization of Israel—the First Census: Mobilizing God's People for the March to the Promised Land, 1:1-2:34

(1:1-2:34) **Introduction—Promised Land—Enemies, of Believers, List of—Pitfalls, List of—Believers, Need of, Other Believers—Mobilization, of Believers—Believers, Described as, Army—Enemies, of Life—Enemies, Victory over**: the promised land is the great hope of the believer. As the believer marches through this world, he is to be ever pressing on to the promised land of God. What is the promised land? What is the great hope God has given to the believer? The promised land means at least two things:

- First, the promised land means conquest and rest. It means conquering all the enemies, trials, and temptations of this life. It also means spiritual rest, learning to rest in God—to be free from all the guilt and anxiety, loneliness and emptiness, sin and shame of this world. As stated, the promised land means conquest and rest. It means being victorious over all the enemies of life and possessing spiritual rest, the rest of God Himself (see *Special Features*, pt.26—Introduction to Numbers for more discussion).
- Second, the promised land means heaven itself, living forever in the eternal presence of God—in the new heavens and earth (2 Pt.3:10-13; Rev.21:1-4; Is.65:17; 66:22).

NUMBERS 1:1-2:34

Throughout life, the believer is to stay focused upon the promised land of heaven. He is to march forth day by day, keeping his eyes focused upon the great hope God has given. But as he marches, he must realize one fact: he cannot march alone. He does not live in a vacuum. He is not alone on the earth. He needs to walk side by side with other believers. Mobilization is needed. Believers must be mobilized as they walk together throughout this life.

Life is filled with pitfalls and enemies, enemies that will attack and destroy us unless we are mobilized, prepared to conquer them. What pitfalls and what enemies?

There are pitfalls such as...

- greed
- covetousness
- materialism
- humanism
- pornography
- lust
- illicit sex
- lying
- stealing
- cheating
- anger
- malice
- idolatry
- unbelief
- murmuring
- complaining
- gluttony

There are enemies such as...

- those who ridicule and persecute
- those who oppose and create problems
- those who hate and despise
- those who abuse and assault
- those who are lawless and violent
- those who are murderers and war-mongers
- those who are selfish and hoarding
- those who are mean-spirited and spiteful
- those who are wicked and evil
- those who seek to destroy

The list could go on and on. The pitfalls and enemies against the believer are innumerable. This is the reason the believer must stand with other believers, mobilized together with them as they all march to the promised land of heaven. The believer can never stand alone and be victorious. He can never triumph over the pitfalls and enemies of this life alone. He must stand with other believers, stand in the church of the living God, stand mobilized with God's people to march forth to the promised land of God, heaven itself.

This is the subject of this passage. It shows how God mobilized His people (the Israelites) to march forth to the promised land. By mobilizing them, God gave us a picture of the church. He has shown us how to mobilize the church—all believers together—in order to be victorious over the pitfalls and enemies of this life. He has shown us how to mobilize as we march together—side by side—to the promised land of God. Note the outline points, how God tells us to mobilize: *The Organization of Israel—the First Census: Mobilizing God's People for the March to the Promised Land*, 1:1-2:34.

1. The strong emphasis: "The LORD spoke"—guided, directed His people (statement used over 150 times in 20 plus ways) (v.1).
2. The military census: the people of God must prepare for warfare (v.2-3).
3. The selection of leaders: some must be willing to serve as leaders (v.4-16).
4. The results of the census: every believer must believe God and serve in the army of God (v.17-46).
5. The setting apart of the Levites to the sacred task of the Tabernacle: some must serve God in special ministries (v.47-54).
6. The placement of the Tabernacle in the center of the camp: all must know that God dwells in the midst of His people and guides them as they march to the promised land (Ch.6:1-2).
7. The placement of the tribes around the Tabernacle, each man under his banner: each believer must take his place under the standard of Christ and stand fast under the banner of God's family (v.2-33).
8. The obedience of God's people: every believer must do everything God commands (v.34).

1 (1:1) **Word of God, Purpose—Guidance, of God—Leadership, of God**: there was the strong emphasis, "The LORD spoke" to His people. That is, He gave instructions, guided and directed His people as they marched to the promised land of God. This statement, "The LORD spoke," is used over 150 times in twenty plus ways in the Book of Numbers alone. This fact points strongly to the inspiration of Numbers, that the book is "God-breathed" (2 Tim.3:16). God guided His people by speaking to Moses and by having Moses declare His Word to the people.

OUTLINE	SCRIPTURE
1. The strong emphasis: "The LORD spoke"—guided, directed His people (statement used over 150 times in 20 plus ways) a. Spoke in the Tent of Meeting b. Spoke in the desert wilderness c. Spoke 13 months after the deliverance from Egyptian slavery	And the LORD spake unto Moses in the wilderness of Sinai, in the tabernacle of the congregation, on the first day of the second month, in the second year after they were come out of the land of Egypt, saying,

God is the Great Communicator. God communicates with His people in the same way that men communicate with men, by word of mouth. As stated, God spoke to Moses, and Moses declared God's Word to the people. God's Word—His speaking to men—is one of the great proofs that He is the living and true God. Other gods are mute, silent—never speaking directly to men. They are false gods. Note where and when God spoke.

1. God spoke to Moses in the Tent of Meeting. This refers to "the tabernacle" (v.51) or to "the tabernacle of the Testimony" (v.50, 53). The Tabernacle was the worship center of that day (see Exodus, Chapters 25-40 for more discussion). The meaning of the word "tabernacle" (miskan) means dwelling. It was the very dwelling place of God Himself, a symbol of His very presence. It was, therefore, only natural that God would meet Moses and speak with him in the Tabernacle or Tent of Meeting.

2. God spoke with Moses in the desert or wilderness. The Israelites were still camped at the foot of Mt. Sinai. It was while the people were in the wilderness that God confronted and spoke with Moses.

3. God spoke thirteen months after the deliverance of His people from Egyptian slavery. Note this: God's people had been camped at the foot of Mt. Sinai for thirteen months (Ex.19:1). During the thirteen months—just a little more than one year—God had given His people the law, led them to construct the Tabernacle, and formed them into a great nation of people. Only one thing remained to be done before they could begin their march to the promised land: they must be mobilized and organized into a great army of people for God. Remember, the population of the Israelites was over two to three million at this time. They could not march and survive through the desert wilderness as vagabonds, as a loosely knit, drifting group of people with little bands of people wandering off, moving about as they wished. Organization and mobilization were necessary. This was the reason God was now meeting with Moses, to give him guidance and direction in mobilizing the people.

Thought 1. God speaks to us. He guides and directs us day by day. God loves us and wants us to conquer all the pitfalls and enemies of this life. As we march toward the promised land of heaven...
⇒ God will meet and speak with us *in the church.*
⇒ God will meet and speak with us *in the desert or wilderness.*

No matter where we are, God will meet and speak with us. We simply have to be available, as Moses was. We need to get alone in the church or out in the desert or wilderness to seek the face of God. We need to ask God to meet and speak with us, to guide and direct us. When we seek God, He meets and speaks to us.

"He shall call upon me, and I will answer him: I *will be* with him in trouble; I will deliver him, and honour him" (Ps.91:15).

"Then shalt thou call, and the LORD shall answer; thou shalt cry, and he shall say, Here I *am.* If thou take away from the midst of thee the yoke, the putting forth of the finger, and speaking vanity..." (Is.58:9).

"And it shall come to pass, that before they call, I will answer; and while they are yet speaking, I will hear" (Is.65:24).

"Call unto me, and I will answer thee, and show thee great and mighty things, which thou knowest not" (Jer.33:3).

"And I say unto you, Ask, and it shall be given you; seek, and ye shall find; knock, and it shall be opened unto you" (Lk.11:9).

"If ye abide in me, and my words abide in you, ye shall ask what ye will, and it shall be done unto you" (Jn.15:7).

"All scripture *is* given by inspiration of God, and *is* profitable for doctrine, for reproof, for correction, for instruction in righteousness" (2 Tim.3:16).

"For this God *is* our God for ever and ever: he will be our guide *even* unto death" (Ps.48:14).

"Thou shalt guide me with thy counsel, and afterward receive me *to* glory" (Ps.73:24).

"And thine ears shall hear a word behind thee, saying, This *is* the way, walk ye in it, when ye turn to the right hand, and when ye turn to the left" (Is.30:21).

"Howbeit when he, the Spirit of truth, is come, he will guide you into all truth: for he shall not speak of himself; but whatsoever he shall hear, *that* shall he speak: and he will show you things to come" (Jn.16:13).

2 (1:2-3) **Israel, Census of—Military, Census of—Warfare, Spiritual—Spiritual Warfare—Census, of Israel**: there was the military census. The people of God had to be prepared for warfare as they marched to the promised land.

OUTLINE	SCRIPTURE
2. The military census: The people of God must prepare for warfare a. To take a census of all Israelites: Listing every man by name	2 Take ye the sum of all the congregation of the children of Israel, after their families, by the house of their fathers, with the number of their names, every male by their polls;
b. To identify all men able to serve in the army—20 years old & above	3 From twenty years old and upward, all that are able to go forth to war in Israel: thou and Aaron shall number them by their armies.

They were to take a census of all Israelites. Note that every man was to be listed by name, one by one. Every man twenty years old or older was to be identified and mobilized to serve in the army. No person was allowed to opt out, not if he was physically fit and able. To refuse to serve in God's army was a great sin, bringing severe judgment (Num.14:1f; Dt.20:3-4). Every able-bodied man had to serve and was expected to fight against the enemies of God's people.

Thought 1. Believers must be prepared for warfare as they march to the promised land. Why? Because we are in a spiritual warfare. We do not wrestle against flesh and blood, but against principalities and powers and spiritual wickedness in high places. The spiritual pitfalls and enemies of life seek to captivate and destroy every one of us. We must, therefore, be mobilized and prepared for warfare. How can we be prepared? By putting on the whole armor of God. This is exactly what God declares in His holy Word.

"Finally, my brethren, be strong in the LORD, and in the power of his might. Put on the whole armour of God, that ye may be able to stand against the wiles of the devil. For we wrestle not against flesh and blood, but against principalities, against powers, against the rulers of the darkness of this world, against spiritual wickedness in high *places*. Wherefore take unto you the whole armour of God, that ye may be able to withstand in the evil day, and having done all, to stand. Stand therefore, having your loins girt about with truth, and having on the breastplate of righteousness; And your feet shod with the preparation of the gospel of peace; Above all, taking the shield of faith, wherewith ye shall be able to quench all the fiery darts of the wicked. And take the helmet of salvation, and the sword of the Spirit, which is the word of God: Praying always with all prayer and supplication in the Spirit, and watching thereunto with all perseverance and supplication for all saints" (Eph.6:10-18).

"Thou therefore endure hardness, as a good soldier of Jesus Christ. No man that warreth entangleth himself with the affairs of *this* life; that he may please him who hath chosen him to be a soldier" (2 Tim.2:3-4).

"Fight the good fight of faith, lay hold on eternal life, whereunto thou art also called, and hast professed a good profession before many witnesses" (1 Tim.6:12).

"(For the weapons of our warfare *are* not carnal, but mighty through God to the pulling down of strong holds)" (2 Cor.10:4).

"This charge I commit unto thee, son Timothy, according to the prophecies which went before on thee, that thou by them mightest war a good warfare" (1 Tim.1:18).

3 (1:4-16) **Leaders, Appointment of—Leadership, Appointment of—Leaders, Willingness to Serve—Church, Leadership of—Church, Need of**: there was the selection of leaders. Some of the people had to be willing to serve as leaders.

OUTLINE	SCRIPTURE	SCRIPTURE	OUTLINE
3. The selection of leaders: Some must be willing to serve as leaders	4 And with you there shall be a man of every tribe; every one head of the house of his fathers.	son of Ammihud: of Manasseh; Gamaliel the son of Pedahzur.	Elishama 2) Tribe of Manasseh: Gamaliel
a. Tribe of Reuben: Elizur	5 And these are the names of the men that shall stand with you: of the tribe of Reuben; Elizur the son of Shedeur.	11 Of Benjamin; Abidan the son of Gideoni.	g. Tribe of Benjamin: Abidan
b. Tribe of Simeon: Shelumiel	6 Of Simeon; Shelumiel the son of Zurishaddai.	12 Of Dan; Ahiezer the son of Ammishaddai.	h. Tribe of Dan: Ahiezer
c. Tribe of Judah: Nahshon	7 Of Judah; Nahshon the son of Amminadab.	13 Of Asher; Pagiel the son of Ocran.	i. Tribe of Asher: Pagiel
d. Tribe of Issachar: Nethanel	8 Of Issachar; Nethaneel the son of Zuar.	14 Of Gad; Eliasaph the son of Deuel.	j. Tribe of Gad: Eliasaph
e. Tribe of Zebulun: Eliab	9 Of Zebulun; Eliab the son of Helon.	15 Of Naphtali; Ahira the son of Enan.	k. Tribe of Naphtali: Ahira
f. Tribe from Joseph 1) Tribe of Ephraim:	10 Of the children of Joseph: of Ephraim; Elishama the	16 These were the renowned of the congregation, princes of the tribes of their fathers, heads of thousands in Israel.	l. These were the tribal leaders, the chiefs or heads of the clans of Israel

God told Moses to select one man from each tribe to help him in taking the census (v.4). These men were to be the leaders of each tribe, men who were to serve as the assistants to Moses. They were his partners in the ministry of mobilizing the people. The point to see is their willingness to serve. They were willing to serve both as the leaders of the tribes and in this particular ministry of mobilizing the people.

Thought 1. Some people must step forth as leaders. Leaders are desperately needed as God's people march to the promised land of heaven. Leaders are needed to guide God's people, to protect them from the pitfalls and enemies of this life. The church of God needs leaders, people who step forth and proclaim loudly and clearly, "I will help. I will accept the position. I will take the leadership role. I will give guidance to those who need direction."

"Go ye therefore, and teach all nations, baptizing them in the name of the Father, and of the Son, and of the Holy Ghost: Teaching them to observe all things whatsoever I have commanded you: and, lo, I am with you alway, *even* unto the end of the world. Amen" (Mt.28:19-20).

"Also I heard the voice of the LORD, saying, Whom shall I send, and who will go for us? Then said I, Here *am* I; send me" (Is.6:8).

"But rise, and stand upon thy feet: for I have appeared unto thee for this purpose, to make thee a minister and a witness both of these things which thou hast seen, and of those things in the which I will appear unto thee" (Acts 26:16).

"For we are labourers together with God" (1 Cor.3:9).

"Jesus saith unto them, My meat is to do the will of him that sent me, and to finish his work" (Jn.4:34).

"Be not thou therefore ashamed of the testimony of our LORD, nor of me his prisoner: but be thou partaker of the afflictions of the gospel according to the power of God" (2 Tim.1:8).

"And the things that thou hast heard of me among many witnesses, the same commit thou to faithful men, who shall be able to teach others also. Thou therefore endure hardness, as a good soldier of Jesus Christ" (2 Tim.2:2-3).

4 (1:17-46) **Census, of Israel—Israel, Census of—Service, Duty of—Ministry, Duty of—Army, of God—Military, of God**: there were the results of the census. Every believer was to believe God and serve in the army of God.

OUTLINE	SCRIPTURE	SCRIPTURE	OUTLINE
4. The results of the census: Every believer must believe God & serve in the army of God a. The leaders compiling the census 1) All men 20 years old or older were listed by name, one by one	17 And Moses and Aaron took these men which are expressed by their names: 18 And they assembled all the congregation together on the first day of the second month, and they declared their pedigrees after their families, by the house of their fathers, according to the number of the names, from twenty years old and upward, by their polls.	by their generations, after their families, by the house of their fathers, according to the number of the names, from twenty years old and upward, all that were able to go forth to war; 25 Those that were numbered of them, even of the tribe of Gad, were forty and five thousand six hundred and fifty.	
2) The census was taken just as the LORD commanded in the Desert of Sinai	19 As the LORD commanded Moses, so he numbered them in the wilderness of Sinai.	26 Of the children of Judah, by their generations, after their families, by the house of their fathers, according to the number of the names, from twenty years old and upward, all that were able to go forth to war; 27 Those that were numbered of them, even of the tribe of Judah, were threescore and fourteen thousand and six hundred.	4) The tribe of Judah: 74,600
b. The number of men from each tribe who were able to serve in the army 1) The tribe of Reuben: 46,500	20 And the children of Reuben, Israel's eldest son, by their generations, after their families, by the house of their fathers, according to the number of the names, by their polls, every male from twenty years old and upward, all that were able to go forth to war; 21 Those that were numbered of them, even of the tribe of Reuben, were forty and six thousand and five hundred.	28 Of the children of Issachar, by their generations, after their families, by the house of their fathers, according to the number of the names, from twenty years old and upward, all that were able to go forth to war; 29 Those that were numbered of them, even of the tribe of Issachar, were fifty and four thousand and four hundred.	5) The tribe of Issachar: 54, 400
2) The tribe of Simeon: 59,300	22 Of the children of Simeon, by their generations, after their families, by the house of their fathers, those that were numbered of them, according to the number of the names, by their polls, every male from twenty years old and upward, all that were able to go forth to war; 23 Those that were numbered of them, even of the tribe of Simeon, were fifty and nine thousand and three hundred.	30 Of the children of Zebulun, by their generations, after their families, by the house of their fathers, according to the number of the names, from twenty years old and upward, all that were able to go forth to war;	6) The tribe of Zebulun: 57,400
3) The tribe of Gad: 45,650	24 Of the children of Gad,	31 Those that were num-	

OUTLINE	SCRIPTURE	SCRIPTURE	OUTLINE
	bered of them, even of the tribe of Zebulun, were fifty and seven thousand and four hundred.	upward, all that were able to go forth to war; 39 Those that were numbered of them, even of the tribe of Dan, were threescore and two thousand and seven hundred.	
7) The tribe of Ephraim: 40, 500	32 Of the children of Joseph, namely, of the children of Ephraim, by their generations, after their families, by the house of their fathers, according to the number of the names, from twenty years old and upward, all that were able to go forth to war; 33 Those that were numbered of them, even of the tribe of Ephraim, were forty thousand and five hundred.	40 Of the children of Asher, by their generations, after their families, by the house of their fathers, according to the number of the names, from twenty years old and upward, all that were able to go forth to war; 41 Those that were numbered of them, even of the tribe of Asher, were forty and one thousand and five hundred.	11) The tribe of Asher: 41,500
8) The tribe of Manasseh: 32,200	34 Of the children of Manasseh, by their generations, after their families, by the house of their fathers, according to the number of the names, from twenty years old and upward, all that were able to go forth to war; 35 Those that were numbered of them, even of the tribe of Manasseh, were thirty and two thousand and two hundred.	42 Of the children of Naphtali, throughout their generations, after their families, by the house of their fathers, according to the number of the names, from twenty years old and upward, all that were able to go forth to war; 43 Those that were numbered of them, even of the tribe of Naphtali, were fifty and three thousand and four hundred.	12) The tribe of Naphtali: 53,400
9) The tribe of Benjamin: 35,400	36 Of the children of Benjamin, by their generations, after their families, by the house of their fathers, according to the number of the names, from twenty years old and upward, all that were able to go forth to war; 37 Those that were numbered of them, even of the tribe of Benjamin, were thirty and five thousand and four hundred.	44 These are those that were numbered, which Moses and Aaron numbered, and the princes of Israel, being twelve men: each one was for the house of his fathers.	c. The accuracy & total of the men 1) The men were counted by Moses & Aaron & the twelve leaders of Israel
		45 So were all those that were numbered of the children of Israel, by the house of their fathers, from twenty years old and upward, all that were able to go forth to war in Israel;	2) The men were counted by families
10) The tribe of Dan: 62,700	38 Of the children of Dan, by their generations, after their families, by the house of their fathers, according to the number of the names, from twenty years old and	46 Even all they that were numbered were six hundred thousand and three thousand and five hundred and fifty.	3) The total number: 603,550

Note that the number of men able to fight were listed tribe by tribe. As stated, every man was to be listed in a register by name, identifying him as a legitimate member of his particular tribe (v.2). A record of each individual was to be very important when they reached the promised land. Each tribe was to receive so much of the promised land as an inheritance from God. And within each tribe, every individual family was to receive a certain inheritance. It was critical, therefore, to know one's lineage or ancestry, that one belonged to a particular tribe. Every person had to be registered, had to have his name written in the book of God's people in order to receive his share of the promised land.

Note the total number of men twenty years old and older: 603,550 (v.46). No doubt, this meant a population of two to four million, depending upon how many children were figured for each family. What a strong declaration of God's faithfulness! He was fulfilling His promise to Abraham...

- that He would bless Abraham with a great nation of people
- that He would send through the descendants of Abraham the promised seed of the Messiah, the Savior of the world
- that He would use Abraham's descendants to bless the world—to be His people, His missionary force and witnesses upon the earth (see outline and notes—Gen. 12:1-3)

NUMBERS 1:1-2:34

Note that the census was begun on the very day that God commanded it to be taken (v.1, 18). A deep sense of God's faithfulness to His people is immediately seen by glancing at the total number of fighting men within each tribe (twenty years old or older). Note the following chart:

⇒	Reuben	*46,500*	⇒	Ephraim	*40,500*
⇒	Simeon	*59,300*	⇒	Manasseh	*32,200*
⇒	Gad	*45,650*	⇒	Benjamin	*35,400*
⇒	Judah	*74,600*	⇒	Dan	*62,700*
⇒	Issachar	*54,400*	⇒	Asher	*41,500*
⇒	Zebulun	*57,400*	⇒	Naphtali	*53,400*
				TOTAL:	***603,550***

Thought 1. There are three strong lessons in this passage:

1) Every believer must believe God. He must be registered in the Book of Life and claim God and the family of God as his lineage and ancestry. He will never reach the promised land of God unless he believes God. God keeps a register, a Book of Life, in which the name of every true believer is written.

"Notwithstanding in this rejoice not, that the spirits are subject unto you; but rather rejoice, because your names are written in heaven" (Lk.10:20).

"He that overcometh, the same shall be clothed in white raiment; and I will not blot out his name out of the book of life, but I will confess his name before my Father, and before his angels" (Rev. 3:5).

"And I saw the dead, small and great, stand before God; and the books were opened: and another book was opened, which is *the book* of life: and the dead were judged out of those things which were written in the books, according to their works" (Rev. 20:12).

"And there shall in no wise enter into it any thing that defileth, neither *whatsoever* worketh abomination, or *maketh* a lie: but they which are written in the Lamb's book of life" (Rev. 21:27).

"And if any man shall take away from the words of the book of this prophecy, God shall take away his part out of the book of life, and out of the holy city, and *from* the things which are written in this book" (Rev. 22:19).

"Yet now, if thou wilt forgive their sin—; and if not, blot me, I pray thee, out of thy book which thou hast written. And the LORD said unto Moses, Whosoever hath sinned against me, him will I blot out of my book" (Ex.32:32-33).

"The LORD shall count, when he writeth up the people, that this man was born there. Selah" (Ps.87:6).

"And it shall come to pass, *that he that is* left in Zion, and *he that* remaineth in Jerusalem, shall be called holy, *even* every one that is written among the living in Jerusalem" (Is.4:3).

"And at that time shall Michael stand up, the great prince which standeth for the children of thy people: and there shall be a time of trouble, such as never was since there was a nation *even* to that same time: and at that time thy people shall be delivered, every one that shall be found written in the book" (Dan.12:1).

"Then they that feared the LORD spake often one to another: and the LORD hearkened, and heard *it*, and a book of remembrance was written before him for them that feared the LORD, and that thought upon his name" (Mal.3:16).

2) Every believer must serve in the army of God. He must demonstrate that he truly believes in God by fighting against the enemies of life and the enemies of God. He must be in a constant battle against the evil and lawlessness of this world, against the greed and lust of the wicked.

"The night is far spent, the day is at hand: let us therefore cast off the works of darkness, and let us put on the armour of light" (Ro.13:12).

"For we wrestle not against flesh and blood, but against principalities, against powers, against the rulers of the darkness of this world, against spiritual wickedness in high *places*" (Eph.6:12).

"Fight the good fight of faith, lay hold on eternal life, whereunto thou art also called, and hast professed a good profession before many witnesses" (1 Tim.6:12).

"Thou therefore endure hardness, as a good soldier of Jesus Christ. No man that warreth entangleth himself with the affairs of *this* life; that he may please him who hath chosen him to be a soldier" (2 Tim.2:3-4).

"Be sober, be vigilant; because your adversary the devil, as a roaring lion, walketh about, seeking whom he may devour" (1 Pt.5:8).

"But let us, who are of the day, be sober, putting on the breastplate of faith and love; and for an helmet, the hope of salvation" (1 Th.5:8).

3) God is faithful. He fulfills His promises to His people.

"Know therefore that the LORD thy God, he *is* God, the faithful God, which keepeth covenant and mercy with them that love him and keep his commandments to a thousand generations" (Dt.7:9).

"Blessed *be* the LORD, that hath given rest unto his people Israel, according to all that he promised:

there hath not failed one word of all his good promise, which he promised by the hand of Moses his servant" (1 Ki.8:56).

"Thy mercy, O LORD, *is* in the heavens; *and* thy faithfulness *reacheth* unto the clouds" (Ps.36:5).

"God *is* faithful, by whom ye were called unto the fellowship of his Son Jesus Christ our LORD" (1 Cor.1:9).

"That by two immutable things, in which *it was* impossible for God to lie, we might have a strong consolation, who have fled for refuge to lay hold upon the hope set before us" (Heb.6:18).

"Wherefore let them that suffer according to the will of God commit the keeping of their souls *to him* in well doing, as unto a faithful Creator" (1 Pt.4:19).

5 (1:47-54) **Levites, Duty of—Tabernacle, Protection of—Laymen, Duties of—Church, Duties of Laymen Within**: there was the setting apart of the Levites to the sacred task of the Tabernacle. Some of God's people had to serve God in special ministries. The Levites were appointed for the spiritual service of the Tabernacle, as helpers or assistants to the priests.

OUTLINE	SCRIPTURE	SCRIPTURE	OUTLINE
5. The setting apart of the Levites to the sacred task of the Tabernacle: Some must serve God in special ministries a. They were excluded from the military b. They were placed in charge of the Tabernacle 1) In charge of materials & furnishings 2) In charge of transporting it 3) In charge of taking it down & erecting it c. They were in charge of pro-	47 But the Levites after the tribe of their fathers were not numbered among them. 48 For the LORD had spoken unto Moses, saying, 49 Only thou shalt not number the tribe of Levi, neither take the sum of them among the children of Israel: 50 But thou shalt appoint the Levites over the tabernacle of testimony, and over all the vessels thereof, and over all things that belong to it: they shall bear the tabernacle, and all the vessels thereof; and they shall minister unto it, and shall encamp round about the tabernacle. 51 And when the tabernacle setteth forward, the Levites shall take it down: and when	the tabernacle is to be pitched, the Levites shall set it up: and the stranger that cometh nigh shall be put to death. 52 And the children of Israel shall pitch their tents, every man by his own camp, and every man by his own standard, throughout their hosts. 53 But the Levites shall pitch round about the tabernacle of testimony, that there be no wrath upon the congregation of the children of Israel: and the Levites shall keep the charge of the tabernacle of testimony. 54 And the children of Israel did according to all that the LORD commanded Moses, so did they.	tecting the Tabernacle: To execute anyone who went near, profaned, or plundered it (a symbol of the church) d. They were to camp around the Tabernacle 1) To set their tents by divisions with each man under his own standard 2) The purpose: • To prevent God's wrath from falling upon the people due to their neglect of the Tabernacle & their allowing it to be abused or robbed • To teach people to approach God with fear & reverence

1. The Levites were excluded from the military (v.49). Why? Because they were the ones in charge of the spiritual service of the Tabernacle. They were not, therefore, included in the military census just taken.

2. The Levites were placed in charge of the Tabernacle itself. They were in charge of all the materials and furnishings and everything else that belonged to the Tabernacle. Moreover, they were in charge of taking the Tabernacle down, transporting it, and erecting it at the new campsites.

3. The Levites were in charge of protecting the Tabernacle (v.51). They were to execute any unauthorized person who went near the Tabernacle, any who profaned or plundered it.

4. The Levites were to camp around the Tabernacle (v.52-53). They were the protectors of the Tabernacle; therefore, they had to camp close by to keep it from being plundered, robbed, abused, or profaned. There were certain preparations that had to be made for a person to approach the Tabernacle. The Levites had to make sure that no one approached it unprepared. It was their duty to keep God's wrath from falling upon the people because of some neglect or because someone came unprepared. It was their duty to teach the people to approach God with fear and reverence. *The Expositor's Bible Commentary* makes the point that God's presence was both a blessing and a curse:

- a blessing for all those who approached God with reverence and respect
- a curse for all those who approached God without respect or reverence[1]

Thought 1. The Levites were appointed to a very special ministry among God's people. There are always special ministries, special needs that must be met. The church needs people to step forth and accept the challenge of these special ministries.

Just think of the needs existing within every community of the world...

- the needs of the orphans, widows, and widowers
- the needs of the prisoners, broken-hearted, and backslidden
- the needs of the diseased, suffering, and hospitalized
- the needs of the hungry, thirsty, and poor
- the needs of the empty, lonely, and purposeless
- the needs of the lost, dying, and doomed

1 *The Expositor's Bible Commentary*, Vol.2. Frank E. Gaebelein, Editor, p. 711.

Some people need to step forth and accept the challenge. Dedication and commitment are needed. The special needs of the world must be met.

"The Spirit of the LORD is upon me, because he hath anointed me to preach the gospel to the poor; he hath sent me to heal the brokenhearted, to preach deliverance to the captives, and recovering of sight to the blind, to set at liberty them that are bruised" (Lk.4:18).

"Even as the Son of man came not to be ministered unto, but to minister, and to give his life a ransom for many" (Mt.20:28).

"Then shall the King say unto them on his right hand, Come, ye blessed of my Father, inherit the kingdom prepared for you from the foundation of the world: For I was an hungred, and ye gave me meat: I was thirsty, and ye gave me drink: I was a stranger, and ye took me in: Naked, and ye clothed me: I was sick, and ye visited me: I was in prison, and ye came unto me" (Mt.25:34-36).

"Whosoever will be great among you, shall be your minister: And whosoever of you will be the chiefest, shall be servant of all" (Mk.10:43-44).

"If I then, *your* LORD and Master, have washed your feet; ye also ought to wash one another's feet" (Jn.13:14).

"He saith to him again the second time, Simon, *son* of Jonas, lovest thou me? He saith unto him, Yea, LORD; thou knowest that I love thee. He saith unto him, Feed my sheep" (Jn.21:16).

"Bear ye one another's burdens, and so fulfil the law of Christ" (Gal.6:2).

"As we have therefore opportunity, let us do good unto all *men,* especially unto them who are of the household of faith" (Gal.6:10).

"And whosoever shall give to drink unto one of these little ones a cup of cold *water* only in the name of a disciple, verily I say unto you, he shall in no wise lose his reward" (Mt.10:42).

"With good will doing service, as to the LORD, and not to men" (Eph.6:7).

"Charge them that are rich in this world, that they be not highminded, nor trust in uncertain riches, but in the living God, who giveth us richly all things to enjoy; That they do good, that they be rich in good works, ready to distribute, willing to communicate" (1 Tim.6:17-18).

6 (2:1-2) **Tabernacle, Placement of—Guidance, of God—Promised Land**: there was the placement of the Tabernacle in the center of the camp. The people were to know one supreme fact: God dwells in the midst of His people and guides them as they march to the promised land. (Pictures of *The Tabernacle, The Encampment of the Tribes,* and *The Marching Positions of the Tribes* are being placed at the end of this commentary.)

OUTLINE	SCRIPTURE
6. The placement of the Tabernacle in the center of the camp: All must know that God dwells in the midst of His people & guides them as they march to the promised land	And the LORD spake unto Moses and unto Aaron, saying, 2 Every man of the children of Israel shall pitch by his own standard, with the ensign of their father's house: far off about the tabernacle of the congregation shall they pitch.

The relationship of God to His people is the stress here. The Tabernacle sat right in the middle of the camp with all the tribes placed equally around it. The picture was that of a square formation: three tribes were placed on each of the four sides of the Tabernacle, some distance from it. The point is this: the presence of God—the Tabernacle—sat right in the midst of His people. God was equally present to help any and all. He was equally present to guide any and all. One person could reach God as easily as the next person. God was available, right in the midst of His people. And He would be available until they reached the promised land. This was to be His permanent position: the Tabernacle was always to sit in the midst of the people.

Thought 1. God dwells in the midst of His people; He dwells in the midst of the church. He is always available to help and guide His people. This is the strong declaration of Scripture.
1) God guides His people.

"He maketh me to lie down in green pastures: he leadeth me beside the still waters" (Ps.23:2).

"The meek will he guide in judgment: and the meek will he teach his way" (Ps.25:9).

"For this God *is* our God for ever and ever: he will be our guide *even* unto death" (Ps.48:14).

"Thou shalt guide me with thy counsel, and afterward receive me *to* glory" (Ps.73:24).

"And thine ears shall hear a word behind thee, saying, This *is* the way, walk ye in it, when ye turn to the right hand, and when ye turn to the left" (Is.30:21).

"And I will bring the blind by a way *that* they knew not; I will lead them in paths *that* they have not known: I will make darkness light before them, and crooked things straight. These things will I do unto them, and not forsake them" (Is.42:16).

"To give light to them that sit in darkness and *in* the shadow of death, to guide our feet into the way of peace" (Lk.1:79).

"Howbeit when he, the Spirit of truth, is come, he will guide you into all truth: for he shall not speak of himself; but whatsoever he shall hear, *that* shall he speak: and he will show you things to come" (Jn.16:13).

2) God is our helper.

"So that we may boldly say, The LORD *is* my helper, and I will not fear what man shall do unto me" (Heb.13:6).

"And, behold, I *am* with thee, and will keep thee in all *places* whither thou goest, and will bring thee again into this land; for I will not leave thee, until I have done *that* which I have spoken to thee of" (Gen.28:15).

"The LORD *is* my strength and my shield; my heart trusted in him, and I am helped: therefore my heart greatly rejoiceth; and with my song will I praise him" (Ps.28:7).

"For the LORD loveth judgment, and forsaketh not his saints; they are preserved for ever: but the seed of the wicked shall be cut off" (Ps.37:28).

"But I *am* poor and needy; *yet* the LORD thinketh upon me: thou *art* my help and my deliverer; make no tarrying, O my God" (Ps.40:17).

"Be merciful unto me, O God, be merciful unto me: for my soul trusteth in thee: yea, in the shadow of thy wings will I make my refuge, until *these* calamities be overpast" (Ps.57:1).

"Fear thou not; for I *am* with thee: be not dismayed; for I *am* thy God: I will strengthen thee; yea, I will help thee; yea, I will uphold thee with the right hand of my righteousness" (Is.41:10).

"And *even* to *your* old age I *am* he; and *even* to hoar [gray] hairs will I carry *you:* I have made, and I will bear; even I will carry, and will deliver *you"* (Is.46:4).

"And he said, My presence shall go *with thee,* and I will give thee rest" (Ex.33:14).

"When thou passest through the waters, I *will be* with thee; and through the rivers, they shall not overflow thee: when thou walkest through the fire, thou shalt not be burned; neither shall the flame kindle upon thee" (Is.43:2).

Thought 2. One thing makes the church advance: giving God and His Word the prominent place in the midst of His people. The church has to listen to God—pay attention to His Word—in order to be guided and blessed by God. God guides and blesses only those who listen to Him, only those who follow His instructions and walk in the direction He points. The church that follows God's Word...

- is the church that marches forth like a mighty army, victorious and triumphant over the enemies of the world
- is the conquering church that conquers all the pitfalls and enemies of the world

"Now ye are clean through the word which I have spoken unto you" (Jn.15:3).

"Sanctify them through thy truth: thy word is truth" (Jn.17:17).

"But these are written, that ye might believe that Jesus is the Christ, the Son of God; and that believing ye might have life through his name" (Jn.20:31).

"For I am not ashamed of the gospel of Christ: for it is the power of God unto salvation to every one that believeth; to the Jew first, and also to the Greek" (Ro.1:16).

"All scripture *is* given by inspiration of God, and *is* profitable for doctrine, for reproof, for correction, for instruction in righteousness" (2 Tim.3:16).

"For the word of God *is* quick, and powerful, and sharper than any twoedged sword, piercing even to the dividing asunder of soul and spirit, and of the joints and marrow, and *is* a discerner of the thoughts and intents of the heart" (Heb.4:12).

"As newborn babes, desire the sincere milk of the word, that ye may grow thereby" (1 Pt.2:2).

"Wherewithal shall a young man cleanse his way? by taking heed *thereto* according to thy word" (Ps.119:9).

"Thy word *is* a lamp unto my feet, and a light unto my path" (Ps.119:105).

"The entrance of thy words giveth light; it giveth understanding unto the simple" (Ps.119:130).

"For the commandment *is* a lamp; and the law *is* light; and reproofs of instruction *are* the way of life" (Pr.6:23).

"*Is* not my word like as a fire? saith the LORD; and like a hammer *that* breaketh the rock in pieces? (Jer.23:29).

7 (2:2-33) **Tabernacle, Placement of—Standing Fast—Perseverance—Family of God—Church—Relationships—God, Presence of**: there was placement of the tribes around the Tabernacle, each man under his banncr. The lesson of this point is striking: each believer must take his place under the standard of Christ and stand fast under the banner of God's family. (See pictures of *The Encampment of the Tribes* and *The Tabernacle*—Num.2:2-33, notes 9-10.)

OUTLINE	SCRIPTURE	SCRIPTURE	OUTLINE
7. The placement of the tribes around the Tabernacle, each man under his banner: Each believer must take his place under the standard of Christ & stand fast under the ban-	2 Every man of the children of Israel shall pitch by his own standard, with the ensign of their father's house: far off about the tabernacle of the congregation	shall they pitch. 3 And on the east side toward the rising of the sun shall they of the standard of the camp of Judah pitch throughout their armies: and	**ner of God's family** a. On the east: 1) The division of Judah • The leader: Nahshon

NUMBERS 1:1-2:34

OUTLINE

- Division number: 74,600

2) The division of Issachar
- The leader: Nethanel
- Division number: 54,400

3) The division of Zebulun
- The leader: Eliab
- Division number: 57,400

4) The total of the three divisions: 186,400

5) The marching position: In the forefront—to lead the way

b. On the south

1) The division of Reuben
- The leader: Elizur
- Division number: 46,500

2) The division of Simeon
- The leader: Shelumiel
- Division number 59, 300

3) The division of Gad
- The leader: Eliasaph
- Division number: 45,650

4) The total of three divisions: 151,450

5) The marching position:

SCRIPTURE

Nahshon the son of
Amminadab shall be captain
of the children of Judah.
4 And his host, and those
that were numbered of them,
were threescore and fourteen
thousand and six hundred.
5 And those that do pitch
next unto him shall be the
tribe of Issachar: and
Nethaneel the son of Zuar
shall be captain of the children of Issachar.
6 And his host, and those
that were numbered thereof,
were fifty and four thousand
and four hundred.
7 Then the tribe of Zebulun:
and Eliab the son of Helon
shall be captain of the children of Zebulun.
8 And his host, and those
that were numbered thereof,
were fifty and seven thousand and four hundred.
9 All that were numbered in
the camp of Judah were an
hundred thousand and
fourscore thousand and six
thousand and four hundred,
throughout their armies.
These shall first set forth.
10 On the south side shall
be the standard of the camp
of Reuben according to their
armies: and the captain of
the children of Reuben shall
be Elizur the son of Shedeur.
11 And his host, and those
that were numbered thereof,
were forty and six thousand
and five hundred.
12 And those which pitch
by him shall be the tribe of
Simeon: and the captain of
the children of Simeon shall
be Shelumiel the son of
Zurishaddai.
13 And his host, and those
that were numbered of them,
were fifty and nine thousand
and three hundred.
14 Then the tribe of Gad:
and the captain of the sons of
Gad shall be Eliasaph the
son of Reuel.
15 And his host, and those
that were numbered of them,
were forty and five thousand
and six hundred and fifty.
16 All that were numbered
in the camp of Reuben were
an hundred thousand and
fifty and one thousand and
four hundred and fifty,
throughout their armies. And
they shall set forth in the

SCRIPTURE

second rank.
17 Then the tabernacle of
the congregation shall set
forward with the camp of the
Levites in the midst of the
camp: as they encamp, so
shall they set forward, every
man in his place by their
standards.
18 On the west side shall be
the standard of the camp of
Ephraim according to their
armies: and the captain of
the sons of Ephraim shall be
Elishama the son of
Ammihud.
19 And his host, and those
that were numbered of them,
were forty thousand and five
hundred.
20 And by him shall be the
tribe of Manasseh: and the
captain of the children of
Manasseh shall be Gamaliel
the son of Pedahzur.
21 And his host, and those
that were numbered of them,
were thirty and two thousand and two hundred.
22 Then the tribe of
Benjamin: and the captain of
the sons of Benjamin shall
be Abidan the son of
Gideoni.
23 And his host, and those
that were numbered of them,
were thirty and five thousand and four hundred.
24 All that were numbered
of the camp of Ephraim
were an hundred thousand
and eight thousand and an
hundred, throughout their
armies. And they shall go
forward in the third rank.
25 The standard of the
camp of Dan shall be on the
north side by their armies:
and the captain of the children of Dan shall be Ahiezer
the son of Ammishaddai.
26 And his host, and those
that were numbered of them,
were threescore and two
thousand and seven hundred.
27 And those that encamp
by him shall be the tribe of
Asher: and the captain of the
children of Asher shall be
Pagiel the son of Ocran.
28 And his host, and those
that were numbered of them,
were forty and one thousand
and five hundred.
29 Then the tribe of
Naphtali: and the captain of
the children of Naphtali

OUTLINE

Second in line

c. In the center: The Tabernacle & the Levites—marched in the same order as they camped

d. On the west

1) The division of Ephraim
- The leader: Elishama
- Division number: 40,500

2) The division of Manasseh
- The leader: Gamaliel
- Division number: 32,200

3) The division of Benjamin
- The leader: Abidan
- Division number: 35,400

4) The total of the these divisions: 108,100

5) The marching position: Third in line

e. On the north

1) The division of Dan
- The leader: Ahiezer
- Division number: 62,700

2) The division of Asher
- The leader: Pagiel
- Division number: 41,500

3) The division of Naphtali
- The leader: Ahira

OUTLINE	SCRIPTURE	SCRIPTURE	OUTLINE
• Division number: 53,400 4) The total of the three divisions: 157,600 5) The marching position: Fourth in line	shall be Ahira the son of Enan. 30 And his host, and those that were numbered of them, were fifty and three thousand and four hundred. 31 All they that were numbered in the camp of Dan were an hundred thousand and fifty and seven thousand and six hundred. They shall go hindmost with their standards.	32 These are those which were numbered of the children of Israel by the house of their fathers: all those that were numbered of the camps throughout their hosts were six hundred thousand and three thousand and five hundred and fifty. 33 But the Levites were not numbered among the children of Israel; as the LORD commanded Moses.	f. The accuracy & total of the men 1) The way they were counted: By families 2) The total numbered: 603,550 3) The Levites were not counted

The people of God were to camp around the Tabernacle in a square formation. They were also to march in the same formation, a formation that placed the Tabernacle in the very middle of God's people. Everyone had to know his or her relationship to the others. Each individual had to know his place within the tribe, and each tribe had to know its place in relationship to the other tribes. But most important, everyone had to know his or her place in relation to the Tabernacle, the symbol of God's very presence. The presence of God was the focus:

⇒ It was He who was going to lead His people to the promised land.
⇒ It was He who was going to give them the strength to conquer the pitfalls and enemies along the way.
⇒ It was He who was going to give them the help and guidance they needed.

Therefore, each individual had to know—beyond any question—his relationship to God. He had to know where he stood among God's people; he had to know under what banner he was to march. Note: this is exactly what Scripture says: each man was to stand under his standard with the banners of the tribe waving in the wind (v.2). Note the word "host" or "division" (saba) running throughout this passage (v.4, 6, 8, etc.). The word means unit, troop, band, host, division, or army. The idea is that of a military camp or a pilgrim camp. God's people can be pictured either as an army or as pilgrims. They are pilgrims or an army marching to the promised land of God.

Note that God's people were to camp some distance away from the Tabernacle. Scripture says elsewhere that the tribes were to be one thousand yards from the Tabernacle (Josh.3:4). The Levites were to camp between the secular tribes and the Tabernacle in order to protect the abuse of God's presence (v.3, 23, 29, 35).

Thought 1. Two descriptive pictures of believers are seen in this point.

1) Believers are like pilgrims walking through the desert and wilderness of this world. They are marching to the promised land of heaven.

"These all died in faith, not having received the promises, but having seen them afar off, and were persuaded of *them,* and embraced *them,* and confessed that they were strangers and pilgrims on the earth" (Heb.11:13).

"Let us go forth therefore unto him without the camp, bearing his reproach. For here have we no continuing city, but we seek one to come" (Heb.13:13-14).

"Dearly beloved, I beseech *you* as strangers and pilgrims, abstain from fleshly lusts, which war against the soul" (1 Pt.2:11).

"And Jacob said unto Pharaoh, The days of the years of my pilgrimage *are* an hundred and thirty years: few and evil have the days of the years of my life been, and have not attained unto the days of the years of the life of my fathers in the days of their pilgrimage" (Gen.47:9).

"And I have also established my covenant with them, to give them the land of Canaan, the land of their pilgrimage, wherein they were strangers" (Ex.6:4).

"For we *are* strangers before thee, and sojourners [pilgrims], as *were* all our fathers: our days on the earth *are* as a shadow, and *there is* none abiding" (1 Chron. 29:15).

"Hear my prayer, O LORD, and give ear unto my cry; hold not thy peace at my tears: for I *am* a stranger with thee, *and* a sojourner [pilgrims], as all my fathers *were.* O spare me, that I may recover strength, before I go hence, and be no more" (Ps.39:12-13).

2) Believers are like soldiers in the desert and wilderness of this world. They are soldiers marching forth to conquer all the pitfalls and enemies of this world, marching forth to the promised land of God.

"For we wrestle not against flesh and blood, but against principalities, against powers, against the rulers of the darkness of this world, against spiritual wickedness in high *places.* Wherefore take unto you the whole armour of God, that ye may be able to withstand in the evil day, and having done all, to stand" (Eph. 6:12-13).

"Thou therefore endure hardness, as a good soldier of Jesus Christ. No man that warreth entangleth himself with the affairs of *this* life; that he may please him who hath chosen him to be a soldier" (2 Tim.2:3-4).

"(For the weapons of our warfare *are* not carnal, but mighty through God to the pulling down of strong holds;)" (2 Cor.10:4).

"Fight the good fight of faith, lay hold on eternal life, whereunto thou art also called, and hast professed a good profession before many witnesses" (1 Tim.6:12).

"And take the helmet of salvation, and the sword of the Spirit, which is the word of God" (Eph.6:17).

"For the word of God *is* quick, and powerful, and sharper than any twoedged sword, piercing even to the dividing asunder of soul and spirit, and of the joints and marrow, and *is* a discerner of the thoughts and intents of the heart" (Heb.4:12).

"And they overcame him by the blood of the Lamb, and by the word of their testimony; and they loved not their lives unto the death" (Rev.12:11).

"By the word of truth, by the power of God, by the armour of righteousness on the right hand and on the left" (2 Cor.6:7).

"But let us, who are of the day, be sober, putting on the breastplate of faith and love; and for an helmet, the hope of salvation" (1 Th.5:8).

Thought 2. Every believer has his appointed place in the army of God. Each believer is related to other believers, and all believers are related to Christ. We are the family of God, standing under the great standard of Christ and the great banner of God. Following Him, we must proclaim our loyalty to Him, giving strong testimony to His great salvation.

1) Every believer has his own place under the great standard of Christ and banner of God.

"Ye have not chosen me, but I have chosen you, and ordained you, that ye should go and bring forth fruit, and *that* your fruit should remain: that whatsoever ye shall ask of the Father in my name, he may give it you" (Jn.15:16).

"Let every man abide in the same calling wherein he was called" (1 Cor.7:20).

"Now ye are the body of Christ, and members in particular [individually]" (1 Cor.12:27).

"For as we have many members in one body, and all members have not the same office: So we, *being* many, are one body in Christ, and every one members one of another" (Ro.12:4-5).

"Ye *are* my witnesses, saith the LORD, and my servant whom I have chosen: that ye may know and believe me, and understand that I *am* he: before me there was no God formed, neither shall there be after me" (Is.43:10).

2) We are to proclaim the standard of Christ and the banner of God—bear strong witness and testimony for Him.

"Go ye therefore, and teach all nations, baptizing them in the name of the Father, and of the Son, and of the Holy Ghost: Teaching them to observe all things whatsoever I have commanded you: and, lo, I am with you alway, *even* unto the end of the world. Amen" (Mt.28:19-20).

"But ye shall receive power, after that the Holy Ghost is come upon you: and ye shall be witnesses unto me both in Jerusalem, and in all Judaea, and in Samaria, and unto the uttermost part of the earth" (Acts 1:8).

"For we cannot but speak the things which we have seen and heard" (Acts 4:20).

"Go, stand and speak in the temple to the people all the words of this life" (Acts 5:20).

"We having the same spirit of faith, according as it is written, I believed, and therefore have I spoken; we also believe, and therefore speak" (2 Cor.4:13).

"Be not thou therefore ashamed of the testimony of our LORD, nor of me his prisoner: but be thou partaker of the afflictions of the gospel according to the power of God" (2 Tim.1:8).

"But sanctify the LORD God in your hearts: and *be* ready always to *give* an answer to every man that asketh you a reason of the hope that is in you with meekness and fear" (1 Pt.3:15).

Thought 3. The Tabernacle was placed right in the middle of God's people for one reason and one reason only: so that God could dwell with His people and guide them as they marched to the promised land. So it is with us.

1) Jesus Christ became flesh and dwelt among us.

"And the Word was made flesh, and dwelt among us, (and we beheld his glory, the glory as of the only begotten of the Father,) full of grace and truth" (Jn.1:14).

2) The Spirit of God dwells within the church.

"Know ye not that ye [plural, the church as a whole] are the temple of God, and *that* the Spirit of God dwelleth in you?" (1 Cor.3:16).

"For as the body is one, and hath many members, and all the members of that one body, being many, are one body: so also *is* Christ. For by one Spirit are we all baptized into one body, whether *we be* Jews or Gentiles, whether *we be* bond or free; and have been all made to drink into one Spirit. For the body is not one member, but many. If the foot shall say, Because I am not the hand, I am not of the body; is it therefore not of the body? And if the ear shall say, Because I am not the eye, I am not of the body; is it therefore not of the body? If the whole body *were* an eye, where *were* the hearing? If the whole *were* hearing, where *were* the smelling? But now hath God set the members every one of them in the body, as it hath pleased him" (1 Cor.12:12-18).

3) The Spirit of God dwells within the body of every individual believer.

"What? know ye not that your body is the temple of the Holy Ghost *which is* in you, which ye have of God, and ye are not your own? For ye are bought with a price: therefore glorify God in your body, and in your spirit, which are God's" (1 Cor.6:19-20).

"And I will pray the Father, and he shall give you another Comforter, that he may abide with you for ever; *Even* the Spirit of truth; whom the world cannot receive, because it seeth him not, neither knoweth him: but ye know him; for he dwelleth with you, and shall be in you" (Jn.14:16-17).

"But ye are not in the flesh, but in the Spirit, if so be that the Spirit of God dwell in you. Now if any man have not the Spirit of Christ, he is none of his" (Ro.8:9).

"That good thing which was committed unto thee keep by the Holy Ghost which dwelleth in us" (2 Tim.1:14).

"But the anointing which ye have received of him abideth in you, and ye need not that any man teach you: but as the same anointing teacheth you of all things, and is truth, and is no lie, and even as it hath taught you, ye shall abide in him" (1 Jn.2:27).

8 (2:34) **Obedience—Commandments, of God**: there was the obedience of God's people. They did everything that God commanded. They camped exactly as God commanded, and they marched exactly as God commanded.

OUTLINE	SCRIPTURE
8. The obedience of God's people: Every believer must do everything God commands a. They camped as God commanded b. They marched as God commanded	34 And the children of Israel did according to all that the LORD commanded Moses: so they pitched by their standards, and so they set forward, every one after their families, according to the house of their fathers.

Thought 1. God's people must obey God and do exactly what He says. There must be absolute compliance in following God, in obeying His Word. The individual believer must obey God, and the church as a whole must obey God. When the believer and the church are obedient—when they obey God exactly as He says—then they will walk triumphantly over the pitfalls and enemies of this life. They will be mobilized, ready to fight the good fight of faith. They will be victorious as they march to the promised land of heaven.

"Not every one that saith unto me, LORD, LORD, shall enter into the kingdom of heaven; but he that doeth the will of my Father which is in heaven" (Mt.7:21).

"Jesus answered and said unto him, If a man love me, he will keep my words: and my Father will love him, and we will come unto him, and make our abode with him" (Jn.14:23).

"If ye keep my commandments, ye shall abide in my love; even as I have kept my Father's commandments, and abide in his love" (Jn.15:10).

"Ye are my friends, if ye do whatsoever I command you" (Jn.15:14).

"Blessed *are* they that do his commandments, that they may have right to the tree of life, and may enter in through the gates into the city" (Rev.22:14).

"This day the LORD thy God hath commanded thee to do these statutes and judgments: thou shalt therefore keep and do them with all thine heart, and with all thy soul" (Dt.26:16).

"This book of the law shall not depart out of thy mouth; but thou shalt meditate therein day and night, that thou mayest observe to do according to all that is written therein: for then thou shalt make thy way prosperous, and then thou shalt have good success" (Josh.1:8).

(See following 3 pages for Pictures of *The Tabernacle, The Encampment of the Tribes*, and *The Marching Positions of the Tribes.*)

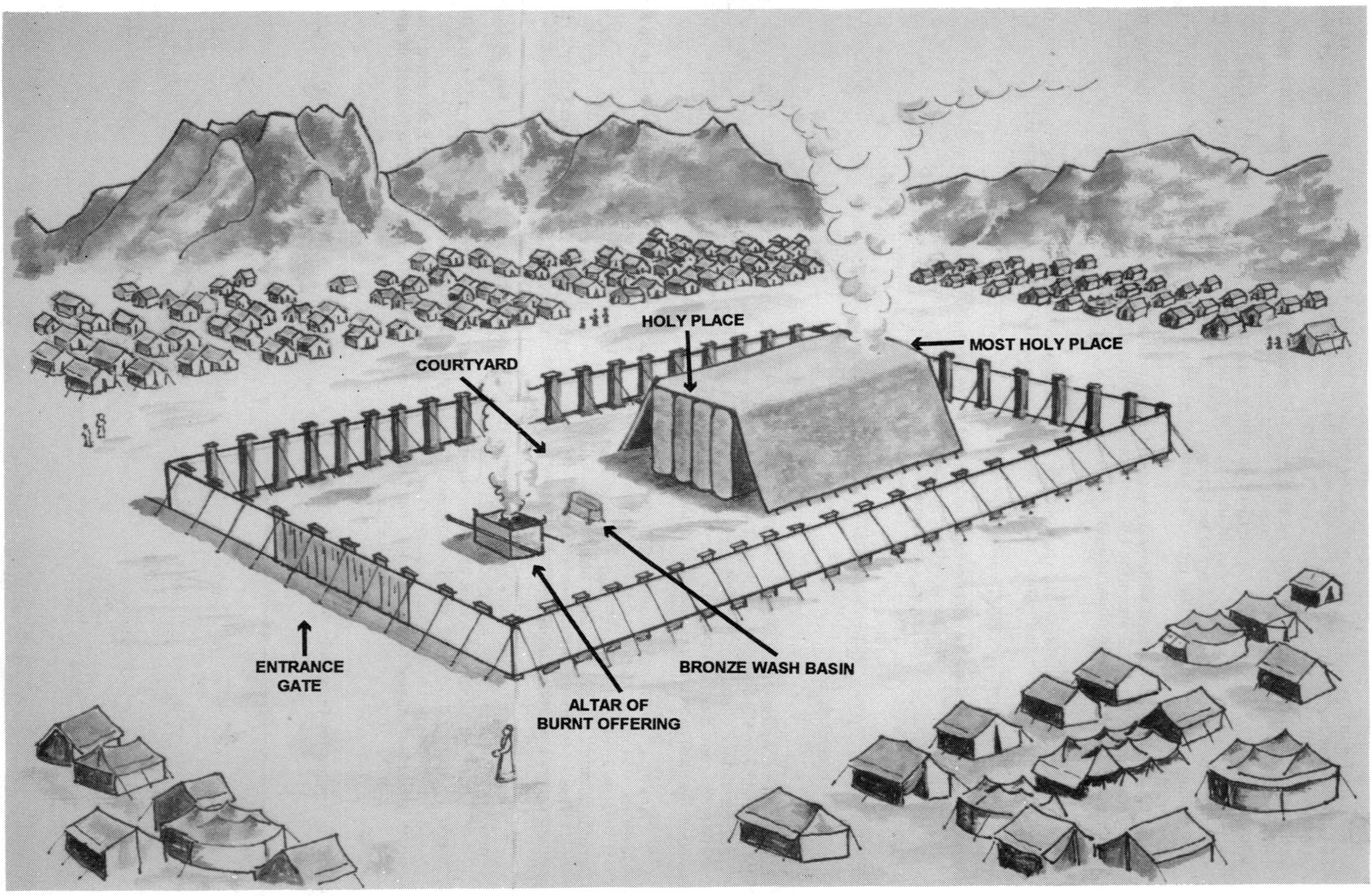

THE TABERNACLE IN THE WILDERNESS

THE TABERNACLE

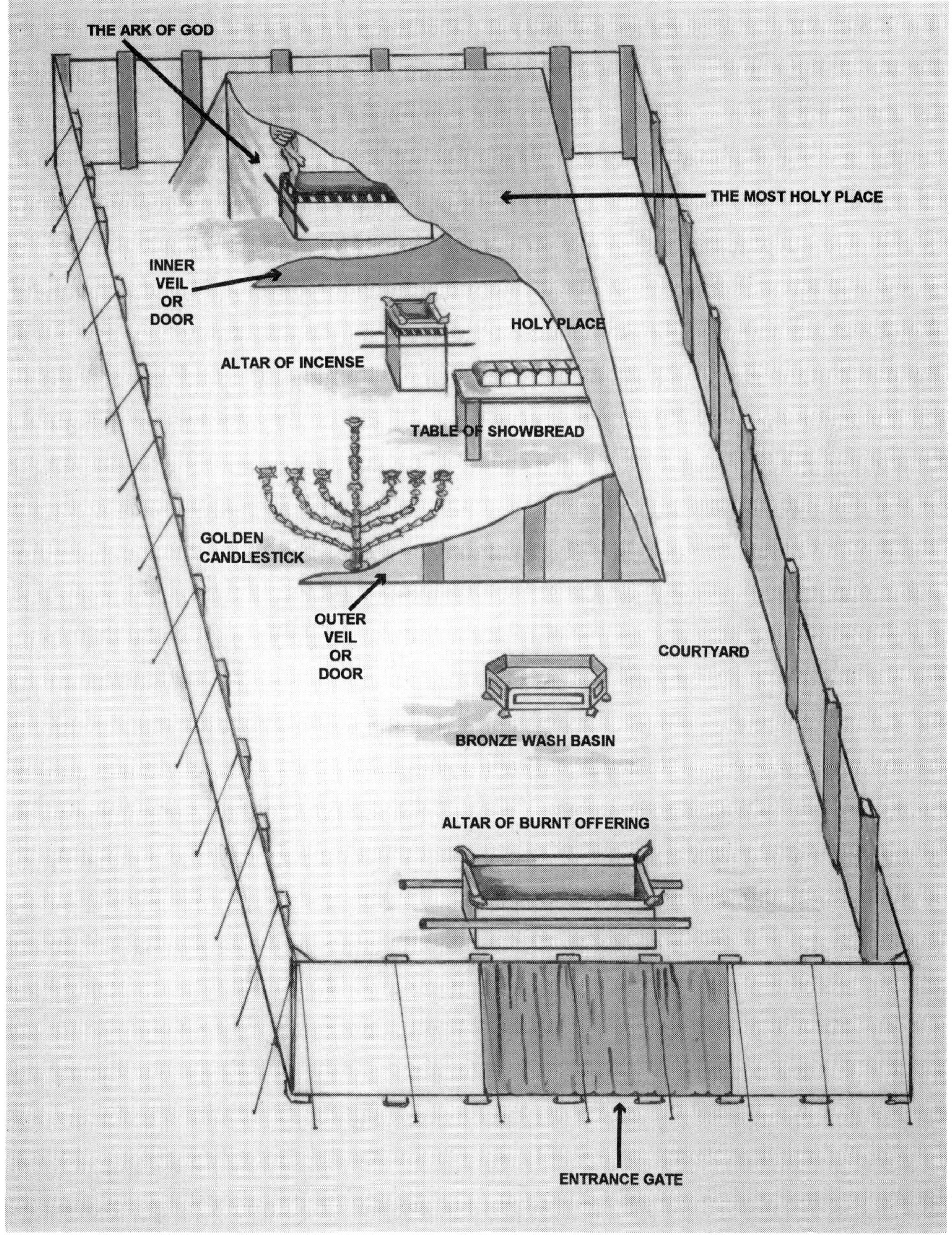
THE ARK OF GOD
THE MOST HOLY PLACE
INNER VEIL OR DOOR
HOLY PLACE
ALTAR OF INCENSE
TABLE OF SHOWBREAD
GOLDEN CANDLESTICK
OUTER VEIL OR DOOR
COURTYARD
BRONZE WASH BASIN
ALTAR OF BURNT OFFERING
ENTRANCE GATE

(2:2-33) **Picture—Israel, Encampment of**:

The Encampment of the Tribes

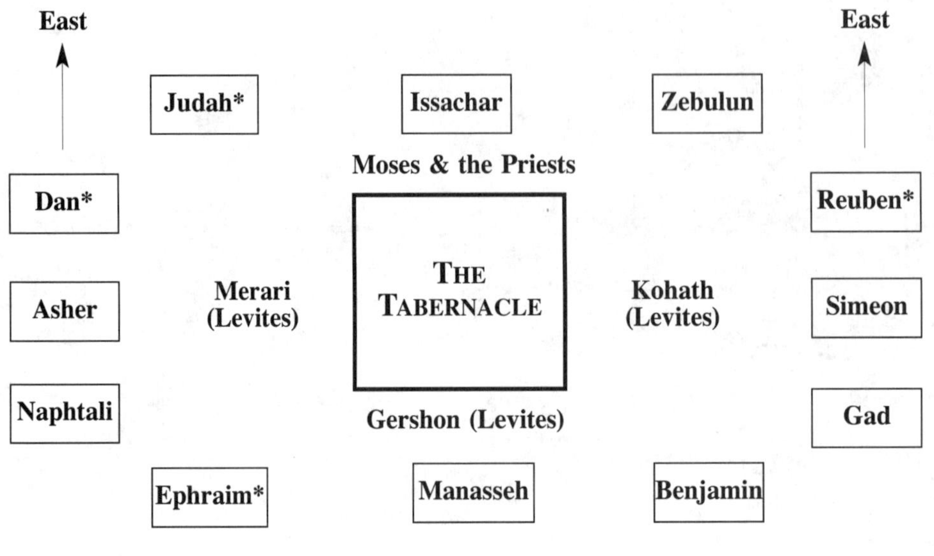

(* *The leading tribe of the group*)

The Marching Positions of the Tribes [2]

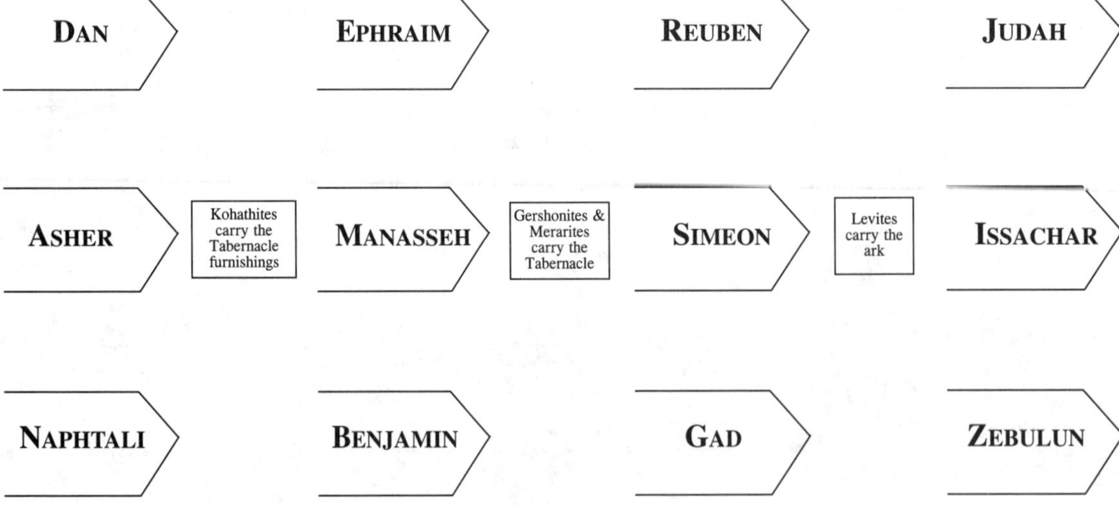

2 The idea for the Marching Positions of the Tribes is taken from the *New International Version Study Bible*. (Grand Rapids, MI: Zondervan Bible Publishers, 1985), p.192.

TYPES, SYMBOLS, AND PICTURES
(Numbers 1:1-2:34)

Historical Term	Type or Picture (Scriptural Basis for Each)	Life Application for Today's Believer	Biblical Application
The Promised Land Num.1:1-2:34; 5:1-31; 34:1-15	*The promised land definitely refers to Palestine, the land of Canaan or of Israel. But the promised land also refers to heaven. The promised land of Canaan is a symbol (a type, a picture, an illustration) of heaven, of God's promise to the believer that he will inherit heaven, the new heavens and earth. The promised land represented many things to Abraham.* *1. The promised land was the assurance of a personal inheritance: the possession of a new country, of his own property with all its good land, wealth, and rights. Abraham believed that he would live in a new city within his own land and country—all given by God Himself. And the land was to be forever, for it was promised by the eternal God Himself.* *2. The promised land was the assurance of conquest and rest, of spiritual victory and spiritual rest. The promised land was to bring a God-given peace and security, freedom and liberty, deliverance and salvation to Abraham.* *3. The promised land was the assurance of God's own presence, that is, of God's love, care, provision, and protection. Abraham was bound to know this: if God was going to give him the promised land, then God must love and care for him. God would therefore provide and protect him no matter what lay ahead. God—His strong presence—would be with him through all the trials and struggles of life.* **"Doubtless ye shall not come into the land, *concerning* which I sware to make you dwell therein, save Caleb the son of Jephunneh, and Joshua the son of Nun." (Num.14:30).**	⇒ It is the obedient who will receive the inheritance of God, the promised land that flows with milk and honey. The obedient person is the person who lives a life of separation, a life that is entirely different from the immoral and lawless people of the earth.	***"Wherefore come out from among them, and be ye separate, saith the Lord, and touch not the unclean thing; and I will receive you" (2 Cor.6:17).*** ***"And take heed to yourselves, lest at any time your hearts be overcharged with surfeiting, and drunkenness, and cares of this life, and so that day come upon you unawares" (Lk.21:34).*** ***"And with many other words did he testify and exhort, saying, Save yourselves from this untoward generation" (Acts 2:40).*** ***"I beseech you therefore, brethren, by the mercies of God, that ye present your bodies a living sacrifice, holy, acceptable unto God, which is your reasonable service. And be not conformed to this world: but be ye transformed by the renewing of your mind, that ye may prove what is that good, and acceptable, and perfect, will of God" (Ro.12:1-2).*** ***"And have no fellowship with the unfruitful works of darkness, but rather reprove them" (Eph.5:11).*** ***"But seek ye first the kingdom of God, and his righteousness; and all these things shall be added unto you" (Mt.6:33).*** ***"Lo, I am with you alway, even unto the end of the world" (Mt.28:20).***

Historical Term	Type or Picture (Scriptural Basis for Each)	Life Application for Today's Believer	Biblical Application
The Tabernacle Num.1:47-54; 4:1-20 (See also Lev.17:3-9)	*The Tabernacle symbolizes or pictures three major things:* *1. The Tabernacle symbolizes or pictures the ministry of Jesus Christ. The materials used to construct the Tabernacle are pictures of God's redemption in Jesus Christ. The various furnishings show God's great plan of salvation for the repentant sinner. (See all notes—Ex.25:1-9; 10-22; 23-30; 31-40; 27:1-21; 30:1-10).* *2. The Tabernacle symbolizes or pictures the ministry of the church. The Tabernacle was a worship center in which God dwelt, and the Tabernacle stood as a witness to the world. So does the church.* *3. The Tabernacle symbolizes or pictures the Christian believer, the person who truly follows God. The Tabernacle was the dwelling place for God's presence upon earth, standing as a strong witness to the LORD.* **"But thou shalt appoint the Levites over the tabernacle of testimony, and over all the vessels thereof, and over all things that *belong* to it: they shall bear the tabernacle, and all the vessels thereof; and they shall minister unto it, and shall encamp round about the tabernacle" (Num.1:50).**	1. The Tabernacle of Moses reveals every aspect of Jesus Christ and His work as the Word who became flesh and dwelt ("tabernacled") among us (John 1:14; see note—Heb.9:1-14). 2. God's presence and witness dwell within the church in two ways: ⇒ God's Spirit dwells within believers. ⇒ God's Spirit dwells among—within the very presence of—believers when two or three of them gather together. 3. The believer—his body—is the very temple of God, the sanctuary and dwelling place for the presence and witness of God upon earth.	***"What? know ye not that your body is the temple of the Holy Ghost which is in you, which ye have of God, and ye are not your own? For ye are bought with a price: therefore glorify God in your body, and in your spirit, which are God's" (1 Cor.6:19-20).*** ***"For where two or three are gathered together in my name, there am I in the midst of them" (Mt.18:20).*** ***"Know ye not that ye [plural, referring to the church, the body or assembly of believers] are the temple of God, and that the Spirit of God dwelleth in you?" (1 Cor.3:16).*** ***"In whom ye [plural] also are builded together for an habitation of God through the Spirit" (Ephes. 2:22).*** ***"Your life is hid with Christ in God" (Col. 3:3).*** ***"I in them, and thou in me, that they may be made perfect in one; and that the world may know that thou hast sent me, and hast loved them, as thou hast loved me" (Jn. 17:23; see also 1 Cor. 6:19-20; 2 Cor. 6:16; Gal.2:20; Col. 1:27).***

B. The Organization of the Priests, the Levites & the Firstborn—the Second & Third Census Records: Called to Be Assistants, 3:1-51

1. The family line of Aaron & Moses: Some are anointed & ordained to serve God

a. The four sons of Aaron—Nadab (the firstborn), Abihu, Eleazar, & Ithamar—were anointed & ordained to serve as priests

b. The two oldest sons (Nadab & Abihu) had been struck dead by the LORD (Lev.10:1-2)
   1) Had offered unauthorized fire: Approached God in a wrong way
   2) Had left no sons to continue their names among the priests

c. The two youngest sons served as priests

2. The appointment of the Levites: Some are set apart to be assistants

a. Called to be the assistants to the High Priest, Aaron (a symbol of Christ)
   1) To take care of all the work of the Tabernacle itself
   2) To take care of all the furnishings of the Tabernacle
   3) To be totally given over to assist the High Priest
   4) To protect the sanctity of the sanctuary: Guard it against the abuse of intruders

b. Called by God to a very special position: To become the substitute, the replacement for the firstborn sons—to be given to the service of God instead of the firstborn sons
   1) The special position: "The Levites are mine"

These also are the generations of Aaron and Moses in the day that the LORD spake with Moses in mount Sinai.

2 And these are the names of the sons of Aaron; Nadab the firstborn, and Abihu, Eleazar, and Ithamar.

3 These are the names of the sons of Aaron, the priests which were anointed, whom he consecrated to minister in the priest's office.

4 And Nadab and Abihu died before the LORD, when they offered strange fire before the LORD, in the wilderness of Sinai, and they had no children: and Eleazar and Ithamar ministered in the priest's office in the sight of Aaron their father.

5 And the LORD spake unto Moses, saying,

6 Bring the tribe of Levi near, and present them before Aaron the priest, that they may minister unto him.

7 And they shall keep his charge, and the charge of the whole congregation before the tabernacle of the congregation, to do the service of the tabernacle.

8 And they shall keep all the instruments of the tabernacle of the congregation, and the charge of the children of Israel, to do the service of the tabernacle.

9 And thou shalt give the Levites unto Aaron and to his sons: they are wholly given unto him out of the children of Israel.

10 And thou shalt appoint Aaron and his sons, and they shall wait on their priest's office: and the stranger that cometh nigh shall be put to death.

11 And the LORD spake unto Moses, saying,

12 And I, behold, I have taken the Levites from among the children of Israel instead of all the firstborn that openeth the matrix among the children of Israel: therefore the Levites shall be mine;

13 Because all the firstborn are mine; for on the day that I smote all the firstborn in the land of Egypt I hallowed unto me all the firstborn in Israel, both man and beast: mine shall they be: I am the LORD.

14 And the LORD spake unto Moses in the wilderness of Sinai, saying,

15 Number the children of Levi after the house of their fathers, by their families: every male from a month old and upward shalt thou number them.

16 And Moses numbered them according to the word of the LORD, as he was commanded.

17 And these were the sons of Levi by their names; Gershon, and Kohath, and Merari.

18 And these are the names of the sons of Gershon by their families; Libni, and Shimei.

19 And the sons of Kohath by their families; Amram, and Izehar, Hebron, and Uzziel.

20 And the sons of Merari by their families; Mahli, and Mushi. These are the families of the Levites according to the house of their fathers.

21 Of Gershon was the family of the Libnites, and the family of the Shimites: these are the families of the Gershonites.

22 Those that were numbered of them, according to the number of all the males, from a month old and upward, even those that were numbered of them were seven thousand and five hundred.

23 The families of the Gershonites shall pitch behind the tabernacle westward.

24 And the chief of the house of the father of the Gershonites shall be Eliasaph the son of Lael.

25 And the charge of the sons of Gershon in the tabernacle of the congregation shall be the tabernacle, and the tent, the covering thereof, and the hanging for the door of the tabernacle of the congregation,

   2) The authority of the call
      - The historical fact: God had set apart the firstborn to serve Him since Egypt (Ex.13:2f; 22:29; 34:19f)
      - The sovereignty of God

3. The census, placement, & duties of the Levites: A picture of doing one's job well

a. The LORD's charge to Moses
   1) To count every male one month old or older
   2) The picture of total obedience: Moses did exactly what God commanded

b. The overall view of the Levites
   1) The three sons of Levi: Gershon, Kohath, & Merari
   2) The Gershonite clans: Libni & Shimei
   3) The Kohathite clans: Amram, Izhar, Hebron, & Uzziel
   4) The Merarite clans: Mahli & Mushi

c. The detailed look at the Gershonites
   1) The clans: Libnites & Shimeites
   2) Their census number: 7,500
   3) Their camp: To the west behind the Tabernacle
   4) Their leader: Eliasaph, son of Lael
   5) Their duties: To take care of the tent of the Tabernacle, its coverings & curtains
      - the entrance curtain
      - the courtyard curtains

- the entrance curtain to the courtyard
- the ropes & all else related to the coverings & curtains

d. The detailed look at the Kohathites
  1) Their clans: Amramites, Izhorites, Hebronites, Uzzielites
  2) Their census number: 8,600
  3) Their overall responsibility: The care of the sanctuary
  4) Their camp: The south side of the Tabernacle
  5) Their leader: Elizaphan, son of Uzziel
  6) Their duties: To take care of...
     - the Ark, the table, & the lampstand
     - the altars & utensils
     - the inner curtain & all else related to their use
  7) The chief administrator over all the Levites was given special oversight over the sanctuary & the Kohathites: Eleazar, son of Aaron

e. The detailed look at the Merarites
  1) Their clans: The Mahlites & the Mushites
  2) Their census number: 6,200
  3) Their leader: Zuriel, son of Abihail
  4) Their camp: The north side of the Tabernacle
  5) Their duties: To take care of...
     - the supporting frames of the Tabernacle, crossbars, posts, bases, & all else related to their use
     - the posts of the courtyard with their bases, pegs, & ropes

f. The detailed look at Moses & Aaron
  1) Their camp: To the east toward the sunrise, in front of the Tabernacle
  2) Their duties: Had overall responsibility for the sanctuary—in behalf of the people
  3) The warning: Anyone other than a priest or Levite who approached the sanctuary was to be executed

g. The total number of Levites one month old or older: 22,000

26 And the hangings of the court, and the curtain for the door of the court, which is by the tabernacle, and by the altar round about, and the cords of it for all the service thereof.

27 And of Kohath was the family of the Amramites, and the family of the Izeharites, and the family of the Hebronites, and the family of the Uzzielites: these are the families of the Kohathites.

28 In the number of all the males, from a month old and upward, were eight thousand and six hundred, keeping the charge of the sanctuary.

29 The families of the sons of Kohath shall pitch on the side of the tabernacle southward.

30 And the chief of the house of the father of the families of the Kohathites shall be Elizaphan the son of Uzziel.

31 And their charge shall be the ark, and the table, and the candlestick, and the altars, and the vessels of the sanctuary wherewith they minister, and the hanging, and all the service thereof.

32 And Eleazar the son of Aaron the priest shall be chief over the chief of the Levites, and have the oversight of them that keep the charge of the sanctuary.

33 Of Merari was the family of the Mahlites, and the family of the Mushites: these are the families of Merari.

34 And those that were numbered of them, according to the number of all the males, from a month old and upward, were six thousand and two hundred.

35 And the chief of the house of the father of the families of Merari was Zuriel the son of Abihail: these shall pitch on the side of the tabernacle northward.

36 And under the custody and charge of the sons of Merari shall be the boards of the tabernacle, and the bars thereof, and the pillars thereof, and the sockets thereof, and all the vessels thereof, and all that serveth thereto,

37 And the pillars of the court round about, and their sockets, and their pins, and their cords.

38 But those that encamp before the tabernacle toward the east, even before the tabernacle of the congregation eastward, shall be Moses, and Aaron and his sons, keeping the charge of the sanctuary for the charge of the children of Israel; and the stranger that cometh nigh shall be put to death.

39 All that were numbered of the Levites, which Moses and Aaron numbered at the commandment of the LORD, throughout their families, all the males from a month old and upward, were twenty and two thousand.

40 And the LORD said unto Moses, Number all the firstborn of the males of the children of Israel from a month old and upward, and take the number of their names.

41 And thou shalt take the Levites for me (I am the LORD) instead of all the firstborn among the children of Israel; and the cattle of the Levites instead of all the firstlings among the cattle of the children of Israel.

42 And Moses numbered, as the LORD commanded him, all the firstborn among the children of Israel.

43 And all the firstborn males by the number of names, from a month old and upward, of those that were numbered of them, were twenty and two thousand two hundred and threescore and thirteen.

44 And the LORD spake unto Moses, saying,

45 Take the Levites instead of all the firstborn among the children of Israel, and the cattle of the Levites instead of their cattle; and the Levites shall be mine: I am the LORD.

46 And for those that are to be redeemed of the two hundred and threescore and thirteen of the firstborn of the children of Israel, which are more than the Levites;

47 Thou shalt even take five shekels apiece by the poll, after the shekel of the sanctuary shalt thou take them: (the shekel is twenty gerahs:)

48 And thou shalt give the

4. The census of the firstborn & their replacement by the Levites: A picture of redemption

a. The LORD's charge: To count all the firstborn sons in Israel: One month old or older
  1) To substitute the Levites for all the firstborn of Israel, to replace them as the servants of God
  2) To substitute the livestock of the Levites for the firstborn livestock of Israel (to be used in the sacrifices)

b. The strict obedience of Moses

c. The number of firstborn sons one month old or older: 22,273

d. The special charge
  1) To substitute the Levites for the firstborn Israelites: The Levites were thereafter to be the LORD's, His servants
  2) To redeem the 273, pay the price for the firstborn sons who exceeded the number of Levites
     - To collect five pieces of silver for each one
     - To give the redemption

money to the priests (Aaron & his sons)	money, wherewith the odd number of them is to be redeemed, unto Aaron and to his sons.	money; a thousand three hundred and threescore and five shekels, after the shekel of the sanctuary:	pounds of silver)
3) The obedience of Moses: He collected the redemption money • He collected 1,365 shekels (about 34	49 And Moses took the redemption money of them that were over and above them that were redeemed by the Levites: 50 Of the firstborn of the children of Israel took he the	51 And Moses gave the money of them that were redeemed unto Aaron and to his sons, according to the word of the LORD, as the LORD commanded Moses.	• He gave the money to the priests, Aaron & his sons • He was careful to obey God—totally

DIVISION I

THE PREPARATION FOR THE MARCH TO THE PROMISED LAND, 1:1-10:36

B. The Organization of the Priests, the Levites, and the Firstborn—the Second and Third Census Records: Called to Be Assistants, 3:1-51

(3:1-51) **Introduction—Ministry, Work of—Assistants, Needed—Ministers, Needed—Work, of the Ministry:** the magnitude of the ministry is overwhelming. No matter the size of the church, the work never is done. There are always people to see, places to go, and work to be done. There are always people who need encouragement, counseling, visiting, and a closer walk with the LORD—some help in some way. Beyond this, there is the task of constantly reaching out to the lost who do not know Christ. Then there is the regular and ongoing administrative care of the church, looking after the buildings, grounds, purchasing, and finances. Moreover, the minister has to live in God's Word—reading and studying—always preparing to preach and teach. This is an endless task that demands a great deal of time every day if anointed messages and lessons are to be used by God to bless His people. On and on the list could go, for the task of the church and of God's minister never ends.

This fact tells us something: there is a need for assistants. The minister and the church need helpers, a large number of helpers to minister to people within the church and to reach out to the lost of the world—carrying out all the functions of the church. God expects every church and every minister to get the job done. But the task cannot be done without assistants stepping forth and committing themselves to the ministry.

This is the subject of this particular Scripture: "Called to be assistants." God was mobilizing His people for the march to the promised land.

⇒ In chapters 1 and 2, the people of God were counted and organized into military divisions. The people of God were mobilized into a great army and given a banner or standard to identify their tribes, the great family to which they belonged. They were then arranged around the Tabernacle and given their permanent positions for camping and marching. The people of God—each person—knew his place within the army of God, knew exactly where he was to march and what he was to do—all except the Levites.

⇒ Now, in chapter 3, the Levites were to be counted and organized by their tribes and assigned their tasks. The Levites had been set apart to the service of God. Consequently, they were not counted with the secular tribes or army divisions.

The Levites would not be fighting in the wars; they would be carrying on the ministry of the Tabernacle for God and His people. The Levites were called to be the assistants to the priests.

This is the subject of this great passage: *The Organization of the Priests, the Levites, and the Firstborn—the Second and Third Census Records: Called to Be Assistants,* 3:1-51.

1. The family line of Aaron and Moses: some are anointed and ordained to serve God (v.1-4).
2. The appointment of the Levites: some are set apart to be assistants (v.5-13).
3. The census, placement, and duties of the Levites: a picture of doing one's job well (v.14-39).
4. The census of the firstborn and their replacement by the Levites: a picture of redemption (v.40-51).

1 (3:1-4) **Ministers, Called—Ministers, Warning to—Warning, to Ministers—Anointing, of Ministers—Ordination, of Ministers—Aaron, Sons of**: there was the family line of Aaron and Moses. Aaron and his sons were anointed and ordained to serve God. Note that the family line of Moses was not given. The focus was upon Aaron and his sons who were to serve as priests.

OUTLINE	SCRIPTURE	SCRIPTURE	OUTLINE
1. The family line of Aaron & Moses: Some are anointed & ordained to serve God a. The four sons of Aaron—Nadab (the firstborn), Abihu,	These also are the generations of Aaron and Moses in the day that the LORD spake with Moses in mount Sinai. 2 And these are the names of the sons of Aaron; Nadab	the firstborn, and Abihu, Eleazar, and Ithamar. 3 These are the names of the sons of Aaron, the priests which were anointed, whom he consecrated to minister in the priest's office.	Eleazar, & Ithamar—were anointed & ordained to serve as priests

OUTLINE	SCRIPTURE	SCRIPTURE	OUTLINE
b. The two oldest sons (Nadab & Abihu) had been struck dead by the LORD (Lev.10:1-2) 1) Had offered unauthorized fire: Approached God in a	4 And Nadab and Abihu died before the LORD, when they offered strange fire before the LORD, in the wilderness of Sinai, and they	had no children: and Eleazar and Ithamar ministered in the priest's office in the sight of Aaron their father.	wrong way 2) Had left no sons to continue their names among the priests c. The two youngest sons served as priests

1. The four sons of Aaron were Nadab (the firstborn), Abihu, Eleazar, and Ithamar (v.1). All four sons were anointed and ordained to serve as priests, the ministers of God to His people (v.3). The anointing and consecration set them apart from the secular world. They were to have a very special commitment to God. They were appointed to be the official teachers of God's people. But more than this, God ordained the priests to be a type, a picture of the coming Savior and Messiah of the world. The people of that day did not know this: nevertheless, the New Testament clearly states this fact (Heb.2:17; 4:14-15; 5:5; 6:20; 7:26; 8:1). Moreover, the work of the priests clearly shows this. As Gordon Wenham points out, the priests were the only ones who "had the right to handle the blood, to touch the altar, and to enter the tent of Meeting."[1] This clearly symbolizes what Jesus Christ Himself did:

⇒ Christ is the only who had the right to handle the sacrificial blood. In fact, He Himself was the sacrifice who shed His blood for the sins of the world.
⇒ Christ alone has the right to touch the altar: no other person—no other sacrifice lying upon the altar—could please God other than the perfect person and sacrifice, Christ Himself.
⇒ Christ alone has the right to enter the tent of meeting, the inner sanctuary of God: no other person is acceptable other than the perfect, sinless Son of God.

In addition to all this, the priests were ordained to be the official mediators standing between God and the people. They were to represent God before the people and represent the people before God. Again, the priests were a symbol, a picture of Christ who stands before God as our Mediator (1 Tim.2:5; Heb.8:6; 9:15, 24; 12:24; 1 Jn.2:1).

The point is this: the priests were set apart from the secular world. They were no longer ordinary: they stood before God in a very special position, appointed to a very special ministry. They were appointed to the service of God, appointed to minister to the people of God. They were to be a testimony to the world—a testimony that God is holy and can be approached only through the sacrifice with no defect (a symbol of Christ). This they were to proclaim both to God's people and to the pagan nations that surrounded them.

2. Note that the two oldest sons of Aaron, Nadab and Abihu, had been struck dead by the LORD (Lev.10:1-2). These two priests—and keep in mind that they were *ordained priests*—offered unauthorized fire before the LORD. What does this mean? Briefly stated, they approached God in a wrong way, contrary to His direct command. They offered a false worship to God: a self-made worship, a worship created in their own minds, a worship of self-righteousness. There is also the possibility that the two priests went into the Most Holy Place; and no person was allowed to enter this hallowed, holy room except the High Priest, and he only once a year. Then there is the possibility that the two priests entered the Tabernacle while drunk or intoxicated (see outline and notes—Lev.10:1-2; 10:4-11 for more discussion). No matter the case, because of their terrible sin, God struck them dead. Obviously, a lightning bolt of fire from God's glory shot out and burned them. They died before the LORD (see outline and note—Lev.10:1-2 for more discussion).

Note the other terrible tragedy mentioned about these two priests: they had no sons. There was no one to continue their names among the priests. When they died, their family name or line died. Their story ended.

3. The two youngest sons were the only sons who served as priests during Aaron's lifetime (v.4). This is significant: at this particular time in the history of Israel, there were only three priests ministering to God's people. An impossible task: serving a population of two to four million. They needed help—desperately. They needed assistants, a large body of laypersons who would step forth and accept the challenge, appointed by God to help in the ministry.

Thought 1. Some persons are anointed and ordained to serve God: the ministers who fill the pulpits of the world. They break the bread of life to us and minister to our needs. But note: they cannot do the task alone. The magnitude of the ministry is too overwhelming. There is simply too much to be done. They need help: they need assistants who will stand in the gap with them.

"Ye have not chosen me, but I have chosen you, and ordained you, that ye should go and bring forth fruit, and *that* your fruit should remain: that whatsoever ye shall ask of the Father in my name, he may give it you" (Jn.15:16).

"But the LORD said unto him, Go thy way: for he is a chosen vessel unto me, to bear my name before the Gentiles, and kings, and the children of Israel" (Acts 9:15).

"Then departed Barnabas to Tarsus, for to seek Saul: And when he had found him, he brought him unto Antioch. And it came to pass, that a whole year they assembled themselves with the church, and taught much people. And the disciples were called Christians first in Antioch" (Acts 11:25-26).

"But rise, and stand upon thy feet: for I have appeared unto thee for this purpose, to make thee a minister and a witness both of these things which thou hast seen, and of those things in the which I will appear unto thee" (Acts 26:16).

"Who also hath made us able ministers of the new testament; not of the letter, but of the spirit: for the letter killeth, but the spirit giveth life" (2 Cor.3:6).

"Therefore seeing we have this ministry, as we have received mercy, we faint not" (2 Cor.4:1).

1 Wenham, Gordon J. *The Book of Numbers*. "The New International Commentary on the Old Testament." (Grand Rapids, MI: Eerdmans Publishing Co., 1979), p.69.

"And all things *are* of God, who hath reconciled us to himself by Jesus Christ, and hath given to us the ministry of reconciliation" (2 Cor.5:18).

"Whereof I was made a minister, according to the gift of the grace of God given unto me by the effectual working of his power" (Eph.3:7).

"If ye continue in the faith grounded and settled, and *be* not moved away from the hope of the gospel, which ye have heard, *and* which was preached to every creature which is under heaven; whereof I Paul am made a minister" (Col.1:23).

"And I thank Christ Jesus our LORD, who hath enabled me, for that he counted me faithful, putting me into the ministry" (1 Tim.1:12).

"Whereunto I am appointed a preacher, and an apostle, and a teacher of the Gentiles" (2 Tim.1:11).

"So he departed thence, and found Elisha the son of Shaphat, who *was* plowing *with* twelve yoke *of oxen* before him, and he with the twelfth: and Elijah passed by him, and cast his mantle upon him" (1 Ki.19:19).

"Also I heard the voice of the LORD, saying, Whom shall I send, and who will go for us? Then said I, Here *am* I; send me" (Is.6:8).

Thought 2. The two priests, Nadab and Abihu, stand as a stark warning to the ministers of God. The work of the ministry is serious business, and the task of the minister is of critical importance. Human life and destiny are at stake; consequently, the responsibility of the minister is enormously heavy. God holds the minister accountable for the souls and lives of people—all because the fruitfulness of life and the eternal fate of people lie in his hands. Therefore, the minister must make absolutely sure that he approaches God exactly as God says:

⇒ not in a worship created by his own mind
⇒ not in self-righteousness
⇒ not in a self-made worship
⇒ not in a self-made worship
⇒ not in laziness
⇒ not abusing authority
⇒ not with disrespect and irreverence
⇒ not in drunkenness and intoxication
⇒ not having been a glutton
⇒ not having stolen
⇒ not with greed
⇒ not living in lust and immorality

The minister of God must approach God exactly as God says: he must demonstrate that he reveres the holy presence of God by approaching God through God's son, the Lord Jesus Christ. Moreover, he must teach people to approach God exactly as God dictates, through the Lord Jesus Christ. And he must teach people to respect and revere the holy presence of God. Again, this passage stands as a stark warning to the ministers of God. In the words of *The Expositor's Bible Commentary*:

> "The deaths of Aaron's newly consecrated sons should warn God's ministers of the awesome seriousness of their task....seemingly the most common reports of failure we hear of God's ministers in our day are of their malfeasance, indolence, greed, lust, and abuse of power. Tragically the lessons of the past are forgotten with frightful ease. The spiritual descendants of Nadab and Abihu continue to occupy the ranks of the 'ministers' of God."[2]

2 (3:5-13) **Assistants—Laymen, Calling of—Call, of Laypersons—Levites, Calling of—Levites, Duty of**: there was the appointment of the Levites. They were set apart to be assistants to the priests.

OUTLINE	SCRIPTURE	SCRIPTURE	OUTLINE
2. The appointment of the Levites: Some are set apart to be assistants a. Called to be the assistants to the High Priest, Aaron (a symbol of Christ) 1) To take care of all the work of the Tabernacle itself 2) To take care of all the furnishings of the Tabernacle	5 And the LORD spake unto Moses, saying, 6 Bring the tribe of Levi near, and present them before Aaron the priest, that they may minister unto him. 7 And they shall keep his charge, and the charge of the whole congregation before the tabernacle of the congregation, to do the service of the tabernacle. 8 And they shall keep all the instruments of the tabernacle of the congregation, and the charge of the children of Israel, to do the service of the tabernacle.	9 And thou shalt give the Levites unto Aaron and to his sons: they are wholly given unto him out of the children of Israel. 10 And thou shalt appoint Aaron and his sons, and they shall wait on their priest's office: and the stranger that cometh nigh shall be put to death. 11 And the LORD spake unto Moses, saying, 12 And I, behold, I have taken the Levites from among the children of Israel instead of all the firstborn that openeth the matrix among the children of Israel:	3) To be totally given over to assist the High Priest 4) To protect the sanctity of the sanctuary: Guard it against the abuse of intruders b. Called by God to a very special position: To become the substitute, the replacement for the firstborn sons—to be given to the service of God instead of the firstborn sons 1) The special position: "The Levites are mine"

2 *The Expositor's Bible Commentary*, Vol.2. Frank E. Gaebelein, Editor, p.721.

OUTLINE	SCRIPTURE	SCRIPTURE	OUTLINE
2) The authority of the call • The historical fact: God had set apart the first-	therefore the Levites shall be mine; 13 Because all the firstborn are mine; for on the day that I smote all the firstborn in	the land of Egypt I hallowed unto me all the firstborn in Israel, both man and beast: mine shall they be: I am the LORD.	born to serve Him since Egypt (Ex.13:2f; 22:29; 34:19f) • The sovereignty of God

1. The Levites were called to be assistants to the High Priest, Aaron, and to the other priests. Keep in mind that the priests were a symbol of Christ. This particular Scripture makes a clear distinction between the priests and their assistants. The priests were the anointed, ordained ministers of God, ultimately responsible for the people and for the Tabernacle of God (a symbol of the church). The Levites were laypersons called by God to step forth and serve as assistants to the priests. They were called out of the secular world just as the priests had been to give full time to the service of God. But their call and work was to be helpers, assistants to the priests. Their ministry was distinct, set apart from the secular world, but it was to be under the supervision of the priests. Note exactly what their work was:

a. They were to take care of all the work of the Tabernacle itself (v.7). They performed whatever duties the priests and the worshippers needed.
b. They were to take care of all the furnishings of the Tabernacle (v.8). This, of course, included day-to-day care and maintenance, but it also included the moving of the Tabernacle from campsite to campsite. They were responsible for taking it apart, packing, transporting, and erecting the Tabernacle as God's people marched to the promised land (Num.1:50-51).
c. They were to be totally given over to assist the High Priest and the other priests (v.9). Note how the privilege of their call was stressed: among all the people of God, they were the ones chosen to serve as assistants to God.
d. They were to protect the sanctity of the sanctuary, to guard it against the abuse of intruders and robbers (v.10; cp. Num.1:51). Note the word "stranger" (zar): the word means unauthorized, illegitimate, a person outside the family, a foreigner. Simply stated, the Levites were to keep any unauthorized person away from the Tabernacle. If a person did not belong at the Tabernacle, he was to be kept away. The Levites even had the right to execute an intruder.

2. The Levites were called by God to a very special position, a very meaningful position. Note this: they became the substitute, the replacement for the firstborn sons. They were to be given to the service of God *instead of* the firstborn sons. Note how meaningful this was to God: "the Levites are mine." They were His because all the firstborn had been His. Ever since the deliverance from Egypt, the firstborn had been appointed to serve God within each family. The firstborn son was also responsible for the service of God among the people of God. When God executed judgment upon Egypt by striking down the firstborn son, He laid claim to the firstborn sons of Israel. He had delivered the firstborn sons of Israel from judgment; therefore, He had the right to lay claim to their lives. After Egypt, they were appointed to serve God as the servants of his ministry. They were to take care of God's people, to be His ministers among the people. In the firstborn son, each family had a picture or symbol of the great salvation of God when He delivered them from the slavery of Egypt (a symbol of the world).

But now, the Levites were being set apart as the substitute, the replacement for the firstborn sons. Note the stress upon the sovereignty of God: they are to be His. "I am the LORD." God is sovereign; therefore, He has the right to replace the firstborn with the Levites. He has the right to call whom He wills to serve His people.

Thought 1. The need is great. At every turn of life people are crying for help. All over the world people are crying:

• the orphans	• the suffering	• the purposeless
• the widows	• the hungry	• the dying
• the widowers	• the thirsty	• the sick
• the prisoners	• the poor	• the hospitalized
• the brokenhearted	• the empty	• the lost
• the backslidden	• the lonely	• the doomed

The list of people crying for help and needing help is beyond imagination. The ministers of God—most of them—are doing everything they can. But they need help. They need men and women who will step forth and be assistants, helpers in the ministry. The person called must step forth and accept the call, not reject it.

"But what think ye? A *certain* man had two sons; and he came to the first, and said, Son, go work to day in my vineyard. He answered and said, I will not: but afterward he repented, and went. And he came to the second, and said likewise. And he answered and said, I *go,* sir: and went not" (Mt.21:28-30).

"He also that had received two talents came and said, LORD, thou deliveredst unto me two talents: behold, I have gained two other talents beside them. His lord said unto him, Well done, good and faithful servant; thou hast been faithful over a few things, I will make thee ruler over many things: enter thou into the joy of thy lord" (Mt.25:22-23).

"And went to *him,* and bound up his wounds, pouring in oil and wine, and set him on his own beast, and brought him to an inn, and took care of him" (Lk.10:34).

"For unto whomsoever much is given, of him shall be much required: and to whom men have committed much, of him they will ask the more" (Lk.12:48).

"I beseech you therefore, brethren, by the mercies of God, that ye present your bodies a living sacrifice, holy, acceptable unto God, *which is* your reasonable service" (Ro.12:1).

"Therefore, my beloved brethren, be ye stedfast, unmovable, always abounding in the work of the

LORD, forasmuch as ye know that your labour is not in vain in the LORD" (1 Cor.15:58).

"And I intreat thee also, true yokefellow, help those women which laboured with me in the gospel, with Clement also, and *with* other my fellowlabourers, whose names *are* in the book of life" (Ph.4:3).

"If any man speak, *let him speak* as the oracles of God; if any man minister, *let him do it* as of the ability which God giveth: that God in all things may be glorified through Jesus Christ, to whom be praise and dominion for ever and ever. Amen" (1 Pt.4:11).

"For Moses had said, Consecrate yourselves to day to the LORD" (Ex.32:29).

"I was eyes to the blind, and feet *was* I to the lame" (Job 29:15).

"My son, give me thine heart, and let thine eyes observe my ways" (Pr.23:26).

"She stretcheth out her hand to the poor; yea, she reacheth forth her hands to the needy" (Pr.31:20).

"Also I heard the voice of the LORD, saying, Whom shall I send, and who will go for us? Then said I, Here *am* I; send me" (Is.6:8).

"The LORD GOD hath given me the tongue of the learned, that I should know how to speak a word in season to *him that is* weary: he wakeneth morning by morning, he wakeneth mine ear to hear as the learned" (Is.50:4).

"Yet now be strong, O Zerubbabel, saith the LORD; and be strong, O Joshua, son of Josedech, the high priest; and be strong, all ye people of the land, saith the LORD, and work: for *I am* with you, saith the LORD of hosts" (Hag.2:4).

3 (3:14-39) **Census, of Levites—Levites, Census of—Levites, Duties of—Levites, Placement of—Assistants, Duties of—Ministers, Assistants to**: there were the census, placement, and duties of the Levites. This is a picture of knowing one's job and doing it well. The Levites needed to be numbered just as the other tribes of God's people were. Just how many men were available for God's service needed to be known. They were to be ministers of God's people, scattered out among them (Num.35:1-8). Therefore, the leadership had to know how many Levites were available for the ministry.

OUTLINE	SCRIPTURE	SCRIPTURE	OUTLINE
3. The census, placement, & duties of the Levites: A picture of doing one's job well a. The LORD's charge to Moses 1) To count every male one month old or older	14 And the LORD spake unto Moses in the wilderness of Sinai, saying, 15 Number the children of Levi after the house of their fathers, by their families: every male from a month old and upward shalt thou number them.	five hundred. 23 The families of the Gershonites shall pitch behind the tabernacle westward. 24 And the chief of the house of the father of the Gershonites shall be Eliasaph the son of Lael.	3) Their camp: To the west behind the Tabernacle 4) Their leader: Eliasaph, son of Lael
2) The picture of total obedience: Moses did exactly what God commanded	16 And Moses numbered them according to the word of the LORD, as he was commanded.	25 And the charge of the sons of Gershon in the tabernacle of the congregation shall be the tabernacle, and	5) Their duties: To take care of the tent of the Tabernacle, its coverings & curtains
b. The overall view of the Levites 1) The three sons of Levi: Gershon, Kohath, & Merari 2) The Gershonite clans: Libni & Shimei 3) The Kohathite clans: Amram, Izhar, Hebron, & Uzziel	17 And these were the sons of Levi by their names; Gershon, and Kohath, and Merari. 18 And these are the names of the sons of Gershon by their families; Libni, and Shimei. 19 And the sons of Kohath by their families; Amram, and Izehar, Hebron, and Uzziel.	the tent, the covering thereof, and the hanging for the door of the tabernacle of the congregation, 26 And the hangings of the court, and the curtain for the door of the court, which is by the tabernacle, and by the altar round about, and the cords of it for all the service thereof.	• the entrance curtain • the courtyard curtains • the entrance curtain to the courtyard • the ropes & all else related to the coverings & curtains
4) The Merarite clans: Mahli & Mushi	20 And the sons of Merari by their families; Mahli, and Mushi. These are the families of the Levites according to the house of their fathers.	27 And of Kohath was the family of the Amramites, and the family of the Izeharites, and the family of the Hebronites, and the family of the Uzzielites: these are the families of the Kohathites.	d. The detailed look at the Kohathites 1) Their clans: Amramites, Izhorites, Hebronites, Uzzielites
c. The detailed look at the Gershonites 1) The clans: Libnites & Shimeites 2) Their census number: 7,500	21 Of Gershon was the family of the Libnites, and the family of the Shimites: these are the families of the Gershonites. 22 Those that were numbered of them, according to the number of all the males, from a month old and upward, even those that were numbered of them were seven thousand and	28 In the number of all the males, from a month old and upward, were eight thousand and six hundred, keeping the charge of the sanctuary. 29 The families of the sons of Kohath shall pitch on the side of the tabernacle southward. 30 And the chief of the	2) Their census number: 8,600 3) Their overall responsibility: The care of the sanctuary 4) Their camp: The south side of the Tabernacle 5) Their leader: Elizaphan,

OUTLINE	SCRIPTURE	SCRIPTURE	OUTLINE
son of Uzziel	house of the father of the families of the Kohathites shall be Elizaphan the son of Uzziel.	of the tabernacle northward.	
6) Their duties: To take care of... • the Ark, the table, & the lampstand • the altars & utensils • the inner curtain & all else related to their use	31 And their charge shall be the ark, and the table, and the candlestick, and the altars, and the vessels of the sanctuary wherewith they minister, and the hanging, and all the service thereof.	36 And under the custody and charge of the sons of Merari shall be the boards of the tabernacle, and the bars thereof, and the pillars thereof, and the sockets thereof, and all the vessels thereof, and all that serveth thereto,	5) Their duties: To take care of... • the supporting frames of the Tabernacle, crossbars, posts, bases, & all else related to their use
7) The chief administrator over all the Levites was given special oversight over the sanctuary & the Kohathites: Eleazar, son of Aaron	32 And Eleazar the son of Aaron the priest shall be chief over the chief of the Levites, and have the oversight of them that keep the charge of the sanctuary.	37 And the pillars of the court round about, and their sockets, and their pins, and their cords.	• the posts of the courtyard with their bases, pegs, & ropes
e. The detailed look at the Merarites 1) Their clans: The Mahlites & the Mushites	33 Of Merari was the family of the Mahlites, and the family of the Mushites: these are the families of Merari.	38 But those that encamp before the tabernacle toward the east, even before the tabernacle of the congregation eastward, shall be Moses, and Aaron and his sons, keeping the charge of the sanctuary for the charge of the children of Israel; and the stranger that cometh nigh shall be put to death.	f. The detailed look at Moses & Aaron 1) Their camp: To the east toward the sunrise, in front of the Tabernacle 2) Their duties: Had overall re-sponsibility for the sanctuary—in behalf of the people 3) The warning: Anyone other than a priest or Levite who approached the sanctuary was to be executed
2) Their census number: 6,200	34 And those that were numbered of them, according to the number of all the males, from a month old and upward, were six thousand and two hundred.	39 All that were numbered of the Levites, which Moses and Aaron numbered at the commandment of the LORD, throughout their families, all the males from a month old and upward, were twenty and two thousand.	g. The total number of Levites one month old or older: 22,000
3) Their leader: Zuriel, son of Abihail 4) Their camp: The north side of the Tabernacle	35 And the chief of the house of the father of the families of Merari was Zuriel the son of Abihail: these shall pitch on the side		

1. The LORD charged Moses to count every male Levite who was one month old or older (v.15). Note the total, explicit obedience of Moses: he did exactly what God commanded (v.16). He took a census of the Levites in order to find out how many were available for the ministry.

2. The overall view of the Levites includes just three sons of Levi: Gershon, Kohath, and Merari (v.17-20).

3. The detailed look at the Gershonites is clearly seen in the Scripture and outline (v.21-26). The Gershonites were responsible for taking care of the tent of the Tabernacle: its covers and curtains (v.25-26). There were three curtains that served as entrances to the Tabernacle: a curtain covering the entrance to the court (v.26; 4:26); a second curtain at the entrance to the tent itself (v.25, 31, 4:25); and a third curtain that set apart the Most Holy Place from everything else within the Tabernacle (v.4-5).

4. A detailed look at the Kohathites is also clearly seen in the Scripture and outline (v.27-32). Note that Eleazar was the chief supervisor for the Gershonites (v.32). Most likely this was because the Gershonites were in charge of the ark and the other major furnishings of the Tabernacle.

5. A detailed look at the Merarites is also clearly seen in the Scripture and outline (v.33-37).

6. Note the detailed look at Moses and Aaron (v.38-39). Moses and Aaron camped in the most honored location, east of the Tabernacle, facing the sun. The morning sun would rise and shine on the entrance to the Tabernacle, symbolizing the life-giving light of God that shone upon His people.[3] Moses and Aaron camped at this honored location because of their responsibility to work in and around the Tabernacle.

Note that the total number of Levites one month old or older was 22,000 (v.39). This means that the number of adults available for service was a very small number.

> **Thought 1**. Every Levite had his place of service; he had a particular job to do for God and for His people. His duties were spelled out in detail. So it should be with every assistant, every helper in the service of God. He should be assigned particular duties to perform for God. Once assigned, the assistant must fulfill his ministry. He must do the work, do it faithfully and well—do it with all his heart and mind.
>
> **"Jesus saith unto them, My meat is to do the will of him that sent me, and to finish his work" (Jn.4:34).**
>
> **"I have glorified thee on the earth: I have finished the work which thou gavest me to do" (Jn.17:4).**
>
> **"And whatsoever ye do in word or deed, *do* all in the name of the LORD Jesus, giving thanks to God and the Father by him" (Acts 20:24).**
>
> **"And whatsoever ye do in word or deed, *do* all in the name of the LORD Jesus, giving thanks to God and the Father by him" (Col.3:17).**

3 *The Expositor's Bible Commentary*, Vol.2. Frank E. Gaebelein, Editor, p.727.

"And whatsoever ye do, do *it* heartily, as to the LORD, and not unto men" (Col.3:23).

"Therefore, my beloved brethren, be ye stedfast, unmovable, always abounding in the work of the LORD, forasmuch as ye know that your labour is not in vain in the LORD" (1 Cor.15:58).

"For I am now ready to be offered, and the time of my departure is at hand. I have fought a good fight, I have finished *my* course, I have kept the faith" (2 Tim.4:6-7).

"With good will doing service, as to the LORD, and not to men" (Eph.6:7).

"Wherefore we receiving a kingdom which cannot be moved, let us have grace, whereby we may serve God acceptably with reverence and godly fear" (Heb.12:28).

"Serve the LORD with fear, and rejoice with trembling" (Ps.2:11).

4 (3:40-51) **Firstborn, Census of—Census, of the Firstborn—Redemption, Picture of**: there was the census of the firstborn and their replacement by the Levites. Note: this is a picture of redemption. Remember that the Levites were to become the substitute, the replacement for the firstborn sons (Num.3:11-13). The Levites were counted by God as a redemption for the firstborn of the Israelites. Throughout history, God had accepted the firstborn of animals to be sacrificed to Him, but He had never approved the sacrifice of persons as an offering. Something else was always substituted for a person. In the present Scripture, a Levite was substituted for the firstborn son as an offering to the service of God. Note that the firstborn of livestock was also included in the substitutionary arrangement. A Levite was substituted for the firstborn, and a Levite's livestock was substituted for the firstborn livestock.[4]

OUTLINE	SCRIPTURE	SCRIPTURE	OUTLINE
4. The census of the firstborn & their replacement by the Levites: A picture of redemption a. The LORD's charge: To count all the firstborn sons in Israel: One month old or older	40 And the LORD said unto Moses, Number all the firstborn of the males of the children of Israel from a month old and upward, and take the number of their names.	46 And for those that are to be redeemed of the two hundred and threescore and thirteen of the firstborn of the children of Israel, which are more than the Levites;	2) To redeem the 273, pay the price for the firstborn sons who exceeded the number of Levites
1) To substitute the Levites for all the firstborn of Israel, to replace them as the servants of God 2) To substitute the livestock of the Levites for the firstborn livestock of Israel (to be used in the sacrifices)	41 And thou shalt take the Levites for me (I am the LORD) instead of all the firstborn among the children of Israel; and the cattle of the Levites instead of all the firstlings among the cattle of the children of Israel.	47 Thou shalt even take five shekels apiece by the poll, after the shekel of the sanctuary shalt thou take them: (the shekel is twenty gerahs:)	• To collect five pieces of silver for each one
b. The strict obedience of Moses	42 And Moses numbered, as the LORD commanded him, all the firstborn among the children of Israel.	48 And thou shalt give the money, wherewith the odd number of them is to be redeemed, unto Aaron and to his sons.	• To give the redemption money to the priests (Aaron & his sons)
c. The number of firstborn sons one month old or older: 22,273	43 And all the firstborn males by the number of names, from a month old and upward, of those that were numbered of them, were twenty and two thousand two hundred and threescore and thirteen.	49 And Moses took the redemption money of them that were over and above them that were redeemed by the Levites:	3) The obedience of Moses: He collected the redemption money
d. The special charge	44 And the LORD spake unto Moses, saying,	50 Of the firstborn of the children of Israel took he the money; a thousand three hundred and threescore and five shekels, after the shekel of the sanctuary:	• He collected 1,365 shekels (about 34 pounds of silver)
1) To substitute the Levites for the firstborn Israelites: The Levites were thereafter to be the LORD's, His servants	45 Take the Levites instead of all the firstborn among the children of Israel, and the cattle of the Levites instead of their cattle; and the Levites shall be mine: I am the LORD.	51 And Moses gave the money of them that were redeemed unto Aaron and to his sons, according to the word of the LORD, as the LORD commanded Moses.	• He gave the money to the priests, Aaron & his sons • He was careful to obey God—totally

1. Note the LORD's charge: to count all the firstborn sons in Israel one month old or older (v.40-41). Remember, the firstborn had been responsible for the spiritual welfare of God's people (v.11-13). Now the Levites were to replace the firstborn as the servants of God. As pointed out above, the livestock of the Levites was also to be substituted for the livestock of the firstborn. This meant that the livestock of the Levites was to be used in the sacrifices offered up to God.

2. Note the strict obedience of Moses: he took a census of all the firstborn sons in Israel, one month old or older.

3. The number of firstborn sons—one month old or older—was 22,273. Note that there were 273 more firstborn sons than there were Levites (22,000).

4. Now comes the special charge from the LORD to Moses: he was to substitute the Levites for the firstborn Israelites. The Levites thereafter were to be the LORD's, His servants (v.44-51).

But what about the 273 firstborn sons who exceeded the number of Levites (v.46-47)? They had to be redeemed; that

4 *The Expositor's Bible Commentary*, Vol.2. Frank E. Gaebelein, Editor, p.728-729.

is, the ransom price had to be paid for them. The price of redemption was five pieces of silver for each one. Note that the ransom price was to be given to the priest for the service of God (v.48).

Again, the obedience of Moses was stressed. He collected the ransom money for each person. He collected about 34 pounds of silver and gave the money to the priest for the service of God. Note the reemphasis: he was careful to obey God—totally (v.51).

Thought 1. This is clearly a picture of redemption. The Levites were servants of God who redeemed the firstborn sons of Israel. As such, they are pictures of the Lord Jesus Christ who paid the redemption price for His people. But note: Jesus Christ did not pay silver and gold to redeem His people. He ransomed His people by substituting His own life for them. Jesus Christ died and paid the ransom price with His own precious blood.

"For all have sinned, and come short of the glory of God; Being justified freely by his grace through the redemption that is in Christ Jesus" (Ro.3:23-24).

"But of him are ye in Christ Jesus, who of God is made unto us wisdom, and righteousness, and sanctification, and redemption" (1 Cor.1:30).

"Christ hath redeemed us from the curse of the law, being made a curse for us: for it is written, Cursed *is* every one that hangeth on a tree" (Gal.3:13).

"In whom we have redemption through his blood, the forgiveness of sins, according to the riches of his grace" (Eph.1:7).

"In whom we have redemption through his blood, *even* the forgiveness of sins" (Col.1:14).

"For the grace of God that bringeth salvation hath appeared to all men, Teaching us that, denying ungodliness and worldly lusts, we should live soberly, righteously, and godly, in this present world; Looking for that blessed hope, and the glorious appearing of the great God and our Saviour Jesus Christ; Who gave himself for us, that he might redeem us from all iniquity, and purify unto himself a peculiar people, zealous of good works" (Tit.2:11-14).

"Neither by the blood of goats and calves, but by his own blood he entered in once into the holy place, having obtained eternal redemption *for us*" (Heb.9:12).

"Forasmuch as ye know that ye were not redeemed with corruptible things, *as* silver and gold, from your vain conversation *received* by tradition from your fathers; But with the precious blood of Christ, as of a lamb without blemish and without spot" (1 Pt.1:18-19).

"And they sung a new song, saying, Thou art worthy to take the book, and to open the seals thereof: for thou wast slain, and hast redeemed us to God by thy blood out of every kindred, and tongue, and people, and nation; And hast made us unto our God kings and priests: and we shall reign on the earth" (Rev.5:9-10).

TYPES, SYMBOLS, AND PICTURES
(Numbers 3:1-51)

Historical Term	Type or Picture (Scriptural Basis for Each)	Life Application for Today's Believer	Biblical Application
The High Priest Num.3:5-13; 4:1-20 (See also Lev.16:3, 6)	*The High Priest is a symbol of Jesus Christ. But keep this fact in mind: the High Priest had to approach God through the Sin Offering and Burnt Offering. He himself had to be cleansed from sin before he could make sacrifice for the sins of the people. Once his sins had been forgiven, he stood sinless and perfect before God. He was then able to represent the people before God. This is a symbol of Jesus Christ, the High Priest of God, who stood sinless and perfect before God, offering Himself as the sacrifice for sin.* **"And thou shalt appoint Aaron and his sons, and they shall wait on their priest's office: and the stranger that cometh nigh shall be put to death" (Num.3:10).**	⇒ Sin has separated and alienated man from God. Sin has created a veil, a curtain, between God and man. The curtain of sin cannot be removed by man, no matter how much he tries. No matter how righteous man seeks to be, his righteousness cannot break through the curtain of sin that separates him and God. But thank God! Jesus Christ—our Great High Priest—has ripped the curtain of sin from top to bottom, opening the way into God's presence. Man now has access into the presence of God. All of us—without exception—can now enter the presence of God, all because of what Jesus Christ has done.	***"Having therefore, brethren, boldness to enter into the holiest by the blood of Jesus, By a new and living way, which he hath consecrated for us, through the veil, that is to say, his flesh; And having an high priest over the house of God; Let us draw near with a true heart in full assurance of faith, having our hearts sprinkled from an evil conscience, and our bodies washed with pure water" (Heb.10:19-22).*** ***"But your iniquities have separated between you and your God, and your sins have hid his face from you, that he will not hear" (Is.59:2).*** ***"Jesus, when he had cried again with a loud voice, yielded up the ghost. And, behold, the veil of the***

Historical Term	Type or Picture (Scriptural Basis for Each)	Life Application for Today's Believer	Biblical Application
			temple was rent in twain from the top to the bottom; and the earth did quake, and the rocks rent" (Mt.27:50-51).
Egypt Num. 3:5-13; 9:1-14 (See also Lev. 11:44-47; 19:33-34)	*Egypt is a symbol of the world. God had saved His people from the slavery of the world (Egypt), from the slavery of its sin and death. Note why:* *1. He saved them to be their God.* *2. He saved them to be set apart as His holy people.* **"And the LORD spake unto Moses in the wilderness of Sinai, in the first month of the second year after they were come out of the land of Egypt, saying," (Num.9:1).** **"For I *am* the LORD that bringeth you up out of the land of Egypt, to be your God: ye shall therefore be holy, for I *am* holy" (Lev.11:45).**	⇒ The application and lesson for us is clear: 1. We must declare that God is the Savior of the world, the Savior who delivered us from the world (Egypt). We must bear testimony, strong testimony, that God is building a new race of people, a people... • who will let Him be their God • who will be set apart and live as the holy people of God To be holy means that we must learn to discern more and more between the clean and unclean, the holy and unholy. We must sharpen our power to discern, learn to distinguish between right and wrong, the just and unjust, the moral and immoral, the kind and unkind, the selfish and unselfish. 2. We must be holy because God is holy. As believers, we have no choice: the command is direct and forceful. We must be like God: consecrated — set apart — holy.	***"That he would grant unto us, that we being delivered out of the hand of our enemies might serve him without fear, In holiness and righteousness before him, all the days of our life" (Lk.1:74-75).*** ***"Having therefore these promises, dearly beloved, let us cleanse ourselves from all filthiness of the flesh and spirit, perfecting holiness in the fear of God" (2 Cor. 7:1).*** ***"Follow peace with all men, and holiness, without which no man shall see the Lord" (Heb.12:14).*** ***"But sanctify [set apart as holy, pure] the Lord God in your hearts: and be ready always to give an answer to every man that asketh you a reason of the hope that is in you with meekness and fear" (1 Pt.3:15).*** ***"But the natural man receiveth not the things of the Spirit of God: for they are foolishness unto him: neither can he know them, because they are spiritually discerned" (1 Cor.2:14).*** ***"But strong meat belongeth to them that are of full age, even those who by reason of use have their senses exercised to discern both good and evil" (Heb.5:14).*** ***"Give therefore thy servant an understanding heart to judge thy people, that I may discern between good and bad: for who is able to judge this thy so great a people?" (1 Ki.3:9).***
Sunrise on the Tabernacle's Entrance Num.3:14-39	*The morning sun that struck the entrance of the Tabernacle symbolized the life-giving light of God that shone on His people. This symbol later became a picture of Jesus Christ, God who came in the flesh of mankind, the Light of the world.* **"But those that encamp before the tabernacle**	⇒ Jesus Christ is said to be the *Light of men* (John 1:4) and the *Light of the world* (John 8:12; John 9:5; John 12:46). It is possible for the Light, Jesus Himself, to be *in men* (John 11:10; cp. Col. 1:27), and for men to become children of Light (see POSB note—John 12:34-36).	***"The people that walked in darkness have seen a great light: they that dwell in the land of the shadow of death, upon them hath the light shined" (Is. 9:2).*** ***"In him was life; and the life was the light of men" (Jn. 1:4).*** ***"Then spake Jesus again unto them, saying, I am the light of the world: he that***

Historical Term	Type or Picture (Scriptural Basis for Each)	Life Application for Today's Believer	Biblical Application
	toward the east, *even* before the tabernacle of the congregation eastward, *shall be* Moses, and Aaron and his sons, keeping the charge of the sanctuary for the charge of the children of Israel; and the stranger that cometh nigh shall be put to death" (Num.3:38).	Apparently, Jesus Christ used the word *light* often. John uses the word about twenty-one times. What is meant by calling Jesus the Light? 1. Jesus Christ, the Light, is light by nature. Light is what He is within Himself, within His being, His nature, His essence, His character. Scripture says... • that "God is Light" (1 John 1:5); • that Jesus Christ is "the image of the invisible God" (Col. 1:15); • therefore, "Jesus Christ is Light." He is "the Light of the world." 2. Jesus Christ, the Light, tells us that He is holy, righteous, and pure. Light is the symbol of purity and holiness. Light means the absence of darkness and blindness; it has no spots of darkness or blackness, nor of sin and shame. 3. Jesus Christ, the Light, reveals. His light clearly shows the nature, the meaning, and the destiny of all things. His light shines in, spots, opens up, identifies, illuminates, and shows things as they really are. The light of Jesus Christ shows the truth about the world and man and God. The light of Jesus Christ reveals that He loves and cares for man and wants man to love and care for Him. 4. Jesus Christ, the Light, guides. His light allows a man to walk out of darkness. Man no longer has to grope, grasp, and stumble about trying to find his way through life. The path of life can now be clearly seen. 5. Jesus Christ, the Light, does away with darkness and with chaos. His light routs, wipes out, strips away and erases the darkness. The empty chaos of creation was routed by	***followeth me shall not walk in darkness, but shall have the light of life" (Jn. 8:12).*** ***"Then Jesus said unto them, Yet a little while is the light with you. Walk while ye have the light, lest darkness come upon you: for he that walketh in darkness knoweth not whither he goeth" (Jn. 12:35).*** ***"The LORD is my light and my salvation; whom shall I fear? the LORD is the strength of my life; of whom shall I be afraid?" (Ps. 27:1).*** ***"For the LORD God is a sun and shield: the LORD will give grace and glory: no good thing will he withhold from them that walk uprightly" (Ps. 84:11).*** ***"Thy sun shall no more go down; neither shall thy moon withdraw itself: for the LORD shall be thine everlasting light, and the days of thy mourning shall be ended" (Is. 60:20).*** ***"This then is the message which we have heard of him, and declare unto you, that God is light, and in him is no darkness at all" (1 Jn. 1:5).*** ***"And there shall be no night there; and they need no candle, neither light of the sun; for the Lord God giveth them light: and they shall reign for ever and ever" (Rev. 22:5).***

Historical Term	Type or Picture (Scriptural Basis for Each)	Life Application for Today's Believer	Biblical Application
		the light given by God (Genesis 1:3). Jesus Christ is the Light that can save man from chaos (John 14:1, 17; John 12:46; John 16:33).	
The Census of the Firstborn and Their Replacement by the Levites Num.3:40-51	*The census of the firstborn and their replacement by the Levites is a picture of redemption.* **"Take the Levites instead of all the firstborn among the children of Israel, and the cattle of the Levites instead of their cattle; and the Levites shall be mine: I *am* the LORD. And for those that are to be redeemed of the two hundred and threescore and thirteen of the firstborn of the children of Israel, which are more than the Levites" (Num.3:45-46).**	The Levites were servants of God who redeemed the first-born sons of Israel. As such, they are pictures of the Lord Jesus Christ who paid the redemption price for His people. But note: Jesus Christ did not pay silver and gold to redeem His people. He ransomed His people by substituting His own life for them. Jesus Christ died, paid the ransom price, with His own precious blood.	***"For all have sinned, and come short of the glory of God; Being justified freely by his grace through the redemption that is in Christ Jesus" (Ro.3:23-24).*** ***"But of him are ye in Christ Jesus, who of God is made unto us wisdom, and righteousness, and sanctification, and redemption" (1 Cor.1:30).*** ***"Christ hath redeemed us from the curse of the law, being made a curse for us: for it is written, Cursed is every one that hangeth on a tree" (Gal.3:13).*** ***"In whom we have redemption through his blood, the forgiveness of sins, according to the riches of his grace" (Eph.1:7).*** ***"In whom we have redemption through his blood, even the forgiveness of sins" (Col.1:14 See also Tit.2:11-14; Heb.9:12; 1 Pt. 1:18-19; Rev.5:9-10).***

C. The Organization of the Mature Levites & Their Duties—the Fourth Census: Knowing One's Job & Doing It, 4:1-49

1. The charge to count the available workers & assign the duties to the Kohathite clans: Stresses the warning of God to respect His holiness
- a. The charge: Must know the number of workers: Take a census, count all the men from thirty to fifty years old
- b. The work: To take care of the most holy things
- c. The critical importance of the most holy things: Can be prepared only by the priests (a symbol of Christ)
  - 1) The Ark
    - To cover it with the Inner Veil or Curtain
    - To then cover this with hides of goats or sea cows, then with a blue cloth
    - To put the poles in place
  - 2) The Table of the Presence
    - To spread a blue cloth over it
    - To place all accessories & the bread upon the blue cloth
    - To cover these with a scarlet cloth & then hides of cows
    - To then put the poles in place
  - 3) The lampstand and all its accessories
    - To wrap in a blue cloth
    - To then wrap these in the hides of goats or sea cows
  - 4) The gold altar
    - To wrap the altar in a blue cloth, then with hides of goats or sea cows & put the poles in place

And the LORD spake unto Moses and unto Aaron, saying,

2 Take the sum of the sons of Kohath from among the sons of Levi, after their families, by the house of their fathers,

3 From thirty years old and upward even until fifty years old, all that enter into the host, to do the work in the tabernacle of the congregation.

4 This shall be the service of the sons of Kohath in the tabernacle of the congregation, about the most holy things:

5 And when the camp setteth forward, Aaron shall come, and his sons, and they shall take down the covering vail, and cover the ark of testimony with it:

6 And shall put thereon the covering of badgers' skins, and shall spread over it a cloth wholly of blue, and shall put in the staves thereof.

7 And upon the table of shewbread they shall spread a cloth of blue, and put thereon the dishes, and the spoons, and the bowls, and covers to cover withal: and the continual bread shall be thereon:

8 And they shall spread upon them a cloth of scarlet, and cover the same with a covering of badgers' skins, and shall put in the staves thereof.

9 And they shall take a cloth of blue, and cover the candlestick of the light, and his lamps, and his tongs, and his snuffdishes, and all the oil vessels thereof, wherewith they minister unto it:

10 And they shall put it and all the vessels thereof within a covering of badgers' skins, and shall put it upon a bar.

11 And upon the golden altar they shall spread a cloth of blue, and cover it with a covering of badgers' skins, and shall put to the staves thereof:

12 And they shall take all the instruments of ministry, wherewith they minister in the sanctuary, and put them in a cloth of blue, and cover them with a covering of badgers' skins, and shall put them on a bar:

13 And they shall take away the ashes from the altar, and spread a purple cloth thereon:

14 And they shall put upon it all the vessels thereof, wherewith they minister about it, even the censers, the fleshhooks, and the shovels, and the basons, all the vessels of the altar; and they shall spread upon it a covering of badgers' skins, and put to the staves of it.

15 And when Aaron and his sons have made an end of covering the sanctuary, and all the vessels of the sanctuary, as the camp is to set forward; after that, the sons of Kohath shall come to bear it: but they shall not touch any holy thing, lest they die. These things are the burden of the sons of Kohath in the tabernacle of the congregation.

16 And to the office of Eleazar the son of Aaron the priest pertaineth the oil for the light, and the sweet incense, and the daily meat offering, and the anointing oil, and the oversight of all the tabernacle, and of all that therein is, in the sanctuary, and in the vessels thereof.

17 And the LORD spake unto Moses and unto Aaron, saying,

18 Cut ye not off the tribe of the families of the Kohathites from among the Levites:

19 But thus do unto them, that they may live, and not die, when they approach unto the most holy things: Aaron and his sons shall go in, and appoint them every one to his service and to his burden:

20 But they shall not go in to see when the holy things are covered, lest they die.

21 And the LORD spake unto Moses, saying,

22 Take also the sum of the

- To take a blue cloth & wrap all the articles used for ministering in the sanctuary, then wrap these with hides of goats or sea cows
  - 5) The bronze altar of Burnt Offering
    - To remove the ashes & put a purple cloth on it
    - To place all accessories on the purple cloth & then cover everything with hides of goats or sea cows
    - To put the poles in place for carrying
- d. The strong, emphatic warning to respect the holiness of God: Must never touch the holy things or they will be stricken dead
  - 1) Stricken dead if they touch when preparing for moving
  - 2) Stricken dead if they touch while carrying the holy things (cp. 2 Sam.6:6-7)
- e. The person placed in charge of the entire Tabernacle, everything in it: Eleazar the priest
  - 1) To personally care for the oil for the lampstand, the incense, the regular Grain Offering, & the anointing oil
  - 2) To oversee everything else in the Tabernacle
- f. The strong, emphatic warning restated—far more forcefully: The workers must be protected from the penalty of being cut off, stricken dead
  - 1) They must never be allowed to approach the holy things alone: Are to be led into the sanctuary & assigned their work by the priests
  - 2) The warning: Will be stricken dead if they even look at the holy things of God—must acknowledge God's holiness

2. The charge to count the available workers & assign the duties to the Gershonite

clans: Stresses the need for a willingness to do anything (general work or service)

a. The charge: Must know the number of workers 30 to 50 years old

b. The service of the workers: To do general work—pack, unpack, & transport certain parts of the Tabernacle

1) The curtains of the Tabernacle itself: Included the outer covering of goat or sea cow hides, & the curtain for the entrance

2) The curtains of the courtyard walls that surrounded the Tabernacle & altar: Included the curtain for the courtyard entrance, the ropes & all the altar's accessories

c. The importance of the service

1) Was to be supervised & assigned by the priests

2) Was to be under the general direction of Ithamar the priest, the son of Aaron

3. The charge to count the available workers & assign the duties to the Merarite clans: Stresses the importance of each person's service

a. The charge: Must know the available workers 30 to 50 years old

b. The service of the workers: To pack, unpack, & transport the frame of the Tabernacle & the surrounding courtyard

- crossbars
- posts & bases
- tent pegs & ropes
- other equipment

c. The importance of each person's service

1) Each person was to be assigned & made responsible for a particular task

sons of Gershon, throughout the houses of their fathers, by their families;

23 From thirty years old and upward until fifty years old shalt thou number them; all that enter in to perform the service, to do the work in the tabernacle of the congregation.

24 This is the service of the families of the Gershonites, to serve, and for burdens:

25 And they shall bear the curtains of the tabernacle, and the tabernacle of the congregation, his covering, and the covering of the badgers' skins that is above upon it, and the hanging for the door of the tabernacle of the congregation,

26 And the hangings of the court, and the hanging for the door of the gate of the court, which is by the tabernacle and by the altar round about, and their cords, and all the instruments of their service, and all that is made for them: so shall they serve.

27 At the appointment of Aaron and his sons shall be all the service of the sons of the Gershonites, in all their burdens, and in all their service: and ye shall appoint unto them in charge all their burdens.

28 This is the service of the families of the sons of Gershon in the tabernacle of the congregation: and their charge shall be under the hand of Ithamar the son of Aaron the priest.

29 As for the sons of Merari, thou shalt number them after their families, by the house of their fathers;

30 From thirty years old and upward even unto fifty years old shalt thou number them, every one that entereth into the service, to do the work of the tabernacle of the congregation.

31 And this is the charge of their burden, according to all their service in the tabernacle of the congregation; the boards of the tabernacle, and the bars thereof, and the pillars thereof, and sockets thereof,

32 And the pillars of the court round about, and their sockets, and their pins, and their cords, with all their instruments, and with all their service: and by name ye shall reckon the instruments of the charge of their burden.

33 This is the service of the families of the sons of Merari, according to all their service, in the tabernacle of the congregation, under the hand of Ithamar the son of Aaron the priest.

34 And Moses and Aaron and the chief of the congregation numbered the sons of the Kohathites after their families, and after the house of their fathers,

35 From thirty years old and upward even unto fifty years old, every one that entereth into the service, for the work in the tabernacle of the congregation:

36 And those that were numbered of them by their families were two thousand seven hundred and fifty.

37 These were they that were numbered of the families of the Kohathites, all that might do service in the tabernacle of the congregation, which Moses and Aaron did number according to the commandment of the LORD by the hand of Moses.

38 And those that were numbered of the sons of Gershon, throughout their families, and by the house of their fathers,

39 From thirty years old and upward even unto fifty years old, every one that entereth into the service, for the work in the tabernacle of the congregation,

40 Even those that were numbered of them, throughout their families, by the house of their fathers, were two thousand and six hundred and thirty.

41 These are they that were numbered of the families of the sons of Gershon, of all that might do service in the tabernacle of the congregation, whom Moses and Aaron did number according to the commandment of the LORD.

42 And those that were numbered of the families of the sons of Merari, throughout their families, by the house of their fathers,

2) The service was to be under the general direction of Ithamar the priest, the son of Aaron

4. The description & results of the census: Stresses obedience

a. The number of the Kohathite clans

1) Counted all men between 30 to 50 years of age who were eligible for service

2) Numbered 2750 men

3) The obedience of the leaders: Counted in obedience to the LORD's command

b. The number of the Gershonite clans

1) Counted all men between 30 to 50 years of age who were eligible for service

2) Numbered 2630 men

3) The obedience of the leaders: Counted in obedience to the LORD's command

c. The number of the Merarite clans

1) Counted all men between 30 to 50 years of age who were eligible for service 2) Numbered 3200 men 3) The obedience of the leaders: Counted in obedience to the LORD's command d. The summary of the census 1) Counted all the Levites by clans & families	43 From thirty years old and upward even unto fifty years old, every one that entereth into the service, for the work in the tabernacle of the congregation, 44 Even those that were numbered of them after their families, were three thousand and two hundred. 45 These be those that were numbered of the families of the sons of Merari, whom Moses and Aaron numbered according to the word of the LORD by the hand of Moses. 46 All those that were numbered of the Levites, whom Moses and Aaron and the chief of Israel numbered, after their families, and after	the house of their fathers, 47 From thirty years old and upward even unto fifty years old, every one that came to do the service of the ministry, and the service of the burden in the tabernacle of the congregation, 48 Even those that were numbered of them, were eight thousand and five hundred and fourscore. 49 According to the commandment of the LORD they were numbered by the hand of Moses, every one according to his service, and according to his burden: thus were they numbered of him, as the LORD commanded Moses.	2) Counted all men between 30 to 50 years of age who were eligible for the work of serving & carrying the Tabernacle 3) Totaled 8580 4) The strong example of obedience • They did their work as assigned, as commanded • They were counted just as the LORD commanded

DIVISION I

THE PREPARATION FOR THE MARCH TO THE PROMISED LAND, 1:1-10:36

C. The Organization of the Mature Levites and Their Duties—the Fourth Census: Knowing One's Job and Doing It, 4:1-49

(4:1-49) **Introduction—Needs, of the World, List of—Laborors, Need for—Ministering, Need for—World, Needs of—Ministry, Need for**: the world is reeling under a weight of desperate need, crying out for help. The harvest is ripe, but the laborers are few. Workers are desperately needed. Many need to step forth and commit their lives to the service of God, to meet the desperate needs of the world. Just think of the desperate needs that surround any one of us, the needs of...

- the orphans, widows, and widowers
- the brokenhearted, backslidden, and diseased
- the suffering, hungry, and thirsty
- the poor, homeless, and destitute
- the empty, lonely, and purposeless
- the blind, deaf, deformed, and handicapped
- the hospitalized, bedridden, and shut-in
- the lost, dying, and doomed

The needs are grave. People are hurting all around us. Laborers are needed, people who will step forth to do the work of the ministry. This is the challenge of the hour, the call of God Himself to everyone of us: "Step forth! Accept the challenge of My call! Meet the needs of this earth! Make a commitment! Reach out to your neighbor. To your fellow worker. To your school mate. To your family. Do the work of the ministry. This is My call to you."

Knowing one's job and doing it—this is the practical subject of this passage. The Israelites knew how many Levites there were from one month old and older, but they did not know how many Levites were available to serve in the ministry of the LORD. Therefore, another census was needed to determine the number of mature Levites aged thirty to fifty. Moreover, the task of transporting the Tabernacle from campsite to campsite was the duty of the Levites. The specific task and details involved in tearing down and erecting the Tabernacle at the new campsites needed to be assigned. Every Levite needed to know his job, and he needed to do it and do it well. This is the subject of this important Scripture: *The Organization of the Mature Levites and Their Duties—the Fourth Census: Knowing One's Job and Doing It*, 4:1-49.

1. The charge to count the available workers and assign the duties in the Kohathite clans: stresses the warning of God to respect His holiness (v.1-20).
2. The charge to count the available workers and assign the duties to the Gershonite clans: stresses the need for a willingness to do anything (general work or service) (v.21-28).
3. The charge to count the available workers and assign the duties to the Merarite clans: stresses the importance of each person's service (v.29-33).
4. The description and results of the census: stresses obedience (v.34-49).

1 (4:1-20) **Holiness, of God—God, Holiness of—Laborers, Duty of—Ministers, Duty of—Kohathite, Clan of Levites—Levites, Kohathite Clan of—Levites, Duties of—Church, Care of**: there was the charge to count the available workers and assign the duties to the Kohathite clan. The work assigned stresses the warning of God, the warning to respect His holiness (v.15-20).

OUTLINE	SCRIPTURE
1. The charge to count the available workers & assign the duties to the Kohathite clans: Stresses the warning of God to respect His holiness	And the LORD spake unto Moses and unto Aaron, saying,
a. The charge: Must know the number of workers: Take a census, count all the men from thirty to fifty years old	2 Take the sum of the sons of Kohath from among the sons of Levi, after their families, by the house of their fathers, 3 From thirty years old and upward even until fifty years old, all that enter into the host, to do the work in the tabernacle of the congregation.
b. The work: To take care of the most holy things	4 This shall be the service of the sons of Kohath in the tabernacle of the congregation, about the most holy things:
c. The critical importance of the most holy things: Can be prepared only by the priests (a symbol of Christ) 1) The Ark • To cover it with the Inner Veil or Curtain • To then cover this with hides of goats or sea cows, then with a blue cloth • To put the poles in place	5 And when the camp setteth forward, Aaron shall come, and his sons, and they shall take down the covering vail, and cover the ark of testimony with it: 6 And shall put thereon the covering of badgers' skins, and shall spread over it a cloth wholly of blue, and shall put in the staves thereof.
2) The Table of the Presence • To spread a blue cloth over it • To place all accessories & the bread upon the blue cloth • To cover these with a scarlet cloth & then hides of cows • To then put the poles in place	7 And upon the table of shewbread they shall spread a cloth of blue, and put thereon the dishes, and the spoons, and the bowls, and covers to cover withal: and the continual bread shall be thereon: 8 And they shall spread upon them a cloth of scarlet, and cover the same with a covering of badgers' skins, and shall put in the staves thereof.
3) The lampstand and all its accessories • To wrap in a blue cloth • To then wrap these in the hides of goats or sea cows	9 And they shall take a cloth of blue, and cover the candlestick of the light, and his lamps, and his tongs, and his snuffdishes, and all the oil vessels thereof, wherewith they minister unto it: 10 And they shall put it and all the vessels thereof within a covering of badgers' skins, and shall put it upon a bar.
4) The gold altar • To wrap the altar in a blue cloth, then with hides of goats or sea cows & put the poles in place • To take a blue cloth & wrap all the articles used for ministering in the sanctuary, then wrap these with hides of goats or sea cows	11 And upon the golden altar they shall spread a cloth of blue, and cover it with a covering of badgers' skins, and shall put to the staves thereof: 12 And they shall take all the instruments of ministry, wherewith they minister in the sanctuary, and put them in a cloth of blue, and cover them with a covering of badgers' skins, and shall put them on a bar:
5) The bronze altar of Burnt Offering • To remove the ashes & put a purple cloth on it • To place all accessories on the purple cloth & then cover everything with hides of goats or sea cows • To put the poles in place for carrying	13 And they shall take away the ashes from the altar, and spread a purple cloth thereon: 14 And they shall put upon it all the vessels thereof, wherewith they minister about it, even the censers, the fleshhooks, and the shovels, and the basons, all the vessels of the altar; and they shall spread upon it a covering of badgers' skins, and put to the staves of it.
d. The strong, emphatic warning to respect the holiness of God: Must never touch the holy things or they will be stricken dead 1) Stricken dead if they touch when preparing for moving 2) Stricken dead if they touch while carrying the holy things (cp. 2 Sam.6:6-7)	15 And when Aaron and his sons have made an end of covering the sanctuary, and all the vessels of the sanctuary, as the camp is to set forward; after that, the sons of Kohath shall come to bear it: but they shall not touch any holy thing, lest they die. These things are the burden of the sons of Kohath in the tabernacle of the congregation.
e. The person placed in charge of the entire Tabernacle, everything in it: Eleazar the priest 1) To personally care for the oil for the lampstand, the incense, the regular Grain Offering, & the anointing oil 2) To oversee everything else in the Tabernacle	16 And to the office of Eleazar the son of Aaron the priest pertaineth the oil for the light, and the sweet incense, and the daily meat offering, and the anointing oil, and the oversight of all the tabernacle, and of all that therein is, in the sanctuary, and in the vessels thereof.
f. The strong, emphatic warning restated—far more forcefully: The workers must be protected from the penalty of being cut off, stricken dead	17 And the LORD spake unto Moses and unto Aaron, saying, 18 Cut ye not off the tribe of the families of the Kohathites from among the Levites:
1) They must never be allowed to approach the holy things alone: Are to be led into the sanctuary & assigned their work by the priests	19 But thus do unto them, that they may live, and not die, when they approach unto the most holy things: Aaron and his sons shall go in, and appoint them every one to his service and to his burden:
2) The warning: Will be stricken dead if they even look at the holy things of God—must acknowledge God's holiness	20 But they shall not go in to see when the holy things are covered, lest they die.

1. There was the clear charge given to Moses and Aaron: they must know the number of available workers. Therefore, they were to take a census, count all the men from thirty to fifty years old (v.3). In chapter 3, the census had counted all the Levites over the age of one month (Num.3:15). Children, of course, were not available to serve in the Tabernacle. This

was the reason for this particular census, to learn the number of available workers, just how many were old enough to serve in the Tabernacle. Note that the years of service were from thirty to fifty years of age. Another Scripture mentions that the actual beginning age of service was twenty-five (Num.8:24). The first five years were most likely a training period, an apprenticeship for the Levite.

2. The work assigned to these clans was to take care of the most holy things (v.4). This is important to note: the primary care of the most holy things was placed into the hands of the Kohathites. How men treat the holy things of God is of critical importance to God: this is clearly seen in the restrictions placed upon the Kohathites. They themselves were not allowed to touch the holy things (v.15), nor were they allowed to even look upon the holy things (v.20). The warning and judgment were forceful: if they touched or looked upon the holy things of God, the blaze of God's holiness would flash forth like a lightning bolt and strike them dead (v.15, 20; cp. 3, 4; Lev.10:1-2). In the words of *The Expositor's Bible Commentary*:

> "As the holy angels who surround the throne of the Divine Presence shield their faces and feet from his presence (cf. Is.6:1-3), so the Kohathites were to shield themselves from too familiar an approach to the holiest of things (v.5); for most holy things symbolize the presence of the most holy God"[1]

3. The critical importance of the most holy things is seen in this fact: the most holy things could be prepared only by the priests. Remember that the priests stood as a symbol or picture of Christ. Only Christ can prepare the holy things and make them acceptable to God. Only the priests themselves were allowed to look upon and handle the holy things. No person could approach the holiness of God nor approach the things that represented His holiness, not without being stricken dead. The only person who is acceptable to God, who can approach God, is the perfect person, Christ Himself, or the person representing the perfect person, the priest. For this reason, the Kohathites were not allowed to touch nor look upon the holy things of God. The priests alone were allowed to enter the inner sanctuary of the Tabernacle, the symbol of the very presence of God Himself. The priests were responsible for covering and wrapping all the holy furnishing of the Tabernacle:

a. The priests covered and wrapped the Ark (v.5-6).
b. The priests covered and wrapped the Table of the Presence or the Table of Showbread (v.7-8).
c. The priests covered and wrapped the lampstand and all its accessories (v.9-10).
d. The priests covered and wrapped the gold altar (v.11-12).
e. The priests covered and wrapped the bronze altar of Burnt Offering (v.13-14).

4. The strong, emphatic warning to respect the holiness of God is stressed: the Kohathites must never touch the holy things or they would be stricken dead (v.15). Note how strict God was:

⇒ They would be stricken dead if they touched any item while preparing it to be moved.
⇒ They would be stricken dead if they touched any item while carrying the holy things (cp. 2 Sam.6:6-7).

5. The person placed in charge of the entire Tabernacle—everything in it—was Eleazar, the priest who was the son of Aaron (v.16). Note that he was personally to care for the oil for the lampstand, the incense, the regular Grain Offering, and the anointing oil. This was all he was to handle personally. He was to oversee or supervise everything else in the Tabernacle.

6. The strong, emphatic warning was restated and reemphasized—far more forcefully: the workers must be protected from the penalty of being cut off, that is, stricken dead (v.17-20). They absolutely must never be allowed to approach the holy things alone. They were to be led into the sanctuary and assigned their work by the priests (v.19). The warning was clear and forceful: they would be stricken dead if they even looked at the holy things of God. It was essential that they acknowledge, respect, and revere the holiness of God (v.20).

Thought 1. The stress of this point is forceful: God demands that the holiness of His presence be respected and revered. He demands that the holy things of God—the things set apart to God and His service—be respected and revered. The declaration and warning of God is clear: He is holy and the things of God are holy. Therefore, He demands that we respect and revere His holiness and the holy things committed to His service.

⇒ the church and its furnishings

"Know ye not that ye [plural, the church] are the temple of God, and *that* the Spirit of God dwelleth in you?" (1 Cor.3:16).

⇒ the physical body of the believer, that is, the temple of the Holy Spirit

"What? know ye not that your body is the temple of the Holy Ghost *which is* in you, which ye have of God, and ye are not your own? For ye are bought with a price: therefore glorify God in your body, and in your spirit, which are God's" (1 Cor.6:19-20).

⇒ the gifts of money, property, and anything else that is set apart to the worship or service of God

"And said unto them that sold doves, Take these things hence; make not my Father's house an house of merchandise" (Jn.2:16).

"And he said, Draw not nigh hither: put off thy shoes from off thy feet, for the place whereon thou standest is holy ground" (Ex.3:5).

"Ye shall keep my sabbaths, and reverence my sanctuary: I *am* the LORD" (Lev.19:30).

"And the captain of the LORD'S host said unto Joshua, Loose thy shoe from off thy foot; for the place whereon thou standest *is* holy. And Joshua did so" (Josh.5:15).

---

1 *The Expositor's Bible Commentary*, Vol.2. Frank E. Gaebelein, Editor, p.734.

"Stand in awe, and sin not: commune with your own heart upon your bed, and be still. Selah" (Ps.4:4).

"O send out thy light and thy truth: let them lead me; let them bring me unto thy holy hill, and to thy tabernacles" (Ps.43:8).

"God is greatly to be feared in the assembly of the saints, and to be had in reverence of all *them that are* about him" (Ps.89:7).

"Keep thy foot when thou goest to the house of God, and be more ready to hear, than to give the sacrifice of fools" (Eccl.5:1).

"But the LORD *is* in his holy temple: let all the earth keep silence before him" (Hab.2:20).

Thought 2. The Levites went through a five year training or apprenticeship (v.3). They trained for five years and served for twenty. This speaks to the church. People need to learn the Word of God before they can preach or teach the Word; they need to learn how to minister so they can be more effective in ministering; they need to learn how to reach people so more people can be won to Christ; they need to learn how to minister to the sick and poor and dying so their ministry will be more encouraging and strengthening. Far, far too often a novice—a new believer—is put into a position of leadership in a teaching or preaching ministry, and the result is catastrophic.

"Go ye therefore, and teach all nations, baptizing them in the name of the Father, and of the Son, and of the Holy Ghost: Teaching them to observe all things whatsoever I have commanded you: and, lo, I am with you alway, *even* unto the end of the world. Amen" (Mt.28:19-20).

"Not a novice, lest being lifted up with pride he fall into the condemnation of the devil" (1 Tim. 3:6).

"Till I come, give attendance to reading, to exhortation, to doctrine. Neglect not the gift that is in thee, which was given thee by prophecy, with the laying on of the hands of the presbytery. Meditate upon these things; give thyself wholly to them; that thy profiting may appear to all. Take heed unto thyself, and unto the doctrine; continue in them: for in doing this thou shalt both save thyself, and them that hear thee" (1 Tim.4:13-16).

"And the things that thou hast heard of me among many witnesses, the same commit thou to faithful men, who shall be able to teach others also" (2 Tim.2:2).

"Study to show thyself approved unto God, a workman that needeth not to be ashamed, rightly dividing the word of truth" (2 Tim.2:15).

2 (4:21-28) **Ministers, Duties of—Service, Dedication—Commitment, Duty to—Gershonites, a Levite Clan—Levites, Clans of**: there was the charge to count the available workers and assign the duties to the Gershonite clans. The work assigned stresses the need for a willingness to do anything, that is, to do general work and service for the LORD.

OUTLINE	SCRIPTURE	SCRIPTURE	OUTLINE
2. The charge to count the available workers & assign the duties to the Gershonite clans: Stresses the need for a willingness to do anything (general work or service) a. The charge: Must know the number of workers 30 to 50 years old b. The service of the workers: To do general work—pack, unpack, & transport certain parts of the Tabernacle 1) The curtains of the Tabernacle itself: Included the outer covering of goat or sea cow hides, & the curtain for the entrance	21 And the LORD spake unto Moses, saying, 22 Take also the sum of the sons of Gershon, throughout the houses of their fathers, by their families; 23 From thirty years old and upward until fifty years old shalt thou number them; all that enter in to perform the service, to do the work in the tabernacle of the congregation. 24 This is the service of the families of the Gershonites, to serve, and for burdens: 25 And they shall bear the curtains of the tabernacle, and the tabernacle of the congregation, his covering, and the covering of the badgers' skins that is above upon it, and the hanging for the door of the tabernacle of the congregation,	26 And the hangings of the court, and the hanging for the door of the gate of the court, which is by the tabernacle and by the altar round about, and their cords, and all the instruments of their service, and all that is made for them: so shall they serve. 27 At the appointment of Aaron and his sons shall be all the service of the sons of the Gershonites, in all their burdens, and in all their service: and ye shall appoint unto them in charge all their burdens. 28 This is the service of the families of the sons of Gershon in the tabernacle of the congregation: and their charge shall be under the hand of Ithamar the son of Aaron the priest.	2) The curtains of the courtyard walls that surrounded the Tabernacle & altar: Included the curtain for the courtyard entrance, the ropes & all the altar's accessories c. The importance of the service 1) Was to be supervised & assigned by the priests 2) Was to be under the general direction of Ithamar the priest, the son of Aaron

1. The charge from God was clear: the number of available workers needed to be known. Therefore, they were to count all the men in the Gershonite clans between the ages of thirty and fifty for service in the Tabernacle.

2. The service of these workers was to do the general work of the Tabernacle: they were to pack, unpack, and transport the outer walls or curtains and hides of the Tabernacle (v.24-26). Remember: the Kohathite workers were not allowed to touch the furnishings of the Tabernacle because of their holy nature. But now, the Gershonite workers were permitted to touch the outer curtains of the Tabernacle. They personally packed and unpacked the parts for which they were responsible.

3. The importance of this work is seen in that it was to be supervised by the priests (v.27-28). The general superintendent of these workers was Ithamar, the priest and son of Aaron (v.28).

Thought 1. The willingness to do any task is desperately needed within the church. People need to step forth and do the general work in their service for the church. No matter what the work is, it is important to God, and it has to be done:

⇒ The small, insignificant, unknown, unrecognizable work has to be done.
⇒ The menial, manual work has to be done.
⇒ The cleaning and maintenance have to be done.
⇒ The straightening of chairs, books, tables, and podiums has to be done.
⇒ The picking up of paper and trash has to be done.
⇒ The turning on and off of lights has to be done.
⇒ The visiting of the sick, shut-ins, and dying has to be done.
⇒ The commitment of hours to study and prepare for preaching and teaching has to be done.
⇒ The witnessing and bearing of testimony to the lost at work, school, play, and home have to be done.

The point is forceful: a willingness to do any task is desperately needed within the church today. People who are willing to do anything for God—no matter how small or unseen—must step forth for God.

"And whosoever shall give to drink unto one of these little ones a cup of cold *water* only in the name of a disciple, verily I say unto you, he shall in no wise lose his reward" (Mt.10:42).

"Even as the Son of man came not to be ministered unto, but to minister, and to give his life a ransom for many" (Mt.20:28).

"Whosoever of you will be the chiefest, shall be servant of all" (Mk.10:43-44).

"Which now of these three, thinkest thou, was neighbour unto him that fell among the thieves? And he said, He that showed mercy on him. Then said Jesus unto him, Go, and do thou likewise" (Lk.10:36-37).

"For whether *is* greater, he that sitteth at meat, or he that serveth? *is* not he that sitteth at meat? but I am among you as he that serveth" (Lk.22:27).

"He riseth from supper, and laid aside his garments; and took a towel, and girded himself. After that he poureth water into a bason, and began to wash the disciples' feet, and to wipe *them* with the towel wherewith he was girded" (Jn.13:4-5).

"If I then, *your* Lord and Master, have washed your feet; ye also ought to wash one another's feet" (Jn.13:14).

"He saith to him again the second time, Simon, *son* of Jonas, lovest thou me? He saith unto him, Yea, Lord; thou knowest that I love thee. He saith unto him, Feed my sheep" (Jn.21:16).

"Therefore, my beloved brethren, be ye stedfast, unmovable, always abounding in the work of the Lord, forasmuch as ye know that your labour is not in vain in the Lord" (1 Cor.15:58).

"As we have therefore opportunity, let us do good unto all *men,* especially unto them who are of the household of faith" (Gal.6:10).

"With good will doing service, as to the Lord, and not to men" (Eph.6:7).

"But made himself of no reputation, and took upon him the form of a servant, and was made in the likeness of men" (Ph.2:7).

"But to do good and to communicate [give] forget not: for with such sacrifices God is well pleased" (Heb.13:16).

"Therefore to him that knoweth to do good, and doeth *it* not, to him it is sin" (Jas.4:17).

3 (4:29-33) **Service, Duty of—Service, Importance of—Merarites, a Major Levite Family—Levites, Families of**: there was the charge to count the available workers and assign the duties to the Merarite clans. This work stresses the need and importance of each person's service.

OUTLINE	SCRIPTURE	SCRIPTURE	OUTLINE
3. The charge to count the available workers & assign the duties to the Merarite clans: Stresses the importance of each person's service a. The charge: Must know the available workers 30 to 50 years old b. The service of the workers: To pack, unpack, & transport the frame of the Tabernacle & the surrounding courtyard • crossbars • posts & bases • tent pegs & ropes • other equipment c. The importance of each per-	29 As for the sons of Merari, thou shalt number them after their families, by the house of their fathers; 30 From thirty years old and upward even unto fifty years old shalt thou number them, every one that entereth into the service, to do the work of the tabernacle of the congregation. 31 And this is the charge of their burden, according to all their service in the tabernacle of the congregation; the boards of the tabernacle, and the bars thereof, and the pil-	lars thereof, and sockets thereof, 32 And the pillars of the court round about, and their sockets, and their pins, and their cords, with all their instruments, and with all their service: and by name ye shall reckon the instruments of the charge of their burden. 33 This is the service of the families of the sons of Merari, according to all their service, in the tabernacle of the congregation, under the hand of Ithamar the son of Aaron the priest.	son's service 1) Each person was to be assigned & made responsible for a particular task 2) The service was to be under the general direction of Ithamar the priest, the son of Aaron

1. The charge was again essential: the number of available workers had to be known, those between the ages of thirty and fifty (v.30).

2. The work of these particular men was to pack, unpack, and transport the frame of the Tabernacle and the surrounding courtyard (v.31-32). This, of course, included the crossbars, post and bases, tent pegs and ropes, and other equipment.

3. The importance of each person's service was clearly seen in this one fact: each person was to be assigned and made responsible for the specific things he was to carry (v.32). Imagine being responsible for carrying a tent peg! What was so important about carrying a tent peg? If one tent peg had been lost, then the Tabernacle wall could not have been erected and worship could not have been held, not without first making another tent peg. Each person's task was of critical importance. Nothing, absolutely nothing, could be lost or mishandled. The work had to be done, every single task, in order for the worship and ministry of God to be carried out. The importance of each person's service was also stressed by the fact that it was under the general direction of the priest, Ithamar, the son of Aaron (v.33).

Thought 1. Every believer has a duty, a role of responsibility to God. Each believer's service is important and needed—desperately needed—by God. To God, responsible service is what the work of each believer is. In the eyes of God, each believer is to be a responsible person, a person committed to fulfilling his service and fulfilling it well and faithfully. Carrying the tent pegs of the church is of critical importance to God, for the ministry cannot go forth unless the tent peg is carried. What God needs is for people to step forth, people who are willing to carry the tent pegs of the church...

- to wash the sinks and clean the floors
- to pay for the supplies
- to build the buildings
- to support the missionaries
- to teach
- to pray
- to visit
- to witness and bear testimony
- to spend hours in study
- to greet people
- to usher
- to keep books and records
- to turn lights on and off

On and on the list could go, for the tent pegs of the church and the ministry are innumerable. But the challenge is ever before God's people. What is needed is for people to step forth to carry the pegs of the church and the ministry. The hour is desperate: the cry of the world is for help. People are brokenhearted, backslidden, diseased, suffering, poor, empty, dying—and in many cases without Christ. The cry of God is, "Step forth! I beg you in the name of My Son, step forth! Carry this tent peg for Me! For My church! For My people who desperately need your help!"

"Even as the Son of man came not to be ministered unto, but to minister, and to give his life a ransom for many" (Mt.20:28).

"For I say, through the grace given unto me, to every man that is among you, not to think of himself more highly than he ought to think; but to think soberly, according as God hath dealt to every man the measure of faith. For as we have many members in one body, and all members have not the same office: So we, being many, are one body in Christ, and every one members one of another. Having then gifts differing according to the grace that is given to us, whether prophecy, let us prophesy according to the proportion of faith; Or ministry, let us wait on our ministering: or he that teacheth, on teaching; Or he that exhorteth, on exhortation: he that giveth, let him do it with simplicity; he that ruleth, with diligence; he that showeth mercy, with cheerfulness" (Ro.12:3-8).

"Bear ye one another's burdens, and so fulfil the law of Christ" (Gal.6:2).

"And let us not be weary in well doing: for in due season we shall reap, if we faint not" (Gal.6:9).

"The people willingly offered themselves" (Judg.5:2).

"If ye be willing and obedient, ye shall eat the good of the land:" (Is.1:19).

4 (4:34-49) **Obedience—Census, of the Levites—Levites, Census of**: there was the description and the results of the census. The point to note throughout this passage is the *obedience* of everyone involved. Obedience to the LORD's command is mentioned four times (v.37, 41, 45, 49).

OUTLINE	SCRIPTURE	SCRIPTURE	OUTLINE
4. The description & results of the census: Stresses obedience a. The number of the Kohathite clans	34 And Moses and Aaron and the chief of the congregation numbered the sons of the Kohathites after their families, and after the house of their fathers,	entereth into the service, for the work in the tabernacle of the congregation:	
		36 And those that were numbered of them by their families were two thousand seven hundred and fifty.	2) Numbered 2750 men
1) Counted all men between 30 to 50 years of age who were eligible for service	35 From thirty years old and upward even unto fifty years old, every one that	37 These were they that were numbered of the fami-	3) The obedience of the leaders: Counted in obedience

OUTLINE	SCRIPTURE	SCRIPTURE	OUTLINE
to the LORD's command	lies of the Kohathites, all that might do service in the tabernacle of the congregation, which Moses and Aaron did number according to the commandment of the LORD by the hand of Moses.	years old, every one that entereth into the service, for the work in the tabernacle of the congregation,	were eligible for service
b. The number of the Gershonite clans	38 And those that were numbered of the sons of Gershon, throughout their families, and by the house of their fathers,	44 Even those that were numbered of them after their families, were three thousand and two hundred.	2) Numbered 3200 men
1) Counted all men between 30 to 50 years of age who were eligible for service	39 From thirty years old and upward even unto fifty years old, every one that entereth into the service, for the work in the tabernacle of the congregation,	45 These be those that were numbered of the families of the sons of Merari, whom Moses and Aaron numbered according to the word of the LORD by the hand of Moses.	3) The obedience of the leaders: Counted in obedience to the LORD's command
2) Numbered 2630 men	40 Even those that were numbered of them, throughout their families, by the house of their fathers, were two thousand and six hundred and thirty.	46 All those that were numbered of the Levites, whom Moses and Aaron and the chief of Israel numbered, after their families, and after the house of their fathers,	d. The summary of the census 1) Counted all the Levites by clans & families
3) The obedience of the leaders: Counted in obedience to the LORD's command	41 These are they that were numbered of the families of the sons of Gershon, of all that might do service in the tabernacle of the congregation, whom Moses and Aaron did number according to the commandment of the LORD.	47 From thirty years old and upward even unto fifty years old, every one that came to do the service of the ministry, and the service of the burden in the tabernacle of the congregation, 48 Even those that were numbered of them, were eight thousand and five hundred and fourscore.	2) Counted all men between 30 to 50 years of age who were eligible for the work of serving & carrying the Tabernacle 3) Totaled 8580
c. The number of the Merarite clans	42 And those that were numbered of the families of the sons of Merari, throughout their families, by the house of their fathers,	49 According to the commandment of the LORD they were numbered by the hand of Moses, every one according to his service, and according to his burden: thus were they numbered of him, as the LORD commanded	4) The strong example of obedience • They did their work as assigned, as commanded • They were counted just as the LORD commanded
1) Counted all men between 30 to 50 years of age who	43 From thirty years old and upward even unto fifty	Moses.	

1. Note the number of the Kohathite clans: it totaled 2,750 men (v.34-37). The obedience of the leaders is stressed: they counted in obedience to the LORD's command (v.37)

2. Note the number of the Gershonite clans: they totaled 2,630 men (v.38-41). Again, note the obedience of the leaders: they counted in obedience to the LORD's command (v.41).

3. Note the total number of the Merarite clans: they numbered 3,200 men (v.42-45). For the third time, the obedience of the leaders is stressed: they again counted in obedience to the LORD's command (v.45).

4. Note the summary of the census (v.46-49):
   a. The leaders counted all Levites by clans and families (v.46).
   b. They counted all the men between the ages of thirty and fifty who were eligible for the work of serving and carrying the Tabernacle (v.47).
   c. The total number of the census was 8,580 (v.48).
   d. The strong example of obedience is stressed throughout the entire passage (v.49).
      1) The workers did the task as assigned, as commanded.
      2) The workers were counted by Moses and the leaders—just as the LORD commanded.

Thought 1. Where is the obedience today? The obedience to do the work of the ministry? The world is reeling in a state of desperate need, crying out for help. The harvest is ripe and ready to be gathered, but the laborers are few, ever so few. Many have been called and are still being called, but few are chosen. Few are making the commitment. Few are stepping forth to serve in the ministry of the Lord Jesus Christ. Few are willing to help the crying needs of the world, the needs...

- of the orphans, widows, and widowers
- of the prisoners, brokenhearted, and backslidden
- of the diseased, poor, and suffering
- of the empty, lonely, and purposeless
- of the lost, dying, and doomed—eternally

When God calls, obedience is demanded. Where are the obedient? So few can be found. Where is your obedience? Where is my obedience? The cry of the hour is for obedience.

"Not every one that saith unto me, Lord, Lord, shall enter into the kingdom of heaven; but he that doeth the will of my Father which is in heaven" (Mt.7:21).

"For whosoever shall do the will of my Father which is in heaven, the same is my brother, and sister, and mother" (Mt.12:50).

"Say not ye, There are yet four months, and then cometh harvest? behold, I say unto you, Lift up your eyes, and look on the fields; for they are white already to harvest. And he that reapeth receiveth wages, and gathereth fruit unto life eternal: that both he that soweth and he that reapeth may rejoice together" (Jn.4:35-36).

"Then Peter and the other apostles answered and said, We ought to obey God rather than men" (Acts 5:29).

"I beseech you therefore, brethren, by the mercies of God, that ye present your bodies a living sacrifice, holy, acceptable unto God, which is your reasonable service. And be not conformed to this world: but be ye transformed by the renewing of your mind, that ye may prove what is that good, and acceptable, and perfect, will of God" (Ro.12:1-2).

"But God hath chosen the foolish things of the world to confound the wise; and God hath chosen the weak things of the world to confound the things which are mighty; And base things of the world, and things which are despised, hath God chosen, yea, and things which are not, to bring to nought things that are: That no flesh should glory in his presence" (1 Cor.1:27-29).

"Be not thou therefore ashamed of the testimony of our Lord, nor of me his prisoner: but be thou partaker of the afflictions of the gospel according to the power of God" (2 Tim.1:8).

"Then said he, Lo, I come to do thy will, O God" (Heb.10:9).

"And Samuel said, Hath the Lord as great delight in burnt offerings and sacrifices, as in obeying the voice of the Lord? Behold, to obey is better than sacrifice, and to hearken than the fat of rams" (1 Sam.15:22).

"My son, give me thine heart, and let thine eyes observe my ways" (Pr.23:26).

"If ye be willing and obedient, ye shall eat the good of the land" (Is.1:19).

"Also I heard the voice of the Lord, saying, Whom shall I send, and who will go for us? Then said I, Here am I; send me" (Is.6:8).

D. The Basic Laws That Keep God's People United & Pure: God's People Must Live Pure Lives, 5:1-31

1. There was the law of separation—the unclean were removed from the camp: A picture of spiritual separation
   a. The unclean identified (cp. Lev.13:1-59)
      1) A person with a contagious skin disease or discharge
      2) A person who came in contact with death
   b. The purpose: A picture of preventing the spread of sin
      1) To prevent the spread to others
      2) To keep from defiling the camp, the place where God is
   c. The obedience of the people: Removed the unclean

2. There was the law that controlled doing any wrong against another person
   a. The primary charge: Was counted as being unfaithful to the LORD—was guilty before God
   b. The remedy
      1) Must confess to God
      2) Must make restitution
         • To add one fifth to the property stolen
         • To give the payment of restitution to the priest if the person was dead & had no close relative
      3) Must approach God through the sacrifice of the Guilt Offering: Approach for atonement
   c. The important reminder
      1) All sacred gifts—once promised or given—belonged to the priests
      2) No gift—once promised or given—was ever to be withdrawn, neither publicly nor secretly

3. There was the law controlling the suspicion & jealousy of sexual unfaithfulness
   a. The case: A man's wife went astray & was unfaithful
      1) The immorality, impurity was undetected: There was no witness
      2) The husband became suspicious, jealous: Strife, accusations, threats occurred—a broken relationship became a possibility
      3) The law was to be followed—even if the wife knew she was not guilty or defiled
   b. The couple was to seek the counsel & help of the priest (minister)
      1) To bring an offering of barley flour (two quarts) to the LORD
      2) Not to pour oil nor put incense on it: A symbol of being anointed & of one's prayers pleasing the LORD
         • Bc. it was not a Grain Offering of thanksgiving but an Investigation Offering to discern guilt
   c. The priest was to present the wife to the LORD
      1) The priest (minister) was to warn her of God's judgment
         • To mix some dust from the Tabernacle floor (holy dust) in some holy water
         • To loosen the woman's hair
         • To place the Investigation Offering in her hands
      2) The priest (minister) was to put the woman under oath
         • If she was not guilty of immorality, she would not suffer God's judgment or curse
         • If she was guilty of immorality—was defiled—she would suffer the judgment & curse of God: She would become infertile, unable to bear children; & if pregnant, she would suffer a miscarriage

And the LORD spake unto Moses, saying,

2 Command the children of Israel, that they put out of the camp every leper, and every one that hath an issue, and whosoever is defiled by the dead:

3 Both male and female shall ye put out, without the camp shall ye put them; that they defile not their camps, in the midst whereof I dwell.

4 And the children of Israel did so, and put them out without the camp: as the LORD spake unto Moses, so did the children of Israel.

5 And the LORD spake unto Moses, saying,

6 Speak unto the children of Israel, When a man or woman shall commit any sin that men commit, to do a trespass against the LORD, and that person be guilty;

7 Then they shall confess their sin which they have done: and he shall recompense his trespass with the principal thereof, and add unto it the fifth part thereof, and give it unto him against whom he hath trespassed.

8 But if the man have no kinsman to recompense the trespass unto, let the trespass be recompensed unto the LORD, even to the priest; beside the ram of the atonement, whereby an atonement shall be made for him.

9 And every offering of all the holy things of the children of Israel, which they bring unto the priest, shall be his.

10 And every man's hallowed things shall be his: whatsoever any man giveth the priest, it shall be his.

11 And the LORD spake unto Moses, saying,

12 Speak unto the children of Israel, and say unto them, If any man's wife go aside, and commit a trespass against him,

13 And a man lie with her carnally, and it be hid from the eyes of her husband, and be kept close, and she be defiled, and there be no witness against her, neither she be taken with the manner;

14 And the spirit of jealousy come upon him, and he be jealous of his wife, and she be defiled: or if the spirit of jealousy come upon him, and he be jealous of his wife, and she be not defiled:

15 Then shall the man bring his wife unto the priest, and he shall bring her offering for her, the tenth part of an ephah of barley meal; he shall pour no oil upon it, nor put frankincense thereon; for it is an offering of jealousy, an offering of memorial, bringing iniquity to remembrance.

16 And the priest shall bring her near, and set her before the LORD:

17 And the priest shall take holy water in an earthen vessel; and of the dust that is in the floor of the tabernacle the priest shall take, and put it into the water:

18 And the priest shall set the woman before the LORD, and uncover the woman's head, and put the offering of memorial in her hands, which is the jealousy offering: and the priest shall have in his hand the bitter water that causeth the curse:

19 And the priest shall charge her by an oath, and say unto the woman, If no man have lain with thee, and if thou hast not gone aside to uncleanness with another instead of thy husband, be thou free from this bitter water that causeth the curse:

20 But if thou hast gone aside to another instead of thy husband, and if thou be defiled, and some man have lain with thee beside thine husband:

21 Then the priest shall charge the woman with an oath of cursing, and the priest shall say unto the woman, The LORD make thee a curse and an oath among thy people, when the LORD doth make thy thigh to rot, and thy belly to swell;

- The woman was forced to think through the oath & situation: She was asked to say "Amen"—to confess or to call God's curse down upon herself

3) The priest (minister) was to write God's curses upon a leather scroll & then wash them off in the water: The woman then drank the water

4) The priest (minister) took the Grain Offering from the woman & waved it before the LORD

5) The priest (minister) then burned a handful of the offering upon the altar

6) The priest (minister) then had the woman drink the bitter water

- If she was defiled—had been sexually unfaithful—the water would cause bitter suffering: Her abdomen would swell & her thigh would waste away (a picture of being pregnant illegitimately or made infertile) & she would be accused among people (declared infertile, unblessed by God)
- If she was innocent & pure, she would be cleared of all charges & able to bear children

d. The purpose of the law is restated: This was the law to control sexual suspicion & jealousy

1) The entire law was to be applied to the woman

2) The husband was innocent of any wrong-doing

3)The woman would be held accountable for her sin (Lev.20:10; Dt.22:22)

22 And this water that
causeth the curse shall
go into thy bowels, to make
thy belly to swell, and
thy thigh to rot: And the
woman shall say, Amen,
amen.
23 And the priest shall write
these curses in a book, and
he shall blot them out with
the bitter water:
24 And he shall cause the
woman to drink the bitter
water that causeth the curse:
and the water that causeth
the curse shall enter into her,
and become bitter.
25 Then the priest shall take
the jealousy offering out of
the woman's hand, and shall
wave the offering before the
LORD, and offer it upon the
altar:
26 And the priest shall take
an handful of the offering,
even the memorial thereof,
and burn it upon the altar,
and afterward shall cause
the woman to drink the
water.
27 And when he hath made
her to drink the water, then
it shall come to pass, that, if
she be defiled, and have
done trespass against
her husband, that the water
that causeth the curse shall
enter into her, and become
bitter, and her belly shall
swell, and her thigh shall
rot: and the woman shall
be a curse among her
people.
28 And if the woman be not
defiled, but be clean; then
she shall be free, and shall
conceive seed.
29 This is the law of jeal-
ousies, when a wife goeth
aside to another instead
of her husband, and is
defiled;
30 Or when the spirit
of jealousy cometh upon
him, and he be jealous
over his wife, and shall
set the woman before the
LORD, and the priest shall
execute upon her all this
law.
31 Then shall the man be
guiltless from iniquity, and
this woman shall bear her
iniquity.

DIVISION I

THE PREPARATION FOR THE MARCH TO THE PROMISED LAND

D. The Basic Laws That Keep God's People United and Pure: God's People Must Live Pure Lives, 5:1-31

(5:1-31) **Introduction—Unified, Duty to Be—One, Duty to Be—Pure, Duty to Be—Holy, Duty to Be—Believers, Duty of**: the human race has the greatest hope that could ever be given, the hope of the promised land. Keep in mind what the promised land means: it means...

- the promised land of conquest over all the pitfalls and enemies of life
- the promised land of heaven, of living forever in the presence of God Himself (Jehovah, Yahweh—the only living and true God)

This is the message of the great Book of Numbers: the march of God's people to the promised land. Once a person begins to follow God, he immediately becomes a part of God's people—a member of God's family, of the church itself. God demands one basic thing of the new believer, the very thing He demands of all His people: that they be united and pure. God's people are to walk together as one, living pure and clean lives before Him. God is holy; therefore, He expects His people to be holy. The overall objective and goal of God's people is to reach the promised land; therefore, as they march, God expects them to march together, walking in formation step by step. They are to be united together as a great force of marching soldiers. Moreover, as God's people march to the promised land, God expects His people to be distinct and different from the secular world. They are soldiers of God, disciplined, following in the footsteps of their Commander-in-Chief, the Lord Jesus Christ. Christ the Commander lived a pure life before God; therefore, the army of Christ is expected to live a pure life. This is the great subject of this passage: *The Basic Laws That Keep God's People United and Pure: God's People Must Live Pure Lives*, 5:1-31.

1. There was the law of separation—the unclean were removed from the camp: a picture of spiritual separation (v.1-4).
2. There was the law that controlled doing any wrong against another person (v.5-10).
3. There was the law controlling the suspicion and jealousy of sexual unfaithfulness (v.11-31).

1 (5:1-4) **Separation, Spiritual—Spiritual Separation—Church Discipline—Uncleanness, Spiritual—Uncleanness, Ceremonial—Ceremonial Uncleanness—Ritual Uncleanness—Disease, of Skin—Leprosy, Symbol of—Infectious Skin Disease, Symbol of—Death, Ceremonial Uncleanness of**: there was the law of separation: the unclean were removed from the camp. This is a picture of spiritual separation. As God's people marched to the promised land, the unclean were to be removed from the camp. The presence of the unclean among God's people was a serious situation. Note how forcefully this was stressed: the Hebrew word for "put out" or "sent away" or "remove" (salah) means just what it says, to expel the unclean person from the camp of God's people. The forcefulness of the command is seen in the fact that it is mentioned no less than four times in these four verses. Just who were the unclean who were to be expelled? Note the Scripture and outline:

OUTLINE	SCRIPTURE
1. There was the law of separation—the unclean were removed from the camp: A picture of spiritual separation a. The unclean identified (cp. Lev.13:1-59) 1) A person with a contagious skin disease or discharge 2) A person who came in contact with death b. The purpose: A picture of preventing the spread of sin 1) To prevent the spread to others 2) To keep from defiling the camp, the place where God is c. The obedience of the people: Removed the unclean	And the LORD spake unto Moses, saying, 2 Command the children of Israel, that they put out of the camp every leper, and every one that hath an issue, and whosoever is defiled by the dead: 3 Both male and female shall ye put out, without the camp shall ye put them; that they defile not their camps, in the midst whereof I dwell. 4 And the children of Israel did so, and put them out without the camp: as the LORD spake unto Moses, so did the children of Israel.

1. The unclean were identified (v.2). A person with leprosy or a contagious skin disease or discharge was counted unclean (v.2). The Hebrew word for leper or leprosy (sara`at) means all kinds of serious or contagious skin diseases or discharges. When a person was seen to have some kind of skin disease, he was to be removed from the community. A person who came in contact with death was also counted unclean (v.2) (see outline and notes—Leviticus, chapters 13-14 for more discussion).

2. The purpose for removing the unclean persons from the camp was twofold. One purpose was to prevent the spread of disease within the camp. Remember, the people of that day did not have the medical knowledge nor medicine to combat disease. The epidemics that have wiped out millions throughout past generations is clear demonstration of this fact. Therefore, one of the purposes of God in having the unclean removed from the camp was to prevent the spread of disease. But there was another reason, a symbolic reason why God wanted the unclean separated from His people. God Himself dwelt within the camp (v.3). His very presence dwelt within the Tabernacle. God had to teach His people that He was holy and that they must live holy, pure, and clean lives before Him. Therefore all uncleanness was to be removed from Him and from His people—lest they both become contaminated by uncleanness and impurity.

3. The obedience of the people is stressed: they removed the unclean from the camp.

Thought 1. God has called His people to spiritual separation, to be totally set apart from the sin and shame of the world. This is the point behind this Scripture. The issue is not whether God cares for the diseased and for those who hurt and suffer. God cares for the suffering and the afflicted; this has been proven throughout the generations of human history. God loves the human race, every single person upon planet earth. Moreover, He loves those who suffer and hurt with a very special love. This has been demonstrated perfectly in Christ Jesus during His walk here upon earth. As stated, God's love for the suffering and hurting is not the issue: the issue is spiritual separation from the sin and darkness of this world. God has called His people to be a distinct people, a people who are set apart totally to Him in purity of heart and behavior. God's people are to be distinct in this one fact: they do not live in the immorality, lawlessness, and violence of this world. The Israelites were not to live as the other nations who surrounded them. They were not to worship the false gods of those nations nor to engage in their lawless, violent, and immoral ways. We too are to be distinct and different in this one area: that of holiness—living pure and clean lives. Our conduct and behavior are to be moral, lawful, and peaceful—not following the ways of immorality, lawlessness, and violence. We are to be totally separated from such, living distinct and separate lives from the world.

"And take heed to yourselves, lest at any time your hearts be overcharged with surfeiting, and drunkenness, and cares of this life, and so that day come upon you unawares" (Lk.21:34).

"If ye were of the world, the world would love his own: but because ye are not of the world, but I have chosen you out of the world, therefore the world hateth you" (Jn.15:19).

"And with many other words did he testify and exhort, saying, Save yourselves from this untoward generation" (Acts 2:40).

"I beseech you therefore, brethren, by the mercies of God, that ye present your bodies a living sacrifice, holy, acceptable unto God, which is your reasonable service. And be not conformed to this world: but be ye transformed by the renewing of your mind, that ye may prove what is that good, and acceptable, and perfect, will of God" (Ro.12:1-2).

"Wherefore come out from among them, and be ye separate, saith the LORD, and touch not the unclean thing; and I will receive you, And will be a Father unto you, and ye shall be my sons and daughters, saith the LORD Almighty" (2 Cor.6:17-18).

"And have no fellowship with the unfruitful works of darkness, but rather reprove them" (Eph.5:11).

"Now we command you, brethren, in the name of our Lord Jesus Christ, that ye withdraw yourselves from every brother that walketh disorderly, and not after the tradition which he received of us" (2 Th.3:6).

"No man that warreth entangleth himself with the affairs of this life; that he may please him who hath chosen him to be a soldier" (2 Tim.2:4).

"Love not the world, neither the things that are in the world. If any man love the world, the love of the Father is not in him. For all that is in the world, the lust of the flesh, and the lust of the eyes, and the pride of life, is not of the Father, but is of the world" (1 Jn.2:15-16).

"Depart ye, depart ye, go ye out from thence, touch no unclean thing; go ye out of the midst of her; be ye clean, that bear the vessels of the LORD" (Is.52:11).

Thought 2. There is a clear lesson here for the church. The church must discipline members who become engaged in serious sin. As Matthew Henry points out, "scandalous persons" must be separated from God's people, lest others become infected and defiled.[1] (See outline and notes—Mt.18:15-20; 1 Cor.5:1-5; 1 Cor.5:6-13 for more discussion.)

"Moreover if thy brother shall trespass against thee, go and tell him his fault between thee and him alone: if he shall hear thee, thou hast gained thy brother. But if he will not hear thee, then take with thee one or two more, that in the mouth of two or three witnesses every word may be established. And if he shall neglect to hear them, tell it unto the church: but if he neglect to hear the church, let him be unto thee as an heathen man and a publican" (Mt.18:15-17).

"Take heed to yourselves: If thy brother trespass against thee, rebuke him; and if he repent, forgive him" (Lk.17:3).

"In the name of our Lord Jesus Christ, when ye are gathered together, and my spirit, with the power of our Lord Jesus Christ, To deliver such an one unto Satan for the destruction of the flesh, that the spirit may be saved in the day of the LORD Jesus. Your glorying is not good. Know ye not that a little leaven leaveneth the whole lump? Purge out therefore the old leaven, that ye may be a new lump, as ye are unleavened. For even Christ our passover is sacrificed for us" (1 Cor.5:4-7).

"Holding faith, and a good conscience; which some having put away concerning faith have made shipwreck: Of whom is Hymenaeus and Alexander; whom I have delivered unto Satan, that they may learn not to blaspheme" (1 Tim.1:19-20).

"Them that sin rebuke before all, that others also may fear" (1 Tim.5:20).

"A man that is an heretic after the first and second admonition reject; Knowing that he that is such is subverted, and sinneth, being condemned of himself" (Tit.3:10-11).

"Preach the word; be instant in season, out of season; reprove, rebuke, exhort with all longsuffering and doctrine" (2 Tim.4:2).

"But hath in due times manifested his word through preaching, which is committed unto me according to the commandment of God our Saviour" (Tit.1:3).

"These things speak, and exhort, and rebuke with all authority. Let no man despise thee" (Tit.2:15).

2 (5:5-10) **Neighbor, Sin against—Believer, Sin against—Believer, Wrong Committed against—Restitution—Confession, of Sin—Law, Controlling Wrong against Others**: there was the law that controlled doing wrong against another person. Most commentators deal with this passage as though it refers only to stolen property. Perhaps this is the correct interpretation, but the law of restitution applies to other cases as well:

⇒ A person was to pay restitution if he injured another person (Ex.21:18-19). The restitution included the payment for all lost time and income from employment as well as all medical costs.
⇒ A person was to pay restitution if he or anything he owned damaged the property of another person (Ex.22:5).
⇒ A person was to pay restitution if a fire started by him got out of hand, damaging another man's property (Ex.22:6).

These are just a few examples. There are many ways that a person can do wrong against others, but this Scripture is clear: any wrong—no matter what it is—is a trespass against another person. *Trespass* differs from *sin*. Trespass involves injury, injury to another person. Keep in mind that a person can injure God as well as man. In fact, everytime we trespass against another person, we trespass against God: we injure God—hurt Him, cut His heart—because we have injured a fellow human being. Note the Scripture and outline:

OUTLINE	SCRIPTURE	SCRIPTURE	OUTLINE
2. There was the law that controlled doing any wrong against another person a. The primary charge: Was counted as being unfaithful to the LORD—was guilty before God	5 And the LORD spake unto Moses, saying, 6 Speak unto the children of Israel, When a man or woman shall commit any sin that men commit, to do a trespass against the LORD, and that person be guilty;	7 Then they shall confess their sin which they have done: and he shall recompense his trespass with the principal thereof, and add unto it the fifth part thereof, and give it unto him against whom he hath trespassed.	b. The remedy 1) Must confess to God 2) Must make restitution • To add one fifth to the property stolen

1 Matthew Henry. *Matthew Henry's Commentary*. Volume 1. (Old Tappan, NJ: Fleming H. Revell Co.), p.580.

OUTLINE	SCRIPTURE	SCRIPTURE	OUTLINE
• To give the payment of restitution to the priest if the person were dead & had no close relative 3) Must approach God through the sacrifice of the Guilt Offering: Approach for atonement c. The important reminder	8 But if the man have no kinsman to recompense the trespass unto, let the trespass be recompensed unto the LORD, even to the priest; beside the ram of the atonement, whereby an atonement shall be made for him. 9 And every offering of all	the holy things of the children of Israel, which they bring unto the priest, shall be his. 10 And every man's hallowed things shall be his: whatsoever any man giveth the priest, it shall be his.	1) All sacred gifts—once promised or given—belonged to the priests 2) No gift—once promised or given—was ever to be withdrawn, neither publicly nor secretly

1. The charge of this passage is stunning: if a person wrongs another, it is counted as being unfaithful to the LORD. The person stands guilty before God, guilty of some damaging, dreadful, lawless, or violent act—not only against another person, but against God Himself.

Among God's people, doing wrong against another person is a terrible trespass (maal). The word means to be unfaithful; to betray the LORD; to commit a serious, grievous transgression. It means to break faith with another person, and by breaking faith with that person, one breaks faith with God Himself. Both man and God have been violated, seriously and grievously violated. As God's people marched to the promised land, He could not allow them to break faith with one another, to do wrong against one another. Lawlessness, violence, injury—harming one another—would create social disorder. Social disorder—doing wrong against one another—would destroy God's people.

2. The remedy for doing wrong against another person involves three steps.

a. The offender must confess his sin to God. No matter what the sin is, it must be confessed to God:
- ⇒ some physical abuse, injury, or harm
- ⇒ some property damage or destruction
- ⇒ any harmful, lawless, or violent act against a person or his property

b. The offender was not only to confess his sin, he was to make restitution. Restitution was just as important as confession. Full restitution plus one fifth (20%) had to be paid for whatever wrong had been done. Note: if the injured person had been killed or were no longer living, or if he had no living relative, the restitution was to be paid to the priests (v.8).

c. The person who wronged others must approach God through the sacrifice of the Guilt Offering (v.8). He had to seek atonement, that is, reconciliation with God and with the offended party. Atonement was an absolute essential.

3. There is an important reminder here for God's people. All sacred gifts, once promised or given, belonged to the priests (v.9). No gift, once it had been promised or given, was ever to be withdrawn—neither publicly nor secretly (v.10). The person making the offering to the LORD could not deceive nor cheat the LORD: he could not publicly present his offering to the LORD and then secretly or quietly withdraw it when others would not know.

Thought 1. The person who wrongs other people must take the same three steps spelled out in this passage:
1) He must confess his sin to God.

"I will arise and go to my father, and will say unto him, Father, I have sinned against heaven, and before thee" (Lk.15:18).

"Repent ye therefore, and be converted, that your sins may be blotted out, when the times of refreshing shall come from the presence of the LORD" (Acts 3:19).

"If we confess our sins, he is faithful and just to forgive us our sins, and to cleanse us from all unrighteousness" (1 Jn.1:9).

"Now therefore make confession unto the LORD God of your fathers, and do his pleasure: and separate yourselves from the people of the land, and from the strange wives" (Ezra 10:11).

"He that covereth his sins shall not prosper: but whoso confesseth and forsaketh them shall have mercy" (Pr.28:13).

"Let the wicked forsake his way, and the unrighteous man his thoughts: and let him return unto the LORD, and he will have mercy upon him; and to our God, for he will abundantly pardon" (Is.55:7).

"Only acknowledge thine iniquity, that thou hast transgressed against the LORD thy God, and hast scattered thy ways to the strangers under every green tree, and ye have not obeyed my voice, saith the LORD" (Jer.3:13).

2) He must make restitution.

"And Zacchaeus stood, and said unto the LORD; Behold, LORD, the half of my goods I give to the poor; and if I have taken any thing from any man by false accusation, I restore him fourfold. And Jesus said unto him, This day is salvation come to this house" (Lk.19:8-9).

"Then it shall be, because he hath sinned, and is guilty, that he shall restore that which he took violently away, or the thing which he hath deceitfully gotten, or that which was delivered him to keep, or the lost thing which he found" (Lev.6:4).

"And when the king asked the woman, she told him. So the king appointed unto her a certain officer, saying, Restore all that was hers, and all the fruits of the field since the day that she left the land, even until now" (2 Ki.8:6).

"Restore, I pray you, to them, even this day, their lands, their vineyards, their oliveyards, and their houses, also the hundredth part of the money, and of the corn, the wine, and the oil, that ye exact of them. Then said they, We will restore them, and will require nothing of them; so will we do as thou sayest. Then I called the priests, and took an oath of them, that they should do according to this promise" (Neh.5:11-12).

"Men do not despise a thief, if he steal to satisfy his soul when he is hungry; But if he be found, he shall restore sevenfold; he shall give all the substance of his house" (Pr.6:30-31).

"But if the wicked will turn from all his sins that he hath committed, and keep all my statutes, and do that which is lawful and right, he shall surely live, he shall not die" (Ezk.18:21).

"Again, when I say unto the wicked, Thou shalt surely die; if he turn from his sin, and do that which is lawful and right; If the wicked restore the pledge, give again that he had robbed, walk in the statutes of life, without committing iniquity; he shall surely live, he shall not die" (Ezk.33:14-15).

3) He must approach God for the atonement or reconciliation through the sacrifice of the Lord Jesus Christ. God accepts only those who approach Him through His Son, the Lord Jesus Christ. There is cleansing from sin only through Him.

"Being justified freely by his grace through the redemption that is in Christ Jesus" (Ro.3:24).

"Much more then, being now justified by his blood, we shall be saved from wrath through him" (Ro.5:9).

"In whom we have redemption through his blood, the forgiveness of sins, according to the riches of his grace" (Eph.1:7).

"In whom we have redemption through his blood, even the forgiveness of sins" (Col.1:14).

"For the grace of God that bringeth salvation hath appeared to all men, Teaching us that, denying ungodliness and worldly lusts, we should live soberly, righteously, and godly, in this present world; Looking for that blessed hope, and the glorious appearing of the great God and our Saviour Jesus Christ; Who gave himself for us, that he might redeem us from all iniquity, and purify unto himself a peculiar people, zealous of good works" (Tit.2:11-14).

"How much more shall the blood of Christ, who through the eternal Spirit offered himself without spot to God, purge your conscience from dead works to serve the living God?" (Heb.9:14).

"Forasmuch as ye know that ye were not redeemed with corruptible things, as silver and gold, from your vain conversation received by tradition from your fathers; But with the precious blood of Christ, as of a lamb without blemish and without spot"(1 Pt.1:18-19).

"But if we walk in the light, as he is in the light, we have fellowship one with another, and the blood of Jesus Christ his Son cleanseth us from all sin" (1 Jn.1:7).

Thought 2. In dealing with restitution, James Phillip makes a statement that needs to be heeded by the legal systems of nations today.

"As to restitution, we may observe that the Mosaic law is considerably in advance of our own. Restitution has hardly figured at all in our criminal law until comparatively recently. If one's house is burgled, and valuables stolen, the thief when caught will receive a prison sentence, but we may never recover our lost property, and our courts have been very slow to help with any compensation. It is, of course, open to us to take the criminal to the civil court and sue him for damages, but the process is so cumbersome that it could take years for the case even to be heard"[2]

3 (5:11-31) **Suspicion, of Sexual Unfaithfulness—Marriage, Sexual Unfaithfulness—Jealousy, of Sexual Unfaithfulness—Israel, Laws of—Immorality—Husband, Suspicion of Unfaithfulness—Wife, Suspicion of Unfaithfulness**: there was the law controlling the suspicion and jealousy of sexual unfaithfulness. Sexual unfaithfulness is a destructive sin, very destructive. It cuts deep, ripping and tearing at the heart of the spouse. Sexual unfaithfulness damages lives and families, sometimes destroying them. Families are the foundation of society itself; therefore, sexual unfaithfulness erodes the very foundation of society. As goes the family, so goes society. If the family is strong, the society is strong. If the family is weak, society is weak. If the family is destroyed, society is destroyed. How can such a sweeping statement be made? Because this is the way God has made human life and society. God has established the family to be the foundation of society. Just think about the fact, about what is destroyed when sexual unfaithfulness destroys families. There is the destruction of the great values and virtues of human life, the destruction of...

- trust
- loyalty
- faithfulness
- love
- joy
- gentleness
- goodness
- control
- peace
- security
- self-esteem
- fulfillment
- satisfaction
- respect

The commandment against adultery is one of the major commandments, one of the Ten Commandments. God gave this commandment to preserve our lives, to preserve the great qualities that bring love, joy, peace, trust, and loyalty to the lives of all of us as well as to society itself. Marital faithfulness builds a healthy mind and heart and a secure, strong society. This was the reason God gave this law controlling the suspicion and jealousy of sexual unfaithfulness. Note the Scripture and outline:

---

2 James Philip. *Mastering the Old Testament, Vol.4: Numbers*. (Dallas, TX: Word Publishing, 1990), p.72-73.

OUTLINE	SCRIPTURE	SCRIPTURE	OUTLINE
3. There was the law controlling the suspicion & jealousy of sexual unfaithfulness a. The case: A man's wife went astray & was unfaithful 1) The immorality, impurity was undetected: There was no witness 2) The husband became suspicious, jealous: Strife, accusations, threats occurred—a broken relationship became a possibility 3) The law was to be followed—even if the wife knew she was not guilty or defiled b. The couple was to seek the counsel & help of the priest (minister) 1) To bring an offering of barley flour (two quarts) to the LORD 2) Not to pour oil nor put incense on it: A symbol of being anointed & of one's prayers pleasing the LORD • Bc. it was not a Grain Offering of thanksgiving but an Investigation Offering to discern guilt c. The priest was to present the wife to the LORD 1) The priest (minister) was to warn her of God's judgment • To mix some dust from the Tabernacle floor (holy dust) in some holy water • To loosen the woman's hair • To place the Investigation Offering in her hands 2) The priest (minister) was to put the woman under oath • If she was not guilty of immorality, she would not suffer God's judgment or curse • If she was guilty of immorality—was defiled—she would suffer the judgment & curse of God: She	11 And the LORD spake unto Moses, saying, 12 Speak unto the children of Israel, and say unto them, If any man's wife go aside, and commit a trespass against him, 13 And a man lie with her carnally, and it be hid from the eyes of her husband, and be kept close, and she be defiled, and there be no witness against her, neither she be taken with the manner; 14 And the spirit of jealousy come upon him, and he be jealous of his wife, and she be defiled: or if the spirit of jealousy come upon him, and he be jealous of his wife, and she be not defiled: 15 Then shall the man bring his wife unto the priest, and he shall bring her offering for her, the tenth part of an ephah of barley meal; he shall pour no oil upon it, nor put frankincense thereon; for it is an offering of jealousy, an offering of memorial, bringing iniquity to remembrance. 16 And the priest shall bring her near, and set her before the LORD: 17 And the priest shall take holy water in an earthen vessel; and of the dust that is in the floor of the tabernacle the priest shall take, and put it into the water: 18 And the priest shall set the woman before the LORD, and uncover the woman's head, and put the offering of memorial in her hands, which is the jealousy offering: and the priest shall have in his hand the bitter water that causeth the curse: 19 And the priest shall charge her by an oath, and say unto the woman, If no man have lain with thee, and if thou hast not gone aside to uncleanness with another instead of thy husband, be thou free from this bitter water that causeth the curse: 20 But if thou hast gone aside to another instead of thy husband, and if thou be defiled, and some man have lain with thee beside thine	husband: 21 Then the priest shall charge the woman with an oath of cursing, and the priest shall say unto the woman, The LORD make thee a curse and an oath among thy people, when the LORD doth make thy thigh to rot, and thy belly to swell; 22 And this water that causeth the curse shall go into thy bowels, to make thy belly to swell, and thy thigh to rot: And the woman shall say, Amen, amen. 23 And the priest shall write these curses in a book, and he shall blot them out with the bitter water: 24 And he shall cause the woman to drink the bitter water that causeth the curse: and the water that causeth the curse shall enter into her, and become bitter. 25 Then the priest shall take the jealousy offering out of the woman's hand, and shall wave the offering before the LORD, and offer it upon the altar: 26 And the priest shall take an handful of the offering, even the memorial thereof, and burn it upon the altar, and afterward shall cause the woman to drink the water. 27 And when he hath made her to drink the water, then it shall come to pass, that, if she be defiled, and have done trespass against her husband, that the water that causeth the curse shall enter into her, and become bitter, and her belly shall swell, and her thigh shall rot: and the woman shall be a curse among her people. 28 And if the woman be not defiled, but be clean; then she shall be free, and shall conceive seed. 29 This is the law of jealousies, when a wife goeth aside to another instead of her husband, and is defiled; 30 Or when the spirit of jealousy cometh upon him, and he be jealous over his wife, and shall	would become infertile, unable to bear children; & if pregnant, she would suffer a miscarriage • The woman was forced to think through the oath & situation: She was asked to say "Amen"—to confess or to call God's curse down upon herself 3) The priest (minister) was to write God's curses upon a leather scroll & then wash them off in the water: The woman then drank the water 4) The priest (minister) took the Grain Offering from the woman & waved it before the LORD 5) The priest (minister) then burned a handful of the offering upon the altar 6) The priest (minister) then had the woman drink the bitter water • If she was defiled—had been sexually unfaithful—the water would cause bitter suffering: Her abdomen would swell & her thigh would waste away (a picture of being pregnant illegitimately or made infertile) & she would be accused among people (declared infertile, unblessed by God) • If she was innocent & pure, she would be cleared of all charges & able to bear children d. The purpose of the law is restated: This was the law to control sexual suspicion & jealousy 1) The entire law was to be applied to the woman

OUTLINE	SCRIPTURE	SCRIPTURE	OUTLINE
2) The husband was innocent	set the woman before the LORD, and the priest shall execute upon her all this law.	31 Then shall the man be guiltless from iniquity, and this woman shall bear her iniquity.	of any wrong-doing 3)The woman would be held accountable for her sin (Lev.20:10; Dt.22:22)

1. The case given to illustrate the law is simply stated: a man's wife went astray and was unfaithful (v.12-14).
   a. The immorality and impurity were undetected: there was no witness, and the husband was not sure about his wife, whether she had been faithful or unfaithful.
   b. But the husband was suspicious (v.14). Strife, accusations, and threats occurred. A broken relationship became a live possibility. What was to be done?
   c. The law was to be followed even if the wife knew that she was not guilty or defiled. She was still to obey the law in order to solve the problem, alleviating the suspicion and jealousy of her husband.

   Note how this law gave strong protection to the women among God's people. The husband could not strike out against his wife, abusing or committing some act of violence against her. This law was of critical importance in the ancient world, for women were counted as nothing more than chattel property. Among pagans, women existed for the pleasure of men, for the rearing of families, and for little else. But this was not to be so among God's people. They were to be a people of the law, controlled not by emotional outrages but by rationality and the rule of law.

2. The couple was to seek the counsel and help of the priest (a symbol of the minister) (v.15). Note that the couple was to take an offering to the LORD as well. The offering was to be two quarts of barley flour, but neither oil nor incense was to be mixed with it. This was usually done when making a Grain Offering of thanksgiving, but this was an investigative offering to discern guilt, not a thanksgiving offering. The oil and incense were a symbol of being anointed or blessed by God, of prayers being lifted up to God as a sweet aroma that pleased Him. However, in this case, God was not pleased. The issue was the possibility of sexual unfaithfulness, of suspicion and jealousy; therefore, as stated, this was an investigative offering to discern guilt. An offering was required, but not an offering that pleased the LORD.

3. The priest (minister) was to present the wife to the LORD (v.16-28). These verses involved a ritual that the suspected wife had to undergo. Note how the ritual stressed the seriousness of sexual unfaithfulness and stood as a strong warning to all against sexual unfaithfulness.
   a. The priest (minister) was to warn the suspected wife of God's judgment (v.17-18). He was to mix some dust from the Tabernacle floor (holy dust) in some holy water, that is, water taken from inside the Tabernacle. This act was to stress the holiness of the situation, a situation that was being brought before the LORD Himself. The priest was then to loosen the woman's hair (v.18). This was probably a symbol of the woman opening up her life before the LORD and requesting that the LORD open up the truth to her husband.[3] The priest then placed the investigative offering, the Grain Offering, in her hands (v.18).
   b. The priest was to put the woman under oath (v.19-22). The priest stated these facts: if she were not guilty of immorality, she would not suffer God's judgment or curse (v.19). But if she were guilty of immorality and had defiled herself, she would suffer the judgment and curse of God. Just what this meant is unknown. Most commentators feel that the curse meant that she would become infertile, unable to bear children, and if pregnant, she would suffer a miscarriage. If she were guilty of sexual unfaithfulness, there was, of course, the possibility that she would become pregnant. Note that she was forced to think through the oath and situation: she was asked to say "Amen"; that is, to confess or to call God's curse down upon herself (v.22).
   c. The priest was to write God's curses upon a piece of leather and then wash them off in the water. The woman was then to drink the water (v.23-24).
   d. The priest took the Grain Offering from the woman and waved it before the LORD (v.25).
   e. The priest then burned a handful of the offering upon the altar (v.26).
   f. The priest then had the woman drink the bitter water (v.26-28). If she were defiled—had been sexually unfaithful—the water would cause bitter suffering. Note how descriptive the bitter suffering is pictured: her abdomen would swell and her thigh would waste away. This is a picture of being pregnant illegitimately or made infertile. It is also stated that she would be accursed among people; that is, declared infertile, unblessed by God. But note: if she were innocent and pure, she would be cleared of all charges and be able to bear children (v.28).

4. The purpose of the law is restated: to control sexual suspicion and jealousy (v.29-31). Simply stated, the entire law was to be applied to the woman (v.30). The husband was innocent of any wrongdoing in this particular case (v.31). The woman was to be held accountable for her sin (Lev.20:10; Dt.22:22).

Thought 1. When a man or woman goes astray or is even thought to be guilty of sexual unfaithfulness, suspicion and jealousy arise. Strife, accusations, and threats occur. Often a broken relationship results, and the couple is ripped apart. Sexual immorality always causes problems...

- guilt
- jealousy
- unwanted pregnancies
- broken marriages
- insecurity
- a false sense of security
- unhappiness
- disease
- a cheapening of sex
- broken trust
- selfishness
- loss of esteem
- loss of respect for others
- loss of respect by others
- problems with children
- emotional problems
- disloyalty
- a lack of fulfillment
- loss of affection in relationships

3 *The Expositor's Bible Commentary*, Frank E. Gaebelein, Editor, p.746.

Because of these problems and so many more, God demands faithfulness between husband and wife. The sanctity of marriage is to be kept. The health and security of God's people and of society are at stake. The foundation of the family, of children, and of society must not be undermined by sexual unfaithfulness. The family and children are to have a fundamental place in society, and the family and children are to be respected and built up, not torn down. The marriage bond is far more than just a civil contract that can be broken anytime a person wishes. The marriage bond is a contract made between two persons before God Himself. He unites the two persons into one flesh. James Phillips points out what "one flesh" means: it means that a new person—a totally new person—has been brought into being by God. Therefore, it is impossible to think of a husband and wife as two individuals; they are one person created by God into "one flesh"—a totally new person. It is, therefore, against God's will for a couple to tear themselves into pieces. The picture is descriptive: the person who divorces rips and tears apart his own body.[4] The Word of God is clear:

"Ye have heard that it was said by them of old time, Thou shalt not commit adultery: But I say unto you, That whosoever looketh on a woman to lust after her hath committed adultery with her already in his heart" (Mt.5:27-28).

"It is not lawful for thee to have her" (Mt.14:4).

"Know ye not that the unrighteous shall not inherit the kingdom of God? Be not deceived: neither fornicators, nor idolaters, nor adulterers, nor effeminate, nor abusers of themselves with mankind" (1 Cor.6:9).

"Now the works of the flesh are manifest, which are *these;* Adultery, fornication, uncleanness, lasciviousness, Idolatry, witchcraft, hatred, variance, emulations, wrath, strife, seditions, heresies, Envyings, murders, drunkenness, revellings, and such like: of the which I tell you before, as I have also told *you* in time past, that they which do such things shall not inherit the kingdom of God" (Gal.5:19-21).

"Having eyes full of adultery, and that cannot cease from sin; beguiling unstable souls: an heart they have exercised with covetous practices; cursed children" (2 Pt.2:14).

"Thou shalt not commit adultery" (Ex.20:14).

"And the man that committeth adultery with *another* man's wife, *even he* that committeth adultery with his neighbour's wife, the adulterer and the adulteress shall surely be put to death" (Lev.20:10).

"The eye also of the adulterer waiteth for the twilight, saying, No eye shall see me: and disguiseth *his* face" (Job 24:15).

TYPES, SYMBOLS, AND PICTURES
(Numbers 5:1-31)

Historical Term	Type or Picture (Scriptural Basis for Each)	Life Application for Today's Believer	Biblical Application
Leprosy or Infectious Skin Disease Num.5:1-4; 12:13-16 (See also Lev. 13:1-59)	*These contagious diseases symbolize the disease of sin, how contagious it is, and the need to prevent the spread of sin.* **"And the cloud departed from off the tabernacle; and, behold, Miriam *became* leprous, *white* as snow: and Aaron looked upon Miriam, and, behold, *she was* leprous" (Num.12:10).**	⇒ God gave Israel the law governing leprosy or infectious skin disease because He loves His people. God loves us and cares for us; therefore He wants us healthy—physically & spiritually. He wants us experiencing the fullness of life, worshipping and serving Him. He wants us bearing strong testimony to a world lost and reeling under the weight of desperate need. He wants all of His people throughout all generations healthy.	***"The Spirit of the Lord is upon me, because he hath anointed me to preach the gospel to the poor; he hath sent me to heal the brokenhearted, to preach deliverance to the captives, and recovering of sight to the blind, to set at liberty them that are bruised" (Lk.4:18).*** ***"When Jesus heard it, he saith unto them, They that are whole have no need of the physician, but they that are sick: I came not to call the righteous, but sinners to repentance" (Mk.2:17).*** ***"Beloved, I wish above all things that thou mayest prosper and be in health, even as thy soul prospereth" (3 Jn.1:2).*** ***"And said, If thou wilt diligently hearken to the voice of the LORD thy God, and wilt do that which is right in his sight, and wilt give ear to his command-***

4 James Philip. *Mastering the Old Testament, Vol.4: Numbers*, p.78.

Historical Term	Type or Picture (Scriptural Basis for Each)	Life Application for Today's Believer	Biblical Application
			ments, and keep all his statutes, I will put none of these diseases upon thee, which I have brought upon the Egyptians: for I am the LORD that healeth thee" (Ex.15:26). ***"And the LORD will take away from thee all sickness, and will put none of the evil diseases of Egypt, which thou knowest, upon thee; but will lay them upon all them that hate thee" (Dt.7:15).*** ***"For I will restore health unto thee, and I will heal thee of thy wounds, saith the LORD; because they called thee an Outcast, saying, This is Zion, whom no man seeketh after" (Jer.30:17).*** ***"Come, and let us return unto the LORD: for he hath torn, and he will heal us; he hath smitten, and he will bind us up" (Hos.6:1).***
The Priest Loosening the Woman's Hair Num.5:11-31, esp. v.18	*This was probably a symbol of the woman (suspected of unfaithfulness) opening up her life before the LORD and requesting that the LORD open up the truth to her husband.*[5] *The priest (minister) was to present the wife to the LORD (v.16-28). These verses involved a ritual that the suspected wife had to undergo. Note how the ritual stressed the seriousness of sexual unfaithfulness and stood as a strong warning to all others against sexual unfaithfulness.* *The priest (minister) was to warn the suspected wife of God's judgment (v.17-18). He was to mix some dust from the Tabernacle floor (holy dust) in some holy water, that is, water taken from inside the Tabernacle. This act was to stress the holiness of the situation, a situation that was being brought before the LORD Himself. The priest was then to loosen the woman's hair (v.18). The priest then placed the investigation offering, the*	What is the duty of the Christian wife to her husband and of the Christian husband to his wife? If a woman wants to give her life to God, she has to give herself to her husband. Scripture says that she has to do five specific things. 1. Live in subjection to her own husband (1 Pt.3:1). 2. Live a chaste life (1 Pt. 3:2). 3. Live a reverent life before God (1 Pt.3:2). 4. Not dress to attract attention (1 Pt.3:3). 5. Adorn her heart with a meek and quiet spirit (1 Pt.3:4-6).	***"Likewise, ye wives, be in subjection to your own husbands; that, if any obey not the word, they also may without the word be won by the conversation [behavior, conduct] of the wives" (1 Pt.3:1).*** ***"And unto the married I command, yet not I, but the Lord, Let not the wife depart from her husband" (1 Cor. 7:10).*** ***"Even so must their wives be grave, not slanderers, sober, faithful in all things" (1 Tim. 3:11).*** ***"Blessed are the pure in heart: for they shall see God" (Mt.5:8).*** ***"For this is the will of God, even your sanctification, that ye should abstain from fornication" (1 Thes. 4:3).*** ***"Now the end of the commandment is charity out of a pure heart, and of a good conscience, and of faith unfeigned" (1 Tim. 1:5).*** ***"That they may teach the young women to be sober, to love their husbands, to love their children, to be discreet, chaste, keepers at home,***

5 *The Expositor's Bible Commentary*, Frank E. Gaebelein, Editor, p.746.

Historical Term	Type or Picture (Scriptural Basis for Each)	Life Application for Today's Believer	Biblical Application
	Grain Offering, in her hands (v.18). **"And the priest shall set the woman before the LORD, and uncover the woman's head, and put the offering of memorial in her hands, which *is* the jealousy offering: and the priest shall have in his hand the bitter water that causeth the curse" (Num. 5:18).**		***good, obedient to their own husbands, that the word of God be not blasphemed" (Tit. 2:4-5).*** ***"Wives, submit yourselves unto your own husbands, as it is fit in the Lord" (Col. 3:18).*** ***"She looketh well to the ways of her household, and eateth not the bread of idleness" (Pr.31:27).*** ***"These are they which were not defiled with women; for they are virgins. These are they which follow the Lamb whithersoever he goeth. These were redeemed from among men, being the firstfruits unto God and to the Lamb" (Rev. 14:4).***

1. The purpose for the vow: A strong desire to draw closer to the Lord—to be separated, totally set apart to the Lord

2. The obligations of the special vow to the LORD

a. He must abstain from all intoxicating drink: To keep his mind clear & focused upon the LORD
   1) From wine & other fermented drinks
   2) From anything that comes from the vine: A caution to prevent temptation

b. He must not cut his hair: To be the mark of his vow
   1) That he was committed to live a life of holiness & separation to God
   2) That he was committed to keep his mind focused upon God

c. He must not go near a dead body, not even of his family: A symbol of becoming defiled & corrupted—spiritually or ceremonially unclean
   1) The reason:
      - Being the Lord's, he was to be totally focused upon the LORD (not upon earthly things, not even the most dear things)
      - Being the Lord's, he was to have no contact with death
   2) The provision for cleansing if a person unexpectedly died in his presence
      - Must shave his head on the 7th day, removing the mark of his vow—for it was defiled
      - Must come to God for cleansing through the sacrifice of the Sin Offering: A symbol of Christ
      - Must approach God for atonement, reconciliation through the sacrifice of the Burnt Offering: A symbol of Christ
      - Must rededicate himself to the LORD for the full term of his vow
      - Must seek freedom from guilt through the sacrifice of the Guilt Offering: A symbol of Christ

E. The Special Provision Instituted for Drawing Closer to God—the Nazirite Vow & the Special Benediction of God: The Importance & Seriousness of Vows, 6:1-27

And the LORD spake unto
Moses, saying,
2 Speak unto the children of
Israel, and say unto them,
When either man or woman
shall separate themselves to
vow a vow of a Nazarite, to
separate themselves unto the
LORD:
3 He shall separate himself
from wine and strong drink,
and shall drink no vinegar of
wine, or vinegar of strong
drink, neither shall he drink
any liquor of grapes, nor eat
moist grapes, or dried.
4 All the days of his separation shall he eat nothing that
is made of the vine tree, from
the kernels even to the husk.
5 All the days of the vow of
his separation there shall no
razor come upon his head:
until the days be fulfilled, in
the which he separateth himself unto the LORD, he shall
be holy, and shall let the
locks of the hair of his head
grow.
6 All the days that he separateth himself unto the LORD
he shall come at no dead
body.
7 He shall not make himself
unclean for his father, or for
his mother, for his brother,
or for his sister, when
they die: because the consecration of his God is upon
his head.
8 All the days of his separation he is holy unto the
LORD.
9 And if any man die very
suddenly by him, and he hath
defiled the head of his consecration; then he shall shave
his head in the day of his
cleansing, on the seventh day
shall he shave it.
10 And on the eighth day he
shall bring two turtles, or
two young pigeons, to the
priest, to the door of the tabernacle of the congregation:
11 And the priest shall offer
the one for a sin offering,
and the other for a burnt
offering, and make an atonement for him, for that he
sinned by the dead, and shall
hallow his head that same
day.
12 And he shall consecrate
unto the LORD the days of his
separation, and shall bring a
lamb of the first year for a
trespass offering: but the
days that were before shall
be lost, because his separation was defiled.
13 And this is the law of the
Nazarite, when the days of
his separation are fulfilled:
he shall be brought unto the
door of the tabernacle of the
congregation:
14 And he shall offer his
offering unto the LORD, one
he lamb of the first year
without blemish for a burnt
offering, and one ewe lamb
of the first year without
blemish for a sin offering,
and one ram without blemish
for peace offerings,
15 And a basket of unleavened bread, cakes of fine
flour mingled with oil, and
wafers of unleavened bread
anointed with oil, and their
meat offering, and their
drink offerings.
16 And the priest shall bring
them before the LORD, and
shall offer his sin offering,
and his burnt offering:
17 And he shall offer the
ram for a sacrifice of peace
offerings unto the LORD,
with the basket of unleavened bread: the priest shall
offer also his meat offering,
and his drink offering.
18 And the Nazarite shall
shave the head of his separation at the door of the tabernacle of the congregation,
and shall take the hair of the
head of his separation, and
put it in the fire which is
under the sacrifice of the
peace offerings.
19 And the priest shall take
the sodden shoulder of the
ram, and one unleavened
cake out of the basket, and
one unleavened wafer, and
shall put them upon the
hands of the Nazarite, after
the hair of his separation is
shaven:
20 And the priest shall wave
them for a wave offering
before the LORD: this is holy
for the priest, with the wave
breast and heave shoulder:

3. The worship required after the fulfillment of the vow

a. He must approach & present his offerings to the LORD
   1) The Burnt Offering: Acknowledged the atonement
   2) The Sin Offering: Acknowledged the need for cleansing
   3) The Peace or Fellowship Offering: Acknowledged the need to grow in peace & fellowship with God
   4) The Grain & Drink Offerings: A person thanked & praised the LORD, dedicating himself—pouring his life out before God

b. He must have the priest make the offerings in his behalf
   1) The Sin Offering & Burnt Offering
   2) The Fellowship or Peace Offering
   3) The Grain & Drink Offering

c. He must shave off his hair & burn it under the sacrifice of the Fellowship Offering: A symbol for a continued commitment & closer fellowship with the Lord

d. The priest then had to place in the Nazarites' hands the boiled shoulder of the ram & one unleavened cake & wafer from the basket
   1) The priest was to offer these as a wave offering to the LORD
   2) The priest was to receive these along with the breast & thigh pieces as the LORD's portion

e. The Nazarite could then drink wine **4. The seriousness & heavy weight of the vow** a. This is a law, the law of the Nazarite vow: A complete & total separation to the LORD b. This vow must be kept, fulfilled **5. The great priestly benediction** a. Promised by God Himself	and after that the Nazarite may drink wine. 21 This is the law of the Nazarite who hath vowed, and of his offering unto the LORD for his separation, beside that that his hand shall get: according to the vow which he vowed, so he must do after the law of his separation. 22 And the LORD spake unto Moses, saying, 23 Speak unto Aaron and unto his sons, saying, On this	wise ye shall bless the children of Israel, saying unto them, 24 The LORD bless thee, and keep thee: 25 The LORD make his face shine upon thee, and be gracious unto thee: 26 The LORD lift up his countenance upon thee, and give thee peace. 27 And they shall put my name upon the children of Israel; and I will bless them.	 1) His blessing 2) His protection, security 3) His face, special presence 4) His grace 5) His acceptance, approval, pleasure (smile) 6) His peace b. The result: The blessings identified the Israelites as God's people, as belonging to Him

DIVISION I

THE PREPARATION FOR THE MARCH TO THE PROMISED LAND

E. The Special Provision Instituted for Drawing Closer to God—the Nazarite Vow and the Special Benediction of God: The Importance and Seriousness of Vows, 6:1-27

(6:1-27) **Introduction—Vow, Importance of—Nazarite Vow—Vow, Nazarite—Devotion, Desire for—Communion, Desire for—Commitment, Deeper, Desire for**: desperate circumstances often stir people to pray and make vows to God. Severe illness, accidents, marital problems, parental problems, school problems, business difficulties, threats, war, and a host of other circumstances can cause people to make vows and promises to God. Every promise and vow is important to God, and God takes the vow seriously. He expects the person to fulfill his or her vows. But there is one vow that is very, very special to God: the Nazarite vow. What is the Nazarite vow? It is a vow that seeks a deeper life with God. The person wants a closer walk with God; therefore, he sets aside a period of time to seek the LORD as never before. He seeks a closer walk with the LORD, a deeper communion and fellowship with Him. He takes more time to study the Word of God, to pray and seek the face of God. He seeks to be more conformed to the image of God. He wants to grow in holiness, to be more totally separated from the world and set apart to God. He wants to be a stronger witness and testimony for God. The passion that burns in his heart is a passion to know God more and more, to be conformed to the very image of God.

This is the great subject of this important passage of Scripture: *The Special Provision Instituted for Drawing Closer to God—the Nazarite Vow and the Special Benediction of God: The Importance and Seriousness of Vows*, 6:1-27.

1. The reason for the vow: a strong desire to draw closer to the LORD—to be separated, totally set apart to the LORD (v.1-2).
2. The obligations of the special vow to the LORD (v.3-12).
3. The fulfillment of and the discharge from the vow (v.13-20).
4. The seriousness and heavy weight of the vow (v.21).
5. The great priestly benediction (v.22-27).

1 (6:1-2) **Vow, Reason for—Separation, to the LORD—Walk, Spiritual, Duty—Walk, Spiritual, Desire for**: the purpose for the vow was a closer walk with the LORD. The Nazarite wanted to draw closer to the LORD—to be separated, totally set apart to Him. The Hebrew word for "shall separate themselves" or "wants to make a special vow" or "to set themselves apart" (pala) means to make a hard, difficult vow; to make a singular, distinctive, different vow; a vow that differs from the usual vows.[1] The idea is striking: the Nazarite vow was different from the common, day-to-day vow. This person had a strong, strong desire to draw closer to the LORD. He was driven to know the LORD more and more personally, to know Him intimately. He had a passionate desire to be totally devoted to the LORD, totally separated and set apart to Him. The very word Nazarite (nazir) means a person who has set his life apart to God. The period of dedication was usually for a specific period of time. However, a few persons apparently were set apart for the Nazarite vow for life. For example, Samson was a Nazarite from the day of his birth (Judg.13:7), and so was Samuel (1 Sam.1:11, 28).

OUTLINE	SCRIPTURE
1. The purpose for the vow: A strong desire to draw closer to the Lord—to be separated, totally set apart to the Lord	And the LORD spake unto Moses, saying, 2 Speak unto the children of Israel, and say unto them, When either man or woman shall separate themselves to vow a vow of a Nazarite, to separate themselves unto the LORD:

1 James Strong. *Strong's Exhaustive Concordance of the Bible*. (Nashville, TN: Thomas Nelson, Inc., 1990).

Thought 1. The longing, the passion, the intense desire to know the LORD more and more is the point to see in the Nazarite vow. The person was driven to seek a closer walk, a deeper devotion, and more and more communion with the LORD. He craved a continued, unbroken consciousness of the Lord's presence, a moment-by-moment fellowship with Him. Moreover, he wanted to be a stronger witness and testimony for the LORD. What a dynamic, strong example for us.

"I beseech you therefore, brethren, by the mercies of God, that ye present your bodies a living sacrifice, holy, acceptable unto God, which is your reasonable service" (Ro.12:1).

"But what things were gain to me, those I counted loss for Christ. Yea doubtless, and I count all things but loss for the excellency of the knowledge of Christ Jesus my Lord: for whom I have suffered the loss of all things, and do count them but dung, that I may win Christ" (Ph.3:7-8).

"That I may know him, and the power of his resurrection, and the fellowship of his sufferings, being made conformable unto his death" (Ph.3:10).

"Let us draw near with a true heart in full assurance of faith, having our hearts sprinkled from an evil conscience, and our bodies washed with pure water" (Heb.10:22).

"Draw nigh to God, and he will draw nigh to you" (Jas.4:8).

"Behold, I stand at the door, and knock: if any man hear my voice, and open the door, I will come in to him, and will sup with him, and he with me" (Rev.3:20).

"I have set the Lord always before me: because he is at my right hand, I shall not be moved" (Ps.16:8).

"My son, give me thine heart, and let thine eyes observe my ways" (Pr.23:26).

"The Lord is nigh unto them that are of a broken heart; and saveth such as be of a contrite spirit" (Ps.34:18).

"But it is good for me to draw near to God: I have put my trust in the Lord God, that I may declare all thy works" (Ps.73:28).

"The Lord is nigh unto all them that call upon him, to all that call upon him in truth" (Ps.145:18).

"Ye are my witnesses, saith the Lord, and my servant whom I have chosen: that ye may know and believe me, and understand that I am he: before me there was no God formed, neither shall there be after me" (Is.43:10).

"Then shall we know, if we follow on to know the Lord: his going forth is prepared as the morning; and he shall come unto us as the rain, as the latter and former rain unto the earth" (Hos.6:3).

2 (6:3-12) **Vow—Drunkenness—Alcohol—Wine—Dedication—Uncleanness, Ceremonial—Uncleanness, Spiritual—Ritual, Laws of Uncleanness—Laws, of Uncleanness—Nazarite, Vow of**: there were three special obligations of the Nazarite vow, three very special commitments the person made to the LORD. Note that the three commitments involved diet, appearance, and associations.[2]

OUTLINE	SCRIPTURE	SCRIPTURE	OUTLINE
2. The obligations of the special vow to the LORD a. He must abstain from all intoxicating drink: To keep his mind clear & focused upon the LORD 1) From wine & other fermented drinks 2) From anything that comes from the vine: A caution to prevent temptation	3 He shall separate himself from wine and strong drink, and shall drink no vinegar of wine, or vinegar of strong drink, neither shall he drink any liquor of grapes, nor eat moist grapes, or dried. 4 All the days of his separation shall he eat nothing that is made of the vine tree, from the kernels even to the husk.	or for his sister, when they die: because the consecration of his God is upon his head. 8 All the days of his separation he is holy unto the LORD. 9 And if any man die very suddenly by him, and he hath defiled the head of his consecration; then he shall shave his head in the day of	to be totally focused upon the LORD (not upon earthly things, not even the most dear things) • Being the Lord's, he was to have no contact with death 2) The provision for cleansing if a person unexpectedly died in his presence • Must shave his head on the 7th day, removing
b. He must not cut his hair: To be the mark of his vow 1) That he was committed to live a life of holiness & separation to God 2) That he was committed to keep his mind focused upon God	5 All the days of the vow of his separation there shall no razor come upon his head: until the days be fulfilled, in the which he separateth himself unto the LORD, he shall be holy, and shall let the locks of the hair of his head grow.	his cleansing, on the seventh day shall he shave it. 10 And on the eighth day he shall bring two turtles, or two young pigeons, to the priest, to the door of the tabernacle of the congregation: 11 And the priest shall offer	the mark of his vow—for it was defiled • Must come to God for cleansing through the sacrifice of the Sin Offering: A symbol of Christ
c. He must not go near a dead body, not even of his family: A symbol of becoming defiled & corrupted—spiritually or ceremonially unclean 1) The reason: • Being the Lord's, he was	6 All the days that he separateth himself unto the LORD he shall come at no dead body. 7 He shall not make himself unclean for his father, or for his mother, for his brother,	the one for a sin offering, and the other for a burnt offering, and make an atonement for him, for that he sinned by the dead, and shall hallow his head that same day. 12 And he shall consecrate	• Must approach God for atonement, reconciliation through the sacrifice of the Burnt Offering: A symbol of Christ • Must rededicate him-

2 *The Expositor's Bible Commentary*, Frank E. Gaebelein, Editor, p.749.

OUTLINE	SCRIPTURE	SCRIPTURE	OUTLINE
self to the LORD for the full term of his vow • Must seek freedom from guilt through the	unto the LORD the days of his separation, and shall bring a lamb of the first year for a trespass offering:	but the days that were before shall be lost, because his separation was defiled.	sacrifice of the Guilt Offering: A symbol of Christ

1. The person was to abstain from all intoxicating drink (v.3-4). This included any and all kinds of drugs or intoxicating drinks. In fact, anything that came from the vine or was made from the fruit of the vine such as grapes, juice, jams, seeds, or skins—all this and anything else—was prohibited. A person was to keep his mind clear, free from any intoxicating numbness or dullness. He was to focus upon the LORD with a clear, sharp mind. The person's mental faculties were needed to meditate upon the Word of God, to commune and fellowship with the LORD, to bear testimony and witness for the LORD.

2. The person must not cut his hair (v.5). Uncut hair was the *public mark* of his vow. He was declaring the awesome importance of being committed to a life of holiness and separation to God, the importance of keeping one's mind focused upon God. Uncut hair was a distinctive witness for God, a witness that a person was committed to a life of holiness, committed to keeping his mind focused upon the LORD.

3. The person must not go near a dead body, not even if it was a family member (v.6-12). Contact with a dead body was a symbol of becoming defiled, unclean, corrupted—of becoming ceremonially, spiritually unclean. Death is the end of life: it is the corruption and decay of the human body. Death is, therefore, the symbol of corruption, decay, and defilement. The person who took the Nazarite vow was, therefore, to have nothing to do with death. He was to be an example of life, not of death. This stern restriction proclaimed the wonderful life that God gives not the death and corruption that sin brings. The person had committed himself totally to the LORD; therefore, he was to be totally set apart and focused upon the LORD, not upon the things of the earth—not even upon the most dear things to his heart.

But what happened if a person unexpectedly died in the Nazarite's presence? In such a circumstance, there was a provision for cleansing (v.9-12).

⇒ He had to shave his head on the seventh day, removing the mark of his vow, of his holiness (devotion to God). (v.9). Because he had become defiled, corrupted, the person had to remove his hair.

⇒ He had to come to God for cleansing through the sacrifice of the Sin Offering (v.10). Remember, the sacrifice is a symbol of the sacrifice of Christ. Only Christ can forgive sins.

⇒ He had to approach God for atonement (reconciliation) through the sacrifice of the Burnt Offering (v.11). This sacrifice is also a symbol of Christ's sacrifice. We receive the atonement, reconciliation with God, through Christ and Christ alone.

⇒ He had to rededicate himself to the LORD for the full term of his vow (v.12). Why the full term? Because the period of his vow and dedication had been disrupted. Consequently, the person had to recommit himself just as he had originally done, for the full term of his vow.

⇒ He had to seek freedom from guilt through the sacrifice of the Guilt Offering (v.12). Again, the sacrifice made was a symbol of Christ's sacrifice. It is only through Christ that guilt can be removed.

Thought 1. The obligation of the Nazarite vow clearly speaks to the heart and life of the believer. The lessons are forceful:

1) The believer must abstain from all intoxicating drinks. He must keep his mind clear and focused totally upon the LORD. The believer must not allow drugs and drink to dull or numb or damage his mind. He must keep his mind healthy, alert, and sharp to focus upon God and the promised land toward which he is marching.

"And take heed to yourselves, lest at any time your hearts be overcharged with surfeiting, and drunkenness, and cares of this life, and so that day come upon you unawares" (Lk.21:34).

"Let us walk honestly, as in the day; not in rioting and drunkenness, not in chambering and wantonness, not in strife and envying" (Ro.13:13).

"Now the works of the flesh are manifest, which are these; Adultery, fornication, uncleanness, lasciviousness, Idolatry, witchcraft, hatred, variance, emulations, wrath, strife, seditions, heresies, Envyings, murders, drunkenness, revellings, and such like: of the which I tell you before, as I have also told you in time past, that they which do such things shall not inherit the kingdom of God" (Gal.5:19-21).

"And be not drunk with wine, wherein is excess; but be filled with the Spirit" (Eph.5:18).

"Wine is a mocker, strong drink is raging: and whosoever is deceived thereby is not wise" (Pr.20:1).

"Be not among winebibbers" (Pr.23:20).

"Who hath woe? who hath sorrow? who hath contentions? who hath babbling? who hath wounds without cause? who hath redness of eyes? They that tarry long at the wine; they that go to seek mixed wine. Look not thou upon the wine when it is red, when it giveth his colour in the cup, when it moveth itself aright" (Pr.23:29-31).

"Woe unto them that rise up early in the morning, that they may follow strong drink; that continue until night, till wine inflame them" (Is.5:11).

"Woe unto him that giveth his neighbour drink, that puttest thy bottle to him, and makest him drunken also, that thou mayest look on their nakedness" (Hab.2:15).

2) The believer must keep his mind clear and focused upon the LORD.

"Casting down imaginations, and every high thing that exalteth itself against the knowledge of God, and bringing into captivity every thought to the obedience of Christ" (2 Cor.10:5).

"Finally, brethren, whatsoever things are true, whatsoever things are honest, whatsoever things are

just, whatsoever things are pure, whatsoever things are lovely, whatsoever things are of good report; if there be any virtue, and if there be any praise, think on these things" (Ph.4:8).

"For it is sanctified by the word of God and prayer" (1 Tim.4:5).

"This book of the law shall not depart out of thy mouth; but thou shalt meditate therein day and night, that thou mayest observe to do according to all that is written therein: for then thou shalt make thy way prosperous, and then thou shalt have good success" (Josh.1:8).

"But his delight is in the law of the Lord; and in his law doth he meditate day and night" (Ps.1:2).

"Let the words of my mouth, and the meditation of my heart, be acceptable in thy sight, O Lord, my strength, and my redeemer" (Ps.19:14).

"My soul shall be satisfied as with marrow and fatness; and my mouth shall praise thee with joyful lips: When I remember thee upon my bed, and meditate on thee in the night watches" (Ps.63:5-6).

"My meditation of him shall be sweet: I will be glad in the Lord" (Ps.104:34).

"Mine eyes prevent [precede] the night watches, that I might meditate in thy word" (Ps.119:148).

3) The Nazarite was not allowed to shave his head because his hair was the mark of his vow to God. His hair was the mark of his holiness and separation to God. So it must be with the believer. The believer must bear the mark of holiness and separation to God. The believer must bear the mark of being totally committed to God, the mark of a holy life before God. The believer must keep his mind totally focused upon the LORD, not upon earthly things, not even upon the things that might be thought most dear. As the believer marches to the promised land, living a holy life is to be the mark of his life.

"That he would grant unto us, that we being delivered out of the hand of our enemies might serve him without fear, In holiness and righteousness before him, all the days of our life" (Lk.1:74-75).

"Having therefore these promises, dearly beloved, let us cleanse ourselves from all filthiness of the flesh and spirit, perfecting holiness in the fear of God" (2 Cor.7:1).

"Follow peace with all men, and holiness, without which no man shall see the Lord" (Heb.12:14).

"But as he which hath called you is holy, so be ye holy in all manner of conversation; Because it is written, Be ye holy; for I am holy" (1 Pt.1:15-16).

"Seeing then that all these things shall be dissolved, what manner of persons ought ye to be in all holy conversation and godliness, Looking for and hasting unto the coming of the day of God, wherein the heavens being on fire shall be dissolved, and the elements shall melt with fervent heat? Nevertheless we, according to his promise, look for new heavens and a new earth, wherein dwelleth righteousness. Wherefore, beloved, seeing that ye look for such things, be diligent that ye may be found of him in peace, without spot, and blameless" (2 Pt.3:11-14).

"For I am the Lord that bringeth you up out of the land of Egypt, to be your God: ye shall therefore be holy, for I am holy" (Lev.11:45).

"Exalt the Lord our God, and worship at his holy hill; for the Lord our God is holy" (Ps.99:9).

4) The Nazarite could not touch a dead body because it symbolized corruption and decay, defilement and uncleanness. So it must be with the believer. The believer must not become corrupted and defiled by sin and shame. Sin and shame bring lawlessness, violence, and death to the earth. The believer is to symbolize life, not corruption and death. The believer is to have nothing to do with corruption and defilement. He is to be totally set apart and focused upon the LORD, not upon the things of this earth. He is to live a life that is totally separated and set apart to God.

"And with many other words did he testify and exhort, saying, Save yourselves from this untoward generation" (Acts 2:40).

"I beseech you therefore, brethren, by the mercies of God, that ye present your bodies a living sacrifice, holy, acceptable unto God, which is your reasonable service. And be not conformed to this world: but be ye transformed by the renewing of your mind, that ye may prove what is that good, and acceptable, and perfect, will of God" (Ro.12:1-2).

"But now I have written unto you not to keep company, if any man that is called a brother be a fornicator, or covetous, or an idolater, or a railer, or a drunkard, or an extortioner" (1 Cor.5:11).

"Be ye not unequally yoked together with unbelievers: for what fellowship hath righteousness with unrighteousness? and what communion hath light with darkness" (2 Cor.6:14).

"Wherefore come out from among them, and be ye separate, saith the Lord, and touch not the unclean thing; and I will receive you, And will be a Father unto you, and ye shall be my sons and daughters, saith the Lord Almighty" (2 Cor.6:17-18).

"And have no fellowship with the unfruitful works of darkness, but rather reprove them" (Eph.5:11).

"Now we command you, brethren, in the name of our Lord Jesus Christ, that ye withdraw yourselves from every brother that walketh disorderly, and not after the tradition which he received of us" (2 Th.3:6).

"Love not the world, neither the things that are in the world. If any man love the world, the love of the Father is not in him. For all that is in the world, the lust of the flesh, and the lust of the eyes, and the pride of life, is not of the Father, but is of the world" (1 Jn.2:15-16).

"Depart ye, depart ye, go ye out from thence, touch no unclean thing; go ye out of the midst of her; be ye clean, that bear the vessels of the Lord" (Is.52:11).

"Blessed is the man that walketh not in the counsel of the ungodly, nor standeth in the way of sinners, nor sitteth in the seat of the scornful" (Ps.1:1).

Thought 2. There is cleansing from sin. God has made provision for cleansing. No matter what a person has done—no matter how defiled or corrupted or unclean a person is—God has made provision. What is that provision? How can a person be cleansed from sin, no matter how terrible? Through the sacrifice of the Lord Jesus Christ. Through Jesus Christ, a person…
- can be forgiven his sins
- can receive the atonement, be reconciled to God
- can have his guilt removed, be set entirely free from guilt and shame

"For God so loved the world, that he gave his only begotten Son, that whosoever believeth in him should not perish, but have everlasting life" (Jn.3:16).

"For when we were yet without strength, in due time Christ died for the ungodly" (Ro.5:6).

"Much more then, being now justified by his blood, we shall be saved from wrath through him" (Ro.5:9).

"And not only so, but we also joy in God through our Lord Jesus Christ, by whom we have now received the atonement [reconciliation]" (Ro.5:11).

"For I delivered unto you first of all that which I also received, how that Christ died for our sins according to the scriptures" (1 Cor.15:3).

"In whom we have redemption through his blood, the forgiveness of sins, according to the riches of his grace" (Eph.1:7).

"Who his own self bare our sins in his own body on the tree, that we, being dead to sins, should live unto righteousness: by whose stripes ye were healed" (1 Pt.2:24).

"For Christ also hath once suffered for sins, the just for the unjust, that he might bring us to God, being put to death in the flesh, but quickened by the Spirit" (1 Pt.3:18).

"But if we walk in the light, as he is in the light, we have fellowship one with another, and the blood of Jesus Christ his Son cleanseth us from all sin" (1 Jn.1:7).

"But he was wounded for our transgressions, he was bruised for our iniquities: the chastisement of our peace was upon him; and with his stripes we are healed" (Is.53:5).

3 (6:13-20) **Vow, Fulfillment of—Law, of Nazarite Vow—Nazarite, Vow of**: there was extensive worship required after the fulfillment of the vow. Naturally, the person was to continue to follow and to be totally committed to the LORD. This was the reason for this extensive worship service that marked the completion of the vow.

OUTLINE	SCRIPTURE	SCRIPTURE	OUTLINE
3. The worship required after the fulfillment of the vow a. He must approach & present his offerings to the LORD 1) The Burnt Offering: Acknowledged the atonement 2) The Sin Offering: Acknowledged the need for cleansing 3) The Peace or Fellowship Offering: Acknowledged the need to grow in peace & fellowship with God 4) The Grain & Drink Offerings: A person thanked & praised the LORD, dedicating himself—pouring his life out before God b. He must have the priest make the offerings in his behalf 1) The Sin Offering & Burnt Offering 2) The Fellowship or Peace Offering 3) The Grain & Drink Offering	13 And this is the law of the Nazarite, when the days of his separation are fulfilled: he shall be brought unto the door of the tabernacle of the congregation: 14 And he shall offer his offering unto the LORD, one he lamb of the first year without blemish for a burnt offering, and one ewe lamb of the first year without blemish for a sin offering, and one ram without blemish for peace offerings, 15 And a basket of unleavened bread, cakes of fine flour mingled with oil, and wafers of unleavened bread anointed with oil, and their meat offering, and their drink offerings. 16 And the priest shall bring them before the LORD, and shall offer his sin offering, and his burnt offering: 17 And he shall offer the ram for a sacrifice of peace offerings unto the LORD,	with the basket of unleavened bread: the priest shall offer also his meat offering, and his drink offering. 18 And the Nazarite shall shave the head of his separation at the door of the tabernacle of the congregation, and shall take the hair of the head of his separation, and put it in the fire which is under the sacrifice of the peace offerings. 19 And the priest shall take the sodden shoulder of the ram, and one unleavened cake out of the basket, and one unleavened wafer, and shall put them upon the hands of the Nazarite, after the hair of his separation is shaven: 20 And the priest shall wave them for a wave offering before the LORD: this is holy for the priest, with the wave breast and heave shoulder: and after that the Nazarite may drink wine.	c. He must shave off his hair & burn it under the sacrifice of the Fellowship Offering: A symbol for a continued commitment & closer fellowship with the Lord d. The priest then had to place in the Nazarites' hands the boiled shoulder of the ram & one unleavened cake & wafer from the basket 1) The priest was to offer these as a wave offering to the LORD 2) The priest was to receive these along with the breast & thigh pieces as the LORD's portion e. The Nazarite could then drink wine

1. The person had to approach and present his offerings to the LORD (v.13-15). He had to present the Burnt Offering acknowledging his continued need for the atonement (reconciliation with God). He was acknowledging that he was totally dependent upon the redemption of God (v.14).

a. He presented the Sin Offering to God: acknowledging his need for continued cleansing (v.14).
b. He presented the Peace or Fellowship Offering: acknowledging his need for more and more fellowship and peace with God (v.14).
c. He presented the Grain and Drink Offerings to God (v.15). The Grain Offering was a thanksgiving offering praising God for the atonement and for forgiveness and fellowship with God. The Drink Offering was a picture of the believer pouring out his life in continued dedication to God.

2. The person had the priest make the offerings in his behalf (v.16-17).

3. The person shaved off his hair and burned it under the sacrifice of the Fellowship Offering (v.18). Remember, his hair was the mark of his vow and devotion to God. By burning his hair under the Fellowship Offering, he was symbolizing that he wanted a continued commitment and close fellowship with the LORD.

4. The priest then placed in the Nazarite's hands the boiled shoulder of the ram and one each of an unleavened cake and wafer from the basket (v.19-20). These were to be offered by the priest as a wave offering to the LORD. The priest was then to receive these along with the breast and thigh pieces as the LORD's portion, that is, as a part of his livelihood.

5. Note that the Nazarite could then drink wine (v.20).

Thought 1. There are two strong lessons for the believer in this point.

1) The believer is totally dependent upon Christ throughout all of life. No matter how dedicated or holy a believer is, no matter how devoted or committed, he is still dependent upon the sacrifice of Jesus Christ—totally dependent. He must still approach God through Christ and Christ alone. He is still dependent upon Christ for atonement (reconciliation), for forgiveness of sins, and for fellowship and peace with God. His righteousness and sufficiency are and always will be in Christ, just as they always have been.

"Jesus saith unto him, I am the way, the truth, and the life: no man cometh unto the Father, but by me" (Jn.14:6).

"Therefore if any man be in Christ, he is a new creature: old things are passed away; behold, all things are become new. And all things are of God, who hath reconciled us to himself by Jesus Christ, and hath given to us the ministry of reconciliation; To wit, that God was in Christ, reconciling the world unto himself, not imputing their trespasses unto them; and hath committed unto us the word of reconciliation. Now then we are ambassadors for Christ, as though God did beseech you by us: we pray you in Christ's stead, be ye reconciled to God. For he hath made him to be sin for us, who knew no sin; that we might be made the righteousness of God in him" (2 Cor.5:17-21).

"For all have sinned, and come short of the glory of God; Being justified freely by his grace through the redemption that is in Christ Jesus: Whom God hath set forth to be a propitiation through faith in his blood, to declare his righteousness for the remission of sins that are past, through the forbearance of God" (Ro.3:23-25).

"For there is one God, and one mediator between God and men, the man Christ Jesus; Who gave himself a ransom for all, to be testified in due time" (1 Tim.2:5-6).

"Neither by the blood of goats and calves, but by his own blood he entered in once into the holy place, having obtained eternal redemption for us. For if the blood of bulls and of goats, and the ashes of an heifer sprinkling the unclean, sanctifieth to the purifying of the flesh: How much more shall the blood of Christ, who through the eternal Spirit offered himself without spot to God, purge your conscience from dead works to serve the living God" (Heb.9:12-14).

"For Christ is not entered into the holy places made with hands, which are the figures of the true; but into heaven itself, now to appear in the presence of God for us" (Heb.9:24).

"My little children, these things write I unto you, that ye sin not. And if any man sin, we have an advocate with the Father, Jesus Christ the righteous: And he is the propitiation for our sins: and not for ours only, but also for the sins of the whole world" (1 Jn.2:1-2).

2) The believer must continue to live a life of commitment and holiness before God. The Nazarite burned his hair under the Fellowship Offering, symbolizing that he wanted a continued commitment and closer fellowship with the LORD. So it must be with the believer. No matter what the believer vows to the LORD, no matter how closely he may walk with the LORD, he must still seek a deeper commitment and fellowship with the LORD; therefore, he must never cease to grow in Christ. He cannot even come close to reaching the maturity of Christ. His journey to the promised land is an ongoing process, a seeking...

- to grow more and more into the image of Christ
- to gain more and more spiritual strength so he can overcome the pitfalls and enemies of this life

"This I say then, Walk in the Spirit, and ye shall not fulfil the lust of the flesh" (Gal.5:16).

"I therefore, the prisoner of the Lord, beseech you that ye walk worthy of the vocation wherewith ye are called" (Eph.4:1).

"But speaking the truth in love, may grow up into him in all things, which is the head, even Christ" (Eph.4:15).

"See then that ye walk circumspectly, not as fools, but as wise" (Eph.5:15).

"As ye have therefore received Christ Jesus the Lord, so walk ye in him: Rooted and built up in him, and stablished in the faith, as ye have been taught, abounding therein with thanksgiving" (Col.2:6-7).

"And the Lord make you to increase and abound in love one toward another, and toward all men, even as we do toward you" (1 Th.3:12).

"Now the end of the commandment is charity out of a pure heart, and of a good conscience, and of faith unfeigned" (1 Tim.1:5).

"Therefore leaving the principles of the doctrine of Christ, let us go on unto perfection; not laying again the foundation of repentance from dead works, and of faith toward God" (Heb.6:1).

"Seeing ye have purified your souls in obeying the truth through the Spirit unto unfeigned love of the brethren, see that ye love one another with a pure heart fervently" (1 Pt.1:22).

"As newborn babes, desire the sincere milk of the word, that ye may grow thereby: If so be ye have tasted that the Lord is gracious" (1 Pt.2:2-3).

"And beside this, giving all diligence, add to your faith virtue; and to virtue knowledge; And to knowledge temperance; and to temperance patience; and to patience godliness" (2 Pt.1:5-6).

"Nevertheless we, according to his promise, look for new heavens and a new earth, wherein dwelleth righteousness. Wherefore, beloved, seeing that ye look for such things, be diligent that ye may be found of him in peace, without spot, and blameless" (2 Pt.3:13-14).

"But grow in grace, and in the knowledge of our Lord and Saviour Jesus Christ. To him be glory both now and for ever. Amen" (2 Pt.3:18).

"But if we walk in the light, as he is in the light, we have fellowship one with another, and the blood of Jesus Christ his Son cleanseth us from all sin" (1 Jn.1:7).

"He that saith he abideth in him ought himself also so to walk, even as he walked" (1 Jn.2:6).

4 (6:21) **Vow, Seriousness of**: note the seriousness and heavy weight of the Nazarite vow. The Nazarite vow is a law, a law established by God Himself.

OUTLINE	SCRIPTURE
4. The seriousness & heavy weight of the vow a. This is a law, the law of the Nazarite vow: A complete & total separation to the LORD b. This vow must be kept, fulfilled	21 This is the law of the Nazarite who hath vowed, and of his offering unto the LORD for his separation, beside that that his hand shall get: according to the vow which he vowed, so he must do after the law of his separation.

The commitment of the vow is significant to God, so significant that He established a law to control the vow. The vow declared a person's desire to draw closer to the LORD, a deep desire to be separated, totally set apart to God. God accepts all vows as serious commitments, but the Nazarite vow was very special to Him. The Nazarite vow was a personal commitment to seek a closer walk with the LORD: to seek a deeper commitment, a closer fellowship and communion with the LORD. It was a commitment...

- to live increasingly in God's law or Word
- to obey God as never before
- to be totally devoted to God
- to love and worship God more and more
- a commitment to live in prayer, in an unbroken consciousness of God's presence
- to bear strong witness and testimony for God

The Nazarite vow had to be kept and fulfilled before God. The person making the vow was responsible for completing the vow. A heavy responsibility and accountability lay upon his shoulders. It was not a vow to be taken lightly. If a person made the commitment and took the time to draw closer to the LORD, the LORD accepted the commitment, the vow, and expected the person to complete it to the fullest.

Thought 1. All vows are serious to God. He accepts the commitment of any vow. But the commitment to draw closer to God—to seek a greater fellowship and communion with Him, to live more than ever before in His Word, to pray more and to bear a stronger witness and testimony for Him—has a very special meaning to God. Therefore, the person must live a holy life before God, be totally separated and set apart to God. The person must follow after God with his whole heart and life. He must be totally devoted and given over to the LORD.

"I beseech you therefore, brethren, by the mercies of God, that ye present your bodies a living sacrifice, holy, acceptable unto God, which is your reasonable service. And be not conformed to this world: but be ye transformed by the renewing of your mind, that ye may prove what is that good, and acceptable, and perfect, will of God" (Ro.12:1-2).

"If a man vow a vow unto the Lord, or swear an oath to bind his soul with a bond; he shall not break his word, he shall do according to all that proceedeth out of his mouth" (Num.30:2).

"When thou shalt vow a vow unto the Lord thy God, thou shalt not slack to pay it: for the Lord thy God will surely require it of thee; and it would be sin in thee" (Dt.23:21).

"Keep thy tongue from evil, and thy lips from speaking guile [a deceptive vow]" (Ps.34:13)

"When thou vowest a vow unto God, defer not to pay it; for he hath no pleasure in fools: pay that which thou hast vowed" (Eccl.5:4).

5 (6:22-27) **Blessing, of God—Security, Source—Protection, Source—Grace, Source—Peace, Source—Blessing, Source—Benediction, the Great Priestly—Benediction, the Aaronic**: note the great priestly benediction of God.

OUTLINE	SCRIPTURE	SCRIPTURE	OUTLINE
5. The great priestly benediction	22 And the LORD spake	face shine upon thee,	3) His face, special presence
a. Promised by God Himself	unto Moses, saying,	and be gracious unto	4) His grace
	23 Speak unto Aaron and	thee:	
	unto his sons, saying, On	26 The LORD lift up his	5) His acceptance, approval,
	this wise ye shall bless the	countenance upon thee, and	pleasure (smile)
	children of Israel, saying	give thee peace.	6) His peace
	unto them,	27 And they shall put my	b. The result: The blessings
1) His blessing	24 The LORD bless thee, and	name upon the children	identified the Israelites as
	keep thee:	of Israel; and I will bless	God's people, as belonging
2) His protection, security	25 The LORD make his	them.	to Him

This prayer is sometimes called the Aaronic benediction because it was to be pronounced by Aaron the High Priest, pronounced over God's people as they marched toward the promised land. It is interesting that the benediction follows immediately after the Nazarite vow. The point of the benediction or prayer is striking: God wants to bless all His people as they march to the promised land. He wants to fulfill His covenant promise to the fullest if His people will only fulfill their part of the promise, to follow Him with all their hearts.

This is one of the most beautiful prayers in the Bible and is one of if not the most quoted benedictions of Scripture. *The Expositor's Bible Commentary* makes this statement:

> "[This benediction] may be thought of as the LORD's prayer of the Old Testament (see Mt.6:9). The priests were told how to pray for God's blessing on the people in the same way that the disciples were instructed by the Savior how to pray for God's blessing in their lives."[3]

1. The benediction was promised by God Himself (v.23-26). God instructed Moses to instruct the priest to use this benediction on behalf of His people as they marched to the promised land. Note the points of the benediction or prayer.

a. The LORD promised His blessing: "The LORD bless you" (v.24). The idea is that God pours out His blessing upon His people. He blesses them abundantly, exceedingly. God provides all the necessities of life for His people: food, shelter, and clothing.

"But seek ye first the kingdom of God, and his righteousness; and all these things shall be added unto you" (Mt.6:33).

"But my God shall supply all your need according to his riches in glory by Christ Jesus" (Ph.4:19).

"And ye shall serve the Lord your God, and he shall bless thy bread, and thy water; and I will take sickness away from the midst of thee" (Ex.23:25).

"And the Lord thy God will make thee plenteous in every work of thine hand, in the fruit of thy body, and in the fruit of thy cattle, and in the fruit of thy land, for good: for the Lord will again rejoice over thee for good, as he rejoiced over thy fathers" (Dt.30:9).

"Thou preparest a table before me in the presence of mine enemies: thou anointest my head with oil; my cup runneth over" (Ps.23:5).

"Oh how great is thy goodness, which thou hast laid up for them that fear thee; which thou hast wrought for them that trust in thee before the sons of men" (Ps.31:19).

"Thou visitest the earth, and waterest it: thou greatly enrichest it with the river of God, which is full of water: thou preparest them corn, when thou hast so provided for it" (Ps.65:9).

"Blessed be the Lord, who daily loadeth us with benefits, even the God of our salvation. Selah" (Ps.68:19).

"I will abundantly bless her provision: I will satisfy her poor with bread" (Ps.132:15).

"The Lord hath been mindful of us: he will bless us; he will bless the house of Israel; he will bless the house of Aaron" (Ps.115:12).

"Then shall he give the rain of thy seed, that thou shalt sow the ground withal; and bread of the increase of the earth, and it shall be fat and plenteous: in that day shall thy cattle feed in large pastures" (Is.30:23).

"Bring ye all the tithes into the storehouse, that there may be meat in mine house, and prove me now herewith, saith the Lord of hosts, if I will not open you the windows of heaven, and pour you out a blessing, that there shall not be room enough to receive it" (Mal.3:10).

b. The LORD promised His protection and security: "The LORD...keep you" (v.24). God has the power to keep His people as they march to the promised land. He has the power to deliver His people from all the pitfalls and enemies of this life.

"But there shall not an hair of your head perish" (Lk.21:18).

"And now I am no more in the world, but these are in the world, and I come to thee. Holy Father, keep through thine own name those whom thou hast given me, that they may be one, as we are" (Jn.17:11).

---

3 *The Expositor's Bible Commentary*, Frank E. Gaebelein, Editor, p.754.

"There hath no temptation taken you but such as is common to man: but God is faithful, who will not suffer you to be tempted above that ye are able; but will with the temptation also make a way to escape, that ye may be able to bear it" (1 Cor.10:13).

"Being confident of this very thing, that he which hath begun a good work in you will perform it until the day of Jesus Christ" (Ph.1:6).

"For the which cause I also suffer these things: nevertheless I am not ashamed: for I know whom I have believed, and am persuaded that he is able to keep that which I have committed unto him against that day" (2 Tim.1:12).

"So that we may boldly say, The Lord is my helper, and I will not fear what man shall do unto me" (Heb.13:6).

"Who are kept by the power of God through faith unto salvation ready to be revealed in the last time" (1 Pt.1:5).

"And who is he that will harm you, if ye be followers of that which is good" (1 Pt.3:13).

"Now unto him that is able to keep you from falling, and to present you faultless before the presence of his glory with exceeding joy" (Jude 24).

"And, behold, I am with thee, and will keep thee in all places whither thou goest, and will bring thee again into this land; for I will not leave thee, until I have done that which I have spoken to thee of" (Gen.28:15).

"The Lord shall fight for you, and ye shall hold your peace" (Ex.14:14).

"For the eyes of the Lord run to and fro throughout the whole earth, to show himself strong in the behalf of them whose heart is perfect toward him. Herein thou hast done foolishly: therefore from henceforth thou shalt have wars" (2 Chron.16:9).

"And thou shalt be secure, because there is hope; yea, thou shalt dig about thee, and thou shalt take thy rest in safety" (Job 11:18).

"He shall cover thee with his feathers, and under his wings shalt thou trust: his truth shall be thy shield and buckler" (Ps.91:4).

"Thou shalt not be afraid for the terror by night; nor for the arrow that flieth by day" (Ps.91:5).

"He shall not be afraid of evil tidings: his heart is fixed, trusting in the Lord" (Ps.112:7).

"Behold, he that keepeth Israel shall neither slumber nor sleep" (Ps.121:4).

"When thou liest down, thou shalt not be afraid: yea, thou shalt lie down, and thy sleep shall be sweet" (Pr.3:24).

c. The LORD promised that His face would shine upon His people, that His very special presence would be with them: "The LORD make His face shine upon you" (v.25). The LORD is always facing His people; His face is always shining upon them. This simply means that God's presence is always with His people. This is a beautiful, descriptive picture of God's presence with His people. The Hebrew literally means that God smiles upon His people: He is pleased with their faith and obedience in following Him.

"For where two or three are gathered together in my name, there am I in the midst of them" (Mt.18:20).

"Lo, I am with you alway, even unto the end of the world. Amen" (Mt.28:20).

"And, behold, I am with thee, and will keep thee in all places whither thou goest, and will bring thee again into this land; for I will not leave thee, until I have done that which I have spoken to thee of" (Gen.28:15).

"And he said, My presence shall go with thee, and I will give thee rest" (Ex.33:14).

"When thou goest out to battle against thine enemies, and seest horses, and chariots, and a people more than thou, be not afraid of them: for the Lord thy God is with thee, which brought thee up out of the land of Egypt" (Dt.20:1).

"The eternal God is thy refuge, and underneath are the everlasting arms: and he shall thrust out the enemy from before thee; and shall say, Destroy them" (Dt.33:27).

"I have set the Lord always before me: because he is at my right hand, I shall not be moved" (Ps.16:8).

"Thou hast also given me the shield of thy salvation: and thy right hand hath holden me up, and thy gentleness hath made me great" (Ps.18:35).

"But I am poor and needy; yet the Lord thinketh upon me: thou art my help and my deliverer; make no tarrying, O my God" (Ps.40:17).

"Fear thou not; for I am with thee: be not dismayed; for I am thy God: I will strengthen thee; yea, I will help thee; yea, I will uphold thee with the right hand of my righteousness" (Is.41:10).

"When thou passest through the waters, I will be with thee; and through the rivers, they shall not overflow thee: when thou walkest through the fire, thou shalt not be burned; neither shall the flame kindle upon thee" (Is.43:2).

"And even to your old age I am he; and even to hoar [gray] hairs will I carry you: I have made, and I will bear; even I will carry, and will deliver you" (Is.46:4).

d. The LORD promised that His grace would be showered upon His people: "The LORD...be gracious to you" (v.25). Grace means that God favors His people and strengthens them to conquer all the pitfalls and enemies of this life. Both favor and strength are included in the meaning of the word grace.

"Being justified freely by his grace through the redemption that is in Christ Jesus" (Ro.3:24).

"I thank my God always on your behalf, for the grace of God which is given you by Jesus Christ; That in every thing ye are enriched by him, in all utterance, and in all knowledge" (1 Cor.1:4-5).

"For our rejoicing is this, the testimony of our conscience, that in simplicity and godly sincerity, not with fleshly wisdom, but by the grace of God, we have had our conversation [behavior] in the world" (2 Cor.1:12).

"In whom we have redemption through his blood, the forgiveness of sins, according to the riches of his grace" (Eph.1:7).

"That in the ages to come he might show the exceeding riches of his grace in his kindness toward us through Christ Jesus" (Eph.2:7).

"For by grace are ye saved through faith; and that not of yourselves: it is the gift of God: Not of works, lest any man should boast" (Eph.2:8-9).

"For the grace of God that bringeth salvation hath appeared to all men" (Tit.2:11).

"That being justified by his grace, we should be made heirs according to the hope of eternal life" (Tit.3:7).

e. God gives His attention, His approval, His pleasure to His people: "The LORD lift up His countenance upon you" (v.26). God never turns His face away from His people. They always have His attention. He sees everything that goes on in their lives: every threat, every temptation, every trial. The believer has the attention of God and the approval and pleasure of God. Therefore, He lifts up His countenance—turns His face—to them. He is their helper in all things.

"But even the very hairs of your head are all numbered. Fear not therefore: ye are of more value than many sparrows" (Lk.12:7).

"Thou hast made known to me the ways of life; thou shalt make me full of joy with thy countenance" (Acts 2:28).

"So that we may boldly say, The Lord is my helper, and I will not fear what man shall do unto me" (Heb.13:6).

"Casting all your care upon him; for he careth for you" (1 Pt.5:7).

"For thou hast made him most blessed for ever: thou hast made him exceeding glad with thy countenance" (Ps.21:6).

"But I am poor and needy; yet the Lord thinketh upon me: thou art my help and my deliverer; make no tarrying, O my God" (Ps.40:17).

"Be merciful unto me, O God, be merciful unto me: for my soul trusteth in thee: yea, in the shadow of thy wings will I make my refuge, until these calamities be overpast" (Ps.57:1).

"For thou hast been a strength to the poor, a strength to the needy in his distress, a refuge from the storm, a shadow from the heat, when the blast of the terrible ones is as a storm against the wall" (Is.25:4).

"Fear thou not; for I am with thee: be not dismayed; for I am thy God: I will strengthen thee; yea, I will help thee; yea, I will uphold thee with the right hand of my righteousness" (Is.41:10).

f. The LORD gave His peace to His people: "The LORD...give you peace" (v.26). God's peace includes *peace with God* and the *peace of God*. People who reject God, who rebel against and curse Him, need to make peace with God. If they fail to make *peace with God*, they are doomed eternally. However, when a person makes *peace with God*, he comes to know the *peace of God*. God's peace floods his heart and life. He has the perfect assurance that he belongs to God, that God looks after and cares for him. He knows that he has the hope of eternal life and that he is marching to the promised land of heaven. God floods him with a great sense of triumph, conquest, and victory—triumph over all the pitfalls and enemies of this life, even the enemy of death. The believer knows that when his moment comes to die, God will transport him right into His presence. He knows that he will live eternally in the promised land of heaven, in the presence of God Himself. God gives this kind of peace to His people, to those who truly trust Him. The *peace of God* floods the believer's heart and life.

"Peace I leave with you, my peace I give unto you: not as the world giveth, give I unto you. Let not your heart be troubled, neither let it be afraid" (Jn.14:27).

"These things I have spoken unto you, that in me ye might have peace. In the world ye shall have tribulation: but be of good cheer; I have overcome the world" (Jn.16:33).

"And the peace of God, which passeth all understanding, shall keep your hearts and minds through Christ Jesus" (Ph.4:7).

"The Lord will give strength unto his people; the Lord will bless his people with peace" (Ps.29:11).

"Great peace have they which love thy law: and nothing shall offend them" (Ps.119:165).

"Thou wilt keep him in perfect peace, whose mind is stayed on thee: because he trusteth in thee" (Is.26:3).

"O that thou hadst hearkened to my commandments! then had thy peace been as a river, and thy righteousness as the waves of the sea" (Is.48:18).

2. Note the result of God's blessings: the blessings of God actually identify a person as belonging to God. When the blessings of God are seen upon a person's life, that person is identified as a believer. It is clearly seen that he is a follower of God. What a glorious testimony: to walk around with the blessings of God upon one's life, to be blessed so much that the blessings actually identify one as belonging to God.

"And ye also shall bear witness, because ye have been with me from the beginning" (Jn.15:27).

"And they were all filled with the Holy Ghost, and began to speak with other tongues, as the Spirit gave them utterance" (Acts 2:4).

"For we cannot but speak the things which we have seen and heard" (Acts 4:20).

"For as many as are led by the Spirit of God, they are the sons of God" (Ro.8:14).

"For thou art an holy people unto the Lord thy God, and the Lord hath chosen thee to be a peculiar people unto himself, above all the nations that are upon the earth" (Dt.14:2).

"Ye are my witnesses, saith the Lord, and my servant whom I have chosen: that ye may know and believe me, and understand that I am he: before me there was no God formed, neither shall there be after me" (Is.43:10).

TYPES, SYMBOLS, AND PICTURES
(Numbers 6:1-27)

Historical Term	Type or Picture (Scriptural Basis for Each)	Life Application for Today's Believer	Biblical Application
Contact with a Dead Body Num.6:3-12 (See also Lev. 10:4-5)	*A symbol of becoming defiled, unclean, corrupted—of becoming ceremonially or spiritually unclean.* *The person who took the Nazarite vow was to have nothing to do with death. He was to be an example of life, not of death. This stern restriction proclaimed the wonderful life that God gives, not the death and corruption that sin brings. The person had committed himself totally to the* LORD; *therefore, he was to be totally set apart and focused upon the* LORD, *not upon the things of the earth—not even upon the most dear things to his heart such as family. If a family member died, he was not allowed to go near nor touch the dead body lest he become defiled by death.* **"All the days that he separateth *himself* unto the LORD he shall come at no dead body" (Num.6:6).**	⇒ The Nazarite could not touch a dead body because it symbolized corruption and decay, defilement and uncleanness. So it must be with the believer. The believer must not become corrupted and defiled by sin and shame. Sin and shame bring lawlessness, violence and death to the earth. The believer is to symbolize life, not corruption and death. The believer is to have nothing to do with corruption and defilement. He is to be totally set apart and focused upon the LORD, not upon the things of this earth. He is to live a life that is totally separated and set apart to God.	***"Looking diligently lest any man fail of the grace of God; lest any root of bitterness springing up trouble you, and thereby many be defiled" (Heb.12:15).*** ***"And the tongue is a fire, a world of iniquity: so is the tongue among our members, that it defileth the whole body, and setteth on fire the course of nature; and it is set on fire of hell" (Jas.3:6).*** ***"All these evil things come from within, and defile the man" (Mk.7:23).*** ***"Having therefore these promises, dearly beloved, let us cleanse ourselves from all filthiness of the flesh and spirit, perfecting holiness in the fear of God" (2 Cor. 7:1).*** ***"Draw nigh to God, and he will draw nigh to you. Cleanse your hands, ye sinners; and purify your hearts, ye double minded" (Jas.4:8).*** ***"If a man therefore purge himself from these, he shall be a vessel unto honour, sanctified, and meet for the master's use, and prepared unto every good work" (2 Tim.2:21).***
The Sin Offering Num.6:3-12; 28:11-15 (See also Lev. 4:1-5:13. 6:24-30; 8:14-17; 9:2; 9:15; 10:17; 16:3-22)	*The Sin Offering is a type of Christ, a symbol or picture of Christ. When a person sensed the need for forgiveness of sins, he approached God through the sacrifice of the Sin Offering.* **"And the priest shall offer the one for a sin offering, and the other for a burnt offering, and make**	⇒ Jesus Christ is the Savior of the world, the One who provides the way of forgiveness for us. This He does through His sacrifice upon the cross. Through His blood we are cleansed from sin, cleansed from all unrighteousness.	***"If we confess our sins, he is faithful and just to forgive us our sins, and to cleanse us from all unrighteousness" (1 Jn.1:9).*** ***"Who his own self bare our sins in his own body on the tree, that we, being dead to sins, should live unto righteousness: by whose stripes ye were healed"***

Historical Term	Type or Picture (Scriptural Basis for Each)	Life Application for Today's Believer	Biblical Application
	an atonement for him, for that he sinned by the dead, and shall hallow his head that same day" (Num.6:11).		***(1 Pt.2:24).*** ***"For Christ also hath once suffered for sins, the just for the unjust, that he might bring us to God, being put to death in the flesh, but quickened by the Spirit" (1 Pt.3:18).*** ***"But he was wounded for our transgressions, he was bruised for our iniquities: the chastisement of our peace was upon him; and with his stripes we are healed" (Is.53:5).*** ***"And thou shalt offer every day a bullock for a sin offering for atonement: and thou shalt cleanse the altar, when thou hast made an atonement for it, and thou shalt anoint it, to sanctify it. Seven days thou shalt make an atonement for the altar, and sanctify it; and it shall be an altar most holy: whatsoever toucheth the altar shall be holy) (Ex.29:36-37).*** ***"And he shall do with the bullock as he did with the bullock for a sin offering, so shall he do with this: and the priest shall make an atonement for them, and it shall be forgiven them" (Lev. 4:20).***
The Burnt Offering Num.6:3-12; 15:1-16; 28:11-15 (See also Lev. 1:1-17; 6:8-13; 8:18-21; 16:24)	*A symbol of atonement, reconciliation with God:* *The Burnt Offering is a type of Christ, a symbol or picture of Christ dying as the substitute sacrifice for us. By dying for us:* ⇒ *Christ bore the full judgment of God against sin—paid the ransom price to deliver us from sin and death.* ⇒ *Christ secured the atonement for us, reconciling us to God.* **"And in the beginnings of your months ye shall offer a burnt offering unto the LORD; two young bullocks, and one ram, seven lambs of the first year without spot" (Num.28:11)**	⇒ Jesus Christ died for us as our substitute sacrifice. He died to secure the atonement or reconciliation with God for us. A person can now approach God and be reconciled with God; a person can now become acceptable to God. How? By approaching God through the sacrifice of Christ.	***"But God commendeth his love toward us, in that, while we were yet sinners, Christ died for us. Much more then, being now justified by his blood, we shall be saved from wrath through him. For if, when we were enemies, we were reconciled to God by the death of his Son, much more, being reconciled, we shall be saved by his life. And not only so, but we also joy in God through our Lord Jesus Christ, by whom we have now received the atonement." (Ro.5:8-11).*** ***"And he shall put his hand upon the head of the burnt offering; and it shall be accepted for him to make atonement for him" (Lev. 1:4).*** ***"Wherefore in all things it behooved him to be made like unto his brethren, that he might be a merciful and faithful high priest in things pertaining to God, to make***

Historical Term	Type or Picture (Scriptural Basis for Each)	Life Application for Today's Believer	Biblical Application
			reconciliation for the sins of the people" (Heb. 2:17
The Guilt Offering Num.6:3-12 (See also Lev. 5:14-6:7)	*The Guilt Offering symbolized Jesus Christ. He is the way for a person to be set free from the weight and anguish of guilt, the pricking of conscience.* **"And he shall consecrate unto the LORD the days of his separation, and shall bring a lamb of the first year for a trespass [guilt] offering: but the days that were before shall be lost, because his separation was defiled" (Num.6:12).**	⇒ Jesus Christ bore our guilt, bore the judgment and condemnation of our sin. His sacrifice has made atonement with God, forgiving the sin and erasing the guilt of the person who comes to Him.	***"For he hath made him to be sin for us, who knew no sin; that we might be made the righteousness of God in him" (2 Cor.5:21).).*** ***"Who gave himself for our sins, that he might deliver us from this present evil world, according to the will of God and our Father" (Gal.1:4).*** ***"Christ hath redeemed us from the curse of the law, being made a curse for us: for it is written, Cursed is every one that hangeth on a tree" (Gal.3:13).*** ***"Having a good conscience; that, whereas they speak evil of you, as of evildoers, they may be ashamed that falsely accuse your good conversation in Christ" (1 Pt.3:16).***
The Fellowship or Peace Offering Num.6:13-20; 15:1-16 (See also Lev. 3:1-17)	*The Fellowship or Peace Offering is a type of Christ, a symbol or picture of Christ, the One who died on the cross bearing the judgment of God for man. The sacrifice of Christ made peace between a holy God and an alienated, fallen, depraved people. The sacrifice of Christ and Christ alone brings peace and fellowship between man and God.* **"And he shall offer his offering unto the LORD, one he lamb of the first year without blemish for a burnt offering, and one ewe lamb of the first year without blemish for a sin offering, and one ram without blemish for peace offerings" (Num.6:14).**	⇒ How do we grow in the fellowship and peace of God? Very simply, by seeking more of the fellowship and peace of God. We must stand upon the completed work of Christ's sacrifice on the cross. Because of Christ... • we can enjoy the fellowship of the Lord • we can experience the peace of God	***"That which we have seen and heard declare we unto you, that ye also may have fellowship with us: and truly our fellowship is with the Father, and with his Son Jesus Christ" (1 Jn.1:3).*** ***"But if we walk in the light, as he is in the light, we have fellowship one with another, and the blood of Jesus Christ his Son cleanseth us from all sin" (1 Jn. 1:7).*** ***"Therefore being justified by faith, we have peace with God through our Lord Jesus Christ" (Ro.5:1).*** ***"And, having made peace through the blood of his cross, by him to reconcile all things unto himself; by him, I say, whether they be things in earth, or things in heaven" (Col.1:20).***
The Drink Offering Num.6:13-20; 15:1-16, esp. v.7	*The Drink Offering is a picture of the believer pouring out his life in continued dedication to God.* **"And a basket of unleavened bread, cakes of fine flour mingled with oil, and wafers of unleavened bread anointed with oil, and their meat offering, and their drink offerings" (Num.6:15).**	⇒ The application for today's believer is clear and striking: he must pour out his life in continued dedication to God.	***"I beseech you therefore, brethren, by the mercies of God, that ye present your bodies a living sacrifice, holy, acceptable unto God, which is your reasonable service" (Ro. 12:1).*** ***"Knowing this, that our old man is crucified with him, that the body of sin might be destroyed, that henceforth we should not***

Historical Term	Type or Picture (Scriptural Basis for Each)	Life Application for Today's Believer	Biblical Application
			serve sin" (Ro. 6:6). *"I am crucified with Christ: nevertheless I live; yet not I, but Christ liveth in me: and the life which I now live in the flesh I live by the faith of the Son of God, who loved me, and gave himself for me" (Gal.2:20).* *"But if we walk in the light, as he is in the light, we have fellowship one with another, and the blood of Jesus Christ his Son cleanseth us from all sin" (1 Jn. 1:7).*
The Nazarite Burning His Hair under the Fellowship Offering Num.6:13-20	*The Nazarite who burned his hair was symbolizing that he wanted a continued commitment and close fellowship with the LORD.* **"And the Nazarite shall shave the head of his separation *at* the door of the tabernacle of the congregation, and shall take the hair of the head of his separation, and put *it* in the fire which *is* under the sacrifice of the peace offerings" (Num.6:18).**	⇒ The believer must continue to live a life of commitment and holiness before God. The Nazarite burned his hair under the Fellowship Offering, symbolizing that he wanted a continued commitment and closer fellowship with the LORD. So it must be with the believer. No matter what the believer vows to the LORD, no matter how closely he may walk with the LORD—he must still seek a deeper commitment and fellowship with the LORD. He must never cease to grow in Christ. He cannot even come close to reaching the maturity of Christ; therefore, his journey to the promised land is an ongoing process. The believer must seek... • to grow more and more into the image of Christ • to gain more and more spiritual strength so that he can overcome the pitfalls and enemies of this life	*"This I say then, Walk in the Spirit, and ye shall not fulfil the lust of the flesh" (Gal.5:16).* *"I therefore, the prisoner of the Lord, beseech you that ye walk worthy of the vocation wherewith ye are called" (Eph.4:1).* *"But speaking the truth in love, may grow up into him in all things, which is the head, even Christ" (Eph.4:15).* *"See then that ye walk circumspectly, not as fools, but as wise" (Eph.5:15).* *"As ye have therefore received Christ Jesus the Lord, so walk ye in him: Rooted and built up in him, and stablished in the faith, as ye have been taught, abounding therein with thanksgiving" (Col.2:6-7).* *"And the Lord make you to increase and abound in love one toward another, and toward all men, even as we do toward you" (1 Th. 3:12).* *"Now the end of the commandment is charity out of a pure heart, and of a good conscience, and of faith unfeigned" (1 Tim. 1:5).* *"Therefore leaving the principles of the doctrine of Christ, let us go on unto perfection; not laying again the foundation of repentance from dead works, and of faith toward God" (Heb.6:1).*

F. The Spontaneous Offerings at the Dedication of the Tabernacle: Supporting God's Work & Approaching Him Exactly as He Says, 7:1-89

1. The gifts for transporting the Tabernacle, that of carts & oxen: Demonstrated the need for joyful, spontaneous support of God's work
   a. The gifts were given right after the dedication of the Tabernacle
      1) The gifts were given by the twelve tribal leaders
      2) The gifts were spontaneously offered to the Lord at the Tabernacle door: Six covered wagons or carts & twelve oxen
   b. The Lord instructed Moses to accept the gifts & to distribute them as needed
   c. The gifts were distributed to the Levites, the assistants responsible for transporting the Tabernacle
      1) The Gershonites received 2 carts & 4 oxen (for transporting all the curtains). Got just what they needed
      2) The Merarites received 4 carts & 8 oxen (for transporting the frame): Got just what they needed
      3) The priest Ithamar supervised the transporting of the Tabernacle
      4) The Kohathites received no carts, for they were to carry the sacred furnishings on their shoulders: They needed none of the gifts

2. The magnificent offerings presented at the dedication of the altar—presented by each tribal leader on different days—in obedience to God's instructions: Demonstrated the need to approach God exactly as He says

And it came to pass on the
day that Moses had fully set
up the tabernacle, and had
anointed it, and sanctified it,
and all the instruments thereof, both the altar and all the
vessels thereof, and had
anointed them, and sanctified them;
2 That the princes of Israel,
heads of the house of their
fathers, who were the princes
of the tribes, and were over
them that were numbered,
offered:
3 And they brought their
offering before the LORD, six
covered wagons, and twelve
oxen; a wagon for two of the
princes, and for each one an
ox: and they brought them
before the tabernacle.
4 And the LORD spake unto
Moses, saying,
5 Take it of them, that they
may be to do the service of
the tabernacle of the congregation; and thou shalt give
them unto the Levites, to
every man according to his
service.
6 And Moses took the wag-
ons and the oxen, and gave
them unto the Levites.
7 Two wagons and four oxen
he gave unto the sons of
Gershon, according to their
service:
8 And four wagons and eight
oxen he gave unto the sons
of Merari, according unto
their service, under the hand
of Ithamar the son of Aaron
the priest.
9 But unto the sons of
Kohath he gave none:
because the service of
the sanctuary belonging
unto them was that they
should bear upon their
shoulders.
10 And the princes offered
for dedicating of the altar in
the day that it was anointed,
even the princes offered their
offering before the altar.
11 And the LORD said unto
Moses, They shall offer their
offering, each prince on his
day, for the dedicating of the
altar.
12 And he that offered his
offering the first day was
Nahshon the son of
Amminadab, of the tribe of
Judah:
13 And his offering was one
silver charger, the weight
thereof was an hundred and
thirty shekels, one silver
bowl of seventy shekels,
after the shekel of the sanctuary; both of them were full
of fine flour mingled with oil
for a meat offering:
14 One spoon of ten shekels
of gold, full of incense:
15 One young bullock, one
ram, one lamb of the first
year, for a burnt offering:
16 One kid of the goats for a
sin offering:
17 And for a sacrifice of
peace offerings, two oxen,
five rams, five he goats, five
lambs of the first year: this
was the offering of Nahshon
the son of Amminadab.
18 On the second day
Nethaneel the son of Zuar,
prince of Issachar, did offer:
19 He offered for his offering one silver charger, the
weight whereof was an hundred and thirty shekels, one
silver bowl of seventy
shekels, after the shekel of
the sanctuary; both of them
full of fine flour mingled
with oil for a meat offering:
20 One spoon of gold of ten
shekels, full of incense:
21 One young bullock, one
ram, one lamb of the first
year, for a burnt offering:
22 One kid of the goats for a
sin offering:
23 And for a sacrifice of
peace offerings, two oxen,
five rams, five he goats, five
lambs of the first year: this
was the offering of
Nethaneel the son of Zuar.
24 On the third day Eliab
the son of Helon, prince of
the children of Zebulun, did
offer:
25 His offering was one silver charger, the weight
whereof was an hundred and
thirty shekels, one silver
bowl of seventy shekels,
after the shekel of the sanctuary; both of them full of
fine flour mingled with oil
for a meat offering:
26 One golden spoon of
ten shekels, full of in-

a. The offering of the first day: Was brought by Nahshon, leader of the tribe of Judah
   1) One silver plate—weighing 130 shekels (about 3¼ pounds)
   2) One silver sprinkling bowl—weighing 70 shekels (about 1¾ pounds)
      • Each was filled with fine flour mixed with oil as a Grain Offering
   3) One gold dish—weighing 10 shekels (about 4 ounces)
      • Filled with incense
   4) Animals for the offerings
      • A Burnt Offering: Acknowledging the atonement
      • A Sin Offering: Seeking cleansing
      • A Fellowship or Peace Offering: Seeking more & more of the fellowship & peace of God

b. The offering on the second day: Was brought by Nethanel, leader of the tribe of Issachar
   1) One silver plate—weighing 130 shekels (about 3¼ pounds)
   2) One silver sprinkling bowl—weighing 70 shekels (about 1¾ pounds)
      • Each was filled with fine flour mixed with oil as a Grain Offering
   3) One gold dish—weighing 10 shekels (about 4 ounces)
      • Filled with incense
   4) Animals for the offerings
      • A Burnt Offering: Seeking the atonement (reconciliation)
      • A Sin Offering: Seeking cleansing
      • A Fellowship or Peace Offering: Seeking more & more of the fellowship & peace of God

c. The offering on the third day: Was brought by Eliab, leader of the tribe of Zebulun
   1) One silver plate—weighing 130 shekels (about 3¼ pounds)
   2) One silver sprinkling bowl—weighing 70 shekels (about 1¾ pounds)
      • Each was filled with fine flour mixed with oil as a Grain Offering
   3) One gold dish—weighing 10 shekels (about 4 ounces)

- Filled with incense
4) Animals for the offerings
   - A Burnt Offering: Seeking the atonement (reconciliation)
   - A Sin Offering: Seeking cleansing
   - A Fellowship or Peace Offering: Seeking more & more of the fellowship & peace of God

d. The offering on the fourth day: Was brought by Elizur, leader of the tribe of Reuben

1) One silver plate—weighing 130 shekels (about 3¼ pounds)
2) One silver sprinkling bowl—weighing 70 shekels (about 1¾ pounds)
   - Each was filled with fine flour mixed with oil as a Grain Offering
3) One gold dish—weighing 10 shekels (about 4 ounces)
   - Filled with incense
4) Animals for the offerings
   - A Burnt Offering: Seeking the atonement (reconciliation)
   - A Sin Offering: Seeking cleansing
   - A Fellowship or Peace Offering: Seeking more & more of the fellowship & peace of God

e. The offering on the fifth day: Was brought by Shelumiel, leader of the tribe of Simeon
1) One silver plate—weighing 130 shekels (about 3¼ pounds)
2) One silver sprinkling bowl—weighing 70 shekels (about 1¾ pounds)
   - Each was filled with fine flour mixed with oil as a Grain Offering
3) One gold dish—weighing 10 shekels (about 4 ounces)
   - Filled with incense
4) Animals for the offerings
   - A Burnt Offering: Seeking the atonement (reconciliation)
   - A Sin Offering: Seeking cleansing
   - A Fellowship or Peace Offering: Seeking more & more of the fellowship & peace of God

cense:
27 One young bullock, one ram, one lamb of the first year, for a burnt offering:
28 One kid of the goats for a sin offering:
29 And for a sacrifice of peace offerings, two oxen, five rams, five he goats, five lambs of the first year: this was the offering of Eliab the son of Helon.
30 On the fourth day Elizur the son of Shedeur, prince of the children of Reuben, did offer:
31 His offering was one silver charger of the weight of an hundred and thirty shekels, one silver bowl of seventy shekels, after the shekel of the sanctuary; both of them full of fine flour mingled with oil for a meat offering:
32 One golden spoon of ten shekels, full of incense:
33 One young bullock, one ram, one lamb of the first year, for a burnt offering:
34 One kid of the goats for a sin offering:
35 And for a sacrifice of peace offerings, two oxen, five rams, five he goats, five lambs of the first year: this was the offering of Elizur the son of Shedeur.
36 On the fifth day Shelumiel the son of Zurishaddai, prince of the children of Simeon, did offer:
37 His offering was one silver charger, the weight whereof was an hundred and thirty shekels, one silver bowl of seventy shekels, after the shekel of the sanctuary; both of them full of fine flour mingled with oil for a meat offering:
38 One golden spoon of ten shekels, full of incense:
39 One young bullock, one ram, one lamb of the first year, for a burnt offering:
40 One kid of the goats for a sin offering:
41 And for a sacrifice of peace offerings, two oxen, five rams, five he goats, five lambs of the first year: this was the offering of Shelumiel the son of Zurishaddai.

42 On the sixth day Eliasaph the son of Deuel, prince of the children of Gad, offered:
43 His offering was one silver charger of the weight of an hundred and thirty shekels, a silver bowl of seventy shekels, after the shekel of the sanctuary; both of them full of fine flour mingled with oil for a meat offering:
44 One golden spoon of ten shekels, full of incense:
45 One young bullock, one ram, one lamb of the first year, for a burnt offering:
46 One kid of the goats for a sin offering:
47 And for a sacrifice of peace offerings, two oxen, five rams, five he goats, five lambs of the first year: this was the offering of Eliasaph the son of Deuel.
48 On the seventh day Elishama the son of Ammihud, prince of the children of Ephraim, offered:
49 His offering was one silver charger, the weight whereof was an hundred and thirty shekels, one silver bowl of seventy shekels, after the shekel of the sanctuary; both of them full of fine flour mingled with oil for a meat offering:
50 One golden spoon of ten shekels, full of incense:
51 One young bullock, one ram, one lamb of the first year, for a burnt offering:
52 one kid of the goats for a sin offering:
53 And for a sacrifice of peace offerings, two oxen, five rams, five he goats, five lambs of the first year: this was the offering of Elishama the son of Ammihud.
54 On the eighth day offered Gamaliel the son of Pedahzur, prince of the children of Manasseh:
55 His offering was one silver charger of the weight of an hundred and thirty shekels, one silver bowl of seventy shekels, after the shekel of the sanctuary; both of them full of fine flour mingled with oil for a meat offering:
56 One golden spoon of ten shekels, full of incense:

f. The offering on the sixth day: Was brought by Eliasaph, leader of the tribe of Gad
1) One silver plate—weighing 130 shekels (about 3¼ pounds)
2) One silver sprinkling bowl—weighing 70 shekels (about 1¾ pounds)
   - Each was filled with fine flour mixed with oil as a Grain Offering
3) One gold dish—weighing 10 shekels (about 4 ounces)
   - Filled with incense
4) Animals for the offerings
   - A Burnt Offering: Seeking the atonement (reconciliation)
   - A Sin Offering: Seeking cleansing
   - A Fellowship or Peace Offering: Seeking more & more of the fellowship & peace of God

g. The offering on the seventh day: Was brought by Elishama, leader of the tribe of Ephraim
1) One silver plate—weighing 130 shekels (about 3¼ pounds)
2) One silver sprinkling bowl—weighing 70 shekels (about 1¾ pounds)
   - Each was filled with fine flour mixed with oil as a Grain Offering
3) One gold dish—weighing 10 shekels (about 4 ounces)
   - Filled with incense
4) Animals for the offerings
   - A Burnt Offering: Seeking the atonement (reconciliation)
   - A Sin Offering: Seeking cleansing
   - A Fellowship or Peace Offering: Seeking more & more of the fellowship & peace of God

h. The offering on the eighth day: Was brought by Gamaliel, leader of the tribe of Manasseh
1) One silver plate—weighing 130 shekels (about 3¼ pounds)
2) One silver sprinkling bowl—weighing 70 shekels (about 1¾ pounds)
   - Each was filled with fine flour mixed with oil as a Grain Offering
3) One gold dish—weighing 10 shekels (about 4 ounces)

4) Filled with incense
Animals for the offerings
- A Burnt Offering: Seeking the atonement (reconciliation)
- A Sin Offering: Seeking cleansing
- A Fellowship or Peace Offering: Seeking more & more of the fellowship & peace of God

i. The offering on the ninth day: Was brought by Abidan, leader of the tribe of Benjamin
1) One silver plate—weighing 130 shekels (about 3¼ pounds)
2) One silver sprinkling bowl—weighing 70 shekels (about 1¾ pounds)
- Each was filled with fine flour mixed with oil as a Grain Offering

3) One gold dish—weighing 10 shekels (about 4 ounces)
- Filled with incense

4) Animals for the offerings
- A Burnt Offering: Seeking the atonement (reconciliation)
- A Sin Offering: Seeking cleansing
- A Fellowship or Peace Offering: Seeking more & more of the fellowship & peace of God

j. The offering on the tenth day: Was brought by Ahiezer, leader of the tribe of Dan
1) One silver plate—weighing 130 shekels (about 3¼ pounds)
2) One silver sprinkling bowl—weighing 70 shekels (about 1¾ pounds)
- Each was filled with fine flour mixed with oil as a Grain Offering

3) One gold dish—weighing 10 shekels (about 4 ounces)
- Filled with incense

4) Animals for the offerings
- A Burnt Offering: Seeking the atonement (reconciliation)
- A Sin Offering: Seeking cleansing
- A Fellowship or Peace Offering: Seeking more & more of the fellowship & peace of God

k. The offering on the eleventh day: Was brought by Pagiel, leader of the tribe of Asher

57 One young bullock, one
ram, one lamb of the first
year, for a burnt offering:
58 One kid of the goats for a
sin offering:
59 And for a sacrifice of
peace offerings, two oxen,
five rams, five he goats, five
lambs of the first year: this
was the offering of Gamaliel
the son of Pedahzur.
60 On the ninth day Abidan
the son of Gideoni, prince of
the children of Benjamin,
offered:
61 His offering was one silver charger, the weight
whereof was an hundred and
thirty shekels, one silver
bowl of seventy shekels,
after the shekel of the sanctuary; both of them full of
fine flour mingled with oil
for a meat offering:
62 One golden spoon of ten
shekels, full of incense:
63 One young bullock, one
ram, one lamb of the first
year, for a burnt offering:
64 One kid of the goats for a
sin offering:
65 And for a sacrifice of
peace offerings, two oxen,
five rams, five he goats, five
lambs of the first year: this
was the offering of Abidan
the son of Gideoni.
66 On the tenth day Ahiezer
the son of Ammishaddai,
prince of the children of
Dan, offered:
67 His offering was one silver charger, the weight
whereof was an hundred and
thirty shekels, one silver
bowl of seventy shekels,
after the shekel of the sanctuary; both of them full of
fine flour mingled with oil
for a meat offering:
68 One golden spoon of ten
shekels, full of incense:
69 One young bullock, one
ram, one lamb of the
first year, for a burnt offering:
70 One kid of the goats for a
sin offering:
71 And for a sacrifice of
peace offerings, two oxen,
five rams, five he goats,
five lambs of the first year:
this was the offering of
Ahiezer the son of
Ammishaddai.
72 On the eleventh day
Pagiel the son of Ocran,
prince of the children of
Asher, offered:
73 His offering was one silver charger, the weight
whereof was an hundred and
thirty shekels, one silver
bowl of seventy shekels,
after the shekel of the sanctuary; both of them full of
fine flour mingled with oil
for a meat offering:
74 One golden spoon of ten
shekels, full of incense:
75 One young bullock, one
ram, one lamb of the first
year, for a burnt offering:
76 One kid of the goats for a
sin offering:
77 And for a sacrifice of
peace offerings, two oxen,
five rams, five he goats, five
lambs of the first year: this
was the offering of Pagiel the
son of Ocran.
78 On the twelfth day Ahira
the son of Enan, prince of the
children of Naphtali, offered:
79 His offering was one silver charger, the weight
whereof was an hundred and
thirty shekels, one silver
bowl of seventy shekels,
after the shekel of the sanctuary; both of them full of
fine flour mingled with oil
for a meat offering:
80 One golden spoon of ten
shekels, full of incense:
81 One young bullock, one
ram, one lamb of the first
year, for a burnt offering:
82 One kid of the goats for a
sin offering:
83 And for a sacrifice of
peace offerings, two oxen,
five rams, five he goats, five
lambs of the first year: this
was the offering of Ahira the
son of Enan.
84 This was the dedication
of the altar, in the day when
it was anointed, by the
princes of Israel: twelve
chargers of silver, twelve silver bowls, twelve spoons of
gold:
85 Each charger of silver
weighing an hundred and
thirty shekels, each bowl
seventy: all the silver vessels
weighed two thousand and
four hundred shekels, after
the shekel of the sanctuary:
86 The golden spoons were
twelve, full of incense,
weighing ten shekels apiece,
after the shekel of the sanctuary: all the gold of the
spoons was an hundred and

1) One silver plate—weighing 130 shekels (about 3¼ pounds)
2) One silver sprinkling bowl—weighing 70 shekels (about 1¾ pounds)
- Each was filled with fine flour mixed with oil as a Grain Offering

3) One gold dish—weighing 10 shekels (about 4 ounces)
- Filled with incense

4) Animals for the offerings
- A Burnt Offering: Seeking the atonement (reconciliation)
- A Sin Offering: Seeking cleansing
- A Fellowship or Peace Offering: Seeking more & more of the fellowship & peace of God

l. The offering on the twelfth day: Was brought by Ahira, leader of the tribe of Naphtali
1) One silver plate—weighing 130 shekels (about 3¼ pounds)
2) One silver sprinkling bowl—weighing 70 shekels (about 1¾ pounds)
- Each was filled with fine flour mixed with oil as a Grain Offering

3) One gold dish—weighing 10 shekels (about 4 ounces)
- Filled with incense

4) Animals for the offerings
- A Burnt Offering: Seeking the atonement (reconciliation)
- A Sin Offering: Seeking cleansing
- A Fellowship or Peace Offering: Seeking more & more of the fellowship & peace of God

m. The totals & value of the offerings
1) There were 12 silver plates, 12 silver bowls, & 12 gold dishes
- The silver plates & bowls weighed about 2400 shekels (about 60 pounds)
- The gold containers with incense weighed 120 shekels (about 3 pounds)

2) There were a large number of animals offered • The Burnt Offering: 12 young bulls, 12 rams, 12 male lambs with their Grain Offering • The Sin Offering: 12 male goats • The Fellowship or Peace Offering: 24 oxen, 60 rams, 60 male goats, 60 male lambs	twenty shekels. 87 All the oxen for the burnt offering were twelve bullocks, the rams twelve, the lambs of the first year twelve, with their meat offering: and the kids of the goats for sin offering twelve. 88 And all the oxen for the sacrifice of the peace offerings were twenty and four bullocks, the rams sixty, the he goats sixty, the lambs of the first year sixty.	This was the dedication of the altar, after that it was anointed. 89 And when Moses was gone into the tabernacle of the congregation to speak with him, then he heard the voice of one speaking unto him from off the mercy seat that was upon the ark of testimony, from between the two cherubims:and he spake unto him.	**3. The great assurance of God: Permanent access into His presence—His communion & guidance** a. The approach of Moses: Approached as he felt the need b. The faithfulness of God: Spoke from between the cherubim on the Ark—communed with & directed His people

DIVISION I

THE PREPARATION FOR THE MARCH TO THE PROMISED LAND, 1:1-10:36

F. The Spontaneous Offerings at the Dedication of the Tabernacle: Supporting God's Work and Approaching Him Exactly as He Says, 7:1-89

(7:1-89) **Introduction—Enemies, of Life—Victory, over Enemies of life—Stewardship, Duty of—Support, Financial, Duty of —Finances, Duty to Give—Ministry, Duty to Support**: the enemies of life are many and terrible, terrible in the sense that they can eventually capture and enslave every human being upon the earth. The attack by an enemy of life is sometimes visible and expected; at other times it is totally unexpected and shocking. Sometimes the attack is silent, lurking, slyly waiting for the opportunity to move against us. At any moment, at any time an enemy can attack and threaten our lives, an enemy such as...

- an unexpected disease or accident
- an intruder into our home or office
- a thief or swindler
- a rapist or sex offender
- a silent urge to steal or lie
- an attraction or passion for illicit sex
- adultery or unfaithfulness
- anger or abuse
- a consuming covetousness or greed
- gluttony, craving more and more
- uncontrolled passion that lusts for more and more
- addiction or drunkenness
- lawlessness or violence
- hatred or malice
- loneliness or emptiness
- lack of meaning or purpose
- lack of fulfillment or satisfaction

The enemies of life are many and varied. They repeatedly attack man until they eventually drag man into that last great enemy, the pit of death and hell—unless a person knows Christ.

What man needs is the power to conquer the enemies of life and gain the victory over them. This is exactly what God wants for the believer as he marches to the promised land: triumph and victory over all the enemies that attack him. This is the message that must be carried to the world: the enemies of life can be conquered and triumphed over. Man can be victorious throughout all of life. Man can conquer all the foes that seek to enslave and destroy him, even the last foe—death itself. This is the message of the gospel that must be carried forth: victory is in Christ Jesus our Lord.

But note this fact: money is needed to carry the message of Christ to the world. God's work needs financial support. People are needed to step forth to support God's work throughout the world: support the preachers, the evangelists, the missionaries, and the teachers of the Word. Financial support is an absolute essential, for while the gospel is free, the cost of taking it to the world is not! There is only way to approach God: through the Lord Jesus Christ. If a person does not approach God through the sacrifice of His Son, he is doomed to an eternity of separation from God. God accepts no person except through the sacrifice of His Son. Christ Himself declared this fact. There is no alternative. Believers have no choice as they march to the promised land. They must support God's work and continue to support it until they reach the promised land of heaven. This is the subject of this great passage: *The Spontaneous Offerings at the Dedication of the Tabernacle: Supporting God's Work and Approaching Him Exactly as He Says*, 7:1-89.

1. The gifts for transporting the Tabernacle, that of carts and oxen: demonstrated the need for joyful, spontaneous support of God's work (v.1-9).
2. The magnificent offerings presented at the dedication of the altar—presented by each tribal leader on different days: demonstrated the need to approach God exactly as He says (v.10-88).
3. The great assurance of God: permanent access into His presence—His communion and guidance (v.89).

1 (7:1-9) **Offerings, Voluntary and Spontaneous—Giving, to the Lord—Stewardship, Duty of—Tabernacle, Dedication of—Church, Dedication of—Dedication, of Tabernacle—Gifts, Voluntary and Spontaneous—Giving, How to Give**: there were the gifts for transporting the Tabernacle, the gifts of carts and oxen. These gifts demonstrated the need for joyful, spontaneous support of God's work. Note the Scripture and outline:

NUMBERS 7:1-89

OUTLINE

1. The gifts for transporting the Tabernacle, that of carts & oxen: Demonstrated the need for joyful, spontaneous support of God's work

a. The gifts were given right after the dedication of the Tabernacle
   1) The gifts were given by the twelve tribal leaders
   2) The gifts were spontaneously offered to the Lord at the Tabernacle door: Six covered wagons or carts & twelve oxen

b. The Lord instructed Moses to accept the gifts & to distribute them as needed

SCRIPTURE

And it came to pass on the
day that Moses had fully set
up the tabernacle, and had
anointed it, and sanctified it,
and all the instruments
thereof, both the altar and all
the vessels thereof, and had
anointed them, and sanctified them;
2 That the princes of Israel,
heads of the house of their
fathers, who were the
princes of the tribes, and
were over them that were
numbered, offered:
3 And they brought their
offering before the LORD,
six covered wagons, and
twelve oxen; a wagon for
two of the princes, and for
each one an ox: and they
brought them before the tabernacle.
4 And the LORD spake unto
Moses, saying,
5 Take it of them, that they
may be to do the service of
the tabernacle of the congregation; and thou shalt give
them unto the Levites, to
every man according to his
service.
6 And Moses took the wag-
ons and the oxen, and gave
them unto the Levites.
7 Two wagons and four oxen
he gave unto the sons of
Gershon, according to their
service:
8 And four wagons and eight
oxen he gave unto the sons
of Merari, according unto
their service, under the hand
of Ithamar the son of Aaron
the priest.
9 But unto the sons of
Kohath he gave none:
because the service of the
sanctuary belonging unto
them was that they should
bear upon their shoul-
ders.

OUTLINE

c. The gifts were distributed to the Levites, the assistants responsible for transporting the Tabernacle
   1) The Gershonites received 2 carts & 4 oxen (for transporting all the curtains): Got just what they needed
   2) The Merarites received 4 carts & 8 oxen (for transporting the frame): Got just what they needed
   3) The priest Ithamar supervised the transporting of the Tabernacle
   4) The Kohathites received no carts, for they were to carry the sacred furnishings on their shoulders: They needed none of the gifts

1. The magnificent gifts were given by the leaders right after the dedication of the Tabernacle (v.1). Exodus chapter 40 describes the completion and dedication of the Tabernacle. It was at that time that the presence of God descended upon the Tabernacle in the cloud of His glory, symbolized in the pillar of cloud (Ex.40:34-35). This present passage (Numbers chapter 7) shows the joyful, spontaneous response of the tribal leaders right after the dedication of the Tabernacle.

Also note this fact: all the events from Exodus chapter 40 through Numbers chapter 9 describe what happened within a *one month* period. The one month stretched from the dedication of the Tabernacle (Exodus chapter 40) through all the events in Leviticus up through Numbers chapter 10. All these events took place in a period of just 1 month. How do we know this? Because the events are dated in Exodus chapter 40 to Numbers chapter 10. Note these dated events: [1]

Date (in second year)	Event	Text
Day 1, first month	Completion of tabernacle	Ex.40:2; Num.7:1
	Laws for offerings begin	Lev.1:1
	Offerings for altar begin	Num.7:3
	Ordination of priests begins	Lev.8:1
Day 8, first month	Ordination of priests completed	Lev.9:1
Day 12, first month	Offerings for altar completed	Num.7:78
	Appointment of Levites	Num.8:5
Day 14, first month	Second Passover	Num.9:2
Day 1, second month	Census begins	Num.1:1
Day 14, second month	Passover for the unclean	Num.9:11
Day 20, second month	The cloud moves, the camp begins its trek	Num.10:11

The point to see is the glorious worship that surrounded the dedication of the Tabernacle. The leaders of the people were deeply moved, filled with joy and rejoicing, stirred to make some wonderful gifts to the Lord and His Tabernacle. Note that the leaders gave the gifts spontaneously. They offered the gifts to the Lord at the Tabernacle door itself: they gave six covered wagons or carts and twelve oxen (v.3).

2. The Lord instructed Moses to accept the gifts and to distribute them as needed (v.4-5).
3. The gifts were distributed by Moses to the Levites, the assistants responsible for transporting the Tabernacle (v.6-9).
   a. The Gershonites were given two carts and four oxen for transporting all the curtains: they received just what they needed for their work (v.7).
   b. The Merarites were given four carts and eight oxen for transporting the frame of the Tabernacle: they, too, received just what their work required (v.8).

---

1 This chart is taken from *The Expositor's Bible Commentary*, Vol.2. Frank E. Gaebelein, Editor, p.757, which in turn is based upon Gordon J. Wenham's chart in *The Book of Numbers*, p.91. Credit is hereby given to both commentaries.

c. The priest Ithamar supervised the transporting of the Tabernacle (v.8).
d. Note that the Kohathites were given no carts, for they were to carry the sacred furnishings on their shoulders. They needed none of the gifts that were brought by the leaders (v.9).

Thought 1. What happened to these leaders is exciting. Just think: How could the heavy curtains and the heavy framing of the Tabernacle ever be transported without wagons and oxen? There was no way. The need—a dire need—existed. A great dedication service of the Tabernacle had just taken place, a glorious and joyful celebration. There was a deep sense of the presence of God. Yet there was a dire need, a need so great that the people could not begin their march to the promised land until the need was met. The Tabernacle could not be transported without oxen and wagons, and the wagons had to be covered to protect the Tabernacle during bad weather. Obviously, at some point during the dedication service, the heart of some leader was gripped with the need, and he shared it with the other leaders. Together, they stepped forth and met the need. Joyfully and spontaneously, they supported the work of God. What a lesson for us! How desperately the needs of the church need to be met! How desperately men and women need to step forth to meet the needs of the church! To give spontaneously and joyfully to the work of the Lord!

> **"Give, and it shall be given unto you; good measure, pressed down, and shaken together, and running over, shall men give into your bosom. For with the same measure that ye mete withal it shall be measured to you again" (Lk.6:38).**
> **"Sell that ye have, and give alms; provide yourselves bags which wax not old, a treasure in the heavens that faileth not, where no thief approacheth, neither moth corrupteth" (Lk.12:33).**
> **"And he looked up, and saw the rich men casting their gifts into the treasury. And he saw also a certain poor widow casting in thither two mites. And he said, Of a truth I say unto you, that this poor widow hath cast in more than they all: For all these have of their abundance cast in unto the offerings of God: but she of her penury hath cast in all the living that she had" (Lk.21:1-4).**
> **"Neither was there any among them that lacked: for as many as were possessors of lands or houses sold them, and brought the prices of the things that were sold, And laid *them* down at the apostles' feet: and distribution was made unto every man according as he had need" (Acts 4:34-35).**
> **"I have showed you all things, how that so labouring ye ought to support the weak, and to remember the words of the Lord Jesus, how he said, It is more blessed to give than to receive" (Acts 20:35).**
> **"But this *I say,* He which soweth sparingly shall reap also sparingly; and he which soweth bountifully shall reap also bountifully" (2 Cor.9:6).**
> **"And they spake unto Moses, saying, The people bring much more than enough for the service of the work, which the LORD commanded to make" (Ex.36:5).**
> **"Moreover, because I have set my affection to the house of my God, I have of mine own proper good, of gold and silver, *which* I have given to the house of my God, over and above all that I have prepared for the holy house" (1 Chron.29:3).**
> **"And all the princes and all the people rejoiced, and brought in, and cast into the chest, until they had made an end" (2 Chron.24:10).**
> **"The liberal soul shall be made fat: and he that watereth shall be watered also himself" (Pr.11:25).**
> **"He that hath a bountiful eye shall be blessed; for he giveth of his bread to the poor" (Pr.22:9).**
> **"Bring ye all the tithes into the storehouse, that there may be meat in mine house, and prove me now herewith, saith the LORD of hosts, if I will not open you the windows of heaven, and pour you out a blessing, that *there shall* not *be room* enough *to receive it*" (Mal.3:10).**

2 (7:10-88) **Offerings, Duty to Give—Giving, Duty of—Dedication, of the Tabernacle—Church, Dedication of—Gifts, Duty to Offer—Approach, to God—Sacrifice, the Way to Approach God**: there were the magnificent offerings presented at the dedication of the altar. (Due to the length of the outline points beside this section of Scripture, they are not being repeated here.) Note: the offerings were presented by each tribal leader on different days in obedience to God's instructions. This demonstrated the need to approach God exactly as He says. Twelve of the most majestic, meaningful worship services ever held now occurred—stretched out over 12 days. Each of the 12 leaders majestically brought his gifts on a different day for the dedication of the altar (v.11). What were the worship services like on each of the days? The fact that each leader's offering is repeated for 12 consecutive days indicates a spectacular, meaningful worship service:

⇒ worship service of pomp and ceremony, of majesty and glory, of pageantry and celebration
⇒ a worship service of meaning, significance, and purpose
⇒ a worship service of joy and rejoicing
⇒ a worship service of deep dedication and commitment
⇒ a worship service acknowledging God's great gift of the atonement, of the forgiveness of sin, and of fellowship and peace with Him

1. Note the offering of the first day: it was brought by Nahshon, leader of the great tribe of Judah (v.12-17).
   a. He brought one silver plate, weighing about 3¼ pounds (v.13). This plate was probably for the Table of Showbread, to be used with the Bread of the Presence.
   b. He brought one silver sprinkling bowl or basin that weighed about 1¾ pounds (v.13). This was probably used for the blood that was to be sprinkled upon the altar. Note that both the silver plate and the silver bowl were filled with Grain Offerings of choice flour mixed with olive oil.
   c. He brought one gold dish that weighed about 4 ounces (v.13). This was filled with incense which probably means that it was used for this very purpose day by day.
   d. He brought the animals necessary to approach God through the blood of the sacrifice (v.15-17). Note:

⇒ He approached God through the Burnt Offering, acknowledging the atonement or reconciliation that God had provided for him and his tribal people.
⇒ He approached God through the Sin Offering, seeking forgiveness of sin (v.16).
⇒ He approached God through the Fellowship or Peace Offering, seeking more of the fellowship and peace of God for himself and his tribe (v.17).

Each of the 12 leaders brought the very *same gifts* as this leader from the tribe of Judah. Each tribal leader had his day before God, his day to present his gifts and offerings to the Lord. Obviously, each leader's heart was filled with joy and rejoicing, praise and honor—all lifted up to the Lord God who had saved and delivered him from the bondage of Egypt (a symbol of the world with all its enslavements). Because each of the 12 days is simply repeated with the gifts offered, the text of the other tribal leader's offerings is not being covered, nor are the Scripture and outline being repeated. The reader can easily glance back at the Scripture and outline at the beginning of this particular study.

Note the totals and great value of the offerings.

a. There were 12 silver plates, 12 silver bowls, and 12 gold dishes. The silver plates and bowls weighed about 2400 shekels or about 60 pounds. The gold containers with incense weighed one hundred twenty shekels or about 3 pounds (v.84-86).
b. There were a large number of animals offered:
   ⇒ For the Burnt Offering, there were 12 young bulls, 12 rams, and 12 male lambs sacrificed with their Grain Offering (v.87).
   ⇒ For the Sin Offering, there were 12 male goats sacrificed (v.87).
   ⇒ For the Fellowship or Peace Offering, there were 24 oxen, 60 rams, 60 male goats, and 60 male lambs sacrificed (v.88).

Thought 1. The tribal leaders of Israel set a dynamic example for us.

1) They were the leaders of the people. As leaders, they took the lead in supporting God's work. The leaders of the church must step forth to take the lead. They are in leadership positions for this very purpose: to lead God's people. Money or financial support is a part of God's work. Therefore, the leaders of the church must take the lead in meeting the financial needs of the church.

"For *the kingdom of heaven is* as a man travelling into a far country, *who* called his own servants, and delivered unto them his goods. And unto one he gave five talents, to another two, and to another one; to every man according to his several ability; and straightway took his journey" (Mt.25:14-15).

"But God said unto him, *Thou* fool, this night thy soul shall be required of thee: then whose shall those things be, which thou hast provided?" (Lk.12:20).

"For unto whomsoever much is given, of him shall be much required: and to whom men have committed much, of him they will ask the more" (Lk.12:48).

"I have showed you all things, how that so labouring ye ought to support the weak, and to remember the words of the Lord Jesus, how he said, It is more blessed to give than to receive" (Acts 20:35).

"Moreover it is required in stewards, that a man be found faithful" (1 Cor.4:2).

"As every man hath received the gift, *even so* minister the same one to another, as good stewards of the manifold grace of God" (1 Pt.4:10).

"And all the princes and all the people rejoiced, and brought in, and cast into the chest, until they had made an end" (2 Chron.24:10).

2) The tribal leaders of Israel approached God exactly as He said: through the substitute sacrifice of the offerings. This is exactly how we must approach God, exactly as He says: through the sacrifice of His Son, the Lord Jesus Christ. There is no other approach to God other than through His Son.

"For God so loved the world, that he gave his only begotten Son, that whosoever believeth in him should not perish, but have everlasting life" (Jn.3:16).

"I said therefore unto you, that ye shall die in your sins: for if ye believe not that I am *he,* ye shall die in your sins" (Jn.8:24).

"Jesus saith unto him, I am the way, the truth, and the life: no man cometh unto the Father, but by me" (Jn.14:6).

"Neither is there salvation in any other: for there is none other name under heaven given among men, whereby we must be saved" (Acts 4:12).

"For other foundation can no man lay than that is laid, which is Jesus Christ" (1 Cor.3:11).

"For *there is* one God, and one mediator between God and men, the man Christ Jesus; Who gave himself a ransom for all, to be testified in due time" (1 Tim.2:5-6).

"But now hath he obtained a more excellent ministry, by how much also he is the mediator of a better covenant, which was established upon better promises" (Heb.8:6).

"And for this cause he is the mediator of the new testament, that by means of death, for the redemption of the transgressions *that were* under the first testament, they which are called might receive the promise of eternal inheritance" (Heb.9:15).

"For Christ is not entered into the holy places made with hands, *which are* the figures of the true; but into heaven itself, now to appear in the presence of God for us" (Heb.9:24).

"And to Jesus the mediator of the new covenant, and to the blood of sprinkling, that speaketh better things than *that of* Abel" (Heb.12:24).

"My little children, these things write I unto you, that ye sin not. And if any man sin, we have an advocate with the Father, Jesus Christ the righteous: And he is the propitiation for our sins: and not for ours only, but also for *the sins of* the whole world" (1 Jn.2:1-2).

3) The tribal leaders approached God for 12 consecutive days, leader after leader—all through the substitute sacrifice. Note the emphasis upon the substitute sacrifice (Num.7:15-17, 21-23, 27-29, 33-35, 39-41, 45-47, 51-53, 57-59, 63-65, 69-71, 75-77, 81-83, 87-88). Scripture declares that the substitute sacrifice is a symbol, a picture of the sacrifice of the Lord Jesus Christ. Jesus Christ is our substitute Sacrifice.

"Who gave himself for our sins, that he might deliver us from this present evil world, according to the will of God and our Father" (Gal.1:4).

"Christ hath redeemed us from the curse of the law, being made a curse for us: for it is written, Cursed is every one that hangeth on a tree" (Gal.3:13).

"And walk in love, as Christ also hath loved us, and hath given himself for us an offering and a sacrifice to God for a sweetsmelling savour" (Eph.5:2).

"Who gave himself for us, that he might redeem us from all iniquity, and purify unto himself a peculiar people, zealous of good works" (Tit.2:14).

"But we see Jesus, who was made a little lower than the angels for the suffering of death, crowned with glory and honour; that he by the grace of God should taste death for every man" (Heb.2:9).

"Forasmuch as ye know that ye were not redeemed with corruptible things, as silver and gold, from your vain conversation received by tradition from your fathers; But with the precious blood of Christ, as of a lamb without blemish and without spot" (1 Pt.1:18-19).

"Who his own self bare our sins in his own body on the tree, that we, being dead to sins, should live unto righteousness: by whose stripes ye were healed" (1 Pt.2:24).

"For Christ also hath once suffered for sins, the just for the unjust, that he might bring us to God, being put to death in the flesh, but quickened by the Spirit" (1 Pt.3:18).

"Hereby perceive we the love of God, because he laid down his life for us: and we ought to lay down our lives for the brethren" (1 Jn.3:16).

3 (7:89) **Assurance, of Access to God—Access, to God—Presence, of God—God, Presence of—Communion, with God—Guidance, of God**: there was the great assurance of God, the assurance of permanent access into His presence—the assurance of His communion and guidance day by day.

OUTLINE	SCRIPTURE
3. The great assurance of God: Permanent access into His presence—His communion & guidance a. The approach of Moses: Approached as he felt the need b. The faithfulness of God: Spoke from between the cherubim on the Ark—communed with & directed His people	89 And when Moses was gone into the tabernacle of the congregation to speak with him, then he heard the voice of one speaking unto him from off the mercy seat that was upon the ark of testimony, from between the two cherubims: and he spake unto him.

The twelve days of glorious worship seemed to roll in one upon another, and then it happened: Climatic! Astounding! Moses entered the Tabernacle to pray. He spoke with the Lord and, astonishingly, he actually heard the voice of God speaking to him. The voice came from between the two cherubim above the Atonement Cover on the Ark of the Testimony. God Himself actually showered His grace upon Moses and communed with him. Remember: the dedication of the Tabernacle and God's glorious presence descending upon the Tabernacle in the cloud had just taken place a few days earlier. The leaders had just made their spectacular, spontaneous offerings to the Lord on 12 consecutive days. Then Moses entered the Tabernacle, and there God poured His presence out upon Moses, speaking to him from between the two cherubim above the Ark. God was giving great assurance of His presence—of His communion and guidance—that He was going to give His people day by day as they marched to the promised land.

Thought 1. God gave Moses two great assurances: the assurance of permanent access into God's presence and the assurance of God's guidance. The very same two assurances are given to every believer upon the earth.

1) There is assurance of permanent access into God's presence.

"Ask, and it shall be given you; seek, and ye shall find; knock, and it shall be opened unto you" (Mt.7:7).

"I am the door: by me if any man enter in, he shall be saved, and shall go in and out, and find pasture" (Jn.10:9).

"Hitherto have ye asked nothing in my name: ask, and ye shall receive, that your joy may be full" (Jn.16:24).

"Therefore being justified by faith, we have peace with God through our Lord Jesus Christ: By whom also we have access by faith into this grace wherein we stand, and rejoice in hope of the glory of God" (Ro.5:1-2).

"For through him we both have access by one Spirit unto the Father" (Eph.2:18).

"In whom we have boldness and access with confidence by the faith of him" (Eph.3:12).

"For the law made nothing perfect, but the bringing in of a better hope *did;* by the which we draw nigh unto God" (Heb.7:19).

"Let us draw near with a true heart in full assurance of faith, having our hearts sprinkled from an evil conscience, and our bodies washed with pure water" (Heb.10:22).

"Draw nigh to God, and he will draw nigh to you. Cleanse *your* hands, *ye* sinners; and purify *your* hearts, *ye* double minded" (Jas.4:8).

"Behold, I stand at the door, and knock: if any man hear my voice, and open the door, I will come in to him, and will sup with him, and he with me" (Rev.3:20).

"Seek the LORD and his strength, seek his face continually" (1 Chron.16:11).

"Who shall ascend into the hill of the LORD? or who shall stand in his holy place? He that hath clean hands, and a pure heart; who hath not lifted up his soul unto vanity, nor sworn deceitfully" (Ps.24:3-4).

"But *it is* good for me to draw near to God: I have put my trust in the Lord GOD, that I may declare all thy works" (Ps.73:28).

"Thou wilt keep *him* in perfect peace, *whose* mind *is* stayed *on thee:* because he trusteth in thee" (Is.26:3).

2) There is the assurance of God's communion and guidance day by day.

"Lo, I am with you alway, *even* unto the end of the world. Amen" (Mt.28:20).

"Howbeit when he, the Spirit of truth, is come, he will guide you into all truth: for he shall not speak of himself; but whatsoever he shall hear, *that* shall he speak: and he will show you things to come" (Jn.16:13).

"That which we have seen and heard declare we unto you, that ye also may have fellowship with us: and truly our fellowship *is* with the Father, and with his Son Jesus Christ" (1 Jn.1:3).

"Behold, I stand at the door, and knock: if any man hear my voice, and open the door, I will come in to him, and will sup with him, and he with me" (Rev.3:20).

"And, behold, I *am* with thee, and will keep thee in all *places* whither thou goest, and will bring thee again into this land; for I will not leave thee, until I have done *that* which I have spoken to thee of" (Gen.28:15).

"And he said, My presence shall go *with thee,* and I will give thee rest" (Ex.33:14).

"When thou goest out to battle against thine enemies, and seest horses, and chariots, *and* a people more than thou, be not afraid of them: for the LORD thy God *is* with thee, which brought thee up out of the land of Egypt" (Dt.20:1).

"He maketh me to lie down in green pastures: he leadeth me beside the still waters" (Ps.23:2).

"The meek will he guide in judgment: and the meek will he teach his way" (Ps.25:9

"For this God *is* our God for ever and ever: he will be our guide *even* unto death" (Ps.48:14).

"Thou shalt guide me with thy counsel, and afterward receive me *to* glory" (Ps.73:24).

"And thine ears shall hear a word behind thee, saying, This *is* the way, walk ye in it, when ye turn to the right hand, and when ye turn to the left" (Is.30:21).

"And I will bring the blind by a way *that* they knew not; I will lead them in paths *that* they have not known: I will make darkness light before them, and crooked things straight. These things will I do unto them, and not forsake them" (Is.42:16).

"When thou passest through the waters, I *will be* with thee; and through the rivers, they shall not overflow thee: when thou walkest through the fire, thou shalt not be burned; neither shall the flame kindle upon thee" (Is.43:2).

1. The placement of the lampstand—to light the area in the Holy Place: A symbol of Christ, the Light of the world

a. Aaron obeyed: Set the lamps & focused the light
   1) On the 12 loaves of showbread: Symbolized the tribes, God's people
   2) On the Altar of Incense: Symbolized prayer, access

b. The great value of the lampstand
   1) Was made of hammered gold
   2) Was made exactly as God designed

2. The dedication of the Levites: A picture of laypersons being set apart to God

a. The Levites must be ceremonially, spiritually cleansed
   1) To be sprinkled with the water of cleansing
   2) To shave their whole heads
   3) To wash their clothes
   4) To make preparation to approach the LORD: Through the Burnt Offering with its Grain Offering & through the Sin Offering

b. The Levites must be presented to the LORD—at the front of the Tabernacle—& the people of God must be assembled
   1) To have the people identify with them—by laying their hands upon them
   2) To wave them (their shoulders) back & forth as a wave offering before the LORD
   3) To have the Levites identify with the sacrifice (a symbol of Christ)
   4) To then offer the sacrifice of the Sin Offering & of the Burnt Offering: To secure forgiveness & to make atonement (reconciliation)
   5) To again present them as a wave offering before the LORD

c. The Levites are to be set apart from other people, set apart to be God's people, to do a special work for God
   1) They are to be set apart only after their purification; then they are to begin their service
   2) They are the ones who are set apart by God Himself, to take the place of the firstborn son
      - Every firstborn son had been set apart by God to be His, set apart when God delivered His people from Egypt
      - Now God replaces the first-born sons with the Levites
   3) They are set apart to be the assistants to the priests
      - To do the work needed at the Tabernacle
      - To make atonement—take care of the offerings—for the people
      - To protect the people by keeping them from abusing the Tabernacle

d. The obedience of everyone: They all set the Levites apart just as God commanded
   1) The Levites purified themselves & washed their clothes
   2) The High Priest presented them to the LORD & made atonement for them: To cleanse them spiritually
   3) The Levites began their work as assistants to the priests

G. The Placement of the Lampstand & the Setting Apart of the Levites to Serve God: Standing Forth as Lights & Servants of God, 8:1-26

And the LORD spake unto
Moses, saying,
2 Speak unto Aaron, and say
unto him, When thou lightest
the lamps, the seven lamps
shall give light over against
the candlestick.
3 And Aaron did so; he
lighted the lamps thereof
over against the candlestick,
as the LORD commanded
Moses.
4 And this work of the candlestick was of beaten gold,
unto the shaft thereof, unto
the flowers thereof, was
beaten work: according unto
the pattern which the LORD
had shewed Moses, so he
made the candlestick.
5 And the LORD spake unto
Moses, saying,
6 Take the Levites from
among the children of Israel,
and cleanse them.
7 And thus shalt thou do unto
them, to cleanse them:
Sprinkle water of purifying
upon them, and let them
shave all their flesh, and let
them wash their clothes, and
so make themselves clean.
8 Then let them take a young
bullock with his meat offering, even fine flour mingled
with oil, and another young
bullock shalt thou take for a
sin offering.
9 And thou shalt bring the
Levites before the tabernacle
of the congregation: and
thou shalt gather the whole
assembly of the children of
Israel together:
10 And thou shalt bring the
Levites before the LORD: and
the children of Israel shall
put their hands upon the
Levites:
11 And Aaron shall offer
the Levites before the LORD
for an offering of the children of Israel, that they may
execute the service of the
LORD.
12 And the Levites shall lay
their hands upon the heads of
the bullocks: and thou shalt
offer the one for a sin offering, and the other for a burnt
offering, unto the LORD, to
make an atonement for the
Levites.
13 And thou shalt set the
Levites before Aaron, and
before his sons, and offer
them for an offering unto the
LORD.
14 Thus shalt thou separate
the Levites from among the
children of Israel: and the
Levites shall be mine.
15 And after that shall the
Levites go in to do the service of the tabernacle of the
congregation: and thou shalt
cleanse them, and offer them
for an offering.
16 For they are wholly
given unto me from among
the children of Israel; instead
of such as open every womb,
even instead of the firstborn
of all the children of Israel,
have I taken them unto me.
17 For all the firstborn of
the children of Israel are
mine, both man and beast: on
the day that I smote every
firstborn in the land of Egypt
I sanctified them for myself.
18 And I have taken the
Levites for all the firstborn
of the children of Israel.
19 And I have given the
Levites as a gift to Aaron
and to his sons from among
the children of Israel, to do
the service of the children of
Israel in the tabernacle of the
congregation, and to make
an atonement for the children of Israel: that there be
no plague among the chil-
dren of Israel, when the children of Israel come nigh
unto the sanctuary.
20 And Moses, and Aaron,
and all the congregation of
the children of Israel, did to
the Levites according unto
all that the LORD commanded Moses concerning the
Levites, so did the children
of Israel unto them.
21 And the Levites were
purified, and they washed
their clothes; and Aaron
offered them as an offering
before the LORD; and Aaron
made an atonement for them
to cleanse them.
22 And after that went the
Levites in to do their service
in the tabernacle of the congregation before Aaron, and
before his sons: as the LORD
had commanded Moses con-

e. The Levites' length of service or retirement years 1) They are to serve in the heavy work between the ages of 25 to 50 years old	cerning the Levites, so did they unto them. 23 And the LORD spake unto Moses, saying, 24 This is it that belongeth unto the Levites: from twenty and five years old and upward they shall go in to wait upon the service of the tabernacle of the congregation:	25 And from the age of fifty years they shall cease waiting upon the service thereof, and shall serve no more: 26 But shall minister with their brethren in the tabernacle of the congregation, to keep the charge, and shall do no service. Thus shalt thou do unto the Levites touching their charge.	2) They must retire from the heavy work after 50 years of age 3)They may assist the younger men after 50, but not do the heavy work themselves

DIVISION I

THE PREPARATION FOR THE MARCH TO THE PROMISED LAND, 1:1-10:36

G. The Placement of the Lampstand and the Setting Apart of the Levites to Serve God: Standing Forth as Lights and Servants of God, 8:1-26

(8:1-26) **Introduction—Needy, the, List of—Laborers, Need for**: people are lost and separated from God, dying and doomed to spend eternity apart from God. But these are not the only tragedies that confront man. Tragedies attack people day after day, tragedies that cause enormous problems and difficulties. Just think of the problems and difficulties that constantly attack…

- the orphans and children of single parents
- the widows and widowers
- the brokenhearted and hurting
- the backslidden and half-hearted
- the diseased and dying
- the suffering and hospitalized
- the hungry and thirsty
- the homeless and unemployed
- the injured and handicapped
- the empty and lonely
- the lawless and prisoners
- the emotionally and mentally disturbed

All around us there are people who need help, yet the laborers are few. Few people step forth to help. There is a desperate need for people to step forth and become servants of God, a need for messengers of light and ministry who will meet the desperate needs of the world. There is a need for laborers. This is the subject of this great Scripture: *The Placement of the Lampstand and the Setting Apart of the Levites to Serve God: Standing Forth as Lights and Servants of God*, 8:1-26.

1. The placement of the lampstand—to light the area in front: a symbol of Christ, the Light of the world (v.1-4).
2. The dedication ceremony of the Levites: a picture of laypersons being set apart to God (v.5-26).

1 (8:1-4) **Lampstand, Symbol of—Jesus Christ, Symbolized by—Light, a Symbol of—Symbol, of the Lampstand**: there was the placement of the lampstand within the Tabernacle. The lampstand was to give light to the holy place within the Tabernacle. Remember, the lampstand is a symbol of Christ, the Light of the world. Note the Scripture and the outline:

OUTLINE	SCRIPTURE	SCRIPTURE	OUTLINE
1. The placement of the lampstand—to light the area in the Holy Place: A symbol of Christ, the Light of the world a. Aaron obeyed: Set the lamps & focused the light 1) On the 12 loaves of show-	And the LORD spake unto Moses, saying, 2 Speak unto Aaron, and say unto him, When thou lightest the lamps, the seven lamps shall give light over against the candlestick. 3 And Aaron did so; he lighted the lamps thereof over against the candlestick,	as the LORD commanded Moses. 4 And this work of the candlestick was of beaten gold, unto the shaft thereof, unto the flowers thereof, was beaten work: according unto the pattern which the LORD had shewed Moses, so he made the candlestick.	bread (symbolized the tribes, God's people) 2) On the Altar of Incense: Symbolized prayer, access b. The great value of the lampstand 1) Was made of hammered gold 2) Was made exactly as God designed

The lampstand apparently sat close by the entrance into the holy place; therefore, when it was focused in front, it lit up everything in the room of the holy place. This meant that its beams of light focused upon both the Table of Showbread and the Altar of Incense, a significant fact. Remember that 12 loaves of bread sat upon the Table of Showbread and that the 12 loaves represented the 12 tribes of Israel. That is, the 12 loaves represented God's people. The symbolism is clear: the light of God's presence is always shining upon His people. God cares for His people and looks after them.

Remember also that the Altar of Incense was constantly burning and sending out a sweet aroma ascending up toward heaven. This was a symbol that prayer should continually ascend up to God. The incense was like a sweet aroma, very pleasing to Him. The light of the lampstand gave focus to prayer: it emphasized prayer—that God's people should continually pray.

1. Note that Aaron obeyed: he faced the lamps forward, focusing them upon the 12 loaves of showbread and the Altar of Incense. The message was immediately conveyed: the Light of the world—God Himself—was focusing upon His peo-

ple. He was focusing His presence and love, His guidance and protection upon them. Moreover, He was focusing upon their prayers, receiving their prayers and accepting them as a sweet aroma, very pleasing to Him.

2. Note the great value of the lampstand (v.4). It was a beautiful, exquisite furnishing, very valuable. It was made of pure hammered gold in the form of a seven-branched tree that flowered. There was, of course, a base with one major shaft. Three branches extended out on each side of the shaft. There were cups shaped like almond blossoms and buds running up and decorating the shaft and branches of the lampstand (see outline and notes—Ex.25:31-40 for more discussion).

Note the emphasis that the lampstand had been made exactly as God Himself had designed it (v.4). This stresses the great value of the lampstand: it was the lampstand of God Himself, for God had designed and overseen the making of it through His servant Moses.

Thought 1. Four clear lessons are seen in this passage.

1) Jesus Christ is the Light of the world. As we march toward the promised land, believers must have the light of Christ to conquer the pitfalls and enemies of this life. Again, Christ is the Light of the world.

"In him was life; and the life was the light of men" (Jn.1:4).

"Then spake Jesus again unto them, saying, I am the light of the world: he that followeth me shall not walk in darkness, but shall have the light of life" (Jn.8:12).

"Then Jesus said unto them, Yet a little while is the light with you. Walk while ye have the light, lest darkness come upon you: for he that walketh in darkness knoweth not whither he goeth" (Jn.12:35).

"I am come a light into the world, that whosoever believeth on me should not abide in darkness" (Jn.12:46).

"For God, who commanded the light to shine out of darkness, hath shined in our hearts, to *give* the light of the knowledge of the glory of God in the face of Jesus Christ" (2 Cor.4:6).

"Wherefore he saith, Awake thou that sleepest, and arise from the dead, and Christ shall give thee light" (Eph.5:14).

"The people that walked in darkness have seen a great light: they that dwell in the land of the shadow of death, upon them hath the light shined" (Is.9:2).

2) The light of the lampstand focused upon the 12 loaves of showbread, a symbol of the 12 tribes of Israel (God's people). The light of God's presence shines upon the true believer. God gives light to His people: His love, care, provision, direction, guidance, knowledge, and wisdom. God's light gives whatever is necessary to overcome the pitfalls and enemies of this life.

"To give light to them that sit in darkness and *in* the shadow of death, to guide our feet into the way of peace" (Lk.1:79).

"That which we have seen and heard declare we unto you, that ye also may have fellowship with us: and truly our fellowship *is* with the Father, and with his Son Jesus Christ. And these things write we unto you, that your joy may be full. This then is the message which we have heard of him, and declare unto you, that God is light, and in him is no darkness at all" (1 Jn.1:3-5).

"And there shall be no night there; and they need no candle, neither light of the sun; for the Lord God giveth them light: and they shall reign for ever and ever" (Rev.22:5).

"He maketh me to lie down in green pastures: he leadeth me beside the still waters" (Ps.23:2).

"For this God *is* our God for ever and ever: he will be our guide *even* unto death" (Ps.48:14).

"Thou shalt guide me with thy counsel, and afterward receive me *to* glory" (Ps.73:24).

"For the LORD God *is* a sun and shield: the LORD will give grace and glory: no good *thing* will he withhold from them that walk uprightly" (Ps.84:11).

"And thine ears shall hear a word behind thee, saying, This *is* the way, walk ye in it, when ye turn to the right hand, and when ye turn to the left" (Is.30:21).

"And I will bring the blind by a way *that* they knew not; I will lead them in paths *that* they have not known: I will make darkness light before them, and crooked things straight. These things will I do unto them, and not forsake them" (Is.42:16).

"Thy sun shall no more go down; neither shall thy moon withdraw itself: for the LORD shall be thine everlasting light, and the days of thy mourning shall be ended" (Is.60:20).

"Rejoice not against me, O mine enemy: when I fall, I shall arise; when I sit in darkness, the LORD *shall be* a light unto me" (Mic.7:8).

3) The lampstand focused upon the Altar of Incense, symbolizing the importance of prayer. The light of God shines upon the prayers of His people, showing us that we have access into His presence—continued, unbroken access. We can approach God anytime with anything, and He hears us.

"Ask, and it shall be given you; seek, and ye shall find; knock, and it shall be opened unto you" (Mt.7:7).

"If ye abide in me, and my words abide in you, ye shall ask what ye will, and it shall be done unto you" (Jn.15:7).

"Hitherto have ye asked nothing in my name: ask, and ye shall receive, that your joy may be full" (Jn.16:24).

"Pray without ceasing" (1 Th.5:17).

"Is any among you afflicted? let him pray. Is any merry? let him sing psalms" (Jas.5:13).

"Seek the LORD and his strength, seek his face continually" (1 Chron.16:11).

"He shall call upon me, and I will answer him: I *will be* with him in trouble; I will deliver him, and honour him" (Ps.91:15).

"Then shalt thou call, and the LORD shall answer; thou shalt cry, and he shall say, Here I *am.* If thou take away from the midst of thee the yoke, the putting forth of the finger, and speaking vanity" (Is.58:9).

"And it shall come to pass, that before they call, I will answer; and while they are yet speaking, I will hear" (Is.65:24).

"Call unto me, and I will answer thee, and show thee great and mighty things, which thou knowest not" (Jer.33:3).

4) The lampstand had to be focused by Aaron. God used one of His servants to give light to the loaves (His people) and to the Altar of Incense (the importance of prayer). So it is with us. God has called His people to lift up and focus the light of the Lord Jesus Christ before the world. In fact, the Scripture declares that God's people are the light of the world. Therefore, as we march to the promised land, we must lift up the light of the Lord Jesus Christ to the surrounding people and nations of the world.

"Ye are the light of the world. A city that is set on an hill cannot be hid" (Mt.5:14).

"For so hath the Lord commanded us, *saying,* I have set thee to be a light of the Gentiles, that thou shouldest be for salvation unto the ends of the earth" (Acts 13:47).

"For ye were sometimes darkness, but now *are ye* light in the Lord: walk as children of light" (Eph.5:8).

"That ye may be blameless and harmless, the sons of God, without rebuke, in the midst of a crooked and perverse nation, among whom ye shine as lights in the world" (Ph.2:15).

2 (8:5-26) **Dedication, of the Levites—Levites, Dedication of—Ceremony, Dedication—Dedication, Ceremony of**: there was the dedication of the Levites. Remember, the Levites were laypersons set apart by God to be assistants to the priests. This passage is a picture of laypersons being set apart to God, to His service. There is a sharp distinction between the Levites and the priests, a distinction that stresses the difference between a layperson who serves as an assistant and the priest or minister of God. *The Expositor's Bible Commentary* points out these differences:

"The Priests were made holy, the Levites clean; the priests were anointed and washed, the Levites sprinkled; the priests were given new garments, the Levites washed theirs; blood was applied to the priests, it was waved over the Levites."[1]

OUTLINE	SCRIPTURE
2. The dedication of the Levites: A picture of laypersons being set apart to God	5 And the LORD spake unto Moses, saying, 6 Take the Levites from among the children of Israel, and cleanse them.
a. The Levites must be ceremonially, spiritually cleansed 1) To be sprinkled with the water of cleansing 2) To shave their whole heads 3) To wash their clothes	7 And thus shalt thou do unto them, to cleanse them: Sprinkle water of purifying upon them, and let them shave all their flesh, and let them wash their clothes, and so make themselves clean.
4) To make preparation to approach the LORD: Through the Burnt Offering with its Grain Offering & through the Sin Offering	8 Then let them take a young bullock with his meat offering, even fine flour mingled with oil, and another young bullock shalt thou take for a sin offering.
b. The Levites must be presented to the LORD—at the front of the Tabernacle—& the people of God must be assembled	9 And thou shalt bring the Levites before the tabernacle of the congregation: and thou shalt gather the whole assembly of the children of Israel together:
1) To have the people identify with them—by laying their hands upon them	10 And thou shalt bring the Levites before the LORD: and the children of Israel shall put their hands upon the Levites:
2) To wave them (their shoulders) back & forth as	11 And Aaron shall offer the Levites before the LORD

SCRIPTURE	OUTLINE
for an offering of the children of Israel, that they may execute the service of the LORD.	a wave offering before the LORD
12 And the Levites shall lay their hands upon the heads of the bullocks: and thou shalt offer the one for a sin offering, and the other for a burnt offering, unto the LORD, to make an atonement for the Levites.	3) To have the Levites identify with the sacrifice (a symbol of Christ) 4) To then offer the sacrifice of the Sin Offering & of the Burnt Offering: To secure forgiveness & to make atonement (reconciliation)
13 And thou shalt set the Levites before Aaron, and before his sons, and offer them for an offering unto the LORD.	5) To again present them as a wave offering before the LORD
14 Thus shalt thou separate the Levites from among the children of Israel: and the Levites shall be mine. 15 And after that shall the Levites go in to do the service of the tabernacle of the congregation: and thou shalt cleanse them, and offer them for an offering.	c. The Levites are to be set apart from other people, set apart to be God's people, to do a special work for God 1) They are to be set apart only after their purification; then they are to begin their service
16 For they are wholly given unto me from among the children of Israel; instead of such as open	2) They are the ones who are set apart by God Himself, to take the place of the firstborn son

1 *The Expositor's Bible Commentary*, Frank E. Gaebelein, Editor, p.766.

OUTLINE	SCRIPTURE	SCRIPTURE	OUTLINE
	every womb, even instead of	purified, and they washed	themselves & washed
	the firstborn of all the chil-	their clothes; and Aaron	their clothes
	dren of Israel, have I taken	offered them as an offering	2) The High Priest presented
	them unto me.	before the LORD; and Aaron	them to the LORD & made
• Every firstborn son had	17 For all the firstborn of	made an atonement for them	atonement for them: To
been set apart by God	the children of Israel are	to cleanse them.	cleanse them spiritually
to be His, set apart	mine, both man and beast:	22 And after that went the	3) The Levites began their
when God delivered	on the day that I smote every	Levites in to do their service	work as assistants to the
His people from Egypt	firstborn in the land of Egypt	in the tabernacle of the con-	priests
	I sanctified them for myself.	gregation before Aaron, and	
• Now God replaces the	18 And I have taken the	before his sons: as the LORD	
first-born sons with the	Levites for all the firstborn	had commanded Moses con-	
Levites	of the children of Israel.	cerning the Levites, so did	
3) They are set apart to be	19 And I have given the	they unto them.	
the assistants to the priests	Levites as a gift to Aaron	23 And the LORD spake	e. The Levites' length of serv-
• To do the work needed	and to his sons from among	unto Moses, saying,	ice or retirement years
at the Tabernacle	the children of Israel, to do	24 This is it that belongeth	1) They are to serve in the
• To make atonement—	the service of the children of	unto the Levites: from twen-	heavy work between the
take care of the offer-	Israel in the tabernacle of the	ty and five years old and	ages of 25 to 50 years old
ings—for the people	congregation, and to make	upward they shall go in to	
• To protect the people	an atonement for the chil-	wait upon the service of the	
by keeping them from	dren of Israel: that there be	tabernacle of the congrega-	
abusing the Tabernacle	no plague among the chil-	tion:	
	dren of Israel, when the chil-	25 And from the age of fifty	2) They must retire from the
	dren of Israel come nigh	years they shall cease	heavy work after 50 years
	unto the sanctuary.	waiting upon the service	of age
d. The obedience of everyone:	20 And Moses, and Aaron,	thereof, and shall serve no	
They all set the Levites apart	and all the congregation of	more:	
just as God commanded	the children of Israel, did to	26 But shall minister with	3)They may assist the
	the Levites according unto	their brethren in the taberna-	younger men after 50, but
	all that the LORD command-	cle of the congregation, to	not do the heavy work
	ed Moses concerning the	keep the charge, and shall do	themselves
	Levites, so did the children	no service. Thus shalt thou	
	of Israel unto them.	do unto the Levites touching	
1) The Levites purified	21 And the Levites were	their charge.	

1. The Levites had to be ceremonially, spiritually cleansed (v.6-8). They had to be sprinkled with the water of cleansing, shave their whole heads, and wash their clothes. This was a symbol of being spiritually cleansed or purified from sin. But this was not all: they were also to make preparation to approach the Lord through the Burnt Offering and the Sin Offering. Keep in mind that the Burnt Offering secured the atonement and reconciliation with God, and the Sin Offering secured the forgiveness of sin. The Grain Offering was laid upon the sacrifice burning upon the altar and symbolized the offering of thanksgiving and of one's life to God (see outline and notes—Lev.1:1-17; 2:1-16; 4:1-5:13).

2. The Levites had to be presented to the Lord at the front of the Tabernacle, and the people of God had to be assembled for the dedication service (v.9-13).

   a. The people were to identify with the Levites by laying their hands upon them (v.10). Of course, just the tribal leaders did this, as the representatives of the people. This symbolized that the Levites were to be the servants of God in behalf of the people. They were to be the people's representatives, their substitutes in serving God day by day in the Tabernacle.
   b. The Levites were to be waved back and forth as a wave offering before the Lord (v.11). Obviously, Aaron took them by the shoulders and waved them back and forth or either side to side. This was a symbol that they were being offered as living sacrifices to God (Ro.12:1-2).
   c. The Levites were then to identify with the sacrifice (v.12). The sacrifice was being substituted for the Levites, bearing the judgment of God that was due the Levites and redeeming them from the wrath of God. Again, remember that the sacrifice was a symbol of Christ.
   d. The Levites were then to offer the sacrifice of the Sin Offering and of the Burnt Offering (v.12). This was to secure forgiveness and to make atonement (reconciliation) for them.
   e. The Levites were then to be presented a second time as a wave offering before the Lord (v.13).

3. The Levites were to be set apart from other people, set apart to be God's servants. They were to do a very special work for God (v.14-19). Note exactly what God says: the Levites *will be His*. The Levites belonged to God, belonged to the full-time service of God.

   a. But note: the Levites were to be set apart only after their purification. Once they had been cleansed and purified, they were then to begin their service (v.15).
   b. Note this important fact as well: the Levites were the ones who were set apart by God Himself to take the place of the firstborn son (v.16-18; see outline and notes—Num.3:11-13 for more discussion). Remember, every first born son had been set apart by God to be His and to serve Him. They were set apart when God delivered His people from Egypt (v.17). God had saved the firstborn sons of Israel when His judgment fell upon Egypt. Therefore, all the firstborn sons belonged to Him and His service. Now God replaced the firstborn sons with the Levites (v.18).

c. The Levites were set apart to be the assistants to the priests (v.19). They were to do whatever work was needed at the Tabernacle. They were to make atonement, that is, to take care of the offerings for the people. They were also to protect the people by keeping them from abusing the Tabernacle. This was essential, for if a person abused the Tabernacle—the symbol of God's holy presence—the judgment of God fell upon His people.
d. Note the obedience of everyone involved in the dedication service: Moses, Aaron, and the whole community of believers set the Levites apart just as God commanded (v.20-22).
   1) The Levites purified themselves and washed their clothes (v.21).
   2) The High Priest presented them to the Lord and made atonement for them: to cleanse them spiritually (v.21).
   3) The Levites began their work as assistants to the priests (v.22).
e. Note the Levites' length of service or retirement years (v.23-26). They were to serve in the heavy work of transporting the Tabernacle between the ages of 25 and 50 years old (v.24). But they had to retire from the heavy work of the Tabernacle after 50 years of age (v.25). However, they could assist the younger men in the lighter work after 50 (v.26).

Thought 1. The laborers are few. Lift up your eyes and look upon the fields, for they are ripe to harvest. Yet there are few workers reaping the harvest. Most of the harvest is going to die and decay in the fields. Most of the harvest will never fulfill the purpose for which it was planted: it will never be reaped or used. The hour is late, and the need for workers is desperate. People desperately need to step forth and join the force of workers. So much of the harvest will be lost unless thousands upon thousands step forth and join the force of God's workers. When God called and challenged the Levites, they stepped forth. God is calling and challenging you and me to step forth, challenging us as His servants to help those who are ministering the Word of Life to the world, the preachers and ministers of God.

"And he saith unto them, Follow me, and I will make you fishers of men" (Mt.4:19).

"Then saith he unto his disciples, The harvest truly *is* plenteous, but the labourers *are* few; Pray ye therefore the Lord of the harvest, that he will send forth labourers into his harvest" (Mt.9:37-38).

"But so shall it not be among you: but whosoever will be great among you, shall be your minister: And whosoever of you will be the chiefest, shall be servant of all" (Mk.10:43-44).

"He first findeth his own brother Simon, and saith unto him, We have found the Messias, which is, being interpreted, the Christ. And he brought him to Jesus. And when Jesus beheld him, he said, Thou art Simon the son of Jona: thou shalt be called Cephas, which is by interpretation, A stone" (Jn.1:41-42).

"Philip findeth Nathanael, and saith unto him, We have found him, of whom Moses in the law, and the prophets, did write, Jesus of Nazareth, the son of Joseph" (Jn.1:45).

"Say not ye, There are yet four months, and *then* cometh harvest? behold, I say unto you, Lift up your eyes, and look on the fields; for they are white already to harvest. And he that reapeth receiveth wages, and gathereth fruit unto life eternal: that both he that soweth and he that reapeth may rejoice together" (Jn.4:35-36).

"He saith to him again the second time, Simon, *son* of Jonas, lovest thou me? He saith unto him, Yea, Lord; thou knowest that I love thee. He saith unto him, Feed my sheep" (Jn.21:16).

"Then departed Barnabas to Tarsus, for to seek Saul: And when he had found him, he brought him unto Antioch. And it came to pass, that a whole year they assembled themselves with the church, and taught much people. And the disciples were called Christians first in Antioch" (Acts 11:25-26).

"For though I be free from all *men,* yet have I made myself servant unto all, that I might gain the more. And unto the Jews I became as a Jew, that I might gain the Jews; to them that are under the law, as under the law, that I might gain them that are under the law" (1 Cor.9:19-20).

"Bear ye one another's burdens, and so fulfil the law of Christ" (Gal.6:2).

"As we have therefore opportunity, let us do good unto all *men,* especially unto them who are of the household of faith" (Gal.6:10).

"And others save with fear, pulling *them* out of the fire; hating even the garment spotted by the flesh" (Jude 23).

"The fruit of the righteous *is* a tree of life; and he that winneth souls *is* wise" (Pr.11:30).

"And they that be wise shall shine as the brightness of the firmament; and they that turn many to righteousness as the stars for ever and ever" (Dan.12:3).

Thought 2. One thing is absolutely essential before serving God: approaching God through the sacrifice of the Lord Jesus Christ. The Levites had to approach God through the sacrifice laid upon the altar. That sacrifice was a symbol of Christ's sacrifice. Before a person serves God, he must make sure that he has been cleansed from sin and has received the atonement or reconciliation with God. Forgiveness and atonement come only through the blood of Christ. God accepts only those who come to Him through Christ. Christ alone bore the judgment of God against sin for us—which was death. Christ died for us. Therefore, a person must accept the death of Christ as his substitute, in his place. Once he identifies with Christ, he is accepted by God. The person is then ready to step forth to serve God.

"The next day John seeth Jesus coming unto him, and saith, Behold the Lamb of God, which taketh away the sin of the world" (Jn.1:29).

"Purge out therefore the old leaven, that ye may be a new lump, as ye are unleavened. For even Christ our passover is sacrificed for us" (1 Cor.5:7).

"Christ hath redeemed us from the curse of the law, being made a curse for us: for it is written, Cursed *is* every one that hangeth on a tree" (Gal.3:13).

"And walk in love, as Christ also hath loved us, and hath given himself for us an offering and a sacrifice to God for a sweetsmelling savour" (Eph.5:2).

"Forasmuch then as the children are partakers of flesh and blood, he also himself likewise took part of the same; that through death he might destroy him that had the power of death, that is, the devil; And deliver them who through fear of death were all their lifetime subject to bondage" (Heb.2:14-15).

"So Christ was once offered to bear the sins of many; and unto them that look for him shall he appear the second time without sin unto salvation" (Heb.9:28).

"Forasmuch as ye know that ye were not redeemed with corruptible things, *as* silver and gold, from your vain conversation *received* by tradition from your fathers; But with the precious blood of Christ, as of a lamb without blemish and without spot" (1 Pt.1:18-19).

"Who his own self bare our sins in his own body on the tree, that we, being dead to sins, should live unto righteousness: by whose stripes ye were healed" (1 Pt.2:24).

"For Christ also hath once suffered for sins, the just for the unjust, that he might bring us to God, being put to death in the flesh, but quickened by the Spirit" (1 Pt.3:18).

"But he *was* wounded for our transgressions, *he was* bruised for our iniquities: the chastisement of our peace *was* upon him; and with his stripes we are healed" (Is.53:5).

TYPES, SYMBOLS, AND PICTURES (Numbers 8:1-26)

Historical Term	Type or Picture (Scriptural Basis for Each)	Life Application for Today's Believer	Biblical Application
The Lampstand Num. 8:1-4 (See also Lev. 24:1-4)	*The lampstand is a symbol that the way into God's presence always shines brightly—is always open for people to approach God. The lampstand is a symbol of Christ, the Light of the world. Jesus Christ gives a clear light and open access into the presence of God.* **"Speak unto Aaron, and say unto him, When thou lightest the lamps, the seven lamps shall give light over against the candlestick" (Num.8:2).**	⇒ The way into God's presence can be clearly seen through Jesus Christ. In fact, the brightest light ever lived is the light of Christ that shows the way into God's presence. Through Christ, the way into God's presence has been lit so brightly that it is wide open. There is not a single barrier, not even the slightest shadow of a barrier, between man and God. Again, the most brightly lit light every created has been set ablaze by Christ Jesus, the Son of God Himself. He is the Light of the universe, giving light into God's presence.	***"In him was life; and the life was the light of men" (Jn.1:4).*** ***"Then spake Jesus again unto them, saying, I am the light of the world: he that followeth me shall not walk in darkness, but shall have the light of life" (Jn.8:12).*** ***"I am come a light into the world, that whosoever believeth on me should not abide in darkness" (Jn. 12:46).*** ***"For God, who commanded the light to shine out of darkness, hath shined in our hearts, to give the light of the knowledge of the glory of God in the face of Jesus Christ" (2 Cor.4:6).*** ***"And the city had no need of the sun, neither of the moon, to shine in it: for the glory of God did lighten it, and the Lamb is the light thereof" (Rev.21:23).***
12 Loaves of Showbread Num.8:1-4	*The light of the lampstand focused upon the 12 loaves of showbread, a symbol of the 12 tribes of Israel (God's people).* **And upon the table of showbread they shall spread a cloth of blue, and put thereon the dishes, and the spoons, and the bowls, and covers to cover withal: and the continual bread shall be thereon: Numbers 4:7**	⇒ The light of God's presence shines upon the true believer. God gives light to His people: His love, care, provision, direction, guidance, knowledge, wisdom. God's light gives whatever is necessary to overcome the pitfalls and enemies of this life.	***"The LORD hath been mindful of us: he will bless us; he will bless the house of Israel; he will bless the house of Aaron" (Ps.115:12).*** ***"Fear thou not; for I am with thee: be not dismayed; for I am thy God: I will strengthen thee; yea, I will help thee; yea, I will uphold thee with the right hand of my righteousness" (Is. 41:10).*** ***"(For after all these things do the Gentiles seek:) for your heavenly Father***

Historical Term	Type or Picture (Scriptural Basis for Each)	Life Application for Today's Believer	Biblical Application
			knoweth that ye have need of all these things" (Mt.6:32). ***"But even the very hairs of your head are all numbered. Fear not therefore: ye are of more value than many sparrows" (Lk. 12:7).*** ***"Casting all your care upon him; for he careth for you" (1 Pt. 5:7).***
The Dedication of the Levites Num.8:5-26	*The dedication of the Levites is a picture of laypersons being set apart to God, to His service.* *There is a sharp distinction between the Levites and the priests, a distinction that stresses the difference between a layperson who serves as an assistant and the priest or minister of God.* *The Expositor's Bible Commentary points out these differences:* *"The Priests were made holy, the Levites clean; the priests were anointed and washed, the Levites sprinkled; the priests were given new garments, the Levites washed theirs; blood was applied to the priests, it was waved over the Levites."*[2] **"This *is it* that *belongeth* unto the Levites: from twenty and five years old and upward they shall go in to wait upon the service of the tabernacle of the congregation" (Num.8:24).**	⇒ Each believer, each layperson, has been given the glorious privilege... • of being given a very special task upon earth. • of being given purpose and meaning and significance in life. • of being given a very special gift or gifts to fulfill his task on earth.	***"And now, Israel, what doth the Lord thy God require of thee, but to fear the Lord thy God, to walk in all his ways, and to love him, and to serve the Lord thy God with all thy heart and with all thy soul" (Dt. 10:12).*** ***"For we are labourers together with God: ye are God's husbandry, ye are God's building" (1 Cor. 3:9).*** ***"With good will doing service, as to the Lord, and not to men" (Eph. 6:7).*** ***"So being affectionately desirous of you, we were willing to have imparted unto you, not the gospel of God only, but also our own souls, because ye were dear unto us" (1 Th. 2:8).*** ***"Wherefore we receiving a kingdom which cannot be moved, let us have grace, whereby we may serve God acceptably with reverence and godly fear" (Heb.12:28).***
The Levites Had to Be Sprinkled with the Water of Cleansing, Shave Their Whole Heads, and Wash Their Clothes Num.8:5-26	*This was a symbol of being spiritually cleansed or purified from sin.* **"Take the Levites from among the children of Israel, and cleanse them. And thus shalt thou do unto them, to cleanse them: Sprinkle water of purifying upon them, and let them shave all their flesh, and let them wash their clothes, and *so* make themselves clean" (Num.8:6-7).**	⇒ No person can cleanse himself, not spiritually, not from sin. Only God's mediator, Jesus Christ, can wash and cleanse a person spiritually. This He does through the blood of His cross.	***"And now why tarriest thou? arise, and be baptized, and wash away thy sins, calling on the name of the Lord" (Acts 22:16).*** ***"In whom we have redemption through his blood, the forgiveness of sins, according to the riches of his grace" (Eph.1:7).*** ***"How much more shall the blood of Christ, who through the eternal Spirit offered himself without spot to God, purge your conscience from dead works to serve the living God?" (Heb.9:14).***

2 *The Expositor's Bible Commentary*. Frank E. Gaebelein, Editor, p.766.

1. The provision of the Passover: A symbol of God's great deliverance
- a. God's command to keep the Passover: Given in the 1st month of the 2nd year
  - 1) To be celebrated at the appointed time: At twilight of the 1st month, the 14th day
  - 2) To be careful—follow all the rules governing the Passover
  - 3) The obedience: Moses & the people did everything exactly as the LORD commanded
- b. God's compassion & grace—a very special provision for the unclean & the traveler
  - 1) The problem: Some persons were unable to celebrate the Passover because they had been in touch with a dead body & were counted unclean (ceremonially, spiritually)
    - They wanted to participate, so they approached Moses
    - Moses told them to wait until he could seek the LORD's will
  - 2) The compassion & grace of God—a very special provision was made for the unclean & for the person away on a journey
    - They may celebrate the Passover one month later (after they are declared cleansed)
    - They must be careful to follow all the regulations: To eat the lamb with unleavened bread & bitter herbs, not leaving any of it until morning nor breaking any of its bones
- c. God's strong warning: The Passover is of critical importance—a person must keep it (a picture of the importance of the LORD's Supper)
  - 1) The person who deliberately failed to keep it: To be cut off
  - 2) The person will suffer God's judgment
- d. God's open invitation to all, to the alien or foreigner
  - 1) The open door: Any person could observe the Passover
  - 2) The one restriction: He must be a believer (Ex.12:48) & observe the Passover as instructed

2. The provision of the fiery cloud: A symbol of God's presence & guidance[DS1]
- a. The cloud came down & hovered above the Tabernacle
- b. The cloud changed into a fiery cloud at night—so the people could continue to see it: Symbolized the continued, unbroken presence & guidance of God
- c. The cloud guided the Israelites
  - 1) If it lifted & moved, the people followed
  - 2) If it settled, the people camped
- d. The cloud was one of the ways the LORD commanded or spoke to His people: At His command, they would either set out or stop & camp
  - 1) If the cloud stayed over the Tabernacle, God was commanding His people to remain in camp
    - Sometimes for long periods of time
    - Sometimes for only a few days
    - Sometimes for only

H. The Three Special Provisions of God: God's Great Deliverance, His Guidance, & His Call to Arise & Follow Him, 9:1-10:10

And the LORD spake unto
Moses in the wilderness of
Sinai, in the first month of
the second year after they
were come out of the land of
Egypt, saying,
2 Let the children of Israel
also keep the passover at his
appointed season.
3 In the fourteenth day of
this month, at even, ye shall
keep it in his appointed season: according to all the rites
of it, and according to all the
ceremonies thereof, shall ye
keep it.
4 And Moses spake unto the
children of Israel, that they
should keep the passover.
5 And they kept the passover
on the fourteenth day of the
first month at even in the
wilderness of Sinai: according to all that the LORD commanded Moses, so did the
children of Israel.
6 And there were certain
men, who were defiled by
the dead body of a man, that
they could not keep the
passover on that day: and
they came before Moses and
before Aaron on that day:
7 And those men said unto
him, We are defiled by the
dead body of a man: wherefore are we kept back, that
we may not offer an offering
of the LORD in his appointed
season among the children of
Israel?
8 And Moses said unto them,
Stand still, and I will hear
what the LORD will com-
mand concerning you.
9 And the LORD spake unto
Moses, saying,
10 Speak unto the children
of Israel, saying, If any man
of you or of your posterity
shall be unclean by reason of
a dead body, or be in a journey afar off, yet he shall
keep the passover unto the
LORD.
11 The fourteenth day of the
second month at even they
shall keep it, and eat it with
unleavened bread and bitter
herbs.
12 They shall leave none of
it unto the morning, nor
break any bone of it: according to all the ordinances of
the passover they shall keep
it.
13 But the man that is clean,
and is not in a journey, and
forbeareth to keep the
passover, even the same soul
shall be cut off from among
his people: because he
brought not the offering of
the LORD in his appointed
season, that man shall bear
his sin.
14 And if a stranger shall
sojourn among you, and will
keep the passover unto the
LORD; according to the ordinance of the passover, and
according to the manner
thereof, so shall he do: ye
shall have one ordinance,
both for the stranger, and for
him that was born in the
land.
15 And on the day that the
tabernacle was reared up the
cloud covered the tabernacle, namely, the tent of the
testimony: and at even there
was upon the tabernacle as it
were the appearance of fire,
until the morning.
16 So it was alway: the
cloud covered it by day, and
the appearance of fire by
night.
17 And when the cloud was
taken up from the tabernacle,
then after that the children of
Israel journeyed: and in the
place where the cloud abode,
there the children of Israel
pitched their tents.
18 At the commandment of
the LORD the children of
Israel journeyed, and at the
commandment of the LORD
they pitched: as long as the
cloud abode upon the tabernacle they rested in their
tents.
19 And when the cloud tarried long upon the tabernacle
many days, then the children
of Israel kept the charge of
the LORD, and journeyed
not.
20 And so it was, when the
cloud was a few days upon
the tabernacle; according to
the commandment of the
LORD they abode in their
tents, and according to the
commandment of the LORD
they journeyed.
21 And so it was, when the

one night
2) If the cloud lifted by day or by night, they followed
3) If the cloud stayed above the Tabernacle for two days or one month or one year, they stayed & did not move; but if it lifted, they followed
4) The people obeyed the LORD's command
- Obeyed God's command to camp or travel
- Obeyed God's Word—the movement of the cloud—when instructed by Moses, God's servant

3. The provision of two silver trumpets: A symbol of God's call to arise & follow Him
a. The command to fashion the trumpets of hammered silver
b. The three general purposes for the trumpets
1) To call the whole community of believers together (blew both trumpets)
2) To call only the leaders

cloud abode from even unto
the morning, and that the
cloud was taken up in the
morning, then they jour-
neyed: whether it was by day
or by night that the cloud
was taken up, they jour-
neyed.
22 Or whether it were two
days, or a month, or a year,
that the cloud tarried upon
the tabernacle, remaining
thereon, the children of
Israel abode in their tents,
and journeyed not: but when
it was taken up, they journeyed.
23 At the commandment of
the LORD they rested in the
tents, and at the commandment of the LORD they journeyed: they kept the charge
of the LORD, at the com-
mandment of the LORD by
the hand of Moses.

CHAPTER 10

And the LORD spake unto
Moses, saying,
2 Make thee two trumpets of
silver; of a whole piece shalt
thou make them: that thou
mayest use them for the calling of the assembly, and for
the journeying of the camps.
3 And when they shall blow
with them, all the assembly
shall assemble themselves to
thee at the door of the tabernacle of the congregation.
4 And if they blow but with
one trumpet, then the
princes, which are heads of
the thousands of Israel, shall
gather themselves unto thee.
5 When ye blow an alarm,
then the camps that lie on the
east parts shall go forward.
6 When ye blow an alarm the
second time, then the camps
that lie on the south side
shall take their journey: they
shall blow an alarm for their
journeys.
7 But when the congregation
is to be gathered together, ye
shall blow, but ye shall not
sound an alarm.
8 And the sons of Aaron, the
priests, shall blow with the
trumpets; and they shall be
to you for an ordinance for
ever throughout your generations.
9 And if ye go to war in your
land against the enemy that
oppresseth you, then ye shall
blow an alarm with the trumpets; and ye shall be remembered before the LORD your
God, and ye shall be saved
from your enemies.
10 Also in the day of your
gladness, and in your solemn
days, and in the beginnings
of your months, ye shall
blow with the trumpets over
your burnt offerings, and
over the sacrifices of your
peace offerings; that they
may be to you for a memorial before your God: I am the
LORD your God.

together (blew only one trumpet)
3) To signal the tribes when to begin marching
- One blast signaled the tribes on the east to march
- Another blast signaled the tribes on the south to march
- The point: A different signal or blast was to be used for each purpose

c. The only persons allowed to blow the trumpets—the priests, the true sons of Aaron: This was to be a permanent law for all generations
d. The three very special purposes for the trumpets
1) To sound the alarm for war
2) To sound the alarm for prayer: For God to remember, rescue, & deliver His people
3) To blow in times of joy & rejoicing—at the appointed feasts & New Moon festivals
- To sound over the Burnt Offerings & Fellowship or Peace Offerings
- To be a memorial, a reminder of God's covenant

DIVISION I

THE PREPARATION FOR THE MARCH TO THE PROMISED LAND, 1:1-10:36

H. The Three Special Provisions of God—the Passover, the Fiery Cloud and the Silver Trumpets: Acknowledging God's Great Deliverance, His Guidance, and His Call to Arise and Follow Him, 9:1-10:10

(9:1-10:10) **Introduction—Deliverance, from Enemies—Guidance, of God—Challenge, Need For**: three of the greatest needs people have are the need for deliverance, for guidance, and for a strong challenge. Why do we need deliverance? Because we are enslaved by the enemies of this life, enemies such as…

- cancer
- heart disease
- diabetes
- other diseases
- drugs
- alcohol
- immorality
- pornography
- sin
- greed
- anger
- malice
- death

In addition to deliverance, people need guidance throughout life as they confront the pitfalls and enemies of this life. Decisions often have to be made, decisions that arouse a desire for some guidance that will tell us what to do. But not only do people need deliverance and guidance, they also need a strong challenge in order to give them fulfillment throughout life. People need a sense of purpose, meaning, and significance throughout life. They need to have a sense of satisfaction and fulfillment, a sense that they are accomplishing something in life, making a contribution to loved ones and to society.

What is needed is the very special provision of God Himself. God provides deliverance. He wants to deliver us from the enslavements of this life, deliver us from sin and death to live eternally in the promised land of heaven. But this is not all:

God wants to guide us in every decision and step we take day by day. God wants us to have the security and assurance that we are making the right decisions and taking the right steps throughout life. But even this is not all: God wants to challenge us, to give us the greatest challenge that could possibly be given in life. God wants to extend a call to us, a call to arise and follow Him—for He has the greatest purpose, the most meaningful and significant call in all of life. This is the subject of this great passage: *The Three Special Provisions of God—the Passover, the Fiery Cloud, and the Silver Trumpets: Acknowledging God's Great Deliverance, His Guidance, and His Call to Arise and Follow Him*, 9:1-10:10.

1. The provision of the Passover: to remember God's great deliverance (v.1-14).
2. The provision of the fiery cloud: a symbol of God's presence and guidance (v.15-23).
3. The provision of two silver trumpets: a symbol of God's call to arise and follow Him (ch.10:1-10).

1 (9:1-14) **Passover—LORD's Supper, Importance of—Salvation, Celebration of—Deliverance, Celebration of**: the first provision of God focused upon deliverance, the provision of the Passover. The Passover celebrated the great exodus from Egypt, God's great deliverance of His people from Egyptian slavery. Remember that Egypt is a symbol of the world with all its bondages and enslavements. The Passover was instituted by God to stir His people to remember their great deliverance from the slavery of Egypt (the world). Note the Scripture and outline:

OUTLINE	SCRIPTURE	SCRIPTURE	OUTLINE
1. The provision of the Passover: A symbol of God's great deliverance a. God's command to keep the Passover: Given in the 1st month of the 2nd year 1) To be celebrated at the appointed time: At twilight of the 1st month, the 14th day 2) To be careful—follow all the rules governing the Passover 3) The obedience: Moses & the people did everything exactly as the LORD commanded b. God's compassion & grace—a very special provision for the unclean & the traveler 1) The problem: Some persons were unable to celebrate the Passover because they had been in touch with a dead body & were counted unclean (ceremonially, spiritually) • They wanted to participate, so they approached Moses • Moses told them to wait until he could seek	And the LORD spake unto Moses in the wilderness of Sinai, in the first month of the second year after they were come out of the land of Egypt, saying, 2 Let the children of Israel also keep the passover at his appointed season. 3 In the fourteenth day of this month, at even, ye shall keep it in his appointed season: according to all the rites of it, and according to all the ceremonies thereof, shall ye keep it. 4 And Moses spake unto the children of Israel, that they should keep the passover. 5 And they kept the passover on the fourteenth day of the first month at even in the wilderness of Sinai: according to all that the LORD commanded Moses, so did the children of Israel. 6 And there were certain men, who were defiled by the dead body of a man, that they could not keep the passover on that day: and they came before Moses and before Aaron on that day: 7 And those men said unto him, We are defiled by the dead body of a man: wherefore are we kept back, that we may not offer an offering of the LORD in his appointed season among the children of Israel? 8 And Moses said unto them, Stand still, and I will	hear what the LORD will command concerning you. 9 And the LORD spake unto Moses, saying, 10 Speak unto the children of Israel, saying, If any man of you or of your posterity shall be unclean by reason of a dead body, or be in a journey afar off, yet he shall keep the passover unto the LORD. 11 The fourteenth day of the second month at even they shall keep it, and eat it with unleavened bread and bitter herbs. 12 They shall leave none of it unto the morning, nor break any bone of it: according to all the ordinances of the passover they shall keep it. 13 But the man that is clean, and is not in a journey, and forbeareth to keep the passover, even the same soul shall be cut off from among his people: because he brought not the offering of the LORD in his appointed season, that man shall bear his sin. 14 And if a stranger shall sojourn among you, and will keep the passover unto the LORD; according to the ordinance of the passover, and according to the manner thereof, so shall he do: ye shall have one ordinance, both for the stranger, and for him that was born in the land.	the LORD's will 2) The compassion & grace of God—a very special provision was made for the unclean & for the person away on a journey • They may celebrate the Passover one month later (after they are declared cleansed) • They must be careful to follow all the regulations: To eat the lamb with unleavened bread & bitter herbs, not leaving any of it until morning nor breaking any of its bones c. God's strong warning: The Passover is of critical importance—a person must keep it (a picture of the importance of the LORD's Supper) 1) The person who deliberately failed to keep it: To be cut off 2) The person will suffer God's judgment d. God's open invitation to all, to the alien or foreigner 1) The open door: Any person could observe the Passover 2) The one restriction: He must be a believer (Ex.12:48) & observe the Passover as instructed

1. God Himself commanded His people to keep the Passover (v.1-5). It had been one year since God's people had left Egypt, one year since they had celebrated the first Passover. At that time, back in Egypt, God had commanded His people to keep the Passover and to do so every year thereafter. He had established the feast to be a memorial, an annual celebration to remember their great deliverance from Egyptian slavery (Ex.12:2-3, 14). Why, then, was God now having to remind His people to celebrate the Passover? Were the people going to remember—going to take the initiative on their own—to

celebrate the feast? Or were the people careless? Lax? Negligent? Indifferent? Failing? Scripture does not say: it simply says that God once again commanded His people to keep the Passover, the commemoration of their great deliverance from Egyptian slavery.

a. The people were to celebrate the Passover at the appointed time: at twilight of the first month, the fourteenth day (v.2-3).

b. The people were to be careful: make sure that they followed all the rules governing the Passover (v.3).

c. Note the obedience of Moses and the people: they did everything exactly as the LORD commanded. They kept the Passover (v.4-5).

2. God showed great compassion and grace in the Passover: He made a very special provision for the unclean and the traveler (v.6-12).

a. A very special problem arose at this particular Passover. Some persons were unable to celebrate the Feast because they had been in contact with a dead body and were counted unclean (ceremonially, spiritually unclean). Death is the result of sin, a symbol of corruption and decay. Therefore to illustrate this truth, a person who came in contact with death was counted spiritually unclean. The ceremonial laws of uncleanness stressed the importance of being spiritually clean, the importance of having one's sins forgiven.

These persons wanted to participate in the Passover, so they approached Moses. Moses simply told them to wait until he could seek the LORD's will (v.8).

b. Note the compassion and grace of God: a very special provision was made for the unclean and for the person away on a journey (v.9-12). These persons could celebrate one month later, after they had been declared cleansed. However, they had to be careful to follow all the regulations: to eat the lamb with unleavened bread and bitter herbs, not leaving any of it until morning nor breaking any of its bones (v.12).

3. God issued a strong warning: the Passover was of critical importance. A person must keep it (v.13). This is a picture of the importance of the LORD's Supper. God declared that any person who deliberately failed to keep the Passover was to be cut off. A person will suffer God's judgment. As Gordon J. Wenham points out: "This is a threat of death by the hand of God and of eternal judgment."[1]

4. God extended an open invitation to all, to the alien or foreigner as well as to the native-born (v.14). There was an open door for any person to celebrate the Passover, as long as the person had become a true believer and member of His people. There was only one condition for any person—any foreigner or any native-born—to become a member of God's people: that condition was faith in God, believing and following God exactly as He dictated, approaching Him for the atonement (reconciliation) and forgiveness of sin through the blood of the sacrifice. This was the very purpose for the Abrahamic covenant, to bless all the people and nations of the world (Gen.12:1-3). Therefore, any person who came to God through the blood of the Passover Lamb was acceptable to God.

Thought 1. There are four significant lessons for us in this passage.

1) Jesus Christ is the true Passover Lamb, the Lamb of God who takes away the sin of the world.

"The next day John seeth Jesus coming unto him, and saith, Behold the Lamb of God, which taketh away the sin of the world" (Jn.1:29).

"Purge out therefore the old leaven, that ye may be a new lump, as ye are unleavened. For even Christ our passover is sacrificed for us" (1 Cor.5:7).

"Forasmuch as ye know that ye were not redeemed with corruptible things, as silver and gold, from your vain conversation received by tradition from your fathers; But with the precious blood of Christ, as of a lamb without blemish and without spot: " (1 Pt.1:18-19).

"But he was wounded for our transgressions, he was bruised for our iniquities: the chastisement of our peace was upon him; and with his stripes we are healed. He was oppressed, and he was afflicted, yet he opened not his mouth: he is brought as a lamb to the slaughter, and as a sheep before her shearers is dumb, so he openeth not his mouth" (Is.53:5, 7).

2) God commanded His people in the Old Testament to acknowledge His great deliverance through celebrating the Passover. God commands us to acknowledge His great deliverance by Christ through celebrating the LORD's Supper.

"And as they were eating, Jesus took bread, and blessed it, and brake it, and gave it to the disciples, and said, Take, eat; this is my body. And he took the cup, and gave thanks, and gave it to them, saying, Drink ye all of it; For this is my blood of the new testament, which is shed for many for the remission of sins" (Mt.26:26-28; cp. Mk.14:22-24; Lk.22:19-20).

"For I have received of the Lord that which also I delivered unto you, That the Lord Jesus the same night in which he was betrayed took bread: And when he had given thanks, he brake it, and said, Take, eat: this is my body, which is broken for you: this do in remembrance of me. After the same manner also he took the cup, when he had supped, saying, This cup is the new testament in my blood: this do ye, as oft as ye drink it, in remembrance of me. For as often as ye eat this bread, and drink this cup, ye do show the Lord's death till he come" (1 Cor.11:23-26).

3) God issues a strong warning about the LORD's Supper; the LORD's Supper is of critical importance to Him: a person must not approach nor partake of the LORD's Supper in an unworthy manner. If he does, he brings judgment upon himself. This is exactly what Scripture declares:

"For he that eateth and drinketh unworthily, eateth and drinketh damnation to himself, not discerning the Lord's body. For this cause many are weak and sickly among you, and many sleep" (1 Cor.11:29-30).

---

1 Gordon J. Wenham. *The Book of Numbers*, p.99

4) God extends an invitation to every person to celebrate the LORD's Supper. There is only one condition: believing God, approaching Him for the atonement (reconciliation) and forgiveness of sin through the shed blood of Christ. God opens the door into His presence for any person to be saved and delivered from sin—through the sacrifice of His Son. There is an open invitation to all.

"Come unto me, all ye that labour and are heavy laden, and I will give you rest" (Mt.11:28).

"In the last day, that great day of the feast, Jesus stood and cried, saying, If any man thirst, let him come unto me, and drink" (Jn.7:37).

"For I delivered unto you first of all that which I also received, how that Christ died for our sins according to the scriptures; And that he was buried, and that he rose again the third day according to the scriptures" (1 Cor.15:3-4).

"Who will have all men to be saved, and to come unto the knowledge of the truth. For there is one God, and one mediator between God and men, the man Christ Jesus; Who gave himself a ransom for all, to be testified in due time" (1 Tim.2:4-6).

"But we see Jesus, who was made a little lower than the angels for the suffering of death, crowned with glory and honour; that he by the grace of God should taste death for every man" (Heb.2:9).

"Come now, and let us reason together, saith the Lord: though your sins be as scarlet, they shall be as white as snow; though they be red like crimson, they shall be as wool" (Is.1:18).

"Look unto me, and be ye saved, all the ends of the earth: for I am God, and there is none else" (Is.45:22).

2 (9:15-23) **Cloud, Pillar of—Guidance, of God—God, Guidance of**: there was the provision of the fiery cloud, that is, the cloud that guided God's people throughout their wilderness wanderings. The cloud was a striking symbol of God's presence and guidance. Note the Scripture and outline:

OUTLINE	SCRIPTURE	SCRIPTURE	OUTLINE
2. The provision of the fiery cloud: A symbol of God's presence & guidance a. The cloud came down & hovered above the Tabernacle b. The cloud changed into a fiery cloud at night—so the people could continue to see it: Symbolized the continued, unbroken presence & guidance of God c. The cloud guided the Israelites 1) If it lifted & moved, the people followed 2) If it settled, the people camped d. The cloud was one of the ways the LORD commanded or spoke to His people: At His command, they would either set out or stop & camp 1) If the cloud stayed over the Tabernacle, God was commanding His people to remain in camp • Sometimes for long periods of time • Sometimes for only a	15 And on the day that the tabernacle was reared up the cloud covered the taberna- cle, namely, the tent of the testimony: and at even there was upon the tabernacle as it were the appearance of fire, until the morning. 16 So it was alway: the cloud covered it by day, and the appearance of fire by night. 17 And when the cloud was taken up from the taberna- cle, then after that the chil- dren of Israel journeyed: and in the place where the cloud abode, there the children of Israel pitched their tents. 18 At the commandment of the LORD the children of Israel journeyed, and at the commandment of the LORD they pitched: as long as the cloud abode upon the taber- nacle they rested in their tents. 19 And when the cloud tar- ried long upon the taberna- cle many days, then the chil- dren of Israel kept the charge of the LORD, and journeyed not. 20 And so it was, when the	cloud was a few days upon the tabernacle; according to the commandment of the LORD they abode in their tents, and according to the commandment of the LORD they journeyed. 21 And so it was, when the cloud abode from even unto the morning, and that the cloud was taken up in the morning, then they jour- neyed: whether it was by day or by night that the cloud was taken up, they journeyed. 22 Or whether it were two days, or a month, or a year, that the cloud tarried upon the tabernacle, remaining thereon, the children of Israel abode in their tents, and journeyed not: but when it was taken up, they jour- neyed. 23 At the commandment of the LORD they rested in the tents, and at the com- mandment of the LORD they journeyed: they kept the charge of the LORD, at the commandment of the LORD by the hand of Moses.	few days • Sometimes for only one night 2) If the cloud lifted by day or by night, they followed 3) If the cloud stayed above the Tabernacle for two days or one month or one year, they stayed & did not move; but if it lifted, they followed 4) The people obeyed the LORD's command • Obeyed God's command to camp or travel • Obeyed God's Word—the movement of the cloud—when instructed by Moses, God's servant

1. The cloud came down and hovered above the Tabernacle right after the Tabernacle's dedication (see outline and note—Ex.40:34-38 for more discussion).

2. The cloud changed its appearance at night, changed into a fiery cloud so the people could continue to see it. This symbolized the continued, unbroken presence and guidance of God (v.15-16). Hovering above the Tabernacle by day and turning into a blazing fire by night—the cloud must have been a striking, awesome sight. Obviously, it gave a great sense of assurance, confidence, comfort, and security. The people knew beyond any question that God was present with them, there to guide and protect them by day and by night.

3. The cloud guided the Israelites (v.17). If it lifted and moved, the people followed. If it settled, the people camped.
4. Note the clear statement of this point: the cloud was one of the ways the LORD commanded His people—one of the ways He spoke to His people. At His command, that is, as the cloud moved, the people would either set out or stop and camp (v.18)-23).

a. If the cloud stayed over the Tabernacle, God was commanding His people to remain in the camp (v.18-21). Sometimes they remained in camp for long periods of time; sometimes they stayed for only a few days; and sometimes they remained for only one night. Simply stated, the cloud was one of the ways God used to speak to His people and guide them to the promised land.
b. If the cloud lifted by day or by night, they followed (v.21).
c. If the cloud stayed above the Tabernacle for two days or one month or one year, the people stayed and did not move. But if the cloud lifted, they followed it (v.22).
d. The people obeyed the LORD's command by the movement of the cloud (v.23). They obeyed God's command to camp or travel as He willed. They obeyed God's Word—the movement of the cloud—when instructed by Moses, God's servant.

Thought 1. The fiery cloud was a striking, awesome picture of God's presence and guidance.

1) God is present with His people, always present. God never leaves the side of a person who truly believes in Him. God is always with us in an unbroken fellowship until we reach the promised land of heaven. His presence walks with us day by day.

"For where two or three are gathered together in my name, there am I in the midst of them" (Mt.18:20).

"Lo, I am with you alway, even unto the end of the world. Amen" (Mt.28:20).

"And, behold, I am with thee, and will keep thee in all places whither thou goest, and will bring thee again into this land; for I will not leave thee, until I have done that which I have spoken to thee of" (Gen.28:15).

"And he said, My presence shall go with thee, and I will give thee rest" (Ex.33:14).

"When thou goest out to battle against thine enemies, and seest horses, and chariots, and a people more than thou, be not afraid of them: for the Lord thy God is with thee, which brought thee up out of the land of Egypt" (Dt.20:1).

"When thou passest through the waters, I will be with thee; and through the rivers, they shall not overflow thee: when thou walkest through the fire, thou shalt not be burned; neither shall the flame kindle upon thee" (Is.43:2).

2) God guides His people, always guides us. If a person truly believes and follows God, God guides his every step day by day. God guides us every step of the way as we march to the promised land of heaven.

"Howbeit when he, the Spirit of truth, is come, he will guide you into all truth: for he shall not speak of himself; but whatsoever he shall hear, that shall he speak: and he will show you things to come" (Jn.16:13).

"He maketh me to lie down in green pastures: he leadeth me beside the still waters" (Ps.23:2).

"The meek will he guide in judgment: and the meek will he teach his way" (Ps.25:9).

"For this God is our God for ever and ever: he will be our guide even unto death" (Ps.48:14).

"Thou shalt guide me with thy counsel, and afterward receive me to glory" (Ps.73:24).

"And thine ears shall hear a word behind thee, saying, This is the way, walk ye in it, when ye turn to the right hand, and when ye turn to the left" (Is.30:21).

DEEPER STUDY # 1

(9:15-23) **God, Presence of—Glory, of God—Pillar of Cloud—Cloud, Pillar of—Shekinah Glory**: the cloud of God's presence hovered, settled, rested, dwelt above the Tabernacle. The Hebrew word is *shakan* or *sakan*. This was the Shekinah Glory, the very glory of God dwelling in the midst of His people. The Shekinah Glory was the cloud that symbolized God's holy presence. It was the very cloud that had guided Israel out of Egypt and that was to rest upon the Tabernacle as long as His people remained totally obedient to Him (Ex.40:34-38). The Shekinah Glory also rested above the Mercy Seat in the Most Holy Place of the Tabernacle. Scripture describes the Shekinah Glory of the LORD as follows:

1. The glory of the Lord is like a consuming fire.

"And the sight of the glory of the LORD was like devouring fire on the top of the mount in the eyes of the children of Israel" (Ex.24:17).

2. The glory of the Lord is like a pillar of fire that radiates light.

"And the LORD went before them by day in a pillar of a cloud, to lead them the way; and by night in a pillar of fire, to give them light; to go by day and night: He took not away the pillar of the cloud by day, nor the pillar of fire by night, from before the people" (Ex.13:21-22).

3. The glory of the Lord is like a fiery furnace.

> **"For ye are not come unto the mount that might be touched, and that burned with fire, nor unto blackness, and darkness, and tempest....For our God is a consuming fire" (Heb.12:18, 29).**
>
> 4. The glory of the Lord is like a light that radiates splendor, a light that is so full of splendor that Peter called it "the excellent glory."
>
> **"For he received from God the Father honour and glory, when there came such a voice to him from the excellent glory, This is my beloved Son, in whom I am well pleased" (2 Pt.1:17).**
>
> 5. The glory of the Lord is a light so glorious and brilliant that there is no need for a sun.
>
> **"Having the glory of God: and her light was like unto a stone most precious, even like a jasper stone, clear as crystal....And the city had no need of the sun, neither of the moon, to shine in it: for the glory of God did lighten it, and the Lamb is the light thereof" (Rev.21:11, 23).**
>
> 6. The glory of the Lord is a light so brilliant that no man can approach it.
>
> **"Who only hath immortality, dwelling in the light which no man can approach unto; whom no man hath seen, nor can see: to whom be honour and power everlasting" (1 Tim.6:16).**

3 (10:1-10) **Provision, of God—God, Provision of—Trumpets, the Two Silver**: there was the provision of two silver trumpets, a symbol of God's call to arise and follow Him. The Israelites were just about ready to begin their great march to the promised land. One final thing remained: the making of two silver trumpets to control and coordinate the people as they marched through the wilderness to the promised land. Other trumpeters were, no doubt, strategically stationed throughout the tribal camps to pass the signal along to those on the outer edges. Keep in mind that there were at least two to three million Israelites camped around the Tabernacle. It was only natural that the two main trumpets stationed at the Tabernacle, the hub of activity, would be very special trumpets.

OUTLINE	SCRIPTURE	SCRIPTURE	OUTLINE
3. The provision of two silver trumpets: A symbol of God's call to arise & follow Him a. The command to fashion the trumpets of hammered silver b. The three general purposes for the trumpets 1) To call the whole community of believers together (blew both trumpets) 2) To call only the leaders together (blew only one trumpet) 3) To signal the tribes when to begin marching • One blast signaled the tribes on the east to march • Another blast signaled the tribes on the south to march • The point: A different	And the LORD spake unto Moses, saying, 2 Make thee two trumpets of silver; of a whole piece shalt thou make them: that thou mayest use them for the calling of the assembly, and for the journeying of the camps. 3 And when they shall blow with them, all the assembly shall assemble themselves to thee at the door of the tabernacle of the congregation. 4 And if they blow but with one trumpet, then the princes, which are heads of the thousands of Israel, shall gather themselves unto thee. 5 When ye blow an alarm, then the camps that lie on the east parts shall go forward. 6 When ye blow an alarm the second time, then the camps that lie on the south side shall take their journey: they shall blow an alarm for their journeys. 7 But when the congregation	is to be gathered together, ye shall blow, but ye shall not sound an alarm. 8 And the sons of Aaron, the priests, shall blow with the trumpets; and they shall be to you for an ordinance for ever throughout your generations. 9 And if ye go to war in your land against the enemy that oppresseth you, then ye shall blow an alarm with the trumpets; and ye shall be remembered before the LORD your God, and ye shall be saved from your enemies. 10 Also in the day of your gladness, and in your solemn days, and in the beginnings of your months, ye shall blow with the trumpets over your burnt offerings, and over the sacrifices of your peace offerings; that they may be to you for a memorial before your God: I am the LORD your God.	signal or blast was to be used for each purpose c. The only persons allowed to blow the trumpets—the priests, the true sons of Aaron: This was to be a permanent law for all generations d. The three very special purposes for the trumpets 1) To sound the alarm for war 2) To sound the alarm for prayer: For God to remember, rescue, & deliver His people 3) To blow in times of joy & rejoicing—at the appointed feasts & New Moon festivals • To sound over the Burnt Offerings & Fellowship or Peace Offerings • To be a memorial, a reminder of God's covenant

1. God Himself gave the command to fashion the trumpets. They were to be made of hammered silver (v.2). No one knows exactly how they were shaped; but it is generally felt they were long, straight pipes, with a flared opening at the end. They could be blown to make different sounds or signals.

2. There were three *general purposes* for the trumpets (v.3-7).
   a. The trumpets were used to call the whole community of believers for general assemblies. Note that both trumpets were blown to call the people together.

b. The trumpets were used to call only the leaders together. Only one trumpet was used to signal the leaders (v.4).
c. The trumpets were used to signal the tribes when to begin marching (v.5-7). Note that one blast signaled the tribes on the east to march; another blast signaled the tribes on the south to march. That is, a different signal or blast was used for each purpose.

3. Note that the only persons allowed to blow the trumpets were the priests, the true sons of Aaron. This was to be a permanent law for all generations (v.8).

4. There were three very *special purposes* for the trumpets (v.9-10). Keep in mind that we have already looked at three *general purposes*; now, Scripture gives three very *special purposes* for the trumpets.

a. The trumpets were to sound the alarm for war (v.9). Both trumpets were to be used to sound forth the battle cry for mobilization against an enemy.
b. The trumpets were to sound the alarm for prayer: this is a picture of prayer arousing God to remember, rescue, and deliver His people.
c. The trumpets were used to blow in times of joy and rejoicing—at the appointed feasts and New Moon festival (v.10). The trumpets were to be sounded over the Burnt Offerings and the Fellowship or Peace Offerings. They were to be a memorial, a reminder of God's covenant with His people and their covenant with Him.

Note the strong declaration: "I am the LORD your God." God is declaring that He is the Sovereign, Omnipotent, Omniscient LORD God of the universe. He is the only living and true God with the power to rescue and deliver His people. Therefore they must sound the trumpet alarm for prayer: for Him to arouse Himself and act in behalf of His people—rescuing and delivering them from their enemies.

Thought 1. The trumpets were a picture of God calling His people to arise and follow Him. So it is with us. God calls us to arise and follow Him to the promised land of God, to heaven itself.

"Then spake Jesus again unto them, saying, I am the light of the world: he that followeth me shall not walk in darkness, but shall have the light of life" (Jn.8:12).

"My sheep hear my voice, and I know them, and they follow me" (Jn.10:27).

"If any man serve me, let him follow me; and where I am, there shall also my servant be: if any man serve me, him will my Father honour" (Jn.12:26).

"(For we walk [follow] by faith, not by sight)" (2 Cor.5:7).

"This I say then, Walk in the Spirit, and ye shall not fulfil the lust of the flesh" (Gal.5:16).

"I therefore, the prisoner of the Lord, beseech you that ye walk worthy of the vocation wherewith ye are called" (Eph.4:1).

"And walk in love, as Christ also hath loved us, and hath given himself for us an offering and a sacrifice to God for a sweetsmelling savour" (Eph.5:2).

"See then that ye walk circumspectly, not as fools, but as wise" (Eph.5:15).

"As ye have therefore received Christ Jesus the Lord, so walk ye in him" (Col.2:6).

"For even hereunto were ye called: because Christ also suffered for us, leaving us an example, that ye should follow his steps" (1 Pt.2:21).

"But if we walk in the light, as he is in the light, we have fellowship one with another, and the blood of Jesus Christ his Son cleanseth us from all sin" (1 Jn.1:7).

Thought 2. What a strong exhortation for believers today: to sound the alarm for prayer, to cry out to God for Him to rescue and deliver us from the pitfalls and enemies of life.

"Ask, and it shall be given you; seek, and ye shall find; knock, and it shall be opened unto you" (Mt.7:7).

"Watch and pray, that ye enter not into temptation: the spirit indeed is willing, but the flesh is weak" (Mt.26:41).

"And he spake a parable unto them to this end, that men ought always to pray, and not to faint" (Lk.18:1).

"If ye abide in me, and my words abide in you, ye shall ask what ye will, and it shall be done unto you" (Jn.15:7).

"Praying always with all prayer and supplication in the Spirit, and watching thereunto with all perseverance and supplication for all saints" (Eph.6:18).

"Pray without ceasing" (1 Th.5:17).

"But if from thence thou shalt seek the Lord thy God, thou shalt find him, if thou seek him with all thy heart and with all thy soul" (Dt.4:29).

"Seek the Lord and his strength, seek his face continually" (1 Chron.16:11).

"This poor man cried, and the Lord heard him, and saved him out of all his troubles" (Ps.34:6).

"From the end of the earth will I cry unto thee, when my heart is overwhelmed: lead me to the rock that is higher than I" (Ps.61:2).

"He shall call upon me, and I will answer him: I will be with him in trouble; I will deliver him, and honour him" (Ps.91:15).

"Then shalt thou call, and the Lord shall answer; thou shalt cry, and he shall say, Here I am. If thou take away from the midst of thee the yoke, the putting forth of the finger, and speaking vanity" (Is.58:9).

TYPES, SYMBOLS, AND PICTURES
(Numbers 9:1-10:10)

Historical Term	Type or Picture (Scriptural Basis for Each)	Life Application for Today's Believer	Biblical Application
The Passover Num.9:1-14 (See also Lev. 23:5)	*The Passover is a symbol of Christ our Passover who was sacrificed for us.* **"And Moses spake unto the children of Israel, that they should keep the passover. And they kept the passover on the fourteenth day of the first month at even in the wilderness of Sinai: according to all that the LORD commanded Moses, so did the children of Israel" (Num.9:4-5).**	⇒ The believer who lives and walks in Christ will be directed by God. 1. He will know God's purpose for his life (see all notes— Matthew 4:12-17). 2. He will know when to go forth to his task, when to carry out God's purpose for his life—just as Christ knew.	***"The next day John seeth Jesus coming unto him, and saith, Behold the Lamb of God, which taketh away the sin of the world" (Jn.1:29).*** ***"...For even Christ our passover is sacrificed for us" (1 Cor.5:7).*** ***"He was oppressed, and he was afflicted, yet he opened not his mouth: he is brought as a lamb to the slaughter, and as a sheep before her shearers is dumb, so he openeth not his mouth" (Is.53:7).***
Pillar of Cloud Num.9:15-23	*The pillar of cloud was a symbol of God's presence and guidance.* **"And *so* it was, when the cloud abode from even unto the morning, and *that* the cloud was taken up in the morning, then they journeyed: whether *it was* by day or by night that the cloud was taken up, they journeyed. Or *whether it were* two days, or a month, or a year, that the cloud tarried upon the tabernacle, remaining thereon, the children of Israel abode in their tents, and journeyed not: but when it was taken up, they journeyed" (Num.9:21-22).**	⇒ Jesus Christ is the perfect fulfillment of the Passover Lamb that was slain in behalf of God's people. Through the blood of Jesus Christ, a person escapes the judgment of God. God accepts the blood of His Son—the blood of the substitute sacrifice—as full payment for a person's sin and rebellion against God.	***"Who gave himself for our sins, that he might deliver us from this present evil world, according to the will of God and our Father" (Gal.1:4).*** ***"Howbeit when he, the Spirit of truth, is come, he will guide you into all truth: for he shall not speak of himself; but whatsoever he shall hear, that shall he speak: and he will show you things to come" (Jn. 16:13).*** ***"The meek will he guide in judgment: and the meek will he teach his way" (Ps.25:9).*** ***"For this God is our God for ever and ever: he will be our guide even unto death" (Ps.48:14).*** ***"Thou shalt guide me with thy counsel, and afterward receive me to glory" (Ps.73:24).*** ***"And thine ears shall hear a word behind thee, saying, This is the way, walk ye in it, when ye turn to the right hand, and when ye turn to the left" (Is.30:21).*** ***"And I will bring the blind by a way that they knew not; I will lead them in paths that they have not known: I will make darkness light before them, and crooked things straight. These things will I do unto them, and not forsake them" (Is.42:16).*** ***"Thus saith the LORD, thy Redeemer, the Holy One of Israel; I am the LORD thy God which teacheth thee to profit, which leadeth thee by the way that thou shouldest go" (Is.48:17).***

I. The Great March to the Promised Land Finally Begins: A Picture of the Believer Finally Beginning His March to the Promised Land of Heaven, 10:11-36

1. The great day to begin the march arrived: A picture of great hope for the promised land
- a. The date: The cloud lifted on the 20th day of the 2nd month (spent about 11 months at Mt. Sinai)
- b. The first part of the journey: Traveled from place to place until they reached the Desert of Paran

2. The great army of God's people marched forth division by division—as commanded: A picture of obeying God as one marches to the promised land
- a. First, the divisions of Judah led the march under their standard: Commanded by Nahshon
  - 1) The division of Issachar marched with Judah: Commanded by Nethanel
  - 2) The division of Zebulun marched with Judah: Commanded by Eliab
- b. Second, the Gershonites & the Merarites followed with the carts & oxen transporting the frame & curtains of the Tabernacle
- c. Third, the divisions of Reuben marched under their standard: Commanded by Elizur
  - 1) The division of Simeon marched with Reuben: Commanded by Shelumiel
  - 2) The division of Gad marched with Reuben: Commanded by Eliasaph
- d. Fourth, the Kohathites followed carrying the holy things of the Tabernacle: It was to be set up when they arrived
- e. Fifth, the divisions of Ephraim marched under their standard: Commanded by Elishama
  - 1) The division of Manasseh marched with Ephraim: Commanded by Gamaliel
  - 2) The division of Benjamin marched with Ephraim: Commanded by Abidan
- f. Finally, the divisions of Dan marched as the rear guard, under its standard: Commanded by Ahiezer
  - 1) The division of Asher marched with Dan: Commanded by Pagiel
  - 2) The division of Naphtali marched with Dan: Commanded by Ahira

3. The appeal of Moses to his brother-in-law to join the march to the promised land: A picture of reaching out to family members to follow after the promised land of God, the promise of heaven
- a. The brother-in-law rejected the appeal: His old life appealed to him
- b. The second appeal of Moses
  - 1) Challenged his brother-in-law to serve as a guide to the people of God
  - 2) Promised to share the good things of the LORD with him

4. The faithfulness of God in leading His people
- a. The first part of the journey lasted three days
- b. The ark of the covenant was carried out front, ahead of all the tribes: A symbol of the LORD's leadership step by step
- c. The fiery cloud of the LORD led them

5. The battle cry—the great

11 And it came to pass on
the twentieth day of the second month, in the second
year, that the cloud was
taken up from off the tabernacle of the testimony.
12 And the children of
Israel took their journeys out
of the wilderness of Sinai;
and the cloud rested in the
wilderness of Paran.
13 And they first took their
journey according to the
commandment of the LORD
by the hand of Moses.
14 In the first place went the
standard of the camp of the
children of Judah according
to their armies: and over his
host was Nahshon the son of
Amminadab.
15 And over the host of the
tribe of the children of
Issachar was Nethaneel the
son of Zuar.
16 And over the host of the
tribe of the children of
Zebulun was Eliab the son of
Helon.
17 And the tabernacle was
taken down; and the sons
of Gershon and the sons
of Merari set forward,
bearing the tabernacle.
18 And the standard of the
camp of Reuben set forward
according to their armies:
and over his host was Elizur
the son of Shedeur.
19 And over the host of the
tribe of the children of
Simeon was Shelumiel the
son of Zurishaddai.
20 And over the host of the
tribe of the children of Gad
was Eliasaph the son of
Deuel.
21 And the Kohathites set
forward, bearing the sanctuary: and the other did set up
the tabernacle against they
came.
22 And the standard of the
camp of the children of
Ephraim set forward according to their armies: and over
his host was Elishama the
son of Ammihud.
23 And over the host of the
tribe of the children of
Manasseh was Gamaliel the
son of Pedahzur.
24 And over the host of the
tribe of the children of
Benjamin was Abidan the
son of Gideoni.
25 And the standard of the
camp of the children of Dan
set forward, which was the
rereward of all the camps
throughout their hosts: and
over his host was Ahiezer
the son of Ammishaddai.
26 And over the host of the
tribe of the children of Asher
was Pagiel the son of Ocran.
27 And over the host of the
tribe of the children of
Naphtali was Ahira the son
of Enan.
28 Thus were the journey-
ings of the children of Israel
according to their armies,
when they set forward.
29 And Moses said unto
Hobab, the son of Raguel the
Midianite, Moses' father in
law, We are journeying unto
the place of which the LORD
said, I will give it you: come
thou with us, and we will do
thee good: for the LORD hath
spoken good concerning
Israel.
30 And he said unto him, I
will not go; but I will depart
to mine own land, and to my
kindred.
31 And he said, Leave us
not, I pray thee; forasmuch
as thou knowest how we are
to encamp in the wilderness,
and thou mayest be to us
instead of eyes.
32 And it shall be, if thou go
with us, yea, it shall be, that
what goodness the LORD
shall do unto us, the same
will we do unto thee.
33 And they departed from
the mount of the LORD three
days' journey: and the ark of
the covenant of the LORD
went before them in the three
days' journey, to search out a
resting place for them.
34 And the cloud of the
LORD was upon them by day,
when they went out of the
camp.
35 And it came to pass,

expectation & cry of Moses: Victory & rest a. When the ark set out: That God would give a victorious march	when the ark set forward, that Moses said, Rise up, LORD, and let thine enemies be scattered; and let them that hate thee flee before	thee. 36 And when it rested, he said, Return, O LORD, unto the many thousands of Israel.	b. When the ark was set down: That God would come among His people & give them rest—both physical & spiritual rest

DIVISION I

THE PREPARATION FOR THE MARCH TO THE PROMISED LAND, 1:1-10:36

I. The Great March to the Promised Land Finally Begins: A Picture of the Believer Finally Beginning His March to the Promised Land of Heaven, 10:11-36

(10:11-36) **Introduction—Destiny, of Man—Destiny, of the World—Promised Land, Hope For—Future, Destiny of**: What is the destiny of man? More technological and scientific and medical advances? No doubt, this will be true and will come to pass. Will there be pure air and pure water to drink? Will there be plenty of food for all the people of the earth? Some authorities say this is questionable. Pollution could contaminate the water we drink and the air we breathe. Greed and selfishness and war could, as they always have, affect the amount of food we have and whether or not everyone in the world will have enough to eat. Will there be peace and security in the world? Will lawlessness and violence continue to increase throughout the world? Will terrorist acts increase or decrease?

What is the destiny of man, of the world, out in the future? Is man's destiny bleak and dismal or hopeful? Or is it both? No person has the answer about the future, not totally. Even the most intelligent among us can only speculate and guess at what will happen. This is particularly true when the long-range future is evaluated. However, there is one destiny that awaits every human being, one terrible event that will happen to every one of us: death. It is the destiny of every man to die and then to face the judgment of God. But this is not the final word, thankfully. God declares a wonderful truth: there is the promised land of heaven lying out in the future. Moreover, every human being can enter the promised land and live eternally in God's presence. God declares that He is going to destroy the present heavens and earth, that all the elements are going to melt with fervent heat (2 Pt.3:10-13). Moreover, God declares that He is going to make a new heavens and earth and that every genuine believer is going to be a citizen of that new world. This is the great hope and expectation of the promised land of heaven. When God speaks of heaven, He is talking about a new heavens and earth—a new world.

The point is this: God longs for every human being to live with Him in the promised land of heaven. But to do this a person has to approach God through the sacrifice of His Son, to approach Him for the atonement (reconciliation with God) and for forgiveness. God longs for every human being to join believers in their march to the promised land of heaven. God wants to guide and help every human being as he marches through this life. God wants to give triumph and victory over all the pitfalls and enemies of this life. But He can help only those who will let Him help, only those who will come to Him through Christ, and join in the great march to the promised land of heaven. This is the subject of this great passage of Scripture: *The Great March to the Promised Land Finally Begins: A Picture of the Believer Finally Beginning His March to the Promised Land of Heaven*, 10:11-36.

1. The great day to begin the march arrived: a picture of great hope for the promised land (v.11-12).
2. The great army of God's people marched forth division by division—as commanded: a picture of obeying God as one marches to the promised land (v.13-28).
3. The appeal of Moses to his brother-in-law to join the march to the promised land: a picture of reaching out to family members to follow after the promised land of God, the promise of heaven (v.29-32).
4. The faithfulness of God in leading His people (v.33 34).
5. The battle cry—the great expectation and cry of Moses: victory and rest (v.35-36).

1 (10:11-12) **March, to the Promised Land—Land, the Promised—Promised Land, March to—Great Days—Symbol, of Salvation**: the great day to begin the march to the promised land finally arrived. At last, God's people were to move out and begin their triumphant journey to the promised land. This was a day for which the Israelites had longed with great expectation and hope, a day that would be inscribed on their minds forever. For believers of every generation, this is a picture of great expectation and hope for the promised land, the great expectation and hope of living forever with God.

OUTLINE	SCRIPTURE
1. The great day to begin the march arrived: A picture of great hope for the promised land a. The date: The cloud lifted on the 20th day of the 2nd month (spent about 11 months at Mt. Sinai) b. The first part of the journey: Traveled from place to place until they reached the Desert of Paran	11 And it came to pass on the twentieth day of the second month, in the second year, that the cloud was taken up from off the tabernacle of the testimony. 12 And the children of Israel took their journeys out of the wilderness of Sinai; and the cloud rested in the wilderness of Paran.

1. Note the date of departure for the promised land: the cloud lifted on the 20th day of the 2nd month. This means that they had spent about 11 months at Mt. Sinai. This was a day that would never be forgotten by God's people, the day when the cloud of His presence indicated that their march to the promised land was now to begin.

2. Note the first part of the journey: they traveled from place to place until they reached the Desert of Paran (v.12). The Israelites made at least three stops on this leg of their journey: Taberah (11:3), Kibroth Hattaavah (11:35), and Hazeroth (11:35). (See Map—Num.33:5-49 for the location of each and the Wilderness Wanderings.)

Thought 1. The Israelites had a great hope for the promised land, a great expectation of reaching the promised land of God. This is a great lesson for believers of all generations. We are to hold a great expectation and hope for the promised land of heaven, for living forever in the presence of God. With great expectation and hope, we are to look for the return of our Lord Jesus Christ.

"In my Father's house are many mansions: if it were not so, I would have told you. I go to prepare a place for you. And if I go and prepare a place for you, I will come again, and receive you unto myself; that where I am, there ye may be also" (Jn.14:2-3).

"But he, being full of the Holy Ghost, looked up stedfastly into heaven, and saw the glory of God, and Jesus standing on the right hand of God, And said, Behold, I see the heavens opened, and the Son of man standing on the right hand of God" (Acts 7:55-56).

"For we know that if our earthly house of this tabernacle were dissolved, we have a building of God, an house not made with hands, eternal in the heavens" (2 Cor.5:1).

"For our conversation is in heaven; from whence also we look for the Saviour, the Lord Jesus Christ: Who shall change our vile body, that it may be fashioned like unto his glorious body, according to the working whereby he is able even to subdue all things unto himself" (Ph.3:20-21).

"Teaching us that, denying ungodliness and worldly lusts, we should live soberly, righteously, and godly, in this present world; Looking for that blessed hope, and the glorious appearing of the great God and our Saviour Jesus Christ" (Tit.2:12-13).

"By faith Abraham, when he was called to go out into a place which he should after receive for an inheritance, obeyed; and he went out, not knowing whither he went. By faith he sojourned in the land of promise, as in a strange country, dwelling in tabernacles with Isaac and Jacob, the heirs with him of the same promise: For he looked for a city which hath foundations, whose builder and maker is God" (Heb.11:8-10).

"These all died in faith, not having received the promises, but having seen them afar off, and were persuaded of them, and embraced them, and confessed that they were strangers and pilgrims on the earth. For they that say such things declare plainly that they seek a country. And truly, if they had been mindful of that country from whence they came out, they might have had opportunity to have returned. But now they desire a better country, that is, an heavenly: wherefore God is not ashamed to be called their God: for he hath prepared for them a city" (Heb.11:13-16).

"Blessed be the God and Father of our Lord Jesus Christ, which according to his abundant mercy hath begotten us again unto a lively hope by the resurrection of Jesus Christ from the dead, To an inheritance incorruptible, and undefiled, and that fadeth not away, reserved in heaven for you" (1 Pt.1:3-4).

"Nevertheless we, according to his promise, look for new heavens and a new earth, wherein dwelleth righteousness. Wherefore, beloved, seeing that ye look for such things, be diligent that ye may be found of him in peace, without spot, and blameless" (2 Pt.3:13-14).

2 (10:13-28) **March, of God's People—Obedience Land, the Promised—Army, of God's People—Believers, Title of**: the great army of God's people marched forth division by division—as commanded by God. The cloud hovering above the Tabernacle that symbolized God's presence had moved. He was now ready to guide His people to the promised land. The servant of God, Moses, had issued orders. The trumpets had sounded. The people had broken camp and taken their positions in their various divisions, tribe by tribe. Then, all of a sudden, the trumpets blasted forth the long-awaited sound for the march to begin. And the people set out. The journey had at long last begun. (See note, *Picture of the Marching Order of the Tribes*—Num.2:2-33.) The outline and Scripture show the marching order of the movement—division by division, tribe by tribe.

OUTLINE	SCRIPTURE	SCRIPTURE	OUTLINE
2. The great army of God's people marched forth division by division—as commanded: A picture of obeying God as one marches to the promised land a. First, the divisions of Judah led the march under their standard: Commanded by Nahshon	13 And they first took their journey according to the commandment of the LORD by the hand of Moses. 14 In the first place went the standard of the camp of the children of Judah according to their armies: and over his host was Nahshon the son of Amminadab.	16 And over the host of the tribe of the children of Zebulun was Eliab the son of Helon. 17 And the tabernacle was taken down; and the sons of Gershon and the sons of Merari set forward, bearing the tabernacle. 18 And the standard of the camp of Reuben set forward according to their armies: and over his host was Elizur the son of Shedeur.	2) The division of Zebulun marched with Judah: Commanded by Eliab b. Second, the Gershonites & the Merarites followed with the carts & oxen transporting the frame & curtains of the Tabernacle c. Third, the divisions of Reuben marched under their standard: Commanded by Elizur
1) The division of Issachar marched with Judah: Commanded by Nethanel	15 And over the host of the tribe of the children of Issachar was Nethaneel the son of Zuar.	19 And over the host of the	1) The division of Simeon

OUTLINE	SCRIPTURE	SCRIPTURE	OUTLINE
marched with Reuben: Commanded by Shelumiel	tribe of the children of Simeon was Shelumiel the son of Zurishaddai.	24 And over the host of the tribe of the children of Benjamin was Abidan the son of Gideoni.	2) The division of Benjamin marched with Ephraim: Commanded by Abidan
2) The division of Gad marched with Reuben: Commanded by Eliasaph	20 And over the host of the tribe of the children of Gad was Eliasaph the son of Deuel.	25 And the standard of the camp of the children of Dan set forward, which was the rereward of all the camps throughout their hosts: and over his host was Ahiezer the son of Ammishaddai.	f. Finally, the divisions of Dan marched as the rear guard, under its standard: Commanded by Ahiezer
d. Fourth, the Kohathites followed carrying the holy things of the Tabernacle: It was to be set up when they arrived	21 And the Kohathites set forward, bearing the sanctuary: and the other did set up the tabernacle against they came.		
e. Fifth, the divisions of Ephraim marched under their standard: Commanded by Elishama	22 And the standard of the camp of the children of Ephraim set forward according to their armies: and over his host was Elishama the son of Ammihud.	26 And over the host of the tribe of the children of Asher was Pagiel the son of Ocran. 27 And over the host of the tribe of the children of Naphtali was Ahira the son of Enan.	1) The division of Asher marched with Dan: Commanded by Pagiel 2) The division of Naphtali marched with Dan: Commanded by Ahira
1) The division of Manasseh marched with Ephraim: Commanded by Gamaliel	23 And over the host of the tribe of the children of Manasseh was Gamaliel the son of Pedahzur.	28 Thus were the journeyings of the children of Israel according to their armies, when they set forward.	

Thought 1. The lesson in this note is obedience to God. Verse 13 makes this clear. When God commanded the people to break camp and set out for the promised land, they immediately obeyed. So it must be with us. As we march to the promised land of God, we must obey God. The only way we can conquer the pitfalls and enemies of this life is to obey God, to do exactly as He says. He alone knows the way to bypass the pitfalls and the high ground that must be taken to conquer the enemies of this life. God must be obeyed.

"Not every one that saith unto me, Lord, Lord, shall enter into the kingdom of heaven; but he that doeth the will of my Father which is in heaven" (Mt.7:21).

"If ye keep my commandments, ye shall abide in my love; even as I have kept my Father's commandments, and abide in his love" (Jn.15:10).

"Ye are my friends, if ye do whatsoever I command you" (Jn.15:14).

"But whoso looketh into the perfect law of liberty, and continueth therein, he being not a forgetful hearer, but a doer of the work, this man shall be blessed in his deed" (Jas.1:25).

"Blessed are they that do his commandments, that they may have right to the tree of life, and may enter in through the gates into the city" (Rev.22:14).

"Now therefore, if ye will obey my voice indeed, and keep my covenant, then ye shall be a peculiar [special] treasure unto me above all people: for all the earth is mine" (Ex.19:5).

"O that there were such an heart in them, that they would fear me, and keep all my commandments always, that it might be well with them, and with their children for ever!" (Dt.5:29).

"This day the Lord thy God hath commanded thee to do these statutes and judgments: thou shalt therefore keep and do them with all thine heart, and with all thy soul " (Dt.26:16).

"This book of the law shall not depart out of thy mouth; but thou shalt meditate therein day and night, that thou mayest observe to do according to all that is written therein: for then thou shalt make thy way prosperous, and then thou shalt have good success" (Josh.1:8).

3 (10:29-32) **Family, Witnessing to—Witnessing, to Family Members—Testimony, to Family Members—Evangelism, to Family Members—Moses, Brother-in-Law—Hobab, Brother-in-Law to Moses—Reuel, Son of**: note that Moses appealed to his brother-in-law to join the march to the promised land.

OUTLINE	SCRIPTURE	SCRIPTURE	OUTLINE
3. The appeal of Moses to his brother-in-law to join the march to the promised land: A picture of reaching out to family members to follow after the promised land of God, the promise of heaven	29 And Moses said unto Hobab, the son of Raguel the Midianite, Moses' father in law, We are journeying unto the place of which the LORD said, I will give it you: come thou with us, and we will do thee good: for the LORD hath spoken good concerning Israel.	kindred. 31 And he said, Leave us not, I pray thee; forasmuch as thou knowest how we are to encamp in the wilderness, and thou mayest be to us instead of eyes.	b. The second appeal of Moses 1) Challenged his brother-in-law to serve as a guide to the people of God
a. The brother-in-law rejected the appeal: His old life appealed to him	30 And he said unto him, I will not go; but I will depart to mine own land, and to my	32 And it shall be, if thou go with us, yea, it shall be, that what goodness the LORD shall do unto us, the same will we do unto thee.	2) Promised to share the good things of the LORD with him

This is a picture of reaching out to family members to seek the promised land of God, the promise of heaven. The name of the brother-in-law was Hobab, the son of Reuel or Jethro the Midianite, Moses' father-in-law (v.29). Moses had married Reuel's or Jethro's daughter. No doubt, Moses did just what any of us would do: used his personal relationship to appeal to Hobab. But notice the other appeal he used: the promised land of God itself. Moses promised his brother-in-law an inheritance in the land and the blessings of God if he would join them in the march to the promised land (v.29).

1. The brother-in-law rejected the appeal (v.30). His old life appealed to him too much. Joining the march to the promised land meant leaving the pleasures, provisions, joy, and bright lights of the world he had known. He would need to undergo a radical change of life. He would need to leave behind his old family and become a part of a new family. He would have to turn away from his religion and follow the Lord God Almighty who claimed to be the only living and true God (Jehovah, Yahweh). To his mind, this was just too much to give up.

2. Note the second appeal of Moses (v.31-32). He challenged his brother-in-law to serve as a guide to the people of God. With strong urging, Moses challenged him to be the "eyes" for the people of God. Hobab was a Midianite from a tribe of people who lived out in the desert or wilderness. His knowledge and ability as a guide would make a significant contribution to the people of God as they marched in the wilderness. To some degree, he would know where to find water and other supplies and provisions. He might also be able to give some insight about the places to which God would be leading them and the others places they would pass through on their journey.

Note also that Moses repeated his promise to share the good things of the Lord with him: an inheritance in the promised land as well as the blessings of God (v.32). Although it is not mentioned here, Hobab did accept the appeal of Moses. He did accept the challenge to follow God and to serve as a guide for the people of God (Judg.1:16).

Thought 1. The lesson is clear: we must reach out to our family members. We must challenge them to join the march to the promised land of God, the promise of heaven. We must do all we can to bear strong witness and testimony to the saving grace of the Lord Jesus Christ. We must challenge them to approach God through the sacrifice of Christ, asking God for the atonement (reconciliation) and for forgiveness of sin. We must reach our family members for Christ. They are doomed to die in this world and be separated forever from God if we fail to reach them. This lays a heavy burden upon us, the burden to do everything we can to reach them, a burden that Moses himself must have felt for his brother-in-law. Note that Moses made two appeals, two direct attempts back-to-back to reach his brother-in-law. We, too, must make concentrated, focused efforts to reach our family for Christ.

"Howbeit Jesus suffered him not, but saith unto him, Go home to thy friends, and tell them how great things the Lord hath done for thee, and hath had compassion on thee" (Mk.5:19).

"But ye shall receive power, after that the Holy Ghost is come upon you: and ye shall be witnesses unto me both in Jerusalem [right at home], and in all Judaea, and in Samaria, and unto the uttermost part of the earth" (Acts 1:8).

"For we cannot but speak the things which we have seen and heard" (Acts 4:20).

"And, ye fathers, provoke not your children to wrath: but bring them up in the nurture and admonition of the Lord" (Eph.6:4).

"When I call to remembrance the unfeigned faith that is in thee, which dwelt first in thy grandmother Lois, and thy mother Eunice; and I am persuaded that in thee also" (2 Tim.1:5).

"And that from a child thou hast known the holy scriptures, which are able to make thee wise unto salvation through faith which is in Christ Jesus" (2 Tim.3:15).

"That they may teach the young women to be sober, to love their husbands, to love their children" (Tit.2:4).

"But sanctify the Lord God in your hearts: and be ready always to give an answer to every man that asketh you a reason of the hope that is in you with meekness and fear " (1 Pt.3:15).

"And these words, which I command thee this day, shall be in thine heart: And thou shalt teach them diligently unto thy children, and shalt talk of them when thou sittest in thine house, and when thou walkest by the way, and when thou liest down, and when thou risest up. And thou shalt bind them for a sign upon thine hand, and they shall be as frontlets between thine eyes. And thou shalt write them upon the posts of thy house, and on thy gates" (Dt.6:6-9).

"Come and hear, all ye that fear God, and I will declare what he hath done for my soul" (Ps.66:16).

"Train up a child in the way he should go: and when he is old, he will not depart from it" (Pr.22:6).

4 (10:33-34) **Faithfulness, of God—God, Faithfulness of—Guidance, of God—God, Guidance of**: the faithfulness of God in leading His people is striking.

OUTLINE	SCRIPTURE
4. The faithfulness of God in leading His people a. The first part of the journey lasted three days b. The ark of the covenant was carried out front, ahead of all the tribes: A symbol of the LORD's leadership step by step c. The fiery cloud of the LORD led them	33 And they departed from the mount of the LORD three days' journey: and the ark of the covenant of the LORD went before them in the three days' journey, to search out a resting place for them. 34 And the cloud of the LORD was upon them by day, when they went out of the camp.

1. The first part of the journey lasted three days (v.33). This was the first *organized march* of God's people. When they first fled from the slavery of Egypt to Mt. Sinai, they were just a misplaced group of people who had been living as slaves for four hundred years. Then, all of a sudden, they were freed; but they were disorganized, disorderly, and fleeing for their lives from the pursuing Egyptian army. Now they were organized into a great army of military divisions, and they had been marching for three days. However, keep in mind that this was the first *organized march*, their very first experience in marching in military divisions.

2. The Ark of the Covenant was carried out front, ahead of all the tribes. Note that the Tabernacle and the holy furnishings within the Tabernacle were carried in the midst of the tribes as they marched, not out front (v.17, 21). However, it is stated that the Ark of the Covenant "went before them." This is interpreted differently by various commentators. Some commentators feel that the words "before them" mean "in their presence." For example, there are passages where God instructs Joshua or Moses to "go before" the people, but the meaning is clearly for them to operate from the midst of the people. They only "go before" in the sense of being visible and leading the people from "the midst of the people." Whatever the case, the Ark of the Covenant—the symbol of God's very presence, the very throne of God itself—went before the people, giving them great assurance and courage to march forward triumphantly.

3. However, the assurance and courage of the people did not come just from the Ark of the Covenant. The fiery cloud of God's holy presence led the people. The cloud of God's Shekinah Glory hovered above the people throughout the day as they marched to the promised land. God was faithful in leading His people step by step, day by day.

Thought 1. God is faithful in leading and guiding us step by step and day by day. Moreover, God promises to be faithful through the whole journey until we reach that glorious destination, the promised land of heaven itself.

1) God is faithful. He keeps His Word and promises.

"Heaven and earth shall pass away: but my words shall not pass away" (Lk.21:33).

"Howbeit when he, the Spirit of truth, is come, he will guide you into all truth: for he shall not speak of himself; but whatsoever he shall hear, that shall he speak: and he will show you things to come" (Jn.16:13).

"God is faithful, by whom ye were called unto the fellowship of his Son Jesus Christ our Lord" (1 Cor.1:9).

"Wherein God, willing more abundantly to show unto the heirs of promise the immutability of his counsel, confirmed it by an oath: That by two immutable things, in which it was impossible for God to lie, we might have a strong consolation, who have fled for refuge to lay hold upon the hope set before us: Which hope we have as an anchor of the soul, both sure and stedfast, and which entereth into that within the veil; Whither the forerunner is for us entered, even Jesus, made an high priest for ever" (Heb.6:17-20).

"Know therefore that the Lord thy God, he is God, the faithful God, which keepeth covenant and mercy with them that love him and keep his commandments to a thousand generations" (Dt.7:9).

"Blessed be the Lord, that hath given rest unto his people Israel, according to all that he promised: there hath not failed one word of all his good promise, which he promised by the hand of Moses his servant" (1 Ki.8:56).

"Thy mercy, O Lord, is in the heavens; and thy faithfulness reacheth unto the clouds" (Ps.36:5).

"I will sing of the mercies of the Lord for ever: with my mouth will I make known thy faithfulness to all generations"(Ps.89:1).

"And thine ears shall hear a word behind thee, saying, This is the way, walk ye in it, when ye turn to the right hand, and when ye turn to the left" (Is.30:21).

"And I will bring the blind by a way that they knew not; I will lead them in paths that they have not known: I will make darkness light before them, and crooked things straight. These things will I do unto them, and not forsake them" (Is.42:16).

"For I am the Lord: I will speak, and the word that I shall speak shall come to pass...." (Ezk.12:25).

2) God guides us step by step until we reach the promised land of heaven.

"To give light to them that sit in darkness and in the shadow of death, to guide our feet into the way of peace" (Lk.1:79).

"Howbeit when he, the Spirit of truth, is come, he will guide you into all truth: for he shall not speak of himself; but whatsoever he shall hear, that shall he speak: and he will show you things to come" (Jn.16:13).

"For this God is our God for ever and ever: he will be our guide even unto death" (Ps.48:14).

"Thou shalt guide me with thy counsel, and afterward receive me to glory" (Ps.73:24).

"And thine ears shall hear a word behind thee, saying, This is the way, walk ye in it, when ye turn to the right hand, and when ye turn to the left" (Is.30:21).

"And I will bring the blind by a way that they knew not; I will lead them in paths that they have not known: I will make darkness light before them, and crooked things straight. These things will I do unto them, and not forsake them" (Is.42:16).

5 (10:35-36) **Victory, Assurance of—Rest, Spiritual—Assurance, of Victory—Spiritual Rest**: the battle cry—the great expectation and cry of Moses—was for victory and rest.

OUTLINE	SCRIPTURE
5. The battle cry—the great expectation & cry of Moses: Victory & rest a. When the ark set out: That God would give a victorious march b. When the ark was set down: That God would come among His people & give them rest—both physical & spiritual rest	35 And it came to pass, when the ark set forward, that Moses said, Rise up, LORD, and let thine enemies be scattered; and let them that hate thee flee before thee. 36 And when it rested, he said, Return, O LORD, unto the many thousands of Israel.

1. This must have been a dramatic scene: there was Moses standing before the Ark of God's throne with all the tribes surrounding the Tabernacle. They were all ready to begin their march. Then it happened: Moses shouted out the great battle cry, "Rise up O Lord! Scatter your enemies! Make your foes flee before you!" (a paraphrased translation). The great battle cry was a direct appeal to God: a cry for the protection and the security of God Himself. It was declaring that God's people were totally dependent upon the strength and power of God to deliver them, to give them the triumphant victory over their enemies. They were marching in unknown terrain, a wilderness and a desert they knew absolutely nothing about. Enemies could be lurking anyplace, ready to launch a surprise attack at any time. They desperately needed the presence, guidance, and protection of God. Therefore, before Moses dared lead the people forward, he shouted out the great battle cry. God must give His people a triumphant victory as they confronted the enemies on their way to the promised land.

2. When the Ark was set down for the evening or during the day for the people to rest, Moses again shouted out: "Return, O Lord, to the many thousands, the countless thousands of Israel." He was crying for God to come among His people and give them rest throughout the night, both physical and spiritual rest. They needed to be refreshed. Their strength needed to be renewed so they could face tomorrow as they continued their march to the promised land of God.

Thought 1. God promises His people both victory and rest.

1) God promises His people victory as they march to the promised land. He assures us: we will be triumphant, victorious over all the pitfalls and enemies of this life.

"Who shall separate us from the love of Christ? shall tribulation, or distress, or persecution, or famine, or nakedness, or peril, or sword? Nay, in all these things we are more than conquerors through him that loved us. For I am persuaded, that neither death, nor life, nor angels, nor principalities, nor powers, nor things present, nor things to come, Nor height, nor depth, nor any other creature, shall be able to separate us from the love of God, which is in Christ Jesus our Lord " (Ro.8:35, 37-39).

"There hath no temptation taken you but such as is common to man: but God is faithful, who will not suffer you to be tempted above that ye are able; but will with the temptation also make a way to escape, that ye may be able to bear it" (1 Cor.10:13).

"Now thanks be unto God, which always causeth us to triumph in Christ, and maketh manifest the savour of his knowledge by us in every place" (2 Cor.2:14).

"For though we walk in the flesh, we do not war after the flesh: (For the weapons of our warfare are not carnal, but mighty through God to the pulling down of strong holds)" (2 Cor.10:3-4).

"Wherefore take unto you the whole armour of God, that ye may be able to withstand in the evil day, and having done all, to stand" (Eph.6:13).

"The Lord knoweth how to deliver the godly out of temptations, and to reserve the unjust unto the day of judgment to be punished" (2 Pt.2:9).

"For whatsoever is born of God overcometh the world: and this is the victory that overcometh the world, even our faith. Who is he that overcometh the world, but he that believeth that Jesus is the Son of God?" (1 Jn.5:4-5).

"The Lord shall fight for you, and ye shall hold your peace" (Ex.14:14).

"I will send my fear before thee, and will destroy all the people to whom thou shalt come, and I will make all thine enemies turn their backs unto thee" (Ex.23:27).

"Through thee will we push down our enemies: through thy name will we tread them under that rise up against us" (Ps.44:5).

2) God promises His people rest, both physical and spiritual rest. God promises a peaceful rest and a restful peace for the souls of His dear people as they march to the promised land.

"Come unto me, all ye that labour and are heavy laden, and I will give you rest. Take my yoke upon you, and learn of me; for I am meek and lowly in heart: and ye shall find rest unto your souls " (Mt.11:28-29).

"Peace I leave with you, my peace I give unto you: not as the world giveth, give I unto you. Let not your heart be troubled, neither let it be afraid" (Jn.14:27).

"These things I have spoken unto you, that in me ye might have peace. In the world ye shall have tribulation: but be of good cheer; I have overcome the world" (Jn.16:33).

"For to be carnally minded is death; but to be spiritually minded is life and peace" (Ro.8:6).

"Be careful for nothing; but in every thing by prayer and supplication with thanksgiving let your requests be made known unto God. And the peace of God, which passeth all understanding, shall keep your hearts and minds through Christ Jesus" (Ph.4:6-7).

"Those things, which ye have both learned, and received, and heard, and seen in me, do: and the God of peace shall be with you" (Ph.4:9).

"For we which have believed do enter into rest, as he said, As I have sworn in my wrath, if they shall enter into my rest: although the works were finished from the foundation of the world" (Heb.4:3).

"And he said, My presence shall go with thee, and I will give thee rest" (Ex.33:14).

"Return unto thy rest, O my soul; for the Lord hath dealt bountifully with thee" (Ps.116:7).

"I will both lay me down in peace, and sleep: for thou, Lord, only makest me dwell in safety"(Ps.4:8).

"The Lord will give strength unto his people; the Lord will bless his people with peace" (Ps.29:11).

"A Psalm of David. The Lord is my shepherd; I shall not want. He maketh me to lie down in green pastures: he leadeth me beside the still waters. He restoreth my soul: he leadeth me in the paths of righteousness for his name's sake. Yea, though I walk through the valley of the shadow of death, I will fear no evil: for thou art with me; thy rod and thy staff they comfort me. Thou preparest a table before me in the presence of mine enemies: thou anointest my head with oil; my cup runneth over. Surely goodness and mercy shall follow me all the days of my life: and I will dwell in the house of the Lord for ever" (Ps.23:1-6).

"And it shall come to pass in the day that the Lord shall give thee rest from thy sorrow, and from thy fear, and from the hard bondage wherein thou wast made to serve" (Is.14:3).

"Thou wilt keep him in perfect peace, whose mind is stayed on thee: because he trusteth in thee" (Is.26:3).

"For thus saith the Lord God, the Holy One of Israel; In returning and rest shall ye be saved; in quietness and in confidence shall be your strength" (Is.30:15).

TYPES, SYMBOLS, AND PICTURES
(Numbers 10:11-36)

Historical Term	Type or Picture (Scriptural Basis for Each)	Life Application for Today's Believer	Biblical Application
The Great March to the Promised Land Finally Begins Num.10:11-36	*The Great March to the promised land is a picture...* • *of the believer finally beginning his march to the promised land of heaven* • *of the believer's great hope for the promised land* **"And it came to pass on the twentieth *day* of the second month, in the second year, that the cloud was taken up from off the tabernacle of the testimony. And the children of Israel took their journeys out of the wilderness of Sinai; and the cloud rested in the wilderness of Paran. And they first took their journey according to the commandment of the LORD by the hand of Moses" (Num.10:11-13).**	⇒ Man must do two things. 1. Man must "get out" of his present surroundings and leave the world and its material comforts and corruptions. 2. Man must believe in the promise of God, that is, in the *promised land* of heaven.	***"And with many other words did he testify and exhort, saying, Save yourselves from this untoward generation" (Acts 2:40).*** ***"Wherefore come out from among them, and be ye separate, saith the Lord, and touch not the unclean thing; and I will receive you, and will be a Father unto you, and ye shall be my sons and daughters, saith the Lord Almighty" (2 Cor. 6:17-18).*** ***"And have no fellowship with the unfruitful works of darkness, but rather reprove them" (Ephes. 5:11).*** ***"Love not the world, neither the things that are in the world. If any man love the world, the love of the Father is not in him. For all that is in the world, the lust of the flesh, and the lust of the eyes, and the pride of life, is not of the Father, but is of the world" (1 John 2:15-16).*** ***"For he looked for a city which hath foundations,***

Historical Term	Type or Picture (Scriptural Basis for Each)	Life Application for Today's Believer	Biblical Application
			whose builder and maker is God" (Heb.11:10). ***"And I saw a new heaven and a new earth: for the first heaven and the first earth were passed away" (Rev. 21:1). (See also Heb.11:13-16; 12:22; 13:14).***
The Great Army of God's People Marched Forth Division by Division—as Commanded Num.10:13-28	*The people of God marching by divisions is a picture of obeying God as one marches to the promised land* **"Thus *were* the journeyings of the children of Israel according to their armies, when they set forward" (Num.10:28).**	⇒ When God commanded the people to break camp and set out for the promised land, they immediately obeyed. So it must be with us. As we march to the promised land of God and of heaven, we must obey God. The only way we can conquer the pitfalls and enemies of this life is to obey God, to do exactly as He says. He alone knows the way to bypass the pitfalls and the high ground that must be taken to conquer the enemies of this life. God must be obeyed.	***"I delight to do thy will, O my God: yea, thy law is within my heart" (Psalm 40:8).*** ***"I beseech you therefore, brethren, by the mercies of God, that ye present your bodies a living sacrifice, holy, acceptable unto God, which is your reasonable service. And be not conformed to this world: but be ye transformed by the renewing of your mind, that ye may prove what is that good, and acceptable, and perfect, will of God" (Ro. 12:1-2).*** ***"For this is the will of God, even your sanctification, that ye should abstain from fornication" (1 Thes. 4:3).*** ***"In every thing give thanks: for this is the will of God in Christ Jesus concerning you" (1 Thes. 5:18).*** ***"[This] is the will of God, that with well doing ye may put to silence the ignorance of foolish men" (1 Pt.2:15).*** ***"That he no longer should live the rest of his time in the flesh to the lusts of men, but to the will of God" (1 Pt.4:2).***
The Appeal of Moses to His Brother-In-Law to Join the March to the Promised Land Num10:29-32	*Moses' appeal is a picture of reaching out to family members to follow after the promised land of God, the promise of heaven.* **"And Moses said unto Hobab, the son of Raguel the Midianite, Moses' father in law, We are journeying unto the place of which the LORD said, I will give it you: come thou with us, and we will do thee good: for the LORD hath spoken good concerning Israel" (Num.10:29).**	⇒ The lesson is clear: we must reach out to our family members. We must challenge them to join the march to the promised land of God, the promise of heaven. We must do all we can to bear strong witness and testimony to the saving grace of the Lord Jesus Christ. We must challenge them to approach God through the sacrifice of Christ, asking God for atonement (reconciliation) and for forgiveness of sin. We must reach our family members for Christ. They are doomed to die in this	***"Howbeit Jesus suffered him not, but saith unto him, Go home to thy friends, and tell them how great things the Lord hath done for thee, and hath had compassion on thee" (Mk.5:19).*** ***"But ye shall receive power, after that the Holy Ghost is come upon you: and ye shall be witnesses unto me both in Jerusalem [right at home], and in all Judaea, and in Samaria, and unto the uttermost part of the earth" (Acts 1:8).*** ***"For we cannot but speak the things which we have seen and heard" (Acts 4:20).*** ***"And, ye fathers, provoke not your children to wrath:***

Historical Term	Type or Picture (Scriptural Basis for Each)	Life Application for Today's Believer	Biblical Application
		world and be separated forever from God if we fail to reach them. This lays a heavy burden upon us, the burden to do everything we can to reach them, a burden that Moses himself must have felt for his brother-in-law. Note that Moses made two appeals, two direct attempts back-to-back to reach his brother-in-law. We, too, must make concentrated, focused efforts to reach our family for Christ.	***but bring them up in the nurture and admonition of the Lord" (Eph.6:4).*** ***"When I call to remembrance the unfeigned faith that is in thee, which dwelt first in thy grandmother Lois, and thy mother Eunice; and I am persuaded that in thee also" (2 Tim. 1:5).*** ***"And that from a child thou hast known the holy scriptures, which are able to make thee wise unto salvation through faith which is in Christ Jesus" (2 Tim. 3:15).*** ***"That they may teach the young women to be sober, to love their husbands, to love their children," (Tit.2:4).*** ***"But sanctify the Lord God in your hearts: and be ready always to give an answer to every man that asketh you a reason of the hope that is in you with meekness and fear " (1 Pt. 3:15).*** ***"Train up a child in the way he should go: and when he is old, he will not depart from it" (Pr.22:6).***
The Ark or Chest Num.10:33-34 (See also Exodus 25:10-22; 40:20; 35:12; 37:1-5; 39:35; 40:3, 20-21)	*The Ark was the very special place where God's Holy presence was manifested.*	What the Ark of the Covenant taught:	
	1. *The Ark was the symbol of God's presence. A very special manifestation of God's presence dwelt right above the Ark, right between the two cherubim.*	1. God reveals His presence to believers in a very special way: • When people need a special sense of God's presence—when they need to feel a special closeness to God—they can go directly into the presence of God. They can worship and seek the Lord personally. How is this possible? Because of the great sacrifice of God's Son, the Lord Jesus Christ.	***"And he said, My presence shall go with thee, and I will give thee rest" (Ex.33:14).*** ***"When thou passest through the waters, I will be with thee; and through the rivers, they shall not overflow thee: when thou walkest through the fire, thou shalt not be burned; neither shall the flame kindle upon thee" (Is.43:2).*** ***"He that hath my commandments, and keepeth them, he it is that loveth me: and he that loveth me shall be loved of my Father, and I will love him, and will manifest myself to him" (Jn. 14:21).***
	2. *The Mercy Seat sat on top of the Ark; therefore, the Ark was a symbol of God's mercy.*	2. God covers our lives with His mercy: • Believers are to understand that the blood	***"But the mercy of the LORD is from everlasting to everlasting upon them that fear him, and his righteous-***

Historical Term	Type or Picture (Scriptural Basis for Each)	Life Application for Today's Believer	Biblical Application
		shed upon the cross makes atonement for their sins, that the blood reconciles them to God. • Believers are to learn that the mercy of God is to be showered upon them because of the blood, because they believe and trust the blood of the sacrifice (Jesus Christ) to cover their sins.	***ness unto children's children" (Ps. 103:17).*** ***"But God, who is rich in mercy, for his great love wherewith he loved us, Even when we were dead in sins, hath quickened us together with Christ, (by grace ye are saved;) And hath raised us up together, and made us sit together in heavenly places in Christ Jesus" (Eph. 2:4-6).***
	3. The Ark was the symbol of the very throne of God. It was the place where the people sought the guidance and instruction of God.	3. God instructs and guides His people from His heavenly throne. From that position, God speaks to His people, gives them His commandments, instructions, and guidance; therefore, when God's people need help or guidance, they are to come directly to the throne of mercy, come and find grace to help in time of need.	***"The meek will he guide in judgment: and the meek will he teach his way" (Ps.25:9).*** ***"I will instruct thee and teach thee in the way which thou shalt go: I will guide thee with mine eye" (Ps. 32:8).*** ***"For we have not an high priest which cannot be touched with the feeling of our infirmities; but was in all points tempted like as we are, yet without sin. Let us therefore come boldly unto the throne of grace, that we may obtain mercy, and find grace to help in time of need" (Heb. 4:15-16).***
	4. The Ark was the symbol of God's Law, holding the Ten Commandments.	4. God gave the Ten Commandments so we would know how to live and relate to God and to one another—so we would know how to build a just and peaceful society.	***"For this is the love of God, that we keep his commandments: and his commandments are not grievous" (1 Jn. 5:3).*** ***"Righteousness exalteth a nation: but sin is a reproach to any people" (Pr.14:34).***
	5. The Ark was the symbol of Christ, of the very presence of Christ personally fulfilling every picture of the Ark. Remember, the word "tabernacle" means to dwell, to abide in the midst of.	5. How Christ fulfilled the symbolism of the Ark of God: ⇒ Jesus Christ promises to be with His people always	***"For where two or three are gathered together in my name, there am I in the midst of them" (Mt.18:20).*** ***"Teaching them to observe all things whatsoever I have commanded you: and, lo, I am with you alway, even unto the end of the world. Amen" (Mt.28:20).***
	"And they departed from the mount of the LORD three days' journey: and the ark of the covenant of the LORD went before them in the three days' journey, to search out a resting place for them" (Num.10:33).	⇒ Jesus Christ shed His blood in order to have mercy upon us and to cleanse us from our sins.	***"Who his own self bare our sins in his own body on the tree, that we, being dead to sins, should live unto righteousness: by whose stripes ye were healed" (1 Pt. 2:24).*** ***"For Christ also hath once suffered for sins, the just for the unjust, that he***

Historical Term	Type or Picture (Scriptural Basis for Each)	Life Application for Today's Believer	Biblical Application
		⇒ Jesus Christ is the Good Shepherd, the One who leads, protects, and guides His people. ⇒ Jesus Christ kept the law of the covenant that was kept in the Ark, kept the law perfectly, without sin.	*might bring us to God, being put to death in the flesh, but quickened by the Spirit" (1 Pt. 3:18).* *"Unto him that loved us, and washed us from our sins in his own blood" (Rev. 1:5).* *"Lo, I am with you alway, [even] unto the end of the world. Amen" (Mt.28:20).* *I am the good shepherd: the good shepherd giveth his life for the sheep" (Jn. 10:11).* *"Let your conversation be without covetousness; and be content with such things as ye have: for he hath said, I will never leave thee, nor forsake thee" (Heb. 13:5).* *"For we have not an high priest which cannot be touched with the feeling of our infirmities; but was in all points tempted like as we are, yet without sin" (Heb. 4:15).*

DIVISION II

THE TRAGIC, DEVASTATING FAILURE OF ISRAEL: WHY PEOPLE FORFEIT THEIR RIGHT TO ENTER THE PROMISED LAND, 11:1-14:45

(11:1—14:45) **DIVISION OVERVIEW—Israel, Failure of—Israel, Privileges of—Israel, Sins of—Promised Land, March to**: totally unexpected—the heart of the first generation of believers is now exposed. They had been prepared as much as a people could be for the promised land, blessed beyond imagination, given privilege after privilege:

⇒ given the adoption: adopted by God Himself to be His holy people, His sons and daughters
⇒ given the care of God: provided for, looked after, taken care of by God Himself—never going without anything
⇒ given the law, the very Word of God Himself
⇒ given the covenant: a contract with God Himself, a contract that guarantees every good and perfect gift imaginable
⇒ given the hope of the promised land: the assurance of living a full and victorious life, conquering all the enemies of life, and the glorious promise of rest, peace, and eternal life with God
⇒ given the service of God: the wonderful privilege of serving the Creator and Sustainer of the universe, the Lord God Himself (Jehovah, Yahweh)
⇒ given the staggering hope of the promised seed: the coming Messiah and Savior of the world
⇒ given the very presence and guidance of God by day and by night: symbolized in the cloud and the Tabernacle
⇒ given all the promises of God: the perfect assurance, confidence, and conviction that all the promises would be fulfilled by God

All this had been given to the first generation. They had been prepared to march to the promised land and to conquer all the enemies of life who opposed them. Their pilgrimage, their march was to be a march of victory and triumph. But tragedy struck. The truth of their hearts was exposed. Unbelief, grumbling, and murmuring filled their hearts, not God. A spirit of selfishness and rebellion was rooted in their hearts. The first generation was not God-centered; they were self-centered: filled with all kinds of immoral, lawless passions and fleshly lusts.

As shocking as this fact is, there is even a more unbelievable fact: they rebelled within *three days*. Only *three days*—that was all it took before they exposed their true, hypocritical hearts—their hearts of unbelief. The march had barely begun and they immediately began to grumble and murmur against God and His dear servant Moses.

Now begins a series of repeated acts of unbelief and rebellion. Now begins the tragic, devastating failure that brought the judgment of God upon Israel. The first generation lost their inheritance. They were shut out—excluded—never allowed to enter the promised land. This is the stunning, bewildering story of these chapters.

THE TRAGIC, DEVASTATING FAILURE OF ISRAEL: WHY PEOPLE FORFEIT THEIR RIGHT TO ENTER THE PROMISED LAND, 11:1-14:45

II. THE TRAGIC, DEVASTATING FAILURE OF ISRAEL: WHY PEOPLE FORFEIT THEIR RIGHT TO ENTER THE PROMISED LAND, 11:1-14:45

A. The First Tragic Failure Seen in the People: Distrusting God—Complaining & Grumbling, Craving & Lusting, 11:1-35

1. Complaining & grumbling about hardships: Not trusting God & losing sight of His guidance
- a. The LORD heard the grumbling & was angered: His judgment fell upon them; some fire burned the outskirts of the camp
- b. The people & the servant of God cried out & prayed
  - 1) The LORD heard the prayer
  - 2) The fire was extinguished
- c. The place was named Taberah, which means "burning," a place of awful judgment

2. Complaining & murmuring about food: Not trusting God, craving & lusting after the food & appetites of the world
- a. The ringleaders: The rabble
- b. The complaint: Had only *manna* to eat
  - 1) Longed for the food of Egypt but exaggerated it
  - 2) Had lost their appetite: Were tired of "this manna"
    - It was like coriander seed
    - It looked like resin
    - It was gathered & ground in a handmill or crushed in a mortar
    - It was cooked in a pot or made into cakes
    - It tasted like something made with olive oil
    - It was miraculously given by God: Fell from the sky as the dew settled on the camp at night
- c. The terrible influence of the grumbling: Every person began to complain & murmur
- d. The response of the LORD & Moses: The LORD became angry & Moses was deeply troubled
  - 1) Moses questioned, poured out his heart to the LORD
    - Why had God allowed so much trouble?
    - Why was God so displeased?
    - Why had God put the burden of the people on him?
    - Had he, Moses, conceived & given birth to the people?
    - Why had God chosen him to carry the people—like babies—to the promised land?
    - Where could he conceivably get enough meat for the people?
  - 2) Moses cried for God to raise up others to help him: The burden was too heavy—he simply could not continue to lead them by himself
    - Cried for God to take him unless He gave him help
    - Cried for God to keep him from ruin
  - 3) The LORD met the need of Moses
    - Instructed Moses to bring 70 elders to the Tabernacle
    - Promised to anoint the elders with God's Spirit, with the very same Spirit Moses had: They would help carry the burden of the people, help deal with their problems
- e. The message of God's judgment to be given to the people
  - 1) To consecrate themselves: Prepare to have their complaint & grumbling answered—the complaint that they were better off in Egypt (a symbol of the world)
  - 2) To know that the Lord would give them meat: Not just for days, but for a whole month—so much meat they would loathe it
  - 3) The reason:
    - Because they had rejected the LORD
    - Because they desired to be back in Egypt (a

And when the people com-
plained, it displeased the
LORD: and the LORD heard it;
and his anger was kindled;
and the fire of the LORD
burnt among them, and consumed them that were in the
uttermost parts of the camp.
2 And the people cried unto
Moses; and when Moses
prayed unto the LORD, the
fire was quenched.
3 And he called the name of
the place Taberah: because
the fire of the LORD burnt
among them.
4 And the mixt multitude
that was among them fell a
lusting: and the children of
Israel also wept again, and
said, Who shall give us flesh
to eat?
5 We remember the fish,
which we did eat in Egypt
freely; the cucumbers, and
the melons, and the leeks,
and the onions, and the garlick:
6 But now our soul is dried
away: there is nothing at all,
beside this manna, before
our eyes.
7 And the manna was as
coriander seed, and the
colour thereof as the colour
of bdellium.
8 And the people went about,
and gathered it, and ground it
in mills, or beat it in a mortar, and baked it in pans, and
made cakes of it: and the
taste of it was as the taste of
fresh oil.
9 And when the dew
fell upon the camp in the
night, the manna fell upon
it.
10 Then Moses heard the
people weep throughout
their families, every man in
the door of his tent: and the
anger of the LORD was kindled greatly; Moses also was
displeased.
11 And Moses said unto
the LORD, Wherefore hast
thou afflicted thy servant?
and wherefore have I not
found favour in thy sight,
that thou layest the burden
of all this people upon
me?
12 Have I conceived all this
people? have I begotten
them, that thou shouldest say
unto me, Carry them in thy
bosom, as a nursing father
beareth the sucking child,
unto the land which thou
swarest unto their fathers?
13 Whence should I have
flesh to give unto all this
people? for they weep unto
me, saying, Give us flesh,
that we may eat.
14 I am not able to bear all
this people alone, because it
is too heavy for me.
15 And if thou deal thus
with me, kill me, I pray thee,
out of hand, if I have found
favour in thy sight; and let
me not see my wretchedness.
16 And the LORD said unto
Moses, Gather unto me seventy men of the elders of
Israel, whom thou knowest
to be the elders of the people,
and officers over them; and
bring them unto the tabernacle of the congregation, that
they may stand there with
thee.
17 And I will come down
and talk with thee there: and
I will take of the spirit which
is upon thee, and will put it
upon them; and they shall
bear the burden of the people
with thee, that thou bear it
not thyself alone.
18 And say thou unto the
people, Sanctify yourselves
against to morrow, and ye
shall eat flesh: for ye have
wept in the ears of the LORD,
saying, Who shall give us
flesh to eat? for it was well
with us in Egypt: therefore
the LORD will give you flesh,
and ye shall eat.
19 Ye shall not eat one day,
nor two days, nor five days,
neither ten days, nor twenty
days;
20 But even a whole month,
until it come out at your nostrils, and it be loathsome
unto you: because that ye
have despised the LORD

symbol of the world)

4) The stress & questioning of Moses
- How could God provide meat for several million?
- Would there be enough even if they slaughtered all their flocks & herds? Or if they had all the fish in the sea?

5) The LORD's rebuke to Moses: The LORD's arm (power) is not too short; He will do exactly what He says

f. The obedience of Moses
1) He declared the LORD's message to the people
2) He summoned the 70 elders to the Tabernacle
3) The faithfulness of the LORD
- He put His Spirit on the 70 elders
- They prophesied this one time, but never again

g. The true spirit of Moses: The spirit of a humble minister, a true servant of God
1) Two elders had remained in camp & did not go to the Tabernacle: The Spirit also came upon them & they prophesied
- A young man ran & told Moses

which is among you, and have wept before him, saying, Why came we forth out of Egypt?
21 And Moses said, The people, among whom I am, are six hundred thousand footmen; and thou hast said, I will give them flesh, that they may eat a whole month.
22 Shall the flocks and the herds be slain for them, to suffice them? or shall all the fish of the sea be gathered together for them, to suffice them?
23 And the LORD said unto Moses, Is the LORD's hand waxed short? thou shalt see now whether my word shall come to pass unto thee or not.
24 And Moses went out, and told the people the words of the LORD, and gathered the seventy men of the elders of the people, and set them round about the tabernacle.
25 And the LORD came down in a cloud, and spake unto him, and took of the spirit that was upon him, and gave it unto the seventy elders: and it came to pass, that, when the spirit rested upon them, they prophesied, and did not cease.
26 But there remained two of the men in the camp, the name of the one was Eldad, and the name of the other Medad: and the spirit rested upon them; and they were of them that were written, but went not out unto the tabernacle: and they prophesied in the camp.
27 And there ran a young man, and told Moses, and said, Eldad and Medad do prophesy in the camp.
28 And Joshua the son of Nun, the servant of Moses, one of his young men, answered and said, My lord Moses, forbid them.
29 And Moses said unto him, Enviest thou for my sake? would God that all the LORD'S people were prophets, and that the LORD would put his spirit upon them!
30 And Moses gat him into the camp, he and the elders of Israel.
31 And there went forth a wind from the LORD, and brought quails from the sea, and let them fall by the camp, as it were a day's journey on this side, and as it were a day's journey on the other side, round about the camp, and as it were two cubits high upon the face of the earth.
32 And the people stood up all that day, and all that night, and all the next day, and they gathered the quails: he that gathered least gathered ten homers: and they spread them all abroad for themselves round about the camp.
33 And while the flesh was yet between their teeth, ere it was chewed, the wrath of the LORD was kindled against the people, and the LORD smote the people with a very great plague.
34 And he called the name of that place Kibroth-hattaavah: because there they buried the people that lusted.
35 And the people journeyed from Kibroth-hattaavah unto Hazeroth; and abode at Hazeroth.

- Joshua, Moses' aide, insisted that Moses stop them

2) Moses' true servant spirit: His desire was for the LORD's Spirit to be upon all believers & for all to be prophets

3) Moses & the elders returned to the camp

h. The judgment of God: The complaint of the people was granted
1) Three feet deep & extended a whole day's walk in every direction
2) The people gathered quail for two days & one night: Every person gathered no less than 10 homers (50 bushels)
3) The people acted like gluttons: Gorged themselves

i. The anger of the LORD: Was aroused, burned against the people
1) He struck them with a severe plague
2) The place was named Kibroth Hattaavah, which means "graves of craving"

j. The march of the people: Camped at Hazeroth

DIVISION II

THE TRAGIC, DEVASTATING FAILURE OF ISRAEL: WHY PEOPLE FORFEIT THEIR RIGHT TO ENTER THE PROMISED LAND, 11:1-14:45

A. The First Tragic Failure Seen in the People: Distrusting God—Complaining and Grumbling, Craving and Lusting, 11:1-35

(11:1-35) **Introduction—Negativism, Age of—Complaining, Age of—Grumbling, Age of—Murmuring, Age of—Trials, Reaction to**: this is an age of negativism—of complaining, grumbling, and murmuring. No matter where we turn, people are being negative or complaining about something:

⇒ work	⇒ a husband	⇒ a manager	⇒ food
⇒ school	⇒ a parent	⇒ an employer	⇒ clothing
⇒ a wife	⇒ a child	⇒ an employee	⇒ shelter

⇒ personal problems	⇒ unemployment	⇒ disappointments	⇒ suffering
⇒ financial problems	⇒ foiled plans	⇒ sorrows	⇒ ill health
⇒ personal hardships	⇒ frustrations	⇒ despondency	⇒ position or status
⇒ accidents	⇒ failures	⇒ rejection	

Bitter trials are the normal experience of human life. They confront us all, and they perplex and puzzle us. We often ask, "Why has God let this happen to me?" Trials are common to all people (1 Cor.10:13). When they strike us, the question is: How are we going to react? Are we going to trust God to help and strengthen us, or grumble and complain and perhaps curse God? Complaining, grumbling, and murmuring hurt and cause pain for others. But more than this, complaining and grumbling show a great distrust in God:

⇒ They show that we do not trust God to meet our needs, to provide the necessities of life.
⇒ They show that we do not trust the goodness and power of God, that He will work things out and give us victory over the pitfalls and enemies of life.

This is the subject of this important passage of Scripture. It covers the first tragic failure seen in the people of God as they began their march to the promised land. Within three days after beginning their march, they demonstrated tragic distrust of God. They immediately began to complain and grumble against God. Moreover, the Israelites began to crave and lust after the food and appetites of Egypt. Keep in mind that Egypt is a type or symbol of the world and its enslavements. This is: *The First Tragic Failure Seen in the People: Distrusting God—Complaining and Grumbling, Craving and Lusting,* 11:1-35.

1. Complaining and grumbling about hardships: not trusting God and losing sight of His guidance (v. 1-3).
2. Complaining and murmuring about food: not trusting God, craving and lusting after the food and appetites of the world (v.4-35).

1 (11:1-3) **Complaining—Grumbling—Murmuring—Criticism, Spirit of—Discontentment, Spirit of—Hardships—Problems—Difficulties—Distrust—Unbelief—Judgment, of God—Israel, Sins of—Israel, Unbelief of—Taberah, Campsite of Israel**: there was the complaining and murmuring about hardships.

OUTLINE	SCRIPTURE
1. Complaining & grumbling about hardships: Not trusting God & losing sight of His guidance a. The LORD heard the grumbling & was angered: His judgment fell upon them; some fire burned the outskirts of the camp b. The people & the servant of God cried out & prayed 1) The LORD heard the prayer 2) The fire was extinguished c. The place was named Taberah, which means "burning," a place of awful judgment	And when the people complained, it displeased the LORD: and the LORD heard it; and his anger was kindled; and the fire of the LORD burnt among them, and consumed them that were in the uttermost parts of the camp. 2 And the people cried unto Moses; and when Moses prayed unto the LORD, the fire was quenched. 3 And he called the name of the place Taberah: because the fire of the LORD burnt among them.

The people failed to trust God, and they lost sight of God's guidance. Shocking! Inexcusable! The people were only three days into their march. Remember, the Israelites had just left Mt. Sinai where they had been camped for eleven months. They had just begun their great march to the promised land, the day for which they had longed with great expectation. Yet within three days, they were complaining and grumbling about the hardships they were facing along the march. They were complaining to the LORD, questioning why He would allow such hardships and difficulties. Why would He not make their march to the promised land smoother and easier, with less difficulty and hardship? They were gripped by a spirit of discontentment with their lives, a critical spirit. They were complaining and grumbling about the bad things that were happening to them. Life was hard and toilsome, and they blamed God.

1. The LORD heard their grumbling and was angry. His judgment fell upon them: a fire was ignited and burned the outskirts of the camp (v.1). Note that the fire was definitely from the LORD. This probably means that God caused a bolt of lightning to strike, igniting a fire that burned some of the property and tents on the outskirts of the camp.
2. The people and Moses cried out to God for help (v.2-3). Note that the LORD immediately heard their prayer and the fire was extinguished.
3. The place was named Taberah, which means "burning." This was a place of awful judgment, a place that needed to stand as a warning to all people in the future. God judges those who complain, grumble, and murmur against Him because of hardships.

> **Thought 1**. The Israelites were immature believers: unspiritual, unstable, and carnal (fleshly). Their carnal hearts of unbelief took over; and they complained, grumbled, and murmured against God because of the hardships. This was a terrible sin of Israel, and it was a sin that was committed by them time and again. In fact, practically every time they faced a crisis of hardship, they complained and grumbled. Note these examples:

1) They complained and grumbled because they had no food.

"And the whole congregation of the children of Israel murmured against Moses and Aaron in the wilderness: And the children of Israel said unto them, Would to God we had died by the hand of the Lord in the land of Egypt, when we sat by the flesh pots, and when we did eat bread to the full; for ye have brought us forth into this wilderness, to kill this whole assembly with hunger" (Ex.16:2-3).

2) They complained and grumbled because they had no water.

"And the people thirsted there for water; and the people murmured against Moses, and said, Wherefore is this that thou hast brought us up out of Egypt, to kill us and our children and our cattle with thirst" (Ex.17:3).

3) They complained and grumbled because of the trials they were facing throughout their wilderness wanderings: they wished to return to Egypt.

"And all the children of Israel murmured against Moses and against Aaron: and the whole congregation said unto them, Would God that we had died in the land of Egypt! or would God we had died in this wilderness! And wherefore hath the Lord brought us unto this land, to fall by the sword, that our wives and our children should be a prey? were it not better for us to return into Egypt? And they said one to another, Let us make a captain, and let us return into Egypt" (Num.14:2-4).

4) They complained and grumbled because they became tired of their leaders, tired of Moses and Aaron's leadership.

"And they gathered themselves together against Moses and against Aaron, and said unto them, Ye take too much upon you, seeing all the congregation are holy, every one of them, and the Lord is among them: wherefore then lift ye up yourselves above the congregation of the Lord....For which cause both thou and all thy company are gathered together against the Lord: and what is Aaron, that ye murmur against him" (Num.16:3, 11).

5) They complained and grumbled because of God's judgment, because God executed justice upon the Israelites who sinned.

"But on the morrow all the congregation of the children of Israel murmured against Moses and against Aaron, saying, Ye have killed the people of the Lord" (Num.16:41).

Thought 2. Complaining and grumbling are signs of distrust, of terrible unbelief in God. When we complain and grumble, we reveal a heart of unbelief and distrust. We reveal that we do not believe God's power and goodness. We do not believe that God is in control, that He will work the situation and hardship out. A heart that trusts God will always pray, asking God to help. The trusting heart never complains nor grumbles against people and situations, especially against fellow believers—certainly not against God nor His servants. Note what Scripture declares about complaining and grumbling.

1) Complaining and grumbling are not against the hardships themselves nor against other people, but against the LORD Himself.

"And Moses said, This shall be, when the Lord shall give you in the evening flesh to eat, and in the morning bread to the full; for that the Lord heareth your murmurings which ye murmur against him: and what are we? your murmurings are not against us, but against the Lord" (Ex.16:8).

2) Complaining and grumbling are often due to a person's lack of faith in God's Word, his refusal to listen to God's voice.

"Yea, they despised the pleasant land, they believed not his word: But murmured in their tents, and hearkened not unto the voice of the Lord" (Ps.106:24-25).

3) Complaining and grumbling are often due to the foolishness and sin of man.

"The foolishness of man perverteth his way: and his heart fretteth against the Lord" (Pr.19:3).
"Wherefore doth a living man complain, a man for the punishment of his sins" (Lam.3:39).

4) Complaining and grumbling are to have no part in the believer's life.

"Do all things without murmurings and disputings" (Ph.2:14).

5) Complaining and grumbling will be severely judged by God.

"Neither murmur ye, as some of them also murmured, and were destroyed of the destroyer" (1 Cor.10:10).
"Behold, the Lord cometh with ten thousands of his saints, To execute judgment upon all, and to convince all that are ungodly among them of all their ungodly deeds which they have ungodly commit-

ted, and of all their hard speeches which ungodly sinners have spoken against him. These are murmurers, complainers, walking after their own lusts; and their mouth speaketh great swelling words, having men's persons in admiration because of advantage (Jude 1:14-16).

2 (11:4-35) **Complaining—Grumbling—Murmuring—Food, Complaining about—Unbelief—Craving—Lusting**: the people complained and grumbled about their food. They did not trust God, and they craved or lusted after the food and provisions of Egypt (a symbol of the world).

How could the people conceivably be failing so soon after their rebellion and the correction of God at Taberah? Apparently, this rebellion took place at the very next campsite, although this is not clearly stated. The fact that these two passages are linked together seems to indicate this. Whatever the case, the reader is again shocked and left wondering how a people could be so carnal and unbelieving. How could the Israelites be so unbelieving and stumble so often when God had done so much for them? Is the human heart that depraved? Or were their hearts that selfish and unbelieving, hard-hearted and stubborn, resistant to God?

1. The complaining and grumbling were stirred up by certain ringleaders, the rabble among them. This is a reference to the mixed group of people (non-Israelite) who joined God's people during the exodus from Egypt (cp. Ex.12:38; Lev.24:10). Note that it was the rabble who actually began to lust and crave after the food of Egypt, in particular the meat of Egypt.

OUTLINE	SCRIPTURE
2. Complaining & murmuring about food: Not trusting God, craving & lusting after the food & appetites of the world a. The ringleaders: The rabble	4 And the mixt multitude that was among them fell a lusting: and the children of Israel also wept again, and said, Who shall give us flesh to eat?

2. The complaint focused upon their diet: they had only *manna* to eat (v.5-9). They craved and lusted after the meat and vegetables of Egypt. In Egypt they had been able to fish in the rivers and streams and grow fresh vegetables such as cucumbers, melons, leeks, onions, and garlic (v.5). Out in the desert, they were unable to plant gardens; and, of course, there were no streams or rivers from which to catch fish. The people were, as they complained, tired of "this manna." They had lost their appetite for "this manna." Keep in mind that the *manna* was the provision of God, a miraculous provision of food. It was also a delicious food (see outline and notes—Ex.16:10-26 for more discussion).

OUTLINE	SCRIPTURE	SCRIPTURE	OUTLINE
b. The complaint: Had only *manna* to eat 1) Longed for the food of Egypt but exaggerated it 2) Had lost their appetite: Were tired of "this manna" • It was like coriander seed • It looked like resin	5 We remember the fish, which we did eat in Egypt freely; the cucumbers, and the melons, and the leeks, and the onions, and the garlick: 6 But now our soul is dried away: there is nothing at all, beside this manna, before our eyes. 7 And the manna was as coriander seed, and the colour thereof as the colour	of bdellium. 8 And the people went about, and gathered it, and ground it in mills, or beat it in a mortar, and baked it in pans, and made cakes of it: and the taste of it was as the taste of fresh oil. 9 And when the dew fell upon the camp in the night, the manna fell upon it.	• It was gathered & ground in a hand-mill or crushed in a mortar • It was cooked in a pot or made into cakes • It tasted like something made with olive oil • It was miraculously given by God: Fell from the sky as the dew settled on the camp at night

Note the people's reference to the manna as "this manna." A bitter, sarcastic complaint! This was a spirit of discontentment, of dissatisfaction with God's provision, an act of unbelief and rebellion against God. An act of unbelief and rebellion against God. Just think how they had forgotten their real condition in Egypt: they had been slaves and mistreated with brutal savagery. As slaves they had known the horrors of abuse, torture, overwork, hunger, thirst, beatings, and death. They were exaggerating the food they had in Egypt, looking back into the past with unwarranted optimism. This was tragic, for the manna was God's provision. The manna was one of the gracious provisions to keep His people alive as they marched to the promised land. Note the description of the manna, how delicious and sufficient a provision it was:

⇒ It was like coriander seed (a small spicy seed taken from a plant of the carrot family. It was used as seasoning and for medicinal purposes.)
⇒ It looked like resin from a plant or tree (v.7).
⇒ It was gathered and ground in a handmill or crushed in a mortar (v.8).
⇒ It was cooked in a pot or made into cakes.
⇒ It tasted like something made with olive oil.
⇒ It was miraculously given by God: it fell daily from the sky as the dew settled on the camp at night (v.9).

3. The grumbling had a terrible and powerful influence: it spread rapidly throughout the whole camp. Note that every family began to complain, murmur, and grumble (v.10).

OUTLINE	SCRIPTURE
c. The terrible influence of the grumbling: Every person began to complain & murmur	10 Then Moses heard the people weep throughout their families, every man in the door of his tent: and the anger of the LORD was kindled greatly; Moses also was displeased.

4. The response of the LORD and Moses was to be expected. The LORD became very angry and Moses was deeply troubled (v.10-17).

OUTLINE	SCRIPTURE	SCRIPTURE	OUTLINE
d. The response of the LORD & Moses: The LORD became angry & Moses was deeply troubled	10 Then Moses heard the people weep throughout their families, every man in the door of his tent: and the anger of the LORD was kindled greatly; Moses also was displeased.	14 I am not able to bear all this people alone, because it is too heavy for me. 15 And if thou deal thus with me, kill me, I pray thee, out of hand, if I have found favour in thy sight; and let me not see my wretchedness.	2) Moses cried for God to raise up others to help him: The burden was too heavy—he simply could not continue to lead them by himself • Cried for God to take him unless He gave him help • Cried for God to keep him from ruin
1) Moses questioned, poured out his heart to the LORD • Why had God allowed so much trouble? • Why was God so displeased? • Why had God put the burden of the people on him? • Had he, Moses, conceived & given birth to the people? • Why had God chosen him to carry the people—like babies—to the promised land? • Where could he conceivably get enough meat for the people?	11 And Moses said unto the LORD, Wherefore hast thou afflicted thy servant? and wherefore have I not found favour in thy sight, that thou layest the burden of all this people upon me? 12 Have I conceived all this people? have I begotten them, that thou shouldest say unto me, Carry them in thy bosom, as a nursing father beareth the sucking child, unto the land which thou swarest unto their fathers? 13 Whence should I have flesh to give unto all this people? for they weep unto me, saying, Give us flesh, that we may eat.	16 And the LORD said unto Moses, Gather unto me seventy men of the elders of Israel, whom thou knowest to be the elders of the people, and officers over them; and bring them unto the tabernacle of the congregation, that they may stand there with thee. 17 And I will come down and talk with thee there: and I will take of the spirit which is upon thee, and will put it upon them; and they shall bear the burden of the people with thee, that thou bear it not thyself alone.	3) The LORD met the need of Moses • Instructed Moses to bring 70 elders to the Tabernacle • Promised to anoint the elders with God's Spirit, with the very same Spirit Moses had: They would help carry the burden of the people, help deal with their problems

a. Moses questioned, poured out his heart to the LORD (v.11-13).
   ⇒ Why had God allowed so much trouble?
   ⇒ Why was God so displeased?
   ⇒ Why had God put the burden of the people on him?
   ⇒ Was it Moses who had conceived and given birth to the people? Was it not God who had conceived and given them birth?
   ⇒ Why had God chosen him to carry the people in his arms—as a nurse carries a child—to the promised land?
   ⇒ Where could he conceivably get enough meat for the people?

b. Moses cried for God to raise up others to help him (v.14-15). The burden was too heavy and was crushing him under its weight. He could not continue to lead the people by himself. At this point, Moses became intense and desperate: he asked God either to help him or take him. Why? Because he felt that he would die right there upon the spot from the intense pressure he was feeling.
c. Note that the LORD met the need of His dear servant Moses (v.16-17). The LORD instructed Moses to bring seventy elders to the Tabernacle. God promised to anoint the elders with His Spirit, with the very same Spirit He had given to Moses. The elders would help carry the burden of the people, help deal with the problems of the people. As always, God met the desperate need of His dear servant. God had earlier appointed some leaders to help Moses in the administrative duties of the people (Ex.18:13f); now God was appointing seventy elders to help His dear servant in the spiritual ministry of the people (cp. Ex.24:9). The intense pressure and distress of Moses were being relieved by the LORD. The enormous weight of the ministry that Moses was sensing was being lifted. As stated, God was meeting the need of His dear servant.

5. Note the message of God's judgment to be given to the people by Moses (v.18-23).

OUTLINE	SCRIPTURE	SCRIPTURE	OUTLINE
e. The message of God's judgment to be given to the people 1) To consecrate themselves: Prepare to have their complaint & grumbling answered—the complaint that they were better off in Egypt (a symbol of the world)	18 And say thou unto the people, Sanctify yourselves against to morrow, and ye shall eat flesh: for ye have wept in the ears of the LORD, saying, Who shall give us flesh to eat? for it was well with us in Egypt: therefore the LORD will give you flesh, and ye shall eat.	ing, Why came we forth out of Egypt? 21 And Moses said, The people, among whom I am, are six hundred thousand footmen; and thou hast said, I will give them flesh, that they may eat a whole month.	4) The stress & questioning of Moses • How could God provide meat for several million?
2) To know that the Lord would give them meat: Not just for days, but for a whole month—so much meat they would loathe it	19 Ye shall not eat one day, nor two days, nor five days, neither ten days, nor twenty days;	22 Shall the flocks and the herds be slain for them, to suffice them? or shall all the fish of the sea be gathered together for them, to suffice them?	• Would there be enough even if they slaughtered all their flocks & herds? Or if they had all the fish in the sea?
3) The reason: • Because they had rejected the LORD • Because they desired to be back in Egypt (a symbol of the world)	20 But even a whole month, until it come out at your nostrils, and it be loathsome unto you: because that ye have despised the LORD which is among you, and have wept before him, say-	23 And the LORD said unto Moses, Is the LORD'S hand waxed short? thou shalt see now whether my word shall come to pass unto thee or not.	5) The LORD's rebuke to Moses: The LORD's arm (power) is not too short; He will do exactly what He says

a. The people were to sanctify or consecrate themselves (v.18). They were to prepare to have their complaining and grumbling answered—the complaint that they were better off in Egypt.
b. The people were to know that the LORD was going to give them meat: not just for days, but for a whole month (v.18-20). They were going to receive just what they grumbled about: meat. In fact, they were going to receive so much meat that they would loathe it. This blessing—an overabundance of meat—was to be a judgment. The people would have all the meat they had wanted and then some! They insisted that they simply had to have meat. So God was going to give them meat. They were going to receive so much meat and be so gluttonous about it that they would spew the meat out of their nostrils—loathing and despising it.
c. Note the reason why: because they had rejected the LORD. They had craved and desired to go back to Egypt (v.20). Keep in mind that Egypt is a symbol of the world with all of its lusts and cravings. The judgment of God was bound to fall upon these unbelievers, these complainers and grumblers who were rejecting God and rebelling against Him.
d. Note the stressful questioning by Moses (v.21-22); Moses was shaken:
   ⇒ How could God possibly provide meat for several million people?
   ⇒ Would there be enough meat even if they slaughtered all their flocks and herds? Or if they had all the fish in the sea?
e. Note the LORD's rebuke to Moses: the LORD's arm (power) is not too short; He will do exactly what He says (v.23). He has the power and the knowledge to do anything. Nothing is too hard for the LORD. The promise may be staggering and seem impossible to people, but He was the LORD God Himself (Jehovah, Yahweh).

6. Note the obedience of Moses (v.24-25).

OUTLINE	SCRIPTURE
f. The obedience of Moses 1) He declared the LORD's message to the people 2) He summoned the 70 elders to the Tabernacle	24 And Moses went out, and told the people the words of the LORD, and gathered the seventy men of the elders of the people, and set them round about the tabernacle.
3) The faithfulness of the LORD • He put His Spirit on the 70 elders • They prophesied this one time, but never again	25 And the LORD came down in a cloud, and spake unto him, and took of the spirit that was upon him, and gave it unto the seventy elders: and it came to pass, that, when the spirit rested upon them, they prophesied, and did not cease.

Moses declared the LORD's message to the people; then he summoned the seventy elders to the Tabernacle (v.24). As soon as Moses proved his obedience, the LORD was faithful (v.25). The LORD came down in the cloud of His Shekinah Glory and spoke with Moses. Furthermore, He did just what He had promised: the Spirit of God came upon the seventy elders, and they prophesied. But note, this was a one-of-a-kind experience. They never again prophesied.

7. Note the true spirit of Moses, the spirit of a humble minister, of a true servant of God (v.26-30).

OUTLINE	SCRIPTURE	SCRIPTURE	OUTLINE
g. The true spirit of Moses: The spirit of a humble minister, a true servant of God 1) Two elders had remained in camp & did not go to the Tabernacle: The Spirit also came upon them & they prophesied • A young man ran & told Moses	26 But there remained two of the men in the camp, the name of the one was Eldad, and the name of the other Medad: and the spirit rested upon them; and they were of them that were written, but went not out unto the tabernacle: and they prophesied in the camp. 27 And there ran a young man, and told Moses, and said, Eldad and Medad do prophesy in the camp.	28 And Joshua the son of Nun, the servant of Moses, one of his young men, answered and said, My lord Moses, forbid them. 29 And Moses said unto him, Enviest thou for my sake? would God that all the LORD'S people were prophets, and that the LORD would put his spirit upon them! 30 And Moses gat him into the camp, he and the elders of Israel.	• Joshua, Moses' aide, insisted that Moses stop them 2) Moses' true servant spirit: His desire was for the LORD'S Spirit to be upon all believers & for all to be prophets 3) Moses & the elders returned to the camp

a. Two elders had remained in camp and not responded to Moses' summons to come to the Tabernacle. However, the Spirit also came upon them, and they prophesied (v.26-28). A young man witnessed the experience and ran to tell Moses. Joshua, who was Moses' aide and standing close by, insisted that Moses stop the two elders from prophesying. Why? Perhaps Joshua felt that the two men had disobeyed by not accepting the summons of Moses; therefore, they should not be appointed as assistants to him. Or perhaps he felt the two men might be personal threats to Moses. If they had received the gift of God's Spirit outside the Tabernacle and away from Moses, this would downplay the gift of Moses. People might begin to feel that God could raise up someone else to be their leader and turn to either one of these two elders or other elders for leadership.

b. But note the spirit of Moses, the spirit of a true servant of God. This was just what he wanted: he prayed for the LORD'S Spirit to come upon all believers, for all believers to be prophets (v.29). He wanted all believers to be filled with the fullness of God, to experience the full presence and provision of God.

c. Moses and the elders then returned to the camp (v.30).

8. Note the judgment of God: the complaint of the people was granted (v.31-33).

OUTLINE	SCRIPTURE	SCRIPTURE	OUTLINE
h. The judgment of God: The complaint of the people was granted 1) Three feet deep & extended a whole day's walk in every direction 2) The people gathered quail for two days & one night:	31 And there went forth a wind from the LORD, and brought quails from the sea, and let them fall by the camp, as it were a day's journey on this side, and as it were a day's journey on the other side, round about the camp, and as it were two cubits high upon the face of the earth. 32 And the people stood up all that day, and all that	night, and all the next day, and they gathered the quails: he that gathered least gathered ten homers: and they spread them all abroad for themselves round about the camp. 33 And while the flesh was yet between their teeth, ere it was chewed, the wrath of the LORD was kindled against the people, and the LORD smote the people with a very great plague.	Every person gathered no less than 10 homers (50 bushels) 3) The people acted like gluttons: Gorged themselves

a. A wind drove quail in from the sea. Miraculously, the quail were three feet deep and extended a whole day's walk in every direction—enough quail to feed two to four million people (v.31).

b. The people gathered quail for two days and one night. Every person gathered no less than ten homers (almost 60 bushels). A staggering amount of meat! God provided far more quail than the people could possibly eat (v.32).

c. Note the animalistic, uncivilized, and savage behavior of the people. The people acted like gluttons: they gorged themselves (v.33). *The Expositor's Bible Commentary* describes it well:

> "The scene must have been similar to a riot: people screaming, birds flapping their wings, everywhere the pell-mell movement of a meat-hungry people in a sea of birds. Dare we picture people ripping at the birds, eating flesh before cooking it, bestial in behavior?"[1]

9. Note the anger of the LORD (v.33-34).

---

[1] *The Expositor's Bible Commentary*. Frank E. Gaebelein, Editor, p.795.

OUTLINE	SCRIPTURE	SCRIPTURE	OUTLINE
i. The anger of the LORD: Was aroused, burned against the people 1) He struck them with a severe plague	33 And while the flesh was yet between their teeth, ere it was chewed, the wrath of the LORD was kindled against the people, and the LORD smote the people with a very	great plague. 34 And he called the name of that place Kibroth-hat-taavah: because there they buried the people that lusted.	2) The place was named Kibroth Hattaavah, which means "graves of craving"

His anger was aroused and burned against the people. He struck them with a severe plague. Note when: "while the meat was still between their teeth" (v.33). Obviously, a plague of choking on the meat struck the people. Before they could swallow the meat, they choked. They were choking on their craving, their lusting, their gluttony. They had cursed and rebelled against the name of God, craving and lusting after flesh to eat. Consequently, God gave them up to their craving and lusting (cp.Ro.1:24-28). They received just what their flesh craved and lusted after: meat. Their fleshly appetite had run wild. As a result, they were given up to their fleshly appetite. And the very thing they had craved and lusted after choked them to death. They had brought the judgment of God upon themselves. Note that the place was named Kibroth Hattaavah which means "graves of craving" (v.34).

10. The people then departed and renewed their march to the promised land. But tragically, their hearts were still hard and stubborn, still filled with unbelief and grumbling. This will be seen in the next three chapters, especially chapter 14. But for now they marched on and camped at Hazeroth (v.35).

OUTLINE	SCRIPTURE
j. The march of the people: Camped at Hazeroth	35 And the people journeyed from Kibroth-hat-taavah unto Hazeroth; and abode at Hazeroth.

Thought 1. Note several strong lessons in this passage (v.4-35).

1) Seeking to fulfill one's appetites—craving and lusting after the things of the world—is wrong. Giving way to the lusts of the flesh arouses the judgment of God against us.

"Wherefore God also gave them up to uncleanness through the lusts of their own hearts, to dishonour their own bodies between themselves: Who changed the truth of God into a lie, and worshipped and served the creature more than the Creator, who is blessed for ever. Amen" (Ro.1:24-25).

"Being filled with all unrighteousness, fornication, wickedness, covetousness, maliciousness; full of envy, murder, debate, deceit, malignity; whisperers, Backbiters, haters of God, despiteful, proud, boasters, inventors of evil things, disobedient to parents, Without understanding, covenantbreakers, without natural affection, implacable, unmerciful: Who knowing the judgment of God, that they which commit such things are worthy of death, not only do the same, but have pleasure in them that do them" (Ro.1:29-32).

"Now the works of the flesh are manifest, which are these; Adultery, fornication, uncleanness, lasciviousness, Idolatry, witchcraft, hatred, variance, emulations, wrath, strife, seditions, heresies, Envyings, murders, drunkenness, revellings, and such like: of the which I tell you before, as I have also told you in time past, that they which do such things shall not inherit the kingdom of God" (Gal.5:19-21).

2) Seeking to fulfill the appetites of the flesh—lusting and craving after the world and its things—is not the call of God. The call of God is to a life of separation from the world. The believer is to live a life that is holy, righteous, and pure. He is to live a life that is totally separated to God, separated from the lusts and evil of this world.

"And take heed to yourselves, lest at any time your hearts be overcharged with surfeiting, and drunkenness, and cares of this life, and so that day come upon you unawares" (Lk.21:34).

"I beseech you therefore, brethren, by the mercies of God, that ye present your bodies a living sacrifice, holy, acceptable unto God, which is your reasonable service. And be not conformed to this world: but be ye transformed by the renewing of your mind, that ye may prove what is that good, and acceptable, and perfect, will of God" (Ro.12:1-2).

"Wherefore come out from among them, and be ye separate, saith the Lord, and touch not the unclean thing; and I will receive you, And will be a Father unto you, and ye shall be my sons and daughters, saith the Lord Almighty" (2 Cor.6:17-18).

"And have no fellowship with the unfruitful works of darkness, but rather reprove them" (Eph.5:11).

"No man that warreth entangleth himself with the affairs of this life; that he may please him who hath chosen him to be a soldier" (2 Tim.2:4).

"Love not the world, neither the things that are in the world. If any man love the world, the love of the Father is not in him. For all that is in the world, the lust of the flesh, and the lust of the eyes, and the pride of life, is not of the Father, but is of the world" (1 Jn.2:15-16).

"Depart ye, depart ye, go ye out from thence, touch no unclean thing; go ye out of the midst of her; be ye clean, that bear the vessels of the Lord" (Is.52:11).

3) Complaining and murmuring because of food is wrong. It is sin. Why? Because God promises to meet our needs, to give us all the necessities of life. But there is one condition: we must seek first the kingdom of God and His righteousness.

"But seek ye first the kingdom of God, and his righteousness; and all these things shall be added unto you" (Mt.6:33).

"Now unto him that is able to do exceeding abundantly above all that we ask or think, according to the power that worketh in us" (Eph.3:20).

"But my God shall supply all your need according to his riches in glory by Christ Jesus" (Ph.4:19).

"And ye shall serve the Lord your God, and he shall bless thy bread, and thy water; and I will take sickness away from the midst of thee" (Ex.23:25).

"And the Lord thy God will make thee plenteous in every work of thine hand, in the fruit of thy body, and in the fruit of thy cattle, and in the fruit of thy land, for good: for the Lord will again rejoice over thee for good, as he rejoiced over thy fathers" (Dt.30:9).

"Blessed be the Lord, who daily loadeth us with benefits, even the God of our salvation. Selah" (Ps.68:19).

"He should have fed them also with the finest of the wheat: and with honey out of the rock should I have satisfied thee" (Ps.81:16).

"I will abundantly bless her provision: I will satisfy her poor with bread" (Ps.132:15).

"Then shall he give the rain of thy seed, that thou shalt sow the ground withal; and bread of the increase of the earth, and it shall be fat and plenteous: in that day shall thy cattle feed in large pastures" (Is.30:23).

"Bring ye all the tithes into the storehouse, that there may be meat in mine house, and prove me now herewith, saith the Lord of hosts, if I will not open you the windows of heaven, and pour you out a blessing, that there shall not be room enough to receive it" (Mal.3:10).

4) Seeking to fulfill the appetites of the flesh—craving and lusting after the things of the world, complaining and grumbling about food—is wrong for one clear and fundamental reason: man shall not live by bread alone. Man has to have spiritual food. He must be fed by God. He must eat, partake of the *manna* from heaven, the Word of God.

"But he answered and said, It is written, Man shall not live by bread alone, but by every word that proceedeth out of the mouth of God" (Mt.4:4).

"As newborn babes, desire the sincere milk of the word, that ye may grow thereby: If so be ye have tasted that the Lord is gracious" (1 Pt.2:2-3).

"And he humbled thee, and suffered thee to hunger, and fed thee with manna, which thou knewest not, neither did thy fathers know; that he might make thee know that man doth not live by bread only, but by every word that proceedeth out of the mouth of the Lord doth man live" (Dt.8:3).

"Neither have I gone back from the commandment of his lips; I have esteemed the words of his mouth more than my necessary food" (Job 23:12).

"How sweet are thy words unto my taste! yea, sweeter than honey to my mouth" (Ps.119:103).

"Thy words were found, and I did eat them; and thy word was unto me the joy and rejoicing of mine heart: for I am called by thy name, O Lord God of hosts" (Jer.15:16).

5) Seeking to fulfill the appetites of the flesh—craving and lusting after the things of the world, complaining and grumbling about food—is sin for one clear and obvious reason: man shall not live by bread alone. He must have and partake of the bread that God sent down *out of* heaven. The bread that God sent *out of* heaven is the Lord Jesus Christ Himself. He is the Bread of Life. A person must eat or partake of Him in order to have his appetites satisfied and fulfilled. Jesus Christ alone can satisfy the hunger of man.

"Then Jesus said unto them, Verily, verily, I say unto you, Moses gave you not that bread from heaven; but my Father giveth you the true bread from heaven. For the bread of God is he which cometh down from heaven, and giveth life unto the world. Then said they unto him, Lord, evermore give us this bread. And Jesus said unto them, I am the bread of life: he that cometh to me shall never hunger; and he that believeth on me shall never thirst" (Jn.6:32-35).

"I am that bread of life. Your fathers did eat manna in the wilderness, and are dead. This is the bread which cometh down from heaven, that a man may eat thereof, and not die. I am the living bread which came down from heaven: if any man eat of this bread, he shall live for ever: and the bread that I will give is my flesh, which I will give for the life of the world" (Jn.6:48-51).

"This is that bread which came down from heaven: not as your fathers did eat manna, and are dead: he that eateth of this bread shall live for ever" (Jn.6:58).

6) Seeking to fulfill the appetites of the flesh—craving and lusting after the things of the world, doubting, complaining, grumbling, and murmuring—is the tragic failure of Israel. It has been recorded in Scripture for one undeniable purpose: to teach us not to lust after evil things as they lusted.

"Moreover, brethren, I would not that ye should be ignorant, how that all our fathers were under the cloud, and all passed through the sea; And were all baptized unto Moses in the cloud and in the sea; And did all eat the same spiritual meat; And did all drink the same spiritual drink: for they drank of

that spiritual Rock that followed them: and that Rock was Christ. But with many of them God was not well pleased: for they were overthrown in the wilderness. Now these things were our examples, to the intent we should not lust after evil things, as they also lusted. Neither be ye idolaters, as were some of them; as it is written, The people sat down to eat and drink, and rose up to play. Neither let us commit fornication, as some of them committed, and fell in one day three and twenty thousand. Neither let us tempt Christ, as some of them also tempted, and were destroyed of serpents. Neither murmur ye, as some of them also murmured, and were destroyed of the destroyer. Now all these things happened unto them for ensamples: and they are written for our admonition, upon whom the ends of the world are come" (1 Cor.10:1-11).

B. The Second Tragic Failure Seen in Two Leaders, Miriam & Aaron: Distrusting God—Criticizing & Questioning the Call of God's Servant, 12:1-16

1. The criticism & questioning of God's servant
   a. The criticizing of Moses' wife: She was of a different race
   b. The questioning of his unique call & mission: He was not the only leader or spokesman—God also chose & spoke through them
   c. The warning: The LORD heard them complain
   d. The response of Moses: Not reactionary nor combative but humble—he did not answer

2. The chastisement & judgment of God
   a. God instructed Moses, Aaron, & Miriam to go to the Tabernacle
      1) They obeyed
      2) He descended in the pillar of cloud & stood at the entrance
      3) He summoned Aaron & Miriam to step forward
   b. God strongly rebuked them & defended His unique call to His servant
      1) God spoke to His prophets through visions & dreams
      2) God called Moses to minister to all God's house
         • Moses was faithful
         • God spoke with Moses directly, not in riddles
         • Moses actually saw the form of God
      3) God's rebuke: They should have feared questioning the mission of God's servant
   c. God's anger burned against Miriam & Aaron & He chastised them
      1) God left them, lifted the cloud from the Tabernacle
      2) Miriam was afflicted with leprosy-like skin
      3) Aaron was stricken with terrible fear
         • He cried to Moses for mercy, confessing their sin against him
         • He cried for the healing of Miriam, that her flesh not be eaten away

3. The great mercy & compassion of God
   a. Moses interceded, cried out for Miriam: "Heal her!"
   b. God healed her, but she still had to be disciplined: To undergo the waiting period of the unclean—to be cut off from God's people for seven days (cp. Lev.13:4-6, 21, 26-27, 31-33, etc.)
   c. The overflowing mercy of God
      1) God led His people to wait on Miriam until she could return & rejoin the march to the promised land
      2) God led His people to the Desert of Paran: The staging area for entering the promised land

And Miriam and Aaron
spake against Moses because
of the Ethiopian woman
whom he had married: for he
had married an Ethiopian
woman.
2 And they said, Hath the
LORD indeed spoken only by
Moses? hath he not spoken
also by us? And the LORD
heard it.
3 (Now the man Moses was
very meek, above all the men
which were upon the face of
the earth.)
4 And the LORD spake sud-
denly unto Moses, and unto
Aaron, and unto Miriam,
Come out ye three unto the
tabernacle of the congregation. And they three came
out.
5 And the LORD came down
in the pillar of the cloud, and
stood in the door of the tabernacle, and called Aaron
and Miriam: and they both
came forth.
6 And he said, Hear now my
words: If there be a prophet
among you, I the LORD will
make myself known unto
him in a vision, and will
speak unto him in a dream.
7 My servant Moses is not
so, who is faithful in all mine
house.
8 With him will I speak
mouth to mouth, even apparently, and not in dark speeches; and the similitude of the
LORD shall he behold:
wherefore then were ye not
afraid to speak against my
servant Moses?
9 And the anger of the LORD
was kindled against them;
and he departed.
10 And the cloud departed
from off the tabernacle; and,
behold, Miriam became leprous, white as snow: and
Aaron looked upon Miriam,
and, behold, she was leprous.
11 And Aaron said unto
Moses, Alas, my lord, I
beseech thee, lay not the sin
upon us, wherein we have
done foolishly, and wherein
we have sinned.
12 Let her not be as one
dead, of whom the flesh is
half consumed when he
cometh out of his mother's
womb.
13 And Moses cried unto
the LORD, saying, Heal her
now, O God, I beseech thee.
14 And the LORD said unto
Moses, If her father had but
spit in her face, should she
not be ashamed seven days?
let her be shut out from the
camp seven days, and after
that let her be received in
again.
15 And Miriam was shut out
from the camp seven days:
and the people journeyed not
till Miriam was brought in
again.
16 And afterward the people
removed from Hazeroth, and
pitched in the wilderness of
Paran.

DIVISION II

THE TRAGIC, DEVASTATING FAILURE OF ISRAEL: WHY PEOPLE FORFEIT THEIR RIGHT TO ENTER THE PROMISED LAND, 11:1-14:45

B. The Second Tragic Failure Seen in Two Leaders, Miriam and Aaron: Distrusting God—Criticizing and Questioning the Call of God's Servant, 12:1-16

(12:1-16) **Introduction—Criticism, Spirit of—Grumbling, Spirit of—Murmuring, Spirit of—Minister, Criticism of**: a spirit of criticism and grumbling is sweeping the earth today. Almost everyone is caught up in the spirit. A critical spirit has infiltrated the attitude and speech of most people. People are criticizing, grumbling, and murmuring against…

- employer
- employee
- neighbor
- spouse
- parent
- family members
- politicians
- government
- taxes
- teachers
- school
- businesses
- friends
- money
- health
- bad luck
- the media

The list could go on and on. But there is one person who is criticized and grumbled about as much as any other person or professional: the minister of God. True, the minister is in a high profile profession and is usually held to a higher standard than most professionals. But there is more behind the criticism than just this: there is a spiritual warfare launched against the minister because of his call to serve God and His people. In fact, one of the major strategies of the devil is to arouse criticism and complaints against the minister of God. Sometimes the criticism is even launched by a family member. This is the subject of the present passage: *The Second Tragic Failure Seen in Two Leaders, Miriam and Aaron: Distrusting God—Criticizing and Questioning the Call of God's Servant,* 12:1-16.

1. The criticism and questioning of God's servant (v.1-3).
2. The chastisement and judgment of God (v.4-12).
3. The great mercy and compassion of God (v.13-16).

1 (12:1-3) **Criticism, of Ministers—Grumbling, against Ministers—Complaining, against Ministers—Miriam - Aaron, Questioned Moses' Leadership—Moses, Opposition to—Family, Criticism of—Minister, Opposition to**: there was the criticism and questioning of God's servant, Moses. What happened was heartbreaking. The very sister and brother of Moses stood against him, challenging his leadership. Keep in mind what Moses had just gone through. The people had at long last begun their march to the promised land, just within the past week. But within three days...

- the people had complained about their hardships, so much so that God was forced to chastise and judge them (Num.11:1-3).
- the people had complained about not having enough variety in their food—not enough meat or fresh vegetables—complained so much that God was forced for a second time to chastise them (Num.11:4-35).

Remember: Moses had become deeply discouraged by the people's constant criticism and complaining. The grumbling and murmuring got to Moses. He became deeply troubled, distressed to the point that he wanted God to remove him and get him out of the situation. He just wanted God to go ahead and take him home, that is, to die (Num.11:10-15). Now, apparently just a few days later, the very sister and brother of Moses began to criticize and attack him. Heartbreaking! Distressing! Discouraging! Cut to the core of his being, Moses was bound to be sensing deep, troubling emotions. This was his own sister and brother, and here they were attacking him immediately after his most distressing experience with the people.

OUTLINE	SCRIPTURE	SCRIPTURE	OUTLINE
1. The criticism & questioning of God's servant a. The criticizing of Moses' wife: She was of a different race b. The questioning of his unique call & mission: He was not the only leader or	**A**nd Miriam and Aaron spake against Moses because of the Ethiopian woman whom he had married: for he had married an Ethiopian woman. 2 And they said, Hath the	LORD indeed spoken only by Moses? hath he not spoken also by us? And the LORD heard it. 3 (Now the man Moses was very meek, above all the men which were upon the face of the earth.)	spokesman—God also chose & spoke through them c. The warning: The LORD heard them complain d. The response of Moses: Not reactionary nor combative but humble—he did not answer

1. Miriam and Aaron criticized Moses because of his wife, apparently because she was of a different race (v.1). Miriam apparently took the lead in the attack. The placement of her name first would seem to indicate this. But obviously, Aaron willingly went along with the criticism against his brother. The seriousness of this attack against God's servant is clearly seen by remembering who Miriam and Aaron were. They were both leaders among God's people. Miriam was a prophetess; in fact, she was the leader among the spirit-filled women of Israel (Ex.15:20-22). And Aaron was the High Priest, the supreme leader of Israel next to Moses. What was happening was incomprehensible, totally irresponsible. Here they were criticizing the servant of God, interrupting and detracting him from his ministry because he had married a Cushite, a woman who was not of Israel. Who was this woman? Is this a reference to Zipporah, Moses' wife (cp. Ex.2:15-22)? Moses' wife was from Midian, which is sometimes identified as Cush or Cushan (Hab.3:7; cp. Ex.2:16f). Was the skin of Zipporah different in any way from the skin of the Israelites? Or, had Zipporah died, and Moses married another woman from Cush?

The present passage seems to indicate that Moses indeed had married another woman, a Cushite. Moreover, if Miriam and Aaron were going to criticize Moses' marriage to Zipporah, they would most likely have done it years before, not now—not years later. It seems far more likely that they would be criticizing him for a recent marriage, a marriage which they opposed. The literal language of this verse seems to indicate a recent marriage to the Cushite woman. Note the literal translation of verse one: "Concerning the issue of the Cushite woman that he had married, for it was a Cushite woman whom he had married."[1]

The point to see is that Miriam and Aaron were cutting the heart of their brother Moses, the servant of God. They were distracting and interrupting his ministry, breaking his focus of thought, troubling and distressing his heart and mind. Moses was as any of us would be: heartbroken, distressed, deeply troubled emotionally and mentally, cut to the core of his being—all because his own sister and brother were now criticizing and murmuring against him.

2. Miriam and Aaron also questioned the unique call and mission of Moses (v.2). To them, Moses was not the only leader or spokesman chosen by God. God had also chosen and spoken through them. Note: they were not criticizing the right of Moses to be a leader nor grumbling against his position of leadership. They were grumbling because their call and position were not as honored or recognized as his. They wanted their position and call to be more recognized and honored among the people. They prided themselves in their abilities, in their call and position, and they felt that the people should give more respect and recognition to their service for the LORD. As stated, they did not want to replace Moses: they accepted his call and position before God. They just wanted equal respect, recognition, and honor for their call and position.

3. Note the warning: the LORD heard them complain (v.2). The implication is that the LORD hears everything. Nothing is said or done upon earth that passes His notice. He hears every criticism and attack, every grumbling and murmuring.

1 *The Expositor's Bible Commentary*, Frank E. Gaebelein, Editor, p.798.

And He saw Miriam and Moses and the primary call and ministry of His dear servant. The idea is that God stood ready to defend and execute justice on behalf of His servant.

4. Note the response of Moses (v.3): it was not reactionary nor combative, but humble. He said nothing, answered nothing to his attackers. He remained silent. Note why: he was meek and humble, more so than anyone else on the face of the earth (v.3). Remember, Moses was not eloquent: he was slow of speech and tongue. He was not fluent, not skillful with words, not expressive nor persuasive. He did not speak with ease (see outline and note—Ex.4:10-12 for more discussion). As so many who have this problem know, this probably means that Moses recoiled, withdrew as much as possible from criticism. Grumbling and murmuring upset him so much that he tried to avoid facing the situation whenever he could. He felt incapable of handling such situations because of his speech impediment. He felt that he could not adequately argue or present positions in a tense situation. Perhaps this is what was happening here: he was silent, not knowing exactly what to say to these two outstanding leaders. He knew they were wrong, but he did not know how to argue the point.

Note this fact as well: there is the possibility that Moses simply did not want to argue with his sister and brother. An argument might have severed the relationship they had with one another. Despite their obvious pride and focus upon themselves, Moses did not want to hurt them nor degrade them before one another and perhaps before other leaders who might have been present. Moses was a very meek and humble man.

Thought 1. Note two significant lessons:

1) Criticism, grumbling, and murmuring against God's servant is forbidden by God. Attacking God's minister is a sin. They are to be honored, not attacked.

"Judge not, that ye be not judged" (Mt.7:1).

"Therefore thou art inexcusable, O man, whosoever thou art that judgest: for wherein thou judgest another, thou condemnest thyself; for thou that judgest doest the same things" (Ro.2:1).

"Who art thou that judgest another man's servant [God's servant]? to his own master [God] he standeth or falleth. Yea, he shall be holden up: for God is able to make him stand" (Ro.14:4).

"Let a man so account of us, as of the ministers of Christ, and stewards of the mysteries of God" (1 Cor.4:1).

"Let nothing be done through strife or vainglory; but in lowliness of mind let each esteem other better than themselves. Look not every man on his own things, but every man also on the things of others" (Ph.2:3-4).

"Wherefore comfort yourselves together, and edify one another, even as also ye do And we beseech you, brethren, to know them which labour among you, and are over you in the Lord, and admonish you" (1 Th.5:11-12).

"There is one lawgiver, who is able to save and to destroy: who art thou that judgest another" (Jas.4:12).

2) The servant of God is not to react against criticism, not to be combative. In the face of criticism, the minister is to be meek and humble—totally submissive and dependent upon God.

"Whosoever therefore shall humble himself as this little child, the same is greatest in the kingdom of heaven" (Mt.18:4).

"For I say, through the grace given unto me, to every man that is among you, not to think of himself more highly than he ought to think; but to think soberly, according as God hath dealt to every man the measure of faith" (Ro.12:3).

"Let this mind be in you, which was also in Christ Jesus: Who, being in the form of God, thought it not robbery to be equal with God: But made himself of no reputation, and took upon him the form of a servant, and was made in the likeness of men: And being found in fashion as a man, he humbled himself, and became obedient unto death, even the death of the cross" (Ph.2:5-8).

"Humble yourselves in the sight of the Lord, and he shall lift you up" (Jas.4:10).

"Likewise, ye younger, submit yourselves unto the elder. Yea, all of you be subject one to another, and be clothed with humility: for God resisteth the proud, and giveth grace to the humble Humble yourselves therefore under the mighty hand of God, that he may exalt you in due time" (1 Pt.5:5-6).

"He hath showed thee, O man, what is good; and what doth the Lord require of thee, but to do justly, and to love mercy, and to walk humbly with thy God" (Mic.6:8).

2 (12:4-12) **Chastisement, of God—Judgment, of God—Discipline, of God—Miriam—Aaron—Intercession—Moses, Intercession of**: there was the chastisement and judgment of God upon Miriam and Aaron. Note that God immediately took over the situation. The words "at once" (pit om) mean immediately, suddenly, unexpectedly, abruptly—the LORD spoke before anyone even had time to think about what was happening. Note the Scripture and outline:

OUTLINE	SCRIPTURE	SCRIPTURE	OUTLINE
2. The chastisement & judgment of God a. God instructed Moses, Aaron, & Miriam to go to the Tabernacle 1) They obeyed 2) He descended in the pillar of cloud & stood at the	4 And the LORD spake suddenly unto Moses, and unto Aaron, and unto Miriam, Come out ye three unto the tabernacle of the congregation. And they three came out. 5 And the LORD came down in the pillar of the cloud, and	stood in the door of the tabernacle, and called Aaron and Miriam: and they both came forth. 6 And he said, Hear now my words: If there be a prophet among you, I the LORD will make myself known unto him in a vision, and will	entrance 3) He summoned Aaron & Miriam to step forward b. God strongly rebuked them & defended His unique call to His servant 1) God spoke to His prophets through visions & dreams

OUTLINE	SCRIPTURE	SCRIPTURE	OUTLINE
2) God called Moses to minister to all God's house • Moses was faithful • God spoke with Moses directly, not in riddles • Moses actually saw the form of God 3) God's rebuke: They should have feared questioning the mission of God's servant c. God's anger burned against Miriam & Aaron & He chastised them 1) God left them, lifted the	speak unto him in a dream. 7 My servant Moses is not so, who is faithful in all mine house. 8 With him will I speak mouth to mouth, even apparently, and not in dark speeches; and the similitude of the LORD shall he behold: wherefore then were ye not afraid to speak against my servant Moses? 9 And the anger of the LORD was kindled against them; and he departed. 10 And the cloud departed	from off the tabernacle; and, behold, Miriam became leprous, white as snow: and Aaron looked upon Miriam, and, behold, she was leprous. 11 And Aaron said unto Moses, Alas, my lord, I beseech thee, lay not the sin upon us, wherein we have done foolishly, and wherein we have sinned. 12 Let her not be as one dead, of whom the flesh is half consumed when he cometh out of his mother's womb.	cloud from the Tabernacle 2) Miriam was afflicted with leprosy-like skin 3) Aaron was stricken with terrible fear • He cried to Moses for mercy, confessing their sin against him • He cried for the healing of Miriam, that her flesh not be eaten away

1. God summoned Moses, Aaron, and Miriam to go to the Tabernacle (v.4-5). All three were obviously together, which means that Miriam and Aaron were most definitely criticizing Moses face-to-face. Note what happened when they reached the Tabernacle: the cloud of the Shekinah Glory—the very presence of God—dramatically descended, not to show mercy but wrath. God stood at the entrance of the Tabernacle to exercise judgment. Stricken with fear and terror, Miriam and Aaron were summoned to step forward toward God.

2. God strongly rebuked them and defended His unique call to His dear servant (v.6-8). Note the first thing God said: "Listen to my words. Hear, heed what I say."

a. God spoke to His prophets through visions and dreams, but this was not so with Moses.

b. God had called Moses to minister to all of God's house, to all of God's people (v.6-7). Three things in particular set Moses apart from all other prophets:

⇒ First, Moses was extremely faithful to the LORD and the ministry to which God called him (v.7).
⇒ Second, God spoke with Moses directly, not in riddles (v.8).
⇒ Third, Moses actually saw the form of God (v.8).

What does this mean, Moses saw the "form" (tmonah) of God? It does not mean that he saw the *unveiled* presence of God. It means that Moses saw a form, a shape, a cloudy image of God, not the very being of God.

c. Note God's rebuke of Miriam and Aaron. They should have feared questioning the mission of God's servant: "Why were you not afraid to speak against my servant?"

3. God's anger burned against Miriam and Aaron, and He chastised them (v.9-12).

a. God left them: the cloud of His presence abruptly lifted from the Tabernacle (v.10). The confrontation had taken place. The judgment had been pronounced.

b. Miriam—because she was apparently the instigator of the attack upon God's servant—was immediately afflicted with leprosy-like skin (v.10). She had committed a terrible sin; consequently, she was afflicted with the very disease that symbolized the sinful nature of man.

c. Aaron was stricken with terrible fear (v.10-12). When he turned, he saw the ghastly disease that had suddenly covered Miriam's body. Stricken with horror, he cried out to Moses for mercy, confessing his and Miriam's sin against him (v.11). He cried for the healing of Miriam, that her flesh not be eaten away (v.12).

Thought 1. God judges or chastises His people. When we sin, God disciplines and corrects us.

"Every branch in me that beareth not fruit he taketh away: and every branch that beareth fruit, he purgeth it, that it may bring forth more fruit" (Jn.15:2).

"But when we are judged, we are chastened of the Lord, that we should not be condemned with the world" (1 Cor.11:32).

"And ye have forgotten the exhortation which speaketh unto you as unto children, My son, despise not thou the chastening of the Lord, nor faint when thou art rebuked of him: For whom the Lord loveth he chasteneth, and scourgeth every son whom he receiveth" (Heb.12:5-6).

"Thou shalt also consider in thine heart, that, as a man chasteneth his son, so the Lord thy God chasteneth thee" (Dt.8:5).

"Blessed is the man whom thou chastenest, O Lord, and teachest him out of thy law" (Ps.94:12).

"My son, despise not the chastening of the Lord; neither be weary of his correction: For whom the Lord loveth he correcteth; even as a father the son in whom he delighteth" (Pr.3:11-12).

Thought 2. Aaron feared the anger and judgment of God. We, too, must fear the anger and judgment of God. God is going to judge us, judge everything that we do—all our works. No matter what people think or say, this is the strong declaration of Scripture.

"For the Son of man shall come in the glory of his Father with his angels; and then he shall reward every man according to his works" (Mt.16:27).

"For we must all appear before the judgment seat of Christ; that every one may receive the things done in his body, according to that he hath done, whether it be good or bad" (2 Cor.5:10).

"And if ye call on the Father, who without respect of persons judgeth according to every man's work, pass the time of your sojourning here in fear" (1 Pt.1:17).

"And, behold, I come quickly; and my reward is with me, to give every man according as his work shall be" (Rev.22:12).

"Also unto thee, O Lord, belongeth mercy: for thou renderest to every man according to his work" (Ps.62:12).

"I the Lord search the heart, I try the reins, even to give every man according to his ways, and according to the fruit of his doings" (Jer.17:10).

Thought 3. God calls and gifts believers differently. Every believer is called to a distinct, specific service. Moses was called to his particular ministry; Miriam and Aaron to theirs. So it is with all believers. God calls every one of us to serve Him and to serve Him faithfully in the ministry given us.

"Having then gifts differing according to the grace that is given to us, whether prophecy, let us prophesy according to the proportion of faith; Or ministry, let us wait on our ministering: or he that teacheth, on teaching; Or he that exhorteth, on exhortation: he that giveth, let him do it with simplicity; he that ruleth, with diligence; he that showed mercy, with cheerfulness" (Ro.12:6-8).

"But unto every one of us is given grace according to the measure of the gift of Christ" (Eph.4:7).

"And he gave some, apostles; and some, prophets; and some, evangelists; and some, pastors and teachers; For the perfecting of the saints, for the work of the ministry, for the edifying of the body of Christ: Till we all come in the unity of the faith, and of the knowledge of the Son of God, unto a perfect man, unto the measure of the stature of the fulness of Christ" (Eph.4:11-13).

"Now there are diversities of gifts, but the same Spirit. And there are differences of administrations, but the same Lord. And there are diversities of operations, but it is the same God which worketh all in all. But the manifestation of the Spirit is given to every man to profit withal. For to one is given by the Spirit the word of wisdom; to another the word of knowledge by the same Spirit; To another faith by the same Spirit; to another the gifts of healing by the same Spirit; To another the working of miracles; to another prophecy; to another discerning of spirits; to another divers kinds of tongues; to another the interpretation of tongues: But all these worketh that one and the selfsame Spirit, dividing to every man severally as he will" (1 Cor.12:4-11).

"Moreover it is required in stewards [servants] of God, that a man be found faithful" (1 Cor.4:2).

3 (12:13-16) **Mercy, of God—Compassion, of God—Prayer, Intercession—Intercession**: there was the great mercy and compassion of God. Note the Scripture and outline:

OUTLINE	SCRIPTURE	SCRIPTURE	OUTLINE
3. The great mercy & compassion of God a. Moses interceded, cried out for Miriam: "Heal her!" b. God healed her, but she still had to be disciplined: To undergo the waiting period of the unclean—to be cut off from God's people for seven days (cp. Lev.13:4-6, 21, 26-	13 And Moses cried unto the LORD, saying, Heal her now, O God, I beseech thee. 14 And the LORD said unto Moses, If her father had but spit in her face, should she not be ashamed seven days? let her be shut out from the camp seven days, and after that let her be received in	again. 15 And Miriam was shut out from the camp seven days: and the people journeyed not till Miriam was brought in again. 16 And afterward the people removed from Hazeroth, and pitched in the wilderness of Paran.	27, 31-33, etc.) c. The overflowing mercy of God 1) God led His people to wait on Miriam until she could return & rejoin the march to the promised land 2) God led His people to the Desert of Paran: The staging area for entering the promised land

1. Moses interceded, cried out from the depths of his heart, cried out to God for his sister Miriam: "O God, please heal her!" (v.3). The chastisement or the affliction had immediately stricken Miriam. The need was desperate. Miriam was suffering, apparently doomed to a life of alienation and death unless God immediately had mercy on her. Moses was helpless except for prayer. He and Aaron both knew this. Therefore, Moses cried out, "O God, please heal her!"
2. God acted: He healed her. But she was still to be disciplined (v.14). She had committed a serious offense; therefore, she needed to learn that a person reaps what he sows, that she must not be critical and prideful, but instead meek and humble. Thus, God insisted that she undergo the waiting period for the ceremonially unclean. For seven days, she had to be put out of the camp, cut off from God's people (cp. Lev.13:4-6, 21, 26-27, 31-33). Remember, leprosy or serious skin disease was a symbol of sin. Therefore, the discipline of Miriam—being removed from God's people—is a picture of the church exercising discipline when members commit serious sin.
3. Note the overflowing mercy of God (v.15-16).
    a. God led His people to wait on her until she returned and could rejoin the march to the promised land. (v.15).
    b. God led His people to the Desert of Paran which was to be the staging area for entering the promised land (v.16).

Thought 1. Note two strong lessons for every generation of people.

1) God hears prayer. If a believer cries out to the LORD—cries out from the depths of his heart—God hears and answers. Oh, how believers must cry out for their families, their brothers and sisters, their parents and children.

"Ask, and it shall be given you; seek, and ye shall find; knock, and it shall be opened unto you" (Mt.7:7).

"Watch and pray, that ye enter not into temptation: the spirit indeed is willing, but the flesh is weak" (Mt.26:41).

"And I say unto you, Ask, and it shall be given you; seek, and ye shall find; knock, and it shall be opened unto you" (Lk.11:9).

"If ye abide in me, and my words abide in you, ye shall ask what ye will, and it shall be done unto you" (Jn.15:7).

"Hitherto have ye asked nothing in my name: ask, and ye shall receive, that your joy may be full" (Jn.16:24).

"And this is the confidence that we have in him, that, if we ask any thing according to his will, he heareth us: And if we know that he hear us, whatsoever we ask, we know that we have the petitions that we desired of him" (1 Jn.5:14-15).

"He shall call upon me, and I will answer him: I will be with him in trouble; I will deliver him, and honour him" (Ps.91:15).

"Then shalt thou call, and the Lord shall answer; thou shalt cry, and he shall say, Here I am. If thou take away from the midst of thee the yoke, the putting forth of the finger, and speaking vanity" (Is.58:9).

"And it shall come to pass, that before they call, I will answer; and while they are yet speaking, I will hear" (Is.65:24).

2) God is merciful and compassionate. He forgave Miriam's sin and met her need. He will forgive our sins and cleanse us—if only we will call out to Him.

"In whom we have redemption through his blood, the forgiveness of sins, according to the riches of his grace"(Eph.1:7).

"If we confess our sins, he is faithful and just to forgive us our sins, and to cleanse us from all unrighteousness"(1 Jn.1:9).

"My little children, these things write I unto you, that ye sin not. And if any man sin, we have an advocate with the Father, Jesus Christ the righteous: And he is the propitiation for our sins: and not for ours only, but also for the sins of the whole world"(1 Jn.2:1-2).

"But he, being full of compassion, forgave their iniquity, and destroyed them not: yea, many a time turned he his anger away, and did not stir up all his wrath" (Ps.78:38).

"But thou, O Lord, art a God full of compassion, and gracious, longsuffering, and plenteous in mercy and truth" (Ps.86:15).

"And it shall come to pass, after that I have plucked them out I will return, and have compassion on them, and will bring them again, every man to his heritage, and every man to his land" (Jer.12:15).

"It is of the Lord's mercies that we are not consumed, because his compassions fail not" (Lam.3:22).

"But though he cause grief, yet will he have compassion according to the multitude of his mercies" (Lam.3:32).

"I drew them with cords of a man, with bands of love: and I was to them as they that take off the yoke on their jaws, and I laid meat unto them" (Hos.11:4).

"And rend your heart, and not your garments, and turn unto the Lord your God: for he is gracious and merciful, slow to anger, and of great kindness, and repenteth him of the evil" (Joel 2:13).

"Who is a God like unto thee, that pardoneth iniquity, and passeth by the transgression of the remnant of his heritage? he retaineth not his anger for ever, because he delighteth in mercy. He will turn again, he will have compassion upon us; he will subdue our iniquities; and thou wilt cast all their sins into the depths of the sea" (Mic.7:18-19).

C. The Final Tragic Failure that Dooms the People—the Twelve Spies & Their Mixed Report: Distrusting God—Being Negative, Fearful, & Defeated, Disbelieving & Rebelling against God, 13:1-14:45

1. The command to send 12 men to spy out the land of Canaan

a. The men selected were to be leaders, one from each tribe
   1) The spies were sent out from the Desert of Paran
   2) The spies were different leaders than the tribal chiefs
      - From the tribe of Reuben: Shammua
      - From the tribe of Simeon: Shaphat
      - From the tribe of Judah: Caleb
      - From the tribe of Issachar: Igal
      - From the tribe of Ephraim: Hoshea (Joshua)
      - From the tribe of Benjamin: Palti
      - From the tribe of Zebulun: Gaddiel
      - From the tribe of Manasseh: Gaddi
      - From the tribe of Dan: Ammiel
      - From the tribe of Asher: Sethur
      - From the tribe of Naphtali: Nahbi
      - From the tribe of Gad: Geuel
   3) The name of the personal assistant to Moses was changed from Hoshea to Joshua
      - Hoshea means "salvation"
      - Joshua means "God saves"

b. The mission given to the spies: To spy out the most southern part of Canaan, the Negev, & then move north through the hill country
   1) To see if the people were strong or weak, few or many

And the LORD spake unto
Moses, saying,
2 Send thou men, that they
may search the land of
Canaan, which I give unto
the children of Israel: of
every tribe of their fathers
shall ye send a man, every
one a ruler among them.
3 And Moses by the commandment
of the LORD sent
them from the wilderness of
Paran: all those men were
heads of the children of
Israel.
4 And these were their
names: of the tribe of
Reuben, Shammua the son of
Zaccur.
5 Of the tribe of Simeon,
Shaphat the son of Hori.
6 Of the tribe of Judah,
Caleb the son of Jephunneh.
7 Of the tribe of Issachar,
Igal the son of Joseph.
8 Of the tribe of Ephraim,
Oshea the son of Nun.
9 Of the tribe of Benjamin,
Palti the son of Raphu.
10 Of the tribe of Zebulun,
Gaddiel the son of Sodi.
11 Of the tribe of Joseph,
namely, of the tribe of
Manasseh, Gaddi the son of
Susi.
12 Of the tribe of Dan,
Ammiel the son of Gemalli.
13 Of the tribe of Asher,
Sethur the son of Michael.
14 Of the tribe of Naphtali,
Nahbi the son of Vophsi.
15 Of the tribe of Gad,
Geuel the son of Machi.
16 These are the names of
the men which Moses sent to
spy out the land. And Moses
called Oshea the son of Nun
Jehoshua.
17 And Moses sent them to
spy out the land of Canaan,
and said unto them, Get you
up this way southward, and
go up into the mountain:
18 And see the land, what it
is; and the people that
dwelleth therein, whether
they be strong or weak, few
or many;
19 And what the land is that
they dwell in, whether it be
good or bad; and what cities
they be that they dwell in,
whether in tents, or in strong
holds;
20 And what the land is,
whether it be fat or lean,
whether there be wood therein,
or not. And be ye of good
courage, and bring of the
fruit of the land. Now the
time was the time of the first
ripe grapes.
21 So they went up, and
searched the land from the
wilderness of Zin unto
Rehob, as men come to
Hamath.
22 And they ascended by
the south, and came unto
Hebron; where Ahiman,
Sheshai, and Talmai, the
children of Anak, were.
(Now Hebron was built
seven years before Zoan in
Egypt.)
23 And they came unto the
brook of Eshcol, and cut
down from thence a branch
with one cluster of grapes,
and they bare it between two
upon a staff; and they
brought of the pomegranates,
and of the figs.
24 The place was called the
brook Eshcol, because of the
cluster of grapes which the
children of Israel cut down
from thence.
25 And they returned from
searching of the land after
forty days.
26 And they went and came
to Moses, and to Aaron, and
to all the congregation of the
children of Israel, unto the
wilderand.
27 And they told him, and
said, We came unto the land
whither thou sentest us, and
surely it floweth with milk
and honey; and this is the
fruit of it.
28 Nevertheless the people
be strong that dwell in the
land, and the cities are
walled, and very great: and
moreover we saw the children
of Anak there.
29 The Amalekites dwell in
the land of the south: and the
Hittites, and the Jebusites,
and the Amorites, dwell in
the mountains: and the
Canaanites dwell by the sea,
and by the coast of Jordan.

   2) To see what the land was like, good or bad
   3) To see if the towns were fortified or unwalled reports
   4) To check the soil to see if it was fertile or poor, barren or full of trees
   5) To bring back samples of the fruit (it was grape season)

c. The mission carried out: Began at the Desert of Zin & spied as far as Rehob[DS1] near Lebo Hamath[DS2] (cp. 34:8)
   1) The first city they spied out: Hebron[DS3]
      - Was inhabited by the Anakites (giants, a tall people, cp. v.28, 33)
      - Had been built seven years before Zoan[DS4] in Egypt
   2) The Valley of Eshcol was very fruitful
      - A single cluster of grapes was so large that it had to be carried on a pole by two men, along with other fruit
      - The valley was given the name *Eshcol* by the Israelites because of the large grapes: "The Valley of the Cluster"
   3) The spies returned after a 40-day mission

2. The report & different conclusion of the spies

a. The report was given to Moses, Aaron, & the whole community; then the fruit was shown to them

b. The report of the spies
   1) The positive factors: The land flowed with milk & honey; the fruit was proof
   2) The negative factors
      - The people were powerful & the cities fortified
      - The descendants of Anak (giants) lived there
      - The Amalekites were in the Negev
      - The Hittites, Jebusites, & Amorites in the hill country
      - The Canaanites along the sea & the Jordan River

c. The different conclusions
  1) The conclusion of Caleb
    - Silenced the people
    - Declared that they should go up & take the land
  2) The conclusion of ten spies (not Joshua)—declared that they could not attack, for the nations were stronger: Began to spread unbelief & exaggerated, discouraging
    - The land—its harsh environment—consumed its inhabitants
    - The people—all of them—were huge, gigantic
    - The Nephilim—descendants of Anak (the giants)—were there: The Israelites were like grasshoppers before them

3. The fatal response of the people: Grumbling, fear, unbelief, & rebellion
a. The grumbling unbelief emphasized: "All the people," "all the Israelites," "the whole assembly"
  1) Were against the leaders
  2) Felt death in Egypt or the desert would have been better
  3) Accused the LORD of forsaking them & their families
  4) Questioned if it would not be better to return to Egypt
  5) Suggested that a new leader be chosen who would lead them back to Egypt (cp. Neh. 9:17, he was actually chosen)
b. The response of Moses & Aaron: Fell face down before the people—helpless, submissive before God
c. The response of Joshua & Caleb: Tore their clothes & declared the truthful facts about the land they had spied out
  1) The land was exceedingly good (would not consume them as the other spies had claimed)

30 And Caleb stilled the
people before Moses, and
said, Let us go up at once,
and possess it; for we are
well able to overcome it.
31 But the men that went up
with him said, We be not
able to go up against the people; for they are stronger
than we.
32 And they brought up an
evil report of the land which
they had searched unto the
children of Israel, saying,
The land, through which we
have gone to search it, is a
land that eateth up the inhabitants thereof; and all the
people that we saw in it are
men of a great stature.
33 And there we saw the
giants, the sons of Anak,
which come of the giants:
and we were in our own
sight as grasshoppers, and so
we were in their sight.

CHAPTER 14

And all the congregation
lifted up their voice, and
cried; and the people wept
that night.
2 And all the children of
Israel murmured against
Moses and against Aaron:
and the whole congregation
said unto them, Would God
that we had died in the land
of Egypt! or would God we
had died in this wilderness!
3 And wherefore hath the
LORD brought us unto this
land, to fall by the sword,
that our wives and our children should be a prey? were
it not better for us to return
into Egypt?
4 And they said one to another, Let us make a captain,
and let us return into
Egypt.
5 Then Moses and Aaron fell
on their faces before all the
assembly of the congrega-
tion of the children of Israel.
6 And Joshua the son of
Nun, and Caleb the son of
Jephunneh, which were of
them that searched the land,
rent their clothes:
7 And they spake unto all the
company of the children of
Israel, saying, The land,
which we passed through to
search it, is an exceeding
good land.
8 If the LORD delight in us,
then he will bring us into this
land, and give it us; a land
which floweth with milk and
honey.
9 Only rebel not ye against
the LORD, neither fear ye the
people of the land; for they
are bread for us: their
defense is departed from
them, and the LORD is with
us: fear them not.
10 But all the congregation
bade stone them with stones.
And the glory of the LORD
appeared in the tabernacle of
the congregation before all
the children of Israel.
11 And the LORD said unto
Moses, How long will this
people provoke me? and
how long will it be ere they
believe me, for all the signs
which I have shewed among
them?
12 I will smite them with
the pestilence, and disinherit
them, and will make of thee
a greater nation and mightier
than they.
13 And Moses said unto the
LORD, Then the Egyptians
shall hear it, (for thou
broughtest up this people in
thy might from ness of
Paran, to Kadesh; and
brought back word unto
them, and unto all the congregation, and shewed them
the fruit of the 1 among
them;)
14 And they will tell it to
the inhabitants of this land:
for they have heard that thou
LORD art among this people,
that thou LORD art seen face
to face, and that thy cloud
standeth over them, and that
thou goest before them, by
daytime in a pillar of a cloud,
and in a pillar of fire by
night.
15 Now if thou shalt kill all
this people as one man, then
the nations which have heard
the fame of thee will speak,
saying,
16 Because the LORD was
not able to bring this people
into the land which he sware
unto them, therefore he hath
slain them in the wilderness.
17 And now, I beseech thee,
let the power of my Lord be
great, according as thou hast
spoken, saying,
18 The LORD is longsuffer-

  2) The LORD would lead & give them the land
  3) The people must not rebel against the LORD nor be afraid of the inhabitants
    - They would swallow up the inhabitants
    - The LORD was with them
d. The fatal rejection: They plotted to stone the godly leaders

4. The anger & fierce judgment of the LORD & the intercession of Moses
a. The glory of the LORD burst forth at the Tabernacle before all
  1) Questioned how long the people would treat God with contempt: Refuse to believe in Him & the miracles He had performed
  2) Threatened to destroy them with a plague: To use Moses to build a new race of people, greater & stronger
b. The intercession, the pleading of Moses
  1) The reputation of God was at stake: The Egyptians would hear about Israel's destruction & tell the Canaanites about it
    - The Canaanites had already heard that the God of the Israelites guided & protected them
    - The Canaanites would question the power & promises of God to His people
    - The strength of God must be demonstrated, His Word kept
  2) The love & forgiveness of

God were at stake, as well as the discipline or chastisement of God: Moses understood this (God was both loving & just)

3) The cry of Moses for God to forgive the sin of the people: Just as He had since their deliverance from Egyptian slavery

c. The astounding forgiveness of the LORD

d. The sure judgment—discipline, chastisement—of the Lord: Was carried out without reservation upon every adult who disobeyed & tested God time and again (note: ten times)[DS5]

1) The first discipline, chastisement: Not one of the adults would see the promised land—were to die in the wilderness or desert

2) The one exception, Caleb (& Joshua, v.38): Because they were loyal, followed the LORD wholeheartedly

3) The second discipline, chastisement: To turn back toward the Red Sea, to wander about in the wilderness or desert

5. The declaration of God's charge & judgment (discipline, chastisement)

a. God's charge against the people: Unbelief—grumbling, complaining against Him

b. God's judgment against the people: To reap the very things they had said (the just or judicial judgment of God)

1) Their bodies would die in the wilderness or desert
   - Every adult 20 years old or older—everyone who grumbled
   - Not a person would ever enter the promised land: Except Caleb & Joshua

2) Their children would be brought into the land & enjoy it: Not enslaved (their false charge against God letting this happen, v.3)
   - The parents would die in the desert
   - The children would be shepherds, having to suffer & wander about in the desert for 40 years: Because of the parents' unfaithfulness

3) Their judgment would cover a 40 year span: One year for each of the 40 days they spied out the land of Canaan
   - Because they had sinned
   - Because God had to discipline & chastise them

4) Their fate was sealed, set in the concrete of God's Word—all because they had banded together against God: They were to meet their end in the desert; they were to die there

c. God's judgment against the ten unbelieving spies

1) The reason
   - Because they misled the people to distrust & grumble against God
   - Because they spread disbelief, an exaggerated report

2) The judgment: Stricken with a plague & died

3) The judgment of God spared Joshua & Caleb: Among the spies, they alone survived

d. The response of the people to the declaration of God's judgment: Sorrow, bitter mourning

6. The incomplete confession & defeat of Israel, acting without God

a. The incomplete confession: No repentance

b. The disobedience:

1) Refusing to turn around & march toward the Red Sea (v.25)

2) Planning to march into the promised land

c. The clear, strong warning of Moses: Would not succeed, but would be defeated by the inhabitants of Canaan

ing, and of great mercy, forgiving iniquity and transgression, and by no means
clearing the guilty, visiting
the iniquity of the fathers
upon the children unto the
third and fourth generation.
19 Pardon, I beseech thee,
the iniquity of this people
according unto the greatness
of thy mercy, and as thou
hast forgiven this people,
from Egypt even until now.
20 And the LORD said, I
have pardoned according to
thy word:
21 But as truly as I live, all
the earth shall be filled with
the glory of the LORD.
22 Because all those men
which have seen my glory,
and my miracles, which I did
in Egypt and in the wilderness, and have tempted me
now these ten times, and
have not hearkened to my
voice;
23 Surely they shall not see
the land which I sware unto
their fathers, neither shall
any of them that provoked
me see it:
24 But my servant Caleb,
because he had another spirit
with him, and hath followed
me fully, him will I bring
into the land whereinto he
went; and his seed shall possess it.
25 (Now the Amalekites
and the Canaanites dwelt in
the valley.) To morrow turn
you, and get you into the
wilderness by the way of the
Red sea.
26 And the LORD spake unto
Moses and unto Aaron, saying,
27 How long shall I bear
with this evil congregation,
which murmur against me? I
have heard the murmurings
of the children of Israel,
which they murmur against
me.
28 Say unto them, As truly
as I live, saith the LORD, as
ye have spoken in mine ears,
so will I do to you:
29 Your carcasses shall fall
in this wilderness; and all
that were numbered of you,
according to your whole
number, from twenty years
old and upward, which have
murmured against me,
30 Doubtless ye shall not
come into the land, concerning which I sware to make
you dwell therein, save
Caleb the son of Jephunneh,
and Joshua the son of Nun.
31 But your little ones,
which ye said should be a
prey, them will I bring in,
and they shall know the land
which ye have despised.
32 But as for you, your carcasses, they shall fall in this
wilderness.
33 And your children shall
wander in the wilderness
forty years, and bear your
whoredoms, until your carcasses be wasted in the
wilderness.
34 After the number of the
days in which ye searched
the land, even forty days,
each day for a year, shall ye
bear your iniquities, even
forty years, and ye shall
know my breach of promise.
35 I the LORD have said, I
will surely do it unto all this
evil congregation, that are
gathered together against
me: in this wilderness they
shall be consumed, and there
they shall die.
36 And the men, which
Moses sent to search the
land, who returned, and
made all the congregation to
murmur against him, by
bringing up a slander upon
the land,
37 Even those men that did
bring up the evil report upon
the land, died by the plague
before the LORD.
38 But Joshua the son of
Nun, and Caleb the son of
Jephunneh, which were of
the men that went to search
the land, lived still.
39 And Moses told these
sayings unto all the children
of Israel: and the people
mourned greatly.
40 And they rose up early in
the morning, and gat them up
into the top of the mountain,
saying, Lo, we be here, and
will go up unto the place
which the LORD hath prom-
ised: for we have sinned.
41 And Moses said,
Wherefore now do ye transgress the commandment of
the LORD? but it shall not
prosper.
42 Go not up, for the LORD is
not among you; that ye be not
smitten before your enemies.
43 For the Amalekites and

1) Because they had turned away from the LORD 2) Because He would not be with them d. The people disobeyed: Marched toward the hill country without Moses or the	the Canaanites are there before you, and ye shall fall by the sword: because ye are turned away from the LORD, therefore the LORD will not be with you. 44 But they presumed to go up unto the hill top: nevertheless the ark of the	covenant of the LORD, and Moses, departed not out of the camp. 45 Then the Amalekites came down, and the Canaanites which dwelt in that hill, and smote them, and discomfited them, even unto Hormah.	Ark of the Covenant (a symbol of God's presence & power) e. The result: The Amalekites & Canaanites attacked them & sent them fleeing as far as Hormah[DS6]

DIVISION II

THE TRAGIC, DEVASTATING FAILURE OF ISRAEL: WHY PEOPLE FORFEIT THEIR RIGHT TO ENTER THE PROMISED LAND, 11:1-14:45

C. The Final Tragic Failure that Dooms the People—the Twelve Spies and Their Mixed Report: Distrusting God—Being Negative and Defeated, Fearful and Unbelieving—Rejecting and Rebelling against God, 13:1-14:45

(13:1-14:45) **Introduction—Negativism, Attitude of—Defeatism, Attitude of—Unbelief, Attitude of—Israel, Failure of**: there is an attitude that will defeat and sometimes destroy a person—that of negativism. There are several words that describe a negative attitude:

⇒ defeated ⇒ unbelieving ⇒ pessimistic
⇒ fearful ⇒ cynical ⇒ despairing

A negative attitude is often unwilling to face the facts, to face the truth of a situation. In fact, a negative attitude that is deeply rooted will often lead to rebellion, an unwillingness to listen and follow the truth.

This was the fundamental problem with Israel: a negative, defeatist, fearful, unbelieving attitude. The result was tragic: rebellion against God and His dear servant Moses.

This present passage is the climax to the history of the first generation of Israelites. This rebellion was the final blow, the tenth rebellion of unbelief and grumbling within two years. However, in this rebellion, God knew their hearts would never change, never trust Him and His Word—not fully, not completely, not like they should. God had no choice. God had to judge His people and judge them permanently. Negativism, defeatism, unbelief, fear, and rebellion were all embedded too deeply within their hearts. They were self-willed, stubborn, and stiff-necked, grounded as hard as concrete in their refusal to follow God. They simply refused to enter the promised land as God demanded: through sheer faith in His Word, believing the promises of God—in particular the promises of the promised land and the promised seed (a symbol of the coming Savior of the world, Christ Jesus Himself).

Again, this is the climactic passage that dooms the first generation of Israelites from ever entering the promised land. This is: *The Final Tragic Failure that Dooms the People—the Twelve Spies and Their Mixed Report: Distrusting God—Being Negative and Defeated, Fearful and Unbelieving—Rejecting and Rebelling against God,* 13:1-14:45

1. The command to send 12 men to spy out the land of Canaan (v.1-25).
2. The report and different conclusion of the spies (v. 26-33).
3. The fatal response of the people: grumbling, fear, unbelief, and rebellion (v.1-10).
4. The anger and fierce judgment of the Lord and the intercession of Moses (v.10-25).
5. The declaration of God's charge and judgment (discipline, chastisement) (v.26-39).
6. The incomplete confession and defeat of Israel acting without God (v.40-45).

1 (13:1-25) **Joshua, Name of—Spies, the Twelve—Israel, Leaders of, Weak—Canaan, Land of**: there was the command to send twelve men to spy out the land of Canaan. At last, the Israelites had reached the Desert of Paran that was to be the launching point for entering the promised land. The journey had been long and difficult, primarily because of the unbelief—the grumbling and complaining of the people. So many of them had caused problem after problem with their complaints and divisiveness, arousing the chastisement of God against them. But now—at long last—here they stood ready to enter the promised land, ready to experience the fulfillment of all their hopes and dreams. But before they entered, they needed to spy out the land. They needed to gather all the tactical information they could about the land and the people living there, to learn all they could about what pitfalls and enemies might lie ahead. Note the Scripture and outline:

OUTLINE	SCRIPTURE	SCRIPTURE	OUTLINE
1. The command to send 12 men to spy out the land of Canaan a. The men selected were to be leaders, one from each tribe	And the LORD spake unto Moses, saying, 2 Send thou men, that they may search the land of Canaan, which I give unto the children of Israel: of every tribe of their fathers	shall ye send a man, every one a ruler among them. 3 And Moses by the commandment of the LORD sent them from the wilderness of Paran: all those men were heads of the children of	1) The spies were sent out from the Desert of Paran 2) The spies were different leaders than the tribal chiefs

OUTLINE	SCRIPTURE	SCRIPTURE	OUTLINE
	Israel.	or many;	
• From the tribe of Reuben: Shammua	4 And these were their names: of the tribe of Reuben, Shammua the son of Zaccur.	19 And what the land is that they dwell in, whether it be good or bad; and what cities they be that they dwell in, whether in tents, or in strong holds;	2) To see what the land was like, good or bad 3) To see if the towns were fortified or unwalled reports
• From the tribe of Simeon: Shaphat	5 Of the tribe of Simeon, Shaphat the son of Hori.		
• From the tribe of Judah: Caleb • From the tribe of Issachar: Igal • From the tribe of Ephraim: Hoshea (Joshua) • From the tribe of Benjamin: Palti	6 Of the tribe of Judah, Caleb the son of Jephunneh. 7 Of the tribe of Issachar, Igal the son of Joseph. 8 Of the tribe of Ephraim, Oshea the son of Nun. 9 Of the tribe of Benjamin, Palti the son of Raphu.	20 And what the land is, whether it be fat or lean, whether there be wood therein, or not. And be ye of good courage, and bring of the fruit of the land. Now the time was the time of the first ripe grapes.	4) To check the soil to see if it was fertile or poor, barren or full of trees 5) To bring back samples of the fruit (it was grape season)
• From the tribe of Zebulun: Gaddiel • From the tribe of Manasseh: Gaddi	10 Of the tribe of Zebulun, Gaddiel the son of Sodi. 11 Of the tribe of Joseph, namely, of the tribe of Manasseh, Gaddi the son of Susi.	21 So they went up, and searched the land from the wilderness of Zin unto Rehob, as men come to Hamath.	c. The mission carried out: Began at the Desert of Zin & spied as far as Rehob near Lebo Hamath (cp. 34:8)
• From the tribe of Dan: Ammiel • From the tribe of Asher: Sethur • From the tribe of Naphtali: Nahbi • From the tribe of Gad: Geuel	12 Of the tribe of Dan, Ammiel the son of Gemalli. 13 Of the tribe of Asher, Sethur the son of Michael. 14 Of the tribe of Naphtali, Nahbi the son of Vophsi. 15 Of the tribe of Gad, Geuel the son of Machi.	22 And they ascended by the south, and came unto Hebron; where Ahiman, Sheshai, and Talmai, the children of Anak, were. (Now Hebron was built seven years before Zoan in Egypt.)	1) The first city they spied out: Hebron • Was inhabited by the Anakites (giants, a tall people, cp. v.28, 33) • Had been built seven years before Zoan in Egypt
3) The name of the personal assistant to Moses was changed from Hoshea to Joshua • Hoshea means "salvation" • Joshua means "God saves"	16 These are the names of the men which Moses sent to spy out the land. And Moses called Oshea the son of Nun Jehoshua.	23 And they came unto the brook of Eshcol, and cut down from thence a branch with one cluster of grapes, and they bare it between two upon a staff; and they brought of the pomegranates, and of the figs.	2) The Valley of Eshcol was very fruitful • A single cluster of grapes was so large that it had to be carried on a pole by two men, along with other fruit
b. The mission given to the spies: To spy out the most southern part of Canaan, the Negev, & then move north through the hill country	17 And Moses sent them to spy out the land of Canaan, and said unto them, Get you up this way southward, and go up into the mountain:	24 The place was called the brook Eshcol, because of the cluster of grapes which the children of Israel cut down from thence.	• The valley was given the name *Eshcol* by the Israelites because of the large grapes: "The Valley of the Cluster"
1) To see if the people were strong or weak, few or many	18 And see the land, what it is; and the people that dwelleth therein, whether they be strong or weak, few	25 And they returned from searching of the land after forty days.	3) The spies returned after a 40-day mission

1. The men selected as spies were to be leaders, one from each of the twelve tribes (v.2-15). They were sent out from their present position, the Desert of Paran (v.3). Note that the spies were selected from the leadership of each tribe. They were obviously outstanding young men, men of courage with spirits of adventure. Such traits within these young men had apparently caught the eye of Moses and the tribal leaders. They were:

⇒ from the tribe of Reuben: Shamuua (v.4)
⇒ from the tribe of Simeon: Shaphat (v.5)
⇒ from the tribe of Judah: Caleb (v.6)
⇒ from the tribe of Issachar: Igal v.7)
⇒ from the tribe of Ephraim: Hoshea (Joshua) (v.8)
⇒ from the tribe of Benjamin: Palti (v.9)
⇒ from the tribe of Zebulun: Gaddiel (v.10)
⇒ from the tribe of Manasseh: Gaddi (v.11)
⇒ from the tribe of Dan: Ammiel (v.12)
⇒ from the tribe of Asher: Sethur (v.13)
⇒ from the tribe of Naphtali: Nahbi (v.14)
⇒ from the tribe of Gad: Geuel (v.15)

Note that the name of Joshua, the assistant to Moses, was changed from Hoshea to Joshua (v.16). There is tenderness and destiny in this fact. Tenderness is seen in that it was Moses who actually changed Joshua's name. This points to a close, father-like relationship between Moses and Joshua. The destiny is also seen in the fact that Moses changed Joshua's name. By changing his name, Moses was pointing the people to Joshua as a future leader. Note the two names of Joshua: Hoshea means *salvation*; Joshua means *God saves*. His very name pictured the great salvation God was going to provide for His people in the promised land.

2. The mission of the spies was clear and thorough: they were to spy out the most southern part of Canaan, the Negev, and then move north through the hill country (v.17-20). Their mission involved spying out most of the land of Canaan. Gordon J. Wenham says that Canaan would include modern-day Israel, Lebanon, and much of southern Syria.[1] (See outline and note—Num.34:1-15, *Map*.) The spies were...

- to see if the people were strong or weak, few or many (v.18)
- to see what the land was like, good or bad (v.19)
- to see if the towns were fortified or unwalled (v.19)
- to check the soil to see if it was fertile or poor, barren or full of trees (v.20)
- to bring back samples of the fruit (it was grape season) (v.20)

3. The mission was carried out. The spies launched their mission from the southern border at the Desert of Zin. This was just northeast of Kadesh (cp. Num.20:1; Josh.15:1). They spied as far north as Rehob near Lebo Hamath which was at the northern frontier (cp. Num.34:8) (v.21-25). The distance from south to north was about 250 miles, a total of about 500 miles, so the mission took them 40 days.[2]

a. The first city they spied out was Hebron (v.22). What they found shocked them:
 ⇒ The Amalekites lived there, that is, the giants of the land, the huge, towering people.
 ⇒ The city of Hebron had been built seven years before Zoan in Egypt. This emphasis probably means that the city was a large, well-fortified city with large buildings.[3]

Note the report on Hebron: the spies said nothing about the part the city and area had played in the history of Abraham and the great promises God had made to him:[4]
 ⇒ God made His promise to Abraham near Hebron, that he would inherit the promised land (Gen.13:14-18).
 ⇒ Abraham camped in the area of Hebron. It became his base of operations in rescuing Lot and defeating the coalition of kings who had conquered Sodom and Gomorrah and other surrounding areas (Gen.14:13f).
 ⇒ Abraham purchased some land in Hebron and buried his wife Sara there. Moreover, other patriarchs were later buried there—all believing in the great hope of the promised land (Gen.23:1f; 25:9; 35:27f; 50:13).

b. The spies explored the unusually fruitful Valley of Eshcol (v.23-24). This valley was so productive, so fruitful that it was almost unbelievable. A single cluster of grapes was so large that it had to be carried, along with other fruit, on a pole by two men. The valley was given the name Eshcol by the Israelites because of the large grapes. The word Eshcol means "the valley of the cluster" (v.24).

c. The spies returned after a 40 day mission (v.25).

Thought 1. God is no respecter of persons. However, God does choose some persons to be leaders. He sees the human heart—and He knows who has the courage, strength, humility, and willingness to lead. This is the person whom God chooses and equips to lead.

1) God is no respecter of persons.

"Then Peter opened his mouth, and said, Of a truth I perceive that God is no respecter of persons: But in every nation he that feareth him, and worketh righteousness, is accepted with him" (Acts 10:34-35).

"For there is no difference between the Jew and the Greek: for the same Lord over all is rich unto all that call upon him" (Ro.10:12).

2) God calls some to be leaders.[5]

a) God called Abraham to be a leader.

"Now the Lord had said unto Abram, Get thee out of thy country, and from thy kindred, and from thy father's house, unto a land that I will show thee" (Gen.12:1).

b) God called Moses to be a leader.

"Come now therefore, and I will send thee unto Pharaoh, that thou mayest bring forth my people the children of Israel out of Egypt" (Ex.3:10).

c) God called Gideon to be a leader.

"And the Lord looked upon him, and said, Go in this thy might, and thou shalt save Israel from the hand of the Midianites: have not I sent thee" (Judg.6:14).

d) God called Elisha to be a leader.

---

1 Gordon J. Wenham. *The Book of Numbers*, p.117.
2 Ibid., p.118.
3 *The Expositor's Bible Commentary*, Vol.2. Frank E. Gaebelein, Editor, p.810.
4 Gordon J. Wenham. *The Book of Numbers*, p.118-119.
5 *The New Thompson Chain Reference Bible*, Condensed Cyclopedia. (Indianapolis, IN: B.B. Kirkbride Bible Co., Inc., 1964), #1790.

"So he departed thence, and found Elisha the son of Shaphat, who was plowing with twelve yoke of oxen before him, and he with the twelfth: and Elijah passed by him, and cast his mantle upon him" (1 Ki.19:19).

e) God called Isaiah to be a leader.

"Also I heard the voice of the Lord, saying, Whom shall I send, and who will go for us? Then said I, Here am I; send me" (Is.6:8).

f) God called Paul to be a leader.

"But rise, and stand upon thy feet: for I have appeared unto thee for this purpose, to make thee a minister and a witness both of these things which thou hast seen, and of those things in the which I will appear unto thee" (Acts 26:16).

g) God calls many today to be leaders.

"Ye have not chosen me, but I have chosen you, and ordained you, that ye should go and bring forth fruit, and that your fruit should remain: that whatsoever ye shall ask of the Father in my name, he may give it you" (Jn.15:16).

"For I say, through the grace given unto me, to every man that is among you, not to think of himself more highly than he ought to think; but to think soberly, according as God hath dealt to every man the measure of faith. For as we have many members in one body, and all members have not the same office: So we, being many, are one body in Christ, and every one members one of another. Having then gifts differing according to the grace that is given to us, whether prophecy, let us prophesy according to the proportion of faith; Or ministry, let us wait on our ministering: or he that teacheth, on teaching; Or he that exhorteth, on exhortation: he that giveth, let him do it with simplicity; he that ruleth, with diligence; he that shows mercy, with cheerfulness" (Ro.12:3-8).

"And he gave some, apostles; and some, prophets; and some, evangelists; and some, pastors and teachers; For the perfecting of the saints, for the work of the ministry, for the edifying of the body of Christ: Till we all come in the unity of the faith, and of the knowledge of the Son of God, unto a perfect man, unto the measure of the stature of the fulness of Christ" (Eph.4:11-13).

Thought 2. There is a need for unbelievers to do just what the spies did: spy out and investigate the promised land of God. Unbelievers need to know that the promised land…

- is a land that flows with milk and honey, with all the provisions of God, all that man ever needs or could want
- is a land that assures conquest over all the pitfalls and enemies of life
- is a land that brings rest, both physical and spiritual rest, to the body and soul
- is a land that guarantees eternal life with God Himself

1) This is the land that the unbeliever needs to explore and investigate. This is heaven itself, the new heavens and earth promised by God.

"But the day of the Lord will come as a thief in the night; in the which the heavens shall pass away with a great noise, and the elements shall melt with fervent heat, the earth also and the works that are therein shall be burned up. Seeing then that all these things shall be dissolved, what manner of persons ought ye to be in all holy conversation and godliness, Looking for and hasting unto the coming of the day of God, wherein the heavens being on fire shall be dissolved, and the elements shall melt with fervent heat? Nevertheless we, according to his promise, look for new heavens and a new earth, wherein dwelleth righteousness" (2 Pt.3:10-13).

"And I saw a new heaven and a new earth: for the first heaven and the first earth were passed away; and there was no more sea" (Rev.21:1).

"For, behold, I create new heavens and a new earth: and the former shall not be remembered, nor come into mind" (Is.65:17).

"For as the new heavens and the new earth, which I will make, shall remain before me, saith the Lord, so shall your seed and your name remain" (Is.66:22).

2) The unbeliever needs to investigate and seek out the promised land of God.

"Come unto me, all ye that labour and are heavy laden, and I will give you rest" (Mt.11:28).

"Again, he sent forth other servants, saying, Tell them which are bidden, Behold, I have prepared my dinner: my oxen and my fatlings are killed, and all things are ready: come unto the marriage" (Mt.22:4).

"But if from thence thou shalt seek the Lord thy God, thou shalt find him, if thou seek him with all thy heart and with all thy soul" (Dt.4:29).

"Come now, and let us reason together, saith the Lord: though your sins be as scarlet, they shall be as white as snow; though they be red like crimson, they shall be as wool" (Is.1:18).

"Ho, every one that thirsteth, come ye to the waters, and he that hath no money; come ye, buy, and eat; yea, come, buy wine and milk without money and without price" (Is.55:1).

"Seek ye the Lord while he may be found, call ye upon him while he is near" (Is.55:6).

"And ye shall seek me, and find me, when ye shall search for me with all your heart" (Jer.29:13).

Thought 3. Moses changed Hosea's name to Joshua because Joshua was the appointed leader to lead God's people into the promised land (v.16). The Greek name for Joshua is *Jesus*. Both Joshua and Jesus mean *God saves*. Joshua is a type of Christ. Jesus Christ is the person who saves us and leads us into the promised land of heaven.

"For unto you is born this day in the city of David a Saviour, which is Christ the Lord" (Lk.2:11).

"For the Son of man is come to seek and to save that which was lost" (Lk.19:10).

"For God sent not his Son into the world to condemn the world; but that the world through him might be saved" (Jn.3:17).

"I am the door: by me if any man enter in, he shall be saved, and shall go in and out, and find pasture" (Jn.10:9).

"Jesus saith unto him, I am the way, the truth, and the life: no man cometh unto the Father, but by me" (Jn.14:6).

"Neither is there salvation in any other: for there is none other name under heaven given among men, whereby we must be saved" (Acts 4:12).

"This is a faithful saying, and worthy of all acceptation, that Christ Jesus came into the world to save sinners; of whom I am chief" (1 Tim.1:15).

"Wherefore he is able also to save them to the uttermost that come unto God by him, seeing he ever liveth to make intercession for them" (Heb.7:25).

DEEPER STUDY # 1

(Num.13:21) **Rehob, City of**: it was located in upper Galilee and was the farthest point of the twelve spies' mission. (See Map—Numbers 33:5-49, end of commentary.) The Hebrew meaning of Rehob is "broad or open place." Rehob was assigned to the Levites (Josh.12:31; 1 Chron.6:75)

See other Scripture references for study:

Joshua 19:28; Joshua 19:30; Judges 1:31; Judges 18:28; Numbers 13:21; Joshua 19:28; Joshua 19:30; Joshua 21:31; Judges 1:31; Judges 18:28; 2 Samuel 8:3; 2 Samuel 8:12; 2 Samuel 10:6; 2 Samuel 10:8; 1 Chron. 6:75

DEEPER STUDY # 2

(Num.13:21) **Lebo-Hamath, City of**: it was located on the northern boundary of Canaan, the promised land. (See Map—Numbers 33:5-49, end of commentary.) The Hebrew meaning of Lebo-Hamath is "entrance to or to come to Hamath."

See other Scripture references for study:

Numbers 13:21; Numbers 34:7-8; Joshua 13:5; Judges 3:3; 1 Kings 8:65; 2 Kings 14:25; 1 Chron. 13:5; 2 Chron. 7:8; Ezekiel 47:15; Ezekiel 47:20; Ezekiel 48:1; Amos 6:14

DEEPER STUDY # 3

(Num.13:22) **Hebron, City of**: it was located in the hill country of Judah about nineteen miles south of Jerusalem and fifteen miles west of the Dead Sea. (See Map—Numbers 33:5-49, end of commentary.) The Hebrew meaning of Hebron is "association" or "league." Hebron possessed plenty of water and fertile soil. It was inhabited by the tribe of Anak. Hebron was built seven years prior to the building of the Egyptian city of Tanis (Num.13:22)

See other Scripture references for study:

Genesis 13:18; Genesis 23:2; Genesis 23:19; Genesis 35:27; Genesis 37:14; Joshua 10:3; Joshua 10:5; Joshua 10:23; Joshua 10:36; Joshua 10:39; Joshua 11:21; Joshua 12:10; Joshua 14:13-15; Joshua 15:13; Joshua 15:54; Joshua 19:28; Joshua 20:7; Joshua 21:11; Joshua 21:13; Judges 1:10; Judges 1:20; Judges 16:3; 1 Samuel 30:31; 2 Samuel 2:1; 2 Samuel 2:3; 2 Samuel 2:11; 2 Samuel 2:32; 2 Samuel 3:2; 2 Samuel 3:5; 2 Samuel 3:19-20; 2 Samuel 3:22; 2 Samuel 3:27; 2 Samuel 3:32; Samuel 4:1; 2 Samuel 4:8; 2 Samuel 4:12-5:1; 2 Samuel 5:3; 2 Samuel 5:5; 2 Samuel 5:13; 2 Samuel 15:7; 2 Samuel 15:9-10; 1 Kings 2:11; 1 Chron. 2:42-43; 1 Chron. 3:1; 1 Chron. 3:4; 1 Chron. 6:55; 1 Chron. 6:57; 1 Chron. 11:1; 1 Chron. 11:3; 1 Chron. 12:23; 1 Chron. 12:38; 1 Chron. 29:27; 2 Chron. 11:10

DEEPER STUDY # 4

(Num.13:22) Zoan, City of: it was located in Egypt on a Tanitic branch of the Nile River. (See Map—Numbers 33:5-49, end of commentary.) Zoan was the Hebrew name for the Egyptian city of Tanis. It was also the setting for several miracles (see Ps.78:12; Ps.78:43). Zoan was a royal city of storage. It was a point of reference that the Old Testament prophets used to speak against the Egyptian government and its actions (see Is.19:11; Is.19:13; Is.30:4; Ezek.30:14)

See other Scripture references for study:

Psalm 78:12; Psalm 78:43; Isaiah 19:11; Isaiah 19:13; Isaiah 30:4; Ezekiel 30:14

2 (13:26-33) **Spies, the Twelve—Joshua—Caleb—Unbelief—Canaan, Described—Promised Land, Described**: there was the spirit and the different conclusions of the spies. The spy mission had been a success: not a single soldier had been lost, and a complete surveillance of the promised land had been made. The spies had carried out their mission and returned after 40 exhausting days in enemy territory. Now, the people were anxiously waiting on their report, filled with excitement and great expectation. They were soon to begin their march into the promised land of God. But unknown to them, a crushing and horrible shock was coming. Some of the spies were gripped with unbelief and were to give a negative report, a *defeatist* report.

OUTLINE	SCRIPTURE	SCRIPTURE	OUTLINE
2. The report & different conclusion of the spies a. The report was given to Moses, Aaron, & the whole community; then the fruit was shown to them b. The report of the spies 1) The positive factors: The land flowed with milk & honey; the fruit was proof 2) The negative factors • The people were powerful & the cities fortified • The descendants of Anak (giants) lived there • The Amalekites were in the Negev • The Hittites, Jebusites, & Amorites in the hill country • The Canaanites along the sea & the Jordan River c. The different conclusions	26 And they went and came to Moses, and to Aaron, and to all the congregation of the children of Israel, unto the wilderand. 27 And they told him, and said, We came unto the land whither thou sentest us, and surely it floweth with milk and honey; and this is the fruit of it. 28 Nevertheless the people be strong that dwell in the land, and the cities are walled, and very great: and moreover we saw the chil- dren of Anak there. 29 The Amalekites dwell in the land of the south: and the Hittites, and the Jebusites, and the Amorites, dwell in the mountains: and the Canaanites dwell by the sea, and by the coast of Jordan. 30 And Caleb stilled the	people before Moses, and said, Let us go up at once, and possess it; for we are well able to overcome it. 31 But the men that went up with him said, We be not able to go up against the people; for they are stronger than we. 32 And they brought up an evil report of the land which they had searched unto the children of Israel, saying, The land, through which we have gone to search it, is a land that eateth up the inhab- itants thereof; and all the people that we saw in it are men of a great stature. 33 And there we saw the giants, the sons of Anak, which come of the giants: and we were in our own sight as grasshoppers, and so we were in their sight.	1) The conclusion of Caleb • Silenced the people • Declared that they should go up & take the land 2) The conclusion of ten spies (not Joshua)—declared that they could not attack, for the nations were stronger: Began to spread unbelief & exaggerated, discouraging • The land—its harsh environment—consumed its inhabitants • The people—all of them—were huge, gigantic • The Nephilim—descendants of Anak (the giants)—were there: The Israelites were like grasshoppers before them

1. The report was given to Moses, Aaron, and the entire community; then the fruit was shown to them (v.26-29).

2. Note that the report given by the spies was mixed (v.27-29). There was one strong, positive factor about the land: the land flowed with milk and honey. The proof was seen in the fruit they brought back (v.27). The land was fertile, very productive and fruitful. It would abundantly feed the people and their livestock, giving them all they could ever need or desire.

But note what then happened: some of the spies were gripped with an attitude of *defeat*. They stressed the shocking, negative factors and then embellished the facts. Of course, they should report the truth about the land, but we know from the response to their report that they gave the account in a negative, pessimistic way. Note how they continually stressed the negative:

⇒ The people who lived there were powerful and the cities fortified (be surot) and very large (v.28). The idea of the Hebrew is that the cities were fortresses, impregnable—that they could not be taken.
⇒ The descendants of Anak, the giants, lived there (v.28).
⇒ The Amalekites lived in the Negev (v.29).
⇒ The Hittites, Jebusites, and Amorites occupied the hill country.
⇒ The Canaanites occupied land along the seacoast (Mediterranean) and along the Jordan River (v.29).

3. The conclusions reached by the spies were very divisive (v.30-33). In fact, the negative, defeatist attitude of ten spies was so distrusting of God that their report is called a *bad, evil report* (v.32).

a. The conclusion of one spy—Caleb—was that of courage and strong faith. Note that he had to silence the leaders who stood around Moses before he could speak. As would be the case with any group of leaders who had heard such a negative, defeatist report, they had begun to murmur and discuss the issues among themselves. Boldly, forcefully—Caleb declared...
- that they should go up and take possession of the promised land
- that they could defeat the enemies of the promised land

b. But the conclusion of the ten spies prevailed (v.31-33). They continued to hold to their negative, unbelieving, defeatist position. They could not attack the enemies of the promised land, for they were stronger.

Then the unimaginable happened: a terrible, evil spirit of divisiveness took over the ten spies. They began to spread their bad, evil report (dibbah) among the people (v.32). Note how they stressed, exaggerated, and distorted the negative factors:

⇒ The land—its hostile environment—consumed, swallowed up the people living there. The environment was hostile: it took a high toll upon human life (v.32).
⇒ The people—all of them—were gigantic, absolutely huge: a complete distortion to arouse and win people to their defeatist, unbelieving position (v.32).
⇒ The Nephilim, the descendants of Anak the giant, were there: the Israelites were like grasshoppers before them (v.33).

This negative, defeatist attitude and this exaggerated, distorted report of the ten spies were to doom both the spies and the people. Imagine how Moses' heart was cut standing there before the spies, listening to their negativism and their unbelief and then hearing about them spreading their evil report among the people. Imagine how the heart of God was cut as He witnessed such irresponsible behavior and unbelief. The ten spies were declaring that God could not fulfill His promise to give them the promised land, that the power of God was not great enough to conquer the enemies of the promised land.

Thought 1. Three strong lessons are seen in this point.

1) The ten spies spread an evil report among the people. They exaggerated and distorted the truth. They became stumblingblocks to Israel. Scripture is clear: we are not to be stumblingblocks, not to cause people to stumble and fall.

"But woe unto you, scribes and Pharisees, hypocrites! for ye shut up the kingdom of heaven against men: for ye neither go in yourselves, neither suffer ye them that are entering to go in" (Mt.23:13).

"Let us not therefore judge one another any more: but judge this rather, that no man put a stumblingblock or an occasion to fall in his brother's way" (Ro.14:13).

"But if thy brother be grieved with thy meat, now walkest thou not charitably. Destroy not him with thy meat, for whom Christ died" (Ro.14:15).

"But take heed lest by any means this liberty of yours become a stumblingblock to them that are weak" (1 Cor.8:9).

"Wherefore, if meat make my brother to offend, I will eat no flesh while the world standeth, lest I make my brother to offend" (1 Cor.8:13).

"Ye did run well; who did hinder you that ye should not obey the truth? This persuasion cometh not of him that calleth you. A little leaven leaveneth the whole lump" (Gal.5:7-9).

"And shall say, Cast ye up, cast ye up, prepare the way, take up the stumblingblock out of the way of my people" (Is.57:14).

"For the priest's lips should keep knowledge, and they should seek the law at his mouth: for he is the messenger of the Lord of hosts. But ye are departed out of the way; ye have caused many to stumble at the law; ye have corrupted the covenant of Levi, saith the Lord of hosts" (Mal.2:7-8).

2) The ten spies were gripped with fear and cowardice. Scripture is clear: believers are not to fear.

"Fear ye not therefore, ye are of more value than many sparrows" (Mt.10:31).

"Nevertheless among the chief rulers also many believed on him; but because of the Pharisees they did not confess him, lest they should be put out of the synagogue" (Jn.12:42).

"For God hath not given us the spirit of fear; but of power, and of love, and of a sound mind" (2 Tim.1:7).

"And the Lord appeared unto him the same night, and said, I am the God of Abraham thy father: fear not, for I am with thee, and will bless thee, and multiply thy seed for my servant Abraham's sake" (Gen.26:24).

"And the officers shall speak further unto the people, and they shall say, What man is there that is fearful and fainthearted? let him go and return unto his house, lest his brethren's heart faint as well as his heart" (Dt.20:8).

"The fear of man bringeth a snare: but whoso putteth his trust in the Lord shall be safe" (Pr.29:25).

"Fear thou not; for I am with thee: be not dismayed; for I am thy God: I will strengthen thee; yea, I will help thee; yea, I will uphold thee with the right hand of my righteousness" (Is.41:10).

"Fear not: for I have redeemed thee, I have called thee by thy name; thou art mine" (Is.43:1).

"When thou passest through the waters, I will be with thee; and through the rivers, they shall not overflow thee: when thou walkest through the fire, thou shalt not be burned; neither shall the flame kindle upon thee" (Is.43:2).

"I, even I, am he that comforteth you: who art thou, that thou shouldest be afraid of a man that shall die, and of the son of man which shall be made as grass" (Is.51:12).

3) The testimony of Caleb was that of strength and courage. Believers are to be strong and courageous.

"Watch ye, stand fast in the faith, quit you like men, be strong" (1 Cor.16:13).

"Finally, my brethren, be strong in the Lord, and in the power of his might" (Eph.6:10).

"Thou therefore, my son, be strong in the grace that is in Christ Jesus" (2 Tim.2:1).

"Thou therefore endure hardness, as a good soldier of Jesus Christ. No man that warreth entangleth himself with the affairs of this life; that he may please him who hath chosen him to be a soldier" (2 Tim.2:3-4).

"Be strong and of a good courage, fear not, nor be afraid of them: for the Lord thy God, he it is that doth go with thee; he will not fail thee, nor forsake thee" (Dt.31:6).

"I go the way of all the earth: be thou strong therefore, and show thyself a man" (1 Ki.2:2).

"I will not be afraid of ten thousands of people, that have set themselves against me round about" (Ps.3:6).

"A Psalm of David. The Lord is my light and my salvation; whom shall I fear? the Lord is the strength of my life; of whom shall I be afraid? When the wicked, even mine enemies and my foes, came upon me to eat up my flesh, they stumbled and fell. Though an host should encamp against me, my heart shall not fear: though war should rise against me, in this will I be confident" (Ps.27:1-3).

"Thou shalt not be afraid for the terror by night; nor for the arrow that flieth by day" (Ps.91:5).
"The Lord is on my side; I will not fear: what can man do unto me" (Ps.118:6).
"Withhold not good from them to whom it is due, when it is in the power of thine hand to do it" (Pr.3:27).
"Behold, God is my salvation; I will trust, and not be afraid: for the Lord Jehovah is my strength and my song; he also is become my salvation" (Is.12:2).
"And I sought for a man among them, that should make up the hedge, and stand in the gap before me for the land, that I should not destroy it: but I found none" (Ezk.22:30).

3 (14:1-10) **Unbelief—Grumbling—Murmuring—Complaining—Rebellion, Against God—Israel, Failure - Errors of**: there was the fatal response of the people. They grumbled, doubted, and feared. They failed to believe God and rebelled against Him. The negative, unbelieving, and defeatist report of the ten spies spread among the people like wildfire on a rampage, consuming everything in its path. What happened then was the fatal climax to a whole generation of people. *The Expositor's Bible Commentary* gives a descriptive picture of the scene that is well worth quoting in full:

> "The malicious report of the ten spies (13:26-33) spread throughout the populace like a vicious virus on rampage. The words of Caleb and Joshua were not heard. Everywhere people heard of walled cities, strong men, giants, and the fabled Nephilim. The giant clusters of grapes were a portent of doom. If clusters of grapes were as great as these, imagine what the people would be like! No one talked about God's grace. None recited his miracles. Forgotten was the act of God where the most powerful nation of their world was stymied at the rushing of waters back to their beds. The thunder of Sinai, the fire of God, that he had spoken and delivered and graced his people beyond imagination—all these things were forgotten in their...fear. Fear unchecked becomes its own fuel, a self-propelling force that expands as it expends. The words of a mid-twentieth-century American president, 'The only thing we have to fear is fear itself,' have their outworking in the self-consumptive absorption with terror that raged through the camps that night."[6]

OUTLINE	SCRIPTURE	SCRIPTURE	OUTLINE
3. The fatal response of the people: Grumbling, fear, unbelief, & rebellion	And all the congregation lifted up their voice, and cried; and the people wept that night.	Nun, and Caleb the son of Jephunneh, which were of them that searched the land, rent their clothes:	Caleb: Tore their clothes & declared the truthful facts about the land they had spied out
a. The grumbling unbelief emphasized: "All the people," "all the Israelites," "the whole assembly" 1) Were against the leaders	2 And all the children of Israel murmured against Moses and against Aaron: and the whole congregation said unto them, Would God that we had died in the land of Egypt! or would God we had died in this wilderness!	7 And they spake unto all the company of the children of Israel, saying, The land, which we passed through to search it, is an exceeding good land.	1) The land was exceedingly good (would not consume them as the other spies had claimed)
2) Felt death in Egypt or the desert would have been better 3) Accused the LORD of forsaking them & their families 4) Questioned if it would not be better to return to Egypt	3 And wherefore hath the LORD brought us unto this land, to fall by the sword, that our wives and our children should be a prey? were it not better for us to return into Egypt?	8 If the LORD delight in us, then he will bring us into this land, and give it us; a land which floweth with milk and honey.	2) The LORD would lead & give them the land
5) Suggested that a new leader be chosen who would lead them back to Egypt (cp. Neh. 9:17, he was actually chosen)	4 And they said one to another, Let us make a captain, and let us return into Egypt.	9 Only rebel not ye against the LORD, neither fear ye the people of the land; for they are bread for us: their defense is departed from them, and the LORD is with us: fear them not.	3) The people must not rebel against the LORD nor be afraid of the inhabitants • They would swallow up the inhabitants • The LORD was with them
b. The response of Moses & Aaron: Fell face down before the people—helpless, submissive before God c. The response of Joshua &	5 Then Moses and Aaron fell on their faces before all the assembly of the congregation of the children of Israel. 6 And Joshua the son of	10 But all the congregation bade stone them with stones. And the glory of the LORD appeared in the tabernacle of the congregation before all the children of Israel.	d. The fatal rejection: They plotted to stone the godly leaders

1. The grumbling unbelief of the people is emphasized: "all the people," "all the Israelites," "the whole assembly"—every adult was grumbling in unbelief. Not a single person was trusting God, believing that He could lead them into the promised land (v.1-4). Note that they raised their voices and wept aloud (v.1). The entire community was "wailing, as only people in the east can do....We are to imagine the worst sort of rage, a picture of screaming, rending, throwing, cursing anger—an intoxication of grief."[7]

a. The people railed against Moses and Aaron.
b. The people felt that death in Egypt or the desert would have been better.
c. The people accused the LORD of forsaking them and their families (v.3). They accused the LORD of bringing them up to the promised land only to let them be destroyed or enslaved by their enemies (v.3).

---

6 *The Expositor's Bible Commentary*, Vol.2. Frank E. Gaebelein, Editor, p.813.
7 Ibid., p.813.

d. The people questioned if it would not be better to return to Egypt.
e. The people, in fact, suggested that a new leader be chosen who would lead them back to Egypt (v.4). We know from Nehemiah that the people actually chose a leader to stand opposed to Moses (Neh.9:17). This shows that a riot was taking place. The people had made their decision: they wanted nothing else to do with Moses or God. They were in total rebellion against God and His appointed leader. They were on a rampage, storming about and making preparation to return back to Egypt. Since an opposition leader had already been chosen, the lives of Moses and Aaron were threatened. Again, *The Expositor's Bible Commentary* gives an excellent picture of the scene:

"The more the people wailed, the more excessive their words. The more the people cried, the more they outreached one another in protests of rage. This is the crowd psychology that leads to riots, lynchings, stormings, and rampages. Now they begin to aim their anger more directly at Yahweh himself. Moses and Aaron were the fall guys, but the Lord was the one really to blame; he had delivered them from Egypt. He had brought Pharaoh to his knees, had cast horse and rider into the sea, had led them through a barren land, and had provided bread from heaven and water from a gushing rock. He had spoken, revealing grace and wonder, power and gentleness, direction and Torah [law]. God was the one at fault! And they began to curse him, to contemn his goodness, to reject his grace.

"Forgetful of God's power against Egypt...the people worked themselves into such a frenzy of fear that they wished that God had not brought them here at all. Why had he not just left them alone? Slavery began to look good to them. The hovels in Egypt became home again. The memory of a variety of food made the memory of oppressive taskmasters less fearsome.

"So it was that the frightening words of the faithless spies led to the mourning of the entire community and to their great rebellion against the Lord. They forgot all the miracles that the Lord had done for them; they contemned his mercies and spurned his might. In their ingratitude they preferred death (v.2). Unfortunately, it was death they deserved and death they were to get. The most reprehensible charge against the grace of God was that concerning their children (see vv.31-33). Only their children would survive. All the rest would die in the desert they had chosen over the Land of Promise."[8]

2. Moses and Aaron did all they could: they fell face down before the people, helpless and submissive before God (v.5). No doubt they did just what any committed believers would do under such circumstances: they prayed, seeking deliverance through the power of God.

3. The response of Joshua and Caleb was different (v.6-9). These two young men tore their clothes in a symbol of ritual mourning. Then they declared the truthful facts about the land they had spied out: the land was exceedingly good. It would not consume the people as the other spies had claimed (v.7).

⇒ The LORD would lead His people into the promised land if they would only obey and please Him. God would give the land—a land that flowed with milk and honey (v.8).

⇒ The people must not rebel against the LORD nor be afraid of the inhabitants of the land (v.9). God's people would swallow the inhabitants up, for the LORD was with His people.

4. But note what happened: the fatal rejection. The people plotted to assassinate, to stone the four godly leaders (v.10).

Thought 1. Unbelief and rebellion are very serious offenses against God, very serious. God will not tolerate unbelief and rebellion from any person.

1) Scripture is clear: unbelief is condemned.

"He that believeth on the Son hath everlasting life: and he that believeth not the Son shall not see life; but the wrath of God abideth on him" (Jn.3:36).

"I said therefore unto you, that ye shall die in your sins: for if ye believe not that I am he, ye shall die in your sins" (Jn.8:24).

"Take heed, brethren, lest there be in any of you an evil heart of unbelief, in departing from the living God" (Heb.3:12).

"Let us labour therefore to enter into that rest, lest any man fall after the same example of unbelief [Israel's unbelief]" (Heb.4:11).

"I will therefore put you in remembrance, though ye once knew this, how that the Lord, having saved the people out of the land of Egypt, afterward destroyed them that believed not" (Jude 5).

2) Scripture is clear: rebellion against God is condemned.

"Let no man deceive you with vain words: for because of these things cometh the wrath of God upon the children of disobedience [rebellion]" (Eph.5:6).

"In flaming fire taking vengeance on them that know not God, and that obey not the gospel of our Lord Jesus Christ" (2 Th.1:8).

"For if the word spoken by angels was stedfast, and every transgression and disobedience [rebellion] received a just recompence of reward; How shall we escape, if we neglect so great salvation; which at the first began to be spoken by the Lord, and was confirmed unto us by them that heard him" (Heb.2:2-3).

"Ye have been rebellious against the Lord from the day that I knew you" (Dt.9:24).

"For rebellion is as the sin of witchcraft, and stubbornness is as iniquity and idolatry. Because thou hast rejected the word of the Lord, he hath also rejected thee from being king" (1 Sam.15:23).

"Woe to the rebellious children, saith the Lord, that take counsel, but not of me; and that cover

---

[8] *The Expositor's Bible Commentary*, Vol.2. Frank E. Gaebelein, Editor, p.814.

with a covering, but not of my spirit, that they may add sin to sin" (Is.30:1).

"I have spread out my hands all the day unto a rebellious people, which walketh in a way that was not good, after their own thoughts" (Is.65:2).

"And he said unto me, Son of man, I send thee to the children of Israel, to a rebellious nation that hath rebelled against me: they and their fathers have transgressed against me, even unto this very day" (Ezk.2:3).

"Son of man, thou dwellest in the midst of a rebellious house, which have eyes to see, and see not; they have ears to hear, and hear not: for they are a rebellious house" (Ezk.12:2).

4 (14:10-25) **Judgment, of God—Judgment, Mitigated—Anger, of God—Intercession—Moses, Intercession of—Chastisement, of God—Discipline, of Believers—Israel, Judgment of**: there was the anger and fierce judgment of the LORD and the intercession of Moses.

OUTLINE	SCRIPTURE	SCRIPTURE	OUTLINE
4. The anger & fierce judgment of the LORD & the intercession of Moses a. The glory of the LORD burst forth at the Tabernacle before all	10 But all the congregation bade stone them with stones. And the glory of the LORD appeared in the tabernacle of the congregation before all the children of Israel.	17 And now, I beseech thee, let the power of my Lord be great, according as thou hast spoken, saying,	• The strength of God must be demonstrated, His Word kept
1) Questioned how long the people would treat God with contempt: Refuse to believe in Him & the miracles He had performed	11 And the LORD said unto Moses, How long will this people provoke me? and how long will it be ere they believe me, for all the signs which I have shewed among them?	18 The LORD is longsuffering, and of great mercy, forgiving iniquity and transgression, and by no means clearing the guilty, visiting the iniquity of the fathers upon the children unto the third and fourth generation.	2) The love & forgiveness of God were at stake, as well as the discipline or chastisement of God: Moses understood this (God was both loving & just)
2) Threatened to destroy them with a plague: To use Moses to build a new race of people, greater & stronger	12 I will smite them with the pestilence, and disinherit them, and will make of thee a greater nation and mightier than they.	19 Pardon, I beseech thee, the iniquity of this people according unto the greatness of thy mercy, and as thou hast forgiven this people, from Egypt even until now.	3) The cry of Moses for God to forgive the sin of the people: Just as He had since their deliverance from Egyptian slavery
b. The intercession, the pleading of Moses 1) The reputation of God was at stake: The Egyptians would hear about Israel's destruction & tell the Canaanites about it	13 And Moses said unto the LORD, Then the Egyptians shall hear it, (for thou broughtest up this people in thy might from ness of Paran, to Kadesh; and brought back word unto them, and unto all the congregation, and shewed them the fruit of the l among them;)	20 And the LORD said, I have pardoned according to thy word: 21 But as truly as I live, all the earth shall be filled with the glory of the LORD. 22 Because all those men which have seen my glory, and my miracles, which I did in Egypt and in the wilderness, and have tempted me now these ten times, and have not hearkened to my voice;	c. The astounding forgiveness of the LORD d. The sure judgment—discipline, chastisement—of the Lord: Was carried out without reservation upon every adult who disobeyed & tested God time and again (note: ten times)
• The Canaanites had already heard that the God of the Israelites guided & protected them	14 And they will tell it to the inhabitants of this land: for they have heard that thou LORD art among this people, that thou LORD art seen face to face, and that thy cloud standeth over them, and that thou goest before them, by daytime in a pillar of a cloud, and in a pillar of fire by night.	23 Surely they shall not see the land which I sware unto their fathers, neither shall any of them that provoked me see it: 24 But my servant Caleb, because he had another spirit with him, and hath followed me fully, him will I bring into the land whereinto he went; and his seed shall possess it.	1) The first discipline, chastisement: Not one of the adults would see the promised land—were to die in the wilderness or desert 2) The one exception, Caleb (& Joshua, v.38): Because they were loyal, followed the LORD wholeheartedly
• The Canaanites would question the power & promises of God to His people	15 Now if thou shalt kill all this people as one man, then the nations which have heard the fame of thee will speak, saying, 16 Because the LORD was not able to bring this people into the land which he sware unto them, therefore he hath slain them in the wilderness.	25 (Now the Amalekites and the Canaanites dwelt in the valley.) To morrow turn you, and get you into the wilderness by the way of the Red sea.	3) The second discipline, chastisement: To turn back toward the Red Sea, to wander about in the wilderness or desert

1. The glory of the LORD burst forth—right at the peak of the people's rage and threatened assault against God's four servants. God's glory burst forth at the Tabernacle in the sight of all the people (v.11-12).

a. God questioned Moses: How long would the people treat the LORD with contempt? How long would they refuse to believe in Him and the miraculous signs He had performed? The word for contempt (naʕas) means to spurn, despise, revile, reject; to treat with utter disregard—to the point of provoking God.

b. God threatened to destroy the people with a plague. Moreover, He threatened to use Moses to build a new race of people, a greater and stronger race. The anger of God against rebellion and unbelief had reached a fevered pitch: it was time for the justice of God to fall and judgment to be executed.

2. Note the intercession, the pleading of Moses for the people of God who had committed such gross sins (v.13-19). He cried out for God to consider three critical points:

a. God must remember that His own reputation and character were at stake: the Egyptians would hear about Israel's destruction and tell the Canaanites about it (v.13-17). God must not let this happen! God's character and reputation were worth more than Moses and the people themselves. They were not worth the destruction of God's character in the eyes of the Egyptians and Canaanites.

⇒ The Canaanites had already heard that the LORD had delivered His people from Egyptian slavery, guiding and protecting them up to the present moment (v.14).

⇒ The Canaanites would question the power and promises of God to His people if God now destroyed His people (v.15-16). The strength of God must be demonstrated, His Word kept (v.17).

b. God must show love and forgiveness (for both were at stake) as well as the discipline (chastisement) of God. Note how Moses understood that God was both loving and just, and he declared both in appealing for the lives of God's people (v.18). God is both loving and just.

c. God must forgive the sin of His people, just as He had been forgiving them since their deliverance from Egyptian slavery (v.19).

3. The forgiveness of the LORD was astounding (v.20). God declared a marvelous truth: God forgave their sins, as awful and terrible as they were. Note why: because Moses had prayed, interceded for the people, asking God to forgive them. And God heard the prayer for forgiveness.

4. The judgment (discipline) and chastisement of the LORD were sure, certain (v.21-25). Note that the judgment was carried out without reservation upon every adult who had disobeyed and tested God time and again. In fact, God stated that the people had tested Him ten different times (see DEEPER STUDY # 1—Num.14:22 for more discussion). Because of the people's continued disobedience and rebellion, God executed His perfect justice and judgment:

a. The first judgment was to be a tragic chastisement: none of the adults—not a single one—would ever see the promised land. They were to die in the wilderness or desert (v.23). Note: this is a picture of *mitigated judgment;* that is, God put a 'check' on His judgment, diminished or softened His judgment because of His dear servant's prayer and intercession. This is an excellent picture of the power of intercessory prayer. Abraham's prayer and intercession for Sodom needs to be compared with this passage (Gen.18:16-33).

b. There was to be one exception to God's discipline and chastisement, that of Caleb and Joshua (v.24, cp. with v.38). These two dear servants were to enter the promised land because they had been loyal and followed the LORD wholeheartedly, believing in Him totally. Note what God says: the "seed" or descendants of Caleb will inherit the promised land. This is one step in the fulfillment of God's wonderful promise concerning *the Promised Seed*, a symbol of the coming Savior of the world, Christ Jesus Himself.

c. The second discipline or chastisement was a move by God to protect His people from the enemies of the promised land (v.25). God told Moses to turn the people back toward the Red Sea, to wander about in the wilderness or desert. This was a necessary step because the Amalekites and Canaanites were living in the valleys right below where the Israelites were camped. The people had marched right up to the border of the promised land. They were so close and yet so far away. Their unbelief and rebellion against God had placed an impassable gulf between them and God. Their unbelief and rebellion had separated them from God. Instead of entering the promised land, they were to wander about in the wilderness for a total of 40 years. The desert was to be the gravesite of these unbelieving, rebellious people.

Thought 1. There are two clear and forceful lessons in this point for us:

1) God judges and chastises (disciplines) His people when they sin—when they fail to believe and follow Him.

"For the Son of man shall come in the glory of his Father with his angels; and then he shall reward every man according to his works" (Mt.16:27).

"Every branch in me that beareth not fruit he taketh away: and every branch that beareth fruit, he purgeth it, that it may bring forth more fruit" (Jn.15:2).

"But when we are judged, we are chastened of the Lord, that we should not be condemned with the world" (1 Cor.11:32).

"For we must all appear before the judgment seat of Christ; that every one may receive the things done in his body, according to that he hath done, whether it be good or bad" (2 Cor.5:10).

"And ye have forgotten the exhortation which speaketh unto you as unto children, My son, despise not thou the chastening of the Lord, nor faint when thou art rebuked of him: For whom the Lord loveth he chasteneth, and scourgeth every son whom he receiveth" (Heb.12:5-6).

"And if ye call on the Father, who without respect of persons judgeth according to every man's work, pass the time of your sojourning here in fear" (1 Pt.1:17).

"And, behold, I come quickly; and my reward is with me, to give every man according as his work shall be" (Rev.22:12).

"Also unto thee, O Lord, belongeth mercy: for thou renderest to every man according to his work" (Ps.62:12).

"My son, despise not the chastening of the Lord; neither be weary of his correction: For whom the Lord loveth he correcteth; even as a father the son in whom he delighteth" (Pr.3:11-12).

"I the Lord search the heart, I try the reins, even to give every man according to his ways, and according to the fruit of his doings" (Jer.17:10).

2) God hears the prayers of His people in behalf of others. Intercessory prayer is like sweet incense ascending up and pleasing God. God loves, accepts, and answers intercessory prayer.

"Ask, and it shall be given you; seek, and ye shall find; knock, and it shall be opened unto you" (Mt.7:7).

"If ye abide in me, and my words abide in you, ye shall ask what ye will, and it shall be done unto you" (Jn.15:7).

"Him hath God exalted with his right hand to be a Prince and a Saviour, for to give repentance to Israel, and forgiveness of sins" (Acts 5:31).

"Praying always with all prayer and supplication in the Spirit, and watching thereunto with all perseverance and supplication for all saints" (Eph.6:18).

"If we confess our sins, he is faithful and just to forgive us our sins, and to cleanse us from all unrighteousness" (1 Jn.1:9).

"My little children, these things write I unto you, that ye sin not. And if any man sin, we have an advocate with the Father, Jesus Christ the righteous: And he is the propitiation for our sins: and not for ours only, but also for the sins of the whole world" (1 Jn.2:1-2).

"And it shall come to pass, that before they call, I will answer; and while they are yet speaking, I will hear" (Is.65:24).

DEEPER STUDY # 5

(14:22) **Israel, Failure of, Ten Failures—Israel, Sins of**: the Israelites failed God, continually failed Him. Here God says that they tested and provoked Him, failed to believe Him, grumbling and murmuring ten different times. The ten times are probably as follows:

1. At the Red Sea, the people complained, grumbled, and murmured instead of trusting God.

"And when Pharaoh drew nigh, the children of Israel lifted up their eyes, and, behold, the Egyptians marched after them; and they were sore afraid: and the children of Israel cried out unto the LORD. And they said unto Moses, Because *there were* no graves in Egypt, hast thou taken us away to die in the wilderness? wherefore hast thou dealt thus with us, to carry us forth out of Egypt? *Is* not this the word that we did tell thee in Egypt, saying, Let us alone, that we may serve the Egyptians? For *it had been* better for us to serve the Egyptians, than that we should die in the wilderness" (Ex.14:10-12).

2. At Marah, the people complained because the water was bitter and they had no water. They failed to trust God.

"And when they came to Marah, they could not drink of the waters of Marah, for they *were* bitter: therefore the name of it was called Marah. And the people murmured against Moses, saying, What shall we drink?" (Ex.15:23-24).

3. In the wilderness or Desert of Sin, the people complained because of no food instead of crying out to God and trusting Him.

"And they took their journey from Elim, and all the congregation of the children of Israel came unto the wilderness of Sin, which *is* between Elim and Sinai, on the fifteenth day of the second month after their departing out of the land of Egypt. And the whole congregation of the children of Israel murmured against Moses and Aaron in the wilderness: And the children of Israel said unto them, Would to God we had died by the hand of the LORD in the land of Egypt, when we sat by the flesh pots, *and* when we did eat bread to the full; for ye have brought us forth into this wilderness, to kill this whole assembly with hunger" (Ex.16:1-3).

4. In the wilderness or Desert of Sin, the people tragically disobeyed God.

"And Moses said, Let no man leave of it till the morning. Notwithstanding they hearkened not unto Moses; but some of them left of it until the morning, and it bred worms, and stank: and Moses was wroth with them" (Ex.16:19-20).

5. In the wilderness or Desert of Sin, the people disobeyed God for a second time.

"Six days ye shall gather it; but on the seventh day, *which is* the sabbath, in it there shall be none. And it came to pass, *that* there went out *some* of the people on the seventh day for to gather, and they found none. And the LORD said unto Moses, How long refuse ye to keep my commandments and my laws?" (Ex.16:26-28).

6. At Rephidim, the people complained and quarrelled with Moses and God because they had no water.

"And all the congregation of the children of Israel journeyed from the wilderness of Sin, after their

journeys, according to the commandment of the LORD, and pitched in Rephidim: and *there was* no water for the people to drink. Wherefore the people did chide with Moses, and said, Give us water that we may drink. And Moses said unto them, Why chide ye with me? wherefore do ye tempt the LORD? And the people thirsted there for water; and the people murmured against Moses, and said, Wherefore *is* this *that* thou hast brought us up out of Egypt, to kill us and our children and our cattle with thirst? And Moses cried unto the LORD, saying, What shall I do unto this people? they be almost ready to stone me" (Ex.17:1-4).

7. At the foot of Mt. Sinai, the people turned to idolatry, the worship of the golden calf.

"And when the people saw that Moses delayed to come down out of the mount, the people gathered themselves together unto Aaron, and said unto him, Up, make us gods, which shall go before us; for *as for* this Moses, the man that brought us up out of the land of Egypt, we wot not what is become of him. And Aaron said unto them, Break off the golden earrings, which *are* in the ears of your wives, of your sons, and of your daughters, and bring *them* unto me. And all the people brake off the golden earrings which *were* in their ears, and brought *them* unto Aaron. And he received *them* at their hand, and fashioned it with a graving tool, after he had made it a molten calf: and they said, These *be* thy gods, O Israel, which brought thee up out of the land of Egypt" (Ex.32:1-4).

8. Within three days after leaving Sinai and beginning their march to the promised land—at Taberah—the people complained and grumbled because of their hardships.

"And *when* the people complained, it displeased the LORD: and the LORD heard *it;* and his anger was kindled; and the fire of the LORD burnt among them, and consumed *them that were* in the uttermost parts of the camp. And the people cried unto Moses; and when Moses prayed unto the LORD, the fire was quenched. And he called the name of the place Taberah: because the fire of the LORD burnt among them" (Num.11:1-3).

9. Soon after the above event—at Kibroth Hattaavah—the people complained and grumbled about food, grumbled about having enough variety, grumbled against the heavenly manna.

"And the mixt multitude that *was* among them fell a lusting: and the children of Israel also wept again, and said, Who shall give us flesh to eat? We remember the fish, which we did eat in Egypt freely; the cucumbers, and the melons, and the leeks, and the onions, and the garlick: But now our soul *is* dried away: *there is* nothing at all, beside this manna, *before* our eyes" (Num.11:4-6).

10. At Kadesh (the present passage) the report of the ten spies threw the people into a raging frenzy of unbelief and rebellion.

"And all the congregation lifted up their voice, and cried; and the people wept that night. And all the children of Israel murmured against Moses and against Aaron: and the whole congregation said unto them, Would God that we had died in the land of Egypt! or would God we had died in this wilderness! And wherefore hath the LORD brought us unto this land, to fall by the sword, that our wives and our children should be a prey? were it not better for us to return into Egypt? And they said one to another, Let us make a captain, and let us return into Egypt" (Num.14:1-4).

In addition to the above ten episodes of unbelief and rebellion by the people, there was the opposition against Moses by his very own sister and brother, Miriam and Aaron.

"And Miriam and Aaron spake against Moses because of the Ethiopian woman whom he had married: for he had married an Ethiopian woman. And they said, Hath the LORD indeed spoken only by Moses? hath he not spoken also by us? And the LORD heard it" (Num.12:1-2).

5 (14:26-39) **Judgment, of God—Discipline, of God—Chastisement, of God—Judgment, Judicial—Wilderness Wanderings, the—Spies, the Ten**: there was the declaration of God's charge and judgment (His discipline or chastisement). For the most part, this point elaborates on the judgment just passed upon the people.

OUTLINE	SCRIPTURE	SCRIPTURE	OUTLINE
5. The declaration of God's charge & judgment (discipline, chastisement) a. God's charge against the people: Unbelief—grumbling, complaining against Him	26 And the LORD spake unto Moses and unto Aaron, saying, 27 How long shall I bear with this evil congregation, which murmur against me? I have heard the murmurings of the children of Israel,	which they murmur against me. 28 Say unto them, As truly as I live, saith the LORD, as ye have spoken in mine ears, so will I do to you: 29 Your carcasses shall fall in this wilderness; and all	b. God's judgment against the people: To reap the very things they had said (the just or judicial judgment of God) 1) Their bodies would die in the wilderness or desert

OUTLINE	SCRIPTURE	SCRIPTURE	OUTLINE
• Every adult 20 years old or older—everyone who grumbled • Not a person would ever enter the promised land: Except Caleb & Joshua 2) Their children would be brought into the land & enjoy it: Not enslaved (their false charge against God letting this happen, v.3) • The parents would die in the desert • The children would be shepherds, having to suffer & wander about in the desert for 40 years: Because of the parents' unfaithfulness 3) Their judgment would cover a 40 year span: One year for each of the 40 days they spied out the land of Canaan	that were numbered of you, according to your whole number, from twenty years old and upward, which have murmured against me, 30 Doubtless ye shall not come into the land, concern- ing which I sware to make you dwell therein, save Caleb the son of Jephunneh, and Joshua the son of Nun. 31 But your little ones, which ye said should be a prey, them will I bring in, and they shall know the land which ye have despised. 32 But as for you, your car- casses, they shall fall in this wilderness. 33 And your children shall wander in the wilderness forty years, and bear your whoredoms, until your car- casses be wasted in the wilderness. 34 After the number of the days in which ye searched the land, even forty days, each day for a year, shall ye	bear your iniquities, even forty years, and ye shall know my breach of promise. 35 I the LORD have said, I will surely do it unto all this evil congregation, that are gathered together against me: in this wilderness they shall be consumed, and there they shall die. 36 And the men, which Moses sent to search the land, who returned, and made all the congregation to murmur against him, by bringing up a slander upon the land, 37 Even those men that did bring up the evil report upon the land, died by the plague before the LORD. 38 But Joshua the son of Nun, and Caleb the son of Jephunneh, which were of the men that went to search the land, lived still. 39 And Moses told these sayings unto all the children of Israel: and the people mourned greatly.	• Because they had sinned • Because God had to discipline & chastise them 4) Their fate was sealed, set in the concrete of God's Word—all because they had banded together against God: They were to meet their end in the desert; they were to die there c. God's judgment against the ten unbelieving spies 1) The reason • Because they misled the people to distrust & grumble against God • Because they spread disbelief, an exaggerated report 2) The judgment: Stricken with a plague & died 3) The judgment of God spared Joshua & Caleb: Among the spies, they alone survived d. The response of the people to the declaration of God's judgment: Sorrow, bitter mourning

1. God's charge against the people was clear: they were guilty of unbelief—of grumbling and complaining against Him (v.27). God clearly says that He hears the complaints of His grumbling people.

2. God's judgment against the people was also clear: they were to reap the very things they had said (v.28). This is the just or judicial judgment of God: what a person sows, that shall he also reap (Gal.6:7) (see outline and DEEPER STUDY # 1—Jn.12:39-41 for more discussion).

a. Their bodies would die in the wilderness or desert (v.29-30). They had complained and grumbled that they would rather die in the desert than to have to face the enemies of the promised land. God executed perfect justice: this was exactly the discipline or chastisement pronounced by God. Every adult twenty years old or older—everyone who had grumbled against God—would die in the desert. Not a single person who had ever grumbled or complained against God would ever enter the promised land, except Caleb and Joshua (v.30).

b. However, the children of the Israelites would be brought into the promised land and enjoy it (v.31-33). Not a single child would ever be enslaved. Remember, the people had made this false charge against God, that He was going to let their children become slaves of their enemies (Num.14:3). But God again executed perfect justice: the parents would be the one's who died in the desert and the children would enter the promised land. However, the children would have to live like shepherds, having to suffer and wander about in the desert with their parents for 40 years—all because of the parents' unfaithfulness (v.33). God would use this time to strengthen, toughen, discipline, and teach the children to follow Him with their whole hearts. For 40 long years, this people—these unbelievers and rebellious sinners—would be forced to remember their terrible sin against their LORD who had done so much for them.

c. Note that their judgment would cover a 40 year span. The people were to wander about in the wilderness for 40 long, hard years—one year for each of the 40 days the unbelieving spies had explored the land of Canaan (v.34). The people—the unbelieving and rebellious sinners—were to suffer through the wilderness wanderings because they had tragically sinned, rebelling against God. It must never be forgotten by any people: God has to discipline and chastise those who sin and rebel against His love and goodness, against the great promise of the promised land.

d. The people's fate was sealed, set in the concrete of God's Holy Word—all because they had banded together against God. They were to meet their end in the desert: they were to die there (v.35). Only the younger generation twenty years old or younger would be allowed to enter the promised land.

3. Note God's judgment against the ten unbelieving spies (v.36-38): the people had received a lighter judgment, but not the ten unbelieving spies. The spies had misled the people, become a stumblingblock to them. Through exaggeration and distortion of the facts, they had misled the people to distrust and grumble against God. They had spread unbelief and a frenzy of fear among the people, causing them to go into a fit of rage and rioting, even threatening the very lives of God's servants. The ten unbelieving spies were totally irresponsible. Obviously, there was no other alternative: they had to be severely judged. Perfect justice had to be executed; therefore, God's judgment fell, and they were stricken with a plague and died (v.37). But note: the judgment of God spared Joshua and Caleb, for they believed God, believed in His gift of the promised land. Among the ten spies, they alone survived.

4. Note what happened when Moses declared the judgment of God to the people: they were gripped with sorrow and

bitter mourning (v.39). But it was too late. The people had gone too long and too far in sin. Within just two years, the people had committed ten grievous sins of unbelief and rebellion against God, ten grievous episodes of complaining, grumbling, and murmuring against God and His dear servant Moses—an astounding episode of rebellion against God about every two months.

Thought 1. There is to be a day of judgment out in the future, a day when God will judge every human being who has ever lived.

"And as it is appointed unto men once to die, but after this the judgment" (Heb.9:27).

"When the Son of man shall come in his glory, and all the holy angels with him, then shall he sit upon the throne of his glory: And before him shall be gathered all nations: and he shall separate them one from another, as a shepherd divideth his sheep from the goats: And he shall set the sheep on his right hand, but the goats on the left" (Mt.25:31-33).

"And to you who are troubled rest with us, when the Lord Jesus shall be revealed from heaven with his mighty angels, In flaming fire taking vengeance on them that know not God, and that obey not the gospel of our Lord Jesus Christ" (2 Th.1:7-8).

"The Lord knoweth how to deliver the godly out of temptations, and to reserve the unjust unto the day of judgment to be punished" (2 Pt.2:9).

"But the heavens and the earth, which are now, by the same word are kept in store, reserved unto fire against the day of judgment and perdition of ungodly men" (2 Pt.3:7).

"Behold, the Lord cometh with ten thousands of his saints, To execute judgment upon all, and to convince all that are ungodly among them of all their ungodly deeds which they have ungodly committed, and of all their hard speeches which ungodly sinners have spoken against him" (Jude 14-15).

"Behold, he cometh with clouds; and every eye shall see him, and they also which pierced him: and all kindreds of the earth shall wail because of him. Even so, Amen" (Rev.1:7).

"Before the Lord: for he cometh, for he cometh to judge the earth: he shall judge the world with righteousness, and the people with his truth" (Ps.96:13).

"I said in mine heart, God shall judge the righteous and the wicked: for there is a time there for every purpose and for every work" (Eccl.3:17).

6 (14:40-45) **Confession—Israel, Defeat of—Rebellion, Against God—Repentance, False—Confession, False**: there was the incomplete confession of the Israelites and their defeat because they had acted without God. What happened was tragic: the people continued in their unbelief and rebellion. They heard what Moses said about the judgment of God, that they were to die and only their children would be allowed to enter the promised land. But they did not really believe the judgment of God.

OUTLINE	SCRIPTURE	SCRIPTURE	OUTLINE
6. The incomplete confession & defeat of Israel, acting without God a. The incomplete confession: No repentance b. The disobedience:	40 And they rose up early in the morning, and gat them up into the top of the mountain, saying, Lo, we be here, and will go up unto the place which the LORD hath promised: for we have sinned.	before you, and ye shall fall by the sword: because ye are turned away from the LORD, therefore the LORD will not be with you.	1) Because they had turned away from the LORD 2) Because He would not be with them
1) Refusing to turn around & march toward the Red Sea (v.25) 2) Planning to march into the promised land	41 And Moses said, Wherefore now do ye transgress the commandment of the LORD? but it shall not prosper.	44 But they presumed to go up unto the hill top: nevertheless the ark of the covenant of the LORD, and Moses, departed not out of the camp.	d. The people disobeyed: Marched toward the hill country without Moses or the Ark of the Covenant (a symbol of God's presence & power)
c. The clear, strong warning of Moses: Would not succeed, but would be defeated by the inhabitants of Canaan	42 Go not up, for the LORD is not among you; that ye be not smitten before your enemies. 43 For the Amalekites and the Canaanites are there	45 Then the Amalekites came down, and the Canaanites which dwelt in that hill, and smote them, and discomfited them, even unto Hormah.	e. The result: The Amalekites & Canaanites attacked them & sent them fleeing as far as Hormah

1. They made an incomplete, partial, false confession; that is, they confessed their sin, but they did not repent. They did not turn to God and accept or trust what He had said (v.40). Obviously, they were sensing deep sorrow for their sin. But the sorrow they felt was a worldly sorrow, not a godly sorrow that leads to repentance. They were sorry that they were missing out on the promised land, not that they had sinned and cut the heart of God. This was a selfish, self-centered people, totally focused upon themselves and their own fleshly desires.

2. Note the tragic disobedience, an astonishing disobedience in light of what had just happened (v.40): the people refused to turn around and march into the wilderness toward the Red Sea (v.25). Instead, they planned to march into the promised land. A foolish, rash, totally disobedient action! A deliberate act of unbelief and rebellion against God!

3. The clear, strong warning of Moses was forceful: the people would not succeed. They would be defeated by the enemies of Canaan. The Amalekites and Canaanites would face them in the valleys and defeat them. Note why: because they had turned away from the LORD, and the LORD would not be with them (v.43).

4. The warning fell upon deaf ears: the people were caught up in a spirit of disobedience and rebellion against God. They marched in the arm of the flesh—marched toward the hill country without Moses or the Ark of the Covenant, the

symbol of the presence and power of God (v.44).

5. The result was predictable: just as God through Moses had declared, the Amalekites and Canaanites attacked them. The enemies of the promised land sent them fleeing as far as Hormah (v.45).

Thought 1. True confession always involves repentance, a turning away from sin to God. A person who repents and turns to God follows God. He obeys God. He does not disobey God and turn away from what God has instructed. True repentance listens to God's Word and does exactly what God's Word says. As stated, true repentance obeys God—explicitly obeys. This is the only confession that receives the forgiveness of sin.

"Then Peter said unto them, Repent, and be baptized every one of you in the name of Jesus Christ for the remission of sins, and ye shall receive the gift of the Holy Ghost" (Acts 2:38).

"Repent ye therefore, and be converted, that your sins may be blotted out, when the times of refreshing shall come from the presence of the Lord" (Acts 3:19).

"Repent therefore of this thy wickedness, and pray God, if perhaps the thought of thine heart may be forgiven thee" (Acts 8:22).

"If we confess our sins, he is faithful and just to forgive us our sins, and to cleanse us from all unrighteousness" (1 Jn.1:9).

"If my people, which are called by my name, shall humble themselves, and pray, and seek my face, and turn from their wicked ways; then will I hear from heaven, and will forgive their sin, and will heal their land" (2 Chron.7:14).

"Let the wicked forsake his way, and the unrighteous man his thoughts: and let him return unto the Lord, and he will have mercy upon him; and to our God, for he will abundantly pardon" (Is.55:7).

"But if the wicked will turn from all his sins that he hath committed, and keep all my statutes, and do that which is lawful and right, he shall surely live, he shall not die" (Ezk.18:21).

"Cast away from you all your transgressions, whereby ye have transgressed; and make you a new heart and a new spirit: for why will ye die, O house of Israel" (Ezk.18:31).

DEEPER STUDY # 6

(Num.14:45) **Hormah, City of**: it was located in the territory assigned to the tribe of Simeon (Joshua 19:4). The Hebrew meaning of Hormah is "split rock" or "cursed for destruction." The city of Hormah marked the limits to which the Canaanites had driven the Israelites.

See other Scripture references for study:

Deut. 1:44; Joshua 12:14; Joshua 15:30; Joshua 19:4; Judges 1:17; 1 Samuel 30:30; 1 Chron. 4:30

TYPES, SYMBOLS, AND PICTURES
(Numbers 13:1-14:45)

Historical Term	Type or Picture (Scriptural Basis for Each)	Life Application for Today's Believer	Biblical Application
Joshua Num.13:1-25; 27:18	*Joshua is a type or picture of Christ, the Person who saves us and leads us into the promised land forever. His very name pictured the great salvation that God was going to provide for His dear people in the promised land.* **"And the LORD said unto Moses, Take thee Joshua the son of Nun, a man in whom *is* the spirit, and lay thine hand upon him" (Num.27:18).**	The Greek name for Joshua is *Jesus*. Both Joshua and Jesus mean *God saves*. Moses changed "Hosea's" name to *Joshua* because Joshua was the appointed leader to lead God's people into the promised land (v.16). Joshua is a type of Christ. Jesus Christ is the Person who saves us and leads us into the promised land of heaven.	***"For unto you is born this day in the city of David a Saviour, which is Christ the Lord" (Lk.2:11).*** ***"For the Son of man is come to seek and to save that which was lost" (Lk. 19:10).*** ***"For God sent not his Son into the world to condemn the world; but that the world through him might be saved" (Jn.3:17).*** ***"I am the door: by me if any man enter in, he shall be saved, and shall go in and out, and find pasture" (Jn.10:9).*** ***"Jesus saith unto him, I am the way, the truth, and the life: no man cometh unto the Father, but by me" (Jn.14:6).***

Historical Term	Type or Picture (Scriptural Basis for Each)	Life Application for Today's Believer	Biblical Application
			"Neither is there salvation in any other: for there is none other name under heaven given among men, whereby we must be saved" (Acts 4:12). ***"This is a faithful saying, and worthy of all acceptation, that Christ Jesus came into the world to save sinners; of whom I am chief" (1 Tim.1:15).*** ***"Wherefore he is able also to save them to the uttermost that come unto God by him, seeing he ever liveth to make intercession for them" (Heb.7:25).***
Tearing of Clothes Num.14:1-10, esp. v.6	*The tearing of clothes was a symbol of ritual mourning.* **"And Joshua the son of Nun, and Caleb the son of Jephunneh, *which were* of them that searched the land, rent their clothes" (Num.14:6).**	Who is it that mourns? Who is it so full of grief that he cries and weeps and utters groanings deep from within? There are three persons who mourn and utter such groanings. 1. The person who is desperately sorry for his sins and feels ever so unworthy before the LORD. He has such a sense of sin that his heart is just broken. (Luke 18:13) 2. The person who really feels the desperate plight and terrible suffering of others. The tragedies, the problems, the sinful behavior of others—the state, the condition, the lostness of the world—all weigh ever so heavily upon the heart of the mourner. 3. The person who experiences personal tragedy and intense trauma.	***"And the publican, standing afar off, would not lift up so much as his eyes unto heaven, but smote upon his breast, saying, God be merciful to me a sinner" (Luke 18:13).*** ***"But when he saw the multitudes, he was moved with compassion on them, because they fainted, and were scattered abroad, as sheep having no shepherd" (Matthew 9:36).*** ***"And Jesus went forth, and saw a great multitude, and was moved with compassion toward them, and he healed their sick" (Matthew 14:14).*** ***"Like as a father pitieth his children, so the LORD pitieth them that fear him" (Psalm 103:13).*** ***"In all their affliction he was afflicted, and the angel of his presence saved them: in his love and in his pity he redeemed them; and he bare them, and carried them all the days of old" (Isaiah 63:9).***

DIVISION III

THE FORTY LONG YEARS OF WILDERNESS WANDERINGS: A PICTURE OF THE BELIEVER'S PILGRIMAGE THROUGH THIS WORLD AS HE PREPARES TO ENTER THE PROMISED LAND 15:1-25:18

(15:1—25:18) **DIVISION OVERVIEW—Wilderness Wanderings—Desert Journeys—Israel, Wilderness Wanderings of—Israel, Second Generation, Preparation of**: "the Wilderness Wanderings"—"the Desert Journeys": this is the all-important subject of this division of Numbers. One of the most fascinating, captivating, and intriguing subjects in all of Scripture. The first generation of Israelites have just committed the final, tragic rebellion that dooms them to wander about in the desert wilderness until they die (chapters 13-14). Now, chapter 15 begins as though nothing has happened. Why? One reason: the second generation—the children twenty years old or younger—now have to be prepared to conquer and claim the inheritance of the promised land. They have to be taught the laws of the land, strengthened, disciplined, and toughened. They must become the best soldiers possible: strong enough to endure the march and to defeat and conquer all the enemies who will oppose them.

God takes the forty years of *wilderness wanderings* and uses them for good. He takes these years of chastisement against the first generation and uses them to prepare their children to claim the inheritance the parents had forfeited by their evil unbelief and rebellion.

Immediately after the final, tragic failure of the first generation, God gave the laws covered in chapter 15. The laws were to help govern the second generation of believers after they entered the promised land. This is surprising; most of these laws would not be needed for about forty years. Why give the laws now, forty years ahead of time? To encourage the parents—who had just failed so miserably—and the children who were the hope of the future. God was encouraging them all, declaring that the promised land was real, so real that He was going to begin training the children in the laws of the land now—immediately. The parents were not to live defeated lives, spending the rest of their days depressed, angry, and discouraged. They were to place their hope in their children. About forty years from then, the children would march into the promised land. Here were laws they would need to govern them during those days. This is exactly what God says in 15:2: "After you come into the land I am giving you," you are to do this and that.

As one reads through the *wilderness wanderings*, a surprising fact emerges: little is really said about the long, hard years of suffering. A few events are shared, but only a few. Considering that the time frame of the *wilderness wanderings* covers about thirty-eight years, we are left wondering what happened during all the silent, unrecorded time.

The point that must be kept in mind during the reading of the *wilderness wanderings* is this: the events that were recorded are for us. They stand as a warning to us: that we must escape the evil of the Israelites. We must not wallow around in unbelief, grumbling, and complaining against God. We must not curse God nor rebel against Him. This fact is the clear declaration of Scripture:

> **"For whatsoever things were written aforetime were written for our learning, that we through patience and comfort of the scriptures might have hope" (Ro.15:4).**
>
> **"Now these things were our examples, to the intent we should not lust after evil things, as they also lusted. Neither be ye idolaters, as *were* some of them; as it is written, The people sat down to eat and drink, and rose up to play. Neither let us commit fornication, as some of them committed, and fell in one day three and twenty thousand. Neither let us tempt Christ, as some of them also tempted, and were destroyed of serpents. Neither murmur ye, as some of them also murmured, and were destroyed of the destroyer. Now all these things happened unto them for ensamples: and they are written for our admonition, upon whom the ends of the world are come" (1 Cor.10:6-11).**

THE FORTY LONG YEARS OF WILDERNESS WANDERINGS: A PICTURE OF THE BELIEVER'S PILGRIMAGE THROUGH THIS WORLD AS HE PREPARES TO ENTER THE PROMISED LAND 15:1-25:18

A. Event 1—God Gave Various Laws to Help Govern His People: Being Reassured and Prepared for the Promised Land, 15:1-41

B. Event 2: A Dangerous Rebellion by Korah and His Allies: God Judges All Grumbling and Unbelief, All Rebellion and Unauthorized Approaches, 16:1-50

C. Event 3—The Budding of Aaron's Staff: The Test to Vindicate God's Priest and His Ministry (a Symbol of Christ or of the Minister), 17:1-13

D. Event 4—God Spelled Out the Service of the Priests and Levites: The Duties, Support, and Tithing of God's Ministers, 18:1-32

E. Event 5—God Gave the Law to Govern the Offering of the Red Heifer and the Cleansing Water: A Symbol of Christ, His Sacrifice and Cleansing Power, 19:1-22

F. Event 6—the Last Year of Israel in the Wilderness: Five Sad Events, 20:1-29

G. Event 7—the First Military Victories the Bronze Snake: A Picture of Desperate Vows, of Christ the Savior, and of God's Protection and Victory, 21:1-3521:1-35

H. Event 8—the Story of Balaam, His Donkey, and His Three Encounters with God (Part 1): A Picture of the Unseen, Unknown Attempts by the Powers of Darkness to Defeat God's People, 22:1-41

I. Event 9—the Story of Balaam and the Seven Startling Oracles or Prophecies Pronounced by Him: The Blessings of God and a Glimpse into the Future, 23:1-24:25

J. Event 10: The Ultimate Rebellion of God's People and the End of the Forty Years of Wilderness Wanderings: Apostasy—Turning to Worldliness, to the Worship of Sex and Other Gods, 25:1-18

III. THE FORTY LONG YEARS OF WILDERNESS WANDERINGS: A PICTURE OF THE BELIEVER'S PILGRIMAGE THROUGH THIS WORLD AS HE PREPARES TO ENTER THE PROMISED LAND

A. Event 1—God Gave Various Laws to Help Govern His People: Being Reassured & Prepared for the Promised Land, 15:1-41

1. The law governing special Grain & Drink Offerings: A symbol of dedication & of thanking God for Christ's sacrifice
- a. When to present the offerings
  - 1) After entering the promised land
  - 2) When offering sacrifices "made by fire" (the Burnt & the Peace Offerings)
    - Because they pleased the LORD
    - Because they involved vows & freewill or festival occasions
- b. The amount to offer
  - 1) When sacrificing a lamb: A symbol of Christ's sacrifice
    - The Grain Offering: 2 qts. of flour mixed with 1 qt. of oil (a symbol of dedication & of thanking God)
    - The Drink Offering: 1 qt. of wine (a symbol of pouring out one's life to God)
  - 2) When sacrificing a ram: A symbol of Christ's sacrifice
    - The Grain Offering: 3 qts. of flour mixed with 2½ pints of oil
    - The Drink Offering: 2½ pints of wine (a symbol of Christ's sacrifice)
    - The result: An aroma that pleases the LORD
  - 3) When sacrificing a young bull: A symbol of Christ's sacrifice
    - The Grain Offering: 5 qts. of flour mixed with 2 qts. of oil (a symbol of giving thanks for the sacrifice)
    - The Drink Offering: 2 qts. of wine (a symbol of pouring out one's life to God)

And the LORD spake unto
Moses, saying,
2 Speak unto the children
of Israel, and say unto
them, When ye be come
into the land of your habitations,
which I give unto
you,
3 And will make an offering
by fire unto the LORD, a
burnt offering, or a sacrifice
in performing a vow, or in a
freewill offering, or in your
solemn feasts, to make a
sweet savour unto the LORD,
of the herd, or of the flock:
4 Then shall he that offereth
his offering unto the LORD
bring a meat offering of a
tenth deal of flour mingled
with the fourth part of an hin
of oil.
5 And the fourth part of
an hin of wine for a drink
offering shalt thou prepare
with the burnt offering
or sacrifice, for one lamb.
6 Or for a ram, thou shalt
prepare for a meat offering
two tenth deals of flour mingled
with the third part of an
hin of oil.
7 And for a drink offering
thou shalt offer the third
part of an hin of wine, for
a sweet savour unto the
LORD.
8 And when thou preparest a
bullock for a burnt offering,
or for a sacrifice in performing
a vow, or peace offerings
unto the LORD:
9 Then shall he bring with a
bullock a meat offering of
three tenth deals of flour
mingled with half an hin of
oil.
10 And thou shalt bring for
a drink offering half an hin
of wine, for an offering made
by fire, of a sweet savour
unto the LORD.
11 Thus shall it be done for
one bullock, or for one ram,
or for a lamb, or a kid.
12 According to the number
that ye shall prepare, so shall
ye do to every one according
to their number.
13 All that are born of the
country shall do these
things after this manner,
in offering an offering
made by fire, of a
sweet savour unto the
LORD.
14 And if a stranger sojourn
with you, or whosoever be
among you in your generations,
and will offer an offering
made by fire, of a sweet
savour unto the LORD; as ye
do, so he shall do.
15 One ordinance shall be
both for you of the congregation,
and also for the stranger
that sojourneth with you, an
ordinance for ever in your
generations: as ye are, so
shall the stranger be before
the LORD.
16 One law and one manner
shall be for you, and for the
stranger that sojourneth with
you.
17 And the LORD spake unto
Moses, saying,
18 Speak unto the children
of Israel, and say unto them,
When ye come into the land
whither I bring you,
19 Then it shall be, that,
when ye eat of the bread of
the land, ye shall offer up an
heave offering unto the
LORD.
20 Ye shall offer up a cake
of the first of your dough for
an heave offering: as ye do
the heave offering of the
threshingfloor, so shall ye
heave it.
21 Of the first of your
dough ye shall give unto
the LORD an heave offering
in your generations.
22 And if ye have erred, and
not observed all these commandments,
which the LORD
hath spoken unto Moses,
23 Even all that the LORD
hath commanded you by the
hand of Moses, from the day
that the LORD commanded
Moses, and henceforward
among your generations;
24 Then it shall be, if ought
be committed by ignorance

- The result: An aroma that pleases the LORD
- c. The absolute necessity for obedience: Must be strictly followed with each sacrifice
- d. The persons who must obey
  - 1) The native-born: Must dedicate himself & present praise to God—a Grain & Drink Offering—when approaching God through the sacrifices (a symbol of Christ)
  - 2) The alien or anyone else: Must dedicate himself & offer praise to God—a Grain or Drink Offering—when approaching God thru the sacrifices (a symbol of Christ)
  - 3) The point stressed: The same rules apply to everyone
  - 4) The law is to be a permanent law
  - 5) The love of God declared:
    - Everyone is the same, equal before the LORD
    - The same law & regulation applies to everyone, native-born & foreigner

2. The law governing the firstfruits: A picture of tithes & offerings
- a. When to present the offering: After entering the promised land & eating the food of the land
- b. What to present
  - 1) A portion of what one eats
  - 2) A cake made from the first of the ground meal—made from the grain harvest
- c. The importance of the law stressed
  - 1) To be a permanent law
  - 2) To be presented from the very first of the ground meal

3. The law governing forgiveness for unintentional sin
- a. The whole community of believers can be forgiven
  - 1) The two conditions for forgiveness:
    - First, the sin must be unintentional—committed in ignorance, being unaware of the sin
    - Second, the community must approach God for

forgiveness thru the sacrifice of the Burnt Offering & the Sin Offering (a symbol of approaching God thru Christ, our sacrifice)

2) The promise of God:
- He will accept the sacrifice as atonement (reconciliation) & forgive the community (a symbol of accepting Christ as the basis for atonement & forgiveness)
- He will forgive the entire community, native-born & foreigner: Because the sin was unintentional

b. The individual can be forgiven
1) The 2 conditions:
- The sin must be unintentional
- The person must come to God thru the sacrifice of the Sin Offering (a symbol of Christ's sacrifice)

2) The promise of God:
- He accepts the sacrifice as atonement & forgives
- He forgives any person who approaches Him as stipulated by this law, whether native-born or foreigner

4. The law governing deliberate, defiant, or brazen sin—sin that dares to presume upon God

a. The nature of defiant sin
1) Blasphemes the LORD
2) Despises God's Word
3) Deliberately breaks God's commandments

without the knowledge of the
congregation, that all the
congregation shall offer one
young bullock for a burnt
offering, for a sweet savour
unto the LORD, with his meat
offering, and his drink offering, according to the manner,
and one kid of the goats for a
sin offering.
25 And the priest shall make
an atonement for all the congregation of the children of
Israel, and it shall be forgiv-
en them; for it is ignorance:
and they shall bring their
offering, a sacrifice made by
fire unto the LORD, and their
sin offering before the LORD,
for their ignorance:
26 And it shall be forgiven
all the congregation of the
children of Israel, and the
stranger that sojourneth
among them; seeing all
the people were in igno-
rance.
27 And if any soul sin
through ignorance, then he
shall bring a she goat of the
first year for a sin offering.
28 And the priest shall make
an atonement for the soul
that sinneth ignorantly, when
he sinneth by ignorance
before the LORD, to make an
atonement for him; and it
shall be forgiven him.
29 Ye shall have one law for
him that sinneth through
ignorance, both for him that
is born among the children
of Israel, and for the stranger
that sojourneth among them.
30 But the soul that doeth
ought presumptuously,
whether he be born in the
land, or a stranger, the same
reproacheth the LORD; and
that soul shall be cut off from
among his people.
31 Because he hath despised
the word of the LORD, and
hath broken his command-
ment, that soul shall utterly
be cut off; his iniquity shall
be upon him.
32 And while the children
of Israel were in the wilderness, they found a man that
gathered sticks upon the sabbath day.
33 And they that found him
gathering sticks brought him
unto Moses and Aaron, and
unto all the congregation.
34 And they put him in
ward, because it was not
declared what should be
done to him.
35 And the LORD said unto
Moses, The man shall be
surely put to death: all the
congregation shall stone him
with stones without the
camp.
36 And all the congregation
brought him without the
camp, and stoned him with
stones, and he died; as the
LORD commanded Moses.
37 And the LORD spake unto
Moses, saying,
38 Speak unto the children
of Israel, and bid them
that they make them fringes
in the borders of their garments throughout their generations, and that they
put upon the fringe of
the borders a ribband of
blue:
39 And it shall be unto you
for a fringe, that ye may look
upon it, and remember all the
commandments of the LORD,
and do them; and that
ye seek not after your own
heart and your own eyes,
after which ye use to go a
whoring:
40 That ye may remember,
and do all my command-
ments, and be holy unto your
God.
41 I am the LORD your God,
which brought you out of the
land of Egypt, to be your
God: I am the LORD your
God.

b. The judgment: Must be cut off—completely, eternally

c. The example of deliberate, defiant sin: A man gathered wood on the Sabbath—defiantly broke the law of the Sabbath
1) He was arrested & brought to the authorities, Moses & Aaron, & before all the people
2) He was held in custody until Moses could seek the Lord about what should be done
3) He was sentenced to death by the LORD: To be stoned in the presence of the entire assembly—outside the camp
4) He was executed as the LORD commanded

5. The law instructing the believer to wear tassels on the hem of his clothing—attached with a blue cord: Pictures the need to live a holy, godly life

a. The importance of the law: To be a permanent law

b. The purpose:
1) To stir the believer to remember God's commandments
2) To stir the believer to live a life of separation from the world: Not to prostitute himself through fleshly lusts
3) To stir the believer to obey all God's commands: To be totally committed to God

c. The authority behind the laws
1) "The LORD": The only living & true God
2) "The LORD your God": Personal
3) "The LORD who [saved] you"

DIVISION III

THE FORTY LONG YEARS OF WILDERNESS WANDERINGS: A PICTURE OF THE BELIEVER'S PILGRIMAGE THROUGH THIS WORLD AS HE PREPARES TO ENTER THE PROMISED LAND

A. Event 1—God Gave Various Laws to Help Govern His People: Being Reassured and Prepared for the Promised Land, 15:1-41

(15:1-41) **Introduction—Assurance, Importance of—Confidence, Importance of**: assurance is a wonderful thing. If a person feels assured, he walks with confidence throughout life, conquering the problems and difficulties, the trials and temptations of life. He is victorious over all the pitfalls and enemies of life. This is what makes assurance so important.

Assurance makes us confident, confident that we can conquer all.

But note: this kind of assurance—this confidence—comes only from God. Without God, we know that no matter how strong we are, disease or accident and eventually death will take us to the grave. Only God can conquer death, and only God can give us the perfect assurance to conquer all the pitfalls and enemies of life. Once a person genuinely comes to God through Jesus Christ, God saves that person and places His precious Holy Spirit within the new believer. The Holy Spirit gives the believer whatever assurance and confidence is needed to walk triumphantly throughout life. Moreover, the Spirit of God assures the believer of the promised land, of living forever in the presence of God.

This is the subject of the present passage. The Israelites had just committed the gross, terrible sin of unbelief and apostasy against God. (See outlines and notes—Num.13:1-14:45 for more discussion.) They even elected a new leader to replace God's servant Moses and were about to kill the four godly leaders: Moses, Aaron, Joshua, and Caleb. The people had gone too far, beyond repentance, beyond ever following God with a heart of true belief and righteousness. God knew this; consequently, He had to step in and judge the Israelites. This He did: the people were barred from entering the promised land. They were to die out in the desert or wilderness—wandering about for a total of 40 years until all the adults twenty years old or older had died. Only the children under twenty years old would be allowed to enter the promised land. The people were, of course, discouraged. They sensed defeat, failure, and some sorrow for their sin.

But into the midst of their discouragement and loss of heart God came. God filled their hearts with His grace, assuring them that their children would enter the promised land. The land would be their inheritance, the inheritance of the children.

How could God take a people so gripped with a spirit of despondency and raise their spirits, lifting them as high as the eagle soars? How could God place a deep-seated assurance within the hearts of His people, an assurance so strong that they could go on living and rearing their children—in order that their children might have a better life than the poor life they were having to live? God did one simple but powerful thing: He gave them several major laws that were to govern the children after they entered the land. It was to be about 40 years before the children would ever need some of these laws. But the day was coming when they would be needed, the day when the children would enter the promised land. Therefore, the adults were to teach these laws to their children. Hereafter, their task as adults was to focus almost entirely upon their children: to prepare their children to enter the promised land.

This is the subject of this passage of Scripture: *Event 1—God Gave Various Laws to Help Govern His People: Being Reassured and Prepared for the Promised Land,* 15:1-41.

1. The law governing special Grain and Drink Offerings: a symbol of dedication and of thanking God for Christ's sacrifice (v.1-16).
2. The law governing the firstfruits: a picture of tithes and offerings (v.17-21).
3. The law governing forgiveness for unintentional sin (v.22-29).
4. The law governing deliberate, defiant, brazen sin—sin that dares to presume upon God (v.30-36).
5. The law instructing the believer to wear tassels on the hem of his clothing—attached with a blue cord: pictures the need to live a holy, godly life (v.37-41).

1 (15:1-16) **Dedication, to God—Submission, to God—Thanksgiving, to God—Praise, to God—Offerings, When to Present—Grain Offering—Drink Offering—Symbol, of Dedication—Symbol, of Submission**: God gave a law that governed special Grain and Drink Offerings. These offerings were a symbol of dedication and submission to God. They were also a symbol of thanking God for the atonement or reconciliation made through the substitute sacrifice.

⇒ Remember this about the Grain Offering: when a person laid his Grain Offering upon the burning sacrifice, he was offering his grain to God as a symbol of himself—of all he had and was. This was a picture of dedication, of laying all he had upon God. But dedication was not the only picture seen in his offering: by laying his grain upon the substitute sacrifice, he was thanking God for the sacrifice, that the sacrifice made atonement for him, reconciling him to God. Thus, the Grain Offering was an offering of dedication and thanksgiving to God, especially for the atonement (see outline and notes—Lev.2:1-16 for more discussion).

⇒ Remember this about the Drink Offering: when the wine was poured out upon the altar, the person was symbolizing that he was pouring out the best he had to offer before God, pouring out his life before God—submitting himself totally to God.

A quick glance at the Scripture and outline will show the points covered by the law. Keep in mind that the Grain Offerings were important to God, very important, for they exposed the human heart of a person. The offerings revealed the true response of the person's heart to the sacrifice being made in his behalf. The sacrifice was a symbol of God's dear Son, the Lord Jesus Christ, who was to sacrifice His life for us all. It was this—the person's response to the sacrifice, a symbol of God's Son—that made the Grain and Drink Offerings so important to God. God gave His Son, the Lord Jesus Christ, to die for the sins of the world so that man would respond to Him, respond in love and obedience.

OUTLINE	SCRIPTURE	SCRIPTURE	OUTLINE
1. The law governing special Grain & Drink Offerings: A symbol of dedication & of thanking God for Christ's sacrifice a. When to present the offerings 1) After entering the promised land	And the LORD spake unto Moses, saying, 2 Speak unto the children of Israel, and say unto them, When ye be come into the land of your habitations, which I give unto you, 3 And will make an offering by fire unto the LORD,	a burnt offering, or a sacrifice in performing a vow, or in a freewill offering, or in your solemn feasts, to make a sweet savour unto the LORD, of the herd, or of the flock: 4 Then shall he that offereth	2) When offering sacrifices "made by fire" (the Burnt & the Peace Offerings) • Because they pleased the LORD • Because they involved vows & freewill or festival occasions b. The amount to offer

OUTLINE	SCRIPTURE	SCRIPTURE	OUTLINE
1) When sacrificing a lamb: A symbol of Christ's sacrifice • The Grain Offering: 2 qts. of flour mixed with 1 qt. of oil (a symbol of dedication & of thanking God) • The Drink Offering: 1 qt. of wine (a symbol of pouring out one's life to God)	his offering unto the LORD bring a meat offering of a tenth deal of flour mingled with the fourth part of an hin of oil. 5 And the fourth part of an hin of wine for a drink offering shalt thou prepare with the burnt offering or sacrifice, for one lamb.	savour unto the LORD. 11 Thus shall it be done for one bullock, or for one ram, or for a lamb, or a kid. 12 According to the number that ye shall prepare, so shall ye do to every one according to their number.	that pleases the LORD c. The absolute necessity for obedience: Must be strictly followed with each sacrifice
2) When sacrificing a ram: A symbol of Christ's sacrifice • The Grain Offering: 3 qts. of flour mixed with 2½ pints of oil • The Drink Offering: 2½ pints of wine (a symbol of Christ's sacrifice) • The result: An aroma that pleases the LORD	6 Or for a ram, thou shalt prepare for a meat offering two tenth deals of flour mingled with the third part of an hin of oil. 7 And for a drink offering thou shalt offer the third part of an hin of wine, for a sweet savour unto the LORD.	13 All that are born of the country shall do these things after this manner, in offering an offering made by fire, of a sweet savour unto the LORD. 14 And if a stranger sojourn with you, or whosoever be among you in your generations, and will offer an offering made by fire, of a sweet savour unto the LORD; as ye do, so he shall do.	d. The persons who must obey 1) The native-born: Must dedicate himself & present praise to God—a Grain & Drink Offering—when approaching God through the sacrifices (a symbol of Christ) 2) The alien or anyone else: Must dedicate himself & offer praise to God—a Grain or Drink Offering—when approaching God thru the sacrifices (a symbol of Christ)
3) When sacrificing a young bull: A symbol of Christ's sacrifice • The Grain Offering: 5 qts. of flour mixed with 2 qts. of oil (a symbol of giving thanks for the sacrifice) • The Drink Offering: 2 qts. of wine (a symbol of pouring out one's life to God) • The result: An aroma	8 And when thou preparest a bullock for a burnt offering, or for a sacrifice in performing a vow, or peace offerings unto the LORD: 9 Then shall he bring with a bullock a meat offering of three tenth deals of flour mingled with half an hin of oil. 10 And thou shalt bring for a drink offering half an hin of wine, for an offering made by fire, of a sweet	15 One ordinance shall be both for you of the congregation, and also for the stranger that sojourneth with you, an ordinance for ever in your generations: as ye are, so shall the stranger be before the LORD. 16 One law and one manner shall be for you, and for the stranger that sojourneth with you.	3) The point stressed: The same rules apply to everyone 4) The law is to be a permanent law 5) The love of God declared: • Everyone is the same, equal before the LORD • The same law & regulation applies to everyone, native-born & foreigner

1. Note when the offerings were to be presented (v.2-3).
   a. They were to present the Grain and Drink Offerings after entering the promised land. This was a glorious promise: the people were going to enter the promised land. Remember, the people had just committed gross sins against God, rebelling against Him and threatening to kill Moses, Aaron, Joshua, and Caleb (Num.13:1-14:45). The result was catastrophic: the judgment of God had fallen and the older generation—twenty years old and older—was condemned never to enter the promised land. Only their children would inherit the land. But God was giving assurance here: the children—the second generation of God's people—would inherit the land. The day would come, and when it came, they were to present the Grain and Drink Offerings to God. Even in the midst of judgment, the grace of God flows out to His people: great assurance is given to them. Their children will enter the promised land. The Word of God guarantees it.

      Note this fact: the people were unable to offer the Grain and Drink Offerings out in the desert or wilderness. They would not have the fields of grain nor the vines of grapes until they settled down in the promised land. This fact reinforces the grace and encouragement of God to His people. There was no apparent need to give this law to His people at this time. God could easily have waited and given it to them when they were going to need the law—some 38 years later, right before they were to enter the promised land. But here God was showering His grace upon His people, using the law as a clear means to encourage them. They could rest assured: their children would enter the promised land. Here was a law they would need when they settled in the land, a law they would need some 38 years in the future. Giving this law then gave assurance—absolute assurance—that God was going to lead the children, the second generation, into the promised land of God.

   b. They were to present the Grain and Drink Offerings with every sacrifice "made by fire" (v.3). This term "made by fire" refers to the Burnt Offering and the Peace or Fellowship Offering (cp. v.3, 8). (See outlines and notes—Lev.1:1-17; 3:1-17 for more discussion.) The whole sacrifice of the Burnt Offering was burned on the altar, but just a part of the sacrifice was burned in the Peace or Fellowship Offering. The rest of the animal was shared between the priest and the worshippers. This is the first mention in Scripture that the wine offerings were to be offered with all Burnt Offerings and Peace or Fellowship Offerings. The picture was this:

      ⇒ When a person wanted to seek atonement or reconciliation with God, he approached God through the sacrifice of the Burnt Offering (a symbol of Christ's sacrifice). The sacrifice bore the penalty for sin that was due the person: the sacrifice paid the ransom, redeemed the person. The sacrifice made atonement, reconciled the person to God. Therefore, in thanksgiving for the atoning sacrifice, the person offered himself—all he was and had—to God. This act of dedication was symbolized by laying the Grain Offering upon the burning sacrifice (a picture of dying with the sacrifice, dying to self). Moreover, the person poured wine out upon the altar to symbolize that he was pouring out his life as an offering to God, submitting himself to God—all he was and had.

⇒ When a person wanted to grow in the peace and fellowship of God, he approached God through the sacrifice of the Peace or Fellowship Offering. The peace and fellowship of God came through the sacrifice. By bringing the sacrifice, a person's mind stayed focused upon seeking more and more of the peace and fellowship of God. Once again, the person was to offer the Grain and Drink Offerings...
- to express both thanksgiving and dedication
- to seek more and more of the peace and fellowship of God

Now, note why a person was to offer the Grain and Drink Offerings with these two particular sacrifices: because these two sacrifices pleased the LORD in a very special way. The sacrifice of the Burnt Offering secured atonement and reconciliation for His dear people, and the sacrifice of the Peace or Fellowship Offering enabled His people to experience and grow in peace and fellowship with Him.

But this was not all: these two sacrifices were offered during meaningful occasions. They were offered when making special vows, or freewill or festival offerings—times that involved special periods of dedication and thanksgiving. It was, therefore, only natural to offer Grain and Drink Offerings along with the sacrifices made during these occasions.

2. Note the amount of grain and drink that was to be offered with each sacrifice (v.4-10). The Scripture and outline above gives the amount, making it unnecessary to repeat here. Note this one fact about the flour in the Grain Offering (v.4, 6, 9): the flour was not to be the regular, ordinary flour used day by day. It was to be "fine, choice flour" (solet), the very best flour that could be made. A person was to give his very best to God, the best he had.

3. Note the absolute necessity for obedience: each sacrifice had to be prepared in this way—without exception (v.11-12). The sacrifice was of critical importance to God, for the sacrifice was a symbol, a type of the sacrifice of His dear Son, the Lord Jesus Christ. Therefore, everything about the sacrifice—every single preparation—had to be carried out exactly as God dictated. Everything had to be done in the order and way He prescribed. Nothing else was acceptable.

4. Note that persons must approach God in this way: through the substitute sacrifice and the Grain and Drink Offerings (v.13-14). Both the native-born Israelite and the foreigner or anyone else living among God's people had to approach God in this way. Atonement or reconciliation with God came only through the substitute sacrifice of the Burnt Offering. Peace and fellowship with God comes only through the substitute sacrifice of the Peace or Fellowship Offering. There was no other approach to God other than through the substitute sacrifice, no other approach that was acceptable to God. This was the way approaching God had to be, for the sacrifice represented the sacrifice of His dear Son who was to die for the world as the Lamb of God, die in order to take away the sin of the world.

Moreover, when a person approached God through the substitute sacrifice, he had to be genuine—completely sincere: he had to dedicate himself to God and be thankful for what God was doing for him through the substitute sacrifice. No matter who the person was—native-born or foreigner or anyone else—this was the only way he could approach God. This and this alone was the way he had to approach God if he wanted to be acceptable to Him.

The point is stressed and reemphasized: the same rules apply to everyone, no matter who he is—native-born or foreigner (v.15). No person—no matter who he is—is ever acceptable to God unless he follows these rules. He must approach God through the substitute sacrifice and be sincere enough to dedicate his life to God, offering thanksgiving for the atonement (reconciliation).

This law was established as a permanent law (v.15). It even applies to us and to all future generations. To be acceptable to God, we have to approach Him through the substitute sacrifice of His dear Son, the Lord Jesus Christ. Moreover, common sense tells us we must be sincere in our approach. We must be sincere enough to dedicate our lives to God, offering thanksgiving and praise to Him for what He does for us through Christ (atonement, reconciliation).

Note the great love of God declared by God Himself (v.15-16): everyone is the same in approaching God. All are equal before the LORD: there are no favorites with God, no partiality shown by God. The same law and regulation applies to everyone. Each person must approach God through the substitute sacrifice. Each person must dedicate himself to God, offering thanksgiving and praise to Him for what He does for His people.

Thought 1. Scripture makes it perfectly clear: there is only one approach to God, only one way to become acceptable to Him—through the substitute sacrifice of Jesus Christ. This is the very reason Christ died upon the cross; this is the meaning of the cross.

1) Jesus Christ died as our substitute sacrifice to secure atonement for us. Through His sacrificial death, we are ransomed, redeemed, reconciled to God.

"For when we were yet without strength, in due time Christ died for the ungodly" (Ro.5:6).

"For if, when we were enemies, we were reconciled to God by the death of his Son, much more, being reconciled, we shall be saved by his life. And not only so, but we also joy in God through our Lord Jesus Christ, by whom we have now received the atonement" (Ro.5:10-11).

"Purge out therefore the old leaven, that ye may be a new lump, as ye are unleavened. For even Christ our passover is sacrificed for us" (1 Cor.5:7).

"Christ hath redeemed us from the curse of the law, being made a curse for us: for it is written, Cursed is every one that hangeth on a tree" (Gal.3:13).

"And walk in love, as Christ also hath loved us, and hath given himself for us an offering and a sacrifice to God for a sweetsmelling savour" (Eph.5:2).

"Who gave himself for us, that he might redeem us from all iniquity, and purify unto himself a peculiar people, zealous of good works" (Tit.2:14).

"Forasmuch as ye know that ye were not redeemed with corruptible things, as silver and gold, from your vain conversation received by tradition from your fathers; But with the precious blood of Christ, as of a lamb without blemish and without spot" (1 Pt.1:18-19).

"For Christ also hath once suffered for sins, the just for the unjust, that he might bring us to God, being put to death in the flesh, but quickened by the Spirit" (1 Pt.3:18).

"Hereby perceive we the love of God, because he laid down his life for us: and we ought to lay down our lives for the brethren" (1 Jn.3:16).

2) Jesus Christ died as our substitute to secure peace and fellowship with God for us.

"For God so loved the world, that he gave his only begotten Son, that whosoever believeth in him should not perish, but have everlasting life" (Jn.3:16).
"The word which God sent unto the children of Israel, preaching peace by Jesus Christ: (he is Lord of all" (Acts 10:36).
"Therefore being justified by faith, we have peace with God through our Lord Jesus Christ" (Ro.5:1).
"But God commendeth his love toward us, in that, while we were yet sinners, Christ died for us" (Ro.5:8).
"For he is our peace, who hath made both one, and hath broken down the middle wall of partition between us" (Eph.2:14).
"And, having made peace through the blood of his cross, by him to reconcile all things unto himself; by him, I say, whether they be things in earth, or things in heaven" (Col.1:20).
"That which we have seen and heard declare we unto you, that ye also may have fellowship with us: and truly our fellowship is with the Father, and with his Son Jesus Christ" (1 Jn.1:3).
"But he was wounded for our transgressions, he was bruised for our iniquities: the chastisement of our peace was upon him; and with his stripes we are healed" (Is.53:5).

Thought 2. The only approach to God is through the sacrifice of His dear Son, the Lord Jesus Christ. God accepts no other approach.

"Jesus answered them, Verily, verily, I say unto you, Whosoever committeth sin is the servant of sin" (Jn.8:34).
"Jesus saith unto him, I am the way, the truth, and the life: no man cometh unto the Father, but by me" (Jn.14:6).
"Neither is there salvation in any other: for there is none other name under heaven given among men, whereby we must be saved" (Acts 4:12).
"For other foundation can no man lay than that is laid, which is Jesus Christ" (1 Cor.3:11).
"For there is one God, and one mediator between God and men, the man Christ Jesus; Who gave himself a ransom for all, to be testified in due time" (1 Tim.2:5-6).
"My little children, these things write I unto you, that ye sin not. And if any man sin, we have an advocate with the Father, Jesus Christ the righteous: And he is the propitiation for our sins: and not for ours only, but also for the sins of the whole world" (1 Jn.2:1-2).

Thought 3. When we approach God, we must be sincere, genuinely sincere. We must be willing to give our lives totally to Him:

1) We must be willing to dedicate ourselves to Him just as the Old Testament believers symbolized in the Grain Offering. We must give our whole hearts to God.

"I beseech you therefore, brethren, by the mercies of God, that ye present your bodies a living sacrifice, holy, acceptable unto God, which is your reasonable service. And be not conformed to this world: but be ye transformed by the renewing of your mind, that ye may prove what is that good, and acceptable, and perfect, will of God" (Ro.12:1-2).
"And thou shalt love the Lord thy God with all thine heart, and with all thy soul, and with all thy might" (Dt.6:5).
"My son, give me thine heart, and let thine eyes observe my ways" (Pr.23:26).
"Trust in the Lord with all thine heart; and lean not unto thine own understanding" (Pr.3:5).
"And ye shall seek me, and find me, when ye shall search for me with all your heart" (Jer.29:13).
"Therefore also now, saith the Lord, turn ye even to me with all your heart, and with fasting, and with weeping, and with mourning" (Joel 2:12).

2) We must be willing to pour out our lives to God, totally surrender and submit ourselves to Him. This is perhaps the same as being totally dedicated to God. However, being totally surrendered and submissive to God is another way to see exactly what God demands. Therefore, to help the reader see both pictures of God's demand, surrender to God is being treated as a different subject from dedication.

"Neither yield ye your members as instruments of unrighteousness unto sin: but yield yourselves unto God, as those that are alive from the dead, and your members as instruments of righteousness unto God" (Ro.6:13).
"I beseech you therefore, brethren, by the mercies of God, that ye present your bodies a living sacrifice, holy, acceptable unto God, which is your reasonable service. And be not conformed to this world: but be ye transformed by the renewing of your mind, that ye may prove what is that good, and acceptable, and perfect, will of God" (Ro.12:1-2).
"Submit yourselves therefore to God. Resist the devil, and he will flee from you" (Jas.4:7).

3) We must thank God for the sacrifice of His dear Son, Christ Jesus the LORD. We must thank God for all He does for us through Christ, for the atonement (reconciliation) and for the peace and fellowship with God that Christ has brought about.

"Giving thanks always for all things unto God and the Father in the name of our Lord Jesus Christ" (Eph.5:20).

"Be careful for nothing; but in every thing by prayer and supplication with thanksgiving let your requests be made known unto God. And the peace of God, which passeth all understanding, shall keep your hearts and minds through Christ Jesus" (Ph.4:6-7).

"Giving thanks unto the Father, which hath made us meet to be partakers of the inheritance of the saints in light" (Col.1:12).

"And whatsoever ye do in word or deed, do all in the name of the Lord Jesus, giving thanks to God and the Father by him" (Col.3:17).

"In every thing give thanks: for this is the will of God in Christ Jesus concerning you" (1 Th.5:18).

"Enter into his gates with thanksgiving, and into his courts with praise: be thankful unto him, and bless his name" (Ps.100:4).

"And let them sacrifice the sacrifices of thanksgiving, and declare his works with rejoicing" (Ps.107:22).

2 (15:17-21) **Tithing—Offerings, to God—Firstfruits, Offering of**: God gave the law to govern the offering of the firstfruits. This was a picture of tithing one's income to the LORD as well as giving other offerings to the LORD. Whatever a person received, it was a gift from God. Therefore, the firstfruit—the first part—of whatever one received was to be given to God.

OUTLINE	SCRIPTURE	SCRIPTURE	OUTLINE
2. The law governing the firstfruits: A picture of tithes & offerings a. When to present the offering: After entering the promised land & eating the food of the land	17 And the LORD spake unto Moses, saying, 18 Speak unto the children of Israel, and say unto them, When ye come into the land whither I bring you, 19 Then it shall be, that, when ye eat of the bread of the land, ye shall offer up an heave offering unto the LORD.	20 Ye shall offer up a cake of the first of your dough for an heave offering: as ye do the heave offering of the threshingfloor, so shall ye heave it. 21 Of the first of your dough ye shall give unto the LORD an heave offering in your generations.	b. What to present 1) A portion of what one eats 2) A cake made from the first of the ground meal—made from the grain harvest c. The importance of the law stressed 1) To be a permanent law 2) To be presented from the very first of the ground meal

1. Note when the offering was to be presented to God (v.18). The firstfruit offering was to begin after the people entered and settled in the promised land, after they reaped their first crops and were ready to begin eating the food.

Again, God's wonderful grace just flows out upon His dear people. For the second time in these laws, He is giving them great assurance, encouraging and shoring up their hearts: their children would enter the promised land. It is a guaranteed fact: they will come to the day when they must begin offering the firstfruit of their crops to the LORD. They will be settled in the promised land and able to eat the food from their own fields. How merciful God is! How gracious and encouraging! The adults had hard, stubborn, immovable, and unyielding hearts—hearts of unbelief and rebellion against God. God knew they would never repent and follow Him—not completely, not in full dedication and surrender. Consequently, He had to judge them by keeping them out of the promised land. But not their precious children. The children would enter the promised land. Note how this would give some encouragement to the adults as well as the older children. The adults at least knew that their children would have a much better life than they.

2. God spelled out exactly what was to be presented as the firstfruit offering (v.19-20). The people were actually to offer a portion of what they ate, that is, a cake from the very first of their flour or dough.

3. Note the importance of the law: it was to be a permanent offering (v.21). The very first of their ground meal was to be given to the LORD.

Thought 1. The lesson is clear: we are to give tithes and offerings to God. In fact, we are to give the firstfruit, the very first of our income and the very first of whatever we receive to God. Why? Because all things come from God. Everything we have—much or little—comes from God. He is the Source of every good and perfect gift.

"Every good gift and every perfect gift is from above, and cometh down from the Father of lights, with whom is no variableness, neither shadow of turning" (Jas.1:17).

"Then the disciples, every man according to his ability, determined to send relief unto the brethren which dwelt in Judaea" (Acts 11:29).

"Upon the first day of the week let every one of you lay by him in store, as God hath prospered him, that there be no gatherings when I come" (1 Cor.16:2).

"For if there be first a willing mind, it is accepted according to that a man hath, and not according to that he hath not" (2 Cor.8:12).

"Every man according as he purposeth in his heart, so let him give; not grudgingly, or of necessity: for God loveth a cheerful giver" (2 Cor.9:7).

"Every man shall give as he is able, according to the blessing of the Lord thy God which he hath given thee" (Dt.16:17).

"And all the tithe of the land, whether of the seed of the land, or of the fruit of the tree, is the Lord's: it is holy unto the Lord" (Lev.27:30).

"They gave after their ability unto the treasure of the work" (Ezra 2:69).

"Honour the Lord with thy substance, and with the firstfruits of all thine increase" (Pr.3:9).

"Bring ye all the tithes into the storehouse, that there may be meat in mine house, and prove me now herewith, saith the Lord of hosts, if I will not open you the windows of heaven, and pour you out a blessing, that there shall not be room enough to receive it" (Mal.3:10).

3 (15:22-29) **Forgiveness, of Sin—Sin, Forgiveness of—Sin, Unintentional—Sin, in Ignorance—Sin, Unknown**: God gave the law that controlled forgiveness for the sins of ignorance or unintentional sins. A whole community of believers can sin unintentionally and need forgiveness as well as individuals. God covers both cases in this Scripture:

OUTLINE	SCRIPTURE	SCRIPTURE	OUTLINE
3. The law governing forgiveness for unintentional sin a. The whole community of believers can be forgiven 1) The two conditions for forgiveness: • First, the sin must be unintentional—committed in ignorance, being unaware of the sin • Second, the community must approach God for forgiveness thru the sacrifice of the Burnt Offering & the Sin Offering (a symbol of approaching God thru Christ, our sacrifice) 2) The promise of God: • He will accept the sacrifice as atonement (reconciliation) & forgive the community (a symbol of accepting Christ as the basis for	22 And if ye have erred, and not observed all these commandments, which the LORD hath spoken unto Moses, 23 Even all that the LORD hath commanded you by the hand of Moses, from the day that the LORD commanded Moses, and henceforward among your generations; 24 Then it shall be, if ought be committed by ignorance without the knowledge of the congregation, that all the congregation shall offer one young bullock for a burnt offering, for a sweet savour unto the LORD, with his meat offering, and his drink offering, according to the manner, and one kid of the goats for a sin offering. 25 And the priest shall make an atonement for all the congregation of the children of Israel, and it shall be forgiven them; for it is ignorance: and they shall bring their offering, a sacrifice	made by fire unto the LORD, and their sin offering before the LORD, for their ignorance: 26 And it shall be forgiven all the congregation of the children of Israel, and the stranger that sojourneth among them; seeing all the people were in ignorance. 27 And if any soul sin through ignorance, then he shall bring a she goat of the first year for a sin offering. 28 And the priest shall make an atonement for the soul that sinneth ignorantly, when he sinneth by ignorance before the LORD, to make an atonement for him; and it shall be forgiven him. 29 Ye shall have one law for him that sinneth through ignorance, both for him that is born among the children of Israel, and for the stranger that sojourneth among them.	atonement & forgiveness) • He will forgive the entire community, native-born & foreigner: Because the sin was unintentional b. The individual can be forgiven 1) The 2 conditions: • The sin must be unintentional • The person must come to God thru the sacrifice of the Sin Offering (a symbol of Christ's sacrifice) 2) The promise of God: • He accepts the sacrifice as atonement & forgives • He forgives any person who approaches Him as stipulated by this law, whether native-born or foreigner

1. The whole community of believers could be forgiven if they broke the law of God. Note exactly what is said: if the community of believers failed to keep any of God's commandments, they could be forgiven (v.22-26). There were two conditions for forgiveness. First, the sin must be unintentional—committed in ignorance. The people had to be totally unaware that they were sinning. The sin had to be inadvertent: accidental, not on purpose, unmindful, unthinking, unthoughtful. If the sin was unintentional—committed in ignorance—God would forgive the whole community of believers.

Second, the community must approach God for forgiveness through the substitute sacrifice—the sacrifice of the Grain Offering and the Sin Offering (v.24). Remember, the substitute sacrifice is a symbol or type of the sacrifice of the LORD Jesus Christ.

2. The promise of God was and still is wonderful (v.25-26). God promised two marvelous things:
   ⇒ God would accept the substitute sacrifice as atonement or reconciliation and would forgive the community. Note how this is a clear picture of our need to accept Christ as the basis for atonement and forgiveness of sin.
   ⇒ God would forgive the entire community, both native-born and foreigner—all because the sin was unintentional, done in ignorance, not knowing that it was sin (v.26).
3. The individual believer could be forgiven if he broke the law of God (v.27-29).
   a. But note: the same two conditions applied to the individual.

      First, the sin had to be unintentional—committed in ignorance. The individual believer had to be totally unaware that he was sinning (v.27).

      Second, the believer had to come to God for forgiveness—had to come through the substitute sacrifice of the sin offering (v.27-28). Again, the substitute sacrifice is a symbol of the sacrifice of Jesus Christ for the sins of the world. When we sin, we must come to God for forgiveness, come through the substitute sacrifice of Christ.
   b. The promises of God to the individual believer were most wonderful (v.27-28). Any believer who had sinned unintentionally could be forgiven. God accepted the substitute sacrifice as atonement or reconciliation and forgave the

sinning believer. No matter who the believer was—native-born or foreigner—he was forgiven if he came to God as stipulated by this law (v.29).

Thought 1. We often sin. In fact, we cannot keep from sinning. Why? Because we are "short of God's glory"—flawed, imperfect beings. We are defective and blemished, both morally and righteously. Consequently, we sin: fail and come short of God's glory, short of what God demands. Usually we are not even aware of the sins we commit. We sin unintentionally and in ignorance. But note: God forgives unintentional sins, sins that we know nothing about—if we will do one thing: come to Him through the substitute sacrifice of Jesus Christ and confess our sin, repenting and turning to Him in renewed dedication. This is the strong declaration of Scripture:

"The next day John seeth Jesus coming unto him, and saith, Behold the Lamb of God, which taketh away the sin of the world" (Jn.1:29).

"Repent ye therefore, and be converted, that your sins may be blotted out, when the times of refreshing shall come from the presence of the Lord" (Acts 3:19).

"Him hath God exalted with his right hand to be a Prince and a Saviour, for to give repentance to Israel, and forgiveness of sins" (Acts 5:31).

"Be it known unto you therefore, men and brethren, that through this man is preached unto you the forgiveness of sins" (Acts 13:38).

"In whom we have redemption through his blood, the forgiveness of sins, according to the riches of his grace" (Eph.1:7).

"If we confess our sins, he is faithful and just to forgive us our sins, and to cleanse us from all unrighteousness" (1 Jn.1:9).

"He that covereth his sins shall not prosper: but whoso confesseth and forsaketh them shall have mercy" (Pr.28:13).

4 (15:30-36) **Sin, Defiant—Sin, Deliberate—Sin, Brazen—Sin, Presumptuous—Sin, Blasphemy—Sin, Presuming upon God—Sin, Despising God's Word**: God gave the law that controlled defiant, deliberate, brazen sin—sin that dares or presumes upon God or thinks that God will not judge or condemn. This law stands as a severe warning to every person within every generation. The word for "defiant" (yad) means with a high hand. Therefore, the person who commits this sin does so with a *high hand*, a hand lifted up in the face of God. This is...

- defiant sin
- deliberate sin
- brazen sin
- presumptuous sin (sin that assumes or thinks God will not judge, that dares God

God has a strong warning to the defiant sinner, to the person who goes out and deliberately sins, knowing full well that he is sinning. Note the Scripture and outline:

OUTLINE	SCRIPTURE	SCRIPTURE	OUTLINE
4. The law governing deliberate, defiant, or brazen sin—sin that dares to presume upon God a. The nature of defiant sin 1) Blasphemes the LORD 2) Despises God's Word 3) Deliberately breaks God's commandments b. The judgment: Must be cut off—completely, eternally c. The example of deliberate, defiant sin: A man gathered wood on the Sabbath—defiantly broke the law of the Sabbath 1) He was arrested &	30 But the soul that doeth ought presumptuously, whether he be born in the land, or a stranger, the same reproacheth the LORD; and that soul shall be cut off from among his people. 31 Because he hath despised the word of the LORD, and hath broken his commandment, that soul shall utterly be cut off; his iniquity shall be upon him. 32 And while the children of Israel were in the wilderness, they found a man that gathered sticks upon the sabbath day. 33 And they that found him	gathering sticks brought him unto Moses and Aaron, and unto all the congregation. 34 And they put him in ward, because it was not declared what should be done to him. 35 And the LORD said unto Moses, The man shall be surely put to death: all the congregation shall stone him with stones without the camp. 36 And all the congregation brought him without the camp, and stoned him with stones, and he died; as the LORD commanded Moses.	brought to the authorities, Moses & Aaron, & before all the people 2) He was held in custody until Moses could seek the Lord about what should be done 3) He was sentenced to death by the LORD: To be stoned in the presence of the entire assembly—outside the camp 4) He was executed as the LORD commanded

1. Note the nature of defiant, deliberate sin (v.30-31). In very simple terms, God spells out exactly what He means. Defiant, deliberate, presumptuous sin means...

- to blaspheme the LORD (v.29)
- to despise God's Word (v.30)
- to deliberately break God's commandments (v.30)

2. Severe judgment is to fall upon the defiant sinner (v.31). God's warning is clear: the defiant sinner must be completely cut off. The idea is eternal separation from God and His people. The person will join all defiant sinners and unbe-

lievers someplace totally apart from God, out of God's presence forever. The defiant sinner wanted nothing to do with God during this earthly life. Therefore, God will give him his wish: the defiant sinner will have nothing to do with God throughout eternity. The sinner has condemned himself to be cut off—to be separated from God eternally.

"And then shall appear the sign of the Son of man in heaven: and then shall all the tribes of the earth mourn, and they shall see the Son of man coming in the clouds of heaven with power and great glory" (Mt.24:30).

"When the Son of man shall come in his glory, and all the holy angels with him, then shall he sit upon the throne of his glory: And before him shall be gathered all nations: and he shall separate them one from another, as a shepherd divideth his sheep from the goats: And he shall set the sheep on his right hand, but the goats on the left" (Mt.25:31-33).

"Whosoever therefore shall be ashamed of me and of my words in this adulterous and sinful generation; of him also shall the Son of man be ashamed, when he cometh in the glory of his Father with the holy angels" (Mk.8:38).

"And to you who are troubled rest with us, when the Lord Jesus shall be revealed from heaven with his mighty angels, In flaming fire taking vengeance on them that know not God, and that obey not the gospel of our Lord Jesus Christ" (2 Th.1:7-8).

"And as it is appointed unto men once to die, but after this the judgment" (Heb.9:27).

"The Lord knoweth how to deliver the godly out of temptations, and to reserve the unjust unto the day of judgment to be punished" (2 Pt.2:9).

"But the heavens and the earth, which are now, by the same word are kept in store, reserved unto fire against the day of judgment and perdition of ungodly men" (2 Pt.3:7).

"Behold, the Lord cometh with ten thousands of his saints, To execute judgment upon all, and to convince all that are ungodly among them of all their ungodly deeds which they have ungodly committed, and of all their hard speeches which ungodly sinners have spoken against him" (Jude 14-15).

"Behold, he cometh with clouds; and every eye shall see him, and they also which pierced him: and all kindreds of the earth shall wail because of him. Even so, Amen" (Rev.1:7).

"And I saw a great white throne, and him that sat on it, from whose face the earth and the heaven fled away; and there was found no place for them. And I saw the dead, small and great, stand before God; and the books were opened: and another book was opened, which is the book of life: and the dead were judged out of those things which were written in the books, according to their works. And the sea gave up the dead which were in it; and death and hell delivered up the dead which were in them: and they were judged every man according to their works. And death and hell were cast into the lake of fire. This is the second death. And whosoever was not found written in the book of life was cast into the lake of fire" (Rev.20:11-15).

3. A clear example of deliberate, defiant sin is given (v.32-36). The picture is that of a man who defiantly raised his fist in the face of God, who deliberately broke the Sabbath law of God. Remember this fact: the Sabbath law was of critical importance to God's people. Resting and meeting together for worship were essential to hold the community of believers together and for carrying on their mission assigned by God. Therefore, for this man to defiantly and deliberately break the Sabbath law was a gross, terrible offense against God and His people. Note what happened:

a. The sinner was arrested and brought to the authorities, Moses and Aaron, and before all the people.
b. The sinner was held in custody until Moses could seek the LORD about what should be done.
c. The sinner was sentenced to death by the LORD: to be stoned in the presence of the entire assembly—outside the camp.
d. The sinner was executed as the LORD commanded.

Thought 1. The Sabbath or Sunday is of critical importance to God and His people. Preserving a day for rest and worship is an absolute essential. The day is so important that it is one of the Ten Commandments. Why is it so important?

⇒ Because the human body needs one day of every seven for rest, relaxation, and recreation. The human body breaks down without a period of rest. (See outline and notes—Ex.20:11 for more discussion.)

⇒ Because God's people need to worship together and carry out the ministry of the LORD together. Simply stated, the task cannot be done by individual believers acting alone. The task requires the church—all of God's people—worshipping and reaching out together.

This was the reason God established the Sabbath, the reason why He set aside one day for rest and worship. For this reason, the day of rest and worship must be preserved and respected.

"How much then is a man better than a sheep? Wherefore it is lawful to do well on the sabbath days" (Mt.12:12).

"And he came to Nazareth, where he had been brought up: and, as his custom was, he went into the synagogue on the sabbath day, and stood up for to read" (Lk.4:16).

"And it was the sabbath day when Jesus made the clay, and opened his eyes" (Jn.9:14).

"And on the sabbath we went out of the city by a river side, where prayer was wont to be made; and we sat down, and spake unto the women which resorted thither" (Acts 16:13).

"And Paul, as his manner was, went in unto them, and three sabbath days reasoned with them out of the scriptures" (Acts 17:2).

"And upon the first day of the week, when the disciples came together to break bread, Paul

preached unto them, ready to depart on the morrow; and continued his speech until midnight" (Acts 20:7).

"Not forsaking the assembling of ourselves together, as the manner of some is; but exhorting one another: and so much the more, as ye see the day approaching" (Heb.10:25).

"Remember the sabbath day, to keep it holy" (Ex.20:8).

"Six days thou shalt work, but on the seventh day thou shalt rest: in earing time and in harvest thou shalt rest" (Ex.34:21).

"Ye shall keep the sabbath therefore; for it is holy unto you: every one that defileth it shall surely be put to death: for whosoever doeth any work therein, that soul shall be cut off from among his people" (Ex.31:14).

"And if the people of the land bring ware or any victuals on the sabbath day to sell, that we would not buy it of them on the sabbath, or on the holy day" (Neh.10:31).

"In those days saw I in Judah some treading winepresses on the sabbath, and bringing in sheaves, and lading asses; as also wine, grapes, and figs, and all manner of burdens, which they brought into Jerusalem on the sabbath day: and I testified against them in the day wherein they sold victuals" (Neh.13:15).

"Blessed is the man that doeth this, and the son of man that layeth hold on it; that keepeth the sabbath from polluting it, and keepeth his hand from doing any evil" (Is.56:2).

"If thou turn away thy foot from the sabbath, from doing thy pleasure on my holy day; and call the sabbath a delight, the holy of the Lord, honourable; and shalt honour him, not doing thine own ways, nor finding thine own pleasure, nor speaking thine own words: Then shalt thou delight thyself in the Lord; and I will cause thee to ride upon the high places of the earth, and feed thee with the heritage of Jacob thy father: for the mouth of the Lord hath spoken it" (Is.58:13-14).

"But the house of Israel rebelled against me in the wilderness: they walked not in my statutes, and they despised my judgments, which if a man do, he shall even live in them; and my sabbaths they greatly polluted: then I said, I would pour out my fury upon them in the wilderness, to consume them" (Ezk.20:13).

5 (15:37-41) **Holiness, of Life—Holy, Duty to Be—Mind, Duty to Protect—Thoughts, Duty to Protect—Mind, Duty to Concentrate—Concentration, Duty to—Commandments, Duty to Remember—Separation, Spiritual**: God gave the law that instructed the believer to wear tassels on the hem of his clothing—attached with a blue cord. Note that this pictured the need for all believers to live a holy, godly life. *The Expositor's Bible Commentary* points out that this law is the basis for wearing the traditional prayer shawl of Israel, and that the prayer shawl is the pattern for the flag of the state of Israel today. Note the Scripture and outline:

OUTLINE	SCRIPTURE	SCRIPTURE	OUTLINE
5. The law instructing the believer to wear tassels on the hem of his clothing—attached with a blue cord: Pictures the need to live a holy, godly life a. The importance of the law: To be a permanent law b. The purpose: 1) To stir the believer to remember God's commandments	37 And the LORD spake unto Moses, saying, 38 Speak unto the children of Israel, and bid them that they make them fringes in the borders of their garments throughout their generations, and that they put upon the fringe of the borders a ribband of blue: 39 And it shall be unto you for a fringe, that ye may look upon it, and remember all the commandments of the	LORD, and do them; and that ye seek not after your own heart and your own eyes, after which ye use to go a whoring: 40 That ye may remember, and do all my commandments, and be holy unto your God. 41 I am the LORD your God, which brought you out of the land of Egypt, to be your God: I am the LORD your God.	2) To stir the believer to live a life of separation from the world: Not to prostitute himself through fleshly lusts 3) To stir the believer to obey all God's commands: To be totally committed to God c. The authority behind the laws 1) "The LORD": The only living & true God 2) "The LORD your God": Personal 3) "The LORD who [saved] you"

1. The importance of the law is seen in that it was established as a permanent law (v.38).
2. The purpose was threefold:
   ⇒ to stir the believer to remember God's commandments (v.39)
   ⇒ to stir the believer to live a life of separation from the world: not to prostitute himself through fleshly lusts (v.39)
   ⇒ to stir the believer to obey all God's commands: to be totally committed to God (v.40)

As a believer moved through the day, the tassels would be flapping about, occasionally attracting his attention. At that point he was to focus—for just a moment—upon the fact that he was to obey God's commandments and live a life of separation from the world. He was to live a holy life, not going after the lusts of his own selfish, fleshly heart and eyes. Note how this is described: the believer was not to live a life of spiritual prostitution, not to turn away from his devotion to God, not to turn to the world with all its fleshly lusts and false gods.

3. The authority behind the laws given in this passage is the LORD Himself (v.41).
   a. The person who gave the laws is "the LORD": the only living and true God.
   b. The person who gave the laws is "the LORD *your* God": He is personal—has established a personal relationship with the believer.
   c. He is "the LORD who [saved] you"—"who brought you out of Egypt" [a symbol of the world]: the only living God who has the power to truly save His people from the world and all its enslavements.

Thought 1. Note several significant lessons:
1) We must control our minds and think of God throughout the day. We must train our minds to think of Him at set times throughout the day—after every so many minutes—to focus upon Him for just a moment.

"Casting down imaginations, and every high thing that exalteth itself against the knowledge of God, and bringing into captivity every thought to the obedience of Christ" (2 Cor.10:5).
"For to be carnally minded is death; but to be spiritually minded is life and peace" (Ro.8:6).
"Let this mind be in you, which was also in Christ Jesus" (Ph.2:5).
"Meditate upon these things; give thyself wholly to them; that thy profiting may appear to all" (1 Tim.4:15).
"For this is the covenant that I will make with the house of Israel after those days, saith the Lord; I will put my laws into their mind, and write them in their hearts: and I will be to them a God, and they shall be to me a people" (Heb.8:10; cp. Heb.10:16).
"This book of the law shall not depart out of thy mouth; but thou shalt meditate therein day and night, that thou mayest observe to do according to all that is written therein: for then thou shalt make thy way prosperous, and then thou shalt have good success" (Josh.1:8).
"But his delight is in the law of the Lord; and in his law doth he meditate day and night" (Ps.1:2).
"Stand in awe, and sin not: commune with your own heart upon your bed, and be still. Selah" (Ps.4:4).
"Let the words of my mouth, and the meditation of my heart, be acceptable in thy sight, O Lord, my strength, and my redeemer" (Ps.19:14).
"Wherewithal shall a young man cleanse his way? by taking heed thereto according to thy word" (Ps.119:9).
"Thy word have I hid in mine heart, that I might not sin against thee" (Ps.119:11).

2) We must remember and obey God's commandments throughout the day.

"Not every one that saith unto me, Lord, Lord, shall enter into the kingdom of heaven; but he that doeth the will of my Father which is in heaven" (Mt.7:21).
"Jesus answered and said unto him, If a man love me, he will keep my words: and my Father will love him, and we will come unto him, and make our abode with him" (Jn.14:23).
"If ye keep my commandments, ye shall abide in my love; even as I have kept my Father's commandments, and abide in his love" (Jn.15:10).
"Ye are my friends, if ye do whatsoever I command you" (Jn.15:14).
"Blessed are they that do his commandments, that they may have right to the tree of life, and may enter in through the gates into the city" (Rev.22:14).
"And thou shalt love the Lord thy God with all thine heart, and with all thy soul, and with all thy might. And these words, which I command thee this day, shall be in thine heart: And thou shalt teach them diligently unto thy children, and shalt talk of them when thou sittest in thine house, and when thou walkest by the way, and when thou liest down, and when thou risest up. And thou shalt bind them for a sign upon thine hand, and they shall be as frontlets between thine eyes. And thou shalt write them upon the posts of thy house, and on thy gates" (Dt.6:5-9).
"This day the Lord thy God hath commanded thee to do these statutes and judgments: thou shalt therefore keep and do them with all thine heart, and with all thy soul" (Dt.26:16).
"Be ye therefore very courageous to keep and to do all that is written in the book of the law of Moses, that ye turn not aside therefrom to the right hand or to the left" (Josh.23:6).
"And Samuel said, Hath the Lord as great delight in burnt offerings and sacrifices, as in obeying the voice of the Lord? Behold, to obey is better than sacrifice, and to hearken than the fat of rams" (1 Sam.15:22).

3) We must keep our minds focused upon living a holy life throughout the day—a life of separation from the world.

"And with many other words did he testify and exhort, saying, Save yourselves from this untoward generation" (Acts 2:40).
"And be not conformed to this world: but be ye transformed by the renewing of your mind, that ye may prove what is that good, and acceptable, and perfect, will of God" (Ro.12:2).
"But now I have written unto you not to keep company, if any man that is called a brother be a fornicator, or covetous, or an idolater, or a railer, or a drunkard, or an extortioner; with such an one no not to eat" (1 Cor.5:11).
"Be ye not unequally yoked together with unbelievers: for what fellowship hath righteousness with unrighteousness? and what communion hath light with darkness" (2 Cor.6:14).
"Wherefore come out from among them, and be ye separate, saith the Lord, and touch not the unclean thing; and I will receive you, And will be a Father unto you, and ye shall be my sons and daughters, saith the Lord Almighty" (2 Cor.6:17-18).
"And have no fellowship with the unfruitful works of darkness, but rather reprove them" (Eph.5:11).
"Now we command you, brethren, in the name of our Lord Jesus Christ, that ye withdraw yourselves from every brother that walketh disorderly, and not after the tradition which he received of us" (2 Th.3:6).

NUMBERS 15:1-41

"Thou shalt not follow a multitude to do evil; neither shalt thou speak in a cause to decline after many to wrest judgment" (Ex.23:2).

"Take heed to thyself, lest thou make a covenant with the inhabitants of the land whither thou goest, lest it be for a snare in the midst of thee" (Ex.34:12).

"I will meditate in thy precepts, and have respect unto thy ways" (Ps.119:15).

"Enter not into the path of the wicked, and go not in the way of evil men" (Pr.4:14).

"Depart ye, depart ye, go ye out from thence, touch no unclean thing; go ye out of the midst of her; be ye clean, that bear the vessels of the Lord" (Is.52:11).

TYPES, SYMBOLS, AND PICTURES
(Numbers 15:1-41)

Historical Term	Type or Picture (Scriptural Basis for Each)	Life Application for Today's Believer	Biblical Application
Grain Offering Num.15:1-16 (See also Lev. 2:3)	*The Grain Offering is a symbol of three things:* *1. A symbol of joy and* thanksgiving *to God...* • *for the joy of atonement: salvation, redemption, reconciliation* • *for one's livelihood: the harvest, crops, rain, sunshine, housing, clothing* *2. A symbol of an act of dedication and dependence upon God* *3. A symbol of Christ, the Bread of Life.* **"Or for a ram, thou shalt prepare *for* a meat [Grain] offering two tenth deals of flour mingled with the third *part* of an hin of oil" (Num.15:6).**	⇒ The symbol of the Grain Offering teaches us three things: 1. We are to offer the joy and thanksgiving of our hearts to God for everything: a. For the joy of the atonement: salvation, redemption, reconciliation b. For our livelihood: the harvest food, crops, rain, sunshine, housing, clothing 2. It is God who has given us life: air, water, sun, moon, stars, crops, food, clothing, housing—all the necessities of life. God created the materials of the universe, everything that sustains our lives and keeps us going. We owe God everything we are and have: we must, therefore, give the offering of dedication to God and declare our dependence upon Him. 3. Jesus Christ is the Bread of Life... • who feeds us • who nourishes us • who sustains us with Himself	***"For the bread of God is he which cometh down from heaven, and giveth life unto the world. Then said they unto him, LORD, evermore give us this bread. And Jesus said unto them, I am the bread of life: he that cometh to me shall never hunger; and he that believeth on me shall never thirst" (Jn.6:33-35).*** ***"Verily, verily, I say unto you, He that believeth on me hath everlasting life. I am that bread of life" (Jn.6:47-48).*** ***"I am the living bread which came down from heaven: if any man eat of this bread, he shall live for ever: and the bread that I will give is my flesh, which I will give for the life of the world" (Jn.6:51).*** ***"This is that bread which came down from heaven: not as your fathers did eat manna, and are dead: he that eateth of this bread shall live for ever" (Jn.6:58).*** ***"And as they did eat, Jesus took bread, and blessed, and brake it, and gave to them, and said, Take, eat: this is my body" (Mk. 14:22).***
Firstfruits Num.15:17-21	*The firstfruits is a picture of tithing one's income as well as other offerings to the Lord. Whatever a person received, it was a gift from God. Therefore, the firstfruit—the first part—of whatever one received was to be given to God.* **"Ye shall offer up a cake of the first of your dough**	⇒ The lesson is clear: we are to give tithes and offerings to God. In fact, we are to give the firstfruit, the very first of our income and the very first of whatever we receive to God. Why? Because all things come from God. Everything we have—much or little—comes from God. He is	***"Every good gift and every perfect gift is from above, and cometh down from the Father of lights, with whom is no variableness, neither shadow of turning" (Jas.1:17).*** ***"Then the disciples, every man according to his ability, determined to send relief unto the brethren which dwelt in Judaea" (Acts 11:29).***

Historical Term	Type or Picture (Scriptural Basis for Each)	Life Application for Today's Believer	Biblical Application
	for **an heave offering: as** ***ye do*** **the heave offering of the threshingfloor, so shall ye heave it. Of the first of your dough ye shall give unto the LORD an heave offering in your generations" (Num.15:20-21).**	the Source of every good and perfect gift.	***"Upon the first day of the week let every one of you lay by him in store, as God hath prospered him, that there be no gatherings when I come" (1 Cor.16:2).*** ***"For if there be first a willing mind, it is accepted according to that a man hath, and not according to that he hath not" (2 Cor.8:12).*** ***"Every man according as he purposeth in his heart, so let him give; not grudgingly, or of necessity: for God loveth a cheerful giver" (2 Cor.9:7 See also Dt.16:17; Lev.27:30; Ezra 2:69; Pr.3:9; Mal.3:10).***

B. Event 2—A Dangerous Rebellion by Korah & His Allies: God Judges All Grumbling & Unbelief, All Rebellion & Unauthorized Approaches 16:1-50

1. The revolt & the issues at stake
- a. The rebels or conspirators
  - 1) Korah: A Levite & a cousin to Moses—their fathers were brothers
  - 2) Dathan, Abiram & On: Reubenites
  - 3) 250 well-known leaders, official representatives of the nation: Some were Levites, religious workers (cp. v.8-11)
- b. The issue or protest: Opposition to Moses & Aaron
  - 1) Their charge: Assumed too much authority—had gone too far by turning from the promised land.
  - 2) Their desire: The power of leadership & the priesthood (v.7-14)
- c. The reaction of Moses: He fell face down—seeking God
  - 1) He arose & challenged Korah & his allies: To let the LORD choose His own leader—show who really belonged to God & who could approach Him for leadership in guiding God's people
    - To prove themselves by taking censers & burning incense before the LORD
    - To prove themselves by letting the LORD choose His leader, the one who was truly holy, set apart
  - 2) He rebuked, warned the Levites
    - They were the ones who had gone too far (v.7)
    - They were guilty of abusing & trampling underfoot God's call to them: To serve as Levites, the privilege of being set apart to serve God & His people
    - They were guilty of seeking the priesthood itself—seeking position that should come only from God never from selfish effort
    - They were revolting against the LORD not against Aaron

Now Korah, the son of Izhar, the son of Kohath, the son of Levi, and Dathan and Abiram, the sons of Eliab, and On, the son of Peleth, sons of Reuben, took men:

2 And they rose up before Moses, with certain of the children of Israel, two hundred and fifty princes of the assembly, famous in the congregation, men of renown:

3 And they gathered themselves together against Moses and against Aaron, and said unto them, Ye take too much upon you, seeing all the congregation are holy, every one of them, and the LORD is among them: wherefore then lift ye up yourselves above the congregation of the LORD?

4 And when Moses heard it, he fell upon his face:

5 And he spake unto Korah and unto all his company, saying, Even to morrow the LORD will shew who are his, and who is holy; and will cause him to come near unto him: even him whom he hath chosen will he cause to come near unto him.

6 This do; Take you censers, Korah, and all his company;

7 And put fire therein, and put incense in them before the LORD to morrow: and it shall be that the man whom the LORD doth choose, he shall be holy: ye take too much upon you, ye sons of Levi.

8 And Moses said unto Korah, Hear, I pray you, ye sons of Levi:

9 Seemeth it but a small thing unto you, that the God of Israel hath separated you from the congregation of Israel, to bring you near to himself to do the service of the tabernacle of the LORD, and to stand before the congregation to minister unto them?

10 And he hath brought thee near to him, and all thy brethren the sons of Levi with thee: and seek ye the priesthood also?

11 For which cause both thou and all thy company are gathered together against the LORD: and what is Aaron, that ye murmur against him?

12 And Moses sent to call Dathan and Abiram, the sons of Eliab: which said, We will not come up:

13 Is it a small thing that thou hast brought us up out of a land that floweth with milk and honey, to kill us in the wilderness, except thou make thyself altogether a prince over us?

14 Moreover thou hast not brought us into a land that floweth with milk and honey, or given us inheritance of fields and vineyards: wilt thou put out the eyes of these men? we will not come up.

15 And Moses was very wroth, and said unto the LORD, Respect not thou their offering: I have not taken one ass from them, neither have I hurt one of them.

16 And Moses said unto Korah, Be thou and all thy company before the LORD, thou, and they, and Aaron, to morrow:

17 And take every man his censer, and put incense in them, and bring ye before the LORD every man his censer, two hundred and fifty censers; thou also, and Aaron, each of you his censer.

18 And they took every man his censer, and put fire in them, and laid incense thereon, and stood in the door of the tabernacle of the congregation with Moses and Aaron.

19 And Korah gathered all the congregation against them unto the door of the tabernacle of the congregation: and the glory of the LORD appeared unto all the congregation.

20 And the LORD spake unto Moses and unto Aaron, saying,

21 Separate yourselves from

- d. The confrontation, contempt, & defiance of Dathan & Abiram
  - 1) They rejected the summons, refused to meet with Moses
  - 2) They exaggerated their former life & provision in Egypt
  - 3) They blamed Moses for their plight in the wilderness
  - 4) They accused him of lording it over them
  - 5) They blamed him for failing to enter the promised land
  - 6) They charged him with abuse of power—with deception, ulterior motives
  - 7) They repeated their outrage, their contempt & defiance: would not meet with Moses
- e. The angry reaction of Moses
  - 1) Cried out for God not to accept the incense offering of the rebels
  - 2) Declared he was innocent: Had not misused his office for gain nor wronged anyone

2. The showdown & the judgment of the rebels
- a. The challenge to Korah & his allies repeated
  - 1) To approach the LORD tomorrow
  - 2) To have each man take his censer & present incense before the LORD—all 250 of the rebels
  - 3) To include Korah & Aaron
- b. The arrogant, defiant stand of the rebels against Moses & Aaron: At the entrance to the Tabernacle
  - 1) The response of the LORD
    - Suddenly, immediately—the glory of the LORD flashed & burst forth, visible to everyone
    - The LORD threatened to destroy the nation—at once, immediately

2) The response of Moses & Aaron: They fell face down before God, crying out in prayer
- To the Creator: "God of the spirits of all mankind"
- Begged God not to destroy all bc. of one man's sins

3) The warning of the LORD: Charge the people to move away from the tents of the rebel ringleaders—Korah, Dathan, & Abiram

c. The catastrophic judgment upon Dathan, Abiram, & Korah: The ringleaders were confronted by the true servants of God, Moses & the elders of Israel

1) The people were warned to move back, out of the presence of these wicked men
- They must separate themselves totally from the wicked: Not touch anything of theirs
- They obeyed the warning

2) The two ringleaders had come out with their families to confront & stand against God's leaders, Moses & the elders

3) The judgment of God would validate or prove that Moses was God's servant: He proposed a test
- If God's judgment did not fall upon the rebels—that would prove that Moses was not God's choice for a leader
- If God's judgment fell in some spectacular way, that would validate Moses as God's servant

4) The judgment of God would fall in a spectacular way
- The earth would open up & swallow the rebels & all their belongings
- They would go down alive into the grave

5) The catastrophic judgment fell—suddenly, immediately
- The ground split open
- The earth swallowed them, their households, the followers standing with them, & their possessions
- They fell alive into the grave: The earth closed over them & they perished

among this congregation, that I may consume them in a moment.

22 And they fell upon their faces, and said, O God, the God of the spirits of all flesh, shall one man sin, and wilt thou be wroth with all the congregation?

23 And the LORD spake unto Moses, saying,

24 Speak unto the congregation, saying, Get you up from about the tabernacle of Korah, Dathan, and Abiram.

25 And Moses rose up and went unto Dathan and Abiram; and the elders of Israel followed him.

26 And he spake unto the congregation, saying, Depart, I pray you, from the tents of these wicked men, and touch nothing of theirs, lest ye be consumed in all their sins.

27 So they gat up from the tabernacle of Korah, Dathan, and Abiram, on every side: and Dathan and Abiram came out, and stood in the door of their tents, and their wives, and their sons, and their little children.

28 And Moses said, Hereby ye shall know that the LORD hath sent me to do all these works; for I have not done them of mine own mind.

29 If these men die the common death of all men, or if they be visited after the visitation of all men; then the LORD hath not sent me.

30 But if the LORD make a new thing, and the earth open her mouth, and swallow them up, with all that appertain unto them, and they go down quick into the pit; then ye shall understand that these men have provoked the LORD.

31 And it came to pass, as he had made an end of speaking all these words, that the ground clave asunder that was under them:

32 And the earth opened her mouth, and swallowed them up, and their houses, and all the men that appertained unto Korah, and all their goods.

33 They, and all that appertained to them, went down alive into the pit, and the earth closed upon them: and they perished from among the congregation.

34 And all Israel that were round about them fled at the cry of them: for they said, Lest the earth swallow us up also.

35 And there came out a fire from the LORD, and consumed the two hundred and fifty men that offered incense.

36 And the LORD spake unto Moses, saying,

37 Speak unto Eleazar the son of Aaron the priest, that he take up the censers out of the burning, and scatter thou the fire yonder; for they are hallowed.

38 The censers of these sinners against their own souls, let them make them broad plates for a covering of the altar: for they offered them before the LORD, therefore they are hallowed: and they shall be a sign unto the children of Israel.

39 And Eleazar the priest took the brasen censers, wherewith they that were burnt had offered; and they were made broad plates for a covering of the altar:

40 To be a memorial unto the children of Israel, that no stranger, which is not of the seed of Aaron, come near to offer incense before the LORD; that he be not as Korah, and as his company: as the LORD said to him by the hand of Moses.

41 But on the morrow all the congregation of the children of Israel murmured against Moses and against Aaron, saying, Ye have killed the people of the LORD.

42 And it came to pass, when the congregation was gathered against Moses and against Aaron, that they looked toward the tabernacle of the congregation: and, behold, the cloud covered it, and the glory of the LORD appeared.

43 And Moses and Aaron came before the tabernacle of the congregation.

44 And the LORD spake unto Moses, saying,

6) The fear of the people: They fled as they heard the screams & commotion of the earthquake

d. The terrifying judgment upon the 250 men offering false incense: Fire blazed forth from God's presence & burned them up

3. The step taken to stir the memory of this judgment

a. The command of the LORD

1) To save the censers of the 250 wicked men who were judged: The censers were holy, had been set apart to God

2) To hammer the censers into sheets of metal & use them to overlay the altar

3) The purpose: To be a warning of God's judgment

b. The obedience of Eleazar the priest, the son of Aaron

1) He collected the censers & had them hammered out to overlay the altar

2) The purpose: To remind the people...
- that no unauthorized person could approach God
- that an unauthorized approach to God would be judged—just as Korah & his allies had been

4. The staggering unbelief of the people: Murmured & grumbled against God's servants—the very next day

a. The false charge: Accused them of causing the rebels' deaths—gathered to oppose them

b. The intervention of God: The cloud covered the Tabernacle & the glory of the LORD burst forth—giving the appearance & threat of judgment

1) The servants of God approached God's presence

2) The threat of God: He was instantly going to destroy the people

c. The response of Moses & Aaron: Fell down in prayer	45 Get you up from among this congregation, that I may consume them as in a moment. And they fell upon their faces.	gation; and, behold, the plague was begun among the people: and he put on incense, and made an atonement for the people.	made atonement for them
d. The judgment of God: A plague 1) Moses gave quick instructions to Aaron • To take his censer with incense & burning coals from the altar • To rush among the people, make atonement • The reason: God's judgment—a plague—had already started 2) Aaron obeyed • Rushed to the people • Offered incense &	46 And Moses said unto Aaron, Take a censer, and put fire therein from off the altar, and put on incense, and go quickly unto the congregation, and make an atonement for them: for there is wrath gone out from the LORD; the plague is begun. 47 And Aaron took as Moses commanded, and ran into the midst of the congre-	48 And he stood between the dead and the living; and the plague was stayed. 49 Now they that died in the plague were fourteen thousand and seven hundred, beside them that died about the matter of Korah. 50 And Aaron returned unto Moses unto the door of the tabernacle of the congregation: and the plague was stayed.	• Stood between the living & the dead: The judgment (plague) was stopped 3) The result of God's judgment • 14,700 people died plus Korah & his allies • Aaron returned to Moses at the Tabernacle (no doubt, to thank God for delivering them & sparing the people)

DIVISION III

THE FORTY LONG YEARS OF WILDERNESS WANDERINGS: A PICTURE OF THE BELIEVER'S PILGRIMAGE THROUGH THIS WORLD AS HE PREPARES TO ENTER THE PROMISED LAND 15:1-25:18

B. Event 2—A Dangerous Rebellion by Korah and His Allies: God Judges All Grumbling and Unbelief, All Rebellion and Unauthorized Approaches, 16:1-50

(16:1-50) **Introduction—Power, Seeking—Position, Seeking—Self-seeking, Example of**: seeking power and authority, position and rule, honor and recognition—all these are sought by people and sought often. But in seeking these things, the motive is often wrong. The motive must always be to serve people, not to rule and lord authority over people. The motive must be to help and to make a contribution to society, not to hold positions in order to receive more money or the esteem and honor of men. It is wrong to covet positions for selfish purposes. Selfishness leads to strife and division, disintegration and destruction. Seeking position, authority, or rule for selfish purposes can destroy lives, corrupt organizations and cause revolt and rebellion within nations. Selfishness and self-seeking lie at the root of so many of the problems we see throughout society.

What happens now to Israel paints a clear picture of what selfishness and self-seeking can do to disrupt the lives of people. Because of their terrible unbelief and rebellion against God, the people were forced to turn back from the promised land and wander about in the desert wilderness. Because of this drastic change of plans, a group of leaders banded together to lead a revolt against God's dear servants, Moses and Aaron. This passage covers this dangerous rebellion, a rebellion that suffered a horrible, terrifying judgment. This is: *Event 2— a Dangerous Rebellion by Korah and His Allies: God Judges All Grumbling and Unbelief, All Rebellion and Unauthorized Approaches,* 16:1-50.

1. The revolt and the issues at stake (v.1-15).
2. The showdown and the judgment of the rebels (v.16-35).
3. The step taken to stir the memory of this judgment (v.36-40).
4. The staggering unbelief of the people: murmured and grumbled against God's servants—the very next day (v.41-50).

1 (16:1-15) **Unbelief, Example of—Grumbling, Against the Minister—Complaining, Against the Minister—Rebellion, Against God—Approach, To God, Wrong—Conspiracy, Against the Minister—Korah—Opposition, to the Minister—Moses, Opposition to**: there was the revolt and the issues at stake. In all revolts or rebellions there are critical issues at stake, strong differences that lead to division and usually to injury, slaughter, and death. Revolts are caused by such things as…

- broken promises
- injustice
- greed
- a true heart for service
- dissatisfaction with leadership or policies
- lust for power
- selfishness
- a belief that one can actually do a better job than the present leader

In the present situation, Korah and his allies were disgusted with the leadership of Moses and Aaron. Remember: under God's direction, Moses had just turned Israel around from the promised land back into the desert wilderness. The adults twenty years old or older were condemned to wander about and die in the wilderness over the next 38 years—all because of their terrible sin (see outline and notes—Num13:1-14:45 for more discussion). Korah and his allies were ready to take action, and take action they did. They conspired and incited a coup against Moses and Aaron. Rebellion, revolt, and insurrection against God and His leaders were actually taking place. Korah and his allies were fed up, filled with anger and wrath, fire and fury against Moses and Aaron. They blamed Moses and Aaron for not fulfilling the promise to take the

Israelites into the promised land. If Moses would not take the leadership reins, then they would. By force they would take over the leadership role and lead the people into the promised land.

The charges against Moses and Aaron are scattered throughout the chapter. For this reason, they are being listed here in one place for a quicker, better understanding. Korah and his allies...

- opposed the leadership of Moses, wanting to replace him—craving the power of the national leader (v.3, 13-14)
- wanted the Levites promoted as priests (v.3, 7)
- craved the priesthood, the power of the High Priest (v.10)
- blamed Moses for failing to enter the promised land (v.14)

OUTLINE	SCRIPTURE	SCRIPTURE	OUTLINE
1. The revolt & the issues at stake a. The rebels or conspirators 1) Korah: A Levite & a cousin to Moses—their fathers were brothers 2) Dathan, Abiram & On: Reubenites 3) 250 well-known leaders, official representatives of the nation: Some were Levites, religious workers (cp. v.8-11) b. The issue or protest: Opposition to Moses & Aaron 1) Their charge: Assumed too much authority—had gone too far by turning from the promised land. 2) Their desire: The power of leadership & the priesthood (v.7-14) c. The reaction of Moses: He fell face down—seeking God 1) He arose & challenged Korah & his allies: To let the LORD choose His own leader—show who really belonged to God & who could approach Him for leadership in guiding God's people • To prove themselves by taking censers & burning incense before the LORD • To prove themselves by letting the LORD choose His leader, the one who was truly holy, set apart 2) He rebuked, warned the Levites	Now Korah, the son of Izhar, the son of Kohath, the son of Levi, and Dathan and Abiram, the sons of Eliab, and On, the son of Peleth, sons of Reuben, took men: 2 And they rose up before Moses, with certain of the children of Israel, two hun- dred and fifty princes of the assembly, famous in the con- gregation, men of renown: 3 And they gathered them- selves together against Moses and against Aaron, and said unto them, Ye take too much upon you, seeing all the congregation are holy, every one of them, and the LORD is among them: where- fore then lift ye up your- selves above the congrega- tion of the LORD? 4 And when Moses heard it, he fell upon his face: 5 And he spake unto Korah and unto all his company, saying, Even to morrow the LORD will shew who are his, and who is holy; and will cause him to come near unto him: even him whom he hath chosen will he cause to come near unto him. 6 This do; Take you censers, Korah, and all his company; 7 And put fire therein, and put incense in them before the LORD to morrow: and it shall be that the man whom the LORD doth choose, he shall be holy: ye take too much upon you, ye sons of Levi. 8 And Moses said unto Korah, Hear, I pray you, ye sons of Levi:	9 Seemeth it but a small thing unto you, that the God of Israel hath separated you from the congregation of Israel, to bring you near to himself to do the service of the tabernacle of the LORD, and to stand before the con- gregation to minister unto them? 10 And he hath brought thee near to him, and all thy brethren the sons of Levi with thee: and seek ye the priesthood also? 11 For which cause both thou and all thy company are gathered together against the LORD: and what is Aaron, that ye murmur against him? 12 And Moses sent to call Dathan and Abiram, the sons of Eliab: which said, We will not come up: 13 Is it a small thing that thou hast brought us up out of a land that floweth with milk and honey, to kill us in the wilderness, except thou make thyself altogether a prince over us? 14 Moreover thou hast not brought us into a land that floweth with milk and honey, or given us inheri- tance of fields and vine- yards: wilt thou put out the eyes of these men? we will not come up. 15 And Moses was very wroth, and said unto the LORD, Respect not thou their offering: I have not taken one ass from them, neither have I hurt one of them.	• They were the ones who had gone too far (v.7) • They were guilty of abusing & trampling underfoot God's call to them: To serve as Levites, the privilege of being set apart to serve God & His people • They were guilty of seeking the priesthood itself—seeking position that should come only from God never from selfish effort • They were revolting against the LORD not against Aaron d. The confrontation, contempt, & defiance of Dathan & Abiram 1) They rejected the summons, refused to meet with Moses 2) They exaggerated their former life & provision in Egypt 3) They blamed Moses for their plight in the wilderness 4) They accused him of lording it over them 5) They blamed him for failing to enter the promised land 6) They charged him with abuse of power—with deception, ulterior motives 7) They repeated their outrage, their contempt & defiance: would not meet with Moses e. The angry reaction of Moses 1) Cried out for God not to accept the incense offering of the rebels 2) Declared he was innocent: Had not misused his office for gain nor wronged anyone

1. Note that the rebels are conspirators (v.1-2). Korah was the ringleader of the coup. He was a Levite and, interestingly, a cousin to Moses. Their fathers were brothers. Three other brothers of the tribe of Reuben were also ringleaders: Dathan, Abiram, and On. Korah was from the Kohathite clan. The Kohathites and the tribe of Reuben camped on the south side of the Tabernacle, camped side by side. Living close together and being friends and co-leaders gave them ample opportunity to sit around in the evenings grumbling, murmuring, and sharing their complaints and disappointments. About what? About having turned away from the promised land to wander about in the desert, a journey that Moses had said would be a 40 year wilderness wandering. Somehow, some way, at some point in time, the four ringleaders shared their complaints and grumbling and began to plot a revolt against the leaders of God, Moses and Aaron. At some point in time, 250 well-known leaders were incited to join the revolt. Note that these were official representatives, appointed members of the coun-

cil of rulers. Some were even Levites, the religious leaders of the nation who worked under Aaron the priest (cp. v.8-11).

2. Note that the issue of protest was opposition to the leadership of Moses and Aaron (v.3). Their charge was a pointed attack against the authority of Moses and Aaron. The charge was direct and sharp: the two leaders had assumed too much authority—had gone too far this time by turning them away from the promised land. The Israelites were a holy people, not unholy, and certainly not so unholy and sinful that they could be kept from entering the promised land. The LORD was among them and with them. Why then did Moses set himself above the assembly as having the authority to turn them away from the promised land, dashing their hopes upon the rocks of despair?

This was the thrust of the rebel attack against Moses and Aaron. Simply stated, Korah and his allies lusted after the power and authority of leadership. They were after the position and power of Moses (v.7, 12-14) and the position and power of the priesthood (v.3, 9-10). Note that the whole group stood face to face against Moses and Aaron, full of fire and fury, ready to take over the reins of government and rule over the people.

3. Note the reaction of Moses: he fell face down, seeking God (v.4-11). How long he stayed upon his face seeking the LORD is not stated. But falling prostrate apparently so startled the rebels that they temporarily held their peace, somewhat backing off until he arose from the ground. Note that Moses did not lash out nor retaliate against the rebels. When they first confronted him face to face, he simply fell prostrate to the ground—in great meekness and humility—and took the matter to the LORD.

a. When Moses arose, he posed a challenge to Korah and his allies (v.5-7). He suggested a *test by fire*: to let the LORD choose His own leader—to show who really belonged to God and who could really approach Him for leadership in guiding God's people (v.5). The test by fire was simple: they would all prove themselves by taking censers and burning incense before the LORD (v.6). Only the priests were allowed to burn incense before the LORD, so this would give God a dramatic opportunity to show just who He wanted in the leadership positions. Remember that two priests, Nadab and Abihu, had offered "strange fire" in burning incense and been stricken dead because of their false approach to God (see outline and note—Lev.10:1-2 for more discussion). Obviously, what Moses was suggesting here was a dramatic demonstration of God's will. God would show exactly whom He wanted to serve as leaders of His people. If Korah and his allies survived *the trial by fire*, then the leadership positions would be theirs. They would immediately become the leaders of God's people. Moses declared that the result would be final: the LORD would definitely show His leader by this *test by fire*. The LORD would choose the one who was truly holy (set apart by God) to be the leader of His people (v.7).

b. Moses rebuked and warned the Levites, Korah, and the other Levites among the 250 rebels (v.7-11). Note that Moses was hot, fiery hot. He shouted:

⇒ They were the ones who had gone too far. He used their own charge against them (v.7, cp. v.3). They were guilty of abusing and trampling underfoot God's call to them to serve as Levites (v.8-9). They had personally been given the privilege of being set apart to serve God and His people. This should have been enough: they were already leaders and servants of God, appointed to lead God's people as directed by Him.

⇒ They were guilty of seeking the priesthood itself—seeking a much higher position that should come only from God, never from selfish effort (v.10).

⇒ They were revolting against the LORD Himself, banding together against Him not against Aaron (v.11).

4. Note the confrontation, contempt, and defiance of Dathan and Abiram (v.12-14). Obviously someone had mentioned to Moses that Dathan and Abiram were also part of the conspiracy. Therefore, Moses summoned them to meet with him.

a. They rejected the summons, refusing to meet with Moses (v.12). Note their outrage: "We will not come!" Anger, wrath, fury, contempt—all the emotions of a rebellious heart flooded their souls. Two times they expressed their contempt and defiance, declaring that they absolutely would not come! (v.12-14).

b. They exaggerated their former life and provision in Egypt (v.13). With hearts full of contempt, they described Egypt as the true land that flows with milk and honey.

c. They blamed Moses for their plight in the wilderness (v.13).

d. They accused Moses of lording it over them (v.13).

e. They blamed Moses for failing to lead them into the promised land as he had promised (v.14).

f. They charged him with abuse of power—with ulterior motives, with deceiving the people (v.14).

g. They repeated their outrage, their contempt and disdain: they would not meet with Moses (v.14).

5. Note the angry reaction of Moses (v.15). He cried out to God not to accept the incense offering of the rebels. He declared that he was innocent: he had not misused his office for any gain nor had he wronged anyone.

Thought 1. There are several important lessons for us in this point:

1) Seeking to be great or seeking positions of power is wrong. A person must seek to serve people, not to hold positions of power. A person after position demonstrates selfish motives and will be severely judged by God.

"And he said unto her, What wilt thou? She saith unto him, Grant that these my two sons may sit, the one on thy right hand, and the other on the left, in thy kingdom" (Mt.20:21).

"And whosoever shall exalt himself shall be abased; and he that shall humble himself shall be exalted" (Mt.23:12).

"And there was also a strife among them, which of them should be accounted the greatest" (Lk.22:24).

"How can ye believe, which receive honour one of another, and seek not the honour that cometh from God only" (Jn.5:44).

"For all that is in the world, the lust of the flesh, and the lust of the eyes, and the pride of life, is not of the Father, but is of the world" (1 Jn.2:16).

"And Absalom rose up early, and stood beside the way of the gate: and it was so, that when any

man that had a controversy came to the king for judgment, then Absalom called unto him, and said, Of what city art thou? And he said, Thy servant is of one of the tribes of Israel. Absalom said moreover, Oh that I were made judge in the land, that every man which hath any suit or cause might come unto me, and I would do him justice" (2 Sam.15:2, 4).

"Then Adonijah the son of Haggith exalted himself, saying, I will be king: and he prepared him chariots and horsemen, and fifty men to run before him" (1 Ki.1:5).

"Therefore pride compasseth them about as a chain; violence covereth them as a garment" (Ps.73:6).

"When pride cometh, then cometh shame: but with the lowly is wisdom" (Pr.11:2).

"Pride goeth before destruction, and an haughty spirit before a fall" (Pr.16:18).

"Put not forth thyself in the presence of the king, and stand not in the place of great men: For better it is that it be said unto thee, Come up hither; than that thou shouldest be put lower in the presence of the prince whom thine eyes have seen" (Pr.25:6-7).

"He that is of a proud heart stirreth up strife: but he that putteth his trust in the LORD shall be made fat" (Pr.28:25).

"For thou hast said in thine heart, I will ascend into heaven, I will exalt my throne above the stars of God: I will sit also upon the mount of the congregation, in the sides of the north: I will ascend above the heights of the clouds; I will be like the most High" (Is.14:13-14).

"Son of man, say unto the prince of Tyrus, Thus saith the LORD God; Because thine heart is lifted up, and thou hast said, I am a God, I sit in the seat of God, in the midst of the seas; yet thou art a man, and not God, though thou set thine heart as the heart of God....Therefore thus saith the LORD God; Because thou hast set thine heart as the heart of God; Behold, therefore I will bring strangers upon thee, the terrible of the nations: and they shall draw their swords against the beauty of thy wisdom, and they shall defile thy brightness. They shall bring thee down to the pit, and thou shalt die the deaths of them that are slain in the midst of the seas" (Ezk.28:2, 6-8).

"Though thou exalt thyself as the eagle, and though thou set thy nest among the stars, thence will I bring thee down, saith the LORD" (Obad 4).

2) When opposition arises, a godly leader must not strike back nor attack the opposition. He must first go before the LORD and do two things:
   a) He must seek the LORD to make sure his leadership has been pure and just, to make sure he has worked hard and fulfilled his service before the LORD and the people.

"Not slothful in business; fervent in spirit; serving the LORD" (Ro.12:11).

"Moreover it is required in stewards, that a man be found faithful" (1 Cor.4:2).

"Therefore, my beloved brethren, be ye stedfast, unmovable, always abounding in the work of the LORD, forasmuch as ye know that your labour is not in vain in the LORD" (1 Cor.15:58).

"And whatsoever ye do in word or deed, do all in the name of the LORD Jesus, giving thanks to God and the Father by him" (Col.3:17).

"And whatsoever ye do, do it heartily, as to the LORD, and not unto men" (Col.3:23).

"As every man hath received the gift, even so minister the same one to another, as good stewards of the manifold grace of God" (1 Pt.4:10).

"Wherefore, beloved, seeing that ye look for such things, be diligent that ye may be found of him in peace, without spot, and blameless" (2 Pt.3:14).

"Seest thou a man diligent in his business? he shall stand before kings; he shall not stand before mean men" (Pr.22:29).

"Whatsoever thy hand findeth to do, do it with thy might; for there is no work, nor device, nor knowledge, nor wisdom, in the grave, whither thou goest" (Eccl.9:10).

   b) The leader must seek the LORD and handle the opposition in a humble, loving, and just way.

"For every one that asketh receiveth; and he that seeketh findeth; and to him that knocketh it shall be opened" (Lk.11:10).

"If ye abide in me, and my words abide in you, ye shall ask what ye will, and it shall be done unto you" (Jn.15:7).

"Seek the LORD and his strength, seek his face continually" (1 Chron.16:11).

"He shall call upon me, and I will answer him: I will be with him in trouble; I will deliver him, and honour him" (Ps.91:15).

"Seek the LORD, and his strength: seek his face evermore" (Ps.105:4).

"And it shall come to pass, that before they call, I will answer; and while they are yet speaking, I will hear" (Is.65:24).

"And I will bring the third part through the fire, and will refine them as silver is refined, and will try them as gold is tried: they shall call on my name, and I will hear them: I will say, It is my people: and they shall say, The LORD is my God" (Zech.13:9).

3) Godly leaders must live meek, humble lives, seeking to serve others.

"But when thou art bidden, go and sit down in the lowest room; that when he that bade thee cometh, he may say unto thee, Friend, go up higher: then shalt thou have worship in the presence of them that

sit at meat with thee" (Lk. 14:10).

"But ye shall not be so: but he that is greatest among you, let him be as the younger; and he that is chief, as he that doth serve" (Lk.22:26).

"For I say, through the grace given unto me, to every man that is among you, not to think of himself more highly than he ought to think; but to think soberly, according as God hath dealt to every man the measure of faith" (Ro.12:3).

"Let nothing be done through strife or vainglory; but in lowliness of mind let each esteem other better than themselves" (Ph.2:3).

"Humble yourselves in the sight of the LORD, and he shall lift you up" (Jas.4:10).

"Likewise, ye younger, submit yourselves unto the elder. Yea, all of you be subject one to another, and be clothed with humility: for God resisteth the proud, and giveth grace to the humble" (1 Pt.5:5).

"He hath showed thee, O man, what is good; and what doth the LORD require of thee, but to do justly, and to love mercy, and to walk humbly with thy God" (Mic.6:8).

4) Believers must not complain, grumble, or murmur against their leaders. Scripture is clear: grumbling, murmuring, and causing strife is forbidden.

"Neither murmur ye, as some of them also murmured, and were destroyed [the Israelites] of the destroyer" (1 Cor.10:10).

"Let nothing be done through strife or vainglory; but in lowliness of mind let each esteem other better than themselves" (Ph.2:3).

"Do all things without murmurings and disputings" (Ph.2:14).

"Of these things put them in remembrance, charging them before the LORD that they strive not about words to no profit, but to the subverting of the hearers" (2 Tim.2:14).

"And the servant of the LORD must not strive; but be gentle unto all men, apt to teach, patient" (2 Tim.2:24).

"A wrathful man stirreth up strife: but he that is slow to anger appeaseth strife" (Pr.15:18).

"He loveth transgression that loveth strife: and he that exalteth his gate seeketh destruction" (Pr.17:19).

"A fool's lips enter into contention, and his mouth calleth for strokes" (Pr.18:6).

"As coals are to burning coals, and wood to fire; so is a contentious man to kindle strife" (Pr.26:21).

2 (16:16-35) **Rebellion—Strife—Contention—Judgment, Of God—Korah, Judgment of—Unbelief, Judgment of—Approach, To God—Judgment, Of False Approaches to God**: there was the showdown and the judgment of the rebels. The *trial by fire* was set. Korah and his allies had accepted the challenge. Now the LORD would dramatically show who His leaders were to be.

OUTLINE	SCRIPTURE	SCRIPTURE	OUTLINE
2. The showdown & the judgment of the rebels a. The challenge to Korah & his allies repeated 1) To approach the LORD tomorrow 2) To have each man take his censer & present incense before the LORD—all 250 of the rebels 3) To include Korah & Aaron	16 And Moses said unto Korah, Be thou and all thy company before the LORD, thou, and they, and Aaron, to morrow: 17 And take every man his censer, and put incense in them, and bring ye before the LORD every man his censer, two hundred and fifty censers; thou also, and Aaron, each of you his censer.	saying, 21 Separate yourselves from among this congregation, that I may consume them in a moment. 22 And they fell upon their faces, and said, O God, the God of the spirits of all flesh, shall one man sin, and wilt thou be wroth with all the congregation?	once, immediately 2) The response of Moses & Aaron: They fell face down before God, crying out in prayer • To the Creator: "God of the spirits of all mankind" • Begged God not to destroy all bc. of one man's sins
b. The arrogant, defiant stand of the rebels against Moses & Aaron: At the entrance to the Tabernacle	18 And they took every man his censer, and put fire in them, and laid incense thereon, and stood in the door of the tabernacle of the congregation with Moses and Aaron.	23 And the LORD spake unto Moses, saying, 24 Speak unto the congregation, saying, Get you up from about the tabernacle of Korah, Dathan, and Abiram.	3) The warning of the LORD: Charge the people to move away from the tents of the rebel ringleaders—Korah, Dathan, & Abiram
1) The response of the LORD • Suddenly, immediately—the glory of the LORD flashed & burst forth, visible to everyone • The LORD threatened to destroy the nation—at	19 And Korah gathered all the congregation against them unto the door of the tabernacle of the congregation: and the glory of the LORD appeared unto all the congregation. 20 And the LORD spake unto Moses and unto Aaron,	25 And Moses rose up and went unto Dathan and Abiram; and the elders of Israel followed him. 26 And he spake unto the congregation, saying, Depart, I pray you, from the tents of these wicked men, and touch nothing of theirs, lest ye be consumed in all	c. The catastrophic judgment upon Dathan, Abiram, & Korah: The ringleaders were confronted by the true servants of God, Moses & the elders of Israel 1) The people were warned to move back, out of the presence of these wicked men

OUTLINE	SCRIPTURE	SCRIPTURE	OUTLINE
• They must separate themselves totally from the wicked: Not touch anything of theirs • They obeyed the warning 2) The two ringleaders had come out with their families to confront & stand against God's leaders, Moses & the elders	their sins. 27 So they gat up from the tabernacle of Korah, Dathan, and Abiram, on every side: and Dathan and Abiam came out, and stood in the door of their tents, and their wives, and their sons, and their little children.	men have provoked the LORD. 31 And it came to pass, as he had made an end of speaking all these words, that the ground clave asunder that was under them:	• They would go down alive into the grave 5) The catastrophic judgment fell—suddenly, immediately
3) The judgment of God would validate or prove that Moses was God's servant: He proposed a test	28 And Moses said, Hereby ye shall know that the LORD hath sent me to do all these works; for I have not done them of mine own mind.	32 And the earth opened her mouth, and swallowed them up, and their houses, and all the men that appertained unto Korah, and all their goods.	• The ground split open • The earth swallowed them, their households, the followers standing with them, & their possessions
• If God's judgment did not fall upon the rebels—that would prove that Moses was not God's choice for a leader	29 If these men die the common death of all men, or if they be visited after the visitation of all men; then the LORD hath not sent me.	33 They, and all that appertained to them, went down alive into the pit, and the earth closed upon them: and they perished from among the congregation.	• They fell alive into the grave: The earth closed over them & they perished
• If God's judgment fell in some spectacular way, that would validate Moses as God's servant	30 But if the LORD make a new thing, and the earth open her mouth, and swallow them up, with all that appertain unto them, and they go down quick into the pit; then ye shall understand that these	34 And all Israel that were round about them fled at the cry of them: for they said, Lest the earth swallow us up also.	6) The fear of the people: They fled as they heard the screams & commotion of the earthquake
4) The judgment of God would fall in a spectacular way • The earth would open up & swallow the rebels & all their belongings		35 And there came out a fire from the LORD, and consumed the two hundred and fifty men that offered incense.	d. The terrifying judgment upon the 250 men offering false incense: Fire blazed forth from God's presence & burned them up

1. The challenge to Korah and his allies was repeated (v.16-17). They were all to approach the LORD the next day. Note that each individual was stressed: "every man" or "each man" was to take his censer and put incense in it—all 250 of the rebels (v.17). Note also that both Korah and Aaron, were to take their censers.

2. The most arrogant, defiant stand was taken by the rebels against Moses and Aaron (v.18-24). Note that the "test by fire" would take place at the entrance of the Tabernacle. It was there that God would choose which men were to be His leaders.

a. The response of the LORD was sudden, immediate: the glory of the LORD flashed or burst forth, visible to everyone (v.19-20). The LORD addressed Moses and Aaron and His message was clear, spelling out doom for all the people. Note this fact: the LORD threatened to destroy the entire nation—at once, immediately (v.20-21). Not only were the rebels to be destroyed, but the whole nation of people as well. This fact indicates that multitudes supported the cause of the rebels. Remember that the rebels were official representatives of the nation, community leaders who had been members of the ruling council of the nation. Obviously, they had been sent to Moses by the vast, vast majority of the people. Again, most of the people obviously supported the cause of the rebel leadership. The rebels were representing the people in their attempt to overthrow the leadership of Moses and Aaron.

b. The response of Moses and Aaron demonstrated godly character: they fell face down before God, crying out in prayer (v.22). Note how they addressed God: as the Creator, the "God of the spirits of all mankind." They begged God not to destroy all the people because of one man's sins. Note that Moses lay most of the blame for the revolt on Korah. But there is the possibility that this was a rhetorical question as well; that is, that the words "one man" referred to the four ringleaders of the revolt (Korah, Dathan, Abiram, and On).

c. The LORD answered the prayer but warned Moses that judgment was still going to fall. He charged Moses to move the people away from the tents of the rebel ringleaders (v.23-24).

3. The catastrophic judgment fell upon Dathan, Abiram, and Korah. Korah, with some of his men, had obviously joined this rebellious group (v.25; cp. v.32; 26:10-11). The ringleaders were confronted by the true servants of God, Moses and the elders of Israel.

a. The people were warned to move back, out of the presence of these wicked men (v.26-27). The instructions were strong: they must separate themselves totally from the wicked, not touch anything of theirs. Hearing these words, the people obeyed the warning.

b. Note that the two ringleaders had come out of their tents. They were standing with their families to confront and stand against God's leaders (v.27).

c. But Moses was courageous and bold: he declared that the judgment of God would validate or prove that he was God's servant (v.28-30). Then Moses proposed a test:

⇒ If God's judgment did not fall upon the rebels, that would prove that Moses was not God's choice for leader (v.29).

⇒ If God's judgment fell in some spectacular way, that would validate Moses as God's servant (v.30).

d. The declaration by Moses was bold: he declared that the judgment of God would fall in a spectacular way (v.30). He even spelled out exactly what the judgment was going to be: the earth would open up, swallowing the rebels and all their belongings. They would go down alive into the grave (Sheol).

e. The catastrophic judgment fell—suddenly, immediately (v.31-33). Just as soon as Moses had finished speaking, the most horrible and frightening thing happened. The ground split open and the earth swallowed the rebels, their households, the followers standing with them, and all their possessions. Miraculously, a great earthquake opened the jaws of the earth, and these rebels fell alive into the grave. The earth closed over them, and they perished and were gone forever from the community of God's believers (v.33).

f. Note the fear of the people: they fled as they heard the screams of the rebels and commotion of the earthquake (v.44).

4. Immediately, the terrifying judgment also fell upon the 250 men offering false incense at the Tabernacle: fire blazed forth from God's presence and burned them up (v.35). A lightning bolt from God's glory flashed forth and scorched them alive.

Note this fact: some of Korah's family survived the judgment (Num. 26:10-11). Obviously, they were not involved in the revolt nor did they support it or else God's judgment would have fallen upon them as well. It is interesting to note that some of Korah's descendants composed several of the Psalms (see the headings to Psalm 42; 44-49; 84-85; 87-88; cp. Ex.6:21, 24; 1 Chron.6:22-31).[1]

Thought 1. God's judgment is just, perfectly just. Only unbelievers are to suffer the eternal judgment of God. Children and spouses do not have to follow in the footsteps of ungodly, wicked mothers and fathers. God will judge all unbelief and rebellion against Him and His appointed leaders. Believers must pray for and support their leaders, not criticize and attack them. The leaders of both the church and the government need our prayers and support, not the complaints of a selfish heart.

1) The judgment of God against unbelief and rebellion is sure. All unbelievers and rebellious hearts will suffer the judgment of God.

"He that believeth on him is not condemned: but he that believeth not is condemned already, because he hath not believed in the name of the only begotten Son of God" (Jn.3:18).

"He that believeth on the Son hath everlasting life: and he that believeth not the Son shall not see life; but the wrath of God abideth on him" (Jn.3:36).

"I said therefore unto you, that ye shall die in your sins: for if ye believe not that I am he, ye shall die in your sins" (Jn.8:24).

"Because he hath appointed a day, in the which he will judge the world in righteousness by that man whom he hath ordained; whereof he hath given assurance unto all men, in that he hath raised him from the dead" (Acts 17:31).

"And to you who are troubled rest with us, when the LORD Jesus shall be revealed from heaven with his mighty angels, In flaming fire taking vengeance on them that know not God, and that obey not the gospel of our Lord Jesus Christ" (2 Th.1:7-8).

"Take heed, brethren, lest there be in any of you an evil heart of unbelief, in departing from the living God" (Heb.3:12).

"The LORD knoweth how to deliver the godly out of temptations, and to reserve the unjust unto the day of judgment to be punished" (2 Pt.2:9).

"But the heavens and the earth, which are now, by the same word are kept in store, reserved unto fire against the day of judgment and perdition of ungodly men" (2 Pt.3:7).

"Behold, the LORD cometh with ten thousands of his saints, To execute judgment upon all, and to convince all that are ungodly among them of all their ungodly deeds which they have ungodly committed, and of all their hard speeches which ungodly sinners have spoken against him" (Jude 14-15).

"Before the LORD: for he cometh, for he cometh to judge the earth: he shall judge the world with righteousness, and the people with his truth" (Ps.96:13).

"I said in mine heart, God shall judge the righteous and the wicked: for there is a time there for every purpose and for every work" (Eccl.3:17).

2) We must pray for and support all leaders, both church and government leaders. Scripture is clear about this:

"Then said Paul, I wist [knew] not, brethren, that he was the high priest: for it is written, Thou shalt not speak evil of the ruler of thy people" (Acts 23:5).

"Let every soul be subject unto the higher powers. For there is no power but of God: the powers that be are ordained of God" (Ro.13:1).

"I exhort therefore, that, first of all, supplications, prayers, intercessions, and giving of thanks, be made for all men; For kings, and for all that are in authority; that we may lead a quiet and peaceable life in all godliness and honesty. For this is good and acceptable in the sight of God our Saviour; Who will have all men to be saved, and to come unto the knowledge of the truth" (1 Tim.2:1-4).

"Put them in mind to be subject to principalities and powers, to obey magistrates, to be ready to every good work" (Tit.3:1).

"Honour all men. Love the brotherhood. Fear God. Honour the king" (1 Pt.2:17).

"Thou shalt not...curse the ruler of thy people" (Ex.22:28).

3 (16:36-40) **Judgment, Duty to Remember—Censers, the Incense—Rebellion, Judgment Of—Warning, Of Judgment**: there was the step to stir the memory of this judgment.

[1] *The Expositor's Bible Commentary*. Frank E. Gaebelein, Editor, p.841.

OUTLINE	SCRIPTURE	SCRIPTURE	OUTLINE
3. The step taken to stir the memory of this judgment a. The command of the LORD 1) To save the censers of the 250 wicked men who were judged: The censers were holy, had been set apart to God 2) To hammer the censers into sheets of metal & use them to overlay the altar 3) The purpose: To be a warning of God's judgment	36 And the LORD spake unto Moses, saying, 37 Speak unto Eleazar the son of Aaron the priest, that he take up the censers out of the burning, and scatter thou the fire yonder; for they are hallowed. 38 The censers of these sinners against their own souls, let them make them broad plates for a covering of the altar: for they offered them before the LORD, therefore they are hallowed: and they shall be a sign unto the children of Israel.	39 And Eleazar the priest took the brasen censers, wherewith they that were burnt had offered; and they were made broad plates for a covering of the altar: 40 To be a memorial unto the children of Israel, that no stranger, which is not of the seed of Aaron, come near to offer incense before the LORD; that he be not as Korah, and as his company: as the LORD said to him by the hand of Moses.	b. The obedience of Eleazar the priest, the son of Aaron 1) He collected the censers & had them hammered out to overlay the altar 2) The purpose: To remind the people... • that no unauthorized person could approach God • that an unauthorized approach to God would be judged—just as Korah & his allies had been

1. The LORD gave a command that was to serve as a warning to the people (v.37-38). Eleazar, the son of Aaron the priest, was to save the censers of the 250 men who were judged. Note that the censers are said to have been holy, that is, set apart to God for special service. For this reason, they had to be saved. All holy things have to be treated as holy—always. Therefore, Eleazar was to walk among the charred bodies of the rebels and save the censers. But note what he was to do with the burning coals: he was to take them some distance away and dispose of them. These burning coals were "strange fire" (see outline and notes—Lev.10:1-2 for more discussion). The censers were to be hammered into sheets of metal and used to overlay the altar (v.38). They were to be a sign, a warning to the people of God's judgment.

2. The obedience of Eleazar is stressed: he did exactly what God had instructed (v.39-40). He collected the censers and had them hammered to overlay the altar. The purpose is clearly stated: the censors were to remind the people...

- that no unauthorized person could approach God
- that an unauthorized approach would be judged, just as Korah's and his allies' approach was judged

In mercy, God wanted to prevent any future unbelief and rebellion against Him. He wanted to keep people from approaching Him in a false, unauthorized way. No person could approach God with the burning incense other than the priest. Keep in mind that the priest is a symbol of the Lord Jesus Christ, and that the incense is a symbol of prayers being offered up to God. All this is a symbol that only Jesus Christ can make prayer acceptable to God. The believer must approach God through Christ and Christ alone for his prayers to be answered.

Thought 1. The judgment of God must be remembered. God warns all people: He judges all false and unauthorized approaches to Him. There is only one approach that is acceptable: the approach that comes through Jesus Christ. Christ is the only Mediator who stands between God and man. Christ alone is the way into God's presence.

"I am the door: by me if any man enter in, he shall be saved, and shall go in and out, and find pasture" (Jn.10:9).

"Jesus saith unto him, I am the way, the truth, and the life: no man cometh unto the Father, but by me" (Jn.14:6).

"Neither is there salvation in any other: for there is none other name under heaven given among men, whereby we must be saved" (Acts 4:12).

"By whom also we have access by faith into this grace wherein we stand, and rejoice in hope of the glory of God" (Ro.5:2).

"Who is he that condemneth? It is Christ that died, yea rather, that is risen again, who is even at the right hand of God, who also maketh intercession for us" (Ro.8:34).

"For through him we both have access by one Spirit unto the Father" (Eph.2:18).

"In whom we have boldness and access with confidence by the faith of him" (Eph.3:12).

"For there is one God, and one mediator between God and men, the man Christ Jesus; Who gave himself a ransom for all, to be testified in due time" (1 Tim.2:5-6).

"Wherefore in all things it behoved him to be made like unto his brethren, that he might be a merciful and faithful high priest in things pertaining to God, to make reconciliation for the sins of the people" (Heb.2:17).

"Seeing then that we have a great high priest, that is passed into the heavens, Jesus the Son of God, let us hold fast our profession. For we have not an high priest which cannot be touched with the feeling of our infirmities; but was in all points tempted like as we are, yet without sin" (Heb.4:14-15).

"Wherefore he is able also to save them to the uttermost that come unto God by him, seeing he ever liveth to make intercession for them" (Heb.7:25).

"For such an high priest became us, who is holy, harmless, undefiled, separate from sinners, and made higher than the heavens" (Heb.7:26).

"Now of the things which we have spoken this is the sum: We have such an high priest, who is set on the right hand of the throne of the Majesty in the heavens" (Heb.8:1).

4 (16:41-50) **Unbelief, Of Israel—Israel, Unbelief of—Complaining, against God's Servants—Murmuring, against God's Servants—Minister, Grumbling against**: the staggering unbelief of the people shows just how hard the human heart can become. Overnight the people began to murmur and grumble against Moses and Aaron again. Note that Scripture says it was the very next day.

OUTLINE	SCRIPTURE
4. The staggering unbelief of the people: Murmured & grumbled against God's servants—the very next day	41 But on the morrow all the congregation of the children of Israel murmured against Moses and against Aaron, saying, Ye have killed the people of the LORD.
a. The false charge: Accused them of causing the rebels' deaths—gathered to oppose them b. The intervention of God: The cloud covered the Tabernacle & the glory of the LORD burst forth—giving the appearance & threat of judgment	42 And it came to pass, when the congregation was gathered against Moses and against Aaron, that they looked toward the tabernacle of the congregation: and, behold, the cloud covered it, and the glory of the LORD appeared.
1) The servants of God approached God's presence	43 And Moses and Aaron came before the tabernacle of the congregation.
2) The threat of God: He was instantly going to destroy the people c. The response of Moses & Aaron: Fell down in prayer d. The judgment of God: A plague	44 And the LORD spake unto Moses, saying, 45 Get you up from among this congregation, that I may consume them as in a moment. And they fell upon their faces.
1) Moses gave quick instructions to Aaron • To take his censer with	46 And Moses said unto Aaron, Take a censer, and put fire therein from off the

SCRIPTURE	OUTLINE
altar, and put on incense, and go quickly unto the congregation, and make an atonement for them: for there is wrath gone out from the LORD; the plague is begun.	incense & burning coals from the altar • To rush among the people, make atonement • The reason: God's judgment— a plague—had already started
47 And Aaron took as Moses commanded, and ran into the midst of the congregation; and, behold, the plague was begun among the people: and he put on incense, and made an atonement for the people.	2) Aaron obeyed • Rushed to the people • Offered incense & made atonement for them
48 And he stood between the dead and the living; and the plague was stayed.	• Stood between the living & the dead: The judgment (plague) was stopped
49 Now they that died in the plague were fourteen thousand and seven hundred, beside them that died about the matter of Korah.	3) The result of God's judgment • 14,700 people died plus Korah & his allies
50 And Aaron returned unto Moses unto the door of the tabernacle of the congregation: and the plague was stayed.	• Aaron returned to Moses at the Tabernacle (no doubt, to thank God for delivering them & sparing the people)

1. Note the false charge: they accused Moses and Aaron of causing the death of the rebels (v.41). The people still did not interpret the judgment of God correctly. They still did not understand unbelief, that unbelief was the rejection of God's Word and refusing to follow Him, failing to do exactly what He says. They still did not understand that grumbling and murmuring against God's leaders and servants were wrong. They still did not understand that they must not stand in opposition to God's leader. Their minds were blinded to the truth of God's Word, blinded to obedience, blinded against following God in a spirit of love and service as He demanded. Consequently, the very next day the whole community grumbled against Moses and Aaron—not just some of the people, but all of the people. They had actually gathered in opposition to these two dear servants of God.

2. The intervention of God was quick and dramatic: the cloud of God's presence covered the Tabernacle and the Glory of the LORD burst forth. This gave the appearance and threat of judgment about to fall (v.42-45). But again, note the character of Moses and Aaron: instead of striking back in anger at the people, these two dear servants approached God's presence in front of the Tabernacle (v.43). It was then that God spoke, threatening the people: He was instantly going to destroy them (v.44-45). He told Moses and Aaron to move away, to leave the people so He could put an end to them immediately.

3. As stated, the response of Moses and Aaron revealed a true character of ministry: they fell down upon their faces in prayer (v.45-50). The bursting forth of God's glory had obviously stricken fear and terror among the people, stopping them dead in their tracks and keeping them from attacking the two servants of God.

4. Nevertheless, the judgment of God fell. Without warning, a plague instantly struck the people (v.46-50).

a. Moses knew immediately what was happening and gave quick instructions to Aaron (v.46). He instructed Aaron to do the work of the *atoning priest:*

⇒ He was to take his censer with incense and place burning coals on it from the altar.

⇒ He was to rush among the people and make atonement for them.

This was necessary because God's judgment had already started. A severe plague—a rapidly spreading plague—had already broken out among the people and they were dropping like flies.

b. Aaron immediately obeyed and rushed to the people, offering incense and making atonement for them (v.47-48). Remember that Aaron was most likely eighty-plus years old at this time; nevertheless, he ran among the people as the High Priest who alone could make atonement for the people, as the High Priest who alone could deliver the people from disease and death. Scripture is clear: the High Priest appointed by God stood between the living and the dead, and the judgment of God was stopped (v.48).

c. Note the result of God's judgment, the result of the rapidly spreading plague: 14,700 people died in addition to Korah and his allies (v.49). After Aaron completed his atoning work, he returned to Moses at the Tabernacle. No doubt he and Moses thanked God for delivering them and sparing some of the people (v.50).

Thought 1. The staggering unbelief of so many people is difficult to understand. God has given evidence after evidence of His existence. Only a fool says, "There is no God" (Ps.14:1; 53:1). Moreover, God has given His Word to reveal the truth to us and to give us the commandments to live by (2 Tim.3:16). But far more than this, God has sent His Son, the Lord Jesus Christ, to reveal the truth of life to man. God has given us far more than just written words to understand the truth; He has given us His very own Son to live the truth out before us. With so much evidence of God's existence and will for man, it is most difficult to understand the hardness of heart, the stubborn will of man that causes him to stand in unbelief and rebellion. Just as God warned the people of Israel, He warns us in the Holy Scripture:

"He that believeth on the Son hath everlasting life: and he that believeth not the Son shall not see life; but the wrath of God abideth on him" (Jn.3:36).

"I said therefore unto you, that ye shall die in your sins: for if ye believe not that I am he, ye shall die in your sins" (Jn.8:24).

"For the heart of this people is waxed gross, and their ears are dull of hearing, and their eyes have they closed; lest they should see with their eyes, and hear with their ears, and understand with their heart, and should be converted, and I should heal them" (Acts 28:27).

"But after thy hardness and impenitent heart treasurest up unto thyself wrath against the day of wrath and revelation of the righteous judgment of God" (Ro.2:5).

"Who being past feeling have given themselves over unto lasciviousness, to work all uncleanness with greediness" (Eph.4:19).

"Take heed, brethren, lest there be in any of you an evil heart of unbelief, in departing from the living God. But exhort one another daily, while it is called To day; lest any of you be hardened through the deceitfulness of sin" (Heb.3:12-13).

"The fool hath said in his heart, There is no God. They are corrupt, they have done abominable works, there is none that doeth good. The LORD looked down from heaven upon the children of men, to see if there were any that did understand, and seek God. They are all gone aside, they are all together become filthy: there is none that doeth good, no, not one" (Ps.14:1-3).

"Be ye not as the horse, or as the mule, which have no understanding: whose mouth must be held in with bit and bridle, lest they come near unto thee. Many sorrows shall be to the wicked: but he that trusteth in the LORD, mercy shall compass him about" (Ps.32:9-10).

"The fool hath said in his heart, There is no God. Corrupt are they, and have done abominable iniquity: there is none that doeth good. God looked down from heaven upon the children of men, to see if there were any that did understand, that did seek God. Every one of them is gone back: they are altogether become filthy; there is none that doeth good, no, not one" (Ps.53:1-3).

"And might not be as their fathers, a stubborn and rebellious generation; a generation that set not their heart aright, and whose spirit was not stedfast with God" (Ps.78:8).

"Harden not your heart, as in the provocation, and as in the day of temptation in the wilderness: When your fathers tempted me, proved me, and saw my work. Forty years long was I grieved with this generation, and said, It is a people that do err in their heart, and they have not known my ways: Unto whom I sware in my wrath that they should not enter into my rest" (Ps.95:8-11).

"He, that being often reproved hardeneth his neck, shall suddenly be destroyed, and that without remedy" (Pr.29:1).

"Hearken unto me, ye stouthearted, that are far from righteousness" (Is.46:12).

"If ye will not hear, and if ye will not lay it to heart, to give glory unto my name, saith the LORD of hosts, I will even send a curse upon you, and I will curse your blessings: yea, I have cursed them already, because ye do not lay it to heart" (Mal.2:2).

TYPES, SYMBOLS, AND PICTURES (Numbers 16:1-50)

Historical Term	Type or Picture (Scriptural Basis for Each)	Life Application for Today's Believer	Biblical Application
Censers Num.16:36-40	*The censers are a picture of acceptable prayer to God: only Christ can make prayer acceptable to God.* **"And Eleazar the priest took the brasen censers, wherewith they that were burnt had offered; and they were made broad** ***plates for*** **a covering of the altar:** ***To be*** **a memorial**	⇒ Keep in mind that the priest is a symbol of the Lord Jesus Christ, and that the incense is a symbol of prayers being offered up to God. All this is a symbol that Jesus Christ alone can make prayer acceptable to God. The believer must approach God through Christ and	***"And whatsoever ye shall ask in my name, that will I do, that the Father may be glorified in the Son" (Jn.14:13).*** ***"Ye have not chosen me, but I have chosen you, and ordained you, that ye should go and bring forth fruit, and that your fruit should remain: that whatsoever ye shall ask of the Father in my***

Historical Term	Type or Picture (Scriptural Basis for Each)	Life Application for Today's Believer	Biblical Application
	unto the children of Israel, that no stranger, which is not of the seed of Aaron, come near to offer incense before the LORD; that he be not as Korah, and as his company: as the LORD said to him by the hand of Moses" (Num.16:39-40).	Christ alone for his prayers to be answered.	***name, he may give it you" (Jn.15:16).*** ***At that day ye shall ask in my name: and I say not unto you, that I will pray the Father for you"" (Jn.16:26).*** ***And this did she many days. But Paul, being grieved, turned and said to the spirit, I command thee in the name of Jesus Christ to come out of her. And he came out the same hour"" (Acts 16:18).*** ***"Giving thanks always for all things unto God and the Father in the name of our Lord Jesus Christ" (Eph.5:20).***

C. Event 3—The Budding of Aaron's Staff: The Test to Vindicate God's Priest & His Ministry (a Symbol of Christ or of the Minister), 17:1-13

1. The test was set up by God Himself

2. The test was to vindicate the priest, to prove that he was God's choice (a symbol of Christ or of the minister)
   a. To secure 12 staffs, one from the leader of each tribe
   b. To put their names on the staffs
   c. To write Aaron's name on the staff of Levi: He was the head of the priestly tribe (a symbol of Christ)
   d. To place the 12 staffs in the Tabernacle, in front of the Ark of the Covenant
   e. The purpose
      1) To cause the staff of God's servant to sprout (produce life, fruit)
      2) To stop all opposition

3. The test was carried out: Moses obeyed God
   a. The 12 staffs were secured, one from each tribal leader

And the LORD spake unto
Moses, saying,
2 Speak unto the children of
Israel, and take of every one
of them a rod according to
the house of their fathers, of
all their princes according to
the house of their fathers
twelve rods: write thou every
man's name upon his rod.
3 And thou shalt write
Aaron's name upon the rod
of Levi: for one rod shall be
for the head of the house of
their fathers.
4 And thou shalt lay them up
in the tabernacle of the congregation before the testimony, where I will meet with
you.
5 And it shall come to pass,
that the man's rod, whom I
shall choose, shall blossom:
and I will make to cease
from me the murmurings of
the children of Israel, whereby they murmur against you.
6 And Moses spake unto the
children of Israel, and every
one of their princes gave him
a rod apiece, for each prince
one, according to their
fathers' houses, even twelve
rods: and the rod of Aaron
was among their rods.
7 And Moses laid up the rods
before the LORD in the tabernacle of witness.
8 And it came to pass, that
on the morrow Moses went
into the tabernacle of witness; and, behold, the rod of
Aaron for the house of Levi
was budded, and brought
forth buds, and bloomed
blossoms, and yielded al-
monds.
9 And Moses brought out all
the rods from before the
LORD unto all the children
of Israel: and they looked,
and took every man his
rod.
10 And the LORD said unto
Moses, Bring Aaron's rod
again before the testimony,
to be kept for a to-ken
against the rebels; and thou
shalt quite take away their
murmurings from me, that
they die not.
11 And Moses did so: as the
LORD commanded him, so
did he.
12 And the children of Israel
spake unto Moses, saying,
Behold, we die, we perish,
we all perish.
13 Whosoever cometh any
thing near unto the tabernacle of the LORD shall die:
shall we be consumed with
dying?

   b. The 12 staffs were placed before the Lord (the Ark) in the Tabernacle
   c. The next day, the staff of God's true priest had been given life—sprouted, budded, blossomed, & produced almonds (a symbol of Christ or the minister bearing fruit & life by God's miraculous power)
   d. The result: The leaders knew that Aaron was the true priest or servant of God (a symbol of Christ or of the minister): Knew by the life & fruit produced—through God's power

4. The staff of Aaron was kept as a permanent sign & warning of God's power
   a. Power to vindicate His name & His servant (Christ or the minister)
   b. Power to judge—stop & wipe out rebellion & grumbling
   c. The response of the grumbling, rebellious people
      1) Sensed deep guilt & failure
      2) Sensed a deep fear of God's judgment & power

DIVISION III

THE FORTY LONG YEARS OF WILDERNESS WANDERINGS: A PICTURE OF THE BELIEVER'S PILGRIMAGE THROUGH THIS WORLD AS HE PREPARES TO ENTER THE PROMISED LAND 15:1-25:18

C. Event 3—The Budding of Aaron's Staff: The Test to Vindicate God's Priest and His Ministry (a Symbol of Christ or of the Minister), 17:1-13

(17:1-13) **Introduction—Minister, Opposition to—Grumbling, against Ministers—Criticism, of Ministers—Ministers, Criticism of**: grumbling and murmuring against God's minister are constant occurrences throughout society, and far too often within the church itself. Many people frankly feel they have a right to grumble against their minister and sometimes even to oppose and rebel against him. But seldom if ever is the will of God sought by these same people: little time is spent in prayer to seek God's will in the issue or difference.

Grumbling against and attacking the minister of God is a critical issue to God. The minister is God's servant, appointed by God. He serves under God, being totally responsible to God. Because of His appointment and responsibility, he is held to a much higher accountability by God. God is able to take care of His minister, whether to discipline and chastise or approve him. However, when His minister is criticized and attacked, God wants His people to know one thing: He has the power to vindicate His minister, the power to protect him and deliver him through the grumbling and the opposition. But He also has the power to judge—to stop and wipe out all grumbling and rebellion against His dear servant. This is the subject of this great passage of Scripture. Aaron, God's dear servant, had just been attacked. Some of God's people had banded together to stand in opposition to Aaron and his priesthood. They had attempted to remove Aaron from the ministry and to place their own man in the priesthood. The judgment of God had fallen upon the grumbling, rebellious opposition. Now God wanted to warn His people and to give them an eternal warning: He is able to vindicate and protect His chosen servant, and He will do just that. This is: *Event 3—the Budding of Aaron's Staff: The Test to Vindicate God's Priest and His Ministry (a Symbol of Christ or of the Minister),* 17:1-13.

1. The test was set up by God Himself (v.1).
2. The test was to vindicate the priest, to prove that he was God's choice (a symbol of Christ or of the minister) (v.2-5).
3. The test was carried out: Moses obeyed God (v.6-9).
4. The staff of Aaron was kept as a permanent sign and warning of God's power (v.10-13).

1 (17:1) **Test, of Minister—Minister, Proof of—Vindication, of Minister—Proof, of Minister's Call—Israel, Priesthood of—Priesthood, Vindication Of**: the test was set up by God Himself. God loved the priest (minister) with a very special love because He had called the priest to a very special ministry.

OUTLINE	SCRIPTURE
1. The test was set up by God Himself	And the LORD spake unto Moses, saying,

Remember that the priest was a symbol or type of Christ. God had called the priest to be His representative upon the earth, to be the mediator between man and God. The priest was called to share the Word of God and to minister to God's people. How people treated the priest (minister) was, therefore, of critical concern to God. There had just been two attempts to remove Aaron from the priesthood, one by Korah and his allies and the other by the people themselves (Num.16:1-35; 16:36-50). God was determined to stop the opposition against His dear servant, stop their grumbling and murmuring against him. Aaron was His minister, appointed by Him to stand as the High Priest between God and man. Aaron was a type of the perfect High Priest who was yet to come, and who alone could secure eternal salvation for God's people. Therefore, the High Priesthood had to be protected as God had established, for it was to give man a picture of the High Priesthood of His dear Son, the Lord Jesus Christ, who was to be the perfect Representative, the great Mediator who stands between God and man.

The Israelites had attacked the High Priesthood of His dear servant Aaron too many times. Therefore, God set up a test to prove forever that Aaron and his descendants were His appointed priests. They and they alone were the line of descendants who were to serve as priests until the Perfect Priest came, the Lord Jesus Christ Himself. Only the Perfect Priest could represent man perfectly before God.

Thought 1. Jesus Christ is the Perfect Priest. He and He alone stands in perfection, perfectly representing God to man and man to God. Jesus Christ alone has established the perfect priesthood:

⇒ the perfect approach to God
⇒ the perfect way to reveal God
⇒ the perfect way to make people acceptable to God
⇒ the perfect way to share the Word of God
⇒ the perfect way to minister and to help people
⇒ the perfect way to pray and make intercession for people
⇒ the perfect way to conquer sin and death
⇒ the perfect way to live victoriously over the pitfalls and enemies of this life
⇒ the perfect way to experience the abundance of life, life now and life eternally

"Who is he that condemneth? It is Christ that died, yea rather, that is risen again, who is even at the right hand of God, who also maketh intercession for us" (Ro.8:34).

"Wherefore in all things it behooved him to be made like unto his brethren, that he might be a merciful and faithful high priest in things pertaining to God, to make reconciliation for the sins of the people" (Heb 2:17).

"Seeing then that we have a great high priest, that is passed into the heavens, Jesus the Son of God, let us hold fast our profession. For we have not an high priest which cannot be touched with the feeling of our infirmities; but was in all points tempted like as we are, yet without sin" (Heb.4:14-15).

"For every high priest taken from among men is ordained for men in things pertaining to God, that he may offer both gifts and sacrifices for sins: Who can have compassion on the ignorant, and on them that are out of the way; for that he himself also is compassed with infirmity. And by reason hereof he ought, as for the people, so also for himself, to offer for sins. And no man taketh this honour unto himself, but he that is called of God, as was Aaron. So also Christ glorified not himself to be made an high priest; but he that said unto him, Thou art my Son, to day have I begotten thee" (Heb.5:1-5).

"That....we might have a strong consolation, who have fled for refuge to lay hold upon the hope set before us: Which hope we have as an anchor of the soul, both sure and stedfast, and which entereth into that within the veil; Whither the forerunner is for us entered, even Jesus, made an high priest for ever after the order of Melchisedec" (Heb.6:18-20).

"Wherefore he is able also to save them to the uttermost that come unto God by him, seeing he ever liveth to make intercession for them. For such an high priest became us, who is holy, harmless, undefiled, separate from sinners, and made higher than the heavens; Who needeth not daily, as those high priests, to offer up sacrifice, first for his own sins, and then for the people's: for this he did once, when he offered up himself. For the law maketh men high priests which have infirmity; but the word of the oath, which was since the law, maketh the Son, who is consecrated for evermore" (Heb.7:25-28).

"Now of the things which we have spoken this is the sum: We have such an high priest, who is set on the right hand of the throne of the Majesty in the heavens" (Heb.8:1).

2 (17:2-5) **Vindication, of the Minister—Priest, Vindication of—Ministry, Vindication of—Aaron, Vindication of—High Priesthood, Vindication of—Proof, of the Minister**: the test was to vindicate the priest, to prove that he was God's choice to serve the people. Remember that the priest was a symbol of Christ or of the minister. The test needed to be strong, so strong that it would settle the issue forever in the minds of the people. Aaron and his descendants were God's choice to fill the position of High Priest, standing between God and man. The people needed to learn this fact once and for all: there was to be no grumbling or murmuring, no opposition to His dear servant, the High Priest (a symbol of Christ or of the minister). Note the test as spelled out in the Scripture and outline:

OUTLINE	SCRIPTURE	SCRIPTURE	OUTLINE
2. The test was to vindicate the priest, to prove that he was God's choice (a symbol of Christ or of the minister) a. To secure 12 staffs, one from the leader of each tribe b. To put their names on the staffs c. To write Aaron's name on the staff of Levi: He was the head of the priestly tribe	2 Speak unto the children of Israel, and take of every one of them a rod according to the house of their fathers, of all their princes according to the house of their fathers twelve rods: write thou every man's name upon his rod. 3 And thou shalt write Aaron's name upon the rod of Levi: for one rod shall be for the head of the house of their fathers.	4 And thou shalt lay them up in the tabernacle of the congregation before the testimony, where I will meet with you. 5 And it shall come to pass, that the man's rod, whom I shall choose, shall blossom: and I will make to cease from me the murmurings of the children of Israel, whereby they murmur against you.	(a symbol of Christ) d. To place the 12 staffs in the Tabernacle, in front of the Ark of the Covenant e. The purpose 1) To cause the staff of God's servant to sprout (produce life, fruit) 2) To stop all opposition

Far too often people grumble and murmur against the minister, even attacking him. Sometimes the attack is...
- against him as a person
- against his family
- against his preaching or teaching ability
- against some idea or program he is trying to get started
- against some position he has taken

On and on the list could go. All grumbling against and opposition to God's dear servant are troubling concerns to God. The opposition to Aaron concerned God deeply, just as any attack against a minister of God concerns Him. This was the reason God was setting up this test: to stop the irrational, demonic grumbling and attacks against His dear servant, to stop the opposition once and for all. The test was a simple one, but it would prove once and for all that Aaron was God's dear servant. The outline lays out the test explicitly:

⇒ Moses was to secure twelve staffs, one from the leader of each tribe (v.2).
⇒ Moses was to write the names of each leader on the staffs (v.3).
⇒ Moses was to write Aaron's name on the staff of Levi: Aaron was the head of the priestly tribe that was always to fill the position of High Priest. Therefore, Aaron was not standing alone but, rather, standing for the whole tribe of Levi (v.3).
⇒ Moses was to place the twelve staffs in the Tabernacle, right in front of the Ark of the Covenant (v.4).
⇒ The purpose is clearly stated: the staff that belonged to the man whom God chose would sprout. It would produce fruit (v.5). But note, this was not the only purpose God had for the test. God clearly stated that one purpose for the test was to stop the grumbling, the opposition against His dear servant. God was out to establish forever the Aaronic priesthood. The line or descendants of Aaron were to be a type of the Perfect Priesthood of the Lord Jesus Christ.

Thought 1. Grumbling and murmuring against God's servant must be stopped, in fact, must never be allowed. The person truly chosen and appointed by God is God's dear servant. He stands totally accountable *to* God, and he will be held accountable *by* God. In fact, his judgment will be far more severe than that of others. This is the clear teaching of Scripture. He will be held accountable by God not man. There is a clear reason for this: no man sees perfectly nor understands perfectly. The minister sometimes fails and comes short, just as all men do. We all stumble as we seek to do the best we can before our Lord. This is the reason God forbids His people to grumble and murmur—not just against the minister but against one another as well. God is against all grumbling and murmuring against any person. Complaining and strife are not of God; they are of self and of the world, even of the evil one, Satan himself. For this reason, all grumbling and murmuring must be stopped.

"And when the Pharisees saw it, they said unto his disciples, Why eateth your Master with publicans and sinners? But when Jesus heard that, he said unto them, They that be whole need not a physician, but they that are sick. But go ye and learn what that meaneth, I will have mercy, and not sacrifice: for I am not come to call the righteous, but sinners to repentance" (Mt.9:11-13).

"But when the Pharisees saw it, they said unto him, Behold, thy disciples do that which is not lawful to do upon the sabbath day. But he said unto them, Have ye not read what David did, when he was an hungred, and they that were with him; How he entered into the house of God, and did eat the showbread, which was not lawful for him to eat, neither for them which were with him, but only for the priests" (Mt.12:2-4).

"Why do thy disciples transgress the tradition of the elders? for they wash not their hands when they eat bread" (Mt.15:2).

"Why doth this man thus speak blasphemies? who can forgive sins but God only? And immediately when Jesus perceived in his spirit that they so reasoned within themselves, he said unto them, Why reason ye these things in your hearts? Whether is it easier to say to the sick of the palsy, Thy sins be forgiven thee; or to say, Arise, and take up thy bed, and walk? But that ye may know that the Son of man hath power on earth to forgive sins, (he saith to the sick of the palsy,) I say unto thee, Arise, and take up thy bed, and go thy way into thine house" (Mk.2:7-11).

"And when the scribes and Pharisees saw him eat with publicans and sinners, they said unto his disciples, How is it that he eateth and drinketh with publicans and sinners? When Jesus heard it, he saith unto them, They that are whole have no need of the physician, but they that are sick: I came not to call the righteous, but sinners to repentance" (Mk.2:16-17).

"And when they saw some of his disciples eat bread with defiled, that is to say, with unwashen, hands, they found fault" (Mk.7:2).

"And the Pharisees and scribes murmured, saying, This man receiveth sinners, and eateth with them" (Lk.15:2).

"And when they saw it, they all murmured, saying, That he was gone to be guest with a man that is a sinner" (Lk.19:7).

"The Jews then murmured at him, because he said, I am the bread which came down from heaven. And they said, Is not this Jesus, the son of Joseph, whose father and mother we know? how is it then that he saith, I came down from heaven? Jesus therefore answered and said unto them, Murmur not among yourselves. No man can come to me, except the Father which hath sent me draw him: and I will raise him up at the last day" (Jn.6:41-44).

"Neither murmur ye, as some of them also murmured, and were destroyed of the destroyer. Now all these things happened unto them for ensamples: and they are written for our admonition, upon whom the ends of the world are come. Wherefore let him that thinketh he standeth take heed lest he fall" (1 Cor.10:10-12).

"Do all things without murmurings and disputings: That ye may be blameless and harmless, the sons of God, without rebuke, in the midst of a crooked and perverse nation, among whom ye shine as lights in the world" (Ph.2:14-15).

"The foolishness of man perverteth his way: and his heart fretteth against the Lord" (Pr.19:3).

Thought 2. The minister of God is God's chosen instrument. He has been chosen by God to declare the Word of God to God's people. Moreover, he has been called to minister to God's people, encouraging and strengthening them in the faith and doing all he can to conform them to the image of Christ. But this is not all: he has been called to lead God's people to reach out to the lost of the world. But even this is not all: he has been called to bear the authority and weight of all the duties of the church itself, both the spiritual and the administrative duties. The weight of the dear minister is heavy with responsibility and accountability before God. Nevertheless, he has to minister because he is the chosen instrument of God. God wants His people to know, respect, and honor this.

"The kingdom of heaven is like unto a certain king, which made a marriage for his son, And sent forth his servants to call them that were bidden to the wedding: and they would not come" (Mt.22:2-3).

"Ye have not chosen me, but I have chosen you, and ordained you, that ye should go and bring forth fruit, and that your fruit should remain: that whatsoever ye shall ask of the Father in my name, he may give it you" (Jn.15:16).

"But the Lord said unto him, Go thy way: for he is a chosen vessel unto me, to bear my name before the Gentiles, and kings, and the children of Israel" (Acts 9:15).

"But rise, and stand upon thy feet: for I have appeared unto thee for this purpose, to make thee a minister and a witness both of these things which thou hast seen, and of those things in the which I will appear unto thee" (Acts 26:16).

"But God hath chosen the foolish things of the world to confound the wise; and God hath chosen the weak things of the world to confound the things which are mighty; And base things of the world, and things which are despised, hath God chosen, yea, and things which are not, to bring to nought things that are: That no flesh should glory in his presence" (1 Cor.1:27-29).

"Now then we are ambassadors for Christ, as though God did beseech you by us: we pray you in Christ's stead, be ye reconciled to God. For he hath made him to be sin for us, who knew no sin; that we might be made the righteousness of God in him" (2 Cor.5:20-21).

"And he gave some, apostles; and some, prophets; and some, evangelists; and some, pastors and teachers; For the perfecting of the saints, for the work of the ministry, for the edifying of the body of Christ" (Eph.4:11-12).

"Obey them that have the rule over you, and submit yourselves: for they watch for your souls, as they that must give account, that they may do it with joy, and not with grief: for that is unprofitable for you" (Heb.13:17).

"Also I heard the voice of the Lord, saying, Whom shall I send, and who will go for us? Then said I, Here am I; send me" (Is. 6:8).

"I have sent also unto you all my servants the prophets, rising up early and sending them, saying, Return ye now every man from his evil way, and amend your doings, and go not after other gods to serve them, and ye shall dwell in the land which I have given to you and to your fathers: but ye have not inclined your ear, nor hearkened unto me" (Jer.35:15).

"Son of man, I have made thee a watchman unto the house of Israel: therefore hear the word at my mouth, and give them warning from me" (Ezk. 3:17).

3 (17:6-9) **Ministry, Fruit of—Fruit, of Ministry—Ministry, Proof of—Minister, Proof of—Vindication, of Minister—Israel, Priesthood of, Established—Priesthood, of Aaron, Established—Aaron, Staff of—Staff, of Aaron**: Moses obeyed God explicitly, without reservation. What happened then gave unequivocal proof, convincing evidencc that Aaron was God's man. Aaron was God's choice to be the priest, the minister who was to stand in the gap between God and man. The Scripture and outline show us exactly what happened:

OUTLINE	SCRIPTURE	SCRIPTURE	OUTLINE
3. The test was carried out: Moses obeyed God a. The 12 staffs were secured, one from each tribal leader b. The 12 staffs were placed before the Lord (the Ark) in the Tabernacle c. The next day, the staff of God's true priest had been	6 And Moses spake unto the children of Israel, and every one of their princes gave him a rod apiece, for each prince one, according to their fathers' houses, even twelve rods: and the rod of Aaron was among their rods. 7 And Moses laid up the rods before the LORD in the tabernacle of witness. 8 And it came to pass, that on the morrow Moses went	into the tabernacle of witness; and, behold, the rod of Aaron for the house of Levi was budded, and brought forth buds, and bloomed blossoms, and yielded almonds. 9 And Moses brought out all the rods from before the LORD unto all the children of Israel: and they looked, and took every man his rod.	given life—sprouted, budded, blossomed, & produced almonds (a symbol of Christ or the minister bearing fruit & life by God's miraculous power) d. The result: The leaders knew that Aaron was the true priest or servant of God (a symbol of Christ or of the minister): Knew by the life & fruit produced—through God's power

Note that something happened to Aaron's rod that did not happen to the rods of the other tribal leaders. Aaron's rod sprouted, budded, blossomed, and produced almonds (v.8). It is impossible for a dead piece of wood in the shape of a staff to sprout and produce fruit—an absolute impossibility. This was the miraculous power of God, a convincing, indisputable demonstration of God's power. James Phillips points out two things about the rod:

First, the rod was a symbol of God's power and authority. By giving life to the rod, God was showing that His authority to serve as the priest or minister of His people was being given to Aaron. The very authority and power of God Himself was being placed upon Aaron.

Second, the rod bore fruit by the hand of God. It sprouted, budded, blossomed, and produced almonds—all by the hand and blessing of God Himself. This was a sign that the ministry of Aaron (his priesthood) would be a life-giving ministry, a ministry that would bear fruit and bring life to the people he served.[1]

The budding of Aaron's rod was a symbol of Christ or of the minister bearing fruit and bringing life to people—all through God's miraculous power! The budding of the rod was not by chance; it was by the miraculous power of God. The budding of the rod produced life and fruit: it was a clear symbol that Aaron was to produce life and fruit in his ministry by the hand of God. An astonishing miracle! An indisputable sign that Aaron was a true servant and minister of God, the man who was to stand as the High Priest between God and His people.

Note the result of the miracle: the leaders knew beyond question that Aaron was the true priest or servant of God (v.9). They knew by the life and fruit produced through the power of God. Never again could any of the tribal leaders legitimately question the choice of Aaron as God's minister. Note that Moses brought all the staffs out from the presence of the Lord and returned them to each of the tribal leaders. Scripture says that each man looked at his staff and saw that it was *dead,* that it bore no fruit. Each man knew that he was not God's choice to bear the fruit of God's Word among God's people. Aaron was. Note that each man took his own staff back home with him. All tribal leaders knew with finality—clearly and unequivocally that Aaron was God's choice to be the priest and minister of God to the people.

Thought 1. The budding staff of Aaron bore fruit and gave life. This was the proof of Aaron's ministry and priesthood. By the authority and power of God, Aaron's ministry was appointed to give life and bear fruit among God's people. The power of God is to rest upon every minister and servant of God. Every minister and servant is to share the Word of life and bear fruit among God's people. What does it mean to say that a minister must bear fruit?
1) Bearing fruit means to bear converts.

"And he saith unto them, Follow me, and I will make you fishers of men" (Mt.4:19).

"Then saith he unto his disciples, The harvest truly is plenteous, but the labourers are few; Pray ye therefore the Lord of the harvest, that he will send forth labourers into his harvest" (Mt.9:37-38).

"But when the fruit is brought forth, immediately he putteth in the sickle, because the harvest is come" (Mk.4:29).

"Therefore said he unto them, The harvest truly is great, but the labourers are few: pray ye therefore the Lord of the harvest, that he would send forth labourers into his harvest" (Lk10:2).

"Say not ye, There are yet four months, and then cometh harvest? behold, I say unto you, Lift up your eyes, and look on the fields; for they are white already to harvest. And he that reapeth receiveth wages, and gathereth fruit unto life eternal: that both he that soweth and he that reapeth may rejoice together" (Jn.4:35-36).

"Now I would not have you ignorant, brethren, that oftentimes I purposed to come unto you, (but was let [hindered] hitherto,) that I might have some fruit [converts] among you also, even as among other Gentiles" (Ro.1:13).

1 James Philip. *Mastering the Old Testament, Vol.4, Numbers*, p. 200.

"And let us not be weary in well doing: for in due season we shall reap, if we faint not" (Gal.6:9).
"The fruit of the righteous is a tree of life; and he that winneth souls is wise" (Pr.11:30).

2) Bearing fruit means to bear righteousness, to bear a holy life.

"For I say unto you, That except your righteousness shall exceed the righteousness of the scribes and Pharisees, ye shall in no case enter into the kingdom of heaven" (Mt.5:20).
"That he would grant unto us, that we being delivered out of the hand of our enemies might serve him without fear, In holiness and righteousness before him, all the days of our life" (Lk.1:74-75).
"What fruit had ye then in those things whereof ye are now ashamed? for the end of those things is death. But now being made free from sin, and become servants to God, ye have your fruit unto holiness, and the end everlasting life. For the wages of sin is death; but the gift of God is eternal life through Jesus Christ our Lord" (Ro.6:21-23).
"Awake to righteousness, and sin not; for some have not the knowledge of God: I speak this to your shame" (1 Cor.15:34).
"Being filled with the fruits of righteousness, which are by Jesus Christ, unto the glory and praise of God" (Ph.1:11).
"Follow peace with all men, and holiness, without which no man shall see the Lord" (Heb.12:14).
"But as he which hath called you is holy, so be ye holy in all manner of conversation [conduct]; Because it is written, Be ye holy; for I am holy" (1 Pt.1:15-16).
"Seeing then that all these things shall be dissolved, what manner of persons ought ye to be in all holy conversation and godliness, Looking for and hasting unto the coming of the day of God, wherein the heavens being on fire shall be dissolved, and the elements shall melt with fervent heat? Nevertheless we, according to his promise, look for new heavens and a new earth, wherein dwelleth righteousness. Wherefore, beloved, seeing that ye look for such things, be diligent that ye may be found of him in peace, without spot, and blameless" (2 Pt.3:11-14).

3) Bearing fruit means to bear the Christian character or the fruit of the Spirit.

"But the fruit of the Spirit is love, joy, peace, longsuffering, gentleness, goodness, faith, Meekness, temperance: against such there is no law" (Gal.5:22-23).
"For ye were sometimes darkness, but now are ye light in the Lord: walk as children of light: (For the fruit of the Spirit is in all goodness and righteousness and truth;) Proving what is acceptable unto the Lord. And have no fellowship with the unfruitful works of darkness, but rather reprove them. For it is a shame even to speak of those things which are done of them in secret" (Eph.5:8-12).
"But the wisdom that is from above is first pure, then peaceable, gentle, and easy to be intreated, full of mercy and good fruits, without partiality, and without hypocrisy" (Jas.3:17).

4 (17:10-13) **Warning, of God's Power—Warning, against Grumbling and Rebellion—Grumbling, Warning against—Rebellion, Warning against—Staff of Aaron—Aaron, Staff of—Signs, to Prove God's Ministry**: the staff of Aaron was kept as a permanent sign and warning of God's power. The rods of the tribal leaders were returned to them, but not Aaron's. Aaron was not allowed to keep his rod. It was to be placed in the Tabernacle, in the Ark of the Covenant itself. Remember that the Ten Commandments (the tables of law) had already been placed into the Ark of the Covenant and so had a jar of manna (Ex.25.16;16.33-34). Now Aaron's rod was to be the third item placed into the Ark of the Covenant. All three were to serve as a memorial, a reminder of three great and significant events in the lives of God's people. God's people were always to remember the Ten Commandments and the great provision of God, that He continually feeds His people both physically (manna, bread) and spiritually (the Word of God). Now they were never to forget that God did the choosing of His priests, His ministers. Man did not choose God's servants: God did. Note the Scripture and outline:

OUTLINE	SCRIPTURE	SCRIPTURE	OUTLINE
4. The staff of Aaron was kept as a permanent sign & warning of God's power a. Power to vindicate His name & His servant (Christ or the minister) b. Power to judge—stop & wipe out rebellion & grumbling	10 And the LORD said unto Moses, Bring Aaron's rod again before the testimony, to be kept for a to-ken against the rebels; and thou shalt quite take away their murmurings from me, that they die not. 11 And Moses did so: as the LORD commanded him, so	did he. 12 And the children of Israel spake unto Moses, saying, Behold, we die, we perish, we all perish. 13 Whosoever cometh any thing near unto the tabernacle of the LORD shall die: shall we be consumed with dying?	c. The response of the grumbling, rebellious people 1) Sensed deep guilt & failure 2) Sensed a deep fear of God's judgment & power

1. The staff of Aaron was a sign of God's power to vindicate His name and His servant (v.10). Remember that the priest was a symbol of Christ or of the minister. The grumblers, unbelievers, and rebellious of the world—both within and without the church—must heed the warning: God has the power to vindicate His own name and the name of His servant.

2. The staff of Aaron was a sign of God's power to judge all who grumble against Him and His dear servant. God has the power to stop and wipe out all rebellion and grumbling. The budding staff of Aaron stands as a warning to all who grumble and rebel: they need not die. They can live if they will only stop their grumbling and rebellion against Him and His servant. This was the very reason the budding staff was being placed as a memorial in the Ark of the Covenant.

3. Note the response of the Israelites, the grumbling and rebellious people (v.12-13). They sensed deep guilt and failure, and they feared God's judgment and power. They began to cry out, fearing that they were going to die under the hand of God's judgment. God could strike out against them in the fury of His holiness just as He had done against the rebellion launched by Korah. They felt what they should have felt: that they were alienated, cut off from the Tabernacle, from the very presence of God Himself. Their sin had, in fact, alienated and separated them from God's presence, and they were sensing the alienation and separation. As with us, this would lead to genuine repentance. At long last, it seemed as though they grasped the glorious truth...

- that God is the Preeminent, Holy One
- that God can be approached only as He dictates
- that there is only one appointed High Priest who can stand in God's presence on behalf of people
- that no person can approach God except through the High Priest

The High Priesthood was established forever in the minds of God's people: there was only one man appointed to be the High Priest, and only one man through whom a person could approach God. No person must ever dare to grumble or rebel against the priest or minister appointed by God. To grumble and rebel against God's appointed servant would arouse the judgment of God.

Thought 1. Note two clear and strong lessons:

1) The staff of Aaron is a memorial to God's power to protect His name and His servant. Any who grumble or rebel against God or His servant will face the judgment of God.

"And whosoever shall not receive you, nor hear you, when ye depart thence, shake off the dust under your feet for a testimony against them. Verily I say unto you, It shall be more tolerable for Sodom and Gomorrha in the day of judgment, than for that city" (Mk.6:11).

"Whosoever therefore shall be ashamed of me and of my words in this adulterous and sinful generation; of him also shall the Son of man be ashamed, when he cometh in the glory of his Father with the holy angels" (Mk.8:38).

"Because he hath appointed a day, in the which he will judge the world in righteousness by that man whom he hath ordained; whereof he hath given assurance unto all men, in that he hath raised him from the dead" (Acts 17:31).

"In the day when God shall judge the secrets of men by Jesus Christ according to my gospel" (Ro.2:16).

"And to you who are troubled rest with us, when the Lord Jesus shall be revealed from heaven with his mighty angels, In flaming fire taking vengeance on them that know not God, and that obey not the gospel of our Lord Jesus Christ" (2 Th.1:7-8).

"And as it is appointed unto men once to die, but after this the judgment" (Heb.9:27).

"The Lord knoweth how to deliver the godly out of temptations, and to reserve the unjust unto the day of judgment to be punished" (2 Pt.2:9).

"But the heavens and the earth, which are now, by the same word are kept in store, reserved unto fire against the day of judgment and perdition of ungodly men" (2 Pt.3:7).

"Behold, the Lord cometh with ten thousands of his saints, To execute judgment upon all, and to convince all that are ungodly among them of all their ungodly deeds which they have ungodly committed, and of all their hard speeches which ungodly sinners have spoken against him" (Jude 14-15).

"And I saw the dead, small and great, stand before God; and the books were opened: and another book was opened, which is the book of life: and the dead were judged out of those things which were written in the books, according to their works" (Rev.20:12).

"Before the Lord: for he cometh, for he cometh to judge the earth: he shall judge the world with righteousness, and the people with his truth" (Ps.96:13).

"To every thing there is a season, and a time to every purpose under the heaven" (Eccl.3:17).

"I the Lord search the heart, I try the reins, even to give every man according to his ways, and according to the fruit of his doings" (Jer.17:10).

2) Any person who has grumbled and rebelled against God or His minister must confess and repent of his sin. He must turn back to God—totally and wholly—doing all he can to help the minister in the work of the church. The grumbling and rebellious person must sense deep guilt and failure, sense a deep fear of God's judgment and power. God is going to judge all grumbling and murmuring and rebellion. We must, therefore, repent, turning totally and wholly to God. We must support the ministers of God who proclaim the Word of God to us and bear the enormous responsibility of leading us as we carry out the mission of the church.

"Repent therefore of this thy wickedness, and pray God, if perhaps the thought of thine heart may be forgiven thee" (Acts 8:22).

"Now I beseech you, brethren, for the Lord Jesus Christ's sake, and for the love of the Spirit, that ye strive together with me in your prayers to God for me" (Ro.15:30).

"That ye submit yourselves unto such, and to every one that helpeth with us, and laboureth" (1 Cor.16:16).

"But when the fulness of the time was come, God sent forth his Son, made of a woman, made under the law" (Gal.4:4).

"Receive him therefore in the Lord with all gladness; and hold such in reputation" (Ph.2:29).

"And we beseech you, brethren, to know them which labour among you, and are over you in the

Lord, and admonish you; And to esteem them very highly in love for their work's sake. And be at peace among yourselves" (1 Th.5:12-13).

"Remember them which have the rule over you, who have spoken unto you the word of God: whose faith follow, considering the end of their conversation" (Heb.13:7).

"If we confess our sins, he is faithful and just to forgive us our sins, and to cleanse us from all unrighteousness" (1 Jn.1:9).

"If my people, which are called by my name, shall humble themselves, and pray, and seek my face, and turn from their wicked ways; then will I hear from heaven, and will forgive their sin, and will heal their land" (2 Chron.7:14).

"Let the wicked forsake his way, and the unrighteous man his thoughts: and let him return unto the Lord, and he will have mercy upon him; and to our God, for he will abundantly pardon" (Is 55:7).

"But if the wicked will turn from all his sins that he hath committed, and keep all my statutes, and do that which is lawful and right, he shall surely live, he shall not die" (Ezk.18:21).

"Cast away from you all your transgressions, whereby ye have transgressed; and make you a new heart and a new spirit: for why will ye die" (Ezk.18:31).

TYPES, SYMBOLS, AND PICTURES
(Numbers 17:1-13)

Historical Term	Type or Picture (Scriptural Basis for Each)	Life Application for Today's Believer	Biblical Application
The Test to Vindicate the Priest, to Prove That He Was God's Choice Num.17:2-5	*The priest was a symbol of Christ or the minister. The test to prove Aaron's call and ministry needed to be strong, so strong that it would settle the issue forever in the minds of the people. Aaron and his descendants were God's choice to fill the position of High Priest, standing between God and man. The people needed to learn this fact once and for all: there was to be no grumbling or murmuring, no opposition to His dear servant, the High Priest (a symbol of Christ or of the minister).* **"And it shall come to pass, *that* the man's rod, whom I shall choose, shall blossom: and I will make to cease from me the murmurings of the children of Israel, whereby they murmur against you" (Num.17:5).**	The minister of God is God's chosen instrument. He has been chosen by God to declare the Word of God to God's people. Moreover, he has been called to minister to God's people, encouraging and strengthening them in the faith and doing all he can to conform them to the image of Christ. But this is not all: he has been called to reach out and to lead God's people to reach out to the lost of the world. But even this is not all: he has been called to bear the authority and weight of all the duties of the church itself, both the spiritual and administrative duties. The weight of the dear minister is heavy, weighed down with responsibility and accountability before God. Nevertheless, he has to minister because he is the chosen instrument of God. This God wants His people to know, respect, and honor.	***"But the Lord said unto him, Go thy way: for he is a chosen vessel unto me, to bear my name before the Gentiles, and kings, and the children of Israel" (Acts 9:15).*** ***"But rise, and stand upon thy feet: for I have appeared unto thee for this purpose, to make thee a minister and a witness both of these things which thou hast seen, and of those things in the which I will appear unto thee" (Acts 26:16).*** ***"But God hath chosen the foolish things of the world to confound the wise; and God hath chosen the weak things of the world to confound the things which are mighty; And base things of the world, and things which are despised, hath God chosen, yea, and things which are not, to bring to nought things that are: That no flesh should glory in his presence" (1 Cor.1:27-29).*** ***"Now then we are ambassadors for Christ, as though God did beseech you by us: we pray you in Christ's stead, be ye reconciled to God. For he hath made him to be sin for us, who knew no sin; that we might be made the righteousness of God in him. (2 Cor.5:19-20).*** ***"And he gave some,***

Historical Term	Type or Picture (Scriptural Basis for Each)	Life Application for Today's Believer	Biblical Application
			apostles; and some, prophets; and some, evangelists; and some, pastors and teachers; For the perfecting of the saints, for the work of the ministry, for the edifying of the body of Christ" (Eph.4:11-12 See also Heb. 13:17; Is. 6:8; Jer.35:15; Ezk. 3:17).
Aaron's Staff Num.17:6-9	*Aaron's staff or rod is a symbol of God's power & authority; of the authority of Christ or the minister to bear fruit and bring life to people. The budding of the rod was not by chance; it was by the miraculous power of God. The budding of the rod produced life and fruit: it was a clear symbol that Aaron was to produce life and fruit in his ministry by the hand of God. An astonishing miracle! An indisputable sign that Aaron was a true servant and minister of God, the man who was to stand as the High Priest between God and His people.* **"And it came to pass, that on the morrow Moses went into the tabernacle of witness; and, behold, the rod of Aaron for the house of Levi was budded, and brought forth buds, and bloomed blossoms, and yielded almonds" (Num. 17:8).**	The budding staff of Aaron bore fruit and gave life. This was the proof of Aaron's ministry and priesthood. By the authority and power of God, Aaron's ministry was appointed to give life and bear fruit among God's people. The power of God is to rest upon every minister and servant of God. Every minister and servant is to share the Word of life and bear fruit among God's people. What does it mean to say that a minister must bear fruit? 1. Bearing fruit means to bear converts. 2. Bearing fruit means to bear righteousness, to bear a holy life. 3. Bearing fruit means to bear the Christian character or the fruit of the Spirit.	*"And he saith unto them, Follow me, and I will make you fishers of men" (Mt. 4:19).* *"But when the fruit is brought forth, immediately he putteth in the sickle, because the harvest is come" (Mk.4:29).* *"Say not ye, There are yet four months, and then cometh harvest? Behold, I say unto you, Lift up your eyes, and look on the fields; for they are white already to harvest. And he that reapeth receiveth wages, and gathereth fruit unto life eternal: that both he that soweth and he that reapeth may rejoice together" (Jn.4:35-36 See also Ro.1:13; Gal.6:9; Pr.11:30).* *"What fruit had ye then in those things whereof ye are now ashamed? For the end of those things is death. But now being made free from sin, and become servants to God, ye have your fruit unto holiness, and the end everlasting life. For the wages of sin is death; but the gift of God is eternal life through Jesus Christ our Lord" (Rom.6:21-23).* *"But the fruit of the Spirit is love, joy, peace, longsuffering, gentleness, goodness, faith, Meekness, temperance: against such there is no law" (Gal.5:22-23).*

D. Event 4—God Spelled Out the Service of the Priests & Levites: The Duties, Support, & Tithing of God's Ministers, 18:1-32

1. The duties of the priests & Levites (a picture of ministers)
- a. Duty 1:To be responsible along with their assistants (the Levites) for any offense against the sanctuary
- b. Duty 2: To be personally responsible for any offense against the priesthood
- c. Duty 3: To be responsible for supervising or overseeing their assistants, the Levites
  - 1) The assistants were to perform all the manual work
  - 2) The assistants were never to go near the sacred objects or altar
  - 3) The warning: If the sacred objects were violated, God's judgment fell (death)
- d. Duty 4: To be responsible, along with their assistants, for the care & protection of the Tabernacle
  - 1) Must make absolutely sure no one ever violates its precincts
  - 2) The reason: To prevent the judgment of God—His anger & wrath—from falling upon the violators
- e. Duty 5: To accept their fellow assistants (the Levites) as a gift from God: They were dedicated to the LORD & His service
- f. Duty 6: To accept the priesthood (God's call & ministry) as a gift from God
  - 1) Must personally handle all the sacred service: Anything associated with the altar & inside the inner curtain
  - 2) The reason: God's judgment death for any violator

2. The support or income of the priests & Levites (ministers)
- a. The priests (God's ministers) were to receive support or income, a share of the holy offerings given by the people

And the LORD said unto Aaron, Thou and thy sons and thy father's house with thee shall bear the iniquity of the sanctuary: and thou and thy sons with thee shall bear the iniquity of your priesthood.

2 And thy brethren also of the tribe of Levi, the tribe of thy father, bring thou with thee, that they may be joined unto thee, and minister unto thee: but thou and thy sons with thee shall minister before the tabernacle of witness.

3 And they shall keep thy charge, and the charge of all the tabernacle: only they shall not come nigh the vessels of the sanctuary and the altar, that neither they, nor ye also, die.

4 And they shall be joined unto thee, and keep the charge of the tabernacle of the congregation, for all the service of the tabernacle: and a stranger shall not come nigh unto you.

5 And ye shall keep the charge of the sanctuary, and the charge of the altar: that there be no wrath any more upon the children of Israel.

6 And I, behold, I have taken your brethren the Levites from among the children of Israel: to you they are given as a gift for the LORD, to do the service of the tabernacle of the congregation.

7 Therefore thou and thy sons with thee shall keep your priest's office for every thing of the altar, and within the vail; and ye shall serve: I have given your priest's office unto you as a service of gift: and the stranger that cometh nigh shall be put to death.

8 And the LORD spake unto Aaron, Behold, I also have given thee the charge of mine heave offerings of all the hallowed things of the children of Israel; unto thee have I given them by reason of the anointing, and to thy sons, by an ordinance for ever.

9 This shall be thine of the most holy things, reserved from the fire: every oblation of theirs, every meat offering of theirs, and every sin offering of theirs, and every trespass offering of theirs, which they shall render unto me, shall be most holy for thee and for thy sons.

10 In the most holy place shalt thou eat it; every male shall eat it: it shall be holy unto thee.

11 And this is thine; the heave offering of their gift, with all the wave offerings of the children of Israel: I have given them unto thee, and to thy sons and to thy daughters with thee, by a statute for ever: every one that is clean in thy house shall eat of it.

12 All the best of the oil, and all the best of the wine, and of the wheat, the firstfruits of them which they shall offer unto the LORD, them have I given thee.

13 And whatsoever is first ripe in the land, which they shall bring unto the LORD, shall be thine; every one that is clean in thine house shall eat of it.

14 Every thing devoted in Israel shall be thine.

15 Every thing that openeth the matrix in all flesh, which they bring unto the LORD, whether it be of men or beasts, shall be thine: nevertheless the firstborn of man shalt thou surely redeem, and the firstling of unclean beasts shalt thou redeem.

16 And those that are to be redeemed from a month old shalt thou redeem, according to thine estimation, for the money of five shekels, after the shekel of the sanctuary, which is twenty gerahs.

17 But the firstling of a cow, or the firstling of a sheep, or the firstling of a goat, thou shalt not redeem; they are holy: thou shalt sprinkle their blood upon the altar, and shalt burn their fat for an offering made by fire, for a sweet savour unto the LORD.

18 And the flesh of them shall be thine, as the wave breast and as the right shoul-

- 1) The portion that was not used or burned in the sacrifices
  - This included portions from the Grain, Sin, & Guilt Offerings
  - This food (income) was to be treated & eaten as something most holy: Because it had been given to God for His service
- 2) The wave offerings (offerings of thanksgiving)
  - This provision (income) was for the entire family
  - is was to be used or eaten only by the ceremonially clean (again, because it was a holy offering, given to God for His service)
- 3) The firstfruit offering—all of the first harvest that was given to God
  - The finest olive oil, new wine, & grain
  - The one restriction: Only the ceremonially clean could use or eat what had been presented to the LORD
- 4) The gifts that were devoted or set apart to God
- 5) The firstborn male of every human or animal that was offered to the LORD
  - The firstborn sons & the firstborn males of unclean animals were to be redeemed: The redemption price was five pieces of silver
  - The firstborn of clean animals such as oxen, sheep, or goats was not to be redeemed: It was holy & was to be sacrificed as instructed, & a portion of its meat was to be given to the priests

b. The importance of the priest (minister) receiving support & income
   1) The law of support was laid down by God Himself
   2) The law of support was established by God as a covenant of salt (an unbreakable covenant)
   3) The priests were not to inherit or own any of the land of Canaan because they were to receive a very special share & inheritance: The LORD Himself

c. The Levites (assistant ministers) were to receive support or income: All the tithes
   1) Because they deserved to be paid for their work
   2) Because they guarded the Tabernacle & shielded the people from the blazing judgment of God's holiness
   3) Because they bore heavy responsibility: They were accountable for any offenses against the sanctuary
   4) Because the law of support was established by God as a permanent law
   5) Because they were not to receive any share or inheritance of the land
   6) Because the law of daily support & income replaces the inheritance of the land they would otherwise be receiving

3. The contributions or tithes of the Levites (assistant ministers)

a. They must tithe one tenth of their income, the support they received from the people
   1) Would be counted as their Grain Offering from the harvest
   2) Would be counted as their gift or offering to the LORD

b. They must give the tithe to the LORD's representative, the priest (minister)

c. They must give the best portion of the tithe to the LORD
   - The spirit of giving the best was counted as the offering of the firstfruit: Accepted, blessed by God
   - The rest of the support or income was counted as the person's wages

d. They must heed the warning: They must tithe the best or stand guilty of defiling the holy offerings & face the eternal judgment of God

der are thine.
19 All the heave offerings
of the holy things, which the
children of Israel offer unto
the LORD, have I given thee,
and thy sons and thy daughters with thee, by a statute
for ever: it is a covenant of
salt for ever before the LORD
unto thee and to thy seed
with thee.
20 And the LORD spake unto
Aaron, Thou shalt have no
inheritance in their land, neither shalt thou have any part
among them: I am thy part
and thine inheritance among
the children of Israel.
21 And, behold, I have
given the children of Levi all
the tenth in Israel for an
inheritance, for their service
which they serve, even the
service of the tabernacle of
the congregation.
22 Neither must the children
of Israel henceforth come
nigh the tabernacle of the
congregation, lest they bear
sin, and die.
23 But the Levites shall do
the service of the tabernacle
of the congregation, and they
shall bear their iniquity: it
shall be a statute for ever
throughout your generations,
that among the children of
Israel they have no inheritance.
24 But the tithes of the children of Israel, which they
offer as an heave offering
unto the LORD, I have given
to the Levites to inherit:
therefore I have said unto
them, Among the children of
Israel they shall have no
inheritance.
25 And the LORD spake unto
Moses, saying,
26 Thus speak unto the
Levites, and say unto them,
When ye take of the children
of Israel the tithes which I
have given you from them
for your inheritance, then ye
shall offer up an heave offering of it for the LORD, even a
tenth part of the tithe.
27 And this your heave
offering shall be reckoned
unto you, as though it were
the corn of the thresh-
ingfloor, and as the fulness
of the winepress.
28 Thus ye also shall offer
an heave offering unto the
LORD of all your tithes,
which ye receive of the children of Israel; and ye shall
give thereof the LORD'S
heave offering to Aaron the
priest.
29 Out of all your gifts ye
shall offer every heave offering of the LORD, of all the
best thereof, even the hallowed part thereof out of it.
30 Therefore thou shalt say
unto them, When ye have
heaved the best thereof from
it, then it shall be counted
unto the Levites as the
increase of the thresh-
ingfloor, and as the increase
of the winepress.
31 And ye shall eat it in
every place, ye and your
households: for it is your
reward for your service in
the tabernacle of the congregation.
32 And ye shall bear no sin
by reason of it, when ye have
heaved from it the best of it:
neither shall ye pollute the
holy things of the children of
Israel, lest ye die.

DIVISION III

THE FORTY LONG YEARS OF WILDERNESS WANDERINGS: A PICTURE OF THE BELIEVER'S PILGRIMAGE THROUGH THIS WORLD AS HE PREPARES TO ENTER THE PROMISED LAND 15:1-25:18

D. Event 4—God Spelled Out the Service of the Priests and Levites: The Duties, Support, and Tithing of God's Ministers, 18:1-32

(18:1-32) **Introduction—Support, of Ministers—Stewardship, Support of Ministers**: it is absolutely essential to support the ministers of God. God demands that His people support them, give them an income for their labor. Why? Because the minister of God serves the people of God. He is to spend as much time as possible in the ministry, every conceivable hour possible. The minister is called by God to proclaim the Word of God. Hour after hour of prayer and preparation is required. But in addition to these long hours, the minister is called to serve people…

- visiting in their homes
- motivating support for missions and outreach
- visiting the shut-ins
- counseling those with problems
- visiting the church members
- reaching out to the lost

- visiting the hospitals
- marrying the young
- visiting the grief-stricken and bereaved
- nurturing, nourishing, and growing people
- visiting the leadership
- overseeing the finances and distribution of moneys
- burying the dead
- overseeing all the committees and administrative work of the church

On and on the list could go: the work of the ministry never ends. It is a constant battle for the minister to merely stay afloat, for the work is constant, hard, and long. On top of all the work, he has to spend hour after hour in prayer and Bible study in order to victoriously lead the people of God on their march to the promised land of God. The pastor earns his keep, his income. He is to be compensated as well as possible for his ministry to God's people. This is the subject of this great passage of Scripture: *Event 4—God Spelled Out the Service of the Priests and Levites: The Duties, Support, and Tithing of God's Ministers,* 18:1-32.

1. The duties of the priests and Levites (a picture of ministers) (v.1-7).
2. The support or income of the priests and Levites (ministers) (v.8-24).
3. The contributions or tithes of the Levites (assistant ministers) (v.25-32).

1 (18:1-7) **Ministers, Duties Of—Priests, Duties Of—Levites, Duties Of—Layman, Service Of—Church, Protection Of—Ministry, A Gift or Privilege From God**: the duties of the priests and the Levites are spelled out. Note that God is speaking only to Aaron throughout this passage. As the leader and High Priest, it was his duty to teach and supervise the other priests in the work of the ministry.

Remember: within the past two days, the people had seen the judgment of God fall upon a revolt against Aaron's priesthood. Moreover, they had witnessed the power of God in causing the staff of Aaron to bud and bear fruit, indicating his call and ministry. These two events had stricken a terrifying fear in the hearts of the people, a fear that kept them from approaching the sanctuary or presence of God. They feared, for they saw no way to be reconciled to God, no way to approach God. This is part of what God is doing in this passage. God is declaring that He has provided exactly what the people are crying out for. He has provided a High Priest who stands between God and man, a High Priest who can approach God on their behalf, a High Priest who can protect them from the holiness and judgment of God, a High Priest who can save them and give them life. But there is more in this passage: the duties and responsibilities of the priests and Levites (ministers) are also being spelled out. Note the six duties spelled out in the Scripture and Outline:

OUTLINE	SCRIPTURE	SCRIPTURE	OUTLINE
1. The duties of the priests &	And the LORD said unto	the congregation, for all the	the Tabernacle
Levites (a picture of ministers)	Aaron, Thou and thy sons	service of the tabernacle:	1) Must make absolutely
a. Duty 1:To be responsible	and thy father's house with	and a stranger shall not	sure no one ever violates
along with their assistants	thee shall bear the iniquity	come nigh unto you.	its precincts
(the Levites) for any offense	of the sanctuary: and thou	5 And ye shall keep the	2) The reason: To prevent
against the sanctuary	and thy sons with thee shall	charge of the sanctuary, and	the judgment of God—His
b. Duty 2: To be personally	bear the iniquity of your	the charge of the altar: that	anger & wrath—from
responsible for any offense	priesthood.	there be no wrath any more	falling upon the violators
against the priesthood	2 And thy brethren also of	upon the children of	
c. Duty 3: To be responsible for	the tribe of Levi, the tribe of	Israel.	
supervising or overseeing	thy father, bring thou with	6 And I, behold, I have taken	e. Duty 5: To accept their fel-
their assistants, the Levites	thee, that they may be joined	your brethren the Levites	low assistants (the Levites)
	unto thee, and minister unto	from among the children of	as a gift from God: They
	thee: but thou and thy sons	Israel: to you they are given	were dedicated to the LORD
	with thee shall minister	as a gift for the LORD, to do	& His service
	before the tabernacle of wit-	the service of the tabernacle	
	ness.	of the congregation.	
1) The assistants were to perform	3 And they shall keep thy	7 Therefore thou and thy	f. Duty 6: To accept the priest-
all the manual work	charge, and the charge of all	sons with thee shall keep	hood (God's call & ministry)
2) The assistants were never to go	the tabernacle: only they	your priest's office for every	as a gift from God
near the sacred objects or altar	shall not come nigh the ves-	thing of the altar, and within	1) Must personally handle all
3) The warning: If the sacred	sels of the sanctuary and the	the vail; and ye shall serve: I	the sacred service:
objects were violated,	altar, that neither they, nor	have given your priest's	Anything associated with
God's judgment fell (death)	ye also, die.	office unto you as a service	the altar & inside the
d. Duty 4: To be responsible,	4 And they shall be joined	of gift: and the stranger that	inner curtain
along with their assistants,	unto thee, and keep the	cometh nigh shall be put to	2) The reason: God's judgment
for the care & protection of	charge of the tabernacle of	death.	death for any violator

1. First, the priests were responsible, along with their assistants (the Levites), for any offense against the sanctuary (v.1). Note the word "iniquity" or "offenses" (avown): it means fault, mischief, sin. It is a general word that applies to all kinds of sin or offenses against the sanctuary of God. The primary duty to protect the sanctuary, God's very presence, was the responsibility of the priests along with the Levites. No person was to make a wrong approach into God's presence: it was the priests' duty to teach the people how to approach God and to prevent them from approaching Him in their own self-righteous ways. No person was to be allowed to defile, damage, or destroy the sanctuary.

2. Second, the priests were personally responsible for any offense against the priesthood (v.1). No person was to be allowed to destroy the priesthood that had been established by God. No grumbling, no attack, and no opposition were to

be allowed. The call and ministry of the priest was to be protected at all costs, for it had been established by God. The priest had been called and appointed by God. He was the minister of God to the people of God:

⇒ to represent God before the people and the people before God
⇒ to declare the Word of God to the people
⇒ to counsel and give guidance to the people
⇒ to minister to the needs of people

No person was to attack the priesthood; no person was to seek to destroy the priest or his ministry. It was the duty of the priest to prevent this. He was personally responsible to protect his call and ministry before God.

3. Third, the priests were responsible for supervising their assistants, the Levites (v.2-3). The Levite assistants were to perform all the manual work around the Tabernacle. But note: they were never to go near the sacred objects or altar. If they ever violated the sacred objects, God's judgment would fall upon them (v.3). The Levite assistants were never to usurp the call or ministry of the priests. They themselves were not the priests; this was not their call. They had their own call: a different and distinctive service to do for God. They were to be faithful to their call, never trying to replace the priest. If they did, the warning was clear: the judgment of God would fall and they would die.

4. Fourth, the priests were responsible, along with the Levite assistants, for the care and protection of the Tabernacle (v.4-5). They were to make absolutely sure that no one ever violated its precincts. Note the reason: to prevent the judgment of God, His anger and wrath, from falling upon the violators (v.5). If a person approached God's holy presence in a wrong way—in his own self-righteous way—the fire of God's holiness would flash out and strike him in judgment. There was only one way to approach God: through the ministry of the priest (a symbol of the ministry of Jesus Christ).

5. Fifth, the priests were to accept their fellow assistants (the Levites) as a gift from God. The Levites were given by God to be their assistants. The Levites were dedicated to the LORD and His service just as the priests were. Each had his own service, his own work to do for the LORD; therefore, the priests were to respect and honor the Levite assistants. They were never to downplay the assistants nor their work for God, never degrade them in any way. They were a very special gift from God to carry on the work and service of God, assisting the priests.

6. Sixth, the priests were responsible for accepting the priesthood as a gift from God (v.7). It was God who had called and given them the ministry of the priesthood; therefore, they were to honor the ministry. They had been highly privileged by God, given the privilege to serve God and God's people. No greater call or ministry could ever be endowed upon a person. The priests and all others were to know this fact: God loves His people; therefore, He wants them cared for and looked after with all diligence.

There is a strong lesson here that points to Christ. Of all people, Aaron alone could approach God. He alone stood between God and man, representing God to man and man to God. He and he alone had been appointed to stand between God and man. This is a clear and descriptive picture of Jesus Christ and His High Priesthood. Note that the priest personally had to handle all the sacred service. The sacred service included anything that was associated with the altar and that was inside the inner curtain. The privilege of entering inside the Holy of Holies and of approaching God through the sacrifice laid upon the altar was a priceless gift. The priest was to accept this priceless gift as coming from God and from Him alone. Note that anyone else who came near the sanctuary was to be put to death. The judgment of God was to fall upon him.

Thought 1. There are at least five strong lessons in this point for the minister of God.

1) The minister of God is ultimately responsible for the church and its care. Just as the priest was responsible for any offense against the sanctuary, so the minister is responsible for any sin committed against Christ and His church. It is the duty of the minister to teach people to respect Christ and the church. Christ is not to be dishonored and the church is not to be disturbed or abused, neither verbally or physically. The lives of God's people are not to be destroyed, neither is the property of God's church to be abused or destroyed. The minister is to protect and care for the church, including the people of God and the property of God's church.

"For we are labourers together with God: ye are God's husbandry, ye are God's building. According to the grace of God which is given unto me, as a wise masterbuilder, I have laid the foundation, and another buildeth thereon. But let every man take heed how he buildeth thereupon. For other foundation can no man lay than that is laid, which is Jesus Christ. Now if any man build upon this foundation gold, silver, precious stones, wood, hay, stubble; Every man's work shall be made manifest: for the day shall declare it, because it shall be revealed by fire; and the fire shall try every man's work of what sort it is. If any man's work abide which he hath built thereupon, he shall receive a reward. If any man's work shall be burned, he shall suffer loss: but he himself shall be saved; yet so as by fire" (1 Cor.3:9-15).

"Know ye [plural, the church] not that ye are the temple of God, and that the Spirit of God dwelleth in you? If any man defile the temple of God, him shall God destroy; for the temple of God is holy, which temple ye are" (1 Cor.3:16-17).

"Now therefore ye are no more strangers and foreigners, but fellowcitizens with the saints, and of the household of God; And are built upon the foundation of the apostles and prophets, Jesus Christ himself being the chief corner stone; In whom all the building fitly framed together groweth unto an holy temple in the LORD: In whom ye also are builded together for an habitation of God through the Spirit" (Eph.2:19-22).

"Ye also, as lively stones, are built up a spiritual house, an holy priesthood, to offer up spiritual sacrifices, acceptable to God by Jesus Christ" (1 Pt.2:5).

2) The minister of God is to be diligent in performing his duties. He is to be very responsible. He is to work hard, be steadfast and persevering, working his fingers to the bone to get the work of the ministry done.

> **"Moreover it is required in stewards, that a man be found faithful" (1 Cor.4:2).**
>
> **"Therefore, my beloved brethren, be ye stedfast, unmovable, always abounding in the work of the LORD, forasmuch as ye know that your labour is not in vain in the LORD" (1 Cor.15:58).**
>
> **"And whatsoever ye do in word or deed, do all in the name of the LORD Jesus, giving thanks to God and the Father by him" (Col.3:17).**
>
> **"And whatsoever ye do, do it heartily, as to the LORD, and not unto men" (Col.3:23).**
>
> **"This is a faithful saying and worthy of all acceptation. For therefore we both labour and suffer reproach, because we trust in the living God, who is the Saviour of all men, specially of those that believe. These things command and teach. Let no man despise thy youth; but be thou an example of the believers, in word, in conversation, in charity, in spirit, in faith, in purity. Till I come, give attendance to reading, to exhortation, to doctrine. Neglect not the gift that is in thee, which was given thee by prophecy, with the laying on of the hands of the presbytery. Meditate upon these things; give thyself wholly to them; that thy profiting may appear to all. Take heed unto thyself, and unto the doctrine; continue in them: for in doing this thou shalt both save thyself, and them that hear thee" (1 Tim.4:9-16).**
>
> **"Preach the word; be instant in season, out of season; reprove, rebuke, exhort with all longsuffering and doctrine. For the time will come when they will not endure sound doctrine; but after their own lusts shall they heap to themselves teachers, having itching ears; And they shall turn away their ears from the truth, and shall be turned unto fables. But watch thou in all things, endure afflictions, do the work of an evangelist, make full proof of thy ministry. For I am now ready to be offered, and the time of my departure is at hand. I have fought a good fight, I have finished my course, I have kept the faith: Henceforth there is laid up for me a crown of righteousness, which the LORD, the righteous judge, shall give me at that day: and not to me only, but unto all them also that love his appearing" (2 Tim.4:2-8).**
>
> **"Wherefore, beloved, seeing that ye look for such things, be diligent that ye may be found of him in peace, without spot, and blameless" (2 Pt.3:14).**

3) The minister is to point people to the Lord Jesus Christ as the Perfect Priest. Jesus Christ is the One who stands between God and man, stands in perfection as the Perfect Intercessor and Mediator. Jesus Christ is the only person who can eternally and perfectly satisfy the holiness of God. He is the only One who is perfectly acceptable to God. The minister must point to Jesus Christ as the Perfect Priest who stands before God, representing God to man and man to God. Jesus Christ is the only person who can bring us to God and make us acceptable to Him.

> **"Wherefore in all things it behooved him to be made like unto his brethren, that he might be a merciful and faithful high priest in things pertaining to God, to make reconciliation for the sins of the people" (Heb.2:17).**
>
> **"Seeing then that we have a great high priest, that is passed into the heavens, Jesus the Son of God, let us hold fast our profession. For we have not an high priest which cannot be touched with the feeling of our infirmities; but was in all points tempted like as we are, yet without sin" (Heb.4:14-15).**
>
> **"For every high priest taken from among men is ordained for men in things pertaining to God, that he may offer both gifts and sacrifices for sins: Who can have compassion on the ignorant, and on them that are out of the way; for that he himself also is compassed with infirmity. And by reason hereof he ought, as for the people, so also for himself, to offer for sins. And no man taketh this honour unto himself, but he that is called of God, as was Aaron. So also Christ glorified not himself to be made an high priest; but he that said unto him, Thou art my Son, to day have I begotten thee" (Heb.5:1-5).**
>
> **"Which hope we have as an anchor of the soul, both sure and stedfast, and which entereth into that within the veil; Whither the forerunner is for us entered, even Jesus, made an high priest for ever after the order of Melchisedec" (Heb.6:19-20).**
>
> **"Wherefore he is able also to save them to the uttermost that come unto God by him, seeing he ever liveth to make intercession for them. For such an high priest became us, who is holy, harmless, undefiled, separate from sinners, and made higher than the heavens; Who needeth not daily, as those high priests, to offer up sacrifice, first for his own sins, and then for the people's: for this he did once, when he offered up himself" (Heb.7:25-27).**
>
> **"Now of the things which we have spoken this is the sum: We have such an high priest, who is set on the right hand of the throne of the Majesty in the heavens" (Heb.8:1).**

4) The minister must know that he represents Christ before the people of the world. He himself must, therefore, live a holy and pure life before God. He must guard himself day by day, making absolutely sure that he walks righteously and godly before people.

> **"For I say unto you, That except your righteousness shall exceed the righteousness of the scribes and Pharisees, ye shall in no case enter into the kingdom of heaven" (Mt.5:20).**
>
> **"That he would grant unto us, that we being delivered out of the hand of our enemies might serve him without fear, In holiness and righteousness before him, all the days of our life" (Lk.1:74-75).**

"Awake to righteousness, and sin not; for some have not the knowledge of God: I speak this to your shame" (1 Cor.15:34).

"Having therefore these promises, dearly beloved, let us cleanse ourselves from all filthiness of the flesh and spirit, perfecting holiness in the fear of God" (2 Cor.7:1).

"Stand therefore, having your loins girt about with truth, and having on the breastplate of righteousness" (Eph.6:14).

"Being filled with the fruits of righteousness, which are by Jesus Christ, unto the glory and praise of God" (Ph.1:11).

"Now the end of the commandment is charity out of a pure heart, and of a good conscience, and of faith unfeigned" (1 Tim.1:5).

"But thou, O man of God, flee these things; and follow after righteousness, godliness, faith, love, patience, meekness" (1 Tim.6:11).

"For the grace of God that bringeth salvation hath appeared to all men, Teaching us that, denying ungodliness and worldly lusts, we should live soberly, righteously, and godly, in this present world" (Tit.2:11-12).

"Follow peace with all men, and holiness, without which no man shall see the LORD" (Heb.12:14).

"Pure religion and undefiled before God and the Father is this, To visit the fatherless and widows in their affliction, and to keep himself unspotted from the world" (Jas.1:27).

"But as he which hath called you is holy, so be ye holy in all manner of conversation; Because it is written, Be ye holy; for I am holy" (1 Pt.1:15-16).

"Seeing then that all these things shall be dissolved, what manner of persons ought ye to be in all holy conversation and godliness, Looking for and hasting unto the coming of the day of God, wherein the heavens being on fire shall be dissolved, and the elements shall melt with fervent heat? Nevertheless we, according to his promise, look for new heavens and a new earth, wherein dwelleth righteousness. Wherefore, beloved, seeing that ye look for such things, be diligent that ye may be found of him in peace, without spot, and blameless" (2 Pt. 3:11-14).

"For I am the LORD that bringeth you up out of the land of Egypt, to be your God: ye shall therefore be holy, for I am holy" (Lev.11:45).

5) The minister of God must accept his call and ministry as a gift from God. He must know that he is called by God and that his ministry has been given by God. Therefore, he must honor and highly esteem his call and ministry. He must recognize that he has been highly privileged, but even more than this, he must know that he has been given an awesome responsibility and will be held more accountable than any other individual. He has been entrusted with the awesome responsibility of God's Holy Word—to proclaim it—and the care and nurturing of God's people. God loves His people above and beyond anything we can possibly imagine. He gave His very own Son to die in their behalf. He allowed His own Son to bear the judgment of God that was due His people, allowed His Son to bear their sin in order to save them. God loves His dear people so much that He has appointed a profession of people—the ministers of God—to look after and care for them. No person dare fail in the call and ministry of God. To fail will be to face the awesome, terrifying judgment of God. No greater call could be extended to a person than to be called to the ministry of God. It is a privilege, but it is also an awesome responsibility. The ministry and its call is the gift of God. This the minister is to honor.

"Moreover it is required in stewards, that a man be found faithful" (1 Cor.4:2).

"To wit, that God was in Christ, reconciling the world unto himself, not imputing their trespasses unto them; and hath committed unto us the word of reconciliation. Now then we are ambassadors for Christ, as though God did beseech you by us: we pray you in Christ's stead, be ye reconciled to God. For he hath made him to be sin for us, who knew no sin; that we might be made the righteousness of God in him" (2 Cor.5:19-21).

"Whereof I was made a minister, according to the gift of the grace of God given unto me by the effectual working of his power. Unto me, who am less than the least of all saints, is this grace given, that I should preach among the Gentiles the unsearchable riches of Christ" (Eph.3:7-8).

"Whereof I am made a minister, according to the dispensation of God which is given to me for you, to fulfil the word of God" (Col.1:25).

"And I thank Christ Jesus our LORD, who hath enabled me, for that he counted me faithful, putting me into the ministry" (1 Tim.1:12).

"Whereunto I am appointed a preacher, and an apostle, and a teacher of the Gentiles. For the which cause I also suffer these things: nevertheless I am not ashamed: for I know whom I have believed, and am persuaded that he is able to keep that which I have committed unto him against that day" (2 Tim.1:11-12).

2 (18:8-24) **Support, of Ministers—Ministers, Support of—Priests, Support of—Levites, Support of**: there was the support or income of the priests and Levites that was spelled out in detail. Keep in mind that the priests and Levites were a symbol of the minister of God. God's people are to support the servants of God around the world. This is a strong message to the priests and Levites, a strong message to the ministers of God: they were to earn their living. They were to work and work hard for their livelihood. In honor of their service and ministry, the people were to support them. The provision of their support is clearly and fully spelled out in this passage.

OUTLINE	SCRIPTURE	SCRIPTURE	OUTLINE
2. The support or income of the priests & Levites (ministers) a. The priests (God's ministers) were to receive support or income, a share of the holy offerings given by the people 1) The portion that was not used or burned in the sacrifices • This included portions from the Grain, Sin, & Guilt Offerings • This food (income) was to be treated & eaten as something most holy: Because it had been given to God for His service 2) The wave offerings (offerings of thanksgiving) • This provision (income) was for the entire family • This was to be used or eaten only by the ceremonially clean (again, because it was a holy offering, given to God for His service) 3) The firstfruit offering—all of the first harvest that was given to God • The finest olive oil, new wine, & grain • The one restriction: Only the ceremonially clean could use or eat what had been presented to the LORD 4) The gifts that were devoted or set apart to God 5) The firstborn male of every human or animal that was offered to the LORD • The firstborn sons & the firstborn males of unclean animals were to be redeemed: The redemption price was five pieces of silver	8 And the LORD spake unto Aaron, Behold, I also have given thee the charge of mine heave offerings of all the hal- lowed things of the children of Israel; unto thee have I given them by reason of the anointing, and to thy sons, by an ordinance for ever. 9 This shall be thine of the most holy things, reserved from the fire: every oblation of theirs, every meat offer- ing of theirs, and every sin offering of theirs, and every trespass offering of theirs, which they shall render unto me, shall be most holy for thee and for thy sons. 10 In the most holy place shalt thou eat it; every male shall eat it: it shall be holy unto thee. 11 And this is thine; the heave offering of their gift, with all the wave offerings of the children of Israel: I have given them unto thee, and to thy sons and to thy daughters with thee, by a statute for ever: every one that is clean in thy house shall eat of it. 12 All the best of the oil, and all the best of the wine, and of the wheat, the first- fruits of them which they shall offer unto the LORD, them have I given thee. 13 And whatsoever is first ripe in the land, which they shall bring unto the LORD, shall be thine; every one that is clean in thine house shall eat of it. 14 Every thing devoted in Israel shall be thine. 15 Every thing that openeth the matrix in all flesh, which they bring unto the LORD, whether it be of men or beasts, shall be thine: never- theless the firstborn of man shalt thou surely redeem, and the firstling of unclean beasts shalt thou redeem. 16 And those that are to be redeemed from a month old shalt thou redeem, according to thine estimation, for the money of five shekels, after the shekel of the sanctuary,	which is twenty gerahs. 17 But the firstling of a cow, or the firstling of a sheep, or the firstling of a goat, thou shalt not redeem; they are holy: thou shalt sprinkle their blood upon the altar, and shalt burn their fat for an offering made by fire, for a sweet savour unto the LORD. 18 And the flesh of them shall be thine, as the wave breast and as the right shoul- der are thine. 19 All the heave offerings of the holy things, which the children of Israel offer unto the LORD, have I given thee, and thy sons and thy daugh- ters with thee, by a statute for ever: it is a covenant of salt for ever before the LORD unto thee and to thy seed with thee. 20 And the LORD spake unto Aaron, Thou shalt have no inheritance in their land, neither shalt thou have any part among them: I am thy part and thine inheritance among the children of Israel. 21 And, behold, I have given the children of Levi all the tenth in Israel for an inheritance, for their service which they serve, even the service of the tabernacle of the congregation. 22 Neither must the chil- dren of Israel henceforth come nigh the tabernacle of the congregation, lest they bear sin, and die. 23 But the Levites shall do the service of the tabernacle of the congregation, and they shall bear their iniquity: it shall be a statute for ever throughout your genera- tions, that among the chil- dren of Israel they have no inheritance. 24 But the tithes of the chil- dren of Israel, which they offer as an heave offering unto the LORD, I have given to the Levites to inherit: therefore I have said unto them, Among the children of Israel they shall have no inheritance.	• The firstborn of clean animals such as oxen, sheep, or goats was not to be redeemed: It was holy & was to be sacrificed as instructed, & a portion of its meat was to be given to the priests b. The importance of the priest (minister) receiving support & income 1) The law of support was laid down by God Himself 2) The law of support was established by God as a covenant of salt (an unbreakable covenant) 3) The priests were not to inherit or own any of the land of Canaan because they were to receive a very special share & inheritance: The LORD Himself c. The Levites (assistant ministers) were to receive support or income: All the tithes 1) Because they deserved to be paid for their work 2) Because they guarded the Tabernacle & shielded the people from the blazing judgment of God's holiness 3) Because they bore heavy responsibility: They were accountable for any offenses against the sanctuary 4) Because the law of support was established by God as a permanent law 5) Because they were not to receive any share or inheritance of the land 6) Because the law of daily support & income replaces the inheritance of the land they would otherwise be receiving

1. The priests (God's ministers) were to receive support or income from the holy offerings given by the people (v.8-18).
   a. The portion of meat that was not used in the sacrifices offered upon the altar was to be the priest's (v.9-10). This included portions from the Grain, Sin, and Guilt Offerings. Note that this food or income was to be treated as something most holy. Keep in mind that anything offered and given to God is considered holy, that is, set apart

for His service. When the holy food or income was transferred to the priest, it remained holy. It did not lose its holiness. The priest was, therefore, to count his food or income as holy; and he was to use it only for holy purposes. He was never to allow the food or income to be used in some worldly occasion or endeavor.

b. The wave offerings were part of the support and income of the priest (v.11). Note that this provision was for the entire family of the priest. However, if a family member was ceremonially or spiritually unclean, he could not eat the food or use the income. Why? Because it was a holy offering, given to God only for His service. Again, the food or income must not be used for any unclean or worldly purpose (see outline and notes—Lev.22:1-9, for God's provision for cleansing).

c. The firstfruit offering—all of the harvest that was given to God—became part of the food or income of the priest (v.12-13). This included the finest olive oil, new wine, and grain. But again note the one restriction: only the family member who was ceremonially or spiritually clean could eat what had been presented to the Lord.

Note the word "best" or "finest": only the finest of the firstfruit was to be offered to God. This meant that both God and the priest received the best of the first.[1] The first and the best of the harvest were given to God, which meant that the first and best became part of the support or income of the priest. God's dear minister was to be cared for and looked after, highly honored and supported by the people.

d. The gifts that were devoted (herem) or set apart to God were to be a part of the income of the priest. The Hebrew word has the idea of being under a ban, prohibited from being used for anything else. The gift was given to God and it was to remain in the possession of God. As the representative of God, the priest had the right to use the gift. But no one else had that right. It was under the ban, consecrated totally to the service of God and to be used only by the minister of God.

e. The firstborn male of every human or animal that was offered to the Lord became part of the income of the priest (v.15-18). (Also see outline and note—Ex.13:1-16 for more discussion.)

1) Note that the firstborn sons and the firstborn males of unclean animals were to be redeemed. God never has and never will accept the human sacrifice of a person or the sacrifice of an unclean animal. The very idea of a human being sacrificed in order to appease God's wrath and judgment has always been repulsive to God. The only approach that God accepts is through the substitute sacrifice of His dear Son. Prior to the coming of Christ, God did establish the sacrifice of clean animals to be a picture of the true approach to God, that of a person approaching Him through His Son, the Promised Seed and Saviour of the world. But note: only a clean animal could be offered, an animal with no defect whatsoever. No unclean animal was ever accepted as a substitute sacrifice for the sins of man. This is the reason that both the firstborn sons and the firstborn males of unclean animals were to be redeemed. The redemption price was five pieces of silver. This, too, became part of the income of the priest.

2) The firstborn of clean animals such as an ox, sheep, or goat was not to be redeemed. Why? Because they were already counted holy and were to be sacrificed as instructed, and a portion of their meat was to be given to the priest (v. 17-18).

2. Note the importance of the priest receiving support and income from the people of God (v.19-20). God is clear: the law of supporting the minister has been laid down by God Himself. God has established the law of support as strongly as a covenant of salt. A covenant of salt simply means an unbreakable, indestructible covenant. It is established forever; God's people are to support the priests and ministers of God. This is an absolute essential. Note why: because the priests were not to inherit any of the land within the promised land (v.20). However, the priest or minister shares an inheritance: the LORD Himself. The priest was given a very special relationship with God, a relationship of love and intimacy, of deep communion and fellowship. The priest or minister was to devote his time to nurturing this relationship not to looking after property and material things.

3. Note that the Levites (assistant ministers) were also to receive support or income from the people. In fact, they were to receive all the *tithes* given to the work of God. The financial support of the Levites or assistant ministers was a new law being established by God. Note why the assistant ministers were to be supported by God's people.

a) The assistant ministers were to be supported because they deserved to be paid for their work (v.21). They served and ministered to God's people within the Tabernacle. Because they worked within the worship center of God, they were to be compensated for their work.

b) The assistant ministers were to be supported because they protected the Tabernacle and shielded the people from the blazing judgment of God's holiness (v.22). It was their duty to keep people from approaching God in their own self-righteous ways, to make sure the people approached God only through the priest. They kept people from coming near the Tabernacle lest the fury of God's holiness strike them dead.

c) The assistant ministers were to receive support because they bore heavy responsibility. They were personally accountable for any offenses against the sanctuary (v.23). This would include any abuse or destruction of the sanctuary.

d) The assistant ministers were to be supported because the law of support was established by God as a permanent law. It was to last for all generations to come. God's people were always to support the assistant ministers serving in His worship center.

e) The assistant ministers were to be supported because they were not to receive any share or inheritance in the promised land (v.23).

f) The assistant ministers were to be supported because the law of daily support and income replaced the inheritance of the land they would otherwise have been receiving (v.24). Simply stated, the assistant ministers had no income apart from the support of God's people. When they arrived in the promised land, they would own no land to farm or produce food. They were totally dependent upon the tithes of the people.

---

1 *The Expositor's Bible Commentary*, Frank E. Gaebelein, Editor, p. 853.

Thought 1. Financial support for the minister of God is an absolute essential. The people of God are the ones responsible for supporting the minister. The minister serves the people of God, proclaiming the Word of God to them and ministering to their needs:

⇒ nurturing and nourishing the people
⇒ caring for the sick and dying
⇒ looking after the hospitalized
⇒ marrying the young
⇒ visiting the membership and the lost of the world
⇒ giving oversight to the finances of the church
⇒ motivating commitment to the mission work of the church
⇒ overseeing and giving direction to all the committees and administrative work of the church.

On and on the list could go, for the work of the ministry never ends. But no matter how much work is involved, the minister of God still has to spend hour after hour in prayer and in the study of God's Word. He has to preach and teach, instructing and rooting the people in the Holy Word of God. Above all else, he must proclaim the unsearchable riches of Christ, rooting people in the righteousness of God Himself. It is this that pleases God first and foremost.

The minister of God earns his income. If he is really committed to the LORD and to the ministry, he more than earns it. In fact, he could never be compensated anywhere close to what he deserves. The truth is this: he is not in the ministry for money or gain, but for God and for the people of God whom he loves with all his heart. It is the love of people in particular that causes him to devote his life to them. The love of Christ compels him to love the people of God, making sure that he proclaims the unsearchable riches of Christ to them and ministers to their needs.

The point is this: the people of God are to support the minister of God financially. God has established this law forever: financial support is to be given to the minister of God.

> **"Provide neither gold, nor silver, nor brass in your purses, Nor scrip for your journey, neither two coats, neither shoes, nor yet staves: for the workman is worthy of his meat" (Mt.10:9-10).**
>
> **"Do ye not know that they which minister about holy things live of the things of the temple? and they which wait at the altar are partakers with the altar? Even so hath the LORD ordained that they which preach the gospel should live of the gospel" (1 Cor.9:13-14).**
>
> **"Upon the first day of the week let every one of you lay by him in store, as God hath prospered him, that there be no gatherings when I come" (1 Cor.16:2).**
>
> **"Let him that is taught in the word communicate [give support] unto him that teacheth in all good things" (Gal.6:6).**
>
> **"Notwithstanding ye have well done, that ye did communicate with my affliction" (Ph.4:14).**
>
> **"Let the elders that rule well be counted worthy of double honour, especially they who labour in the word and doctrine. For the scripture saith, Thou shalt not muzzle the ox that treadeth out the corn. And, The labourer is worthy of his reward" (1 Tim.5:17-18).**

3 (18:25-32) **Ministers, Duty to Tithe—Tithing, Of Ministers—Assistant Ministers, Duty to Tithe**: there were the contributions or tithes of the Levites (assistant ministers) (v.25-32). The minister of God is to tithe his income just as everyone else does. *The Expositor's Bible Commentary* makes an excellent comment that speaks to the heart of the minister:

> "There is a tendency, then and now, for persons to believe that if their lives are spent in the Lord's work, then they are exempt from contributing to that work. This leads to a concept, lamentably, more and more observed in our own day, that payment for ministry is something deserved and is something to be demanded."[2]

This is a direct commandment from God to the Levites or assistant ministers: "you must tithe" (v.26). This is a direct commandment that speaks to all the ministers of God down through all generations: you must tithe just as everyone else is required to tithe. Note the Scripture and outline:

OUTLINE	SCRIPTURE	SCRIPTURE	OUTLINE
3. The contributions or tithes of the Levites (assistant ministers) a. They must tithe one tenth of their income, the support they received from the people 1) Would be counted as their Grain Offering from the harvest	25 And the LORD spake unto Moses, saying, 26 Thus speak unto the Levites, and say unto them, When ye take of the children of Israel the tithes which I have given you from them for your inheritance, then ye shall offer up an heave offering of it for the LORD, even a tenth part of the tithe. 27 And this your heave offering shall be reckoned unto you, as though it were the corn of the thresh-	ingfloor, and as the fulness of the winepress. 28 Thus ye also shall offer an heave offering unto the LORD of all your tithes, which ye receive of the children of Israel; and ye shall give thereof the LORD's heave offering to Aaron the priest. 29 Out of all your gifts ye shall offer every heave offering of the LORD, of all the best thereof, even the hallowed part thereof out of it.	 2) Would be counted as their gift or offering to the LORD b. They must give the tithe to the LORD's representative, the priest (minister) c. They must give the best portion of the tithe to the LORD

2 *The Expositor's Bible Commentary*, Frank E. Gaebelein, Editor, p. 857.

OUTLINE	SCRIPTURE	SCRIPTURE	OUTLINE
• The spirit of giving the best was counted as the offering of the first-fruit: Accepted, blessed by God	30 Therefore thou shalt say unto them, When ye have heaved the best thereof from it, then it shall be counted unto the Levites as the increase of the threshingfloor, and as the increase	of the winepress. 31 And ye shall eat it in every place, ye and your households: for it is your reward for your service in the tabernacle of the congregation.	• The rest of the support or income was counted as the person's wages

1. The Levites (assistant ministers) were to tithe one tenth of their support or income (v.26-28). Note an interesting statement: God would accept their tithe as their Grain Offering from the harvest. Their tithe would be counted as their gift or offering to the LORD. When the Levites reached the promised land, they were to receive no inheritance of land; consequently, they would not be able to give a Grain Offering from the harvest. But God would accept or count their tithe as a Grain Offering from the harvest.

2. The Levites (assistant ministers) must give the tithe to the LORD's representatives, that is, the priests (v.28). The priest was God's representative upon the earth, overseeing the operation of the Tabernacle or worship center. He was responsible to see that the tithes of everyone were used for the work of God. Therefore, the assistant ministers were to make their tithe to the LORD's representative, the priest.

3. The Levites (assistant ministers) must give the best portion of the tithe to the LORD (v.29-31). The people were going to be giving the best possessions as tithes to the LORD, which in turn were to be given to the Levites or assistant ministers. Therefore the assistant ministers must give the best portion of their income to the LORD. Note that the spirit of giving the best was counted as the offering of the firstfruit: it was accepted and blessed by God (v.30). Keep in mind that the Levite would have no land or crops to give a firstfruit offering to God. But God would accept the best portion of his income as a firstfruit offering. Note the clear statement of God: the rest of the income of the Levite or assistant minister was counted as his wages. He could keep and use the food or income as he wished.

4. The Levites (assistant ministers) must heed the warning: they must tithe the best or stand guilty of defiling the holy offerings and be forced to face the eternal judgment of God (v.32). Under no circumstances could the leftovers or the last fruits be given to God. God was to be given the first and the best.

Thought 1. The minister of God is to tithe just as everyone else tithes. He is more responsible to tithe and support God's work than the average person. Why? Because he has been appointed by God to be the minister of God, to get the Word of God out and to meet the desperate needs of people both within and without the church.

"And, behold, one came and said unto him, Good Master, what good thing shall I do, that I may have eternal life?….Jesus said unto him, If thou wilt be perfect, go and sell that thou hast, and give to the poor, and thou shalt have treasure in heaven: and come and follow me" (Mt.19:16, 21).

"And went to him, and bound up his wounds, pouring in oil and wine, and set him on his own beast, and brought him to an inn, and took care of him. And on the morrow when he departed, he took out two pence, and gave them to the host, and said unto him, Take care of him; and whatsoever thou spendest more, when I come again, I will repay thee" (Lk.10:34-35).

"Sell that ye have, and give alms; provide yourselves bags which wax not old, a treasure in the heavens that faileth not, where no thief approacheth, neither moth corrupteth" (Lk.12:33).

"And he looked up, and saw the rich men casting their gifts into the treasury. And he saw also a certain poor widow casting in thither two mites. And he said, Of a truth I say unto you, that this poor widow hath cast in more than they all: For all these have of their abundance cast in unto the offerings of God: but she of her penury hath cast in all the living that she had" (Lk.21:1-4).

"Neither was there any among them that lacked: for as many as were possessors of lands or houses sold them, and brought the prices of the things that were sold, And laid them down at the apostles' feet: and distribution was made unto every man according as he had need" (Acts 4:34-35).

"I have showed you all things, how that so labouring ye ought to support the weak, and to remember the words of the LORD Jesus, how he said, It is more blessed to give than to receive" (Acts 20:35).

"Distributing to the necessity of saints; given to hospitality" (Ro.12:13).

"Upon the first day of the week let every one of you lay by him in store, as God hath prospered him, that there be no gatherings when I come" (1 Cor.16:2).

"As we have therefore opportunity, let us do good unto all men, especially unto them who are of the household of faith" (Gal.6:10).

"And this stone, which I have set for a pillar, shall be God's house: and of all that thou shalt give me I will surely give the tenth unto thee" (Gen.28:22).

"And all the tithe of the land, whether of the seed of the land, or of the fruit of the tree, is the LORD's: it is holy unto the LORD" (Lev.27:30).

"And as soon as the commandment came abroad, the children of Israel brought in abundance the firstfruits of corn, wine, and oil, and honey, and of all the increase of the field; and the tithe of all things brought they in abundantly" (2 Chron.31:5).

"Bring ye all the tithes into the storehouse, that there may be meat in mine house, and prove me now herewith, saith the LORD of hosts, if I will not open you the windows of heaven, and pour you out a blessing, that there shall not be room enough to receive it" (Mal.3:10).

E. Event 5—God Gave the Law to Govern the Offering of the Red Heifer & the Cleansing Water: A Symbol of Christ, His Sacrifice & Cleansing Power, 19:1-22

1. The offering of the red heifer (female cow): A symbol of the sacrifice of Christ cleansing a person defiled by death
   a. To have no defect: A symbol of Christ's perfection
   b. To be unused (never under a yoke): A symbol of freedom, the voluntary sacrifice of Christ
   c. To be put to death outside the camp: A symbol of Christ dying outside the city gate (Heb.13:12)
   d. To sprinkle some blood seven times toward the front of the Tabernacle: A symbol that Christ's sacrifice was being offered to God as full satisfaction for sin
   e. To wholly burn the heifer, all its parts: A symbol of the extreme sufferings of Christ
   f. To burn some cedar wood, hyssop, & scarlet wool with the heifer: A picture of using everything to intensify the *purifying power* of the offering
   g. To have every person involved in the sacrifice cleanse himself & his clothes: A symbol that all, even priests, stood guilty & needed cleansing
      1) The priest had to be cleansed
      2) The person who burned the sacrifice needed to be cleansed
   h. To have a clean person gather up the ashes of the sacrifice & keep them in a clean place outside the camp
      1) The ashes were kept for mixing in the "water of cleansing"—for the purification from sin: A symbol of Christ cleansing man from sin
      2) The man who gathered up the ashes was counted unclean, guilty: He had to wash himself & his clothes
   i. To establish this as a permanent law for Israel & for all foreigners among them: A picture of the eternal sacrifice & cleansing power of Christ

2. The basic cause of uncleanness—being defiled by death: A symbol of sin that causes death
   a. The one strict essential: Had to be purified with the cleansing water twice, on the 3rd & 7th days (a symbol of being totally defiled and of the power of Christ to fully & completely cleanse a person)
   b. The strong warning: A person who had been in contact with death defiled the Lord's Tabernacle, the very presence of God, & was cut off (a symbol of eternal judgment if one refuses to be cleansed by Christ)
   c. The caution against day-to-day uncleanness
      1) Must guard against being defiled by death within the tent
      2) Must guard against being defiled by death out in the open

3. The way to secure cleansing
   a. To have the unclean person mix some ashes from the sacrificed heifer in a jar of water
   b. To have a clean person take some hyssop & sprinkle the "cleansing water" upon all that was defiled by death
      1) All that was defiled with a tent
      2) All that was defiled out in the open
   c. To have the clean person sprinkle the unclean person on the 3rd & 7th days; also to have the unclean person wash himself & his clothes on the 7th day: A symbol of full & complete cleansing through the sacrifice & power of Christ

4. The strong warning reemphasized
   a. The person who was unclean & refused to be cleansed: Was to be cut off from the community
      1) Because he defiled the sanctuary
      2) Because he had not been

And the LORD spake unto Moses and unto Aaron, saying,

2 This is the ordinance of the law which the LORD hath commanded, saying, Speak unto the children of Israel, that they bring thee a red heifer without spot, wherein is no blemish, and upon which never came yoke:

3 And ye shall give her unto Eleazar the priest, that he may bring her forth without the camp, and one shall slay her before his face:

4 And Eleazar the priest shall take of her blood with his finger, and sprinkle of her blood directly before the tabernacle of the congregation seven times:

5 And one shall burn the heifer in his sight; her skin, and her flesh, and her blood, with her dung, shall he burn:

6 And the priest shall take cedar wood, and hyssop, and scarlet, and cast it into the midst of the burning of the heifer.

7 Then the priest shall wash his clothes, and he shall bathe his flesh in water, and afterward he shall come into the camp, and the priest shall be unclean until the even.

8 And he that burneth her shall wash his clothes in water, and bathe his flesh in water, and shall be unclean until the even.

9 And a man that is clean shall gather up the ashes of the heifer, and lay them up without the camp in a clean place, and it shall be kept for the congregation of the children of Israel for a water of separation: it is a purification for sin.

10 And he that gathereth the ashes of the heifer shall wash his clothes, and be unclean until the even: and it shall be unto the children of Israel, and unto the stranger that sojourneth among them, for a statute for ever.

11 He that toucheth the dead body of any man shall be unclean seven days.

12 He shall purify himself with it on the third day, and on the seventh day he shall be clean: but if he purify not himself the third day, then the seventh day he shall not be clean.

13 Whosoever toucheth the dead body of any man that is dead, and purifieth not himself, defileth the tabernacle of the LORD; and that soul shall be cut off from Israel: because the water of separation was not sprinkled upon him, he shall be unclean; his uncleanness is yet upon him.

14 This is the law, when a man dieth in a tent: all that come into the tent, and all that is in the tent, shall be unclean seven days.

15 And every open vessel, which hath no covering bound upon it, is unclean.

16 And whosoever toucheth one that is slain with a sword in the open fields, or a dead body, or a bone of a man, or a grave, shall be unclean seven days.

17 And for an unclean person they shall take of the ashes of the burnt heifer of purification for sin, and running water shall be put thereto in a vessel:

18 And a clean person shall take hyssop, and dip it in the water, and sprinkle it upon the tent, and upon all the vessels, and upon the persons that were there, and upon him that touched a bone, or one slain, or one dead, or a grave:

19 And the clean person shall sprinkle upon the unclean on the third day, and on the seventh day: and on the seventh day he shall purify himself, and wash his clothes, and bathe himself in water, and shall be clean at even.

20 But the man that shall be unclean, and shall not purify himself, that soul shall be cut off from among the congregation, because he hath defiled the sanctuary of the LORD: the water of separation hath not been

cleansed by the "cleansing water" b. The law of cleansing is a permanent law: A symbol that all need to be cleansed c. The people involved in handling the water: All were	sprinkled upon him; he is unclean. 21 And it shall be a perpetual statute unto them, that he that sprinkleth the water of separation shall wash his clothes; and he that touch-	eth the water of separation shall be unclean until even. 22 And whatsoever the unclean person toucheth shall be unclean; and the soul that toucheth it shall be unclean until even.	unclean & needed cleansing 1) The person who sprinkled it 2) Any person who touched it 3) Anyone & anything who became unclean by touching a defiled person or object

DIVISION III

THE FORTY LONG YEARS OF WILDERNESS WANDERINGS: A PICTURE OF THE BELIEVER'S PILGRIMAGE THROUGH THIS WORLD AS HE PREPARES TO ENTER THE PROMISED LAND 15:1-25:18

E. Event 5—God Gave the Law to Govern the Offering of the Red Heifer and the Cleansing Water: A Symbol of Christ, His Sacrifice and Cleansing Power, 19:1-22

(19:1-22) **Introduction–Death, Caused by–Death, Results of–Death, Defilement of–Death, Corruption of–Defilement, of Death**: death is the ultimate defilement, the ultimate defilement or corruption of man. Man was never created to die but rather to live eternally in all the abundance of life. Man was created to worship and serve God, living in perfect communion and fellowship with Him. But selfishness and sin changed man. Selfishness and sin corrupted man, planting the seed of deterioration and decay, of death itself, within man. The result of selfishness and sin is death: corruption, deterioration, and decay. Nothing defiles a man like death. Death is the ultimate defilement. Death is contrary to God's purpose for man, totally contrary to man's reason for existing. This is the great concern of the present Scripture: how to be cleansed from the defilement of death. God wants man to live eternally with him, fulfilling his purpose to the fullest. God wants man living in all the abundance of life, being victorious and triumphant over all the enemies of life that drag him down into the pit of corruption and decay. God wants man to conquer death and to live eternally with Him.

The glorious news is just this: God has provided a way for man to be cleansed from defilement, even from the defilement of death. Cleansing from defilement was pictured or symbolized in the offering of the red heifer (a red female cow). The red heifer symbolized the cleansing power of Jesus Christ, the power of His sacrifice to cleanse from the defilement of sin and death. This is the great subject of this passage: *Event 5—God Gave the Law to Govern the Offering of the Red Heifer and the Cleansing Water: A Symbol of Christ, His Sacrifice and Cleansing Power,* 19:1-22.

1. The offering of the red heifer (female cow): a symbol of the sacrifice of Christ cleansing a person defiled by death (v.11-10).
2. The basic cause of uncleanness—being defiled by death: a symbol of sin that causes death (v.11-16).
3. The way to secure cleansing (v.17-19).
4. The strong warning reemphasized (v.20-22).

1 (19:1-10) **Red Heifer–Sacrifice, of Red Heifer–Cleansing, from Sin–Sin, Cleansing from–Symbol, of Christ's Sacrifice–Sacrifice, of Christ, Symbol of–Forgiveness, of Sin–Defilement, by Death–Death, Causes Defilement**: there was the offering of the red heifer (a red female cow). The offering of the red heifer was instituted by God for a good reason: it met a dire need of the people. If a person sinned while the Israelites were marching along, Moses could not stop the march in its tracks, put up the Tabernacle, then go through the ritual of approaching God for forgiveness through the substitute sacrifice. What, then, was a person to do if he sinned while marching along the way? The answer lay in the offering of the red heifer: the priest would take a small amount of ashes from the red heifer and mix those ashes with fresh water. Then the priest would take some hyssop, dip it in the mixed water, and sprinkle the person who had sinned. Keep in mind that this is a picture of the cleansing, purifying power of Christ's sacrifice. Note the Scripture and outline:

OUTLINE	SCRIPTURE	SCRIPTURE	OUTLINE
1. The offering of the red heifer (female cow): A symbol of the sacrifice of Christ cleansing a person defiled by death a. To have no defect: A symbol of Christ's perfection b. To be unused (never under a yoke): A symbol of freedom, the voluntary sacrifice of Christ	And the LORD spake unto Moses and unto Aaron, saying, 2 This is the ordinance of the law which the LORD hath commanded, saying, Speak unto the children of Israel, that they bring thee a red heifer without spot, wherein is no blemish, and upon which never came yoke:	4 And Eleazar the priest shall take of her blood with his finger, and sprinkle of her blood directly before the tabernacle of the congregation seven times: 5 And one shall burn the heifer in his sight; her skin, and her flesh, and her blood, with her dung, shall he burn:	d. To sprinkle some blood seven times toward the front of the Tabernacle: A symbol that Christ's sacrifice was being offered to God as full satisfaction for sin e. To wholly burn the heifer, all its parts: A symbol of the extreme sufferings of Christ
c. To be put to death outside the camp: A symbol of Christ dying outside the city gate (Heb.13:12)	3 And ye shall give her unto Eleazar the priest, that he may bring her forth without the camp, and one shall slay her before his face:	6 And the priest shall take cedar wood, and hyssop, and scarlet, and cast it into the midst of the burning of the heifer.	f. To burn some cedar wood, hyssop, & scarlet wool with the heifer: A picture of using everything to intensify the *purifying power* of the offering

OUTLINE	SCRIPTURE	SCRIPTURE	OUTLINE
g. To have every person involved in the sacrifice cleanse himself & his clothes: A symbol that all, even priests, stood guilty & needed cleansing 1) The priest had to be cleansed 2) The person who burned the sacrifice needed to be cleansed h. To have a clean person gather up the ashes of the sacrifice & keep them in a clean place out-	7 Then the priest shall wash his clothes, and he shall bathe his flesh in water, and afterward he shall come into the camp, and the priest shall be unclean until the even. 8 And he that burneth her shall wash his clothes in water, and bathe his flesh in water, and shall be unclean until the even. 9 And a man that is clean shall gather up the ashes of the heifer, and lay them up	without the camp in a clean place, and it shall be kept for the congregation of the chil- dren of Israel for a water of separation: it is a purifica- tion for sin. 10 And he that gathereth the ashes of the heifer shall wash his clothes, and be unclean until the even: and it shall be unto the children of Israel, and unto the stranger that sojourneth among them, for a statute for ever.	side the camp 1) The ashes were kept for mixing in the "water of cleansing"—for the purification from sin: A symbol of Christ cleansing man from sin 2) The man who gathered up the ashes was counted unclean, guilty: He had to wash himself & his clothes i. To establish this as a permanent law for Israel & for all foreigners among them: A picture of the eternal sacrifice & cleansing power of Christ

1. The red heifer was to have no defect or blemish: it was to be a perfect offering. This was a symbol of the perfection of Jesus Christ. He was the sinless, perfect sacrifice offered up to God (v.2).

> **"For he hath made him to be sin for us, who knew no sin; that we might be made the righteousness of God in him" (2 Cor.5:21).**
>
> **"For it became him, for whom are all things, and by whom are all things, in bringing many sons unto glory, to make the captain of their salvation perfect through sufferings" (Heb.2:10).**
>
> **"For we have not an high priest which cannot be touched with the feeling of our infirmities; but was in all points tempted like as we are, yet without sin" (Heb.4:15).**
>
> **"And being made perfect, he became the author of eternal salvation unto all them that obey him" (Heb.5:9).**
>
> **"For such an high priest became us, who is holy, harmless, undefiled, separate from sinners, and made higher than the heavens" (Heb.7:26).**
>
> **"For the law maketh men high priests which have infirmity; but the word of the oath, which was since the law, maketh the Son, who is consecrated for evermore" (Heb.7:28).**

2. The red heifer was to be unused, that is, an animal that had never been worked with a yoke around its neck. It had always been a free animal. This was a symbol of Christ being free to choose or voluntarily sacrifice Himself for the sins of the human race (v.2).

> **"For the Son of man is come to seek and to save that which was lost" (Lk.19:10).**
>
> **"This is a faithful saying, and worthy of all acceptation, that Christ Jesus came into the world to save sinners; of whom I am chief" (1 Tim.1:15).**
>
> **"Wherefore when he cometh into the world, he saith, Sacrifice and offering thou wouldest not, but a body hast thou prepared me: In burnt offerings and sacrifices for sin thou hast had no pleasure. Then said I, Lo, I come (in the volume of the book it is written of me,) to do thy will, O God. Above when he said, Sacrifice and offering and burnt offerings and offering for sin thou wouldest not, neither hadst pleasure therein; which are offered by the law; Then said he, Lo, I come to do thy will, O God. He taketh away the first, that he may establish the second. By the which will we are sanctified through the offering of the body of Jesus Christ once for all" (Heb.10:5-10).**
>
> **"And ye know that he was manifested to take away our sins; and in him is no sin" (1 Jn.3:5).**
>
> **"For the zeal of thine house hath eaten me up; and the reproaches of them that reproached thee are fallen upon me" (Ps.69:9).**

3. The red heifer was to be put to death outside the camp. This was a symbol of Christ being put to death outside the city gate.

> **"Wherefore Jesus also, that he might sanctify the people with his own blood, suffered without the gate" (Heb.13:12).**

4. Some blood of the red heifer was to be sprinkled seven times toward the front of the Tabernacle. Remember that the number seven was a symbol of full and complete acceptance. The blood of the red heifer was being accepted by God as full and complete satisfaction for sin. Of course, this was a symbol that Christ's sacrifice was being offered to God as complete satisfaction for sin. God accepts the sacrifice of Christ fully and completely. Our sins are fully and completely forgiven—all through Christ (v.4).

> **"Him hath God exalted with his right hand to be a Prince and a Saviour, for to give repentance to Israel, and forgiveness of sins" (Acts.5:31).**
>
> **"And walk in love, as Christ also hath loved us, and hath given himself for us an offering and a sacrifice to God for a sweetsmelling [pleasing] savour" (Eph.5:2).**

5. The red heifer was to be wholly burned, all its parts. The burning of the entire heifer was a symbol of the extreme sufferings of Christ (v.5).

> **"And at the ninth hour Jesus cried with a loud voice, saying, Eloi, Eloi, lama sabachthani? which is, being interpreted, My God, my God, why hast thou forsaken me" (Mk.15:34).**
> **"And being in an agony he prayed more earnestly: and his sweat was as it were great drops of blood falling down to the ground" (Lk.22:44).**
> **"I gave my back to the smiters, and my cheeks to them that plucked off the hair: I hid not my face from shame and spitting" (Is.50:6).**

6. The priest was to burn some cedar wood, hyssop, and scarlet wool with the red heifer. All these materials were considered to have some cleansing elements or properties (cp. Lev.14:4). This was a picture of using everything to intensify the purifying power of the offering (v.6).

> **"In whom we have redemption through his blood, the forgiveness of sins, according to the riches of his grace" (Eph.1:7).**
> **"Wash me throughly from mine iniquity, and cleanse me from my sin....Purge me with hyssop, and I shall be clean: wash me, and I shall be whiter than snow" (Ps.51:2, 7).**
> **"Come now, and let us reason together, saith the Lord: though your sins be as scarlet, they shall be as white as snow; though they be red like crimson, they shall be as wool" (Is.1:18).**

7. Note that everyone who had anything to do with the sacrifice had to cleanse himself and his clothes. This is a symbol that everyone, including priests, stands guilty before God and must be cleansed (v.7-8).

> **"As it is written, There is none righteous, no, not one: There is none that understandeth, there is none that seeketh after God. They are all gone out of the way, they are together become unprofitable; there is none that doeth good, no, not one" (Ro.3:10-12).**
> **"For all have sinned, and come short of the glory of God"(Ro.3:23).**

8. Note that a clean person was to gather up the ashes of the sacrifice and keep them in a clean place outside the camp (v.9-10). The ashes were to be kept for future use, for mixing in the water of cleansing. "The mixture was to be used in the ritual of purification. This is a symbol of Christ cleansing us from sin (v.9). Note that the man who gathered up the ashes was counted unclean, guilty. He, too, had to wash himself and his clothes (v.10).

9. The offering of the red heifer was established as a permanent law for Israel and for all foreigners among them. By being established as a permanent law, this was a picture of the permanent, eternal sacrifice and cleansing power of Christ (v.10).

> **"Knowing that Christ being raised from the dead dieth no more; death hath no more dominion over him. For in that he died, he died unto sin once: but in that he liveth, he liveth unto God" (Ro.6:9-10).**
> **"Neither by the blood of goats and calves, but by his own blood he entered in once into the holy place, having obtained eternal redemption for us. For if the blood of bulls and of goats, and the ashes of an heifer sprinkling the unclean, sanctifieth to the purifying of the flesh: How much more shall the blood of Christ, who through the eternal Spirit offered himself without spot to God, purge your conscience from dead works to serve the living God" (Heb.9:12-14).**
> **"So Christ was once offered to bear the sins of many; and unto them that look for him shall he appear the second time without sin unto salvation" (Heb.9:28).**
> **"For Christ also hath once suffered for sins, the just for the unjust, that he might bring us to God, being put to death in the flesh, but quickened by the Spirit" (1 Pt.3:18).**

2 (19:11-16) **Uncleanness, Cause of—Defilement, Caused by—Death, Caused by**: the basic cause of uncleanness or defilement is death. Man is unclean just by being born and living in a corruptible world. Positionally—standing in the world as a human being—man is defiled. This is what is known as *positional defilement. Positionally* man sins; *positionally* man dies. Furthermore, man becomes even more defiled as he walks throughout life. Every time man sins, he defiles himself. But the basic cause of defilement is death itself. Death is the ultimate defilement, the ultimate enemy of life. Death takes man down into the grave to waste away and decay. Again, death is the ultimate, final defilement. This was the major focus of the red heifer offering: to cleanse man from all defilement, but in particular from the ultimate defilement of death. All this was pictured in the ritual of the red heifer. Any person who came in contact with death by any means was to be cleansed through the ritual of the red heifer. Keep in mind that this ritual was a symbol of man's need to be cleansed, a symbol of the power of Christ's sacrifice to cleanse him.

OUTLINE	SCRIPTURE	SCRIPTURE	OUTLINE
2. The basic cause of uncleanness—being defiled by death: A symbol of sin that causes death a. The one strict essential: Had to be purified with the cleansing water twice, on the 3rd & 7th days (a symbol of being	11 He that toucheth the dead body of any man shall be unclean seven days. 12 He shall purify himself with it on the third day, and on the seventh day he shall be clean: but if he purify not	himself the third day, then the seventh day he shall not be clean. 13 Whosoever toucheth the dead body of any man that is dead, and purifieth not himself, defileth the tabernacle	totally defiled and of the power of Christ to fully & completely cleanse a person) b. The strong warning: A person who had been in contact with death defiled the Lord's Tabernacle, the very pres-

OUTLINE	SCRIPTURE	SCRIPTURE	OUTLINE
ence of God, & was cut off (a symbol of eternal judgment if one refuses to be cleansed by Christ) c. The caution against day-to-day uncleanness 1) Must guard against being defiled by death within	of the LORD; and that soul shall be cut off from Israel: because the water of separation was not sprinkled upon him, he shall be unclean; his uncleanness is yet upon him. 14 This is the law, when a man dieth in a tent: all that come into the tent, and all that is in the tent, shall be	unclean seven days. 15 And every open vessel, which hath no covering bound upon it, is unclean. 16 And whosoever toucheth one that is slain with a sword in the open fields, or a dead body, or a bone of a man, or a grave, shall be unclean seven days.	the tent 2) Must guard against being defiled by death out in the open

1. There was one strict essential in order to be cleansed: the unclean person had to be purified with the cleansing water on the third and seventh days (v.12). He was counted unclean for the full seven days, but he had to be sprinkled with the cleansing water on two different occasions. This was a symbol of the person's being totally defiled and of the power of Christ to completely cleanse him.

2. Note the strong warning: a person who had been in contact with death defiled the Lord's Tabernacle. He defiled the very presence of God Himself. Consequently, he was to be cut off (v.13). He was to be removed from the people, put outside the camp. He was unclean, defiled, and could not approach God nor fellowship with the people of God until he had been cleansed. This is a symbol of eternal judgment, of being cut off and separated from God eternally if a person refuses to be cleansed by Christ.

3. Note the caution against day-to-day uncleanness (v.14-16). A person was to guard against becoming defiled by death within his home or tent. Sometimes this could not be prevented, for family members did die. However, family members or close friends who came in contact with the dead relative were still counted unclean for seven days. In addition, any container or coffin that was left open was counted as defiled. The people also had to guard against being defiled by death out in the open, outside the home (v.16). If a person touched someone who had been killed by any means or had died a natural death, or if he touched a human bone or grave—he himself would be unclean for seven days.

Death is the ultimate defilement of man, so God gave His people a picture, a strong caution to fight against sin and death. Man is to do all he can to struggle, to conquer, to triumph, to gain the victory over sin and death. This is what God was picturing through these cautions.

Thought 1. There are two strong lessons in this point:

1) We must understand that people are totally defiled. We are all sinful, short of God's glory, standing in need of cleansing.

"As it is written, There is none righteous, no, not one: There is none that understandeth, there is none that seeketh after God. They are all gone out of the way, they are together become unprofitable; there is none that doeth good, no, not one. Their throat is an open sepulchre; with their tongues they have used deceit; the poison of asps is under their lips: Whose mouth is full of cursing and bitterness: Their feet are swift to shed blood: Destruction and misery are in their ways: And the way of peace have they not known: There is no fear of God before their eyes" (Ro.3:10-18).

"For all have sinned, and come short of the glory of God" (Ro.3:23).

"If we say that we have no sin, we deceive ourselves, and the truth is not in us" (1 Jn.1:8).

"And God saw that the wickedness of man was great in the earth, and that every imagination of the thoughts of his heart was only evil continually" (Gen.6:5).

"There is no man that sinneth not" (1 Ki.8:46).

"Who can say, I have made my heart clean, I am pure from my sin" (Pr.20:9).

"All we like sheep have gone astray; we have turned every one to his own way; and the Lord hath laid on him the iniquity of us all" (Is.53:6).

"But we are all as an unclean thing, and all our righteousnesses are as filthy rags; and we all do fade as a leaf; and our iniquities, like the wind, have taken us away" (Is.64:6).

2) We must guard against defilement and uncleanness. We must seek cleansing through the Lord Jesus Christ and seek to stay clean and undefiled.

"For this is my blood of the new testament, which is shed for many for the remission of sins" (Mt.26:28).

"And now why tarriest thou? arise, and be baptized, and wash away thy sins, calling on the name of the Lord" (Acts 22:16).

"Having therefore these promises, dearly beloved, let us cleanse ourselves from all filthiness of the flesh and spirit, perfecting holiness in the fear of God" (2 Cor.7:1).

"In whom we have redemption through his blood, the forgiveness of sins, according to the riches of his grace" (Eph.1:7).

"Draw nigh to God, and he will draw nigh to you. Cleanse your hands, ye sinners; and purify your hearts, ye double minded" (Jas.4:8).

"Unto him that loved us, and washed us from our sins in his own blood" (Rev.1:5).

"Wash you, make you clean; put away the evil of your doings from before mine eyes; cease to do evil" (Is.1:16).

"Wash thine heart from wickedness, that thou mayest be saved. How long shall thy vain thoughts lodge within thee" (Jer.4:14).

3 (19:17-19) **Cleansing, How to Secure—Forgiveness, How to Secure**: the way to secure cleansing was spelled out explicitly. These verses explain the actual ritual involving the red heifer, the ritual that a person went through to secure cleansing. Keep this fact in mind: the ritual or symbol was being used just like all rituals or symbols are used by men, to picture some truth. For example, the flag of nations symbolizes loyalty and devotion; the wine and bread symbolize the blood and body of Jesus Christ; the waters of baptism symbolize identification with Christ—all these symbols are pictures of some truth. So it is with the ritual or symbol of the red heifer. The red heifer symbolized the way to secure cleansing from defilement, in particular how to be cleansed from the ultimate defilement, death itself.

OUTLINE	SCRIPTURE	SCRIPTURE	OUTLINE
3. The way to secure cleansing a. To have the unclean person mix some ashes from the sacrificed heifer in a jar of water b. To have a clean person take some hyssop & sprinkle the "cleansing water" upon all that was defiled by death 1) All that was defiled with a tent	17 And for an unclean person they shall take of the ashes of the burnt heifer of purification for sin, and running water shall be put thereto in a vessel: 18 And a clean person shall take hyssop, and dip it in the water, and sprinkle it upon the tent, and upon all the vessels, and upon the persons that were there, and	upon him that touched a bone, or one slain, or one dead, or a grave: 19 And the clean person shall sprinkle upon the unclean on the third day, and on the seventh day: and on the seventh day he shall purify himself, and wash his clothes, and bathe himself in water, and shall be clean at even.	2) All that was defiled out in the open c. To have the clean person sprinkle the unclean person on the 3rd & 7th days; also to have the unclean person wash himself & his clothes on the 7th day: A symbol of full & complete cleansing through the sacrifice & power of Christ

1. The unclean person was to mix some ashes from this heifer in a jar of water (v.17).
2. The unclean person was to secure the help of a friend who was clean (ceremonially, spiritually clean). The clean person was to take some hyssop and sprinkle the "cleansing water" upon anyone who had been defiled by coming in contact with death (v.18-19). Note that all who had been defiled by death, either within or without their homes, were to be cleansed.
3. The clean person was to sprinkle the unclean person on the third and seventh days. Then the unclean person was to wash himself and his clothes on the seventh day (v.19). The number seven was a symbol of full and complete cleansing through the sacrifice of Christ.

Thought 1. The only way to secure cleansing is through the sacrifice and power of Christ. No person can make himself acceptable to God. No person can sacrifice enough to cleanse himself, no matter what he does. Man can picture every sacrifice he knows and come to only one conclusion: there is no perfect sacrifice known to man. There is no perfect sacrifice any place in this world. Consequently, man is confronted with the most serious problem imaginable: his sacrifice can never be acceptable to a perfect God. The reason: man is imperfect and therefore cannot provide a perfect sacrifice to stand in his place before the perfect, holy God. Man's only hope is for God Himself to provide the perfect sacrifice who can stand as man's substitute, making him acceptable to God. This perfect sacrifice is Christ, who died for the sins of man. The only way to secure cleansing from sin is through the sacrifice of Christ. To become acceptable to God, a person must approach God through Christ and Christ alone. It is His sacrifice that atones for the sins of man, that satisfies the justice and judgment of God against sin.

"For this is my blood of the new testament, which is shed for many for the remission of sins" (Mt.26:28).

"Who gave himself for our sins, that he might deliver us from this present evil world, according to the will of God and our Father" (Gal.1:4).

"Christ hath redeemed us from the curse of the law, being made a curse for us: for it is written, Cursed is every one that hangeth on a tree" (Gal.3:13).

"In whom we have redemption through his blood, the forgiveness of sins, according to the riches of his grace" (Eph.1:7).

"Who gave himself for us, that he might redeem us from all iniquity, and purify unto himself a peculiar people, zealous of good works" (Tit.2:14).

"So Christ was once offered to bear the sins of many; and unto them that look for him shall he appear the second time without sin unto salvation" (Heb.9:28).

"Who his own self bare our sins in his own body on the tree, that we, being dead to sins, should live unto righteousness: by whose stripes ye were healed" (1 Pt.2:24).

"For Christ also hath once suffered for sins, the just for the unjust, that he might bring us to God, being put to death in the flesh, but quickened by the Spirit" (1 Pt.3:18).

"But if we walk in the light, as he is in the light, we have fellowship one with another, and the blood of Jesus Christ his Son cleanseth us from all sin" (1 Jn.1:7).

"And ye know that he was manifested to take away our sins; and in him is no sin" (1 Jn.3:5).

4 (19:20-22) **Warning, against Rejection—Defilement, Warning against—Uncleanness, Warning against—Rejection, Warning against—Rebellion, Warning against—Sin, Warning against**: the strong warning is reemphasized, stressed even more forcefully. The failure to be cleansed from defilement causes man to face the most serious consequences. Note the Scripture and outline:

OUTLINE	SCRIPTURE	SCRIPTURE	OUTLINE
4. The strong warning reemphasized a. The person who was unclean & refused to be cleansed: Was to be cut off from the community 1) Because he defiled the sanctuary 2) Because he had not been cleansed by the "cleansing water" b. The law of cleansing is a	20 But the man that shall be unclean, and shall not purify himself, that soul shall be cut off from among the congregation, because he hath defiled the sanctu- ary of the LORD: the water of separation hath not been sprinkled upon him; he is unclean. 21 And it shall be a perpet-	ual statute unto them, that he that sprinkleth the water of separation shall wash his clothes; and he that touch- eth the water of separation shall be unclean until even. 22 And whatsoever the unclean person toucheth shall be unclean; and the soul that toucheth it shall be unclean until even.	permanent law: A symbol that all need to be cleansed c. The people involved in handling the water: All were unclean & needed cleansing 1) The person who sprinkled it 2) Any person who touched it 3) Anyone & anything who became unclean by touching a defiled person or object

1. The person who was unclean and refused to be cleansed was to be cut off from the community of believers (v.20). There was a clear reason for this judgment:

⇒ because the person defiled the sanctuary of God's presence. His uncleanness contaminated or polluted the ground and atmosphere of God's presence. This could not be allowed, for God is holy, dwelling in perfect righteousness and purity. The ground of the sanctuary was holy ground, ground that had been set apart for the service and worship of God. No defiled person was ever to be allowed in the presence of the holy and perfect God.

⇒ because the person had not been cleansed by the "cleansing water." The person had deliberately chosen to remain defiled and unclean. Through carelessness, neglect, hardness of heart, or deliberate decision, the defiled person failed to be cleansed.

2. There was no other choice. The defiled and unclean person was to be condemned, cut off from the presence of God and from the community of believers. He was to be put *outside the camp*, not allowed to worship God nor to fellowship with God's people. He was "cut off," ostracized, separated, alienated from God and God's people. Note what else is reemphasized: the law of cleansing was to be a permanent law. Remember this was a symbol that every person needed to be cleansed by Christ (v.21).

3. All the people involved in handling the ritual were counted unclean and needed to be cleansed (v.21-22). This included...

- the person who sprinkled the cleansing water
- the person who touched the water of cleansing
- anyone and anything that became unclean by touching a defiled person (v.22)

Thought 1. The judgment of God is going to fall upon every unclean and defiled person. God is going to execute justice against all defilement and uncleanness. There will be no escape. The holiness of God will not be violated; the presence of God will not be contaminated. God could never allow this to happen. God will not allow pollution in His presence, no injustice or immorality, no defilement or uncleanness whatsoever. The defiled person will be judged if he refuses to be cleansed. This is the warning of God to every person who is unclean or defiled.

"For the Son of man shall come in the glory of his Father with his angels; and then he shall reward every man according to his works" (Mt.16:27).

"Because he hath appointed a day, in the which he will judge the world in righteousness by that man whom he hath ordained [Christ]; whereof he hath given assurance unto all men, in that he hath raised him from the dead" (Acts 17:31).

"And as it is appointed unto men once to die, but after this the judgment" (Heb.9:27).

"The Lord knoweth how to deliver the godly out of temptations, and to reserve the unjust unto the day of judgment to be punished" (2 Pt.2:9).

"But the heavens and the earth, which are now, by the same word are kept in store, reserved unto fire against the day of judgment and perdition of ungodly men" (2 Pt.3:7).

"Behold, the Lord cometh with ten thousands of his saints, To execute judgment upon all, and to convince all that are ungodly among them of all their ungodly deeds which they have ungodly committed, and of all their hard speeches which ungodly sinners have spoken against him" (Jude 14-15).

"And I saw the dead, small and great, stand before God; and the books were opened: and another book was opened, which is the book of life: and the dead were judged out of those things which were written in the books, according to their works" (Rev.20:12).

"Before the Lord: for he cometh, for he cometh to judge the earth: he shall judge the world with righteousness, and the people with his truth" (Ps.96:13).

TYPES, SYMBOLS, AND PICTURES
(Numbers 19:1-22)

Historical Term	Type or Picture (Scriptural Basis for Each)	Life Application for Today's Believer	Biblical Application
Offering of the Red Heifer (A Red Female Cow) Num.19:1-22	*The red heifer symbolized the cleansing power of Jesus Christ, the power of His sacrifice to cleanse from the defilement of sin and death.* *The offering of the red heifer was instituted by God for a good reason: it met a dire need of the people. If a person sinned while the Israelites were marching along, Moses could not stop the march in its tracks, put up the Tabernacle, then go through the ritual of approaching God for forgiveness through the substitute sacrifice. What then was a person to do if he sinned while marching along the way? The answer lay in the offering of the red heifer: they would take a small amount of ashes from the red heifer and mix those ashes with fresh water. Then they would take some hyssop, dip it in the mixed water, and sprinkle the person who had sinned. Keep in mind that this is a picture of the cleansing, purifying power of Christ's sacrifice* **"This *is* the ordinance of the law which the LORD hath commanded, saying, Speak unto the children of Israel, that they bring thee a red heifer without spot, wherein *is* no blemish, *and* upon which never came yoke" (Num.19:2).**	As the believer walks throughout life—marching to the promised land of God—he becomes contaminated by the pollutions of this world. He must be cleansed from the pollution of sin. Cleansing is through the sacrifice of Jesus Christ. Jesus Christ cleanses us from all sin.	***"In whom we have redemption through his blood, the forgiveness of sins, according to the riches of his grace" (Eph. 1:7).*** ***"And such were some of you: but ye are washed, but ye are sanctified, but ye are justified in the name of the Lord Jesus, and by the Spirit of our God" (1 Cor. 6:11).*** ***"If we confess our sins, he is faithful and just to forgive us our sins, and to cleanse us from all unrighteousness" (1 Jn. 1:9).***
The Red Heifer Was to Have No Defect or Blemish Num.19:1-10, esp. v.2	*The perfect red heifer was a symbol of the perfection of Jesus Christ.* **"This is the ordinance of the law which the Lord hath commanded, saying, Speak unto the children of Israel, that they bring thee a red heifer without spot, wherein is no blemish, and upon which never came yoke" (Num. 19:2).**	⇒ Jesus Christ was the sinless, perfect sacrifice offered up to God.	***"For he hath made him to be sin for us, who knew no sin; that we might be made the righteousness of God in him" (2 Cor.5:21).*** ***"For it became him, for whom are all things, and by whom are all things, in bringing many sons unto glory, to make the captain of their salvation perfect through sufferings" (Heb. 2:10).*** ***"For we have not an high priest which cannot be touched with the feeling of***

Historical Term	Type or Picture (Scriptural Basis for Each)	Life Application for Today's Believer	Biblical Application
			our infirmities; but was in all points tempted like as we are, yet without sin" (Heb. 4:15). *"And being made perfect, he became the author of eternal salvation unto all them that obey him" (Heb. 5:9).* *"For the law maketh men high priests which have infirmity; but the word of the oath, which was since the law, maketh the Son, who is consecrated for evermore" (Heb.7:28).* *"For such an high priest became us, who is holy, harmless, undefiled, separate from sinners, and made higher than the heavens" (Heb.7:26).*
An Unused Red Heifer Num.19:1-10, esp. v.2	*This was a symbol of Christ being free to choose or voluntarily sacrifice Himself for the sins of the human race. The red heifer was to be unused, that is, an animal that had never been worked with a yoke around its neck. it had always been a free animal.* **"This *is* the ordinance of the law which the LORD hath commanded, saying, Speak unto the children of Israel, that they bring thee a red heifer without spot, wherein *is* no blemish, *and* upon which never came yoke" (Num. 19:2).**	Jesus Christ willingly, voluntarily died for us. This He did in obedience to God. He obeyed God perfectly. He ignored and despised the shame of the cross in order to finish the race of perfect obedience to God. And because He was perfectly obedient, He has blazed the path of perfect righteousness, of the very faith that makes us acceptable to God. The Christian race exists because Jesus Christ disciplined Himself; He obeyed God perfectly, even to the extent of dying for us. This He willingly did, and because He did, He is the supreme example for us. We should endure in our belief and obedience to God no matter the cost or price we have to pay, even if it means martyrdom.	*"For the Son of man is come to seek and to save that which was lost" (Lk. 19:10).* *"This is a faithful saying, and worthy of all acceptation, that Christ Jesus came into the world to save sinners; of whom I am chief" (1 Tim.1:15).* *"Wherefore when he cometh into the world, he saith, Sacrifice and offering thou wouldest not, but a body hast thou prepared me: In burnt offerings and sacrifices for sin thou hast had no pleasure. Then said I, Lo, I come (in the volume of the book it is written of me,) to do thy will, O God. Above when he said, Sacrifice and offering and burnt offerings and offering for sin thou wouldest not, neither hadst pleasure therein; which are offered by the law; Then said he, Lo, I come to do thy will, O God. He taketh away the first, that he may establish the second. By the which will we are sanctified through the offering of the body of Jesus Christ once for all" (Heb. 10:5-10).* *"And ye know that he was manifested to take away our sins; and in him is no sin" (1 Jn.3:5).* *"For the zeal of thine house hath eaten me up; and the reproaches of them that reproached thee are fallen upon me" (Ps.69:9).*

Historical Term	Type or Picture (Scriptural Basis for Each)	Life Application for Today's Believer	Biblical Application
The Red Heifer Was to Be Put to Death Outside the Camp Num.19:1-10, esp. v.3	*This was a symbol of Christ being put to death outside the city gate.* **"And ye shall give her unto Eleazar the priest, that he may bring her forth without the camp, and *one* shall slay her before his face" (Num. 19:3).**	Under the Old Testament or covenant, the sacrificial animals were burned outside and away from the camp. This shows how perfectly Jesus Christ fulfilled the type and symbol of the Lamb of God. Jesus Christ was crucified outside the city of Jerusalem and away from the temple just as the animals suffered outside the camp. Jesus Christ was the Perfect Sacrifice, fulfilling the sacrificial type perfectly.	***"Wherefore Jesus also, that he might sanctify the people with his own blood, suffered without the gate" (Heb.13:12.).*** ***"For I delivered unto you first of all that which I also received, how that Christ died for our sins according to the scriptures" (1 Cor. 15:3).*** ***"And that he died for all, that they which live should not henceforth live unto themselves, but unto him which died for them, and rose again" (2 Cor. 5:15).*** ***"Who gave himself for our sins, that he might deliver us from this present evil world, according to the will of God and our Father" (Gal.1:4).*** ***"And walk in love, as Christ also hath loved us, and hath given himself for us an offering and a sacrifice to God for a sweet-smelling savour" (Eph. 5:2).*** ***"Who gave himself for us, that he might redeem us from all iniquity, and purify unto himself a peculiar people, zealous of good works" (Tit. 2:14).***
Some Blood of the Red Heifer Was to Be Sprinkled Seven Times at the Front of the Tabernacle Num.19:1-10, esp. v.4	*The number seven is a symbol of full and complete acceptance. The blood of the red heifer was being accepted by God as full and complete satisfaction for sin. Of course, this was a symbol that Christ's sacrifice was being offered to God as complete satisfaction for sin.* **"And Eleazar the priest shall take of her blood with his finger, and sprinkle of her blood directly before the tabernacle of the congregation seven times" (Num. 19:4).**	God accepts the sacrifice of Christ fully and completely. Our sins are fully and completely forgiven—all through Christ.	***"Him hath God exalted with his right hand to be a Prince and a Saviour, for to give repentance to Israel, and forgiveness of sins" (Acts.5:31).*** ***"And walk in love, as Christ also hath loved us, and hath given himself for us an offering and a sacrifice to God for a sweet-smelling [pleasing] savour" (Eph.5:2).*** ***For God so loved the world, that he gave his only begotten Son, that whosoever believeth in him should not perish, but have everlasting life. John 3:16***
The Red Heifer Was to Be Wholly Burned, All Its Parts Num.19:1-10, esp. v.5	*The burning of the entire heifer was a symbol of the extreme sufferings of Christ.* **"And *one* shall burn the heifer in his sight; her skin, and her flesh, and her blood, with her dung, shall he burn" (Num. 19:5).**	Words could never express what Christ experienced. Words are just totally inadequate. Using all the descriptive words in the world would be insufficient in describing the sufferings of Christ as using a syringe to drain an ocean.	***"And at the ninth hour Jesus cried with a loud voice, saying, Eloi, Eloi, lama sabachthani? which is, being interpreted, My God, my God, why hast thou forsaken me" (Mk.15:34).*** ***"And being in an agony he prayed more earnestly:***

Historical Term	Type or Picture (Scriptural Basis for Each)	Life Application for Today's Believer	Biblical Application
		1. There was the *mental and emotional agony*: the weight, pressure, anguish, sorrow, and excessive strain such as no man has ever experienced. 2. There was the *physical experience of death while being the Son of God.* 3. There was *the spiritual experience of death* while being the Son of Man (see note—Matthew 5:17-18; Deeper Study #3—Matthew 8:20; note—Romans 8:2-4).	***and his sweat was as it were great drops of blood falling down to the ground" (Lk.22:44).*** ***"I gave my back to the smiters, and my cheeks to them that plucked off the hair: I hid not my face from shame and spitting" (Is.50:6).*** ***"Though he were a Son, yet learned he obedience by the things which he suffered; and being made perfect, he became the author of eternal salvation unto all them that obey him" (Hebrews 5:8-9).*** ***"In due time Christ died for the ungodly" (Romans 5:6).*** ***"But he was wounded for our transgressions, he was bruised for our iniquities: the chastisement of our peace was upon him; and with his stripes we are healed" (Isaiah 53:5).***
The Priest Was to Burn Some Cedar Wood, Hyssop and Scarlet Wool with the Red Heifer Num.19:1-10, esp. v.6	*This was a picture of using everything [cedar wood, hyssop and scarlet wool] to intensify the purifying power of the offering. Note: All these materials were considered to have some cleansing elements or properties (cp. Lev.14:4).* **"And the priest shall take cedar wood, and hyssop, and scarlet, and cast *it* into the midst of the burning of the heifer" (Num. 19:6).**	A person is cleansed or made pure by the blood of Jesus Christ. The cleansing, purifying power to forgive sins is found in Him and Him alone.	***"In whom we have redemption through his blood, the forgiveness of sins, according to the riches of his grace" (Eph.1:7).*** ***"Wash me throughly from mine iniquity, and cleanse me from my sin....Purge me with hyssop, and I shall be clean: wash me, and I shall be whiter than snow" (Ps.51:2, 7).*** ***"Come now, and let us reason together, saith the Lord: though your sins be as scarlet, they shall be as white as snow; though they be red like crimson, they shall be as wool" (Is.1:18).***
Everyone Who Had Anything to Do with the Sacrifice Had to Cleanse Himself and His Clothes Num.19:1-10, esp. v.7-8	*This is a symbol that everyone, including priests, stands guilty before God and must be cleansed.* **"Then the priest shall wash his clothes, and he shall bathe his flesh in water, and afterward he shall come into the camp, and the priest shall be unclean until the even. And he that burneth her shall wash his clothes in water,**	The only way to secure cleansing is through the sacrifice and power of Christ. No person can make himself acceptable to God. No person can sacrifice enough to cleanse himself, no matter what he does. Man can picture every sacrifice he knows and come to only one conclusion: there is no perfect sacrifice known to man. There is no perfect sacrifice anyplace in this world. Consequently,	***"As it is written, There is none righteous, no, not one: There is none that understandeth, there is none that seeketh after God. They are all gone out of the way, they are together become unprofitable; there is none that doeth good, no, not one" (Ro.3:10-12).*** ***"For all have sinned, and come short of the glory of God"(Ro.3:23).*** ***"For this is my blood of***

Historical Term	Type or Picture (Scriptural Basis for Each)	Life Application for Today's Believer	Biblical Application
	and bathe his flesh in water, and shall be unclean until the even" (Num. 19:7-8).	man is confronted with the most serious problem imaginable: his sacrifice can never be acceptable to a *perfect* God. The reason: man is imperfect and therefore cannot provide a perfect sacrifice to stand in his place before the perfect, holy God. Man's only hope is for God Himself to provide the perfect sacrifice, a perfect sacrifice that can stand as man's substitute, making him acceptable to God. This perfect sacrifice is Christ, who died for the sins of man.	***the new testament, which is shed for many for the remission of sins" (Mt.26:28).*** ***"Who gave himself for our sins, that he might deliver us from this present evil world, according to the will of God and our Father" (Gal.1:4).*** ***"Christ hath redeemed us from the curse of the law, being made a curse for us: for it is written, Cursed is every one that hangeth on a tree" (Gal.3:13).*** ***"In whom we have redemption through his blood, the forgiveness of sins, according to the riches of his grace" (Eph.1:7).***
A Clean Person Was to Gather Up the Ashes of the Sacrifice and Keep Them In a Clean Place Outside the Camp Num.19:1-10, esp. v.9-10	*This is a symbol of Christ cleansing us from sin (v.9). The ashes were to be kept for future use, for mixing in the water of cleansing. Note that the man who gathered up the ashes was counted unclean, guilty. He, too, had to wash himself and his clothes (v.10).* **"And a man *that is* clean shall gather up the ashes of the heifer, and lay *them* up without the camp in a clean place, and it shall be kept for the congregation of the children of Israel for a water of separation: it *is* a purification for sin" (Num. 19:9).**	The only way to secure cleansing from sin is through the sacrifice of Christ. To become acceptable to God a person must approach God through Christ and Christ alone. It is His sacrifice that atones for the sins of man, that satisfies the justice and judgment of God against sin.	***"So Christ was once offered to bear the sins of many; and unto them that look for him shall he appear the second time without sin unto salvation" (Heb.9.28).*** ***"Who gave himself for us, that he might redeem us from all iniquity, and purify unto himself a peculiar people, zealous of good works" (Tit.2:14).*** ***"Who his own self bare our sins in his own body on the tree, that we, being dead to sins, should live unto righteousness: by whose stripes ye were healed" (1 Pt.2:24).*** ***"For Christ also hath once suffered for sins, the just for the unjust, that he might bring us to God, being put to death in the flesh, but quickened by the Spirit" (1 Pt.3:18).***
The Offering of the Red Heifer Was Established As a Permanent Law for Israel and for All Foreigners Among Them Num.19:1-10, esp. v.10	*By being established as a permanent law, this was a picture of the permanent, eternal sacrifice and cleansing power of Christ (v.10).* **"And he that gathereth the ashes of the heifer shall wash his clothes, and be unclean until the even: and it shall be unto the children of Israel, and unto the stranger that sojourneth among them, for a statute for ever" (Num. 19:10).**	Christ was once offered to bear the sins and judgment of many. Christ has taken our sins upon Himself. He has sacrificed Himself for our sins and borne our judgment for us. We no longer have to bear the judgment for our sins and imperfections. If we believe—truly trust Jesus Christ to bear our sins and judgment—then God counts our sins as having been borne by Christ. God counts us as being free from sin—as being perfect and acceptable to Him. Therefore, we never	***"Knowing that Christ being raised from the dead dieth no more; death hath no more dominion over him. For in that he died, he died unto sin once: but in that he liveth, he liveth unto God" (Ro.6:9-10).*** ***"So Christ was once offered to bear the sins of many; and unto them that look for him shall he appear the second time without sin unto salvation" (Heb.9:28).*** ***"Neither by the blood of goats and calves, but by his own blood he entered in***

Historical Term	Type or Picture (Scriptural Basis for Each)	Life Application for Today's Believer	Biblical Application
		have to be judged and condemned for sin. But note: this glorious salvation is not brought about in the lives of all people. A person has to believe and trust in the sacrifice of Jesus Christ. This is only reasonable: if a person does not believe in something, he does not allow it to work *for* him. But if he does believe, he does allow it to work *for* him. When we believe—really believe—then the sacrifice of Jesus Christ works *for* us. His sacrifice covers our sins and we become acceptable to God. We never have to face the judgment and condemnation for our sins.	***once into the holy place, having obtained eternal redemption for us. For if the blood of bulls and of goats, and the ashes of an heifer sprinkling the unclean, sanctifieth to the purifying of the flesh: How much more shall the blood of Christ, who through the eternal Spirit offered himself without spot to God, purge your conscience from dead works to serve the living God" (Heb.9:12-14).*** ***"For Christ also hath once suffered for sins, the just for the unjust, that he might bring us to God, being put to death in the flesh, but quickened by the Spirit" (1 Pt.3:18).***
Death Num.19:11-16	*Death is a type or symbol of uncleanness.* *Man is unclean just by being born and living in a corruptible world. Positionally—standing in the world as a human being—man is defiled. This is what is known as* positional defilement. *Positionally man sins; positionally man dies. Furthermore, man becomes even more defiled as he walks throughout life. Every time man sins, he defiles himself. But the basic cause of defilement is death itself. Death is the ultimate defilement, the ultimate enemy of life. Death takes man down into the grave to waste away and decay. Again, death is the ultimate, final defilement. This was the major focus of the red heifer offering: to cleanse man from all defilement, but in particular from the ultimate defilement of death.* **"Whosoever toucheth the dead body of any man that is dead, and purifieth not himself, defileth the tabernacle of the LORD; and that soul shall be cut off from Israel: because the water of separation was not sprinkled upon him, he shall be unclean; his uncleanness *is* yet upon him" (Num. 19:13).**	There are two strong lessons in this point: ⇒ We must understand that people are totally defiled. We are all sinful, short of God's glory, standing in need of cleansing. ⇒ We must guard against defilement and uncleanness. We must seek to stay clean and undefiled, seeking cleansing through the Lord Jesus Christ.	***"As it is written, There is none righteous, no, not one: There is none that understandeth, there is none that seeketh after God. They are all gone out of the way, they are together become unprofitable; there is none that doeth good, no, not one. Their throat is an open sepulchre; with their tongues they have used deceit; the poison of asps is under their lips: Whose mouth is full of cursing and bitterness: Their feet are swift to shed blood: Destruction and misery are in their ways: And the way of peace have they not known: There is no fear of God before their eyes" (Ro.3:10-18).*** ***"For all have sinned, and come short of the glory of God" (Ro.3:23).*** ***"If we say that we have no sin, we deceive ourselves, and the truth is not in us" (1 Jn.1:8).*** ***"In whom we have redemption through his blood, the forgiveness of sins, according to the riches of his grace" (Eph.1:7).*** ***"Unto him that loved us, and washed us from our sins in his own blood" (Rev.1:5).*** ***"For this is my blood of the new testament, which is shed for many for the remission of sins" (Mt.26:28).***

Historical Term	Type or Picture (Scriptural Basis for Each)	Life Application for Today's Believer	Biblical Application
The Unclean Person Had to Be Purified With the Cleansing Water On the Third and Seventh Days Num.19:11-16, esp. v.12	*This was a picture of the person being totally defiled and of the power of Christ to completely cleanse him. The unclean person was counted unclean for the full seven days, but he had to be sprinkled with the cleansing water on two different occasions.* **"He shall purify himself with it on the third day, and on the seventh day he shall be clean: but if he purify not himself the third day, then the seventh day he shall not be clean" (Num.19:12).**	⇒ There are two strong lessons in this point: 1. We must understand that people are totally defiled. We are all sinful, short of God's glory, standing in need of cleansing (Ro. 3:23). 2. We must guard against defilement and uncleanness. We must seek cleansing through the Lord Jesus Christ and seek to stay clean and undefiled.	***"As it is written, There is none righteous, no, not one: There is none that understandeth, there is none that seeketh after God. They are all gone out of the way, they are together become unprofitable; there is none that doeth good, no, not one. Their throat is an open sepulchre; with their tongues they have used deceit; the poison of asps is under their lips: Whose mouth is full of cursing and bitterness: Their feet are swift to shed blood: Destruction and misery are in their ways: And the way of peace have they not known: There is no fear of God before their eyes" (Ro.3:10-18).*** ***"For all have sinned, and come short of the glory of God" (Ro.3:23).*** ***"In whom we have redemption through his blood, the forgiveness of sins, according to the riches of his grace" (Eph.1:7).*** ***"Unto him that loved us, and washed us from our sins in his own blood" (Rev.1:5).***
A Person Who Had Been In Contact With Death Defiled the Lord's Tabernacle: He Was to Be Cut Off Num.19:11-16, esp. v.13	*This is a picture of eternal judgment, of being cut off and separated from God eternally if a person refuses to be cleansed by Christ. He was to be removed from the people, put outside the camp. He was unclean, defiled, and could not approach God nor fellowship with the people of God until he had been cleansed.* **"Whosoever toucheth the dead body of any man that is dead, and purifieth not himself, defileth the tabernacle of the LORD; and that soul shall be cut off from Israel: because the water of separation was not sprinkled upon him, he shall be unclean; his uncleanness *is* yet upon him" (Num.19:13)**	It is critical to note the words of Christ: "These shall go away into everlasting punishment" (Mt.25:46). The judgment is for eternity. There is no second chance; judgment is unchangeable.	***"And cast ye the unprofitable servant into outer darkness: there shall be weeping and gnashing of teeth" (Mt. 25:30).*** ***"Then said the king to the servants, Bind him hand and foot, and take him away, and cast him into outer darkness; there shall be weeping and gnashing of teeth" (Mt. 22:13; cp. Mt.25:30).*** ***"Then shall he say also unto them on the left hand, Depart from me, ye cursed, into everlasting fire, prepared for the devil and his angels" (Mt.25:41).*** ***"And the devil that deceived them was cast into the lake of fire and brimstone, where the beast and the false prophet are, and shall be tormented day and night for ever and ever. And I saw the dead, small and great, stand before God; and the books were opened: and another book was opened,***

Historical Term	Type or Picture (Scriptural Basis for Each)	Life Application for Today's Believer	Biblical Application
			which is the book of life: and the dead were judged out of those things which were written in the books, according to their works. And the sea gave up the dead which were in it; and death and hell delivered up the dead which were in them: and they were judged every man according to their works. And death and hell were cast into the lake of fire. This is the second death. And whosoever was not found written in the book of life was cast into the lake of fire" (Rev.20:10-15; cp. Mt.25:41).

F. Event 6—the Last Year of Israel in the Wilderness: Five Sad Events, 20:1-29

1. The sad death of Miriam
- a. In the first month (early spring)
- b. In the Desert of Zin, at Kadesh

2. The sad, continued grumbling of the people over having no food & no water
- a. The confrontation: Gathered to oppose Moses & Aaron
  - 1) Blamed God: Shouted they would have preferred to die with their brothers under God's judgment than suffer in the wilderness
  - 2) Rioted & blamed Moses
    - For bringing them into this wilderness where they & their livestock were facing death from no water
    - For leading them out of Egypt, away from the land of plenty—taking them to this terrible place with no affluence & no water
- b. The response of Moses & Aaron
  - 1) They went to the Tabernacle & fell face down
  - 2) The glory of the LORD appeared to them

3. The sad, tragic failure & sin of Moses
- a. The clear instructions of the LORD
  - 1) To take the staff & gather the people together
  - 2) To speak to the rock that God identified as being the source of water
  - 3) The result: Water would flow
- b. The response of Moses
  - 1) Obeyed God: Took the staff & gathered the people together in front of the rock
  - 2) Disobeyed God:
    - By speaking to the people & not the rock
    - By not giving God the full credit & honor: "Must 'we' bring you water?"
    - By striking the rock (twice) instead of speaking to it as commanded: He failed to trust God's Word
- c. The response of the Lord
  - 1) He gave water from the rock
  - 2) He charged Moses & Aaron
    - With failing to trust Him
    - With not honoring Him as holy before the people
  - 3) He chastised Moses: Would not be allowed to enter the promised land
- d. The naming of the place: Meribah, meaning a place of strife, arguing, or grumbling

4. The sad, arrogant resistance of Edom
- a. The appeal to the king of Edom for safe passage through his land
  - 1) Addressed Edom as Israel's brother (through Esau)
  - 2) Mentioned the predicament & hardships that Israel had suffered under Egyptian slavery
  - 3) Acknowledged that the LORD had delivered Israel
  - 4) Stated their present location
  - 5) Requested permission to pass through his country
  - 6) Promised & gave assurance
    - That they would not damage any of the land nor forage any of the crops
    - That they would travel only along the king's highway, that they would not veer off any whatsoever
- b. The answer or response of the king: Rejection—a hostile, blunt refusal & a rash threat of war
- c. The counter-request & assurances
  - 1) Would travel only the main road
  - 2) Would pay for any water used
  - 3) Had no hidden motive: No plan to conquer Edom
- d. The absolute rejection of Edom & the abrupt show of force
- e. The backing off of Israel & the march to Mount Hor

Then came the children of
Israel, even the whole congregation, into the desert of
Zin in the first month: and
the people abode in Kadesh;
and Miriam died there, and
was buried there.
2 And there was no water for
the congregation: and they
gathered themselves together
against Moses and against
Aaron.
3 And the people chode with
Moses, and spake, saying,
Would God that we had died
when our brethren died
before the LORD!
4 And why have ye brought
up the congregation of the
LORD into this wilderness,
that we and our cattle should
die there?
5 And wherefore have ye
made us to come up out of
Egypt, to bring us in unto
this evil place? it is no place
of seed, or of figs, or of
vines, or of pomegranates;
neither is there any water to
drink.
6 And Moses and Aaron
went from the presence of
the assembly unto the door
of the tabernacle of the congregation, and they fell upon
their faces: and the glory of
the LORD appeared unto
them.
7 And the LORD spake unto
Moses, saying,
8 Take the rod, and gather
thou the assembly together,
thou, and Aaron thy brother,
and speak ye unto the rock
before their eyes; and it shall
give forth his water, and thou
shalt bring forth to them
water out of the rock: so thou
shalt give the congregation
and their beasts drink.
9 And Moses took the rod
from before the LORD, as he
commanded him.
10 And Moses and Aaron
gathered the congregation
together before the rock, and
he said unto them, Hear now,
ye rebels; must we fetch you
water out of this rock?
11 And Moses lifted up his
hand, and with his rod he
smote the rock twice: and the
water came out abundantly,
and the congregation drank,
and their beasts also.
12 And the LORD spake unto
Moses and Aaron, Because
ye believed me not, to sanctify me in the eyes of the
children of Israel, therefore
ye shall not bring this congregation into the land which
I have given them.
13 This is the water of
Meribah; because the children of Israel strove with the
LORD, and he was sanctified
in them.
14 And Moses sent messen-
gers from Kadesh unto the
king of Edom, Thus saith thy
brother Israel, Thou knowest
all the travail that hath
befallen us:
15 How our fathers went
down into Egypt, and we
have dwelt in Egypt a long
time; and the Egyptians
vexed us, and our fathers:
16 And when we cried unto
the LORD, he heard our
voice, and sent an angel, and
hath brought us forth out of
Egypt: and, behold, we are in
Kadesh, a city in the uttermost of thy border:
17 Let us pass, I pray thee,
through thy country: we will
not pass through the fields,
or through the vineyards,
neither will we drink of
the water of the wells: we
will go by the king's high
way, we will not turn to the
right hand nor to the left,
until we have passed thy
borders.
18 And Edom said unto
him, Thou shalt not pass by
me, lest I come out against
thee with the sword.
19 And the children of
Israel said unto him, We will
go by the high way: and if I
and my cattle drink of thy
water, then I will pay for it: I
will only, without doing any
thing else, go through on my
feet.
20 And he said, Thou shalt
not go through. And Edom
came out against him with
much people, and with a
strong hand.
21 Thus Edom refused to
give Israel passage through
his border: wherefore Israel
turned away from him.
22 And the children of
Israel, even the whole congregation, journeyed from

5. The sad, touching death of Aaron a. The LORD Himself informed Moses & Aaron of Aaron's inpending death 1) He was to be "gathered to his people": A picture of joining former believers in the presence of God 2) He would not enter the promised land: Because he & Moses had disobeyed God 3) He & his son Eleazar & Moses were to climb Mt. Hor 4) Moses was to transfer the power of the High Priest from Aaron to Eleazar:	Kadesh, and came unto mount Hor. 23 And the LORD spake unto Moses and Aaron in mount Hor, by the coast of the land of Edom, saying, 24 Aaron shall be gathered unto his people: for he shall not enter into the land which I have given unto the children of Israel, because ye rebelled against my word at the water of Meribah. 25 Take Aaron and Eleazar his son, and bring them up unto mount Hor: 26 And strip Aaron of his garments, and put them upon Eleazar his son: and Aaron	shall be gathered unto his people, and shall die there. 27 And Moses did as the LORD commanded: and they went up into mount Hor in the sight of all the congregation. 28 And Moses stripped Aaron of his garments, and put them upon Eleazar his son; and Aaron died there in the top of the mount: and Moses and Eleazar came down from the mount. 29 And when all the congregation saw that Aaron was dead, they mourned for Aaron thirty days, even all the house of Israel.	Symbolized by putting Aaron's garments on Eleazar b. The obedience of Moses 1) He led the two priests up Mt. Hor 2) He transferred the power of the High Priest from Aaron to Eleazar c. The death of Aaron on top of Mt. Hor: Obviously buried by Moses & Eleazar d. The mourning of Israel for Aaron: Thirty days

DIVISION III

THE FORTY LONG YEARS OF WILDERNESS WANDERINGS: A PICTURE OF THE BELIEVER'S PILGRIMAGE THROUGH THIS WORLD AS HE PREPARES TO ENTER THE PROMISED LAND 15:1-25:18

F. Event 6—the Last Year of Israel in the Wilderness: Five Sad Events: 20:1-29

(20:1-29) **Introduction—Unhappiness, Caused by—Sad - Sadness, Caused by**: unhappy, sad events are a common occurrence. The daily news media are filled with such reports. If the truth were known, many people are so depressed, downcast, and heartsick that the pain is almost unbearable. They are hurting due to the grief of some sad, unhappy experience—an experience so intense—they can hardly go on. The unfortunate experience may be caused...

- by the death of a loved one
- by unfaithfulness or adultery
- by being abandoned or forsaken
- by the news of some serious disease
- by suffering a critical accident
- by losing one's job
- by having one's money stolen or lost
- by going bankrupt
- by losing one's closest and dearest friend
- by sensing no purpose, significance, or meaning in life
- by suffering some deep depression or discouragement
- by not securing an expected promotion or raise
- by suffering some catastrophic holocaust

It is impossible to walk through life without suffering sad, unhappy experiences. We all suffer the most sad experiences known to man: severe diseases and sicknesses and then eventually death. None of these are escaped by any of us. But there is glorious news: in the midst of the deepest moments of sadness and unhappiness, God promises deliverance. There is victory and triumph over all the enemies that attempt to sap the life out of us. This is the thrust of this particular chapter of Holy Scripture. Five sad, unhappy events take place in the life of Israel. And note: all five unhappy events take place within the span of one year. This is Israel's fortieth year in the wilderness. During the last year, five of the saddest experiences that could happen to a nation of people took place in the life of the Israelites. This is the subject of this present Scripture.
Event 6—the Last Year of Israel in the Wilderness: Five Sad Events, 20:1-29

1. The sad death of Miriam (v.1).
2. The sad, continued grumbling of the people over no food and no water (v.2-6).
3. The sad, tragic failure and sin of Moses (v.7-13).
4. The sad, arrogant resistance of Edom (v.14-22).
5. The sad, touching death of Aaron (v.23-29).

1 (20:1) **Death, of Miriam—Miriam, Death of**: there was the sad death of Miriam. Remember, Miriam was the sister of Moses and Aaron. She was the leader among the women of the nation. Three facts show us this:

⇒ First, Miriam was the person who led all the women in singing praise to God after their great deliverance from Egyptian slavery.

"And Miriam the prophetess, the sister of Aaron, took a timbrel in her hand; and all the women went out after her with timbrels and with dances. And Miriam answered them, Sing ye to the LORD, for

he hath triumphed gloriously; the horse and his rider hath he thrown into the sea" (Ex.15:20-21).

⇒ The Lord Himself identifies Miriam as being a leader right alongside Moses and Aaron.

"For I brought thee up out of the land of Egypt, and redeemed thee out of the house of servants; and I sent before thee Moses, Aaron, and Miriam" (Mic.6:4).

⇒ Miriam took the lead in challenging the leadership and authority of Moses, attempting to secure some of the authority for herself and her older brother Aaron.

"And Miriam and Aaron spake against Moses because of the Ethiopian woman whom he had married: for he had married an Ethiopian woman. And they said, Hath the Lord indeed spoken only by Moses? hath he not spoken also by us? And the Lord heard it" (Num.12:1-2).

It was this rebellion against God and His appointed minister that kept Miriam from ever entering the promised land. This is the reason she was now dying out in the wilderness or desert. She died in the wilderness and was buried in the wilderness, not in the promised land of God. Note when she died: in the first month, which was early spring out in the desert of Zin, at Kadesh. The year is not given in this verse, but we know from other passages that it was in the fortieth year after the Exodus (cp. Num.20:22-29 with Num.33:38). Remember that the wilderness wanderings or desert journeys lasted for forty years. This means that most of the first generation of Israelites had already died off, as dictated by God's judgment (see outline and note—Num.14:26-39 for more discussion). The new generation was on the verge of being ready to enter the promised land. But not Miriam. Because of her rebellion against God and His dear servant, she died and was buried in the sands of the desert wilderness. She was not allowed to enter the promised land.

OUTLINE	SCRIPTURE
1. The sad death of Miriam a. In the first month (early spring) b. In the Desert of Zin, at Kadesh	Then came the children of Israel, even the whole congregation, into the desert of Zin in the first month: and the people abode in Kadesh; and Miriam died there, and was buried there.

Thought 1. The enemies of life conquered Miriam, instead of her conquering them. She gave in to the enemy of grumbling and unbelief to the point of actually rebelling against God's dear servant. Because of unbelief and rebellion, she never entered the spiritual rest and conquest of the promised land. She never received the inheritance of God's rest and victory over the enemies of life. She never received an inheritance in the promised land.

Grumbling, unbelief, and rebellion will keep any of us out of the promised land. Only God can give us victory over the enemies of life, for only He has the power to conquer and triumph. If we allow the enemy of unbelief and rebellion to take hold of our hearts, then we will be as Miriam: dying out in the wilderness and desert of this world. We will be doomed, never allowed to enter the promised land of spiritual rest and victory.

"Take heed, brethren, lest there be in any of you an evil heart of unbelief, in departing from the living God. But exhort one another daily, while it is called To day; lest any of you be hardened through the deceitfulness of sin" (Heb.3:12-13).

"Let us therefore fear, lest, a promise being left us of entering into his rest, any of you should seem to come short of it. For unto us was the gospel preached, as well as unto them: but the word preached did not profit them, not being mixed with faith in them that heard it. For we which have believed do enter into rest, as he said, As I have sworn in my wrath, if they shall enter into my rest" (Heb.4:1-3).

"Let us labour therefore to enter into that rest, lest any man fall after the same example of unbelief" (Heb.4:11).

"I will therefore put you in remembrance, though ye once knew this, how that the Lord, having saved the people out of the land of Egypt, afterward destroyed them that believed not" (Jude 5).

"Return unto thy rest, O my soul; for the Lord hath dealt bountifully with thee" (Ps.116:7).

"To whom he said, This is the rest wherewith ye may cause the weary to rest; and this is the refreshing: yet they would not hear" (Is.28:12).

"For thus saith the Lord God, the Holy One of Israel; In returning and rest shall ye be saved; in quietness and in confidence shall be your strength: and ye would not" (Is.30:15).

2 (20:2-6) **Complaining—Grumbling—Opposition, Against God's Servant—Unbelief—Israel, Sins of, Complaining and Grumbling—Water, Grumbling Over**: there was the sad, continued grumbling of the people over no food and no water. This was a clear picture of how children follow in the footsteps of their parents. On several occasions the parents had grumbled over inadequate food and water supplies (see outline and notes Ex.15:22-27; Ex.16:1-36; Ex.17:1-7; Num.11:1-35; Num.21:4-9). They had demonstrated little faith in God and His gracious provision. Their unbelief cut the heart of God, causing great pain for Him, for He loved them dearly. They allowed a seed of unbelief, stubbornness, resistance, and hardness of heart to take root against God. It was this unbelief that kept the first generation—the parents—out of the promised land. It was this unbelief that doomed them to die out in the desert wilderness. Now the same threat of unbelief was seen in the children. They were walking in the footsteps of their parents, failing to trust the promise of God—that He would provide the necessities of life as they marched to the promised land. Note the Scripture and outline:

OUTLINE	SCRIPTURE	SCRIPTURE	OUTLINE
2. The sad, continued grumbling of the people over having no food & no water a. The confrontation: Gathered to oppose Moses & Aaron 1) Blamed God: Shouted they would have preferred to die with their brothers under God's judgment than suffer in the wilderness 2) Rioted & blamed Moses • For bringing them into this wilderness where they & their livestock were facing death from no water	2 And there was no water for the congregation: and they gathered themselves together against Moses and against Aaron. 3 And the people chode with Moses, and spake, saying, Would God that we had died when our brethren died before the LORD! 4 And why have ye brought up the congregation of the LORD into this wilderness, that we and our cattle should die there?	5 And wherefore have ye made us to come up out of Egypt, to bring us in unto this evil place? it is no place of seed, or of figs, or of vines, or of pomegranates; neither is there any water to drink. 6 And Moses and Aaron went from the presence of the assembly unto the door of the tabernacle of the congregation, and they fell upon their faces: and the glory of the LORD appeared unto them.	• For leading them out of Egypt, away from the land of plenty—taking them to this terrible place with no affluence & no water b. The response of Moses & Aaron 1) They went to the Tabernacle & fell face down 2) The glory of the LORD appeared to them

1. Note the confrontation: the people gathered in opposition to Moses and Aaron, arguing against Moses (v.2-5). The younger generation of believers blamed God for not having adequate water and food supplies. They shouted out against God, they would have preferred to die with their brothers under God's judgment than to suffer in the wilderness (v.3). But they were not only accusing God of failing them; they also attacked Moses. They blamed Moses for bringing them into the wilderness where they and their livestock were facing death from lack of water. They blamed him for taking them out of Egypt, the land of plenty, where they had all the delicious luxuries they ever wanted. They blamed Moses for taking them out of the wonderful land of Egypt to this terrible place with no luxuries and no water (v.4-5).
2. Note the response of Moses and Aaron (v.6): they went to the Tabernacle and fell face down before the Lord. As always, the Lord met their need. The glory of the Lord appeared to them.

Thought 1. Grumbling against God and against His dear servant is a terrible sin. Grumbling reveals a heart of unbelief, a distrust of God. Grumbling stands up in the face of God and declares: "I do not like what is happening to me in life. Not enough good things are happening. I am not getting enough good breaks nor enough of the good things in life. God's provision to me is too meager, His supplies too few. I do not have enough money, food, clothing, housing, property, recognition, esteem, honor, or position."

Not trusting God and His provision and care for us arouses grumbling and unbelief. It was grumbling and unbelief that kept God's people from entering the promised land. A believer never learns to walk victoriously through life as long as he grumbles and fails to trust God. He never conquers the pitfalls and enemies of this life. He never learns to rest and trust in the provision of God. He never has fellowship and communion with God, never knows God personally and intimately, never knows what it is to be carried along and sustained by God day by day. Unbelief and grumbling keep a person out of the promised land.

"Jesus therefore answered and said unto them, Murmur not among yourselves" (Jn.6:43).

"Neither murmur ye, as some of them also murmured, and were destroyed of the destroyer" (1 Cor.10:10).

"Do all things without murmurings and disputings" (Ph.2:14).

"Take heed, brethren, lest there be in any of you an evil heart of unbelief, in departing from the living God" (Heb.3:12).

"Let us labour therefore to enter into that rest, lest any man fall after the same example of unbelief" (Heb.4:11).

"I will therefore put you in remembrance, though ye once knew this, how that the Lord, having saved the people out of the land of Egypt, afterward destroyed them that believed not" (Jude 5).

"The foolishness of man perverteth his way: and his heart fretteth against the Lord" (Pr.19:3).

3 (20:7-13) **Moses, Sin of—Believers, Failure of—Sin, Example of, Moses**: there was the sad, tragic failure and sin of Moses. What happened next breaks the heart of the reader who has truly followed the life of Moses through Exodus, Leviticus, and now Numbers. This dear servant of God finally exploded. In utter frustration and anger, he struck out against the people. For the first time in his ministry, he committed a terrible, serious offense against God. He disobeyed God, failing to trust Him. He did not honor God before the people, did not give God the full credit and honor for meeting their needs. For this failure, the heart of this dear servant was crushed. He had failed to follow the Lord who had loved and cared for him through all the years, looking after his every need. Consequently, he lost that which he most wanted and for which he had so long sought: the promised land. He lost the privilege of entering the promised land, of leading the people to victory over the enemies of life. He lost the privilege of experiencing the spiritual rest and conquest of the promised land, the spiritual rest that the promised land brings to the human soul. A crushing blow to the soul of one of the dearest servants of God who has ever lived! He would live with God eternally, but he had lost one of the privileges of ministry, the privilege of leading the people in their conquest of the promised land. He had lost the privilege of leading the people to victory over the enemies of life.

OUTLINE	SCRIPTURE	SCRIPTURE	OUTLINE
3. The sad, tragic failure & sin of Moses a. The clear instructions of the LORD 1) To take the staff & gather the people together 2) To speak to the rock that God identified as being the source of water 3) The result: Water would flow b. The response of Moses 1) Obeyed God: Took the staff & gathered the people together in front of the rock 2) Disobeyed God: • By speaking to the people & not the rock • By not giving God the full credit & honor: "Must	7 And the LORD spake unto Moses, saying, 8 Take the rod, and gather thou the assembly together, thou, and Aaron thy brother, and speak ye unto the rock before their eyes; and it shall give forth his water, and thou shalt bring forth to them water out of the rock: so thou shalt give the congregation and their beasts drink. 9 And Moses took the rod from before the LORD, as he commanded him. 10 And Moses and Aaron gathered the congregation together before the rock, and he said unto them, Hear now, ye rebels; must we fetch you water out of this	rock? 11 And Moses lifted up his hand, and with his rod he smote the rock twice: and the water came out abundantly, and the congregation drank, and their beasts also. 12 And the LORD spake unto Moses and Aaron, Because ye believed me not, to sanctify me in the eyes of the children of Israel, therefore ye shall not bring this congregation into the land which I have given them. 13 This is the water of Meribah; because the children of Israel strove with the LORD, and he was sanctified in them.	'we' bring you water?" • By striking the rock (twice) instead of speaking to it as commanded: He failed to trust God's Word c. The response of the Lord 1) He gave water from the rock 2) He charged Moses & Aaron • With failing to trust Him • With not honoring Him as holy before the people 3) He chastised Moses: Would not be allowed to enter the promised land d. The naming of the place: Meribah, meaning a place of strife, arguing or grumbling

1. The instructions of the Lord were clear, perfectly clear: Moses was to take his staff and gather the people together. He was then to speak to the rock that God identified as being the source of water, the source of living water—the water that would keep them alive. Note how this is a clear symbol of Jesus Christ, the source of living water. The Scripture also declares that Jesus Christ was that rock (Jn.7:38; 1 Cor.10:4). God made a phenomenal promise to Moses, a glorious event would happen: water would miraculously flow from the rock (v.8)

2. The response of Moses began in obedience: he took the staff from the Lord's presence in the Tabernacle and gathered the people just as God had commanded (v.9-10). But then the tragedy happened; he exploded and burst out against the people. He committed three gross errors of disobedience:

⇒ He spoke to the people and not to the rock (v.10). Remember that God had given clear instructions: Moses was to address the rock.

⇒ He did not give God the full credit and honor (v.10). He charged the people with being rebels and asked them, "Must 'we bring' you water out of this rock?" Note that he puts himself on a level with God, suggesting that it was he and God who were going to provide water for them. Standing there before the people, he failed to honor God as the only one who can meet man's need, in particular man's need for *living water*. Moses exalted himself, accepting some of the credit for the miracle that was about to happen.

⇒ He struck the rock (in anger) instead of merely speaking to it as commanded by God. And note: he struck the rock not once but twice. His anger and frustration had taken complete control of his spirit. This dear servant of God had lost control of his behavior (v.11).

3. The response of the Lord was immediate. Moreover, in light of God's love and justice, His response was to be expected (v.11-12). In love God caused water to gush out of the rock. But in justice and chastisement, God made two charges against Moses and Aaron:

⇒ That they had not trusted God, had not obeyed Him as He commanded. Instead of speaking to the rock, Moses had spoken to the people and had reacted in utter frustration and anger.

⇒ That they had not honored God as holy before the people, as the only person who was to be revered as the provision to meet man's needs.

God had no choice: His dear servant had to be chastised. Moses would not be allowed to enter the promised land (v.12). His rash behavior barred him from the glorious privilege of leading the people to victory and rest in the promised land of God.

4. Note that the place was given a name so that it would never be forgotten: Meribah, which means a place of strife, arguing, or grumbling (v.13).

Thought 1. There are two important lessons in this point.
1) God will not share His glory with any person.

"Hallowed be thy name....Give us this day our daily bread" (Mt.6:9, 11).

"Give unto the Lord the glory due unto his name; worship the Lord in the beauty of holiness" (Ps.29:2).

"O magnify the Lord with me, and let us exalt his name together" (Ps.34:3).

"Let them exalt him also in the congregation of the people, and praise him in the assembly of the elders" (Ps.107:32).

"O Lord, thou art my God; I will exalt thee, I will praise thy name; for thou hast done wonderful things; thy counsels of old are faithfulness and truth" (Is.25:1).

"I am the Lord: that is my name: and my glory will I not give to another, neither my praise" (Is.42:8).

2) God chastises the disobedient believer and servant of God. God never allows His dear people to continue in sin without correcting them. To do so would lead to disastrous results:
⇒ the growth of more and more sin
⇒ the misleading of others
⇒ the putting of stumbling blocks in the way of others
⇒ the damaging of our bodies through such things as overeating, drugs, accidents, and reckless living
⇒ the destruction of marriages and homes
⇒ the acts of lawlessness such as stealing and cheating
⇒ the more serious acts such as abuse and violence

On and on the list could go, but the point is well made: if a child of God is allowed to continue in sin without being corrected by God, then sin abounds. Sin grows and grows until it overflows, damaging people well beyond anything ever thought. God chastises the disobedient believer because God loves him. God wants to prevent him from harming himself and others.

"Every branch in me that beareth not fruit he taketh away: and every branch that beareth fruit, he purgeth it, that it may bring forth more fruit" (Jn.15:2).

"And ye have forgotten the exhortation which speaketh unto you as unto children, My son, despise not thou the chastening of the Lord, nor faint when thou art rebuked of him: For whom the Lord loveth he chasteneth, and scourgeth every son whom he receiveth" (Heb.12:5-6).

"Now no chastening for the present seemeth to be joyous, but grievous: nevertheless afterward it yieldeth the peaceable fruit of righteousness unto them which are exercised thereby. Wherefore lift up the hands which hang down, and the feeble knees; And make straight paths for your feet, lest that which is lame be turned out of the way; but let it rather be healed. Follow peace with all men, and holiness, without which no man shall see the Lord: Looking diligently lest any man fail of the grace of God; lest any root of bitterness springing up trouble you, and thereby many be defiled" (Heb.12:11-15).

"Thou shalt also consider in thine heart, that, as a man chasteneth his son, so the Lord thy God chasteneth thee" (Dt.8:5).

"Blessed is the man whom thou chastenest, O Lord, and teachest him out of thy law" (Ps.94:12).

"My son, despise not the chastening of the Lord; neither be weary of his correction: For whom the Lord loveth he correcteth; even as a father the son in whom he delighteth" (Pr.3:11-12).

4 (20:14-22) **Arrogance, Against God's People—Resistance, Against God's People—Edom**: there was the sad, arrogant resistance of Edom against God's people. The events that bring sadness and grief to the human heart continue through this Scripture. God's people were marching to the promised land. As they marched, they approached the border of one of the nations that surrounded the land of Canaan. That nation was the land of Edom. If Edom granted permission to pass through its land, the march to the promised land would be much shorter. Receiving the inheritance of the promised land—that for which the Israelites had hoped so long—would be fulfilled much quicker. God's people could enter the promised land much sooner if Edom would just grant the right of *safe passage* through their land. To secure this permission, Moses sent a diplomatic letter to the king of Edom. Note the Scripture and outline:

OUTLINE	SCRIPTURE	SCRIPTURE	OUTLINE
4. The sad, arrogant resistance of Edom a. The appeal to the king of Edom for safe passage through his land 1) Addressed Edom as Israel's brother (through Esau) 2) Mentioned the predicament & hardships that Israel had suffered under Egyptian slavery 3) Acknowledged that the LORD had delivered Israel 4) Stated their present location 5) Requested permission to pass through his country 6) Promised & gave assurance • That they would not damage any of the land	14 And Moses sent messengers from Kadesh unto the king of Edom, Thus saith thy brother Israel, Thou knowest all the travail that hath befallen us: 15 How our fathers went down into Egypt, and we have dwelt in Egypt a long time; and the Egyptians vexed us, and our fathers: 16 And when we cried unto the LORD, he heard our voice, and sent an angel, and hath brought us forth out of Egypt: and, behold, we are in Kadesh, a city in the uttermost of thy border: 17 Let us pass, I pray thee, through thy country: we will not pass through the fields, or through the vineyards, neither will we drink	of the water of the wells: we will go by the king's high way, we will not turn to the right hand nor to the left, until we have passed thy borders. 18 And Edom said unto him, Thou shalt not pass by me, lest I come out against thee with the sword. 19 And the children of Israel said unto him, We will go by the high way: and if I and my cattle drink of thy water, then I will pay for it: I will only, without doing any thing else, go through on my feet. 20 And he said, Thou shalt not go through. And Edom came out against him with much people, and with a strong hand. 21 Thus Edom refused to	nor forage any of the crops • That they would travel only along the king's highway, that they would not veer off any whatsoever b. The answer or response of the king: Rejection—a hostile, blunt refusal & a rash threat of war c. The counter-request & assurances 1) Would travel only the main road 2) Would pay for any water used 3) Had no hidden motive: No plan to conquer Edom d. The absolute rejection of Edom & the abrupt show of force e. The backing off of Israel &

OUTLINE	SCRIPTURE	SCRIPTURE	OUTLINE
the march to Mount Hor	give Israel passage through his border: wherefore Israel turned away from him. 22 And the children of	Israel, even the whole congregation, journeyed from Kadesh, and came unto mount Hor.	

1. Note the appeal to the king of Edom for *safe passage* through his land (v.14-17). Moses referred to Edom as Israel's brother. This was because Edom was a descendant of Esau, a brother of Jacob (Gen.27:30; 32:28; 36:1). Moses then mentioned the predicament and hardships that Israel had suffered under Egyptian slavery, acknowledging that the Lord Himself had been the One who delivered Israel (v.15-16). Note that Moses then gave the present location where the Israelites were camped (v.16). Finally Moses came to the heart of the matter: he requested permission to pass safely through the country of Edom (v.17). Moses did a wise thing: he promised and gave assurance...

- that Israel would not damage any of the land nor forage any of the crops
- that Israel would travel only along the king's highway, that they would not veer off the main highway any whatsoever (v.17)

2. The answer or response of the king was rejection: a hostile, blunt refusal and a rash threat of war (v.18).
3. However, Moses made the counter-request and did all he could to reassure Edom: Israel would travel only along the main road, and they would pay for any water used. He assured the king that the Israelites had no hidden motive, no plan to conquer Edom (v.19).
4. Note the absolute rejection of Edom and the abrupt show of force. The king mobilized his army and actually marched out against Israel. Scripture says that the army was large and powerful, a dangerous threat to God's people.
5. Israel immediately backed off and marched in order to escape the threat of Edom. God's people marched to Mount Hor (v.21-22).

Thought 1. God protects His people. We may have to go through trials and sufferings, threats and dangers throughout life, but God protects us and looks after us. He delivers us from all evil, even saving us from the most terrible evil, that of death. God will protect us and deliver us from every evil until we reach the promised land of heaven.

"There hath no temptation taken you but such as is common to man: but God is faithful, who will not suffer you to be tempted above that ye are able; but will with the temptation also make a way to escape, that ye may be able to bear it" (1 Cor.10:13).

"Who delivered us from so great a death, and doth deliver: in whom we trust that he will yet deliver us" (2 Cor.1:10).

"And the Lord shall deliver me from every evil work, and will preserve me unto his heavenly kingdom: to whom be glory for ever and ever. Amen" (2 Tim.4:18).

"Forasmuch then as the children are partakers of flesh and blood, he also himself likewise took part of the same; that through death he might destroy him that had the power of death, that is, the devil; And deliver them who through fear of death were all their lifetime subject to bondage" (Heb.2:14-15).

"The Lord knoweth how to deliver the godly out of temptations, and to reserve the unjust unto the day of judgment to be punished" (2 Pt.2:9).

"And he said, The Lord is my rock, and my fortress, and my deliverer" (2 Sam.22:2).

"Surely he shall deliver thee from the snare of the fowler, and from the noisome pestilence" (Ps.91:3).

"And even to your old age I am he; and even to hoar [gray] hairs will I carry you: I have made, and I will bear; even I will carry, and will deliver you" (Is.46:4).

"Be not afraid of their faces: for I am with thee to deliver thee, saith the Lord" (Jer.1:8).

Thought 2. James Phillip has an excellent application dealing with God's protection of the Israelites. Although long, the quotation is well worth quoting in full:

"He who touches God's people touches the apple of His eye. *God* could chastise His people,, judge them or discipline them, but woe betide any one *else* who did them harm and ill....This also is the grace of God: He would buffet and bruise them, sending judgment after judgment upon them, but He cared for them. He would never let them go, and He would allow no other to touch them with impunity. This is a phenomenon that has remained true throughout history to the present time. In our own day any nation that has done despite to God's covenant people has fallen into trouble.

"The following quotation serves to underline the miraculous preservation of God's people, against all the attempts of their enemies to destroy them:

'Four hundred years in Egypt; forty in the wilderness; a long dark and terrible period of warfare, backsliding and idolatry; a brief gleam of sunshine in the reigns of David and Solomon, a rapid downward career of apostacy, discord and sin, to the time of the Babylonian captivity; seventy years' exile, a long interval of darkness and oppression; the great rejection of the Lord of glory, the frightful sufferings and downfall of Jerusalem, and nineteen centuries of shame, oppression, dispersion, and above all, unbelief, blindness, hatred to God's dear Son, the only Saviour....

'Why do they exist after all the persecutions that they have endured? Pharaoh tried to drown them, but they could not be drowned; Nebuchadnezzar tried to burn them, but they could not be burned; Haman tried to hang them, but it was of no avail. All the nations of the earth have persecuted them, but here they are, and more numerous at the present day than ever before. Why? Because God calls them an everlasting nation.'[1]

"And we could well add to these words the horrors of the Holocaust and Nazi Germany's 'final solution,' to which the answer of God has been the establishment of modern Israel as a nation, after so many centuries of dispersion."[2]

5 (20:23-29) **Aaron, Death of—Priesthood, of Eleazar—Eleazar, Priesthood of—High Priest, Transferring Power of—Heaven, Hope of—"Gathered to His People," Meaning—Hope, for Heaven**: there was the sad, touching death of Aaron. Despite the sadness and grief of this experience, there is a preciousness and tenderness about what happened. Aaron did not die suddenly, with no indication that death was pending. To the contrary, the Lord Himself prepared His dear servant for departing this world. In tenderness and love, compassion and mercy, God reached down and strengthened His dear servant for the experience of death. Note exactly what happened:

OUTLINE	SCRIPTURE	SCRIPTURE	OUTLINE
5. The sad, touching death of Aaron a. The LORD Himself informed Moses & Aaron of Aaron's inpending death 1) He was to be "gathered to his people": A picture of joining former believers in the presence of God 2) He would not enter the promised land: Because he & Moses had disobeyed God 3) He & his son Eleazar & Moses were to climb Mt. Hor 4) Moses was to transfer the power of the High Priest from Aaron to Eleazar: Symbolized by putting	23 And the LORD spake unto Moses and Aaron in mount Hor, by the coast of the land of Edom, saying, 24 Aaron shall be gathered unto his people: for he shall not enter into the land which I have given unto the children of Israel, because ye rebelled against my word at the water of Meribah. 25 Take Aaron and Eleazar his son, and bring them up unto mount Hor: 26 And strip Aaron of his garments, and put them upon Eleazar his son: and Aaron shall be gathered unto	his people, and shall die there. 27 And Moses did as the LORD commanded: and they went up into mount Hor in the sight of all the congregation. 28 And Moses stripped Aaron of his garments, and put them upon Eleazar his son; and Aaron died there in the top of the mount: and Moses and Eleazar came down from the mount. 29 And when all the congregation saw that Aaron was dead, they mourned for Aaron thirty days, even all the house of Israel.	Aaron's garments on Eleazar b. The obedience of Moses 1) He led the two priests up Mt. Hor 2) He transferred the power of the High Priest from Aaron to Eleazar c. The death of Aaron on top of Mt. Hor: Obviously buried by Moses & Eleazar d. The mourning of Israel for Aaron: Thirty days

1. The Lord Himself informed both Moses and Aaron of Aaron's impending death (v.23-26). The scene is tender, and God is handling His two dear servants with the care of a father for his child. By this time Aaron was elderly, 123 years old (Num.33:39). He had walked with the Lord many years, sometimes failing rather seriously; nevertheless, he had remained true to the faith, persevered to the end. Despite his enormous failures, God still loved His dear servant, loved him deeply. The journey had been long and difficult and would have taken its toll upon anyone. This was proven by the fact that not a single adult who had started out on the journey from the slavery of Egypt was allowed to enter the promised land, not even Moses. Even he had committed a serious act of disobedience. Only two men who started out on the journey would enter the promised land: Caleb and Joshua. The point is this: Aaron had failed God and failed Him miserably on several occasions. But in every instance, Aaron had repented—genuinely repented—and God had forgiven him his sins. God had restored him and used him more mightily than ever before, using his position as High Priest to be the prime symbol of God's dear Son who was yet to come into the world. Because Aaron kept the faith and persevered to the end, God held him ever so dear to His heart. Therefore, when it came time to depart this world, his departure was to be a very special occasion between God and Aaron and his dear brother, Moses. Words are really inadequate to express the tenderness of the occasion, the face-to-face meeting between God and His dear servant Aaron. The first man ever chosen to fill the position of High Priest, the symbol of God's own beloved Son, was coming home. God reached out with all the tenderness, compassion, and mercy that filled His heart and prepared His dear servant for the glorious occasion.

a. Note what God said: Aaron was to be "gathered to his people." This is a picture of Aaron joining former believers in the presence of God (see outline and notes, point 3—Gen.25:7-10 for more discussion).

b. However, Aaron would not be allowed to enter the promised land because he and Moses had disobeyed God (v.24).

c. Aaron, his son Eleazar, and Moses were to climb Mount Hor (v.25). The purpose for this is seen in the next point.

d. Moses was to transfer the power of the High Priest from Aaron to Eleazar (v.26). The transfer of power was to be symbolized by putting Aaron's garments on Eleazar.

2. Note the obedience of Moses (v.27-28). Moses led the two priests up Mount Hor and did exactly what God had said: he transferred the power of the High Priest from Aaron to Eleazar. Remember that it was the special clothing that identified the High Priest. The clothing was the symbol of the official position of the High Priest (see outline and notes—Vol.2, Ex.29:29-30 for more discussion).

3. Aaron then died on top of Mount Hor and was obviously buried there by Moses and Eleazar the new High Priest, the son of Aaron (v.28).

4. Note that Israel mourned for Aaron for thirty days (v.29).

---

1 Adolph Saphir. *Christ and Israel.* (Grand Rapids, MI: Kregel Publications), p.165.

2 James Philip. *Mastering the Old Testament, Vol.4, Numbers*, p.226-227.

Thought 1. The death of God's dear people is very precious to God. The death of any believer is a tender moment to the Lord, for one of God's dear servants is coming home to be with Him. The believer must always remember this fact about death: to be absent from the body is to be present with the Lord. When a believer's moment comes to leave this earth, quicker than the eye can blink God transfers the believer right into His presence. Suddenly, immediately, the believer is face-to-face with the Father and His dear Son, the Lord Jesus Christ. The believer is perfected, living in perfect fellowship and communion with God, ready to begin his eternal worship and service for God. Eternal life—living face-to-face with God in heaven—is a living reality. This is the strong declaration of Scripture.

"For God so loved the world, that he gave his only begotten Son, that whosoever believeth in him should not perish, but have everlasting life" (Jn.3:1).

"Notwithstanding in this rejoice not, that the spirits are subject unto you; but rather rejoice, because your names are written in heaven" (Lk 10:20).

"He that believeth on the Son hath everlasting life" (Jn.3:36).

"In my Father's house are many mansions: if it were not so, I would have told you. I go to prepare a place for you. And if I go and prepare a place for you, I will come again, and receive you unto myself; that where I am, there ye may be also" (Jn.14:2-3).

"And this is life eternal, that they might know thee the only true God, and Jesus Christ, whom thou hast sent" (Jn.17:3).

"For we know that if our earthly house of this tabernacle were dissolved, we have a building of God, an house not made with hands, eternal in the heavens" (2 Cor.5:1).

"For our conversation [citizenship] is in heaven; from whence also we look for the Saviour, the Lord Jesus Christ: Who shall change our vile body, that it may be fashioned like unto his glorious body, according to the working whereby he is able even to subdue all things unto himself" (Ph.3:20-21).

"By faith Abraham, when he was called to go out into a place which he should after receive for an inheritance, obeyed; and he went out, not knowing whither he went. By faith he sojourned in the land of promise, as in a strange country, dwelling in tabernacles with Isaac and Jacob, the heirs with him of the same promise: For he looked for a city which hath foundations, whose builder and maker is God" (Heb.11:8-10).

"These all died in faith, not having received the promises, but having seen them afar off, and were persuaded of them, and embraced them, and confessed that they were strangers and pilgrims on the earth. For they that say such things declare plainly that they seek a country....But now they desire a better country, that is, an heavenly: wherefore God is not ashamed to be called their God: for he hath prepared for them a city" (Heb.11:13-14, 16).

"Blessed be the God and Father of our Lord Jesus Christ, which according to his abundant mercy hath begotten us again unto a lively hope by the resurrection of Jesus Christ from the dead, To an inheritance incorruptible, and undefiled, and that fadeth not away, reserved in heaven for you" (1 Pt. 1:3-4).

"Wherefore the rather, brethren, give diligence to make your calling and election sure: for if ye do these things, ye shall never fall: For so an entrance shall be ministered unto you abundantly into the everlasting kingdom of our Lord and Saviour Jesus Christ" (2 Pt.1:10-11).

"But the day of the Lord will come as a thief in the night; in the which the heavens shall pass away with a great noise, and the elements shall melt with fervent heat, the earth also and the works that are therein shall be burned up. Seeing then that all these things shall be dissolved, what manner of persons ought ye to be in all holy conversation and godliness, Looking for and hasting unto the coming of the day of God, wherein the heavens being on fire shall be dissolved, and the elements shall melt with fervent heat? Nevertheless we, according to his promise, look for new heavens and a new earth, wherein dwelleth righteousness" (2 Pt.3:10-13).

TYPES, SYMBOLS, AND PICTURES
(Numbers 20:1-29)

Historical Term	Type or Picture (Scriptural Basis for Each)	Life Application for Today's Believer	Biblical Application
Gathered to His People Num.20:23-29	*A picture of joining former believers in the presence of God.* **"Aaron shall be gathered unto his people: for he shall not enter into the land which I have given unto the children of Israel, because ye rebelled against my word at the water of Meribah" (Num.20:24)**	The death of God's dear people is very precious to God. The death of any believer is a tender moment to the Lord, for one of God's dear servants is coming home to be with Him. The believer must always remember this fact about death: to be absent from the body is to be present with the Lord. When a believer's moment	***"Precious in the sight of the LORD is the death of his saints" (Ps. 116:15).*** ***"For God so loved the world, that he gave his only begotten Son, that whosoever believeth in him should not perish, but have everlasting life" (Jn.3:16).*** ***"Notwithstanding in this rejoice not, that the spirits are subject unto you; but rather rejoice, because your***

Historical Term	Type or Picture (Scriptural Basis for Each)	Life Application for Today's Believer	Biblical Application
		comes to leave this earth, quicker than the eye can blink God transfers the believer right into His presence. Suddenly, immediately, the believer is face-to-face with the Father and His dear Son, the Lord Jesus Christ. The believer is perfected, living in perfect fellowship and communion with God, ready to begin his eternal worship and service for God. Eternal life—living face-to-face with God in heaven—is a living reality. This is the strong declaration of Scripture.	***names are written in heaven" (Lk.10:20).*** ***"He that believeth on the Son hath everlasting life" (Jn.3:36).*** ***"In my Father's house are many mansions: if it were not so, I would have told you. I go to prepare a place for you. And if I go and prepare a place for you, I will come again, and receive you unto myself; that where I am, there ye may be also" (Jn.14:2-3).*** ***"Blessed be the God and Father of our Lord Jesus Christ, which according to his abundant mercy hath begotten us again unto a lively hope by the resurrection of Jesus Christ from the dead, To an inheritance incorruptible, and undefiled, and that fadeth not away, reserved in heaven for you" (1 Pt. 1:3-4).***
Putting Aaron's Garments on Eleazar Num.20:23-29	*A symbol of transferring the power of the High Priest.* **"And Moses stripped Aaron of his garments, and put them upon Eleazar his son; and Aaron died there in the top of the mount: and Moses and Eleazar came down from the mount" (Num.20:28).**	Remember that it was the special clothing that identified the High Priest. The symbol of the High Priest's special call was his clothing. The purpose of his clothing was to stir dignity and honor for God's call and for the Priestly office. When the High Priest *put on* these holy garments, it lent dignity to his work. In the same sense, when the believer *puts on holy garments* it also lends dignity to his work for the Lord. ⇒ The believer is to put on Christ (Gal.3:27). ⇒ The believer is to put on the new man (Eph.4:24; Col.3:10). ⇒ The believer is to put on the armor of God, the whole armor (Eph.6:11). ⇒ The believer is to put on the armor of light (Ro.13:12). ⇒ The believer is to put on love (Col.3:14). ⇒ The believer is to put on compassion, kindness, humility, gentleness, and patience (Col. 3:12). ⇒ The believer is to put on incorruption and immortality (1 Cor.15:53-54).	***"For as many of you as have been baptized into Christ have put on Christ" (Gal.3:27).*** ***"And that ye put on the new man, which after God is created in righteousness and true holiness" (Eph.4:24).*** ***"And have put on the new man, which is renewed in knowledge after the image of him that created him" (Col. 3:10).*** ***"Put on the whole armour of God, that ye may be able to stand against the wiles of the devil" (Eph. 6:11).*** ***"The night is far spent, the day is at hand: let us therefore cast off the works of darkness, and let us put on the armour of light" (Ro.13:12).*** ***"And above all these things put on charity, which is the bond of perfectness" (Col. 3:14).*** ***"Put on therefore, as the elect of God, holy and beloved, bowels of mercies, kindness, humbleness of mind, meekness, longsuffering" (Col. 3:12).*** ***"For this corruptible must put on incorruption, and this mortal must put on immortality. So when this corruptible shall have put on incorruption, and this mortal shall have put on immortality, then shall be brought to pass the saying that is written, Death is swallowed up in victory" (1 Cor.15:53-54).***

1. The first military victory: A picture of making & fulfilling vows
- a. The Canaanite king of Arad[DS1] heard that the Israelites were traveling close by: He secretly attacked & captured some of them
- b. The reaction of Israel: A courageous determination & faith
  - 1) They made a vow: If God would give victory, they would destroy them
  - 2) They were heard by the LORD: He gave them victory
  - 3) They fulfilled their vow: Completely destroyed the savage, evil attackers (cp. Gen.15:16)[DS2]

2. The bronze snake: A picture of unbelief & of Christ the Savior
- a. The tragic situation
  - 1) Had to bypass Edom, a long distance out of the way
  - 2) Grew impatient & grumbled against God & Moses
    - Asked why they had led them out of Egypt into the desert to die: Had no bread & no water
    - Stated they detested the "worthless manna"
- b. The judgment, chastisement of the LORD
  - 1) He sent snakes among them
  - 2) Many died
- c. The confession & repentance of the people
  - 1) They confessed their sin
  - 2) They asked Moses, their mediator, to pray for God to take away the snakes
  - 3) Moses prayed for them
- d. The answer of the LORD
  - 1) To make a replica of a snake & hang it on a high pole
  - 2) The condition for deliverance: Must look at it to live
- e. The obedience of Moses: Hung a bronze snake on a pole
- f. The deliverance: Some looked, believed, & lived (a picture of deliverance by looking at Christ, Jn.3:14-15)

G. Event 7—the First Military Victories & the Bronze Snake: A Picture of Desperate Vows, of Christ the Savior, & of God's Protection & Victory, 21:1-35

And when king Arad
the Canaanite, which dwelt
in the south, heard tell
that Israel came by the
way of the spies; then he
fought against Israel, and
took some of them prisoners.
2 And Israel vowed a vow
unto the LORD, and said, If
thou wilt indeed deliver this
people into my hand, then I
will utterly destroy their
cities.
3 And the LORD hearkened to
the voice of Israel, and delivered
up the Canaanites; and
they utterly destroyed them
and their cities: and he called
the name of the place
Hormah.
4 And they journeyed from
mount Hor by the way of the
Red sea, to compass the land
of Edom: and the soul of the
people was much discouraged
because of the way.
5 And the people spake
against God, and against
Moses, Wherefore have ye
brought us up out of Egypt to
die in the wilderness? for
there is no bread, neither is
there any water; and our soul
loatheth this light bread.
6 And the LORD sent fiery
serpents among the people,
and they bit the people; and
much people of Israel died.
7 Therefore the people came
to Moses, and said, We have
sinned, for we have spoken
against the LORD, and
against thee; pray unto the
LORD, that he take away the
serpents from us. And Moses
prayed for the people.
8 And the LORD said unto
Moses, Make thee a fiery
serpent, and set it upon a
pole: and it shall come to
pass, that every one that is
bitten, when he looketh upon
it, shall live.
9 And Moses made a serpent
of brass, and put it upon a
pole, and it came to pass,
that if a serpent had bitten
any man, when he beheld the
serpent of brass, he lived.
10 And the children of
Israel set forward, and
pitched in Oboth.
11 And they journeyed from
Oboth, and pitched at Ije-abarim,
in the wilderness
which is before Moab,
toward the sunrising.
12 From thence they removed,
and pitched in the
valley of Zared.
13 From thence they removed,
and pitched on the
other side of Arnon, which is
in the wilderness that cometh
out of the coasts of the
Amorites: for Arnon is the
border of Moab, between
Moab and the Amorites.
14 Wherefore it is said in
the book of the wars of the
LORD, What he did in the
Red sea, and in the brooks of
Arnon,
15 And at the stream of the
brooks that goeth down to
the dwelling of Ar, and lieth
upon the border of Moab.
16 And from thence they
went to Beer: that is the well
whereof the LORD spake unto
Moses, Gather the people
together, and I will give
them water.
17 Then Israel sang this
song, Spring up, O well; sing
ye unto it:
18 The princes digged the
well, the nobles of the people
digged it, by the direction of
the lawgiver, with their
staves. And from the wilderness
they went to Mattanah:
19 And from Mattanah to
Nahaliel: and from Nahaliel
to Bamoth:
20 And from Bamoth in the
valley, that is in the country
of Moab, to the top of
Pisgah, which looketh
toward Jeshimon.
21 And Israel sent messengers
unto Sihon king of the
Amorites, saying,
22 Let me pass through thy
land: we will not turn into
the fields, or into the vineyards;
we will not drink of
the waters of the well: but
we will go along by the
king's high way, until we be
past thy borders.
23 And Sihon would not
suffer Israel to pass through
his border: but Sihon gathered
all his people together,
and went out against Israel

3. The march around Moab: A picture of progress—marching forth from place to place in a spirit of strong assurance
- a. They camped at Oboth (v.10)
- b. They camped at Iye Abarim
- c. They camped at the Zered Valley
- d. They camped alongside the Arnon River
  - 1) It flowed into Amorite territory
  - 2) It was the border between Moab & the Amorites
  - 3) It was a famous river: A place where significant battles had been fought
- e. They camped at the well Beer
  - 1) The well was dug in obedience to the LORD's instructions
  - 2) The gift of water led God's people to compose a song of joy, the "Song of the Well"
- f. They camped at Mattanah
- g. They camped at Nahaliel
- h. They camped at Bamoth
- i. They camped in Moab in the valley below Pisgah Peak—an excellent lookout to spy out the land

4. The military victory over Sihon, the king of the Amorites: A picture of God's protection when attacked by enemies
- a. The diplomatic, non-threatening request by Israel for safe passage
- b. The hostile attack against Israel at Jahaz[DS3]

c. The great victory of Israel
  1) Conquered all the Amorite territory
  2) Stopped at the Ammonite border: Because the border was fortified
  3) Captured & occupied all the cities of the Amorites: Included Heshbon[DS4] & its surrounding villages

d. The significance of the victory: A great victory over a celebrated king & army had been achieved
  - This is seen in the conquest of the great city of Heshbon: It was the capital of the Amorites
  - This is seen in the great king Sihon: He had formerly conquered Moab, a conquest so great that it had been celebrated by ancient poets

into the wilderness: and he came to Jahaz, and fought against Israel.
24 And Israel smote him with the edge of the sword, and possessed his land from Arnon unto Jabbok, even unto the children of Ammon: for the border of the children of Ammon was strong.
25 And Israel took all these cities: and Israel dwelt in all the cities of the Amorites, in Heshbon, and in all the villages thereof.
26 For Heshbon was the city of Sihon the king of the Amorites, who had fought against the former king of Moab, and taken all his land out of his hand, even unto Arnon.
27 Wherefore they that speak in proverbs say, Come into Heshbon, let the city of Sihon be built and prepared:
28 For there is a fire gone out of Heshbon, a flame from the city of Sihon: it hath consumed Ar of Moab, and the lords of the high places of Arnon.
29 Woe to thee, Moab! thou art undone, O people of Chemosh: he hath given his sons that escaped, and his daughters, into captivity unto Sihon king of the Amorites.
30 We have shot at them; Heshbon is perished even unto Dibon, and we have laid them waste even unto Nophah, which reacheth unto Medeba.
31 Thus Israel dwelt in the land of the Amorites.
32 And Moses sent to spy out Jaazer, and they took the villages thereof, and drove out the Amorites that were there.
33 And they turned and went up by the way of Bashan: and Og the king of Bashan went out against them, he, and all his people, to the battle at Edrei.
34 And the LORD said unto Moses, Fear him not: for I have delivered him into thy hand, and all his people, and his land; and thou shalt do to him as thou didst unto Sihon king of the Amorites, which dwelt at Heshbon.
35 So they smote him, and his sons, and all his people, until there was none left him alive: and they possessed his land.

  - Now Israel had proven stronger than the Amorites

e. The victory was even extended: Sent spies to Jazer & captured the towns, driving out the Amorite citizens

5. The military victory over Og, the king of Bashan: A picture of victory through the power of God (Gen.15:16; Ps.136:19)

a. The attack of Og: Marched his whole army against Israel at Edrei[DS5]

b. The strong assurance of victory from the LORD
  1) God's people were not to fear their enemy: Total & complete victory was assured
  2) God's people were to use the same pattern as before: Pursuit & total conquest

c. The obedience & victory
  1) They struck down all the wicked: Their "cup was full of sin," had "reached its full measure" (Gen.15:16)
  2) They occupied the land

DIVISION III

THE FORTY LONG YEARS OF WILDERNESS WANDERINGS: A PICTURE OF THE BELIEVER'S PILGRIMAGE THROUGH THIS WORLD AS HE PREPARES TO ENTER THE PROMISED LAND 15:1-25:18

G. Event 7—the First Military Victories and the Bronze Snake: A Picture of Desperate Vows, of Christ the Savior, and of God's Protection and Victory, 21:1-35

(21:1-35) **Introduction—Vows, Reasons for Making—Crises, List of**: when facing a desperate crisis, people often make vows. They promise to do certain things if God will only deliver them through the crisis. The crisis may be created by...

- war
- abuse
- financial problems
- disease
- accident
- unfaithfulness
- family problems
- unemployment
- unwanted pregnancy
- mismanagement by self or others
- drugs
- alcohol

Crises are serious matters to God. God expects us to fulfill the vows and promises we make during crises. But making vows is only one picture seen in the events of this Scripture. There are two others:

⇒ the picture of Christ the Savior
⇒ the picture of God's protection and victory against the enemies that attack His dear people as they march to the promised land

This is a passage that speaks to the deepest needs of man, a passage that needs to be heeded by us all. This is: *Event 7—the First Military Victories and the Bronze Snake: A Picture of Desperate Vows, of Christ the Savior, and of God's Protection and Victory*, 21:1-35.

1. The first military victory: a picture of making and fulfilling vows (v.1-3).
2. The bronze snake: a picture of unbelief and of Christ the Savior (v.4-9).
3. The march around Moab: a picture of progress—marching forth from place to place in a spirit of strong assurance (v.10-20).

4. The military victory over Sihon, the king of the Amorites: a picture of God's protection when attacked by enemies (v.21-32).
5. The military victory over Og, the king of Bashan: a picture of victory through the power of God (Gen.15:16; Ps.136:19) (v.33-35).

1 (21:1-3) **Victory, Over Enemies—Faith, Courageous—Triumph, Over Enemies—Conquest, of Enemies—Israel, Conquest of Enemies—Canaanites, Conquest of—Arad, Conquered by Israel**: there was the first military victory of Israel, a victory over the Canaanite king of Arad. This is a clear picture of making vows to God and fulfilling the vows. This was the launch of a new day in the history of Israel. After wandering about in the wilderness for forty years, they experienced their very first military victory, a victory over one of the Canaanite nations. Remember, the Canaanite nations were so savage, evil, and corrupt that they were beyond repair or repentance (cp. Gen.15:16; see outline and note, pt.4, d—Gen.15:7-21 for more discussion). Forty years earlier, from this same area, Israel had attempted to enter the promised land. This was right after the spies had returned from their mission of spying out the land. But as we have seen, because of the terrible unbelief of the spies and the people, the march into the promised land had to be aborted. The people were condemned to spend forty years wandering about in the wilderness until the entire first generation of faithless believers had died. For forty years the people of God had been wandering about in the wilderness of this world. They were defeated, disappointed, frustrated, beaten down—all because of unbelief, grumbling, and murmuring against God and His dear servant Moses. They had failed to lay hold of the promises of God, that He would give them victory over the pitfalls and enemies of this life. As a result, they were unable to enter the promised land. But now their children, the second generation, were about ready to enter. The new day was dawning; here they were on the threshold of claiming the great promise of God, the hope of the promised land. Here is the very first military victory, a victory over a formidable enemy, an enemy that was set on destroying them. Note the Scripture and outline:

OUTLINE	SCRIPTURE	SCRIPTURE	OUTLINE
1. The first military victory: A picture of making & fulfilling vows a. The Canaanite king of Arad heard that the Israelites were traveling close by: He secretly attacked & captured some of them b. The reaction of Israel: A courageous determination & faith	And when king Arad the Canaanite, which dwelt in the south, heard tell that Israel came by the way of the spies; then he fought against Israel, and took some of them prisoners. 2 And Israel vowed a vow unto the LORD, and said, If thou wilt indeed deliver this	people into my hand, then I will utterly destroy their cities. 3 And the LORD hearkened to the voice of Israel, and delivered up the Canaanites; and they utterly destroyed them and their cities: and he called the name of the place Hormah.	1) They made a vow: If God would give victory, they would destroy them 2) They were heard by the LORD: He gave them victory 3) They fulfilled their vow: Completely destroyed the savage, evil attackers (cp. Gen.15:16)

1. The Canaanite king of Arad heard that Israel was traveling close by (v.1). For some reason, he launched a savage, secret attack against the Israelites. He apparently attacked some of the Israelites on the outskirts of the campsite. His armed forces were apparently not large enough to launch an all out attack against the military of Israel. Whatever the case, he captured some of the Israelites and took them back to the capital of Arad.

2. Note the reaction of Israel: a courageous determination and faith (v.2-3). They made a *vow* to the Lord that if God would give them victory, they would totally destroy the Arads. God heard the prayer of their *vow* and He gave them victory. Note the total obedience of the people in fulfilling their vow: they completely destroyed the savage, evil Canaanites (v.3) (see DEEPER STUDY # 1—Num.21:2-3 for more discussion).

Thought 1. Making vows is a serious matter. When we make a vow, God expects us to keep the vow. He expects us to fulfill what we promise. This was true with Israelites, and it is true with us. We must fulfill our vows, the promises we make to the Lord.

"If a man vow a vow unto the Lord, or swear an oath to bind his soul with a bond; he shall not break his word, he shall do according to all that proceedeth out of his mouth" (Num.30:2).

"When thou shalt vow a vow unto the Lord thy God, thou shalt not slack to pay it: for the Lord thy God will surely require it of thee; and it would be sin in thee. But if thou shalt forbear to vow, it shall be no sin in thee. That which is gone out of thy lips thou shalt keep and perform; even a freewill offering, according as thou hast vowed unto the Lord thy God, which thou hast promised with thy mouth" (Dt.23:21-23).

"Thou shalt make thy prayer unto him, and he shall hear thee, and thou shalt pay thy vows" (Job 22:27).

"Offer unto God thanksgiving; and pay thy vows unto the most High" (Ps.50:14).

"Vow, and pay unto the Lord your God: let all that be round about him bring presents unto him that ought to be feared" (Ps.76:11).

"When thou vowest a vow unto God, defer not to pay it; for he hath no pleasure in fools: pay that which thou hast vowed. Better is it that thou shouldest not vow, than that thou shouldest vow and not pay. Suffer not thy mouth to cause thy flesh to sin; neither say thou before the angel, that it was an error: wherefore should God be angry at thy voice, and destroy the work of thine hands" (Eccl.5:4-6).

DEEPER STUDY # 1
(Num.21:1) **Arad, City of**: it was located in the Negev in the southern extreme of Judah's territory. (See Map—Numbers 33:5-49, end of commentary.) Arad was a Canaanite city about eleven miles west southwest of Beersheba. It was also the headquarters of the Canaanite king of Arad and the scene of Israel's first military victory.
See other Scripture references for study:
Numbers 33:40; Joshua 12:14; Judges 1:16

DEEPER STUDY # 2
(21:2-3) **Iniquity, Cup of—Nations, Destruction of—Nations, Savage and Evil—Nations, Judgment of—Canaanites, Destruction of**: the words "utterly, totally, completely destroy" (harami or charam) mean to annihilate, exterminate, eliminate, or abolish. The word is related to the Hebrew *herem* which means "to devote to the ban."[1] Once something had been promised or devoted to God, it was placed under the ban: it could not be removed. If it was a gift, it had to be given to God. If it was the promise to do something, then it had to be done. If it was a vow to devote something to destruction, then it had to be destroyed or exterminated. In ancient days, this was known as the *herem principal or law*. Once a person or thing had been *devoted* to the LORD, it could not be removed. It went to the LORD.

In the present case, Israel made a promise to God: if God would give them victory over the savage Canaanites, they would totally destroy the Canaanite cities. (See note, pt.4, d—Gen.15:7-21 for more discussion.)

The very idea that God and moral people would be set on the total destruction of a people is offensive to some persons. How could God and moral people possibly endorse such an act? In looking at this, certain factors need to be kept in mind:

1. People can become so savage, evil, and corrupt that they are beyond repair or repentance, beyond hope or correction. This is what is known as the "cup of iniquity being full"—filled to the point that it overflows and continues to overflow with…

- savagery
- violence
- brutality
- slavery
- ruthlessness
- lawlessness
- abuse
- cruelty
- atrocities
- barbarism
- corruption
- evil
- immorality
- injustice

History has shown that such behavior can be true of both individuals and nations. A person's or a nation's "cup of iniquity" can become full—well beyond repair or repentance, well beyond hope or correction. God declares this fact time and again as the Scriptures below show (Gen.15:16).

God wants justice executed against these people. Scripture is clear about this fact: this is the very purpose for the judgment of God.

> **"But in the fourth generation they shall come hither again: for the iniquity of the Amorites is not yet full" (Gen.15:16).**
>
> **"Defile not ye yourselves in any of these things: for in all these the nations are defiled which I cast out before you: And the land is defiled: therefore I do visit the iniquity thereof upon it, and the land itself vomiteth out her inhabitants" (Lev.18:24-25).**
>
> **"And ye shall not walk in the manners of the nation, which I cast out before you: for they committed all these things, and therefore I abhorred them" (Lev.20:23).**
>
> **"Speak not thou in thine heart, after that the Lord thy God hath cast them out from before thee, saying, For my righteousness the Lord hath brought me in to possess this land: but for the wickedness of these nations the Lord doth drive them out from before thee. Not for thy righteousness, or for the uprightness of thine heart, dost thou go to possess their land: but for the wickedness of these nations the LORD thy God doth drive them out from before thee, and that he may perform the word which the LORD sware unto thy fathers, Abraham, Isaac, and Jacob" (Dt.9:4-5).**
>
> **"And he did that which was evil in the sight of the Lord, after the abominations of the heathen, whom the Lord cast out before the children of Israel" (2 Ki.21:2).**
>
> **"Moreover he burnt incense in the valley of the son of Hinnom, and burnt his children in the fire, after the abominations of the heathen whom the Lord had cast out before the children of Israel" (2 Chron.28:3).**
>
> **"But did that which was evil in the sight of the Lord, like unto the abominations of the heathen, whom the Lord had cast out before the children of Israel" (2 Chron.33:2).**
>
> **"And shed innocent blood, even the blood of their sons and of their daughters, whom they sacrificed unto the idols of Canaan: and the land was polluted with blood" (Ps.106:38).**
>
> **"The earth also is defiled under the inhabitants thereof; because they have transgressed the laws, changed the ordinance, broken the everlasting covenant" (Is.24:5).**
>
> **"…thou hast polluted the land with thy whoredoms and with thy wickedness" (Jer.3:2).**
>
> **"And first I will recompense their iniquity and their sin double; because they have defiled my land, they have filled mine inheritance with the carcases of their detestable and abominable things" (Jer.16:18).**

2. God is a just God as well as a God of love. God loves all people—every individual and all the people of every nation upon earth. His love continually flows out to everyone. But God is also a just God, the Sovereign Lord who executes justice upon the earth. God is not an *indulgent grandfather* type of person who pampers the evil and savage of this world. To allow injustice to go unpunished, He would be a God of evil, a God who showed partiality and favoritism. He would

1 *The Expositor's Bible Commentary*. Frank E. Gaebelein, Editor, p.874.

be favoring the evil of the earth by allowing them to go unpunished and showing injustice to the moral of the earth by allowing them to continue to suffer under the injustices of evil people.

When the "cup of iniquity becomes full"—well beyond repair or repentance, well beyond hope or correction—that person or people are to be judged. Justice is to be executed upon them. God wants justice executed against such persons. This is the reason He has appointed a day in which He will judge the world.

"For the Son of man shall come in the glory of his father with his angels; and then he shall reward every man according to his works" (Mt.16:27).

"When the Son of man shall come in his glory, and all the holy angels with him, then shall he sit upon the throne of his glory: And before him shall be gathered all nations: and he shall separate them one from another, as a shepherd divideth his sheep from the goats: And he shall set the sheep on his right hand, but the goats on the left" (Mt.25:31-33).

"Because he hath appointed a day, in the which he will judge the world in righteousness by that man whom he hath ordained; whereof he hath given assurance unto all men, in that he hath raised him from the dead" (Acts 17:31).

"In the day when God shall judge the secrets of men by Jesus Christ according to my gospel" (Ro.2:16).

"I charge thee therefore before God, and the Lord Jesus Christ, who shall judge the quick and the dead at his appearing and his kingdom" (2 Tim.4:1).

"And as it is appointed unto men once to die, but after this the judgment" (Heb.9:27).

"The Lord knoweth how to deliver the godly out of temptations, and to reserve the unjust unto the day of judgment to be punished" (2 Pt.2:9).

"The Lord is not slack concerning his promise, as some men count slackness; but is longsuffering to us-ward, not willing that any should perish, but that all should come to repentance" (2 Pt.3:9).

"And Enoch also, the seventh from Adam, prophesied of these, saying, Behold, the Lord cometh with ten thousands of his saints, To execute judgment upon all, and to convince all that are ungodly among them of all their ungodly deeds which they have ungodly committed, and of all their hard speeches which ungodly sinners have spoken against him" (Jude 14-15).

"And I saw the dead, small and great, stand before God; and the books were opened: and another book was opened, which is the book of life: and the dead were judged out of those things which were written in the books, according to their works" (Rev.20:12).

3. Israel was used by God as His instrument of justice and judgment against the nations of Canaan. The Israelites did not receive the promised land of Canaan because of some merit or value within themselves nor because of their own strength or power. In justice and judgment, God Himself destroyed the Canaanites, and it was because of their wickedness that He destroyed them.

Again, it is critical to note this fact: Israel as a people did not receive the promised land because of their merit or value nor because of some righteousness they possessed. The Canaanites were destroyed because they were evil and their "cup of iniquity" had been filled to the brim. They reached the point of no repentance; they were beyond correction. Moses himself declared to the Israelites:

a. "It is not because of any personal righteousness within you, not because you have pure hearts, that you inherit the promised land (Dt.9:5). The enemies of the land are to be conquered and destroyed for two reasons:
   ⇒ Because of their wickedness and because they are an evil people; their 'cup of iniquity' is full.
   ⇒ Because God is faithful; He fulfills His promise to the forefathers, to Abraham, Isaac, and Jacob. God has promised to give the promised land to their descendants, to all those down through the centuries who believe His Word, His promises."

b. "Understand this warning: it is not because of your righteousness that God gives you the promised land. On the contrary, you are a stiff-necked, stubborn people (Dt.9:6). You are a sinful people. You have no righteousness within yourselves that merits God's favor. Your hearts are not upright nor pure enough to make God accept you and give you the victory over the enemies of the promised land. You are a stiff-necked, stubborn people."

"Not for thy righteousness, or for the uprightness of thine heart, dost thou go to possess their land: but for the wickedness of these nations the LORD thy God doth drive them out from before thee, and that he may perform the word which the LORD sware unto thy fathers, Abraham, Isaac, and Jacob. Understand therefore, that the LORD thy God giveth thee not this good land to possess it for thy righteousness; for thou *art* a stiffnecked people" (Dt.9:5-6).

Thought 1. James Philip makes an excellent statement on the justice and judgment of God that is well worth quoting in full.

"God was using His people as the rod of His anger against peoples whose cup of iniquity was full to overflowing. They were being judged for their sins and their depravities. This is, of course, stated explicitly more than once in the Old Testament itself (cf. Gen. 15:16 and Lev. 18:24-30). The time of their destruction was ripe. This is why they were thus dealt with, and it was no arbitrary act of injustice that drove them out of their land. They had forfeited the right to live as nations in Canaan by the extremes of their debauchery and depravity, just as Sodom and Gomorrah had done (Gen. 19), and just as the Cainite civilization as a whole had done, bringing upon itself the judgment of the Flood (Gen. 6). Furthermore, it should be remembered that God dealt with His own people in similar fashion when they proved themselves unworthy to life in the land of promise, and He brought them into the captivity of Babylon in 586 B.C. To understand God's burning passion for righteousness in His creatures is to understand the basic reason for these judgments upon men and nations that refused to be righteous, and who rendered themselves incapable of being so by their continued sin."[2]

2 (21:4-9) **Bronze Snake**: the bronze snake is a picture of unbelief and of Christ the Savior. Marching out in the wilderness was hard and difficult. At the end of each day, the people were bound to be tired, exhausted, and bone-weary. This passage shows how fatigue and exhaustion got to the people, how they had become so bone-weary that they lapsed back into their grumbling and unbelief. They began once again to attack God and His dear servant. The Scripture and outline clearly paint the picture:

OUTLINE	SCRIPTURE	SCRIPTURE	OUTLINE
2. The bronze snake: A picture of unbelief & of Christ the Savior a. The tragic situation 1) Had to bypass Edom, a long distance out of the way 2) Grew impatient & grumbled against God & Moses • Asked why they had led them out of Egypt into the desert to die: Had no bread & no water • Stated they detested the "worthless manna" b. The judgment, chastisement of the LORD 1) He sent snakes among them 2) Many died c. The confession & repentance	4 And they journeyed from mount Hor by the way of the Red sea, to compass the land of Edom: and the soul of the people was much discouraged because of the way. 5 And the people spake against God, and against Moses, Wherefore have ye brought us up out of Egypt to die in the wilderness? for there is no bread, neither is there any water; and our soul loatheth this light bread. 6 And the LORD sent fiery serpents among the people, and they bit the people; and much people of Israel died. 7 Therefore the people came	to Moses, and said, We have sinned, for we have spoken against the LORD, and against thee; pray unto the LORD, that he take away the serpents from us. And Moses prayed for the people. 8 And the LORD said unto Moses, Make thee a fiery serpent, and set it upon a pole: and it shall come to pass, that every one that is bitten, when he looketh upon it, shall live. 9 And Moses made a serpent of brass, and put it upon a pole, and it came to pass, that if a serpent had bitten any man, when he beheld the serpent of brass, he lived.	of the people 1) They confessed their sin 2) They asked Moses, their mediator, to pray for God to take away the snakes 3) Moses prayed for them d. The answer of the LORD 1) To make a replica of a snake & hang it on a high pole 2) The condition for deliverance: Must look at it to live e. The obedience of Moses: Hung a bronze snake on a pole f. The deliverance: Some looked, believed, & lived (a picture of deliverance by looking at Christ, Jn.3:14-15)

1. Note the tragic situation: the people had to bypass or detour around Edom. This was a long distance out of the way (v.4-5). Remember, Moses had sent two diplomatic letters to the king of Edom asking permission to pass through their land. The king had rejected the appeal and had even gone so far as to threaten attack against the Israelites. Therefore, Moses had to lead the people on a detour around the land of Edom. As stated, this was a long distance out of the way for the people to travel. Fatigue and exhaustion set in, and they grew impatient. They began to grumble and murmur against God and against Moses:

⇒ They asked why they had been led out of Egypt into the desert wilderness to die: there was no bread and no water in the desert wilderness.

⇒ They stated that they detested the "worthless manna." Remember that the *manna* was the bread from heaven, the bread that God Himself had provided to feed the people through their wilderness wanderings. The word the people used to describe the "manna" was *ballehem haqqeloqel*. This means "contemptible, worthless bread"; it means miserable, wretched, despicable, cheap bread. It even has the idea of cursing the heavenly bread, the bread that had been provided by God Himself.[3] The people had constantly grumbled about God's gracious provision during their 40 year wilderness wandering, but this time it was different. They actually stated that they detested the *manna*, and they cursed it. It was despicable, worthless, at best *junk food*. This time, the people had gone too far. God had no choice but to judge and chastise them and to do so severely.

2. Note the judgment, the chastisement of the Lord: He sent snakes among them, and many of them died (v.6). They were "fiery serpents," that is, *poisonous snakes*. The poison was obviously strong, very potent—the kind of venom that causes a horrible, agonizing death. This is indicated by the fact that many of the people subsequently died.

3. Note the confession and repentance of the people: they confessed their sin and asked Moses to pray for them, asking God to take away the snakes (v.7). This Moses did. He was the servant of God, so he once again forgave them for their attacks against him and the Lord. As their minister, he loved them, so he again became their intercessor and mediator before God. No doubt, he begged God to forgive the sin of the people and to have mercy upon them.

4. Note the surprising answer of the Lord (v.8): the Lord told Moses to make a replica of a snake and hang it on a high pole. Then God spelled out a condition for deliverance and healing: a person had to look at the snake hanging upon the pole. If he looked, he would be healed and would live.

This is one of the great symbols of Jesus Christ in the Scripture—His being hung upon the cross for the sins of the world. This is exactly what Christ Himself said:

---

2 James Philip. *Mastering The Old Testament, Vol.4, Numbers*, p.311.
3 *The Expositor's Bible Commentary*. Frank E. Gaebelein, Editor, p.879.

"And as Moses lifted up the serpent in the wilderness, even so must the Son of man be lifted up: That whosoever believeth in him should not perish, but have eternal life. For God so loved the world, that he gave his only begotten Son, that whosoever believeth in him should not perish, but have everlasting life" (Jn.3:14-16).

5. Now, note the obedience of Moses: he hung a bronze snake on a pole just as instructed by God (v.9).
6. The people were delivered, but only some. Only those who looked at the snake and believed the promise of God lived (v.9). Keep in mind, this is a picture of deliverance by looking at (believing in) the cross of Jesus Christ (Jn.3:14-15).

Thought 1. There are three significant lessons in this point for us.

1) Jesus Christ is the manna, the bread from heaven. God has given Jesus Christ to feed the souls of people. People hunger and crave for the food of purpose, meaning, and significance in life. Christ and Christ alone can meet the hunger of the human soul. Jesus Christ is the Bread of Life.

"But seek ye first the kingdom of God, and his righteousness; and all these things shall be added unto you" (Mt.6:33).

"Then Jesus said unto them, Verily, verily, I say unto you, Moses gave you not that bread from heaven; but my Father giveth you the true bread from heaven. For the bread of God is he which cometh down from heaven, and giveth life unto the world. Then said they unto him, Lord, evermore give us this bread. And Jesus said unto them, I am the bread of life: he that cometh to me shall never hunger; and he that believeth on me shall never thirst" (Jn.6:32-35).

"I am that bread of life. Your fathers did eat manna in the wilderness, and are dead. This is the bread which cometh down from heaven, that a man may eat thereof, and not die. I am the living bread which came down from heaven: if any man eat of this bread, he shall live for ever: and the bread that I will give is my flesh, which I will give for the life of the world" (Jn.6:48-51).

"This is that bread which came down from heaven: not as your fathers did eat manna, and are dead: he that eateth of this bread shall live for ever" (Jn.6:58).

"He that hath an ear, let him hear what the Spirit saith unto the churches; To him that overcometh will I give to eat of the tree of life, which is in the midst of the paradise of God" (Rev.2:7).

"Wherefore do ye spend money for that which is not bread? and your labour for that which satisfieth not? hearken diligently unto me, and eat ye that which is good, and let your soul delight itself in fatness" (Is.55:2).

2) The Israelites cursed the bread of God which was a symbol of Jesus Christ. Any person who curses Jesus Christ will be judged by God, severely judged. Any person who looks upon Jesus Christ as contemptible, worthless, wretched—as being useless—is going to face the wrath of God, a judgment beyond comprehension.

"He that believeth on the Son hath everlasting life: and he that believeth not the Son shall not see life; but the wrath of God abideth on him" (Jn.3:36).

"For the wrath of God is revealed from heaven against all ungodliness and unrighteousness of men, who hold the truth in unrighteousness" (Ro.1:18).

"But unto them that are contentious, and do not obey the truth, but obey unrighteousness, indignation and wrath" (Ro.2:8).

"Be ye therefore followers of God, as dear children; And walk in love, as Christ also hath loved us, and hath given himself for us an offering and a sacrifice to God for a sweetsmelling savour. But fornication, and all uncleanness, or covetousness, let it not be once named among you, as becometh saints; Neither filthiness, nor foolish talking, nor jesting, which are not convenient: but rather giving of thanks. For this ye know, that no whoremonger, nor unclean person, nor covetous man, who is an idolater, hath any inheritance in the kingdom of Christ and of God. Let no man deceive you with vain words: for because of these things cometh the wrath of God upon the children of disobedience" (Eph.5:1-6).

"And to you who are troubled rest with us, when the Lord Jesus shall be revealed from heaven with his mighty angels, In flaming fire taking vengeance on them that know not God, and that obey not the gospel of our Lord Jesus Christ" (2 Th.1:7-8).

"The Lord knoweth how to deliver the godly out of temptations, and to reserve the unjust unto the day of judgment to be punished" (2 Pt.2:9).

"But the heavens and the earth, which are now, by the same word are kept in store, reserved unto fire against the day of judgment and perdition of ungodly men" (2 Pt.3:7).

"Behold, the Lord cometh with ten thousands of his saints, To execute judgment upon all, and to convince all that are ungodly among them of all their ungodly deeds which they have ungodly committed, and of all their hard speeches which ungodly sinners have spoken against him" (Jude 14-15).

"Behold, he cometh with clouds; and every eye shall see him, and they also which pierced him: and all kindreds of the earth shall wail because of him. Even so, Amen" (Rev.1:7).

"Kiss the Son, lest he be angry, and ye perish from the way, when his wrath is kindled but a little. Blessed are all they that put their trust in him" (Ps.2:12).

3) Jesus Christ has been lifted up as the Savior of the world. God lifted up Christ just as the serpent was lifted up, as a symbol of deliverance. Any person who looks upon Christ and believes in Him will be delivered, that is, saved.

"And as Moses lifted up the serpent in the wilderness, even so must the Son of man be lifted up: That whosoever believeth in him should not perish, but have eternal life. For God so loved the world,

that he gave his only begotten Son, that whosoever believeth in him should not perish, but have everlasting life" (Jn.3:14-16).

"Verily, verily, I say unto you, He that heareth my word, and believeth on him that sent me, hath everlasting life, and shall not come into condemnation; but is passed from death unto life" (Jn.5:24).

"Jesus said unto her, I am the resurrection, and the life: he that believeth in me, though he were dead, yet shall he live" (Jn.11:25).

"I am come a light into the world, that whosoever believeth on me should not abide in darkness" (Jn.12:46).

"But these are written, that ye might believe that Jesus is the Christ, the Son of God; and that believing ye might have life through his name" (Jn.20:31).

"That if thou shalt confess with thy mouth the Lord Jesus, and shalt believe in thine heart that God hath raised him from the dead, thou shalt be saved. For with the heart man believeth unto righteousness; and with the mouth confession is made unto salvation" (Ro.10:9-10).

3 (21:10-20) **March, the Believer's—Walk, the Believer's—Confidence—Assurance**: there was the march around Moab. This is a picture of progress, of marching forth from place to place in a spirit of strong assurance. Now the people were ready for their final march right up to the border of the promised land. At last, they were on the verge of reaching their destination. As they marched along, the excitement of their hearts could be seen in a faster pace: the tempo of their steps increased as they marched day by day. Note how Scripture paints the scene with a graphic fast-paced stroke.

OUTLINE	SCRIPTURE	SCRIPTURE	OUTLINE
3. The march around Moab: A picture of progress—marching forth from place to place in a spirit of strong assurance a. They camped at Oboth (v.10)	10 And the children of Israel set forward, and pitched in Oboth.	the dwelling of Ar, and lieth upon the border of Moab.	
b. They camped at Iye Abarim	11 And they journeyed from Oboth, and pitched at Ije-abarim, in the wilderness which is before Moab, toward the sunrising.	16 And from thence they went to Beer: that is the well whereof the LORD spake unto Moses, Gather the people together, and I will give them water.	e. They camped at the well Beer 1) The well was dug in obedience to the LORD's instructions
c. They camped at the Zered Valley	12 From thence they removed, and pitched in the valley of Zared.	17 Then Israel sang this song, Spring up, O well; sing ye unto it:	2) The gift of water led God's people to compose a song of joy, the "Song of the Well"
d. They camped alongside the Arnon River 1) It flowed into Amorite territory 2) It was the border between Moab & the Amorites	13 From thence they removed, and pitched on the other side of Arnon, which is in the wilderness that cometh out of the coasts of the Amorites: for Arnon is the border of Moab, between Moab and the Amorites.	18 The princes digged the well, the nobles of the people digged it, by the direction of the lawgiver, with their staves. And from the wilderness they went to Mattanah:	f. They camped at Mattanah
3) It was a famous river: A place where significant battles had been fought	14 Wherefore it is said in the book of the wars of the LORD, What he did in the Red sea, and in the brooks of Arnon,	19 And from Mattanah to Nahaliel: and from Nahaliel to Bamoth:	g. They camped at Nahaliel h. They camped at Bamoth
	15 And at the stream of the brooks that goeth down to	20 And from Bamoth in the valley, that is in the country of Moab, to the top of Pisgah, which looketh toward Jeshimon.	i. They camped in Moab in the valley below Pisgah Peak—an excellent lookout to spy out the land

1. The Israelites camped at Oboth (v.10).
2. The Israelites camped at Iye Abarim (v.11).
3. The Israelites camped at the Zered Valley (v.12).
4. The Israelites camped alongside the Arnon River (v.13-15). This was one of the famous rivers of ancient history, a river that flowed into Amorite territory. The river was actually the border between Moab and the Amorite territory. A large number of significant battles had been fought in the area around the river (v.14-15). Note the reference to the "Book of the Wars of the Lord." This is actually the only mention of this book, the only thing we know about it. Obviously, it was a book of songs about famous battles and wars that had been fought in those days.
5. The Israelites camped at the well Beer (v.16-17). The people again were apparently without water, but the Lord stepped into the situation and told them where they could dig a well and hit water. Note that the gift of water led God's people to compose a song of joy, the "Song of the Well."
6. The Israelites camped at Mattanah (v.18).
7. The Israelites camped at Nahaliel (v.19).
8. The Israelites camped at Bamoth (v.19).
9. The Israelites camped in Moab in the valley below Pisgah peak, an excellent location to spy out the land of Canaan (v.20).

Thought 1. This is a different picture of God's people than seen before. Up until now, the picture painted has been that of an unbelieving people, a grumbling people, a people who lacked assurance and confidence in the Lord. They just did not believe He had the power to carry them into the promised land. But this scene of Scripture is entirely different: it is a picture of a quick pace, an excitement to reach their destination. The picture painted is that of breaking camp, marching, stopping, and setting up camp; then again breaking camp, marching, stopping, and setting up camp; then again breaking camp, marching, stopping, and setting up camp; and on and on. The idea is that of a fast pace, of purpose and motivation, of enthusiasm and excitement. This has not been seen before, but now the people are rapidly approaching the promised land. They seem to be trusting God more than ever before. Therefore, God pours out His grace upon them, providing for them and meeting their need for water and all else.

The lesson for us is this: we must be diligent as we march to the promised land of God. We need a quick, fast pace in trusting and obeying God, in following the leadership of God as He leads us to the promised land.

> **"By faith Abraham, when he was called to go out into a place which he should after receive for an inheritance, obeyed; and he went out, not knowing whither he went. By faith he sojourned in the land of promise, as in a strange country, dwelling in tabernacles with Isaac and Jacob, the heirs with him of the same promise: For he looked for a city which hath foundations, whose builder and maker is God" (Heb.11:8-10).**
>
> **"These all died in faith, not having received the promises, but having seen them afar off, and were persuaded of them, and embraced them, and confessed that they were strangers and pilgrims on the earth. For they that say such things declare plainly that they seek a country" (Heb.11:13-14).**
>
> **"But the day of the Lord will come as a thief in the night; in the which the heavens shall pass away with a great noise, and the elements shall melt with fervent heat, the earth also and the works that are therein shall be burned up. Seeing then that all these things shall be dissolved, what manner of persons ought ye to be in all holy conversation and godliness, Looking for and hasting unto the coming of the day of God, wherein the heavens being on fire shall be dissolved, and the elements shall melt with fervent heat? Nevertheless we, according to his promise, look for new heavens and a new earth, wherein dwelleth righteousness. Wherefore, beloved, seeing that ye look for such things, be diligent that ye may be found of him in peace, without spot, and blameless" (2 Pt.3:10-14).**
>
> **"Blessed are they that do his commandments, that they may have right to the tree of life, and may enter in through the gates into the city" (Rev.22:14).**
>
> **"But if from thence thou shalt seek the Lord thy God, thou shalt find him, if thou seek him with all thy heart and with all thy soul" (Dt.4:29).**
>
> **"Seek ye the Lord while he may be found, call ye upon him while he is near" (Is.55:6).**
>
> **"And ye shall seek me, and find me, when ye shall search for me with all your heart" (Jer.29:13).**

DEEPER STUDY # 3

(Num.21:23) **Jahaz, City of (See other spellings—Jahaza, Jahazah)**: the exact location is unknown. Jahaz became part of the tribal territory of Reuben (Joshua 13:18). Sihon the Amorite was defeated there after attacking Israel. It became a city of the Levites (Joshua 21:36).

See other Scripture references for study:

Deut. 2:32; Joshua 13:18; Joshua 21:36; Judges 11:20; Isaiah 15:4; Jeremiah 48:21; Jeremiah 48:34

DEEPER STUDY # 4

(Num.21:25-30; Num.32:37-38) **Heshbon, City of**: it was located east of the Dead Sea and north of the Arnon River in Moab. (See Map—Numbers 33:5-49, end of commentary.) The Hebrew meaning of Heshbon is "reckoning." It was assigned to the tribe of Reuben and later chosen to be a Levitical city (Joshua 13:27-28; Joshua 21:38-39).

See other Scripture references for study:

Numbers 21:25-28; Numbers 21:30; Numbers 21:34; Numbers 32:3; Numbers 32:37; Deut. 1:4; Deut. 2:24; Deut. 2:26; Deut. 2:30; Deut. 3:2; Deut. 3:6; Deut. 4:46; Deut. 29:7; Joshua 9:10; Joshua 12:2; Joshua 12:5; Joshua 13:10; Joshua 13:17; Joshua 13:21; Joshua 13:26-27; Joshua 21:39; Judges 11:19; Judges 11:26; 1 Chron. 6:81; Neh. 9:22; Song 7:4; Isaiah 15:4; Isaiah 16:8-9; Jeremiah 48:2; Jeremiah 48:34; Jeremiah 48:45; Jeremiah 49:3

4 (21:21-32) **Victory, Military—Victory, over Enemies—Enemies, Victory over—Justice, of God—Faithfulness, of God—Amorites, Conquered by Israel—Israel, Conquest of Amorites—Sihon**: there was the military victory over Sihon, the king of the Amorites. This is a picture of God's protection when attacked by enemies (Gen.15:16; Ps.136:19). As the Israelites marched to the promised land, they came to the border of the Amorite nation. The land of the Amorites stood between them and the promised land. God's people had no choice: if they were going to continue their journey to the promised land, they had to pass through the land of the Amorites. What happened is most interesting:

OUTLINE	SCRIPTURE	SCRIPTURE	OUTLINE
4. The military victory over Sihon, the king of the Amorites: A picture of God's protection when attacked by enemies a. The diplomatic, non-threatening request by Israel for	21 And Israel sent messengers unto Sihon king of the Amorites, saying, 22 Let me pass through thy land: we will not turn into the fields, or into the vineyards; we will not drink of	the waters of the well: but we will go along by the king's high way, until we be past thy borders. 23 And Sihon would not suffer Israel to pass through his border: but Sihon gath-	safe passage b. The hostile attack against Israel at Jahaz

OUTLINE	SCRIPTURE	SCRIPTURE	OUTLINE
	ered all his people together, and went out against Israel into the wilderness: and he came to Jahaz, and fought against Israel.	Sihon be built and prepared: 28 For there is a fire gone out of Heshbon, a flame from the city of Sihon: it hath consumed Ar of Moab, and the lords of the high places of Arnon.	tal of the Amorites • This is seen in the great king Sihon: He had formerly conquered Moab, a conquest so great that it had been celebrated by ancient poets
c. The great victory of Israel 1) Conquered all the Amorite territory 2) Stopped at the Ammonite border: Because the border was fortified	24 And Israel smote him with the edge of the sword, and possessed his land from Arnon unto Jabbok, even unto the children of Ammon: for the border of the children of Ammon was strong.	29 Woe to thee, Moab! thou art undone, O people of Chemosh: he hath given his sons that escaped, and his daughters, into captivity unto Sihon king of the Amorites.	
3) Captured & occupied all the cities of the Amorites: Included Heshbon & its surrounding villages	25 And Israel took all these cities: and Israel dwelt in all the cities of the Amorites, in Heshbon, and in all the villages thereof.	30 We have shot at them; Heshbon is perished even unto Dibon, and we have laid them waste even unto Nophah, which reacheth unto Medeba.	
d. The significance of the victory: A great victory over a celebrated king & army had been achieved	26 For Heshbon was the city of Sihon the king of the Amorites, who had fought against the former king of Moab, and taken all his land out of his hand, even unto Arnon.	31 Thus Israel dwelt in the land of the Amorites.	• Now Israel had proven stronger than the Amorites
• This is seen in the conquest of the great city of Heshbon: It was the capi-	27 Wherefore they that speak in proverbs say, Come into Heshbon, let the city of	32 And Moses sent to spy out Jaazer, and they took the villages thereof, and drove out the Amorites that were there.	e. The victory was even extended: Sent spies to Jazer & captured the towns, driving out the Amorite citizens

1. Note the diplomatic, non-threatening request of Israel for safe passage (v.22). Moses promised that the Israelites would not do any damage to the fields or crops or water as they marched through Amorite territory. He promised to stay strictly on the king's highway until they had passed completely through the territory.

2. Note the surprise, hostile attack against Israel (v.23). King Sihon rejected the request of Israel for safe passage. Instead, the king and his officials mobilized their entire army and marched out against Israel. When the Amorites reached Jahaz, they attacked.

3. Despite the surprise attack, Israel was victorious (v.24-25). They routed the Amorite army and pursued them all over Amorite territory, conquering the entire nation. But they stopped at the Amorite border because of the fortifications. However, they did capture and occupy all the cities of the Amorites including the capital of Heshbon and its surrounding villages (v.25).

4. Note the significance of the victory: a great victory over a celebrated king and army had been achieved (v.26-31).
   a. The great victory is seen in the conquest of the great city of Heshbon: as stated, it was the capital of the Amorites' king, Sihon (v.26).
   b. The great victory is also seen in the defeat of the great king Sihon. he had formerly conquered Moab, a conquest so great that it had been celebrated by ancient poets (v.27-31). The thrust of the poem is this: king Sihon had been so powerful that he was able to conquer Moab. Therefore, the people of God must be even more powerful, for they had conquered the great king Sihon. The message was clear: Israel was the super-power of the area, stronger than either the Amorites or the Moabites.

5. The victory was even extended to the major city of Jazer (v.32). Moses sent spies to Jazer and captured the towns surrounding it. He also drove out all the Amorite citizens of that area.

Thought 1. The king of the Amorites launched a surprise, hostile attack against God's people. This is a picture of the world and the enemies of life attacking us as we walk through life. As we march to the promised land of heaven, enemy after enemy will attack us, enemies such as...

• disease	• anger	• unemployment
• accident	• discouragement	• lack of purpose
• immorality	• depression	• loneliness
• greed	• failure	• emptiness
• covetousness	• financial difficulty	• death

Some enemies are small and weak, amounting to nothing more than minor problems or difficulties. Such enemies are easy to conquer, even by the arm of the flesh. But there are other enemies that are far more powerful and brutal in their attack. These enemies can never be defeated by man, such enemies as a terminal disease, a paralyzing accident, or even death. Such enemies as these can be conquered only by the power of God Himself. Note this: God says that He will protect His people when they are attacked by enemies. No matter the size or power of an enemy, God promises to protect His dear people from their attack and onslaught.

"But there shall not an hair of your head perish" (Lk.21:18).

"So that we may boldly say, The Lord is my helper, and I will not fear what man shall do unto me" (Heb.13:6).

"The Lord shall fight for you, and ye shall hold your peace" (Ex.14:14).

"I will send my fear before thee, and will destroy all the people to whom thou shalt come, and I will make all thine enemies turn their backs unto thee" (Ex.23:27).

"For the eyes of the Lord run to and fro throughout the whole earth, to show himself strong in the behalf of them whose heart is perfect toward him" (2 Chron.16:9).

"With him is an arm of flesh; but with us is the Lord our God to help us, and to fight our battles" (2 Chron.32:8).

"For in the time of trouble he shall hide me in his pavilion: in the secret of his tabernacle shall he hide me; he shall set me up upon a rock" (Ps.27:5).

"The Lord is my strength and my shield; my heart trusted in him, and I am helped: therefore my heart greatly rejoiceth; and with my song will I praise him" (Ps.28:7).

"Thou shalt hide them in the secret of thy presence from the pride of man: thou shalt keep them secretly in a pavilion from the strife of tongues" (Ps.31:20).

"The angel of the Lord encampeth round about them that fear him, and delivereth them" (Ps.34:7).

"He shall cover thee with his feathers, and under his wings shalt thou trust: his truth shall be thy shield and buckler" (Ps.91:4).

"Fear thou not; for I am with thee: be not dismayed; for I am thy God: I will strengthen thee; yea, I will help thee; yea, I will uphold thee with the right hand of my righteousness" (Is.41:10).

5 (21:33-35) **Victory, over Enemies—Military, Victory of—Israel, Military Victory of—Triumph, over Enemies—Og, King of Bashan**: there was the military victory over Og, the king of Bashan. This is a clear picture of victory through the power of God. As the Israelites marched to the promised land, their journey took them along the road toward Bashan. Obviously, the king and his officials felt threatened and feared being overthrown just like the Amorite king Sihon. The picture is dramatic:

OUTLINE	SCRIPTURE	SCRIPTURE	OUTLINE
5. The military victory over Og,	33 And they turned	and his land; and thou shalt	assured
the king of Bashan: A picture	and went up by the way of	do to him as thou didst	2) God's people were to use
of victory through the power	Bashan: and Og the king	unto Sihon king of the	the same pattern as before:
of God (Gen.15:16; Ps.136:19)	of Bashan went out	Amorites, which dwelt at	Pursuit & total conquest
a. The attack of Og: Marched his	against them, he, and all	Heshbon.	
whole army against Israel at Edrei	his people, to the battle at	35 So they smote him,	c. The obedience & victory
b. The strong assurance of vic-	Edrei.	and his sons, and all	1) They struck down all the
tory from the LORD	34 And the LORD said unto	his people, until there	wicked: Their "cup was full
1) God's people were not to	Moses, Fear him not: for I	was none left him alive:	of sin," had "reached its
fear their enemy: Total &	have delivered him into thy	and they possessed his	full measure" (Gen.15:16)
complete victory was	hand, and all his people,	land.	2) They occupied the land

1. The king of Og marched his whole army out to attack Israel at Edrei (v.33).
2. But God gave His people strong assurance of victory (v.34). Moses and the people were not to fear their enemy. Total and complete victory was assured. Moreover, God's people were to use the same pattern as before: pursuit and total conquest, just as they had done with Sihon, king of the Amorites. The whole nation of Bashan was to be conquered and the cities destroyed.
3. Note the obedience of God's people and the victory given (v.35). They struck down all the wicked whose "cup was full of sin"—all whose sin had "reached its full measure" (Gen.15:16; see DEEPER STUDY # 1—Num.21:2-3 for more discussion). Once the victory had been achieved, the Israelites occupied the land.

Thought 1. Note verse 34: God told His people not to fear, for He had handed their enemies over to them. He guaranteed total and complete victory over the enemies of His dear people. God promises us victory over the enemies of this life. Total and complete victory is assured. As we march to the promised land of heaven, the enemies of life can be conquered, triumphed over—through the power of God Himself.

"Through thee will we push down our enemies: through thy name will we tread them under that rise up against us" (Ps.44:5).

"Who shall separate us from the love of Christ? shall tribulation, or distress, or persecution, or famine, or nakedness, or peril, or sword....Nay, in all these things we are more than conquerors through him that loved us. For I am persuaded, that neither death, nor life, nor angels, nor principalities, nor powers, nor things present, nor things to come, Nor height, nor depth, nor any other creature, shall be able to separate us from the love of God, which is in Christ Jesus our Lord" (Ro.8:35, 37-39).

"Put on the whole armour of God, that ye may be able to stand against the wiles of the devil. For we wrestle not against flesh and blood, but against principalities, against powers, against the rulers of the darkness of this world, against spiritual wickedness in high places. Wherefore take unto you the whole armour of God, that ye may be able to withstand in the evil day, and having done all, to stand" (Eph.6:11-13).

NUMBERS 21:1-35

"There hath no temptation taken you but such as is common to man: but God is faithful, who will not suffer you to be tempted above that ye are able; but will with the temptation also make a way to escape, that ye may be able to bear it" (1 Cor.10:13).

"For whatsoever is born of God overcometh the world: and this is the victory that overcometh the world, even our faith. Who is he that overcometh the world, but he that believeth that Jesus is the Son of God" (1 Jn.5:4-5).

DEEPER STUDY # 5

(Num.21:33-35) **Edrei, City of**: it was located in the tribal territory of Naphtali, near Kedesh and Hazor (Joshua 19:37). (See Map—Numbers 33:5-49, end of commentary.) The Hebrew meaning of Edrei is "mighty." Edrei was a fortified city. It was the place where Israel won the victory over Og, king of Bashan.

See other Scripture references for study:

Deut. 1:4; Deut. 3:1; Deut. 3:10; Joshua 12:4; Joshua 13:12; Joshua 13:31; Joshua 19:37

TYPES, SYMBOLS, AND PICTURES (Numbers 21:1-35)

Historical Term	Type or Picture (Scriptural Basis for Each)	Life Application for Today's Believer	Biblical Application
Bronze Snake Num.21:4-9	The Bronze snake is a type of Christ the Savior who delivers us from perishing. **"And the LORD said unto Moses, Make thee a fiery serpent, and set it upon a pole: and it shall come to pass, that every one that is bitten, when he looketh upon it, shall live" (Num.21:8).**	This is one of the great symbols of Jesus Christ in the Scripture, of His being hung upon the cross in order to deliver His people from perishing. This is exactly what Christ Himself said (Jn.3:14-16). Jesus Christ has been lifted up as the Savior of the world. God lifted up Christ just as the serpent was lifted up, as a symbol of deliverance. Any person who looks upon Christ and believes in Him will be delivered—saved.	***"And as Moses lifted up the serpent in the wilderness, even so must the Son of man be lifted up: That whosoever believeth in him should not perish, but have eternal life. For God so loved the world, that he gave his only begotten Son, that whosoever believeth in him should not perish, but have everlasting life" (Jn.3:14-16).*** ***"Verily, verily, I say unto you, He that heareth my word, and believeth on him that sent me, hath everlasting life, and shall not come into condemnation; but is passed from death unto life" (Jn.5:24).*** ***"Jesus said unto her, I am the resurrection, and the life: he that believeth in me, though he were dead, yet shall he live" (Jn.11:25).*** ***"I am come a light into the world, that whosoever believeth on me should not abide in darkness" (Jn. 12:46).*** ***"But these are written, that ye might believe that Jesus is the Christ, the Son of God; and that believing ye might have life through his name" (Jn.20:31).*** ***"That if thou shalt confess with thy mouth the Lord Jesus, and shalt believe in thine heart that God hath raised him from the dead, thou shalt be saved. For with the heart man believeth unto righteousness; and with the mouth confession is made unto salvation" (Ro.10:9-10).***

Historical Term	Type or Picture (Scriptural Basis for Each)	Life Application for Today's Believer	Biblical Application
Attack upon Israel (by the Amorites) Num.21:21-32	*An attack upon Israel [by the Amorites] is a picture of the world and the enemies of life attacking as we walk through this life.* **"And Sihon would not suffer Israel to pass through his border: but Sihon gathered all his people together, and went out against Israel into the wilderness: and he came to Jahaz, and fought against Israel. And Israel smote him with the edge of the sword, and possessed his land from Arnon unto Jabbok, even unto the children of Ammon: for the border of the children of Ammon *was* strong" (Num.21:23-24).**	Some enemies are small and weak, amounting to nothing more than minor problems or difficulties. Such enemies are easy to conquer, even by the arm of the flesh. But there are other enemies that are far more powerful and brutal in their attack. These enemies can never be defeated by man, such enemies as a terminal disease, a paralyzing accident, or even death. Such enemies as these can be conquered only by the power of God Himself. Note this: God says that He will protect His people when they are attacked by enemies. No matter the size or power of an enemy, God promises to protect His dear people from their attack and onslaught.	***"But there shall not an hair of your head perish" (Lk.21:18).*** ***"So that we may boldly say, The Lord is my helper, and I will not fear what man shall do unto me" (Heb. 13:6).*** ***"The Lord shall fight for you, and ye shall hold your peace" (Ex.14:14).*** ***"I will send my fear before thee, and will destroy all the people to whom thou shalt come, and I will make all thine enemies turn their backs unto thee" (Ex. 23:27).*** ***"For the eyes of the Lord run to and fro throughout the whole earth, to show himself strong in the behalf of them whose heart is perfect toward him" (2 Chron. 16:9).*** ***"With him is an arm of flesh; but with us is the Lord our God to help us, and to fight our battles" (2 Chron.32:8).*** ***"The Lord is my strength and my shield; my heart trusted in him, and I am helped: therefore my heart greatly rejoiceth; and with my song will I praise him" (Ps.28:7).*** ***"For in the time of trouble he shall hide me in his pavilion: in the secret of his tabernacle shall he hide me; he shall set me up upon a rock" (Ps.27:5).***

H. Event 8—the Story of Balaam, His Donkey, & His Three Encounters with God (Part 1): A Picture of the Unseen, Unknown Attempts by the Powers of Darkness to Defeat God's People, 22:1-41

1. The dramatic background to the encounters with God: A false belief in divination
- a. The Israelites were poised to enter the promised land[DS1]
- b. The king of Moab heard about Israel
  - 1) Heard they were nearby & about their military exploits
  - 2) Was terrified, filled with dread because of the Israelites
- c. The king formed an alliance with the leaders of Midian: Feared Israel would devour everything just like an ox devours grass
- d. The king sought to curse & defeat Israel by pagan divination: He sent for Balaam, a famous diviner with an international reputation[DS2]
  - 1) Related how a horde of people had arrived from Egypt & settled next to him
  - 2) Wanted Balaam to put a curse on them so he could defeat them in battle
  - 3) Stated that he believed strongly in the divination powers of Balaam: The people Balaam blessed were blessed, & those he cursed were cursed

2. The 1st encounter of Balaam with God: A man who earned money dishonestly (2 Pt.2:15)
- a. The officials from both Moab & Midian traveled to see Balaam with the fee for divination
- b. The response of Balaam was immediate: He invited the officials to spend the night while he sought God's will
- c. The 1st encounter with God
  - 1) God asked who the men were visiting him
  - 2) Balaam identified them as officials from Balak, the

And the children of Israel set
forward, and pitched in the
plains of Moab on this side
Jordan by Jericho.
2 And Balak the son of
Zippor saw all that Israel had
done to the Amorites.
3 And Moab was sore afraid
of the people, because they
were many: and Moab was
distressed because of the
children of Israel.
4 And Moab said unto the
elders of Midian, Now shall
this company lick up all that
are round about us, as the ox
licketh up the grass of the
field. And Balak the son of
Zippor was king of the
Moabites at that time.
5 He sent messengers therefore unto Balaam the son of
Beor to Pethor, which is by
the river of the land of the
children of his people, to call
him, saying, Behold, there is
a people come out from
Egypt: behold, they cover
the face of the earth, and
they abide over against me:
6 Come now therefore, I
pray thee, curse me this people; for they are too mighty
for me: peradventure I shall
prevail, that we may smite
them, and that I may drive
them out of the land: for I
wot that he whom thou
blessest is blessed, and he
whom thou cursest is cursed.
7 And the elders of Moab
and the elders of Midian
departed with the rewards of
divination in their hand; and
they came unto Balaam, and
spake unto him the words of
Balak.
8 And he said unto them,
Lodge here this night, and I
will bring you word again, as
the LORD shall speak unto
me: and the princes of Moab
abode with Balaam.
9 And God came unto
Balaam, and said, What men
are these with thee?
10 And Balaam said unto
God, Balak the son of
Zippor, king of Moab, hath
sent unto me, saying,
11 Behold, there is a people
come out of Egypt, which
covereth the face of the
earth: come now, curse me
them; peradventure I shall be
able to overcome them, and
drive them out.
12 And God said unto
Balaam, Thou shalt not go
with them; thou shalt not
curse the people: for they are
blessed.
13 And Balaam rose up in
the morning, and said unto
the princes of Balak, Get you
into your land: for the LORD
refuseth to give me leave to
go with you.
14 And the princes of Moab
rose up, and they went unto
Balak, and said, Balaam
refuseth to come with us.
15 And Balak sent yet again
princes, more, and more
honourable than they.
16 And they came to
Balaam, and said to him,
Thus saith Balak the son of
Zippor, Let nothing, I pray
thee, hinder thee from coming unto me:
17 For I will promote thee
unto very great honour, and I
will do whatsoever thou
sayest unto me: come therefore, I pray thee, curse me
this people.
18 And Balaam answered
and said unto the servants of
Balak, If Balak would give
me his house full of silver
and gold, I cannot go beyond
the word of the LORD my
God, to do less or more.
19 Now therefore, I pray
you, tarry ye also here this
night, that I may know what
the LORD will say unto me
more.
20 And God came unto
Balaam at night, and said
unto him, If the men come to
call thee, rise up, and go with
them; but yet the word which
I shall say unto thee, that
shalt thou do.
21 And Balaam rose up in
the morning, and saddled his
ass, and went with the
princes of Moab.
22 And God's anger was
kindled because he went:
and the angel of the LORD
stood in the way for an
adversary against him. Now
he was riding upon his ass,

king of Edom, & related their request for a curse to be put upon Israel
  - 3) God's warning to Balaam
    - Was not to go with them
    - Was not to curse Israel
    - The reason: They were God's people—blessed
- d. The clear-cut response of Balaam to the confrontation with God
  - 1) He refused to go with the officials
  - 2) The officials returned & related Balaam's refusal to the king

3. The 2nd encounter of Balaam with God: A man who would do anything for money (Jude 11)
- a. The king tried a more urgent request: He sent other officials—a larger number & more distinguished—with a far more appealing offer to Balaam
  - 1) He would reward him well
  - 2) He would do anything
  - 3) He was desperate: Begged Balaam to come & put a curse on Israel
- b. The response of Balaam: Revealed a spirit enslaved by greed
  - 1) He declared that nothing could change his mind, not to go against God's will (not even for a palace filled with silver & gold)
  - 2) He invited the officials to spend the night while he sought God (just in case God would let him go)
- c. The 2nd encounter with God: Gave Balaam over to his greed (Ro.1:28-32)
  - 1) Gave permission to go
  - 2) But warned him: Had better do only what God told him
- d. The response of Balaam to the confrontation: He went with the officials (let greed consume him, v.12)

4. The 3rd encounter of Balaam with God (the story of the donkey): The anger of God over greed & the signs of His anger
- a. The angel of the LORD stood

in the road to block Balaam's way
1) The donkey saw the angel of the Lord blocking theroad with a drawn sword: Turned off the road into a field
2) Balaam beat her to get her back on the road

b. The angel of the LORD blocked the path again, a narrow path with walls on both sides
1) The donkey again saw the angel of the LORD: Tried to squeeze by & crushed Balaam's foot
2) Balaam again beat the animal

c. The angel of the LORD then moved ahead to a place so narrow that the donkey could not get by
1) The donkey saw the angel of the LORD & just lay down under Balaam
2) Balaam, in anger, beat her with his staff

d. The LORD opened the donkey's mouth & the animal miraculously, shockingly spoke to Balaam (cp. 2 Pt.2:16)
1) The donkey complained of Balaam's cruelty
2) Balaam—in a fit of rage—wished he had a sword to kill the animal: Because it had made a fool of him
3) The donkey reasoned with Balaam
- That she was Balaam's property
- That she had always served Balaam well
- That she had never behaved like this before

4) Balaam agreed

e. The LORD opened Balaam's eyes
1) Balaam saw the angel of the Lord standing with his drawn sword (a symbol of God's anger, a strong warning): He fell face down on the ground
2) The angel of the LORD

and his two servants were
with him.
23 And the ass saw the
angel of the LORD standing
in the way, and his sword
drawn in his hand: and the
ass turned aside out of the
way, and went into the field:
and Balaam smote the ass, to
turn her into the way.
24 But the angel of the
LORD stood in a path of the
vineyards, a wall being on
this side, and a wall on that
side.
25 And when the ass saw
the angel of the LORD, she
thrust herself unto the wall,
and crushed Balaam's foot
against the wall: and he
smote her again.
26 And the angel of the
LORD went further, and stood
in a narrow place, where was
no way to turn either to the
right hand or to the left.
27 And when the ass saw
the angel of the LORD, she
fell down under Balaam: and
Balaam's anger was kindled,
and he smote the ass with a
staff.
28 And the LORD opened the
mouth of the ass, and she
said unto Balaam, What have
I done unto thee, that thou
hast smitten me these three
times?
29 And Balaam said unto
the ass, Because thou hast
mocked me: I would there
were a sword in mine hand,
for now would I kill thee.
30 And the ass said unto
Balaam, Am not I thine ass,
upon which thou hast ridden
ever since I was thine unto
this day? was I ever wont to
do so unto thee? And he said,
Nay.
31 Then the LORD opened
the eyes of Balaam, and he
saw the angel of the LORD
standing in the way, and his
sword drawn in his hand:
and he bowed down his
head, and fell flat on his
face.
32 And the angel of the
LORD said unto him,
Wherefore hast thou smitten
thine ass these three times?
behold, I went out to withstand
thee, because thy way
is perverse before me:
33 And the ass saw me, and
turned from me these three
times: unless she had turned
from me, surely now also I
had slain thee, and saved her
alive.
34 And Balaam said unto
the angel of the LORD, I have
sinned; for I knew not that
thou stoodest in the way
against me: now therefore, if
it displease thee, I will get
me back again.
35 And the angel of the
LORD said unto Balaam, Go
with the men: but only the
word that I shall speak unto
thee, that thou shalt speak.
So Balaam went with the
princes of Balak.
36 And when Balak heard
that Balaam was come, he
went out to meet him unto a
city of Moab, which is in the
border of Arnon, which is in
the utmost coast.
37 And Balak said unto
Balaam, Did I not earnestly
send unto thee to call thee?
wherefore camest thou not
unto me? am I not able
indeed to promote thee to
honour?
38 And Balaam said unto
Balak, Lo, I am come unto
thee: have I now any power
at all to say any thing? the
word that God putteth in my
mouth, that shall I speak.
39 And Balaam went with
Balak, and they came unto
Kirjath-huzoth.
40 And Balak offered oxen
and sheep, and sent to
Balaam, and to the princes
that were with him.
41 And it came to pass on
the morrow, that Balak took
Balaam, and brought him
up into the high places of
Baal, that thence he might
see the utmost part of the
people.

confronted Balaam
- Rebuked him for mistreatment of an animal
- Condemned him because of his reckless, stubborn heart & resistance to God
- Warned him that God would have taken his life by now because of his resistance if the donkey had not stopped

3) Balaam confessed his sin & offered to return (but did not repent)

4) The response of the angel of the LORD: Gave Balaam over to his greed—he could go, but he must speak only what God said

5. The effect of the encounters & warnings upon Balaam

a. The excitement of king Balak at Balaam's coming
1) He traveled all the way to the border to meet Balaam
2) He expressed disappointment at Balaam's refusal of the first request—especially in light of the offer to be so well rewarded

b. The effect of the encounters with the LORD & His warnings: Balaam replied that He had now come, but he could speak only the message God gave him

c. The king celebrated Balaam's coming
1) He offered pagan sacrifices to his gods: Balaam participated with Balak
2) He took Balaam up to Bamoth Baal, some hill or high place where Baal was worshipped: To scan the camp of Israel

DIVISION III

THE FORTY LONG YEARS OF WILDERNESS WANDERINGS: A PICTURE OF THE BELIEVER'S PILGRIMAGE THROUGH THIS WORLD AS HE PREPARES TO ENTER THE PROMISED LAND 15:1-25:18

H. Event 8—the Story of Balaam, His Donkey, and His Three Encounters with God (Part 1): A Picture of the Unseen, Unknown Attempts by the Powers of Darkness to Defeat God's People, 22:1-41

NUMBERS 22:1-41

(22:1-41) **Introduction—Spiritual World, Warfare of —Evil Spirits, Work of—Occult, World of—Sorcery, Evil of —Psychics, Evil of—Diviners, Evil of—Darkness, Powers of, Described**: there is an unseen warfare going on behind the events of world history. This warfare is conducted by the evil spirits of darkness, evil spirits who serve under a supreme power that is identified in the Holy Scripture as Satan or the devil. In deep malice and wrath against God, these evil forces try their best, when possible, to frustrate the plan of God for this world. Evil spirits seek to cut the heart of God because of God's judgment against their arrogance and rejection of Him. The way they seek to hurt God is by taking over the normal desires and the obsessive passions of men, using them to destroy people. They use the passions that enslave people, passions such as…

- greed
- drugs
- alcohol
- gluttony
- lust
- cravings
- vulgarity
- profanity
- pornography
- immorality
- abuse
- killing
- bestiality

If the curtain were rolled back between earth and heaven, man would easily see what lies behind all the sin and evil, all the conflicts and struggles of this world. He would clearly see a horde of evil spirits seeking to cut the heart of God by deceiving people, by turning them away from God (see outline and notes—Lk.8:26-39 for more discussion). One of the ways used by these evil spirits is the world of the occult, the world of the false prophet, the diviner, the sorcerer, the psychic, the palm-reader, the fortune-teller, the astrologer, and a host of others. The leaders of the occult advertise and cry out for the attention of people, claiming that they know the future, can meet needs, and can bring blessings into the lives of people. Some even go so far as to claim that they can control and alter the future, that they can bring blessings upon those whom they bless and cursings upon those whom they curse. Under the power of darkness and spiritual wickedness in high places, they mislead people and cause them to turn away from the only living and true God, the Lord God Himself (Jehovah, Yahweh). The world of the occult is a world controlled by evil spirits who are set upon destroying the lives of people and cutting the heart of God. (See outline and notes—Acts 16:16-17; Rev.12:3-4; 12:9 for more discussion.)

"For we wrestle not against flesh and blood, but aaainst principalities, against powers, against the rulers of the darkness of this world, against spiritual wickedness in high places" (Eph.6:12).

Remember, Israel is camped in the plains of Moab by the Jordan River across from the great city of Jericho. The present Scripture is an event that takes place totally unknown to the Israelites. It is a picture of the unseen, unknown attempts by the powers of darkness and spiritual wickedness in high places—an attempt to destroy the people of God in order to break the heart of God. Keep in mind that Israel is totally unaware of what is happening. But not God. God knows, and God protects His people. He will not allow any person to touch His people, to call a curse of judgment and destruction down upon them. Judgment and destruction are in His hands and no one else's. To curse His people with judgment and destruction will never happen, never be allowed. This is the story of this Scripture: *Event 8—the Story of Balaam, His Donkey, and His Three Encounters with God (Part 1): A Picture of the Unseen, Unknown Attempts by the Powers of Darkness to Defeat God's People*, 22:1-41.

1. The background to the encounters with God: a false belief in divination (v.1-6).
2. The 1st encounter of Balaam with God: a man who earned money dishonestly (2 Pt.2:15) (v.7-14).
3. The 2nd encounter of Balaam with God: a man who would do anything for money (Jude 11) (v.15-21).
4. The 3rd encounter of Balaam with God (the story of the donkey): the anger of God over greed and the signs of His anger (v.22-35).
5. The effect of the encounters and warnings upon Balaam (v.36-41).

1 (22:1-6) **Divination—Sorcery—Occult—Balaam—Balak**: the background to Balaam's encounters with God was dramatic. A false belief in the world of divination, sorcery, and the occult is seen. Note the Scripture and outline:

OUTLINE	SCRIPTURE	SCRIPTURE	OUTLINE
1. The dramatic background to the encounters with God: A false belief in divination a. The Israelites were poised to enter the promised land b. The king of Moab heard about Israel 1) Heard they were nearby & about their military exploits 2) Was terrified, filled with dread because of the Israelites c. The king formed an alliance with the leaders of Midian: Feared Israel would devour everything just like an ox devours grass d. The king sought to curse & defeat Israel by pagan divination: He sent for Balaam,	And the children of Israel set forward, and pitched in the plains of Moab on this side Jordan by Jericho. 2 And Balak the son of Zippor saw all that Israel had done to the Amorites. 3 And Moab was sore afraid of the people, because they were many: and Moab was distressed because of the children of Israel. 4 And Moab said unto the elders of Midian, Now shall this company lick up all that are round about us, as the ox licketh up the grass of the field. And Balak the son of Zippor was king of the Moabites at that time.	5 He sent messengers therefore unto Balaam the son of Beor to Pethor, which is by the river of the land of the children of his people, to call him, saying, Behold, there is a people come out from Egypt: behold, they cover the face of the earth, and they abide over against me: 6 Come now therefore, I pray thee, curse me this people; for they are too mighty for me: peradventure I shall prevail, that we may smite them, and that I may drive them out of the land: for I wot that he whom thou blessest is blessed, and he whom thou cursest is cursed.	a famous diviner with an international reputation 1) Related how a horde of people had arrived from Egypt & settled next to him 2) Wanted Balaam to put a curse on them so he could defeat them in battle 3) Stated that he believed strongly in the divination powers of Balaam: The people Balaam blessed were blessed, & those he cursed were cursed

NUMBERS 22:1-41

1. The Israelites were poised to enter the promised land (v.1). At long last, the Israelites had reached the plains of Moab and camped along the Jordan River right across from the great city of Jericho. From this vantage point, the promised land was in plain view and God's people would soon lay claim to the wonderful inheritance God had promised them. Picture the excitement of the people as they sat around their campfires by night: the children playing, running, and dancing around; the adults sharing their joys and plans for the land they are soon to inherit and the homes they are to build. Excitement, joy, anticipation, great expectation—all the hopes and dreams of a people who had been freed from slavery and were about to return home—were wrapped up in the moment of these days. But behind this scene of great excitement and joy, another dramatic plot was being played out. The unseen, unknown powers of darkness were scheming to destroy God's people.

2. The king of Moab had heard about Israel, that they were camped nearby in the plains of Moab (v.2-3). He of course had also heard about the military exploits of Israel against the Amorites and the kingdom of Bashan. This news struck fear in king Balak and his people. Note what Scripture says: they were terrified, greatly distressed, and filled with dread because of the Israelites. The word "fear," "afraid," or "terrified" (gur) means a dreadful, horrifying fear. It has the idea of being frightened or terrified out of one's mind. But even this does not fully describe the depth of fear they were experiencing. Note the word "distressed" or "dread" (qus): this means a sickening, nauseating, debilitating, incapacitating, hopeless, and helpless fear. The king and his officials saw no way to stop the march of the Israelites. If he launched a military operation against the Israelites, he would be defeated and his nation utterly destroyed. A surprise military action was therefore out of the question. Some other way had to be devised to defeat God's people. No doubt after days of consultation and consideration of contingency plans, the king and his official came up with a devious plot. To modern ears within industrial societies, their devious plot may sound strange, but divination, sorcery, and the world of the occult were a part of everyday society among pagan people in the ancient world. To be honest, the world of the occult—diviners, psychics witch doctors, astrologers, and many others—is just as active today as ever.

3. The king and his advisors formed an alliance with the leaders of Midian (v.4). Note how Balak described the strength of Israel to the Midianites: Israel was so strong and powerful that she was just like an ox that devours grass. It should be noted that this particular plot against God's people by these two nations would fail. However, a later plot by Moab and Midian would succeed, and Balaam—this false prophet—would again be right in the middle of the plot. In fact, he would actually devise the plan and scheme that would overthrow the children of God (Num.25:1-18). Now note the devious and strange sounding plot.

4. The king (in alliance with the Midianites) sought to curse and defeat Israel by pagan divination or sorcery (v.4-6). The king sent messengers to secure the help of Balaam, a famous diviner or sorcerer with an international reputation. The summons sent to the false prophet spelled out exactly what the king wanted:

- ⇒ He related how a horde of people had arrived from Egypt and settled next to him (v.5).
- ⇒ He wanted Balaam to come and put a curse on them so he could defeat them in battle (v.6).
- ⇒ He stated that he believed strongly in the divination or sorcery powers of Balaam; that is, the people Balaam blessed were blessed, and those he cursed were cursed (v.6).

The king was desperate: the Israelites were too powerful for him to fight without the help of the "gods." There was no hope for victory unless the gods helped him by cursing the Israelites and blessing his own military forces. Consequently, he summoned one of the famous diviners or psychics of that day and time. Along with so many others down through history and even up until this day, he believed that the gods had gifted some persons who could pronounce cursings or blessings upon people. He believed if Balaam could just pronounce a curse upon the Israelites, either some supernatural event would wipe them out or else he would be able to defeat them in battle.

Thought 1. Psychics, fortune-tellers, palm-readers, sorcerers, diviners, psychics, self-proclaimed prophets of new-age movements or of the zodiac—the whole world of the occult—have all been sought by people down through the centuries of human history. People want to know their destiny, what the future holds. They want the blessings of the gods that be, or else they want some enemy cursed. They want only good things to happen to them, not bad things. They want good experiences, not bad experiences. They want plenty, not the bare necessities. They want more, not less. They want acceptance, not rejection. They want to be highly esteemed, not put down. They want position and power, not servitude and enslavement.

For these reasons and for so many more, people seek the leaders of the occult. They seek the help of any person who claims to have the power of astrology, the power to read the stars, the zodiac, or any other medium. If a person claims to have the answer to the future or to people's problems, they flock to him. But Scripture is clear: the world of the occult is a world of sin and evil. Man is to have nothing—absolutely nothing—to do with the world of the occult.

"And it came to pass, as we went to prayer, a certain damsel possessed with a spirit of divination met us, which brought her masters much gain by soothsaying: The same followed Paul and us, and cried, saying, These men are the servants of the most high God, which show unto us the way of salvation. And this did she many days. But Paul, being grieved, turned and said to the spirit, I command thee in the name of Jesus Christ to come out of her. And he came out the same hour. And when her masters saw that the hope of their gains was gone, they caught Paul and Silas, and drew them into the marketplace unto the rulers" (Acts 16:16-19).

"Now the works of the flesh are manifest, which are these; Adultery, fornication, uncleanness, lasciviousness, Idolatry, witchcraft, hatred, variance, emulations, wrath, strife, seditions, heresies, Envyings, murders, drunkenness, revellings, and such like: of the which I tell you before, as I have also told you in time past, that they which do such things shall not inherit the kingdom of God" (Gal 5:19-21).

"But the fearful, and unbelieving, and the abominable, and murderers, and whoremongers, and sorcerers, and idolaters, and all liars, shall have their part in the lake which burneth with fire and brimstone: which is the second death" (Rev.21:8).

"When thou art come into the land which the Lord thy God giveth thee, thou shalt not learn to do

after the abominations of those nations. There shall not be found among you any one that maketh his son or his daughter to pass through the fire, or that useth divination, or an observer of times, or an enchanter, or a witch, Or a charmer, or a consulter with familiar spirits, or a wizard, or a necromancer. For all that do these things are an abomination unto the Lord: and because of these abominations the Lord thy God doth drive them out from before thee. Thou shalt be perfect with the Lord thy God" (Dt.18:9-13).

"And they caused their sons and their daughters to pass through the fire, and used divination and enchantments, and sold themselves to do evil in the sight of the Lord, to provoke him to anger" (2 Ki.17:17).

"And he [king Manasseh] made his son pass through the fire, and observed times, and used enchantments, and dealt with famiiiar spirits and wizards: he wrought much wickedness in the sight of the Lord, to provoke him to anger" (2 Ki.21:6).

"But these two things shall come to thee in a moment in one day, the loss of children, and widowhood: they shall come upon thee in their perfection for the multitude of thy sorceries, and for the great abundance of thine enchantments" (Is.47:9).

"Likewise, thou son of man, set thy face against the daughters of thy people, which prophesy out of their own heart; and prophesy thou against them, And say, Thus saith the Lord GOD; Woe to the *women* that sew pillows to all armholes, and make kerchiefs upon the head of every stature to hunt souls! Will ye hunt the souls of my people, and will ye save the souls alive *that come* unto you?...Because with lies ye have made the heart of the righteous sad, whom I have not made sad; and strengthened the hands of the wicked, that he should not return from his wicked way, by promising him life: Therefore ye shall see no more vanity, nor divine divinations: for I will deliver my people out of your hand: and ye shall know that I *am* the LORD" (Ezk.13:17-18, 22-23).

"And I will cut off witchcrafts out of thine hand; and thou shalt have no more soothsayers" (Mic.5:12).

"For the idols have spoken vanity, and the diviners have seen a lie, and have told false dreams; they comfort in vain: therefore they went their way as a flock, they were troubled, because there was no shepherd" (Zech.10:2).

"And now we call the proud happy; yea, they that work wickedness are set up; yea, they that tempt God are even delivered" (Mal.3:15).

DEEPER STUDY # 1
(Num.22:1) **Jericho, City of**: it was located in the lower Jordan River valley, on the plains of Moab. The Hebrew meaning of Jericho is "moon city" or possibly "place of fragrance." (See Map—Numbers 33:5-49, end of commentary.) It is here, in Numbers, where Jericho is first mentioned in the Bible. Israel camped across from Jericho before entering into the promised land. It was a fortified city whose walls tumbled down before God's chosen people. In New Testament times, Jericho was known for its aromatic gum that was used for medical purposes.
See other Scripture references for study:

Numbers 26:3; Numbers 26:63; Numbers 31:12; Numbers 33:48; Numbers 33:50; Numbers 34:15; Numbers 35:1; Numbers 36:13; Deut. 32:49; Deut. 34:1; Deut. 34:3; Joshua 2:1-3; Joshua 3:16; Joshua 4:13; Joshua 4:19; Joshua 5:10; Joshua 5:13; Joshua 6:1-2; Joshua 6:25-26; Joshua 7:2; Joshua 8:2; Joshua 9:3; Joshua 10:1; Joshua 10:28; Joshua 10:30; Joshua 12:9; Joshua 13:32; Joshua 16:1; Joshua 16:7; Joshua 18:12; Joshua 18:21; Joshua 20:8; Joshua 24:11; 2 Samuel 10:5; 1 Kings 16:34; 2 Kings 2:4-5; 2 Kings 2:15; 2 Kings 2:18; 2 Kings 25:5; 1 Chron. 6:78; 1 Chron. 19:5; 2 Chron. 28:15; Ezra 2:34; Neh. 3:2; Neh. 7:36; Jeremiah 39:5; Jeremiah 52:8; Matthew 20:29; Mark 10:46; Luke 10:30; Luke 18:35; Luke 19:1; Hebrews 11:30

DEEPER STUDY # 2
(Num.22:5) **Pethor, City of**: it was located twelve miles south of Carchemish in Mesopotamia near the meeting of the Sajur and Euphrates rivers (See Map—Numbers 33:5-49, end of commentary.) The Hebrew meaning of Pethor is "soothsayer." Pethor was the home of Balaam.
See other Scripture reference for study:

Deut. 23:4

2 (22:7-14) **Encounter, with God—Confrontation, with God—Warning, of God—Balaam, Warned by God—Money, Earned Dishonestly—Divination, Evil of—Sorcery, Evil of**: the first encounter of Balaam with God was a warning. This false prophet, this diviner, needed a severe warning. He was a man who earned money the wrong way, by dishonesty.

"Which have forsaken the right way, and are gone astray, following the way of Balaam the son of Bosor, who loved the wages of unrighteousness [by divination, sorcery]" (2 Pt.2:15).

He earned a living by playing off the fears, sufferings, and hopes of people—claiming to have the answer to whatever they wanted or needed. He could bless and a person would be blessed, or he could curse and a person would be cursed. He could help people, give them exactly what they needed. But for his help he was to receive a fee, obviously a large fee because of his international reputation. God condemns diviners, sorcerers, mystics, or anyone else who preys upon people seeking direction or help. Note the Scripture and outline:

OUTLINE	SCRIPTURE	SCRIPTURE	OUTLINE
2. The 1st encounter of Balaam with God: A man who earned money dishonestly (2 Pt.2:15) a. The officials from both Moab & Midian traveled to see Balaam with the fee for divination b. The response of Balaam was immediate: He invited the officials to spend the night while he sought God's will c. The 1st encounter with God 1) God asked who the men were visiting him 2) Balaam identified them as officials from Balak, the king of Edom, & related their request for a curse to be put upon Israel	7 And the elders of Moab and the elders of Midian departed with the rewards of divination in their hand; and they came unto Balaam, and spake unto him the words of Balak. 8 And he said unto them, Lodge here this night, and I will bring you word again, as the LORD shall speak unto me: and the princes of Moab abode with Balaam. 9 And God came unto Balaam, and said, What men are these with thee? 10 And Balaam said unto God, Balak the son of Zippor, king of Moab, hath sent unto me, saying, 11 Behold, there is a people	come out of Egypt, which covereth the face of the earth: come now, curse me them; peradventure I shall be able to overcome them, and drive them out. 12 And God said unto Balaam, Thou shalt not go with them; thou shalt not curse the people: for they are blessed. 13 And Balaam rose up in the morning, and said unto the princes of Balak, Get you into your land: for the LORD refuseth to give me leave to go with you. 14 And the princes of Moab rose up, and they went unto Balak, and said, Balaam refuseth to come with us.	3) God's warning to Balaam • Was not to go with them • Was not to curse Israel • The reason: They were God's people—blessed d. The clear-cut response of Balaam to the confrontation with God 1) He refused to go with the officials 2) The officials returned & related Balaam's refusal to the king

1. The officials from both Moab and Midian traveled to see Balaam. Special attention is called to the fact that they took with them a large *fee for divination* (v.7). This fact suggests that Balaam had a heart consumed with greed, the desire for money and possessions—the things of this world (1 Jn.2:15-16).

2. The response of Balaam was immediate: he invited the officials to spend the night while he sought God's will (v.8). Note that he was going to seek God during the night, while the others were asleep.

3. Note the first confrontation with God. Balaam got the surprise of his life: shockingly, astoundingly, the Lord Himself (Jehovah, Yahweh) confronted this false prophet, this seer, this diviner, this psychic, this sorcerer.

a. God asked who the men were visiting Balaam (v.9).
b. No doubt in shock, Balaam identified them as officials from Balak, the king of Edom. He related their request for a curse to be put upon Israel so that the king might fight and drive them out of his land (v.10-11).
c. Upon hearing the word "curse," God immediately issued a strong warning to Balaam:
⇒ He was not to go with the messengers to the king.
⇒ He was not under any circumstance to "curse" Israel.
⇒ The reason was clearly stated: they were God's people, especially blessed by God Himself (v.12).

God loves His dear people, for they bear His name and stand as a strong testimony to His name. They live righteous and godly lives before God, proclaiming the absolute necessity for man to live righteously and godly. God loves His dear people because they are the heirs of the Abrahamic covenant, the great covenant God made with His people through Abraham:

⇒ the promise of the promised seed
⇒ the promise of the promised land (see outline and notes—Gen.12:1-3 for more discussion)

4. The response of Balaam to the confrontation with God was decisive, clear-cut: he refused to go with the officials, and the officials returned to relate the refusal to the king (v.13-14).

Thought 1. God's people are very special to Him, a very special treasure (Ex.19:5). What makes them so special is God's call: the fact that He has called and set them apart to be His followers. Simply stated, genuine believers live holy and righteous lives before God. They seek with all their hearts to live lives...

- of morality and purity
- of honesty and fairness
- of truthfulness and integrity
- of giving and sharing
- of service and ministry
- of healing and helping
- of encouragement and consolation
- of strengthening and equipping
- of generosity and good will
- of supporting and building up
- of preaching and teaching
- of witnessing and sharing Christ

For these reasons and for many others, God loves His dear people. He has called and appointed them to be His witnesses upon this earth, just as He had the Israelites. No person can call upon God to curse His people. Once God has called a person and set that person apart to become a member of His people, that person cannot be cursed. He is destined to live eternally—some day out in the future—with God Himself, face-to-face. The believer is God's heritage, God's treasure, God's chosen, God's elect, God's heir, God's adopted son or daughter—very, very special to God!

"Ye have not chosen me, but I have chosen you, and ordained you, that ye should go and bring forth fruit, and that your fruit should remain: that whatsoever ye shall ask of the Father in my name, he may

give it you" (Jn.15:16).

"Who shall lay any thing to the charge of God's elect? It is God that justifieth. Who is he that condemneth? It is Christ that died, yea rather, that is risen again, who is even at the right hand of God, who also maketh intercession for us" (Ro.8:33-34).

"But when the fulness of the time was come, God sent forth his Son, made of a woman, made under the law, To redeem them that were under the law, that we might receive the adoption of sons. And because ye are sons, God hath sent forth the Spirit of his Son into your hearts, crying, Abba, Father" (Gal.4:4-6).

"According as he hath chosen us in him before the foundation of the world, that we should be holy and without blame before him in love" (Eph.1:4).

"Blessed is the man that endureth temptation: for when he is tried, he shall receive the crown of life, which the Lord hath promised to them that love him" (Jas.1:12).

"Behold, what manner of love the Father hath bestowed upon us, that we should be called the sons of God: therefore the world knoweth us not, because it knew him not" (1 Jn.3:1).

"Now therefore, if ye will obey my voice indeed, and keep my covenant, then ye shall be a peculiar treasure unto me above all people: for all the earth is mine" (Ex.19:5).

3 (22:15-21) **Encounter, with God—Greed—Money, Lust for—Judgment, Judicial—Judicial Judgment—Balaam**: the second encounter of Balaam with God was stunning and revealing: it revealed a double-minded, hypocritical, and greedy heart. This encounter with God exposed a man who would do anything for money.

"Woe unto them! for they have gone in the way of Cain, and ran greedily after the error of Balaam for reward, and perished in the gainsaying of Core" (Jude 11).

OUTLINE	SCRIPTURE	SCRIPTURE	OUTLINE
3. The 2nd encounter of Balaam with God: A man who would do anything for money (Jude 11) a. The king tried a more urgent request: He sent other officials—a larger number & more distinguished—with a far more appealing offer to Balaam 1) He would reward him well 2) He would do anything 3) He was desperate: Begged Balaam to come & put a curse on Israel b. The response of Balaam: Revealed a spirit enslaved by greed 1) He declared that nothing could change his mind,	15 And Balak sent yet again princes, more, and more honourable than they. 16 And they came to Balaam, and said to him, Thus saith Balak the son of Zippor, Let nothing, I pray thee, hinder thee from coming unto me: 17 For I will promote thee unto very great honour, and I will do whatsoever thou sayest unto me: come therefore, I pray thee, curse me this people. 18 And Balaam answered and said unto the servants of Balak, If Balak would give me his house full of silver	and gold, I cannot go beyond the word of the LORD my God, to do less or more. 19 Now therefore, I pray you, tarry ye also here this night, that I may know what the LORD will say unto me more. 20 And God came unto Balaam at night, and said unto him, If the men come to call thee, rise up, and go with them; but yet the word which I shall say unto thee, that shalt thou do. 21 And Balaam rose up in the morning, and saddled his ass, and went with the princes of Moab.	not to go against God's will (not even for a palace filled with silver & gold) 2) He invited the officials to spend the night while he sought God (just in case God would let him go) c. The 2nd encounter with God: Gave Balaam over to his greed (Ro.1:28-32) 1) Gave permission to go 2) But warned him: Had better do only what God told him d. The response of Balaam to the confrontation: He went with the officials (let greed consume him, v.12)

1. The king was not going to give up, for he was desperate. He tried a more urgent request with Balaam: he sent other officials, a larger number and more distinguished. Note that he also sent a far more appealing offer:

⇒ The king would pay him well, in essence, pay Balaam whatever he desired.
⇒ The king would do anything, bestow whatever honor Balaam desired.
⇒ The king was desperate: he begged Balaam to come and put a curse on Israel (v.17).

Note how the king appealed to the greed and covetousness of the human heart. He offered this false prophet, this diviner, this sorcerer, this psychic anything he wanted—any amount of money and any honor. He appealed to his greed, his pride, and his ambition. The king was desperate: this diviner must come and put a curse on God's people so that he could defeat them and drive them out of his country (cp. v.6).

2. The response of Balaam revealed a spirit that was totally enslaved by greed (v.18-19). Note how Balaam's actions were for appearance only. He only seemed to be resisting the summons and offer of the king.

a. Balaam declared that nothing could change his mind, not to go against God's will. He would not even go against God's will for a palace filled with silver and gold (v.18). Remember, God had already revealed His will: the false prophet was not to go (v.12). He knew exactly what God wanted him to do: he was not to curse Israel. They were God's people, followers of the only living and true God. Therefore, there was no chance that God was going to curse His people nor allow anyone else to put a true curse upon them. No one would ever be allowed to defeat His people nor to curse His people to the judgment of death. Only the Lord God Himself (Jehovah, Yahweh) had the power to curse and judge people to death. No one else had this power. Consequently, there was no chance that God was going to judge His own people, those who sought to follow after Him. Moreover, there was no chance that He was going to allow Balaam or anyone else to curse His dear people. All this Balaam already knew. God had revealed it to him, forbidding him from going and attempting to curse God's people. But note how wavering, double-minded, and hypocritical Balaam was.

b. He told the officials to stay and spend the night while he sought God, just in case God would give him another message and allow him to go (v.19). This shows a strong, strong urge and intention to accept the offer. This was a terrible reflection upon God, as though God were double-minded and would change His mind, allowing him to go and put a curse upon the people of God. The heart and mind of this man were so corrupt and twisted that he played the role of a hypocrite, of a double-minded man himself. Deceiving and misleading the officials were nothing to him. He would not go against God's will even for a palace filled with silver and gold, but he would take the night to seek God just in case God would let him go. He was play-acting with the name of God, preying upon the needs, the hopes, and the dreams of people—all for money and profit. Obviously to him, God was little higher than man himself who wavered back and forth, changing his mind day by day. Simply stated, he already knew God's will. He knew that he was not to go, for God had already told him that he was not to go nor to put a curse upon the precious people of God.

3. Note the second encounter with God: God gave Balaam over to his greed, gave him up to the lusts of his own heart (Ro.1:28-32). Balaam's heart was set on going. He lusted to go, craved after the wealth and honors offered by the king. The lust and greed had enslaved his heart. His mind had already made the decision: he was going. But note what happened when he got alone that night: God came to Balaam and gave him a severe warning: "Since these men had come to summon him—since he had determined to go with them—he could go. But he had better do only what God told him" (v.20). The decision to rebel against God by going was made by Balaam. The permission to allow Balaam to follow through was given by God. Balaam was permitted to go, but he was warned and warned severely: he must do only what God told him to do.

4. The response of Balaam to the confrontation with God was just what would be expected from a greedy heart: he got up in the morning and went with the officials. He still had the freedom to obey God, the ability to choose not to go, not to put a curse upon God's people. But the choice was made, driven by the consuming passion of greed, the lust after money and honor.

Thought 1. Greed and covetousness are wrong; they are sin before God and man. A covetous, greedy person violates the very commandment of God Himself. Moreover, the covetous, greedy person causes suffering by not sharing and distributing to those who are in need. And sometimes, by stealing from the needy and poor, covetousness and greed consume a person, eating away at his spirit and life. A greedy, covetous person actually falls into many foolish and hurtful passions, doing many foolish and hurtful things. Greed and covetousness actually plunge men into destruction and doom.

"And he [Judas] cast down the pieces of silver in the temple, and departed, and went and hanged himself" (Mt.27:5).

"And he said unto them, Take heed, and beware of covetousness: for a man's life consisteth not in the abundance of the things which he possesseth" (Lk.12:15).

"Mortify therefore your members which are upon the earth; fornication, uncleanness, inordinate affection, evil concupiscence, and covetousness, which is idolatry" (Col.3:5).

"But they that will be rich fall into temptation and a snare, and into many foolish and hurtful lusts, which drown men in destruction and perdition. For the love of money is the root of all evil: which while some coveted after, they have erred from the faith, and pierced themselves through with many sorrows" (1 Tim.6:9-10).

"Your gold and silver is cankered; and the rust of them shall be a witness against you, and shall eat your flesh as it were fire. Ye have heaped treasure together for the last days" (Jas.5:3).

"Behold, the hire of the labourers who have reaped down your fields, which is of you kept back by fraud, crieth: and the cries of them which have reaped are entered into the ears of the Lord of sabaoth" (Jas.5:4).

"Thou shalt not covet thy neighbour's house, thou shalt not covet thy neighbour's wife, nor his manservant, nor his maidservant, nor his ox, nor his ass, nor any thing that is thy neighbour's" (Ex.20:17).

"He that is greedy of gain troubleth his own house; but he that hateth gifts shall live" (Pr.15:27).

"Better is a little with righteousness than great revenues without right" (Pr.16:8).

"The getting of treasures by a lying tongue is a vanity tossed to and fro of them that seek death" (Pr.21:6).

"He that oppresseth the poor to increase his riches, and he that giveth to the rich, shall surely come to want" (Pr.22:16).

"He that loveth silver shall not be satisfied with silver; nor he that loveth abundance with increase: this is also vanity" (Eccl.5:10).

"As the partridge sitteth on eggs, and hatcheth them not; so he that getteth riches, and not by right, shall leave them in the midst of his days, and at his end shall be a fool" (Jer.17:11).

"Woe unto him that buildeth his house by unrighteousness, and his chambers by wrong; that useth his neighbour's service without wages, and giveth him not for his work" (Jer.22:13).

"And they come unto thee as the people cometh, and they sit before thee as my people, and they hear thy words, but they will not do them: for with their mouth they show much love, but their heart goeth after their covetousness" (Ezk.33:31).

"And they covet fields, and take them by violence; and houses, and take them away: so they oppress a man and his house, even a man and his heritage" (Mic.2:2).

"Woe to him that coveteth an evil covetousness to his house, that he may set his nest on high, that he may be delivered from the power of evil! Thou hast consulted shame to thy house by cutting off many people, and hast sinned against thy soul" (Hab.2:9-10).

4 (22:22-35) **Greed, Results—Anger, of God—God, Anger of—Balaam, Story of the Donkey—Encounter, with God—Money, Love of**: the third encounter of Balaam with God aroused the anger of God. This is the story of Balaam and the donkey, a story that reveals the anger of God over greed. Simply stated, God used the donkey as a sign of His anger against the greed of this false prophet. God used the donkey as a warning of judgment if the false prophet did not do exactly what God instructed. This is a dramatic lesson that shows God's anger and displeasure with the world of the occult. God stands opposed to any false prophet, diviner, sorcerer, psychic, palm-reader, fortune-teller, or astrologer. God is angry with any person who uses the fears and hopes of people to gain profit or money. The leaders of the occult world are stumblingblocks to people: they lead people into a false belief, away from the only living and true God (Jehovah, Yahweh). But even more terrible than this, they doom people to an eternity of separation from God in the judgment to come. This is the reason God is angry with the world of the occult, the reason He is going to severely judge the world of the occult. This was certainly part of the reason God spoke through the donkey to Balaam. In this dramatic event of the donkey speaking, God was warning Balaam, giving him a severe warning: he must do exactly what God says. This dramatic experience emphasized the point to Balaam, gave him an experience that he could not ignore. Note exactly what Scripture says: God's anger was aroused because Balaam went (v.22). Balaam had known exactly what God's will was; nevertheless, he ignored God and went anyway. But this one thing God determined: this false prophet was not going to curse the dear people of God.

OUTLINE	SCRIPTURE	SCRIPTURE	OUTLINE
4. The 3rd encounter of Balaam with God (the story of the donkey): The anger of God over greed & the signs of His anger a. The angel of the LORD stood in the road to block Balaam's way 1) The donkey saw the angel of the Lord blocking theroad with a drawn sword: Turned off the road into a field 2) Balaam beat her to get her back on the road	22 And God's anger was kindled because he went: and the angel of the LORD stood in the way for an adversary against him. Now he was riding upon his ass, and his two servants were with him. 23 And the ass saw the angel of the LORD standing in the way, and his sword drawn in his hand: and the ass turned aside out of the way, and went into the field: and Balaam smote the ass, to turn her into the way.	hast mocked me: I would there were a sword in mine hand, for now would I kill thee. 30 And the ass said unto Balaam, Am not I thine ass, upon which thou hast ridden ever since I was thine unto this day? was I ever wont to do so unto thee? And he said, Nay. 31 Then the LORD opened the eyes of Balaam, and he saw the angel of the LORD standing in the way, and his sword drawn in his hand: and he bowed down his head, and fell flat on his face.	sword to kill the animal: Because it had made a fool of him 3) The donkey reasoned with Balaam • That she was Balaam's property • That she had always served Balaam well • That she had never behaved like this before 4) Balaam agreed e. The LORD opened Balaam's eyes 1) Balaam saw the angel of the Lord standing with his drawn sword (a symbol of God's anger, a strong warning): He fell face down on the ground
b. The angel of the LORD blocked the path again, a narrow path with walls on both sides 1) The donkey again saw the angel of the LORD: Tried to squeeze by & crushed Balaam's foot 2) Balaam again beat the animal	24 But the angel of the LORD stood in a path of the vineyards, a wall being on this side, and a wall on that side. 25 And when the ass saw the angel of the LORD, she thrust herself unto the wall, and crushed Balaam's foot against the wall: and he smote her again.	32 And the angel of the LORD said unto him, Wherefore hast thou smitten thine ass these three times? behold, I went out to withstand thee, because thy way is perverse before me:	2) The angel of the LORD confronted Balaam • Rebuked him for mistreatment of an animal • Condemned him because of his reckless, stubborn heart & resistance to God
c. The angel of the LORD then moved ahead to a place so narrow that the donkey could not get by 1) The donkey saw the angel of the LORD & just lay down under Balaam 2) Balaam, in anger, beat her with his staff	26 And the angel of the LORD went further, and stood in a narrow place, where was no way to turn either to the right hand or to the left. 27 And when the ass saw the angel of the LORD, she fell down under Balaam: and Balaam's anger was kindled, and he smote the ass with a staff.	33 And the ass saw me, and turned from me these three times: unless she had turned from me, surely now also I had slain thee, and saved her alive. 34 And Balaam said unto the angel of the LORD, I have sinned; for I knew not that thou stoodest in the way against me: now therefore, if it displease thee, I will get me back again.	• Warned him that God would have taken his life by now because of his resistance if the donkey had not stopped 3) Balaam confessed his sin & offered to return (but did not repent)
d. The LORD opened the donkey's mouth & the animal miraculously, shockingly spoke to Balaam (cp. 2 Pt.2:16) 1) The donkey complained of Balaam's cruelty 2) Balaam—in a fit of rage—wished he had a	28 And the LORD opened the mouth of the ass, and she said unto Balaam, What have I done unto thee, that thou hast smitten me these three times? 29 And Balaam said unto the ass, Because thou	35 And the angel of the LORD said unto Balaam, Go with the men: but only the word that I shall speak unto thee, that thou shalt speak. So Balaam went with the princes of Balak.	4) The response of the angel of the LORD: Gave Balaam over to his greed—he could go, but he must speak only what God said

1. In anger, the angel of the Lord stood in the road to block Balaam's way (v.22-23). This blind, false prophet was so blinded by his covetousness and greed that he could not see the angel of the Lord. But the donkey saw the angel standing

with a drawn sword in the middle of the road. Frightened, the donkey turned off the road into a field. Balaam beat the donkey to get her back on the road.

2. But again, the angel of the Lord blocked the path, a narrow path with walls on both sides (v.24-25). The result was the same: the donkey saw the angel with his sword drawn and tried to squeeze by, crushing Balaam's foot against one of the walls. Balaam again beat the animal.

3. The angel of the Lord then moved ahead to a place so narrow that the donkey simply could not get by (v.26-27). This time the donkey saw the angel of the Lord and simply lay down under Balaam. In anger, Balaam struck the donkey, beating her with his staff.

4. Then it was that the drama began: in dramatic fashion God opened the donkey's mouth. The animal miraculously, shockingly spoke to Balaam (cp. 2 Pt.2:16). The reader must keep this fact in mind: the donkey did not speak by its own power; it spoke by the power of God. This was a miracle, a miracle brought about by the hand of God Himself. Note what the donkey did:

a. The donkey did what any living creature would do if it could speak: it complained of Balaam's cruelty (v.28).
b. Balaam flew into a fit of rage, stating that he wished he had a sword to kill the animal. The animal had made a fool out of him (v.29).
c. But note how the donkey miraculously reasoned with Balaam (v.30). She argued that she was Balaam's property and that she had always served Balaam well. Moreover, she had never behaved like this before (v.30).
d. Balaam, obviously stunned and amazed at the dumb animal speaking to him, could only agree.

5. At this point, the Lord opened Balaam's eyes (v.31-35).

a. Balaam immediately saw the angel of the Lord standing with his sword drawn. The drawn sword was a symbol of God's anger, a strong warning to Balaam. Stricken with fear, he fell face down on the ground.
b. The angel of the Lord then confronted this obstinate, hard-hearted false prophet who was so consumed with greed (v.32-33). The Lord immediately rebuked him for mistreating an animal. Then it happened: God condemned him because of his reckless, stubborn heart, because of his resistance to God. Balaam had chosen to follow the sinful way of greed, the stubborn, reckless way that stands in opposition to God. God warned Balaam in no uncertain terms: God would have taken his life by now because of his stubborn, disobedient resistance if the donkey had not stopped (v.33). (See DEEPER STUDY # 1—Num.22:15-21 for more discussion.)
c. Balaam confessed his sin and offered to return (v.34). But note: he did not repent. This was only a partial confession, for true confession involves repentance. Repentance is the turning back to God, obeying God totally, fully, and completely—doing exactly what God commands. If Balaam had been sincere, he would have truly repented, returned home, and given his life to God, becoming a follower of the only living and true God. But this Balaam did not do. With one eye on the sword in the hand of the angel and with a heart filled with greed, he half-heatedly said that he would return if he had displeased the Lord. Of this, there was no question. The Lord had already told him never to leave to go to king Balak. Balaam had disobeyed the instructions of the Lord, and he was continuing to disobey them: all because his heart was full of greed and covetousness.
d. Note the response of the angel of the Lord: he gave Balaam over to his greed (Ro.1:28-32). He could go, but he must speak only what God told him (v.35).

Thought 1. There are two clear lessons for us in this point:

1) God had the power to speak through the donkey of Balaam. God has the power to perform miracles in order to achieve His purposes upon this earth. One of His purposes is the same purpose that He was working out through Balaam: the purpose of protecting His dear people. God has the power to protect His precious people and protect them He will. God's power is unlimited, and He will use whatever amount of power is needed to protect and take care of His dear people.

"But Jesus beheld them, and said unto them, With men this is impossible; but with God all things are possible" (Mt.19:26).

"For with God nothing shall be impossible" (Lk.1:37).

"Now to him that is of power to stablish you according to my gospel, and the preaching of Jesus Christ, according to the revelation of the mystery, which was kept secret since the world began" (Ro.16:25).

"Now unto him that is able to do exceeding abundantly above all that we ask or think, according to the power that worketh in us" (Eph.3:20).

"Being confident of this very thing, that he which hath begun a good work in you will perform it until the day of Jesus Christ" (Ph.1:6).

"For our conversation [behavior, conduct] is in heaven; from whence also we look for the Saviour, the Lord Jesus Christ: Who shall change our vile body, that it may be fashioned like unto his glorious body, according to the working whereby he is able even to subdue all things unto himself" (Ph.3:20-21).

"And the Lord shall deliver me from every evil work, and will preserve me unto his heavenly kingdom: to whom be glory for ever and ever. Amen" (2 Tim.4:18).

"So that we may boldly say, The Lord is my helper, and I will not fear what man shall do unto me" (Heb.13:6).

"Now unto him that is able to keep you from falling, and to present you faultless before the presence of his glory with exceeding joy" (Jude 24).

"And he said, The Lord is my rock, and my fortress, and my deliverer" (2 Sam.22:2).

"I know that thou canst do every thing, and that no thought can be withholden from thee" (Job 42:2).

"But I am poor and needy; yet the Lord thinketh upon me: thou art my help and my deliverer; make no tarrying, O my God" (Ps.40:17).

"But our God is in the heavens: he hath done whatsoever he hath pleased" (Ps.115:3).

"Fear thou not; for I am with thee: be not dismayed; for I am thy God: I will strengthen thee; yea, I will help thee; yea, I will uphold thee with the right hand of my righteousness" (Is.41:10).

"Yea, before the day was I am he; and there is none that can deliver out of my hand: I will work, and who shall let [hinder, prevent] it" (Is.43:13).

"Be not afraid of their faces: for I am with thee to deliver thee, saith the Lord" (Jer.1:8).

2) The heart of Balaam was reckless, stubborn, and resistant to God. He was a hard-hearted person whose mind was set on the things of this world, its money and possessions. He was possessed by greed and covetousness. As a result, his heart was hard and stubborn against God. Scripture declares in no uncertain terms: a stubborn, hard heart is condemned by God. A hard-hearted, stubborn person will face the judgment of God and be eternally separated from God—tragically, all because the person resists the salvation of God provided through Christ Jesus. Hardness of heart condemns a person.

"But after thy hardness and impenitent heart treasurest up unto thyself wrath against the day of wrath and revelation of the righteous judgment of God" (Ro.2:5).

"But exhort one another daily, while it is called To day; lest any of you be hardened through the deceitfulness of sin" (Heb.3:13).

"For rebellion is as the sin of witchcraft, and stubbornness is as iniquity and idolatry. Because thou hast rejected the word of the Lord, he hath also rejected thee" (1 Sam.15:23).

"Happy is the man that feareth alway: but he that hardeneth his heart shall fall into mischief" (Pr.28:14).

"He, that being often reproved hardeneth his neck, shall suddenly be destroyed, and that without remedy" (Pr.29:1).

"If ye will not hear, and if ye will not lay it to heart, to give glory unto my name, saith the Lord of hosts, I will even send a curse upon you, and I will curse your blessings: yea, I have cursed them already, because ye do not lay it to heart" (Mal 2:2).

5 (22:36-41) **Encounter, with God—Warning, of God—Sacrifices, Pagan**: the effect of God's encounters and warnings upon Balaam was a lesson that was going to be heeded. Remember what God had just told Balaam along the journey: He had considered striking Balaam dead (v.33). This threat and the experience with the donkey had gotten across to Balaam. Balaam was to be an instrument, a mouth-piece for God to share some very special messages with the world. Balaam did not yet know this, but he soon would. This false prophet was ready to share with the king only what God Himself revealed.

OUTLINE	SCRIPTURE	SCRIPTURE	OUTLINE
5. The effect of the encounters & warnings upon Balaam a. The excitement of king Balak at Balaam's coming 1) He traveled all the way to the border to meet Balaam 2) He expressed disappointment at Balaam's refusal of the first request—especially in light of the offer to be so well rewarded b. The effect of the encounters with the LORD & His warnings: Balaam replied that He had now come, but he could	36 And when Balak heard that Balaam was come, he went out to meet him unto a city of Moab, which is in the border of Arnon, which is in the utmost coast. 37 And Balak said unto Balaam, Did I not earnestly send unto thee to call thee? wherefore camest thou not unto me? am I not able indeed to promote thee to honour? 38 And Balaam said unto Balak, Lo, I am come unto thee: have I now any power at all to say any thing? the	word that God putteth in my mouth, that shall I speak. 39 And Balaam went with Balak, and they came unto Kirjath-huzoth. 40 And Balak offered oxen and sheep, and sent to Balaam, and to the princes that were with him. 41 And it came to pass on the morrow, that Balak took Balaam, and brought him up into the high places of Baal, that thence he might see the utmost part of the people.	speak only the message God gave him c. The king celebrated Balaam's coming 1) He offered pagan sacrifices to his gods: Balaam participated with Balak 2) He took Balaam up to Bamoth Baal, some hill or high place where Baal was worshipped: To scan the camp of Israel

1. Note the excitement and expectation of king Balak at the coming of Balaam (v.36-37). He traveled all the way to the border to meet Balaam. After their greetings, the king expressed disappointment in Balaam's refusal of his first request. He could not understand the refusal in light of the rich rewards he had so willingly offered Balaam.

2. Note the effect of Balaam's encounters with the Lord, the effect of God's warnings to him (v.38). Balaam replied to the king that he had now come despite his earlier reluctance. But Balaam added that he still could speak only the message that God gave him. No doubt, the image of the drawn sword in the hand of the angel dominated the thoughts of Balaam. Stricken with the fear of the angel and the threat of God, Balaam was determined to share only the message God wanted shared.

3. Note how the king celebrated Balaam's coming (v.39-41). The king offered pagan sacrifices of sheep and goats to his "gods." Note that Balaam participated with Balak, eating the meat that was sacrificed. The king then took Balaam up to Bamoth Baal, that is, some hill or high place where Baal was worshipped. He did this so that they could scan the camp of Israel together.

Thought 1. God is sovereign, in total control of the universe and of all that happens within the universe. This does not mean that God overrides the free will of people; rather it means that God works all things out for good...
- in order to achieve His eternal purpose
- in order to look after His people and conform them to the image of His dear Son

God takes all the events throughout the universe, twisting and turning and working them out for the good of those who love Him, those who have been called according to His eternal purpose. This is exactly what God was doing with Balaam: twisting and turning and using the experiences of Balaam to protect His dear people. Moreover, He was going to use Balaam to proclaim some glorious messages to the world. God is God; that is, He is Sovereign, Almighty, able to do exactly what He wills. Therefore, God overrode Balaam's greed and covetousness, determining to use him to bless God's dear people instead of cursing them.

The point to see is this: God is sovereign, in control of all things. Therefore, God works all things out for the good of His dear people, for the good of all those who love Him and are called by Him.

"And we know that all things work together for good to them that love God, to them who are the called according to his purpose" (Ro.8:28).

"For our light affliction, which is but for a moment, worketh for us a far more exceeding and eternal weight of glory" (2 Cor.4:17).

"And he said unto me, My grace is sufficient for thee: for my strength is made perfect in weakness. Most gladly therefore will I rather glory in my infirmities, that the power of Christ may rest upon me" (2 Cor.12:9).

"Beloved, think it not strange concerning the fiery trial which is to try you, as though some strange thing happened unto you: But rejoice, inasmuch as ye are partakers of Christ's sufferings; that, when his glory shall be revealed, ye may be glad also with exceeding joy" (1 Pt.4:12-13).

"In his favour is life: weeping may endure for a night, but joy cometh in the morning" (Ps.30:5).

"Many are the afflictions of the righteous: but the Lord delivereth him out of them all" (Ps.34:19).

"The Lord will strengthen him upon the bed of languishing: thou wilt make all his bed in his sickness" (Ps.41:3).

"For thou art the God of my strength: why dost thou cast me off? why go I mourning because of the oppression of the enemy" (Ps.43:2).

"And call upon me in the day of trouble: I will deliver thee, and thou shalt glorify me" (Ps.50:15).

"Though I walk in the midst of trouble, thou wilt revive me: thou shalt stretch forth thine hand against the wrath of mine enemies, and thy right hand shall save me" (Ps.138:7).

TYPES, SYMBOLS, AND PICTURES
(Numbers 22:1-41)

Historical Term	Type or Picture (Scriptural Basis for Each)	Life Application for Today's Believer	Biblical Application
The Sword of the Angel of the Lord Num.22:22-35	*A type or symbol of God's anger and warning. Balaam immediately saw the angel of the Lord standing with his sword drawn. The sword was a strong warning to Balaam.* **"And the ass saw the angel of the LORD standing in the way, and his sword drawn in his hand: and the ass turned aside out of the way, and went into the field: and Balaam smote the ass, to turn her into the way" (Num.22:23).**	God is angry with men... • who are ungodly, who do not love and obey God. • who are unrighteous, who do not love and treat others as they should. • who hold the truth to themselves while they live ungodly and unrighteous lives.	***"But when he saw many of the Pharisees and Sadducees come to his baptism, he said unto them, O generation of vipers, who hath warned you to flee from the wrath to come?" (Mt.3:7).*** ***"For the wrath of God is revealed from heaven against all ungodliness and unrighteousness of men, who hold the truth in unrighteousness" (Ro.1:18).*** ***"But unto them that are contentious, and do not obey the truth, but obey unrighteousness, indignation and wrath, tribulation and anguish, upon every soul of man that doeth evil, of the Jew first, and also of the Gentile" (Ro.2:8-9).*** ***"Among whom also we all had our conversation in***

Historical Term	Type or Picture (Scriptural Basis for Each)	Life Application for Today's Believer	Biblical Application
			times past in the lusts of our flesh, fulfilling the desires of the flesh and of the mind; and were by nature the children of wrath, even as others" (Eph.2:3). *"Let no man deceive you with vain words: for because of these things cometh the wrath of God upon the children of disobedience" (Eph.5:6; cp. Col. 3:6).* *"Kiss the Son, lest he be angry, and ye perish from the way, when his wrath is kindled but a little. Blessed are all they that put their trust in him" (Psalm 2:12).* *"So I sware in my wrath, They shall not enter into my rest" (Heb.3:11).*

1. The 1st prophecy: The blessings of God's people
- a. The preparation for the prophecy
  - 1) Balaam requested that seven altars be built for sacrifice
  - 2) Balaam & the king offered pagan sacrifice: To secure the favor of their gods (24:1)
  - 3) Balaam then climbed a high hill to be alone, hoping the LORD would meet him
    - Instructed the king to wait beside his offering
    - Promised to tell the king whatever the LORD revealed
  - 4) God met with Balaam
    - Balaam immediately sought God's favor: Told God that he had offered seven sacrifices
    - God ignored the sacrifices
    - God did, however, give Balaam a message for king Balak
  - 5) Balaam returned to the king: Found him still standing by his offering with all the officials of Moab
- b. The prophecy Balaam declared: The blessings of Israel (a symbol of God's people)
  - 1) They were an innocent, secure people (a justified people): God had not cursed nor denounced them; therefore, he could not do so
  - 2) They were a new, separated, distinctive people
  - 3) They were a numerous people
  - 4) They were a righteous people with eternal hope: He wished to share in their destiny
- c. The result of the prophecy
  - 1) Balak was enraged, furious:Reproached Balaam

I. Event 9—the Story of Balaam & the Seven Startling Oracles or Prophecies Pronounced by Him: The Blessings of God & a Glimpse into the Future[1], 23:1-24:25

And Balaam said unto Balak, Build me here seven altars, and prepare me here seven oxen and seven rams.

2 And Balak did as Balaam had spoken; and Balak and Balaam offered on every altar a bullock and a ram.

3 And Balaam said unto Balak, Stand by thy burnt offering, and I will go: peradventure the LORD will come to meet me: and whatsoever he sheweth me I will tell thee. And he went to an high place.

4 And God met Balaam: and he said unto him, I have prepared seven altars, and I have offered upon every altar a bullock and a ram.

5 And the LORD put a word in Balaam's mouth, and said, Return unto Balak, and thus thou shalt speak.

6 And he returned unto him, and, lo, he stood by his burnt sacrifice, he, and all the princes of Moab.

7 And he took up his parable, and said, Balak the king of Moab hath brought me from Aram, out of the mountains of the east, saying, Come, curse me Jacob, and come, defy Israel.

8 How shall I curse, whom God hath not cursed? or how shall I defy, whom the LORD hath not defied?

9 For from the top of the rocks I see him, and from the hills I behold him: lo, the people shall dwell alone, and shall not be reckoned among the nations.

10 Who can count the dust of Jacob, and the number of the fourth part of Israel? Let me die the death of the righteous, and let my last end be like his!

11 And Balak said unto Balaam, What hast thou done unto me? I took thee to curse mine enemies, and, behold, thou hast blessed them altogether.

12 And he answered and said, Must I not take heed to speak that which the LORD hath put in my mouth?

13 And Balak said unto him, Come, I pray thee, with me unto another place, from whence thou mayest see them: thou shalt see but the utmost part of them, and shalt not see them all: and curse me them from thence.

14 And he brought him into the field of Zophim, to the top of Pisgah, and built seven altars, and offered a bullock and a ram on every altar.

15 And he said unto Balak, Stand here by thy burnt offering, while I meet the LORD yonder.

16 And the LORD met Balaam, and put a word in his mouth, and said, Go again unto Balak, and say thus.

17 And when he came to him, behold, he stood by his burnt offering, and the princes of Moab with him. And Balak said unto him, What hath the LORD spoken?

18 And he took up his parable, and said, Rise up, Balak, and hear; hearken unto me, thou son of Zippor:

19 God is not a man, that he should lie; neither the son of man, that he should repent: hath he said, and shall he not do it? or hath he spoken, and shall he not make it good?

20 Behold, I have received commandment to bless: and he hath blessed; and I cannot reverse it.

21 He hath not beheld iniquity in Jacob, neither hath he seen perverseness in Israel: the LORD his God is with him, and the shout of a king is among them.

22 God brought them out of Egypt; he hath as it were the strength of an unicorn.

23 Surely there is no enchantment against Jacob, neither is there any divination against Israel: according to this time it shall be said of Jacob and of Israel, What hath God wrought!

- 2) Balaam defended himself: As a diviner, he could speak only what God revealed

2. The 2nd prophecy: The source of the blessings, God Himself
- a. The preparation for the prophecy
  - 1) Balak tried a different tactic: Suggested cursing Israel from a site where only a small number could be seen
    - Took Balaam to the top of Mt. Pisgah
    - Built seven altars & offered pagan sacrifices: Sought to secure the favor of the gods
  - 2) Balaam then walked some distance to seek God: Hoping that God would again meet him
  - 3) God met with Balaam: Gave him a message for king Balak
  - 4) Balaam returned: Found king Balak standing beside his offerings with the officials of Moab
- b. The prophecy: The source that guarantees the blessings of God's people
  - 1) God's truthfulness & unchangableness: He does not lie nor change His mind
  - 2) God's faithfulness: He speaks & acts; He promises & fulfills
  - 3) God's promises: His promises & blessings are irrevocable—they cannot be changed
    - No misfortune is seen
    - No misery or trouble is in store
  - 4) God's presence: His presence assures the blessing of His people
  - 5) God's power: His power assures the protection & deliverance of His people
    - Assures deliverance from all sorcery & divination
    - Assures a strong testimony for God

1 Some thoughts and statements for this outline were gleaned from *The Expositor's Bible Commentary*. Frank E. Gaebelein, Editor, p.895-913.

- Assures victory over all enemies

c. The result of the prophecy
1) Balak was desperate: He commanded "Stop! Say nothing! Neither curse nor bless them!"
2) Balaam insisted upon his rights as sorcerer (cp. 24:1)

3. The 3rd prophecy: A picture of how God blesses His people

a. The preparation for the prophecy
1) Balak suggested a third site
- He was desperate—Israel must be cursed
- He took Balaam to the top of Mt. Peor

2) Balaam requested that seven altars be built

3) Balaam offered pagan sacrifices upon the altar

4) Balaam made a significant change: He did not resort to sorcery (chants, spells, charms, magic)

5) Balaam looked out over the camp of Israel tribe by tribe & was stricken by the sight: Suddenly, the Spirit of God came upon him & Balaam declared...
- that his eyes saw clearly
- that he heard the Word of God
- that he saw a vision from the Almighty
- that his eyes were opened

b. The prophecy: A picture of how God blesses His people
1) Their dwelling place—homes & land will be beautiful
2) Their homes & lands will be fruitful before the LORD

3) Their resources will be sufficient & even overflow

24 Behold, the people shall
rise up as a great lion, and
lift up himself as a young
lion: he shall not lie down
until he eat of the prey, and
drink the blood of the slain.
25 And Balak said unto
Balaam, Neither curse them
at all, nor bless them at all.
26 But Balaam answered
and said unto Balak, Told not
I thee, saying, All that the
LORD speaketh, that I must
do?
27 And Balak said unto
Balaam, Come, I pray thee, I
will bring thee unto another
place; peradventure it will
please God that thou mayest
curse me them from thence.
28 And Balak brought
Balaam unto the top of Peor,
that looketh toward Jeshimon.
29 And Balaam said unto
Balak, Build me here seven
altars, and prepare me here
seven bullocks and seven
rams.
30 And Balak did as Balaam
had said, and offered a bullock and a ram on every
altar.

CHAPTER 24

And when Balaam saw that
it pleased the LORD to bless
Israel, he went not, as at
other times, to seek for
enchantments, but he set his
face toward the wilderness.
2 And Balaam lifted up his
eyes, and he saw Israel abiding in his tents according to
their tribes; and the spirit of
God came upon him.
3 And he took up his parable,
and said, Balaam the son of
Beor hath said, and the man
whose eyes are open hath
said:
4 He hath said, which heard
the words of God, which saw
the vision of the Almighty,
falling into a trance, but having his eyes open:
5 How goodly are thy tents,
O Jacob, and thy tabernacles,
O Israel!
6 As the valleys are they
spread forth, as gardens by
the river's side, as the trees
of lign aloes which the LORD
hath planted, and as cedar
trees beside the waters.
7 He shall pour the water out
of his buckets, and his seed
shall be in many waters, and
his king shall be higher than
Agag, and his kingdom shall
be exalted.
8 God brought him forth out
of Egypt; he hath as it were
the strength of an unicorn: he
shall eat up the nations his
enemies, and shall break
their bones, and pierce them
through with his arrows.
9 He couched, he lay down
as a lion, and as a great lion:
who shall stir him up?
Blessed is he that blesseth
thee, and cursed is he that
curseth thee.
10 And Balak's anger was
kindled against Balaam, and
he smote his hands together:
and Balak said unto Balaam,
I called thee to curse mine
enemies, and, behold, thou
hast altogether blessed them
these three times.
11 Therefore now flee thou
to thy place: I thought to promote thee unto great honour;
but, lo, the LORD hath kept
thee back from honour.
12 And Balaam said unto
Balak, Spake I not also to thy
messengers which thou sentest unto me, saying,
13 If Balak would give me
his house full of silver and
gold, I cannot go beyond the
commandment of the LORD,
to do either good or bad of
mine own mind; but what the
LORD saith, that will I
speak?
14 And now, behold, I go
unto my people: come therefore, and I will advertise thee
what this people shall do to
thy people in the latter days.
15 And he took up his parable, and said, Balaam the son
of Beor hath said, and the
man whose eyes are open
hath said:
16 He hath said, which
heard the words of God, and
knew the knowledge of the
most High, which saw the
vision of the Almighty,
falling into a trance, but having his eyes open:
17 I shall see him, but not
now: I shall behold him, but
not nigh: there shall come a
Star out of Jacob, and a
Sceptre shall rise out of
Israel, and shall smite the
corners of Moab, and destroy
all the children of Sheth.
18 And Edom shall be a

4) Their leaders & kingdom will be powerful & exalted

5) Their Deliverer is God Himself
6) Their strength is as an ox
7) Their victory is assured over all hostile enemies

8) Their courage & security are assured
9) Their blessings are guaranteed by the promise of God Himself (cp. Gen.12:2-3)

c. The result of the prophecy
1) Balak flew into a rage, clapped his hands & shouted
- Charged Balaam with breaking their agreement: Was summoned to curse Israel; instead, he had blessed them three times
- Charged Balaam to leave immediately—go home!
- Dismissed him without pay: The ultimate insult to his greed (2 Pt.2:15)

2) Balaam attempted to excuse the disappointment (in his professional pride as a diviner, sorcerer): Reminded Balak of the terms laid down with his officials
- He could only speak what the LORD said
- He was powerless to do anything against the LORD—even if the king gave him a palace filled with gold & silver

4. The 4th prophecy: A picture of the coming Deliverer

a. The preparation for the prophecy
1) Balaam started to leave, but he was suddenly constrained by God to prophesy: About the "days to come"
2) Balaam declared...
- that his eyes saw clearly
- that he heard the Words of God
- that he had knowledge from the Most High
- that he saw a vision from the Almighty
- that his eyes were opened

b. The prophecy: A picture of the coming Deliverer
1) He will come in the future
2) He will be a star & a scepter (have dominion)
3) He will be victorious over all enemies, including Moab & Edom
4) He will guarantee the

growing strength of His people (Israel) 5) He will guarantee the triumph & dominion of God's people **5. The 5th prophecy: A picture of victory over the greatest enemies** a. Balaam saw Amalek & prophesied b. Amalek, the greatest of nations, would be destroyed **6. The 6th prophecy: A picture of the greatest fortresses of the enemy being destroyed** a. Balaam saw the Kenites &	possession, Seir also shall be a possession for his enemies; and Israel shall do valiantly. 19 Out of Jacob shall come he that shall have dominion, and shall destroy him that remaineth of the city. 20 And when he looked on Amalek, he took up his parable, and said, Amalek was the first of the nations; but his latter end shall be that he perish for ever. 21 And he looked on the Kenites, and took up his parable, and said, Strong is thy dwellingplace, and thou	puttest thy nest in a rock. 22 Nevertheless the Kenite shall be wasted, until Asshur shall carry thee away captive. 23 And he took up his parable, and said, Alas, who shall live when God doeth this! 24 And ships shall come from the coast of Chittim, and shall afflict Asshur, and shall afflict Eber, and he also shall perish for ever. 25 And Balaam rose up, and went and returned to his place: and Balak also went his way.	prophesied b. The Kenites & their impregnable fortress would be destroyed by Assyria **7. The 7th prophecy: A picture of God's judgment against all whose "cup is full of iniquity" (has reached the full measure that God allows)** a. Balaam again prophesied the future b. Assyria & Eber would be destroyed: By an invading force coming across the sea c. Balaam & Balak separated & returned home

DIVISION III

THE FORTY LONG YEARS OF WILDERNESS WANDERINGS: A PICTURE OF THE BELIEVER'S PILGRIMAGE THROUGH THIS WORLD AS HE PREPARES TO ENTER THE PROMISED LAND 15:1-25:18

I. Event 9—the Story of Balaam and the Seven Startling Oracles or Prophecies Pronounced by Him: The Blessings of God and a Glimpse into the Future, 23:1-24:25

(23:1-24:25) **Introduction—Future, Question About**: a glimpse into the future—what would a person give to have such a revelation, to be able to see into the future? Would it even be wise to know the future? Would knowing the future bring joy? Sorrow? Pain? Suffering? Anger? Frustration? Loneliness? Unemployment? Divorce? Death? What does lie out in the future? A glimpse into the future is the subject of this passage of Scripture.

Remember what had happened: the king of Moab and his people had become terrified of the Israelites who were camped nearby. They felt hopeless and helpless, so the king sent for a diviner, a sorcerer or false prophet named Balaam who had an international reputation. He wanted Balaam to call upon the "gods" to put a curse upon the Israelites. He felt the curse would help him defeat the Israelites in battle (Num.22:6). This chapter focuses upon Balaam trying to curse Israel, God's people. However, God stops Balaam in his tracks. God refuses to let Balaam curse His people. Instead, God takes control of Balaam's tongue and makes seven astounding prophecies about His people, prophecies that speak to all of God's people down through human history. This is: *Event 9—the Story of Balaam and the Seven Startling Oracles or Prophecies Pronounced by Him: The Blessings of God and a Glimpse into the Future*, 23:1-24:25.

1. The 1st prophecy: the blessings of God's people (v.1-12).
2. The 2nd prophecy: the source of the blessings, God Himself (v.13-26).
3. The 3rd prophecy: a picture of how God blesses His people (ch. 23:27-24:13).
4. The 4th prophecy: a picture of the coming Deliverer (v.14 19).
5. The 5th prophecy: a picture of victory over the greatest enemies (v.20).
6. The 6th prophecy: a picture of the greatest fortresses of the enemy being defeated (v.21-22).
7. The 7th prophecy: a picture of God's judgment against all whose "cup is full of iniquity" (has reached the full measure that God allows) (v.23-25).

1 (23:1-12) **Blessings, of God's People—Believers, Blessings of—Israel, Blessings of—Prophecy, Concerning God's People**: the first prophecy focuses upon the blessings of God's people. Remember why the king and this false prophet were together: to curse God's people, to call down upon them the judgment and destruction of God. The Israelites were camped in the plain of Moab nearby the Jordan River, camped right across from the great city of Jericho. As stated, king Balak and his people feared the Israelites: a sense of helplessness and hopelessness had swept over the king and his people. To the king, the only hope he and his people had lay in the hands of their gods. In desperation, the king hoped that this diviner could put a curse upon the Israelites, a curse that would allow him to defeat them in battle (Num.22:6). Now, here stood the king and the false prophet on a hill that overlooked the campsites of the Israelites, a high place that was dedicated to the worship of the false god Baal (Num.22:41). The scene is dramatic, for a false prophet of international reputation is ready to call down a terrifying, destructive curse upon the people of God. Note what happened:

OUTLINE	SCRIPTURE	SCRIPTURE	OUTLINE
1. The 1st prophecy: The blessings of God's people a. The preparation for the prophecy 1) Balaam requested that seven altars be built for	And Balaam said unto Balak, Build me here seven altars, and prepare me here seven oxen and seven rams. 2 And Balak did as Balaam	had spoken; and Balak and Balaam offered on every altar a bullock and a ram. 3 And Balaam said unto Balak, Stand by thy burnt	sacrifice 2) Balaam & the king offered pagan sacrifice: To secure the favor of their gods (24:1) 3) Balaam then climbed a high hill to be alone, hoping the

OUTLINE	SCRIPTURE	SCRIPTURE	OUTLINE
LORD would meet him • Instructed the king to wait beside his offering • Promised to tell the king whatever the LORD revealed 4) God met with Balaam • Balaam immediately sought God's favor: Told God that he had offered seven sacrifices • God ignored the sacrifices • God did, however, give Balaam a message for king Balak 5) Balaam returned to the king: Found him still standing by his offering with all the officials of Moab b. The prophecy Balaam declared: The blessings of Israel (a symbol of God's people)	offering, and I will go: per- adventure the LORD will come to meet me: and what- soever he sheweth me I will tell thee. And he went to an high place. 4 And God met Balaam: and he said unto him, I have pre- pared seven altars, and I have offered upon every altar a bullock and a ram. 5 And the LORD put a word in Balaam's mouth, and said, Return unto Balak, and thus thou shalt speak. 6 And he returned unto him, and, lo, he stood by his burnt sacrifice, he, and all the princes of Moab. 7 And he took up his para- ble, and said, Balak the king of Moab hath brought me from Aram, out of the moun- tains of the east, saying, Come, curse me Jacob, and come, defy Israel.	8 How shall I curse, whom God hath not cursed? or how shall I defy, whom the LORD hath not defied? 9 For from the top of the rocks I see him, and from the hills I behold him: lo, the people shall dwell alone, and shall not be reckoned among the nations. 10 Who can count the dust of Jacob, and the number of the fourth part of Israel? Let me die the death of the right- eous, and let my last end be like his! 11 And Balak said unto Balaam, What hast thou done unto me? I took thee to curse mine enemies, and, behold, thou hast blessed them altogether. 12 And he answered and said, Must I not take heed to speak that which the LORD hath put in my mouth?	1) They were an innocent, secure people (a justified people): God had not cursed nor denounced them; therefore, he could not do so 2) They were a new, separated, distinctive people 3) They were a numerous people 4) They were a righteous people with eternal hope: He wished to share in their destiny c. The result of the prophecy 1) Balak was enraged, furious:Reproached Balaam 2) Balaam defended himself: As a diviner, he could speak only what God revealed

1. Note the preparation for the prophecy (v.1-6).
   a. Balaam requested that the king build seven altars for sacrifice (v.1).
   b. Balaam and the king offered pagan sacrifice. This is a pagan sacrifice not the true sacrifice of the LORD God, the only living and true God (Jehovah, Yahweh). They attempted to secure the favor of their gods to curse Israel. This was clearly an act of sorcery (24:1).
   c. Balaam then climbed a high hill, seeking to be alone and hoping that the LORD would meet him (v.3). He instructed the king to wait beside his offering, obviously praying to his gods. He then promised to tell the king whatever the LORD revealed to him up on the mountain.
   d. Note that God met with Balaam (v.4-5). Balaam immediately sought to secure God's favor, to bribe Him. He told God that he had offered seven sacrifices in His name. Keep in mind that this false prophet did not know who God was, not personally. To him, God was only one among many gods. In his mind, this particular god was only the 'god of the Israelites.' Therefore, in order to secure the favor of the Israelite God, he had offered the sacrifices in His name. But note what God did: He completely ignored the sacrifices (v.5). However, He did give this false prophet Balaam a message for the king.
   e. After receiving the message, Balaam returned to the king and found him still standing by his offering with all the other officials of Moab (v.6).

2. Balaam immediately declared the prophecy. Note that the prophecy focused upon the blessings of Israel, but these blessings are also blessings that God has given to all His people down through the ages (v.7-10). Most likely the LORD had taken over the tongue of Balaam just as He had with the donkey. God was speaking through Balaam the message He wanted conveyed to the king and to all succeeding generations. It is most unlikely that Balaam—of his own free will—would dare proclaim these prophecies for fear of the king. Obviously, his tongue was under God's control. Note the blessings of God's people:
   a. God's people are an innocent, secure people (v.8). God had not cursed the people, for they were an innocent, justified people before Him. Since they were innocent or justified, He could not denounce or curse them.
   b. God's people are a new, separated, and distinctive people (v.9). They are distinctive in that they live holy lives, lives that are totally set apart to the LORD God (Jehovah, Yahweh). They live lives that are separated from the people of the world. They are a totally new people, a new race of people. (See outline and note—Eph.4:17-19 for more discussion.)
   c. God's people are a numerous people (v.10). One of the amazing promises of God concerns this very point: by the end of the world they will number as the stars of the sky and as the sands by the seashore. As Balaam asked: "Who can count the dust of Jacob or number even the fourth part of Israel?"
   d. God's people are a righteous people with an eternal hope. Note what Balaam cried out: that he too could wish to die the death of the righteous and to have an end just like theirs (v.10). This is a clear reference to heaven, to living eternally with God.

3. The result of the prophecy is to be expected: Balak was enraged, furious (v.11-12). He severely rebuked and reproached Balaam. But Balaam defended himself: as a diviner, he could only speak what God revealed to him. No doubt, Balaam was fearful of the reaction of Balak and was counting on the king's fear of the gods to protect him.

Thought 1. The blessings of God given in this passage are gifts of God to all His people. Note the blessings one by one.

1) God's people are an innocent, secure people—a people who are justified, eternally secure before God. God has forgiven our sins and justified us, counted us innocent before Him. Moreover, He has given us the greatest security that could be given: the inner witness of His Spirit who assures us of eternal life, of living with Him face to face throughout all of eternity. The person who believes—who truly trusts the Lord Jesus Christ as his Savior—is justified before God, that is, counted innocent and secure forever and ever. God's Spirit guarantees our security.

"And I give unto them eternal life; and they shall never perish, neither shall any man pluck them out of my hand" (Jn.10:28).

"Therefore being justified by faith, we have peace with God through our Lord Jesus Christ" (Ro.5:1).

"The Spirit itself beareth witness with our spirit, that we are the children of God: And if children, then heirs; heirs of God, and joint-heirs with Christ; if so be that we suffer with him, that we may be also glorified together" (Ro.8:16-17).

"Who shall lay any thing to the charge of God's elect? It is God that justifieth" (Ro.8:33).

"And such were some of you: but ye are washed, but ye are sanctified, but ye are justified in the name of the Lord Jesus, and by the Spirit of our God" (1 Cor.6:11).

"Even as Abraham believed God, and it was accounted to him for righteousness" (Gal.3:6).

"And because ye are sons, God hath sent forth the Spirit of his Son into your hearts, crying, Abba, Father" (Gal.4:6).

"Blessed be the God and Father of our Lord Jesus Christ, which according to his abundant mercy hath begotten us again unto a lively hope by the resurrection of Jesus Christ from the dead, To an inheritance incorruptible, and undefiled, and that fadeth not away, reserved in heaven for you, Who are kept by the power of God through faith unto salvation ready to be revealed in the last time" (1 Pt.1:3-5).

"And he that keepeth his commandments dwelleth in him, and he in him. And hereby we know that he abideth in us, by the Spirit which he hath given us" (1 Jn.3:24).

"Hereby know we that we dwell in him, and he in us, because he hath given us of his Spirit" (1 Jn.4:13).

"Now unto him that is able to keep you from falling, and to present you faultless before the presence of his glory with exceeding joy, To the only wise God our Saviour, be glory and majesty, dominion and power, both now and ever. Amen" (Jude 24-25).

"And he believed in the Lord; and he counted it to him for righteousness" (Gen.15:6).

2) God's people are a separated and distinctive people. The genuine believer lives a holy life before God, a life that is pure and righteous, moral and clean, just and fair. The believer lives a life of separation from the world, a life that has nothing to do with…

- stealing
- lying
- cheating
- greed
- covetousness
- sorcery
- divination
- illicit sex
- pornography
- abuse
- revenge
- anger
- the occult

A life of separation—the life that is totally different from the immoral, unjust, and violent of this earth, a life that is totally distinct and different from neighbors and communities who live in disobedience to God—is the call of God to us. We are to be a separated people, a distinctive people in this one fact: we are to live holy, pure, and righteous lives. We are to be strong witnesses for the lost of the world, that they too are to live pure and righteous lives before God. This is the life of separation to which God calls us.

"If ye were of the world, the world would love his own: but because ye are not of the world, but I have chosen you out of the world, therefore the world hateth you" (Jn.15:19).

"But now I have written unto you not to keep company, if any man that is called a brother be a fornicator, or covetous, or an idolater, or a railer, or a drunkard, or an extortioner; with such an one no not to eat" (1 Cor.5:11).

"Therefore if any man be in Christ, he is a new creature: old things are passed away; behold, all things are become new" (2 Cor.5:17).

"Be ye not unequally yoked together with unbelievers: for what fellowship hath righteousness with unrighteousness? and what communion hath light with darkness" (2 Cor.6:14).

"Wherefore come out from among them, and be ye separate, saith the Lord, and touch not the unclean thing; and I will receive you, And will be a Father unto you, and ye shall be my sons and daughters, saith the Lord Almighty" (2 Cor.6:17-18).

"And have no fellowship with the unfruitful works of darkness, but rather reprove them" (Eph.5:11).

"Now we command you, brethren, in the name of our Lord Jesus Christ, that ye withdraw yourselves from every brother that walketh disorderly, and not after the tradition which he received of us" (2 Th.3:6).

"Love not the world, neither the things that are in the world. If any man love the world, the love of the Father is not in him. For all that is in the world, the lust of the flesh, and the lust of the eyes, and the pride of life, is not of the Father, but is of the world" (1 Jn.2:15-16).

"Thou shalt not follow a multitude to do evil; neither shalt thou speak in a cause to decline after many to wrest judgment" (Ex.23:2).

"Take heed to thyself, lest thou make a covenant with the inhabitants of the land whither thou goest, lest it be for a snare in the midst of thee" (Ex.34:12).

"Blessed is the man that walketh not in the counsel of the ungodly, nor standeth in the way of sinners, nor sitteth in the seat of the scornful" (Ps.1:1).

"Enter not into the path of the wicked, and go not in the way of evil men" (Pr.4:14).

"Be not thou envious against evil men, neither desire to be with them" (Pr.24:1).

"Depart ye, depart ye, go ye out from thence, touch no unclean thing; go ye out of the midst of her; be ye clean, that bear the vessels of the Lord" (Is.52:11).

3) God's people are eventually to be a numerous people. This was the promise made to Abraham and his descendants, that is, all the succeeding generations of believers down through the ages. Believers are eventually to number as the stars of the sky and as the sands by the seashore.

"That in blessing I will bless thee, and in multiplying I will multiply thy seed as the stars of the heaven, and as the sand which is upon the sea shore; and thy seed shall possess the gate of his enemies" (Gen.22:17).

"And thou saidst, I will surely do thee good, and make thy seed as the sand of the sea, which cannot be numbered for multitude" (Gen.32:12).

4) God's people are a righteous people with eternal hope. A genuine believer is counted righteous through the righteousness of Jesus Christ. Jesus Christ is the believer's only approach to God. A person can approach God only through Christ, only through His righteousness. When a person comes to God through Christ's righteousness, God accepts that person; God counts that person justified, righteous. Once the person has been justified—counted righteous—he is given the wonderful hope of living eternally with God.

"And as Moses lifted up the serpent in the wilderness, even so must the Son of man be lifted up: That whosoever believeth in him should not perish, but have eternal life" (Jn.3:14-15).

"For God so loved the world, that he gave his only begotten Son, that whosoever believeth in him should not perish, but have everlasting life" (Jn.3:16).

"He that believeth on the Son hath everlasting life: and he that believeth not the Son shall not see life; but the wrath of God abideth on him" (Jn.3:36).

"Verily, verily, I say unto you, If a man keep my saying, he shall never see death" (Jn.8:51).

"And whosoever liveth and believeth in me shall never die. Believest thou this" (Jn.11:26).

"For this corruptible must put on incorruption, and this mortal must put on immortality. So when this corruptible shall have put on incorruption, and this mortal shall have put on immortality, then shall be brought to pass the saying that is written, Death is swallowed up in victory" (1 Cor.15:53-54).

"For we know that if our earthly house of this tabernacle were dissolved, we have a building of God, an house not made with hands, eternal in the heavens" (2 Cor.5:1).

"For the Lord himself shall descend from heaven with a shout, with the voice of the archangel, and with the trump of God: and the dead in Christ shall rise first: Then we which are alive and remain shall be caught up together with them in the clouds, to meet the Lord in the air: and so shall we ever be with the Lord" (1 Th.4:16-17).

2 (23:13-26) **Blessings, Source of—God, Blessings of—Assurance, of God's Faithfulness—Faithfulness, of God**: the second prophecy focused upon the source of the blessings, God Himself. The first attempt to curse God's people backfired. Instead of cursing, the false prophet had declared the blessings of God's people. The power of God had taken control of his tongue and stopped him from cursing Israel. When the king heard the blessings prophesied, he became enraged, furious. Now, note what happened:

OUTLINE	SCRIPTURE	SCRIPTURE	OUTLINE
2. The 2nd prophecy: The source of the blessings, God Himself	13 And Balak said unto him, Come, I pray thee, with	his mouth, and said, Go again unto Balak, and say	king Balak
a. The preparation for the prophecy	me unto another place, from whence thou mayest see	thus. 17 And when he came to	4) Balaam returned: Found king Balak standing
1) Balak tried a different tactic: Suggested cursing Israel from a site where only a small number could be seen	them: thou shalt see but the utmost part of them, and shalt not see them all: and curse me them from thence.	him, behold, he stood by his burnt offering, and the princes of Moab with him. And Balak said unto him,	beside his offerings with the officials of Moab
• Took Balaam to the top of Mt. Pisgah	14 And he brought him into the field of Zophim, to the	What hath the LORD spoken? 18 And he took up his para-	b. The prophecy: The source
• Built seven altars & offered pagan sacrifices: Sought to secure the favor of the gods	top of Pisgah, and built seven altars, and offered a bullock and a ram on every altar.	ble, and said, Rise up, Balak, and hear; hearken unto me, thou son of Zippor: 19 God is not a man, that he	that guarantees the blessings of God's people 1) God's truthfulness &
2) Balaam then walked some distance to seek God: Hoping that God would again meet him	15 And he said unto Balak, Stand here by thy burnt offering, while I meet the LORD yonder.	should lie; neither the son of man, that he should repent: hath he said, and shall he not do it? or hath he spoken, and	unchangableness: He does not lie nor change His mind 2) God's faithfulness: He speaks & acts; He promises & fulfills
3) God met with Balaam: Gave him a message for	16 And the LORD met Balaam, and put a word in	shall he not make it good? 20 Behold, I have received	3) God's promises: His

OUTLINE	SCRIPTURE	SCRIPTURE	OUTLINE
promises & blessings are irrevocable—they cannot be changed • No misfortune is seen • No misery or trouble is in store 4) God's presence: His presence assures the blessing of His people 5) God's power: His power assures the protection & deliverance of His people • Assures deliverance from all sorcery & divination • Assures a strong testimony for God	commandment to bless: and he hath blessed; and I cannot reverse it. 21 He hath not beheld iniq- uity in Jacob, neither hath he seen perverseness in Israel: the LORD his God is with him, and the shout of a king is among them. 22 God brought them out of Egypt; he hath as it were the strength of an unicorn. 23 Surely there is no enchantment against Jacob, neither is there any divina- tion against Israel: according to this time it shall be said of	Jacob and of Israel, What hath God wrought! 24 Behold, the people shall rise up as a great lion, and lift up himself as a young lion: he shall not lie down until he eat of the prey, and drink the blood of the slain. 25 And Balak said unto Balaam, Neither curse them at all, nor bless them at all. 26 But Balaam answered and said unto Balak, Told not I thee, saying, All that the LORD speaketh, that I must do?	• Assures victory over all enemies c. The result of the prophecy 1) Balak was desperate: He commanded "Stop! Say nothing! Neither curse nor bless them!" 2) Balaam insisted upon his rights as sorcerer (cp. 24:1)

1. The preparation for the prophecy was the same as for the first prophecy (v.14-17).
   a. King Balak tried a different tactic: he suggested cursing Israel from a site where only a small number of the people could be seen. By reducing the number that could be seen, he obviously hoped to reduce the impact they might make upon Balaam. Seeing the enormous number of Israelites earlier had, perhaps, aroused a fear within Balaam, a fear that kept him from cursing the king's enemies. Therefore, he took him to the top of Mt. Pisgah, where only a few of the king's enemies could be seen. Note that he again built seven altars and offered pagan sacrifices, seeking to bribe the gods and to secure their favor to curse Israel. Keep in mind that these are pagan offerings not the true worship of God. In fact, Gordon J. Wenham tells us that a Babylonian tablet actually describes a similar pagan offering that was offered up to three Babylonian gods and offered upon seven altars. The pagan offering also made use of seven incense burners and poured out the blood of seven sheep.[2]
   b. Balaam then walked some distance away to seek God, hoping that God would again meet him (v.15). No doubt, Balaam was somewhat concerned for his life, unless God actually allowed him to curse the enemies of the king.
   c. God did meet with Balaam and gave him a message for king Balak (v.16). Note exactly what this verse says: God "put the word, the message, the oracle" in the mouth of the prophet. God was controlling the tongue of the false prophet to speak exactly what God wanted proclaimed.
   d. Balaam then returned and found king Balak standing beside his offerings with the officials of Moab (v.17).

2. The prophecy focused upon the source of the blessings, God Himself (v.18-24). The people of God are blessed because of God not because of man. Kings and advisors, nations and armies are not the source of the blessings that come upon God's people; God is the source of the blessings. Consequently, the blessings can never be removed; the people of God can never be cursed. The people of God are conquerors over all the enemies who stand against them and attempt to curse them. They are victorious and triumphant throughout all of life—all because their source is God Himself. He is the source of all their blessings. This is the prophecy—the word and oracle—now being proclaimed by the false prophet.
   a. God's truthfulness and unchangableness guarantee the blessings of God's people. God does not lie nor change His mind (v.19). God is not like man who sometimes does lie and change his mind.
   b. God's faithfulness guarantees the promises to His people. God speaks and acts; He promises and fulfills. When God says something He carries it through. He acts and does exactly what He says.
   c. God's promises are the guarantee of His blessings. God's promises and blessings are irrevocable: they cannot be changed (v.20-21). God has promised to bless His people; therefore, when trials and problems arise, God strengthens His people to conquer the trials. This is His promise. No misfortune will conquer His people, and no misery or trouble will overcome them. Again, God's promises are irrevocable; therefore, the blessings that are promised to His people are irrevocable.
   d. God's presence guarantees the blessings of His people. The LORD their God is with the Israelites. He is proclaimed to be their King. Moreover, the shout of their King defends them against all enemies. His shout is mighty and powerful, striking fear in the heart of the enemy, routing and defeating them—all on behalf of His people.
   e. God's power guarantees the blessings of Israel. His power assures their protection and deliverance. This was perfectly demonstrated in their deliverance from Egyptian slavery: it was the power of God Himself that brought them out of Egypt. The power of God is like the strength of a wild ox (v.22). Note the great assurance that God's power gives to His people:
      ⇒ the assurance of deliverance from all sorcery and divination (v.23)
      ⇒ the assurance of a strong testimony for God (v.23)
      ⇒ the assurance of victory over all enemies (v.24)

3. Note the result, what happened as soon as Balaam completed the prophecy (v.25-26). In desperation, king Balak cried out: "Stop! Say nothing more! Neither curse nor bless them!" Once again Balaam tried to protect himself by insisting on his rights as a sorcerer (cp. Num.24:1).

> **Thought 1**. Great and wonderful blessings have been promised to God's people, blessings that explode the human imagination. But what guarantee do we have, we who live in this day and time? That we will receive the blessings of

2 Gordon J. Wenham. *The Book of Numbers*, p.172.

God? That the blessings will actually be given to us? As we march to the promised land of heaven, what assurance do we have that God is going to bless us? How can we know that good things are going to happen to us, that we are going to be blessed? We can know because of God, because of who God is. God guarantees His blessings for all generations of believers. If a person truly follows God, God promises to bless him. It is God Himself who guarantees that He will bless the believer. God gives five guarantees to the believer:
1) God's truthfulness and unchangableness guarantee that He will bless His people.

"God forbid: yea, let God be true, but every man a liar; as it is written, That thou mightest be justified in thy sayings, and mightest overcome when thou art judged" (Ro.3:4).

"That by two immutable things, in which it was impossible for God to lie, we might have a strong consolation, who have fled for refuge to lay hold upon the hope set before us" (Heb.6:18).

"Every good gift and every perfect gift is from above, and cometh down from the Father of lights, with whom is no variableness [changing], neither shadow of turning" (Jas.1:17).

"And now, O Lord God, thou art that God, and thy words be true, and thou hast promised this goodness unto thy servant" (2 Sam.7:28).

"Which made heaven, and earth, the sea, and all that therein is: which keepeth truth for ever" (Ps.146:6).

"For I am the Lord, I change not...." (Mal.3:6).

2) God's faithfulness guarantees that He will bless His people.

"God is faithful, by whom ye were called unto the fellowship of his Son Jesus Christ our Lord" (1 Cor.1:9).

"Wherefore let them that suffer according to the will of God commit the keeping of their souls to him in well doing, as unto a faithful Creator" (1 Pt.4:19).

"Know therefore that the Lord thy God, he is God, the faithful God, which keepeth covenant and mercy with them that love him and keep his commandments to a thousand generations" (Dt.7:9).

"I will sing of the mercies of the Lord for ever: with my mouth will I make known thy faithfulness to all generations" (Ps.89:1).

3) God's promises guarantee that He will bless His people.

"He staggered not at the promise of God through unbelief; but was strong in faith, giving glory to God; And being fully persuaded that, what he had promised, he was able also to perform" (Ro.4:20-21).

"For all the promises of God in him are yea, and in him Amen, unto the glory of God by us" (2 Cor.1:20).

"Whereby are given unto us exceeding great and precious promises: that by these ye might be partakers of the divine nature, having escaped the corruption that is in the world through lust" (2 Pt.1:4).

"And this is the promise that he hath promised us, even eternal life" (1 Jn.2:25).

"Blessed be the Lord, that hath given rest unto his people Israel, according to all that he promised: there hath not failed one word of all his good promise, which he promised by the hand of Moses his servant" (1 Ki.8:56).

4) God's presence guarantees and assures the blessings of His people.

"Lo, I am with you alway, even unto the end of the world. Amen" (Mt.28:20).

"And, behold, I am with thee, and will keep thee in all places whither thou goest, and will bring thee again into this land; for I will not leave thee, until I have done that which I have spoken to thee of" (Gen.28:15).

"And he said, My presence shall go with thee, and I will give thee rest" (Ex.33:14).

"When thou goest out to battle against thine enemies, and seest horses, and chariots, and a people more than thou, be not afraid of them: for the Lord thy God is with thee, which brought thee up out of the land of Egypt" (Dt.20:1).

"When thou passest through the waters, I will be with thee; and through the rivers, they shall not overflow thee: when thou walkest through the fire, thou shalt not be burned; neither shall the flame kindle upon thee" (Is.43:2).

5) God's power guarantees that He will bless His people, that He will protect and deliver them.

"But Jesus beheld them, and said unto them, With men this is impossible; but with God all things are possible" (Mt.19:26).

"For with God nothing shall be impossible" (Lk.1:37).

"But there shall not an hair of your head perish" (Lk.21:18).

"Now to him that is of power to stablish you according to my gospel, and the preaching of Jesus Christ, according to the revelation of the mystery, which was kept secret since the world began....To God only wise, be glory through Jesus Christ for ever. Amen" (Ro.16:25, 27).

"Now unto him that is able to do exceeding abundantly above all that we ask or think, according to the power that worketh in us" (Eph.3:20).

"There hath no temptation taken you but such as is common to man: but God is faithful, who will not suffer you to be tempted above that ye are able; but will with the temptation also make a way to escape, that ye may be able to bear it" (1 Cor.10:13).

"And he said unto me, My grace is sufficient for thee: for my strength is made perfect in weakness. Most gladly therefore will I rather glory in my infirmities, that the power of Christ may rest upon me. Therefore I take pleasure in infirmities, in reproaches, in necessities, in persecutions, in distresses for Christ's sake: for when I am weak, then am I strong" (2 Cor.12:9-10).

"And the Lord shall deliver me from every evil work, and will preserve me unto his heavenly kingdom: to whom be glory for ever and ever. Amen" (2 Tim.4:18).

"The Lord knoweth how to deliver the godly out of temptations, and to reserve the unjust unto the day of judgment to be punished" (2 Pt.2:9).

"Both riches and honour come of thee, and thou reignest over all; and in thine hand is power and might; and in thine hand it is to make great, and to give strength unto all" (1 Chron.29:12).

"For the eyes of the Lord run to and fro throughout the whole earth, to show himself strong in the behalf of them whose heart is perfect toward him" (2 Chron.16:9).

"I know that thou canst do every thing, and that no thought can be withholden from thee" (Job 42:2).

"The angel of the Lord encampeth round about them that fear him, and delivereth them" (Ps.34:7).

"Surely he shall deliver thee from the snare of the fowler, and from the noisome pestilence" (Ps.91:3).

"He shall cover thee with his feathers, and under his wings shalt thou trust: his truth shall be thy shield and buckler" (Ps.91:4).

"But our God is in the heavens: he hath done whatsoever he hath pleased" (Ps.115:3).

"Yea, before the day was I am he; and there is none that can deliver out of my hand: I will work, and who shall let [hinder, prevent] it" (Is.43:13).

3 (23:27-24:13) **Blessings, of God's People—Prophecy, of God's Blessings**: the third prophecy focused upon how God blesses His people. The king was desperate, so he could not give up. Somehow, some way, the Israelites had to be cursed. It was the only hope he had of defeating them in battle; therefore he must continue to seek the face of the gods, hoping that they would curse Israel. In desperation, he again appealed to the false prophet Balaam, the diviner who claimed to have the ear of the gods.

OUTLINE	SCRIPTURE	SCRIPTURE	OUTLINE
3. The 3rd prophecy: A picture of how God blesses His people a. The preparation for the prophecy 1) Balak suggested a third site • He was desperate—Israel must be cursed • He took Balaam to the top of Mt. Peor	27 And Balak said unto Balaam, Come, I pray thee, I will bring thee unto another place; peradventure it will please God that thou mayest curse me them from thence. 28 And Balak brought Balaam unto the top of Peor, that looketh toward Jeshimon.	the man whose eyes are open hath said: 4 He hath said, which heard the words of God, which saw the vision of the Almighty, falling into a trance, but having his eyes open:	of God • that he saw a vision from the Almighty • that his eyes were opened
2) Balaam requested that seven altars be built	29 And Balaam said unto Balak, Build me here seven altars, and prepare me here seven bullocks and seven rams.	5 How goodly are thy tents, O Jacob, and thy tabernacles, O Israel! 6 As the valleys are they spread forth, as gardens by the river's side, as the trees of lign aloes which the LORD hath planted, and as cedar trees beside the waters.	b. The prophecy: A picture of how God blesses His people 1) Their dwelling place—homes & land will be beautiful 2) Their homes & lands will be fruitful before the LORD
3) Balaam offered pagan sacrifices upon the altar	30 And Balak did as Balaam had said, and offered a bullock and a ram on every altar. **CHAPTER 24**	7 He shall pour the water out of his buckets, and his seed shall be in many waters, and his king shall be higher than Agag, and his kingdom shall be exalted.	3) Their resources will be sufficient & even overflow 4) Their leaders & kingdom will be powerful & exalted
4) Balaam made a significant change: He did not resort to sorcery (chants, spells, charms, magic)	And when Balaam saw that it pleased the LORD to bless Israel, he went not, as at other times, to seek for enchantments, but he set his face toward the wilderness.	8 God brought him forth out of Egypt; he hath as it were the strength of an unicorn: he shall eat up the nations his enemies, and shall break their bones, and pierce them through with his arrows.	5) Their Deliverer is God Himself 6) Their strength is as an ox 7) Their victory is assured over all hostile enemies
5) Balaam looked out over the camp of Israel tribe by tribe & was stricken by the sight: Suddenly, the Spirit of God came upon him & Balaam declared... • that his eyes saw clearly • that he heard the Word	2 And Balaam lifted up his eyes, and he saw Israel abiding in his tents according to their tribes; and the spirit of God came upon him. 3 And he took up his parable, and said, Balaam the son of Beor hath said, and	9 He couched, he lay down as a lion, and as a great lion: who shall stir him up? Blessed is he that blesseth thee, and cursed is he that curseth thee.	8) Their courage & security are assured 9) Their blessings are guaranteed by the promise of God Himself (cp. Gen.12:2-3)

OUTLINE	SCRIPTURE	SCRIPTURE	OUTLINE
c. The result of the prophecy 1) Balak flew into a rage, clapped his hands & shouted • Charged Balaam with breaking their agreement: Was summoned to curse Israel; instead, he had blessed them three times • Charged Balaam to leave immediately—go home! • Dismissed him without pay: The ultimate insult to his greed (2 Pt.2:15)	10 And Balak's anger was kindled against Balaam, and he smote his hands together: and Balak said unto Balaam, I called thee to curse mine enemies, and, behold, thou hast altogether blessed them these three times. 11 Therefore now flee thou to thy place: I thought to promote thee unto great hon- our; but, lo, the LORD hath kept thee back from	honour. 12 And Balaam said unto Balak, Spake I not also to thy messengers which thou sentest unto me, saying, 13 If Balak would give me his house full of silver and gold, I cannot go beyond the commandment of the LORD, to do either good or bad of mine own mind; but what the LORD saith, that will I speak?	2) Balaam attempted to excuse the disappointment (in his professional pride as a diviner, sorcerer): Reminded Balak of the terms laid down with his officials • He could only speak what the LORD said • He was powerless to do anything against the LORD—even if the king gave him a palace filled with gold & silver

1. Note the preparation for the prophecy (23:27-24:4).
   a. King Balak suggested a third site, hoping that a change of location would make a difference to the gods. He was desperate: a curse must be called down upon Israel. It was the only way his people and nation could be saved from the threat of invasion by the Israelites. Note that he took Balaam to the top of Mt. Peor. This was apparently the center of Baal worship in Moab (Num.25:3).
   b. Balaam again requested that seven altars be built (v.29).
   c. Once again, the false prophet offered pagan sacrifices upon the altar (v.30).
   d. At this point, Balaam made a significant change from what he had been doing: he did not resort to sorcery. He did not begin the usual chants, spells, charms, or magic tricks that were used to deceive the people (24:1).
   e. Instead, Balaam looked out over the camp of Israel tribe by tribe. Obviously, the sight struck him with a deep sense of God's presence among His people, that God was truly protecting them and blessing them beyond all imagination (v.2-4). Suddenly, the Spirit of God came upon the false prophet in some kind of ecstatic trance or control. Under the control of God's Spirit, Balaam declared...
      - that his eyes saw clearly
      - that he heard the Word of God
      - that he saw a vision from the Almighty
      - that his eyes were opened

2. Balaam then proclaimed the prophecy, a prophecy that shows exactly how God blesses His people (v.5-9). Standing there on top of the mountain and looking down upon the campsites of Israel, this false prophet was stricken with the beauty of the sight. What he saw was immediately transferred over into the future. He began to predict what the future blessings of God would be upon His dear people.
   a. God would bless their dwelling places: their homes and lands would be beautiful (v.5).
   b. God would bless the fruitfulness of their homes and lands. Both the people and the land would be very productive and fruitful.
   c. God would bless the resources of the people. There would always be sufficient, overflowing water to take care of the crops and production (v.7). This was a clear promise of God taking care of the necessities of life.
   d. God would bless the leaders and the kingdom of His people. Both the leaders and the kingdom of God's people would be powerful and exalted, far greater than any ruler or kingdom surrounding them (v.7).
   e. God would bless their deliverance, for He Himself was their Deliverer. He would always deliver them from the attacks of their enemies (v.8).
   f. God would bless their strength and make them personally as strong as oxen (v.8).
   g. God would bless their struggle against all enemies. They were assured of complete and total victory (v.8). All enemies would be defeated by His people (v.8).
   h. God would bless their courage and security. They would always be courageous and secure under His watch (v.9). They would be as courageous and secure as a lion who lies down in the deep grass knowing that he is perfectly secure.
   i. God guaranteed the blessings of His people. The guarantee was the promise of God Himself (v.9). Any who blessed His people would be blessed, and any who cursed His people would be cursed. This was the very promise of the Abrahamic covenant (cp. Gen.12:2-3).

3. Note the result of the prophecy: the message could not be missed, neither by the king nor by his officials (v.10-13).
   a. King Balak flew into a rage of anger, clapped his hands and shouted out at Balaam:
      ⇒ He charged Balaam with breaking their agreement. The false prophet had been summoned to curse Israel; instead, he had blessed them three times. He shouted out at Balaam to leave immediately and go home.
      ⇒ He dismissed Balaam without pay. This was the ultimate insult to the greed of this false prophet, this sorcerer who loved to make money through the unrighteous profession of sorcery (2 Pt.2:15).

   b. Balaam attempted to excuse the disappointment of the king in his ability as a diviner or sorcerer. No doubt, Balaam was somewhat concerned about his reputation as a diviner with other leaders and nations. He reminded the king of the terms laid down with his officials when they first summoned him. He had made it perfectly clear that he could speak only what the LORD had said, that he was powerless to do anything against the LORD—even if the king gave him a palace filled with gold and silver (Num.22:18).

Thought 1.The blessings given to Israel are applicable to the believer. God promises to bless the believer with great and wonderful blessings.
1) God blesses the believer with all the necessities of life: with shelter, food, and clothing.

"Therefore take no thought, saying, What shall we eat? or, What shall we drink? or, Wherewithal shall we be clothed? (For after all these things do the Gentiles seek:) for your heavenly Father knoweth that ye have need of all these things. But seek ye first the kingdom of God, and his righteousness; and all these things shall be added unto you" (Mt.6:31-33).

"But my God shall supply all your need according to his riches in glory by Christ Jesus" (Ph.4:19).

2) God blesses His people with a fruitful, overflowing life.

"And ye shall serve the Lord your God, and he shall bless thy bread, and thy water; and I will take sickness away from the midst of thee" (Ex.23:25).

"Thou preparest a table before me in the presence of mine enemies: thou anointest my head with oil; my cup runneth over" (Ps.23:5).

"Oh how great is thy goodness, which thou hast laid up for them that fear thee; which thou hast wrought for them that trust in thee before the sons of men" (Ps.31:19).

"Behold, the days come, saith the Lord, that the plowman shall overtake the reaper, and the treader of grapes him that soweth seed; and the mountains shall drop sweet wine, and all the hills shall melt" (Amos 9:13).

"Bring ye all the tithes into the storehouse, that there may be meat in mine house, and prove me now herewith, saith the Lord of hosts, if I will not open you the windows of heaven, and pour you out a blessing, that there shall not be room enough to receive it" (Mal.3:10).

3) God blesses His people with outstanding leaders and strong church fellowships.

"Take heed therefore unto yourselves, and to all the flock, over the which the Holy Ghost hath made you overseers, to feed the church of God, which he hath purchased with his own blood" (Acts 20:28).

"And he gave some, apostles; and some, prophets; and some, evangelists; and some, pastors and teachers; For the perfecting of the saints, for the work of the ministry, for the edifying of the body of Christ" (Eph.4:11-12).

"Feed the flock of God which is among you, taking the oversight thereof, not by constraint, but willingly; not for filthy lucre, but of a ready mind" (1 Pt.5:2).

"And I will give you pastors according to mine heart, which shall feed you with knowledge and understanding" (Jer.3:15).

"And I will set up shepherds over them which shall feed them: and they shall fear no more, nor be dismayed, neither shall they be lacking, saith the Lord" (Jer.23:4).

4) God blesses the believer with deliverance through all the trials and temptations of life.

"There hath no temptation taken you but such as is common to man: but God is faithful, who will not suffer you to be tempted above that ye are able; but will with the temptation also make a way to escape, that ye may be able to bear it" (1 Cor.10:13).

"And the Lord shall deliver me from every evil work, and will preserve me unto his heavenly kingdom: to whom be glory for ever and ever. Amen" (2 Tim.4:18).

"The Lord knoweth how to deliver the godly out of temptations, and to reserve the unjust unto the day of judgment to be punished" (2 Pt.2:9).

"Surely he shall deliver thee from the snare of the fowler, and from the noisome pestilence" (Ps.91:3).

5) God blesses the believer with strength, both physical and spiritual.

"And he said unto me, My grace is sufficient for thee: for my strength is made perfect in weakness. Most gladly therefore will I rather glory in my infirmities, that the power of Christ may rest upon me. Therefore I take pleasure in infirmities, in reproaches, in necessities, in persecutions, in distresses for Christ's sake: for when I am weak, then am I strong" (2 Cor.12:9-10).

"That he would grant you, according to the riches of his glory, to be strengthened with might by his Spirit in the inner man" (Eph.3:16).

"Who through faith subdued kingdoms, wrought righteousness, obtained promises, stopped the mouths of lions, Quenched the violence of fire, escaped the edge of the sword, out of weakness were made strong, waxed valiant in fight, turned to flight the armies of the aliens" (Heb.11:33-34).

"But they that wait upon the Lord shall renew their strength; they shall mount up with wings as eagles; they shall run, and not be weary; and they shall walk, and not faint" (Is.40:31).

"Fear thou not; for I am with thee: be not dismayed; for I am thy God: I will strengthen thee; yea, I will help thee; yea, I will uphold thee with the right hand of my righteousness" (Is.41:10).

6) God blesses His people with victory over all the pitfalls and enemies of this life.

"Who shall separate us from the love of Christ? shall tribulation, or distress, or persecution, or famine, or nakedness, or peril, or sword" (Ro.8:35).

"Nay, in all these things we are more than conquerors through him that loved us. For I am persuaded, that neither death, nor life, nor angels, nor principalities, nor powers, nor things present, nor things to come, Nor height, nor depth, nor any other creature, shall be able to separate us from the love of God, which is in Christ Jesus our Lord" (Ro.8:37-39)

"For whatsoever is born of God overcometh the world: and this is the victory that overcometh the world, even our faith. Who is he that overcometh the world, but he that believeth that Jesus is the Son of God" (1 Jn.5:4-5).

"Through thee will we push down our enemies: through thy name will we tread them under that rise up against us" (Ps.44:5).

7) God blesses His people with courage and security throughout life.

"So that we may boldly say, The Lord is my helper, and I will not fear what man shall do unto me" (Heb.13:6).

"The Lord is my light and my salvation; whom shall I fear? the Lord is the strength of my life; of whom shall I be afraid? When the wicked, even mine enemies and my foes, came upon me to eat up my flesh, they stumbled and fell. Though an host should encamp against me, my heart shall not fear: though war should rise against me, in this will I be confident" (Ps.27:1-3).

"I will say of the Lord, He is my refuge and my fortress: my God; in him will I trust. Surely he shall deliver thee from the snare of the fowler, and from the noisome pestilence. He shall cover thee with his feathers, and under his wings shalt thou trust: his truth shall be thy shield and buckler. Thou shalt not be afraid for the terror by night; nor for the arrow that flieth by day; Nor for the pestilence that walketh in darkness; nor for the destruction that wasteth at noonday" (Ps.91:2-6).

"The Lord is on my side; I will not fear: what can man do unto me" (Ps.118:6).

"When thou liest down, thou shalt not be afraid: yea, thou shalt lie down, and thy sleep shall be sweet" (Pr.3:24).

"Behold, God is my salvation; I will trust, and not be afraid: for the Lord Jehovah is my strength and my song; he also is become my salvation" (Is.12:2).

8) God guarantees that the believer will be blessed by Him. God will keep His promises to His people and fulfill every promise.

"He staggered not at the promise of God through unbelief; but was strong in faith, giving glory to God; And being fully persuaded that, what he had promised, he was able also to perform" (Ro.4:20-21).

"For all the promises of God in him are yea, and in him Amen, unto the glory of God by us" (2 Cor.1:20).

"Whereby are given unto us exceeding great and precious promises: that by these ye might be partakers of the divine nature, having escaped the corruption that is in the world through lust" (2 Pt.1:4).

"Blessed be the Lord, that hath given rest unto his people Israel, according to all that he promised: there hath not failed one word of all his good promise, which he promised by the hand of Moses his servant" (1 Ki.8:56).

4 (24:14-19) **Prophecy, Concerning the Coming Deliverer—Deliverance, Prophecy Concerning—Jesus Christ, Prophecy Concerning—Prophecy, of Jesus Christ**: the fourth prophecy focused upon the coming Deliverer. This was a picture of the coming of the Lord Jesus Christ as the Messianic Ruler over all the universe.

OUTLINE	SCRIPTURE	SCRIPTURE	OUTLINE
4. The 4th prophecy: A picture of the coming Deliverer a. The preparation for the prophecy 1) Balaam started to leave, but he was suddenly constrained by God to prophesy: About the "days to come" 2) Balaam declared... • that his eyes saw clearly • that he heard the Words of God • that he had knowledge from the Most High • that he saw a vision from the Almighty • that his eyes were opened	14 And now, behold, I go unto my people: come therefore, and I will advertise thee what this people shall do to thy people in the latter days. 15 And he took up his parable, and said, Balaam the son of Beor hath said, and the man whose eyes are open hath said: 16 He hath said, which heard the words of God, and knew the knowledge of the most High, which saw the vision of the Almighty, falling into a trance, but having his eyes open:	17 I shall see him, but not now: I shall behold him, but not nigh: there shall come a Star out of Jacob, and a Sceptre shall rise out of Israel, and shall smite the corners of Moab, and destroy all the children of Sheth. 18 And Edom shall be a possession, Seir also shall be a possession for his enemies; and Israel shall do valiantly. 19 Out of Jacob shall come he that shall have dominion, and shall destroy him that remaineth of the city.	b. The prophecy: A picture of the coming Deliverer 1) He will come in the future 2) He will be a star & a scepter (have dominion) 3) He will be victorious over all enemies, including Moab & Edom 4) He will guarantee the growing strength of His people (Israel) 5) He will guarantee the triumph & dominion of God's people

1. There was the preparation for the prophecy (v.14-16). Just as Balaam turned to leave, suddenly he was constrained by the power of God to begin prophesying. The subject of this prophecy concerned the "latter days," the "days yet to come." Of course this is a reference to the future.

Balaam declared...
- that his eyes saw the future clearly
- that he actually heard the words of God
- that he had knowledge from the Most High
- that he saw a vision from the Almighty
- that his eyes were opened to see into the future

2. The prophecy focused upon the coming Deliverer, the coming Messiah who was to reign as the Sovereign LORD over all (v.17-19). Note exactly what was said:
   a. He would come in the future. The false prophet saw Him but His coming was not yet near (v.17).
   b. He would be a star and a scepter that would come out of Jacob and rise out of Israel. This is a reference to the rule and reign of Jesus Christ during the Messianic Kingdom and throughout all eternity (v.17).
   c. He would be victorious. He would crush both Moab and Edom (v.17). Imagine the impact of these words upon the king of Edom standing right there listening to this prophecy as it was being proclaimed.
   d. He would guarantee the growing strength of His people, Israel. They would grow stronger and stronger (v.18).
   e. He would guarantee the triumph and dominion of God's people. He would lead God's people to destroy all their enemies (v.19).

Thought 1. Jesus Christ is the promised Deliverer, the Messiah and Messianic King who was to come and rule over all the universe. He is the Sovereign LORD and King of the universe.

"And I appoint unto you a kingdom, as my Father hath appointed unto me; That ye may eat and drink at my table in my kingdom, and sit on thrones judging the twelve tribes of Israel" (Lk.22:29-30).

"And he said unto Jesus, Lord, remember me when thou comest into thy kingdom" (Lk.23:42).

"Nathanael answered and saith unto him, Rabbi, thou art the Son of God; thou art the King of Israel" (Jn.1:49).

"These things I have spoken unto you, that in me ye might have peace. In the world ye shall have tribulation: but be of good cheer; I have overcome the world" (Jn.16:33).

"Jesus answered, My kingdom is not of this world: if my kingdom were of this world, then would my servants fight, that I should not be delivered to the Jews: but now is my kingdom not from hence" (Jn.18:36).

"Pilate therefore said unto him, Art thou a king then? Jesus answered, Thou sayest that I am a king. To this end was I born, and for this cause came I into the world, that I should bear witness unto the truth. Every one that is of the truth heareth my voice" (Jn.18:37).

"For as in Adam all die, even so in Christ shall all be made alive. But every man in his own order: Christ the firstfruits; afterward they that are Christ's at his coming. Then cometh the end, when he shall have delivered up the kingdom to God, even the Father; when he shall have put down all rule and all authority and power" (1 Cor.15:22-24).

"For he must reign, till he hath put all enemies under his feet" (1 Cor.15:25).

"To him that overcometh will I grant to sit with me in my throne, even as I also overcame, and am set down with my Father in his throne" (Rev.3:21).

"These shall make war with the Lamb, and the Lamb shall overcome them: for he is Lord of lords, and King of kings: and they that are with him are called, and chosen, and faithful" (Rev.17:14).

"Of the increase of his government and peace there shall be no end, upon the throne of David, and upon his kingdom, to order it, and to establish it with judgment and with justice from henceforth even for ever. The zeal of the Lord of hosts will perform this" (Is.9:7).

"Therefore will I divide him a portion with the great, and he shall divide the spoil with the strong; because he hath poured out his soul unto death: and he was numbered with the transgressors; and he bare the sin of many, and made intercession for the transgressors" (Is.53:12).

"Behold, the days come, saith the Lord, that I will raise unto David a righteous Branch, and a King shall reign and prosper, and shall execute judgment and justice in the earth" (Jer.23:5).

"And there was given him dominion, and glory, and a kingdom, that all people, nations, and languages, should serve him: his dominion is an everlasting dominion, which shall not pass away, and his kingdom that which shall not be destroyed" (Dan.7:14).

5 (24:20) **Victory, over Enemies—Enemies, Victory over—Prophecy, Concerning Victory over Enemies—Amalek, Prophecy Concerning Destruction—Israel, Prophecy of Victories**: the fifth prophecy focused upon the victory of Israel over the greatest of enemies. This prophecy and the final two are brief predictions concerning the enemies of God's people. These prophecies must have shaken the king to the core of his being. His purpose had been to bring a curse upon the Israelites; but instead he was being cursed and, not only him, but all the other enemies who stood opposed to the people of God. They were having the curse or judgment of God cast upon them as well. One thing was sure: it was not wise to oppose God's people. The prophecy was very simple: the false prophet saw Amalek and prophesied that this greatest of nations would be destroyed.

OUTLINE	SCRIPTURE
5. The 5th prophecy: A picture of victory over the greatest enemies a. Balaam saw Amalek & prophesied b. Amalek, the greatest of nations, would be destroyed	20 And when he looked on Amalek, he took up his parable, and said, Amalek was the first of the nations; but his latter end shall be that he perish for ever.

Thought 1. There is one strong lesson in this prophecy: victory is assured to God's people, even over the greatest of enemies. No matter how strong the enemy, no matter how great the assault, no matter how often the attack—victory belongs to God's people. The believer will conquer and triumph over all enemies, even the greatest of enemies.
1) God gives victory over death.

"For God so loved the world, that he gave his only begotten Son, that whosoever believeth in him should not perish, but have everlasting life" (Jn.3:16).

"Let not your heart be troubled: ye believe in God, believe also in me. In my Father's house are many mansions: if it were not so, I would have told you. I go to prepare a place for you" (Jn.14:1-2).

"Forasmuch then as the children are partakers of flesh and blood, he also himself likewise took part of the same; that through death he might destroy him that had the power of death, that is, the devil; And deliver them who through fear of death were all their lifetime subject to bondage" (Heb.2:14-15).

2) God gives victory over the world with all its enslavements and bondages.

"And ye shall know the truth, and the truth shall make you free" (Jn.8:32).

"Likewise reckon ye also yourselves to be dead indeed unto sin, but alive unto God through Jesus Christ our Lord. Let not sin therefore reign in your mortal body, that ye should obey it in the lusts thereof. Neither yield ye your members as instruments of unrighteousness unto sin: but yield yourselves unto God, as those that are alive from the dead, and your members as instruments of righteousness unto God. For sin shall not have dominion over you: for ye are not under the law, but under grace" (Ro.6:11-14).

"I find then a law, that, when I would do good, evil is present with me. For I delight in the law of God after the inward man: But I see another law in my members, warring against the law of my mind, and bringing me into captivity to the law of sin which is in my members. O wretched man that I am! who shall deliver me from the body of this death? I thank God through Jesus Christ our Lord. So then with the mind I myself serve the law of God; but with the flesh the law of sin" (Ro.7:21-25).

"For the law of the Spirit of life in Christ Jesus hath made me free from the law of sin and death" (Ro.8:2).

"For whatsoever is born of God overcometh the world: and this is the victory that overcometh the world, even our faith. Who is he that overcometh the world, but he that believeth that Jesus is the Son of God" (1 Jn.5:4-5).

3) God gives victory over the evil of men, over all who oppose us and stand as enemies against us.

"And the Lord shall deliver me from every evil work, and will preserve me unto his heavenly kingdom: to whom be glory for ever and ever. Amen" (2 Tim.4:18).

"The Lord shall fight for you, and ye shall hold your peace" (Ex.14:14).

"I will send my fear before thee, and will destroy all the people to whom thou shalt come, and I will make all thine enemies turn their backs unto thee" (Ex.23:27).

"Through thee will we push down our enemies: through thy name will we tread them under that rise up against us" (Ps.44:5).

4) God gives victory over the temptations and trials of life.

"There hath no temptation taken you but such as is common to man: but God is faithful, who will not suffer you to be tempted above that ye are able; but will with the temptation also make a way to escape, that ye may be able to bear it" (1 Cor.10:13).

"Many are the afflictions of the righteous: but the Lord delivereth him out of them all" (Ps.34:19).

"The Lord will strengthen him upon the bed of languishing: thou wilt make all his bed in his sickness" (Ps.41:3).

"When thou passest through the waters, I will be with thee; and through the rivers, they shall not overflow thee: when thou walkest through the fire, thou shalt not be burned; neither shall the flame kindle upon thee" (Is.43:2).

5) God gives victory over all the evil powers and rulers of darkness, over all the spiritual wickedness that attacks us.

"Finally, my brethren, be strong in the Lord, and in the power of his might. Put on the whole armour of God, that ye may be able to stand against the wiles of the devil. For we wrestle not against flesh and blood, but against principalities, against powers, against the rulers of the darkness of this

world, against spiritual wickedness in high places. Wherefore take unto you the whole armour of God, that ye may be able to withstand in the evil day, and having done all, to stand" (Eph.6:10-13).

"Submit yourselves therefore to God. Resist the devil, and he will flee from you" (Jas.4:7).

"Be sober, be vigilant; because your adversary the devil, as a roaring lion, walketh about, seeking whom he may devour" (1 Pt.5:8).

"And they overcame him by the blood of the Lamb, and by the word of their testimony; and they loved not their lives unto the death" (Rev.12:11).

6) God gives victory over any person or any thing, in this world and in the spiritual world.

"Who shall separate us from the love of Christ? shall tribulation, or distress, or persecution, or famine, or nakedness, or peril, or sword....Nay, in all these things we are more than conquerors through him that loved us. For I am persuaded, that neither death, nor life, nor angels, nor principalities, nor powers, nor things present, nor things to come, Nor height, nor depth, nor any other creature, shall be able to separate us from the love of God, which is in Christ Jesus our Lord" (Ro.8:35, 37-39).

7) God gives us victory over persecution.

"For our light affliction, which is but for a moment, worketh for us a far more exceeding and eternal weight of glory" (2 Cor.4:17).

"Beloved, think it not strange concerning the fiery trial which is to try you, as though some strange thing happened unto you: But rejoice, inasmuch as ye are partakers of Christ's sufferings; that, when his glory shall be revealed, ye may be glad also with exceeding joy"(1 Pt.4:12-13).

6 (24:21-22) **Victory, over Enemies—Triumph, over Enemies—Prophecy, Victory over Enemies—Israel, Prophecies Concerning—Kenites, Prophecy Concerning—Prophecy, Concerning the Kenites—Assyria, Prophecy Concerning**: the sixth prophecy focused upon the greatest fortresses of the enemy being destroyed. Note that the Kenites were said to be secure, living behind an impregnable fortress. But they would be destroyed.

OUTLINE	SCRIPTURE
6. The 6th prophecy: A picture of the greatest fortresses of the enemy being destroyed a. Balaam saw the Kenites & prophesied b. The Kenites & their impregnable fortress would be destroyed by Assyria	21 And he looked on the Kenites, and took up his parable, and said, Strong is thy dwellingplace, and thou puttest thy nest in a rock. 22 Nevertheless the Kenite shall be wasted, until Asshur shall carry thee away captive.

Someday out in the future, the great nation of Assyria would conquer the Kenites and take them captive. This is a prophecy that was looking ahead to the future, several centuries ahead. Assyria was not yet a powerful nation, not the powerful nation that was to be moving across the face of the earth seeking world domination. It should be noted that some commentators say that Asshur mentioned here was actually a small tribe that lived in northern Sinai (Gen.25:3, 18; 2 Sam.2:9; Ps.83:8). If this is accurate, it means that the Kenites were conquered by a small tribe of people who lived close by. However, this position is most unlikely.

Thought 1. Every believer has certain enemies that seem impregnable, immovable. Certain temptations and trials seem to afflict him time and again. Temptation after temptation and trial after trial seem to lurk behind fortresses that just cannot be torn down. The believer tries to get rid of the temptations or trials, but they seem to be secure, settled in as though behind concrete fortresses—immovable, impregnable. The barrage of temptations and trials seems relentless. At times they attack the mind: the believer tries his best to get rid of the thoughts continually assaulting him. Foul words, lustful thoughts, cravings for food, drugs, or alcohol; seeking recognition or position; coveting more money, possessions, or property—a shower of tempting thoughts assault the believer all throughout the day. No matter how hard he tries, the temptations or trials seem to be impregnable; they cannot be cast down. But note the strong proclamation of Scripture: the greatest fortresses of the enemy can be destroyed. This is the promise of God.

"Who shall separate us from the love of Christ? shall tribulation, or distress, or persecution, or famine, or nakedness, or peril, or sword.... Nay, in all these things we are more than conquerors through him that loved us. For I am persuaded, that neither death, nor life, nor angels, nor principalities, nor powers, nor things present, nor things to come, Nor height, nor depth, nor any other creature, shall be able to separate us from the love of God, which is in Christ Jesus our Lord" (Ro.8:35, 37-39).

"(For the weapons of our warfare are not carnal, but mighty through God to the pulling down of strong holds;) Casting down imaginations, and every high thing that exalteth itself against the knowledge of God, and bringing into captivity every thought to the obedience of Christ" (2 Cor.10:4-5).

"Finally, my brethren, be strong in the Lord, and in the power of his might. Put on the whole armour of God, that ye may be able to stand against the wiles of the devil. For we wrestle not against

flesh and blood, but against principalities, against powers, against the rulers of the darkness of this world, against spiritual wickedness in high places. Wherefore take unto you the whole armour of God, that ye may be able to withstand in the evil day, and having done all, to stand" (Eph.6:10-13).

"For the word of God is quick, and powerful, and sharper than any twoedged sword, piercing even to the dividing asunder of soul and spirit, and of the joints and marrow, and is a discerner of the thoughts and intents of the heart" (Heb.4:12).

"Be sober, be vigilant; because your adversary the devil, as a roaring lion, walketh about, seeking whom he may devour: Whom resist stedfast in the faith, knowing that the same afflictions are accomplished in your brethren that are in the world. But the God of all grace, who hath called us unto his eternal glory by Christ Jesus, after that ye have suffered a while, make you perfect, stablish, strengthen, settle you" (1 Pt.5:8-10).

"Through thee will we push down our enemies: through thy name will we tread them under that rise up against us" (Ps.44:5).

7 (24:23-25) **Judgment, Against All Enemies—Prophecy, of Judgment—Judicial Judgment, of God—Nations, Cup Full of Iniquity—Cup, Full of Iniquity—Judgment, Full Measure of**: the seventh prophecy focused upon God's judgment against all enemies whose "cup was full of iniquity." This simply means that a nation had reached the full measure of evil that God allows. They would not be allowed to go any further, not allowed to continue committing one atrocity after another. They would be judged and destroyed as a nation.

OUTLINE	SCRIPTURE
7. The 7th prophecy: A picture of God's judgment against all whose "cup is full of iniquity" (has reached the full measure that God allows) a. Balaam again prophesied the future b. Assyria & Eber would be destroyed: By an invading force coming across the sea c. Balaam & Balak separated & returned home	23 And he took up his parable, and said, Alas, who shall live when God doeth this! 24 And ships shall come from the coast of Chittim, and shall afflict Asshur, and shall afflict Eber, and he also shall perish for ever. 25 And Balaam rose up, and went and returned to his place: and Balak also went his way.

Note that Balaam again prophesied the future. Assyria and Eber would be destroyed by an invading force coming from across the sea. After this prophecy, Balaam and Balak separated and returned home.

Thought 1. The judgment of God will fall upon the wicked and evil, the lawless and immoral of this earth. There will be no escape. When the "cup of iniquity" is full, when the full measure of sin has been committed by a person—that person will leave this earth and face the judgment of God. But note: this is not only true of individuals, it is also true of nations. When the "cup of iniquity," the full measure of evil and brutality, has been filled to overflowing by nations—that nation will be destroyed by the terrifying hand of God's judgment. This is the record of human history, as any objective and honest historian can testify.

1) God will judge the nations of this earth.

"When the Son of man shall come in his glory, and all the holy angels with him, then shall he sit upon the throne of his glory: And before him shall be gathered all nations: and he shall separate them one from another, as a shepherd divideth his sheep from the goats: And he shall set the sheep on his right hand, but the goats on the left.... Then shall he say also unto them on the left hand, Depart from me, ye cursed, into everlasting fire, prepared for the devil and his angels.... And these shall go away into everlasting punishment: but the righteous into life eternal" (Mt.25:31-33, 41, 46).

"Because he hath appointed a day, in the which he will judge the world in righteousness by that man whom he hath ordained; whereof he hath given assurance unto all men, in that he hath raised him from the dead" (Acts 17:31).

2) God will judge the people of this earth, individual by individual—every one of us.

"In the day when God shall judge the secrets of men by Jesus Christ according to my gospel" (Ro.2:16).

"So then every one of us shall give account of himself to God" (Ro.14:12).

"And as it is appointed unto men once to die, but after this the judgment" (Heb.9:27).

"The Lord knoweth how to deliver the godly out of temptations, and to reserve the unjust unto the day of judgment to be punished" (2 Pt.2:9).

"But the heavens and the earth, which are now, by the same word are kept in store, reserved unto fire against the day of judgment and perdition of ungodly men" (2 Pt.3:7).

NUMBERS 23:1-24:25

"And Enoch also, the seventh from Adam, prophesied of these, saying, Behold, the Lord cometh with ten thousands of his saints, To execute judgment upon all, and to convince all that are ungodly among them of all their ungodly deeds which they have ungodly committed, and of all their hard speeches which ungodly sinners have spoken against him" (Jude 14-15).

TYPES, SYMBOLS, AND PICTURES (Numbers 23:1-24:25)

Historical Term	Type or Picture (Scriptural Basis for Each)	Life Application for Today's Believer	Biblical Application
Israel Num.23:1-12	*Israel is a type or symbol of God's people.* **"And he took up his parable, and said, Balak the king of Moab hath brought me from Aram, out of the mountains of the east, *saying,* Come, curse me Jacob, and come, defy Israel. How shall I curse, whom God hath not cursed? or how shall I defy, *whom* the LORD hath not defied? For from the top of the rocks I see him, and from the hills I behold him: lo, the people shall dwell alone, and shall not be reckoned among the nations. Who can count the dust of Jacob, and the number of the fourth *part* of Israel? Let me die the death of the righteous, and let my last end be like his" (Num.23:7-10)**	The blessings of God given in this passage are gifts of God to all His people (Num.23:1-12). Note the blessings one by one. 1. God's people are an innocent, secure people—a people who are justified, eternally secure before God. God has forgiven our sins and justified us, counted us innocent before Him.	***"And I give unto them eternal life; and they shall never perish, neither shall any man pluck them out of my hand" (Jn.10:28).***
		2. God's people are a separated and distinctive people. The genuine believer lives a holy life before God, a life that is pure and righteous, moral and clean, just and fair. The believer lives a life of separation from the world.	***"If ye were of the world, the world would love his own: but because ye are not of the world, but I have chosen you out of the world, therefore the world hateth you" (Jn.15:19).*** ***"And have no fellowship with the unfruitful works of darkness, but rather reprove them" (Eph.5:11).***
		3. God's people are eventually to be a numerous people. This was the promise made to Abraham and his descendants, that is, all the succeeding generations of believers down through the ages. Believers are eventually to number as the stars of the sky and as the sands by the seashore.	***"That in blessing I will bless thee, and in multiplying I will multiply thy seed as the stars of the heaven, and as the sand which is upon the sea shore; and thy seed shall possess the gate of his enemies" (Gen. 22:17).***
		4. God's people are a righteous people with eternal hope. A genuine believer is counted righteous through the righteousness of Jesus Christ. Jesus Christ is the believer's only approach to God. A person can approach God only through Christ, only through His righteousness. When a person comes to God through Christ's righteousness, God accepts that person; God counts that person justified, righteous. Once the person has been justified—	***"For Christ is the end of the law for righteousness to every one that believeth" (Ro.10:4).*** ***"But of him are ye in Christ Jesus, who of God is made unto us wisdom, and righteousness, and sanctification, and redemption" (1 Cor.1:30).*** ***"And be found in him, not having mine own righteousness, which is of the law, but that which is through the faith of Christ, the righteousness which is of God by faith" (Ph. 3:9).***

Historical Term	Type or Picture (Scriptural Basis for Each)	Life Application for Today's Believer	Biblical Application
		counted righteous—he is given the wonderful hope of living eternally with God.	
The Third Prophecy of Balaam Num.23:27-24:14	*The third prophecy of Balaam is a picture of how God blesses His people.* Balaam began to predict what the future blessings of God would be upon His dear people. 1. God would bless their dwelling places: their homes and lands would be beautiful (v.5). 2. God would bless the fruitfulness of their homes and lands. Both the people and the land would be very productive and fruitful. 3. God would bless the resources of the people. There would always be sufficient, overflowing water to take care of the crops and production (v.7). This was a clear promise of God taking care of the necessities of life. 4. God would bless the leaders and the kingdom of His people. Both the leaders and the kingdom of God's people would be powerful and exalted, far greater than any ruler or kingdom surrounding them (v.7). 5. God would bless their deliverance, for He Himself was their Deliverer. He would always deliver them from the attacks of their enemies (v.8). 6. God would bless their strength and make them personally as strong as oxen (v.8). 7. God would bless their struggle against all enemies. He assured them of complete and total victory (v.8). All enemies would be defeated by His people (v.8). 8. God would bless their courage and security. They were assured that they would always be courageous and secure under His watch (v.9).	The blessings given to Israel are applicable to the believer. God promises to bless the believer with great and wonderful blessings. ⇒ God blesses the believer with all the necessities of life: with shelter, food, and clothing. ⇒ God blesses His people with a fruitful, overflowing life. ⇒ God blesses His people with outstanding leaders and strong church fellowships. ⇒ God blesses the believer with deliverance through all the trials and temptations of life. ⇒ God blesses the believer with strength, both physical and spiritual. ⇒ God blesses His people with victory over all the pitfalls and enemies of this life. ⇒ God blesses His people with courage and security throughout life. ⇒ God guarantees that the believer will be blessed by Him. God will keep His promises to His people and fulfill every promise.	***"Therefore take no thought, saying, What shall we eat? or, What shall we drink? or, Wherewithal shall we be clothed? (For after all these things do the Gentiles seek:) for your heavenly Father knoweth that ye have need of all these things. But seek ye first the kingdom of God, and his righteousness; and all these things shall be added unto you" (Mt.6:31-33).*** ***"And ye shall serve the Lord your God, and he shall bless thy bread, and thy water; and I will take sickness away from the midst of thee" (Ex.23:25).*** ***"Take heed therefore unto yourselves, and to all the flock, over the which the Holy Ghost hath made you overseers, to feed the church of God, which he hath purchased with his own blood" (Acts 20:28).*** ***"There hath no temptation taken you but such as is common to man: but God is faithful, who will not suffer you to be tempted above that ye are able; but will with the temptation also make a way to escape, that ye may be able to bear it" (1 Cor. 10:13).*** ***"That he would grant you, according to the riches of his glory, to be strengthened with might by his Spirit in the inner man" (Eph.3:16).*** ***"Who shall separate us from the love of Christ? shall tribulation, or distress, or persecution, or famine, or nakedness, or peril, or sword" (Ro.8:35).*** ***"So that we may boldly say, The Lord is my helper, and I will not fear what man shall do unto me" (Heb.13:6).*** ***"He staggered not at the promise of God through unbelief; but was strong in faith, giving glory to God; And being fully persuaded***

Historical Term	Type or Picture (Scriptural Basis for Each)	Life Application for Today's Believer	Biblical Application
	They would be as courageous and secure as a lion who lies down in the deep grass knowing that he is perfectly secure. 9. God guaranteed the blessings of His people. The guarantee was the promise of God Himself (v.9). Any who blessed His people would be blessed, and any who cursed His people would be cursed. This was the very promise of the Abrahamic covenant (cp. Gen.12:2-3). **"How goodly are thy tents, O Jacob, *and* thy tabernacles, O Israel! As the valleys are they spread forth, as gardens by the river's side, as the trees of lign aloes which the LORD hath planted, *and* as cedar trees beside the waters. He shall pour the water out of his buckets, and his seed *shall be* in many waters, and his king shall be higher than Agag, and his kingdom shall be exalted" (Num.24:5-7)**		***that, what he had promised, he was able also to perform" (Ro.4:20-21).***
The Coming Deliverer Num.24:14-19	*The coming Deliverer is a symbol of the coming of the Lord Jesus Christ as the Messianic Ruler over all the universe.* The prophecy focused upon the coming Deliverer, the coming Messiah who was to reign as the Sovereign LORD over all (v.17-19). Note exactly what was said: 1. He would come in the future. The false prophet saw Him, but His coming was not yet near (v.17). 2. He would be a star and a scepter that would come out of Jacob and rise out of Israel. This is a reference to the rule and reign of Jesus Christ during the Messianic Kingdom and throughout all eternity (v.17). 3. He would be victorious. He would crush both Moab and Edom (v.17). Imagine the impact of these words upon the king of Edom standing right there listening to this	Jesus Christ is the promised Deliverer, the Messiah and Messianic King who was to come and rule over all the universe. He is the Sovereign LORD and King of the universe.	***"Nathanael answered and saith unto him, Rabbi, thou art the Son of God; thou art the King of Israel" (Jn.1:49).*** ***"These things I have spoken unto you, that in me ye might have peace. In the world ye shall have tribulation: but be of good cheer; I have overcome the world" (Jn.16:33).*** ***"Jesus answered, My kingdom is not of this world: if my kingdom were of this world, then would my servants fight, that I should not be delivered to the Jews: but now is my kingdom not from hence" (Jn.18:36).*** ***"Pilate therefore said unto him, Art thou a king then? Jesus answered, Thou sayest that I am a king. To this end was I born, and for this cause came I into the world, that I should bear witness unto the truth. Every one that is of the truth heareth my voice" (Jn. 18:37).***

Historical Term	Type or Picture (Scriptural Basis for Each)	Life Application for Today's Believer	Biblical Application
	prophecy as it was being proclaimed. 4. He would guarantee the growing strength of His people, Israel. They would grow stronger and stronger (v.18). 5. He would guarantee the triumph and dominion of God's people. He would lead God's people to destroy all their enemies (v.19). **"I shall see him, but not now: I shall behold him, but not nigh: there shall come a Star out of Jacob, and a Sceptre shall rise out of Israel, and shall smite the corners of Moab, and destroy all the children of Sheth" (Num.24:17).**		***"And I appoint unto you a kingdom, as my Father hath appointed unto me; That ye may eat and drink at my table in my kingdom, and sit on thrones judging the twelve tribes of Israel" (Lk.22:29-30).*** ***"For as in Adam all die, even so in Christ shall all be made alive. But every man in his own order: Christ the firstfruits; afterward they that are Christ's at his coming. Then cometh the end, when he shall have delivered up the kingdom to God, even the Father; when he shall have put down all rule and all authority and power" (1 Cor.15:22-24).*** ***"For he must reign, till he hath put all enemies under his feet" (1 Cor.15:25).*** ***"To him that overcometh will I grant to sit with me in my throne, even as I also overcame, and am set down with my Father in his throne" (Rev.3:21).***
Assyria Destroying the Kenites Num.24:21-22	*Assyria Destroying The Kenites is a picture of the greatest fortress of the enemy being defeated. Note that the Kenites were said to be secure, living behind an impregnable fortress. But they would be destroyed.* **"And he looked on the Kenites, and took up his parable, and said, Strong is thy dwellingplace, and thou puttest thy nest in a rock. Nevertheless the Kenite shall be wasted, until Asshur shall carry thee away captive" (Num.24:21-22).**	Every believer has certain enemies that seem impregnable, immovable. Certain temptations and trials seem to afflict him time and again. Temptation after temptation and trial after trial seem to lurk behind fortresses that cannot be torn down. The believer tries to get rid of the temptations or trials, but they seem to be secure, settled in as though behind concrete fortresses—immov-able, impregnable. The barrage of temptations and trials seems relentless. At times they attack the mind: the believer tries his best to get rid of the thoughts continually assaulting him. Foul words, lustful images, cravings for food, drugs, or alcohol; seeking recognition or position; coveting more money, possessions, or property—a shower of tempting thoughts assault the believer all throughout the day. No matter how hard he tries, the temptations or trials seem to be unbeatable; they cannot be cast down. But note the strong proclamation of Scripture: the	***"Who shall separate us from the love of Christ? shall tribulation, or distress, or persecution, or famine, or nakedness, or peril, or sword.... Nay, in all these things we are more than conquerors through him that loved us. For I am persuaded, that neither death, nor life, nor angels, nor principalities, nor powers, nor things present, nor things to come, Nor height, nor depth, nor any other creature, shall be able to separate us from the love of God, which is in Christ Jesus our Lord" (Ro.8:35, 37-39).*** ***"(For the weapons of our warfare are not carnal, but mighty through God to the pulling down of strong holds;) Casting down imaginations, and every high thing that exalteth itself against the knowledge of God, and bringing into captivity every thought to the obedience of Christ" (2 Cor.10:4-5).*** ***"Finally, my brethren, be strong in the Lord, and in***

Historical Term	Type or Picture (Scriptural Basis for Each)	Life Application for Today's Believer	Biblical Application
		greatest fortresses of the enemy can be destroyed. This is the promise of God.	***the power of his might. Put on the whole armour of God, that ye may be able to stand against the wiles of the devil. For we wrestle not against flesh and blood, but against principalities, against powers, against the rulers of the darkness of this world, against spiritual wickedness in high places. Wherefore take unto you the whole armour of God, that ye may be able to withstand in the evil day, and having done all, to stand" (Eph.6:10-13).***

J. Event 10: The Ultimate Rebellion of God's People & the End of the Forty Years of Wilderness Wanderings: Apostasy—Turning to Worldliness, to the Worship of Sex & Other Gods, 25:1-18

1. The cause of the apostasy
- a. Sexual immorality: The men began to have sex with their neighbors, the Moabite women
- b. Worshipping other gods
  - 1) The Moabite women seduced the men to join them in their festivals of worship
  - 2) The men—before long—yielded & joined in their false worship

2. The judgment of God
- a. He was angry: Sent a plague (v.8)
- b. He commanded Moses to execute the ringleaders
  - 1) In broad daylight, publicly, as a strong warning
  - 2) In obedience to the law (Lev.18:24-30; 20:10)
- c. Moses obeyed: Charged the judges to execute all who had worshipped & turned to the false god Baal of Peor

3. The way the judgment was stopped
- a. The zeal of a priest, Phinehas, stopped the judgment
  - 1) An outrageous sin: A man & a pagan woman showed public, sexual affection before Moses & the people as they were praying & weeping
  - 2) The righteous zeal of the priest Phinehas
    - He jumped up & left the prayer assembly, taking a spear
    - He followed the couple who showed such outrageous contempt against God & the people
    - He went into the tent & executed the couple
  - 3) The judgment stopped: The plague ended, but 24,000 people had died
- b. The result of the priest's zeal
  - 1) God stopped the judgment
  - 2) God acknowledged the gr eatness of his zeal: He was zealous for God's honor
  - 3) God made His covenant of peace with Phinehas: His kind of zeal made peace between God & man
  - 4) God established that the High Priest would come from his descendants
  - 5) God accepted his act of zeal as atonement (reconciliation) for the people

4. The dangerous threat of apostasy & immorality
- a. The man & woman would have influenced many to sin
  - 1) He was the son of a prominent leader, the leader of the great tribe of Simeon
  - 2) She was the daughter of a a Midianite (1 Ki.31:8)
- b. The strategy of the Midianites would have destroyed Israel
  - 1) The clear fact: They were enemies & had to be executed
  - 2) The reason: Because their strategy was clearly seen
    - They seduced through illicit sex & the false worship of Baal Peor
    - They had contempt for God & His people: Seen in the outrageous sin of Cozbi (cp. v.6)

And Israel abode in Shittim, and the people began to commit whoredom with the daughters of Moab.
2 And they called the people unto the sacrifices of their gods: and the people did eat, and bowed down to their gods.
3 And Israel joined himself unto Baal-peor: and the anger of the LORD was kindled against Israel.
4 And the LORD said unto Moses, Take all the heads of the people, and hang them up before the LORD against the sun, that the fierce anger of the LORD may be turned away from Israel.
5 And Moses said unto the judges of Israel, Slay ye every one his men that were joined unto Baal-peor.
6 And, behold, one of the children of Israel came and brought unto his brethren a Midianitish woman in the sight of Moses, and in the sight of all the congregation of the children of Israel, who were weeping before the door of the tabernacle of the congregation.
7 And when Phinehas, the son of Eleazar, the son of Aaron the priest, saw it, he rose up from among the congregation, and took a javelin in his hand;
8 And he went after the man of Israel into the tent, and thrust both of them through, the man of Israel, and the woman through her belly. So the plague was stayed from the children of Israel.
9 And those that died in the plague were twenty and four thousand.
10 And the LORD spake unto Moses, saying,
11 Phinehas, the son of Eleazar, the son of Aaron the priest, hath turned my wrath away from the children of Israel, while he was zealous for my sake among them, that I consumed not the children of Israel in my jealousy.
12 Wherefore say, Behold, I give unto him my covenant of peace:
13 And he shall have it, and his seed after him, even the covenant of an everlasting priesthood; because he was zealous for his God, and made an atonement for the children of Israel.
14 Now the name of the Israelite that was slain, even that was slain with the Midianitish woman, was Zimri, the son of Salu, a prince of a chief house among the Simeonites.
15 And the name of the Midianitish woman that was slain was Cozbi, the daughter of Zur; he was head over a people, and of a chief house in Midian.
16 And the LORD spake unto Moses, saying,
17 Vex the Midianites, and smite them:
18 For they vex you with their wiles, wherewith they have beguiled you in the matter of Peor, and in the matter of Cozbi, the daughter of a prince of Midian, their sister, which was slain in the day of the plague for Peor's sake.

DIVISION III

THE FORTY LONG YEARS OF WILDERNESS WANDERINGS: A PICTURE OF THE BELIEVER'S PILGRIMAGE THROUGH THIS WORLD AS HE PREPARES TO ENTER THE PROMISED LAND 15:1-25:18

J. Event 10: The Ultimate Rebellion of God's People and the End of the Forty Years of Wilderness Wanderings: Apostasy—Turning to Worldliness, to the Worship of Sex and Other Gods, 25:1-18

(25:1-18) **Introduction—Sex, Age of—Society, Facts, Bombarded with Sex—Society, Problems of, False Worship—Immorality, Age of**: this is an age that worships sex. It has even been called "the age of the sexual revolution." It is an age when sex is used to advertise practically every product that is sold, certainly most of the products. Newspapers, magazines, films, television, radio, videos—little can be read or seen for more than a few brief moments before some sexual image or insinuation has bombarded the human mind. Society is being taught that all forms of sexual behavior are acceptable:

⇒ adultery	⇒ homosexuality	⇒ sadism
⇒ living together outside of marriage	⇒ pornography	⇒ bestiality
⇒ premarital sex	⇒ sex with children	
⇒ spouse-swapping	⇒ masochism	

All forms of sexual abnormalities and deviancies are being hurled at society today. There seems to be a deliberate attempt to destroy common decency and the control of fleshly lusts and passions. But this is not the only problem faced today: our society also faces the problem of false worship. Scripture is clear: there is only one true and living God, the LORD God Himself (Jehovah, Yahweh). Therefore, there is only one true worship, the worship of Him and Him alone. Any other worship is false. This is the subject of this passage of Scripture, a passage that clearly speaks to all of us: *Event 10: The Ultimate Rebellion of God's People and the End of the Forty Years of Wilderness Wanderings: Apostasy—Turning to Worldliness, to the Worship of Sex and Other Gods*, 25:1-18.

1. The cause of the apostasy (v.1-3).
2. The judgment and chastisement of God (v.4-5).
3. The way the judgment was stopped (v.6-13).
4. The dangerous threat of apostasy and immorality (v.14-18).

1 (25:1-3) **Apostasy, Cause of—Immorality—Israel, Apostasy of—Apostasy, of Israel—Israel, Sins of—Baal of Peor**: the cause of the apostasy was twofold: sexual immorality and false worship. This was the ultimate rebellion of God's people against Him and the end of the forty years of wilderness wanderings. With this rebellion, the last of the first generation died. Tragically, they had all died because of sin and the inevitable judgment of God against sin. It is important to note this fact: all the first generation of Israel had now died; only their children—the second generation—survived. Only the second generation would enter the promised land of God. The first generation that had left Egypt—that had experienced the saving power of God from slavery—had all died in the desert wilderness. Terrible unbelief and grumbling against God and His dear servant had brought the judgment of God upon them. They would never enter the promised land: never know the conquering, victorious power of God over the pitfalls and enemies of this life. They would never know the spiritual rest—the peace, love, and joy—that God gives to the human soul who trusts Him. The first generation of Israelites failed God, miserably failed Him, and they failed to lay hold of the fullness of life. Now, the last of them died, died just as the first of them had—under the hand of God's judgment. However, there is one difference between the two sins they were committing in this current passage and the sins they had committed before: the sins now committed would be the very sins that would eventually bring about the downfall of Israel as a nation—the sins of sexual immorality and apostasy, the worship of false gods. Incomprehensible! Unbelievable! But it did happen. This is seen later on in the Old Testament. But for now, note that some Israelite men began to participate in the false worship of their neighbors—all for sex. The Scripture and outline clearly describe the scene:

OUTLINE	SCRIPTURE
1. The cause of the apostasy a. Sexual immorality: The men began to have sex with their neighbors, the Moabite women	And Israel abode in Shittim, and the people began to commit whoredom with the daughters of Moab.
b. Worshipping other gods 1) The Moabite women seduced the men to join them in their festivals of worship	2 And they called the people unto the sacrifices of their gods: and the people did eat, and bowed down to their gods.
2) The men—before long—yielded & joined in their false worship	3 And Israel joined himself unto Baal-peor: and the anger of the LORD was kindled against Israel.

1. The first terrible cause of apostasy was sexual immorality (v.1). Remember, Israel was camped in the plains of Moab along the Jordan River right across from the great city of Jericho. The area was also called Shittim. What then happened to Israel was a satanic plot devised by the false prophet—the diviner and sorcerer—Balaam. Remember, he had been unable to call down a curse upon God's people. But he came up with another idea, a satanic plot and scheme. He suggested to the king of Moab the following: that Moabite women seduce the Israelite men to have sex. Once they were enslaved to sex, the women could invite them to their festivals of worship, encouraging them to join in the worship of their gods. Obviously, he suggested that this perhaps would arouse the anger of God against the Israelites, causing God to judge and curse them. This satanic plot and scheme was followed through with: the Moabite women became stumblingblocks to the men of Israel. They seduced the men into immorality and no doubt even some of the husbands into committing adultery against their dear wives. As history and human nature show, men have strong sexual urges. The king and the Moabite women used these basic urges to seduce the men, and in the weakness of the flesh the men caved in. They were not focused upon God enough. They were not spiritually strong in their day-to-day walk with God; consequently, they fell into the gross sin of immorality.

As the great book of Proverbs says: they were attracted...
- by the lips and the kisses of the strange woman (Pr.7:13)
- by the beauty of her face and the shape of her body (Pr.7:15)
- by the coverings and the perfume of her bed (Pr.7:16-17)
- by making love with her until the morning (Pr.7:18)
- by her sweet voice and flattering words (Pr.7:21)

Because of the weakness of their flesh, the men crumbled and fell. They were not walking closely enough with God, not day by day. They failed to withstand the seductive, enticing appeal for pleasure. In utter weakness of the flesh, the men forgot God. They ignored and broke the seventh commandment, "You shall not commit adultery" (Ex.20:14).

2. Before long, the men yielded and joined in the false worship of their neighbors (v.2-3). Once the seductive women had the men enslaved to sex, they invited the men to join them at their festival occasions which were centered around their worship. The men soon accepted the invitations and joined the women at the festivals. Once there, it was not long before the men were joining in the worship of their gods, in particular the god known as *Baal of Peor. Peor* was a mountain in Moab that was close to where the Israelites were camped. Most likely because of its high elevation, it had been chosen to be the major site for the worship of the false god Baal. (See DEEPER STUDY # 1—Num.25:3 for more discussion.) Note the word "joined" (tsamad, Strong's; samad, NIV). The word means to be linked together, fastened, framed, joined together. It means to be harnessed, strapped, yoked together. The men had actually attached or joined themselves to the false worship of the people, to the worship of this false god. The women of Moab had been the tempters and conquerors of the men. At first, the men had yielded to the temptations of sex, but now they were yielding to the seductions of *false worship*. In unbelief and disobedience to God, they had slipped back into the world, seduced by the fleshly lusts and false worship of the world.

Thought 1. The lessons for us are clear, and they speak loudly.
1) We must not break the seventh commandment. Scripture is clear: we must not commit adultery.

"But I say unto you, That whosoever looketh on a woman to lust after her hath committed adultery with her already in his heart" (Mt.5:28).

"Wherefore God also gave them up to uncleanness through the lusts of their own hearts, to dishonour their own bodies between themselves....For this cause God gave them up unto vile affections: for even their women did change the natural use into that which is against nature: And likewise also the men, leaving the natural use of the woman, burned in their lust one toward another; men with men working that which is unseemly, and receiving in themselves that recompence of their error which was meet. And even as they did not like to retain God in their knowledge, God gave them over to a reprobate mind, to do those things which are not convenient" (Ro.1:24, 26-28).

"Know ye not that the unrighteous shall not inherit the kingdom of God? Be not deceived: neither fornicators, nor idolaters, nor adulterers, nor effeminate, nor abusers of themselves with mankind, Nor thieves, nor covetous, nor drunkards, nor revilers, nor extortioners, shall inherit the kingdom of God. And such were some of you: but ye are washed, but ye are sanctified, but ye are justified in the name of the Lord Jesus, and by the Spirit of our God" (1 Cor.6:9-11).

"Flee fornication [all forms of illicit sex]. Every sin that a man doeth is without the body; but he that committeth fornication sinneth against his own body" (1 Cor. 6:18).

"But fornication, and all uncleanness, or covetousness, let it not be once named among you, as becometh saints; Neither filthiness, nor foolish talking, nor jesting, which are not convenient: but rather giving of thanks" (Eph.5:3-4).

"For this is the will of God, even your sanctification, that ye should abstain from fornication: That every one of you should know how to possess his vessel in sanctification and honour; Not in the lust of concupiscence, even as the Gentiles which know not God" (1 Th.4:3-5).

"Abstain from all appearance of evil" (1 Th.5:22).

"Marriage is honourable in all, and the bed undefiled: but whoremongers and adulterers God will judge" (Heb.13:4).

"Dearly beloved, I beseech you as strangers and pilgrims, abstain from fleshly lusts, which war against the soul" (1 Pt.2:11).

"But the fearful, and unbelieving, and the abominable, and murderers, and whoremongers, and sorcerers, and idolaters, and all liars, shall have their part in the lake which burneth with fire and brimstone: which is the second death" (Rev.21:8).

"Thou shalt not commit adultery" (Ex.20:14).

"And the man that committeth adultery with another man's wife, even he that committeth adultery with his neighbour's wife, the adulterer and the adulteress shall surely be put to death" (Lev.20:10).

"Lust not after her beauty in thine heart; neither let her take thee with her eyelids" (Pr.6:25).

"But whoso committeth adultery with a woman lacketh understanding: he that doeth it destroyeth his own soul" (Pr.6:32).

2) We must not join in the false worship of the world. We must not worship the false gods of this world. There is only one true and living God, the LORD God Himself (Jehovah, Yahweh). There is only one true approach to God, only one approach that is acceptable to God: the approach through the Lord Jesus Christ, the very Son of God Himself. We must never attempt to approach God through anyone other than the Lord Jesus Christ. Any other approach or any other worship is false. There is only one God and one mediator between God and man, the Lord Jesus Christ.

The Israelite men made a fatal mistake: they joined the false worship of the world. They worshipped the false gods that had been created and formed by the imaginations of men. The people of that day did just what the people of today do: they used the highest, most elevated thoughts they could think, the greatest ideas they could conceive, and they imagined what God was like. They created a god they wanted to follow, a god who would allow them to behave and do the things they wanted. They formed their god around their own morality and ideas of justice. Man is corrupt, filled with immoral, selfish, and unjust thoughts; therefore, when he creates a god to match his behavior and desires—his god is no higher than himself. His god is a man-made god.

This is what the Moabites had done in creating Baal. This was part of the reason the Israelite men gave themselves over to follow the false worship and gods of their neighbors. The false worship allowed them to live immoral lives, to enjoy the bright lights and pleasures of their society. They were able to fulfill the lusts of the flesh, the eyes, and the pride of life. But Scripture is clear: "You shall have no other gods before me" (Ex.20:3). You shall not engage in false worship—the false worship and religions of this world—the false worship created by the imaginations and ideas of men.

"I said therefore unto you, that ye shall die in your sins: for if ye believe not that I am he, ye shall die in your sins" (Jn.8:24).

"For the wrath of God is revealed from heaven against all ungodliness and unrighteousness of men, who hold the truth in unrighteousness; Because that which may be known of God is manifest in them; for God hath showed it unto them. For the invisible things of him from the creation of the world are clearly seen, being understood by the things that are made, even his eternal power and Godhead; so that they are without excuse: Because that, when they knew God, they glorified him not as God, neither were thankful; but became vain in their imaginations, and their foolish heart was darkened. Professing themselves to be wise, they became fools, And changed the glory of the uncorruptible God into an image made like to corruptible man, and to birds, and fourfooted beasts, and creeping things" (Ro.1:18-23).

"For though there be that are called gods, whether in heaven or in earth, (as there be gods many, and lords many,) But to us there is but one God, the Father, of whom are all things, and we in him; and one Lord Jesus Christ, by whom are all things, and we by him" (1 Cor.8:5-6).

"Ye know that ye were Gentiles, carried away unto these dumb idols, even as ye were led" (1 Cor.12:2).

"And for this cause God shall send them strong delusion, that they should believe a lie: That they all might be damned who believed not the truth, but had pleasure in unrighteousness" (2 Th.2:11-12).

"But the fearful, and unbelieving, and the abominable, and murderers, and whoremongers, and sorcerers, and idolaters, and all liars, shall have their part in the lake which burneth with fire and brimstone: which is the second death" (Rev.21:8).

"The fool hath said in his heart, There is no God. They are corrupt, they have done abominable works, there is none that doeth good" (Ps.14:1).

"Their idols are silver and gold, the work of men's hands. They have mouths, but they speak not: eyes have they, but they see not: They have ears, but they hear not: noses have they, but they smell not: They have hands, but they handle not: feet have they, but they walk not: neither speak they through their throat. They that make them are like unto them; so is every one that trusteth in them" (Ps.115:4-8).

"To whom then will ye liken God? or what likeness will ye compare unto him? The workman melteth a graven image, and the goldsmith spreadeth it over with gold, and casteth silver chains. He that is so impoverished that he hath no oblation chooseth a tree that will not rot; he seeketh unto him a cunning workman to prepare a graven image, that shall not be moved" (Is.40:18-20).

"I am the Lord: that is my name: and my glory will I not give to another, neither my praise to graven images" (Is.42:8).

"Assemble yourselves and come; draw near together, ye that are escaped of the nations: they have no knowledge that set up the wood of their graven image, and pray unto a god that cannot save" (Is.45:20).

"Shall a man make gods unto himself, and they are no gods" (Jer.16:20).

"Hath a nation changed their gods, which are yet no gods? but my people have changed their glory for that which doth not profit" (Jer.2:11).

"Thus saith the Lord, Learn not the way of the heathen, and be not dismayed at the signs of heaven; for the heathen are dismayed at them. For the customs of the people are vain: for one cutteth a tree out of the forest, the work of the hands of the workman, with the axe. They deck it with silver and with gold; they fasten it with nails and with hammers, that it move not. They are upright as the palm tree, but speak not: they must needs be borne, because they cannot go. Be not afraid of them; for they cannot do evil, neither also is it in them to do good" (Jer.10:2-5).

2 (25:4-5) **Judgment, of God—Immorality, Judgment of—Idolatry, Judgment of—Worship, False, Judgment of**: the judgment of God was quick and sure. The immoral and the false worshippers were immediately judged. They had broken two of the major commandments of God, two of the Ten Commandments. By their terrible sins, they had aroused the anger of God. Both the holiness and justice of God had been violated. His commandment was ignored and abused. His holy, pure, and righteous nature had to be satisfied. His justice had to be executed. Judgment upon the immoral and false worshippers was carried out:

OUTLINE	SCRIPTURE	SCRIPTURE	OUTLINE
2. The judgment of God a. He was angry: Sent a plague (v.8) b. He commanded Moses to execute the ringleaders 1) In broad daylight, publicly, as a strong warning	4 And the LORD said unto Moses, Take all the heads of the people, and hang them up before the LORD against the sun, that the fierce anger of the LORD	may be turned away from Israel. 5 And Moses said unto the judges of Israel, Slay ye every one his men that were joined unto Baal-peor.	2) In obedience to the law (Lev.18:24-30; 20:10) c. Moses obeyed: Charged the judges to execute all who had worshipped & turned to the false god Baal of Peor

1. God was greatly angered because the people had committed sexual immorality and joined in false worship (v.3). His justice against sin had to be executed; consequently, He sent a plague among them (cp. v.8). There were obviously thousands of people involved in this gross sin, for twenty-four thousand people died in the plague.

2. God commanded Moses to execute the ringleaders (v.4). They were to be executed in broad daylight—publicly—so they would stand as a strong warning to the whole community. Because of the strong sexual drive of many, there was the danger that many others would fall into sexual immorality. Remember, there was a deliberate plot to destroy Israel through the lure of illicit sex and the worship of the false gods of their neighbors—a deliberate plot devised by the false prophet Balaam and the king of Moab. By publicly executing the ringleaders, the people would be warned: they must not cave in to the seduction of sexual immorality nor join in the worship of the false gods of their neighbors. Some commentators think that the execution even involved hanging the ringleaders up on a pole in full sight of all who passed by. However, Scripture seems to indicate elsewhere that a public execution and display of the dead bodies were probably what happened (2 Sam.21:6-13). The penalty for adultery and for false worship or idolatry was death (Lev.18:24-30; 20:10).

3. Moses obeyed God: he charged the judges to execute all who had worshipped and turned to the false god Baal of Peor (v.5).

Thought 1. The focus of this point is the judgment of God, the fact that God judges sin. God is holy, righteous, pure, perfect. The fact that God is holy means that He will someday judge the world. God cannot allow His holy presence to become contaminated, polluted, unclean, or defiled. To allow any sin in His presence would defile the very atmosphere around God. This God must never allow. But God is not only holy; He is just. God dwells in perfect justice. He cannot allow a single act of injustice to exist in His presence. To do so would mean that injustices dwell and defile the very presence and atmosphere surrounding God. This God must never allow.

There is only one solution to the problem created by the sin, the immoralities, and the injustices of the world: that solution is the judgment of God. All the sin and injustices, and all the people who have committed these, must be removed from God's holy and just presence. This is the reason the judgment of God fell upon those who committed sexual immorality and joined in the false worship of their neighbors. Some day every human being who has ever lived will face the judgment of God. God will judge the world in righteousness. The judgment of God is coming just as it came upon the Israelites.

"When the Son of man shall come in his glory, and all the holy angels with him, then shall he sit upon the throne of his glory: And before him shall be gathered all nations: and he shall separate them one from another, as a shepherd divideth his sheep from the goats: And he shall set the sheep on his right hand, but the goats on the left.... Then shall he say also unto them on the left hand, Depart from me, ye cursed, into everlasting fire, prepared for the devil and his angels....And these shall go away into everlasting punishment: but the righteous into life eternal" (Mt.25:31-33, 41, 46).

"For the wrath of God is revealed from heaven against all ungodliness and unrighteousness of men, who hold the truth in unrighteousness" (Ro.1:18).

"But unto them that are contentious, and do not obey the truth, but obey unrighteousness, indignation and wrath" (Ro.2:8).

"But fornication, and all uncleanness, or covetousness, let it not be once named among you, as becometh saints; Neither filthiness, nor foolish talking, nor jesting, which are not convenient: but rather giving of thanks. For this ye know, that no whoremonger, nor unclean person, nor covetous man, who is an idolater, hath any inheritance in the kingdom of Christ and of God. Let no man deceive you with vain words: for because of these things cometh the wrath of God upon the children of disobedience" (Eph.5:3-6).

"And as it is appointed unto men once to die, but after this the judgment" (Heb.9:27).

"The Lord knoweth how to deliver the godly out of temptations, and to reserve the unjust unto the day of judgment to be punished" (2 Pt.2:9).

"But the heavens and the earth, which are now, by the same word are kept in store, reserved unto fire against the day of judgment and perdition of ungodly men" (2 Pt.3:7).

"And Enoch also, the seventh from Adam, prophesied of these, saying, Behold, the Lord cometh with ten thousands of his saints, To execute judgment upon all, and to convince all that are ungodly among them of all their ungodly deeds which they have ungodly committed, and of all their hard speeches which ungodly sinners have spoken against him" (Jude 14-15).

3 (25:6-13) **Immorality, Example of—Affection, Public Display of—Immorality, Public Display of—Disrespect, Example of—Irreverence, Example of—Sin, Irreverence—Zeal, Example of—Phinehas, the Priest**: the judgment was stopped in a dramatic way. The scene needs to be grasped by the mind's eye. While Moses and the people were weeping in prayer, seeking the LORD to stop the plague from among the people, a shocking and outrageous event happened. Note the Scripture and outline:

OUTLINE	SCRIPTURE	SCRIPTURE	OUTLINE
3. The way the judgment was	6 And, behold, one of the	plague were twenty and four	The plague ended, but
stopped	children of Israel came and	thousand.	24,000 people had died
a. The zeal of a priest, Phinehas,	brought unto his brethren a	10 And the LORD spake	b. The result of the priest's zeal
stopped the judgment	Midianitish woman in the	unto Moses, saying,	
1) An outrageous sin: A man	sight of Moses, and in the	11 Phinehas, the son of	1) God stopped the judgment
& a pagan woman	sight of all the congregation	Eleazar, the son of Aaron the	2) God acknowledged the gr
showed public, sexual	of the children of Israel, who	priest, hath turned my wrath	eatness of his zeal: He
affection before Moses &	were weeping before the	away from the children of	was zealous for God's
the people as they were	door of the tabernacle of the	Israel, while he was zealous	honor
praying & weeping	congregation.	for my sake among them,	
2) The righteous zeal of the	7 And when Phinehas, the	that I consumed not the chil-	
priest Phinehas	son of Eleazar, the son of	dren of Israel in my	
• He jumped up & left	Aaron the priest, saw it, he	jealousy.	
the prayer assembly,	rose up from among the con-	12 Wherefore say, Behold, I	3) God made His covenant of
taking a spear	gregation, and took a javelin	give unto him my covenant	peace with Phinehas: His
	in his hand;	of peace:	kind of zeal made peace
• He followed the couple	8 And he went after the man	13 And he shall have it,	between God & man
who showed such out-	of Israel into the tent, and	and his seed after him,	4) God established that the
rageous contempt	thrust both of them through,	even the covenant of an	High Priest would come
against God & the peo-	the man of Israel, and the	everlasting priesthood;	from his descendants
ple	woman through her belly. So	because he was zealous for	5) God accepted his act of
• He went into the tent &	the plague was stayed from	his God, and made an	zeal as atonement (recon-
executed the couple	the children of Israel.	atonement for the children	ciliation) for the people
3) The judgment stopped:	9 And those that died in the	of Israel.	

1. A terrible, outrageous sin took place between a man who professed to be a believer and a pagan woman.
   a. The man and woman showed public, sexual affection before the very eyes of Moses and the people while they were weeping in prayer. The people were praying at the entrance to the Tabernacle, so this meant that the sexual affection and stimulating pleasure took place right there at the Tabernacle. Note what happened: the Israelite man brought the immoral woman to meet his parents in the midst of the prayer meeting. Obviously his parents were involved in the prayer meeting. This young man had no more reverence for the things of God than to show public, sexual affection in the presence of God's people. These two immoral young people...
      - had a contempt for the holy things of God
      - cared nothing for the Word of the LORD
      - scorned the holiness of God
      - showed outrageous, incomprehensible, and unspeakable behavior
      - disgraced the holiness and majesty of God
      - demonstrated the depth of disrespect and irreverence for the people of God

   b. Note the righteous zeal of the priest Phinehas (v.7-8). Obviously, the young couple had left the Tabernacle to go to the young man's tent or home. After thinking for a few minutes about what had happened, Phinehas jumped up and left the prayer meeting, grabbing a spear or javelin as he left. He followed the couple who had shown such outrageous contempt for God and His people. He found them in the man's tent and executed them both (v.8).
   c. Immediately the judgment stopped and the plague ended. But note: twenty-four thousand people had died in the plague. Most likely, the plague had been some sexually transmitted disease that vindicated the warning of God's Holy Word: "Whatsoever a man soweth, that shall he also reap" (Gal.6:7).
2. Note the result of the priest's zeal (v.10-13).
   a. God stopped the judgment, stopped it immediately. God turned His anger away from the sinful and guilty Israelites (v.11).
   b. God acknowledged the great zeal of the young priest: he was zealous for God's honor and had dramatically demonstrated his respect for God and His righteousness (v.11). He stood up for righteousness when no one else would. All the judges and leaders of Israel were most likely in the prayer meeting, certainly most of them. Yet not one jumped to his feet to stand up for the holiness and righteousness of God, only Phinehas. The others were either too embarrassed or afraid to stand up for righteousness. But not this young priest; he had a zeal for God, a very special zeal. As a priest, he represented God before men and men before God. He knew that he was to be a testimony of righteousness before God and the people. He knew that the plague—the hand of God's judgment against the sin—could not be stopped as long as the sin continued to be committed by the people. The sin was the very cause for the judgment of the plague; therefore, the plague could not be stopped until the sin was removed. With holy zeal, this young man, this young priest, stood up for righteousness when others would not. In fact, Scripture declares that God took this act of zeal and counted it to Phinehas for righteousness. Moreover, his zeal for righteousness stands as an example of righteousness forever.

      "Then stood up Phinehas, and executed judgment: and so the plague was stayed. And that was counted unto him for righteousness unto all generations for evermore" (Ps.106:30-31).

   c. God made His covenant of peace with Phinehas: that is, his kind of zeal made peace between God and man (v.12). It was his zeal that had stopped the plague, the hand of God's judgment against the sin. The sin of the people had alienated and separated them from God. The sin had created a great gulf, a chasm of unrighteousness and ungodliness between God and the people. The people were alienated from God and God from the people. But the zeal of this young man to remove the sin brought peace and reconciliation between God and the people. Because of his zeal, God made an eternal covenant of peace with Phinehas; that is, his kind of zeal for righteousness would always bring peace between God and people. What God wants is for people to stand up for righteousness, removing sin from their presence. When a person does this—removes sin from among a group of people—God will take that person's zeal and make peace with the people. Once the sin has been removed, God reconciles the people to Himself.

d. God established that the High Priest would come from the descendants of this young priest (v.13). Phinehas was the son of Eleazar and the grandson of Aaron himself. Remember that the High Priest is a type of Christ and His priesthood. What God was doing was bestowing one of the highest privileges upon this young priest. Phinehas was to stand forth forever as a type of Christ.

e. God accepted the act of this young man's zeal as atonement for the people (v.13). Note this fact: there was *corporate guilt and responsibility* for this sin. All the people stood guilty before God, corporately. They were either guilty of engaging in the sins themselves or else guilty of not stepping in and preventing the sin. Both the sins of *commission* and *omission were committed.* The people—in particular the leadership of the nation—all stood guilty of not having stopped those who were engaging in the sin. The sin should never have been allowed to get a grip on the people. Yet it did. It took control because those who knew about the seduction going on did nothing.

⇒ Silence ruled the day.
⇒ Silence allowed the sin.
⇒ Silence encouraged the sin.
⇒ Silence supported the sin.
⇒ Silence promoted the sin.
⇒ Silence validated the sin.
⇒ Silence affirmed the sin.
⇒ Silence granted the sin.
⇒ Silenced endorsed the sin.
⇒ Silence gave permission for the sin.
⇒ Silence sanctioned the sin.
⇒ Silence tolerated the sin.

All the people were guilty; therefore, all the people stood corporately responsible before God. This was the reason that atonement (reconciliation) had to be made for all the people. The people had to be reconciled as a corporate body. Because of their guilt, all the people were guilty; therefore, all the people had to be reconciled to God. But note: the zeal of this young priest for God and His righteousness was counted as atonement for the people. God accepted his *zeal for righteousness* as atonement, as the act of reconciliation for the people.

Thought 1. Note several lessons for us.

1) The zeal of this young man, this young priest, is a dynamic example for us. We, too, need a strong zeal for God and His righteousness. God calls us to righteousness and He demands righteousness. We must have a zeal for living holy, pure, and righteous lives before God.

"For I say unto you, That except your righteousness shall exceed the righteousness of the scribes and Pharisees, ye shall in no case enter into the kingdom of heaven" (Mt.5:20).

"And his disciples remembered that it was written, The zeal of thine house hath eaten me up" (Jn.2:17).

"Jesus saith unto them, My meat is to do the will of him that sent me, and to finish his work" (Jn.4:34).

"I must work the works of him that sent me, while it is day: the night cometh, when no man can work" (Jn.9:4).

"This man was instructed in the way of the Lord; and being fervent in the spirit, he spake and taught diligently the things of the LORD" (Acts 18:25).

"Brethren, my heart's desire and prayer to God for Israel is, that they might be saved" (Ro.10:1).

"Awake to righteousness, and sin not; for some have not the knowledge of God: I speak this to your shame" (1 Cor.15:34).

"As many as I love, I rebuke and chasten: be zealous therefore, and repent" (Rev.3:19).

"My zeal hath consumed me, because mine enemies have forgotten thy words" (Ps.119:139).

"For Zion's sake will I not hold my peace, and for Jerusalem's sake I will not rest, until the righteousness thereof go forth as brightness, and the salvation thereof as a lamp that burneth" (Is.62:1).

"Wherefore, O king, let my counsel be acceptable unto thee, and break off thy sins by righteousness, and thine iniquities by showing mercy to the poor; if it may be a lengthening of thy tranquility" (Dan.4:27).

2) This young priest was chosen by God to be the next High Priest. He was given the glorious privilege of being a symbol or type of the coming Messiah and His Priesthood. For all generations down through human history, this young man stands forth as a type of the Lord Jesus Christ, the perfect High Priest.

"Wherefore in all things it behoved him to be made like unto his brethren, that he might be a merciful and faithful high priest in things pertaining to God, to make reconciliation for the sins of the people" (Heb.2:17).

"Seeing then that we have a great high priest, that is passed into the heavens, Jesus the Son of God, let us hold fast our profession. For we have not an high priest which cannot be touched with the feeling of our infirmities; but was in all points tempted like as we are, yet without sin" (Heb.4:14-15).

"For every high priest taken from among men is ordained for men in things pertaining to God, that he may offer both gifts and sacrifices for sins: Who can have compassion on the ignorant, and on them

that are out of the way; for that he himself also is compassed with infirmity. And by reason hereof he ought, as for the people, so also for himself, to offer for sins. And no man taketh this honour unto himself, but he that is called of God, as was Aaron. So also Christ glorified not himself to be made an high priest; but he that said unto him, Thou art my Son, to day have I begotten thee" (Heb.5:1-5).

"Which hope we have as an anchor of the soul, both sure and stedfast, and which entereth into that within the veil; Whither the forerunner is for us entered, even Jesus, made an high priest for ever after the order of Melchisedec" (Heb.6:19-20).

"Wherefore he is able also to save them to the uttermost that come unto God by him, seeing he ever liveth to make intercession for them. For such an high priest became us, who is holy, harmless, undefiled, separate from sinners, and made higher than the heavens; Who needeth not daily, as those high priests, to offer up sacrifice, first for his own sins, and then for the people's: for this he did once, when he offered up himself" (Heb.7:25-27).

"Now of the things which we have spoken this is the sum: We have such an high priest, who is set on the right hand of the throne of the Majesty in the heavens" (Heb.8:1).

3) The zeal of this young man, this priest, made atonement or reconciliation for the people. The atonement made by him is a picture of the atonement and reconciliation made by the Lord Jesus Christ. Atonement has been made for us: we are reconciled to God by the zeal of Christ to provide righteousness for us. He provided righteousness for us by living a perfect life, the ideal life of righteousness. As the ideal, His righteousness can stand for us and cover us. Therefore, when God looks at us, He sees us covered, standing in the perfect righteousness of Jesus Christ. God is able to accept us in the ideal righteousness of Christ, able to count us as righteous—all because we stand in His perfect, ideal righteousness.

But this is not all: Jesus Christ secured righteousness for us by dying for us. He took our sin and the punishment due our sin upon Himself. He died for our sin, as our substitute, in our place. His death is the ideal, perfect death in the eyes of God. Therefore, God accepts His death, His substitute sacrifice as our death. When we place our faith in Christ, God counts the death of Christ in our place. Therefore, we do not have to suffer or bear the condemnation and judgment of God. As stated above, we are accepted by God through the righteousness of Jesus Christ. Moreover, we are freed from ever having to suffer the judgment of God through the sacrifice of Jesus Christ.

The zeal for righteousness that the young priest Phinehas had stood as a type of the righteous zeal of Christ. Jesus Christ secured righteousness for man and bore the judgment of God for man. By this zeal, Christ secured atonement and reconciled man to God. Jesus Christ is our atonement, the way we are reconciled to God.

"Therefore being justified by faith, we have peace with God through our Lord Jesus Christ" (Ro.5:1).

"Much more then, being now justified by his blood, we shall be saved from wrath through him. For if, when we were enemies, we were reconciled to God by the death of his Son, much more, being reconciled, we shall be saved by his life. And not only so, but we also joy in God through our Lord Jesus Christ, by whom we have now received the atonement" (Ro.5:9-11).

"For he hath made him to be sin for us, who knew no sin; that we might be made the righteousness of God in him" (2 Cor.5:21).

"Even as Abraham believed God, and it was accounted to him for righteousness" (Gal.3:6).

"Who gave himself for our sins, that he might deliver us from this present evil world, according to the will of God and our Father" (Gal.1:4).

"Who his own self bare our sins in his own body on the tree, that we, being dead to sins, should live unto righteousness: by whose stripes ye were healed" (1 Pt.2:24).

"For Christ also hath once suffered for sins, the just for the unjust, that he might bring us to God, being put to death in the flesh, but quickened by the Spirit" (1 Pt.3:18

4 (25:14-18) **Apostasy, Danger of—Immorality, Danger of—Israel, Failure of, Caused by—Zimri—Cozbi**: the dangerous threat of apostasy and immorality was real. A cesspool of immorality and apostasy had been dug by the people. The corruption had become so pervasive that it threatened to destroy the people. Tragically, many of the leaders themselves had engaged in the sexual immorality and false worship (v.4). When leaders become involved in sin, a much greater threat to survival is created because of the leaders' influence. This is clearly seen in these present verses.

OUTLINE	SCRIPTURE	SCRIPTURE	OUTLINE
4. The dangerous threat of apostasy & immorality a. The man & woman would have influenced many to sin 1) He was the son of a prominent leader, the leader of the great tribe of Simeon 2) She was the daughter of a a Midianite (1 Ki.31:8) b. The strategy of the Midianites would have destroyed Israel	14 Now the name of the Israelite that was slain, even that was slain with the Midianitish woman, was Zimri, the son of Salu, a prince of a chief house among the Simeonites. 15 And the name of the Midianitish woman that was slain was Cozbi, the daughter of Zur; he was head over a people, and of a chief house in Midian.	16 And the LORD spake unto Moses, saying, 17 Vex the Midianites, and smite them: 18 For they vex you with their wiles, wherewith they have beguiled you in the matter of Peor, and in the matter of Cozbi, the daughter of a prince of Midian, their sister, which was slain in the day of the plague for Peor's sake.	1) The clear fact: They were enemies & had to be executed 2) The reason: Because their strategy was clearly seen • They seduced through illicit sex & the false worship of Baal Peor • They had contempt for God & His people: Seen in the outrageous sin of Cozbi (cp. v.6)

1. The man and woman who showed public, sexual affection would have influenced and led many to sin (v.14-15). They were young leaders within their respective communities. Note that his name was Zimri, the son of the leader of the great tribe of Simeon. The young lady was named Cozbi, the daughter of Zur, who was a king of the Midianites (v.15; cp.31:8). Being from prominent families meant that their influence would have been far and wide. They would have led many into sin. This is just one example of influential leaders who had obviously been involved in sexual immorality and false worship. But this was not the only dangerous threat to the survival of the Israelites.

2. The strategy of the Midianites would also have destroyed Israel. This is the reason God commanded that the Midianites be treated as enemies and be executed once they had been conquered in battle (v.16-17). Note that the reason is clearly spelled out: because their strategy was to seduce God's people through illicit sex and the false worship of Baal Peor (v.18). They had shown contempt for God and His people. Therefore, they were to be destroyed for their outrageous sin.

Thought 1. Every believer influences other people. Eyes are always watching our behavior:
⇒ Children watch parents.
⇒ Parents watch children.
⇒ Spouses watch each other.
⇒ Employers watch employees.
⇒ Employees watch employers as well as their co-workers.
⇒ Neighbors watch neighbors.
⇒ Fans watch athletes.
⇒ Athletes watch fellow athletes.

On and on the list could go. How we live influences other people. If we live holy, righteous, and pure lives, we influence people to live lives of holiness, righteousness, and purity. If we live sinful and evil lives, we influence people to live sinful and evil lives. If we break the law, we encourage people to break the law. If we are violent and abusive, we encourage people to be violent and abusive. Our lives influence people either to be good or to be bad. It is that simple. Our lives either build people up or tear people down, either teach people to live for God or to live for the world (against God). We either live for good or for bad, and we influence people to live for good or for bad. If we live sinful lives—engaging in sexual immorality and false worship—we are a threat to other people and to society. We are a danger to other people and to society in that we add more corruption and defilement to the world. And our corruption and defilement in turn multiply and influence at least several others, and through them even more are influenced. It is this, the multiplying effect of sin, that makes the influence of sin such a threat and danger to us all. This is the reason we must guard and protect our testimony for God. We must make sure that we are living holy, righteous, and pure lives before God and the community in which we live. We must never become a dangerous threat, a bad and evil influence, leading others into sin and the condemnation of God's judgment.

"Ye are the salt of the earth: but if the salt have lost his savour, wherewith shall it be salted? it is thenceforth good for nothing, but to be cast out, and to be trodden under foot of men" (Mt.5:13).

"But woe unto you, scribes and Pharisees, hypocrites! for ye shut up the kingdom of heaven against men: for ye neither go in yourselves, neither suffer ye them that are entering to go in" (Mt.23:13).

"Let us not therefore judge one another any more: but judge this rather, that no man put a stumblingblock or an occasion to fall in his brother's way" (Ro.14:13).

"But if thy brother be grieved with thy meat, now walkest thou not charitably. Destroy not him with thy meat, for whom Christ died. Let not then your good be evil spoken of" (Ro.14:15-16).

"Your glorying is not good. Know ye not that a little leaven leaveneth the whole lump? Purge out therefore the old leaven, that ye may be a new lump, as ye are unleavened. For even Christ our passover is sacrificed for us" (1 Cor.5:6-7).

"For if any man see thee which hast knowledge sit at meat in the idol's temple, shall not the conscience of him which is weak be emboldened to eat those things which are offered to idols; And through thy knowledge shall the weak brother perish, for whom Christ died? But when ye sin so against the brethren, and wound their weak conscience, ye sin against Christ. Wherefore, if meat make my brother to offend, I will eat no flesh while the world standeth, lest I make my brother to offend" (1 Cor.8:10-13).

"Ye did run well; who did hinder you that ye should not obey the truth? This persuasion cometh not of him that calleth you. A little leaven leaveneth the whole lump" (Gal.5:7-9).

"He that loveth his brother abideth in the light, and there is none occasion of stumbling in him" (1 Jn.2:10).

"And shall say, Cast ye up, cast ye up, prepare the way, take up the stumblingblock out of the way of my people" (Is.57:14).

"For the priest's lips should keep knowledge, and they should seek the law at his mouth: for he is the messenger of the Lord of hosts. But ye are departed out of the way; ye have caused many to stumble at the law; ye have corrupted the covenant of Levi, saith the Lord of hosts" (Mal.2:7-8).

NUMBERS 25:1-18

TYPES, SYMBOLS, AND PICTURES
(Numbers 25:1-18)

Historical Term	Type or Picture (Scriptural Basis for Each)	Life Application for Today's Believer	Biblical Application
Phinehas Num.25:6-13	*Phinehas as High Priest is a type or symbol of Christ.* God established that the High Priest would come from the descendants of this young priest (v.13). Phinehas was the son of Eleazar and the grandson of Aaron himself. Remember that the High Priest is a type of Christ and His priesthood. What God was doing was bestowing one of the highest privileges upon this young priest. Phinehas was to stand forth forever as a type of Christ. **"Phinehas, the son of Eleazar, the son of Aaron the priest, hath turned my wrath away from the children of Israel, while he was zealous for my sake among them, that I consumed not the children of Israel in my jealousy. Wherefore say, Behold, I give unto him my covenant of peace: And he shall have it, and his seed after him, *even* the covenant of an everlasting priesthood; because he was zealous for his God, and made an atonement for the children of Israel" (Num.25:11-13).**	This young priest was chosen by God to be the next High Priest. He was given the glorious privilege of being a type of the coming Messiah and His Priesthood. For all generations down through human history, this young man stands forth as a type of the Lord Jesus Christ as the perfect High Priest.	***"Wherefore in all things it behoved him to be made like unto his brethren, that he might be a merciful and faithful high priest in things pertaining to God, to make reconciliation for the sins of the people" (Heb.2:17). "Seeing then that we have a great high priest, that is passed into the heavens, Jesus the Son of God, let us hold fast our profession. For we have not an high priest which cannot be touched with the feeling of our infirmities; but was in all points tempted like as we are, yet without sin" (Heb.4:14-15). "For every high priest taken from among men is ordained for men in things pertaining to God, that he may offer both gifts and sacrifices for sins: Who can have compassion on the ignorant, and on them that are out of the way; for that he himself also is compassed with infirmity. And by reason hereof he ought, as for the people, so also for himself, to offer for sins. And no man taketh this honour unto himself, but he that is called of God, as was Aaron. So also Christ glorified not himself to be made an high priest; but he that said unto him, Thou art my Son, to day have I begotten thee" (Heb.5:1-5). "Which hope we have as an anchor of the soul, both sure and stedfast, and which entereth into that within the veil; Whither the forerunner is for us entered, even Jesus, made an high priest for ever after the order of Melchisedec" (Heb.6:19-20 See also Heb.7:25-27). "Now of the things which we have spoken this is the sum: We have such an high priest, who is set on the right hand of the throne of the Majesty in the heavens" (Heb.8:1).***

Historical Term	Type or Picture (Scriptural Basis for Each)	Life Application for Today's Believer	Biblical Application
The Zeal of Phinehas that Made Atonement or Reconciliation for the People Num.25:6-13	*The atonement made by Phinehas is a picture of the atonement and reconciliation made by the Lord Jesus Christ.* **"And he shall have it, and his seed after him, *even* the covenant of an everlasting priesthood; because he was zealous for his God, and made an atonement for the children of Israel" (Num.25:13).**	Atonement has been made for us: we are reconciled to God by the zeal of Christ to provide righteousness for us. He provided righteousness for us by living a perfect life, the ideal life of righteousness. As the ideal, His righteousness can stand for us and cover us. Therefore, when God looks at us, He sees us covered, standing in the perfect righteousness of Jesus Christ. God is able to accept us in the ideal righteousness of Christ, able to count us as righteous—all because we stand in His perfect, ideal righteousness. But this is not all: Jesus Christ secured righteousness for us by dying for us. He took our sin and the punishment due our sin upon Himself. He died for our sin, as our substitute, in our place. His death is the ideal, perfect death in the eyes of God. Therefore, God accepts His death, His substitute sacrifice as our death. When we place our faith in Christ, God counts the death of Christ in our place. Therefore, we do not have to suffer or bear the condemnation and judgment of God. As stated above, we are accepted by God through the righteousness of Jesus Christ. Moreover, we are freed from ever having to suffer the judgment of God through the sacrifice of Jesus Christ.	***"Much more then, being now justified by his blood, we shall be saved from wrath through him. For if, when we were enemies, we were reconciled to God by the death of his Son, much more, being reconciled, we shall be saved by his life. And not only so, but we also joy in God through our Lord Jesus Christ, by whom we have now received the atonement" (Ro.5:9-11).*** ***"For he hath made him to be sin for us, who knew no sin; that we might be made the righteousness of God in him" (2 Cor.5:21).*** ***"Who his own self bare our sins in his own body on the tree, that we, being dead to sins, should live unto righteousness: by whose stripes ye were healed" (1 Pt.2:24).***
Phinehas' Zeal for Righteousness Num.25:6-13	*The zeal for righteousness that the young priest Phinehas had stood as a type of the righteous zeal of Christ.* **"And he shall have it, and his seed after him, *even* the covenant of an everlasting priesthood; because he was zealous for his God, and made an atonement for the children of Israel" (Num.25:13).**	Jesus Christ secured righteousness for man and bore the judgment of God for man. By this zeal, Christ secured atonement and reconciled man to God. Jesus Christ is our atonement, the way we are reconciled to God.	***"Therefore being justified by faith, we have peace with God through our Lord Jesus Christ" (Ro.5:1).*** ***"Even as Abraham believed God, and it was accounted to him for righteousness" (Gal.3:6).*** ***"Who gave himself for our sins, that he might deliver us from this present evil world, according to the will of God and our Father" (Gal.1:4).***

DIVISION IV

THE PREPARATION FOR THE MARCH INTO THE PROMISED LAND, 26:1-36:13

(26:1-36:13) **DIVISION OVERVIEW—Wilderness Wanderings—Desert Journeys—Israel, Second Generation, Preparation of**: the forty years of the wilderness wanderings had now ended. The first generation of Israelites had died off. Tragically, their journey with God had ended just as it had begun: in unbelief and rebellion. They had committed the ultimate rebellion against God, apostasy—turning to worldliness, to the worship of sex and false gods. The result: death. A plague swept through the camp and killed thousands of them. Among the dead were the last of the first generation of Israelites, those whose lives had been so tragic—so marked by unbelief and grumbling.

Now, God is ready to make final preparations for the second generation of believers to enter the promised land and receive their glorious inheritance. As *The Expositor's Bible Commentary* says:

> "The expression 'after the plague' [26:2] is…the turning point from the first generation to the second, the shift from the fathers and mothers to sons and daughters. God was about to begin a new work with a new people. The younger generation would begin to have their day….
>
> "So [we face]…a great, haunting question: What will the children be like? Will they be like their parents? Or will they be like Moses and Aaron, like Joshua and Caleb, like Miriam and others faithful to God? Will they believe in him, obey his commands, and take up their weapons as they march in victory song?"[1]

THE PREPARATION FOR THE MARCH INTO THE PROMISED LAND, 26:1-36:13

A. The Organization of the Second Generation—the Second Nationwide Census: Mobilizing God's People to Enter and Inherit the Promised Land, 26:1-65

B. The Basic Law that Gave Women an Inheritance in the Promised Land: Five Women of Enormous Courage, Faith, and Hope, 27:1-11

C. The Appointment of Joshua as the Successor to Moses: A Strong Picture of God Preparing the Believer for Death 27:12-23

D. The Offerings and Sacrifices Commanded by the Lord: A Picture of Man's Need to Continually Approach and Worship God through the Atonement Secured by the Sacrifice (a Symbol of God's Dear Son, the Lord Jesus Christ), 28:1-29:40

E. The Laws that Govern Vows: The Obligation to Keep Vows and to Consider Others in Making Vows, 30:1-16

F. The Conquest of the Most Dangerous and Threatening of Enemies, the Midianites: A Picture of Conquering the Seductive, Immoral Enemies of the World, 31:1-54

G. The Settlement East of the Jordan River: A Picture of Compromise,Selfishness, Covetousness, Disloyalty, and Half-Hearted Commitment, 32:1-42

---

1 *The Expositor's Bible Commentary*. Frank E. Gaebelein, Editor, p.924-925.

DIVISION IV
26:1-36:13

H. The Review of the Wilderness Wanderings and a Strong Charge to Take Possession of the Promised Land: A Picture of God's Faithfulness and Man's Failure, 33:1-56

I. The Boundaries of Canaan, the Promised Land: The Great Gift and Assurance of God—His People Will Inherit the Promised Land, 34:1-29

J. The Inheritance of the Levites and the Cities of Refuge: The Provision of God for His Ministers and for All Who Need Refuge from the Storms and Threats of Life, 35:1-34

K. The Women Who Inherited Property: A Picture of Strong Faith in the Promised Land of God, 37:1-13

1. The strong emphasis: "The LORD spoke": A picture of God guiding His people

2. The 1st purpose of the census—military: A picture of the people of God preparing for warfare

a. To count all men able to serve 20 years old or older

b. To count while camped by the Jordan across from Jericho

3. The number counted, division by division—counted just as they came out of Egypt: A picture of the faithfulness of God & a strong warning to man

a. The division & tribe of Reuben
   1) The tribal clans
      - The Hanochite clan
      - The Pallu clan
      - The Hezron clan
      - The Carmite clan
   2) The total number: 43,730
   3) The tragic record of Korah's rebellion & the descendants of Reuben who rebelled with Korah (cp. Jude 11)
      - The son of the clan leader Pallu was Eliab
      - Two of the sons of Eliab rebelled with Korah
      - They were severely judged by God along with 250 other rebels (cp. 16:35)
      - They are a warning to all who reject & rebel

IV. THE PREPARATION FOR THE MARCH INTO THE PROMISED LAND, 26:1-36:13

A. The Organization of the Second Generation—the Second Nationwide Census: Mobilizing God's People to Enter & Inherit the Promised Land, 26:1-65

And it came to pass after the
plague, that the LORD spake
unto Moses and unto Eleazar
the son of Aaron the priest,
saying,
2 Take the sum of all the
congregation of the children
of Israel, from twenty years
old and upward, throughout
their fathers' house, all that
are able to go to war in
Israel.
3 And Moses and Eleazar the
priest spake with them in the
plains of Moab by Jordan
near Jericho, saying,
4 Take the sum of the people,
from twenty years old and
upward; as the LORD com-
manded Moses and the children of Israel, which went
forth out of the land of
Egypt.
5 Reuben, the eldest son of
Israel: the children of
Reuben; Hanoch, of whom
cometh the family of the
Hanochites: of Pallu, the
family of the Palluites:
6 Of Hezron, the family of
the Hezronites: of Carmi, the
family of the Carmites.
7 These are the families of
the Reubenites: and they that
were numbered of them were
forty and three thousand and
seven hundred and thirty.
8 And the sons of Pallu;
Eliab.
9 And the sons of Eliab;
Nemuel, and Dathan, and
Abiram. This is that Dathan
and Abiram, which were
famous in the congregation,
who strove against Moses
and against Aaron in the
company of Korah, when
they strove against the LORD:
10 And the earth opened her
mouth, and swallowed them
up together with Korah,
when that company died,
what time the fire devoured
two hundred and fifty men:
and they became a sign.
11 Notwithstanding the
children of Korah died not.
12 The sons of Simeon after
their families: of Nemuel,
the family of the Nemuelites:
of Jamin, the family of the
Jaminites: of Jachin, the
family of the Jachinites:
13 Of Zerah, the family of
the Zarhites: of Shaul, the
family of the Shaulites.
14 These are the families of
the Simeonites, twenty and
two thousand and two hun-
dred.
15 The children of Gad after
their families: of Zephon, the
family of the Zephonites: of
Haggi, the family of the
Haggites: of Shuni, the family of the Shunites:
16 Of Ozni, the family of
the Oznites: of Eri, the family of the Erites:
17 Of Arod, the family of
the Arodites: of Areli, the
family of the Arelites.
18 These are the families of
the children of Gad according to those that were numbered of them, forty thousand and five hundred.
19 The sons of Judah were
Er and Onan: and Er and
Onan died in the land of
Canaan.
20 And the sons of Judah
after their families were; of
Shelah, the family of the
Shelanites: of Pharez, the
family of the Pharzites: of
Zerah, the family of the
Zarhites.
21 And the sons of Pharez
were; of Hezron, the family
of the Hezronites: of Hamul,
the family of the Hamulites.
22 These are the families of
Judah according to those that
were numbered of them,
threescore and sixteen thousand and five hundred.
23 Of the sons of Issachar
after their families: of Tola,
the family of the Tolaites: of
Pua, the family of the
Punites:
24 Of Jashub, the family of
the Jashubites: of Shimron,
the family of the Shimron-
ites.
25 These are the families of
Issachar according to those
that were numbered of them,
threescore and four thousand
and three hundred.
26 Of the sons of Zebulun

against God
- The line of Korah did not die out completely

b. The division & tribe of Simeon
   1) The tribal clans
      - The Nemuelite clan
      - The Jaminite clan
      - The Jakinite clan
      - The Zerahite clan
      - The Shaulite clan
   2) The total number: 22,200

c. The division & tribe of Gad
   1) The tribal clans
      - The Zephonite clan
      - The Haggite clan
      - The Shunite clan
      - The Oznite clan
      - The Erite clan
      - The Arodite clan
      - The Arelite clan
   2) The total number: 40,500

d. The division & tribe of Judah
   1) The two sons of Judah who died in Canaan: Er & Onan
   2) The tribal clans through Judah
      - The Shelanite clan
      - The Perezite clan
      - The Zerahite clan
   3) The tribal clan through Perez
      - The Hezronite clan
      - The Hamulite clan
   4) The total number: 76,500

e. The division & tribe of Issachar
   1) The tribal clans
      - The Tolaite clan
      - The Puite clan
      - The Jashubite clan
      - The Shimronite clan
   2) The total number: 64,300

f. The division & tribe of

Zebulun
1) The tribal clans
- The Seredite clan
- The Elonite clan
- The Jahleelite clan

2) The total number: 60,500

g. The division & tribes of Joseph: He was granted a double honor, two major divisions or tribes (cp. Gen.48:1-6)

h. The division & tribe of Manasseh
1) The tribal clan
- The Makirite clan: The father of Gilead
- The Gileadite clan

2)The tribal clans through Gilead
- The Iezerite clan
- The Helekite clan
- The Asrielite clan
- The Shechemite clan
- The Shemidaite clan
- The Hepherite clan

3) The son of Hepher, Zelophehad, had only daughters

4) The total number: 52,700

i. The divisions & tribes of Ephraim
1) The tribal clans
- The Shuthelahite clan
- The Bekerite clan
- The Tahanite clan

2) The tribal clans through Shuthelah: The Eranite tribe

3) The total number: 32,500

j. The divisions & tribes of Benjamin
1) The tribal clans
- The Belaite clan
- The Ashbelite clan
- The Ahiramite clan
- The Shuphamite clan
- The Huphamite clan

after their families: of Sered,
the family of the Sardites: of
Elon, the family of the
Elonites: of Jahleel, the family of the Jahleelites.
27 These are the families of
the Zebulunites according to
those that were numbered of
them, threescore thousand
and five hundred.
28 The sons of Joseph after
their families were Manasseh and Ephraim.
29 Of the sons of Manasseh:
of Machir, the family of the
Machirites: and Machir
begat Gilead: of Gilead
come the family of the
Gileadites.
30 These are the sons of
Gilead: of Jeezer, the family
of the Jeezerites: of Helek,
the family of the Helekites:
31 And of Asriel, the family
of the Asrielites: and of
Shechem, the family of the
Shechemites:
32 And of Shemida, the
family of the Shemidaites:
and of Hepher, the family of
the Hepherites.
33 And Zelophehad the son
of Hepher had no sons, but
daughters: and the names of
the daughters of Zelophehad
were Mahlah, and Noah,
Hoglah, Milcah, and Tirzah.
34 These are the families of
Manasseh, and those that
were numbered of them, fifty
and two thousand and seven
hundred.
35 These are the sons of
Ephraim after their families:
of Shuthelah, the family of
the Shuthalhites: of Becher,
the family of the Bachrites:
of Tahan, the family of the
Tahanites.
36 And these are the sons of
Shuthelah: of Eran, the family of the Eranites.
37 These are the families of
the sons of Ephraim according to those that were numbered of them, thirty and two
thousand and five hundred.
These are the sons of Joseph
after their families.
38 The sons of Benjamin
after their families: of Bela,
the family of the Belaites: of
Ashbel, the family of the
Ashbelites: of Ahiram, the
family of the Ahiramites:
39 Of Shupham, the family
of the Shuphamites: of
Hupham, the family of the

Huphamites.
40 And the sons of Bela
were Ard and Naaman: of
Ard, the family of the
Ardites: and of Naaman, the
family of the Naamites.
41 These are the sons of
Benjamin after their families: and they that were numbered of them were forty and
five thousand and six hundred.
42 These are the sons of
Dan after their families: of
Shuham, the family of the
Shuhamites. These are the
families of Dan after their
families.
43 All the families of the
Shuhamites, according to
those that were numbered of
them, were threescore and
four thousand and four hundred.
44 Of the children of Asher
after their families: of Jimna,
the family of the Jimnites: of
Jesui, the family of the
Jesuites: of Beriah, the family of the Beriites.
45 Of the sons of Beriah: of
Heber, the family of the
Heberites: of Malchiel, the
family of the Malchielites.
46 And the name of the
daughter of Asher was
Sarah.
47 These are the families of
the sons of Asher according
to those that were numbered
of them; who were fifty and
three thousand and four hundred.
48 Of the sons of Naphtali
after their families: of
Jahzeel, the family of the
Jahzeelites: of Guni, the
family of the Gunites:
49 Of Jezer, the family of
the Jezerites: of Shillem, the
family of the Shillemites.
50 These are the families of
Naphtali according to their
families: and they that were
numbered of them were forty
and five thousand and four
hundred.
51 These were the num-
bered of the children of
Israel, six hundred thousand
and a thousand seven hun-
dred and thirty.
52 And the LORD spake unto
Moses, saying,
53 Unto these the land shall
be divided for an inheritance
according to the number of
names.

2) The tribal clans of Bela
- Through Ard, the Ardite clan
- Through Naaman, the Naamite clan

3) The total number: 45,600

k. The divisions & tribes of Dan
1) The tribal clan numbered just one: The Shuhamite clan

2) The total number: 64,400

l. The division & tribes of Asher
1) The tribal clans
- The Imnite clan
- The Ishvite clan
- The Beriite clan

2) The tribal clans through Beriah
- The Heberite clan
- The Malkielite clan

3) The daughter of Asher: Serah

4) The total number: 53,400

m. The divisions & tribes of Naphtali
1) The tribal clans
- The Jahzeelite clan
- The Gunite clan
- The Jezerite clan
- The Shillemite clan

2) The total number: 45,400

n. The total number of all divisions or tribes: 601,730

4. The 2nd purpose of the census—to divide the inheritance of the promised land: A picture of the believer's assurance of the promised land

a. The size of a tribe deter-

mined the amount of land it inherited
- If large, the tribe received a large inheritance
- If small, the tribe received a small inheritance

b. The land was to be divided by lot
c. The importance of these two regulations reemphasized
   1) The inheritance of each tribe was to be based on the size of each tribe
   2) The land was to be distributed by lot

5. The census of the Levites: A picture of being totally dedicated to God & His service
a. The major clans
- The Gershonite clan
- The Kohathite clan
- The Merarite clan

b. The sub-clans
- The Libnite clan
- The Hebronite clan
- The Mahlite clan
- The Mushite clan
- The Korahite clan

c. The lineage of Moses, Aaron, & Miriam
- Kohath was the forefather of Amram
- Amram & Jochebed were the parents

54 To many thou shalt give
the more inheritance, and to
few thou shalt give the less
inheritance: to every one
shall his inheritance be given
according to those that were
numbered of him.
55 Notwithstanding the land
shall be divided by lot:
according to the names of
the tribes of their fathers
they shall inherit.
56 According to the lot shall
the possession thereof be
divided between many and
few.
57 And these are they that
were numbered of the Lev-
ites after their families: of
Gershon, the family of the
Gershonites: of Kohath, the
family of the Kohathites: of
Merari, the family of the
Merarites.
58 These are the families of
the Levites: the family of the
Libnites, the family of the
Hebronites, the family of the
Mahlites, the family of the
Mushites, the family of the
Korathites. And Kohath
begat Amram.
59 And the name of Am-
ram's wife was Jochebed,
the daughter of Levi,
whom her mother bare to
Levi in Egypt: and she bare
unto Amram Aaron and
Moses, and Miriam their sister.
60 And unto Aaron was
born Nadab, and Abihu,
Eleazar, and Ithamar.
61 And Nadab and Abihu
died, when they offered
strange fire before the LORD.
62 And those that were
numbered of them were
twenty and three thousand,
all males from a month old
and upward: for they were
not numbered among the
children of Israel, because
there was no inheritance
given them among the children of Israel.
63 These are they that were
numbered by Moses and
Eleazar the priest, who numbered the children of Israel
in the plains of Moab by
Jordan near Jericho.
64 But among these there
was not a man of them
whom Moses and Aaron the
priest numbered, when they
numbered the children of
Israel in the wilderness of
Sinai.
65 For the LORD had said of
them, They shall surely die
in the wilderness. And there
was not left a man of them,
save Caleb the son of
Jephunneh, and Joshua the
son of Nun.

d. The descendants of Aaron:
   1) His sons: Nadab, Abihu, Eleazar, & Ithamar
   2) The tragic record of Aaron's family: Nadab & Abihu died under the judgment of God
e. The total number of Levites: 23,000
   1) The number was based upon one month old or older
   2) They were counted separately because they received no inheritance of land

6. The tragic record of the second census: A picture of the sure judgment of God
a. The people were counted right before they were to enter the promised land
b. The tragic fact: Not a single person from the first census was listed
   1) They had all died in the desert wilderness, died because of their unbelief & sin (cp. Num.11:1-14:45)
   2) They had all died except Caleb & Joshua

DIVISION IV

THE PREPARATION FOR THE MARCH INTO THE PROMISED LAND, 26:1-36:13

A. The Organization of the Second Generation—the Second Census: Mobilizing God's People to Enter and Inherit the Promised Land, 26:1-65

(26:1-65) **Introduction—Israel, Judgment of, Death of First Generation—Promised Land, How to Enter**: heaven is real. God has given the great hope of the promised land of heaven. The person who has trusted Jesus Christ as his Savior and truly follows after Him will inherit the promised land of God—heaven itself. This is the great promise of God. But note: it is not the person who *professes* to believe in God and Christ who will inherit the promised land of heaven. It is the person who *follows* after and *obeys* God who will inherit heaven. This is the clear message of this passage.

Note the very first three words of verse one: "After the plague." This is a reference to the plague of the former chapter, the plague that had wiped out the last of the first generation of believers. The people had given themselves over to immorality and false worship; consequently, the judgment of God had fallen. When the plague of God's judgment had ended, the last of the first generation of believers had died out in the desert wilderness—died "outside" the promised land. From this point on, the focus will be upon the second generation of believers, the children of the parents who had failed so miserably in life. In the words of *The Expositor's Bible Commentary*:

> "(This is) the turning point from the first generation to the second, the shift from the fathers and mothers to sons and daughters. God was about to begin a new work with a new people. The younger generation would begin to have their day."[1]

God now begins to mobilize the children, the second generation of believers, to actually enter and inherit the promised land. This is the subject of this passage of Scripture: *The Organization of the Second Generation—the Second Census: Mobilizing God's People to Enter and Inherit the Promised Land*, 26:1-65.

---

1 *The Expositor's Bible Commentary*. FrankE.Gaebelein, Editor, p.924.

1. The strong emphasis: "the LORD spoke": a picture of God guiding His people (v.1).
2. The 1st purpose of the census—military: a picture of the people of God preparing for warfare (v.2-3).
3. The number counted, division by division—counted just as they came out of Egypt: a picture of the faithfulness of God and a strong warning to man (v.4-52).
4. The 2nd purpose of the census—to divide the inheritance of the promised land: a picture of the believer's assurance of the promised land (v.53-56).
5. The census of the Levites: a picture of being totally dedicated to God and His service (v.57-62).
6. The tragic record of the second census: a picture of the sure judgment of God (v.63-65).

1 (26:1) **Word of God, Purpose—Guidance, of God—Leadership, of God**: there was the strong emphasis, "The LORD spoke." This is a picture of God guiding His people—the believers of all generations—as they prepare to march into the promised land.

OUTLINE	SCRIPTURE
1. The strong emphasis: "The LORD spoke": A picture of God guiding His people	And it came to pass after the plague, that the LORD spake unto Moses and unto Eleazar the son of Aaron the priest, saying,

The first generation had died off, every one of them except Joshua and Caleb. They had lived carnal, fleshly lives. Unbelief and grumbling had gripped their lives. They were constantly grumbling about the hardships, the problems, and the difficulties in life. Moreover, they were continually murmuring against and opposing Moses, the servant of God. They never learned to trust God, to believe and rest in Him. Unbelief and grumbling were the dominant traits of their lives. Consequently, they never were able to enter the promised land. Instead they were doomed to wander about in the desert wilderness for forty years until they had all died away. Now they had all gone: the forty years had passed. Only the children—the second generation—survived. It was now time to prepare this second generation of believers to enter the promised land. Therefore, "God spoke." God spoke to Moses and to the new High Priest Eleazar, the son of Aaron. God spoke, giving instructions for preparation, telling His people how to prepare for their entrance into the promised land. The point is this: God guided His people by His Word. Remember, God's guiding His people by *His Word* is one of the strongest emphases of the Book of Numbers. "The LORD spoke"—guided His people—is used over one hundred and fifty times in twenty plus ways in this great book. God guides His people by speaking to them through His precious Word. The second generation of believers had to be prepared to enter the promised land. They had to learn to trust God, learn the *spiritual rest* that God brings to the souls of those who trust Him. If they were to conquer the pitfalls and enemies of the promised land, they had to learn to trust the conquering power of God. Therefore, God spoke in order to begin preparing them to trust Him more and more. God spoke in order to give them all the guidance they needed for preparation.

Thought 1. God guides His people through His precious Holy Word. God has spoken in His precious Holy Word. It is in the Holy Scriptures that we are guided throughout life. In the Holy Scriptures we find out...
- how to live and how not to live
- where to go and where not to go
- what to do and what not to do
- how to speak and how not to speak
- how to approach God and how not to approach God
- how to worship God and how not to worship God

God has spoken to us through the Holy Scriptures. God has given us the Holy Scriptures to guide us throughout life. It is His Word that tells us how to prepare and how to enter the promised land of heaven.

"All scripture is given by inspiration of God, and is profitable for doctrine, for reproof, for correction, for instruction in righteousness" (2 Tim.3:16).

"Study to show thyself approved unto God, a workman that needeth not to be ashamed, rightly dividing the word of truth" (2 Tim.2:15).

"But he answered and said, It is written, Man shall not live by bread alone, but by every word that proceedeth out of the mouth of God" (Mt.4:4).

"For verily I say unto you, Till heaven and earth pass, one jot or one tittle shall in no wise pass from the law, till all be fulfilled" (Mt.5:18).

"Heaven and earth shall pass away, but my words shall not pass away" (Mt.24:35).

"Now ye are clean through the word which I have spoken unto you" (Jn.15:3).

"But these are written, that ye might believe that Jesus is the Christ, the Son of God; and that believing ye might have life through his name" (Jn.20:31).

"For whatsoever things were written aforetime were written for our learning, that we through patience and comfort of the scriptures might have hope" (Ro.15:4).

"Now all these things happened unto them for ensamples: and they are written for our admonition, upon whom the ends of the world are come" (1 Cor.10:11).

"For the word of God is quick, and powerful, and sharper than any twoedged sword, piercing even to the dividing asunder of soul and spirit, and of the joints and marrow, and is a discerner of the thoughts and intents of the heart" (Heb.4:12).

"But the word of the Lord endureth for ever. And this is the word which by the gospel is preached unto you" (1 Pt.1:25).

"As newborn babes, desire the sincere milk of the word, that ye may grow thereby: If so be ye have tasted that the Lord is gracious" (1 Pt.2:2-3).

"We have also a more sure word of prophecy [the Word of God]; whereunto ye do well that ye take heed, as unto a light that shineth in a dark place, until the day dawn, and the day star arise in your hearts: For the prophecy came not in old time by the will of man: but holy men of God spake as they were moved by the Holy Ghost" (2 Pt.1:19, 21).

"These things have I written unto you that believe on the name of the Son of God; that ye may know that ye have eternal life, and that ye may believe on the name of the Son of God" (1 Jn.5:13).

"And he humbled thee, and suffered thee to hunger, and fed thee with manna, which thou knewest not, neither did thy fathers know; that he might make thee know that man doth not live by bread only, but by every word that proceedeth out of the mouth of the Lord doth man live" (Dt.8:3).

"Neither have I gone back from the commandment of his lips; I have esteemed the words of his mouth more than my necessary food" (Job 23:12).

"Wherewithal shall a young man cleanse his way? by taking heed thereto according to thy word" (Ps.119:9).

"Thy word is a lamp unto my feet, and a light unto my path" (Ps.119:105).

"The entrance of thy words giveth light; it giveth understanding unto the simple" (Ps.119:130).

"For the commandment is a lamp; and the law is light; and reproofs of instruction are the way of life" (Pr.6:23).

2 (26:2-3) **Israel, Census of—Military, Census of—Warfare, Spiritual—Spiritual Warfare—Census, of Israel**: there was the first purpose of the census, that of taking a military count. This was a picture of God's people preparing for warfare. Keep this fact in mind: this is a census of the second generation of believers. The first census had been taken by the first generation over thirty-eight years earlier. All that generation had died out in the desert wilderness. Now it was time for their children, the second generation, to prepare to enter and inherit the promised land. But before they could, the leadership needed to know how many men were available to fight. Entering the promised land was to be a hard and difficult struggle. There were pitfalls—traps and snares—that had to be bypassed and guarded against as God's people marched into the promised land. Moreover, there were strong enemies that had to be conquered. How strong was Israel? How many fighting men were available? This fact had to be known before they could even think about entering the promised land. Therefore, the people were to count all the men able to serve in the military who were twenty years old or older. Note: they took the census while they were camped by the Jordan River across from the great city of Jericho.

OUTLINE	SCRIPTURE
2. The 1st purpose of the census—military: A picture of the people of God preparing for warfare a. To count all men able to serve 20 years old or older	2 Take the sum of all the congregation of the children of Israel, from twenty years old and upward, throughout their fathers' house, all that are able to go to war in Israel.
b. To count while camped by the Jordan across from Jericho	3 And Moses and Eleazar the priest spake with them in the plains of Moab by Jordan near Jericho, saying,

Thought 1. The military census is a picture of the people of God preparing for warfare. This is a strong lesson for us: we are engaged in a spiritual warfare. There are pitfalls throughout life—traps and snares—that will trip us up and ruin our lives. Furthermore, there are strong enemies that oppose us, trying to keep us out of the promised land of heaven. There are enemies in this life that strongly oppose God and us, enemies such as...

- humanism
- secularism
- atheism
- agnosticism
- covetousness
- greed
- immorality
- drugs
- alcohol
- peer pressure
- selfishness
- self-centeredness
- pride
- anger
- hostility
- revenge
- adultery
- divorce
- disease
- sorcery
- witchcraft
- psychics
- the world of the occult

The list of pitfalls and enemies that oppose the promised land of heaven is innumerable. These pitfalls and enemies are all around us, confronting us every day of our lives. To conquer, to triumph, to be victorious, we must prepare. We must be prepared for spiritual warfare, prepared to stand by the power of God Himself.

"Casting down imaginations, and every high thing that exalteth itself against the knowledge of God, and bringing into captivity every thought to the obedience of Christ" (2 Cor.10:5).

"Finally, my brethren, be strong in the Lord, and in the power of his might. Put on the whole armour of God, that ye may be able to stand against the wiles of the devil. For we wrestle not against flesh and blood, but against principalities, against powers, against the rulers of the darkness of this

world, against spiritual wickedness in high places. Wherefore take unto you the whole armour of God, that ye may be able to withstand in the evil day, and having done all, to stand" (Eph.6:10-13 cp. v.14-18).

"But let us, who are of the day, be sober, putting on the breastplate of faith and love; and for an helmet, the hope of salvation. For God hath not appointed us to wrath, but to obtain salvation by our Lord Jesus Christ" (1 Th.5:8-9).

"This charge I commit unto thee, son Timothy, according to the prophecies which went before on thee, that thou by them mightest war a good warfare" (1 Tim.1:18).

"But thou, O man of God, flee these things; and follow after righteousness, godliness, faith, love, patience, meekness. Fight the good fight of faith, lay hold on eternal life, whereunto thou art also called, and hast professed a good profession before many witnesses" (1 Tim.6:11-12).

"Thou therefore endure hardness, as a good soldier of Jesus Christ. No man that warreth entangleth himself with the affairs of this life; that he may please him who hath chosen him to be a soldier" (2 Tim.2:3-4).

"Be sober, be vigilant; because your adversary the devil, as a roaring lion, walketh about, seeking whom he may devour: Whom resist stedfast in the faith, knowing that the same afflictions are accomplished in your brethren that are in the world. But the God of all grace, who hath called us unto his eternal glory by Christ Jesus, after that ye have suffered a while, make you perfect, stablish, strengthen, settle you" (1 Pt.5:8-10).

"For whatsoever is born of God overcometh the world: and this is the victory that overcometh the world, even our faith. Who is he that overcometh the world, but he that believeth that Jesus is the Son of God" (1 Jn.5:4-5).

"For the eyes of the Lord run to and fro throughout the whole earth, to show himself strong in the behalf of them whose heart is perfect toward him. Herein thou hast done foolishly: therefore from henceforth thou shalt have wars" (2 Chron.16:9).

"The angel of the Lord encampeth round about them that fear him, and delivereth them" (Ps.34:7).

"He shall cover thee with his feathers, and under his wings shalt thou trust: his truth shall be thy shield and buckler" (Ps.91:4)

3 (26:4-51) **Census, of Israel—Israel, Census of—Army, of God—Military, of God—Faithfulness, of God—Promises, of God—Power, of God**: there was the number counted, division by division—counted just as they came out of Egypt. This census is a picture of the faithfulness of God, and it stands as a strong warning to man. Note three significant facts about this census. First, the clans within each tribe are of Korah's rebellion is recorded for all succeeding generations. Even we today are reading about it. It stands as a strong warning against disbelieving God, against rejecting and rebelling against Him. Thirdly, the total number of people listed in this census is almost the same total counted in the first census: 601,730 compared to 603,550, a difference of only 820 (v.51, cp. 1:46).

This is a strong picture of God's faithfulness. God had promised Abraham that his descendants would become a great nation of people (see outline and notes—Gen.12:1-3 for more discussion). When his grandson Jacob went down into Egypt with his twelve sons, the descendants of Abraham numbered less than one hundred persons. But four hundred years later when God delivered His people out of Egypt, they obviously numbered somewhere between two to four million persons. This is indicated by the military census that numbers over six hundred thousand men alone, men who were of military fighting age—twenty years old or older. An astounding miracle by God! A clear demonstration of God's faithfulness! He was fulfilling His promise given to His dear servant Abraham.

OUTLINE	SCRIPTURE	SCRIPTURE	OUTLINE
3. The number counted, division by division—counted just as they came out of Egypt: A picture of the faithfulness of God & a strong warning to man	4 Take the sum of the people, from twenty years old and upward; as the LORD commanded Moses and the children of Israel, which went forth out of the land of Egypt.	9 And the sons of Eliab; Nemuel, and Dathan, and Abiram. This is that Dathan and Abiram, which were famous in the congregation, who strove against Moses and against Aaron in the company of Korah, when they strove against the LORD:	descendants of Reuben who rebelled with Korah (cp. Jude 11) • The son of the clan leader Pallu was Eliab • Two of the sons of Eliab rebelled with Korah
a. The division & tribe of Reuben 1) The tribal clans • The Hanochite clan • The Pallu clan • The Hezron clan • The Carmite clan	5 Reuben, the eldest son of Israel: the children of Reuben; Hanoch, of whom cometh the family of the Hanochites: of Pallu, the family of the Palluites: 6 Of Hezron, the family of the Hezronites: of Carmi, the family of the Carmites.	10 And the earth opened her mouth, and swallowed them up together with Korah, when that company died, what time the fire devoured two hundred and fifty men: and they became a sign.	• They were severely judged by God along with 250 other rebels (cp. 16:35) • They are a warning to all who reject & rebel against God
2) The total number: 43,730	7 These are the families of the Reubenites: and they that were numbered of them were forty and three thousand and seven hundred and thirty.	11 Notwithstanding the children of Korah died not. 12 The sons of Simeon after their families: of Nemuel, the family of the Nemuelites: of Jamin, the family of the Jaminites: of Jachin,	• The line of Korah did not die out completely b. The division & tribe of Simeon 1) The tribal clans • The Nemuelite clan • The Jaminite clan
3) The tragic record of Korah's rebellion & the	8 And the sons of Pallu; Eliab.		

OUTLINE	SCRIPTURE
• The Jakinite clan • The Zerahite clan • The Shaulite clan	the family of the Jachinites: 13 Of Zerah, the family of the Zarhites: of Shaul, the family of the Shaulites.
2) The total number: 22,200	14 These are the families of the Simeonites, twenty and two thousand and two hun- dred.
c. The division & tribe of Gad 1) The tribal clans • The Zephonite clan • The Haggite clan • The Shunite clan	15 The children of Gad after their families: of Zephon, the family of the Zephonites: of Haggi, the family of the Haggites: of Shuni, the family of the Shunites:
• The Oznite clan • The Erite clan	16 Of Ozni, the family of the Oznites: of Eri, the fami- ly of the Erites:
• The Arodite clan • The Arelite clan	17 Of Arod, the family of the Arodites: of Areli, the family of the Arelites.
2) The total number: 40,500	18 These are the families of the children of Gad accord- ing to those that were num- bered of them, forty thou- sand and five hundred.
d. The division & tribe of Judah 1) The two sons of Judah who died in Canaan: Er & Onan	19 The sons of Judah were Er and Onan: and Er and Onan died in the land of Canaan.
2) The tribal clans through Judah • The Shelanite clan • The Perezite clan • The Zerahite clan	20 And the sons of Judah after their families were; of Shelah, the family of the Shelanites: of Pharez, the family of the Pharzites: of Zerah, the family of the Zarhites.
3) The tribal clan through Perez • The Hezronite clan • The Hamulite clan 4) The total number: 76,500	21 And the sons of Pharez were; of Hezron, the family of the Hezronites: of Hamul, the family of the Hamulites. 22 These are the families of Judah according to those that were numbered of them, threescore and sixteen thou- sand and five hundred.
e. The division & tribe of Issachar 1) The tribal clans • The Tolaite clan • The Puite clan • The Jashubite clan • The Shimronite clan	23 Of the sons of Issachar after their families: of Tola, the family of the Tolaites: of Pua, the family of the Punites: 24 Of Jashub, the family of the Jashubites: of Shimron, the family of the Shimron- ites.
2) The total number: 64,300	25 These are the families of Issachar according to those that were numbered of them, threescore and four thousand and three hundred.
f. The division & tribe of Zebulun 1) The tribal clans • The Seredite clan • The Elonite clan • The Jahleelite clan 2) The total number: 60,500	26 Of the sons of Zebulun after their families: of Sered, the family of the Sardites: of Elon, the family of the Elonites: of Jahleel, the fam- ily of the Jahleelites. 27 These are the families of

SCRIPTURE	OUTLINE
the Zebulunites according to those that were numbered of them, threescore thousand and five hundred.	
28 The sons of Joseph after their families were Manas- seh and Ephraim.	g. The division & tribes of Joseph: He was granted a double honor, two major divisions or tribes (cp. Gen.48:1-6)
29 Of the sons of Manas- seh: of Machir, the family of the Machirites: and Machir begat Gilead: of Gilead come the family of the Gileadites.	h. The division & tribe of Manasseh 1) The tribal clan • The Makirite clan: The father of Gilead • The Gileadite clan
30 These are the sons of Gilead: of Jeezer, the family of the Jeezerites: of Helek, the family of the Helekites: 31 And of Asriel, the family of the Asrielites: and of Shechem, the family of the Shechemites: 32 And of Shemida, the family of the Shemidaites: and of Hepher, the family of the Hepherites.	2)The tribal clans through Gilead • The Iezerite clan • The Helekite clan • The Asrielite clan • The Shechemite clan • The Shemidaite clan • The Hepherite clan 3) The son of Hepher, Zelophehad, had only daughters
33 And Zelophehad the son of Hepher had no sons, but daughters: and the names of the daughters of Zelophehad were Mahlah, and Noah, Hoglah, Milcah, and Tirzah.	
34 These are the families of Manasseh, and those that were numbered of them, fifty and two thousand and seven hundred.	4) The total number: 52,700
35 These are the sons of Ephraim after their families: of Shuthelah, the family of the Shuthalhites: of Becher, the family of the Bachrites: of Tahan, the family of the Tahanites.	i. The divisions & tribes of Ephraim 1) The tribal clans • The Shuthelahite clan • The Bekerite clan • The Tahanite clan
36 And these are the sons of Shuthelah: of Eran, the fam- ily of the Eranites.	2) The tribal clans through Shuthelah: The Eranite tribe
37 These are the families of the sons of Ephraim accord- ing to those that were num- bered of them, thirty and two thousand and five hundred. These are the sons of Joseph after their families.	3) The total number: 32,500
38 The sons of Benjamin after their families: of Bela, the family of the Belaites: of Ashbel, the family of the Ashbelites: of Ahiram, the family of the Ahiramites: 39 Of Shupham, the family of the Shuphamites: of Hupham, the family of the Huphamites.	j. The divisions & tribes of Benjamin 1) The tribal clans • The Belaite clan • The Ashbelite clan • The Ahiramite clan • The Shuphamite clan • The Huphamite clan
40 And the sons of Bela were Ard and Naaman: of Ard, the family of the Ardites: and of Naaman, the	2) The tribal clans of Bela • Through Ard, the Ardite clan • Through Naaman, the

OUTLINE	SCRIPTURE	SCRIPTURE	OUTLINE
Naamite clan 3) The total number: 45,600	family of the Naamites. 41 These are the sons of Benjamin after their families: and they that were numbered of them were forty and five thousand and six hundred.	46 And the name of the daughter of Asher was Sarah. 47 These are the families of the sons of Asher according to those that were numbered of them; who were fifty and three thousand and four hundred.	3) The daughter of Asher: Serah 4) The total number: 53,400
k. The divisions & tribes of Dan 1) The tribal clan numbered just one: The Shuhamite clan 2) The total number: 64,400	42 These are the sons of Dan after their families: of Shuham, the family of the Shuhamites. These are the families of Dan after their families. 43 All the families of the Shuhamites, according to those that were numbered of them, were threescore and four thousand and four hundred.	48 Of the sons of Naphtali after their families: of Jahzeel, the family of the Jahzeelites: of Guni, the family of the Gunites: 49 Of Jezer, the family of the Jezerites: of Shillem, the family of the Shillemites. 50 These are the families of Naphtali according to their families: and they that were numbered of them were forty and five thousand and four hundred.	m. The divisions & tribes of Naphtali 1) The tribal clans • The Jahzeelite clan • The Gunite clan • The Jezerite clan • The Shillemite clan 2) The total number: 45,400
l. The division & tribes of Asher 1) The tribal clans • The Imnite clan • The Ishvite clan • The Beriite clan 2) The tribal clans through Beriah • The Heberite clan • The Malkielite clan	44 Of the children of Asher after their families: of Jimna, the family of the Jimnites: of Jesui, the family of the Jesuites: of Beriah, the family of the Beriites. 45 Of the sons of Beriah: of Heber, the family of the Heberites: of Malchiel, the family of the Malchielites.	51 These were the numbered of the children of Israel, six hundred thousand and a thousand seven hundred and thirty.	n. The total number of all divisions or tribes: 601,730

Thought 1. Note two clear lessons for us.

1) God is faithful, never failing to keep His promises. What God has promised, He will do, do everything He says. Failure is not in the vocabulary of God: the one thing God cannot do is fail to keep His Word. Once God has spoken, He will fulfill His promises to us just as He did to Abraham and to the Israelites. God is faithful, always faithful to His Word, always faithful to do exactly what He promises us.

"God is faithful, by whom ye were called unto the fellowship of his Son Jesus Christ our Lord" (1 Cor.1:9).

"Wherein God, willing more abundantly to show unto the heirs of promise the immutability of his counsel, confirmed it by an oath: That by two immutable things, in which it was impossible for God to lie, we might have a strong consolation, who have fled for refuge to lay hold upon the hope set before us" (Heb.6:17-18).

"Wherefore let them that suffer according to the will of God commit the keeping of their souls to him in well doing, as unto a faithful Creator" (1 Pt.4:19).

"Know therefore that the Lord thy God, he is God, the faithful God, which keepeth covenant and mercy with them that love him and keep his commandments to a thousand generations" (Dt.7:9).

"Blessed be the Lord, that hath given rest unto his people Israel, according to all that he promised: there hath not failed one word of all his good promise, which he promised by the hand of Moses his servant" (1 Ki.8:56).

"Thy mercy, O Lord, is in the heavens; and thy faithfulness reacheth unto the clouds" (Ps.36:5).

"Blessed be the Lord, who daily loadeth us with benefits, even the God of our salvation. Selah" (Ps.68:19).

"I will sing of the mercies of the Lord for ever: with my mouth will I make known thy faithfulness to all generations" (Ps.89:1).

2) Two facts about this census stand as a strong warning to us. First, this is a census of the second generation of believers. The parents failed to believe and follow after God. Consequently, they were disallowed and barred from ever entering the promised land. Second, the rebellion of Korah is recorded in this census. He led an uprising against the servant of God, rejecting and refusing to follow God and His dear servant.

This census stands as a strong warning to us all: being listed in the army of God—having one's name written on the roll—does not guarantee entrance into the promised land.

⇒ A person must *believe* and *follow* God.
⇒ A person must *believe* and *obey* God.
⇒ A person must *possess* Christ as well as *profess* Christ.
⇒ A person must *live for God* and not *live for the world*.
⇒ A person must *walk in Christ* and not *walk in the lust of the flesh*.
⇒ A person must keep his mind upon *spiritual things* and not upon *carnal things*.
⇒ A person must live a life of *faith* and not a life of *unbelief*.

Because of these things, the first generation of believers never entered the promised land of God. They died out in the desert wilderness. This census declares this fact to all succeeding generations: we can miss out on the promised land of God. What we profess is not what matters to God. What matters is what we do, how we live. Do we follow Christ? Are we living holy, righteous, and pure lives? Are we a testimony to God and His saving grace?

God warns us: just because our names are listed in the army of God does not mean that we will enter the promised land of God. We must live out what we profess. To believe means to obey God.

"Not every one that saith unto me, Lord, Lord, shall enter into the kingdom of heaven; but he that doeth the will of my Father which is in heaven" (Mt.7:21).

"He answered and said unto them, Well hath Esaias prophesied of you hypocrites, as it is written, This people honoureth me with their lips, but their heart is far from me" (Mk.7:6).

"Be not deceived; God is not mocked: for whatsoever a man soweth, that shall he also reap" (Gal.6:7).

"They profess that they know God; but in works they deny him, being abominable, and disobedient, and unto every good work reprobate" (Tit.1:16).

"My little children, let us not love in word, neither in tongue; but in deed and in truth" (1 Jn.3:18).

"And they remembered that God was their rock, and the high God their redeemer. Nevertheless they did flatter him with their mouth, and they lied unto him with their tongues" (Ps.78:35-36).

"And they come unto thee as the people cometh, and they sit before thee as my people, and they hear thy words, but they will not do them: for with their mouth they show much love, but their heart goeth after their covetousness" (Ezk.33:31).

4 (26:52-56) **Inheritance, of the Believer—Inheritance, of Israel—Land, the Promised, Inheritance of**: there was the second purpose of the census—to divide the inheritance of the promised land. This is a picture of the believer's assurance of the promised land. This census had two major purposes: to determine the size of the tribes for military purposes and to serve as the basis for dividing up the promised land of God.

OUTLINE	SCRIPTURE	SCRIPTURE	OUTLINE
4. The 2nd purpose of the census—to divide the inheritance of the promised land: A picture of the believer's assurance of the promised land a. The size of a tribe determined the amount of land it inherited • If large, the tribe received a large inheritance • If small, the tribe received	52 And the LORD spake unto Moses, saying, 53 Unto these the land shall be divided for an inheritance according to the number of names. 54 To many thou shalt give the more inheritance, and to few thou shalt give the less inheritance: to every one shall his inheritance be	given according to those that were numbered of him. 55 Notwithstanding the land shall be divided by lot: according to the names of the tribes of their fathers they shall inherit. 56 According to the lot shall the possession thereof be divided between many and few.	a small inheritance b. The land was to be divided by lot c. The importance of these two regulations reemphasized 1) The inheritance of each tribe was to be based on the size of each tribe 2) The land was to be distributed by lot

1. As would be expected, the size of a tribe determined the amount of land it was to inherit. If the tribe was large, it was to receive a large inheritance. A smaller tribe received a smaller inheritance.

2. As would be expected, the land was to be divided and distributed by lot (v.55). This was to prevent any favoritism from being shown when the land was distributed and to prevent any charge of favoritism.

3. As would be expected, the importance of these two regulations was repeated for reemphasis (v.55-56). The inheritance of each tribe was to be based on the size of each tribe, and the land was to be distributed by lot. Inheriting the promised land of God was the longing of God's people, the beat of their hearts. With great expectation, they were waiting for that glorious day when they would receive their inheritance. It was of critical importance that the land be distributed fairly, without partiality or favoritism. The people had to have confidence in the distribution of the land. This was the reason for the census: to give every believer full assurance, complete confidence that he would receive his inheritance in the promised land.

Thought 1. The believer can rest assured: he will receive his inheritance in the promised land of heaven. This glorious fact has been settled by God once and for all: the person who truly believes and follows God will live eternally with God. He will enter the promised land of heaven and serve God forever and ever. This is the assurance, the confidence that God gives the genuine believer.

"For God so loved the world, that he gave his only begotten Son, that whosoever e in him should not perish, but have everlasting life" (Jn.3:16).

"And I give unto them eternal life; and they shall never perish, neither shall any man pluck them out of my hand" (Jn.10:28).

"And now, brethren, I commend you to God, and to the word of his grace, which is able to build you up, and to give you an inheritance among all them which are sanctified" (Acts 20:32).

"To open their eyes, and to turn them from darkness to light, and from the power of Satan unto God, that they may receive forgiveness of sins, and inheritance among them which are sanctified by faith that is in me" (Acts 26:18).

"To them who by patient continuance in well doing seek for glory and honour and immortality, eternal life" (Ro.2:7).

"But now being made free from sin, and become servants to God, ye have your fruit unto holiness, and the end everlasting life" (Ro.6:22).

"The Spirit itself beareth witness with our spirit, that we are the children of God: And if children,then heirs; heirs of God, and joint-heirs with Christ; if so be that we suffer with him, that we may be also glorified together" (Ro.8:16-17).

"For ye are all the children of God by faith in Christ Jesus. For as many of you as have been baptized into Christ have put on Christ. There is neither Jew nor Greek, there is neither bond nor free, there is neither male nor female: for ye are all one in Christ Jesus. And if ye be Christ's, then are ye Abraham's seed, and heirs according to the promise" (Gal.3:26-29).

"Giving thanks unto the Father, which hath made us meet to be partakers of the inheritance of the saints in light" (Col.1:12).

"Knowing that of the Lord ye shall receive the reward of the inheritance: for ye serve the Lord Christ" (Col.3:24).

"Laying up in store for themselves a good foundation against the time to come, that they may lay hold on eternal life" (1 Tim.6:19).

"In hope of eternal life, which God, that cannot lie, promised before the world began" (Tit.1:2).

"That being justified by his grace, we should be made heirs according to the hope of eternal life" (Tit.3:7).

"Blessed be the God and Father of our Lord Jesus Christ, which according to his abundant mercy hath begotten us again unto a lively hope by the resurrection of Jesus Christ from the dead, To an inheritance incorruptible, and undefiled, and that fadeth not away, reserved in heaven for you" (1 Pt.1:3-4).

"But the day of the Lord will come as a thief in the night; in the which the heavens shall pass away with a great noise, and the elements shall melt with fervent heat, the earth also and the works that are therein shall be burned up. Seeing then that all these things shall be dissolved, what manner of persons ought ye to be in all holy conversation and godliness, Looking for and hasting unto the coming of the day of God, wherein the heavens being on fire shall be dissolved, and the elements shall melt with fervent heat? Nevertheless we, according to his promise, look for new heavens and a new earth, wherein dwelleth righteousness" (2 Pt.3:10-13).

"And this is the promise that he hath promised us, even eternal life" (1 Jn.2:25).

"Keep yourselves in the love of God, looking for the mercy of our Lord Jesus Christ unto eternal life" (Jude 21).

"And I saw a new heaven and a new earth: for the first heaven and the first earth were passed away; and there was no more sea.... And God shall wipe away all tears from their eyes; and there shall be no more death, neither sorrow, nor crying, neither shall there be any more pain: for the former things are passed away" (Rev.21:1, 4).

"And at that time shall Michael stand up, the great prince which standeth for the children of thy people: and there shall be a time of trouble, such as never was since there was a nation even to that same time: and at that time thy people shall be delivered, every one that shall be found written in the book" (Dan.12:2).

5 (26:57-62) **Ministers, Appointed—Ministers, Dedication of—Census, of Levites**: there was the census of the Levites. This is a picture of being totally dedicated to God and His service. A new census of the Levites was necessary to determine how many were available to serve in the ministry of the LORD. It was necessary to know this fact because the Levites were going to be scattered throughout the nation as ministers to the people. Forty-eight towns were going to be assigned to the Levites, a certain number within each tribe. This would put the ministers out among the people so they could better minister to them and help them in their moments of need (see outline and notes—Num.35:1-8 for more discussion).

OUTLINE	SCRIPTURE	SCRIPTURE	OUTLINE
5. The census of the Levites: A picture of being totally dedicated to God & His service a. The major clans • The Gershonite clan • The Kohathite clan • The Merarite clan	57 And these are they that were numbered of the Levites after their families: of Gershon, the family of the Gershonites: of Kohath, the family of the Kohathites: of Merari, the family of the Merarites.	59 And the name of Amram's wife was Jochebed, the daughter of Levi, whom her mother bare to Levi in Egypt: and she bare unto Amram Aaron and Moses, and Miriam their sister.	c. The lineage of Moses, Aaron, & Miriam • Kohath was the forefather of Amram • Amram & Jochebed were the parents
b. The sub-clans • The Libnite clan • The Hebronite clan • The Mahlite clan • The Mushite clan • The Korahite clan	58 These are the families of the Levites: the family of the Libnites, the family of the Hebronites, the family of the Mahlites, the family of the Mushites, the family of the Korathites. And Kohath begat Amram.	60 And unto Aaron was born Nadab, and Abihu, Eleazar, and Ithamar. 61 And Nadab and Abihu died, when they offered strange fire before the LORD. 62 And those that were numbered of them were	d. The descendants of Aaron: 1) His sons: Nadab, Abihu, Eleazar, & Ithamar 2) The tragic record of Aaron's family: Nadab & Abihu died under the judgment of God e. The total number of Levites: 23,000

OUTLINE	SCRIPTURE	SCRIPTURE	OUTLINE
1) The number was based upon one month old or older 2) They were counted sepa-	twenty and three thousand, all males from a month old and upward: for they were not numbered among the	children of Israel, because there was no inheritance given them among the children of Israel.	rately because they received no inheritance of land

Thought 1. The minister of God is to be totally dedicated to God, totally dedicated to the call God has given him. His call is to minister to people. In fact, the ministry is people. Without people there would be no ministry. Therefore, the minister is to reach out to those people, helping them and meeting their needs. He is to be totally dedicated to God and to people.

> **"Even as the Son of man came not to be ministered unto, but to minister, and to give his life a ransom for many" (Mt.20:28).**
>
> **"Go ye therefore, and teach all nations, baptizing them in the name of the Father, and of the Son, and of the Holy Ghost: Teaching them to observe all things whatsoever I have commanded you: and, lo, I am with you alway, even unto the end of the world. Amen" (Mt.28:19-20).**
>
> **"Ye have not chosen me, but I have chosen you, and ordained you, that ye should go and bring forth fruit, and that your fruit should remain: that whatsoever ye shall ask of the Father in my name, he may give it you" (Jn.15:16).**
>
> **"He saith unto him the third time, Simon, son of Jonas, lovest thou me? Peter was grieved because he said unto him the third time, Lovest thou me? And he said unto him, Lord, thou knowest all things; thou knowest that I love thee. Jesus saith unto him, Feed my sheep" (Jn.21:17).**
>
> **"But the Lord said unto him, Go thy way: for he is a chosen vessel unto me, to bear my name before the Gentiles, and kings, and the children of Israel" (Acts 9:15).**
>
> **"In meekness instructing those that oppose themselves; if God peradventure will give them repentance to the acknowledging of the truth" (2 Tim.2:25).**
>
> **"Feed the flock of God which is among you, taking the oversight thereof, not by constraint, but willingly; not for filthy lucre, but of a ready mind" (1 Pt.5:2).**
>
> **"And I will set up shepherds over them which shall feed them: and they shall fear no more, nor be dismayed, neither shall they be lacking, saith the Lord" (Jer.23:4).**
>
> **"Son of man, I have made thee a watchman unto the house of Israel: therefore hear the word at my mouth, and give them warning from me" (Ezk.3:17).**
>
> **"But if the watchman see the sword come, and blow not the trumpet, and the people be not warned; if the sword come, and take any person from among them, he is taken away in his iniquity; but his blood will I require at the watchman's hand" (Ezk.33:6).**

6 (26:63-65) **Judgment, of God—Israel, Failure of—Census**: there was the tragic record of the second census. This record is a picture of the sure judgment of God.

OUTLINE	SCRIPTURE	SCRIPTURE	OUTLINE
6. The tragic record of the second census: A picture of the sure judgment of God a. The people were counted right before they were to enter the promised land b. The tragic fact: Not a single person from the first census was listed	63 These are they that were numbered by Moses and Eleazar the priest, who numbered the children of Israel in the plains of Moab by Jordan near Jericho. 64 But among these there was not a man of them whom Moses and Aaron the priest numbered, when they	numbered the children of Israel in the wilderness of Sinai. 65 For the LORD had said of them, They shall surely die in the wilderness. And there was not left a man of them, save Caleb the son of Jephunneh, and Joshua the son of Nun.	1) They had all died in the desert wilderness, died because of their unbelief & sin (cp. Num.11:1-14:45) 2) They had all died except Caleb & Joshua

1. Note that the census was taken right before the people were to enter the promised land. Remember, they were camped on the plains of Moab by the Jordan River, right across from the great city of Jericho (v.63).

2. The tragic record of the second census is this: not a single person from the first census was listed (v.64). Note that this is the clear statement of Scripture, the subject of these two verses. Not a single person from the first generation of believers was allowed to enter the promised land. They had all died in the desert wilderness, died because of their unbelief and sin. (See outline and notes—Num.11:1-14:45.) They had all died except Caleb and Joshua. Only these two had believed in the promises of God, that He would lead them into the promised land. Therefore, they had escaped the judgment of God and were to receive a glorious inheritance in the promised land.

Thought 1. The judgment of God against *unbelief and sin* is sure. Judgment will fall upon every unbeliever and sinner in this world. We will all—every one of us—stand before God and give an account for what we have done. Both believer and unbeliever are going to stand before God. Believers will be judged for the work they have done for God or failed to do. Unbelievers will be judged because they failed to approach God through His Son Jesus Christ, failed to trust the Savior of the world who could have forgiven their sins and made them acceptable to God. Every one of us will stand before God and give an account.

"And as it is appointed unto men once to die, but after this the judgment" (Heb.9:27).

"For the Son of man shall come in the glory of his Father with his angels; and then he shall reward every man according to his works" (Mt.16:27).

"When the Son of man shall come in his glory, and all the holy angels with him, then shall he sit upon the throne of his glory: And before him shall be gathered all nations: and he shall separate them one from another, as a shepherd divideth his sheep from the goats: And he shall set the sheep on his right hand, but the goats on the left" (Mt.25:31-33).

"In the day when God shall judge the secrets of men by Jesus Christ according to my gospel" (Ro.2:16).

"For we must all [believers] appear before the judgment seat of Christ; that every one may receive the things done in his body, according to that he hath done, whether it be good or bad" (2 Cor.5:10).

"And to you who are troubled rest with us, when the Lord Jesus shall be revealed from heaven with his mighty angels, In flaming fire taking vengeance on them that know not God, and that obey not the gospel of our Lord Jesus Christ" (2 Th.1:7-8).

"And if ye call on the Father, who without respect of persons judgeth according to every man's work, pass the time of your sojourning here in fear" (1 Pt.1:17).

"The Lord knoweth how to deliver the godly out of temptations, and to reserve the unjust unto the day of judgment to be punished" (2 Pt.2:9).

"But the heavens and the earth, which are now, by the same word are kept in store, reserved unto fire against the day of judgment and perdition of ungodly men" (2 Pt.3:7).

"Behold, the Lord cometh with ten thousands of his saints, To execute judgment upon all, and to convince all that are ungodly among them of all their ungodly deeds which they have ungodly committed, and of all their hard speeches which ungodly sinners have spoken against him" (Jude 14-15).

"And I saw the dead, small and great, stand before God; and the books were opened: and another book was opened, which is the book of life: and the dead were judged out of those things which were written in the books, according to their works" (Rev.20:12).

"And, behold, I come quickly; and my reward is with me, to give every man according as his work shall be" (Rev.22:12).

"Also unto thee, O Lord, belongeth mercy: for thou renderest to every man according to his work" (Ps.62:12).

"I the Lord search the heart, I try the reins, even to give every man according to his ways, and according to the fruit of his doings" (Jer.17:10).

TYPES, SYMBOLS, AND PICTURES
(Numbers 26:1-65)

Historical Term	Type or Picture (Scriptural Basis for Each)	Life Application for Today's Believer	Biblical Application
Dividing the Inheritance of the Promised Land Num.26:53-56	*The division of the inheritance is a picture of the believer's assurance of the promised land.* **"Unto these the land shall be divided for an inheritance according to the number of names" (Num.26:53).**	The believer can rest assured: he will receive his inheritance in the promised land of heaven. This glorious fact has been settled by God once and for all: the person who truly believes and follows God will live eternally with God. He will enter the promised land of heaven and serve God forever and ever. This is the assurance, the confidence that God gives the genuine believer.	***"For God so loved the world, that he gave his only begotten Son, that whosoever e in him should not perish, but have everlasting life" (Jn.3:16).*** ***"And I give unto them eternal life; and they shall never perish, neither shall any man pluck them out of my hand" (Jn.10:28).*** ***"And now, brethren, I commend you to God, and to the word of his grace, which is able to build you up, and to give you an inheritance among all them which are sanctified" (Acts 20:32).*** ***"But now being made free from sin, and become servants to God, ye have your fruit unto holiness, and the end everlasting life" (Ro.6:22).***

Historical Term	Type or Picture (Scriptural Basis for Each)	Life Application for Today's Believer	Biblical Application
"The LORD Spoke" Num.26:1	*This is a picture of God's Word guiding His people—the believers, all generations—as they prepare to march into the promised land.* **"And it came to pass after the plague, that the LORD spake unto Moses and unto Eleazar the son of Aaron the priest, saying" (Num.26:1).**	God guides His people through His Holy Word. "God has spoken" in His precious Word. It is in the Holy Scriptures that we are guided throughout life. In the Holy Scriptures we find out... • how to live and how not to live • where to go and where not to go • what to do and what not to do • how to speak and how not to speak • how to approach God and how not to approach God • how to worship God and how not to worship God "God has spoken" to us through the Holy Scriptures. God has given us the Holy Scriptures to guide us throughout life. It is His Word that tells us how to prepare and how to enter the promised land of heaven.	***"All scripture is given by inspiration of God, and is profitable for doctrine, for reproof, for correction, for instruction in righteousness" (2 Tim.3:16).*** ***"Study to show thyself approved unto God, a workman that needeth not to be ashamed, rightly dividing the word of truth" (2 Tim.2:15).*** ***"But he answered and said, It is written, Man shall not live by bread alone, but by every word that proceedeth out of the mouth of God" (Mt.4:4).*** ***"Heaven and earth shall pass away, but my words shall not pass away" (Mt.24:35).*** ***"Now ye are clean through the word which I have spoken unto you" (Jn.15:3).*** ***"But these are written, that ye might believe that Jesus is the Christ, the Son of God; and that believing ye might have life through his name" (Jn.20:31).*** ***"For whatsoever things were written aforetime were written for our learning, that we through patience and comfort of the scriptures might have hope" (Ro.15:4).*** ***"Now all these things happened unto them for ensamples: and they are written for our admonition, upon whom the ends of the world are come" (1 Cor.10:11).*** ***"For the word of God is quick, and powerful, and sharper than any twoedged sword, piercing even to the dividing asunder of soul and spirit, and of the joints and marrow, and is a discerner of the thoughts and intents of the heart" (Heb.4:12).*** ***"But the word of the Lord endureth for ever. And this is the word which by the gospel is preached unto you" (1 Pt.1:25).***

B. The Basic Law that Gave Women an Inheritance in the Promised Land: Five Women of Enormous Courage, Faith, & Hope, 27:1-11

1. The godly heritage & the names of the women
- a. Their heritage: Belonged to the tribe of Manasseh, son of Joseph (one of the most godly persons in Scripture, Gen.39:1f)
- b. Their names

2. The courage of the women
- a. They approached the Tabernacle
- b. They approached the highest legal body of the nation, Israel's supreme court

3. The concern, the great faith, & the hope of the women
- a. Their father had died with no sons: Died believing in the promised land, not in Korah's rebellion against God's promises
- b. Their faith in the promised land
  - 1) Wanted their father's name—the testimony of his faith—preserved
  - 2) Requested his inheritance

4. The case was taken to the LORD by Moses: A picture of seeking God for help in solving problems
- a. He granted the request:
  - Gave them their father's inheritance
  - Honored the faith & hope of the women in the promised land
- b. He established the case as a legal precedent for other cases
  - If a man had no son, his inheritance went to his daughter
  - If he had no daughter, it went to his brothers
  - If he had no brothers, it went to his father's brothers
  - If his father had no brothers, it went to the nearest relative in his clan
  - The point: To keep the inheritance as close as possible to the family line

Then came the daughters of
Zelophehad, the son of
Hepher, the son of Gilead,
the son of Machir, the son of
Manasseh, of the families of
Manasseh the son of Joseph:
and these are the names of
his daughters; Mahlah,
Noah, and Hoglah, and
Milcah, and Tirzah.
2 And they stood before
Moses, and before Eleazar
the priest, and before the
princes and all the congregation, by the door of the tabernacle of the congregation,
saying,
3 Our father died in the
wilderness, and he was not in
the company of them that
gathered themselves together
against the LORD in the company of Korah; but died in
his own sin, and had no sons.
4 Why should the name of
our father be done away
from among his family,
because he hath no son?
Give unto us therefore a possession among the brethren
of our father.
5 And Moses brought their
cause before the LORD.
6 And the LORD spake unto
Moses, saying,
7 The daughters of Zelophehad speak right: thou shalt
surely give them a possession of an inheritance among
their father's brethren; and
thou shalt cause the inheritance of their father to pass
unto them.
8 And thou shalt speak unto
the children of Israel, saying,
If a man die, and have no
son, then ye shall cause his
inheritance to pass unto his
daughter.
9 And if he have no daughter, then ye shall give his
inheritance unto his brethren.
10 And if he have no
brethren, then ye shall give
his inheritance unto his
father's brethren.
11 And if his father have no
brethren, then ye shall give
his inheritance unto his kinsman that is next to him of his
family, and he shall possess
it: and it shall be unto the
children of Israel a statute of
judgment, as the LORD commanded Moses.

DIVISION I

THE PREPARATION FOR THE MARCH INTO THE PROMISED LAND, 26:1-36:13

B. The Basic Law that Gave Women an Inheritance in the Promised Land: Five Women of Enormous Courage, Faith, and Hope, 27:1-11

(27:1-11) **Introduction—Rights Equal—Non-Discrimination, Need for—Impartiality, Need for—Prejudice, Trait of Nations—Unbiased, Need for Being—Treatment, Fair, Need for**: throughout history, the rights of minorities have been neglected, ignored, and abused. Even in the twentieth century, most nations and communities still do not give equal rights to minorities. Mistreatment of people still takes place, the abuse of different races, nationalities, religions, and positions. The handicapped or physically deformed are seldom given equal rights within any society. Sometimes unequal rights are deliberately fostered by communities and nations; at other times equal rights are deprived out of ignorance—people simply are not aware that a person is not experiencing equal rights. But there is one person who is aware of mistreatment and abuse: God. Concern for the mistreated is the beat of God's heart. God cares for the helpless and the needy, for the abused and unprotected, for the underprivileged and the people who do not have adequate provision. God cares for every need we have, for the lack of any provision in our lives. This is the subject that is now to be studied: *The Basic Law that Gave Women an Inheritance in the Promised Land: Five Women of Enormous Courage, Faith, and Hope,* 27:1-11.

1. The godly heritage & the names of the women (v.1).
2. The courage of the women (v.2).
3. The concern, the great faith, and the hope of the women (v.3-4).
4. The case was taken to the Lord by Moses: a picture of seeking God for help in solving problems (v.5-11).

1 (27:1) **Heritage, Godly, Importance of—Parents, Godly, Importance of**: there was the godly heritage and the names of the women. They belonged to the tribe of Manasseh who was one of the two sons of Joseph. Remember: one of the most godly persons in Scripture was Joseph (Gen.39:1f). His godly and moral character soared to the highest degree imaginable, just as an eagle soars above the clouds of the earth. Because of his godly character, his son Manasseh lived a godly life; and because Manasseh lived a godly life, his grandson Makir lived a godly life. Because Makir lived a godly life, his son Gilead lived a godly life; and because Gilead lived a godly life, his son Hepher lived a godly life. And because Hepher lived a godly life, Zelophehad lived a godly life. As Zelophehad was the father of these five godly daughter, the godly heritage was carried through the entire line of Manasseh, who had a godly father, Joseph himself. This is the first fact to note about these five women of enormous courage, faith, and hope: they had a godly heritage.

OUTLINE	SCRIPTURE
1. The godly heritage & the names of the women a. Their heritage: Belonged to the tribe of Manasseh, son of Joseph (one of the most godly persons in Scripture, Gen.39:1f) b. Their names	Then came the daughters of Zelophehad, the son of Hepher, the son of Gilead, the son of Machir, the son of Manasseh, of the families of Manasseh the son of Joseph: and these are the names of his daughters; Mahlah, Noah, and Hoglah, and Milcah, and Tirzah.

1. The need for a godly heritage cannot be over-emphasized. Parents need to live godly lives before their children. Children need parents...

- who believe and trust the LORD
- who will love them, nurture and nourish them
- who will take care of them and look after them.
- who will teach and instruct them in the ways of the LORD
- who will encourage them and see that they receive an education
- who will discipline and correct them when they are wrong

Parents need to live holy, pure, and righteous lives for the sake of their children, yes. But this is not all. Society desperately needs the example of a godly heritage. The cry of society is for godly parents, parents who will leave a godly heritage to the world. Lawlessness, violence, immorality, abuse, greed—all the evils of society—will be corrected only through the example of godly parents. A godly heritage cannot be over-emphasized.

> **"And now, brethren, I commend you to God, and to the word of his grace, which is able to build you up, and to give you an inheritance among all them which are sanctified" (Acts 20:32).**
> **"And, ye fathers, provoke not your children to wrath: but bring them up in the nurture and admonition of the Lord" (Eph.6:4).**
> **"When I call to remembrance the unfeigned faith that is in thee, which dwelt first in thy grandmother Lois, and thy mother Eunice; and I am persuaded that in thee also" (2 Tim.1:5).**
> **"And that from a child thou hast known the holy scriptures, which are able to make thee wise unto salvation through faith which is in Christ Jesus" (2 Tim.3:15).**
> **"That they may teach the young women to be sober, to love their husbands, to love their children" (Tit.2:4).**
> **"And thou shalt teach them diligently unto thy children, and shalt talk of them when thou sittest in thine house, and when thou walkest by the way, and when thou liest down, and when thou risest up" (Dt.6:7).**
> **"For thou, O God, hast heard my vows: thou hast given me the heritage of those that fear thy name" (Ps.61:5).**
> **"Train up a child in the way he should go: and when he is old, he will not depart from it" (Pr.22:6).**

2 (27:2) **Courage, Example of—Women, Courage of**: there was the unusual courage of the women. First, their remarkable courage is seen in two facts. First, they approached the Tabernacle, the very place that symbolized God's holy presence. As they approached, they obviously had complete confidence that they were not displeasing God at all. They were well aware that God's holiness struck out and consumed any who violated God's presence, who approached God with hypocritical motives. Obviously, within their hearts, they had prayed and entrusted their case into the hands of God. Second, they approached the highest legal body of the nation, Israel's supreme court. There they stood before Moses himself, Eleazar the priest, and all the other leaders of the whole nation. What enormous courage!

OUTLINE	SCRIPTURE
2. The courage of the women a. They approached the Tabernacle b. They approached the highest legal body of the nation, Israel's supreme court	2 And they stood before Moses, and before Eleazar the priest, and before the princes and all the congregation, by the door of the tabernacle of the congregation, saying,

Thought 1. These dear women—all sisters—stand as a dynamic example of courage for all believers of all generations. They felt that an injustice was being done, not only to them, but to so many other of the women throughout the nation. The injustice will be seen in the next point. For now, the point to see is their courage—their great courage.

Just as these women stood up against injustice, so we must stand up against injustice, so we must stand up and be courageous. We need courage to stand against the injustices, lawlessness, violence, immorality, and sins of society. Courageous people—people who will stand staunchly, with hearts filled with courage—are desperately needed. Fearlessness is needed to combat the evils of this world. Brave, bold, valiant people are needed, people with courage, people who are lionhearted.

"Watch ye, stand fast in the faith, quit you like men, be strong" (1 Cor.16:13).

"Finally, my brethren, be strong in the Lord, and in the power of his might" (Eph.6:10).

"Wherefore take unto you the whole armour of God, that ye may be able to withstand in the evil day, and having done all, to stand" (Eph.6:13).

"Only let your conversation [behavior] be as it becometh the gospel of Christ: that whether I come and see you, or else be absent, I may hear of your affairs, that ye stand fast in one spirit, with one mind striving together for the faith of the gospel; And in nothing terrified by your adversaries: which is to them an evident token of perdition, but to you of salvation, and that of God" (Ph.1:27-28).

"For God hath not given us the spirit of fear; but of power, and of love, and of a sound mind. Be not thou therefore ashamed of the testimony of our Lord, nor of me his prisoner: but be thou partaker of the afflictions of the gospel according to the power of God" (2 Tim.1:7-8).

"Thou therefore, my son, be strong in the grace that is in Christ Jesus" (2 Tim.2:1).

"Thou therefore endure hardness, as a good soldier of Jesus Christ" (2 Tim.2:3).

"Let us therefore come boldly unto the throne of grace, that we may obtain mercy, and find grace to help in time of need" (Heb.4:16).

"Be strong and of a good courage, fear not, nor be afraid of them: for the Lord thy God, he it is that doth go with thee; he will not fail thee, nor forsake thee" (Dt.31:6).

"When thou liest down, thou shalt not be afraid: yea, thou shalt lie down, and thy sleep shall be sweet" (Pr.3:24).

"The Lord is my light and my salvation; whom shall I fear? the Lord is the strength of my life; of whom shall I be afraid? When the wicked, even mine enemies and my foes, came upon me to eat up my flesh, they stumbled and fell. Though an host should encamp against me, my heart shall not fear: though war should rise against me, in this will I be confident" (Ps.27:1-3).

"I will say of the Lord, He is my refuge and my fortress: my God; in him will I trust. Surely he shall deliver thee from the snare of the fowler, and from the noisome pestilence. He shall cover thee with his feathers, and under his wings shalt thou trust: his truth shall be thy shield and buckler. Thou shalt not be afraid for the terror by night; nor for the arrow that flieth by day; Nor for the pestilence that walketh in darkness; nor for the destruction that wasteth at noonday" (Ps.91:2-6).

"The Lord is on my side; I will not fear: what can man do unto me" (Ps.118:6).

"Behold, God is my salvation; I will trust, and not be afraid: for the Lord Jehovah is my strength and my song; he also is become my salvation" (Is.12:2).

3 (27:3-4) **Faith, Great—Hope, Great—Land, the Promised, Faith in—Faith, in the Promised Land**: there was the concern, the great faith, and the hope of the women. In the ancient world, a father's property was divided among his sons. The oldest son received twice as much as the younger sons (Dt.21:15-17; see DEEPER STUDY # 1, **Birthright**—Gen.25:31 for more discussion). Daughters did not receive property. Rather, when they were married, they received a dowry or a wedding present from their father. Of course, what they received depended upon the wealth of the father. Wealthy fathers were known to give large dowries such as expensive clothing, jewelry, perfumes, money, furniture, slave-help, and sometimes even houses and entire cities (Gen.29:24, 29; Judg.1:13-15; 1 Ki.9:16). Once the daughter had married, the father had no more responsibility for her, and she received no inheritance of land or property upon his death. By law she became a full-fledged member of the family into which she married.[1] This was the deep concern that had gripped the hearts of these five dear sisters. The Scripture and outline state in very simple terms the injustice they were feeling, no doubt an injustice that existed with other women throughout the nation.

OUTLINE	SCRIPTURE
3. The concern, the great faith, & the hope of the women a. Their father had died with no sons: Died believing in the promised land, not in Korah's rebellion against God's promises	3 Our father died in the wilderness, and he was not in the company of them that gathered themselves together against the LORD in the company of Korah; but died in his own sin, and had no sons.
b. Their faith in the promised land 1) Wanted their father's name—the testimony of his faith—preserved 2) Requested his inheritance	4 Why should the name of our father be done away from among his family, because he hath no son? Give unto us therefore a possession among the brethren of our father.

1 Gordon J. Wenham. *The Book of Numbers,* p.192.

1. The father of these dear sisters had died with no sons, leaving only them as the surviving members of the family. Note that he had died believing in the promised land, not in Korah's rebellion that sought to replace Moses and to lead the Israelites back to Egypt. Their father had been a true believer in God's promises: he had not been a seeker after the pleasures of Egypt nor of this world. (See outline and notes—Num.16:1-50 for more discussion.)

2. Their faith in the promised land was strong. No doubt their testimony touched the hearts of the judges who sat on the supreme court hearing their case. Note what they wanted: their father's name—the testimony of his faith—preserved. Therefore, they were requesting his inheritance (v.4). Note what they asked the supreme court: Why should the name of their father disappear from history, lose its identity—just because he had no sons? The point to see is the great faith and hope of the women in the promised land. Keep in mind that Israel had not yet entered the promised land, yet these dear women had faith in God. They knew that God was going to lead the Israelites into the promised land and give them their inheritance. Entering and inheriting the promised land was not a question to them. They knew that God was going to fulfill His promise. They were women of deep conviction, faith, and hope in the great inheritance promised by God. Their faith was strong, so strong that they did something that had never been done in the history of the world. They appeared before the supreme court of the land to change one of the most basic and ancient laws in all of history, a history that had been dominated by men. That law was the law of inheritance or of the birthright, a law that gave the inheritance of land *only* to the sons of a family. But these dear women believed God's promise, believed in the promised land so much that they were willing to risk everything in order to secure their inheritance. They wanted the godly heritage and inheritance of their family's name to be carried on through succeeding generations. They wanted their inheritance in the promised land of God.

Thought 1. The only person who will ever enter the promised land of heaven will be the person who follows in the steps of these five dear sisters. Murderers will never enter the promised land of heaven. Neither will the violent, the lawless, the abuser, the drunk, the drug addict, the greedy, the immoral, the hater, the liar, the thief, nor the person who uses profanity and takes God's name in vain—no person who walks or lives in sin will ever enter the promised land of God. As stated, the only person who will ever enter heaven is the person who follows in the steps of these five dear sisters. They believed with all their hearts in God and in the promised land. Their faith in the inheritance promised by God was strong, very strong. Our faith in God and the promised land of heaven must be strong. God promises us an inheritance in the new heavens and earth. By faith, we must lay hold of our inheritance, lay hold of the promised land of heaven.

"But lay up for yourselves treasures in heaven, where neither moth nor rust doth corrupt, and where thieves do not break through nor steal" (Mt.6:20).

"Let not your heart be troubled: ye believe in God, believe also in me. In my Father's house are many mansions: if it were not so, I would have told you. I go to prepare a place for you. And if I go and prepare a place for you, I will come again, and receive you unto myself; that where I am, there ye may be also" (Jn.14:1-3).

"For we know that if our earthly house of this tabernacle were dissolved, we have a building of God, an house not made with hands, eternal in the heavens" (2 Cor.5:1).

"For our conversation [behavior, conduct] is in heaven; from whence also we look for the Saviour, the Lord Jesus Christ: Who shall change our vile body, that it may be fashioned like unto his glorious body, according to the working whereby he is able even to subdue all things unto himself" (Ph.3:20-21).

"By faith Abraham, when he was called to go out into a place which he should after receive for an inheritance, obeyed; and he went out, not knowing whither he went. By faith he sojourned in the land of promise, as in a strange country, dwelling in tabernacles with Isaac and Jacob, the heirs with him of the same promise: For he looked for a city which hath foundations, whose builder and maker is God" (Heb.11:8-10).

"These all [believers] died in faith, not having received the promises, but having seen them afar off, and were persuaded of them, and embraced them, and confessed that they were strangers and pilgrims on the earth. For they that say such things declare plainly that they seek a country. And truly, if they had been mindful of that country from whence they came out, they might have had opportunity to have returned. But now they desire a better country, that is, an heavenly: wherefore God is not ashamed to be called their God: for he hath prepared for them a city" (Heb.11:13-16).

"Blessed be the God and Father of our Lord Jesus Christ, which according to his abundant mercy hath begotten us again unto a lively hope by the resurrection of Jesus Christ from the dead, To an inheritance incorruptible, and undefiled, and that fadeth not away, reserved in heaven for you" (1 Pt.1:3-4).

"But the day of the Lord will come as a thief in the night; in the which the heavens shall pass away with a great noise, and the elements shall melt with fervent heat, the earth also and the works that are therein shall be burned up. Seeing then that all these things shall be dissolved, what manner of persons ought ye to be in all holy conversation and godliness, Looking for and hasting unto the coming of the day of God, wherein the heavens being on fire shall be dissolved, and the elements shall melt with fervent heat? Nevertheless we, according to his promise, look for new heavens and a new earth, wherein dwelleth righteousness" (2 Pt.3:10-13).

"And there shall in no wise enter into it [heaven] any thing that defileth, neither whatsoever worketh abomination, or maketh a lie: but they which are written in the Lamb's book of life" (Rev.21:27).

4 (27:5-11) **Seeking, of God—God, Seeking for—Problems, Seeking Answer to—Prayer, Seeking Answers to**: the case was taken to the LORD by Moses. This is a picture of seeking God for help in solving problems. Keep in mind the earth-shattering case of these dear women, a request to change a law that was commonly known and had been practiced by all civilizations down through human history. At the very least, the judges sitting on the supreme court of the nation were bound to be surprised if not shocked by the request of the women. Most rulers and courts of that day would have reacted against such a request. But note the spiritual sensitivity of God's servant Moses. Obviously, he sensed the deep faith and sincerity of these dear women. Therefore he did not react but, rather, responded. He took their case before the LORD. The Scripture and outline demonstrate a wonderful fact: the love and grace of God are as open to women as they are to men. With God there is no partiality or favoritism, no discrimination whatsoever. There are no minorities: not women or men, not black, red, yellow, or white. There is no race or nationality or sex that stands as a favorite with God. There is no discrimination with God whatsoever. This is the clear teaching of Scripture:

OUTLINE	SCRIPTURE	SCRIPTURE	OUTLINE
4. The case was taken to the LORD by Moses: A picture of seeking God for help in solving problems a. He granted the request: • Gave them their father's inheritance • Honored the faith & hope of the women in the promised land b. He established the case as a legal precedent for other cases • If a man had no son, his inheritance went to his daughter	5 And Moses brought their cause before the LORD. 6 And the LORD spake unto Moses, saying, 7 The daughters of Zelophehad speak right: thou shalt surely give them a possession of an inheritance among their father's brethren; and thou shalt cause the inheritance of their father to pass unto them. 8 And thou shalt speak unto the children of Israel, saying, If a man die, and have no son, then ye shall cause his inheritance to pass unto his daughter.	9 And if he have no daughter, then ye shall give his inheritance unto his brethren. 10 And if he have no brethren, then ye shall give his inheritance unto his father's brethren. 11 And if his father have no brethren, then ye shall give his inheritance unto his kinsman that is next to him of his family, and he shall possess it: and it shall be unto the children of Israel a statute of judgment, as the LORD commanded Moses.	• If he had no daughter, it went to his brothers • If he had no brothers, it went to his father's brothers • If his father had no brothers, it went to the nearest relative in his clan • The point: To keep the inheritance as close as possible to the family line

1. Note that God granted the request of these dear sisters (v.6-7). He gave them their father's inheritance, honored their faith and hope in the promised land.

2. God established the case as a legal precedent for other cases (v.8-11). Simply stated, if a man had no son, his inheritance went to his daughter(s) (v.8). If he had no daughter, then the land passed to his nearest male relative (v.9-11). The point of the law was to keep the inheritance as close as possible to the family line.

Thought 1. This was an earth-shattering case, a case that created a serious problem for Moses. In seeking God, Moses sets a dynamic example for us. When problems confront us, we should seek the face of the LORD. The LORD will help us if only we will seek Him. Too often we attempt to handle problems and circumstances alone, in our own strength. In so doing, we often dig ditches so deep that it is difficult to claw our way out of them. We merely create more and more problems for ourselves. The answer to problems is the Divine Helper, God Himself. God wants to help us. But He wants us first to seek Him, to draw near Him, to fellowship and commune with Him. This was the very purpose for which He created us; therefore, we must first seek Him. When we seek Him, He steps in and helps us conquer the problems of this life. Seeking the LORD is the answer to a victorious life. We triumph over the pitfalls of this life, over the problems and circumstances of this life when we seek the face of the LORD God Himself.

"For every one that asketh receiveth; and he that seeketh findeth; and to him that knocketh it shall be opened" (Lk.11:10).

"Hitherto have ye asked nothing in my name: ask, and ye shall receive, that your joy may be full" (Jn.16:24).

"Be careful for nothing; but in every thing by prayer and supplication with thanksgiving let your requests be made known unto God. And the peace of God, which passeth all understanding, shall keep your hearts and minds through Christ Jesus" (Ph.4:6-7).

"Continue in prayer, and watch in the same with thanksgiving; Withal praying also for us, that God would open unto us a door of utterance, to speak the mystery of Christ, for which I am also in bonds" (Col.4:2-3).

"Is any among you afflicted? let him pray. Is any merry? let him sing psalms. Is any sick among you? let him call for the elders of the church; and let them pray over him, anointing him with oil in the name of the Lord" (Jas.5:13-14).

"But if from thence thou shalt seek the Lord thy God, thou shalt find him, if thou seek him with all thy heart and with all thy soul" (Dt.4:29).

"Seek the Lord and his strength, seek his face continually" (1 Chron.16:11).

"He shall call upon me, and I will answer him: I will be with him in trouble; I will deliver him, and honour him" (Ps.91:15).

"Seek the Lord, and his strength: seek his face evermore" (Ps.105:4).

"Seek ye the Lord while he may be found, call ye upon him while he is near" (Is.55:6).

"Then shalt thou call, and the Lord shall answer; thou shalt cry, and he shall say, Here I am. If thou take away from the midst of thee the yoke, the putting forth of the finger, and speaking vanity" (Is.58:9).

"And it shall come to pass, that before they call, I will answer; and while they are yet speaking, I will hear" (Is.65:24).

"And ye shall seek me, and find me, when ye shall search for me with all your heart" (Jer.29:13).

"For thus saith the Lord unto the house of Israel, Seek ye me, and ye shall live" (Amos 5:4).

"Seek ye the Lord, all ye meek of the earth, which have wrought his judgment; seek righteousness, seek meekness: it may be ye shall be hid in the day of the Lord's anger" (Zeph.2:3).

C. The Appointment of Joshua as the Successor to Moses: A Strong Picture of God Preparing the Believer for Death, 27:12-23

1. God told Moses to prepare for death: A picture of God preparing the believer for death
   a. God granted Moses a glimpse of the promised land
   b. God assured Moses that he "will be gathered to his people": Live with them eternally in the promised land of heaven

2. God reminded Moses why he could not enter the promised land: A picture of the holiness & justice of God against sin
   a. Moses had disobeyed God
   b. Moses had failed to honor God & failed to demonstrate His holiness
   c. Moses responded with broken humility & deep concern
      1) Accepted the judgment
      2) Prayed for the Sovereign LORD to appoint a successor
         • To lead the people
         • To be a shepherd to them—to keep them from being like sheep with no shepherd

12 And the LORD said unto Moses, Get thee up into this mount Abarim, and see the land which I have given unto the children of Israel.

13 And when thou hast seen it, thou also shalt be gathered unto thy people, as Aaron thy brother was gathered.

14 For ye rebelled against my commandment in the desert of Zin, in the strife of the congregation, to sanctify me at the water before their eyes: that is the water of Meribah in Kadesh in the wilderness of Zin.

15 And Moses spake unto the LORD, saying,

16 Let the LORD, the God of the spirits of all flesh, set a man over the congregation,

17 Which may go out before them, and which may go in before them, and which may lead them out, and which may bring them in; that the congregation of the LORD be not as sheep which have no shepherd.

18 And the LORD said unto Moses, Take thee Joshua the son of Nun, a man in whom is the spirit, and lay thine hand upon him;

19 And set him before Eleazar the priest, and before all the congregation; and give him a charge in their sight.

20 And thou shalt put some of thine honour upon him, that all the congregation of the children of Israel may be obedient.

21 And he shall stand before Eleazar the priest, who shall ask counsel for him after the judgment of Urim before the LORD: at his word shall they go out, and at his word they shall come in, both he, and all the children of Israel with him, even all the congregation.

22 And Moses did as the LORD commanded him: and he took Joshua, and set him before Eleazar the priest, and before all the congregation:

23 And he laid his hands upon him, and gave him a charge, as the LORD commanded by the hand of Moses.

3. God instructed Moses to appoint Joshua: A picture of God providing a leader for His people
   a. To know God's Spirit is in Joshua
   b. To identify him as the new leader
   c. To commission him in the presence of everyone: Standing before the High Priest & the entire assembly
   d. To assign some day-to-day authority to him: Gradually transferring authority so the people would follow him
   e. To have him approach God for major decisions through the High Priest: The High Priest was to seek God's will through the Urim (sacred lots)
   f. To have him take over immediate command of the marching divisions
   g. The obedience of Moses
      1) He had Joshua stand before the High Priest, Eleazar, & the entire assembly
      2) He laid his hands on him: Identified him as the new leader
      3) He commissioned him

DIVISION IV

THE PREPARATION FOR THE MARCH INTO THE PROMISED LAND, 26:1-36:13

C. The Appointment of Joshua as the Successor to Moses: A Strong Picture of God Preparing the Believer for Death, 27:12-23

(27:12-23) **Introduction—Death, Experience of—Death, Hope of—Death, of Moses**: death is inevitable. Every person dies—some sooner some later, but the grim hand of death eventually comes. Scripture declares that death is a horrifying experience for any person who has not followed Jesus Christ. But Scripture also declares that death is a glorious experience for the believer, for the person who has truly followed Christ. This glorious experience is seen in the life of Moses. It was time for Moses to leave this earth and go to live with God eternally. God was ready to welcome him and give him a triumphant entrance into the kingdom of heaven. But before God could take him home, a successor had to be appointed to lead God's people into the promised land. This is the subject of this great passage of Scripture: *The Appointment of Joshua as the Successor to Moses: A Strong Picture of God's Grace, Holiness, and Sovereignty,* 27:12-23.

1. God told Moses to prepare for death: a picture of God preparing the believer for death (v.12-13).
2. God reminded Moses why he could not enter the promised land: a picture of the holiness and justice of God against sin (v.14-17).
3. God instructed Moses to appoint Joshua: a picture of God providing a leader for His people (v.18-23).

1 (27:12-13) **Death, of Moses—Death, Preparation for—Grace, of God—Love, of God—Death, of Believer, Preparation for**: God told Moses to prepare for death. This was a strong picture of God preparing the believer for death. Moses was an old man now, almost one hundred and twenty years old. This dear servant of God had served the people for almost forty years, serving them faithfully and well. He had persevered to the end, and now it was about time for him to leave this earth and go home to God. Moses had committed a terrible sin at Kadesh, a sin so terrible that he was disallowed or barred from entering the promised land. This will be seen in point two below. For now, the point to see is God's preparation of Moses for death. Because of his sin, Moses was heartsick, broken-hearted. His heart was heavy, feeling deep pain, hurt, and regret. He was crushed, disappointed, sorrowful, humbled, and subdued. He was a bruised man, hurt and shamed, marked for life by his sin. His sin never left him: it was always before his face and upon his mind. This dear servant had been so faithful through the forty years in leading God's people through the desert wilderness, through some of the most difficult problems and hardships imaginable. By the grace and appointment of God he had taken over two million slaves and led them to freedom. He had molded them into a very distinctive nation of people who were set apart to be the followers of the only living and true God. But there came a day when he failed to control the passions of his flesh, committing a terrible sin before God and the people. Because of his sin, he had forfeited his right to enter the promised land. He was not allowed to lead the people to their spiritual rest, not allowed to lead them through the victorious conquest of their enemies. He would live eternally with God, but his ultimate reward was affected. He had lost the privilege of seeing his dear people receive their inheritance in the promised land, lost the privilege of seeing them enter their spiritual rest. This crushing blow never left Moses: it marked him every day for the rest of his life. As he walked through each day, he felt the pain, hurt, and regret with a heart that was broken, a heart that sensed his failure ever so deeply.

God knew the feelings of Moses, knew exactly how he felt. God's heart went out to His dear servant, a servant who had been so faithful to his call except in this one instance. Therefore when it was time for God to take Moses home, God wanted to make his death a very special occasion, a precious time of communion and intimacy between Him and His dear servant. God determined to do a very special thing for Moses: to give him a glimpse of the promised land.

OUTLINE	SCRIPTURE
1. God told Moses to prepare for death: A picture of God preparing the believer for death a. God granted Moses a glimpse of the promised land b. God assured Moses that he "will be gathered to his people": Live with them eternally in the promised land of heaven	12 And the LORD said unto Moses, Get thee up into this mount Abarim, and see the land which I have given unto the children of Israel. 13 And when thou hast seen it, thou also shalt be gathered unto thy people, as Aaron thy brother was gathered.

1. In mercy, God granted Moses a glimpse of the promised land (v.12). Note that God told Moses to climb to the top of a particular mountain and survey the land which He was giving to the Israelites. Despite the terrible sin of Moses, God poured out His mercy and goodness upon Moses. God showed him great love and compassion. This dear servant was about ready to go home to heaven, and God wanted to be there for him. But before God took His dear servant home, God wanted to reassure and encourage him: his faith in the promised land was a living reality. God gave him a glimpse of the land. Just imagine the assurance that flowed through Moses' heart as he stood on top of the mountain, stood there surveying the promised land lying out before him. Tears, perhaps even a brokenness, poured out from his soul—for there lay before him the inheritance of the promised land given by God to His dear people. Most likely, Moses fell to his knees with a heart filled with mixed emotions: yes, sorrow and regret for his sin that was keeping him from leading the dear people of God into the land. But he also felt joy and rejoicing at the promise of God that was soon becoming a living reality in their hearts and lives. Other Scriptures tell us that Moses begged God to let him cross over the Jordan and survey the promised land before God took him home. But God said, "No." Moses had sinned; therefore the justice and judgment of God had to be executed. His dear servant could not enter the promised land.

2. However, God assured Moses that he would "be gathered to his people." This means that Moses would join all the believers who had gone before him and live with them eternally in the promised land of heaven, face to face with God. God was preparing His dear servant for the moment of death, the moment when He would transfer him from this earth into heaven. In that moment, God wanted to be there for His dear servant. God's heart went out to him and embraced him with feelings of warmth, tenderness, and gentleness. God reached out to prepare His dear servant for the fast-approaching day of his death, reached out to comfort and console him, to give him perfect assurance and confidence.

Thought 1. The death of a believer is a warm, tender, gentle, and touching experience. This is because of Jesus Christ and His death upon the cross. Christ died for us. Because He died for us, we are to live forever, never dying. When we come to that moment that is commonly called "death"—quicker than the eye can blink—God transfers us from this world into His presence. We never taste or experience death. In one moment of time we are on this earth; in the next moment of time we are face to face with God in heaven. In one moment we are in this world, in the physical dimension of being; in the next moment of time we are in the spiritual world, in the spiritual dimension of being. Just as God prepared Moses for heaven, giving him perfect assurance and confidence, so God prepares us. When that moment comes, God will infuse within our beings the greatest assurance and confidence imaginable, yea, perfect assurance and confidence. We will live forever face to face with God in heaven.

"And I give unto them eternal life; and they shall never perish, neither shall any man pluck them out of my hand" (Jn.10:28).

"Let not your heart be troubled: ye believe in God, believe also in me. In my Father's house are many mansions: if it were not so, I would have told you. I go to prepare a place for you. And if I go and prepare a place for you, I will come again, and receive you unto myself; that where I am, there ye may be also" (Jn.14:1-3).

"To them who by patient continuance in well doing seek for glory and honour and immortality, eternal life" (Ro.2:7).

"For none of us liveth to himself, and no man dieth to himself. For whether we live, we live unto the Lord; and whether we die, we die unto the Lord: whether we live therefore, or die, we are the Lord's. For to this end Christ both died, and rose, and revived, that he might be Lord both of the dead and living" (Ro.14:7-9).

"For we know that if our earthly house of this tabernacle were dissolved, we have a building of God, an house not made with hands, eternal in the heavens" (2 Cor.5:1).

"We are confident, I say, and willing rather to be absent from the body, and to be present with the Lord" (2 Cor.5:8).

"For to me to live is Christ, and to die is gain" (Ph.1:21).

"For I am in a strait betwixt two, having a desire to depart, and to be with Christ; which is far better" (Ph.1:23).

"For our conversation [citizenship] is in heaven; from whence also we look for the Saviour, the Lord Jesus Christ: Who shall change our vile body, that it may be fashioned like unto his glorious body, according to the working whereby he is able even to subdue all things unto himself" (Ph.3:20-21).

"In hope of eternal life, which God, that cannot lie, promised before the world began" (Tit.1:2).

"These [believers] all died in faith, not having received the promises, but having seen them afar off, and were persuaded of them, and embraced them, and confessed that they were strangers and pilgrims on the earth. For they that say such things declare plainly that they seek a country" (Heb.11:13-14).

"Blessed be the God and Father of our Lord Jesus Christ, which according to his abundant mercy hath begotten us again unto a lively hope by the resurrection of Jesus Christ from the dead, To an inheritance incorruptible, and undefiled, and that fadeth not away, reserved in heaven for you" (1 Pt.1:3-4).

"And this is the promise that he hath promised us, even eternal life" (1 Jn.2:25).

"And I heard a voice from heaven saying unto me, Write, Blessed are the dead which die in the Lord from henceforth: Yea, saith the Spirit, that they may rest from their labours; and their works do follow them" (Rev.14:13).

"And I saw an angel come down from heaven, having the key of the bottomless pit and a great chain in his hand. And I saw thrones, and they sat upon them, and judgment was given unto them: and I saw the souls of them that were beheaded for the witness of Jesus, and for the word of God, and which had not worshipped the beast, neither his image, neither had received his mark upon their foreheads, or in their hands; and they lived and reigned with Christ a thousand years. But the rest of the dead lived not again until the thousand years were finished. This is the first resurrection. Blessed and holy is he that hath part in the first resurrection: on such the second death hath no power, but they shall be priests of God and of Christ, and shall reign with him a thousand years. And when the thousand years are expired, Satan shall be loosed out of his prison" (Rev.20:1, 4-7).

"Let me die the death of the righteous, and let my last end be like his" (Num.23:10).

"Yea, though I walk through the valley of the shadow of death, I will fear no evil: for thou art with me; thy rod and thy staff they comfort me" (Ps.23:4).

"Precious in the sight of the Lord is the death of his saints" (Ps.116:15).

2 (27:14-17) **Moses, Sin of—Holiness, of God—Justice, of God—Minister, Heart of—Moses, Heart of—Minister, Described as, Shepherd**: God reminded Moses why he could not enter the promised land. This is a strong picture of the holiness and justice of God against sin. Moses and Aaron were both guilty of the sins that are covered in this passage. The Scripture clearly spells out the sins:

OUTLINE	SCRIPTURE	SCRIPTURE	OUTLINE
2. God reminded Moses why he could not enter the promised land: A picture of the holiness & justice of God against sin a. Moses had disobeyed God b. Moses had failed to honor God & failed to demonstrate His holiness c. Moses responded with broken humility & deep concern 1) Accepted the judgment	14 For ye rebelled against my commandment in the desert of Zin, in the strife of the congregation, to sanctify me at the water before their eyes: that is the water of Meribah in Kadesh in the wilderness of Zin. 15 And Moses spake unto the LORD, saying, 16 Let the LORD, the God of	the spirits of all flesh, set a man over the congregation, 17 Which may go out before them, and which may go in before them, and which may lead them out, and which may bring them in; that the congregation of the LORD be not as sheep which have no shepherd.	2) Prayed for the Sovereign LORD to appoint a successor • To lead the people • To be a shepherd to them—to keep them from being like sheep with no shepherd

1. The first sin was disobedience. Moses disobeyed God's command (v.14). Remember, the people needed water. God told Moses to walk over to a particular rock and call for water to gush out. The result would be a wonderful miracle: water would pour out from the rock. Another important command involved the people: Moses was to call the people together so they could be eyewitnesses of the event. They were to know beyond any question that it was God who was meeting their need. God Himself was providing for them. But Moses had disobeyed God. Moses had done the exact opposite of what God had instructed.

2. Moses had failed to honor God and failed to demonstrate His holiness before the people (v.14). Moses had disobeyed God in three ways:

⇒ Moses had spoken to the people in anger instead of addressing the rock as commanded by God. In fact he had lashed out at the people, calling them "rebels."
⇒ Moses had not given God the full credit and honor for providing the water. He took some of the credit himself. In anger, he lashed out at the people, shouting "Must '*we*' bring you water?" By saying "*we,*" Moses was assuming some of the credit himself. This was a serious offense to God, for God will not share His glory with any man.
⇒ Moses struck the rock with his staff instead of speaking to it as God had commanded. In fact, he was so angry that he struck the rock twice.

Note what God then told Moses in this passage: the dear servant had failed to honor God as holy before the eyes of the people (v.14). Moses had failed to acknowledge God as the sole provider for His people. Moses had lost complete control of his emotions, becoming violently angry. He was acting ungodly, unrighteous, and completely out of control before the people. He was doing anything but bringing honor and glory to God. He was demonstrating the very opposite of God's holiness. He had degraded and torn down the image of God in the people's minds, desecrating the holiness of God. Moses had committed the terrible sin of disobedience. This was the reason Moses was disallowed or barred from entering the promised land. The holiness and justice of God against sin had to be executed. The servant of God had gone too far in violating the holiness of God in the eyes of the people. Consequently, he had to be judged, chastised.

3. Moses responded with a broken humility and deep concern for the people of God (v.15-17). Moses accepted the judgment of God and accepted the fact that he was now "to be gathered to his people." The real character and heart of this dear servant of God is clearly seen in what happened next. He immediately began to pray for the Sovereign LORD to appoint a successor. Note how he addressed the LORD: "the LORD, the God of the spirits of all mankind." He was acknowledging that God...

- was the only living and true God
- was the great Creator and Sustainer of all mankind
- was the Giver of all life
- was sovereign over all people
- was the only God who could provide for His people

If Moses was leaving the scene, another leader had to be raised up, another successor had to be appointed. The people would desperately need a leader, a successor to replace Moses. Without a leader, the people would be like sheep with no shepherd. Without a shepherd, they would be wandering about, lost and scattered abroad. God must give a shepherd to continue leading His dear people to the promised land. This was the primary concern that gripped the heart of Moses.

Thought 1. There are two clear lessons for us in this point.

1) God judges sin. His holiness and justice demand that He judge and chastise His people when they sin. This is the clear declaration of Scripture:

"Every branch in me that beareth not fruit he taketh away: and every branch that beareth fruit, he purgeth it, that it may bring forth more fruit" (Jn.15:2).

"For this cause many are weak and sickly among you [believers], and many sleep. For if we would judge ourselves, we should not be judged. But when we are judged, we are chastened of the Lord, that we should not be condemned with the world" (1 Cor.11:30-32).

"And ye have forgotten the exhortation which speaketh unto you as unto children, My son, despise not thou the chastening of the Lord, nor faint when thou art rebuked of him: For whom the Lord loveth he chasteneth, and scourgeth every son whom he receiveth" (Heb.12:5-6).

"As many as I love, I rebuke and chasten: be zealous therefore, and repent" (Rev.3:19).

"Thou shalt also consider in thine heart, that, as a man chasteneth his son, so the Lord thy God chasteneth thee" (Dt.8:5).

"Blessed is the man whom thou chastenest, O Lord, and teachest him out of thy law" (Ps.94:12).

"My son, despise not the chastening of the Lord; neither be weary of his correction: For whom the Lord loveth he correcteth; even as a father the son in whom he delighteth" (Pr.3:11-12).

2) Believers must pray for God to raise up leaders, strong leaders who will serve God's people faithfully. This was the concern of Moses, and it was the concern of the Lord Jesus Christ. In fact, Christ used the very comparison that Moses used in describing the minister as a shepherd. He said that people are as sheep without a shepherd (Mt.9:1, 36-38).

God answers prayer. He moves when His people pray. The challenge of the hour is for leaders, godly leaders. People who are sold out to Jesus Christ and to meeting the needs of people are desperately needed. God will raise up leaders if we pray. The church will have faithful shepherds who will lead and feed the people if we will pray.

"Ask, and it shall be given you; seek, and ye shall find; knock, and it shall be opened unto you" (Mt.7:7).

"But when he saw the multitudes, he was moved with compassion on them, because they fainted, and were scattered abroad, as sheep having no shepherd. Then saith he unto his disciples, The harvest truly is plenteous, but the labourers are few; Pray ye therefore the Lord of the harvest, that he will send forth labourers into his harvest" (Mt.9:36-38).

"And it shall come to pass, that before they call, I will answer; and while they are yet speaking, I will hear" (Is.65:24).

"And I will give you pastors according to mine heart, which shall feed you with knowledge and understanding" (Jer.3:15).

"And I will set up shepherds over them which shall feed them: and they shall fear no more, nor be dismayed, neither shall they be lacking, saith the Lord" (Jer.23:4).

"My sheep wandered through all the mountains, and upon every high hill: yea, my flock was scattered upon all the face of the earth, and none did search or seek after them" (Ezk.34:6).

3 (27:18-23) **Ministers, Appointed by God—Call, of God—Joshua, Appointed by God—Israel, Leaders of—Leaders, Appointment of—Leaders, Example of, Joshua**: God instructed Moses to appoint Joshua as his successor. This is a strong picture of God providing a leader for His people. Remember, Joshua had been the assistant to Moses for many years, probably from his earliest youth (Num.11:28; Ex.17:9f; 24:13; 32:17). Joshua had also been one of the twelve spies who years earlier had spied out the land of Canaan. Along with Caleb, he had stood staunchly against the other ten spies, declaring that Israel could march in and conquer the enemies of the promised land. He had proven to be a strong believer in the great promises of God, a man of strong courage and faith, a leader who soared head and shoulders above other leaders. He was a man after God's own heart. He was, therefore, the choice of God to follow in the footsteps of Moses. He was to be the leader who would take God's dear people into the promised land and give them their inheritance. Remember that Joshua is the Hebrew name *Jesus* in the Greek. He was to be the deliverer of God's people, a type of the coming Deliverer who was to save the whole world, the Lord Jesus Christ Himself. God gave clear instructions to Moses concerning Joshua:

OUTLINE	SCRIPTURE	SCRIPTURE	OUTLINE
3. God instructed Moses to appoint Joshua: A picture of God providing a leader for His people a. To know God's Spirit is in Joshua b. To identify him as the new leader c. To commission him in the presence of everyone: Standing before the High Priest & the entire assembly d. To assign some day-to-day authority to him: Gradually transferring authority so the people would follow him e. To have him approach God for major decisions through the High Priest: The High	18 And the LORD said unto Moses, Take thee Joshua the son of Nun, a man in whom is the spirit, and lay thine hand upon him; 19 And set him before Eleazar the priest, and before all the congregation; and give him a charge in their sight. 20 And thou shalt put some of thine honour upon him, that all the congregation of the children of Israel may be obedient. 21 And he shall stand before Eleazar the priest, who shall ask counsel for	him after the judgment of Urim before the LORD: at his word shall they go out, and at his word they shall come in, both he, and all the children of Israel with him, even all the congregation. 22 And Moses did as the LORD commanded him: and he took Joshua, and set him before Eleazar the priest, and before all the congregation: 23 And he laid his hands upon him, and gave him a charge, as the LORD commanded by the hand of Moses.	Priest was to seek God's will through the Urim (sacred lots) f. To have him take over immediate command of the marching divisions g. The obedience of Moses 1) He had Joshua stand before the High Priest, Eleazar, & the entire assembly 2) He laid his hands on him: Identified him as the new leader 3) He commissioned him

1. Moses was to know that God's Spirit was in Joshua (v.18). No man could lead God's people apart from the Spirit of God. For this reason, God had already placed His Spirit in Joshua. The Holy Spirit was now controlling Joshua's life and preparing him to lead God's people.

2. Moses was to identify Joshua as the new leader of God's people. This was to be done publicly by laying hands on him (v.18).

3. Moses was to commission Joshua in the presence of the people. He was to call the people together and stand Joshua before the High Priest in the sight of everyone. Then he was to commission him *publicly* (v.19).

4. Moses was to assign some day-to-day authority to Joshua. Authority was to be transferred to him gradually so the people would learn to follow him (v.20). This was essential so the people could learn to trust his leadership. They needed to see that he was capable of leading day by day; thereby, they would learn to trust him more and more. Being without Moses, God's great leader for so many years, was going to be a traumatic experience for the people. Following in his footsteps would be difficult for any leader. The gradual transfer of power to Joshua would give the people time to gain confidence in his leadership.

5. Moses was to have Joshua approach God for major decisions through the High Priest. Joshua did not have the same privilege that Moses had, that of approaching God in the Tabernacle. Joshua had to approach God the same as everyone else, through the appointed mediator, Eleazar the priest (a symbol of Christ our High Priest). When Joshua had a decision to make, he was to go to the priest and the priest was to seek God's will in his behalf. Note that he was to use the Urim, which was a sacred lot utilized in seeking God's will. (See note, pt.3, b—Ex.28:15-30 for more discussion.)

6. Moses was to have Joshua take over immediate command of the marching divisions (v.21).

7. Note the obedience of Moses (v.22-23). He had Joshua stand before Eleazar the High Priest and the entire assembly. Then he laid his hands on him, identifying him as the new leader. He commissioned this young man who was to take over the leadership reins of God's dear people.

Thought 1. This is a grave hour, an hour when leaders are desperately needed. Christ Himself said that the fields were ripe, ready for harvest, but the laborers were few. We need laborers, leaders who will step forth and make themselves available to God and His service. Where are such laborers? Where are the people who will step forth? To a large degree, the plight of the world is due to a lack of godly leadership. God's eyes search the earth to find people who will love and obey Him, stepping forth to serve His dear people (2 Chron.16:9). God calls many, but few are chosen (Mt.20:16). Few accept the call and step forth to meet the desperate needs of the world. In searching the earth, who is available? Where are the persons who will make the commitment to serve? Who has rejected the call? God longs to choose, to appoint those who are called to serve Him and His dear people. God wants men and women to make themselves available. God wants to choose and appoint leaders to go and meet the desperate needs of the world.

"So the last shall be first, and the first last: for many be called, but few chosen. (Mt.20:16; cp. Mt.22:14).

"Even as the Son of man came not to be ministered unto, but to minister, and to give his life a ransom for many" (Mt.20:28).

"Go ye therefore, and teach all nations, baptizing them in the name of the Father, and of the Son, and of the Holy Ghost: Teaching them to observe all things whatsoever I have commanded you: and, lo, I am with you alway, even unto the end of the world. Amen" (Mt.28:19-20).

"And he said unto them, Go ye into all the world, and preach the gospel to every creature" (Mk.16:15).

"Ye have not chosen me, but I have chosen you, and ordained you, that ye should go and bring forth fruit, and that your fruit should remain: that whatsoever ye shall ask of the Father in my name, he may give it you" (Jn.15:16).

"Then said Jesus to them again, Peace be unto you: as my Father hath sent me, even so send I you" (Jn.20:21).

"He saith unto him the third time, Simon, son of Jonas, lovest thou me? Peter was grieved because he said unto him the third time, Lovest thou me? And he said unto him, Lord, thou knowest all things; thou knowest that I love thee. Jesus saith unto him, Feed my sheep" (Jn.21:17).

"But the Lord said unto him, Go thy way: for he is a chosen vessel unto me, to bear my name before the Gentiles, and kings, and the children of Israel" (Acts 9:15).

"And I will give you pastors according to mine heart, which shall feed you with knowledge and understanding" (Jer.3:15).

"And I will set up shepherds over them which shall feed them: and they shall fear no more, nor be dismayed, neither shall they be lacking, saith the Lord" (Jer.23:4).

D. The Offerings & Sacrifices Commanded by the LORD: A Picture of Man's Need to Continually Approach & Worship God through the Atonement Secured by the Sacrifice (a Symbol of God's Dear Son, the Lord Jesus Christ), 28:1-29:40

1. The importance of the offerings or sacrifices
- a. Were a clear command of God
- b. Were to be presented exactly at the appointed time
- c. Were an aroma that pleased God

2. The daily sacrifices of the Burnt Offering: A symbol of Christ's sacrifice that secured atonement or reconciliation for man
- a. To sacrifice two lambs: A year old without defect (a symbol of the perfection of Christ)
- b. To sacrifice one in the morning & one in the evening
- c. To offer a Grain Offering with each sacrifice (a symbol of thanking God for the atonement & all else): Two qts. of choice flour mixed with one qt. oil
- d. The result: A pleasing aroma to the LORD (a symbol that God is pleased with the sacrifice of Christ & with a person's faith in Christ)
- e. To offer the Drink Offering (a symbol of dedication, of pouring out one's life to God) DS1
  - 1) One qt. of fermented drink with each sacrifice
  - 2) To be poured out to God
- f. To prepare the 2nd lamb at twilight
  - 1) To offer the same Grain Offering & Drink Offering
  - 2) The result: An aroma pleasing to the LORD

3. The Sabbath Day sacrifices: A symbol of Christ our Sabbath rest (Heb.3:10-4:16)
- a. To sacrifice two lambs: One year old without defect
- b. To offer the Drink Offering
- c. To offer a Grain Offering: Three qts. of flour with oil
- d. To be known as the Sabbath Burnt Offering: An additional offering to the regular Burnt Offering

And the LORD spake unto Moses, saying,
2 Command the children of Israel, and say unto them, My offering, and my bread for my sacrifices made by fire, for a sweet savour unto me, shall ye observe to offer unto me in their due season.
3 And thou shalt say unto them, This is the offering made by fire which ye shall offer unto the LORD; two lambs of the first year without spot day by day, for a continual burnt offering.
4 The one lamb shalt thou offer in the morning, and the other lamb shalt thou offer at even;
5 And a tenth part of an ephah of flour for a meat offering, mingled with the fourth part of an hin of beaten oil.
6 It is a continual burnt offering, which was ordained in mount Sinai for a sweet savour, a sacrifice made by fire unto the LORD.
7 And the drink offering thereof shall be the fourth part of an hin for the one lamb: in the holy place shalt thou cause the strong wine to be poured unto the LORD for a drink offering.
8 And the other lamb shalt thou offer at even: as the meat offering of the morning, and as the drink offering thereof, thou shalt offer it, a sacrifice made by fire, of a sweet savour unto the LORD.
9 And on the sabbath day two lambs of the first year without spot, and two tenth deals of flour for a meat offering, mingled with oil, and the drink offering thereof:
10 This is the burnt offering of every sabbath, beside the continual burnt offering, and his drink offering.
11 And in the beginnings of your months ye shall offer a burnt offering unto the LORD; two young bullocks, and one ram, seven lambs of the first year without spot;
12 And three tenth deals of flour for a meat offering, mingled with oil, for one bullock; and two tenth deals of flour for a meat offering, mingled with oil, for one ram;
13 And a several tenth deal of flour mingled with oil for a meat offering unto one lamb; for a burnt offering of a sweet savour, a sacrifice made by fire unto the LORD.
14 And their drink offerings shall be half an hin of wine unto a bullock, and the third part of an hin unto a ram, and a fourth part of an hin unto a lamb: this is the burnt offering of every month throughout the months of the year.
15 And one kid of the goats for a sin offering unto the LORD shall be offered, beside the continual burnt offering, and his drink offering.
16 And in the fourteenth day of the first month is the passover of the LORD.
17 And in the fifteenth day of this month is the feast: seven days shall unleavened bread be eaten.
18 In the first day shall be an holy convocation; ye shall do no manner of servile work therein:
19 But ye shall offer a sacrifice made by fire for a burnt offering unto the LORD; two young bullocks, and one ram, and seven lambs of the first year: they shall be unto you without blemish:
20 And their meat offering shall be of flour mingled with oil: three tenth deals shall ye offer for a bullock, and two tenth deals for a ram;
21 A several tenth deal shalt thou offer for every lamb, throughout the seven lambs:
22 And one goat for a sin offering, to make an atonement for you.
23 Ye shall offer these beside the burnt offering in the morning, which is for a continual burnt offering.
24 After this manner ye

4. The monthly sacrifices: A symbol of Christ's sacrifice
- a. To present a Burnt Offering on the 1st day of every month: Two bulls, one ram, seven male lambs one year old without defect
- b. To offer a Grain Offering of choice flour mixed with oil for each sacrifice (a symbol of thanking God for the atonement & for all else)
  - 1) Five qts. with each bull
  - 2) Three qts. with the ram
  - 3) Two qts. with each lamb
- c. The result: A Burnt Offering that pleased the Lord (a symbol of God's pleasure with Christ's sacrifice & with one's faith in Christ)
- d. To give a Drink Offering of wine with each sacrifice (a symbol of dedication)
  - 1) Two qts. with each bull
  - 2) Two & one half pints with the ram
  - 3) One qt. with each lamb
- e. To strictly observe the Burnt Offering sacrifice each month (a symbol of the atonement)
- f. To also sacrifice one male goat as a Sin Offering (a symbol of Christ's sacrifice, His dying for sin)

5. The Passover: A symbol of Christ the Lamb of God
- a. The date: 1st month, 14th day
- b. To observe the festival of unleavened bread for seven days (a symbol of rushing to be free from the slavery of this world)
  - 1) On the 15th day
  - 2) Eat no bread with yeast
- c. To call a sacred assembly on the 1st day: Do no work
- d. To present a Burnt Offering on the sacred assembly day: Two bulls, one ram, seven male lambs a year old, without defect (a symbol of Christ's sacrifice)
- e. To offer a Grain Offering with each sacrifice (a symbol of thanking God for the atonement & for all else)
  - 1) Five qts. with each bull
  - 2) Three qts. with the ram
  - 3) Two qts. with each lamb
- f. To also sacrifice a male goat as a Sin Offering: To make atonement (reconciliation)
- g. To be additional sacrifices to the regular morning sacrifice
- h. To offer these Burnt Offer-

ings on each of the seven days (a symbol of the atonement secured by Christ's sacrifice)
   1) Was an aroma pleasing to the Lord
   2) Was in addition to the regular Burnt Offering
 i. To call a sacred assembly day on the 7th day: Do no work

6. The Feast of Weeks or Firstfruits: To thank God for the harvest & dedicate one's life anew (a symbol of Pentecost, the great harvest of souls)
 a. To call a sacred assembly & do no work
 b. To present a Burnt Offering
   1) Two bulls, one ram, seven male lambs a year old
   2) Would be an aroma that pleased the LORD
 c. To offer a Grain Offering of choice flour mixed with oil (a symbol of giving thanks to God for the atonement & for all else)
   1) Five qts. with each bull
   2) Three qts. with the ram
   3) Two qts. with each lamb
 d. To sacrifice one male goat as a Sin Offering (a symbol of atonement made by Christ)
 e. To be in addition to the regular Burnt Offering
 f. To diligently guard one requirement: The sacrifices must be without defect (a symbol of the perfection of Christ)

7. The Feast of Trumpets: To arouse all to trust God more & more (a symbol of salvation & the Rapture—Christ's return)
 a. The date: 7th month, 1st day
 b. To offer a Burnt Offering (a symbol of Christ's sacrifice)
   1) One bull, one ram, seven male lambs with no defect
   2) Result: Pleased the LORD
 c. To offer a Grain Offering of choice flour mixed with oil (a symbol of giving thanks to God for the atonement & for all else)
   1) Five qts. with the bull
   2) Three qts. with the ram
   3) Two qts. with each lamb
 d. To sacrifice one male goat as a Sin Offering (a symbol of atonement made by Christ
 e. To be in addition to the

shall offer daily, throughout
the seven days, the meat of
the sacrifice made by fire, of
a sweet savour unto the
LORD: it shall be offered beside the continual burnt offering, and his drink offering.
25 And on the seventh day
ye shall have an holy convocation; ye shall do no servile
work.
26 Also in the day of the
firstfruits, when ye bring a
new meat offering unto the
LORD, after your weeks be
out, ye shall have an holy
convocation; ye shall do no
servile work:
27 But ye shall offer the
burnt offering for a sweet
savour unto the LORD; two
young bullocks, one ram,
seven lambs of the first year;
28 And their meat offering
of flour mingled with oil,
three tenth deals unto one
bullock, two tenth deals unto
one ram,
29 A several tenth deal unto
one lamb, throughout the
seven lambs;
30 And one kid of the goats,
to make an atonement for
you.
31 Ye shall offer them beside the continual burnt offering, and his meat offering,
(they shall be unto you without blemish) and their drink
offerings.

CHAPTER 29

And in the seventh month,
on the first day of the month,
ye shall have an holy convocation; ye shall do no servile
work: it is a day of blowing
the trumpets unto you.
2 And ye shall offer a burnt
offering for a sweet savour
unto the LORD; one young
bullock, one ram, and seven
lambs of the first year without blemish:
3 And their meat offering
shall be of flour mingled
with oil, three tenth deals for
a bullock, and two tenth
deals for a ram,
4 And one tenth deal for one
lamb, throughout the seven
lambs:
5 And one kid of the goats
for a sin offering, to make an
atonement for you:
6 Beside the burnt offering
of the month, and his meat
offering, and the daily burnt
offering, and his meat offering, and their drink offerings, according unto their
manner, for a sweet savour, a
sacrifice made by fire unto
the LORD.
7 And ye shall have on the
tenth day of this seventh
month an holy convocation;
and ye shall afflict your
souls: ye shall not do any
work therein:
8 But ye shall offer a burnt
offering unto the LORD for a
sweet savour; one young
bullock, one ram, and seven
lambs of the first year; they
shall be unto you without
blemish:
9 And their meat offering
shall be of flour mingled
with oil, three tenth deals to
a bullock, and two tenth
deals to one ram,
10 A several tenth deal for
one lamb, throughout the
seven lambs:
11 One kid of the goats for a
sin offering; beside the sin
offering of atonement, and
the continual burnt offering,
and the meat offering of it,
and their drink offerings.
12 And on the fifteenth day
of the seventh month ye shall
have an holy convocation; ye
shall do no servile work, and
ye shall keep a feast unto the
LORD seven days:
13 And ye shall offer a burnt
offering, a sacrifice made by
fire, of a sweet savour unto
the LORD; thirteen young
bullocks, two rams, and
fourteen lambs of the first
year; they shall be without
blemish:
14 And their meat offering
shall be of flour mingled
with oil, three tenth deals
unto every bullock of the
thirteen bullocks, two tenth
deals to each ram of the two
rams,
15 And a several tenth deal
to each lamb of the fourteen
lambs:
16 And one kid of the goats
for a sin offering; beside the
continual burnt offering, his
meat offering, and his drink
offering.
17 And on the second day
ye shall offer twelve young
bullocks, two rams, fourteen
lambs of the first year with-

monthly & daily Burnt Offerings
 f. Result: All the offerings pleased the LORD (a symbol of pleasure with the sacrifice of Christ & one's faith in Christ)

8. The Day of Atonement or Yom Kippur: Symbolized the only way to approach God—thru the shed blood of Christ
 a. The date: 7th month, 10th day
 b. To offer a Burnt Offering (a symbol of Christ's sacrifice)
   1) One bull, one ram, seven male lambs with no defect
   2) Result: Pleased the LORD
 c. To offer a Grain Offering of choice flour mixed with oil (a symbol of giving thanks to God for the atonement & for all else)
   1) Five qts. with the bull
   2) Three qts. with the ram
   3) Two qts. with each lamb
 d. To sacrifice one male goat as a Sin Offering (a symbol of atonement made by Christ
 e. To be in addition to the other Sin Offering for the atonement (cp. Lev.16) & the regular Burnt Offering: A symbol of Christ's securing atonement for us

9. The Feast of Tabernacles: To thank God for deliverance thru the wilderness wanderings & for the harvest (a symbol of the believer's march thru this world)
 a. The date: 7th month, 15th day
 b. To offer a Burnt Offering (a symbol of Christ's sacrifice securing atonement [reconciliation] for us)
   1) Thirteen bulls, two rams, fourteen lambs with no defect
   2) Result: Pleased the LORD
 c. To offer a Grain Offering of choice flour mixed with oil (a symbol of giving thanks to God for the atonement & for all else)
   1) Five qts. with the bull
   2) Three qts. with the ram
   3) Two qts. with each lamb
 d. To sacrifice a male goat as a Sin Offering (a symbol of Christ dying for sin)
 e. To be in addition to the regular Burnt Offering
 f. To offer a Burnt Offering on the 2nd day of this festival but reduce the bulls by one: Sacrifice only 12 bulls (a symbol of

Christ's atoning sacrifice)
- 1) Offer the Grain Offering & Drink Offerings as specified (a symbol of thanking God & pouring one's life out in dedication to God)
- 2) Sacrifice one male goat as a Sin Offering (a symbol of Christ dying for sin)
- 3) Was to be in addition to the regular Burnt Offering

g. To offer a Burnt Offering on the 3rd day but reduce the bulls by one: Sacrifice 11 bulls (a symbol of Christ's atoning sacrifice)
- 1) Offer the Grain & the Drink Offerings as specified (a symbol of thanking God & pouring one's life out)
- 2) Sacrifice one male goat as a Sin Offering (a symbol of Christ dying for sin)
- 3) Was to be in addition to the regular Burnt Offering

h. To offer a Burnt Offering on the 4th day but reduce the bulls by one: Sacrifice 10 bulls (a symbol of Christ's sacrifice)
- 1) Offer the Grain & the Drink Offerings as specified (a symbol of thanking God & pouring one's life out in dedication to God)
- 2) Sacrifice one male goat as a Sin Offering (a symbol of Christ dying for sin)
- 3) Was to be in addition to the regular Burnt Offering

i. To offer a Burnt Offering on the 5th day but reduce the bulls by one: Sacrifice 9 bulls (a symbol of Christ's sacrifice)
- 1) Offer the Grain & the Drink Offerings as specified (a symbol of thanking God & pouring one's life out in dedication to God)
- 2) Sacrifice one male goat as a Sin Offering (a symbol of Christ dying for sin)
- 3) Was to be in addition to the regular Burnt Offering

j. To offer a Burnt Offering on the 6th day but reduce the bulls by one: Sacrifice 8 bulls

out spot:
18 And their meat offering and their drink offerings for the bullocks, for the rams, and for the lambs, shall be according to their number, after the manner:
19 And one kid of the goats for a sin offering; beside the continual burnt offering, and the meat offering thereof, and their drink offerings.
20 And on the third day eleven bullocks, two rams, fourteen lambs of the first year without blemish;
21 And their meat offering and their drink offerings for the bullocks, for the rams, and for the lambs, shall be according to their number, after the manner:
22 And one goat for a sin offering; beside the continual burnt offering, and his meat offering, and his drink offering.
23 And on the fourth day ten bullocks, two rams, and fourteen lambs of the first year without blemish:
24 Their meat offering and their drink offerings for the bullocks, for the rams, and for the lambs, shall be according to their number, after the manner:
25 And one kid of the goats for a sin offering; beside the continual burnt offering, his meat offering, and his drink offering.
26 And on the fifth day nine bullocks, two rams, and fourteen lambs of the first year without spot:
27 And their meat offering and their drink offerings for the bullocks, for the rams, and for the lambs, shall be according to their number, after the manner:
28 And one goat for a sin offering; beside the continual burnt offering, and his meat offering, and his drink offering.
29 And on the sixth day eight bullocks, two rams, and fourteen lambs of the first year without blemish:
30 And their meat offering and their drink offerings for the bullocks, for the rams, and for the lambs, shall be according to their number, after the manner:
31 And one goat for a sin offering; beside the continual burnt offering, his meat offering, and his drink offering.
32 And on the seventh day seven bullocks, two rams, and fourteen lambs of the first year without blemish:
33 And their meat offering and their drink offerings for the bullocks, for the rams, and for the lambs, shall be according to their number, after the manner:
34 And one goat for a sin offering; beside the continual burnt offering, his meat offering, and his drink offering.
35 On the eighth day ye shall have a solemn assembly: ye shall do no servile work therein:
36 But ye shall offer a burnt offering, a sacrifice made by fire, of a sweet savour unto the LORD: one bullock, one ram, seven lambs of the first year without blemish:
37 Their meat offering and their drink offerings for the bullock, for the ram, and for the lambs, shall be according to their number, after the manner:
38 And one goat for a sin offering; beside the continual burnt offering, and his meat offering, and his drink offering.
39 These things ye shall do unto the LORD in your set feasts, beside your vows, and your freewill offerings, for your burnt offerings, and for your meat offerings, and for your drink offerings, and for your peace offerings.
40 And Moses told the children of Israel according to all that the LORD commanded Moses.

(a symbol of Christ's sacrifice)
- 1) Offer the Grain & the Drink Offerings as specified (a symbol of thanking God & pouring one's life out in dedication to God)
- 2) Sacrifice one male goat as a Sin Offering (a symbol of Christ dying for sin)
- 3) Was to be in addition to the regular Burnt Offering

k. To offer a Burnt Offering on the 7th day but reduce the bulls by one: Sacrifice 7 bulls (a symbol of Christ's sacrifice)
- 1) Offer the Grain & the Drink Offerings as specified (a symbol of thanking God & pouring one's life out in dedication to God)
- 2) Sacrifice one male goat as a Sin Offering (a symbol of Christ dying for sin)
- 3) Was to be in addition to the regular Burnt Offering

l. To call an assembly on the 8th day: Were to do no work
- 1) Present a Burnt Offering (a symbol of Christ's sacrifice)
  - One bull, one ram, seven male lambs: With no defect (a symbol of Christ's perfection)
  - Result: Pleased the LORD
- 2) Offer the Grain & the Drink Offerings as specified (a symbol of thanking God & pouring one's life out in dedication to God)
- 3) Sacrifice one male goat as a Sin Offering (a symbol of Christ dying for sin)
- 4) Was to be in addition to the regular Burnt Offering

10. The awesome importance of the offerings

a. They were additional sacrifices

b. They symbolized Christ
- 1) Burnt Offering: His sacrifice
- 2) Grain Offering: Giving thanks
- 3) Drink Offering: Pouring out, sacrificing one's life to Him
- 4) Fellowship Offering: Seeking more fellowship, v.39

c. They were commanded by God

DIVISION IV

THE PREPARATION FOR THE MARCH INTO THE PROMISED LAND, 26:1-36:13

D. The Offerings and Sacrifices Commanded by the Lord: The Picture of Man's Need to Continually Approach and Worship God through the Atonement Secured by the Sacrifice (a Symbol of God's Dear Son, the Lord Jesus Christ), 28:1-29:40

(28:1-29:40) **Introduction—Approach, to God—Way, Only One—Access, to God**: there is only one way to approach God, only one way that He accepts. There are not many ways—no matter what people may say. No matter how much people may despise the fact or deny and object to the fact—there is only one way to approach God. This is the clear declaration of Scripture from beginning to end. In fact, this is one of the major lessons taught by the offerings and sacrifices of the Old Testament.

Remember, the first generation of Israelites had died out during the forty years of wandering about in the desert wilderness. Now the second generation of believers was about to enter the promised land and receive its inheritance. It had been almost forty years since God had last covered the laws governing the sacrifices and offerings with His people. Before the new generation of believers could ever enter the promised land, He had to teach them this one absolute essential that they must never forget: there is only one approach to God that is acceptable to Him. How was God going to teach this essential truth to them? Through the offerings and sacrifices that He had commanded forty years earlier. Therefore, it was necessary for God to cover the offerings and sacrifices with the new generation of believers. This is the subject of this all-important passage of Scripture: *The Offerings and Sacrifices Commanded by the LORD: A Picture of Man's Need to Continually Approach and Worship God through the Atonement Secured by the Sacrifice (a Symbol of God's Dear Son, the Lord Jesus Christ),* 28:1-29:40.

1. The importance of the offerings or sacrifices (v.1-2).
2. The daily sacrifices of the Burnt Offering: a symbol of Christ's sacrifice that secured atonement or reconciliation for man (v.3-8).
3. The Sabbath Day sacrifices: a symbol of Christ our Sabbath rest (Heb.3:10-4:16) (v.9-10).
4. The monthly sacrifices: a symbol of Christ's sacrifice (v.11-15).
5. The Passover: a symbol of Christ the Lamb of God (v.16-25).
6. The Feast of Weeks or Firstfruits: to thank God for the harvest and dedicate one's life anew (a symbol of Pentecost, the great harvest of souls) (v.26-31).
7. The Feast of Trumpets: to arouse all to trust God more and more, (a symbol of salvation and the Rapture—Christ's return) (ch.29:1-6).
8. The Day of Atonement or Yom Kippur: Symbolized the only way to approach God—through the shed blood of Christ (v.7-11).
9. The Feast of Tabernacles: to thank God for deliverance through the wilderness wanderings and for the harvest (a symbol of the believer's march through this world) (v.12-38).
10. The awesome importance of the offerings (v.39-40).

1 (28:1-2) **Sacrifices, Importance of—Offerings, Importance of—Animal Sacrifices, Importance of**: God Himself spelled out the importance of the offerings or sacrifices. Three clear reasons are given for presenting the offerings or sacrifices to God. Note the Scripture and outline:

OUTLINE	SCRIPTURE
1. The importance of the offerings or sacrifices a. Were a clear command of God b. Were to be presented exactly at the appointed time c. Were an aroma that pleased God	And the LORD spake unto Moses, saying, 2 Command the children of Israel, and say unto them, My offering, and my bread for my sacrifices made by fire, for a sweet savour unto me, shall ye observe to offer unto me in their due season.

1. The offerings and sacrifices were a clear command of God Himself. God had established them to teach men how to approach and worship Him. Each offering or sacrifice taught a different truth about how to approach God. Each symbolized a different feature or attitude needed in worship. When God gave the offerings or sacrifices to man, He knew what He was doing. He knew that man needed to learn how to approach and worship Him. Therefore, God established the sacrifices and offerings as a commandment, a commandment that man was to obey.

2. The offerings or sacrifices were to be presented exactly at the appointed time. This was of critical importance for one central reason: to teach man that certain events had to take place before he could approach God. The approach to God is exact, precise, and very specific. In fact, there is only one acceptable way to approach God: through the *substitute sacrifice*. Therefore the sacrifice first had to be offered before man could approach God and make any other offering he wished to present to God. There was a specific order in which the offerings or sacrifices were to be made. There was a set time, an appointed time, a "fullness of time" for the substitute sacrifice to be offered and for all the other offerings to be presented. Each had its set time in order to teach man when and how to approach and worship God.

3. The offerings or sacrifices were an aroma that pleased God. The aroma that ascended up was a symbol that God was pleased with the offering. He accepted the offering or sacrifice presented by the person.

> **Thought 1**. The offerings or sacrifices symbolized Christ, the coming Savior and Messiah of the world. It was this fact that gave the offerings or sacrifices such importance. Each taught a different truth about Christ, a truth that man had to understand in order to approach God and become acceptable to God. Without grasping the truth of Christ as the Savior of the world, man could never become acceptable to God. He would perish, be doomed to an eternity of separation from God.

"For God so loved the world, that he gave his only begotten Son, that whosoever believeth in him should not perish, but have everlasting life" (Jn.3:16).

"I said therefore unto you, that ye shall die in your sins: for if ye believe not that I am he, ye shall die in your sins" (Jn.8:24).

"Neither is there salvation in any other: for there is none other name under heaven given among men, whereby we must be saved" (Acts 4:12).

2 (28:3-8) **Sacrifice, of Christ—Atonement—Reconciliation—Sacrifice, of the Burnt Offering—Offering, the Burnt—Burnt Offering—Animal Sacrifice, In the Burnt Offering**: the daily sacrifice of the Burnt Offering was the basic offering to be presented by the people. This was a symbol of Christ's sacrifice that secured atonement or reconciliation for man. (See outline and notes—Lev.1:1-17 for more discussion.) The Burnt Offering taught man one essential truth: there is only one way to approach God and become acceptable to Him—through the *substitute sacrifice*. It was the Burnt Offering that made atonement or reconciliation between God and man. Man was reconciled to God through the substitute sacrifice and it alone. Keep in mind that the substitute sacrifice is a symbol of the sacrifice of the Lord Jesus Christ. It was Christ and Christ alone who secured atonement or reconciled man to God. Christ and Christ alone is the only way into the presence of God, the only approach that is acceptable to God. Note the facts about the Burnt Offering:

OUTLINE	SCRIPTURE	SCRIPTURE	OUTLINE
2. The daily sacrifices of the Burnt Offering: A symbol of Christ's sacrifice that secured atonement or reconciliation for man a. To sacrifice two lambs: A year old without defect (a symbol of the perfection of Christ) b. To sacrifice one in the morning & one in the evening c. To offer a Grain Offering with each sacrifice (a symbol of thanking God for the atonement & all else): Two qts. of choice flour mixed with one qt. oil d. The result: A pleasing aroma to the LORD (a symbol that	3 And thou shalt say unto them, This is the offering made by fire which ye shall offer unto the LORD; two lambs of the first year without spot day by day, for a continual burnt offering. 4 The one lamb shalt thou offer in the morning, and the other lamb shalt thou offer at even; 5 And a tenth part of an ephah of flour for a meat offering, mingled with the fourth part of an hin of beaten oil. 6 It is a continual burnt offering, which was ordained	in mount Sinai for a sweet savour, a sacrifice made by fire unto the LORD. 7 And the drink offering thereof shall be the fourth part of an hin for the one lamb: in the holy place shalt thou cause the strong wine to be poured unto the LORD for a drink offering. 8 And the other lamb shalt thou offer at even: as the meat offering of the morning, and as the drink offering thereof, thou shalt offer it, a sacrifice made by fire, of a sweet savour unto the LORD.	God is pleased with the sacrifice of Christ & with a person's faith in Christ) e. To offer the Drink Offering (a symbol of dedication, of pouring out one's life to God) *DS1* 1) One qt. of fermented drink with each sacrifice 2) To be poured out to God f. To prepare the 2nd lamb at twilight 1) To offer the same Grain Offering & Drink Offering 2) The result: An aroma pleasing to the LORD

1. The daily sacrifice of the Burnt Offering required two lambs that were one year old. They were to be without blemish, without any defect whatsoever. This was the significant fact about the lambs, for they symbolized the perfection of Jesus Christ. The only sacrifice acceptable to God was the perfect sacrifice. The perfection of the sacrifice was an absolute essential, for the sacrifice had to be the ideal sacrifice, the pattern of all sacrifices. The sacrifice of Jesus Christ had to be the ideal sacrifice, the pattern that could stand for and represent every human who was ever to be born. As the ideal and the pattern, His sacrifice could cover the sins of every human being. His sacrifice could represent every human being before God, making atonement and reconciling every person to God. This was the reason the lambs of the Burnt Offering had to be without blemish or defect: they were a symbol, a type of the coming Savior of the world who was going to be sacrificed as man's substitute. The Savior was going to make atonement and reconciliation for the people.

"For he hath made him to be sin for us, who knew no sin; that we might be made the righteousness of God in him" (2 Cor.5:21).

"Forasmuch as ye know that ye were not redeemed with corruptible things, as silver and gold, from your vain conversation received by tradition from your fathers; But with the precious blood of Christ, as of a lamb without blemish and without spot" (1 Pt.1:18-19).

2. The Burnt Offering was to be offered in the morning and again in the evening. One lamb was to be sacrificed each time (v.4).

3. A Grain Offering was to be made with both the morning and the evening sacrifices. The Grain Offering was simply two quarts of choice flour mixed with one quart of oil taken from pressed olives. The person simply took the Grain Offering and placed it upon the burning sacrifice lying upon the altar. The Grain Offering was...

- a declaration of thanksgiving to God for the atonement (reconciliation) and for all else God had done
- a declaration of laying one's life upon God—all one was and had—and committing oneself totally to God

When the priests made the sacrifices on behalf of the nation, they were doing two things: offering thanksgiving to God and declaring that the people were dedicating their lives to God. All this was being done on behalf of every Israelite. The Burnt Offering...

- included the atoning sacrifice that made reconciliation with God
- included the Grain Offering that presented thanksgiving to God for the atoning sacrifice and reconciliation

Moreover, by laying the Grain Offering upon the substitute sacrifice, the people were declaring that they owed their lives in dedication to God because of the sacrifice that was being substituted for them.

"Who gave himself for us, that he might redeem us from all iniquity, and purify unto himself a peculiar people, zealous of good works" (Tit.2:14).

"Hereby perceive we the love of God, because he laid down his life for us: and we ought to lay down our lives for the brethren" (1 Jn.3:16).

4. Note the result of the sacrifice in the Burnt Offering: the sacrifice was a pleasing aroma to the Lord. This was a symbol that God is pleased with the sacrifice of Christ and with a person's faith and dedication to Christ.

"And walk in love, as Christ also hath loved us, and hath given himself for us an offering and a sacrifice to God for a sweetsmelling savour" (Eph.5:2).

5. A Drink Offering was also to be presented to the Lord with each sacrifice of the Burnt Offering. The Drink Offering was either poured out upon the altar or, more likely, at the foot of the altar. The Drink Offering…
- was a symbol of the blood of Christ that is pictured in the Lord's Supper
- was a symbol of a person's dedication, of his life being poured out to God

"I beseech you therefore, brethren, by the mercies of God, that ye present your bodies a living sacrifice, holy, acceptable unto God, which is your reasonable service" (Ro.12:1).

"Yea, and if I be offered upon the sacrifice and service of your faith, I joy, and rejoice with you all" (Ph.2:17).

6. The second lamb was to be prepared and offered in the evening, at twilight (v.8). During the evening sacrifice, the same Grain Offering and Drink Offering were to be offered. Once offered, the result was the same: the aroma—the sacrifice—pleased the Lord.

Thought 1. The sacrifice of the Burnt Offering is a symbol of Christ's sacrifice which secured atonement or reconciliation for us. Through the sacrifice of Christ, we received the atonement: we are reconciled to God. Remember: our sins have separated us from God, and we stand condemned before God to an eternity of separation from Him. But Jesus Christ took the judgment of God that was due us and bore that judgment—the judgment of death. Jesus Christ paid the ransom price to deliver us from sin and its penalty. All this He did to make atonement for us, that is, to reconcile us to God.

"For if, when we were enemies, we were reconciled to God by the death of his Son, much more, being reconciled, we shall be saved by his life. And not only so, but we also joy in God through our Lord Jesus Christ, by whom we have now received the atonement" (Ro.5:10-11).

"For Christ also hath once suffered for sins, the just for the unjust, that he might bring us to God, being put to death in the flesh, but quickened by the Spirit" (1 Pt.3:18).

"But he was wounded for our transgressions, he was bruised for our iniquities: the chastisement of our peace was upon him; and with his stripes we are healed" (Is.53:5).

DEEPER STUDY # 1

(28:7) **Drink Offering**: the Drink Offering was first mentioned in Exodus (cp. Ex.29:40; 30:9. Cp. Lev.23:13, 18, 37; Num.6:15; Dt.32:38.) Note these facts.

1. The Drink Offering was usually wine or oil. It was sometimes drunk (Dt.32:38) and sometimes poured out on the altar as a sacrifice (Gen.35:14). However, Scripture seems to indicate that it was to be poured and not drunk (Ex.30:9).
2. The Drink Offering was usually used in connection with other offerings. However, Jacob apparently used it by itself as an independent offering.
3. The Drink Offering was one of the offerings used by Israel (Num 15:5-7), but it was not included in the Levitical offerings (Lev.1-7).
4. The Drink Offering was a type of Christ in that Christ "poured out His soul unto death" (Is.53:12; cp. Ps.22:14).
5. The Drink Offering symbolized the dedication, the giving, the pouring out of one's heart and life to God. It symbolized that a person was offering, sacrificing, and pouring out his whole being in dedication to God and His service.

3 (28:9-10) **Sabbath Day, Sacrifices on—Sacrifices, on Sabbath Day—Jesus Christ, Our Sabbath Rest—Spiritual Rest, Symbol of—Symbol, of Christ Our Spiritual Rest**: there were the Sabbath day sacrifices. These sacrifices were a symbol of Christ, our Sabbath rest (Heb.3:10-4:16). The people rested on the Sabbath day, but not the priest. While the people rested, the priest made a very special Burnt Offering to God. Again, this Burnt Offering included the sacrifice of two lambs, the Drink Offering, and a Grain Offering. But note: this was an additional offering to the regular two Burnt Offerings. This means that the Sabbath day was marked off as a special day of holiness, a day when a very special third Burnt Offering was presented to the Lord. The body and blood of the sacrifice were offered up to God as a special offering on every Sabbath day. This is a strong message, a strong symbol to the people of God: His people are to celebrate their redemption every Sabbath or Sunday. Note the Scripture and outline:

OUTLINE	SCRIPTURE
3. The Sabbath Day sacrifices: A symbol of Christ our Sabbath rest (Heb.3:10-4:16) a. To sacrifice two lambs: One year old without defect b. To offer the Drink Offering c. To offer a Grain Offering: Three qts. of flour with oil d. To be known as the Sabbath Burnt Offering: An additional offering to the regular Burnt Offering	9 And on the sabbath day two lambs of the first year without spot, and two tenth deals of flour for a meat offering, mingled with oil, and the drink offering thereof: 10 This is the burnt offering of every sabbath, beside the continual burnt offering, and his drink offering.

Thought 1. There are two lessons for us in this point:

1) We must do just what the Israelites did: celebrate our redemption on the Sabbath. As commanded in other Scriptures, we must worship the LORD on the Sabbath.
2) Jesus Christ is our Sabbath rest. He gives us rest from all the storms of life; He and He alone brings spiritual rest to the human soul: peace, assurance, confidence, purpose, meaning, significance, security, fulfillment and satisfaction.

"Blessed are they which do hunger and thirst after righteousness: for they shall be filled" (Mt.5:6).

"Take my yoke upon you, and learn of me; for I am meek and lowly in heart: and ye shall find rest unto your souls" (Mt.11:29).

"Peace I leave with you, my peace I give unto you: not as the world giveth, give I unto you. Let not your heart be troubled, neither let it be afraid" (Jn.14:27).

"These things I have spoken unto you, that in me ye might have peace. In the world ye shall have tribulation: but be of good cheer; I have overcome the world" (Jn.16:33).

"For we which have believed do enter into rest, as he said, As I have sworn in my wrath, if they shall enter into my rest: although the works were finished from the foundation of the world" (Heb.4:3).

"For if Jesus had given them rest, then would he not afterward have spoken of another day. There remaineth therefore a rest to the people of God. For he that is entered into his rest, he also hath ceased from his own works, as God did from his" (Heb.4:8-10).

"And I heard a voice from heaven saying unto me, Write, Blessed are the dead which die in the Lord from henceforth: Yea, saith the Spirit, that they may rest from their labours; and their works do follow them" (Rev.14:13).

"And he said, My presence shall go with thee, and I will give thee rest" (Ex.33:14).

"I will both lay me down in peace, and sleep: for thou, Lord, only makest me dwell in safety" (Ps.4:8).

"As for me, I will behold thy face in righteousness: I shall be satisfied, when I awake, with thy likeness" (Ps.17:15).

"For he satisfieth the longing soul, and filleth the hungry soul with goodness" (Ps.107:9).

"Return unto thy rest, O my soul; for the Lord hath dealt bountifully with thee" (Ps.116:7).

"To whom he said, This is the rest wherewith ye may cause the weary to rest; and this is the refreshing: yet they would not hear" (Is.28:12).

"For thus saith the Lord God, the Holy One of Israel; In returning and rest shall ye be saved; in quietness and in confidence shall be your strength: and ye would not" (Is.30:15).

4 (28:11-15) **Monthly Sacrifices—Sacrifices, the Monthly—Animal Sacrifice, In the Monthly Offerings—Offerings, the Monthly—Symbol, of Christ's Sacrifice—Sacrifice, of Christ, Symbol of**: there were the monthly sacrifices that were to be made. These were sometimes referred to as the new moon offerings; that is, they were to be presented to the Lord at every new or full moon. These sacrifices were a clear symbol of the sacrifice of Christ. Note that a much larger number of animals were to be offered at the monthly sacrifice. This meant that a larger Grain Offering and Drink Offering were also to be presented to the Lord. Note also that a Sin Offering was to be presented to God during the monthly sacrifices (v.15). Later in the history of Israel, the new moon festivals were abused. They apparently became festivals for partying, drinking, and immoral behavior (Is.1:13-14).[1]

OUTLINE	SCRIPTURE	SCRIPTURE	OUTLINE
4. The monthly sacrifices: A symbol of Christ's sacrifice a. To present a Burnt Offering on the 1st day of every month: Two bulls, one ram, seven male lambs one year old without defect	11 And in the beginnings of your months ye shall offer a burnt offering unto the LORD; two young bullocks, and one ram, seven lambs of the first year without spot;	12 And three tenth deals of flour for a meat offering, mingled with oil, for one bullock; and two tenth deals of flour for a meat offering, mingled with oil, for one ram;	b. To offer a Grain Offering of choice flour mixed with oil for each sacrifice (a symbol of thanking God for the atonement & for all else) 1) Five qts. with each bull 2) Three qts. with the ram 3) Two qts. with each lamb

1 *The Expositor's Bible Commentary*. Frank E. Gaebelein, Editor, p.951.

OUTLINE	SCRIPTURE	SCRIPTURE	OUTLINE
c. The result: A Burnt Offering that pleased the LORD (a symbol of God's pleasure with Christ's sacrifice & with one's faith in Christ) d. To give a Drink Offering of wine with each sacrifice (a symbol of dedication) 1) Two qts. with each bull	13 And a several tenth deal of flour mingled with oil for a meat offering unto one lamb; for a burnt offering of a sweet savour, a sacrifice made by fire unto the LORD. 14 And their drink offerings shall be half an hin of wine unto a bullock, and the third part of an hin unto a ram,	and a fourth part of an hin unto a lamb: this is the burnt offering of every month throughout the months of the year. 15 And one kid of the goats for a sin offering unto the LORD shall be offered, beside the continual burnt offering, and his drink offering.	2) Two & one half pints with the ram 3) One qt. with each lamb e. To strictly observe the Burnt Offering sacrifice each month (a symbol of the atonement) f. To also sacrifice one male goat as a Sin Offering (a symbol of Christ's sacrifice, His dying for sin)

Thought 1. The sacrifice of the Burnt Offering symbolized the death of Jesus Christ, but so did the Sin Offering. The Sin Offering was a symbol of Christ's sacrifice for the sins of the world. He died to provide forgiveness of sins for us. Through the blood of Christ, we are forgiven for all sin. But note: there is a condition for forgiveness. We must confess and repent of our sins. We must turn away from sin and turn to follow after Christ. Both confession and repentance are essential for forgiveness of sins.

"For this is my blood of the new testament, which is shed for many for the remission of sins" (Mt.26:28).

"Then Peter said unto them, Repent, and be baptized every one of you in the name of Jesus Christ for the remission of sins, and ye shall receive the gift of the Holy Ghost" (Acts 2:38).

"Repent ye therefore, and be converted, that your sins may be blotted out, when the times of refreshing shall come from the presence of the Lord" (Acts 3:19).

"Repent therefore of this thy wickedness, and pray God, if perhaps the thought of thine heart may be forgiven thee" (Acts 8:22).

"In whom we have redemption through his blood, the forgiveness of sins, according to the riches of his grace" (Eph.1:7).

"If we confess our sins, he is faithful and just to forgive us our sins, and to cleanse us from all unrighteousness" (1 Jn.1:9).

"But if we walk in the light, as he is in the light, we have fellowship one with another, and the blood of Jesus Christ his Son cleanseth us from all sin" (1 Jn.1:7).

"Unto him that loved us, and washed us from our sins in his own blood" (Rev.1:5).

"Let the wicked forsake his way, and the unrighteous man his thoughts: and let him return unto the Lord, and he will have mercy upon him; and to our God, for he will abundantly pardon" (Is.55:7).

"But if the wicked will turn from all his sins that he hath committed, and keep all my statutes, and do that which is lawful and right, he shall surely live, he shall not die" (Ezk.18:21).

5 (28:16-25) **Passover—Lamb of God, Symbol of Christ—Christ, the Lamb of God**: there was the Passover, a symbol of Christ the Lamb of God who takes away the sins of the world. The Passover celebrated the great deliverance of God from Egyptian slavery. God freed His people from the world so that they could live life to the fullest in the promised land of God. They were freed to live life to the fullest, freed to worship and serve God fully. They were to live lives that...

- were holy, righteous, and pure
- would be dynamic witnesses to the surrounding nations of unbelievers

This was the very purpose for which God had delivered and given freedom to His people. This was the reason for celebrating the Passover. God's people were never to forget the great deliverance of God: their freedom and liberty to live life to the fullest and the great hope of the promised land were gifts from God.

Note that the Passover was tied to the festival of unleavened bread (v.17f). This was the first of the great national festival that were held each year. It was celebrated in the first month of the year, Nisan, which was somewhere around March or April on our calendar. The facts involved in the Passover and the festival of unleavened bread are clearly seen in the Scripture and outline:

OUTLINE	SCRIPTURE	SCRIPTURE	OUTLINE
5. The Passover: A symbol of Christ the Lamb of God a. The date: 1st month, 14th day b. To observe the festival of unleavened bread for seven days (a symbol of rushing to be free from the slavery of this world) 1) On the 15th day 2) Eat no bread with yeast c. To call a sacred assembly on the 1st day: Do no work d. To present a Burnt Offering on the sacred assembly day:	16 And in the fourteenth day of the first month is the passover of the LORD. 17 And in the fifteenth day of this month is the feast: seven days shall unleavened bread be eaten. 18 In the first day shall be an holy convocation; ye shall do no manner of servile work therein: 19 But ye shall offer a sacrifice made by fire for a burnt	offering unto the LORD; two young bullocks, and one ram, and seven lambs of the first year: they shall be unto you without blemish: 20 And their meat offering shall be of flour mingled with oil: three tenth deals shall ye offer for a bullock, and two tenth deals for a ram; 21 A several tenth deal shalt thou offer for every lamb,	Two bulls, one ram, seven male lambs a year old, without defect (a symbol of Christ's sacrifice) e. To offer a Grain Offering with each sacrifice (a symbol of thanking God for the atonement & for all else) 1) Five qts. with each bull 2) Three qts. with the ram 3) Two qts. with each lamb

OUTLINE	SCRIPTURE	SCRIPTURE	OUTLINE
f. To also sacrifice a male goat as a Sin Offering: To make atonement (reconciliation) g. To be additional sacrifices to the regular morning sacrifice h. To offer these Burnt Offerings on each of the seven	throughout the seven lambs: 22 And one goat for a sin offering, to make an atonement for you. 23 Ye shall offer these beside the burnt offering in the morning, which is for a continual burnt offering. 24 After this manner ye shall offer daily, throughout	the seven days, the meat of the sacrifice made by fire, of a sweet savour unto the LORD: it shall be offered beside the continual burnt offering, and his drink offering. 25 And on the seventh day ye shall have an holy convocation; ye shall do no servile work.	days (a symbol of the atonement secured by Christ's sacrifice) 1) Was an aroma pleasing to the Lord 2) Was in addition to the regular Burnt Offering i. To call a sacred assembly day on the 7th day: Do no work

Thought 1. The Passover was a symbol of Christ and His sacrifice. Note these facts:

1) Jesus Christ referred to His death as an exodus or departure from this world. The word *exodos* actually means death, decease, or departing.

> **"Who appeared in glory, and spake of his decease which he should accomplish at Jerusalem" (Lk.9.31).**

2) One of the requirements of the Passover lamb was that no bone was ever to be broken. This was a picture that pointed to Christ, none of whose bones were ever broken.

> **"For these things were done, that the scripture should be fulfilled, A bone of him shall not be broken" (Jn.19:36).**

3) Leaven was a type of sin; therefore all leaven had to be thrown out of a person's house prior to the Passover. Scripture declares that believers must be ruthless in purging out the old leaven, the sins of their lives.[2]

> **"Purge out therefore the old leaven, that ye may be a new lump, as ye are unleavened. For even Christ our passover is sacrificed for us: Therefore let us keep the feast, not with old leaven, neither with the leaven of malice and wickedness; but with the unleavened bread of sincerity and truth" (1 Cor. 5:7-8).**

4) Jesus Christ is the Passover Lamb, the lamb who takes away the sin of the world.

> **"The next day John seeth Jesus coming unto him, and saith, Behold the Lamb of God, which taketh away the sin of the world" (Jn.1:29).**
>
> **"Purge out therefore the old leaven, that ye may be a new lump, as ye are unleavened. For even Christ our passover is sacrificed for us" (1 Cor.5:7).**
>
> **"Forasmuch as ye know that ye were not redeemed with corruptible things, as silver and gold, from your vain conversation received by tradition from your fathers; But with the precious blood of Christ, as of a lamb without blemish and without spot" (1 Pt.1:18-19).**
>
> **"And I beheld, and, lo, in the midst of the throne and of the four beasts, and in the midst of the elders, stood a Lamb as it had been slain, having seven horns and seven eyes, which are the seven Spirits of God sent forth into all the earth. And he came and took the book out of the right hand of him that sat upon the throne. And when he had taken the book, the four beasts and four and twenty elders fell down before the Lamb, having every one of them harps, and golden vials full of odours, which are the prayers of saints. And they sung a new song, saying, Thou art worthy to take the book, and to open the seals thereof: for thou wast slain, and hast redeemed us to God by thy blood out of every kindred, and tongue, and people, and nation; And hast made us unto our God kings and priests: and we shall reign on the earth" (Rev.5:6-10).**
>
> **"After this I beheld, and, lo, a great multitude, which no man could number, of all nations, and kindreds, and people, and tongues, stood before the throne, and before the Lamb, clothed with white robes, and palms in their hands" (Rev.7:9).**
>
> **"And they sing the song of Moses the servant of God, and the song of the Lamb, saying, Great and marvellous are thy works, Lord God Almighty; just and true are thy ways, thou King of saints" (Rev.15:3).**
>
> **"And I saw no temple therein: for the Lord God Almighty and the Lamb are the temple of it" (Rev.21:22).**
>
> **"He was oppressed, and he was afflicted, yet he opened not his mouth: he is brought as a lamb to the slaughter, and as a sheep before her shearers is dumb, so he openeth not his mouth" (Is.53:7).**

6 (28:26-31) **Feast, of Weeks-—Feast, of Firstfruits—Firstfruits, Feast of—Weeks, Feast of**: there was the Feast of Weeks or Firstfruits. This was a festival to give thanks to God for the harvest and to dedicate one's life anew to God. This

2 The idea for these first three applications comes from Gordon J. Wenham. *The Book of Numbers*, p. 201.

was a symbol of Pentecost, the great harvest of souls and of people giving their lives to God. The festival of firstfruits was held exactly fifty days after the feast of unleavened bread (see outline and notes—Lev.23:15-22 for more discussion). Pentecost took place fifty days after the resurrection of Christ, the great day when the Holy Spirit came upon the disciples and gave a great harvest of souls (Acts 2:1, 4). The very same number of sacrifices was required at this festival as was required at the feast of unleavened bread and at the monthly or new moon offerings.

OUTLINE	SCRIPTURE	SCRIPTURE	OUTLINE
6. The Feast of Weeks or Firstfruits: To thank God for the harvest & dedicate one's life anew (a symbol of Pentecost, the great harvest of souls) a. To call a sacred assembly & do no work b. To present a Burnt Offering 1) Two bulls, one ram, seven male lambs a year old 2) Would be an aroma that pleased the LORD c. To offer a Grain Offering of choice flour mixed with oil (a	26 Also in the day of the firstfruits, when ye bring a new meat offering unto the LORD, after your weeks be out, ye shall have an holy convocation; ye shall do no servile work: 27 But ye shall offer the burnt offering for a sweet savour unto the LORD; two young bullocks, one ram, seven lambs of the first year; 28 And their meat offering of flour mingled with oil,	three tenth deals unto one bullock, two tenth deals unto one ram, 29 A several tenth deal unto one lamb, throughout the seven lambs; 30 And one kid of the goats, to make an atonement for you. 31 Ye shall offer them beside the continual burnt offering, and his meat offering, (they shall be unto you without blemish) and their drink offerings.	symbol of giving thanks to God for the atonement & for all else) 1) Five qts. with each bull 2) Three qts. with the ram 3) Two qts. with each lamb d. To sacrifice one male goat as a Sin Offering (a symbol of atonement made by Christ) e. To be in addition to the regular Burnt Offering f. To diligently guard one requirement: The sacrifices must be without defect (a symbol of the perfection of Christ)

Thought 1. The lesson for the believer is clear: as we march to the promised land, we are constantly to be giving our lives anew to God and bearing strong testimony for Him. We are constantly to be seeking a great harvest of souls.

"And when the day of Pentecost was fully come, they were all with one accord in one place....And they were all filled with the Holy Ghost, and began to speak with other tongues, as the Spirit gave them utterance" (Acts 2:1, 4).

"And he saith unto them, Follow me, and I will make you fishers of men" (Mt.4:19).

"Go ye therefore, and teach all nations, baptizing them in the name of the Father, and of the Son, and of the Holy Ghost: Teaching them to observe all things whatsoever I have commanded you: and, lo, I am with you alway, even unto the end of the world. Amen" (Mt.28:19-20).

"And he said unto them, Go ye into all the world, and preach the gospel to every creature" (Mk.16:15).

"But ye shall receive power, after that the Holy Ghost is come upon you: and ye shall be witnesses unto me both in Jerusalem, and in all Judaea, and in Samaria, and unto the uttermost part of the earth" (Acts 1:8).

"For we cannot but speak the things which we have seen and heard" (Acts 4:20).

"I beseech you therefore, brethren, by the mercies of God, that ye present your bodies a living sacrifice, holy, acceptable unto God, which is your reasonable service" (Ro.12:1).

"For though I be free from all men, yet have I made myself servant unto all, that I might gain the more. And unto the Jews I became as a Jew, that I might gain the Jews; to them that are under the law, as under the law, that I might gain them that are under the law" (1 Cor.9:19-20).

"And others save with fear, pulling them out of the fire; hating even the garment spotted by the flesh" (Jude 23).

"And thou shalt love the Lord thy God with all thine heart, and with all thy soul, and with all thy might" (Dt.6:5).

"Trust in the Lord with all thine heart; and lean not unto thine own understanding" (Pr.3:5).

"The fruit of the righteous is a tree of life; and he that winneth souls is wise" (Pr.11:30).

"My son, give me thine heart, and let thine eyes observe my ways" (Pr.23:26).

"And they that be wise shall shine as the brightness of the firmament; and they that turn many to righteousness as the stars for ever and ever" (Dan.12:3).

7 (29:1-6) **Trumpets, Feast of—Festivals, Trumpets of—Commitment—Dedication—Witnessing, to Christ**: there was the Feast of Trumpets which had a twofold purpose: to arouse the people to trust God more and more, and to proclaim the message of joy for the atonement or reconciliation with God. This feast was held on the first day of the seventh month, which was to be a great month of worship for the people. The Feast of Trumpets is a symbol of salvation and of the Rapture, the glorious day when Christ will return and take believers to be with Him forever. There were actually three major festivals held during this month:

⇒ The Feast of Trumpets was held on the first day of the seventh month (v.1).
⇒ The Day of Atonement was held on the tenth day of the seventh month (v.7).
⇒ The Feast of Tabernacles was held for eight consecutive days beginning on the fifteenth day of the seventh month (v.12, 35).

The Feast of Trumpets eventually became known as Rosh Hashanah, which became the beginning of the new year for the Jewish people. The trumpets are still blown in the synagogue worship on this particular day.

OUTLINE	SCRIPTURE	SCRIPTURE	OUTLINE
7. The Feast of Trumpets: To arouse all to trust God more & more (a symbol of salvation & the Rapture—Christ's return)	And in the seventh month, on the first day of the month, ye shall have an holy convo- cation; ye shall do no servile	deals for a ram, 4 And one tenth deal for one lamb, throughout the seven lambs:	else) 1) Five qts. with the bull 2) Three qts. with the ram 3) Two qts. with each lamb
a. The date: 7th month, 1st day	work: it is a day of blowing the trumpets unto you.	5 And one kid of the goats for a sin offering, to make an	d. To sacrifice one male goat as a Sin Offering (a symbol of
b. To offer a Burnt Offering (a symbol of Christ's sacrifice) 1) One bull, one ram, seven male lambs with no defect 2) Result: Pleased the LORD	2 And ye shall offer a burnt offering for a sweet savour unto the LORD; one young bullock, one ram, and seven lambs of the first year with- out blemish:	atonement for you: 6 Beside the burnt offering of the month, and his meat offering, and the daily burnt offering, and his meat offer- ing, and their drink offer-	atonement made by Christ e. To be in addition to the monthly & daily Burnt Offerings f. Result: All the offerings
c. To offer a Grain Offering of choice flour mixed with oil (a symbol of giving thanks to God for the atonement & for all	3 And their meat offering shall be of flour mingled with oil, three tenth deals for a bullock, and two tenth	ings, according unto their manner, for a sweet savour, a sacrifice made by fire unto the LORD.	pleased the LORD (a symbol of pleasure with the sacrifice of Christ & one's faith in Christ)

Thought 1. The Feast of Trumpets is a clear symbol of salvation and of the Rapture. The glorious day is coming when Christ will return and take believers to be with Him forever. As we march to the promised land of heaven, we are to grow in our trust and joy; we are to be ever maturing, learning to focus and to bear a stronger witness to the atoning sacrifice of Christ. We are to focus upon the Lord and His glorious return.

"For as the lightning cometh out of the east, and shineth even unto the west; so shall also the coming of the Son of man be....But of that day and hour knoweth no man, no, not the angels of heaven, but my Father only" (Mt.24:27, 36).

"Jesus saith unto him, Thou hast said: nevertheless I say unto you, Hereafter shall ye see the Son of man sitting on the right hand of power, and coming in the clouds of heaven" (Mt.26:64).

"Blessed are those servants, whom the lord when he cometh shall find watching: verily I say unto you, that he shall gird himself, and make them to sit down to meat, and will come forth and serve them" (Lk.12:37).

"Be ye therefore ready also: for the Son of man cometh at an hour when ye think not" (Lk.12:40).

"And then shall they see the Son of man coming in a cloud with power and great glory" (Lk.21:27).

"In my Father's house are many mansions: if it were not so, I would have told you. I go to prepare a place for you. And if I go and prepare a place for you, I will come again, and receive you unto myself; that where I am, there ye may be also" (Jn.14:2-3).

"Which also said, Ye men of Galilee, why stand ye gazing up into heaven? this same Jesus, which is taken up from you into heaven, shall so come in like manner as ye have seen him go into heaven" (Acts 1:11).

"For our conversation [citizenship] is in heaven; from whence also we look for the Saviour, the Lord Jesus Christ: Who shall change our vile body, that it may be fashioned like unto his glorious body, according to the working whereby he is able even to subdue all things unto himself" (Ph.3:20-21).

"When Christ, who is our life, shall appear, then shall ye also appear with him in glory" (Col.3:4).

"For the Lord himself shall descend from heaven with a shout, with the voice of the archangel, and with the trump of God: and the dead in Christ shall rise first: Then we which are alive and remain shall be caught up together with them in the clouds, to meet the Lord in the air: and so shall we ever be with the Lord" (1 Th.4:16-17).

"For yourselves know perfectly that the day of the Lord so cometh as a thief in the night" (1 Th.5:2).

"So Christ was once offered to bear the sins of many; and unto them that look for him shall he appear the second time without sin unto salvation" (Heb.9:28).

"And when the chief Shepherd shall appear, ye shall receive a crown of glory that fadeth not away" (1 Pt.5:4).

"Beloved, now are we the sons of God, and it doth not yet appear what we shall be: but we know that, when he shall appear, we shall be like him; for we shall see him as he is" (1 Jn.3:2).

"Behold, I come as a thief. Blessed is he that watcheth, and keepeth his garments, lest he walk naked, and they see his shame" (Rev.16:15).

8 (29:7-11) **Atonement, Day of—Feast, Day of Atonement—Yom Kippur, Festival of—Approach, to God—Symbol, of Christ's Atonement**: there was the Day of Atonement or Yom Kippur. This feast symbolized the only way to approach God, through the shed blood of the *substitute sacrifice*. The substitute sacrifice was a clear symbol of Christ, our substitute sacrifice (see outline and notes—Lev.23:26-32). Note the words "afflict your souls" or "deny yourselves" (NIV) or "humble yourselves" (NASB) or "go without food" (NLT). The Day of Atonement was not to be a day of festivities but rather of denial and fasting. It was to be devoted totally to worship, focusing upon the atonement or reconciliation with God that had been brought about through the substitute sacrifice. A Day of Atonement was established to teach people that there was only one way to become acceptable to God: through the atonement and reconciliation made by the *substitute sacrifice*. The Day of Atonement was the most sacred, holy day of the year. Keep in mind that the Day of Atonement was held only one day of the year: the tenth day of the seventh month.

OUTLINE	SCRIPTURE	SCRIPTURE	OUTLINE
8. The Day of Atonement or Yom Kippur: Symbolized the only way to approach God—thru the shed blood of Christ a. The date: 7th month, 10th day b. To offer a Burnt Offering (a symbol of Christ's sacrifice) 1) One bull, one ram, seven male lambs with no defect 2) Result: Pleased the LORD c. To offer a Grain Offering of	7 And ye shall have on the tenth day of this seventh month an holy convocation; and ye shall afflict your souls: ye shall not do any work therein: 8 But ye shall offer a burnt offering unto the LORD for a sweet savour; one young bullock, one ram, and seven lambs of the first year; they shall be unto you without blemish: 9 And their meat offering	shall be of flour mingled with oil, three tenth deals to a bullock, and two tenth deals to one ram, 10 A several tenth deal for one lamb, throughout the seven lambs: 11 One kid of the goats for a sin offering; beside the sin offering of atonement, and the continual burnt offering, and the meat offering of it, and their drink offerings.	choice flour mixed with oil (a symbol of giving thanks to God for the atonement & for all else) 1) Five qts. with the bull 2) Three qts. with the ram 3) Two qts. with each lamb d. To sacrifice one male goat as a Sin Offering (a symbol of atonement made by Christ e. To be in addition to the other Sin Offering for the atonement (cp. Lev.16) & the regular Burnt Offering: A symbol of Christ's securing atonement for us

Thought 1. Jesus Christ has secured the atonemen or reconciliation with God for us. We are to keep our minds upon the atoning sacrifice of the Lord Jesus Christ. We must never forget that there is only one way to become acceptable to God: through the sacrifice of God's dear Son, the Lord Jesus Christ Himself. It is He who cleanses us from sin and delivers us from the penalty of death.

"For when we were yet without strength, in due time Christ died for the ungodly" (Ro.5:6).

"But God commendeth his love toward us, in that, while we were yet sinners, Christ died for us" (Ro.5:8).

"Much more then, being now justified by his blood, we shall be saved from wrath through him. For if, when we were enemies, we were reconciled to God by the death of his Son, much more, being reconciled, we shall be saved by his life. And not only so, but we also joy in God through our Lord Jesus Christ, by whom we have now received the atonement" (Ro.5:9-11).

"For I delivered unto you first of all that which I also received, how that Christ died for our sins according to the scriptures; And that he was buried, and that he rose again the third day according to the scriptures" (1 Cor.15:3-4).

"Who gave himself for our sins, that he might deliver us from this present evil world, according to the will of God and our Father" (Gal.1:4).

"Christ hath redeemed us from the curse of the law, being made a curse for us: for it is written, Cursed is every one that hangeth on a tree" (Gal.3:13).

"Who his own self bare our sins in his own body on the tree, that we, being dead to sins, should live unto righteousness: by whose stripes ye were healed" (1 Pt.2:24).

"For Christ also hath once suffered for sins, the just for the unjust, that he might bring us to God, being put to death in the flesh, but quickened by the Spirit" (1 Pt.3:18).

"But we see Jesus, who was made a little lower than the angels for the suffering of death, crowned with glory and honour; that he by the grace of God should taste death for every man" (Heb.2:9).

"Neither by the blood of goats and calves, but by his own blood he entered in once into the holy place, having obtained eternal redemption for us. For if the blood of bulls and of goats, and the ashes of an heifer sprinkling the unclean, sanctifieth to the purifying of the flesh: How much more shall the blood of Christ, who through the eternal Spirit offered himself without spot to God, purge your conscience from dead works to serve the living God" (Heb.9:12-14).

9 (29:12-38) **Feast, of Tabernacles—Tabernacles, Festival of—Wilderness Wanderings—Journeys, Wilderness—Heaven, Journey to**: there was the Feast of Tabernacles. This was a festival to thank God for deliverance through the wilderness wanderings and for the harvest. This feast symbolized the believer's march through this world to heaven, a symbol of how temporary the believer's march through the world is (see outline and notes—Lev.23:33-44 for more discussion). This feast was to celebrate the wanderings, when the people lived in tents on their way to the promised land, and to thank God for the harvest. During this period of time, the people lived in temporary tents or booths. Despite the harsh conditions of their lives, they were to be ever thankful to God and to keep their minds focused upon the promised land.

Note this fact: there were far more animals sacrificed during the Festival of Tabernacles than any other festival. In fact, there were more bulls and rams sacrificed than during all the other festivals combined. This festival lasted for a full eight days. Note that thirteen bulls, two rams, and fourteen lambs were sacrificed on the first day (v.13). But the number of bulls was decreased by one each day thereafter. The same number of rams and lambs were sacrificed, but there was a change in the number of bulls offered to the Lord. Scripture does not say why. Perhaps it was because of the extreme cost of a bull. Whatever the reason, this fact needs to be noted. Note one other fact: all these sacrifices were in addition to the regular Burnt Offering (v.38). The importance of the sacrifice of the daily Burnt Offerings—both morning and evening—cannot be over-emphasized. There is only one way to approach God that is acceptable to God: through the *substitute sacrifice*. This one fact must always be kept in mind by believers throughout all generations: there is only one approach to God that is acceptable; that approach is through the atoning sacrifice of the Lord Jesus Christ.

OUTLINE	SCRIPTURE	SCRIPTURE	OUTLINE
9. The Feast of Tabernacles: To thank God for deliverance thru the wilderness wanderings & for the harvest (a symbol of the believer's march thru this world) a. The date: 7th month, 15th day b. To offer a Burnt Offering (a symbol of Christ's sacrifice securing atonement [reconciliation] for us) 1) Thirteen bulls, two rams, fourteen lambs with no defect 2) Result: Pleased the LORD c. To offer a Grain Offering of choice flour mixed with oil (a symbol of giving thanks to God for all) 1) Five qts. with the bull 2) Three qts. with the ram 3) Two qts. with each lamb d. To sacrifice a male goat as a Sin Offering (a symbol of Christ dying for sin) e. To be in addition to the regular Burnt Offering f. To offer a Burnt Offering on the 2nd day of this festival but reduce the bulls by one: Sacrifice only 12 bulls (a symbol of Christ's atoning sacrifice) 1) Offer the Grain Offering & Drink Offerings as specified (a symbol of thanking God & pouring one's life out in dedication to God) 2) Sacrifice one male goat as a Sin Offering (a symbol of Christ dying for sin) 3) Was to be in addition to the regular Burnt Offering g. To offer a Burnt Offering on the 3rd day but reduce the bulls by one: Sacrifice 11 bulls (a symbol of Christ's atoning sacrifice) 1) Offer the Grain & theDrink Offerings as specified (a symbol of thanking God & pouring one's life out) 2) Sacrifice one male goat as a Sin Offering (a symbol of Christ dying for sin) 3) Was to be in addition to the regular Burnt Offering h. To offer a Burnt Offering on the 4th day but reduce the bulls by one: Sacrifice 10 bulls (a symbol of Christ's sacrifice) 1) Offer the Grain & the Drink Offerings as speci-	12 And on the fifteenth day of the seventh month ye shall have an holy convocation; ye shall do no servile work, and ye shall keep a feast unto the LORD seven days: 13 And ye shall offer a burnt offering, a sacrifice made by fire, of a sweet savour unto the LORD; thirteen young bullocks, two rams, and fourteen lambs of the first year; they shall be without blemish: 14 And their meat offering shall be of flour mingled with oil, three tenth deals unto every bullock of the thirteen bullocks, two tenth deals to each ram of the two rams, 15 And a several tenth deal to each lamb of the fourteen lambs: 16 And one kid of the goats for a sin offering; beside the continual burnt offering, his meat offering, and his drink offering. 17 And on the second day ye shall offer twelve young bullocks, two rams, fourteen lambs of the first year without spot: 18 And their meat offering and their drink offerings for the bullocks, for the rams, and for the lambs, shall be according to their number, after the manner: 19 And one kid of the goats for a sin offering; beside the continual burnt offering, and the meat offering thereof, and their drink offerings. 20 And on the third day eleven bullocks, two rams, fourteen lambs of the first year without blemish; 21 And their meat offering and their drink offerings for the bullocks, for the rams, and for the lambs, shall be according to their number, after the manner: 22 And one goat for a sin offering; beside the continual burnt offering, and his meat offering, and his drink offering. 23 And on the fourth day ten bullocks, two rams, and fourteen lambs of the first year without blemish: 24 Their meat offering and their drink offerings for the	bullocks, for the rams, and for the lambs, shall be according to their number, after the manner: 25 And one kid of the goats for a sin offering; beside the continual burnt offering, his meat offering, and his drink offering. 26 And on the fifth day nine bullocks, two rams, and fourteen lambs of the first year without spot: 27 And their meat offering and their drink offerings for the bullocks, for the rams, and for the lambs, shall be according to their number, after the manner: 28 And one goat for a sin offering; beside the continual burnt offering, and his meat offering, and his drink offering. 29 And on the sixth day eight bullocks, two rams, and fourteen lambs of the first year without blemish: 30 And their meat offering and their drink offerings for the bullocks, for the rams, and for the lambs, shall be according to their number, after the manner: 31 And one goat for a sin offering; beside the continual burnt offering, his meat offering, and his drink offering. 32 And on the seventh day seven bullocks, two rams, and fourteen lambs of the first year without blemish: 33 And their meat offering and their drink offerings for the bullocks, for the rams, and for the lambs, shall be according to their number, after the manner: 34 And one goat for a sin offering; beside the continual burnt offering, his meat offering, and his drink offering. 35 On the eighth day ye shall have a solemn assembly: ye shall do no servile work therein: 36 But ye shall offer a burnt offering, a sacrifice made by fire, of a sweet savour unto the LORD: one bullock, one ram, seven lambs of the first year without blemish: 37 Their meat offering and their drink offerings for the bullock, for the ram, and for	fied (a symbol of thanking God & pouring one's life out in dedication to God) 2) Sacrifice one male goat as a Sin Offering (a symbol of Christ dying for sin) 3) Was to be in addition to the regular Burnt Offering i. To offer a Burnt Offering on the 5th day but reduce the bulls by one: Sacrifice 9 bulls (a symbol of Christ's sacrifice) 1) Offer the Grain & the Drink Offerings as specified (a symbol of thanking God & pouring one's life out in dedication to God) 2) Sacrifice one male goat as a Sin Offering (a symbol of Christ dying for sin) 3) Was to be in addition to the regular Burnt Offering j. To offer a Burnt Offering on the 6th day but reduce the bulls by one: Sacrifice 8 bulls (a symbol of Christ's sacrifice) 1) Offer the Grain & the Drink Offerings as specified (a symbol of thanking God & pouring one's life out in dedication to God) 2) Sacrifice one male goat as a Sin Offering (a symbol of Christ dying for sin) 3) Was to be in addition to the regular Burnt Offering k. To offer a Burnt Offering on the 7th day but reduce the bulls by one: Sacrifice 7 bulls (a symbol of Christ's sacrifice) 1) Offer the Grain & the Drink Offerings as specified (a symbol of thanking God & pouring one's life out in dedication to God) 2) Sacrifice one male goat as a Sin Offering (a symbol of Christ dying for sin) 3) Was to be in addition to the regular Burnt Offering l. To call an assembly on the 8th day: Were to do no work 1) Present a Burnt Offering (a symbol of Christ's sacrifice) • One bull, one ram, seven male lambs: With no defect (a symbol of Christ's perfection) • Result: Pleased the LORD 2) Offer the Grain & the Drink Offerings as specified (a symbol of thanking

OUTLINE	SCRIPTURE	SCRIPTURE	OUTLINE
God & pouring one's life out in dedication to God) 3) Sacrifice one male goat as	the lambs, shall be according to their number, after the manner: 38 And one goat for a sin	offering; beside the continual burnt offering, and his meat offering, and his drink offering.	a Sin Offering (a symbol of Christ dying for sin) 4) Was to be in addition to the regular Burnt Offering

Thought 1. The Festival of Tabernacles celebrated the wilderness wanderings when the people lived in tents on their way to the promised land. This is a clear symbol of the believer's march through this world to heaven, a symbol of how short-lived the believer's march through this world is. As the believer marches to heaven, his dwelling upon this earth is only temporary. No matter what kind of house we live in, it is only temporary. It is made out of decaying, corruptible materials. It will waste away and some day, perhaps decades or even a few centuries away, it will cease to be. Earthly homes are only transient structures. Moreover, we are living in mortal bodies, bodies that the Bible describes as a temporary tent or tabernacle. The body is corruptible and will decay and cease to exist. Our journey through this world is only a short-lived pilgrimage. We are marching to our permanent and eternal home in heaven, marching forth to live forever in the presence of God.

"But lay up for yourselves treasures in heaven, where neither moth nor rust doth corrupt, and where thieves do not break through nor steal" (Mt.6:20).

"For we know that if our earthly house of this tabernacle were dissolved, we have a building of God, an house not made with hands, eternal in the heavens" (2 Cor.5:1).

"For our conversation [citizenship] is in heaven; from whence also we look for the Saviour, the Lord Jesus Christ: Who shall change our vile body, that it may be fashioned like unto his glorious body, according to the working whereby he is able even to subdue all things unto himself" (Ph.3:20-21).

"That being justified by his grace, we should be made heirs according to the hope of eternal life" (Tit.3:7).

"For he [Abraham] looked for a city which hath foundations, whose builder and maker is God" (Heb.11:10).

"Blessed be the God and Father of our Lord Jesus Christ, which according to his abundant mercy hath begotten us again unto a lively hope by the resurrection of Jesus Christ from the dead, To an inheritance incorruptible, and undefiled, and that fadeth not away, reserved in heaven for you" (1 Pt.1:3-4).

"Blessed are they that do his commandments, that they may have right to the tree of life, and may enter in through the gates into the city" (Rev.22:14).

10 (29:39-40) **Offerings, Importance of—Sacrifices, Importance of—Symbol, of Christ, Importance of**: there was the awesome importance of the offerings.

OUTLINE	SCRIPTURE
10. The awesome importance of the offerings a. They were additional sacrifices b. They symbolized Christ 1) Burnt Offering: His sacrifice 2) Grain Offering: Giving thanks 3) Drink Offering: Pouring out, sacrificing one's life to Him 4) Fellowship Offering: Seeking more fellowship, v.39 c. They were commanded by God	39 These things ye shall do unto the LORD in your set feasts, beside your vows, and your freewill offerings, for your burnt offerings, and for your meat offerings, and for your drink offerings, and for your peace offerings. 40 And Moses told the children of Israel according to all that the LORD commanded Moses.

1. Note that these offerings were to be additional sacrifices to any other offerings that a person might bring. People who were seeking God often brought offerings, but the offerings spelled out in this chapter were to be additional sacrifices. A constant presentation of sacrifices to God was to be conducted in the Tabernacle. The offering of the *substitute sacrifice* was to be continually upon the minds of the people. They were to know one fact beyond any question: there is only one approach to God—through the *substitute sacrifice*. This one truth was to be driven into their hearts and minds. For this reason, God established all these offerings and sacrifices. Presenting the substitute sacrifices to God was a constant ministry conducted on behalf of the people. When one considers all these offerings and all the voluntary offerings that were brought to the Tabernacle by the people, presenting the substitute sacrifice to God was most likely a continuous, unbroken offering that was being offered up to God. Again, the purpose was to keep this one essential fact before the people: they must approach God through the *substitute sacrifice*. No other approach was acceptable to God. The only way they could ever secure the approval of God was to approach Him through the *substitute sacrifice*.

2. The sacrifice symbolized Christ. Note exactly how:

⇒ The Burnt Offering symbolized the atonement or reconciliation secured by the sacrifice of Christ.

⇒ The Grain Offering symbolized the giving of thanks for the atoning sacrifice and the dedication of one's life because of the atoning sacrifice.

⇒ The Drink Offering symbolized the pouring out, the sacrificing of a person's life in thanksgiving for the substitute sacrifice.

⇒ The Fellowship Offering symbolized the believer seeking to grow in the fellowship and peace of God—all because of the substitute sacrifice that brought about the atonement or reconciliation with God.

3. Note that the offerings and sacrifices were commanded by God.

Thought 1. The offering of the substitute sacrifice was a symbol of the coming Savior of the world. God sent His Son into the world to save us.

"For unto you is born this day in the city of David a Saviour, which is Christ the Lord" (Lk.2:11).

"For the Son of man is come to seek and to save that which was lost" (Lk.19:10).

"For God so loved the world, that he gave his only begotten Son, that whosoever believeth in him should not perish, but have everlasting life. For God sent not his Son into the world to condemn the world; but that the world through him might be saved" (Jn.3:16-17).

"I am the door: by me if any man enter in, he shall be saved, and shall go in and out, and find pasture" (Jn.10:9).

"Him hath God exalted with his right hand to be a Prince and a Saviour, for to give repentance to Israel, and forgiveness of sins" (Acts 5:31).

"But God commendeth his love toward us, in that, while we were yet sinners, Christ died for us. Much more then, being now justified by his blood, we shall be saved from wrath through him. For if, when we were enemies, we were reconciled to God by the death of his Son, much more, being reconciled, we shall be saved by his life. And not only so, but we also joy in God through our Lord Jesus Christ, by whom we have now received the atonement" (Ro.5:8-11).

"This is a faithful saying, and worthy of all acceptation, that Christ Jesus came into the world to save sinners; of whom I am chief" (1 Tim.1:15).

"Though he were a Son, yet learned he obedience by the things which he suffered; And being made perfect, he became the author of eternal salvation unto all them that obey him" (Heb.5:8-9).

"Wherefore he is able also to save them to the uttermost that come unto God by him, seeing he ever liveth to make intercession for them" (Heb.7:25).

"So Christ was once offered to bear the sins of many; and unto them that look for him shall he appear the second time without sin unto salvation" (Heb.9:28).

TYPES, SYMBOLS, AND PICTURES
(Numbers 28:1-29-40)

Historical Term	Type or Picture (Scriptural Basis for Each)	Life Application for Today's Believer	Biblical Application
The Sweet Aroma Num.28:1-2; 28:3-8 (See also Lev. 1:9; 8:21; 16:27-28)	*The aroma ascending up is...* • *a symbol of the person's faith (obedience) in the sacrifice ascending up like a sweet aroma to the LORD* • *a picture of faith and obedience: the sweet aroma of the sacrifice pleased the LORD.* • *a symbol that God was pleased with the offering. He accepted the offering or sacrifice presented by the person.* **"Command the children of Israel, and say unto them, My offering, *and* my bread for my sacrifices made by fire, *for* a sweet savour unto me, shall ye observe to offer unto me in their due season" (Num. 28:2).**	What can we do to please the LORD? We must have faith in the sacrifice of Christ. We must obey God, do exactly what God says: approach Him through the sacrifice of Christ. When we approach God through the sacrifice of Christ, God is pleased and He accepts us. God reconciles us to Him.	***"And walk in love, as Christ also hath loved us, and hath given himself for us an offering and a sacrifice to God for a sweet-smelling savour" (Eph.5:2).*** ***"For if, when we were enemies, we were reconciled to God by the death of his Son, much more, being reconciled, we shall be saved by his life. And not only so, but we also joy in God through our Lord Jesus Christ, by whom we have now received the atonement" (Ro.5:10-11*** ***"For God so loved the world, that he gave his only begotten Son, that whosoever believeth in him should not perish, but have everlasting life" (Jn.3:16).***

Historical Term	Type or Picture (Scriptural Basis for Each)	Life Application for Today's Believer	Biblical Application
Rest, Spiritual Num.28:9-10	*Spiritual rest is a type or symbol of Christ, our spiritual rest.* **"And on the sabbath day two lambs of the first year without spot, and two tenth deals of flour *for* a meat offering, mingled with oil, and the drink offering thereof: *This is* the burnt offering of every sabbath, beside the continual burnt offering, and his drink offering" (Num.28:9-10)**	Jesus Christ is our Sabbath rest. He and He alone brings spiritual rest to the human soul: peace, assurance, confidence, purpose, meaning, significance, security, fulfillment, and satisfaction.	***"Blessed are they which do hunger and thirst after righteousness: for they shall be filled" (Mt.5:6).*** ***"Take my yoke upon you, and learn of me; for I am meek and lowly in heart: and ye shall find rest unto your souls" (Mt. 11:29).*** ***"Peace I leave with you, my peace I give unto you: not as the world giveth, give I unto you. Let not your heart be troubled, neither let it be afraid" (Jn.14:27).*** ***"These things I have spoken unto you, that in me ye might have peace. In the world ye shall have tribulation: but be of good cheer; I have overcome the world" (Jn.16:33).*** ***"For we which have believed do enter into rest, as he said, As I have sworn in my wrath, if they shall enter into my rest: although the works were finished from the foundation of the world" (Heb.4:3).*** ***"For if Jesus had given them rest, then would he not afterward have spoken of another day. There remaineth therefore a rest to the people of God. For he that is entered into his rest, he also hath ceased from his own works, as God did from his" (Heb.4:8-10).*** ***"And I heard a voice from heaven saying unto me, Write, Blessed are the dead which die in the Lord from henceforth: Yea, saith the Spirit, that they may rest from their labours; and their works do follow them" (Rev.14:13).*** ***"And he said, My presence shall go with thee, and I will give thee rest" (Ex.33:14).*** ***"I will both lay me down in peace, and sleep: for thou, Lord, only makest me dwell in safety" (Ps.4:8).***
Monthly Offerings of Animal Sacrifices Num.28:11-15	*A picture of Christ's sacrifice: these were sometimes referred to as the new moon offerings; that is, they were to be presented to the LORD at every new or full moon. These sacrifices were a clear*	The sacrifice of the Burnt Offering symbolized the death of Jesus Christ, but so did the Sin Offering. The Sin Offering was a symbol of Christ's sacrifice for the sins of the world. He died to pro-	***"For this is my blood of the new testament, which is shed for many for the remission of sins" (Mt.26:28).*** ***"Then Peter said unto them, Repent, and be baptized every one of you in the name***

Historical Term	Type or Picture (Scriptural Basis for Each)	Life Application for Today's Believer	Biblical Application
	symbol of the sacrifice of Christ. Note that a much larger number of animals were to be offered at the monthly sacrifice. This meant that a larger Grain Offering and Drink Offering were also to be presented to the LORD. Note also that a Sin Offering was to be presented to God during the monthly sacrifices (v.15). Later in the history of Israel, the new moon festivals were abused. They apparently became festivals for partying involving drink and occasions for immoral behavior (Is.1:13-14).[3] **"And in the beginnings of your months ye shall offer a burnt offering unto the LORD; two young bullocks, and one ram, seven lambs of the first year without spot" (Num.28:11).**	vide forgiveness of sins for us. Through the blood of Christ, we are forgiven for all sin. But note: there is a condition for forgiveness. We must confess and repent of our sins. We must turn away from sin and turn to follow after Christ. Both confession and repentance are essential for forgiveness of sins.	***of Jesus Christ for the remission of sins, and ye shall receive the gift of the Holy Ghost" (Acts 2:38).*** ***"Repent ye therefore, and be converted, that your sins may be blotted out, when the times of refreshing shall come from the presence of the LORD" (Acts 3:19).*** ***"Repent therefore of this thy wickedness, and pray God, if perhaps the thought of thine heart may be forgiven thee" (Acts 8:22).*** ***"In whom we have redemption through his blood, the forgiveness of sins, according to the riches of his grace" (Eph.1:7).*** ***"If we confess our sins, he is faithful and just to forgive us our sins, and to cleanse us from all unrighteousness" (1 Jn.1:9).***
The Passover Num.28:16-25 (See also Lev. 23:5)	*The Passover is a symbol of Christ our Passover who was sacrificed for us.* **"But ye shall offer a sacrifice made by fire *for* a burnt offering unto the LORD; two young bullocks, and one ram, and seven lambs of the first year: they shall be unto you without blemish"(Num.28:19).**	⇒ Jesus Christ is the perfect fulfillment of the Passover Lamb that was slain in behalf of God's people. Through the blood of Jesus Christ, a person escapes the judgment of God. God accepts the blood of His Son—the blood of the substitute sacrifice—as full payment for a person's sin and rebellion against God.	***"The next day John seeth Jesus coming unto him, and saith, Behold the Lamb of God, which taketh away the sin of the world" (Jn.1:29).*** ***"...For even Christ our passover is sacrificed for us" (1 Cor.5:7).*** ***"He was oppressed, and he was afflicted, yet he opened not his mouth: he is brought as a lamb to the slaughter, and as a sheep before her shearers is dumb, so he openeth not his mouth" (Is.53:7).*** ***"Who gave himself for our sins, that he might deliver us from this present evil world, according to the will of God and our Father" (Gal.1:4).***
The Festival of Firstfruits Num.28:26-31 (See also Lev. 23:9-14)	*The Festival of Firstfruits is a symbol of Christ's resurrection: He is the first of the harvest, the first to arise from the dead.* *The Festival of Firstfruits is also a symbol of Pentecost, the great harvest of souls and of people giving their lives to God.* **"Also in the day of the firstfruits, when ye bring a new meat offering unto the LORD, after your weeks *be***	⇒ Christ is the first of the harvest, the first to arise from the dead. It is Jesus Christ and His resurrection that gives the believer hope of arising from the dead and living eternally with God. The prophetic picture of salvation is this: the Passover symbolized the believer's deliverance or redemption from the world; the Festival of Unleavened Bread sym-	***"That Christ should suffer, and that he should be the first that should rise from the dead, and should show light unto the people, and to the Gentiles" (Acts 26:23).*** ***"But now is Christ risen from the dead, and become the firstfruits of them that slept. For since by man came death, by man came also the resurrection of the dead. For as in Adam all die, even so in Christ shall all be made alive. But every man in his own***

3 *The Expositor's Bible Commentary.* Frank E. Gaebelein, Editor, p.951.

Historical Term	Type or Picture (Scriptural Basis for Each)	Life Application for Today's Believer	Biblical Application
	out, **ye shall have an holy convocation; ye shall do no servile work"(Num.28:26).**	bolized the urgency of the believer to leave the world and begin his march to the promised land; and now, the Festival of Firstfruits symbolizes the glorious hope the believer has as he marches toward the promised land, the hope of being raised from the dead and living eternally with God—all because of the resurrection of Christ.	***order: Christ the firstfruits; afterward they that are Christ's at his coming" (1 Cor. 15:20-23).*** ***"Knowing that he which raised up the LORD Jesus shall raise up us also by Jesus, and shall present us with you" (2 Cor.4:14).*** ***"Blessed be the God and Father of our Lord Jesus Christ, which according to his abundant mercy hath begotten us again unto a lively hope by the resurrection of Jesus Christ from the dead, To an inheritance incorruptible, and undefiled, and that fadeth not away, reserved in heaven for you" (1 Pt.1:3-4).***
The Festival of Trumpets Num.29:1-6 (See also Lev. 23:23-25)	*The Festival of Trumpets is a picture of salvation and of the Rapture, the glorious day when Christ will return and take believers—both the living and the dead—to live with Him forever.* **"And in the seventh month, on the first *day* of the month, ye shall have an holy convocation; ye shall do no servile work: it is a day of blowing the trumpets unto you"(Num.29:1).**	⇒ As the believer marches to the promised land, he is to focus upon God, learning to trust God more and more and to heed the message of joy over the atonement or reconciliation with God. God has saved him; consequently, the believer is to joy in his salvation, joy in the atonement and reconciliation with God. Moreover, he is to focus upon God increasingly, learning to trust God more and more. Simply stated, the believer is to grow in his trust and joy; he is to be ever maturing, learning to focus upon the LORD.	***"But I would not have you to be ignorant, brethren, concerning them which are asleep, that ye sorrow not, even as others which have no hope. For if we believe that Jesus died and rose again, even so them also which sleep in Jesus will God bring with him. For this we say unto you by the word of the LORD, that we which are alive and remain unto the coming of the LORD shall not prevent them which are asleep. For the LORD himself shall descend from heaven with a shout, with the voice of the archangel, and with the trump [the trumpet call] of God: and the dead in Christ shall rise first: Then we which are alive and remain shall be caught up together with them in the clouds, to meet the LORD in the air: and so shall we ever be with the LORD. Wherefore comfort one another with these words" (1 Thes. 4:13-18).***
The Day of Atonement Num.29:7-11 (See also Lev. 16:1-34; Lev.23:27)	*The Day of Atonement symbolizes the only way to approach God: through the shed blood of the atoning sacrifice of the Lord Jesus Christ. A person is forgiven his sins and reconciled to God only through the atoning sacrifice of Christ.* **"And ye shall have on the tenth *day* of this seventh**	⇒ The penalty for sin has been paid. How? By Jesus Christ. Jesus Christ died as our atoning sacrifice, reconciling us to God. Hanging upon the cross, Jesus Christ... • bore our sins, taking them away • allowed the justice and judgment of	***"Having therefore, brethren, boldness to enter into the holiest by the blood of Jesus, By a new and living way, which he hath consecrated for us, through the veil, that is to say, his flesh; And having an high priest over the house of God; Let us draw near with a true heart in full assurance of faith, having our hearts sprinkled from an evil con-***

Historical Term	Type or Picture (Scriptural Basis for Each)	Life Application for Today's Believer	Biblical Application
	month an holy convocation; and ye shall afflict your souls: ye shall not do any work *therein*" (Num. 29:7).	God to be executed against Him, suffering the punishment due us • paid the penalty of sin and death, bearing the alienation and separation from God for us	***science, and our bodies washed with pure water" (Heb.10:19-22).*** ***"Therefore being justified by faith, we have peace with God through our Lord Jesus Christ: By whom also we have access by faith into this grace wherein we stand, and rejoice in hope of the glory of God" (Ro.5:1-2).***
The Festival of Tabernacles or Booths or Shelters Num.29:12-38 (See also Lev. 23:33-34)	*The Festival of Tabernacles is a symbol of the believer's short, temporary life and march through this world to the promised land of heaven.* **"And on the fifteenth day of the seventh month ye shall have an holy convocation; ye shall do no servile work, and ye shall keep a feast unto the LORD seven days"(Num.29:12).**	⇒ As the believer marches through this world to the promised land of heaven, his dwelling is only temporary. No matter what kind of house he lives in, it is temporary. It is made out of decaying, corruptible materials. It will waste away and some day, perhaps decades or even centuries away, it will cease to be. Earthly homes are only temporary structures. Moreover, the believer is living in a temporary body, a body that the Bible describes as a temporary tent or tabernacle. The body is corruptible and will decay and cease to exist. The believer's journey or pilgrimage through this world is only temporary. He is marching to his permanent and eternal home in heaven where he will live forever in the presence of God.	***"For we know that if our earthly house of this tabernacle were dissolved, we have a building of God, an house not made with hands, eternal in the heavens" (2 Cor.5:1).*** ***"Of old hast thou laid the foundation of the earth: and the heavens are the work of thy hands. They shall perish, but thou shalt endure: yea, all of them shall wax old like a garment; as a vesture shalt thou change them, and they shall be changed" (Ps.102:25-26).*** ***"And they that use this world, as not abusing it: for the fashion of this world passeth away" (1 Cor.7:31).*** ***"While we look not at the things which are seen, but at the things which are not seen: for the things which are seen are temporal; but the things which are not seen are eternal" (2 Cor. 4:18; cp. 2 Pt. 3:10; Rev. 21:1).***

1. The importance of vows & pledges
   a. Vows & pledges concern the LORD Himself & are governed by the LORD
   b. Vows & pledges must not be broken

2. The vows & pledges of a young woman still living with her parents
   a. The obligation: She must keep her vow or pledge
   b. The one exception: The parents' authority must be respected & followed
      1) If her father approves, the vow stands
      2) If her father objects, the vow is released
      3) The point: The parent must be considered (because of finances, hardship, health—whatever the vow involved)

3. The vows or pledges of a woman who marries while her commitment is still in force
   a. The obligation: Must keep her vow, even rash promises
   b. The one exception: The husband's authority
      1) If her husband approves, the vow or pledge stands
      2) If her husband objects, the vow or pledge is nullified: The LORD releases her
      3) The point: Spouses are tobe considered in vows

E. The Laws that Govern Vows: The Obligation to Keep Vows & to Consider Others in Making Vows, 30:1-16

And Moses spake unto the
heads of the tribes concerning the children of Israel,
saying, This is the thing
which the LORD hath com-
manded.
2 If a man vow a vow unto
the LORD, or swear an oath to
bind his soul with a bond; he
shall not break his word, he
shall do according to all that
proceedeth out of his mouth.
3 If a woman also vow a vow
unto the LORD, and bind herself by a bond, being in her
father's house in her youth;
4 And her father hear her
vow, and her bond where-
with she hath bound her soul,
and her father shall hold his
peace at her: then all her
vows shall stand, and every
bond wherewith she hath
bound her soul shall stand.
5 But if her father disallow
her in the day that he
heareth; not any of her vows,
or of her bonds wherewith
she hath bound her soul,
shall stand: and the LORD
shall forgive her, because her
father disallowed her.
6 And if she had at all an
husband, when she vowed,
or uttered ought out of her
lips, wherewith she bound
her soul;
7 And her husband heard it,
and held his peace at her in
the day that he heard it: then
her vows shall stand, and her
bonds wherewith she bound
her soul shall stand.
8 But if her husband disallowed her on the day that he
heard it; then he shall make
her vow which she vowed,
and that which she uttered
with her lips, wherewith she
bound her soul, of none
effect: and the LORD shall
forgive her.
9 But every vow of a widow,
and of her that is divorced,
wherewith they have bound
their souls, shall stand
against her.
10 And if she vowed in her
husband's house, or bound
her soul by a bond with an
oath;
11 And her husband heard
it, and held his peace at her,
and disallowed her not: then
all her vows shall stand, and
every bond wherewith she
bound her soul shall stand.
12 But if her husband hath
utterly made them void on
the day he heard them; then
whatsoever proceeded out of
her lips concerning her
vows, or concerning the
bond of her soul, shall not
stand: her husband hath
made them void; and the
LORD shall forgive her.
13 Every vow, and every
binding oath to afflict the
soul, her husband may establish it, or her husband may
make it void.
14 But if her husband altogether hold his peace at her
from day to day; then he
establisheth all her vows, or
all her bonds, which are
upon her: he confirmeth
them, because he held his
peace at her in the day that
he heard them.
15 But if he shall any ways
make them void after that he
hath heard them; then he
shall bear her iniquity.
16 These are the statutes,
which the LORD commanded
Moses, between a man and
his wife, between the father
and his daughter, being yet
in her youth in her father's
house.

(because of finances, hardships, health, etc.)

4. The vows or pledges of a widow or divorced woman: Are binding—must still be fulfilled

5. The vows or pledges of a married woman
   a. The obligation: She must keep her vow or pledge
   b. The one exception: The husband's authority
      1) If her husband approves, the vow or pledge stands
      2) If her husband disapproves, the vow or pledge is nullified: The LORD releases her
   c. The point: Consideration must be given to the husband (spouse) when making vows or pledges
      1) He (as family head) has the right to confirm or disallow
      2) He confirms by saying nothing on the day he hears about the vow or pledge
      3) He personally stands guilty before God if he nullifies them some time after hearing about them

6. The concern of God for order in families
   a. These laws build the relationship between man & wife
   b. These laws build the relationship between father & daughter

DIVISION IV

THE PREPARATION FOR THE MARCH INTO THE PROMISED LAND, 26:1-36:13

E. The Laws that Govern Vows: The Obligation to Keep Vows and to Consider Others in Making Vows, 30:1-16

(30:1-16) **Introduction—Non-Profit Organizations—Organizations, Non-Profit—Support, of Non-Profit Organizations—Pledges, to Support Ministries—Church, Support of—Vows, Discussed**: thousands of institutions and non-profit organizations depend upon the vows and pledges of people. If people stopped giving to these organizations, their doors would close. Some of these organizations are meeting desperate needs within their own community while others are meeting desperate needs around the world. They are legitimate organizations that should be supported, even supported to the point of sacrifice. Because they are meeting desperate needs, many of these organizations are very dear to the hearts of people. People pour their hard-earned dollars into meeting the needs of their communities and of the world. They even make pledges and commitments to give something on a regular basis in order to have a part in meeting the continued need that cries out so desperately for help. The point is this: once a vow or pledge has been made, the commitment is to be kept. This is the law of God. This is the discussion of this important passage of Scripture: *The Laws that Govern Vows: The Obligation to Keep Vows and to Consider Others in Making Vows,* 30:1-16.

1. The importance of vows and pledges (v.1-2).
2. The vows and pledges of a young woman still living with her parents (v.3-5).
3. The vows or pledges of a woman who marries while her commitment is still in force (v.6-8).
4. The vows or pledges of a widow or divorced woman: are binding—must still be fulfilled (v.9).
5. The vows or pledges of a married woman (v.10-15).
6. The concern of God for order in families (v.16).

1 (30:1-2) **Vows, Importance of—Pledges, Importance of—Vows, Duty of**: the importance of vows and pledges can be seen in two facts.

OUTLINE	SCRIPTURE
1. The importance of vows & pledges a. Vows & pledges concern the LORD Himself & are governed by the LORD b. Vows & pledges must not be broken	And Moses spake unto the heads of the tribes concerning the children of Israel, saying, This is the thing which the LORD hath commanded. 2 If a man vow a vow unto the LORD, or swear an oath to bind his soul with a bond; he shall not break his word, he shall do according to all that proceedeth out of his mouth

First, vows and pledges concern the LORD Himself and are governed by the LORD (v.1). Anything that concerns God is of critical importance, for the destiny of human life is in His hands. Both blessings and judgment are determined by God. If a person approaches God as he should, he is blessed. But if he approaches God in a wrong or false way, he is condemned and to be judged by God. This is one reason vows and pledges are so important. They involve and concern the LORD; they are offered up to God Himself. This is the reason God gave certain laws to govern vows and pledges. In love, God wants man to understand exactly how vows and pledges are to be made. God loves man and does not want him to come under condemnation. He wants a perfect understanding between Himself and man. He wants man to be blessed, not cursed to face judgment.

The second fact that makes vows and pledges important is this: vows and pledges must not be broken (v.2). A person must be conscientious; he must not break his word when he makes a promise to God. God has declared that a person can make a vow or pledge to Him, but once made, the promise must be kept—absolutely kept. Hypocrisy—a hypocritical approach to God—profanes and defiles God's holy name. It is far better not to make a vow than to break a vow (Eccl.5.5). Man must not deceive himself. Scripture is clear: "God is not mocked: for whatsoever a man soweth, that shall he also reap" (Gal.6:9). A person must keep his vows once they are made. He must not break his word, his promise to God. He must do everything he vowed or pledged.

Thought 1. A person must keep the vows or pledges made to God. Failing to keep his promises, his word, makes a person a liar. But this is not the worst offense: his broken promise profanes and defiles the holy name of God. This God will never tolerate. Once a vow or pledge has been made, it must be kept. This is the strong declaration of Scripture:

"If a man vow a vow unto the Lord, or swear an oath to bind his soul with a bond; he shall not break his word, he shall do according to all that proceedeth out of his mouth" (Num.30:2).

"When thou shalt vow a vow unto the Lord thy God, thou shalt not slack to pay it: for the Lord thy God will surely require it of thee; and it would be sin in thee. But if thou shalt forbear to vow, it shall be no sin in thee. That which is gone out of thy lips thou shalt keep and perform; even a freewill offering, according as thou hast vowed unto the Lord thy God, which thou hast promised with thy mouth" (Dt.23:21-23).

"It is a snare to the man who devoureth that which is holy, and after vows to make enquiry" (Pr.20:25).

"When thou vowest a vow unto God, defer not to pay it; for he hath no pleasure in fools: pay that which thou hast vowed. Better is it that thou shouldest not vow, than that thou shouldest vow and not pay. Suffer not thy mouth to cause thy flesh to sin; neither say thou before the angel, that it was an error: wherefore should God be angry at thy voice, and destroy the work of thine hands" (Eccl.5:4-6).

2 (30:3-5) **Vows, of Children—Pledges, of Children—Vows, of Single Women—Parents, Duties to Children**: there was the law governing the vows and pledges of a daughter who still lived with her parents. The hearts of young people are tender and sensitive, subject to following whatever examples or influences surround them. Hopefully, the example and influence around a young person are godly. When a young person has a godly example, the child often makes vows and pledges to God. This was definitely true with the children of the Israelites. The parents stressed the importance of following God, of learning His commandments and obeying them. Because of this strong instruction in righteousness, children often made vows and pledges to God. The point to see is this: sometimes a child's pledge could cause a serious problem for the family, in particular if the pledge involved an expensive gift or a large quantity of some item. For example, a young daughter might pledge food or clothing to the poor, or a large sum of money that she had saved, or jewelry that was of great value and offered security to the family, or some animal that provided necessary security for her and her family, or any other property or expensive possession she held under her care. There was the possibility that her vow could damage or bring hardship to the family. Since parents usually try to protect their children from crises situations, they seldom discuss crises or genuine hardships with their children. A father could be facing severe loss, even bankruptcy involving the loss of business, house, or property. A young daughter still living at home would likely have no way of knowing this. God knew that situations like this would arise; therefore, with a heart full of grace and love for young children who love Him so much that they would make vows in order to draw closer to Him, He made provision for their safeguard and such dire circumstances. This is clearly seen in the Scripture and outline:

OUTLINE	SCRIPTURE	SCRIPTURE	OUTLINE
2. The vows & pledges of a young woman still living with her parents a. The obligation: She must keep her vow or pledge b. The one exception: The parents' authority must be respected & followed 1) If her father approves, the vow stands	3 If a woman also vow a vow unto the LORD, and bind herself by a bond, being in her father's house in her youth; 4 And her father hear her vow, and her bond wherewith she hath bound her soul, and her father shall hold his peace at her: then all her vows shall stand, and	every bond wherewith she hath bound her soul shall stand. 5 But if her father disallow her in the day that he heareth; not any of her vows, or of her bonds wherewith she hath bound her soul, shall stand: and the LORD shall forgive her, because her father disallowed her.	2) If her father objects, the vow is released 3) The point: The parent must be considered (because of finances, hardship, health—whatever the vow involved)

1. Note the obligation of the young woman who had made a vow or pledge: she must keep the promise she made to God. If a vow or pledge was made, there was no excuse: she had to keep her word.

2. But as stated, with a heart full of love for the young daughter, God made one exception: the parents' authority must be respected and followed. The parents knew whether or not her vow would cause problems or hardships for the family. Therefore, the child was to obey the instructions of her parents. If the father approved, the vow stood. If her father objected, the vow was released from the young woman. She would not face the condemnation and judgment of God. But note: the father had to object to the vow immediately after hearing about it. Once he had heard about the vow, if he said nothing, the vow was to stand. He was not to allow the vow to stand unopposed and then one day object to the vow and disallow it. If the father first allowed the vow and then stepped in and stopped the vow at a later date, he personally became obligated to fulfill the vow himself (cp. v.15).

The point is this: a young daughter must consider her parents when she makes a vow, and she must obey her parents if her parents object to the vow. This is because of finances, hardships, health reasons, or any other factor that might damage the family and its welfare.

Thought 1. Children must obey parents. This is particularly true when making vows or pledges. Only the parent knows the full situation within the family, what problems the family may be facing such as...

- financial difficulty
- loss of employment
- change of employment
- health problems
- relocation
- marital problems
- financial commitments and obligations

The child simply has no way to know the overall picture of the family. Therefore, the child must always obey the parent, in particular when making vows or pledges to the LORD.

"For God commanded, saying, Honour thy father and mother: and, He that curseth father or mother, let him die the death" (Mt.15:4).

"Children, obey your parents in the Lord: for this is right. Honour thy father and mother; (which is the first commandment with promise;) That it may be well with thee, and thou mayest live long on the earth" (Eph.6:1-3).

"Children, obey your parents in all things: for this is well pleasing unto the Lord" (Col.3:20).

"But if any widow have children or nephews, let them learn first to show piety at home, and to requite their parents: for that is good and acceptable before God" (1 Tim.5:4).

"Honour thy father and thy mother: that thy days may be long upon the land which the Lord thy God giveth thee" (Ex.20:12).

"Ye shall fear every man his mother, and his father, and keep my sabbaths: I am the Lord your God" (Lev.19:3).

"Cursed be he that setteth light by his father or his mother. And all the people shall say, Amen" (Dt.27:16).

"My son, hear the instruction of thy father, and forsake not the law of thy mother" (Pr.1:8).

"My son, keep thy father's commandment, and forsake not the law of thy mother" (Pr.6:20).

"The eye that mocketh at his father, and despiseth to obey his mother, the ravens of the valley shall pick it out, and the young eagles shall eat it" (Pr.30:17).

3 (30:6-8) **Vows, Law Governing—Pledges, Law Governing—Women, Duties of, to Keep Vows**: there was the law governing the vows or pledges of a woman who married while her commitment was still in force.

OUTLINE	SCRIPTURE	SCRIPTURE	OUTLINE
3. The vows or pledges of a woman who marries while her commitment is still in force a. The obligation: Must keep her vow, even rash promises b. The one exception: The husband's authority 1) If her husband approves, the vow or pledge stands	6 And if she had at all an husband, when she vowed, or uttered ought out of her lips, wherewith she bound her soul; 7 And her husband heard it, and held his peace at her in the day that he heard it: then her vows shall stand, and her bonds wherewith she bound	her soul shall stand. 8 But if her husband disallowed her on the day that he heard it; then he shall make her vow which she vowed, and that which she uttered with her lips, wherewith she bound her soul, of none effect: and the LORD shall forgive her.	2) If her husband objects, the vow or pledge is nullified: The LORD releases her 3) The point: Spouses are tobe considered in vows (because of finances, hardships, health, etc.)

1. The young woman was obligated to keep her vow (v.6). She had made the vow or pledge in good faith; therefore, she was to keep the promise. She was to fulfill her word, do exactly what she had said. Even if the vow was a rash promise, uttered in an impulsive moment, she was still to keep her promise. Note this is exactly what Scripture says (v.6).

But what happens if her vow creates a hardship for her and her husband? After all, she had made the vow before their marriage, and she had no idea that it would create a hardship upon them. But it had. So what was she to do? God knew the problem this would create for His dear people; therefore, He instituted a law that would release her from her vow.

2. Note the law: this is one exception that is based upon the husband's authority within the family (v.7-8). In ancient society, the husband always managed the property, looked after the finances, and handled the business dealings for the family. Within the family, the husband was the one who knew the overall financial situation. Therefore, if a young woman made a vow before she was married, the husband had the authority either to approve or disapprove the vow after the marriage. If her husband approved the vow, the vow or pledge stood. She could fulfill her promise, keep her word. But if her husband objected, the vow or pledge was nullified. The LORD released her (v.8). The point is this: spouses were to consider one another when evaluating vows and pledges. This was an absolute essential because of finances, business dealings, employment, and a host of other factors that might create hardship upon young people who had just been married.

Thought 1. God cares about young married couples. He wants them to have a full and rich life, establishing godly families upon this earth. He knows that young people have tender hearts and can be challenged to step out in great faith, step out in making strong vows and commitments to follow after Him. The vows or pledges may involve the giving of a certain amount of money, the commitment of a life to missionary service, the commitment of so much time or of certain possessions or a host of other commitments. In facing marriage, sometimes the young person will have to decide between keeping the vow made to God or marriage. A choice will have to be made. For example, a choice may have to be made between missionary service and marriage. But before the marriage is the time for the decision to be made. However, after marriage, if the vow creates a hardship for the young married couple, the young woman is released from her vow. Her first obligation is to her husband. She will not be held guilty by God.

The point to see in this law is God's love and care for His dear people. God knows that we get ourselves into difficult situations sometimes, situations that create hardships. God does not want this. With tenderness and care, He releases a young person from a vow that creates a hardship after marriage. God does not want a young couple suffering under hardship nor any other pressure or strain. He wants young people free from difficult circumstances so they can focus upon building a strong, godly love and family. God is mindful of their needs and He wants to provide for all of them. This is the reason God frees a young person from a vow or pledge after marriage. He loves and He cares for His dear people. This is the strong declaration of Scripture.

"But seek ye first the kingdom of God, and his righteousness; and all these things shall be added unto you" (Mt.6:33).

"But even the very hairs of your head are all numbered. Fear not therefore: ye are of more value than many sparrows" (Lk.12:7).

"Casting all your care upon him; for he careth for you" (1 Pt.5:7).

"The eternal God is thy refuge, and underneath are the everlasting arms" (Dt.33:27).

"The Lord is my strength and my shield; my heart trusted in him, and I am helped: therefore my heart greatly rejoiceth; and with my song will I praise him" (Ps.28:7).

"The Lord hath been mindful of us: he will bless us; he will bless the house of Israel; he will bless the house of Aaron" (Ps.115:12).

"Fear thou not; for I am with thee: be not dismayed; for I am thy God: I will strengthen thee; yea, I will help thee; yea, I will uphold thee with the right hand of my righteousness" (Is.41:10).

4 (30:9) **Vows, of the Divorced—Pledges, of the Divorced—Widows, Vows or Pledges of**: the vows or pledges of a widow or divorced woman are binding. They must still be fulfilled even after divorce or after becoming a widow.

OUTLINE	SCRIPTURE
4. The vows or pledges of a widow or divorced woman: Are binding—must still be fulfilled	9 But every vow of a widow, and of her that is divorced, wherewith they have bound their souls, shall stand against her.

Sometimes a recently widowed or divorced woman would return home to her parents or go live with a child, at least temporarily. In such situations, the woman was still considered to be the sole authority of her own affairs. Neither her father nor son could insist that she break her vow. The divorced or widowed woman was still obligated to fulfill her promise, to make her pledge. She was to be faithful to her word, to do exactly what she had promised.

> **"If a man vow a vow unto the Lord, or swear an oath to bind his soul with a bond; he shall not break his word, he shall do according to all that proceedeth out of his mouth" (Num.30:2).**
> **"When thou shalt vow a vow unto the Lord thy God, thou shalt not slack to pay it: for the Lord thy God will surely require it of thee; and it would be sin in thee" (Dt.23:21).**
> **"When thou vowest a vow unto God, defer not to pay it; for he hath no pleasure in fools: pay that which thou hast vowed" (Eccl.5:4).**

5 (30:10-15) **Vows, of Married Women—Women, Married, Pledges of**: there was the law governing the vows or pledges of a married woman. A woman who follows after the LORD often makes pledges or vows. Seeing and hearing about needs touches her heart, needs such as...

- suffering people
- poor families
- disaster-stricken areas
- disease-stricken children or adults
- fire victims
- the appeals of mission organizations
- opportunities to get the gospel out
- the hungry and homeless
- the poor and destitute
- the suffering and dying

By their very nature, women are nurturing; therefore, they are tenderhearted and often reach out to meet the needs of others. Sometimes the meeting of these needs requires making commitments on a regular basis. If a woman made a vow or pledge without the knowledge of her husband, what was to be done? This law governed the situation:

OUTLINE	SCRIPTURE	SCRIPTURE	OUTLINE
5. The vows or pledges of a married woman a. The obligation: She must keep her vow or pledge b. The one exception: The husband's authority 1) If her husband approves, the vow or pledge stands 2) If her husband disapproves, the vow or pledge is nullified: The LORD releases her	10 And if she vowed in her husband's house, or bound her soul by a bond with an oath; 11 And her husband heard it, and held his peace at her, and disallowed her not: then all her vows shall stand, and every bond wherewith she bound her soul shall stand. 12 But if her husband hath utterly made them void on the day he heard them; then whatsoever proceeded out of her lips concerning her vows, or concerning the bond of her soul, shall not stand: her husband hath made them void; and the	LORD shall forgive her. 13 Every vow, and every binding oath to afflict the soul, her husband may establish it, or her husband may make it void. 14 But if her husband altogether hold his peace at her from day to day; then he establisheth all her vows, or all her bonds, which are upon her: he confirmeth them, because he held his peace at her in the day that he heard them. 15 But if he shall any ways make them void after that he hath heard them; then he shall bear her iniquity.	c. The point: Consideration must be given to the husband (spouse) when making vows or pledges 1) He (as family head) has the right to confirm or disallow 2) He confirms by saying nothing on the day he hears about the vow or pledge 3) He personally stands guilty before God if he nullifies them some time after hearing about them

1. The wife was obligated to keep the vow or pledge. She had made the commitment; therefore she was to fulfill her commitment. She was to keep her vow, do exactly what she had said and promised.

2. But note, there was one exception: the husband's authority (v.11-12). If the husband heard about the vow and said nothing, the vow or pledge stood. But if the husband disapproved, the vow or pledge was nullified. The LORD released the wife from her vow. Remember, the husband managed the finances, looked after the property, and took care of business matters for the family. He was the only family member who saw the overall financial situation of the family. Therefore, he knew whether or not the vow would bring hardship upon the family. He must have a voice in the vow or pledge being made by the wife. If she made the vow on her own, without considering her husband, she had made an unwise decision, a

decision that could bankrupt or create extreme hardship for the family. God knew this and He cared, not wanting the family to live under the strain of hardship or financial difficulty. Therefore, God made provision for the wife to be released from the vow or pledge she made. She would not stand guilty before God if she broke her vow. She was free to listen and follow the request or demand of her husband that the vow be annulled.

3. Note the point: consideration must be given to the husband when making vows or pledges (v.13-15). As stated, in ancient Israel, the husband was the person who managed the finances, property, and business dealings of the family. Therefore, he had the right to confirm or disallow all vows or pledges. He confirmed a vow by saying nothing when he heard about it. The wife was free to fulfill her vow or pledge. But note: if he nullified the vow sometime after having heard about it, he personally stood guilty before God. The guilt for having broken the vow was not counted against the wife but against him. In God's eyes, he was the guilty party; therefore, he was to stand accountable to God in the day of judgment.

Thought 1. Wives and husbands are to consider one another when making vows or pledges to God. No pledge or vow should be made by either party without discussing it first with the other spouse. Once married, a couple is a unit, bound together as one body in the eyes of God. Therefore, whatever one spouse does affects the other spouse, even if the one making the pledge or vow manages the finances and business affairs of the family. Consideration must always be given to the other spouse before making vows and pledges. The other spouse may know something that would create a hardship upon the family, some upcoming misfortune such as...

- health problems
- financial difficulties
- unemployment
- bankruptcy
- loss of property
- dropping stock prices
- lower interest income
- possible relocation

For these and a host of other reasons, spouses must always consider one another when making vows or pledges. God does not want a family going through hardships or financial difficulties. He wants a husband and wife focused upon building a godly family, not focused upon hardships and difficulties that put undue strain upon them. God wants His dear people experiencing the spiritual rest of the promised land, not suffering under the strain and hardships of life. He wants them bound together in love, focused upon Him, one another, and the rest of their family. God wants strong, godly families who know the fullness of life in all of the love and joy of His Spirit. He wants them marching together to the promised land, being victorious over all the hardships and enemies of this life, conquering and triumphing over all. If a couple is living separately and making decisions alone without considering the other spouse, the fullness of life can never be experienced by the family. Therefore, no spouse is to make a vow without considering the other spouse. In making vows and pledges, consideration of the other spouse is always a necessity.

"Wives, submit yourselves unto your own husbands, as unto the Lord" (Eph.5:22).

"Husbands, love your wives, even as Christ also loved the church, and gave himself for it" (Eph.5:25).

"Nevertheless let every one of you in particular so love his wife even as himself; and the wife see that she reverence her husband" (Eph.5:32-33).

"Even so must their wives be grave, not slanderers, sober, faithful in all things" (1 Tim.3:11).

"Likewise, ye husbands, dwell with them according to knowledge, giving honour unto the wife, as unto the weaker vessel, and as being heirs together of the grace of life; that your prayers be not hindered" (1 Pt.3:7).

"Therefore shall a man leave his father and his mother, and shall cleave unto his wife: and they shall be one flesh" (Gen.2:24).

"Let thy fountain be blessed: and rejoice with the wife of thy youth" (Pr.5:18).

6 (30:16) **Families, Order Within—Organization, of Families—Relationships, Between Man and Wife—Relationships, Between Father and Children**: there was the concern of God for order and organization within families. One of the very first institutions ever created was that of the family. Adam was the first man and Eve the first woman upon earth. When they came together to have a child, the first family was instituted. This was the very purpose of God for putting man and woman upon earth, to share together as husband and wife and as the parental heads of the family. God cares about the family, about how it functions, wanting the family to experience the richness and fullness of life. This is the very reason for this present law governing vows made by various family members. As has been seen, these laws built the relationship between man and wife and between father and daughter or children. Note how this is stressed in the Scripture and outline:

OUTLINE	SCRIPTURE
6. The concern of God for order in families a. These laws build the relationship between man & wife b. These laws build the relationship between father & daughter	16 These are the statutes, which the LORD commanded Moses, between a man and his wife, between the father and his daughter, being yet in her youth in her father's house.

Thought 1. This fact is true of the human body: without a head, there is no living body. So it is within any body of

people. There has to be a head who has ultimate authority for any organization to function properly. Without a head, without someone in charge, there is chaos. There is no accountability, no one to make sure that the functions of an organization or project are adequately carried out. Within the family, the head is one of the parents. If the family is a one-parent family, then the one parent is the head. If the family is a two-parent family, then the ultimate responsibility for the love, care, and protection of the family is the father's. He is to love the family to the point of sacrificing himself totally if necessary, just as Christ sacrificed and gave Himself for the church (Eph.5:25). The point to see is this: God is concerned about order in the family; therefore, He gave these laws to build a strong relationship between man and wife and between father and daughter or children. God wants the strongest relationships possible to exist among all family members. This is the clear declaration of Scripture:

"Submitting yourselves one to another in the fear of God. Wives, submit yourselves unto your own husbands, as unto the Lord. For the husband is the head of the wife, even as Christ is the head of the church: and he is the saviour of the body. Therefore as the church is subject unto Christ, so let the wives be to their own husbands in every thing. Husbands, love your wives, even as Christ also loved the church, and gave himself for it" (Eph.5:21-25).

"So ought men to love their wives as their own bodies. He that loveth his wife loveth himself. For no man ever yet hated his own flesh; but nourisheth and cherisheth it, even as the Lord the church: For we are members of his body, of his flesh, and of his bones. For this cause shall a man leave his father and mother, and shall be joined unto his wife, and they two shall be one flesh" (Eph.5:28-31).

"And, ye fathers, provoke not your children to wrath: but bring them up in the nurture and admonition of the Lord" (Eph.6:4).

"Even so must their wives be grave, not slanderers, sober, faithful in all things" (1 Tim.3:11).

"That they may teach the young women to be sober, to love their husbands, to love their children" (Tit.2:4).

"Likewise, ye husbands, dwell with them according to knowledge, giving honour unto the wife, as unto the weaker vessel, and as being heirs together of the grace of life; that your prayers be not hindered" (1 Pt.3:7).

"And thou shalt teach them diligently unto thy children, and shalt talk of them when thou sittest in thine house, and when thou walkest by the way, and when thou liest down, and when thou risest up" (Dt.6:7).

"Train up a child in the way he should go: and when he is old, he will not depart from it" (Pr.22:6).

1. The order to launch the campaign: God judges the evil of this world
   a. The reason: God's justice
      1) The Midianites[DS1] had seduced & tried to destroy God's people
      2) Moses was soon to die
   b. The call to arms by Moses: He charged the people to prepare for war against the Midianites
      1) To carry out God's vengeance on the seductive, immoral enemies
      2) To arm 1000 soldiers from each tribe: A total of 12,000 armed soldiers
      3) To take the priest Phinehas with them
         - With the holy objects of the sanctuary
         - With the trumpets for sounding the charge

2. The victorious campaign: A picture of victory over the evil, seductive, & immoral enemies of life
   a. They triumphed over Midian
      1) The five kings of Midian were killed
      2) The wicked advisor of the evil, seductive plan, Balaam, was killed (22:1-25:18)
   b. They captured the women, children, animals, & possessions—even the women who had seduced & sought to destroy them
   c. They burned all the cities & camps
   d. They triumphantly marched back to their camp with the captives, spoils, & plunder
      1) They expected a triumphant celebration with Moses, Eleazar, & the people

F. The Conquest of the Most Dangerous & Threatening Enemies, the Midianites: A Picture of Conquering the Seductive, Immoral Enemies of the World, 31:1-54

And the LORD spake unto
Moses, saying,
2 Avenge the children of Israel of the Midianites: afterward shalt thou be gathered
unto thy people.
3 And Moses spake unto the
people, saying, Arm some of
yourselves unto the war, and
let them go against the Midianites, and avenge the LORD
of Midian.
4 Of every tribe a thousand,
throughout all the tribes of
Israel, shall ye send to the
war.
5 So there were delivered out
of the thousands of Israel, a
thousand of every tribe,
twelve thousand armed for
war.
6 And Moses sent them to
the war, a thousand of every
tribe, them and Phinehas the
son of Eleazar the priest, to
the war, with the holy instruments, and the trumpets to
blow in his hand.
7 And they warred against
the Midianites, as the LORD
commanded Moses; and they
slew all the males.
8 And they slew the kings of
Midian, beside the rest of
them that were slain; namely,
Evi, and Rekem, and Zur,
and Hur, and Reba, five
kings of Midian: Balaam
also the son of Beor they
slew with the sword.
9 And the children of Israel
took all the women of Midian captives, and their little
ones, and took the spoil of all
their cattle, and all their
flocks, and all their goods.
10 And they burnt all their
cities wherein they dwelt,
and all their goodly castles,
with fire.
11 And they took all the
spoil, and all the prey, both
of men and of beasts.
12 And they brought the
captives, and the prey, and
the spoil, unto Moses, and
Eleazar the priest, and unto
the congregation of the children of Israel, unto the camp
at the plains of Moab, which
are by Jordan near Jericho.
13 And Moses, and Eleazar
the priest, and all the princes
of the congregation, went
forth to meet them without
the camp.
14 And Moses was wroth
with the officers of the host,
with the captains over thousands, and captains over
hundreds, which came from
the battle.
15 And Moses said unto
them, Have ye saved all the
women alive?
16 Behold, these caused the
children of Israel, through
the counsel of Balaam, to
commit trespass against the
LORD in the matter of Peor,
and there was a plague
among the congregation of
the LORD.
17 Now therefore kill every
male among the little ones,
and kill every woman that
hath known man by lying
with him.
18 But all the women children, that have not known a
man by lying with him, keep
alive for yourselves.
19 And do ye abide without
the camp seven days: whosoever hath killed any person,
and whosoever hath touched
any slain, purify both yourselves and your captives on
the third day, and on the seventh day.
20 And purify all your raiment, and all that is made of
skins, and all work of goats'
hair, and all things made of
wood.
21 And Eleazar the priest
said unto the men of war
which went to the battle,
This is the ordinance of the
law which the LORD com-
manded Moses;
22 Only the gold, and the
silver, the brass, the iron, the
tin, and the lead,
23 Every thing that may
abide the fire, ye shall make
it go through the fire, and it
shall be clean: nevertheless it
shall be purified with the
water of separation: and all
that abideth not the fire ye
shall make go through the
water.
24 And ye shall wash your
clothes on the seventh day,
and ye shall be clean, and afterward ye shall come into

      2) Moses, Eleazar, & all the leaders went to meet the victorious army outside the camp

3. The shocking military error: A picture of failing to fully destroy the evil, seductive, & immoral enemies of life
   a. The anger of Moses with the officers & commanders of the army
      1) They had spared some of the most dangerous enemies, the women
      2) The women had seduced them into immoral behavior & false worship in an attempt to destroy them
      3) The women had caused the judgment of God to fall: A plague that killed 21,000 Israelites
   b. The enemies—all who sought or could seek to destroy Israel—had to be destroyed: Women & boys
   c. The innocent & non-threatening girls were saved

4. The purification of the soldiers & the spoils: A reminder that death is the ultimate corruption
   a. They were unclean: Had been in contact with death
      1) Could not go in the camp
      2) Had to cleanse themselves & the captives
      3) Had to cleanse every garment & all else made of leather & cloth
   b. They had to fully obey the law of cleansing in detail: It was God's command
      1) All metal objects had to be cleansed by fire & water: Gold, silver, bronze, iron, tin, & lead objects
      2) All other objects had to be cleansed by water
      3) All personal clothing had to be washed
      4) The result: Could enter camp—be reconciled

5. The division of the spoils: A picture of rewards & of giving thanks to God

a. The command of the LORD
   1) The leaders were to count all the spoils
   2) The leaders were to divide the spoils between the soldiers & the people
   3) The soldiers were to contribute a portion to the LORD
      - To give one out of every 500 of everything
      - To give the LORD's part to the priest: The LORD's representative—His minister to the people
   4) The people were to contribute a portion to the LORD
      - To give one out of every 50 of everything
      - To give to the Levites: The LORD's servants who cared for the Tabernacle

b. The obedience of Moses & Eleazar, the High Priest
   1) They counted the plunder
      - The sheep: 675,000
      - The cattle: 72,000
      - The donkeys: 61,000
      - The innocent women: 32,000
   2) They distributed the soldiers' share
      - The sheep: 337,500 with 675 given to the LORD
      - The cattle: 36,000 with 72 given to the LORD
      - The donkeys: 30,500 with 61 given to the LORD

the camp.

25 And the LORD spake unto Moses, saying,

26 Take the sum of the prey that was taken, both of man and of beast, thou, and Eleazar the priest, and the chief fathers of the congregation:

27 And divide the prey into two parts; between them that took the war upon them, who went out to battle, and between all the congregation:

28 And levy a tribute unto the LORD of the men of war which went out to battle: one soul of five hundred, both of the persons, and of the beeves, and of the asses, and of the sheep:

29 Take it of their half, and give it unto Eleazar the priest, for an heave offering of the LORD.

30 And of the children of Israel's half, thou shalt take one portion of fifty, of the persons, of the beeves, of the asses, and of the flocks, of all manner of beasts, and give them unto the Levites, which keep the charge of the tabernacle of the LORD.

31 And Moses and Eleazar the priest did as the LORD commanded Moses.

32 And the booty, being the rest of the prey which the men of war had caught, was six hundred thousand and seventy thousand and five thousand sheep,

33 And threescore and twelve thousand beeves,

34 And threescore and one thousand asses,

35 And thirty and two thousand persons in all, of women that had not known man by lying with him.

36 And the half, which was the portion of them that went out to war, was in number three hundred thousand and seven and thirty thousand and five hundred sheep:

37 And the LORD's tribute of the sheep was six hundred and threescore and fifteen.

38 And the beeves were thirty and six thousand; of which the LORD's tribute was threescore and twelve.

39 And the asses were thirty thousand and five hundred; of which the LORD's tribute was threescore and one.

40 And the persons were sixteen thousand; of which the LORD's tribute was thirty and two persons.

41 And Moses gave the tribute, which was the LORD's heave offering, unto Eleazar the priest, as the LORD commanded Moses.

42 And of the children of Israel's half, which Moses divided from the men that warred,

43 (Now the half that pertained unto the congregation was three hundred thousand and thirty thousand and seven thousand and five hundred sheep,

44 And thirty and six thousand beeves,

45 And thirty thousand asses and five hundred,

46 And sixteen thousand persons;)

47 Even of the children of Israel's half, Moses took one portion of fifty, both of man and of beast, and gave them unto the Levites, which kept the charge of the tabernacle of the LORD; as the LORD commanded Moses.

48 And the officers which were over thousands of the host, the captains of thousands, and captains of hundreds, came near unto Moses:

49 And they said unto Moses, Thy servants have taken the sum of the men of war which are under our charge, and there lacketh not one man of us.

50 We have therefore brought an oblation for the LORD, what every man hath gotten, of jewels of gold, chains, and bracelets, rings, earrings, and tablets, to make an atonement for our souls before the LORD.

51 And Moses and Eleazar the priest took the gold of them, even all wrought jewels.

52 And all the gold of the offering that they offered up to the LORD, of the captains of thousands, and of the captains of hundreds, was sixteen thousand seven hundred and fifty shekels.

53 (For the men of war had taken spoil, every man for himself.)

      - The people: 16,000 with 32 given to the LORD
      - The strong picture of faithfulness: Gave the LORD's share to the High Priest—just as God commanded
   3) They distributed the people's share: One half of the spoils
      - The sheep: 337,500
      - The cattle 36,000
      - The donkeys: 30,500
      - The people: 16,000
      - The strong picture of faithfulness: Gave the LORD's share to the Levites for the care of the Tabernacle—just as God commanded

c. The very special, spontaneous gifts of the officers & commanders
   1) The astounding, miraculous fact that stirred them to make the very special gift: Had no casualties, not one
   2) The gift of thanksgiving: All the gold articles they had acquired
   3) Their purpose: To make atonement before God—to pay Him for the lives that would have been lost but were saved, all due to Him
   4) The acceptance of the gift by Moses & the High Priest, Eleazar
      - The gold weighed 420 pounds
      - The gold came from the plunder of the officers

5) The gift was taken into the Tabernacle as a memorial: Was a reminder of the great victory God had	54 And Moses and Eleazar the priest took the gold of the captains of thousands and of hundreds, and brought it into	the tabernacle of the congregation, for a memorial for the children of Israel before the LORD.	given over the evil, seductive & immoral enemies who sought to destroy them

DIVISION IV

THE PREPARATION FOR THE MARCH INTO THE PROMISED LAND, 26:1-36:13

F. The Conquest of the Most Dangerous and Threatening Enemies, the Midianites: A Picture of Conquering the Seductive, Immoral Enemies of the World, 31:1-54

(3:1-54) **Introduction—Enemies, Kinds of—Enemies, Evil and Seductive**: There are enemies in the world who are evil, seductive, and immoral. These enemies seek to tempt and lead people astray, to lead them down the road of defilement and uncleanness, of corruption and death. If a person does not stand guard against these enemies, he will be corrupted and enslaved and led down the path of destruction. Just think of the evil, seductive, and immoral enemies that stand opposed to people:

⇒ drunkenness and drug addiction
⇒ adultery and immorality
⇒ pornography and sexual deviancy
⇒ gluttony and other enslaving habits
⇒ false religion and idolatry
⇒ lawlessness and violence
⇒ greed and covetousness
⇒ lusts and enslavements

These are just a few of the evil, seductive, and immoral enemies of the world that can easily destroy the lives of people. This is the discussion of this important passage*: The Conquest of the Most Dangerous and Threatening Enemies, the Midianites: A Picture of Conquering the Seductive, Immoral Enemies of the World,* 31:1-54.

1. The order to launch the campaign: God judges the evil of this world (v.1-6)
2. The victorious campaign: a picture of victory over the evil, seductive, and immoral enemies of life (v.7-13).
3. The shocking military error: a picture of failing to fully destroy the evil, seductive, and immoral enemies of life (v.14-18).
4. The purification of the soldiers and the spoils: a reminder that death is the ultimate corruption (v.19-24).
5. The division of the spoils: a picture of rewards and of the generous thoughts of God (v.25-54).

1 (31:1-6) **Justice, of God—Vengeance, of God—Israel, Conquest of Midianites—Midianites, Conquered By Israel—Wars, of Israel—Nations, Evil, Judged by God—Evil, Judged by God**: there was the order to launch the campaign against the Midianites. This is a picture of God's judgment against the evil of this world.

OUTLINE	SCRIPTURE	SCRIPTURE	OUTLINE
1. The order to launch the campaign: God judges the evil of this world a. The reason: God's justice 1) The Midianites had seduced & tried to destroy God's people 2) Moses was soon to die b. The call to arms by Moses: He charged the people to prepare for war against the Midianites 1) To carry out God's vengeance on the seductive, immoral enemies 2) To arm 1000 soldiers from	And the LORD spake unto Moses, saying, 2 Avenge the children of Israel of the Midianites: afterward shalt thou be gathered unto thy people. 3 And Moses spake unto the people, saying, Arm some of yourselves unto the war, and let them go against the Midianites, and avenge the LORD of Midian. 4 Of every tribe a thousand, throughout all the tribes of	Israel, shall ye send to the war. 5 So there were delivered out of the thousands of Israel, a thousand of every tribe, twelve thousand armed for war. 6 And Moses sent them to the war, a thousand of every tribe, them and Phinehas the son of Eleazar the priest, to the war, with the holy instruments, and the trumpets to blow in his hand.	each tribe: A total of 12,000 armed soldiers 3) To take the priest Phinehas with them • With the holy objects of the sanctuary • With the trumpets for sounding the charge

1. God Himself gave the command for Israel to go to war against the Midianites (v.1-2). God's justice was to be executed against this evil, seductive, and immoral people. Remember, the Midianites had seduced and attempted to destroy God's people. But they were unable to defeat Israel in battle, so they devised a devious scheme to corrupt them. They, along with the Moabites, sent their women and their temple prostitutes to seduce the men of Israel. Once the men were seduced and hooked, they invited them to their festivals of worship which led to false worship and the forsaking of God (see outline and notes—Num.25:1-18 for more discussion).

The Midianites were beyond repair or repentance as a nation of people, beyond hope or correction. Their cup of iniquity or evil was full—filled to the point that it overflowed and would continue to overflow against God's people and the other peoples of the world (see DEEPER STUDY #1—Num.21:2-3 for more discussion). It was time for the justice of God against the Midianites to be executed, time for the judgment of God to fall upon them. Consequently, God gave the orders for the

Midianite nation to be destroyed. Note: the Midianites were to be conquered before Moses died, before he was "gathered to his people." This enemy had attempted to destroy God's people during Moses' leadership: therefore, they were to be conquered during his administration.

2. Note the call to arms by Moses: he charged the people to prepare for war against the Midianites (v.3-6). They were to carry out God's vengeance, His justice upon the evil, seductive, and immoral enemies of God's people. But all they needed was a strike force not the entire army. A small strike force of twelve thousand well-equipped men was all that was needed. The officers were to select one thousand soldiers from each tribe (v.4-5). The evil, seductive, and immoral enemy had threatened the very existence of each tribe; therefore, each tribe was to have a part in the destruction of the evil Midianites.

Note that the priest Phinehas was to go with them. He was to take the holy objects of the sanctuary and the trumpets for sounding the battle charge (v.6, cp.10:9).

Thought 1. The judgment of God is coming. All the evil, seductive, and immoral people and nations of this earth will face the judgment of God. God is going to judge the world in righteousness, judge every human being for all the evil, seductive, and immoral deeds they have done. This is the strong declaration of Holy Scripture:

"And as it is appointed unto men once to die, but after this the judgment" (Heb.9:27).

"For the Son of man shall come in the glory of his Father with his angels; and then he shall reward every man according to his works" (Mt.16:27).

"When the Son of man shall come in his glory, and all the holy angels with him, then shall he sit upon the throne of his glory: And before him shall be gathered all nations: and he shall separate them one from another, as a shepherd divideth his sheep from the goats: And he shall set the sheep on his right hand, but the goats on the left" (Mt.25:31-33).

"Marvel not at this: for the hour is coming, in the which all that are in the graves shall hear his voice, And shall come forth; they that have done good, unto the resurrection of life; and they that have done evil, unto the resurrection of damnation" (Jn.5.28-29).

"The Lord knoweth how to deliver the godly out of temptations, and to reserve the unjust unto the day of judgment to be punished" (2 Pt.2:9).

"But the heavens and the earth, which are now, by the same word are kept in store, reserved unto fire against the day of judgment and perdition of ungodly men" (2 Pt.3:7).

"Behold, the Lord cometh with ten thousands of his saints, To execute judgment upon all, and to convince all that are ungodly among them of all their ungodly deeds which they have ungodly committed, and of all their hard speeches which ungodly sinners have spoken against him" (Jude 14-15).

"And I saw the dead, small and great, stand before God; and the books were opened: and another book was opened, which is the book of life: and the dead were judged out of those things which were written in the books, according to their works" (Rev.20:12).

DEEPER STUDY # 1

(31:1-3) **The Midianites**: these people were a large confederation of tribes who were mainly nomads roaming throughout the Sinai Desert and south of Moab throughout the Negev and East Jordan. They did not merge with the other people of Palestine, but rather formed alliances with them, for example with...

- the Moabites (Num.22:4f)
- the Amalekites (Judg.6:3, 33; 7:12)
- the Ishmaelites (Gen.37:28; Judg.8:22-24)
- Ephah (Gen.25:4; Is.66)

Midian was a son of Abraham and Keturah. When Moses fled from Egypt, he stayed with a Midianite shepherd, Jethro or Reuel. He later married Jethro's daughter, Zipporah (Ex.2:15-3:1). The Midianites are sometimes referred to as the Ishmaelites (Judg.8:24). There was a group of merchants from the tribe of Ishmael who purchased Joseph when he was sold as a slave by his brothers (Gen.37:25f). In confederation with other tribes, the Midianites were to be a constant thorn in Israel's side (Judges, Chapters 6-8). The kings of the Midianites were known for wearing gold rings, earrings, gold chains and the purple clothing so often worn by kings (Judg.8:26).

The Midianites defeated by Moses were those who had formed an alliance with Moab, not the whole confederation of tribes.[1]

2 (31:7-13) **Victory, Over Enemies of This Life—Israel, Victories of, Over the Midianites—Midianites, Conquered by Israel—Baalam, Death of—Judgment, of God**: there was the victorious campaign against the Midianites. This is a picture of a believer's victory over the evil, seductive, and immoral enemies of life. The strike force was successful against the Midianites and a decisive victory was carried out.

OUTLINE	SCRIPTURE	SCRIPTURE	OUTLINE
2. The victorious campaign: A picture of victory over the evil, seductive, & immoral enemies of life a. They triumphed over Midian	7 And they warred against the Midianites, as the LORD commanded Moses; and they slew all the males. 8 And they slew the kings of	Midian, beside the rest of them that were slain; namely, Evi, and Rekem, and Zur, and Hur, and Reba, five kings of Midian: Balaam	1) The five kings of Midian were killed 2) The wicked advisor of the evil, seductive plan, Balaam, was killed (22:1-

[1] Gordon J. Wenham. *The Book of Numbers*, p.209.

OUTLINE	SCRIPTURE	SCRIPTURE	OUTLINE
25:18) b. They captured the women, children, animals, & possessions—even the women who had seduced & sought to destroy them c. They burned all the cities & camps d. They triumphantly marched back to their camp with the	also the son of Beor they slew with the sword. 9 And the children of Israel took all the women of Midian captives, and their little ones, and took the spoil of all their cattle, and all their flocks, and all their goods. 10 And they burnt all their cities wherein they dwelt, and all their goodly castles, with fire. 11 And they took all the spoil, and all the prey, both	of men and of beasts. 12 And they brought the captives, and the prey, and the spoil, unto Moses, and Eleazar the priest, and unto the congregation of the children of Israel, unto the camp at the plains of Moab, which are by Jordan near Jericho. 13 And Moses, and Eleazar the priest, and all the princes of the congregation, went forth to meet them without the camp.	captives, spoils, & plunder 1) They expected a triumphant celebration with Moses, Eleazar, & the people 2) Moses, Eleazar, & all the leaders went to meet the victorious army outside the camp

1. The Israelites triumphed over the evil, seductive, and immoral Midianites (v.7-8). The reference here to killing every man does not mean that every Midianite male citizen was killed, for we find that the Midianites fought against Israel in the days of Gideon (Judg.6:3). Note that five kings of the Midianites were killed as well as Balaam, the wicked adviser who had worked out the evil, seductive plan to destroy God's people (v.16; see outline and notes—Num.22:1-25:18 for more discussion).

2. The Israelites captured the women, children, animals, and possessions (v.9). Among the women would be those who had seduced and sought to destroy them through sexual immorality and false worship.

3. The Israelites burned all the cities and camps of the Midianites (v.10).

4. The Israelites triumphantly marched back to their camp with the captives, spoils, and plunder (v.11-12). The strike force expected a triumphant celebration when they returned with the news of their glorious victory and with the spoils of their conquest. With excitement, Moses, Eleazar the High Priest, and all the leaders went outside the camp to meet the victorious army.

Thought 1. God gives victory over the evil, seductive, and immoral enemies of this life. Some of the most powerful enemies that confront and attack us are...

- adultery
- premarital sex
- homosexuality
- pedophilia
- sexual deviancy
- bestiality
- pornography
- drunkenness
- drug addiction
- gluttony
- false worship
- idolatry
- witchcraft
- sorcery
- astrology
- psychic readings
- divination
- lawless acts
- greed
- covetousness
- lusts
- enslavements

The temptations and attacks of the enemies of this life are innumerable. But victory is assured, victory by the power of God.

"And the Lord said, Simon, Simon, behold, Satan hath desired to have you, that he may sift you as wheat: But I have prayed for thee, that thy faith fail not: and when thou art converted, strengthen thy brethren" (Lk.22:31-32).

"Nay, in all these things we are more than conquerors through him that loved us" (Ro.8:37).

"And the God of peace shall bruise Satan under your feet shortly. The grace of our Lord Jesus Christ be with you. Amen" (Ro.16:20).

"There hath no temptation taken you but such as is common to man: but God is faithful, who will not suffer you to be tempted above that ye are able; but will with the temptation also make a way to escape, that ye may be able to bear it" (1 Cor.10:13).

"Wherefore take unto you the whole armour of God, that ye may be able to withstand in the evil day, and having done all, to stand" (Eph.6:13).

"Wherefore in all things it behoved him to be made like unto his brethren, that he might be a merciful and faithful high priest in things pertaining to God, to make reconciliation for the sins of the people. For in that he himself hath suffered being tempted, he is able to succour them that are tempted" (Heb.2:17-18).

"For we have not an high priest which cannot be touched with the feeling of our infirmities; but was in all points tempted like as we are, yet without sin. Let us therefore come boldly unto the throne of grace, that we may obtain mercy, and find grace to help in time of need" (Heb.4:15-16).

"My brethren, count it all joy when ye fall into divers temptations; Knowing this, that the trying of your faith worketh patience. But let patience have her perfect work, that ye may be perfect and entire, wanting nothing. If any of you lack wisdom, let him ask of God, that giveth to all men liberally, and upbraideth not; and it shall be given him" (Jas.1:2-5).

"Submit yourselves therefore to God. Resist the devil, and he will flee from you" (Jas.4:7).

"The Lord knoweth how to deliver the godly out of temptations, and to reserve the unjust unto the day of judgment to be punished" (2 Pt.2:9).

"For whatsoever is born of God overcometh the world: and this is the victory that overcometh the world, even our faith. Who is he that overcometh the world, but he that believeth that Jesus is the Son of God" (1 Jn.5:4-5)

"Through thee will we push down our enemies: through thy name will we tread them under that rise up against us" (Ps.44:5).
"The Lord shall fight for you, and ye shall hold your peace" (Ex.14:14).

3 (31:14-18) **Military, Error of—Enemies, Failing to Destroy—Judgment, of God—Iniquity, Cup of, Filled—Nations, Savage and Evil—Nations, Destruction of, Total**: there was the shocking military error by the strike force of the Israelites. This is a picture of failing to totally destroy the evil, seductive, and immoral enemies of life. The strike force was expecting a triumphant reception and celebration upon their return. But what they received was an utter shock.

OUTLINE	SCRIPTURE	SCRIPTURE	OUTLINE
3. The shocking military error: A picture of failing to fully destroy the evil, seductive, & immoral enemies of life a. The anger of Moses with the officers & commanders of the army 1) They had spared some of the most dangerous enemies, the women 2) The women had seduced them into immoral behavior & false worship in an attempt to destroy them	14 And Moses was wroth with the officers of the host, with the captains over thousands, and captains over hundreds, which came from the battle. 15 And Moses said unto them, Have ye saved all the women alive? 16 Behold, these caused the children of Israel, through the counsel of Balaam, to commit trespass against the	LORD in the matter of Peor, and there was a plague among the congregation of the LORD. 17 Now therefore kill every male among the little ones, and kill every woman that hath known man by lying with him. 18 But all the women children, that have not known a man by lying with him, keep alive for yourselves.	3) The women had caused the judgment of God to fall: A plague that killed 21,000 Israelites b. The enemies—all who sought or could seek to destroy Israel—had to be destroyed: Women & boys c. The innocent & non-threatening girls were saved

1. Note the anger of Moses with the officers and commanders of the armies (v.14-16). Moses was furious, for the officers had obviously disobeyed orders. They had spared some of the most dangerous of the enemies—the women who had seduced the Israelites into immoral behavior and false worship in an attempt to destroy them. It was these very women who had caused the judgment of God to fall upon the Israelites, a plague that had killed 21,000 people.

2. The enemies of God's people had to be destroyed—all who had sought or could seek in the future to destroy Israel. Note that this included all the women who had slept with an Israelite man and all the boys, for they were potential future enemies of Israel. It was dangerous to let the women live, for they would still be tempting the Israelites to uncleanness and to false worship which would eventually destroy the nation. In fact, we know from future Scripture that it was the evil, seductive immorality of surrounding nations and their false worship that eventually led to the loss of the promised land by the Israelites.

Why was it necessary to execute all the male children? James Philip says this:

> "But little children? Could God have ordained this? Some things need to be said in this connection. We must insist that it was not mere wanton brutality, for the slaughter was not indiscriminate. Not all the children were slain, only the males. They were the future 'Midian,' a potential danger and peril for Israel if allowed to grow up. What we must realize is that there are such things as national character and national traits and propensities. We speak of such and such a people being a military people, and as such liable to be war-like and belligerent. So it was with the Midianites.
>
> "That is the first thing, and the second is this: we have to remember something much closer to our own time, the extirpation and destruction of whole cities during World War II by huge bombing raids on Germany. We estimated, rightly or wrongly, that the only way for the Nazi menace to be destroyed was to have done this, when doing it involved innocent civilians, children included."[2]

3. The innocent and unthreatening girls and young women were saved (v.18). They were adopted by the Israelite families and obviously taught about the only living and true God (Jehovah, Yahweh). They became a part of the great nation of God's people.

Thought 1. The believer must fully—completely and wholly—destroy the evil, seductive, and immoral enemies of life. He must put these enemies to death:
⇒ all forms of immorality and illicit sex
⇒ all pornography: films, audio, music, and reading material
⇒ all drunkenness and drug addictions
⇒ all gluttony and other enslaving habits
⇒ all forms of lusts and enslavements
⇒ all greed and lawlessness

The believer must never play around with such sins, allowing them to entice him. The believer must combat the lust of the flesh and the lust of the eyes and the pride of life (1 Jn.2:15-16). He must not refuse to put these sins to death. By the power of Christ, he must strike a fatal blow against the evil, seductive, and immoral sins that constantly bombard him.

"Ye have heard that it was said by them of old time, Thou shalt not commit adultery: But I say unto you, That whosoever looketh on a woman to lust after her hath committed adultery with her already in his heart. And if thy right eye offend thee, pluck it out, and cast it from thee: for it is profitable for thee

2 James Philip. *Mastering the Old Testament, Vol.4, Numbers,* p.313.

that one of thy members should perish, and not that thy whole body should be cast into hell. And if thy right hand offend thee, cut if off, and cast it from thee: for it is profitable for thee that one of thy members should perish, and not that thy whole body should be cast into hell" (Mt.5:27-30).

"And take heed to yourselves, lest at any time your hearts be overcharged with surfeiting, and drunkenness, and cares of this life, and so that day come upon you unawares" (Lk.21:34).

"Likewise reckon ye also yourselves to be dead indeed unto sin, but alive unto God through Jesus Christ our Lord. Let not sin therefore reign in your mortal body, that ye should obey it in the lusts thereof. Neither yield ye your members as instruments of unrighteousness unto sin: but yield yourselves unto God, as those that are alive from the dead, and your members as instruments of righteousness unto God" (Ro.6:11-13).

"For if ye live after the flesh, ye shall die: but if ye through the Spirit do mortify the deeds of the body, ye shall live" (Ro.8:13).

"But put ye on the Lord Jesus Christ, and make not provision for the flesh, to fulfil the lusts thereof" (Ro.13:14).

"This I say then, Walk in the Spirit, and ye shall not fulfil the lust of the flesh. For the flesh lusteth against the Spirit, and the Spirit against the flesh: and these are contrary the one to the other: so that ye cannot do the things that ye would. But if ye be led of the Spirit, ye are not under the law. Now the works of the flesh are manifest, which are these; Adultery, fornication, uncleanness, lasciviousness, Idolatry, witchcraft, hatred, variance, emulations, wrath, strife, seditions, heresies, Envyings, murders, drunkenness, revellings, and such like: of the which I tell you before, as I have also told you in time past, that they which do such things shall not inherit the kingdom of God" (Gal.5:16-21).

"Mortify therefore your members which are upon the earth; fornication, uncleanness, inordinate affection, evil concupiscence, and covetousness, which is idolatry" (Col.3:5).

"Dearly beloved, I beseech you as strangers and pilgrims, abstain from fleshly lusts, which war against the soul" (1 Pt.2:11).

"That he no longer should live the rest of his time in the flesh to the lusts of men, but to the will of God" (1 Pt.4:2).

"Love not the world, neither the things that are in the world. If any man love the world, the love of the Father is not in him. For all that is in the world, the lust of the flesh, and the lust of the eyes, and the pride of life, is not of the Father, but is of the world" (1 Jn.2:15-16).

4 (31:19-24) **Purification, From Sin—Forgiveness, of Sin—Cleansing, From Sin—Death, Symbol of Corruption—Killing, Result of, Defiled a Person—Warfare, Results of, Defiled a Soldier**: there was the purification of the soldiers and the spoils. This is a reminder that *death* is the ultimate symbol of defilement and uncleanness, of corruption and decay.

OUTLINE	SCRIPTURE	SCRIPTURE	OUTLINE
4. The purification of the soldiers & the spoils: A reminder that death is the ultimate corruption a. They were unclean: Had been in contact with death 1) Could not go in the camp 2) Had to cleanse themselves & the captives 3) Had to cleanse every garment & all else made of leather & cloth	19 And do ye abide without the camp seven days: whosoever hath killed any person, and whosoever hath touched any slain, purify both yourselves and your captives on the third day, and on the seventh day. 20 And purify all your raiment, and all that is made of skins, and all work of goats' hair, and all things made of wood.	manded Moses; 22 Only the gold, and the silver, the brass, the iron, the tin, and the lead, 23 Every thing that may abide the fire, ye shall make it go through the fire, and it shall be clean: nevertheless it shall be purified with the water of separation: and all that abideth not the fire ye shall make go through the water.	1) All metal objects had to be cleansed by fire & water: Gold, silver, bronze, iron, tin, & lead objects 2) All other objects had to be cleansed by water
b. They had to fully obey the law of cleansing in detail: It was God's command	21 And Eleazar the priest said unto the men of war which went to the battle, This is the ordinance of the law which the LORD com-	24 And ye shall wash your clothes on the seventh day, and ye shall be clean, and afterward ye shall come into the camp.	3) All personal clothing had to be washed 4) The result: Could enter camp—be reconciled

1. The soldiers were unclean, for they had been in contact with death (v.19-20). They could not, therefore, go into the camp until they had cleansed themselves and the captives they had taken in battle. They also had to cleanse every garment and all else that had been made out of leather and cloth. Death takes the life out of a person: it is the "catastrophic destruction of God's creation."[3] Death destroys the physical life of a person. Therefore, it is the ultimate defilement and uncleanness, corruption and decay. God wants this fact to stick in the minds of His dear people. For this reason, the soldiers had to be cleansed before they could go into the camp. Uncleanness and defilement, corruption and decay were not to coexist with God's people. The soldiers had to be cleansed before they could be reunited with the society of God's people.

2. The soldiers had to fully obey the law of cleansing in every detail. This was the command of God (v.22-24). All possessions had to be cleansed, for possessions could contaminate and corrupt God's people. Note the command of God:

a. All metal objects had to be cleansed both by fire and by water: all the gold, silver, bronze, iron, tin, and lead objects (v.22).
b. All other objects had to be cleansed by water.

---

3 Gordon J. Wenham. *The Book of Numbers,* p.212.

c. All personal clothing had to be washed (v.24).
d. Note the result: once all this had been done, the soldiers could enter camp and be reconciled with their families and the rest of God's people (v.24).

Thought 1. There is a lesson in this for the church and for individual believers.

1) A person must be cleansed from all defilement and uncleanness, corruption and decay before he is allowed in the camp or membership of God's people. The purity and righteousness of the camp or church body must be protected. The church membership is for genuine believers, those who live holy lives before God, those who have been set apart to live righteous and pure lives. The church membership is a body of believers who have been set apart by God to worship and serve Him and to go out into the world as strong witnesses of His saving grace. The church must make sure that its members have been cleansed from all defilement and uncleanness, corruption and decay.

"And now why tarriest thou? arise, and be baptized, and wash away thy sins, calling on the name of the Lord" (Acts 22:16).

"Know ye not that the unrighteous shall not inherit the kingdom of God? Be not deceived: neither fornicators, nor idolaters, nor adulterers, nor effeminate, nor abusers of themselves with mankind, Nor thieves, nor covetous, nor drunkards, nor revilers, nor extortioners, shall inherit the kingdom of God. And such were some of you: but ye are washed, but ye are sanctified, but ye are justified in the name of the Lord Jesus, and by the Spirit of our God" (1 Cor.6:9-11).

"Husbands, love your wives, even as Christ also loved the church, and gave himself for it; That he might sanctify and cleanse it with the washing of water by the word" (Eph.5:25-26).

"How much more shall the blood of Christ, who through the eternal Spirit offered himself without spot to God, purge your conscience from dead works to serve the living God" (Heb.9:14).

"Draw nigh to God, and he will draw nigh to you. Cleanse your hands, ye sinners; and purify your hearts, ye double minded" (Jas.4:8).

"But if we walk in the light, as he is in the light, we have fellowship one with another, and the blood of Jesus Christ his Son cleanseth us from all sin" (1 Jn.1:7).

"Come now, and let us reason together, saith the Lord: though your sins be as scarlet, they shall be as white as snow; though they be red like crimson, they shall be as wool" (Is.1:18).

2) The possessions and things of this world can defile and make a person unclean. Possessions can take hold of a person and enslave him. Things can arouse greed and covetousness within a person, arouse a passion for more and more. This is the reason our possessions must be dedicated, set apart to God and His service. As the root of all evil, money and possessions can consume the human heart and destroy our lives. Possessions and money must be cleansed, purified, set apart, dedicated, and given over to God. If not, they will consume and destroy us.

"Jesus said unto him, If thou wilt be perfect, go and sell that thou hast, and give to the poor, and thou shalt have treasure in heaven: and come and follow me. But when the young man heard that saying, he went away sorrowful: for he had great possessions. Then said Jesus unto his disciples, Verily I say unto you, That a rich man shall hardly enter into the kingdom of heaven. And again I say unto you, It is easier for a camel to go through the eye of a needle, than for a rich man to enter into the kingdom of God" (Mt.19:21-24).

"And the cares of this world, and the deceitfulness of riches, and the lusts of other things entering in, choke the word, and it becometh unfruitful" (Mk.4:19).

"Mortify therefore your members which are upon the earth; fornication, uncleanness, inordinate affection, evil concupiscence, and covetousness, which is idolatry" (Col.3:5).

"Wherefore come out from among them, and be ye separate, saith the Lord, and touch not the unclean thing; and I will receive you, And will be a Father unto you, and ye shall be my sons and daughters, saith the Lord Almighty" (2 Cor.6:17-18).

"But they that will be rich fall into temptation and a snare, and into many foolish and hurtful lusts, which drown men in destruction and perdition. For the love of money is the root of all evil: which while some coveted after, they have erred from the faith, and pierced themselves through with many sorrows" (1 Tim.6:9-10).

"*Let your* conversation *be* without covetousness; *and be* content with such things as ye have: for he hath said, I will never leave thee, nor forsake thee" (Heb.13:5).

"And when thy herds and thy flocks multiply, and thy silver and thy gold is multiplied, and all that thou hast is multiplied; Then thine heart be lifted up, and thou forget the Lord thy God, which brought thee forth out of the land of Egypt, from the house of bondage" (Dt.8:13-14).

"Trust not in oppression, and become not vain in robbery: if riches increase, set not your heart upon them" (Ps.62:10).

5 (31:25-54) **Spoils, of Warfare—Offerings, Voluntary—Stewardship, of Income—Rewards, For Fighting a Good Warfare—Thanksgiving, to God**: there was the division of the spoils, of the plunder taken from the defeated enemy. This is a picture of the rewards for fighting a good warfare and a picture of giving thanks to God.

OUTLINE	SCRIPTURE	SCRIPTURE	OUTLINE
5. The division of the spoils: A picture of rewards & of giving thanks to God a. The command of the LORD 1) The leaders were to count	25 And the LORD spake unto Moses, saying, 26 Take the sum of the prey that was taken, both of man and of beast, thou, and	Eleazar the priest, and the chief fathers of the congregation: 27 And divide the prey into two parts; between them that	all the spoils 2) The leaders were to divide the spoils between the sol-

NUMBERS 31:1-54

OUTLINE	SCRIPTURE	SCRIPTURE	OUTLINE
diers & the people	took the war upon them, who went out to battle, and between all the congregation:	LORD commanded Moses. 42 And of the children of Israel's half, which Moses divided from the men that warred,	God commanded 3) They distributed the people's share: One half of the spoils
3) The soldiers were to contribute a portion to the LORD • To give one out of every 500 of everything	28 And levy a tribute unto the LORD of the men of war which went out to battle: one soul of five hundred, both of the persons, and of the beeves, and of the asses, and of the sheep:	43 (Now the half that pertained unto the congregation was three hundred thousand and thirty thousand and seven thousand and five hundred sheep,	• The sheep: 337,500
• To give the LORD's part to the priest: The LORD's representative—His minister to the people	29 Take it of their half, and give it unto Eleazar the priest, for an heave offering of the LORD.	44 And thirty and six thousand beeves, 45 And thirty thousand asses and five hundred,	• The cattle 36,000 • The donkeys: 30,500
4) The people were to contribute a portion to the LORD • To give one out of every 50 of everything • To give to the Levites: The LORD's servants who cared for the Tabernacle	30 And of the children of Israel's half, thou shalt take one portion of fifty, of the persons, of the beeves, of the asses, and of the flocks, of all manner of beasts, and give them unto the Levites, which keep the charge of the tabernacle of the LORD.	46 And sixteen thousand persons;) 47 Even of the children of Israel's half, Moses took one portion of fifty, both of man and of beast, and gave them unto the Levites, which kept the charge of the tabernacle of the LORD; as the LORD commanded Moses.	• The people: 16,000 • The strong picture of faithfulness: Gave the LORD's share to the Levites for the care of the Tabernacle—just as God commanded
b. The obedience of Moses & Eleazar, the High Priest	31 And Moses and Eleazar the priest did as the LORD commanded Moses.	48 And the officers which were over thousands of the host, the captains of thousands, and captains of hundreds, came near unto Moses:	c. The very special, spontaneous gifts of the officers & commanders
1) They counted the plunder • The sheep: 675,000 • The cattle: 72,000 • The donkeys: 61,000	32 And the booty, being the rest of the prey which the men of war had caught, was six hundred thousand and seventy thousand and five thousand sheep, 33 And threescore and twelve thousand beeves, 34 And threescore and one thousand asses,	49 And they said unto Moses, Thy servants have taken the sum of the men of war which are under our charge, and there lacketh not one man of us.	1) The astounding, miraculous fact that stirred them to make the very special gift: Had no casualties, not one
• The innocent women: 32,000	35 And thirty and two thousand persons in all, of women that had not known man by lying with him.	50 We have therefore brought an oblation for the LORD, what every man hath gotten, of jewels of gold, chains, and bracelets, rings, earrings, and tablets, to make an atonement for our souls before the LORD.	2) The gift of thanksgiving: All the gold articles they had acquired 3) Their purpose: To make atonement before God—to pay Him for the lives that would have been lost but were saved, all due to Him
2) They distributed the soldiers' share • The sheep: 337,500 with 675 given to the LORD	36 And the half, which was the portion of them that went out to war, was in number three hundred thousand and seven and thirty thousand and five hundred sheep: 37 And the LORD's tribute of the sheep was six hundred and threescore and fifteen.	51 And Moses and Eleazar the priest took the gold of them, even all wrought jewels.	4) The acceptance of the gift by Moses & the High Priest, Eleazar
• The cattle: 36,000 with 72 given to the LORD	38 And the beeves were thirty and six thousand; of which the LORD's tribute was threescore and twelve.	52 And all the gold of the offering that they offered up to the LORD, of the captains of thousands, and of the captains of hundreds, was sixteen thousand seven hundred and fifty shekels.	• The gold weighed 420 pounds
• The donkeys: 30,500 with 61 given to the LORD	39 And the asses were thirty thousand and five hundred; of which the LORD's tribute was threescore and one.	53 (For the men of war had taken spoil, every man for himself.)	• The gold came from the plunder of the officers
• The people: 16,000 with 32 given to the LORD • The strong picture of faithfulness: Gave the LORD's share to the High Priest—just as	40 And the persons were sixteen thousand; of which the LORD's tribute was thirty and two persons. 41 And Moses gave the tribute, which was the LORD's heave offering, unto Eleazar the priest, as the	54 And Moses and Eleazar the priest took the gold of the captains of thousands and of hundreds, and brought it into the tabernacle of the congregation, for a memorial for the children of Israel before the LORD.	5) The gift was taken into the Tabernacle as a memorial: Was a reminder of the great victory God had given over the evil, seductive & immoral enemies who sought to destroy them

The details covered by the Scripture can be clearly seen in the outline above. Note three significant facts about the division of the spoils.

1. First, the rewards of battle were divided equally between the soldiers and the people; that is, half went to the soldiers and half went to the people. Of course, this meant far more rewards for the 12,000 soldiers than for the people, who most likely numbered between two to four million persons. But this was a fair distribution since the soldiers had actually done the fighting, putting their lives at risk for the sake of the nation. A summary of the rewards of battle is given in the following chart:

The Rewards of Battle—
For Fighting a Good Warfare

	Total	Soldier's Share	People's Share	Lord's Tithe	Levites Share
Sheep (incl.goats)	675,000	337,500	337,500	675	6750
Cattle	72,000	36,000	36,000	72	720
Donkeys	61,000	30,500	30,500	61	610
Women (virgins)	32,000	16,000	16,000	32	320

2. The faithfulness of the people in stewardship should be noted. They gave exactly what had been commanded by the Lord: a strong, strong picture of faithfulness in stewardship (v.41-47).

3. The very special and spontaneous gifts of the officers and commanders should also be noted (v.48-54).
   a. There was an astounding, miraculous fact that stirred them to make the very special gift: they had suffered no casualties; not a single soldier had lost his life in the battle against the Midianites (v.48-49). A deep spirit of gratitude swelled up in their hearts for what God had done in protecting them and the strike force of the soldiers under their command.
   b. Note the gift of thanksgiving: they gave all the gold articles they had acquired (v.50).
   c. Their purpose was to make atonement before God, to pay Him for the lives that would have been lost but were saved. The miracle was totally due to Him; therefore, the officers and commanders wanted to make payment—to pay a ransom—in return for all the soldiers that would ordinarily have lost their lives in battle. However, in this case, God had delivered them all and given them back into the hands of His dear people. Therefore they owed Him a ransom, an atonement for His great gift of life.
   d. Note the acceptance of the gift by Moses and the High Priest Eleazar (v.51-53). The gold itself weighed over four hundred and twenty pounds. An enormous gift of gratitude from these officers!
   e. The gift of gold was taken into the Tabernacle by Moses and Eleazar as a memorial. This was a reminder of the great victory God had given over the evil, seductive, and immoral enemies who had sought to destroy God's people (v.54).

Thought 1. There are two strong lessons for us in this point:

1) There are rewards in heaven. Faithful believers are to be rewarded if they fight a good warfare while on this earth. We must, therefore, keep our eyes on the reward that lies out ahead of us, that awaits us when we arrive in heaven. Even Jesus Christ endured the cross and its shame because of the joy of the reward that was set before Him (Heb.12:2). God promises to reward us abundantly if we are faithful. We must, then, follow in the steps of Christ, fix our eyes upon Him: stand fast and persevere to the end—all for the joy of the reward that awaits us in heaven. (See notes—Lk.16:10-12; 1 Cor.13-15; Tit.3:6; 1 Pt.1:4 for more discussion.)

"And whosoever shall give to drink unto one of these little ones a cup of cold water only in the name of a disciple, verily I say unto you, he shall in no wise lose his reward" (Mt.10:42).

"His lord said unto him, Well done, good and faithful servant; thou hast been faithful over a few things, I will make thee ruler over many things: enter thou into the joy of thy lord" (Mt.25:23).

"But love ye your enemies, and do good, and lend, hoping for nothing again; and your reward shall be great, and ye shall be the children of the Highest: for he is kind unto the unthankful and to the evil" (Lk.6:35).

"But glory, honour, and peace, to every man that worketh good, to the Jew first, and also to the Gentile" (Ro.2:10).

"And every man that striveth for the mastery is temperate in all things. Now they do it to obtain a corruptible crown; but we an incorruptible" (1 Cor.9:25).

"Therefore, my beloved brethren, be ye stedfast, unmovable, always abounding in the work of the Lord, forasmuch as ye know that your labour is not in vain in the Lord" (1 Cor.15:58).

"Knowing that whatsoever good thing any man doeth, the same shall he receive of the Lord, whether he be bond or free" (Eph.6:8).

"Henceforth there is laid up for me a crown of righteousness, which the Lord, the righteous judge, shall give me at that day: and not to me only, but unto all them also that love his appearing" (2 Tim.4:8).

"Wherefore seeing we also are compassed about with so great a cloud of witnesses, let us lay aside every weight, and the sin which doth so easily beset us, and let us run with patience the race that is set before us, Looking unto Jesus the author and finisher of our faith; who for the joy that was set before him endured the cross, despising the shame, and is set down at the right hand of the throne of God. For consider him that endured such contradiction of sinners against himself, lest ye be wearied and faint in your minds. Ye have not yet resisted unto blood, striving against sin" (Heb.12:1-4).

"Blessed is the man that endureth temptation: for when he is tried, he shall receive the crown of life, which the Lord hath promised to them that love him" (Jas.1:12).

"And when the chief Shepherd shall appear, ye shall receive a crown of glory that fadeth not away" (1 Pt.5:4).

"Behold, I come quickly: hold that fast which thou hast, that no man take thy crown" (Rev.3:11).

"The four and twenty elders fall down before him that sat on the throne, and worship him that liveth for ever and ever, and cast their crowns before the throne, saying" (Rev.4:10).

"And, behold, I come quickly; and my reward is with me, to give every man according as his work shall be" (Rev.22:12).

2) The commanders and officers were deeply grateful to God for the miracle He had performed for His dear people. Miraculously, not a single soldier had lost his life in the battle. When God does a marvelous thing for us, we should make an offering of thanksgiving to Him. Whatever God gives us, we must do exactly what Scripture teaches: give God His share of the gift He has given us. Whatever God does for us, we must make a gift of thanksgiving to Him for having acted in our behalf. Not only tithes should be given, but additional offerings should be made to God—all in appreciation to God for the very special things He does for us as we march to the promised land of heaven.

"Sell that ye have, and give alms; provide yourselves bags which wax not old, a treasure in the heavens that faileth not, where no thief approacheth, neither moth corrupteth" (Lk.12:33).

"For where your treasure is, there will your heart be also. Let your loins be girded about, and *your* lights burning" (Lk.10:34-35).

"And he looked up, and saw the rich men casting their gifts into the treasury. And he saw also a certain poor widow casting in thither two mites. And he said, Of a truth I say unto you, that this poor widow hath cast in more than they all: For all these have of their abundance cast in unto the offerings of God: but she of her penury hath cast in all the living that she had" (Lk.21:1-4).

"Neither was there any among them that lacked: for as many as were possessors of lands or houses sold them, and brought the prices of the things that were sold, And laid *them* down at the apostles' feet: and distribution was made unto every man according as he had need" (Acts 4:34-35).

"I have showed you all things, how that so labouring ye ought to support the weak, and to remember the words of the Lord Jesus, how he said, It is more blessed to give than to receive" (Acts 20:35).

"Giving thanks always for all things unto God and the Father in the name of our Lord Jesus Christ" (Eph.5:20).

"Giving thanks unto the Father, which hath made us meet to be partakers of the inheritance of the saints in light" (Col.1:12).

"And blessed be the most high God, which hath delivered thine enemies into thy hand. And he gave him tithes of all" (Gen.14:20).

"And they came, both men and women, as many as were willing hearted, *and* brought bracelets, and earrings, and rings, and tablets, all jewels of gold: and every man that offered *offered* an offering of gold unto the LORD" (Ex.35:22).

"And they spake unto Moses, saying, The people bring much more than enough for the service of the work, which the LORD commanded to make" (Ex.36:5).

"But thou shalt remember the Lord thy God: for it is he that giveth thee power to get wealth, that he may establish his covenant which he sware unto thy fathers, as it is this day" (Dt.8:18).

"And they brought their offering before the LORD, six covered wagons, and twelve oxen; a wagon for two of the princes, and for each one an ox: and they brought them before the tabernacle" (Num.7:3).

"Moreover, because I have set my affection to the house of my God, I have of mine own proper good, of gold and silver, *which* I have given to the house of my God, over and above all that I have prepared for the holy house, *Even* three thousand talents of gold, of the gold of Ophir, and seven thousand talents of refined silver, to overlay the walls of the houses *withal*" (1 Chron.29:3-4).

"And all the princes and all the people rejoiced, and brought in, and cast into the chest, until they had made an end" (2 Chron.24:10).

"And all they that *were* about them strengthened their hands with vessels of silver, with gold, with goods, and with beasts, and with precious things, beside all *that* was willingly offered" (Ezra 1:6).

"And let them sacrifice the sacrifices of thanksgiving, and declare his works with rejoicing" (Ps.107:22).

TYPES, SYMBOLS, AND PICTURES
(Numbers 31:1-54)

Historical Term	Type or Picture (Scriptural Basis for Each)	Life Application for Today's Believer	Biblical Application
Conquest of the Midianites Num.31:1-54	*The conquest of the Midianites is a picture of conquering the seductive, immoral enemies of the world.*	There are enemies in the world who are evil, seductive, and immoral. These enemies seek to tempt and lead people astray, to lead them	***"And when the woman saw that the tree was good for food, and that it was pleasant to the eyes, and a tree to be desired to make one wise, she***

Historical Term	Type or Picture (Scriptural Basis for Each)	Life Application for Today's Believer	Biblical Application
	"And they warred against the Midianites, as the LORD commanded Moses; and they slew all the males" (Num. 31:7).	down the road of defilement and uncleanness, of corruption and death. If a person does not stand guard against these enemies, he will be corrupted and enslaved and led down the path of destruction. Just think of the evil, seductive, and immoral enemies that stand opposed to people: ⇒ drunkenness and drug addiction ⇒ adultery and immorality ⇒ pornography and sexual deviancy ⇒ gluttony and other enslaving habits ⇒ false religion and idolatry ⇒ lawlessness and violence ⇒ greed and covetous ⇒ lust and enslavements These are just a few of the evil, seductive, and immoral enemies of the world that can easily destroy the lives of people.	***took of the fruit thereof, and did eat, and gave also unto her husband with her; and he did eat" (Gen. 3:6).*** ***"Stolen waters are sweet, and bread eaten in secret is pleasant" (Pr. 9:17).*** ***"There is a way which seemeth right unto a man, but the end thereof are the ways of death" (Pr.14:12).*** ***"But every man is tempted, when he is drawn away of his own lust, and enticed" (Jas.1:14).*** ***"For when they speak great swelling words of vanity, they allure through the lusts of the flesh, through much wantonness, those that were clean escaped from them who live in error" (2 Pt.2:18).*** ***"My son, if sinners entice thee, consent thou not" (Pr. 1:10).*** ***"Enter not into the path of the wicked, and go not in the way of evil men" (Pr. 4:14).*** ***"Neither yield ye your members as instruments of unrighteousness unto sin: but yield yourselves unto God, as those that are alive from the dead, and your members as instruments of righteousness unto God" (Ro. 6:13).*** ***"Wherefore take unto you the whole armour of God, that ye may be able to withstand in the evil day, and having done all, to stand" (Eph.6:13).***
Israel's Shocking Military Error against Midian Num.31:14-18	*Israel's failure to completely destroy Midian is a picture of failing to fully destroy the evil, seductive, and immoral enemies of life.* **"And Moses was wroth with the officers of the host, with the captains over thousands, and captains over hundreds, which came from the battle. And Moses said unto them, Have ye saved all the women alive? Behold, these caused the children of Israel, through the counsel of Balaam, to commit trespass against the LORD in the matter of Peor, and there was a plague among the congregation of the LORD. Now therefore**	The believer must fully—completely and totally—destroy the evil, seductive, and immoral enemies of life. He must put these enemies to death: ⇒ all forms of immorality and illicit sex ⇒ all pornography: films, audio, music, and reading material ⇒ all drunkenness and drug addictions ⇒ all gluttony and other covetousness habits ⇒ all forms of lust and covetousness ⇒ all acts of greed and lawlessness The believer must never play around with such sins,	***"Ye have heard that it was said by them of old time, Thou shalt not commit adultery: But I say unto you, That whosoever looketh on a woman to lust after her hath committed adultery with her already in his heart. And if thy right eye offend thee, pluck it out, and cast it from thee: for it is profitable for thee that one of thy members should perish, and not that thy whole body should be cast into hell. And if thy right hand offend thee, cut if off, and cast it from thee: for it is profitable for thee that one of thy members should perish, and not that thy whole body should be cast into hell" (Mt.5:27-30).***

Historical Term	Type or Picture (Scriptural Basis for Each)	Life Application for Today's Believer	Biblical Application
	kill every male among the little ones, and kill every woman that hath known man by lying with him" (Num. 31:14-17).	allowing them to entice him. The believer must combat the lust of the flesh and the lust of the eyes and the pride of life (1 Jn.2:15-16). He must not refuse to put these sins to death. By the power of Christ, he must strike a fatal blow against the evil, seductive, and immoral sins that constantly bombard him.	***"And take heed to yourselves, lest at any time your hearts be overcharged with surfeiting, and drunkenness, and cares of this life, and so that day come upon you unawares" (Lk.21:34).*** ***"Likewise reckon ye also yourselves to be dead indeed unto sin, but alive unto God through Jesus Christ our LORD. Let not sin therefore reign in your mortal body, that ye should obey it in the lusts thereof. Neither yield ye your members as instruments of unrighteousness unto sin: but yield yourselves unto God, as those that are alive from the dead, and your members as instruments of righteousness unto God" (Ro.6:11-13; 8:13; 13:14; Gal.5:16-21; Col.3:5).***
Spoils Taken from the Defeated Enemy Num.31:25-54	*The spoils taken from a defeated enemy are a picture of rewards for fighting a good warfare* and *a picture of giving thanks to God.* **"And the LORD spake unto Moses, saying, Take the sum of the prey that was taken, both of man and of beast, thou, and Eleazar the priest, and the chief fathers of the congregation: And divide the prey into two parts; between them that took the war upon them, who went out to battle, and between all the congregation: And levy a tribute unto the LORD of the men of war which went out to battle: one soul of five hundred, both of the persons, and of the beeves, and of the asses, and of the sheep" (Num. 31:25-28).**	There are two strong lessons for us in this point: 1. There are rewards in heaven. Faithful believers are to be rewarded if they fight a good warfare while on this earth. We must therefore keep our eyes on the reward that lies out ahead of us, awaiting us when we arrive in heaven. Even Jesus Christ endured the cross and its shame because of the joy of the reward that was set before Him (Heb.12:2). God promises to reward us abundantly if we are faithful. We must, then, follow in the steps of Christ, fix our eyes upon Him: stand fast and persevere to the end—all for the joy of the reward that awaits us in heaven. (See notes—Lk. 16:10-12; 1 Cor.13-15; Tit.3:6; 1 Pt.1:4 for more discussion.) 2. The commanders and officers were deeply grateful to God for the incomprehensible miracle He had performed for His dear people. Miraculously, not a single soldier had lost his life in the battle. When God does a marvelous thing for us, we should make an offering of thanksgiving to Him.	***"And whosoever shall give to drink unto one of these little ones a cup of cold water only in the name of a disciple, verily I say unto you, he shall in no wise lose his reward" (Mt.10:42).*** ***"His lord said unto him, Well done, good and faithful servant; thou hast been faithful over a few things, I will make thee ruler over many things: enter thou into the joy of thy lord" (Mt.25:23).*** ***"But love ye your enemies, and do good, and lend, hoping for nothing again; and your reward shall be great, and ye shall be the children of the Highest: for he is kind unto the unthankful and to the evil" (Lk.6:35).*** ***"But glory, honour, and peace, to every man that worketh good, to the Jew first, and also to the Gentile" (Ro.2:10).*** ***"And every man that striveth for the mastery is temperate in all things. Now they do it to obtain a corruptible crown; but we an incorruptible" (1 Cor.9:25).*** ***"Giving thanks unto the Father, which hath made us meet to be partakers of the inheritance of the saints in light" (Col.1:12).*** ***"But thou shalt remember the LORD thy God: for it is he***

Historical Term	Type or Picture (Scriptural Basis for Each)	Life Application for Today's Believer	Biblical Application
		Whatever God gives us, we must do exactly what Scripture teaches: give God His share of the gift He has given us. Whatever God does for us, we must make a gift of thanksgiving to Him for having acted in our behalf. Not only tithes should be given, but additional offerings should be made to God—all in appreciation to God for the very special things He does for us as we march to the promised land of heaven.	***that giveth thee power to get wealth, that he may establish his covenant which he sware unto thy fathers, as it is this day" (Dt.8:18).*** ***"And let them sacrifice the sacrifices of thanksgiving, and declare his works with rejoicing" (Ps.107:22).***

1. **The compromise of two tribes: A picture of selfishness, covetousness, disloyalty—half-hearted commitment**
   a. Saw & coveted the fertile land
   b. Considered only their livestock
   c. Went to Moses & the leaders: Stated three points
      1) That the East Jordan land was a gift of God by conquest (21:1-35, 31:1-54)
      2) That the conquered land was fertile, good pastureland for their livestock
      3) That they wanted "this land" as their possession: They did not want to "cross over" the Jordan with the other tribes to fight for the promised land
2. **The angry reaction of Moses: A charge of disloyalty & half-hearted commitment**
   a. Their disloyalty: Wanted to sit while the others fought—this would discourage the others from "crossing over" into the promised land
   b. Their guilt: Guilty of the same sins committed by the 10 spies at Kadesh Barnea: The sins of unbelief, disloyalty—half-hearted commitment (13:1-14:45)
      1) The spies discouraged the former generation from entering the promised land
      2) The spies aroused the Lord's anger
         - God accused them of a half-hearted commitment: They were not following Him wholeheartedly
         - God judged the people: Not one person 20 years old or older was ever allowed to enter the promised land
         - God was going to allow only two exceptions—Caleb & Joshua: Because they followed the Lord with their whole hearts
         - God's anger burned against the half-hearted—all who had sinned against Him—& He severely chastised them: They had to wander in the wilderness for 40 years until all died
   c. Their sin & its consequences
      1) They were a "brood of sinners"
      2) They were arousing the Lord's anger—even more than their fathers
      3) If they turned away from following God into the promised land...
         - The disunity would cause God to chastise the people
         - They would be responsible
3. **The selfish insistence of the two tribes & the forced compromise permitted**
   a. The insistence: The right to build pens for their livestock & fortified cities for their families
   b. The promises
      1) They would fight with the other tribes: Actually take the lead in battle until they secured their inheritance (cp. Josh.4:12f; 22:1f)
         - They wanted their families protected in fortified cities while they were off fighting
         - They would not return until all the people had received their inheritance
      2) They would not lay claim to any inheritance on the "other side" of the Jordan (the boundaries of the promised land: cp. v.20-22, 30, 32; 34:1-12)
   c. The forced compromise by Moses
      1) Moses granted their request: To maintain the unity of the people
         - They must, however, fulfill their promise:
         - They must join the others in fighting until the LORD had defeated His enemies
         - They could then return & claim the East Jordan as their land of the possession

G. The Settlement East of the Jordan River: A Picture of Compromise, Selfishness, Covetousness, Disloyalty & Half-Hearted Commitment, 32:1-42

Now the children of Reuben
and the children of Gad had
a very great multitude of cattle: and when they saw the
land of Jazer, and the land of
Gilead, that, behold, the
place was a place for cattle;
2 The children of Gad and
the children of Reuben came
and spake unto Moses, and
to Eleazar the priest, and
unto the princes of the congregation, saying,
3 Ataroth, and Dibon, and
Jazer, and Nimrah, and Heshbon, and Elealeh, and She-
bam, and Nebo, and Beon,
4 Even the country which
the LORD smote before the
congregation of Israel, is a
land for cattle, and thy servants have cattle:
5 Wherefore, said they, if
we have found grace in thy
sight, let this land be given
unto thy servants for a possession, and bring us not
over Jordan.
6 And Moses said unto the
children of Gad and to the
children of Reuben, Shall
your brethren go to war, and
shall ye sit here?
7 And wherefore discour-
age ye the heart of the children of Israel from going
over into the land which the
LORD hath given them?
8 Thus did your fathers,
when I sent them from
Kadesh-barnea to see the
land.
9 For when they went up
unto the valley of Eshcol,
and saw the land, they discouraged the heart of the
children of Israel, that they
should not go into the land
which the LORD had given
them.
10 And the LORD'S anger
was kindled the same time,
and he sware, saying,
11 Surely none of the
men that came up out of
Egypt, from twenty years old
and upward, shall see the
land which I sware unto
Abraham, unto Isaac, and
unto Jacob; because they
have not wholly followed
me:
12 Save Caleb the son of Jephunneh the Kenezite, and
Joshua the son of Nun: for
they have wholly followed
the LORD.
13 And the LORD'S anger
was kindled against Israel,
and he made them wander
in the wilderness forty
years, until all the generation, that had done evil in the
sight of the LORD, was consumed.
14 And, behold, ye are risen
up in your fathers' stead, an
increase of sinful men,
to augment yet the fierce
anger of the LORD toward Israel.
15 For if ye turn away
from after him, he will
yet again leave them in
the wilderness; and ye
shall destroy all this people.
16 And they came near unto
him, and said, We will build
sheepfolds here for our cattle, and cities for our little
ones:
17 But we ourselves will
go ready armed before
the children of Israel,
until we have brought them
unto their place: and our
little ones shall dwell in
the fenced cities because
of the inhabitants of the
land.
18 We will not return
unto our houses, until the
children of Israel have inherited every man his inheritance.
19 For we will not inherit
with them on yonder
side Jordan, or forward; because our inheritance is fall-
en to us on this side Jordan
eastward.
20 And Moses said unto
them, If ye will do this thing,
if ye will go armed before
the LORD to war,
21 And will go all of you
armed over Jordan before the
LORD, until he hath driven
out his enemies from before
him,
22 And the land be subdued
before the LORD: then
afterward ye shall return,
and be guiltless before the
LORD, and before Israel;
and this land shall be
your possession before the

2) Moses issued a strong warning to the two compromising tribes: If they failed, their sin would find them out (1 Chron.5:18-26)
3) Moses then gave two charges
   - To go & build cities & pens
   - To fulfill their promise
4) The two compromising tribes repeated the conditions of the agreement
   - Their women & children would remain in the cities of Gilead with their livestock
   - They—every soldier—would cross over Jordan & fight

4. The agreement with the two compromising tribes publicly declared & the territory assigned

a. The agreement declared by Moses to all the leadership
   1) If the two compromising tribes "crossed over" the Jordan & joined the other tribes in subduing the promised land, they were to be given the land of Gilead as their inheritance
   2) If the two compromising tribes did not help fight, they had to accept an inheritance inside the promised land

b. The public declaration by the two compromising tribes
   1) They would obey the Lord
   2) They would "cross over" & fight for the promised

LORD.
23 But if ye will not do so,
behold, ye have sinned
against the LORD: and be
sure your sin will find you
out.
24 Build you cities for your
little ones, and folds for your
sheep; and do that which
hath proceeded out of your
mouth.
25 And the children of Gad
and the children of Reuben
spake unto Moses, saying,
Thy servants will do as my
lord commandeth.
26 Our little ones, our wives,
our flocks, and all our cattle,
shall be there in the cities of
Gilead:
27 But thy servants will pass
over, every man armed for
war, before the LORD to battle, as my lord saith.
28 So concerning them
Moses commanded Eleazar
the priest, and Joshua the son
of Nun, and the chief fathers
of the tribes of the children
of Israel:
29 And Moses said unto
them, If the children of Gad
and the children of Reuben
will pass with you over Jordan, every man armed to battle, before the LORD, and the
land shall be subdued before
you; then ye shall give them
the land of Gilead for a possession:
30 But if they will not pass
over with you armed, they
shall have possessions
among you in the land of
Canaan.
31 And the children of Gad
and the children of Reuben
answered, saying, As the
LORD hath said unto thy servants, so will we do.
32 We will pass over armed
before the LORD into the land
of Canaan, that the possession of our inheritance on
this side Jordan may be
ours.
33 And Moses gave unto
them, even to the children of
Gad, and to the children of
Reuben, and unto half the
tribe of Manasseh the son of
Joseph, the kingdom of
Sihon king of the Amorites,
and the kingdom of Og king
of Bashan, the land, with the
cities thereof in the coasts,
even the cities of the country
round about.
34 And the children of Gad
built Dibon, and Ataroth,
and Aroer,
35 And Atroth, Shophan,
and Jaazer, and Jogbehah,
36 And Beth-nimrah, and
Beth-haran, fenced cities:
and folds for sheep.
37 And the children of
Reuben built Heshbon, and
Elealeh, and Kirjathaim,
38 And Nebo, and Baal-
meon, (their names being
changed,) and Shibmah: and
gave other names unto the
cities which they builded.
39 And the children of
Machir the son of Manasseh
went to Gilead, and took it,
and dispossessed the Amorite which was in it.
40 And Moses gave Gilead
unto Machir the son of Manasseh; and he dwelt therein.
41 And Jair the son
of Manasseh went and took
the small towns thereof,
and called them Havoth
jair.
42 And Nobah went
and took Kenath, and the villages thereof, and called
it Nobah, after his own
name.

land
   3) Their inheritance would be on the East side of the Jordan

c. The territory was assigned to the two compromising tribes & to the half-tribe of Manasseh
   1) The territory included the lands of King Sihon of the Amorites & of King Og of Bashan
   2) The Gadites rebuilt nine cities, fortified them, & built pens for their livestock[DS1-8]
   3) The Reubenites rebuilt & renamed six cities[DS9-13]
   4) The descendants of Makir of the tribe of Manasseh conquered Gilead
   5) The people of Jair—a clan of Manasseh—conquered many of the cities & settlements of Gilead: Called them Havvoth Jair[DS14]
   6) A man named Nobah captured Kenath[DS15] & the surrounding villages: Named them Nobah,[DS16] after himself

DIVISION IV

THE PREPARATION FOR THE MARCH INTO THE PROMISED LAND, 26:1-36:13

G. The Settlement, East of the Jordan River: A Picture of Compromise, Selfishness, Covetousness, Disloyalty, and Half-Hearted Commitment, 32:1-42

(32:1-42) **Introduction**: compromising with worldliness can destroy a person. Compromise can put us in jeopardy and endanger us. Compromise can discredit us and put us under suspicion. Compromise can ruin, weaken, and destroy us. The things of the world attract us, appealing to the lust of the eyes, the lust of the flesh, and the pride of life. If we compromise with the things of this world, they will often enslave us, putting us in bondage to them. This is always true with the things of the world, things such as…

- drugs
- alcohol
- illicit sex
- gluttony
- pornography
- lust
- covetousness
- greed
- power
- fame
- false worship
- profanity
- indulgence
- a spirit of disrespect

NUMBERS 32:1-42

Compromise with worldliness always weakens us, leading to disloyalty and half-hearted commitments. This is what happened in the present passage of Scripture. The Israelites were camped by the Jordan River right across from the great city of Jericho. They were poised, almost ready to cross the Jordan into the promised land, when two tribes declared their desire to stay behind. Their proposal was a devastating compromise, a compromise to accept an inheritance in the world instead of the inheritance of the promised land. This is the important subject of the Scripture. *The Settlement East of the Jordan River: A Picture of Compromise, Selfishness, Covetousness, Disloyalty, and Half-Hearted Commitment,* 32:1-42.

1. The compromise of the two tribes: a picture of selfishness, covetousness, disloyalty—half-hearted commitment (v.1-5).
2. The angry reaction of Moses: a charge of disloyalty and half-hearted commitment (v. 6-15).
3. The selfish insistence of the two tribes and the forced compromise permitted (v.16-27).
4. The agreement with the two compromising tribes publicly declared and the territory assigned (v.28-42).

1 (32:1-5) **Selfishness, Example of—Covetousness, Example of—Compromise, Example of—Disloyalty, Example of—Disunity, Example of—Tribe of Reuben, Location of—Tribe of Gad, Location of—Israel, Tribes of, Location of**: there was the compromise of the two tribes. This is a picture of selfishness, covetousness, disloyalty—a half-hearted commitment to the Lord and to the other tribes of Israel. Remember, the Israelites had been camped for some months in the plains of Moab by the River Jordan, right across from the great city of Jericho. They had conquered much of the land east of the Jordan River, including the land of the Amorites, the land of Bashan, and the land of the Midianites. They were sitting there in the comfort and security of conquerors. They and their livestock were enjoying the beauty, tranquillity and fruitfulness of the roaming pasture lands and the production of fertile soil. Then it happened: the value and potential of this land began to prey upon the minds of several tribes, the tribes of Reuben, Gad, and half of the tribe of Manasseh. Note the Scripture and outline:

OUTLINE	SCRIPTURE	SCRIPTURE	OUTLINE
1. The compromise of two tribes: A picture of selfishness, covetousness, disloyalty—half-hearted commitment a. Saw & coveted the fertile land b. Considered only their livestock c. Went to Moses & the leaders: Stated three points 1) That the East Jordan land	Now the children of Reuben and the children of Gad had a very great multitude of cattle: and when they saw the land of Jazer, and the land of Gilead, that, behold, the place was a place for cattle; 2 The children of Gad and the children of Reuben came and spake unto Moses, and to Eleazar the priest, and unto the princes of the congregation, saying, 3 Ataroth, and Dibon, and	Jazer, and Nimrah, and Heshbon, and Elealeh, and Shebam, and Nebo, and Beon, 4 Even the country which the LORD smote before the congregation of Israel, is a land for cattle, and thy servants have cattle: 5 Wherefore, said they, if we have found grace in thy sight, let this land be given unto thy servants for a possession, and bring us not over Jordan.	was a gift of God by conquest (21:1-35, 31:1-54) 2) That the conquered land was fertile, good pastureland for their livestock 3) That they wanted "this land" as their possession: They did not want to "cross over" the Jordan with the other tribes to fight for the promised land

1. These tribes saw and coveted the fertile land of the nations they had conquered. The fertility of the land was obviously as rich as a person could ever desire. The tribes of Reuben and Gad had large herds and flocks of livestock. At some point some of the leaders began to covet the surrounding land. They knew that East Jordan—the land they coveted—was outside Canaan, was not a part of the promised land of God. The south boundary of the promised land began at the Sea of Galilee and stretched northward along the Jordan River. The Jordan River was the eastern frontier of the promised land of Canaan (v.34:3, 12; see outline and note—Num.34:2-15 for more discussion). However, this fact did not stop these two tribes from desiring the land as their own.

⇒ Selfishly, they "saw" the land, that it was very fertile and suitable for livestock (v.1).
⇒ Selfishly, they focused their eyes upon the land, and converted it.
⇒ Selfishly, they were willing to compromise in order to secure the land.

After some time these two tribes sent representatives to Moses and the other leaders, requesting that the land of East Jordan be given them as their inheritance (v.2-5). They stated that it was God who had led them to conquer the land of the East Jordan. They pointed out that the conquered land was fertile, that it would make good pastureland for their livestock; therefore they wanted "this land" as their possession. They then made a statement that exposed hearts of disloyalty to God and to the other tribes, hearts that exposed half-hearted commitment to the call of God and to the promised land: they did not want to "cross over" the Jordan with the other tribes to fight for the promised land (v.5). These two tribes were not only guilty of *compromise* by their desire for an inheritance outside the promised land. They were also guilty of *disloyalty* and of *half-hearted commitment*. They did not want to help the other tribes as the tribes struggled to gain their inheritance, as they fought to conquer the enemies of the promised land. These two tribes were guilty of compromise: they had been gripped by selfishness, covetousness, and disloyalty. They had only a half-hearted commitment to God and to the other tribes, only a half-hearted commitment to the promised land.

> **Thought 1**. God warns a person against compromise. Compromising with the world is sin. Far too many of us lose sight of the promised land of heaven and begin to focus upon the world. We look at the world and see what it has to offer and we begin to covet…

- the pleasures and bright lights of the world
- the stimulations and excitements of the world
- the comforts and recreations of the world
- the properties and land of the world
- the money and wealth of the world
- the possessions and provisions of the world

Covetousness and greed set in and begin consuming our hearts. We want more and more and soon, we lose sight of the promised land of heaven. By focusing upon the things of the world instead of the things of God, we compromise with the world. We accept a lesser inheritance, far fewer riches than what the promised land of heaven has to offer. We become entangled with the things of the world. We compromise and become selfish, covetous, and disloyal to God and to other believers, all because of our attraction to the world and its things. Worldliness stands opposed to God and to the kingdom of heaven. This is the reason God warns us against worldliness.

"For what is a man profited, if he shall gain the whole world, and lose his own soul? or what shall a man give in exchange for his soul" (Mt.16:26).

"And take heed to yourselves, lest at any time your hearts be overcharged with surfeiting, and drunkenness, and cares of this life, and so that day come upon you unawares" (Lk.21.34).

"And be not conformed to this world: but be ye transformed by the renewing of your mind, that ye may prove what is that good, and acceptable, and perfect, will of God" (Ro.12:2).

"And they that use this world, as not abusing it: for the fashion of this world passeth away" (1 Cor.7:31).

"Set your affection on things above, not on things on the earth" (Col.3:2).

"And you hath he quickened, who were dead in trespasses and sins; Wherein in time past ye walked according to the course of this world, according to the prince of the power of the air, the spirit that now worketh in the children of disobedience: Among whom also we all had our conversation in times past in the lusts of our flesh, fulfilling the desires of the flesh and of the mind; and were by nature the children of wrath, even as others" (Eph.2:1-3).

"Teaching us that, denying ungodliness and worldly lusts, we should live soberly, righteously, and godly, in this present world; Looking for that blessed hope, and the glorious appearing of the great God and our Saviour Jesus Christ" (Tit.2:12-13).

"By faith Moses, when he was come to years, refused to be called the son of Pharaoh's daughter; Choosing rather to suffer affliction with the people of God, than to enjoy the pleasures of sin for a season" (Heb.11:24-25).

"Ye adulterers and adulteresses, know ye not that the friendship of the world is enmity with God? whosoever therefore will be a friend of the world is the enemy of God" (Jas.4:4).

"No man that warreth entangleth himself with the affairs of this life; that he may please him who hath chosen him to be a soldier" (2 Tim.2:4).

"For Demas hath forsaken me, having loved this present world, and is departed unto Thessalonica; Crescens to Galatia, Titus unto Dalmatia" (2 Tim.4:10).

"Love not the world, neither the things that are in the world. If any man love the world, the love of the Father is not in him. For all that is in the world, the lust of the flesh, and the lust of the eyes, and the pride of life, is not of the Father, but is of the world" (1 Jn.2:15-16).

"And they rejected his statutes, and his covenant that he made with their fathers, and his testimonies which he testified against them; and they followed vanity, and became vain, and went after the heathen that were round about them, concerning whom the Lord had charged them, that they should not do like them" (2 Ki.17:15).

2 (32:6-15) **Disunity, Example of—Half-hearted, Example of—Commitment, Half-hearted, Example of**: there was the angry reaction of Moses against the representatives of Gad and Reuben. He charged them with a spirit of disunity, with having a half-hearted commitment to God and to the other tribes. This was a severe rebuke of the two tribes. Moses was burning with anger because of their willingness to compromise and their unwillingness to "cross over" the Jordan with the other tribes to fight for the promised land. In a rage of anger, he charged them with disloyalty and issued a strong warning to them: they were as guilty of disloyalty as their fathers were at Kadesh Barnea and were on the verge of arousing God's anger and judgment even as their fathers had. This charge and warning are clearly seen in the Scripture and outline.

OUTLINE	SCRIPTURE	SCRIPTURE	OUTLINE
2. The angry reaction of Moses: A charge of disloyalty & half-hearted commitment	6 And Moses said unto the children of Gad and to the children of Reuben, Shall your brethren go to war, and shall ye sit here?	Kadesh-barnea to see the land. 9 For when they went up unto the valley of Eshcol, and saw the land, they dis-	10 spies at Kadesh Barnea: The sins of unbelief, disloyalty—half-hearted commitment (13:1-14:45)
a. Their disloyalty: Wanted to sit while the others fought—this would discourage the others from "crossing over" into the promised land	7 And wherefore discourage ye the heart of the children of Israel from going over into the land which the LORD hath given them?	couraged the heart of the children of Israel, that they should not go into the land which the LORD had given them.	1) The spies discouraged the former generation from entering the promised land
b. Their guilt: Guilty of the same sins committed by the	8 Thus did your fathers, when I sent them from	10 And the LORD'S anger was kindled the same time,	2) The spies aroused the Lord's anger

OUTLINE	SCRIPTURE	SCRIPTURE	OUTLINE
• God accused them of a half-hearted commitment: They were not following Him wholeheartedly • God judged the people: Not one person 20 years old or older was ever allowed to enter the promised land • God was going to allow only two exceptions—Caleb & Joshua: Because they followed the Lord with their whole hearts • God's anger burned against the half-hearted—all who had sinned	and he sware, saying, 11 Surely none of the men that came up out of Egypt, from twenty years old and upward, shall see the land which I sware unto Abraham, unto Isaac, and unto Jacob; because they have not wholly followed me: 12 Save Caleb the son of Je- phunneh the Kenezite, and Joshua the son of Nun: for they have wholly followed the LORD. 13 And the LORD'S an- ger was kindled against Israel, and he made them	wander in the wilderness forty years, until all the generation, that had done evil in the sight of the LORD, was consum- ed. 14 And, behold, ye are risen up in your fathers' stead, an increase of sinful men, to augment yet the fierce anger of the LORD toward Is- rael. 15 For if ye turn away from after him, he will yet again leave them in the wilderness; and ye shall destroy all this people.	against Him—& He severely chastised them: They had to wander in the wilderness for 40 years until all died c. Their sin & its consequences 1) They were a "brood of sinners" 2) They were arousing the Lord's anger—even more than their fathers 3) If they turned away from following God into the promised land... • The disunity would cause God to chastise the people • They would be responsible

1. Note the charge of disloyalty against the tribe of Reuben and Gad: they wanted to sit while the others fought to conquer the promised land. Their sitting would discourage the people of God from "crossing over" into the promised land. Their desire for comfort and ease was going to influence the lives of many others, discouraging them from continuing on and persevering until they secured their inheritance. This act of disloyalty was dangerous, a threat to the very survival of God's people. They all might begin to desire the ease and comfort of the land "outside" the promised land of God. They all might begin to compromise and give up the struggle against the enemies of the promised land. It would be far easier to accept the ease and comfort "outside" the promised land than to "cross over" the Jordan and have to fight for one's inheritance. This was the threat of this dangerous proposal being made by the two tribes.

2. Note their guilt: they were guilty of the same sins committed by the ten spies at Kadesh Barnea, that is, the sins of unbelief, disloyalty, and half-hearted commitment (v.8-13). By reviewing the story of the ten unfaithful spies, Moses was issuing a strong warning to these two tribes.

a. The ten spies had discouraged the former generation from entering the promised land. This was exactly what these two tribes were in danger of doing: discouraging the other tribes from entering the promised land (v.9).

b. The spies aroused the Lord's anger against them and against the people (v.10-13). God judged the people, not allowing one person twenty years old or older to enter the promised land. There were only two exceptions to this judgment: Caleb and Joshua. God's anger had burned against the ten spies and the people because of their disloyalty and half-hearted commitment.

3. The sins of these two tribes were about to bring the very same consequences upon the people of God (v.14-15). Note what Moses called them: they were a "brood of sinners" who were arousing the Lord's anger even more than their fathers. If they turned away from following God into the promised land, they would cause disunity, cause the people to be disloyal to the Lord. This disunity and disloyalty would cause God to chastise the people and they would personally be responsible.

Thought 1. God warns us against comfort and ease. He has called us to a life of commitment, wholehearted commitment. We are engaged in a spiritual warfare, struggling against the enemies of this life, enemies that keep us out of the promised land:

⇒ compromise	⇒ unbelief	⇒ worldliness
⇒ covetousness	⇒ indifference	⇒ lust of the eyes
⇒ disloyalty	⇒ neglect	⇒ worldly desires
⇒ selfishness	⇒ ignorance	⇒ indulgence
⇒ half-hearted commitment	⇒ comfort and ease	⇒ self-gratification

The enemies of life and of the promised land are many and varied. God warns us: we must conquer these enemies and press on to the promised land. We must not seek the comfort and ease of this world, not compromise with worldliness. We must press on to secure the great inheritance God has promised us.

"And every one that heareth these sayings of mine, and doeth them not, shall be likened unto a foolish man, which built his house upon the sand: And the rain descended, and the floods came, and the winds blew, and beat upon that house; and it fell: and great was the fall of it" (Mt.7:26-27).

"And because iniquity shall abound, the love of many shall wax cold. But he that shall endure unto the end, the same shall be saved" (Mt.24:12-13).

"And that servant, which knew his lord's will, and prepared not himself, neither did according to his will, shall be beaten with many stripes" (Lk.12:47).

"What doth it profit, my brethren, though a man say he hath faith, and have not works? can faith save him" (Jas.2:14).

"Therefore to him that knoweth to do good, and doeth it not, to him it is sin" (Jas.4:17).

"And Joshua said unto the children of Israel, How long are ye slack to go to possess the land, which the Lord God of your fathers hath given you" (Josh.18:3).

"And he did that which was right in the sight of the Lord, but not with a perfect heart" (2 Chron.25:2).

"Our soul is exceedingly filled with the scorning of those that are at ease, and with the contempt of the proud" (Ps.123:4).

"Rise up, ye women that are at ease; hear my voice, ye careless daughters; give ear unto my speech. Many days and years shall ye be troubled, ye careless women: for the vintage shall fail, the gathering shall not come. Tremble, ye women that are at ease; be troubled, ye careless ones" (Is.32:9-11).

"Cursed be he that doeth the work of the Lord deceitfully, and cursed be he that keepeth back his sword from blood" (Jer.48:10).

"Woe to them that are at ease in Zion" (Amos 6:1).

3 (32:16-27) **Compromise—Half-hearted—Commitment, Half-hearted**: there was the selfish insistence of the two tribes and the forced compromise permitted. The representatives from the compromising tribes were most likely shaken at the angry reaction and the severe charge of disloyalty by Moses. Apparently, the two tribes requested permission to withdraw and reconsider their proposal. They just were not willing to lose out on the property: a passion, a covetousness had gripped their hearts for the land of the East Jordan. Within their own minds, they had to figure out some way, some modification to their proposal that Moses would accept. They had to work out a compromise and insist upon it. This was exactly what they did. At some point they returned and made the following modified promises to Moses, a compromised proposal.

OUTLINE	SCRIPTURE	SCRIPTURE	OUTLINE
3. The selfish insistence of the two tribes & the forced compromise permitted a. The insistence: The right to build pens for their livestock & fortified cities for their families b. The promises 1) They would fight with the other tribes: Actually take the lead in battle until they secured their inheritance (cp. Josh.4:12f; 22:1f) • They wanted their families protected in fortified cities while they were off fighting • They would not return until all the people had received their inheritance 2) They would not lay claim to any inheritance on the "other side" of the Jordan (the boundaries of the promised land: cp. v.20-22, 30, 32; 34:1-12) c. The forced compromise by Moses 1) Moses granted their request: To maintain the unity of the people • They must, however, fulfill their promise: • They must join the oth-	16 And they came near unto him, and said, We will build sheepfolds here for our cattle, and cities for our little ones: 17 But we ourselves will go ready armed before the children of Israel, until we have brought them unto their place: and our little ones shall dwell in the fenced cities because of the inhabitants of the land. 18 We will not return unto our houses, until the children of Israel have inherited every man his inheritance. 19 For we will not inherit with them on yonder side Jordan, or forward; because our inheritance is fallen to us on this side Jordan eastward. 20 And Moses said unto them, If ye will do this thing, if ye will go armed before the LORD to war, 21 And will go all of you armed over Jordan before the LORD, until he hath driven out his enemies from be-	fore him, 22 And the land be subdued before the LORD: then afterward ye shall return, and be guiltless before the LORD, and before Israel; and this land shall be your possession before the LORD. 23 But if ye will not do so, behold, ye have sinned against the LORD: and be sure your sin will find you out. 24 Build you cities for your little ones, and folds for your sheep; and do that which hath proceeded out of your mouth. 25 And the children of Gad and the children of Reuben spake unto Moses, saying, Thy servants will do as my lord commandeth. 26 Our little ones, our wives, our flocks, and all our cattle, shall be there in the cities of Gilead: 27 But thy servants will pass over, every man armed for war, before the LORD to battle, as my lord saith.	ers in fighting until the LORD had defeated His enemies • They could then return & claim the East Jordan as their land of the possession 2) Moses issued a strong warning to the two compromising tribes: If they failed, their sin would find them out (1 Chron.5:18-26) 3) Moses then gave two charges • To go & build cities & pens • To fulfill their promise 4) The two compromising tribes repeated the conditions of the agreement • Their women & children would remain in the cities of Gilead with their livestock • They—every soldier—would cross over Jordan & fight

1. The compromising tribes insisted on the right to inherit the land, to build pens for their livestocks and fortified cities for their families (v.16).

2. In return for the right to inherit the land, they would make two strong promises to Moses and the rest of the tribes.

   a. They would fight with the other tribes. They would actually take the lead in battle until the other tribes secured their inheritance. They just wanted their families protected and their cities fortified while they were fighting off then they would not return until all the people of Israel had received their inheritance. They knew that they were just as accountable as the other tribes for fighting against the enemies of the promised land. In no way would they shirk their duty until all the enemies of the promised land had been defeated and conquered. Later history shows that these two tribes did exactly what they had promised (Josh.4:12-13; 22:1f).

   b. They personally would not lay claim to any inheritance on the "other side" of the Jordan. Their inheritance would be on the east side of the Jordan River, not on the west side, not in the promised land of God (cp. 34:1-12).

3. Moses was forced to accept the compromise proposal. What more could he do? The two compromising tribes were insisting that their modified promises, their compromised proposal be accepted (v.20-27).

a. Moses therefore granted their request in order to maintain the unity of the people (v.20-22). However the two compromising tribes must fulfill their promise: they must join the others in fighting until the Lord had defeated His enemies, the enemies who would oppose His people entering the promised land. The two compromising tribes could then return and claim the East Jordan as their possession.

b. But note that Moses issued a strong warning to the two compromising tribes: if they failed to keep their promises, they could rest assured: "Your sin will find you out." The sin of these two compromising tribes did eventually find them out and brought terrible judgment upon them time and time again. By choosing to remain outside the promised land, they were tempted more and more to compromise with the surrounding nations. Moreover, it was far easier for them to be attacked by the enemies of God's people. This is seen time and again in the later history of these compromising tribes (Judg.10:6-9; 10:17-18; 1 Ki.22:3; 2 Ki.10:32-33; 15:27-29; 1 Chron.5:18-26).

c. Moses then gave two charges to these compromising tribes: they were to go build cities and pens for their families and livestock, but they were to make absolutely sure that they fulfilled their promises.

d. The two compromising tribes repeated their promises and the conditions of the agreement. They would do just what they had said: their women and children would remain in the cities of Gilead with their livestock while they every soldier among them—would "cross over" Jordan and fight the enemies of the promised land. This would do for the Lord, just as He had commanded (v.25-27).

Thought 1. The compromising tribes were determined to go their own way. They wanted the inheritance on the east side of the Jordan. They did not want to "cross over" the Jordan into the promised land. They liked what they saw where they were, and they wanted what they saw.

This is just like so many people today: they are determined to go their own way instead of God's way. They like what they see out in the world, and they compromise with the world. But God warns us all: "Your sin will find you out." Compromise and sin will be exposed. It cannot be hid. What we sow, we will reap. This happened to the compromising tribes and it will happen to any of us who compromise with the world and its sin.

"For there is nothing covered, that shall not be revealed; neither hid, that shall not be known" (Lk.12:2).

"Be not deceived; God is not mocked: for whatsoever a man soweth, that shall he also reap" (Gal.6:7).

"Therefore judge nothing before the time, until the Lord come, who both will bring to light the hidden things of darkness, and will make manifest the counsels of the hearts: and then shall every man have praise of God" (1 Cor.4:5).

"But if ye will not do so, behold, ye have sinned against the Lord: and be sure your sin will find you out" (Num.32:23).

"If I sin, then thou markest me, and thou wilt not acquit me from mine iniquity" (Job 10:14).

"For now thou numberest my steps: dost thou not watch over my sin" (Job 14:16).

"The heaven shall reveal his iniquity; and the earth shall rise up against him" (Job.20:27).

"Whose hatred is covered by deceit, his wickedness shall be shown before the whole congregation" (Pr.26:26).

"For God shall bring every work into judgment, with every secret thing, whether it be good, or whether it be evil" (Eccl.12:14).

"For though thou wash thee with nitre, and take thee much sope, yet thine iniquity is marked before me, saith the Lord God" (Jer.2:22).

"For mine eyes are upon all their ways: they are not hid from my face, neither is their iniquity hid from mine eyes" (Jer.16:17).

"I know the things that come into your mind, every one of them" (Ezk.11:5).

"And they consider not in their hearts that I remember all their wickedness: now their own doings have beset them about; they are before my face" (Hos.7:2).

4 (32:28-42) **Reuben, Territory of—Gad, Territory of—Manasseh, Half-tribe of, Territory of**: the agreement with the two compromising tribes was publicly declared and the territory was assigned to them. What then happened was a legal and binding contract between the two compromising tribes and the rest of Israel.

OUTLINE	SCRIPTURE	SCRIPTURE	OUTLINE
4. The agreement with the two compromising tribes publicly declared & the territory assigned a. The agreement declared by Moses to all the leadership 1) If the two compromising tribes "crossed over" the Jordan & joined the other tribes in subduing the promised land, they were	28 So concerning them Moses commanded Eleazar the priest, and Joshua the son of Nun, and the chief fathers of the tribes of the children of Israel: 29 And Moses said unto them, If the children of Gad and the children of Reuben will pass with you over Jordan, every man armed to	battle, before the LORD, and the land shall be subdued before you; then ye shall give them the land of Gilead for a possession: 30 But if they will not pass over with you armed, they shall have possessions among you in the land of Canaan. 31 And the children of Gad	to be given the land of Gilead as their inheritance 2) If the two compromising tribes did not help fight, they had to accept an inheritance inside the promised land b. The public declaration by the

OUTLINE	SCRIPTURE	SCRIPTURE	OUTLINE
two compromising tribes 1) They would obey the Lord 2) They would "cross over" & fight for the promised land 3) Their inheritance would be on the East side of the Jordan	and the children of Reuben answered, saying, As the LORD hath said unto thy ser- vants, so will we do. 32 We will pass over armed before the LORD into the land of Canaan, that the pos- session of our inheritance on this side Jordan may be ours.	Beth-haran, fenced cities: and folds for sheep. 37 And the children of Reuben built Heshbon, and Elealeh, and Kirjathaim, 38 And Nebo, and Baal- meon, (their names being changed,) and Shibmah: and gave other names unto the cities which they builded.	3) The Reubenites rebuilt & renamed six cities
c. The territory was assigned to the two compromising tribes & to the half-tribe of Manasseh 1) The territory included the lands of King Sihon of the Amorites & of King Og of Bashan	33 And Moses gave unto them, even to the children of Gad, and to the children of Reuben, and unto half the tribe of Manasseh the son of Joseph, the kingdom of Sihon king of the Amorites, and the kingdom of Og king of Bashan, the land, with the cities thereof in the coasts, even the cities of the country round about.	39 And the children of Machir the son of Manasseh went to Gilead, and took it, and dispossessed the Amorite which was in it. 40 And Moses gave Gilead unto Machir the son of Ma- nasseh; and he dwelt therein. 41 And Jair the son of Manasseh went and took the small towns thereof,	4) The descendants of Makir of the tribe of Manasseh conquered Gilead 5) The people of Jair—a clan of Manasseh—conquered many of the cities & settlements of Gilead: Called them Havvoth Jair
2) The Gadites rebuilt nine cities, fortified them, & built pens for their livestock	34 And the children of Gad built Dibon, and Ataroth, and Aroer, 35 And Atroth, Shophan, and Jaazer, and Jogbehah, 36 And Beth-nimrah, and	and called them Havoth-jair. 42 And Nobah went and took Kenath, and the vil- lages thereof, and called it Nobah, after his own name.	6) A man named Nobah captured Kenath & the surrounding villages: Named them Nobah, after himself

1. The agreement was declared by Moses to all the leadership of Israel. This included Eleazar the priest, Joshua the son of Nun, and all the tribal leaders of Israel (v.28-30). If the two compromising tribes "crossed over" the Jordan and joined the other tribes in subduing the promised land, they were to be given the land of Gilead as their inheritance. But the two compromising tribes were strongly warned: if they did not "cross over" the Jordan to fight the enemies of God's people, they had to accept an inheritance inside the promised land.

2. The two compromising tribes then made a public declaration to all the leadership (v.31-32): they would obey the Lord and "cross over" to fight against the enemies of the promised land. Their inheritance would be on the east side of the Jordan.

3. The territory was then assigned to the two compromising tribes and to the half-tribe of Manasseh (v.33-42). This is the first time the half-tribe of Manasseh has been mentioned as being a part of the compromise proposal. Most likely they initially feared approaching Moses with the other two tribes, so they waited until the compromise proposal had been accepted before they joined in the contract agreement.

   a. The territory included the lands that had been conquered from Sihon King of the Amorites and from King Og of Bashan (v.33).
   b. The Gadites rebuilt nine cities, fortified them, and built pens for their livestock (v.34-36). Obviously these were exciting and joyful days even for these compromising tribes. Individuals and families are usually most happy when they are working together on projects such as building their own homes. The people of Israel had not owned land nor had homes for generations. Now for the first time they possessed land and were in the process of constructing their homes. What an exciting and joyful occasion this must have been for them.
   c. The Reubenites rebuilt and renamed six cities (v.37-38). In some cases the old names of the cities had been named after false gods such as Baal; therefore the people of God felt compelled to change their names.
   d. The descendants of Makir of the tribe of Manasseh conquered Gilead (v.39-40).
   e. The people of Jair—a clan of Manasseh—conquered many of the cities and settlements of Gilead. These they called Havvoth Jair (v.41).
   f. A man named Nobah captured Kenath and the surrounding villages. These he named Nobah, after himself (v.42).

Thought 1. The lesson to see in this point is the promise of the compromising tribes: they would obey the Lord (v.31). They promised that they would "cross over" and fight with the other tribes against the enemies of the promised land.

The one thing God demands of every believer is obedience. To obey is the supreme demand of God. Obeying God means more to Him than sacrifice, even the sacrifice of one's life to Him. When we declare that we are sacrificing our lives to God, this promise is only profession—only words. If we are sincere in the sacrifice of our lives, we prove our sincerity by obedience. It is the obedience that matters to God, not our words of promise. Our promise is proven by our obedience. It is the obedience that God is after. This was true with these compromising tribes, and it is also true with us. They clearly *stated* that they would obey the Lord when they were *not obeying* the Lord in the first place. They were choosing to compromise with the world, to accept an inheritance "outside" the promised land. It is not our words that matter to God: it is our obedience. First and foremost, God demands that we obey Him.

"And Samuel said, Hath the Lord as great delight in burnt offerings and sacrifices, as in obeying the voice of the Lord? Behold, to obey is better than sacrifice, and to hearken than the fat of rams" (1 Sam.15:22).

"Not every one that saith unto me, Lord, Lord, shall enter into the kingdom of heaven; but he that doeth the will of my Father which is in heaven" (Mt.7:21).

"Jesus answered and said unto him, If a man love me, he will keep my words: and my Father will love him, and we will come unto him, and make our abode with him" (Jn.14:23).

"If ye keep my commandments, ye shall abide in my love; even as I have kept my Father's commandments, and abide in his love" (Jn.15:10).

"Ye are my friends, if ye do whatsoever I command you" (Jn.15:14).

"Blessed are they that do his commandments, that they may have right to the tree of life, and may enter in through the gates into the city" (Rev.22:14).

"This day the Lord thy God hath commanded thee to do these statutes and judgments: thou shalt therefore keep and do them with all thine heart, and with all thy soul" (Dt.26:16).

"But if ye will not obey the voice of the Lord, but rebel against the commandment of the Lord, then shall the hand of the Lord be against you, as it was against your fathers" (1 Sam.12:15).

DEEPER STUDY # 1
(Num.32:34-36) **Dibon, City of (See also Dibon-Gad; Dimonah)**: it was located east of the Jordan River, about thirteen miles east of the Dead Sea. (See Map—Numbers 33:5-49, end of commentary.) The Hebrew meaning of Dibon is "pining away" or "fence of tubes." Dibon was the capital city of the Moabites (Num.21:21-31). It was rebuilt by the tribe of Gad and was later named Dibon-Gad.
See other Scripture references for study:

Numbers 21:30; Numbers 32:3; Numbers 33:45-46; Joshua 13:9; Joshua 13:17; Joshua 15:22; Neh. 11:25; Isaiah 15:2; Isaiah 15:9; Jeremiah 48:18; Jeremiah 48:22

DEEPER STUDY # 2
(Num.32:34-36) **Ataroth, City of**: it was located eight miles northwest of Dibon and eight miles east of the Dead Sea. (See Map—Numbers 33:5-49, end of commentary.) The Hebrew meaning of Ataroth is "crowns." It was rebuilt by the tribe of Gad (Numbers 32:3; Numbers 32:34). There is a different town on the border of Benjamin and Ephraim called Ataroth-addar (Joshua 16:2; Joshua 16:7). Also note that there is a different town called "Ataroth of the house of Joab" in the tribe of Judah, a city founded by the descendants of Salma (1 Chron. 2:54. See also Atroth-Beth-Joab.)
See other Scripture references for study:

Numbers 32:3; Joshua 16:2-3; Joshua 16:5; Joshua 16:7; Joshua 18:13; 1 Chron. 2:54

DEEPER STUDY # 3
(Num.32:34-36) **Aroer, City of**: it was located on the northern bank of the Arnon River, the southernmost town of Israel east of the Jordan River (Joshua 13:9). The Hebrew meaning of Aroer is "juniper" or "nudity." It was the capital city of Shion, king of the Amorites (Joshua 12:2). Aroer was rebuilt by the tribe of Gad (Numbers 32:34)
See other Scripture references for study:

Deut. 2:36; Deut. 3:12; Deut. 4:48; Joshua 12:2; Joshua 13:9; Joshua 13:16; Joshua 13:25; Judges 11:26; Judges 11:33; 1 Samuel 30:28; 2 Samuel 24:5; 2 Kings 10:33; 1 Chron. 5:8; Isaiah 17:2; Jeremiah 48:19

DEEPER STUDY # 4
(Num.32:34-36) **Atroth Shophan, City of**: the location is unknown. It was rebuilt by the tribe of Gad.
See other Scripture references for study:

Numbers 32:35 (Only reference in Scripture)

DEEPER STUDY # 5
(Num.32:34-36) **Jazer, City of**: it was located east of the Jordan River, in or near Gilead, between Dibon and Nimrah. (See Map—Numbers 33:5-49, end of commentary.) The Hebrew meaning of Jazer is "may He help" or "helpful." It was a former Amorite city state conquered by Israel on its march to the promised land. Jazer was rebuilt by the tribe of Gad (Num.32:35). It was later chosen to be a Levitical city (Joshua 21:39).
See other Scripture references for study:

Numbers 32:1; Numbers 32:3; Joshua 13:25; Joshua 21:39; 2 Samuel 24:5; 1 Chron. 6:81; 1 Chron. 26:31; Isaiah 16:8-9; Jeremiah 48:32

DEEPER STUDY # 6
(Num.32:34-36) **Jogbehah, City of**: it was located east of the Jordan River. (See Map—Numbers 33:5-49, end of commentary.) The Hebrew meaning of Jogbehah is "height, little hill" or "hillock." It was rebuilt and settled by the tribe of Gad (Num.32:35). Gideon defeated the kings of Midian at Jogbehah (Judges 8:11).
See other Scripture references for study:

Numbers 32:35; Judges 8:11

DEEPER STUDY # 7
(Num.32:34-36) **Beth Nimrah, City of**: it was located east, about ten miles from the mouth of the Jordan River. (See Map—Numbers 33:5-49, end of commentary.) The Hebrew meaning of Beth Nimrah is "house of the panther" or "house of the leopard." Beth Nimrah was a fenced or fortified city (Num.32:36) It was rebuilt and settled by the tribe of Gad (Num.32:36).
See other Scripture references for study:
Numbers 32:3; Joshua 13:27

DEEPER STUDY # 8
(Num.32:34-36) **Beth Haran, City of (See also Beth-haram)**: it was located east of the Jordan River. (See Map—Numbers 33:5-49, end of commentary.) The Hebrew meaning of Beth Haran is "house of height" or "built." It was rebuilt and settled by the tribe of Gad (Num.32:36). Beth Haran was a fenced or fortified city (Num.32:36).
See other Scripture reference for study:
Joshua 13:27

DEEPER STUDY # 9
(Num.32:37-38) **Elealeh, City of**: it was located east of the Jordan River, a former town of the Amorites. (See Map—Numbers 33:5-49, end of commentary.) The Hebrew meaning of Elealeh is "God has ascended," "God went up," or "high ground." The tribe of Reuben asked Moses for this town. It was rebuilt, strengthened by the tribe of Reuben.
See other Scripture references for study:
Numbers 32:3; Isaiah 15:4; Isaiah 16:9; Jeremiah 48:34

DEEPER STUDY # 10
(Num.32:37-38) **Kiriathaim, City of (See also Kirjathaim; Kartan)**: it was located in the tribal territory of Naphtali (1 Chron.6:76). (See Map—Numbers 33:5-49, end of commentary.) The Hebrew meaning of Kiriathaim is "double city" or "two cities." It was taken from the Amorites and assigned to the tribe of Reuben (Num.32:37; Josh.13:9). Kiriathaim became a Levitical city and a city of refuge.
See other Scripture references for study:
Genesis 14:5; Numbers 32:37; Joshua 13:19; Joshua 21:32; 1 Chron. 6:76; Jeremiah 48:1; Jeremiah 48:23; Ezekiel 25:9

DEEPER STUDY # 11
(Num.32:37-38) **Nebo, City of**: it was located east of the Jordan River, southwest of Heshbon. (See Map—Numbers 33:5-49, end of commentary.) The Hebrew meaning of Nebo is "height." It was a Moabite city assigned to the tribe of Reuben.
See other Scripture references for study:
Numbers 32:3; 1 Chron. 5:8; Isaiah 15:2; Isaiah 46:1; Jeremiah 48:1; Jeremiah 48:22

DEEPER STUDY # 12
(Num.32:37-38) **Baal Meon, City of**: it was located east of the Jordan River, toward the northern border of the tribe of Reuben, about nine miles east of the Dead Sea. (See Map—Numbers 33:5-49, end of commentary.) The Hebrew meaning of Baal Meon is "lord of the residence, dwelling" or "Baal of the residence." It was rebuilt by the tribe of Reuben and renamed (Num.32:38).
See other Scripture references for study:
Joshua 13:17; 1 Chron. 5:8; Ezekiel 25:9

DEEPER STUDY # 13
(Num.32:37-38) **Sibmah, City of (See also Sebam; Shibmah)**: it was located east of the Jordan River. (See Map—Numbers 33:5-49, end of commentary.) The Hebrew meaning of Sibmah is "cold, coolness" or "high." It was assigned to the tribe of Reuben and rebuilt by the tribe of Reuben.
See other Scripture references for study:
Numbers 32:3; Joshua 13:19; Isaiah 16:8-9; Jeremiah 48:32

DEEPER STUDY # 14
(Num.32:41) **Havvoth Jair, City of (See also Havoth Jair)**: it was located in Bashan, east of the Jordan River. (See Map—Numbers 33:5-49, end of commentary.) The Hebrew meaning of Havvoth Jair is "hut, hamlets, tents of Jair." There was a district of villages which Jair, the son of Manasseh, captured and called by his name (Numbers 32:41).
See other Scripture references for study:
Deut. 3:14; Judges 10:4; 1 Chron. 2:23

DEEPER STUDY # 15
(Num.32:42) **Kenath, City of**: it was located in eastern Gilead. (See Map—Numbers 33:5-49, end of commentary.) The Hebrew meaning of Kenath is uncertain.
See other Scripture reference for study:
1 Chron. 2:23

DEEPER STUDY # 16
(Num.32:42) **Nobah, City of**: it was located in eastern Gilead. (See Map—Numbers 33:5-49, end of commentary.) The Hebrew meaning of Nobah is "barking" or "howling." It was Nobah, the leader of the tribe of Manasseh, who conquered Keneth and renamed it after himself.
See other Scripture reference for study:
Judges 8:11

TYPES, SYMBOLS, AND PICTURES
(Numbers 32:1-42)

Historical Term	Type or Picture (Scriptural Basis for Each)	Life Application for Today's Believer	Biblical Application
The Compromise of Gad and Reuben Num.32:1-42	*The compromise of Gad and Reuben is a picture of selfishness, coveteousness, disloyalty and half-hearted commitment.* *Compromise with worldliness always weakens us, leading to disloyalty and half-hearted commitments. This is what happened in the present passage of Scripture. The Israelites were camped by the Jordan River right across from the great city of Jericho. They were poised, almost ready to cross the Jordan into the promised land, when two tribes declared their desire to stay behind. Their proposal was a devastating compromise, a compromise to accept an inheritance in East Jordan, an inheritance in the world instead of the inheritance of the promised land.* **"Wherefore, said they, if we have found grace in thy sight, let this land be given unto thy servants for a possession, and bring us not over Jordan" (Num. 32:5).**	Compromising with worldliness can destroy a person. Compromise can put us in jeopardy and endanger us. Compromise can discredit us and put us under suspicion. Compromise can ruin, weaken, and destroy us. The things of the world attract us, appealing to the lust of the eyes, the lust of the flesh, and the pride of life. If we compromise with the things of this world, they will often enslave us, putting us in bondage to them.	***"For what is a man profited, if he shall gain the whole world, and lose his own soul? or what shall a man give in exchange for his soul" (Mt.16:26).*** ***"And take heed to yourselves, lest at any time your hearts be overcharged with surfeiting, and drunkenness, and cares of this life, and so that day come upon you unawares" (Lk. 21:34).*** ***"Set your affection on things above, not on things on the earth" (Col. 3:2).*** ***"For Demas hath forsaken me, having loved this present world, and is departed unto Thessalonica; Crescens to Galatia, Titus unto Dalmatia" (2 Tim. 4:10).*** ***"Teaching us that, denying ungodliness and worldly lusts, we should live soberly, righteously, and godly, in this present world" (Tit. 2:12).*** ***"Ye adulterers and adulteresses, know ye not that the friendship of the world is enmity with God? whosoever therefore will be a friend of the world is the enemy of God" (Jas. 4:4).***

NUMBERS 33:1-56

1. The faithfulness of God in leading & guiding His people
- a. God led His people out of Egypt (a symbol of the world)
  - 1) Led orderly by divisions
  - 2) Led by Moses & Aaron
- b. God led Moses to record the stages or camps of the march to the promised land
- c. God led His people to march out triumphantly—as a great nation of people
  - 1) On the 15th of the first month
  - 2) In full view of all Egyptians
    - As they were burying their firstborn
    - God had judged them

2. The wilderness wanderings: A picture of man's failure—40 years of no progress[1]
- a. The camps from Rameses to Mt. Sinai: Left Rameses—Egypt
  - 1) Succoth (Ex.13:20)
  - 2) Etham (Ex.13:20): First reference to the cloud
  - 3) Pi Hahiroth (Ex.14:2, 9): The campsite from which they crossed the Red Sea (Ex.14:1f)
  - 4) Marah (Ex.15:23) Bitter waters sweetened by God
  - 5) Elim (Ex.15:27): An oasis in the desert
  - 6) The Red Sea: Not mentioned as a camp
  - 7. Desert of Sin (Ex.16:1)

H. The Review of the Wilderness Wanderings & a Strong Charge to Take Possession of the Promised Land: A Picture of God's Faithfulness & Man's Failure, 33:1-56

These are the journeys of the children of Israel, which went forth out of the land of Egypt with their armies under the hand of Moses and Aaron.

2 And Moses wrote their goings out according to their journeys by the commandment of the LORD: and these are their journeys according to their goings out.

3 And they departed from Rameses in the first month, on the fifteenth day of the first month; on the morrow after the passover the children of Israel went out with an high hand in the sight of all the Egyptians.

4 For the Egyptians buried all their firstborn, which the LORD had smitten among them: upon their gods also the LORD executed judgments.

5 And the children of Israel removed from Rameses, and pitched in Succoth.

6 And they departed from Succoth, and pitched in Etham, which is in the edge of the wilderness.

7 And they removed from Etham, and turned again unto Pi-hahiroth, which is before Baal-zephon: and they pitched before Migdol.

8 And they departed from before Pi-hahiroth, and passed through the midst of the sea into the wilderness, and went three days' journey in the wilderness of Etham, and pitched in Marah.

9 And they removed from Marah, and came unto Elim: and in Elim were twelve fountains of water, and threescore and ten palm trees; and they pitched there.

10 And they removed from Elim, and encamped by the Red sea.

11 And they removed from the Red sea, and encamped in the wilderness of Sin.

12 And they took their journey out of the wilderness of Sin, and encamped in Dophkah.

13 And they departed from Dophkah, and encamped in Alush.

14 And they removed from Alush, and encamped at Rephidim, where was no water for the people to drink.

15 And they departed from Rephidim, and pitched in the wilderness of Sinai.

16 And they removed from the desert of Sinai, and pitched at Kibroth-hattaavah.

17 And they departed from Kibroth-hattaavah, and encamped at Hazeroth.

18 And they departed from Hazeroth, and pitched in Rithmah.

19 And they departed from Rithmah, and pitched at Rimmon-parez.

20 And they departed from Rimmon-parez, and pitched in Libnah.

21 And they removed from Libnah, and pitched at Rissah.

22 And they journeyed from Rissah, and pitched in Kehelathah.

23 And they went from Kehelathah, and pitched in mount Shapher.

24 And they removed from mount Shapher, and encamped in Haradah.

25 And they removed from Haradah, and pitched in Makheloth.

26 And they removed from Makheloth, and encamped at Tahath.

27 And they departed from Tahath, and pitched at Tarah.

28 And they removed from Tarah, and pitched in Mithcah.

29 And they went from Mithcah, and pitched in Hashmonah.

30 And they departed from Hashmonah, and encamped at Moseroth.

31 And they departed from Moseroth, and pitched in Bene-jaakan.

32 And they removed from Bene-jaakan, and encamped at Hor-hagidgad.

33 And they went from Hor-

- 8) Dophkah: No reference in Exodus
- 9) Alush: No reference in Exodus
- 10) Rephidim (Ex.17:1): No water to drink
- 11) Desert of Sinai (Ex.19:2): The law was given

b. The camps from Mt. Sinai to Mt. Hor
- 1) Kibroth Hattaavah (Num. 11:34): Was 3 days from Sinai
- 2) Hazeroth (Num.11:35; 12:16; Dt.1:1)
- 3) Rithmah: No other reference
- 4) Rimmon Perez: No other reference
- 5) Libnab: No other reference
- 6) Rissah: No other reference
- 7) Kehelathah: No other reference
- 8) Mount Shepher: No other reference
- 9) Haradah: No other reference
- 10) Makheloth: No other reference
- 11) Tahath: No other reference
- 12) Terah: No other reference
- 13) Mithcah: No other reference
- 14) Hashmonah: No other reference
- 15) Moseroth (Dt.10:6): Place of Aaron's death (cp. v.38)
- 16) Bene Jaakan (Gen.36:27; Dt.10:6; 1 Chron.1:42)
- 17) Hor Haggidgad (Dt.10:7)
- 18) Jotbathah (Dt.10:7)

1 The brief notes and Scripture cross references for the campsites were gleaned from the *Expositor's Bible Commentary,* p. 987-990.

19) Abronah: No other reference

20) Ezion Geber (Dt.2:8; 1 Ki. 9:26): A well known oasis

21) Kadesh (Num.13:21): Place where 12 spies were sent out & 10 rebelled

c. The campsite at Mt. Hor

1) God took Aaron home to heaven while on Mt. Hor: Died on the 1st day of the 5th month, 40 years after Israel's deliverance (Num.20:23-29)

2) God gave Aaron a long, fruitful life: 123 years

3) God was faithful & gave His people their first military victory at Mt. Hor (Num.21:1-3)

d. The camps from Mt. Hor to the Jordan River across from Jericho

1) Zalmonah: No other reference

2) Punon (Gen.36:41; 1 Chron. 1:52)

3) Oboth (Num.21:10-11)

4) Iye Abarim (Num.21:11): A place on the border of Moab

5) Dibon Gad (Num.21:30; 32:3): Was in Moab

6) Almon Diblathaim (Jer.48:22)

7) Mountains of Abarim, near Nebo (Num.27:12): A range of mountains in NW Moab just NE of the Dead Sea

hagidgad, and pitched in
Jotbathah.
34 And they removed from
Jotbathah, and encamped at
Ebronah.
35 And they departed from
Ebronah, and encamped at
Ezion-gaber.
36 And they removed from
Ezion-gaber, and pitched in
the wilderness of Zin, which
is Kadesh.
37 And they removed from
Kadesh, and pitched in
mount Hor, in the edge of the
land of Edom.
38 And Aaron the priest
went up into mount Hor at
the commandment of the
LORD, and died there, in the
fortieth year after the children of Israel were come out
of the land of Egypt, in the
first day of the fifth month.
39 And Aaron was an hun-
dred and twenty and three
years old when he died in
mount Hor.
40 And king Arad the
Canaanite, which dwelt in
the south in the land of
Canaan, heard of the coming
of the children of Israel.
41 And they departed from
mount Hor, and pitched in
Zalmonah.
42 And they departed from
Zalmonah, and pitched in
Punon.
43 And they departed from
Punon, and pitched in Oboth.
44 And they departed from
Oboth, and pitched in Ije-
abarim, in the border of
Moab.
45 And they departed from
Iim, and pitched in Dibon-
gad.
46 And they removed from
Dibon-gad, and encamped in
Almon-diblathaim.
47 And they removed
from Almon-diblathaim, and
pitched in the mountains of
Abarim, before Nebo.

48 And they departed from
the mountains of Abarim,
and pitched in the plains of
Moab by Jordan near
Jericho.
49 And they pitched by
Jordan, from Beth-jesimoth
even unto Abel-shittim in the
plains of Moab.
50 And the LORD spake unto
Moses in the plains of Moab
by Jordan near Jericho, saying,
51 Speak unto the children
of Israel, and say unto them,
When ye are passed over
Jordan into the land of
Canaan;
52 Then ye shall drive out
all the inhabitants of the land
from before you, and destroy
all their pictures, and destroy
all their molten images, and
quite pluck down all their
high places:
53 And ye shall dispossess
the inhabitants of the land,
and dwell therein: for I have
given you the land to possess
it.
54 And ye shall divide the
land by lot for an inheritance
among your families: and to
the more ye shall give the
more inheritance, and to the
fewer ye shall give the less
inheritance: every man's
inheritance shall be in
the place where his lot falleth; according to the tribes
of your fathers ye shall
inherit.
55 But if ye will not drive
out the inhabitants of the
land from before you; then it
shall come to pass, that those
which ye let remain of them
shall be pricks in your eyes,
and thorns in your sides, and
shall vex you in the land
wherein ye dwell.
56 Moreover it shall come
to pass, that I shall do unto
you, as I thought to do unto
them.

8) The plains of Moab by the Jordan across from Jericho:
- The final staging point for marching into the promised land
- The camp stretched from Beth Jeshimoth to Abel Shittim: Over five miles

3. The charge & warning of God to take possession of the promised land: A picture of spiritual conquest & rest

a. The strong charge: Five strong commands are given

1) To drive out all the enemies who opposed their entering the promised land

2) To destroy all their idols

3) To demolish all the false worship sites

4) To take possession of the promised land & settle it: It was the gift of God, their inheritance

5) To distribute the land by sacred lot
- Give a larger inheritance to the larger tribes
- Give a smaller inheritance to the smaller tribes

b. The strong warning: A failure to drive out the enemies of the land would result in severe judgment

1) The enemies would be constant trouble: Like splinters in one's eye & thorns in one's side

2) The Lord would dispossess & remove His people from the promised land

DIVISION IV

THE PREPARATION FOR THE MARCH INTO THE PROMISED LAND, 26:1-36:13

H. The Review of the Wilderness Wanderings and a Strong Charge to Take Possession of the Promised Land: A Picture of God's Faithfulness and Man's Failure, 33:1-56

(33:1-56) **Introduction—Sin, Enslavement to—Death, Enslavement to—Man, Unbelief of**: man is enslaved to sin and death. In fact, two things are certain in this life: man sins and man dies. But God is faithful: the provision to be delivered from sin and death has been offered to man. No longer do we have to be gripped by sin; neither do we have to die. There is strong deliverance from sin and triumphant, victorious deliverance from death. This is one message in the present Scripture, but there is also another message: man's failure. God has been faithful in making every provision necessary to save man and to give him an abundant life. A life that overflows with love, joy, and peace is now available to man. But man does not believe God. Man curses God, doing the unimaginable, the incomprehensible—taking God's name in vain. But this is not all: man questions and even denies the very existence of God. But even this is not all: the vast majority of people reject God, ignoring and neglecting Him, following after the false worship of gods created by their own imaginations. Man wallows around in unbelief, closing his eyes and refusing to believe the only living and true God, the Lord God Himself (Jehovah, Yahweh). And, tragically, man takes pride in his unbelief, sometimes even boasting and freely discussing his unbelief with others. Unbelief dooms a person to wander about in the wilderness of this world without the help of the only living and true God. An unbeliever does not have God's care, provision, protection, security, nor the indwelling assurance of living eternally with God face to face. Unbelief dooms a person to wander about in the wilderness of this world without the help and support of God. The person has only the help and support that other people can give him. Unbelief shuts God out of a person's life. This is the subject of this passage of Scripture: *The Review of the Wilderness Wanderings and a Strong Charge to Take Possession of the Promised Land: a Picture of God's Faithfulness and Man's Failure,* 33:1-56.

1. The faithfulness of God in leading and guiding His people (v.1-4).
2. The wilderness wanderings: a picture of man's failure—40 years of no progress (v.5-49).
3. The charge and warning of God to take possession of the promised land: a picture of spiritual conquest and rest (v.50-56).

1 (33:1-4) **Faithfulness, of God—Wilderness Wanderings—Campsites, of Israel—Israel, Date of Deliverance**: there was the faithfulness of God in leading and guiding His people from Egyptian slavery. God delivered His people so they could begin their march to the promised land of God. The point of these few verses is clear: if God had the power to lead His people from Egyptian slavery, then He had the power to lead them *into* the promised land. God's guidance and leadership are clearly seen in the Scripture and outline:

OUTLINE	SCRIPTURE	SCRIPTURE	OUTLINE
1. The faithfulness of God in leading & guiding His people a. God led His people out of Egypt (a symbol of the world) 1) Led orderly by divisions 2) Led by Moses & Aaron b. God led Moses to record the stages or camps of the march to the promised land c. God led His people to march	These are the journeys of the children of Israel, which went forth out of the land of Egypt with their armies under the hand of Moses and Aaron. 2 And Moses wrote their goings out according to their journeys by the commandment of the LORD: and these are their journeys according to their goings out. 3 And they departed from	Rameses in the first month, on the fifteenth day of the first month; on the morrow after the passover the children of Israel went out with an high hand in the sight of all the Egyptians. 4 For the Egyptians buried all their firstborn, which the LORD had smitten among them: upon their gods also the LORD executed judgments.	out triumphantly—as a great nation of people 1) On the 15th of the first month 2) In full view of all Egyptians • As they were burying their firstborn • God had judged them

1. God led His people out of Egypt (a symbol of the world). He lead them to march out of Egypt like a mighty army, division by division, marching under the leadership of Moses and Aaron (v.1).

2. God led Moses to record the stages or campsites along the journey. They were marching to the promised land of God; therefore, it was important to have an accurate record of the events that took place along the journey.

3. God led His people to march out triumphantly—as a great nation of people (v.3-4). The exact date that they marched out of Egypt is recorded: the fifteenth of the first month. Note the spirit in which they marched out: they marched out with a bold, courageous, and defiant spirit; not with a fearful, cowering, slavish spirit.

Thought 1. One of the strongest messages of Scripture is this: God is faithful. Day and night, night and day—God is faithful. God is faithful to save us from the enslavements of this world just as He saved Israel from the enslavement of Egypt. We are enslaved to sin and death. No person can keep from sinning nor from dying. We all sin and we all die. We are enslaved to sin and death. But God is faithful: He saves us from sin and death. But this is not all: just as God was faithful to lead and guide the Israelites, so He will lead and guide us to the promised land of heaven. This is the strong declaration of Scripture: God will not fail us. He will lead and guide us every step of the way as we march to the promised land of heaven.

"To give light to them that sit in darkness and in the shadow of death, to guide our feet into the way of peace" (Lk.1:79).

"Howbeit when he, the Spirit of truth, is come, he will guide you into all truth: for he shall not speak of himself; but whatsoever he shall hear, that shall he speak: and he will show you things to come" (Jn.16:13).

"God is faithful, by whom ye were called unto the fellowship of his Son Jesus Christ our Lord" (1 Cor.1:9).

"Know therefore that the Lord thy God, he is God, the faithful God, which keepeth covenant and mercy with them that love him and keep his commandments to a thousand generations" (Dt.7:9).

"And thou shalt remember all the way which the Lord thy God led thee these forty years in the wilderness, to humble thee, and to prove thee, to know what was in thine heart, whether thou wouldest keep his commandments, or no" (Dt.8:2).

"As an eagle stirreth up her nest, fluttereth over her young, spreadeth abroad her wings, taketh them, beareth them on her wings: So the Lord alone did lead him [Israel], and there was no strange god with him" (Dt.32:11-12).

"Blessed be the Lord, that hath given rest unto his people Israel, according to all that he promised: there hath not failed one word of all his good promise, which he promised by the hand of Moses his servant" (1 Ki.8:56).

"The meek will he guide in judgment: and the meek will he teach his way" (Ps.25:9).
"Teach me thy way, O Lord, and lead me in a plain path, because of mine enemies" (Ps.27:11).
"For this God is our God for ever and ever: he will be our guide even unto death" (Ps.48:14).
"Thou shalt guide me with thy counsel, and afterward receive me to glory" (Ps.73:24).
"Thou leddest thy people like a flock by the hand of Moses and Aaron" (Ps.77:20).
"If I take the wings of the morning, and dwell in the uttermost parts of the sea; Even there shall thy hand lead me, and thy right hand shall hold me" (Ps.139:9-10).
"And thine ears shall hear a word behind thee, saying, This is the way, walk ye in it, when ye turn to the right hand, and when ye turn to the left" (Is.30:21).
"And I will bring the blind by a way that they knew not; I will lead them in paths that they have not known: I will make darkness light before them, and crooked things straight. These things will I do unto them, and not forsake them" (Is.42:16).

2 (33:5-49) **Wilderness Wanderings, Failure During—Israel, Failure of—Unbelief, of Believers, Example of**: there was the wilderness wanderings of the Israelites. This is a picture of man's failure, of following after God for *forty long years* and making no progress. Remember, the Israelites had committed the terrible sin of unbelief against God. They had failed to trust the faithfulness of God in leading and guiding them. They had complained, grumbled, and murmured against God time and time again—all because of the hardships of life that confronted them as they marched to the promised land. They grumbled about the things that happened to them, complained because of the bad breaks they received. They felt not enough good things happened to them, that they did not receive enough of the good things of life. They blamed God for the bad and complained because the good was not good enough. Tragically, they refused to believe and trust God; they rebelled against God. They refused to follow His leadership and guidance. Consequently, they were condemned to wander about in the wilderness until the last of the first generation had died.

The following list of campsites covers the desert experience of the Israelites as they wandered about in the wilderness. As the campsites are studied, several difficulties arise. For example, some of the places are not recorded elsewhere in Exodus and Numbers (cp.v.19-29). However, other places that are mentioned in Numbers are not included here (for example, Taberah, 11:3; cp.21:19). Other places given here are mentioned in Deuteronomy, but they are spelled differently (v.30-34 cp.Dt.10:6-7).[2] It is difficult to know the exact location of some of the cities and campsites listed in the Scripture because some of the places no longer exist and others have changed names. Even if the name of a particular city has survived to the present day, it is actually attached to a different city or location.[3] Despite these problems, a map is being included to help the reader as he attempts to grasp the wilderness wanderings of the Israelites (see map of *The Desert or Wilderness Wanderings of Israel*—Num.33:5-49, p.389).

OUTLINE	SCRIPTURE	SCRIPTURE	OUTLINE
2. The wilderness wanderings: A picture of man's failure—40 years of no progress a. The camps from Rameses to Mt. Sinai: Left Rameses—Egypt 1) Succoth (Ex.13:20) 2) Etham (Ex.13:20): First reference to the cloud 3) Pi Hahiroth (Ex.14:2, 9): The campsite from which they crossed the Red Sea (Ex.14:1f)	5 And the children of Israel removed from Rameses, and pitched in Succoth. 6 And they departed from Succoth, and pitched in Etham, which is in the edge of the wilderness. 7 And they removed from Etham, and turned again unto Pi-hahiroth, which is before Baal-zephon: and they pitched before Migdol. 8 And they departed from before Pi-hahiroth, and passed through the midst of the sea into the wilderness, and went three days' journey in the wilderness of Etham, and pitched in Marah.	in the wilderness of Sin. 12 And they took their journey out of the wilderness of Sin, and encamped in Dophkah. 13 And they departed from Dophkah, and encamped in Alush. 14 And they removed from Alush, and encamped at Rephidim, where was no water for the people to drink. 15 And they departed from Rephidim, and pitched in the wilderness of Sinai. 16 And they removed from the desert of Sinai, and pitched at Kibroth-hattaavah.	8) Dophkah: No reference in Exodus 9) Alush: No reference in Exodus 10) Rephidim (Ex.17:1): No water to drink 11) Desert of Sinai (Ex.19:2): The law was given b. The camps from Mt. Sinai to Mt. Hor
4) Marah (Ex.15:23) Bitter waters sweetened by God 5) Elim (Ex.15:27): An oasis in the desert	9 And they removed from Marah, and came unto Elim: and in Elim were twelve fountains of water, and threescore and ten palm trees; and they pitched there.	17 And they departed from Kibroth-hattaavah, and encamped at Hazeroth. 18 And they departed from Hazeroth, and pitched in Rithmah.	1) Kibroth Hattaavah (Num. 11:34): Was 3 days from Sinai 2) Hazeroth (Num.11:35; 12:16; Dt.1:1) 3) Rithmah: No other reference
6) The Red Sea: Not mentioned as a camp	10 And they removed from Elim, and encamped by the Red sea.	19 And they departed from Rithmah, and pitched at Rimmon-parez.	4) Rimmon Perez: No other reference
7. Desert of Sin (Ex.16:1)	11 And they removed from the Red sea, and encamped	20 And they departed from Rimmon-parez, and pitched	5) Libnab: No other reference

2 *The Expositor's Bible Commentary*. Frank E. Gaebelein, Editor, p. 984.
3 Gordon J. Wenham. *The Book of Numbers*, p.220.

OUTLINE	SCRIPTURE
	in Libnah.
6) Rissah: No other reference	21 And they removed from Libnah, and pitched at Rissah.
7) Kehelathah: No other reference	22 And they journeyed from Rissah, and pitched in Kehelathah.
8) Mount Shepher: No other reference	23 And they went from Kehelathah, and pitched in mount Shapher.
9) Haradah: No other reference	24 And they removed from mount Shapher, and encamped in Haradah.
10) Makheloth: No other reference	25 And they removed from Haradah, and pitched in Makheloth.
11) Tahath: No other reference	26 And they removed from Makheloth, and encamped at Tahath.
12) Terah: No other reference	27 And they departed from Tahath, and pitched at Tarah.
13) Mithcah: No other reference	28 And they removed from Tarah, and pitched in Mithcah.
14) Hashmonah: No other reference	29 And they went from Mithcah, and pitched in Hashmonah.
15) Moseroth (Dt.10:6): Place of Aaron's death (cp. v.38)	30 And they departed from Hashmonah, and encamped at Moseroth.
16) Bene Jaakan (Gen.36:27; Dt.10:6; 1 Chron.1:42)	31 And they departed from Moseroth, and pitched in Bene-jaakan.
17) Hor Haggidgad (Dt.10:7)	32 And they removed from Bene-jaakan, and encamped at Hor-hagidgad.
18) Jotbathah (Dt.10:7)	33 And they went from Hor-hagidgad, and pitched in Jotbathah.
19) Abronah: No other reference	34 And they removed from Jotbathah, and encamped at Ebronah.
20) Ezion Geber (Dt.2:8; 1 Ki. 9:26): A well known oasis	35 And they departed from Ebronah, and encamped at Ezion-gaber.
21) Kadesh (Num.13:21): Place where 12 spies were sent out & 10 rebelled	36 And they removed from Ezion-gaber, and pitched in the wilderness of Zin, which is Kadesh.
c. The campsite at Mt. Hor	37 And they removed from Kadesh, and pitched in

SCRIPTURE	OUTLINE
mount Hor, in the edge of the land of Edom.	
38 And Aaron the priest went up into mount Hor at the commandment of the LORD, and died there, in the fortieth year after the children of Israel were come out of the land of Egypt, in the first day of the fifth month.	1) God took Aaron home to heaven while on Mt. Hor: Died on the 1st day of the 5th month, 40 years after Israel's deliverance (Num.20:23-29)
39 And Aaron was an hundred and twenty and three years old when he died in mount Hor.	2) God gave Aaron a long, fruitful life: 123 years
40 And king Arad the Canaanite, which dwelt in the south in the land of Canaan, heard of the coming of the children of Israel.	3) God was faithful & gave His people their first military victory at Mt. Hor (Num.21:1-3)
41 And they departed from mount Hor, and pitched in Zalmonah.	d. The camps from Mt. Hor to the Jordan River across from Jericho
42 And they departed from Zalmonah, and pitched in Punon.	1) Zalmonah: No other reference 2) Punon (Gen.36:41; 1 Chron. 1:52)
43 And they departed from Punon, and pitched in Oboth.	3) Oboth (Num.21:10-11)
44 And they departed from Oboth, and pitched in Ije-abarim, in the border of Moab.	4) Iye Abarim (Num.21:11): A place on the border of Moab
45 And they departed from Iim, and pitched in Dibon-gad.	5) Dibon Gad (Num.21:30; 32:3): Was in Moab
46 And they removed from Dibon-gad, and encamped in Almon-diblathaim.	6) Almon Diblathaim (Jer.48:22)
47 And they removed from Almon-diblathaim, and pitched in the mountains of Abarim, before Nebo.	7) Mountains of Abarim, near Nebo (Num.27:12): A range of mountains in NW Moab just NE of the Dead Sea
48 And they departed from the mountains of Abarim, and pitched in the plains of Moab by Jordan near Jericho.	8) The plains of Moab by the Jordan across from Jericho: • The final staging point for marching into the promised land
49 And they pitched by Jordan, from Beth-jesimoth even unto Abel-shittim in the plains of Moab.	• The camp stretched from Beth Jeshimoth to Abel Shittim: Over five miles

Thought 1. The wilderness wanderings would never have taken place but for one thing: unbelief. A spirit of unbelief gripped the hearts of the Israelites. They refused to believe and trust God. Unbelief is a terrible sin. It is an insult to God: an outrage, an abuse, a slap in the face of God. God promises to save His people, to lead and guide them to the promised land of heaven. He promises to give us victory, a conquering power over all the pitfalls and enemies of this life. Moreover, God promises to give us an abundant life, a life that overflows with love, joy, and peace—a life that is beyond comprehension. Every good thing and every gift that we ever experience come from the hand of God (Jas.1:17). All this is what makes unbelief such a terrible insult against God. Unbelief will keep us in the wilderness of this world, keep us out of the promised land of heaven. Unbelief means that the enemies of life will eventually conquer and gain the victory over us. Unbelief means that we will be enslaved by sin and someday be led into the grave of death. Unbelief means that we will face the terrifying judgment of God and be doomed to an eternity separated from God. Unbelief is the most devastating, destructive position a man can take. Unbelief doomed the Israelites to the wilderness wanderings for over forty years, doomed them to death in the wilderness. Not a single one escaped except Caleb and Joshua who believed and trusted God. All the unbelievers perished in the desert never knowing the victory of God over the enemies of this life. Again, not one of the unbelievers escaped. Unbelief will doom us to perish in the wilderness of this world and doom us to suffer the eternal judgment of God.

"He that believeth on him is not condemned: but he that believeth not is condemned already, because he hath not believed in the name of the only begotten Son of God" (Jn.3:18).

"He that believeth on the Son hath everlasting life: and he that believeth not the Son shall not see life; but the wrath of God abideth on him" (Jn.3:36).

"I said therefore unto you, that ye shall die in your sins: for if ye believe not that I am he, ye shall die in your sins" (Jn.8:24).

"That they all might be damned who believed not the truth, but had pleasure in unrighteousness" (2 Th.2:12).

"Take heed, brethren, lest there be in any of you an evil heart of unbelief, in departing from the living God" (Heb.3:12).

"Let us labour therefore to enter into that rest, lest any man fall after the same example of unbelief" (Heb.4:11).

"I will therefore put you in remembrance, though ye once knew this, how that the Lord, having saved the people out of the land of Egypt, afterward destroyed them that believed not" (Jude 5).

3 (33:50-56) **Warning, of God—Land, the Promised, Duty Toward—Spiritual Victory—Victory, Spiritual—Rest, Spiritual**: there was the charge and warning of God to take possession of the promised land. This was a picture of spiritual conquest and rest. Behind the Israelites lay the terrible tragedy of the wilderness wanderings, but now they sat on the plains of Moab by the Jordan River, directly across from the great city of Jericho. They sat there poised to enter the promised land. But before they could enter, a strong charge and warning had to be given to them.

OUTLINE	SCRIPTURE	SCRIPTURE	OUTLINE
3. The charge & warning of God to take possession of the promised land: A picture of spiritual conquest & rest a. The strong charge: Five strong commands are given	50 And the LORD spake unto Moses in the plains of Moab by Jordan near Jericho, saying, 51 Speak unto the children of Israel, and say unto them, When ye are passed over Jordan into the land of Canaan;	among your families: and to the more ye shall give the more inheritance, and to the fewer ye shall give the less inheritance: every man's inheritance shall be in the place where his lot falleth; according to the tribes of your fathers ye shall inherit.	• Give a larger inheritance to the larger tribes • Give a smaller inheritance to the smaller tribes
1) To drive out all the enemies who opposed their entering the promised land 2) To destroy all their idols 3) To demolish all the false worship sites	52 Then ye shall drive out all the inhabitants of the land from before you, and destroy all their pictures, and destroy all their molten images, and quite pluck down all their high places:	55 But if ye will not drive out the inhabitants of the land from before you; then it shall come to pass, that those which ye let remain of them shall be pricks in your eyes,	b. The strong warning: A failure to drive out the enemies of the land would result in severe judgment 1) The enemies would be constant trouble: Like splinters in one's eye & thorns in one's side
4) To take possession of the promised land & settle it: It was the gift of God, their inheritance	53 And ye shall dispossess the inhabitants of the land, and dwell therein: for I have given you the land to possess it.	and thorns in your sides, and shall vex you in the land wherein ye dwell. 56 Moreover it shall come to pass, that I shall do unto	2) The Lord would dispossess & remove His people from the promised land
5) To distribute the land by sacred lot	54 And ye shall divide the land by lot for an inheritance	you, as I thought to do unto them.	

1. Note the charge: five strong commands were given (v.51-54).
   a. The Israelites were to drive out all the enemies who opposed their entering the promised land (v.52). No unbeliever was to be allowed to live in the promised land. All the enemies who stood opposed to God were to be rejected. God's people were to build a new nation, a nation of people who lived holy lives, lives that were set apart to serve God. They were to live pure and righteous lives and be witnesses to the surrounding nations who lived around them. But the enemies who stood opposed to them and sought to keep God's people out of the promised land were to be destroyed. The promised land was to be the inheritance of God's people; therefore, the Israelites were to drive out all the enemies who opposed God and His people.
   b. The Israelites were to destroy all the idols and false worship that were in the promised land (v.52). Any image and any false worship were to be destroyed. There is only one true and living God, the Lord God Himself (Jehovah, Yahweh). He and He alone is to be worshipped. False gods and false worship are nothing more than the creation of the imaginations of men. They have no life and can hear no prayer; neither can they help any person in time of need. Therefore, the images and idols of all false gods were to be destroyed as well as all false worship.
   c. The Israelites were to demolish all the false worship sites in the promised land (v.52). No false worship whatsoever was to be allowed. So long as worship sites remained, there would be a tendency for the weak and wicked person to seek false worship in order to ease his conscience. For this reason, all the false worship sites were to be demolished.
   d. The Israelites were to take possession of the promised land and settle it. It was the gift of God, their inheritance; therefore, they were not to fear the enemies who would confront them. They were to be courageous and march forth to conquer any who opposed God and their possession of the promised land (v.53).
   e. The Israelites were to distribute the land by sacred lot. Remember, God controlled the roll of the sacred lots. By throwing the lots, there would be no partiality or favoritism shown in the distribution of the land; neither could

there be a charge of favoritism or partiality. The larger tribes were to receive a larger inheritance, and the smaller tribes were to receive a smaller inheritance—all based upon population.

2. God issued a strong, strong warning: a failure to drive out the enemies of the land would result in severe judgment (v.55-56). If the people of God failed to drive out the enemies, the enemies would be constant trouble for them. Note the descriptive picture given: the enemies would be like splinters in one's eye and thorns in one's side. They would be constant trouble, causing a constant flow of tears and flowing blood. But this was not all: the Lord Himself would dispossess and remove His people from the promised land (v.56). God would do to His people exactly what He planned to do to the enemies who stood opposed to Him. Severe judgment would fall upon His people: they would be expelled from the promised land of God.

Thought 1. God's people are to live lives of separation. They are to live holy lives, lives that are totally set apart to God. They are to live righteous and pure lives, seeking to be conformed to the very image of Jesus Christ. This was the reason the Israelites were to drive out all the enemies of the promised land. And this is the reason the believer is to be separated to God, to live a life that is different and distinct from the immoral, lawless, and violent ways of the world. The believer is to be moral, not immoral; to be lawful, not lawless; to make peace, not violence. As the believer marches to the promised land of heaven, he is not to embrace the evil of the unbelievers of this world; rather, he is to be a witness to them. The holiness of God, His demand for righteousness and purity, is to be proclaimed. In all this the believer is to live a life of separation to God, not a life of worldliness. He is not to walk in the lies and deceit of this world but in the light and truth of God. His life is to be given over—totally separated and set apart—to the only living and true God, the Lord God Himself (Jehovah, Yahweh).

"That he would grant unto us, that we being delivered out of the hand of our enemies might serve him without fear, In holiness and righteousness before him, all the days of our life" (Lk.1:74-75).

"If ye were of the world, the world would love his own: but because ye are not of the world, but I have chosen you out of the world, therefore the world hateth you" (Jn.15:19).

"And with many other words did he testify and exhort, saying, Save yourselves from this untoward generation" (Acts 2:40).

"But now I have written unto you not to keep company, if any man that is called a brother be a fornicator, or covetous, or an idolater, or a railer, or a drunkard, or an extortioner; with such an one no not to eat" (1 Cor.5:11).

"Be ye not unequally yoked together with unbelievers: for what fellowship hath righteousness with unrighteousness? and what communion hath light with darkness" (2 Cor.6:14).

"Wherefore come out from among them, and be ye separate, saith the Lord, and touch not the unclean thing; and I will receive you, And will be a Father unto you, and ye shall be my sons and daughters, saith the Lord Almighty" (2 Cor.6:17-18).

"Having therefore these promises, dearly beloved, let us cleanse ourselves from all filthiness of the flesh and spirit, perfecting holiness in the fear of God" (2 Cor.7:1).

"And have no fellowship with the unfruitful works of darkness, but rather reprove them" (Eph.5:11).

"Now we command you, brethren, in the name of our Lord Jesus Christ, that ye withdraw yourselves from every brother that walketh disorderly, and not after the tradition which he received of us" (2 Th.3:6).

"Follow peace with all men, and holiness, without which no man shall see the Lord" (Heb.12:14).

"But as he which hath called you is holy, so be ye holy in all manner of conversation; Because it is written, Be ye holy; for I am holy" (1 Pt.1:15-16).

"Seeing then that all these things shall be dissolved, what manner of persons ought ye to be in all holy conversation and godliness, Looking for and hasting unto the coming of the day of God, wherein the heavens being on fire shall be dissolved, and the elements shall melt with fervent heat? Nevertheless we, according to his promise, look for new heavens and a new earth, wherein dwelleth righteousness. Wherefore, beloved, seeing that ye look for such things, be diligent that ye may be found of him in peace, without spot, and blameless" (2 Pt.3:11-14).

"Who shall not fear thee, O Lord, and glorify thy name? for thou only art holy: for all nations shall come and worship before thee; for thy judgments are made manifest" (Rev.15:4).

"Thou shalt not follow a multitude to do evil; neither shalt thou speak in a cause to decline after many to wrest judgment" (Ex.23:2).

"Take heed to thyself, lest thou make a covenant with the inhabitants of the land whither thou goest, lest it be for a snare in the midst of thee" (Ex.34:12).

"For I am the Lord that bringeth you up out of the land of Egypt, to be your God: ye shall therefore be holy, for I am holy" (Lev.11:45).

"Blessed is the man that walketh not in the counsel of the ungodly, nor standeth in the way of sinners, nor sitteth in the seat of the scornful" (Ps.1:1).

"Enter not into the path of the wicked, and go not in the way of evil men" (Pr.4:14).

"Be not thou envious against evil men, neither desire to be with them" (Pr.24:1).

"Depart ye, depart ye, go ye out from thence, touch no unclean thing; go ye out of the midst of her; be ye clean, that bear the vessels of the Lord" (Is.52:11).

TYPES, SYMBOLS, AND PICTURES (Numbers 33:1-56)

Historical Term	Type or Picture (Scriptural Basis for Each)	Life Application for Today's Believer	Biblical Application
Wilderness Wanderings Num.33:5-49	*A picture of man's failure—40 years of no progress.* **"And they departed from Iim, and pitched in Dibon-gad. And they removed from Dibon-gad, and encamped in Almon-diblathaim. And they removed from Almon-diblathaim, and pitched in the mountains of Abarim, before Nebo. And they departed from the mountains of Abarim, and pitched in the plains of Moab by Jordan near Jericho. And they pitched by Jordan, from Beth-jesimoth even unto Abel-shittim in the plains of Moab" (Num. 33:45-49).**	The wilderness wanderings would never have taken place but for one thing: unbelief. A spirit of unbelief gripped the hearts of the Israelites. They refused to believe and trust God. Unbelief is a terrible sin. It is an insult to God: an outrage, an abuse, a slap in the face of God. God promises to save His people, to lead and guide them to the promised land of heaven. He promises to give us victory, a conquering power over all the pitfalls and enemies of this life. Moreover, God promises to give us an abundant life, a life that overflows with love, joy, and peace—a life that is beyond comprehension. Every good thing and every gift that we ever experience comes from the hand of God (Jas.1:17). All this is what makes unbelief such a terrible insult against God. Unbelief will keep us in the wilderness of this world, keep us out of the promised land of heaven. Unbelief means that the enemies of life will eventually conquer and gain the victory over us. Unbelief means that we will be enslaved by sin and someday be led into the grave of death. Unbelief means that we will face the terrifying judgment of God and be doomed to an eternity separated from God. Unbelief is the most devastating, destructive position a man can take. Unbelief doomed the Israelites to the wilderness wanderings for over forty years, doomed them to death in the wilderness. Not a single one escaped except Caleb and Joshua who believed and trusted God. All the unbelievers perished in the desert never knowing the victory of God over the enemies of this life. Again, not one of the unbelievers escaped. Unbelief will doom us to perish in the wilderness of this world and doom us to suffer the eternal judgment of God.	***"He that believeth on him is not condemned: but he that believeth not is condemned already, because he hath not believed in the name of the only begotten Son of God" (Jn.3:18).*** ***"He that believeth on the Son hath everlasting life: and he that believeth not the Son shall not see life; but the wrath of God abideth on him" (Jn.3:36).*** ***"I said therefore unto you, that ye shall die in your sins: for if ye believe not that I am he, ye shall die in your sins" (Jn.8:24).*** ***"That they all might be damned who believed not the truth, but had pleasure in unrighteousness" (2 Th. 2:12).*** ***"Take heed, brethren, lest there be in any of you an evil heart of unbelief, in departing from the living God" (Heb.3:12).*** ***"Let us labour therefore to enter into that rest, lest any man fall after the same example of unbelief" (Heb.4:11).*** ***"I will therefore put you in remembrance, though ye once knew this, how that the LORD, having saved the people out of the land of Egypt, afterward destroyed them that believed not" (Jude 5).***

(33:5-49) **Map—Israel, Wilderness Wanderings of—Wilderness Wanderings, of Israel—Desert Wanderings, of Israel—Journeys, Desert Wanderings of Israel:**

THE DESERT OR WILDERNESS WANDERINGS OF ISRAEL

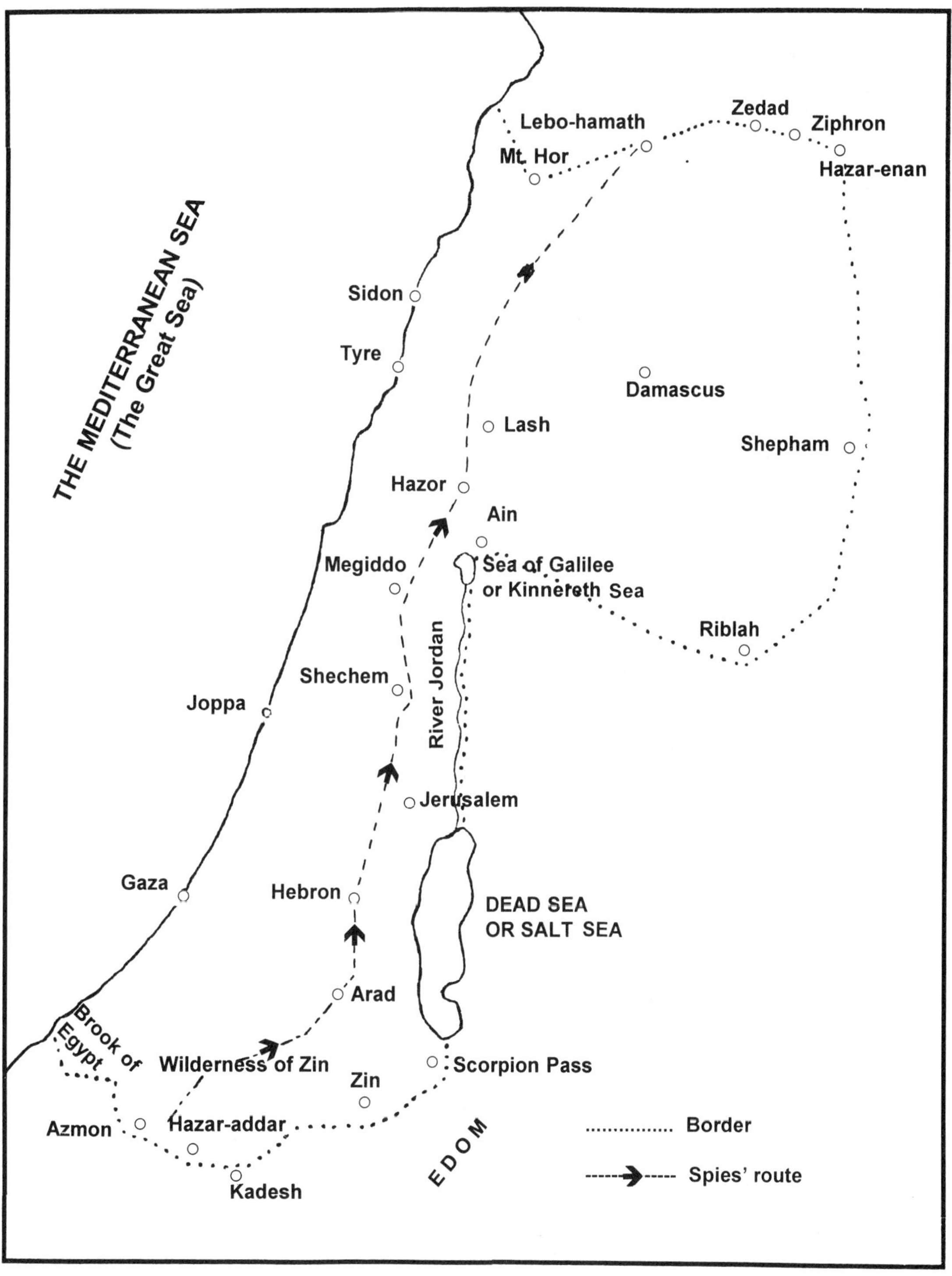

I. The Boundaries of Canaan, the Promised Land: The Great Gift & Assurance of God—His People Will Inherit the Promised Land, 34:1-29

1. The great gift of God: The gift of the promised land (a symbol of spiritual conquest & rest) (Ex.23:31)[DS1]

a. The southern border
   1) Included some of the Desert of Zin near Edom
   2) Started at the Salt Sea
   3) Crossed south of Scorpion Pass & ran to Zin & south of Kadesh Barnea
   4) Went to Hazar Adar & Azmon
   5) Joined the brooks of Egypt
   6) Ended at the Mediterranean Sea

b. The western border: Ran up the coast of the Mediterranean Sea

c. The northern border
   1) Ran along the Great Sea over to Mount Hor
   2) Went to Lebo Hamath then to Zedad
   3) Ran to Ziphron
   4) Ended at Hazar Enan

d. The eastern border
   1) Started at Hazar Enan
   2) Ran to Shepham
   3) Went to Riblah, on the east side of Ain
   4) Ran along the eastern edge of the Sea of Galilee (Kinnereth)
   5) Continued along the Jordan River
   6) Ended at the Dead Sea

And the LORD spake unto
Moses, saying,
2 Command the children of
Israel, and say unto them,
When ye come into the land
of Canaan; (this is the land
that shall fall unto you for an
inheritance, even the land of
Canaan with the coasts
thereof:)
3 Then your south quarter
shall be from the wilderness
of Zin along by the coast of
Edom, and your south border
shall be the outmost coast of
the salt sea eastward:
4 And your border shall turn
from the south to the ascent
of Akrabbim, and pass on to
Zin: and the going forth
thereof shall be from the
south to Kadesh-barnea, and
shall go on to Hazar-addar,
and pass on to Azmon:
5 And the border shall fetch
a compass from Azmon unto
the river of Egypt, and the
goings out of it shall be at the
sea.
6 And as for the western border, ye shall even have the
great sea for a border: this
shall be your west border.
7 And this shall be your
north border: from the great
sea ye shall point out for you
mount Hor:
8 From mount Hor ye shall
point out your border unto
the entrance of Hamath; and
the goings forth of the border
shall be to Zedad:
9 And the border shall go on
to Ziphron, and the goings
out of it shall be at Hazar-
enan: this shall be your north
border.
10 And ye shall point out
your east border from Hazar-
enan to Shepham:
11 And the coast shall go
down from Shepham to
Riblah, on the east side of
Ain; and the border shall
descend, and shall reach unto
the side of the sea of
Chinnereth eastward:
12 And the border shall go
down to Jordan, and the
goings out of it shall be at the
salt sea: this shall be your
land with the coasts thereof
round about.
13 And Moses commanded
the children of Israel, saying,
This is the land which ye
shall inherit by lot, which the
LORD commanded to give
unto the nine tribes, and to
the half tribe:
14 For the tribe of the children of Reuben according to
the house of their fathers,
and the tribe of the children
of Gad according to the
house of their fathers, have
received their inheritance;
and half the tribe of
Manasseh have received
their inheritance:
15 The two tribes and
the half tribe have received
their inheritance on this side
Jordan near Jericho east-
ward, toward the sunris-
ing.
16 And the LORD spake unto
Moses, saying,
17 These are the names of
the men which shall divide
the land unto you: Eleazar
the priest, and Joshua the son
of Nun.
18 And ye shall take one
prince of every tribe, to
divide the land by inheritance.
19 And the names of the
men are these: Of the tribe of
Judah, Caleb the son of
Jephunneh.
20 And of the tribe of the
children of Simeon, Shemuel
the son of Ammihud.
21 Of the tribe of Benjamin,
Elidad the son of Chislon.
22 And the prince of the
tribe of the children of Dan,
Bukki the son of Jogli.
23 The prince of the children of Joseph, for the tribe
of the children of Manasseh,
Hanniel the son of Ephod.
24 And the prince of the
tribe of the children of
Ephraim, Kemuel the son of
Shiphtan.
25 And the prince of the
tribe of the children of
Zebulun, Elizaphan the son
of Parnach.
26 And the prince of the
tribe of the children of
Issachar, Paltiel the son of
Azzan.
27 And the prince of the
tribe of the children of
Asher, Ahihud the son of
Shelomi.
28 And the prince of the

e. The land was to be assigned by lot to the 9½ tribes
   1) The tribes of Reuben, Gad, & the half tribe of Manasseh had received their inheritance (32:1-42)
   2) Their inheritance was on the east side of the Jordan across from Jericho: They settled outside of the promised land because of their compromise (32:1-42)

2. The great assurance of God: The leaders who were to assign the land were appointed ahead of time (a picture of the great assurance of God)

a. The supervisors: Eleazar the priest & Joshua

b. The leaders from each tribe: Some must be willing to lead, handling difficult tasks
   1) Tribe of Judah: Caleb
   2) Tribe of Simeon: Shemuel
   3) Tribe of Benjamin: Elidad
   4) Tribe of Dan: Bukki
   5) Tribe of Manasseh: Hanniel
   6) Tribe of Ephraim: Kemuel
   7) Tribe of Zebulun: Elizaphan
   8) Tribe of Issachar: Paltiel
   9) Tribe of Asher: Ahihud
   10) Tribe of Naphtali: Pedahel

c. The difficult task of dividing	tribe of the children of Naphtali, Pedahel the son of Ammihud. 29 These are they whom the	LORD commanded to divide the inheritance unto the children of Israel in the land of Canaan.	land among heirs: These were the willing leaders appointed to the task

DIVISION IV

THE PREPARATION FOR THE MARCH INTO THE PROMISED LAND, 26:1-36:13

I. The Boundaries of Canaan, the Promised Land: The Great Gift and Assurance of God—His People Will Inherit the Promised Land, 34:1-29

(34:1-29) **Introduction—Eternal Life—Promised Land**: How can a person know that he is going to live forever? Beyond doubt, can we know that there is life eternal? That heaven is real? That the good news is true? That we can live face to face with God forever and ever? Is there such absolute assurance and conviction for the human soul? Scripture declares a resounding "Yes"!

This is the subject of this passage of Scripture. The Israelites were camped on the plains of Moab by the Jordan River across from the great city of Jericho. They were poised, ready to cross over the Jordan into the promised land, but note: they had not yet crossed over nor entered. Yet in this Scripture, God outlines the boundaries of the promised land and appoints the leaders who were to assign the inheritance to each tribe. God outlined the boundaries and appointed the leaders *ahead of time*, before His people ever entered the land. He was giving them assurance and confidence in the promised land. The promised land was as good as theirs: this was the oath, the promise that God was swearing to His people. He had made a covenant, a contract between Himself and His people: if they would follow Him, He would give them the promised land. Here they were camped right across from the land, poised and ready to walk in. Therefore, God was ready to fulfill His promise: they would inherit and possess the land. He flooded their spirits with assurance and conviction: the promised land was real. The inheritance was to be theirs. This is the great subject of this encouraging passage: *The Boundaries of Canaan, the Promised Land: The Great Gift and Assurance of God—His People Will Inherit the Promised Land,* 34:1-29.

1. The great gift of God: the gift of the promised land (a symbol of spiritual conquest and rest) (Ex.23:31) (v.1-15).
2. The great assurance of God: the leaders who were to assign the land were appointed ahead of time (a picture of the great assurance of God) (v.16-29).

1 (34:1-15) **Land, the Promised—Gift, of God, the Promised Land—Spiritual Conquest—Spiritual Rest—Symbol, of Spiritual Conquest and Rest**: the glorious gift of God was the promised land. God's people were to inherit the land of Canaan. The promised land was a symbol of heaven, but also of spiritual conquest and rest. It was a symbol of God's people conquering the enemies of life and finding rest for their souls. (See DEEPER STUDY # 1—Num.34:1-15 for more discussion.) The four boundaries of the promised land are actually spelled out in this passage:

⇒ the southern border (v.3-5)
⇒ the western border (v.6)
⇒ the northern border (v.7-9)
⇒ the eastern border (v.10-12)

OUTLINE	SCRIPTURE	SCRIPTURE	OUTLINE
1. The great gift of God: The gift of the promised land (a symbol of spiritual conquest & rest) (Ex.23:31)	And the LORD spake unto Moses, saying, 2 Command the children of Israel, and say unto them, When ye come into the land of Canaan; (this is the land that shall fall unto you for an inheritance, even the land of Canaan with the coasts thereof:)	and pass on to Azmon: 5 And the border shall fetch a compass from Azmon unto the river of Egypt, and the goings out of it shall be at the sea. 6 And as for the western border, ye shall even have the great sea for a border: this shall be your west border.	5) Joined the brooks of Egypt 6) Ended at the Mediterranean Sea b. The western border: Ran up the coast of the Mediterranean Sea
a. The southern border 1) Included some of the Desert of Zin near Edom 2) Started at the Salt Sea	3 Then your south quarter shall be from the wilderness of Zin along by the coast of Edom, and your south border shall be the outmost coast of the salt sea eastward:	7 And this shall be your north border: from the great sea ye shall point out for you mount Hor: 8 From mount Hor ye shall point out your border unto the entrance of Hamath; and the goings forth of the border shall be to Zedad:	c. The northern border 1) Ran along the Great Sea over to Mount Hor 2) Went to Lebo Hamath then to Zedad
3) Crossed south of Scorpion Pass & ran to Zin & south of Kadesh Barnea 4) Went to Hazar Adar & Azmon	4 And your border shall turn from the south to the ascent of Akrabbim, and pass on to Zin: and the going forth thereof shall be from the south to Kadesh-barnea, and shall go on to Hazar-addar,	9 And the border shall go on to Ziphron, and the goings out of it shall be at Hazar-enan: this shall be your north border.	3) Ran to Ziphron 4) Ended at Hazar Enan

OUTLINE	SCRIPTURE	SCRIPTURE	OUTLINE
d. The eastern border 1) Started at Hazar Enan 2) Ran to Shepham	10 And ye shall point out your east border from Hazar-enan to Shepham:	the LORD commanded to give unto the nine tribes, and to the half tribe:	
3) Went to Riblah, on the east side of Ain 4) Ran along the eastern edge of the Sea of Galilee (Kinnereth)	11 And the coast shall go down from Shepham to Riblah, on the east side of Ain; and the border shall descend, and shall reach unto the side of the sea of Chinnereth eastward:	14 For the tribe of the children of Reuben according to the house of their fathers, and the tribe of the children of Gad according to the house of their fathers, have received their inheritance; and half the tribe of Manasseh have received their inheritance:	1) The tribes of Reuben, Gad, & the half tribe of Manasseh had received their inheritance (32:1-42)
5) Continued along the Jordan River 6) Ended at the Dead Sea	12 And the border shall go down to Jordan, and the goings out of it shall be at the salt sea: this shall be your land with the coasts thereof round about.	15 The two tribes and the half tribe have received their inheritance on this side Jordan near Jericho eastward, toward the sunrising.	2) Their inheritance was on the east side of the Jordan across from Jericho: They settled outside of the promised land because of their compromise (32:1-42)
e. The land was to be assigned by lot to the 9½ tribes	13 And Moses commanded the children of Israel, saying, This is the land which ye shall inherit by lot, which		

The promised land was the glorious gift of God to His people. Years before, God had made this great covenant with Abraham, the covenant of the promised land. If Abraham would follow God with all of his heart, he would receive the great gifts of God, the gift of the promised land and the gift of the promised seed (the Savior and Messiah of the world). The present passage concerns the great gift of the promised land. It is now hundreds of years later, and finally the descendants of Abraham are poised to enter the promised land. Once again, God is spelling out the borders of the land that the Israelites were to inherit. Note several points about the great gift of God, the promised land.

1. First, some of the boundary cities cannot be accurately located because they do not presently exist. However, enough is known about the location of most of the boundary markers to give a fairly accurate map of the promised land (see Map—Num.34:1-15 at the end of this commentary).

2. Second Israel never did claim all of the promised land outlined in this passage. King David did control most of Canaan and most of Transjordan. However, even he failed to conquer and lay claim to the outer reaches of the promised land.[1]

3. Third, God Himself is the One who outlines the boundaries of the promised land (v.1-12). These boundaries are not drawn by a man, nor were they determined by the nation Israel. God Himself had given the promise of the promised land to Abraham and his descendants who truly followed Him. The very existence and idea of the promised land was created in God's mind, not man's. The location, fertility, richness, fruitfulness, environment, quality of life, and everything else about the promised land was conceived in the mind of God, created and controlled by the hand of God. It was God who gave the hope of the promised land to His dear people, the hope of a land that would bring fullness of life, peace, and rest to their bodies and souls (Heb.11:13-16).

4. Fourth, the promise of the promised land is based upon a covenant between God and His people. The gift of God is a contract established by Him, a contract that requires obedience in order to inherit the promised land. (See DEEPER STUDY # 1—Num.34:1-15 for more discussion.)

DEEPER STUDY # 1

(34:1-15) **The Promised Land—Promises of God**: the promise of the *promised land* is based upon a covenant. The covenant or contract between God and man is conditional: a person must obey God in order to enter and inherit the promised land. Scripture has made this clear from the beginning when God initially approached Abraham with the covenant. Note the major references to the covenant, the contract involving the promised land of God:

⇒ Abraham had to obey God, had to leave his old life and follow God in order to inherit the promised land.

> **"Now the Lord had said unto Abram, Get thee out of thy country, and from thy kindred, and from thy father's house, unto a land that I will show thee: And I will make of thee a great nation, and I will bless thee, and make thy name great; and thou shalt be a blessing: And I will bless them that bless thee, and curse him that curseth thee: and in thee shall all families of the earth be blessed" (Gen.12:1-3).**

⇒ Abraham obeyed God; therefore, God reconfirmed His covenant time and again with His dear servant.

> **"And the Lord said unto Abram, after that Lot was separated from him, Lift up now thine eyes, and look from the place where thou art northward, and southward, and eastward, and westward: For all the land which thou seest, to thee will I give it, and to thy seed for ever. And I will make thy seed as the dust of the earth: so that if a man can number the dust of the earth, then shall thy seed also be numbered. Arise, walk through the land in the length of it and in the breadth of it; for I will give it unto thee" (Gen.13:14-17).**
> **"In the same day the Lord made a covenant with Abram, saying, Unto thy seed have I given this land,**

1 Gordon J. Wenham. *The Book of Numbers,* p.232. Also *The Expositor's Bible Commentary*. Frank E. Gaebelein, Editor, p.996.

from the river of Egypt unto the great river, the river Euphrates: The Kenites, and the Kenizzites, and the Kadmonites, And the Hittites, and the Perizzites, and the Rephaims, And the Amorites, and the Canaanites, and the Girgashites, and the Jebusites" (Gen.15:18-21).

"And I will give unto thee, and to thy seed after thee, the land wherein thou art a stranger, all the land of Canaan, for an everlasting possession; and I will be their God" (Gen.17:8).

⇒ Joseph and his eleven brothers, the sons of Jacob, believed God and followed after God during their lives; therefore, God established His promise with them.

"And Joseph said unto his brethren, I die: and God will surely visit you, and bring you out of this land unto the land which he sware to Abraham, to Isaac, and to Jacob" (Gen.50:24).

⇒ Moses obeyed and followed after God; therefore, God established the covenant of the promised land with him.

"And I will bring you in unto the land, concerning the which I did swear to give it to Abraham, to Isaac, and to Jacob; and I will give it you for an heritage: I am the Lord" (Ex.6:8).

⇒ God gave the promise of the promised land to the people of Israel; however, they had to cleave to Him. They had to diligently keep His commandments and love God—with their whole hearts. Then and only then would He strengthen them to defeat the enemies of the promised land.

"I will send my fear before thee, and will destroy all the people to whom thou shalt come, and I will make all thine enemies turn their backs unto thee. And I will send hornets before thee, which shall drive out the Hivite, the Canaanite, and the Hittite, from before thee. I will not drive them out from before thee in one year; lest the land become desolate, and the beast of the field multiply against thee. By little and little I will drive them out from before thee, until thou be increased, and inherit the land. And I will set thy bounds from the Red sea even unto the sea of the Philistines, and from the desert unto the river: for I will deliver the inhabitants of the land into your hand; and thou shalt drive them out before thee. Thou shalt make no covenant with them, nor with their gods. They shall not dwell in thy land, lest they make thee sin against me: for if thou serve their gods, it will surely be a snare unto thee" (Ex.23:27-33).

"Ye shall therefore keep all my statutes, and all my judgments, and do them: that the land, whither I bring you to dwell therein, spue you not out. And ye shall not walk in the manners of the nation, which I cast out before you: for they committed all these things, and therefore I abhorred them. But I have said unto you, Ye shall inherit their land, and I will give it unto you to possess it, a land that floweth with milk and honey: I am the Lord your God, which have separated you from other people" (Lev.20:22-24).

"If the Lord delight in us, then he will bring us into this land, and give it us; a land which floweth with milk and honey" (Num.14:8).

"For if ye shall diligently keep all these commandments which I command you, to do them, to love the Lord your God, to walk in all his ways, and to cleave unto him; Then will the Lord drive out all these nations from before you, and ye shall possess greater nations and mightier than yourselves. Every place whereon the soles of your feet shall tread shall be yours: from the wilderness and Lebanon, from the river, the river Euphrates, even unto the uttermost sea shall your coast be. There shall no man be able to stand before you: for the Lord your God shall lay the fear of you and the dread of you upon all the land that ye shall tread upon, as he hath said unto you" (Dt.11:22-25).

"Now therefore write ye this song for you, and teach it the children of Israel: put it in their mouths, that this song may be a witness for me against the children of Israel. For when I shall have brought them into the land which I sware unto their fathers, that floweth with milk and honey; and they shall have eaten and filled themselves, and waxen fat; then will they turn unto other gods, and serve them, and provoke me, and break my covenant. And it shall come to pass, when many evils and troubles are befallen them, that this song shall testify against them as a witness; for it shall not be forgotten out of the mouths of their seed: for I know their imagination which they go about, even now, before I have brought them into the land which I sware" (Dt.31:19-21).

"For the children of Israel walked forty years in the wilderness, till all the people that were men of war, which came out of Egypt, were consumed, because they obeyed not the voice of the Lord: unto whom the Lord sware that he would not show them the land, which the Lord sware unto their fathers that he would give us, a land that floweth with milk and honey" (Josh.5:6).

"And an angel of the Lord came up from Gilgal to Bochim, and said, I made you to go up out of Egypt, and have brought you unto the land which I sware unto your fathers; and I said, I will never break my covenant with you. And ye shall make no league with the inhabitants of this land; ye shall throw down their altars: but ye have not obeyed my voice: why have ye done this? Wherefore I also said, I will not drive them out from before you; but they shall be as thorns in your sides, and their gods shall be a snare unto you" (Judg.2:1-3).

Thought 1. There are several lessons for us in this point.

1) The great gift of God is the promised land. To the believer, the promised land means several things:
   a) The promised land means heaven itself, the new heavens and new earth that God is going to create for His dear people someday out in the future.

"In my Father's house are many mansions: if it were not so, I would have told you. I go to prepare a place for you. And if I go and prepare a place for you, I will come again, and receive you unto myself; that where I am, there ye may be also" (Jn.14:2-3).

"For we know that if our earthly house of this tabernacle were dissolved, we have a building of God, an house not made with hands, eternal in the heavens" (2 Cor.5:1).

"But the day of the Lord will come as a thief in the night; in the which the heavens shall pass away with a great noise, and the elements shall melt with fervent heat, the earth also and the works that are therein shall be burned up. Seeing then that all these things shall be dissolved, what manner of persons ought ye to be in all holy conversation and godliness, Looking for and hasting unto the coming of the day of God, wherein the heavens being on fire shall be dissolved, and the elements shall melt with fervent heat? Nevertheless we, according to his promise, look for new heavens and a new earth, wherein dwelleth righteousness" (2 Pt.3:10-13).

"And I saw a new heaven and a new earth: for the first heaven and the first earth were passed away; and there was no more sea. And I John saw the holy city, new Jerusalem, coming down from God out of heaven, prepared as a bride adorned for her husband. And I heard a great voice out of heaven saying, Behold, the tabernacle of God is with men, and he will dwell with them, and they shall be his people, and God himself shall be with them, and be their God. And God shall wipe away all tears from their eyes; and there shall be no more death, neither sorrow, nor crying, neither shall there be any more pain: for the former things are passed away" (Rev.21:1-4).

"For, behold, I create new heavens and a new earth: and the former shall not be remembered, nor come into mind" (Is.65:17).

b) The promised land means spiritual conquest and rest. It means that God's people conquer the enemies of life and find rest for their souls.

"Take my yoke upon you, and learn of me; for I am meek and lowly in heart: and ye shall find rest unto your souls" (Mt.11:29).

"Who shall separate us from the love of Christ? shall tribulation, or distress, or persecution, or famine, or nakedness, or peril, or sword?...Nay, in all these things we are more than conquerors through him that loved us. For I am persuaded, that neither death, nor life, nor angels, nor principalities, nor powers, nor things present, nor things to come, Nor height, nor depth, nor any other creature, shall be able to separate us from the love of God, which is in Christ Jesus our Lord" (Ro.8:35, 37-39).

"Let us therefore fear, lest, a promise being left us of entering into his rest, any of you should seem to come short of it. For unto us was the gospel preached, as well as unto them: but the word preached did not profit them, not being mixed with faith in them that heard it. For we which have believed do enter into rest, as he said, As I have sworn in my wrath, if they shall enter into my rest: although the works were finished from the foundation of the world" (Heb.4:1-3).

"Let us labour therefore to enter into that rest, lest any man fall after the same example of unbelief" (Heb.4:11).

"For whatsoever is born of God overcometh the world: and this is the victory that overcometh the world, even our faith. Who is he that overcometh the world, but he that believeth that Jesus is the Son of God" (1 Jn.5:4-5).

"And I heard a voice from heaven saying unto me, Write, Blessed are the dead which die in the Lord from henceforth: Yea, saith the Spirit, that they may rest from their labours; and their works do follow them" (Rev.14:13).

"And he said, My presence shall go with thee, and I will give thee rest" (Ex.33:14).

"Through thee will we push down our enemies: through thy name will we tread them under that rise up against us" (Ps.44:5).

"Return unto thy rest, O my soul; for the Lord hath dealt bountifully with thee" (Ps.116:7).

"To whom he said, This is the rest wherewith ye may cause the weary to rest; and this is the refreshing: yet they would not hear" (Is.28:12).

2) Entrance into the promised land is conditional. A person has to believe God and obey Him in order to enter the promised land of heaven. If a person is covetous, immoral, wicked, lawless, violent, or ungodly, he cannot inherit the kingdom of God, the promised land of heaven. A person has to believe God—trust His dear Son—if he is to inherit the promised land of heaven.

"And this is his commandment, That we should believe on the name of his Son Jesus Christ, and love one another, as he gave us commandment" (1 Jn.3:23).

"And this is his commandment, That we should believe on the name of his Son Jesus Christ, and love one another, as he gave us commandment" (1 Jn.3:23).

"But lay up for yourselves treasures in heaven, where neither moth nor rust doth corrupt, and where thieves do not break through nor steal" (Mt.6:20).

"For God so loved the world, that he gave his only begotten Son, that whosoever believeth in him should not perish, but have everlasting life" (Jn.3:16).

"Now the works of the flesh are manifest, which are these; Adultery, fornication, uncleanness, lasciviousness, Idolatry, witchcraft, hatred, variance, emulations, wrath, strife, seditions, heresies, Envyings, murders, drunkenness, revellings, and such like: of the which I tell you before, as I have also told you in time past, that they which do such things shall not inherit the kingdom of God" (Gal.5:19-21).

"For this ye know, that no whoremonger, nor unclean person, nor covetous man, who is an idolater, hath any inheritance in the kingdom of Christ and of God" (Eph.5:5).

"And there shall in no wise enter into it any thing that defileth, neither whatsoever worketh abomination, or maketh a lie: but they which are written in the Lamb's book of life" (Rev.21:27).

2 (34:16-29) **Assurance, of God—Leaders, of Israel—Israel, Leadership of—Land, the Promised, Assignment of**: the great assurance of God was seen in one clear fact: God appointed the leaders to assign the land before Israel ever entered the land. The day was coming when their inheritance would be assigned to them, and it was coming soon—during their lifetime—for the leaders were being appointed now. What excitement must have filled the hearts of God's people. They were being assured by God that they were on the verge of receiving their inheritance. A sense of full knowledge flooded their souls, the knowledge that they were definitely going to receive their inheritance. No doubt God was flooding their souls with assurance and confidence in the promised land.

OUTLINE	SCRIPTURE	SCRIPTURE	OUTLINE
2. The great assurance of God: The leaders who were to assign the land were appointed ahead of time (a picture of the great assurance of God)	16 And the LORD spake unto Moses, saying,	seh, Hanniel the son of Ephod.	
a. The supervisors: Eleazar the priest & Joshua	17 These are the names of the men which shall divide the land unto you: Eleazar the priest, and Joshua the son of Nun.	24 And the prince of the tribe of the children of Ephraim, Kemuel the son of Shiphtan.	6) Tribe of Ephraim: Kemuel
b. The leaders from each tribe: Some must be willing to lead, handling difficult tasks	18 And ye shall take one prince of every tribe, to divide the land by inheritance.	25 And the prince of the tribe of the children of Zebulun, Elizaphan the son of Parnach.	7) Tribe of Zebulun: Elizaphan
1) Tribe of Judah: Caleb	19 And the names of the men are these: Of the tribe of Judah, Caleb the son of Jephunneh.	26 And the prince of the tribe of the children of Issachar, Paltiel the son of Azzan.	8) Tribe of Issachar: Paltiel
2) Tribe of Simeon: Shemuel	20 And of the tribe of the children of Simeon, Shemuel the son of Ammihud.	27 And the prince of the tribe of the children of Asher, Ahihud the son of Shelomi.	9) Tribe of Asher: Ahihud
3) Tribe of Benjamin: Elidad	21 Of the tribe of Benjamin, Elidad the son of Chislon.	28 And the prince of the tribe of the children of Naphtali, Pedahel the son of Ammihud.	10) Tribe of Naphtali: Pedahel
4) Tribe of Dan: Bukki	22 And the prince of the tribe of the children of Dan, Bukki the son of Jogli.	29 These are they whom the LORD commanded to divide the inheritance unto the children of Israel in the land of Canaan.	c. The difficult task of dividing land among heirs: These were the willing leaders appointed to the task
5) Tribe of Manasseh: Hanniel	23 The prince of the children of Joseph, for the tribe of the children of Manas-		

Thought 1. Assurance, confidence, and conviction in the promised land have been given by God. The person who approaches God through Christ is given the assurance of living forever with God. When a person receives Christ as his Savior, the Holy Spirit of God enters his life. God places His Spirit within the person, and the Spirit of God becomes the guarantee of living forever within the promised land of heaven. The Holy Spirit within a person is the guarantee, the surety of heaven.

"The Spirit itself beareth witness with our spirit, that we are the children of God: And if children, then heirs; heirs of God, and joint-heirs with Christ; if so be that we suffer with him, that we may be also glorified together" (Ro.8:16-17).

"And because ye are sons, God hath sent forth the Spirit of his Son into your hearts, crying, Abba, Father" (Gal.4:6).

"In whom ye also trusted, after that ye heard the word of truth, the gospel of your salvation: in whom also after that ye believed, ye were sealed with that holy Spirit of promise, Which is the earnest of our inheritance until the redemption of the purchased possession, unto the praise of his glory" (Eph.1:13-14).

"I know whom I have believed, and am persuaded that he is able to keep that which I have committed unto him against that day" (2 Tim.1:12).

"Let us draw near with a true heart in full assurance of faith, having our hearts sprinkled from an evil conscience, and our bodies washed with pure water" (Heb.10:22).

"And he that keepeth his commandments dwelleth in him, and he in him. And hereby we know that he abideth in us, by the Spirit which he hath given us" (1 Jn.3:24).

"Hereby know we that we dwell in him, and he in us, because he hath given us of his Spirit" (1 Jn.4:13).

"He that believeth on the Son of God hath the witness in himself: he that believeth not God hath made him a liar; because he believeth not the record that God gave of his Son" (1 Jn.5:10).

"And this is the record, that God hath given to us eternal life, and this life is in his Son. He that hath the Son hath life; and he that hath not the Son of God hath not life" (1 Jn.5:11-12).

(34:1-15) Map—Israel, Boundaries of—Promised Land, Boundaries of—Spies, Twelve, Mission of—Canaan, Boundaries of:

THE BORDERS OF THE PROMISED LAND OF CANAAN AND THE MISSION OF THE TWELVE SPIES

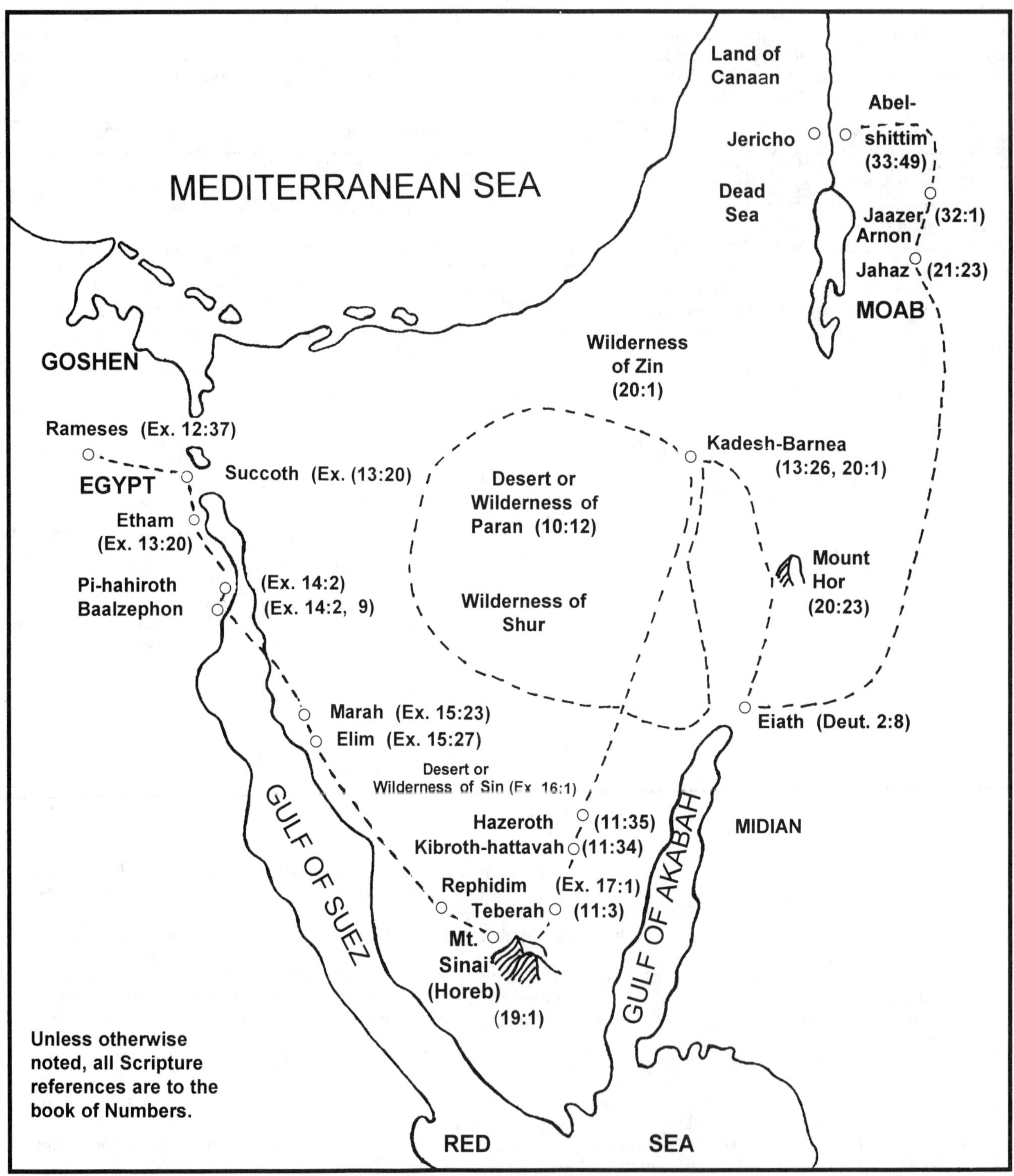

1. **God's provision for the Levites: A picture of ministry & of God's provision of necessities for His servants**
   a. The people were to give towns & pastureland to support His servants, the Levites (cp. 18:1-32)
      1) The purpose
         • To spread them out in the community among the people—for ministry
         • To give them a home & pastureland for their livestock
      2) The size of the pastureland
         • To extend out 1500' from the wall of the town
         • To measure about 3000' on each side with the town in the center (the footage was no doubt enlarged as the town & population grew)
   b. The people were to give six towns as cities of refuge: A place of safety for a person guilty of accidental manslaughter
   c. The people were to give 48 towns total
      • Forty-two homesites
      • Six cities of refuge
   d. The people were to be fair in selecting the towns & land to be given
      1) Fair to God's servants: An understood fact
      2) Fair to each tribe: To give in proportion to the size of the tribe

J. The Inheritance of the Levites & the Cities of Refuge: The Provision of God for His Ministers & for All Who Need Refuge from the Storms & Threats of Life, 35:1-34

And the LORD spake unto
Moses in the plains of Moab
by Jordan near Jericho, saying,
2 Command the children of
Israel, that they give unto the
Levites of the inheritance of
their possession cities to
dwell in; and ye shall give
also unto the Levites suburbs
for the cities round about
them.
3 And the cities shall they
have to dwell in; and the
suburbs of them shall be for
their cattle, and for their
goods, and for all their
beasts.
4 And the suburbs of the
cities, which ye shall give
unto the Levites, shall reach
from the wall of the city and
outward a thousand cubits
round about.
5 And ye shall measure from
without the city on the east
side two thousand cubits,
and on the south side two
thousand cubits, and on the
west side two thousand cubits, and on the north side
two thousand cubits and the
city shall be in the midst: this
shall be to them the suburbs
of the cities.
6 And among the cities
which ye shall give unto the
Levites there shall be six
cities for refuge, which ye
shall appoint for the
manslayer, that he may flee
thither: and to them ye shall
add forty and two cities.
7 So all the cities which ye
shall give to the Levites shall
be forty and eight cities:
them shall ye give with their
suburbs.
8 And the cities which ye
shall give shall be of the possession of the children of Israel: from them that have
many ye shall give many;
but from them that have few
ye shall give few: every one
shall give of his cities unto
the Levites according to his
inheritance which he in-
heriteth.
9 And the LORD spake unto
Moses, saying,
10 Speak unto the children
of Israel, and say unto them,
When ye be come over Jor-
dan into the land of Canaan;
11 Then ye shall appoint
you cities to be cities of
refuge for you; that the slayer may flee thither, which
killeth any person at un-
awares.
12 And they shall be unto
you cities for refuge from the
avenger; that the manslayer
die not, until he stand before
the congregation in judg-
ment.
13 And of these cities which
ye shall give six cities shall
ye have for refuge.
14 Ye shall give three cities
on this side Jordan, and three
cities shall ye give in the
land of Canaan, which shall
be cities of refuge.
15 These six cities shall be
a refuge, both for the children of Israel, and for
the stranger, and for the sojourner among them: that
every one that killeth any
person unawares may flee
thither.
16 And if he smite him with
an instrument of iron, so that
he die, he is a murderer: the
murderer shall surely be put
to death.
17 And if he smite him with
throwing a stone, wherewith
he may die, and he die, he
is a murderer: the mur-
derer shall surely be put to
death.
18 Or if he smite him with
an hand weapon of wood,
wherewith he may die, and
he die, he is a murderer: the
murderer shall surely be put
to death.
19 The revenger of blood
himself shall slay the murderer: when he meeteth him,
he shall slay him.
20 But if he thrust him of
hatred, or hurl at him by
laying of wait, that he
die;
21 Or in enmity smite him
with his hand, that he die: he
that smote him shall surely
be put to death; for he is a
murderer: the revenger of
blood shall slay the murderer, when he meeteth him.

2. **God's provision of refuge—establishing the cities of refuge: A picture of the Lord our Refuge—a refuge from the threats & storms of life**
   a. The basic purpose of the cities of refuge
      1) To be a refuge, an asylum for persons guilty of accidental murder
      2) To be a place to flee from the avenger
      3) To be a place of safety until a trial could be set by community courts
   b. The location of the cities of refuge
      1) Three in Transjordan
      2) Three in Canaan
   c. The open access of the cities of refuge: Any person—native born, foreigner, or traveling merchant—could flee for refuge in the cities (picture that any person can flee to Christ)
   d. The cases of willful murder excluded a person from the cities of refuge
      1) The person who picks up an iron object does so willfully; he is a murderer & is to be executed
      2) The person who picks up a stone does so willfully: He is a murderer & is to be executed
      3) The person who picks up a wooden object does so willfully: He is a murderer & is to be executed
      4) The victim's nearest relative (the avenger of blood) is responsible for the execution
      5) The person who murders someone with premeditated malice by shoving or throwing something is a murderer
      6) The person who angrily kills anyone with his fists is a murderer: He is to be executed by the victim's avenger or nearest relative (5:8; Lev.25:25-26)

Outline	Scripture
e. The cases of murder that allowed a person to flee to a city of refuge: Cases without hostility, that were unintentional, such as accidentally shoving or throwing something or by dropping an object	22 But if he thrust him suddenly without enmity, or have cast upon him any thing without laying of wait, 23 Or with any stone, wherewith a man may die, seeing him not, and cast it upon him, that he die, and was not his enemy, neither sought his harm:
1) The courts must decide between the slayer & the avenger or nearest relative	24 Then the congregation shall judge between the slayer and the revenger of blood according to these judgments:
2) The courts must protect the accused by sending him to a city of refuge 3) The accused must stay in the city of refuge until the death of the High Priest: A picture of deliverance by the death of Christ	25 And the congregation shall deliver the slayer out of the hand of the revenger of blood, and the congregation shall restore him to the city of his refuge, whither he was fled: and he shall abide in it unto the death of the high priest, which was anointed with the holy oil.
f. The strong warning to the accused (a picture of God's warning to the accused sinner) 1) The avenger could execute the accused if the accused ever left the city of refuge	26 But if the slayer shall at any time come without the border of the city of his refuge, whither he was fled; 27 And the revenger of blood find him without the borders of the city of his refuge, and the revenger of blood kill the slayer; he shall not be guilty of blood:
2) The accused must stay in the city of refuge until the death of the High Priest (a symbol of Christ our Refuge, the Deliverer from the avenger of death)	28 Because he should have remained in the city of his refuge until the death of the high priest: but after the death of the high priest the slayer shall return into the land of his possession.
g. The laws governing the cities of refuge were established as permanent laws	29 So these things shall be for a statute of judgment unto you throughout your generations in all your dwellings.
3. God's provision of mercy in dealing with murder a. Two or more witnesses are required to execute a person	30 Whoso killeth any person, the murderer shall be put to death by the mouth of witnesses: but one witness shall not testify against any person to cause him to die.
b. No unequal justice is to be allowed; no ransom is ever to be accepted from a rich murderer: He is to be executed	31 Moreover ye shall take no satisfaction for the life of a murderer, which is guilty of death: but he shall be surely put to death.
c. No ransom is to be accepted from a rich person in a city of refuge: No person is to be allowed to buy his freedom	32 And ye shall take no satisfaction for him that is fled to the city of his refuge, that he should come again to dwell in the land, until the death of the priest.
d. No land is to be polluted by murder • Bloodshed—murder—pollutes the land • Atonement can be made only by the blood or execution of the murderer, the one who shed blood	33 So ye shall not pollute the land wherein ye are: for blood it defileth the land: and the land cannot be cleansed of the blood that is shed therein, but by the blood of him that shed it.
e. God demands justice, demands that the land not be defiled: The reason—He lives there, lives among His people	34 Defile not therefore the land which ye shall inhabit, wherein I dwell: for I the LORD dwell among the children of Israel.

DIVISION IV

THE PREPARATION FOR THE MARCH INTO THE PROMISED LAND, 26:1-36:13

J. The Inheritance of the Levites and the Cities of Refuge: The Provision of God for His Ministers and for All Who Need Refuge from the Storms and Threats of Life, 35:1-34

(35:1-34) **Introduction**: water, food, clothing, and housing—all are necessities that every human being must have in order to survive and sustain life. But physical and material items are not the only things necessary to sustain life. Meaning, significance, purpose, satisfaction, and fulfillment—all these are necessary to live a full and free life upon this earth. The necessities of life are provisions that we absolutely must have in order to live and experience the fullness of life.

When dealing with the necessities of life, there is wonderful, glorious news. God promises to meet every need of human life. There is no need that God does not promise to meet. Provision to meet the needs of every human being is in the hands of God. This is the loud and clear declaration of Scripture: *The Inheritance of the Levites and the Cities of Refuge: the Provision of God for His Ministers and for All Who Need Refuge from the Storms and Threats of Life,* 35:1-34.

1. God's provision for the Levites: a picture of ministry and of God's provision of necessities for His servants (v.1-8).
2. God's provision of refuge—establishing the cities of refuge: a picture of Christ our Refuge—a refuge from the threats and storms of life (v.9-29).
3. God's provision of mercy in dealing with murder (v.30-34).

1 (35:1-8) **Provision, For God's Ministers—Ministers, Provision For—Levites, Provision For—Necessities, Provision of—Provision, of God—Ministers, Ministry of**: there was God's provision for the Levites. This is a picture of ministry and of God's provision for His servants. The Levites were not to inherit any land in Canaan in order that they might focus entirely upon the ministry to the people. If they owned land, they would have to be involved in the business affairs of their property. This was not their call: they were called to serve and minister to the people. This was to be their sole focus. God Himself—His worship and His ministry—was to be their inheritance (Num.18:20-24). However, the Levites and their families needed a place to live and their livestock needed good pastureland. These needs were now met by God:

OUTLINE	SCRIPTURE	SCRIPTURE	OUTLINE
1. God's provision for the Levites: A picture of ministry & of God's provision of necessities for His servants a. The people were to give towns & pastureland to support His servants, the Levites (cp. 18:1-32) 1) The purpose • To spread them out in the community among the people—for ministry • To give them a home & pastureland for their livestock	And the LORD spake unto Moses in the plains of Moab by Jordan near Jericho, say- ing, 2 Command the children of Israel, that they give unto the Levites of the inheritance of their possession cities to dwell in; and ye shall give also unto the Levites sub- urbs for the cities round about them. 3 And the cities shall they have to dwell in; and the suburbs of them shall be for their cattle, and for their goods, and for all their beasts.	bits, and on the north side two thousand cubits and the city shall be in the midst: this shall be to them the sub- urbs of the cities. 6 And among the cities which ye shall give unto the Levites there shall be six cities for refuge, which ye shall appoint for the manslayer, that he may flee thither: and to them ye shall add forty and two cities. 7 So all the cities which ye shall give to the Levites shall be forty and eight cities: them shall ye give with their suburbs.	b. The people were to give six towns as cities of refuge: A place of safety for a person guilty of accidental manslaughter c. The people were to give 48 towns total • Forty-two homesites • Six cities of refuge
2) The size of the pastureland • To extend out 1500' from the wall of the town • To measure about 3000' on each side with the town in the center (the footage was no doubt enlarged as the town & population grew)	4 And the suburbs of the cities, which ye shall give unto the Levites, shall reach from the wall of the city and outward a thousand cubits round about. 5 And ye shall measure from without the city on the east side two thousand cubits, and on the south side two thousand cubits, and on the west side two thousand cu-	8 And the cities which ye shall give shall be of the possession of the children of Israel: from them that have many ye shall give many; but from them that have few ye shall give few: every one shall give of his cities unto the Levites according to his in- heritance which he in- heriteth.	d. The people were to be fair in selecting the towns & land to be given 1) Fair to God's servants: An understood fact 2) Fair to each tribe: To give in proportion to the size of the tribe

1. The people were to give town's and pastureland to support God's servants, the Levites (v.2-5). Keep in mind that the Levites were supported by God's people; therefore they did not need land for a garden nor for farming (see outline and notes—Num.18:8-24 for more discussion).

a. The gift of towns and pastureland was an absolute essential for two purposes. First, there was a need for the Levites to live out among the people within their very communities so that they could minister to them. When the people needed help, the ministers of God needed to be available to help. They were the representatives of God's love and care; therefore they were to be living within the communities of the people and demonstrating God's love and care. They were to be teaching the truth and instructing people in the law of God.

"And that ye [Levites, ministers] may teach the children of Israel all the statutes which the Lord hath spoken unto them by the hand of Moses" (Lev.10:11).

"And Moses wrote this law, and delivered it unto the priests the sons of Levi, which bare the ark of the covenant of the Lord, and unto all the elders of Israel. And Moses commanded them, saying, At the end of every seven years, in the solemnity of the year of release, in the feast of tabernacles, When all Israel is come to appear before the Lord thy God in the place which he shall choose, thou shalt read this law before all Israel in their hearing. Gather the people together, men, and women, and children, and thy stranger that is within thy gates, that they may hear, and that they may learn, and fear the Lord your God, and observe to do all the words of this law: And that their children, which have not known any thing, may hear, and learn to fear the Lord your God, as long as ye live in the land whither ye go over Jordan to possess it" (Dt.31:9-13).

"They shall teach Jacob thy judgments, and Israel thy law: they [Levites] shall put incense before thee, and whole burnt sacrifice upon thine altar" (Dt.33:10).

The second purpose for giving towns and pastureland to the Levites was to provide a home for them, their families and their livestock. Very simply, they needed a place to live. There are several other major passages that deal with the cities and pasturelands of the Levites (Lev.25:32-34; Josh.14:4; 1 Chron.13:2; 2 Chron.11:14; 31:15, 19). There are also other passages that refer to the Levite cities (Ezra 2:70; Neh.7:73; 11:3, 20, 36. Also cp. Ezk.48:8-14.)[1]

b. Note that the amount of land to be given was dictated by God (v.4-5). The pastureland was to extend out 1500 feet from the wall of the town. The surveyor was then to measure about 3000 feet on each side with the town in the center. The footage was no doubt enlarged as the town and population grew. A diagram of the city would look like the drawing on the following page:[2]

1 *The Expositor's Bible Commentary*, Frank E. Gaebelein, Editor, p.999.
2 This diagram is suggested by Gordon J. Wenham. *The Book of Numbers*, p.234.

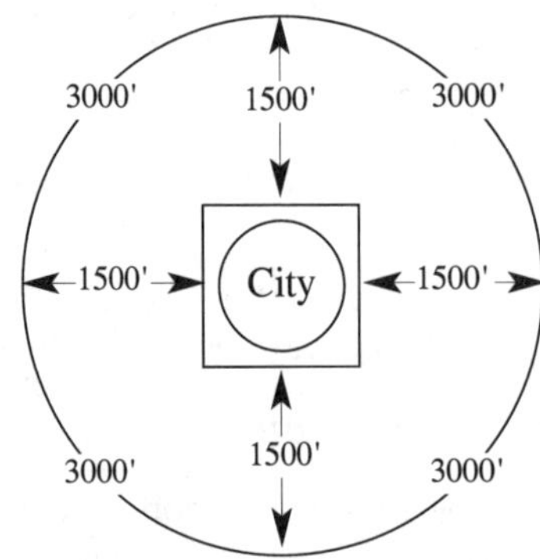

2. The people were also to give six towns as cities of refuge. These cities were a place of safety for a person guilty of accidental manslaughter (v.6). Three cities of refuge were to be located in the promised land of Canaan and three among the two and a half tribes that settled in East Jordan. Joshua tells us that these cities were strategically located throughout the land (Josh.20:1-9). These cities will be discussed in detail in note two (v.9-29).

3. The people were to give a total of forty-eight towns: forty-two homesites for the Levites and six cities of refuge (v.6-7).

4. The people were to be fair in selecting the towns and land to be given. They were to give in proportion to the size of the inheritance of the tribe (v.8).

Thought 1. The minister of God is to be out among people, ministering to them. He is to be available to help in times of need. Moreover, he is to be teaching and instructing God's people in the truth of God's Holy Word, and he is to be reaching out to the lost of the world.

1) The minister of God is to be available to help in times of need, seeking to do good at every opportunity possible.

> **"Even as the Son of man came not to be ministered unto, but to minister, and to give his life a ransom for many" (Mt.20:28).**
>
> **"And whosoever of you will be the chiefest, shall be servant of all" (Mk.10:44).**
>
> **"For whether is greater, he that sitteth at meat, or he that serveth? is not he that sitteth at meat? but I am among you as he that serveth" (Lk.22:27).**
>
> **"If I then, your Lord and Master, have washed your feet; ye also ought to wash one another's feet" (Jn.13:14).**
>
> **"Bear ye one another's burdens, and so fulfil the law of Christ" (Gal.6:2).**
>
> **"As we have therefore opportunity, let us do good unto all men, especially unto them who are of the household of faith" (Gal.6:10).**

2) The minister is to teach and instruct God's people in the truth of God's Word.

> **"Teaching them to observe all things whatsoever I have commanded you: and, lo, I am with you alway, even unto the end of the world. Amen" (Mt.28:20).**
>
> **"He saith unto him the third time, Simon, son of Jonas, lovest thou me? Peter was grieved because he said unto him the third time, Lovest thou me? And he said unto him, Lord, thou knowest all things; thou knowest that I love thee. Jesus saith unto him, Feed my sheep" (Jn.21:17).**
>
> **"Take heed therefore unto yourselves, and to all the flock, over the which the Holy Ghost hath made you overseers, to feed the church of God, which he hath purchased with his own blood" (Acts 20:28).**
>
> **"A bishop then must be blameless, the husband of one wife, vigilant, sober, of good behaviour, given to hospitality, apt to teach" (1 Tim.3:2).**
>
> **"These things command and teach" (1 Tim.4:11).**
>
> **"In meekness instructing those that oppose themselves; if God peradventure will give them repentance to the acknowledging of the truth" (2 Tim.2:25).**
>
> **"Feed the flock of God which is among you, taking the oversight thereof, not by constraint, but willingly; not for filthy lucre, but of a ready mind" (1 Pt.5:2).**
>
> **"And I will give you pastors according to mine heart, which shall feed you with knowledge and understanding" (Jer.3:15).**
>
> **"And I will set up shepherds over them which shall feed them: and they shall fear no more, nor be dismayed, neither shall they be lacking, saith the Lord" (Jer.23:4).**

3) The minister of God is to reach out and bear testimony and witness for Christ.

> **"Go ye therefore, and teach all nations, baptizing them in the name of the Father, and of the Son, and of the Holy Ghost: Teaching them to observe all things whatsoever I have commanded you: and, lo, I am with you alway, *even* unto the end of the world. Amen" (Mt.28:19-20).**
>
> **"And he said unto them, Go ye into all the world, and preach the gospel to every creature" (Mk.16:15).**

"But ye shall receive power, after that the Holy Ghost is come upon you: and ye shall be witnesses unto me both in Jerusalem, and in all Judaea, and in Samaria, and unto the uttermost part of the earth" (Acts 1:8).

"To wit, that God was in Christ, reconciling the world unto himself, not imputing their trespasses unto them; and hath committed unto us the word of reconciliation. Now then we are ambassadors for Christ, as though God did beseech *you* by us: we pray *you* in Christ's stead, be ye reconciled to God" (2 Cor.5:19-20).

"To the one we are the savour of death unto death; and to the other the savour of life unto life. And who is sufficient for these things" (2 Cor.2:16).

"To wit, that God was in Christ, reconciling the world unto himself, not imputing their trespasses unto them; and hath committed unto us the word of reconciliation. Now then we are ambassadors for Christ, as though God did beseech you by us: we pray you in Christ's stead, be ye reconciled to God. For he hath made him to be sin for us, who knew no sin; that we might be made the righteousness of God in him" (2 Cor.5:19-21).

"But watch thou in all things, endure afflictions, do the work of an evangelist, make full proof of thy ministry" (2 Tim.4:5).

"Ye are my witnesses, saith the Lord, and my servant whom I have chosen: that ye may know and believe me, and understand that I am he: before me there was no God formed, neither shall there be after me" (Is.43:10).

"I have set watchmen upon thy walls, O Jerusalem, which shall never hold their peace day nor night: ye that make mention of the Lord, keep not silence" (Is.62:6).

"But if the watchman see the sword come, and blow not the trumpet, and the people be not warned; if the sword come, and take any person from among them, he is taken away in his iniquity; but his blood will I require at the watchman's hand" (Ezk.33:6).

Thought 2. God promises to provide all the necessities of life for His dear people. The person who truly follows God will be looked after by God. God will take care of him, meeting his every need, and often giving him an overflowing provision.

"But seek ye first the kingdom of God, and his righteousness; and all these things shall be added unto you" (Mt.6:33).

"The thief cometh not, but for to steal, and to kill, and to destroy: I am come that they might have life, and that they might have it more abundantly" (Jn.10:10).

"And God is able to make all grace abound toward you; that ye, always having all sufficiency in all things, may abound to every good work" (2 Cor.9:8).

"Now unto him that is able to do exceeding abundantly above all that we ask or think, according to the power that worketh in us" (Eph.3:20).

"But my God shall supply all your need according to his riches in glory by Christ Jesus" (Ph.4:19).

"For so an entrance shall be ministered unto you abundantly into the everlasting kingdom of our Lord and Saviour Jesus Christ" (2 Pt.1:11).

"And ye shall serve the Lord your God, and he shall bless thy bread, and thy water; and I will take sickness away from the midst of thee" (Ex.23:25).

"Blessed be the Lord, who daily loadeth us with benefits, even the God of our salvation. Selah" (Ps.68:19).

"Bring ye all the tithes into the storehouse, that there may be meat in mine house, and prove me now herewith, saith the Lord of hosts, if I will not open you the windows of heaven, and pour you out a blessing, that there shall not be room enough to receive it" (Mal.3:10).

2 (35:9-29) **Refuge, Cities of—Cities of Refuge—Christ, Our Refuge—Symbol, of Christ, Our Refuge**: there was God's provision of refuge, that of establishing the cities of refuge for persons who were guilty of accidental manslaughter. This is a clear picture of Christ, our Refuge from the threats and storms of life. This passage deals with the law governing cases of murder and manslaughter. The grace and mercy of God is clearly seen in setting up the cities of refuge for the murderer.

OUTLINE	SCRIPTURE	SCRIPTURE	OUTLINE
2. God's provision of refuge—establishing the cities of refuge: A picture of the Lord our Refuge—a refuge from the threats & storms of life a. The basic purpose of the cities of refuge 1) To be a refuge, an asylum for persons guilty of accidental murder	9 And the LORD spake unto Moses, saying, 10 Speak unto the children of Israel, and say unto them, When ye be come over Jordan into the land of Canaan; 11 Then ye shall appoint you cities to be cities of refuge for you; that the slayer may flee thither, which killeth any person at unawares.	12 And they shall be unto you cities for refuge from the avenger; that the manslayer die not, until he stand before the congregation in judgment. 13 And of these cities which ye shall give six cities shall ye have for refuge. 14 Ye shall give three cities on this side Jordan, and three cities shall ye give in the	2) To be a place to flee from the avenger 3) To be a place of safety until a trial could be set by community courts b. The location of the cities of refuge 1) Three in Transjordan 2) Three in Canaan

OUTLINE	SCRIPTURE	SCRIPTURE	OUTLINE
c. The open access of the cities of refuge: Any person—native born, foreigner, or traveling merchant—could flee for refuge in the cities (picture that any person can flee to Christ) d. The cases of willful murder excluded a person from the cities of refuge 1) The person who picks up an iron object does so willfully; he is a murderer & is to be executed 2) The person who picks up a stone does so willfully: He is a murderer & is to be executed 3) The person who picks up a wooden object does so willfully: He is a murderer & is to be executed 4) The victim's nearest relative (the avenger of blood) is responsible for the execution 5) The person who murders someone with premeditated malice by shoving or throwing something is a murderer 6) The person who angrily kills anyone with his fists is a murderer: He is to be executed by the victim's avenger or nearest relative (5:8; Lev.25:25-26) e. The cases of murder that allowed a person to flee to a city of refuge: Cases without	land of Canaan, which shall be cities of refuge. 15 These six cities shall be a refuge, both for the chil- dren of Israel, and for the stranger, and for the so- journer among them: that every one that killeth any person unawares may flee thither. 16 And if he smite him with an instrument of iron, so that he die, he is a murderer: the murderer shall surely be put to death. 17 And if he smite him with throwing a stone, wherewith he may die, and he die, he is a murderer: the murderer shall surely be put to death. 18 Or if he smite him with an hand weapon of wood, wherewith he may die, and he die, he is a murderer: the murderer shall surely be put to death. 19 The revenger of blood himself shall slay the mur- derer: when he meeteth him, he shall slay him. 20 But if he thrust him of hatred, or hurl at him by laying of wait, that he die; 21 Or in enmity smite him with his hand, that he die: he that smote him shall surely be put to death; for he is a murderer: the revenger of blood shall slay the murder- er, when he meeteth him. 22 But if he thrust him sud- denly without enmity, or have cast upon him any	thing without laying of wait, 23 Or with any stone, wherewith a man may die, seeing him not, and cast it upon him, that he die, and was not his enemy, neither sought his harm: 24 Then the congregation shall judge between the slay- er and the revenger of blood according to these judg- ments: 25 And the congregation shall deliver the slayer out of the hand of the revenger of blood, and the congregation shall restore him to the city of his refuge, whither he was fled: and he shall abide in it unto the death of the high priest, which was anointed with the holy oil. 26 But if the slayer shall at any time come without the border of the city of his refuge, whither he was fled; 27 And the revenger of blood find him without the borders of the city of his refuge, and the revenger of blood kill the slayer; he shall not be guilty of blood: 28 Because he should have remained in the city of his refuge until the death of the high priest: but after the death of the high priest the slayer shall return into the land of his possession. 29 So these things shall be for a statute of judgment unto you throughout your generations in all your dwellings.	hostility, that were unintentional, such as accidentally shoving or throwing something or by dropping an object 1) The courts must decide between the slayer & the avenger or nearest relative 2) The courts must protect the accused by sending him to a city of refuge 3) The accused must stay in the city of refuge until the death of the High Priest: A picture of deliverance by the death of Christ f. The strong warning to the accused (a picture of God's warning to the accused sinner) 1) The avenger could execute the accused if the accused ever left the city of refuge 2) The accused must stay in the city of refuge until the death of the High Priest (a symbol of Christ our Refuge, the Deliverer from the avenger of death) g. The laws governing the cities of refuge were established as permanent laws

1. Note the basic purpose for the cities of refuge: the cities were to be a refuge, an asylum for persons guilty of accidental murder. They were to provide a place for the murderer to flee from the avenger, a place of safety until a trial could be set by community courts (v.11-12). In ancient days it was the responsibility of the nearest relative to protect the family rights of the victim. The nearest relative was known as the "redeemer" or "kinsman" (goel). The nearest relative or "kinsman" was responsible by law to save his relative from any trouble he faced. Moreover, if the relative had been killed, the "kinsman" became his avenger or the avenger of blood (v.12, 19, 21, 24-25, 27. See also Num.5:8; Lev.25:25-26; Ruth 3:12f; 4:1, 6, 8; Job 19:25; Is.59:20.)[3]

2. The location of the cities of refuge was given: three were to be located in Transjordan and three in Canaan proper or the promised land itself (v.14). These, of course, were to be strategically located so that the people would have equal access to the cities of refuge.

3. Note the open access to the cities of refuge: any person—native-born, foreigner, or traveling merchant—could flee for refuge to the cities (v.15). This is a picture of the wonderful grace of God and a picture that any person can flee to Christ for refuge.

4. Note that the cases of willful murder were excluded from the cities of refuge (v.16-21). Several examples are given to serve as precedence to cover any cases that might arise. The idea behind the six cases given has to do with willful intent, premeditation, or deliberate murder. The six cases are clearly seen by glancing up at the Scripture and outline (v.16-21).

5. Note the cases of murder that allowed a person to flee to a city of refuge (v.22-25).

   a. Persons who had committed murder without hostility—unintentionally or involuntarily—could flee to the city of refuge. For example, if a person accidentally shoved or threw something or dropped an object on a person that

3 Gordon J. Wenham. *The Book of Numbers*, p.236.

killed the victim, he could flee to a city of refuge (v.22-23).

b. In these cases, the courts had to decide between the slayer and the avenger or nearest relative (v.24). If the courts decided that the person had committed deliberate or premeditated murder, he was turned over to the avenger and executed.

c. However, if the courts found the person innocent, the courts sent him to a city of refuge where he would be protected (v.25).

d. But note: the accused had to stay in the city of refuge until the current High Priest had died (v.25). The death of the High Priest was a picture of atonement, of the atoning death of the coming Savior Jesus Christ. Therefore when the High Priest died, the person who had committed accidental, unintentional murder was set free. This was a clear picture of deliverance from sin and death through the sacrifice and death of Jesus Christ. When Jesus Christ died as our High Priest, we were set free from the condemnation of death.

6. Note the strong warning to the accused (v.26-28): the avenger could execute him if he ever left the city of refuge. Therefore, the accused must stay in the city of refuge until the death of the High Priest. Again note the symbolism: this is a clear symbol of Christ our Refuge, the Deliverer from the avenger of death.

7. The laws governing the cities of refuge were established as permanent laws (v.29).

Thought 1. The Lord is our Refuge from the threats and storms of life. Scripture declares four wonderful truths about the protection the Lord gives us.

1) The Lord is our Refuge.

"The eternal God *is thy* refuge, and underneath *are* the everlasting arms: and he shall thrust out the enemy from before thee; and shall say, Destroy *them*" (Dt.33:27).

"God *is* our refuge and strength, a very present help in trouble" (Ps.46:1).

"Be thou my strong habitation, whereunto I may continually resort: thou hast given commandment to save me; for thou *art* my rock and my fortress" (Ps.71:3).

"The name of the LORD *is* a strong tower: the righteous runneth into it, and is safe" (Pr.18:10).

"For thou hast been a strength to the poor, a strength to the needy in his distress, a refuge from the storm, a shadow from the heat, when the blast of the terrible ones *is* as a storm *against* the wall" (Is.25:4).

"Turn you to the strong hold, ye prisoners of hope" (Zech.9:12).

2) The Lord is our Hiding Place.

"Keep me as the apple of the eye, hide me under the shadow of thy wings" (Ps.17:8).

"For in the time of trouble he shall hide me in his pavilion: in the secret of his tabernacle shall he hide me; he shall set me up upon a rock" (Ps.27:5).

"Thou shalt hide them in the secret of thy presence from the pride of man: thou shalt keep them secretly in a pavilion from the strife of tongues" (Ps.31:20).

"Thou *art* my hiding place; thou shalt preserve me from trouble; thou shalt compass me about with songs of deliverance. Selah" (Ps.32:7).

"Hide me from the secret counsel of the wicked; from the insurrection of the workers of iniquity" (Ps.64:2).

"Thou *art* my hiding place and my shield: I hope in thy word" (Ps.119:114).

"Deliver me, O LORD, from mine enemies: I flee unto thee to hide me" (Ps.143:9).

"And a man shall be as an hiding place from the wind, and a covert from the tempest; as rivers of water in a dry place, as the shadow of a great rock in a weary land" (Is.32:2).

3) The Lord is our Shield in protecting us.

"After these things the word of the LORD came unto Abram in a vision, saying, Fear not, Abram: I *am* thy shield, *and* thy exceeding great reward" (Gen.15:1).

"Our soul waiteth for the LORD: he *is* our help and our shield" (Ps.33:20).

"For the LORD God *is* a sun and shield: the LORD will give grace and glory: no good *thing* will he withhold from them that walk uprightly" (Ps.84:11).

"O Israel, trust thou in the LORD: he *is* their help and their shield" (Ps.115:9).

4) The Lord is our Atoning Sacrifice who delivers us from the avenger of death.

"For God so loved the world, that he gave his only begotten Son, that whosoever believeth in him should not perish, but have everlasting life" (Jn.3:16).

"And whosoever liveth and believeth in me shall never die. Believest thou this" (Jn.11:26).

"The last enemy that shall be destroyed is death" (1 Cor.15:26).

"For this corruptible must put on incorruption, and this mortal must put on immortality. So when this corruptible shall have put on incorruption, and this mortal shall have put on immortality, then shall be brought to pass the saying that is written, Death is swallowed up in victory" (1 Cor.15:53-54).

"For we know that if our earthly house of this tabernacle were dissolved, we have a building of God, an house not made with hands, eternal in the heavens" (2 Cor.5:1).

"For the Lord himself shall descend from heaven with a shout, with the voice of the archangel, and with the trump of God: and the dead in Christ shall rise first: then we which are alive and remain shall

be caught up together with them in the clouds, to meet the Lord in the air: and so shall we ever be with the Lord" (1 Th.4:16-17).

"But is now made manifest by the appearing of our Saviour Jesus Christ, who hath abolished death, and hath brought life and immortality to light through the gospel" (2 Tim.1:10).

"But we see Jesus, who was made a little lower than the angels for the suffering of death, crowned with glory and honour; that he by the grace of God should taste death for every man" (Heb.2:9).

"Forasmuch then as the children are partakers of flesh and blood, he also himself likewise took part of the same; that through death he might destroy him that had the power of death, that is, the devil; And deliver them who through fear of death were all their lifetime subject to bondage" (Heb.2:14-15).

"And God shall wipe away all tears from their eyes; and there shall be no more death, neither sorrow, nor crying, neither shall there be any more pain: for the former things are passed away" (Rev.21:4).

"He will swallow up death in victory; and the Lord God will wipe away tears from off all faces; and the rebuke of his people shall he take away from off all the earth: for the Lord hath spoken it" (Is.25:8).

3 (35:30-34) **Mercy, of God—Murder, Laws Governing—Provision, For Murderers**: there is God's provision of mercy in dealing with murder. The laws are clearly seen in the Scripture and outline:

OUTLINE	SCRIPTURE	SCRIPTURE	OUTLINE
3. God's provision of mercy in dealing with murder a. Two or more witnesses are required to execute a person b. No unequal justice is to be allowed; no ransom is ever to be accepted from a rich murderer: He is to be executed c. No ransom is to be accepted from a rich person in a city of refuge: No person is to be allowed to buy his freedom	30 Whoso killeth any person, the murderer shall be put to death by the mouth of witnesses: but one witness shall not testify against any person to cause him to die. 31 Moreover ye shall take no satisfaction for the life of a murderer, which is guilty of death: but he shall be surely put to death. 32 And ye shall take no satisfaction for him that is fled to the city of his refuge, that he should come again to	dwell in the land, until the death of the priest. 33 So ye shall not pollute the land wherein ye are: for blood it defileth the land: and the land cannot be cleansed of the blood that is shed therein, but by the blood of him that shed it. 34 Defile not therefore the land which ye shall inhabit, wherein I dwell: for I the LORD dwell among the children of Israel.	d. No land is to be polluted by murder • Bloodshed—murder—pollutes the land • Atonement can be made only by the blood or execution of the murderer, the one who shed blood e. God demands justice, demands that the land not be defiled: The reason—He lives there, lives among His people

1. Two or more witnesses were required to execute a person. This law was established by God to protect a person from execution based on insufficient evidence. Tragically, down through the centuries, some persons have been condemned and executed on insufficient evidence. Note the Scripture: no person was to be put to death on the testimony of only one witness. At least two witnesses were always necessary.

2. No unequal justice was to be allowed: no ransom was ever to be accepted from a rich murderer (v.31). Justice was to be impartial, showing no favoritism whatsoever to the wealthy. If there were sufficient evidence and the wealthy person was sentenced to death, he was to be executed.

3. Even if a rich person was in a city of refuge and had been temporarily protected, a ransom was not to be accepted from him. No person was ever to be allowed to buy his freedom, not if there was sufficient evidence against him (v.32).

4. No land was to be polluted by murder. Note that bloodshed or murder pollutes the land. Blood pollutes the land because the land belongs to God, and God lives in the land just as His people live in the land. God is holy; therefore He demands that the land be holy. God's very holiness demands that justice be executed against any who commit murder and shed blood. The murderer pollutes the land; consequently, he must be executed. Note that atonement can be made only by the blood or execution of the murderer, the execution of the one who shed blood. Man is made in the image of God; therefore murder is one of the most serious crimes against the sanctity of life (Gen.9:5-6; Ex.21:12-14, 28-32; Dt.19:1-13; 21:1-9).

5. God demands justice, demands that the land not be defiled because He lives in the land, lives among His people (v.34).

Thought 1. God forgives sin. No matter what the sin is—no matter how serious, how unlawful, violent, or abusive—God forgives the sin. But there is a condition for forgiveness: confession and repentance, turning away from the sin and turning to God. A person has to turn his life completely and totally over to God, to live a holy and righteous life. With all his heart, mind, body, and soul, a person must follow God. A person must begin to love and obey God, seeking to be conformed to the very image of Jesus Christ. This is the only way a person can be forgiven: by confessing and repenting, turning his life completely over to the Lord Jesus Christ. This is the great provision of mercy that God has made for murderers and for all other sinners upon this earth: the provision of confession and repentance. Through confession and repentance, we are forgiven our sins.

"And saying, Repent ye: for the kingdom of heaven is at hand" (Mt.3:2).

"I tell you, Nay: but, except ye repent, ye shall all likewise perish" (Lk.13:3).

"Then Peter said unto them, Repent, and be baptized every one of you in the name of Jesus Christ for the remission of sins, and ye shall receive the gift of the Holy Ghost" (Acts 2:38).

"Repent ye therefore, and be converted, that your sins may be blotted out, when the times of refreshing shall come from the presence of the Lord" (Acts 3:19).

"Repent therefore of this thy wickedness, and pray God, if perhaps the thought of thine heart may be forgiven thee" (Acts 8:22).

"If we confess our sins, he is faithful and just to forgive us our sins, and to cleanse us from all unrighteousness" (1 Jn.1:9).

"Now therefore make confession unto the Lord God of your fathers, and do his pleasure: and separate yourselves from the people of the land, and from the strange wives" (Ezra 10:11).

"He that covereth his sins shall not prosper: but whoso confesseth and forsaketh them shall have mercy" (Pr.28:13).

"Let the wicked forsake his way, and the unrighteous man his thoughts: and let him return unto the Lord, and he will have mercy upon him; and to our God, for he will abundantly pardon" (Is.55:7).

"But if the wicked will turn from all his sins that he hath committed, and keep all my statutes, and do that which is lawful and right, he shall surely live, he shall not die" (Ezk.18:21).

"Only acknowledge thine iniquity, that thou hast transgressed against the Lord thy God, and hast scattered thy ways to the strangers under every green tree, and ye have not obeyed my voice, saith the Lord" (Jer.3:13).

TYPES, SYMBOLS, AND PICTURES
(Numbers 35:1-13)

Historical Term	Type or Picture (Scriptural Basis for Each)	Life Application for Today's Believer	Biblical Application
Cities of Refuge Num.35:9-29	*The cities of refuge are a picture of Christ, our refuge from the threats and storms of life.* **"Then ye shall appoint you cities to be cities of refuge for you; that the slayer may flee thither, which killeth any person at unawares" (Num. 35:11).**	The LORD is our Refuge from the threats and storms of life. Scripture declares four wonderful truths about the protection the LORD gives us. 1. The LORD is our Refuge.	***"The eternal God is thy refuge, and underneath are the everlasting arms: and he shall thrust out the enemy from before thee; and shall say, Destroy them" (Dt. 33:27).*** ***The God of my rock; in him will I trust: he is my shield, and the horn of my salvation, my high tower, and my refuge, my saviour; thou savest me from violence" (2 Sam. 22:3).*** ***"The LORD also will be a refuge for the oppressed, a refuge in times of trouble" (Ps.9:9).*** ***"God is our refuge and strength, a very present help in trouble" (Ps.46:1).*** ***"In God is my salvation and my glory: the rock of my strength, and my refuge, is in God" (Ps.62:7).*** ***"Because thou hast made the LORD, which is my refuge, even the most High, thy habitation" Ps.91:9.***
		2. The LORD is our Hiding Place.	***"Thou art my hiding place; thou shalt preserve me from trouble; thou shalt compass me about with songs of deliverance. Selah" (Ps.32:7).*** ***"Thou art my hiding place***

Historical Term	Type or Picture (Scriptural Basis for Each)	Life Application for Today's Believer	Biblical Application
			and my shield: I hope in thy word" (Ps.119:114).
		3. The LORD is our Shield in protecting us.	*"After these things the word of the Lord came unto Abram in a vision, saying, Fear not, Abram: I am thy shield, and thy exceeding great reward" (Gen.15:1).* *"Happy art thou, O Israel: who is like unto thee, O people saved by the Lord, the shield of thy help, and who is the sword of thy excellency! and thine enemies shall be found liars unto thee; and thou shalt tread upon their high places" (Dt. 33:29).* *"The God of my rock; in him will I trust: he is my shield, and the horn of my salvation, my high tower, and my refuge, my saviour; thou savest me from violence" (2 Sam.22:3).* *"Thou hast also given me the shield of thy salvation: and thy gentleness hath made me great" (2 Sam. 22:36).* *"But thou, O Lord, art* a *shield for me; my glory, and the lifter up of mine head" (Ps. 3:3).* *"For thou, Lord, wilt bless the righteous; with favour wilt thou compass him as with a shield" (Ps. 5:12).* *"Thou hast also given me the shield of thy salvation: and thy right hand hath holden me up, and thy gentleness hath made me great" (Ps.18:35).* *"The Lord is my strength and my shield; my heart trusted in him, and I am helped: therefore my heart greatly rejoiceth; and with my song will I praise him" (Ps. 28:7).* *"My goodness, and my fortress; my high tower, and my deliverer; my shield, and he in whom I trust; who subdueth my people under me" (Ps. 144:2).* *"Every word of God is pure: he is a shield unto them that put their trust in him" (Pr.30:5).*
		4. The LORD is our Atoning Sacrifice who delivers us from the avenger of death.	*"For God so loved the world, that he gave his only begotten Son, that whosoever believeth in him should not perish, but have everlasting life" (Jn. 3:16).*

Historical Term	Type or Picture (Scriptural Basis for Each)	Life Application for Today's Believer	Biblical Application
			"And whosoever liveth and believeth in me shall never die. Believest thou this" (Jn.11:26). *"To them who by patient continuance in well doing seek for glory and honour and immortality, eternal life" (Ro.2:7).* *"The last enemy that shall be destroyed is death" (1 Cor. 15:26).*

1. The legal question: What happened to an inheritance if a woman married outside her tribe? (a picture of great humility & faith)
- a. The humble approach to Moses & the leaders
  - 1) Did not complain against the law (27:1-11)
  - 2) Were not anti-feminists: Not against the daughters inheriting their brothers' land
- b. The humble & legitimate question: What happened to the land if a daughter married a man from another tribe
  - 1) The inherited land would go with the daughters
  - 2) The total area of tribal land would decrease
  - 3) The Year of Jubilee would cause the land to be permanently added to the other tribe—lost forever to the ancestral tribe
- c. The great faith in the promised land: Believed—but had not yet entered the land

2. The legal solution: Marrying within one's tribe (a picture of marrying a person with common interests & true faith in the promised land)
- a. The law was expanded
  - 1) The women could marry any man they desired, but the men had to be from their own tribal clan (of common interests & faith)
  - 2) The promised land—the land of inheritance—was not to pass from tribe to tribe
  - 3) The land of every person must be kept in the tribe that inherited the land
- b. The law was set as a precedent
  - The law applied to all women inheriting land
  - Each family was to retain its inheritance in the promised land
  - Each tribe was to preserve the land it inherited

3. The faith of the five daughters (a picture of obedience) (Num.27:1-11)
- a. They married their distant cousins: Men of common interests & true spiritual commitment
- b. They kept their inheritance in the promised land in their father's clan & tribe: A picture of protecting one's inheritance in the promised land by obeying God

4. The commands of God
- a. Given to the people thru Moses the mediator (a symbol of Christ the perfect Mediator)
- b. Given to guide the believer's march to the promised land

K. The Women Who Inherited Property: A Picture of Strong Faith in the Promised Land of God, 36:1-13

And the chief fathers of the families of the children of Gilead, the son of Machir, the son of Manasseh, of the families of the sons of Joseph, came near, and spake before Moses, and before the princes, the chief fathers of the children of Israel:

2 And they said, The LORD commanded my lord to give the land for an inheritance by lot to the children of Israel: and my lord was commanded by the LORD to give the inheritance of Zelophehad our brother unto his daughters.

3 And if they be married to any of the sons of the other tribes of the children of Israel, then shall their inheritance be taken from the inheritance of our fathers, and shall be put to the inheritance of the tribe whereunto they are received: so shall it be taken from the lot of our inheritance.

4 And when the jubile of the children of Israel shall be, then shall their inheritance be put unto the inheritance of the tribe whereunto they are received: so shall their inheritance be taken away from the inheritance of the tribe of our fathers.

5 And Moses commanded the children of Israel according to the word of the LORD, saying, The tribe of the sons of Joseph hath said well.

6 This is the thing which the LORD doth command concerning the daughters of Zelophehad, saying, Let them marry to whom they think best; only to the family of the tribe of their father shall they marry.

7 So shall not the inheritance of the children of Israel remove from tribe to tribe: for every one of the children of Israel shall keep himself to the inheritance of the tribe of his fathers.

8 And every daughter, that possesseth an inheritance in any tribe of the children of Israel, shall be wife unto one of the family of the tribe of her father, that the children of Israel may enjoy every man the inheritance of his fathers.

9 Neither shall the inheritance remove from one tribe to another tribe; but every one of the tribes of the children of Israel shall keep himself to his own inheritance.

10 Even as the LORD commanded Moses, so did the daughters of Zelophehad:

11 For Mahlah, Tirzah, and Hoglah, and Milcah, and Noah, the daughters of Zelophehad, were married unto their father's brothers' sons:

12 And they were married into the families of the sons of Manasseh the son of Joseph, and their inheritance remained in the tribe of the family of their father.

13 These are the commandments and the judgments, which the LORD commanded by the hand of Moses unto the children of Israel in the plains of Moab by Jordan near Jericho.

DIVISION IV

THE PREPARATION FOR THE MARCH INTO THE PROMISED LAND, 26:1-36:13

K. The Women Who Inherited Property: A Picture of Strong Faith in the Promised Land of God Heaven, 36:1-13

(36:1-13) **Introduction—Society, Foundation of—Law, Basis of Society**: legal matters or laws govern everything about us. Buying and selling, driving and walking, food and drink, words and behavior—there are laws to govern practically every act and everything that concerns human life. The laws and regulations that govern society, the way we relate to one another, are important. Without the law, society would disintegrate and every person would go his or her own way. Lawlessness and violence would reign supreme. There would be no respect of property and very little if any reverence for life. Utter chaos would be the way of life. The laws or regulations to control human behavior are absolute essentials for society to exist.

The present Scripture concerns the expansion of a particular law that had just recently been established in the law books of Israel. The problem that arose and the legal solution to the problem are the topics of discussion in this passage. It is a passage that focuses upon the inheritance of women in the promised land, a passage that speaks against anti-feminism and against being anti-any person. This is a passage that is desperately needed by society today: *The Women Who Inherited Property: A Picture of Strong Faith in the Promised Land of God,* 36:1-13.

1. The legal question: What happened to an inheritance if a woman married outside her tribe? (a picture of great humility and faith) (v.1-4).
2. The legal solution: marrying within one's tribe (a picture of marrying a person with common interests and true faith in the promised land) (v. 5-9).
3. The faith of the five daughters (a picture of obedience) (Num.27:1-11), (v.10-12).
4. The commands of God (v.13).

1 (36:1-4) **Humility, Example of—Faith, Example of—Law, Governing Women's Inheritance—Land, the Promised, Law Governing—Inheritance, of Women, Law Governing**: there was the legal question: What happened to an inheritance if a woman married outside her tribe? This event is a picture of great humility and faith. Remember, a law had already been established that allowed women to inherit their father's land if he had no sons (see outline and notes—Num.27:1-11 for more discussion). But there was another problem that arose: if the daughter married outside her family line, the property would pass to her husband's side of the family. This meant that all property like it would be split up all across the nation, that there would be an unequal ownership of the property among the tribal families. God's plan for each tribe to inherit a just and fair amount of land would be upset. The Scripture and outline clearly explain the problem:

OUTLINE	SCRIPTURE	SCRIPTURE	OUTLINE
1. The legal question: What happened to an inheritance if a woman married outside her tribe? (a picture of great humility & faith) a. The humble approach to Moses & the leaders 1) Did not complain against the law (27:1-11) 2) Were not anti-feminists: Not against the daughters inheriting their brothers' land b. The humble & legitimate	And the chief fathers of the families of the children of Gilead, the son of Machir, the son of Manasseh, of the families of the sons of Joseph, came near, and spake before Moses, and before the princes, the chief fathers of the children of Israel: 2 And they said, The LORD commanded my lord to give the land for an inheritance by lot to the children of Israel: and my lord was commanded by the LORD to give the inheritance of Zelophehad our brother unto his daughters. 3 And if they be married to	any of the sons of the other tribes of the children of Israel, then shall their inheritance be taken from the inheritance of our fathers, and shall be put to the inheritance of the tribe whereunto they are received: so shall it be taken from the lot of our inheritance. 4 And when the jubile of the children of Israel shall be, then shall their inheritance be put unto the inheritance of the tribe whereunto they are received: so shall their inheritance be taken away from the inheritance of the tribe of our fathers.	question: What happened to the land if a daughter married a man from another tribe 1) The inherited land would go with the daughters 2) The total area of tribal land would decrease 3) The Year of Jubilee would cause the land to be permanently added to the other tribe—lost forever to the ancestral tribe c. The great faith in the promised land: Believed—but had not yet entered the land

1. Note the humble approach to Moses and the leaders of the nation (v.1-2). Some leaders from the clan of Gilead foresaw the problem created by the newly established law. They did not react by complaining against the law—grumbling and murmuring that it was unfair and unjust. Neither were they anti-feminists, against daughters inheriting their brothers' land. On the contrary, they were humble and considerate, men of great faith in the promised land. This was clearly seen by their humble approach to Moses and the leaders, the supreme court of the nation.

2. Note the humble and legitimate question they asked: What happened to the land if a daughter married a man from another tribe (v.3-4)? They pointed out that the inherited land would go with the daughters, and that the total area of their tribal land would decrease. In the Year of Jubilee, the land would be permanently added to the other tribe, lost forever to the ancestral or family tribe. This was a legitimate problem brought to the attention of the supreme court in a most humble way. But humility is not the only lesson of importance.

3. Note the faith of the family heads of Gilead: they had strong faith in the promised land. They had not yet entered into the promised land, yet they believed this problem would arise. They were going to have to deal with the problem. They believed they were going to enter the promised land and be facing this problem. They had great faith in the promise of God, that they were going to inherit the promised land of God.

Thought 1. There are several lessons in this point for us.

1) Equality before God is a right that is to be given to every human being. These men were not anti-feminists; neither are we to be. Scripture declares that we are not to be anti-*any person*. Every person upon this earth is created equal before God. Of course, there are differences between us. For example, some are short, others are tall; some are good looking, others are not so good looking; some are very intelligent, others are not so intelligent; some are handicapped, others are not. Women are able to bear children, and men are not. Some are born with the genes and brain cells that allow them to progress and achieve far beyond what the rest of us are able to accomplish. Some are driven to work far harder than others; therefore they achieve and secure far more. These persons usually hold positions of wealth and leadership in our communities and nation, just as these leaders from Gilead did and the leaders who sat upon the supreme court of Israel. But Scripture declares this one strong fact: the same spirit of humility and faith that was in the leaders of Gilead is to be within our hearts. There is to be no inequali-

ty, no anti-feminism nor anti-any person. There are to be equal opportunities and equal rights for every human being.

"There is neither Jew nor Greek, there is neither bond nor free, there is neither male nor female: for ye are all one in Christ Jesus" (Gal.3:28).

"But be not ye called Rabbi: for one is your Master, even Christ; and all ye are brethren" (Mt.23:8).

"And he said unto them, Ye know how that it is an unlawful thing for a man that is a Jew to keep company, or come unto one of another nation; but God hath showed me that I should not call any man common or unclean" (Acts 10:28).

"Then Peter opened his mouth, and said, Of a truth I perceive that God is no respecter of persons: But in every nation he that feareth him, and worketh righteousness, is accepted with him" (Acts 10:34-35).

"For there is no difference between the Jew and the Greek: for the same Lord over all is rich unto all that call upon him" (Ro.10:12).

"I charge thee before God, and the Lord Jesus Christ, and the elect angels, that thou observe these things without preferring one before another, doing nothing by partiality" (1 Tim.5:21).

"My brethren, have not the faith of our Lord Jesus Christ, the Lord of glory, with respect of persons. For if there come unto your assembly a man with a gold ring, in goodly apparel, and there come in also a poor man in vile raiment; And ye have respect to him that weareth the gay clothing, and say unto him, Sit thou here in a good place; and say to the poor, Stand thou there, or sit here under my footstool: Are ye not then partial in yourselves, and are become judges of evil thoughts? Hearken, my beloved brethren, Hath not God chosen the poor of this world rich in faith, and heirs of the kingdom which he hath promised to them that love him" (Jas.2:1-5).

"Ye shall do no unrighteousness in judgment: thou shalt not respect the person of the poor, nor honour the person of the mighty: but in righteousness shalt thou judge thy neighbour" (Lev.19:15).

"He will surely reprove you, if ye do secretly accept persons" (Job 13:10).

"The rich and poor meet together: the Lord is the maker of them all" (Pr.22:2).

2) Humility is the demand of God. We are to walk humbly before one another, demonstrating humility in dealing with one another.

"Whosoever therefore shall humble himself as this little child, the same is greatest in the kingdom of heaven" (Mt.18:4).

"But when thou art bidden, go and sit down in the lowest room; that when he that bade thee cometh, he may say unto thee, Friend, go up higher: then shalt thou have worship in the presence of them that sit at meat with thee" (Lk.14:10).

"But ye shall not be so: but he that is greatest among you, let him be as the younger; and he that is chief, as he that doth serve" (Lk.22:26).

"For I say, through the grace given unto me, to every man that is among you, not to think of himself more highly than he ought to think; but to think soberly, according as God hath dealt to every man the measure of faith" (Ro.12:3).

"Humble yourselves in the sight of the Lord, and he shall lift you up" (Jas.4:10).

"Likewise, ye younger, submit yourselves unto the elder. Yea, all of you be subject one to another, and be clothed with humility: for God resisteth the proud, and giveth grace to the humble. Humble yourselves therefore under the mighty hand of God, that he may exalt you in due time" (1 Pt.5:5-6).

"Better it is to be of an humble spirit with the lowly, than to divide the spoil with the proud" (Pr.16:19).

"By humility and the fear of the Lord are riches, and honour, and life" (Pr.22:4).

"A man's pride shall bring him low: but honour shall uphold the humble in spirit" (Pr.29:23).

"For thus saith the high and lofty One that inhabiteth eternity, whose name is Holy; I dwell in the high and holy place, with him also that is of a contrite and humble spirit, to revive the spirit of the humble, and to revive the heart of the contrite ones" (Is.57:15).

"He hath showed thee, O man, what is good; and what doth the Lord require of thee, but to do justly, and to love mercy, and to walk humbly with thy God" (Micah 6:8).

3) There is only one way to enter the promised land of heaven: a person must believe in God and His promises. The men from Gilead believed in God and in the inheritance of the promised land of God. They were just as we are, standing there not yet having entered the promised land. Yet they believed and trusted the promise of God. So it is to be with us: we must believe God and His promises, believe in the promised land of heaven. Faith in God and in His promises is an absolute essential. This is the clear declaration of Scripture:

"For God so loved the world, that he gave his only begotten Son, that whosoever believeth in him should not perish, but have everlasting life" (Jn.3:16).

"Verily, verily, I say unto you, He that heareth my word, and believeth on him that sent me, hath everlasting life, and shall not come into condemnation; but is passed from death unto life" (Jn.5:24).

"Then said they unto him, What shall we do, that we might work the works of God? Jesus answered and said unto them, This is the work of God, that ye believe on him whom he hath sent" (Jn.6:28-29).

"Jesus said unto her, I am the resurrection, and the life: he that believeth in me, though he were dead, yet shall he live" (Jn.11:25).

"But these are written, that ye might believe that Jesus is the Christ, the Son of God; and that believing ye might have life through his name" (Jn.20:31).

"But without faith it is impossible to please him: for he that cometh to God must believe that he is, and that he is a rewarder of them that diligently seek him" (Heb.11:6).

"By faith Noah, being warned of God of things not seen as yet, moved with fear, prepared an ark to the saving of his house; by the which he condemned the world, and became heir of the righteousness which is by faith. By faith Abraham, when he was called to go out into a place which he should after receive for an inheritance, obeyed; and he went out, not knowing whither he went. By faith he sojourned in the land of promise, as in a strange country, dwelling in tabernacles with Isaac and Jacob, the heirs with him of the same promise: For he looked for a city which hath foundations, whose builder and maker is God" (Heb.11:7-10).

"These all died in faith, not having received the promises, but having seen them afar off, and were persuaded of them, and embraced them, and confessed that they were strangers and pilgrims on the earth. For they that say such things declare plainly that they seek a country. And truly, if they had been mindful of that country from whence they came out, they might have had opportunity to have returned. But now they desire a better country, that is, an heavenly: wherefore God is not ashamed to be called their God: for he hath prepared for them a city" (Heb.11:13-16).

"And this is his commandment, That we should believe on the name of his Son Jesus Christ, and love one another, as he gave us commandment" (1 Jn.3:23).

"And they rose early in the morning, and went forth into the wilderness of Tekoa: and as they went forth, Jehoshaphat stood and said, Hear me, O Judah, and ye inhabitants of Jerusalem; Believe in the Lord your God, so shall ye be established; believe his prophets, so shall ye prosper" (2 Chron. 20:20).

2 (36:5-9) **Marriage, Duties of—Inheritance, Laws Governing—Laws, of Inheritance—Women, Inheritance of**: there was the legal solution governing the inheritance of women. This is a picture of marrying a person with common interests and true faith in the promised land. The legal solution to this problem is clearly spelled out by the Scripture and outline:

OUTLINE	SCRIPTURE	SCRIPTURE	OUTLINE
2. The legal solution: Marrying within one's tribe (a picture of marrying a person with common interests & true faith in the promised land) a. The law was expanded 1) The women could marry any man they desired, but the men had to be from their own tribal clan (of common interests & faith) 2) The promised land—the land of inheritance—was not to pass from tribe to tribe 3) The land of every person	5 And Moses commanded the children of Israel according to the word of the LORD, saying, The tribe of the sons of Joseph hath said well. 6 This is the thing which the LORD doth command concerning the daughters of Zelophehad, saying, Let them marry to whom they think best; only to the family of the tribe of their father shall they marry. 7 So shall not the inheritance of the children of Israel remove from tribe to tribe: for every one of the children of Israel shall keep himself to	the inheritance of the tribe of his fathers. 8 And every daughter, that possesseth an inheritance in any tribe of the children of Israel, shall be wife unto one of the family of the tribe of her father, that the children of Israel may enjoy every man the inheritance of his fathers. 9 Neither shall the inheritance remove from one tribe to another tribe; but every one of the tribes of the children of Israel shall keep himself to his own inheritance.	must be kept in the tribe that inherited the land b. The law was set as a precedent • The law applied to all women inheriting land • Each family was to retain its inheritance in the promised land • Each tribe was to preserve the land it inherited

1. The law was expanded by the Lord and related to the people by Moses (v.5-7). The woman could marry any man she desired, but the man had to be from her own tribal or family clan. Note how this is a picture of a young couple considering common interest in faith before marrying. The promised land—the land of inheritance—was not to pass from tribe to tribe. The land of every person was to be kept within the tribe that inherited the land.

2. The law was established as a precedent (v.8-9). The law applied to all women inheriting land. Each family was to retain its inheritance in the promised land, and each tribe was to preserve the land it inherited. Just as a man was to cleave to his wife, so a person was to cleave to the land he or she inherited (Gen.2:24).[1]

Thought 1. Marriage was not to jeopardize the inheritance of a person nor take the inheritance away from the family or out of the tribe. Again, if a woman wished to marry out of her tribe, she could. But she was not able to transfer the property of her inheritance over to the family of her husband.

This is a strong lesson for marriage, a strong lesson for young couples who are considering marriage. A person should never marry anyone who does not believe in the inheritance of God, in the promised land of heaven. But something else is just as important: common interests, purpose, culture, emotional compatibility. All these factors must be considered in order to have a loving and successful marriage. Husband and wife have to be fitted for one another in all these ways in order to adjust and experience the fullness of life together.

1 *The Expositor's Bible Commentary*. Frank E. Gaebelein, Editor, p. 1007.

Consider this fact: many, many people make a mistake in marrying. A large percentage of marriages end in divorce. But this is not all: a great number of spouses stay together who are not happy. Combine the divorces and the unhappy spouses who remain together and only one conclusion can be reached: the vast majority of marriages are unhappy. Believers must always do what this law pictures: marry within the tribe or family of faith. Both spouses must believe in God and His promises, believe in the promised land of heaven. Two persons cannot walk through life divided, one marching to the promised land of heaven and the other marching to a life of separation from God. Both must have their eyes and lives focused upon the inheritance of God, upon His great gift of the promised land of heaven. A divided family equals unhappiness. Division causes discord—trouble, dissension, arguments, conflict, hurt, pain, and regret. Far better to solve this issue while dating than after marriage. This is the important lesson of this point: a person must marry someone with common interests and a true faith in God and the promised land of heaven.

"But seek ye first the kingdom of God, and his righteousness; and all these things shall be added unto you" (Mt.6:33).

"But now I have written unto you not to keep company, if any man that is called a brother be a fornicator, or covetous, or an idolater, or a railer, or a drunkard, or an extortioner; with such an one no not to eat" (1 Cor.5:11).

"Be ye not unequally yoked together with unbelievers: for what fellowship hath righteousness with unrighteousness? and what communion hath light with darkness" (2 Cor.6:14).

"Wherefore come out from among them, and be ye separate, saith the Lord, and touch not the unclean thing; and I will receive you, And will be a Father unto you, and ye shall be my sons and daughters, saith the Lord Almighty" (2 Cor.6:17-18).

"Wives, submit yourselves unto your own husbands, as unto the Lord" (Eph.5:22).

"Husbands, love your wives, even as Christ also loved the church, and gave himself for it" (Eph.5:25).

"I will therefore that the younger women marry, bear children, guide the house, give none occasion to the adversary to speak reproachfully" (1 Tim.5:14).

"Therefore shall a man leave his father and his mother, and shall cleave unto his wife: and they shall be one flesh" (Gen.2:24).

"I am a companion of all them that fear thee, and of them that keep thy precepts" (Ps.119:63).

"That thou mayest walk in the way of good men, and keep the paths of the righteous" (Pr.2:20).

"He that walketh with wise men shall be wise: but a companion of fools shall be destroyed" (Pr.13:20).

3 (36:10-12) **Obedience—Inheritance, Spiritual—Land, the Promised, Protecting One's Inheritance**: there was the obedience of the five daughters of faith. These were the daughters of Zelophehad who had died without sons. Because of this problem, these five daughters had become concerned about their father's inheritance in the promised land. It was their problem that had led to the original law, the law that granted the inheritance of land to daughters who had no brothers. The point to note is the strong faith of these daughters, all five of them. They believed in the promised land, so much so that they were going to obey the new law that had just been established. No matter the cost, they were going to cling to the inheritance promised by God. The Scripture and outline clearly show this:

OUTLINE	SCRIPTURE
3. The faith of the five daughters (a picture of obedience) (Num.27:1-11)	10 Even as the LORD commanded Moses, so did the daughters of Zelophehad:
a. They married their distant cousins: Men of common interests & true spiritual commitment	11 For Mahlah, Tirzah, and Hoglah, and Milcah, and Noah, the daughters of Zelophehad, were married unto their father's brothers' sons:
b. They kept their inheritance in the promised land in their father's clan & tribe: A picture of protecting one's inheritance in the promised land by obeying God	12 And they were married into the families of the sons of Manasseh the son of Joseph, and their inheritance remained in the tribe of the family of their father.

1. The five daughters of faith married within their tribal families, married distant cousins. They married men of common family or tribal interests and men of true spiritual faith and commitment (v.11).
2. These five daughters kept their inheritance in the promised land, kept it in their father's clan and family tribe.

Thought 1. This is a clear picture of a person protecting his inheritance in the promised land by obeying God. Obedience is absolutely necessary in order to receive one's inheritance. This fact cannot be stressed enough in modern society, a society of 'cheap faith.' The meaning of faith is not really understood by many people today; faith is often distorted, twisted, and watered down. It is thought to mean mental *ascent,* simply believing that something is true, that it is historically true. It is thought that faith does not necessarily have a bearing upon a person's behavior, that it makes no difference how a person lives just so he believes. Of course, this is absurd. This is nothing more than the "*emptying*" of faith, taking faith and *emptying* it of all meaning. It is profession *only*, a false profession. It is, quite frankly, only empty, meaningless words. A person who truly believes, obeys. To believe is to obey and to obey is to believe. If a person genuinely believes something, he will act upon it. He will do exactly what his faith says. Obedience is the great lesson taught us by these five women of faith. If we believe in the promised land of heaven, then we will obey God and follow after Him. We will seek after—actively pursue—the righteousness of heaven. We will do all we can to enter the promised land of heaven. We will actively obey God so that He will accept us in that glorious day.

"Not every one that saith unto me, Lord, Lord, shall enter into the kingdom of heaven; but he that doeth the will of my Father which is in heaven" (Mt.7:21).

"Give not that which is holy [faith] unto the dogs, neither cast ye your pearls [faith, belief] before swine, lest they trample them under their feet, and turn again and rend you" (Mk.7:6).

"They profess that they know God; but in works they deny him, being abominable, and disobedient, and unto every good work reprobate" (Tit.1:16).

"Blessed are they that do his commandments, that they may have right to the tree of life, and may enter in through the gates into the city" (Rev.22:14).

"He that hath my commandments, and keepeth them, he it is that loveth me: and he that loveth me shall be loved of my Father, and I will love him, and will manifest myself to him" (Jn.14:21).

"Jesus answered and said unto him, If a man love me, he will keep my words: and my Father will love him, and we will come unto him, and make our abode with him" (Jn.14:23).

"If ye keep my commandments, ye shall abide in my love; even as I have kept my Father's commandments, and abide in his love" (Jn.15:10).

"This day the Lord thy God hath commanded thee to do these statutes and judgments: thou shalt therefore keep and do them with all thine heart, and with all thy soul" (Dt.26:16).

"This book of the law shall not depart out of thy mouth; but thou shalt meditate therein day and night, that thou mayest observe to do according to all that is written therein: for then thou shalt make thy way prosperous, and then thou shalt have good success" (Josh.1:8).

4 (36:13) **Numbers, Conclusion of—Commandments, of God, Purpose for—Pilgrimage, of the Believer—March, of the Believer—Believers, Pilgrimage of—Believers, March of**: there were the commands and regulations of God. This is the conclusion to the great book of Numbers. Remember, the Israelites were camped in the plains of Moab beside the Jordan River, right across from the great city of Jericho. They were poised to "cross over" the Jordan and enter the promised land to claim their inheritance. But keep this fact in mind: this was the second generation of believers, the sons and daughters of the generation that had marched out of Egypt. The march or pilgrimage of the first generation was a miserable failure. Unbelief and rebellion, grumbling and murmuring against God and His dear servant Moses—all the terrible sins that can be imagined—had been the traits, characteristics, and character flaws of the first generation. They had forced the hand of God, forced Him to chastise them. Consequently, they had been condemned to die in the desert wilderness. They were barred, never allowed to enter the promised land of God. The wilderness wanderings—the forty years of wandering about in the desert wilderness—were now over. The new generation of believers now stood poised to "cross over" the Jordan River and claim the inheritance promised by God, to lay hold of the promised land. The tragic pilgrimage of the first generation of believers and the raising up of the second generation of believers has been the story of the great book of Numbers. The first generation has passed from the scene, having been doomed to die in the desert wilderness of this world; now the second generation stands poised to "cross over" the Jordan to claim its inheritance in the promised land of God. Laying hold of the promise of God by this new generation of believers will be the story of the great book of Joshua.

In closing the great book of Numbers, Scripture declares two significant facts:

OUTLINE	SCRIPTURE
4. The commands of God a. Given to the people thru Moses the mediator (a symbol of Christ the perfect Mediator) b. Given to guide the believer's march to the promised land	13 These are the commandments and the judgments, which the LORD commanded by the hand of Moses unto the children of Israel in the plains of Moab by Jordan near Jericho.

1. First, the commandments and regulations of God have been given to the people through Moses, the mediator between God and man.

2. Second, the commandments and regulations of God have been given to guide the believer's march or pilgrimage to the promised land.

Thought 1. Two significant lessons are seen in this point.

1) As mediator, Moses was appointed by God to be a type of Christ. Jesus Christ is the Perfect Mediator who stands between God and man. He is the Perfect Intercessor, the Advocate who stands and pleads our case before God. Jesus Christ is the only Mediator who bridges the great gulf between God and man. No person can approach God apart from Christ and be accepted. God accepts only those who come to Him through His dear Son, the Lord Jesus Christ. Christ and Christ alone is the Mediator who can reconcile people to God.

"Jesus saith unto him, I am the way, the truth, and the life: no man cometh unto the Father, but by me" (Jn.14:6).

"Neither is there salvation in any other: for there is none other name under heaven given among men, whereby we must be saved" (Acts 4:12).

"Who is he that condemneth? It is Christ that died, yea rather, that is risen again, who is even at the right hand of God, who also maketh intercession for us" (Ro.8:34).

"For there is one God, and one mediator between God and men, the man Christ Jesus; Who gave himself a ransom for all, to be testified in due time" (1 Tim.2:5-6).

"Wherefore in all things it behoved him to be made like unto his brethren, that he might be a merciful and faithful high priest in things pertaining to God, to make reconciliation for the sins of the people" (Heb.2:17).

"Seeing then that we have a great high priest, that is passed into the heavens, Jesus the Son of God, let us hold fast our profession. For we have not an high priest which cannot be touched with the feeling of our infirmities; but was in all points tempted like as we are, yet without sin" (Heb.4:14-15).

"For every high priest taken from among men is ordained for men in things pertaining to God, that he may offer both gifts and sacrifices for sins: Who can have compassion on the ignorant, and on them that are out of the way; for that he himself also is compassed with infirmity. And by reason hereof he ought, as for the people, so also for himself, to offer for sins. And no man taketh this honour unto himself, but he that is called of God, as was Aaron. So also Christ glorified not himself to be made an high priest; but he that said unto him, Thou art my Son, to day have I begotten thee" (Heb.5:1-5).

"Which hope we have as an anchor of the soul, both sure and stedfast, and which entereth into that within the veil; Whither the forerunner is for us entered, even Jesus, made an high priest for ever after the order of Melchisedec" (Heb.6:19-20).

"Wherefore he is able also to save them to the uttermost that come unto God by him, seeing he ever liveth to make intercession for them. For such an high priest became us, who is holy, harmless, undefiled, separate from sinners, and made higher than the heavens; Who needeth not daily, as those high priests, to offer up sacrifice, first for his own sins, and then for the people's: for this he did once, when he offered up himself" (Heb.7:25-27).

"But now hath he obtained a more excellent ministry, by how much also he is the mediator of a better covenant, which was established upon better promises" (Heb.8:6).

"And for this cause he is the mediator of the new testament, that by means of death, for the redemption of the transgressions that were under the first testament, they which are called might receive the promise of eternal inheritance" (Heb.9:15).

"For Christ is not entered into the holy places made with hands, which are the figures of the true; but into heaven itself, now to appear in the presence of God for us: Nor yet that he should offer himself often, as the high priest entereth into the holy place every year with blood of others; For then must he often have suffered since the foundation of the world: but now once in the end of the world hath he appeared to put away sin by the sacrifice of himself. And as it is appointed unto men once to die, but after this the judgment: So Christ was once offered to bear the sins of many; and unto them that look for him shall he appear the second time without sin unto salvation" (Heb.9:24-28).

"My little children, these things write I unto you, that ye sin not. And if any man sin, we have an advocate with the Father, Jesus Christ the righteous: And he is the propitiation for our sins: and not for ours only, but also for the sins of the whole world" (1 Jn.2:1-2).

2) The Word of God—His commandments and regulations—guide the believer's pilgrimage as he marches to the promised land of heaven. There are pitfalls and enemies that stand opposed to the promised land of God. As we march throughout life, we need to know how to bypass the pitfalls and how to conquer the enemies who oppose us. There are pitfalls and enemies such as…

- disease
- accident
- financial difficulty
- unemployment
- immorality
- greed
- covetousness
- anger
- discouragement
- emptiness
- loneliness
- failure
- depression
- death
- lack of fulfillment
- lack of purpose

The pitfalls and enemies of life are innumerable. Any one of them can attack us at any time. This is the reason we need the Word of God to guide us.

As we march to the promised land of God, the only way to finish our pilgrimage is to listen to God. We must study, learn, and teach the commandments and regulations of God. We must live in His Word and obey His Word. Above all the lessons in the great book of Numbers, this is the one lesson that has been demonstrated before our very eyes, the one lesson that we ourselves must learn: we must obey God's Holy Word. This is the declaration of this last concluding verse of Numbers: these are the commandments and regulations given by God to His people as they were poised to "cross over" into the promised land. These are the commandments, the Word of God given to guide the believer's pilgrimage or march to the promised land of heaven.

"Now ye are clean through the word which I have spoken unto you" (Jn.15:3).

"Sanctify them through thy truth: thy word is truth" (Jn.17:17).

"But these are written, that ye might believe that Jesus is the Christ, the Son of God; and that believing ye might have life through his name" (Jn.20:31).

"That he might sanctify and cleanse it [the church] with the washing of water by the word" (Eph.5:26).

"Let the word of Christ dwell in you richly in all wisdom; teaching and admonishing one another in psalms and hymns and spiritual songs, singing with grace in your hearts to the Lord" (Col.3:16).

"Study to show thyself approved unto God, a workman that needeth not to be ashamed, rightly dividing the word of truth" (2 Tim.2:15).

"All scripture is given by inspiration of God, and is profitable for doctrine, for reproof, for correction, for instruction in righteousness" (2 Tim.3:16).

"For the word of God is quick, and powerful, and sharper than any twoedged sword, piercing even to the dividing asunder of soul and spirit, and of the joints and marrow, and is a discerner of the thoughts and intents of the heart" (Heb.4:12).

"These things have I written unto you that believe on the name of the Son of God; that ye may know that ye have eternal life, and that ye may believe on the name of the Son of God" (1 Jn.5:13).

"Wherewithal shall a young man cleanse his way? by taking heed thereto according to thy word" (Ps.119:9).

"Thy word have I hid in mine heart, that I might not sin against thee" (Ps.119:11).

"Thy word is a lamp unto my feet, and a light unto my path" (Ps.119:105).

"The entrance of thy words giveth light; it giveth understanding unto the simple" (Ps.119:130).

Thought 2. The great book of Numbers has been written to teach us, so that we might grow in endurance, encouragement, and hope. But this is not the only purpose for the great book of Numbers: it was also written to serve as a warning. The tragic failure of the first generation of believers stands as an example, as a strong warning to us upon whom the end of the world and the fulfillment of the ages has come.

"For whatsoever things were written aforetime were written for our learning, that we through patience and comfort of the scriptures might have hope" (Ro.15:4).

"Now all these things happened unto them for ensamples: and they are written for our admonition, upon whom the ends of the world are come" (1 Cor.10:11).

TYPES, SYMBOLS, AND PICTURES (Numbers 36:1-13)

Historical Term	Type or Picture (Scriptural Basis for Each)	Life Application for Today's Believer	Biblical Application
Moses Num.36:13 (See also Lev. 1:1; 8:1-5)	*A clear type of Jesus Christ, the appointed Mediator, who stood between man and God. As the mediator, he revealed and declared the way to God.* **"These *are* the commandments and the judgments, which the LORD commanded by the hand of Moses unto the children of Israel in the plains of Moab by Jordan *near* Jericho" (Num. 36:13).**	⇒ It is Jesus Christ who is the appointed Mediator. It is Christ, and Christ alone... • who stands in the gap between God and man. Through believing on Jesus Christ (the Mediator) a person believes on God. Through seeing Jesus Christ (the Mediator) a person sees God. • who proclaims the way to God • who opens the way into God's presence	***"For there is one God, and one mediator between God and men, the man Christ Jesus" (1 Tim.2:5).*** ***"God, who at sundry times and in divers manners spake in time past unto the fathers by the prophets, Hath in these last days spoken unto us by his Son, whom he hath appointed heir of all things, by whom also he made the worlds; Who being the brightness of his glory, and the express image of his person, and upholding all things by the word of his power, when he had by himself purged our sins, sat down on the right hand of the Majesty on high" (Heb.1:1-3).*** ***"My little children, these things write I unto you, that ye sin not. And if any man sin, we have an advocate with the Father, Jesus Christ the righteous" (1 Jn.2:1; cp. Jn 14:6).***

THE
OUTLINE & SUBJECT INDEX

REMEMBER: When you look up a subject and turn to the Scripture reference, you have not only the Scripture, you have an outline and a discussion (commentary) of the Scripture and subject.

This is one of the GREAT VALUES of *The Preacher's Outline & Sermon Bible®*. Once you have all the volumes, you will have not only what all other Bible indexes give you, that is, a list of all the subjects and their Scripture references, BUT you will also have...

An outline of every Scripture and subject in the Bible.
A discussion (commentary) on every Scripture and subject.
Every subject supported by other Scriptures or cross references.

DISCOVER THE GREAT VALUE for yourself. Quickly glance below to the very first subject of the Index of Numbers. It is:

AARON
Benediction of. 6:22-27

Turn to the reference. Glance at the Scripture and outline of the Scripture, then read the commentary. You will immediately see the GREAT VALUE of the INDEX of *The Preacher's Outline & Sermon Bible®*.

OUTLINE AND SUBJECT INDEX

INDEX

Of having courage & security throughout life. 23:27-23:13, Thgt.1
Of having deliverance through all the trials & temptations of life. 23:27-23:13, Thgt.1
Of having outstanding leaders & strong church fellowships. 23:27-23:13, Thgt.1
Of having strength, both physical & spiritual. 23:27-23:13, Thgt.1
Of having victory over all the pitfalls of life. 23:27-23:13, Thgt.1
Discussed.
God provides all the necessities of life for His people. 6:22-27
Of God's people. 23:1-12; 23:27-24:13
The blessings of God & a glimpse into the future. 23:1-24:25
The promise of God's **b**. 6:22-27
Kinds of. Of God: Blessing, protection, grace, acceptance, peace. 6:22-27
List of Scriptures. Of blessing. 6:22-27
Results of. The **b**. identified the Israelites as God's people, as belonging to Him. 6:22-27; esp. v.27
Source. God. 6:22-27; 23:13-26

BLOOD
Typed - Pictured - Symbolized. By the Drink Offering: A symbol of the blood of Christ that is pictured in the LORD's Supper. 28:3-8

BONDAGE
Deliverance from. By God. God gives victory over the world with all its enslavements & bondages. 24:20, Thgt.1

BOOK OF LIFE
Fact. God keeps a register in which the name of every true believer is written. 1:17-46, Thgt.1

BOOK OF THE WARS OF THE LORD
Contents of. 21:10-20, esp. v.14

BREAD, HOLY (See **SHOWBREAD**)

BREAD OF THE PRESENCE (See **SHOWBREAD**)

BRONZE SNAKE
Discussed. Purpose of. 21:4-9
Type - Symbol of.
Christ the Savior. 21:4-9
Unbelief. 21:4-9

BUKKI
Appointed by Moses as a supervisor of the promised land. 34:16-29
Led the tribe of Dan into the promised land. 34:16-29

BULL
Sacrifice of. As a sacrifice in the burnt offering. 28:11-15; 28:16-25

BURNT OFFERING
Discussed. The worship required after the fulfillment of the Nazarite vow. 6:13-20
Facts.
Was the basic offering to be presented by the people. 28:3-8
Was to be offered in the morning & again in the evening. 28:3-8, esp. v. 4
Meaning of. 28:3-8
Purpose.
Was part of the Levites' ceremonial, spiritual cleansing. 9:5-26
Was when a person wanted to seek atonement or reconciliation with God. 15:1-16
Results of.
Atonement, reconciliation with God. 6:13-20, esp. v.14
Cleansing. 6:3-12, esp. v.11
Type - Symbol of. Christ's sacrifice (His death) which secured atonement or reconciliation for us. 6:3-12, esp. v.11; 15:1-16; 28:3-8; 28:11-15, Thgt.1; 29:12-38

CALEB
Appointed by Moses as a supervisor of the promised land. 34:16-29
Report of. 13:26-33
Spy from the tribe of Judah. 13:1-25; esp. v.6

CALL - CALLED
Of God.
God called Abraham to be a leader. 13:1-25, Thgt.1
God called Elisha to be a leader. 13:1-25, Thgt.1
God called Gideon to be a leader. 13:1-25, Thgt.1
God called Isaiah to be leader. 13:1-25, Thgt.1
God called Joshua to succeed Moses as leader. 27:18-23
God called Moses to be a leader. 13:1-25, Thgt.1
God called Paul to be a leader. 13:1-25, Thgt.1
God calls & gifts believers differently. 12:4-12, Thgt.3
God calls many today to be leaders. 13:1-25, Thgt.1
Proof of. Minister's **c**. 17:1

CAMPSITES (See **CITIES - AREAS**)
Chart of. 33:1-56, D.S.#1
Fact. Difficult to know the exact location of some **c**. 33:5-49
Of Israel.
Abel Shittim. A camp located between Mt. Hor & the Jordan River across from Jericho. 33:48-49
Abraim, mountains of. A camp located between Mt. Hor & the Jordan River across from Jericho. 33:47-48
Abronah. A camp located between Mt. Sinai & Mt. Hor. 33:34-35
Almon Diblathaim. A camp located between Mt. Hor & the Jordan River across from Jericho. 33:46-47
Alush. A camp located between Rameses & Mt. Sinai. 33:13-14
Bene Jaakan. A camp located between Mt. Sinai & Mt. Hor. 33:31-32
Beth Jeshimoth. A camp located between Mt. Hor & the Jordan River across from Jericho. 33:48-49
Desert of Sin. A camp located between Rameses & Mt. Sinai. 33:11-12
Desert of Sinai. A camp located between Rameses & Mt. Sinai. Discussed. The law was given. 33:15-16
Dibon Gad.
A camp located between Mt. Hor & the Jordan River across from Jericho. 33:45-46; 33:1-56, D.S. #1
Discussed. Was in Moab. 33:45-46
Dophkah. A camp located between Rameses & Mt. Sinai. 33:12-13
Elim. A camp located between Rameses & Mt. Sinai. Discussed. An oasis in the desert. 33:9-10
Etham. A camp located between Rameses & Mt. Sinai. Discussed. First ref. to the cloud. 33:6-7
Ezion-Gaber. A camp located between Mt. Sinai & Mt. Hor. Discussed. A well-known oasis. 33:35-36
Haradah. A camp located between Mt. Sinai & Mt. Hor. 33:24-25
Hashmonah. A camp located between Mt. Sinai & Mt. Hor. 33:29-30
Hazeroth. A camp located between Mt. Sinai & Mt. Hor. 33:17-18
Hor Haggidgad. A camp located between Mt. Sinai & Mt. Hor. 33:32-33
Iye Abarim. A camp located between Mt. Hor & the Jordan River across from Jericho. Discussed. On the border of Moab. 33:44-45
Jotbathah. A camp located between Mt. Sinai & Mt. Hor. 33:33-34
Kadesh. A camp located between Mt. Sinai & Mt. Hor. Discussed. Place where 12 spies were sent out & 10 rebelled. 33:36-37
Kehelathah. A camp located between Mt. Sinai & Mt. Hor. 33:22-23
Kibroth Hattaavah. A camp located between Mt. Sinai & Mt. Hor. Discussed. Was three days from Sinai. 33:16-17
Libnah. A camp located between Mt. Sinai & Mt. Hor. 33:20-21
Makheloth. A camp located between Mt. Sinai & Mt. Hor. 33:25-26
Marah. A camp located between Rameses & Mt. Sinai. Discussed. Bitter waters sweetened by God. 33:8-9
Mithcah. A camp located between Mt. Sinai & Mt. Hor. 33:28-29
Moab, plains of. A camp located between Mt. Hor & the Jordan River across from Jericho.
Camp stretched from Beth Jeshimoth & Abel Shittim (over five miles). 33:48-49
Discussed. By the Jordan, across from Jericho. 33:48-49
Final staging point for marching into the promised land. 33:48-49
Moseroth. A camp located between Mt. Sinai & Mt. Hor. Discussed. Place of Aaron's death. 33:30-31
Mt. Hor. A camp located between Mt. Sinai & Mt. Hor.
Discussed. Place of Israel's first military victory. 33:40
Where Aaron died. 33:37-39
Mt. Shepher. A camp located between Mt. Sinai & Mt. Hor. 33:23-24
Oboth. A camp located between Mt. Hor & the Jordan River across from Jericho. 33:43-44
Pi Hahiroth. A camp located between Rameses & Mt. Sinai. Discussed. **C**.

Edom. Land of. 20:14-22
Edrei.
Discussed. The place where Israel won the victory over Og, the king of Bashan. 21:33-35
Location of. 21:33-35; D.S. #5
Elealeh.
City of. The tribe of Reuben. 32:28-42, esp. v.37-38
Location of. 32:37-38; D.S. #9
Gilead. Territory of. The tribe of Manasseh, descendants of Makir. 32:28-42, esp. v.39-40
Havvoth Jair.
City of. The tribe of Manasseh, people of Jair. 32:28-42, esp. v.41
Location of. 32:41; D.S. #14
Hazeroth.
Campsite of Israel. 11:35
Israel waited here until Miriam's confinement was over. 12:16
Hebron.
Location of. About nineteen miles south of Jerusalem & fifteen miles west of the Dead Sea. 13:22; D.S. #3
Meaning of. "Association" or "league." 13:22
The first city spied out. 13:22
Heshbon.
Location of. 21:25-30; D.S. #4
Territory of. The tribe of Reuben. 32:28-42, esp. v.37-38
The capital of the Amorites. 21:21-32, esp. v.26
Hor, Mount.
Place where Aaron died & was buried. 20:23-29; esp. v.28
Transfer of power of the High Priest. 20:23-29, esp. v.27-28
Hormah.
Discussed. Israel fled to this place after being attacked. 14:45
Israel destroyed the kingdom of Arad. Named it **H**. 21:1-3, esp. v.3
Location of. Uncertain, but in the territory given to Simeon. 14:45; D.S. #6
Meaning of. "Split rock" or "cursed for destruction." 14:45
Iye Abarim. Place where Israel camped on its way to the promised land. 21:10-20, esp. v.11
Jahaz. The place where the Amorites attacked Israel. 21:21-32, esp. v.23; D.S. #3
Jazer.
City of. The tribe of Gad. 32:28-42, esp. v.34-36
Location of. 32:34-36; D.S. #5
Jericho.
City of. Israel camped in the plains of Moab by the Jordan River across from **J**. 22:1-41, esp. v.1
Location of. 22:1; D.S. #1
Jogbehah.
City of. The tribe of Gad. 32:28-42, esp. v.34-36
Location of. 32:34-36; D.S. #6
Kadesh.
Campsite of Israel. 33:36-37; 33:1-56, D.S. #1
In the desert of Zin. Where Miriam died & was buried. 20:1
Place where 12 spies were sent out & 10 rebelled. 33:36-37
Kenath (See Nobah).
Discussed.
Nobah captured the city of Kenath & its surrounding villages. 32:42
Nobah named the city of Kenath after himself. 32:42
Location of. 32:42; D.S. #15
Kibroth Hattaavah. 11:35
Meaning of. "Graves of craving." 11:35
Place of quail judgment. 11:35
Kiriathaim. City of. The tribe of Reuben. 32:28-42, esp. v.37-38
Lebo-Hamath.
Discussed. The 12 spies spied as far as Lebo-Hamath. 13:21
Location of. The northern boundary of Canaan promised to Israel. 13:21; D.S. #2
Meaning of. "Entrance to or to come to Hamath." 13:21
Mattanah. Place where Israel camped on its way to the promised land. 21:10-20, esp. v.18
Moab. Place where Israel camped on its way to the promised land. 21:10-20, esp. v.20
Nahaliel. Place where Israel camped on its way to the promised land. 21:10-20, esp. v.19
Nebo.
City of. The tribe of Reuben. 32:28-42, esp. v.37-38
Fact. Name changed. 32:38
Location of. 32:37-38; D.S. # 11
Nobah (See Kenath).
City of.
Nobah captured the city of Kenath & its surrounding villages. 32:42
Nobah named the city of Kenath after himself. 32:42
Location of. 32:42; D.S. #16
Oboth. Place where Israel camped on its way to the promised land. 21:10-20, esp. v.10
Peor, Mount. The center of Baal worship in Moab. 23:27-24:13; 25:1-3
Pethor.
Home of Balaam. 22:1-6, esp. v.5
Location of. 22:5; D.S. #2
Pisgah Peak.
An excellent place to spy out the promised land. 21:10-20, esp. v.20
Balak took Balaam here to curse Israel. 23:13-26, esp. v.14-17
Place where Israel camped on its way to the promised land. 21:10-20, esp. v.20
Rehob.
Discussed. The furthest point where the 12 spies went. 13:21
Location of. Town in the vicinity of Laish in upper Galilee. 13:21; D.S. #1
Meaning of. "Broad or open place." 13:21
Shittim. Location of. The plains of Moab, right across from the great city of Jericho. 25:1-3, esp. v.1
Sibmah. City of. The tribe of Reuben. 32:28-42, esp. v.37-38
Location of. 32:37-38; D.S. #13
Taberah. 11:3
Campsite of Israel. 11:1-3, esp. v.3
Meaning of. "Burning," a place of awful judgment. 11:1-3, esp. v.3
Zered Valley, The. Place where Israel camped on its way to the promised land. 21:10-20, esp. v.12
Zin, Desert Of.
Southern border of the promised land. 34:3
The place where the mission of the 12 spies began. 13:21
Where Miriam died. 20:1
Where the community rebelled at the waters. 27:14
Zoan.
Hebron was built seven years before Zoan. 13:22
Location of. In Egypt. 13:22; D.S. #4

CITIES OF REFUGE (See **REFUGE, CITIES OF**)

CLEANSING
Discussed. The only way to secure **c.** is through the sacrifice & power of Christ. 19:17-19, Thgt.1
From sin. 31:19-24
How to secure **c.** 19:17-19

CLEANSING, CEREMONIAL
Example of the Levites. 8:1-26

CLEANSING, SPIRITUAL
Discussed. The only way to secure **c.** is through the sacrifice & power of Christ. 19:17-19, Thgt.1
From sin. 19:1-10
How to secure. 19:17-19
Typed - Symbolized - Pictured. By the cleansing of the Levites. 8:5-26

CLOTHES - CLOTHING
Of the High Priest. Symbol of the official position of the High Priest. 20:23-29
Of the Levites. Levites had to wash their clothes. 8:5-26
Of the priests. Priests were given new, clean garments. 8:5-26
Typed - Pictured - Symbolized. By tearing of clothes. A symbol of ritual mourning. 14:1-10, esp. v.7

CLOUD, PILLAR OF (See **PILLAR OF CLOUD**)
Facts.
God guides His people, always guides them. 9:15-23, Thgt.1
God is present with His people, always present. 9:15-23, Thgt.1
Qualities of.
Changed its appearance at night: A fiery cloud. 9:15-23; esp. v.15-16
Contained the glory of God. 7:1-9; esp. v.1; 9:15-23
Guided the Israelites. 9:15-23; esp. v.17
One of the ways God spoke to His people. 9:15-23; esp. v.18-23
The Shekinah Glory. 9:15-23, D.S. #1
Type - Symbol of. God's presence & guidance. 9:15-23

COMFORT
Warning. God warns us against comfort & ease. 32:6-15, Thgt.1

COMMANDS—COMMANDMENTS
Duty.
Must not break the seventh commandment (adultery). 25:1-3, Thgt.1

DAY OF ATONEMENT
Discussed.
Was established to teach people that there was only one way to become acceptable to God. 29:7-11
Was held on the tenth day of the seventh month. 29:7
Was the most sacred, holy day of the year. 29:7-11
Type - Symbol of. The only way to approach God, through the shed blood of the substitute sacrifice (Christ). 29:7-11

DEATH
Caused by. 19:11-16
Discussed.
Causes defilement. 19:1-10
Is the ultimate defilement, corruption of man. 19:1-22, Intro.
The ceremonial uncleanness of. 5:1-4
The death of God's dear people is very precious to God. 20:23-29, Thgt.1
Experience of. 27:12-23, Intro.
Facts.
God gives victory over death. 24:20, Thgt.1
The death of a believer is a warm, tender, gentle & touching experience. 27:12-13, Thgt.1
To be absent from the body is to be present with the LORD. 20:23-29, Thgt.1
Hope of. 27:12-23, Intro.
Of Aaron. 20:23-29
Of Balaam. 31:7-13
Of believer. 27:12-13
Of Miriam. 20:1
Leader of the women of Israel. Three facts. 20:1
Of Moses. 27:12-23, Intro.; 27:12-13
Picture of. God preparing the believer for death: God told Moses to prepare for **d**. 27:12-13
Preparation for.
Death of believer. 27:12-13
Death of Moses. 27:12-13
Type - Symbol of.
Corruption. 31:19-24
Uncleanness. 19:11-16

DEDICATION - DEDICATE
Ceremony of. 8:5-26
Discussed.
Festival of Trumpets. 29:1-6
Three special obligations of the Nazarite vow. 6:3-12
Of Tabernacle. 7:1-9; 7:10-88
Of the Levites. 8:5-26
To God. 15:1-16

DEFIANT SIN
Example of. A picture of a man who defiantly raised his fist in the face of God. 15:30-36
Judgment of. Severe **j**. 15:30-36
Meaning of. 15:30-36

DEFILE - DEFILEMENT
Caused by. 19:11-16
Discussed. By death. 19:1-10
Duty.
Must guard against defilement & uncleanness. 19:11-16, Thgt.1
Must know that people are totally defiled. 19:11-16, Thgt.1
Kind of. Positional **d**. 19:11-16
Typed - Symbolized - Pictured. By the Red Heifer Offering. A symbol of cleansing a person defiled by death. 19:1-10
Warning.
The judgment of God is going to fall upon every unclean & defiled person. 19:20-22, Thgt.1
The possessions & things of this world can defile & make a person unclean. 31:19-24, Thgt.1

DELIVER - DELIVERANCE
Discussed.
Celebration of. 9:1-14
From the enemies of life. 9:1-10:10, Intro.
Prophecy concerning. 24:14-19
Type - Symbol of. The coming Deliverer. The coming of the Lord Jesus Christ as the Messianic Ruler over all the universe. 24:14-19

DESERT OF SIN
Campsite of Israel. 33:11-12; 33:1-56, D.S. #1

DESERT OF SINAI
Campsite of Israel. 33:15-16; 33:1-56, D.S. #1
Fact. Place where the law was given. 33:15-16

DESERT OF ZIN (See **ZIN, DESERT OF**)
Location of. Southern border of the promised land. 34:3
Place where Miriam died. 20:1
Place where the community rebelled at the waters. 27:14
Place where the mission of the 12 spies began. 13:21

DESERTS
Of Paran.
Encamped here after Israel left Hazeroth. 12:16
Spies sent out from **P**. 13:1-25
The cloud came to rest in the desert of **P**. 10:11-12
Of Sin. Christ's sacrifice that secured atonement or reconciliation for man. 28:3-8. 33:11-12:,33:1-56, D.S. #1
Of Sinai. The Israelites set out from the desert of **S**. on their march to the promised land. 10:11-12
Of Zin. The place where the mission of the 12 spies began. 13:21

DESTINY
Of man. 10:11-36, Intro.
Of the world. 10:11-36, Intro.

DEVOTION TO GOD
Discussed. Desire for. 6:1-27, Intro.

DIBON
Location of. 32:37-38; D.S. #1
Territory of. The tribe of Gad.
Cities rebuilt.
Dibon, Ataroth, Aroer, Atroth Shophan, Jazer, Jogbehah, Beth Nimrah & Beth Haran. 32:28-42, esp. v.34-36

DIBON GAD
Campsite of Israel. 33:45-46; 33:1-56, D.S. #1

DIET (See **FOOD**)

DIFFICULTIES
Of Israel. 11:1-3

DISCIPLINE
Of believers. 14:10-25
Of God. 12:4-12; 14:26-39

DISCONTENTMENT
Discussed. Dissatisfaction with God's provision. 11:4-35
Reasons for. Israel's **c**.
Of being tired of leadership. 11:1-3, Thgt.1
Of God's judgment upon sin. 11:1-3, Thgt.1
Of no food. 11:1-3, Thgt.1; 11:4-35
Of no water. 11:1-3, Thgt.1
Of trials in the wilderness wanderings. 11:1-3, Thgt.1
Spirit of. 11:1-3
Warning. Complaining & grumbling are signs of distrust, of terrible unbelief in God. 11:1-3, Thgt.2

DISEASE
Kinds. Of skin. Leprosy. 5:1-4

DISOBEY - DISOBEDIENCE
Warning. Leads to serious consequences. 20:7-13, Thgt.1

DISRESPECT
Example of. 25:6-13

DISTRUST
Of Israel. 11:1-3

DISUNITY
Example of. 32:6-15

DIVINATION
Discussed.
Balaam's false belief in **d**. 22:1-6
Balak sought to curse & defeat Israel by pagan divination or sorcery. 22:1-6, esp. v.4-6
Fee for. 22:7-14, esp. v.7
Evil of. 22:7-14

DIVINERS
Evil of. 22:1-41, Intro.
Warning. God condemns diviners, sorcerers, mystics, or anyone else who preys upon people seeking direction or help. 22:7-14

DIVISION (See **HOST**)
Meaning of. 2:2-33; esp. v.4, 6, 8, etc.

DIVORCE - DIVORCED
Vows of. 30:9

DOCUMENTARY HYPOTHESIS
Discussed. History of. Introduction to Numbers: Author

DONKEY
Discussed. Story of the **d**. 22:22-35
Fact. Did not speak by its own power; it spoke by the power of God. 22:22-35

DOPHKAH
Campsite of Israel. 33:12-13; 33:1-56, D.S. #1

GADDI
Spy from the tribe of Manasseh. 13:1-25; esp. v.11

GADDIEL
Spy from the tribe of Zebulun. 13:1-25; esp. v.10

GAMALIEL
Leader of tribe of Manasseh. 1:4-16; esp. v.10

GATHERED TO HIS PEOPLE
Discussed.
Aaron. 20:23-29
Moses. 27:12-13
Meaning of. 20:23-29; 27:12-13
Type - Symbol of. A picture of joining former believers in the presence of God. 20:23-29

GERSHON - GERSHONITES
Campsite: To the west behind the Tabernacle. 3:14-39, esp. v.23
Census of.
2,630 in number. 4:34-49
All men from thirty to fifty years old. 4:21-28, esp. v.23
Reason: To learn the number of available workers. 4:21-28, esp. v.23
Clans of.
7,500 in number. 3:14-39, esp. v.22
Libnites & Shimeites. 3:14-39, esp. v.21
Duty of. To take care of the tent of the Tabernacle. 3:14-39, esp. v.21-26; 10:13-28, esp. v.17
Leader of: Eliasaph, son of Lael. 3:14-39, esp. v.24

GEUEL
Spy from the tribe of Gad. 13:1-25; esp. v.15

GIDEON
Call of. God called Gideon to be a leader. 13:1-25, Thgt.1

GIFT - GIFTS
Duty. To offer to the LORD. 7:10-88
Fact. All sacred **g.**, once promised or given, belonged to the priests. 5:5-10
Kind. Voluntary & spontaneous **g.** 7:1-9
Of God.
God calls & gifts believers differently. 12:4-12, Thgt.3;
The promised land. 34:1-15

GILEAD
Territory of. Captured by the tribe of Manasseh. Gilead. Descendants of Makir. 32:28-42, esp. v.39-40

GIVE - GIVING
Discussed. How to give. 7:1-9
Duty. To the LORD. 7:1-9; 7:10-88
Kind. Voluntary & spontaneous **g.** 7:1-9

GLORY OF GOD
Typed - Pictured - Symbolized. By the pillar cloud. 7:1-9; esp. v.1; 9:15-23, D.S. #1

GOAT
Type - Symbol of. Christ's sacrifice, His dying for sin: Male goat as a Sin Offering. 28:11-15

GOD
Access to. 15:1-16, Thgt.1
Anger of. 11:1-3; Num.11:4-35, esp. v.33; 12:4-12; 14:10-25; 22:22-35
Approach to. 15:1-16, Thgt.1
Approval of. 6:22-27; esp. v.26
Attention of. 6:22-27; esp. v.26
Blessings of.
Five guarantees to the believer:
God's faithfulness. 23:13-26, Thgt.1
God's power. 23:13-26, Thgt.1
God's presence. 23:13-26, Thgt.1
God's promises. 23:13-26, Thgt.1
God's truthfulness & unchangeableness. 23:13-26, Thgt.1
Call of.
God called Abraham to be a leader. 13:1-25, Thgt.1
God called Elisha to be a leader. 13:1-25, Thgt.1
God called Gideon to be a leader. 13:1-25, Thgt.1
God called Isaiah to be leader. 13:1-25, Thgt.1
God called Moses to be a leader. 13:1-25, Thgt.1
God called Paul to be a leader. 13:1-25, Thgt.1
God calls many today to be leaders. 13:1-25, Thgt.1
Care of. 6:13-20, Thgt.1
Character of. 14:10-25, esp. v.13-17
Chastisement of. 14:10-25; 14:26-39
Compassion of God. 12:13-16
Discipline of. 12:4-12; 14:10-25; 14:26-39
Duty to. (Man's duty to.)
Must acknowledge God & acknowledge Him as holy.
Must approach God in the right way. 7:1-89; 8:5-26, Thgt.2; 15:1-16, Thgt.2
Must be holy. 6:3-12, Thgt.1
Must not turn to idols or false gods. 25:4-5
Must respect God's appointed order within the family. 30:16, Thgt.1
Must seek God. 27:5-11
Must worship on the Sabbath. 15:30-36, Thgt.1
Face of. 6:22-27; esp. v.25
Facts.
God does choose some persons to be leaders. 13:1-25, Thgt.1
God dwells in the midst of His people. 2:1-2
God forgives sin. 35:30-34, Thgt.1
God gives five guarantees to the believer. 23:13-26, Thgt.1
God guides His people as they march to the promised land. 2:1-2
God hears everything (criticism). 11:1-3, esp. v.2
God hears prayer. 12:13-16, Thgt.1
God is faithful in leading & guiding us step by step & day by day. 10:33-34, Thgt.1
God is merciful & compassionate. 12:13-16, Thgt.1
God is no respecter of persons. 13:1-25, Thgt.1
God is the Great Communicator. 1:1
God judges or chastises His people when they sin. 12:4-12, Thgt.1
God's judgment against unbelief & rebellion is sure. 16:16-35, Thgt.1
God promises to provide all the necessities of life for His dear people. 35:1-8, Thgt.2
God protects His people. 20:14-22
God speaks to us. 1:1
God will judge the world in righteousness. 25:4-5, Thgt.1
Source of Laws. 15:41
Faithfulness of. 10:33-34; 33:1-4
Forgiveness of God. 14:10-25, esp. v.13-17
Glory of. 9:15-23, D.S. #1
Grace of. 6:22-27; esp. v.25; 27:12-13
Guidance of. 2:1-2; Num.10:33-34; 26:1
Help of. 2:1-2
Holiness of. 4:1-20
Judgment of. 11:1-3; Num.12:4-12; 14:10-25; 14:26-39; 16:16-35; 31:1-6
Justice of. 21:21-32
Leadership of. 26:1
Love of G. 14:10-25, esp. v.13-17; 27:12-13
Mercy of. 12:13-16; 35:30-34
Peace of. 6:22-27; esp. v.26
Pleasure of. 6:22-27; esp. v.26
Presence of. 2:2-33, Thgt.3; 6:22-27; esp. v.25; 7:89; 9:15-23, D.S. #1
Promises of. (See **PROMISES**)
God gives us victory over persecution. 24:20, Thgt.1
God gives victory over all the evil powers & rulers of darkness, over all the spiritual wickedness that attacks us. 24:20, Thgt.1
God gives victory over any person or any thing in this world & in the spiritual world. 24:20, Thgt.1
God gives victory over death. 24:20, Thgt.1
God gives victory over the evil of men, over evil men who oppose us & stand as enemies against us. 24:20, Thgt.1
God gives victory over the temptations & trials of life. 24:20, Thgt.1
God gives victory over the world with all its enslavements & bondages. 24:20, Thgt.1
Protection of. 20:14-22
Provision of. 9:1-10:10
Sovereignty of. 22:36-41, Thgt.1
Tenderness of. 20:23-29, Thgt.1
Vengeance of. 31:1-6
Warning.
God demands justice. 35:30-34, esp. v.34
God judges all grumbling & unbelief. 16:1-50
God judges all rebellion & unauthorized approaches. 16:1-50
God judges & chastises His people when they sin. 14:10-25, Thgt.1
God judges sin. 27:14-17, Thgt.1
God warns us against comfort & ease. 32:6-15, Thgt.1
God will judge every human being who has ever lived. 14:26-39, Thgt.1
God will judge the nations of this earth. 24:23-35, Thgt.1
God will judge the people of this earth, individual by individual. 24:23-35
God will not share His glory with any person. 20:7-13, Thgt.1
God will not tolerate unbelief & rebellion from any person. 14:1-10, Thgt.1

GOLD
Gift of. 31:25-54

INDEX

INDEX

INDEX

a clean place outside the camp. 19:1-10, esp. v.9-10
Everyone who had anything to do with the sacrifice had to cleanse himself & his clothes. 19:1-10, esp. v.7-8
Some blood of the red heifer was to be sprinkled seven times toward the front of the Tabernacle. 19:1-10, esp. v.4
The priest was to burn some cedar wood, hyssop & scarlet wool with the red heifer. 19:1-10, esp. v.6
Was to be put to death outside the camp. 19:1-10, esp. v.3
Was to be unused, that is, an animal that had never been worked with a yoke around it's neck. 19:1-10, esp. v.2
Was to be wholly burned, all its parts. 19:1-10, esp. v.5
Was to have no defect or blemish. 19:1-10, esp. v.2
Offering of. 19:1-10
Purpose of. Was established as a permanent law for Israel & for all foreigners among them. 19:1-10, esp. v.10
Sacrifice of. 19:1-10
Type - Symbol of.
Of cleansing a person defiled by death. 19:1-10
The cleansing power of Jesus Christ, the power of His sacrifice to cleanse from the defilement of sin & death. 19:1-22, Intro.; 19:1-10

REDEEM - REDEMPTION
Picture of. **R**. Census of the firstborn & their replacement by the Levites. 3:40-51
Price of. 3:40-51

REDEEMER
Meaning of kinsman or **r**. 35:9-29

REFUGE, CITIES OF
Discussed. Provision for all who need refuge from the storms & threats of life. 35:1-34
Location of. 35:9-29
Picture of. Christ, our refuge from the threats & storms of life. 35:9-29
Purpose of. 35:9-29

REHOB
Discussed. The furthest point where the 12 spies went. 13:21
Location of. Town in the vicinity of Laish in upper Galilee. 13:21; D.S. #1
Meaning of. "Broad or open place." 13:21

REJECTION
Against God.
Fatal response of Israel. 14:1-10
Warning against. 19:20-22
Against leaders. Assassination of leaders. 14:1-10, esp. v.10

RELATIONSHIPS
Authority of. There has to be a head who has ultimate authority for any organization or body of people to function properly. 30:16, Thgt.1
Between father & children. 30:16
Between man & wife. 30:16
Duty.
Must stand fast under the banner of God's family. 2:2-33
Must take one's place under the standard of Christ. 2:2-33

REPENT - REPENTANCE
False **r**.
Incomplete confession. 14:40-45
Result of. True confession always involves repentance, a turning away from sin to God. 14:40-45, Thgt.1

REPHIDIM
Campsite of Israel. 33:14-15; 33:1-56, D.S. #1
Discussed. No water to drink. 33:14-15

RESIST - RESISTANCE
Discussed. Against God's people. 20:14-22

REST, PHYSICAL
Discussed. God promises His people rest, both physical & spiritual **r**. 10:35-36, Thgt.1

REST, SPIRITUAL
Discussed.
God promises His people rest, both physical & spiritual **r**. 10:35-36, Thgt.1
The gift of the promised land. 34:1-29
Picture of. Spiritual conquest & rest: Taking possession of the promised land. 33:50-56
Type - Symbol of. Christ, our spiritual rest. 28:9-10

RESTITUTION
Discussed.
Law of **r**. 5:5-10
Superiority of **r**. compared to modern criminal law. 5:5-10, Thgt.2
Duty. Must make **r**. 5:5-10, Thgt.1

REUBEN, TRIBE OF
Census of.
1st census. 46,500 fighting men. 1:7-46, esp. v.21
2nd census. 43, 730 fighting men. 26:4-51, esp. v.6
Leaders of.
Dathan, Abiram, & On. Co-conspirators with Korah. 16:1-15, esp. v.1
Elizur. Helped with the first census. 1:4-16, esp. v.5
Settlement, east of the Jordan River. 32:1-42
Sins of.
Unbelief, disloyalty, & half-hearted commitment. 32:6-15, esp. v.8-13
Wanted to sit while others fought to conquer the promised land. 32:6-15
Spy. Shammua. One of the twelve spies. 13:1-25, esp. v.4
Territory of.
Cities rebuilt.
Heshbon, Elealeh, Kiriathaim, Nebo, Baal Meon, Sibmah 32:28-42, esp. v.37-38
Lands that had been conquered from Shion, king of the Amorites, & from king Og of Bashan. 32:28-42, esp. v.33
Typed - Pictured - Symbolized. A picture of selfishness, coveteousness, disloyalty: The compromise of Gad & Reuben. 32:1-42

REUEL, SON OF
Family of.
Hobab: Brother-in-law of Moses. 10:29-32
Hobab: Son of Reuel. 10:29-32, esp. v.29

REVOLT - REVOLTS
Discussed. Caused by. 16:1-15

REWARD - REWARDS
Discussed. For fighting a good warfare. 31:25-54
Example of. A church that follows God's Word. 2:1-2, Thgt.2
Of battle. 31:25-54
Results of. There are rewards in heaven. 31:25-54, Thgt.1

RIGHTEOUSNESS
Typed - Symbolized - Pictured. By the clothing of the High Priest: A symbol of righteousness. 20:23-29

RIGHTS
Discussed. Equal. 27:1-11, Intro.

RIMMON PEREZ
Campsite of Israel. 33:19-20; 33:1-56, D.S. #1

RISSAH
Campsite of Israel. 33:21-22; 33:1-56, D.S. #1

RITHMAH
Campsite of Israel. 33:18-19

RITUAL UNCLEANNESS (See **CEREMONIAL UNCLEANNESS**)

ROCK
Type - Symbol of. Christ, the source of living water. 20:7-13

ROSH HASHANAH (See **TRUMPETS, FEAST OF**)
Discussed. The beginning of the new year for the Jewish people. 29:1-6

SABBATH
Discussed.
Day. Sacrifices on. 28:9-10
The people rested on the Sabbath day, but not the priest. 28:9-10
Duty. Must celebrate our redemption every Sabbath or Sunday. 28:9-10
Importance of. 15:30-36, Thgt.1
Judgment of. Breaking the **S**. Severe judgment. 15:30-36

SACRIFICE - SACRIFICES (See **OFFERINGS**)
Discussed.
A clear command of God. 28:1-2
Importance of the offerings or sacrifices. 28:1-2
S. on the Sabbath Day. 28:9-10
The way to approach God. 7:10-88
Duty. To be presented at the appointed time. 28:1-2

INDEX

SHOWBREAD (See **BREAD, HOLY**)
Type - Symbol of. A symbol of the 12 tribes of Israel or of God's people. 8:1-4, Thgt.1

SIBMAH
Location of. 32:37-38; D.S. #13
Territory of. The tribe of Reuben.
Cities rebuilt.
Heshbon, Elealeh, Kiriathaim, Nebo, Baal Meon, Sibmah 32:28-42, esp. v.37-38

SIHON
King of Amorites. 21:21-32, esp. v.23

SIMEON, TRIBE OF
Census of.
1st census. 59,300 fighting men. 1:17-46; esp. v.23
2nd census. 22,200 fighting men. 26:4-51, esp. v.14
Leaders of. Shelumiel. Helped with the first census. 1:4-16; esp. v.6
Shemuel.
Appointed by Moses as a supervisor of the promised land. 34:16-29
Led the tribe of Simeon into the promised land. 34:16-29
Spy. Shaphat. One of the twelve spies. 13:1-25; esp. v.5

SINAI, DESERT OF (See **DESERTS**)
Place where the Israelites set out on their march to the promised land. 10:11-12

SIN - SINS
Discussed. In ignorance. 15:22-29
Duty. Must be totally set apart from the sin & shame of the world. 5:1-4, Thgt.1
Example of. Moses. 20:7-13
Facts.
Man is enslaved to sin & death. 33:1-56, Intro.
The whole community of believers could be forgiven if they broke the law of God. 15:22-29
We often sin; we cannot keep from sinning. 15:22-29, Thgt.1
Forgiveness of. 15:22-29
Kinds of.
Against one's neighbor. 5:5-10
Attacking God's minister. 12:1-3, Thgt.1
Blasphemy. 15:30-36
Brazen **s.** 15:30-36
Breaking the commandments of God. 25:4-5
Defiant **s.** 15:30-36
Deliberate **s.** 15:30-36
Despising God's Word. 15:30-36
Ignorance. 15:22-29
Irreverence. 25:6-13
National **s.** 15:30-36
Presumptuous **s.** 15:30-36
Sexual. 25:4-5
S. through ignorance. 15:22-29
Unintentional **s.** 15:22-29
Unknown **s.** 15:22-29
Of Israel.
Not trusting God & losing sight of His guidance. 11:1-3
Why God forgave Israel's sins. Prayers of Moses. 14:10-25, esp. v.13-17
Remedy for.
God forgives sin. 35:30-34, Thgt.1
There is cleansing from sin. 6:3-12, Thgt.2; 19:1-10
True confession always involves repentance, a turning away from sin to God. 14:40-45, Thgt.1
Seriousness of.
God judges sin. 27:14-17, Thgt.1
Must discipline church members who become engaged in serious sin. 5:1-4, Thgt.1
Warning against. 19:20-22

SIN OFFERING, THE
Purpose of.
Was part of the Levites' ceremonial, spiritual cleansing. 9:5-26
Was the worship required after the fulfillment of the Nazarite vow. 6:13-20
Results of.
Cleansing. 6:3-12; esp. v.10
Continual cleansing. 6:13-20; esp. v.14
Type - Symbol of. Christ's sacrifice for the sins of the world. 6:3-12; esp. v.10; 28:11-15, Thgt.1

SMILE
Of God. 6:22-27; esp. v.25

SOCIETY
Problems of.
Bombarded with sex. 25:1-18, Intro.
False worship. 25:1-18, Intro.
Is being taught that all forms of sexual behavior are acceptable. 25:1-18, Intro.

SOLDIERS
Life & walk. Believers are like **s.** walking through the desert & wildernessof this world. 2:2-33, Thgt.1

SORCERY (See **FORTUNE TELLING**)
Evil of. 22:1-41, Intro.; 22:7-14
Example of.
Balaam's false belief in **s.** 22:1-6
Balak sought to curse & defeat Israel by pagan divination or sorcery. 22:1-6, esp. v.4-6
Warning. God condemns diviners, sorcerers, mystics, or anyone else who preys upon people seeking direction or help. 22:7-14

SOVEREIGN - SOVEREIGNTY
Of God. God is **s.**, in total control of the universe & all that happens within the universe. 22:36-41, Thgt.1

SPIES, THE TWELVE
Duty of.
To bring back samples of the fruit. 13:1-25, esp. v.20
To check the soil to see if it was fertile or poor, barren or full of trees. 13:1-25, esp. v.20
To see if the people were strong or weak, few or many. 13:1-25, esp. v.18
To see if the towns were fortified or unwalled. 13:1-25, esp. v.19
To see what the land was like, good or bad. 13:1-25, esp. v.19
Judgment of. Upon the ten unbelieving spies. 14:26-39, esp. v.36-38
List of. One man from each tribe. 13:1-25
Mission of.
Distance of total mission. About 500 miles. 13:1-25
Length of mission in days: 40. 13:1-25, esp. v.25
Spies said nothing about Abraham's relationship to Hebron. 13:1-25
Report of. 13:26-33

SPIRITISTS (See **PSYCHICS**)

SPIRITUAL CONQUEST
Discussed. The gift of the promised land. 34:1-29

SPIRITUAL REST (See **REST, SPIRITUAL**)

SPIRITUAL SEPARATION (See **SEPARATION, SPIRITUAL**)

SPIRITUAL VICTORY
Picture of. Spiritual conquest & rest: Taking possession of the promised land. 33:50-56

SPIRITUAL WARFARE
Warning. Believers must be prepared for **w.** as they march to the promised land. 1:2-3

SPIRITUAL WORLD
Warfare of. 22:1-41, Intro.

SPOILS
Of warfare. 31:25-54
Picture of.
Giving thanks to God: Division of the spoils taken from the defeated enemy. 31:25-54
Rewards for fighting a good warfare: Division of the spoils taken from the defeated enemy. 31:25-54

SPOKE, THE LORD
Examples of.
In the desert or wilderness. 1:1
In the Tent of Meeting. 1:1
Fact. This phrase is used over 150 times in 20 plus ways in the Book of Numbers. 1:1

STAFF, AARON'S
Discussed.
Placed in Ark. Reason why. 17:10-13
Sprouted, budded, blossomed, & produced almonds. 17:6-9
Typed - Symbolized - Pictured.
By Christ or the minister bearing fruit & bringing life to people. 17:6-9
By God's power & authority. 17:6-9

STANDING FAST
Duty.
Must stand fast under the banner of God's family. 2:2-33
Must take one's place under the standard of Christ. 2:2-33

STEWARD - STEWARDSHIP
Duty. To the LORD. 7:1-9
Of income. 31:25-54

STRANGER
Meaning of. 3:5-13

STRIFE
Discussed. The showdown & judgment of Korah & his allies. 16:16-35

INDEX

• PURPOSE STATEMENT •

LEADERSHIP MINISTRIES WORLDWIDE

exists to equip ministers, teachers, and laymen in their understanding, preaching, and teaching of God's Word by publishing and distributing worldwide *The Preacher's Outline & Sermon Bible®* and related *Outline* Bible materials, to reach & disciple men, women, boys, and girls for Jesus Christ.

• MISSION STATEMENT •

1. To make the Bible so understandable - its truth so clear and plain - that men and women everywhere, whether teacher or student, preacher or hearer, can grasp its Message and receive Jesus Christ as Savior; and...
2. To place the Bible in the hands of all who will preach and teach God's Holy Word, verse by verse, precept by precept, regardless of the individual's ability to purchase it.

The ***Outline*** Bible materials have been given to LMW for printing and especially distribution worldwide at/below cost, by those who remain anonymous. One fact, however, is as true today as it was in the time of Christ:

• The Gospel is free, but the cost of taking it is not •

LMW depends on the generous gifts of Believers with a heart for Him and a love and burden for the lost. They help pay for the translating, printing, and distributing of ***Outline*** Bible materials in the hands of God's servants worldwide who will present the Gospel message with clarity, authority and understanding beyond their own.

LMW was incorporated in the state of Tennessee in July 1992 and received IRS 501(c)(3) non-profit status in March 1994. LMW is an international, nondenominational mission organization. All proceeds from USA sales, along with donations from donor partners, go 100% into underwriting our translation and distribution projects of ***Outline*** Bible materials to preachers, church & lay leaders, and Bible students around the world.

2/98

Box 21310 - Chattanooga, TN 37424 • (423) 855-2181 • FAX (423) 855-8616
• E-Mail - outlinebible@compuserve.com — www.outlinebible.org •

Publisher & Distributor of OUTLINE Bible Materials

Currently Available Materials, with New Volumes Releasing Regularly

- **THE PREACHER'S OUTLINE & SERMON BIBLE® — DELUXE EDITION**

  Volume 1 . . . . St. Matthew I (chapters 1-15) 3-Ring, looseleaf binder
  Volume 2 . . . . St. Matthew II (chapters 16-28)
  Volume 3 . . . . St. Mark
  Volume 4 . . . . St. Luke
  Volume 5 . . . . St. John
  Volume 6 . . . . Acts
  Volume 7 . . . . Romans
  Volume 8 . . . . 1 & 2 Corinthians (1 volume)
  Volume 9 . . . . Galatians, Ephesians, Philippians, Colossians (1 volume)
  Volume 10 . . . . 1 & 2 Thessalonians, 1 & 2 Timothy, Titus, Philemon (1 volume)
  Volume 11 . . . . Hebrews -James (1 volume)
  Volume 12 . . . . 1 & 2 Peter, 1,2 & 3 John, Jude (1 volume)
  Volume 13 . . . . Revelation
  Volume 14 . . . . Master Outline & Subject Index
  FULL SET — 14 Volumes

- **THE PREACHER'S OUTLINE & SERMON BIBLE® — OLD TESTAMENT**

  Volume 1 . . . . Genesis I (chapters 1-11)
  Volume 2 . . . . Genesis II (chapters 12-50)
  Volume 3 . . . . Exodus I (chapters 1-18)
  Volume 4 . . . . Exodus II (chapters 19-40)
  Volume 5 . . . . Leviticus
  Volume 6 . . . . Numbers New volumes release periodically

- **THE PREACHER'S OUTLINE & SERMON BIBLE® — SOFTBOUND EDITION**

  Identical content as Deluxe. Lightweight, compact, and affordable for overseas & traveling

- **THE PREACHER'S OUTLINE & SERMON BIBLE® — 3 VOL HARDCOVER w/CD**
- **THE PREACHER'S OUTLINE & SERMON BIBLE® — NIV SOFTBOUND EDITION**
- **THE MINISTER'S PERSONAL HANDBOOK - What the Bible Says . . . to the Minister**

  12 Chapters - 127 Subjects - 400 Verses OUTLINED - Paperback, Leatherette Deluxe

- **THE TEACHER'S OUTLINE & STUDY BIBLE™ • New Testament Books •**

  Complete 45 minute lessons - 4 months of studies/book; 200± pages - Student Journal

- **OUTLINE Bible Studies series: 10 Commandments - The Tabernacle**
- **NEW TESTAMENT PRACTICAL WORD STUDIES - 2,000 Key Words Made Easy**
- **CD-ROM: Preacher, Teacher, and Handbook- (Windows/STEP) - WORDSearch**
- **Translations of Preacher, Teacher, and Minister's Handbook: Limited Quantities**

  Russian - Spanish - Korean - Hindi - Telugu - Tamil - Chinese • *Future: French, Portuguese*

— Contact us for Specific Language Availability and Prices —

For quantity orders and information, please contact either:

LEADERSHIP MINISTRIES WORLDWIDE *or* *Your OUTLINE Bible Bookseller*
PO Box 21310
Chattanooga, TN 37424-0310
(423) 855-2181 (9am - 5pm Eastern) • FAX (423) 855-8616 (24 hours)
E•Mail - outlinebible@compuserve.com.
FREE Download Samples & 24 hr Orders — www.outlinebible.org

• Equipping God's Servants Worldwide with OUTLINE Bible Materials •
LMW is a nonprofit, international, nondenominational mission agency

2/99

Equipping God's Servants Worldwide

1. **PAYMENT PLANS**. Convenient and affordable ways to get/use your FullSet with easy payments.
2. **NEW TESTAMENT**. In 14 volumes. Deluxe version 3-ring binders. Also: SoftBound Set, 3 volume set, and NIV edition. All on 1 CD-ROM disc.
3. **OLD TESTAMENT**. In process; 1 volume releases about every 6-8 months, in sequence.
4. **THE MINISTERS HANDBOOK**. Acclaimed as a "must-have" for every minister or Christian worker. Outlines more than 400 verses into topics like Power, Victory, Encouragement, Security, Restoration, etc. Discount for quantities.
5. **THE TEACHER'S OUTLINE & STUDY BIBLE™**. Verse-by-verse study & teaching; 45 minute lesson or session. Ideal for study, small groups, classes, even home schooling. Each book also offers a STUDENT JOURNAL for study members.
6. **OUTLINE BIBLE CD-ROM.** Includes all current volumes and books; Preacher, Teacher, and Minister Handbook. 1 disc. WORDsearch STEP format. Also 50+ Bible study tools unlockable on same disc.
   FREE Downloads - www.outlinebible.org
7. THE **OUTLINE**. Quarterly newsletter to all users and owners of *POSB*. Complimentary.
8. **LMW AGENT PLAN**. An exciting way any user sells *OUTLINE* materials & earns a second income.
9. **DISTRIBUTION**. Our ultimate mission is to provide *POSB* volumes & materials to preachers, pastors, national church leaders around the world. This is especially for those unable to purchase at U.S. price. USA sales gain goes 100% to provide volumes at affordable prices within the local economy.
10. **TRANSLATIONS**. Korean, Russian, & Spanish are shipping first volumes — Others in-process: Hindi, Tamil, Telugu, Chinese, French, German, Finnish.
11. **FUNDING PARTNERS**. To cover the cost of all the translations, plus print, publish, and distribute around the world is a multi million dollar project.

    Church-to-Church Partners send ***Outline*** Bible books to their missionaries, overseas church leaders, Bible Institues and seminaries...at special prices.
12. **REFERRALS**. Literally thousands (perhaps even you!) first heard of *POSB* from a friend. Now Referral Credit pays $16.00 for each new person who orders from a customer's Referral.
13. **CURRICULUM & COPYRIGHT**. Permission may be given to copy specific portions of *POSB* for special group situations. Write/FAX for details.

9/98

For Information about any of the above, kindly FAX, E-Mail, Call, or Write

Please PRAY 1 Minute/Day for LMW!

PO Box 21310, Chattanooga, TN 37424 • (423) 855-2181 • FAX (423) 855-8616
• E-Mail - outlinebible@compuserve.com — www.outlinebible.org •

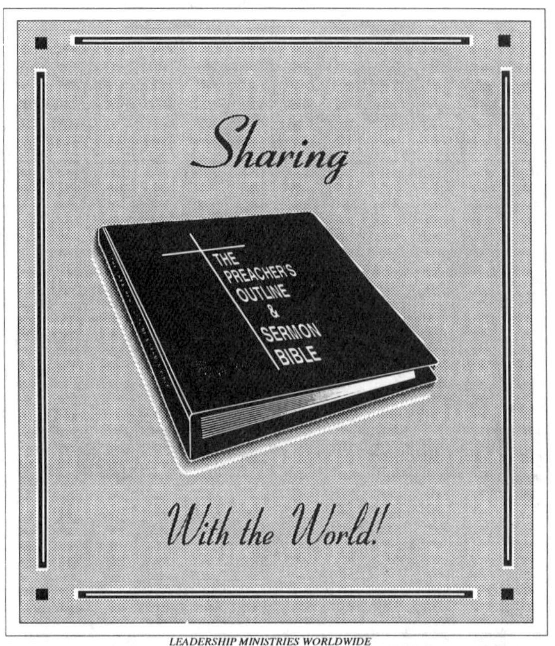

LEADERSHIP MINISTRIES WORLDWIDE
P.O. BOX 21310 Chattanooga, TN 37424 (615) 855-2181 FAX (615) 855-8616

This material, like similar works, has come from imperfect man and is thus susceptible to human error. We are nevertheless grateful to God for both calling us and empowering us through His Holy Spirit to undertake this task. Because of His goodness and grace *The Preacher's Outline & Sermon Bible®* - New Testament is complete in 14 volumes as well as the single volume of **The Minister's Handbook**.

God has given the strength and stamina to bring us this far. Our confidence is that, as we keep our eyes on Him and grounded in the undeniable truths of the Word, we will continue working through the Old Testament Volumes plus introduce the second series known as ***The Teacher's Outline & Study Bible.*** Future materials will include CD-ROM, The Believer's *Outline* NT, and similar ***Outline*** and **Handbook** materials.

To everyone everywhere who preaches and teaches the Word, we offer this material firstly to Him in whose name we labor and serve, and for whose glory it has been produced.

Our daily prayer is that each volume will lead thousands, millions, yes even billions, into a better understanding of the Holy Scriptures and a fuller knowledge of Jesus Christ the incarnate Word, of whom the Scriptures so faithfully testify.

As you have purchased this volume, you will be pleased to know that a portion of the price you have paid has gone to underwrite and provide similar volumes in other languages (Russian, Korean, Spanish and others yet to come) to a preacher, pastor, lay leader, or Bible student somewhere around the world, who will present God's message with clarity, authority, and understanding beyond their own. *Amen.*

For ministry information, prices and shipping details, kindly contact your LMW Agent or:

LEADERSHIP MINISTRIES WORLDWIDE

P.O. Box 21310, 515 Airport Road, Suite 107
Chattanooga, TN 37424-0310
(423) 855-2181 FAX (423) 855-8616
E-Mail 74152.616@compuserve.com
Web site: http://www.outlinebible.org